The Macquarie

THESAURUS

NEW
BUDGET
EDITION

The Macquarie

THESAURUS

NEW
BUDGET
EDITION

THE MACQUARIE LIBRARY

Published by The Macquarie Library Pty. Ltd.
The Macquarie Dictionary, Macquarie University, NSW 2109 Australia
First published 1985
Reprinted 1986, 1988, 1989, 1990

Produced in Australia for the Publisher
Typeset in Australia by Photoset Computer Service, Sydney

Printed by Griffin Press Limited,
Netley, South Australia

National Library of Australia
Cataloguing-in-Publication Data

The Macquarie Thesaurus New Budget Edition
Index
ISBN 0 949757 33 0

1. English language — Dictionaries
2. English language — Australia

A number of words entered in this thesaurus are derived from trademarks. However, the presence or absence of this indication of derivation should not be regarded as affecting the legal status of any trademark.

Contents

Introduction, J.R.L. Bernard vii

How to use this book xiii

The Macquarie Thesaurus New Budget Edition 1

Special lists 449

- Plants 451
- Animals 469
- Matter 483
- Sport 488
- Language 492

Introduction

J.R.L. Bernard
Associate Professor in Linguistics,
Macquarie University
General Editor, The Macquarie Thesaurus

1 The Good-luck Story of an Unlucky Word

Modern English contains a large number of words which have been brought into it from Latin, either by direct borrowing from that language or by indirect borrowing from some intermediary language like French or Italian.

Some of these words, like *opera* and *stimulus,* retain the same visual forms as their Latin originals, but most, like *monastery* (L. monasterium) and *chateau* (L. castellum), to a greater or lesser extent, do not. Nevertheless, in as much that all the words we have in mind here have accepted modern English pronunciations, are all in current use, and are all likely to appear as headwords in English dictionaries, they may be said to have made the move from one language to another with success.

We may regard them in a sense as *lucky words* for they have survived a process of transition and naturalisation which has claimed many casualties. There were great numbers of other Latin words which began this same process but which somehow failed to complete it. These were the *unlucky words.*

The brief histories of their abortive attempts to join the English word stock may most often be sketched out in the period somewhat before the reign of Elizabeth I. At this time English scholars were turning back again to the use of their own language, then in its Early Modern English form, for serious writing and discourse.

English had been very little used for these purposes in the centuries which followed the Norman Conquest, since Latin and French were considered preferable. The native language was, in the main, kept for colloquial and mundane use. As a consequence, those scholarly words which English had had before the Conquest withered for lack of use and fell from it. Moreover, during those Norman centuries, English did not coin new scholarly words in order to equip itself to deal with expanding knowledge and thought.

It is hardly surprising, then, that those pre-Elizabethan scholars who were determined to use English again in their serious writing found it to be deficient. Many of them consciously set about making good the deficit by bringing into their writing suitable words borrowed from Latin and Greek, which they had themselves "Englished" with varying degrees of thoroughness.

Yet of these two (celeritie and slownesse) springeth an excellent vertue, wherunto we lacke a name in englishe. Wherefore I am constrained to usurpe a latine worde, callying it *Maturitie*

Elyot, "The Governour", 1.xxii. 1546

Maturity (L. maturitas) had in fact been coined earlier, but Elyot's words have special interest because they show how the minds of the time worked.

Great numbers of hot-house creations like this ultimately became fixed in the language and are now as familiar to use as *maturity* has become – words like *allusion, capsule* or *dexterity,* all of which come from the same general period.

On the other hand, great numbers of similar creations did not become fixed in the language and disappeared after a brief appearance. These, poor sad creatures like *deruncinate, adjuvate, obtestate* and *collaude,* are now to be found only on those pages from earlier centuries which chance to come to hand. Why they did not appeal, what, if any, were their inherent weaknesses, it is hard to say. On them fortune just did not smile.

At one time one might well have been tempted to include in their unhappy, unlucky band, the word *thesaurus.* This was a Latin word, although itself borrowed beforehand from Greek, and meant *treasure* or *storehouse.*

It had that same flickering and uncertain life which characterised most other "unlucky" words before their extinction, but it seems to have had a greater persistence. *Thesaurus* kept knocking on the door of the English language for centuries without ever being made truly welcome and, curiously, without ever being positively led through to the scrapheap.

Predictably the word first appeared in English guise in the Early Modern English period where fleetingly as *thesaure* it meant *treasure* and where, equally fleetingly, *to thesaurise* meant *to hoard money.*

The Scots were kinder to it than most. At one time they used to speak of their *Thesaury,* or State treasury, and to have the office of *Thesaurer,* or treasurer, on their books. The union with England of 1707 put an end to these two usages which might otherwise have continued.

In the early 19th century, briefly again, archaeologists picked up the word in its Latin shape to mean *storehouse for treasure* and perhaps it was this which led John Stuart Mill to apply it in 1840 to a linguistic context. He spoke of "a thesaurus of commonplaces for the discussion of questions". Alternatively he may have been reviving a use among Elizabethan dictionary writers from that earlier time when they were much more concerned with writing in Latin. In 1565, for example, Thomas Cooper published what he called a *Thesaurus Linguae Romanae et Britannicae,* that is, a *Treasure-house of the Roman and British Tongues.* But this application of the word seems to have had very little currency in Mill's time.

It is possible that the word might have clung on like this, leading a sporadic sort of life, half in and half out of the language and mentioned, if at all, in only the biggest of dictionaries. But this was not to be. Today *thesaurus* is a common enough word and is to be found in quite small dictionaries where it may be glossed perhaps as "an elaborate lexicon" or "a reference book of synonyms and antonyms", perhaps as "a dictionary of selected words or topics".

The change in fortune of this previously unlucky word is due to the work of one man. He was Peter Mark Roget, 1779-1869.

2 Peter Mark Roget

Roget's surname was French because his Calvinist father was a native of French-speaking Geneva. He had settled in London as the pastor of a French Protestant church and had married into a distinguished Huguenot family rather longer established in England. Thus Peter Mark's family was French on both sides but he himself was born in Soho and lived and died as an Englishman through and through, in fact, as an Englishman of considerable distinction.

While quite young by today's standards, he elected to be a doctor and graduated in 1798 when only nineteen. One can follow the bare bones of his medical career from student days at the Edinburgh Infirmary, through the short period as private physician to the Marquess of Lansdowne, to the appointment in 1803 as physician to the Manchester Infirmary and then on to the more expansive days in London which began in 1808.

He was a doctor, and lived by his medical practice as most doctors do, but neither this nor a list of his practices is a full statement, for he was additionally a man of unusually active social conscience and unusually active intellect.

Because of the former he seems to have initiated something worthwhile wherever he was. In his short years in Manchester he helped to found and taught in the Manchester Medical School. In London he helped found the North London Dispensary to which he gave his services for eighteen years without fee, and, more importantly no doubt, he was one of the people who were instrumental in the creation of London University. (There he was also an examiner in physiology and comparative anatomy and a member of the Senate for many years.) He was also Professor of physiology at the Royal Institution but not too proud to serve a term as a prison doctor.

His associates included men of the stature of Sir Humphry Davy the chemist and Jeremy Bentham the principal shaper of London University.

Because of his intellect and scholarly bent, he was much published and much in demand for public lectures. While in Manchester he addressed the Manchester Philosophic and Literary Society and became its vice-president. In London he held the same position in the Medico-Chirurgical Society. He was co-founder of the Society for the Diffusion of Useful Knowledge. He wrote on many subjects besides physiology, including electricity and magnetism. He was thus a man constantly needing to put words together.

He was made a Fellow of the Royal Society because of his invention in 1815 of an unusual slide rule – a device of great utility with which very few people associate his name. In 1852 he gave the world his Thesaurus, another device of great utility but one with which his name is likely forever to be associated. Its publication radically altered the fate of that previously *unlucky* word.

3 Roget's Thesaurus and others

Roget was 70 when in 1849 he began to work in earnest towards the publication of this book but it was a project which had long been in his mind. He had, in fact, written something of the kind for his own use forty and more years before when he was lecturing at the Manchester Medical School.

Like all who compose English either for written publication or verbal delivery, Roget must on occasion have been stuck for a word and have grappled with the annoying awareness that, yes certainly, there was a precisely right word, a mot juste, lurking about somewhere and, although its shape could almost be sensed in a vague way, the word obstinately refused to come to mind. Perhaps Roget suffered more than most of us, perhaps not, but he *did* determine to do something about the problem quite early in life, and in his retirement turned to refining and expanding his efforts prior to offering them to the public.

The purpose of his thesaurus, his treasure-trove of words, is quite clear from the ponderous title: *Thesaurus of English words, Phrases, classified and arranged so as to facilitate the Expression of Ideas and assist in Literary Composition.*

Those who are unfamiliar with what a thesaurus is should bear in mind that it is *not* a dictionary. They might suspect this themselves immediately in the case of Roget's work because the bulk of what it contains is not arranged alphabetically. But this would be to come to a correct conclusion for an incorrect reason. Alphabetical order in dictionaries did not become usual until the latter half of the 16th century and, however useful and usual alphabetical order is now, it is not a necessary feature. The earliest dictionaries, usually Latin/English ones, most often grouped words by general areas of meaning (or semantic field), not by order of initial letter. Thus all the words and their Latin equivalents concerned with *fire* might be together in one place, and all those concerned with *sea* in another.

This is in fact Roget's plan of arrangement. The whole world of ideas is carved up into component parts and the words which belong to each of them are assembled in separate blocks. The whole is not a dictionary with unusual arrangement, however, because there is no attempt to translate or define any word. Rather the words assembled in each block are those which might come to mind when a particular topic is being discussed. They are related to one another by being in the same semantic field and hence are just what the struggling writer might need to prod his or her work along, but they are not necessarily equivalent terms such as a dictionary must limit itself to.

For example, under the headword *busyness* in a thesaurus might appear *quickness, eagerness* and *vigour.* These three words refer to qualities which in some sense relate to, or conceptually abut, the idea of busyness but which are not the same as it and which do not, therefore, define it. Against the entry *busyness* in a dictionary however, some attempt at a definition would have to be made, some attempt to find words which describe an equivalent entity. Perhaps in this case a periphrase like *a state of being attentively engaged* would be needed.

For many people one of the fascinations of Roget's thesaurus is the grand scheme it offers for splitting up the world of thought into component parts. The scheme is perhaps not as complete as it looks but it is a brave attempt to reduce what must seem like near chaos to splendid order.

It is clear however that it is to the book's usefulness as an aid to composition that it has owed its phenomenal success. Twenty-eight editions were published in Peter Roget's lifetime and his son, John Lewis Roget, and his grandson, Samuel Romilly Roget, kept alive a family tradition by bringing out progressively updated versions with the original publishing house. Generations of writers of all types have used it.

Not surprisingly other English publishing houses, seeing the success, have issued their own versions. Some have been simply called "Thesaurus" and some, even when apparently representing independent compilations, mysteriously, "Roget's Thesaurus". Thus gradually the word *thesaurus* has ceased to refer to one book and its lineal descendants, and has taken on those generic senses by which it is today defined in many dictionaries.

Inevitably variations in the categories chosen and in patterns of arrangement appeared and, inevitably also, versions based on American rather than British usage. Some American thesauruses have tended to favour a simpler alphabetical arrangement than Roget and have derived from entirely original work, the source of which has been particular dictionaries of American English.

On a somewhat subtle level some readers claim to be able to trace in American thesauruses patterns of thought, as revealed in the associative connections, which are peculiarly American and at variance with the British.

Until now there has never been a thesaurus based on the English of Australia and New Zealand.

How to use this book

To find all the words for an idea, simply look up the first related word or phrase that comes to mind.

- If this word is followed by an arrow, go to the word it points to, and you will find all the words associated with your idea.
- If your starting word is followed by an arrow and several numbered words, choose the one closest to the meaning you have in mind. Look up that word and you will find all the associated terms.
- If your starting word is in CAPITALS, you have gone directly to the full list of associated words and phrases. Just read the paragraph and choose the expression that best suits your needs.

It's that simple!

Commonly used abbreviations

adj	adjective	*Colloq.*	colloquial
adv	adverb	*Obs.*	obsolete
interj	interjection		
n	noun		
prep	preposition		
pron	pronoun		
v	verb		

Aa

aback *adv* → behind

abacus *n* → 1 computer 2 top

ABANDON *v* defect from, desolate, discontinue *(Law)*, dish, disown, ditch, forsake, give over, give up, give up as a bad job, hand over, jettison, leave someone to their own devices, let down, let go, throw up, wash one's hands of, write off, yield; **renounce,** abjure, abnegate, discard, disclaim, dismiss, dispense with, forgo, have done with, reject, relinquish, repudiate, waive; **jilt,** cast off, drop, throw over; **strand,** expose, maroon; **desert,** bugger off, decamp, leave someone holding the baby, leave someone in the lurch, pike on, rat on, run out on, shoot through, squib on, walk out on

abandon *n* → 1 liberty *v* 2 depart 3 stop

ABANDONED *adj* abject *(Obs.)*, derelict, deserted, desolate, destitute *(Obs.)*, forlorn, forsaken, high and dry, like a shag on a rock, lorn *(Archaic)*, lovelorn, stranded, unredeemed, vacant *(Law)*

ABANDONER *n* defector, deserter, evacuator, quitter, rat, relinquisher, seceder; **jilt,** jilter; **abnegator,** forgoer

ABANDONMENT *n* defection, dereliction, desertion, desolation, evacuation, exposure, relinquishment, resignation, surrender, vacation, waiver; **renunciation,** abdication, abnegation, rejection, shedding; **forsakenness,** desolateness, forlornness, lovelornness

abase *v* → 1 demote 2 humble 3 lower

abashed *adj* → 1 meek 2 penitent

abate *v* → 1 cancel 2 decrease 3 moderate 4 stop 5 subtract 6 wane

ABATEMENT *n* assuagement, attenuation, mitigation, moderation, modulation, palliation, relaxation, relief, remission, remittence, remittency, temperament *(Obs.)*, wane; **pacification,** mollification, tranquillisation

abattoirs *n* → place of killing

abbess *n* → monastic

ABBEY *n* cell, chartreuse, cloister, convent, hermitage, monastery, nunnery, priorate, priory; **ashram.** *See also* PLACE OF WORSHIP; CHURCH; SHRINE

abbot *n* → monastic

ABBREVIATE *v* abridge, condense, cut a long story short, epigrammatise, precis, sum up, summarise, telescope; **abstract,** boil down, digest, encapsulate, formularise, formulate, formulise, make a synopsis of, outline, precis

abbreviate *v* → shorten

abdicate *v* → resign

ABDOMEN *n* belly, gut, hypochondrium, hypogastrium, middle, midriff, pubes, puku *(N.Z.)*, venter, waist, waistline, womb *(Obs.)*; **stomach,** bingie, breadbasket, inner man, maw, tum, tummy; **paunch,** bay window, beer gut, bow window, corporation, pot, potbelly, pukunui *(N.Z.)*, spare tyre; **solar plexus,** mark *(Boxing)*, wind *(Colloq.)*; **entrails,** comic cuts, gizzard, guts, innards, insides, internals, intestines, viscera, vitals; **alimentary canal,** appendix, bowel, bowels, caecum, colon, duodenum, enteron, epigastrium, foregut, ileum, jejunum, large intestine, midgut, oesophagus, omentum, pylorus, rectum, small intestine, vermiform appendix; **navel,** bellybutton, omphalos, umbilicus

abduct *v* → 1 capture 2 diverge 3 rob

aberration *n* → 1 astronomic point 2 deflection 3 illusion 4 madness 5 reflection 6 strangeness 7 wrong

abet *v* → 1 encourage 2 help

abeyance *n* → 1 deferment 2 interruption 3 interval 4 period of inaction 5 rest 6 stoppage

abhor *v* → 1 dislike 2 hate

abhorrent *adj* → 1 hateful 2 unpleasant

abide *v* → 1 be 2 continue 3 inhabit 4 persevere

ability *n* → 1 capability 2 competence

abject *adj* → 1 abandoned 2 bad 3 meek

abjure *v* → 1 abandon 2 cancel 3 deny

ablation *n* → medical treatment

ablaze *adj* → 1 angry 2 enthusiastic

able *adj* → 1 capable 2 competent 3 intelligent 4 knowledgeable

ablution *n* → cleansing

abnegate *v* → 1 abandon 2 refuse

abnormal *adj* → 1 nonconformist 2 strange

aboard *adv* → 1 inside 2 sideways 3 wanderingly

abode *n* → 1 dwelling 2 visit

abolish *v* → 1 cancel 2 destroy 3 finish

abominable *adj* → 1 bad 2 hateful 3 immoral 4 sickening

abomination *n* → 1 bad thing 2 dislike 3 evildoing 4 hate 5 unpleasant thing

aboriginal *adj* → 1 old 2 resident

aborigine *n* → population

ab origine *adv* → firstly

abort *n* → 1 failure *v* 2 be early 3 be infertile 4 fail 5 give birth 6 stop

abortion *n* → 1 birth 2 contraception 3 failure

ABOUND *v* bristle, crowd, flock, formicate, mass, swarm, teem, throng, troop; **oversupply,** congest, overman, overwhelm, snow under

abound *v* → be fertile

about *adj* → 1 awake *adv* 2 almost 3 imprecisely 4 regularly *prep* 5 concerning 6 near

ABOVE *adv* atop, over, overhead

above *adj* → 1 preceding *adv* 2 before 3 superiorly

aboveboard *adj* → 1 forthright 2 honest *adv* 3 honestly

abrade *v* → 1 powder 2 rub

abrasion *n* → rubbing

ABRASIVE *n* abradant, abrader, bath brick *(Metall.)*, emery board, emery cloth, emery paper, emery wheel, floatstone, oilstone, sandblast, sander, sandpaper, steel wool, stone, strop, wet and dry, whetstone; **rasp,** broach, grattoir, rasper, scraper; **scratcher,** back scratcher, strigil

ABRASIVE *adj* abradant, erodent, erosive, grating, scratchy; **frictional,** non-skid, non-slip, tractional

abreast *adv* → 1 equally 2 sideways

abridge *v* → 1 abbreviate 2 decrease

ABRIDGMENT *n* abbreviation, compression, condensation, encapsulation, shortened version; **abstract,** analysis, argument, compendium, digest, epitome, formularisation, formulation, formulisation, highlights, outline, precis, résumé, run-down, summarisation, summary, summing up, synopsis; **epigram,** cameo, capsule, epitaph, essay, haiku, limerick, monostich, mot, news item, novella, short story, vignette; **jottings,** adversaria; **ellipsis,** abbreviation, acronym, blend, brachylogy, elision, portmanteau word, syncope

abroad *adv* → 1 dispersedly 2 outside

abrogate *v* → 1 annihilate 2 cancel

abrupt *adj* → 1 discourteous 2 irregular 3 momentary 4 sloping

abscess *n* → sore

abscond *v* → 1 depart 2 elude 3 escape

ABSENCE *n* blank, blankness, default, dumbness, emptiness, lack, lacuna, loss, non-access, short, vacuity, want, wantage *(U.S.)*; **leave,** furlough, leave of absence, sabbatical, sickie; **absenteeism,** exile, non-appearance, truancy, voidance

absence *n* → non-being

ABSENT *adj* A.W.L., A.W.O.L., absent without leave, ack-willie, away, missing, off, truant; **bereft,** bankrupt, blank, dry, dumb, empty-handed, minus, unprovided for, vacant, wanting; **used up,** out of stock

absent *adj* → 1 forgetful 2 nonexistent

ABSENTEE *n* absenter, exile, interstater, truant, wag

absentee *n* → escapee

absenteeism *n* → absence

ABSENTLY *adv* blankly, dumbly, vacantly; **off,** out

absent-minded *adj* → 1 forgetful 2 inattentive

absolute *adj* → 1 certain 2 most 3 perfect 4 predominant 5 simple 6 unconditional 7 unrelated 8 whole

absolution *n* → 1 acquittal 2 forgiving 3 liberation

absolve *v* → 1 acquit 2 forgive 3 liberate

ABSORB *v* assimilate, blot, digest, occlude, soak up, sop up, sponge up, swab; **consume,** devour, down, drink, eat, engorge, gobble, goof, gulf, gulp, imbibe, ingest, ingurgitate, lap, manducate *(Rare)*, raven *(Obs.)*, sip, sup, swallow, take, taste, whet one's whistle; **take in,** drink, drink in, embrace, engulf, import, receive, ship *(Naut.)*; **respire,** aspirate, gasp, inbreathe, inhale, suck in, whiff

absorb *v* → 1 dry 2 eat 3 engross 4 learn

ABSORBENT *adj* absorptive, bibulous, hygroscopic, leachy, leaky, pervious, porous, receptive, recipient, spongelike, suctorial; **ingestive,** aspiratory, assimilative, assimilatory, digestive, edacious, inspiratory; **diathermanous,** diathermic; **assimilable,** consumable, digestible, respirable

ABSORBER *n* absorbent, consumer, devourer, digester, embracer, imbiber, inhaler, recipient, soak; **sucker,** aspirator, haustellum *(Crustacean Entomol.)*; **sponge,** activated charcoal, blotting paper, mop, pounce, sanitary napkin, tampon, wettex

ABSORPTION *n* consumption, engorgement, imbibition, importation, ingestion, ingurgitation, occlusion, suction; **assimilation,** digestion, embracement, engulfment; **intake,** gasp, in-draught, inhalation, inrush, inrushing, inspiration, puff, pull, suck, whiff; **receptiveness,** absorbency, absorptiveness, absorptivity, receptivity, recipience

absorption *n* → 1 attentiveness 2 learning

ABSTAIN *v* deny oneself, forbear, forgo, hold back, mortify oneself, refrain, resist, restrain oneself; **give up,** be on the wagon, be on the water wagon, cold-turkey, cut, eschew, forswear, kick the habit, renounce, swear off, take the pledge; **fast,** count calories, diet, reduce, watch one's waistline

abstain *v* → 1 be neutral 2 vacillate

ABSTAINER *n* abstinent, eschewer, faster, forgoer, Lysistratan, monk, nun, old maid, Spartan, Victorian; **ascetic,** mortifier, penitent, puritan; **celibate,** cherry, vestal, vestal virgin, virgin, virgo intacta; **dieter,** weight watcher; **teetotaller,** coldwater man *(Obs.)*, lemon avenue, prohibitionist, total abstainer, waterbag, wowser

abstemious *adj* → 1 abstinent 2 thrifty

abstention *n* → 1 abstinence 2 avoidance 3 inaction 4 neutrality

ABSTINENCE *n* austerities, cold-turkey, denial, eschewal, fasting, mortification, penance, self-abnegation, self-denial; **asceticism,** austereness, austerity, monachism, monasticism, puritanism; **abstemiousness,** abnegation, abstention, forbearance, frugality, refrainment, sparingness, Spartanism, temperateness; **celibacy,** chastity, continence, honesty *(Archaic)*, intactness, maidenhead, maidenhood, non-access, virginity; **teetotalism,** Prohibition, soberness, sobriety, temperance, the pledge; **dieting,** banting, weight reduction. *See also* FAST

abstinence *n* → avoidance

ABSTINENT *adj* abstemious, abstentious, puritanical, self-denying, steady, temperate, Victorian, wowserish; **ascetic,** ascetical, austere; **celibate,** chaste, clean, continent, honest, moral, pure; **virgin,** intact, vestal, virginal; **frugal,** spare, sparing, Spartan; **teetotal,** dry, off the grog, on the square, on the wagon, on the water wagon, sober, sober as a judge, stone-cold sober

abstract *n* → 1 abridgment 2 essence 3 idea *v* 4 abbreviate 5 capture 6 etherealise 7 generalise 8 remove 9 rob *adj* 10 artistic 11 conjectural 12 intangible 13 nonexistent 14 unclear

abstraction *n* → 1 conjecture 2 fine arts 3 generalisation 4 idea 5 inattentiveness 6 removal 7 the intangible

abstruse *adj* → 1 hidden 2 unclear

absurd *adj* → 1 foolish 2 humorous 3 illogical 4 impossible 5 nonsensical

ABUNDANCE *n* ampleness, bounteousness, bountifulness, copiousness, foison *(Archaic)*, fulsomeness, plenitude, plenteousness, plentifulness, prodigality, prolificacy, prolificness; **plenty,** bonanza, cornucopia, flood, lashings, milk and honey, more where it came from, outpouring, profusion; **generousness,** heartiness, lavishness

abundance *n* → 1 fertility 2 fullness 3 much 4 numerousness 5 wealth

ABUNDANT *adj* ample, bounteous, bountiful, copious, cornucopian, enough and to spare, overabundant, plenteous, plentiful, polycarpic *(Bot.)*, profuse, prolific, rampant, superabundant, teeming, wealthy; **hearty,** fulsome, generous, lavish; **fat,** bumper, pregnant, prodigal, rich

abundant *adj* → 1 fertile 2 great 3 many

abuse *n* → 1 disapproval 2 misuse 3 slander 4 swearing 5 trickery 6 unfairness 7 wrong *v* 8 act unkindly 9 ill-treat 10 slander 11 swear 12 trick 13 wrong

abut *v* → contact

abysmal *adj* → 1 bad 2 deep

abyss *n* → 1 depth 2 gap 3 hell 4 infinity

academic *n* → 1 intellectual 2 teacher *adj* 3 conjectural 4 conventional 5 educated 6 infertile 7 intellectual

academy *n* → 1 college 2 institute

accede *v* → 1 capitulate 2 promise

ACCELERATE *v* give it herbs, gun *(Aeron.)*, race *(Motor Vehicles)*, rap, rev, step on it, step on the gas *(U.S.)*; **quicken,** pick up, rally *(Theat.)*

accelerate *v* → 1 help 2 increase

ACCELERATOR *n* pedal, quickener, tandem generator, throttle

ACCENT *n* brogue, burr, inflection; **drawl,** drone, gutturalness, hoarseness, monotone, nasality, rhotacism, snuffle, trachyphonia, trill, twang; **dialect,** cockneyism, dialecticism, foreignism, localism, patois; **Received Standard English,** BBC English, cockney, the King's English, the Queen's English; **Australian English,** Broad Australian, Cultivated Australian, General Australian, Modified Australian

accent *n* → 1 assertiveness 2 faulty speech 3 importance 4 speaking *v* 5 emphasise 6 mark

accentuate *v* → 1 emphasise 2 mark

accept *v* → 1 approve 2 assent to 3 believe 4 get 5 know 6 persevere

accepted *adj* → 1 conventional 2 customary

ACCESS *n* fairway, gate *(Archaic)*, pass, passage, thoroughfare, way; **right of way,** dedication of way; **way in,** adit, doorway, dromos, entrance, gateway; **way through,** cluse, defile, ghat *(India)*, notch *(U.S.)*, strait *(Archaic)*; **way out,** débouché, exit; **driveway,** approach, avenue *(Brit.)*, drive; **runway,** airstrip, flare-path, tarmac, taxiway

access *n* → 1 bridge 2 entrance 3 right of way 4 use

accession *n* → 1 addition 2 affirmation 3 convergence 4 increase *v* 5 list

accessory *n* → 1 accomplice 2 addition 3 cooperator 4 criminal 5 equipment *adj* 6 additional

accident *n* → 1 luck 2 misfortune 3 unimportant thing

accidental *n* → 1 unimportant thing *adj* 2 lucky 3 unimportant

acclaim *n* → 1 applause 2 election *v* 3 approve

acclimatise *v* → habituate

accolade *n* → pat

accommodate *v* → 1 conform 2 equip 3 house 4 lend

accommodation *n* → 1 adjustment 2 agreement 3 dwelling 4 evolution 5 expedient 6 help 7 hotel 8 loan 9 space

accompaniment *n* → 1 addition 2 companionship 3 music

ACCOMPANY *v* associate with, assort *(Archaic)*, bear company with, chaperone, companion, company *(Archaic)*, consort, join with, keep company with, run with; **escort,** arm, conduct, convoy, guide, walk; **follow,** dangle, go around with, hang about, hang round, run around with, string along with; **partner,** see, squire, take out

accompany *v* → partner

ACCOMPANYING *adj* appendant, attached, attendant, collateral; **companionate,** associate, associational

ACCOMPLICE *n* abettor, accessory, camorrist, colluder, conspirator, particeps criminis, partner in crime; **ally,** affiliate, aligner, confederate, friend at court; **collaborator,** fellow traveller, fifth columnist, quisling, sympathiser; **factionary,** champion, cultist, factionist, partisan, votary; **follower,** hanger on, henchman, parasite, satellite, stooge, yes-man. *See also* PARTNER

accomplice *n* → cooperator

ACCOMPLISH *v* achieve, act up to, attain, break the back of, compass, deliver the goods, discharge, dispatch, dispose of, do, effect, effectuate, execute, expedite, fulfil, perform, procure, produce, produce the goods, realise, transact, turn the trick; **bring off,** bang over, bring about, button up, carry out, carry through, chalk up, fix up, get over, hurdle, knock off, make, make a good job of, make short work of, pull off, put over, put through, surmount, work, work the oracle; **complete,** bring to a head, cap, cast off *(Knitting)*, clinch, conclude, consummate, crown, culminate, finish, put the capper on *(N.Z.)*, round off, succeed

accomplish *v* → make whole

ACCOMPLISHED *adj* a dab hand at, a good hand at, artful, artistic, fine, handsome *(U.S.)*, hot-shot, light-handed, master, masterful, masterly, nice, notable *(Archaic)*, specialistic, stylish, subtle, virtuoso; **experienced,** au fait, blooded, educated, old, practised, pragmatic, professional, qualified, sure-footed, thoroughbred, thoroughpaced, up-to-date, versed, veteran. *See also* COMPETENT

accomplished *adj* → done

ACCOMPLISHMENT *n* achievement, attainment, discharge, dispatch, effectuation, execution, implementation, performance, procurance, production, time, transaction; **feat,** blow, coup, deed, effort, exploit, fait accompli, masterstroke, res gestae, stroke, success; **completion,** arrival, close, conclusion, culmination, effect, finish, fruition, rounding off, windup; **realisation,** consumation, entelechy, fulfilment

accomplishment *n* → **1** artistry **2** competence

accord *n* → **1** agreement **2** arrangement **3** congruity **4** music *v* **5** agree **6** evolve **7** fit **8** give

according *adj* → in agreement

accordingly *adv* → congruously

ACCORDING TO RULE *adv* according to Hoyle, bureaucratically, constitutionally, preceptively, prescriptively

accost *v* → **1** beg **2** be sociable **3** prostitute oneself

ACCOUNT *n* bank account, budget account, capital account, cash account, debtor and creditor account, deposit account, drawing account *(U.S.)*, expense account, joint account, running account, suspense account; **passbook,** bank passbook, bankbook, tally *(Hist.)*; **balance sheet,** bank statement, contract note, group certificate, profit and loss statement, return, statement; **entry,** balance, credit, debit, double entry, foot *(Obs.)*, item, minute, note, record, single entry, tally, trial balance, write-off; **bill,** bills of lading, invoice, itemised bill, reckoning, score, statement, tab, tally, ticket; **receipt,** warrant; **ledger,** budget, cashbook, daybook, folio, inventory, journal, receipt book, register, the books

ACCOUNT *v* audit, bank, budget, inventory, keep accounts, keep books, take stock; **balance,** balance the books, cast up, make accounts square, make square, make up, settle, square, tally, tot up, wind up; **enter,** bill, capitalise, credit, debit, journalise, log, note, post, record, ring up, set off; **write off,** liquidate

account *n* → **1** importance **2** indebtedness **3** judgment **4** list **5** narrative **6** record **7** reputation

ACCOUNTABILITY *n* accountableness, answerableness, avouchment, blamableness, responsibility; **assignability,** attributiveness, imputativeness; **blameworthiness,** blamefulness, culpability, culpableness, guilt

accountable *adj* → obligated

ACCOUNTANT *n* chartered accountant, cost accountant, public accountant; **bookkeeper,** balancer, purser, tallier; **auditor,** auditor-general, comptroller, controller

ACCOUNTING *n* accountancy, bookkeeping, cost accounting, money matters, reckoning; **budgeting,** allocation, batch costing, costing, factoring, job costing, periodising, process costing; **audit,** auditing

accoutrements *n* → **1** equipment **2** furniture

accredit *v* → **1** authorise **2** depute **3** employ

accretion *n* → **1** addition **2** increase

accrue *v* → **1** get **2** grow

accumulate *v* → **1** become greater **2** gather **3** grow **4** increase

ACCUMULATION *n* agglomerate, agglomeration, aggregate, aggregation, collective, conglomerate, cumulation, deposit, glomeration; **collection,** budget, hoard, miscellanea, miscellanies, odds and sods, omnium gatherum, paraphernalia, rhapsody *(Archaic)*, sundries; **hoardings,** gleanings; **backlog,** bank-up, pile-up; **bundle,** bale, faggot, fardel *(Archaic)*, fascicle, sheaf, wisp; **heap,** congeries, cumulus, drift, haymow, hayrick, haystack, hill, mound, pile, pyre, stack; **cluster,** bob, bunch, clump, clutch, knot, whisk; **batch,** battery, crop; **lot,** boodle *(U.S.)*, book, caboodle, nest, set; **package,** packet, parcel, shiralee, truss; **mass,** forest, wilderness; **accumulativeness,** amassment, crowdedness, cumulativeness

ACCUMULATIVE *adj* agglomerative, aggregative, cumulative; **collective,** congregate, congregative, gregarious; **clustered,** aciniform, agminate; **cumulate,** aggregate; **clustery,** clumpish, clumpy; **conglomerate,** agglomerate, conglomeratic, conglomeritic, glomerate

ACCUMULATIVELY *adv* aggregately, collectively, cumulatively, in the aggregate; **together,** crowdedly, en masse, tout ensemble; **gregariously**

accurate *adj* → **1** precise **2** true

accursed *adj* → **1** cursed **2** hateful **3** immoral **4** irreverent **5** unfortunate

ACCUSATION *n* attack, bill, denunciation *(Obs.)*, impeachment, personal action, prosecution; **charge,** arraign *(Obs.)*, arraignment, blame, complaint, count, crimination, frame-up, gravamen, imputation, incrimination, inculpation, indictment, laying of charges, matter, plaint, quantum meruit, rap, reproach; **countercharge,** appeal *(Obs.)*, recrimination, retort; **denunciation,** delation, denouncement; **allegation,** implication, innuendo, insinuation

ACCUSATORY *adj* accusatorial, accusing, condemnatory, criminative, denunciatory, inculpatory, invective, recriminative, recriminatory; **incriminatory,** incriminating, inculpatory

ACCUSE *v* complain about, oppugn, tax with; **denounce,** delate, denunciate, hammer *(Stock Exchange)*, put someone's pot on, turn queen's evidence against, turn state's evidence against; **criminate,** crust; **finger,** fit, frame, have the wood on, point the bone at, put the finger on; **allege,** imply, insinuate. *See also* LAY CHARGES

accuse *v* → **1** impute **2** litigate

ACCUSED *n* appellee, co-defendant, co-respondent, defendant, prosecutor, respondent, suspect

ACCUSER *n* alleger, arraigner, attacker, charger, complainant, complainer, demandant, impeacher, incriminator, indicter, plaintiff, public prosecutor, taxer; **recriminator,** countercharger; **denouncer,** approver, delator, denunciator, framer, oppugner

accustom *v* → habituate

ace *n* → **1** combat troops **2** expert **3** one **4** pilot **5** small amount **6** winner *adj* **7** good

acerbity *n* → **1** misbehaviour **2** sourness

acetylene *n* → fuel

ACHE *n* pain, pang, qualm, throb, throe, twinge, twitch; **headache,** hemicrania *(Obs.)*, migraine, sick headache, splitting headache; **earache,** toothache; **backache,** Lebanese back, Mediterranean back, shagger's back; **stomach-ache,** colic, collywobbles, gastralgia, gripes, hunger pain, pain in the gut; **afterpains,** growing pains, phantom limb pains, referred pain, teething pains; **cardialgia,** angina; **hyperalgesia,** arthralgia, brachialgia, causalgia, hemialgia, neuralgia, neuritis. *See also* PAIN

ache *n* → **1** desire *v* **2** pain

achieve *v* → **1** accomplish **2** gain

achromatic *adj* → colourless

acknowledge *v* → **1** answer **2** assent to **3** be grateful **4** confess

acme *n* → **1** good thing **2** perfect thing **3** top

acne *n* → **1** disfigurement **2** sore

acolyte *n* → **1** helper **2** partner **3** preacher **4** religious dignitary **5** religious follower

ACOUSTIC *adj* phonic, sonant, sonantal, soniferous, vocal, voiced; **audible,** clear, distinct, heard, plain; **sonic,** infrasonic, subsonic, supersonic; **homophonic,** polyphonic

acoustic *n* → **1** hearing aid *adj* **2** hearing

acoustics *n* → hearing

acquaint *v* → inform

acquaintance *n* → **1** friend **2** friendship **3** knowledge

acquiesce *v* → **1** be willing **2** capitulate

ACQUIESCENCE *n* compliance, obedience; **amenability,** amenableness, corrigibility, ductility, tractability; **passivity,** meekness, non-resistance, passiveness, resignation, resignedness, tameness, yieldingness

acquire *v* → **1** buy **2** gain **3** get **4** rob

acquisitive *adj* → avaricious

ACQUIT *v* assoil *(Archaic)*, compound, discharge, exonerate, forgive, let off, pardon, purge, remit, reprieve, spare; **absolve,** clear, exculpate, excuse, justify, let out, vindicate; **turn up,** compurge, testify for; **get off,** get up

acquit *v* → **1** forgive **2** justify **3** liberate **4** pay

ACQUITTAL *n* absolution, acquittance, clearance, discharge, dismissal, exoneration, pardon, purgation, quittance, release, remission, reprieve; **excusal,** exculpation, vindication; **nolle prosequi,** autrefois acquit, autrefois attaint, non prosequitur; **amnesty,** immunity

ACQUITTED *adj* clear, exonerated, not guilty, uncondemned; **absolvable,** exculpable, excusable, vindicable

acre *n* → **1** area **2** buttocks

acrid *adj* → **1** pungent **2** sharp **3** unsavoury

ACRIMONIOUS *adj* acerbate, bitter, caustic, fierce, heated, maenadic, passionate, peppery, rancorous, shrewish, stinging, vehement, virulent, warm; **resentful,** aggrieved, hurt, indignant, peeved, shat off, sulky, sullen

ACRIMONY *n* acrimoniousness, asperity, bitterness, ill feeling, intolerance, rancorousness, rancour, sourness, verjuice; **sullenness,** sulkiness

acrimony *n* → misbehaviour

acrobat *n* → **1** circus performer **2** defector

acronym *n* → abridgment

across *adv* → deflectively

acrostic *n* → **1** figure of speech **2** poetry **3** puzzle

ACT *n* afterpiece, catastasis, drop scene, episode, induction, love-scene, scena, scene, sequence; **routine,** number, show stopper, showpiece; **interlude,** antic *(Archaic)*, antimasque, ballet, curtain-raiser, entr'acte, episode, hokum *(U.S.)*, inset, intermezzo, lollipop, waits; **character sketch,** duologue, impersonation, monologue, monology *(Obs.)*, personation, rendition, representation, sketch, skit; **curtain call,** curtain speech, epilogue, prologue, protasis

act *n* → **1** action **2** affectation **3** angry act **4** command **5** fake **6** irritation **7** law **8** record *v* **9** attitudinise **10** behave **11** do **12** operate **13** perform

ACT DISCOURTEOUSLY *v* commit a solecism, drop a brick, forget oneself, speak out of turn, speak with one's foot in one's mouth, take a liberty, tread on someone's corns, tread on someone's toes; **talk back,** answer back, give someone a short answer, give someone lip

ACT FOR *v* act on behalf of, deputise for, represent, stand in for, subcontract

ACTING *n* mummery, rendering; **characterisation,** portrayal, representation; **Stanislavsky Method,** epic theatre, the Method; **dramatics,** histrionics, staginess, theatricals; **showmanship,** stagecraft, stardom, theatrecraft

acting *adj* → **1** agential **2** impermanent **3** operating

ACTION *n* act, deed, delaying action, factum, manoeuvre, move, proceeding, stroke, transaction; **feat,** execution, exploit, gest *(Archaic)*, jest *(Obs.)*, performance, stunt; **practice,** exercitation, hands-on experience, praxis, run-through; **process,** function, progress, unit process; **reaction,** reflex

action *n* → **1** act of war **2** energy **3** litigation **4** machine **5** move **6** movement **7** narrative **8** operation **9** power *v* **10** activate

ACTIVATE *v* action, actuate, energise, galvanise, initiate, provoke, put into commission; **animate,** arouse, excite, rouse, wake up, waken; **revive,** reactivate, reanimate, recrudesce, repeat; **crack the whip,** get things moving

activate *v* → **1** air **2** belt into **3** energise **4** militarise

active *adj* → **1** busy **2** energetic **3** influential **4** medicinal **5** speedy

activist *n* → **1** doer **2** encourager **3** hater **4** helper **5** revolutionary

activity *n* → **1** busyness **2** operation **3** power

ACT OF WAR *n* aggression, armed intervention, casus belli, declaration of war, invasion; **battle,** action, armed conflict, brush, charge, clash, combat, contest, dogfight, engagement, fight, fray, incident, melee, pitched battle, raid, rencounter, skirmish, stonk *(Colloq.)*, stoush *(Colloq.)*, toil *(Archaic)*; **war manoeuvre,** combined operations, framework operations, operation, siege, tactic; **campaign,** anabasis, crusade, expedition, mission; **call to arms,** battle cry, cry, marching orders, summons, war cry; **strategy,** battle-orders, commander's concept, concept of operations, deployment, generalship, manoeuvres, orders of the day, plan, tactics; **war game,** field day, naumachia, naumachy; **fortune of war,** outcome of battle; **massacre,** bloodshed, mayhem, pillage; **militarisation,** armament, mobilisation, rearmament, war footing, war measures. *See also* WAR; BATTLEGROUND

ACTOR *n* actress, artist, artiste, character actor, ham, method actor, portrayer, quick-change artist, stager *(Archaic)*, straight man, Thespian, tragedian, tragedienne, trouper; **star,** choragus, co-star, coryphaeus *(Gk. Antiq.)*, film star, lead, leading lady, leading man, matinee idol, megastar, premiere, principal, principal boy, solo, soloist, starlet, superstar; **extra,** bit-player, chorus member, spear-carrier, supernumerary, support, supporting actor, walk-on; **understudy,** double, stand-in, stuntman, substitute; **baddie,** black hat, villain; **feed,** endman; **dame,** figurant, figurante, foil, heavy, ingenue, interlocutor, interlocutress, interlocutrice, interlocutrix, juvenile, pantomime dame, soubrette

actor *n* → **1** affected person **2** agent **3** doer **4** show-off **5** trickster

ACT PRETENTIOUSLY *v* bung on an act, bung on side, give oneself airs, pile on the agony, put on dog, put on jam, put on the dog, show off, swank; **bedizen,** dandify, lairise; **dramatise,** overdress, overwrite, theatricalise

ACT RASHLY *v* count one's chickens before they are hatched, go at something baldheaded, go off half-cocked, go off the deep end, have a death-wish, plunge in, rush in, rush in where angels fear to tread, rush one's fences; **live dangerously,** adventure, buy a pig in a poke, buy into trouble, chance one's arm, give a hostage to fortune, play a dangerous game, play with fire, put all one's eggs in one basket, ride for a fall, risk, stick one's neck out, take a risk, tempt providence; **go to any length,** be extreme, stick at nothing; **burn one's fingers,** get out of one's depth

actual *adj* → **1** current **2** occurrent **3** real **4** true

ACTUALITY *n* actualness, concreteness, entelechy, here, here and now, immediacy, objectivity, reality, realness, solidness, substance, substantiveness, the real, truth, verity; **object,** entity, fact, noumenon, realia, subject, substantial, substratum, thing, thing-in-itself. *See also* REALITY

actuality *n* → truth

ACTUALLY *adv* as a matter of fact, concretely, existentially, factually, for real, in fact, in reality, in substance, in truth, indeed, solidly, substantively

actually *adv* → in fact

actuary *n* → mathematician

actuate *v* → **1** activate **2** arouse **3** operate

ACT UNFAIRLY *v* be on the grouter, come in on the grouter, take advantage, take unfair advantage; **discriminate,** discriminate against, favour, gerrymander, load the scales, rig, rob Peter to pay Paul, stack; **not play the game,** break the rules, commit a foul, hit below the belt

ACT UNKINDLY *v* bear malice towards, cut, disoblige, do someone a bad turn, offend, put someone's nose out of joint; **bully,** abuse, browbeat, hector, victimise; **torment,** bedevil, harry, hound, persecute, play cat and mouse with, torture; **harm,** come the acid over *(N.Z.)*, give no quarter to, give someone hell, hurt, maltreat, ride roughshod over, spitchcock *(Rare)*; **brutalise,** brutify, dehumanise

acuity *n* → sharpness

acumen *n* → intelligence

acupuncture *n* → healing

acute *adj* → **1** bent **2** impermanent **3** important **4** intelligent **5** perceptive **6** pointed **7** sharp **8** shrill **9** unwholesome

adage *n* → proverb

adamant *n* → **1** jewel *adj* **2** dissident **3** hard **4** stubborn

adapt *v* → **1** adjust **2** change **3** evolve **4** make do

ADD *v* admix, annex, append, attach, enlarge, heap, lend, piggyback, postfix, subjoin, suffix, superinduce, tack on, tag, throw in; **add to,** accessorise; **supplement,** accrete, round out, superadd, superimpose on; **interpolate,** grangerise, intercalate, interject, interpose; **footnote,** note; **be additional,** advene, supervene

add *v* → compute

addendum *n* → **1** book part **2** postscript

addict *n* → drug user

ADDITION *n* accession, accruement, additive, adjunct, affix, alts and adds, annexation, annexe, appendance, appendant, appurtenance, appurtenant, attachment, bonus, enlargement, interpolation, mixture, postfix, postscript, prolongation, streak, subjunction, superaddition, superimposition, superinducement, superinduction, supplementation; **total,** subtotal, sum, summation; **appendage,** appendicle, arm, fin, flap, label, lapel, lappet, tab, tag, tailpiece, wing; **accompaniment,** accessory, accretion, accrual, accumulation, admixture, extension, increase, increment, makeweight, trappings. *See also* MORE; POSTSCRIPT

addition *n* → **1** building **2** combination **3** increase **4** name

ADDITIONAL *adj* another, appendiculate, codicillary, follow-up, fresh, incidental, more, new, second, supernumerary; **additive,** accretive, adjunctive, incremental, interpolative; **annexed,** accessorial, accessory, appendant, appertaining, appurtenant, attached, belonging, incident; **supplementary,** ancillary, auxiliary, subsidiary, supplemental; **extra,** bonus, further, over, plus, surplus

ADDITIONALLY *adv* adjunctively, caudally, extensionally, in addition, subscriptively, supplementally, supplementarily; **moreover,** at that, beyond, by the way, farther, further, furthermore, incidentally, more, yea *(Archaic)*; **as well,** also, and all, beside, besides, either, eke *(Archaic)*, else, even, for good measure, into the bargain, item *(Obs.)*, likewise, nay, to boot, too, withal *(Archaic)*, yet; **and so on,** and all that, and all that jazz, and so forth, and then some, and what have you, and what not, et al, et cetera, etc.

additive *n* → **1** addition *adj* **2** additional

address *n* → **1** competence **2** dwelling **3** oration **4** position **5** preparation *v* **6** entreat **7** flirt **8** prepare **9** send a message **10** speak well

adduce *v* → attract

adept *n* → **1** expert *adj* **2** competent

ADEQUACY *n* adequateness, all that could be desired, enough, full measure, reasonableness, satisfaction, store, sufficiency; **quorum,** right number; **repletion,** bellyful, one's fill; **minimum,** least one can do, no less; **competence,** competency, effectuality, effectualness, worthiness; **one's due,** one's just deserts

ADEQUATE *adj* enough, equal to one's needs; **sufficient,** self-sufficient; **satisfactory,** decent, fair, reasonable; **barely sufficient,** bare, scant, scanty; **competent,** effectual, equal to the task

adhere *v* → stick together

adherent *adj* → sticky

ADHESIVE *n* adherer, agglutinant, binding, cohesive, fixative, goo, stick; **binder,** bind, bond, bonder; **uniter,** binder, bonder, gluer; **burr,** clinger; **adhesive tape,** durex, Scotch tape, Sellotape, sticky tape, wafer; **glue,** araldite, arming, birdlime, clag, clearcole, contact cement, contact glue, dextrin, fish glue, gluten, glyptal resin, glyptol, gum, mucilage, original gum, paste, propolis, size, solder, spirit gum, starch-gum; **grout,** luting, putty, sealant, sealing wax, wax; **cement,** compo, concrete, mortar, mud, plaster, ready-mix

adhesive *adj* → sticky

ad hoc *adj* → **1** capricious **2** expedient **3** impermanent **4** momentary **5** particular *adv* **6** particularly **7** temporarily

adipose *n* → **1** fat *adj* **2** fat **3** oily **4** thick

adjacent *adj* → close

adjective *n* → word

adjoin *v* → contact

adjourn *v* → defer

adjudicate *v* → assess

ADJUDICATOR *n* arbitrator, arbitress, concluder, condemner, decider, determiner, disposer, judge, judger, judicator, juror, jury; **referee,** central umpire, field umpire, goal umpire, ref, third man, touch judge, ump, umpie, umpire

adjunct *n* → **1** addition **2** inferior **3** partner

adjure *v* → **1** command **2** entreat

ADJUST *v* adapt, correct *(Physics)*, phase in, regularise, shape; **accomodate,** attune, get it together, move with the times, reconcile; **match,** find one's level, register, synchronise, track

adjust *v* → **1** change **2** pay **3** regularise

ADJUSTMENT *n* accommodation, compromise, conformation, reconcilement, reconciliation, settlement, settling, standardisation, synchronisation

adjutant *n* → **1** helper **2** partner

adlib *v* → be impulsive

ad lib *n* → **1** caprice *adj* **2** capricious *adv* **3** capriciously

administer *v* → **1** give **2** impose **3** legislate **4** manage **5** operate **6** share out

administration *n* → **1** imposition **2** legislation **3** management **4** operation **5** sharing out

ADMINISTRATIVE AREA *n* canton *(Switzerland)*, city, commonwealth, constituency, county, department *(France)*, division, electorate, municipality, oblast *(Russia)*, precinct *(U.S.)*, province, riding, satrapy *(Obs.)*, shire, state, subdivision, town, ward

admirable *adj* → **1** approved **2** reputable

ADMIRABLENESS *n* acceptability, commendableness, exemplariness, favourable-

ness, laudability, laudableness, praiseworthiness, splendidness, unobjectionableness
admiral *n* → 1 ruler 2 seaman
admire *v* → 1 approve 2 desire 3 enjoy
admissible *adj* → permitted
admission *n* → 1 assertion 2 charge 3 cost 4 employment 5 entrance 6 revealing
admit *v* → 1 assent to 2 confess 3 permit
admonish *v* → 1 guide 2 remind 3 scold
ad nauseam *adv* → excessively
ado *n* → 1 excitement 2 turbulence
adobe *n* → 1 building materials 2 house 3 soil
adolescence *n* → youth
ADOLESCENT *n* grommet, juvenile, spring chicken, teenager, teeny-bopper, youngling, youth; **lad,** colt, cub, debutant, fledgling, hobbledehoy, pup, puppy, sapling, shaveling *(Archaic)*, shaver, sprig, stripling, younker *(Archaic)*; **hoodlum,** larrikin, yob; **bodgie,** mod, punk, rocker, skinhead, surfie, ted, teddy boy; **lass,** damsel, debutante, filly, mademoiselle, maid, maiden; **nymphette,** carnie; **widgie,** bobbysoxer *(U.S..)*, bud; **youthful person,** evergreen, Peter Pan, young blood
adopt *v* → 1 assent to 2 elect 3 get 4 take 5 use
adoration *n* → 1 high regard 2 love 3 reverence 4 worship
adore *v* → 1 love 2 respect 3 revere 4 worship
adorn *v* → decorate
adrift *adj* → 1 confused 2 separate
A DRINK *n* drop of the old religion *(Brit.)*, aperitif, bracer, charge, chaser, chug-a-lug, coaster *(Obs.)*, dram, drop, drop of the doings, drop of the needle, gargle, hair of the dog that bit you, heart-starter, hooker, Jimmy Woodser, lace, lacing, leg opener, mickey, Mickey Finn, nightcap, nip, nobbler, one for the bitumen, one for the gutter, one for the road, pipe-opener, potation, quickie, reviver, rosiner, shot *(U.S.)*, slug, snifter, snort, snorter, spot, sting, stirrup cup, sundowner, swig, the other half, tipple, toast, tot
adroit *adj* → competent
adulate *v* → flatter
adult *adj* → aged
adulterate *v* → 1 mix 2 spoil *adj* 3 deteriorated 4 inferior
adultery *n* → 1 betrayal 2 sexual intercourse
ADVANCE *n* advancement, course, distance, going forwards, headway, march, movement, passage, process, progress, progression, race *(Archaic)*, way *(Naut.)*; **encroachment,** invasion, trespass; **surge,** effluxion, floodtide, flow, flux, onrush, press, push, rush, stream, sweep, wave, whirlwind; **forward position,** forefront, forwardness, front, head, lead, van, vanguard; **head start,** lead, lead time, start
ADVANCE *v* amble, continue, cover the ground, follow, go on, jog, make headway, make one's way, make progress, make strides, move, nose forward, precede, press forward, proceed, progress, push forward, shoot along, shoot through, stalk, take, thread, travel ahead, travel on, walk, wend *(Archaic)*; **come up to,** arrive at, breast, come abreast of; **close in,** approach, draw in; **bring up,** bring on, march forward, track in *(Film)*; **encroach,** advance on, head into, head towards, impinge on, impinge upon, invade, make tracks for; **pull ahead,** burn ahead, gain ground, lose, make up leeway, outstrip, overhaul, overtake, pass, plough through *(Naut.)*, stem; **advance relentlessly,** forge ahead, juggernaut, steamroller; **crowd,** hustle, press; **surge,** flood, roll, rush, sweep
advance *n* → 1 combat troops 2 debt 3 improvement 4 income 5 inflation 6 loan 7 promotion 8 signal 9 supply *v* 10 assert 11 attack 12 become greater 13 grow 14 improve 15 lend 16 lift 17 offer 18 pay 19 promote *adj* 20 prototypal
ADVANCED *adj* first, foremost, forward, leading, up; **advancing,** coming, forward moving, go-ahead, ongoing, onward, proceeding, processional, progressing, progressional, progressive, sweeping
ADVANTAGE *n* benefit, profit, vantage; **upper hand,** command, high ground, trump card, vantage ground, vantage point; **flying start,** edge, jump, lead, odds, pull, start; **privilege,** favour; **advantageousness,** desirability, preferability, preferableness
advantage *n* → 1 antecedence 2 expedient 3 good 4 profit 5 usefulness *v* 6 be expedient 7 profit
ADVANTAGEOUS *adj* beneficial, desirable, preferable
advent *n* → 1 arrival 2 occurrence
Advent *n* → fast
adventitious *adj* → 1 foreign 2 lucky 3 misplaced
adventure *n* → 1 attempt 2 danger 3 gamble 4 trade 5 undertaking *v* 6 act rashly
adventurous *adj* → 1 courageous 2 enterprising 3 lucky
adverb *n* → word
adversary *n* → 1 competitor 2 dissident 3 enemy
adverse *adj* → 1 bad 2 calamitous 3 opposite 4 unfriendly
adversity *n* → misfortune
advert *n* → 1 public notice *v* 2 attend to
advertise *v* → 1 encourage 2 inform 3 publicise 4 warn
advertisement *n* → 1 incentive 2 message 3 news item 4 public notice
advice *n* → 1 guidance 2 information
advisable *adj* → expedient
advise *v* → 1 guide 2 inform 3 practise law 4 send a message
advocate *n* → 1 approver 2 guide 3 helper 4 lawyer *v* 5 approve 6 encourage 7 guide 8 offer
adze *n* → 1 chisel *v* 2 cut
aegis *n* → protection
aeon *n* → duration
aerate *v* → 1 air 2 bubble 3 disperse

AERATED *adj* aeriferous, bubbly, carbonated, oxygenated; **inflated,** blown up, puffy; **well-ventilated,** air-conditioned

aerial *adj* → **1** airy **2** beautiful **3** ethereal **4** flying **5** high **6** light **7** resident

aerobatics *n* → flying

aerodrome *n* → airport

aerodynamics *n* → friction

aeronautics *n* → flying

AEROPLANE *n* air ambulance, air-taxi, airbus, airliner, biplane, bird, canard, cantilever, charter plane, convertiplane, fixed-wing aircraft, flying wing, freighter, glider-tug, goony bird, jet, jetliner, jumbo, jump-jet, monocoque, monoplane, penguin, plane, propjet, pusher, semi-monocoque, ski-plane, STOL, stratocruiser, stressed skin, swing-wing, tanker, tractor, transport, triplane, turbojet, turboprop, VTOL, wing; **air force,** bomber, dive-bomber, fighter, fighter-bomber, helicopter gunship, interceptor, pathfinder, spotter, spotter plane, troop-carrier, warplane *(U.S.)*

aerosol *n* → **1** cloud **2** disperser **3** gas

AESTHETE *n* artist, cognoscente, connoisseur, critic, culture-vulture, culturist, epicure, fusspot, gentleman, gourmet, highbrow, judge, lady, virtuoso

aesthetic *adj* → **1** artistic **2** beautiful **3** cultivated

aetiology *n* → **1** causality **2** healing

afar *adv* → remotely

A FEW *n* a handful, just one or two, trickle, two men and a dog; **the few,** minority, remnant

affable *adj* → friendly

AFFAIR *n* business, concern, job, matter, piece, present *(Obs.)*, spin *(Colloq.)*, thing. *See also* OCCURRENCE; SITUATION

affair *n* → **1** flirtation **2** love affair **3** operation **4** sexual relationship **5** undertaking

affect *n* → **1** emotion **2** perception **3** point of view *v* **4** aim at **5** attitudinise **6** be important **7** change **8** elect **9** emotionalise **10** imitate **11** influence **12** inhabit

AFFECTATION *n* beau geste, dramatisation, frill, mannerism, postiche, pretence, pretension; **airs,** airs and graces, dramatics, graces, histrionics; **act,** attitude, manner, pose, side; **schmalz,** bathos, crocodile tears, simper, snivel, sob-stuff, treacle; **varnish,** shoddy, veneer

affectation *n* → **1** arrogance **2** desire

AFFECTED *adj* all piss 'n' wind, artificial, arty, dramatic, exhibitionistic, factitious, forced, hammy, histrionic, laboured, mannered, missish, over-produced, studied, theatrical, unnatural; **pretentious,** arty-crafty, arty-farty, bombastic *(Obs.)*, bombastical *(Obs.)*, flatulent, piss-elegant, prestige, swank, up-market; **snobbish,** condescending, gracious, grand, grandiose, high-sounding, highfalutin, jumped-up, la-di-da, la-di-dady, Pecksniffian, snooty, snotnosed, snotty, snotty-nosed, toffee-nosed *(Brit.)*; **dandyish,** all ponced up, buckish, coxcombical, mincing, minikin, peacockish, peacocky, poncy, sparkish, strutting; **precious,** coy, fallal *(Obs.)*, foppish, niminy-piminy, rosewater, simpering, twee; **schmalzy,** crocodilian, sawney, soppy, soupy, treacly, unctuous; **donnish,** hypercorrect, pedantic, pedantical, precise; **priggish,** dandy, fine, genteel, goody-goody, mealy-mouthed, old-maidish, prim, prissy, proper, prudish, superfine; **hypocritical,** tongue-in-cheek

affected *adj* → **1** bombastic **2** damaged **3** influenced **4** perceptive

AFFECTEDNESS *n* artificiality, artificialness, factitiousness, forcedness, hype, hypocrisy, overelaborateness, studiedness, theatricality, theatricalness, unnaturalness; **pretentiousness,** bombast, condescendence, flatulence, flatulency, graciosity, grandiosity, magniloquence, pomposity, snobbery, stiltedness; **soppiness,** treacliness, unctuosity, unctuousness; **foppery,** coquetry, coxcombry, foppishness; **preciosity,** coyness, preciousness; **pedantry,** donnishness, preciseness, precision; **genteelness,** piss-elegance; **priggery,** priggishness, primness, sanctimony

AFFECTED PERSON *n* actor, actress, affecter, artiste, attitudiniser, drama queen, dramatiser, hypocrite, poser, poseur; **dandy,** adonis, beau, buck, coxcomb, dude *(U.S.)*, exquisite, fop, gay, gay blade, jackanapes, lair, macaroni, masher *(Obs.)*, peacock, ponce, prancer, prig *(Archaic)*, show pony, spark, turkey cock, two-bob lair, ultra; **arty,** culture-vulture; **snob,** buckeen, bunyip aristocracy, his Lordship, Lady Muck, Lord Muck, snoot, snot, snotnose, snotty nose, stuffed shirt; **Grand Pooh-Bah,** panjandrum; **pedant,** bush-lawyer; **sniveller,** crocodile, simperer; **pharisee,** holy Joe, pietist, religionist, Tartuffe

affection *n* → **1** condition **2** emotion **3** illness **4** influence **5** love **6** point of view

affiance *n* → **1** wedding *v* **2** marry

affidavit *n* → **1** assertion **2** evidence

affiliate *n* → **1** accomplice **2** child *v* **3** associate

affinity *n* → **1** congruity **2** point of view **3** relation **4** similarity **5** spouse

affirm *v* → **1** assent to **2** assert **3** testify

AFFIRMATION *n* attestation, confirmation, corroboration, endorsement, homologation, ratification; **approval,** accession, assent, consent, okay, Royal assent, sanction, support; **avowal,** acknowledgment, cognovit, confession, recognition; **acceptance,** accession, acquiescence, adoption, resignation, sanctification, subscription; **the affirmative,** affirmative, amen, ay, placet, pro, the nod, yea, yes. *See also* AGREEMENT

affirmative *n* → **1** affirmation *adj* **2** assenting

affix *n* → **1** addition **2** join *v* **3** fasten **4** impute **5** join **6** press

afflict *v* → **1** defeat **2** pain **3** punish

affluence *n* → **1** flow **2** numerousness **3** wealth

affluent *n* → 1 stream *adj* 2 flowing 3 many 4 wealthy
afford *v* → 1 make possible 2 supply
affront *n* → 1 insult *v* 2 front 3 insult
afield *adv* → 1 away 2 deflectively 3 remotely
afloat *adj* → 1 buoyant 2 nautical 3 operating
afraid *adj* → 1 frightened 2 penitent
afresh *adv* → repeatedly
aft *adj* → 1 rear *adv* 2 behind
AFTER *adv* next, proximately, proximo, second, secondarily, secondly; **afterwards,** since, thereon, thereupon, therewith; **behind,** in the tracks of, in the wake of, posteriorly, postpositively, ulteriorly; **hereunder,** below, et seq, hereinafter, thereinafter; **consequently,** ex post facto, in consequence, subsequently, thus
after *adj* → 1 following 2 future 3 rear *adv* 4 behind 5 imitatively *prep* 6 concerning
afterlife *n* → 1 afterworld 2 future
aftermath *n* → result
AFTERNOON *n* afto, arvo, midafternoon, p.m.
afternoon *n* → 1 finish *adj* 2 daily 3 final
afterwards *adv* → 1 after 2 in the future
AFTERWORLD *n* afterlife, beyond, hereafter, other world, the other side; **underworld,** Hades, limbo, lower world, nether regions, nether world, Shades, Sheol; **Dreamtime,** alchera, alcheringa; **nirvana,** atman, Brahma. *See also* HEAVEN; HELL
again *adv* → repeatedly
against *prep* → 1 opposite *conj* 2 while
agape *n* → 1 love 2 meal 3 religious ceremony *adj* 4 gaping 5 open *adv* 6 in astonishment
agate *n* → marble
AGE *n* chronological age, life-span, longevity, three score and ten; **old age,** eighties, elderliness, Indian summer, nineties, seventies, sixties; **agedness,** ancientness, oldness, senescence; **senility,** anecdotage, dotage, second childhood; **middle age,** certain age, change of life, climacteric, menopause; **autumn,** autumn of life, mellowness; **adulthood,** adultness, age of consent, age of discretion, drinking age, driving age, full age, legal age, majority, manhood, matronage, maturity, prime, prime of life, summer, voting age, womanhood; **maturity,** matureness, ripeness; **marriageability,** marriageableness, nubility; **geratology,** geriatrics, gerontology, nostology; **geriatrician,** gerontologist; **age-group,** generation, peer group
AGE *v* flower, grow old, grow out of, grow up, mature, mellow, number, ripen; **have had a good innings,** have one foot in the grave; **decline,** wane; **outlive,** overlive *(Obs.)*
age *n* → 1 period 2 the public *v* 3 be old 4 deteriorate 5 taste
AGED *adj* advanced in years, ancient, autumnal, elderly, frosty, grey, grey-headed, hoary, in the sere and sallow, long in the tooth, long-lived, longeval, of a ripe old age, old, old as Methuselah, old as the hills, white-haired, white-headed; **anile,** haggish; **senile,** burnt out, decrepit, doddering, doting, gaga, over the hill, past it, past one's prime, run to seed; **ageing,** declining, failing, getting on, in one's declining years, oldish, senescent, with one foot in the grave; **venerable,** matriarchal, patriarchal; **retired,** pensioned off, superannuated; **geriatric,** nostologic; **centenarian,** nonagenary, octogenary, quinquagenary, septuagenary, sexagenary; **mature,** adult, full-grown, fully-fledged, grown, grown-up, mellowed, of age, over-age; **middle-aged,** of a certain age; **menopausal,** menopausic; **marriageable,** nubile, ripe and ready; **elder,** aîné, eldest, major *(Brit.)*, senior
AGEDLY *adv* ; **mellowly** autumnally, maturely, ripely; **on the shady side of,** upwards of
AGENCY *n* instrument, instrumentation, machine, operation, procuration *(Obs.)*; **mission,** brevet, commission, errand; **embassy,** chancellery, consulate, legation, viceconsulate; **assignment,** delegacy
agency *n* → doer
AGENDA *n* docket *(U.S.)*, notice paper *(Parl. Proc.)*, program, schedule, timetable; **repertoire,** repertory, stock *(Theat.)*; **menu,** range of options, set of alternatives; **bill of fare,** carte, diet chart, menu, table d' hôte, tariff; **questionnaire,** ballot paper, survey, unity ticket
agenda *n* → plan
AGENT *n* apparatchik, clerk of works, depositary, mandatary, proctor, receiver, representative, subagent, vicar; **deputy,** appointee, fill-in, spokesman, spokesperson, spokeswoman, substitute, surrogate, vice-chairman; **actor,** coexecutor, coexecutrix, contractor, doer, executor, executor de son tort, executrix, factotum, palatine, performer, practitioner, subcontractor; **viceroy,** crown agent, governor-general, lieutenant governor, state governor, vice-regent, vicegerent. *See also* DELEGATE; AMBASSADOR
agent *n* → 1 doer 2 manager 3 method 4 operator 5 seller 6 trader
AGENTIAL *adj* proctorial, representational, representative, vice-regal, vicegeral; **acting,** deputy; **ambassadorial,** commissarial, consular, diplomatic, legatine, legationary, official, proconsular, vice-consular; **vicarious,** delegated, vicarial
agglomerate *n* → 1 accumulation *v* 2 gather *adj* 3 accumulative
agglutinate *v* → 1 stick together *adj* 2 sticky
aggrandise *v* → 1 be wealthy 2 glorify 3 grow 4 increase
aggravate *v* → 1 annoy 2 irritate
aggregate *n* → 1 accumulation 2 combine 3 computation 4 score *v* 5 gather *adj* 6 accumulative 7 combined
aggression *n* → 1 act of war 2 violence 3 warmongering
AGGRESSIVE *adj* aggro *(Colloq.)*, assailant, belligerent, combative, hawkish, militant,

persecutive, persecutory, spoiling for a fight, truculent; **predatory,** depredatory, incursive, offensive

aggressive *adj* → 1 energetic 2 ferocious 3 unfriendly

aggrieved *adj* → 1 acrimonious 2 discontented 3 repressed

aghast *adj* → 1 astonished 2 frightened

agile *adj* → 1 athletic 2 busy 3 light-footed 4 speedy

agist *v* → 1 farm 2 impose

agistment *n* → farming

AGITATE *v* disturb, startle, tempest *(Obs.)*, traumatise, trouble, unfix, unsettle, wimple; **shake,** jiggle, joggle, succuss, toss about, vex *(Archaic)*; **ferment,** hot up; **beat,** cheddar, churn, cream, mill, move, muddle *(U.S.)*, popple, stir, stoke, whip, whisk; **torment,** disturb, roil, stir, vex, worry

agitate *v* → 1 arouse 2 call attention to 3 excite 4 move 5 politicise 6 revolt

agnostic *n* → 1 doubter 2 irreverent person *adj* 3 doubting 4 irreverent 5 uncertain

ago *adv* → in the past

agog *adj* → 1 astonished 2 curious 3 desirous 4 enthusiastic 5 excited *adv* 6 enthusiastically 7 excitedly 8 expectantly 9 inquisitively

agonise *v* → feel pain

agony *n* → 1 contest 2 excitement 3 pain 4 unfortunateness

A GOOD TIME *n* ball, feast, field day, high time, idyll, picnic, time of one's life; **pastime,** amusement, dissipation, hobby, sport; **red-letter day,** special occasion; **dolce vita,** gracious living, high life, life of Riley; **paradise,** Eden, Elysium, heaven, land of milk and honey, lucky country; **a place in the sun,** a bed of roses, a good scene, clover, featherbed, lap of luxury, the primrose path

agrarian *adj* → 1 farming 2 rural

AGREE *v* arrange, close up on, close with, consent *(Obs.)*, cotton *(Colloq.)*, harmonise, meet, run parallel, see eye to eye, settle, shake, shake hands, unite; **sympathise,** empathise; **accord,** act together, attune, concert

agree *v* → 1 be similar 2 be willing 3 conform 4 fit 5 promise

AGREEABLE *adj* agreeably disposed, amenable, bent upon, complacent *(Archaic)*, complaisant, compliant, desirous, disposed, easygoing, favourably disposed, inclined, minded, of a mind to, predisposed, willing; **happy to,** apt *(Archaic)*, content, fain *(Archaic)*, glad, lief *(Archaic)*, nothing loath, ready; **wholehearted,** ungrudging, unmurmuring; **prompt,** alacritous, spontaneous; **voluntary,** gratuitous, ultroneous *(Rare)*, unasked for, unforced, volunteer

agreeable *adj* → 1 assenting 2 conventional 3 in agreement 4 lenient 5 pleasant 6 tasty

AGREEMENT *n* accord, complaisance, compliance, concord, concurrence, consensus, covenant, facility, general agreement, unanimity; **harmony,** accord, accordance, amity, arrangement, common ground, compatibility, concert, concord, congeniality, consent *(Archaic)*, consentaneity, consentaneousness, consentience, consonance, empathy, esprit de corps, fellow feeling, meeting point, rapport, settlement, solidarity, sympathy, team spirit, understanding, unity; **compliance,** coexistence, conformance, conformity; **reconciliation,** accommodation, atonement *(Obs.)*, détente, rapprochement, reconcilement. *See also* AFFIRMATION

agreement *n* → 1 arrangement 2 conformity 3 congruity 4 contract 5 obligation 6 peace

agriculture *n* → farming

agronomy *n* → farming

ague *n* → 1 coldness 2 fever

ahead *adj* → 1 profitable *adv* 2 first 3 forward 4 frontally

a head *n* → drunkenness

ahoy *interj* → 1 cooee 2 hey

aid *n* → 1 charity 2 help 3 payment 4 supply *v* 5 help

aide-de-camp *n* → 1 helper 2 servant

ail *v* → 1 be ill 2 be out of luck

aileron *n* → 1 steadier 2 steering wheel

AIM *n* ambition, be-all and end-all, errand, ideal, mecca, mission, object, target, view; **goal,** bourn, butt *(Obs.)*, destination; **target,** bird, butt, chase, checkpoint, clay pigeon, dartboard, inner, mark, pin, popinjay, tee; **purpose,** end, intention, purport, sake

aim *n* → 1 conjecture 2 direction *v* 3 direct

AIM AT *v* affect *(Archaic)*, aspire to, intend, meditate, premeditate, pretend to, purpose

AIR *n* air-mass; **fresh air,** open, open air, out-of-doors, ozone, sea air, the great outdoors; **sky,** ether, the blue, the heavens; **thin air,** ethereality, etherealness, rarity; **gas,** compressed air, nitrogen, oxygen

AIR *v* expose, give an airing; **ventilate,** air-condition; **aerate,** activate, carbonate, oxygenate; **blow up,** inflate; **puff up,** balloon out, blouse out

air *n* → 1 appearance 2 behaviour 3 characteristics 4 gas 5 music 6 radio 7 wind

airborne *adj* → 1 airy 2 flying 3 transport

air-conditioning *n* → 1 airing 2 cooling

AIRCRAFT *n* aerodyne, craft, delta wing, flying machine, kite, ship; **helicopter,** autogyro, chopper, copter, egg-beater, gyrocopter, gyroplane, ornithopter, rotary wing aircraft, rotorcraft, whirlybird *(U.S.)*; **flying boat,** amphibian, float plane, hydroplane, seaplane; **glider,** box kite, hang-glider, kite, sailplane, soarer; **parachute,** brolly *(Brit.)*, canopy, chute, drogue; **aerostat,** airship, balloon, blimp, captive balloon, dirigible, kite balloon, montgolfier, sausage, zeppelin; **gondola,** car, nacelle; **UFO,** bogy, flying saucer, magic carpet

aircraft-carrier *n* → watercraft

AIRFLOW *n* advection, air-cushion, current, down draught, in-draught, jet stream, slipstream, thermal, up draught, wind; **turbulence,** air-pocket, airhole, backwash, backwind, bump, burble *(Aeron.)*, dirty wind, downwash, pocket, wash

airforce *n* → armed forces

air force *n* → aeroplane
AIRING *n* air-conditioning, flowthrough ventilation, ventilation
airline *n* → route
airlock *n* → 1 obstacle 2 room 3 wall
airman *n* → 1 combat troops 2 pilot
AIRPORT *n* aerodrome, hangar; **runway,** apron, landing strip, tarmac, threshold; **air traffic control,** control tower, ground control
air-raid *n* → 1 attack *v* 2 fire on 3 irritate
airship *n* → aircraft
airtight *adj* → closed
AIRWAY *n* air-drive, air-duct, air-intake, airshaft, louvre, vent, ventilator; **air-conditioner,** demister, exhaust fan, fan; **inflator,** aerator, bicycle pump, pump; **air-chamber,** air-jacket
AIRY *adj* elemental, elementary, ethereal; **pneumatic,** aerologic, aeromechanic, aeromechanical, aerometric, aerostatic; **aerobiotic,** aerobic; **aerial,** airborne, flying
airy *adj* → 1 apathetic 2 delusive 3 ethereal 4 happy 5 high 6 imprecise 7 insulting 8 light
aisle *n* → path
ajar *adj* → 1 dissonant 2 gaping 3 open *adv* 4 open
akin *adj* → 1 related 2 similar
alabaster *n* → 1 smooth object 2 white *adj* 3 smooth 4 white
alacrity *n* → 1 happiness 2 speed 3 sprightliness 4 willingness
ALARM *v* consternate, disquiet, distress, unhinge, unnerve, unsettle, unstring; **worry,** eat, exercise, trouble
alarm *n* → 1 fright 2 shout 3 signal 4 surprise 5 warning *v* 6 frighten 7 surprise 8 warn
ALAS *interj* alack *(Archaic),* deary-me, heigh-ho, lack a day *(Archaic),* misery me, oh dear, oh no, wellaway *(Archaic),* woe, woe is me
albeit *conj* → still
albino *n* → 1 white 2 woman *adj* 3 white
album *n* → 1 book 2 diary 3 mixture 4 recording
alchemy *n* → 1 change 2 magic 3 metallurgy
ALCOHOL *n* aqua vitae, ardent spirits, bombo, bootleg *(U.S.),* booze, brewage, cordial *(U.S.),* drink, ethanol, ethyl alcohol, firewater, grain alcohol, grave-digger *(Brit. Mil.),* grog, gutrot, hard stuff, home-brew, hooch *(U.S.),* ink, juice, La Perouse, Lady Blamey, liquor, lunatic soup, lush, plonk, pot, purge *(N.Z.),* rotgut, rum *(U.S.),* shicker, skinful, slosh *(Brit.),* snake juice, spirits of wine, stagger juice, swipes, the bottle, turps, waipiro *(N.Z.),* wallop; **intoxicant,** inebriant, stimulant; **sly grog,** hooch *(U.S.),* moonshine, mountain dew, Old Hokanni *(N.Z.),* poteen *(Irish);* **methylated spirits,** bush champagne, jungle juice, metho, musical milk, white angel, white lady. *See also* A DRINK; BEER; WINE
ALCOHOL CONTAINER *n* balthazar, eighteen, keg, nine, pig *(N.Z.),* pipe, wineskin; **beer glass,** bobby *(W.A.),* bumper, butcher *(S.A.),* cruiser, half, handle, jar, lady's waist, long-sleever, middy, pint, pixie *(Vic.),* pony, pot, pottle, schooner, tankard; **stubby,** baby, Darwin stubby, echo *(S.A.),* frostie, glass can; **wine measure,** jigger, noggin, tot; **can,** tinnie, tube
alcoholic *n* → 1 heavy drinker *adj* 2 drunk 3 intoxicating 4 preserved
alcoholism *n* → drunkenness
ALCOTEST *n* Alcolmeter, bag test, blue balloon, booze bus, breathalyser
alcove *n* → niche
alderman *n* → member of parliament
ale *n* → beer
alert *n* → 1 warning *v* 2 warn *adj* 3 attentive 4 light-footed 5 speedy
alfresco *adj* → 1 open-air 2 outside *adv* 3 in the fresh air 4 outside
alga *n* → plant
algebra *n* → mathematics
alias *n* → 1 disguise 2 lie 3 name
alibi *n* → 1 evidence 2 justification
alien *n* → 1 foreigner 2 outsider 3 population *adj* 4 dissident 5 foreign 6 resident
alienate *v* → 1 be unfriendly 2 isolate 3 provoke hatred
alight *v* → 1 arrive 2 dismount *adj* 3 fiery
align *v* → 1 associate 2 line 3 regularise 4 straighten 5 tidy
alike *adj* → 1 similar *adv* 2 equally 3 homogeneously
alimentary canal *n* → abdomen
alimony *n* → 1 charity 2 divorce
alive *adj* → 1 busy 2 energetic 3 living 4 operating
allay *v* → 1 alleviate 2 decrease 3 moderate
allege *v* → 1 accuse 2 assert 3 testify
allegiance *n* → 1 dutifulness 2 faithfulness
allegory *n* → 1 comparison 2 figure of speech 3 representation 4 sign 5 story
allegro *adv* → speedily
alleluia *interj* → 1 hooray 2 well done
Alleluia *n* → religious ceremony
ALLERGY *n* hay fever, hypersensitivity, idiosyncrasy, photoallergy, pollinosis
allergy *n* → hate
ALLEVIANT *adj* alleviative, assuasive, balmy, balsamaceous, balsamic, emollient, lenient *(Archaic),* lenitive, palliative, sooth, soothing; **analgesic,** anodyne, paregoric, sedative; **soothed,** comfortable, easeful, easy
ALLEVIATE *v* addulce *(Obs.),* allay, assuage, ease, lighten, mitigate, palliate, sweeten; **soothe,** attemper, comfort, give comfort to, hush, mollify, pat on the back, pour oil on troubled waters, salve, set at ease, solace; **relieve,** disburden, disembarrass, disencumber, free, reprieve, rescue, respite; **clear the air,** get off someone's back, lay off, smooth the ruffled brow of care, temper the wind to the shorn lamb
alleviate *v* → 1 decrease 2 ease
ALLEVIATOR *n* allayer, assuager, comforter, easer, mitigator, pacifier, palliator, reliever, solacer, soother; **salve,** alleviant, alleviative, balm, balsam, comfort, lenitive *(Rare),* palliative; **analgesic,** anodyne, paregoric, sedative

alley *n* → **1** gambling hall **2** marble **3** path **4** road *v* **5** depart

ALLIANCE *n* coalition, combine, confederacy, confederation, league, pie

alliance *n* → **1** class **2** marriage **3** relation **4** relationship **5** society

allied *adj* → **1** combined **2** cooperative **3** in agreement **4** societal

alliteration *n* → **1** figure of speech **2** rhyme **3** similarity **4** sound

allocate *v* → **1** position **2** share out

allot *v* → **1** separate **2** share out

allotment *n* → **1** garden **2** part **3** share **4** sharing out **5** yard

allow *v* → **1** give **2** have the right **3** make possible **4** permit **5** speak **6** subtract **7** think

ALLOWANCE *n* beer money, expenses, housekeeping, maintenance, pin money, pocket-money, spending money, tip, viaticum; **subsidy,** deficiency payment; **scholarship,** bursary, exhibition; **alms,** charity, collection, maundy *(Brit.)*, maundy money *(Brit.)*, offering; **expenditure,** disbursement. *See also* FUNDS

allowance *n* → **1** charity **2** compensation **3** income **4** more **5** part **6** share **7** supplies **8** surplus

alloy *v* → mix

all right *adj* → **1** approved **2** bribable **3** good **4** healthy **5** safe **6** satisfactory *adv* **7** certainly **8** satisfactorily *interj* **9** yes

ALLURE *n* amiability, animal magnetism, appeal, attraction, charisma, charm, cynosure, fascination, glam, glamour, it, magic, oomph, sex appeal, sunny disposition, winning ways, zest; **draw,** drawcard; **lure,** allurement, attraction, bait, captivation, come-on, counterattraction, enchantment, engagement, enticement, fascination, inducement, magnetism, spell; **seduction,** cajolery, honeyed words, inveiglement, invitation, solicitation, temptation; **entanglement,** ensnarement, entrapment; **trap,** birdlime, booby trap, butterfly net, drawnet, hook, lure, mesh, rat-trap, snare, springe, tin hare, toils, wire

ALLURE *v* attempt *(Archaic)*, attract, becharm, beguile, captivate, charm, court, enamour, enmesh, entice, fascinate, intrigue, inveigle, invite, magnetise *(Obs.)*, make *(Colloq.)*, mesmerise, seduce, smite, tantalise, titillate, toll *(Obs.)*, trepan *(Archaic)*, vamp, wheedle, witch; **lure,** bait, catch, ensnare, entrap, mesh, waylay

allure *v* → attract

ALLURER *n* attractor, bewitcher, captivator, charmer, desirable, dish, dreamboat, enchanter, engager, enthraller, enticer, fascinator, forbidden fruit, inviter, lady-killer, magnet, magnetiser, object of desire, object of lust, seducer, sex object, sex symbol, tempter; **siren,** a bit of fluff, Circe, Delilah, enchantress, femme fatale, mantrap, Mata Hari, nymphette, pin-up, seductress, temptress, twat, vamp, vamper, witch; **stud,** Don Juan, masher *(Archaic)*, rake, sheikh *(Archaic)*, sugar daddy, wolf; **gold-digger,** inveigler; **ensnarer,** entrapper, spider, trapper, waylayer

ALLURING *adj* amorous, appealing, appetising, attractive, bed-worthy, buxom, Circean, come-hither, cuddlesome, cuddly, delectable, desirable, enticing, flirtatious, glam, glamorous, intriguing, inviting, kinky, kissable, kittenish, lush, much in demand, oomphy, pin-up, piquant, provocative, racy, ravishing, seductive, sensual, sexy, siren, stimulating, tantalising, tempting, thrilling, voluptuous, well-endowed, well-hung, well-proportioned, well-rounded, winsome, zesty; **charismatic,** bewitching, captivating, catching, charming, enchanting, engaging, fascinating, fetching, impressive, interesting, irresistible, magic, magnetic, prepossessing, striking, taking, winning, witching

ALLUSION *n* hint, implication, innuendo, insinuation, intimation, rumour, suggestion, undercurrent, word; **connotation,** overtone, predication, sub-text, subaudition; **indication,** adumbration, prefigurement

allusion *n* → figure of speech

ALLUSIVE *adj* allusory, insinuative, oblique, suggestive; **implicational,** connotative, implicative, indicative, predicative; **implicit,** half-spoken, implied, tacit, undeclared, understood, unexpressed, unspoken, unvoiced, unwritten; **latent,** below the surface, doormat, potential, sleeping, underlying, undeveloped, unsuspected; **obscure,** arcane, esoteric, unexplored

ALLUSIVENESS *n* implicitness, obliqueness, obliquity, suggestiveness, tacitness; **latency,** more than meets the eye, potentiality

alluvial *n* → **1** diggings **2** mineral

alluvium *n* → **1** remnant **2** soil

ally *n* → **1** accomplice **2** cooperator **3** friend **4** helper *v* **5** associate **6** be friends **7** join **8** promise **9** relate

almanac *n* → list

almighty *adj* → **1** most **2** powerful *adv* **3** very

almond *n* → **1** oval *adj* **2** brown

almoner *n* → **1** giver **2** helper

ALMOST *adv* about, all but, approximately, chock, for all practical purposes, give or take, most *(U.S.)*, nearly, practically, proximately, pushing, rising, thereabouts, upon the point of, wellnigh. *See also* CLOSELY

alms *n* → **1** allowance **2** charity **3** gift

ALMSHOUSE *n* refuge, settlement, shelter, social settlement

aloft *adj* → **1** high *adv* **2** high

ALONE *adv* like a bandicoot on a burnt ridge, like a country dunny, like a lily on a dirt box, like a lily on a dustbin, like a petunia in an onion patch, like a shag on a rock, on one's ace, on one's own, on one's Pat, on one's Pat Malone, single-handedly, solitarily, solo, solus, with the flies

alone *adv* → **1** negligibly **2** solitarily

along *adv* → **1** forward **2** lengthways

alongside *adv* → sideways

aloof *adj* → 1 apathetic 2 distant 3 elusive 4 reticent 5 solitary 6 unsociable *adv* 7 remotely 8 solitarily
aloud *adv* → loudly
alp *n* → mountain
alpha *n* → start
alphabet *n* → 1 essence 2 letter
ALPHABETICAL *adj* abecedarian, alphabetic, alphanumeric
already *adv* → 1 in the past 2 now
also *adv* → additionally
altar *n* → shrine
alter *v* → 1 change 2 cut off
altercation *n* → 1 argument 2 fight
alter ego *n* → 1 disguise 2 friend 3 similar thing
ALTERNATE *v* interchange, intermit, reciprocate, recur, take turns, vary; **cycle,** circulate, revolve, roll round, rotate, run, turn
alternate *n* → 1 substitute *v* 2 exchange 3 interact *adj* 4 following 5 interactive 6 regular 7 two
alternative *n* → 1 choice *adj* 2 nonconformist 3 optional
although *conj* → still
altitude *n* → 1 erectness 2 height 3 importance 4 length 5 reputation
altogether *n* → 1 whole *adv* 2 wholly
altruism *n* → 1 help 2 kindness
always *adv* → 1 continually 2 eternally
amalgam *n* → combine
amalgamate *v* → 1 combine 2 mix
AMALGAMATION *n* consolidation, embodiment, federalisation, fusion, integration, merger, unification; **affiliation,** filiation, membership; **institutionalism,** officialism, regimentation
amanuensis *n* → 1 recorder 2 writer
amass *v* → 1 gather 2 quantify 3 store
amateur *n* → 1 approver 2 ignoramus 3 novice 4 sportsman 5 unimportant person *adj* 6 ignorant 7 sports
amatory *adj* → 1 flirtatious 2 loving
amaze *n* → 1 astonishment 2 surprise *v* 3 astonish 4 confuse 5 surprise
amazon *n* → 1 fighter 2 good person 3 woman
Amazon *n* → strong person
AMBASSADOR *n* ambassador extraordinary, ambassador plenipotentiary, ambassador-at-large *(U.S.)*, ambassadress, career diplomat, chargé d'affaires, diplomat, diplomatist, high commissioner, minister resident, resident *(Brit.)*; **attaché,** commissioner, consular agent, cultural attache, first secretary, minister, second secretary; **consul,** consul general, proconsul, representative, vice-consul; **papal nuncio,** ablegate, commissary, internuncio, legate, nuncio, vicar; **diplomatic corps,** corps diplomatique; **persona grata,** persona non grata. *See also* AGENT; DELEGATE
ambassador *n* → messenger
amber *n* → 1 orange 2 signal *adj* 3 brown 4 orange
ambidextrous *adj* → 1 competent 2 dishonest 3 equal
ambience *n* → 1 essence 2 surroundings
ambient *adj* → 1 moving 2 surrounding
ambiguous *adj* → 1 imprecise 2 meaningful 3 uncertain
ambit *n* → 1 edge 2 space
ambition *n* → 1 aim 2 desire 3 vitality *v* 4 desire
ambivalence *n* → 1 indecision 2 uncertainty
amble *n* → 1 walking *v* 2 advance 3 go slowly 4 walk
ambrosia *n* → food
ambush *n* → 1 attack 2 hiding place 3 stratagem *v* 4 attack 5 beguile 6 lie low 7 surprise
ameliorate *v* → improve
amen *n* → 1 affirmation 2 finish *v* 3 assent to *interj* 4 yes
amenable *adj* → 1 agreeable 2 influenced 3 obligated 4 obsequious 5 predisposed
AMENABLY *adv* plastically, pliably, pliantly, sensitively, susceptibly
amend *v* → 1 change 2 correct 3 improve
amends *n* → 1 compensation 2 recovery
amethyst *n* → purple
amiable *adj* → 1 friendly 2 kind 3 pleasant
amicable *adj* → 1 friendly 2 peaceful
AMID *prep* amidst, mid, midst
amid *prep* → between
amiss *adj* → incorrect
amity *n* → 1 agreement 2 friendliness
AMMUNITION *n* ammo, munitions; **bullet,** cannonball, cartouche, cartridge, dumdum, magazine, pellet, projectile, rubber bullet, slow bullet, slug, torpedo, tracer bullet; **gunpowder,** cordite, dynamite, explosive, gelignite, guncotton, high explosive, propellant, salt-petre, smokeless powder, T.N.T.; **shot,** canister, cannon shot, case shot, chain-shot, drop shot, dust-shot, grape, grapeshot, langrage, lead, load, round-shot, shrapnel; **percussion cap,** ball, cap, pineapple *(Colloq.)*; **shell,** gas shell, grenade, hand grenade, hangfire, incendiary, rifle grenade, sabot, whizbang; **detonator,** booster; **cannelure,** twist; **nuclear warhead,** nose-cone, war nose, warhead; **chemical weapon,** blister gas, diphosgene, fireball, gas, lewisite, liquid fire, mustard gas, napalm, nerve gas, phosgene, poison gas, stinkpot, vesicant, yellow rain. *See also* BOMB; ARSENAL
ammunition *n* → 1 evidence 2 supplies
amnesia *n* → 1 forgetting 2 psychic disorder
amnesty *n* → 1 acquittal 2 forgiving 3 peace *v* 4 forgive
among *prep* → between
amorous *adj* → 1 alluring 2 flirtatious 3 loving
amorphous *adj* → 1 imprecise 2 shapeless
amortise *v* → pay
AMOUNT *n* complement, matter, number, proportion, quantity, quantum, sum; **batch,** boiling, brewing, cast *(Metall.)*, churning, lot, make, making, measure, pour, shear, shower; **haul,** catch, draught, take; **load,** boatful, cartload *(Obs.)*, keel, lift, pack, pitch, shipload, shipment, wagonload; **supply,** flow, output, yield; **dose,** dosage, overdose; **bagful,** armful, barrelful, basinful,

boxful, dipperful, dishful, fistful, forkful, glassful, handful, hatful, kettleful, lapful, pipeful, plateful, pocketful, potful, sackful, shovelful, spadeful; **miscellaneous quantities,** butt, cordage, escort return, frail, haymow, job lot, pocket *(Tas.)*, reel. *See also* BIT

amour *n* → 1 flirtation 2 love affair 3 sexual relationship

AMPHIBIAN *adj* amphibiotic, amphibious, batrachian; **froglike,** anuran, toadlike

amphibian *n* → 1 aircraft 2 fauna 3 plant

amphitheatre *n* → 1 auditorium 2 hollow

ample *adj* → 1 abundant 2 big 3 enormous 4 great 5 many 6 thick

amplify *v* → 1 clarify 2 exaggerate 3 grow 4 increase 5 waffle

amplitude *n* → 1 acoustics 2 numerousness 3 size 4 thickness

amputate *v* → 1 cut off 2 medicate

AMULET *n* charm, Christopher medal, force-field, palladium, phylactery *(Archaic)*, scarab, scarabaeus, talisman

amulet *n* → magic spell

AMUSE *v* distract, divert, tickle

amuse *v* → 1 engross 2 joke 3 puzzle

AMUSED *adj* distracted, diverted, entertained; **sportive,** frisky, frolicsome, gamesome, larksome, playful, rompish, sportful

AMUSEMENT *n* disport *(Archaic)*, distraction, diversion, divertissement, entertainment, game, pastime, recreation, relaxation, sport; **toy,** plaything, puzzle; **romp,** buffoonery, buster *(U.S.)*, frolic, horseplay, jinks, lark, shine, spree; **sportiveness,** frolicsomeness, gamesomeness, rompishness, sportfulness; **fun and games,** beer and skittles, bobsydie, enjoyment, fun, play, pleasure; **revelry,** carnival, merrymaking, whoopee; **bush week,** capping day *(N.Z.)*, festivities, gaieties, gaudy *(Brit.)*, revels; **playtime,** break

amusement *n* → a good time

AMUSEMENT PARK *n* carnival, fair, fun park, funfair; **fairground amusements,** Aunt Sally *(Brit.)*, big dipper, carousel, coaster *(U.S.)*, coconut shy, Ferris wheel, helter-skelter, merry-go-round, river caves, roller-coaster, roundabout, scenic railway, sideshow, swing boat, switchback, whirlabout, whirligig; **play centre,** creative leisure centre, day centre; **fun parlour,** amusement arcade, casino, midway *(U.S.)*, penny arcade, poolroom; **playroom,** cubbyhouse, nursery, playhouse, rumpus room, Wendy house; **playground,** adventure playground, park, sandpit; **swing,** jungle gym, monkey bars, seesaw, slide, slippery dip

AMUSE ONESELF *v* disport oneself, have fun, play, recreate, sport; **trifle,** dabble, dally, toy, toy with; **romp,** fool around, frisk, frolic, gambol, horse about, play silly buggers, play up, skylark

AMUSING *adj* distractive, diversionary, diverting, divertive, entertaining, fun, light, recreational

anachronism *n* → untimeliness

anaemia *n* → 1 colourlessness 2 weakness

ANAESTHETIC *n* abirritant, anaesthesin, benzocaine, ether, etheriser, ethyl ether, eucaine, fluothane, general, general anaesthetic, halothane, knockout drop, local, local anaesthetic, novocaine, palfium, pethidine, phenacaine, phencyclidine, procaine, tribromoethanol, trichlorethylene; **analgesic,** anodyne, deadener, pain-killer; **laughing gas,** gas, nitrous oxide; **sedative,** chloral, hypnotic, laudanum, Mickey Finn, narcotic, opiate, sleeping-draught, sleeping-drug, sleeping-pill, stupefacient, stupefier, truth drug

ANAESTHETIC *adj* abirritant, analgesic, anodyne, deadening, knockout, sedative

ANAESTHETISE *v* chloroform, etherise, freeze, keep under; **narcotise,** dope, drug, hocus, opiate, stupefy; **knock out,** concuss, daze, flatten, K.O., kayo, king-hit, knock endwise *(N.Z.)*, knock endways, stun; **desensitise,** abirritate, benumb, blur, deaden, dull, numb

anagram *n* → puzzle

analgesic *n* → 1 alleviator 2 anaesthetic *adj* 3 alleviant 4 anaesthetic

analogous *adj* → 1 comparable 2 related

analogue *n* → similar thing

analogy *n* → 1 comparison 2 similarity

analyse *v* → 1 examine 2 inquire into

ANALYSIS *n* appraisal, assay, assessment, breakdown, criticism, critique, diagnosis, methodology; **analytical procedure,** classification, exhaustive study, graphing, ordering, random sampling, reductionism, sifting, sorting, systematisation, tabulating; **microanalysis,** destructive distillation, gas chromatography, gas-liquid chromatography, on-stream analysis, paper chromatography; **dissection,** anatomisation, anatomy, autopsy, biopsy, segmentation; **inquiry,** investigation, review, reviewal, scan, scrutiny, study; **analytics,** critical-path analysis, input-output analysis, marginalism, operations research, principal components analysis, systems analysis, variable rule analysis; **analytical display,** frequency distribution, graph, histogram, record, register, table

analysis *n* → 1 abridgment 2 investigation 3 listing 4 measurement 5 psychotherapy 6 separation

ANALYST *n* analyser, appraiser, assayer, assessor, deriver, dissector, nuts-and-bolts man, prosector, reductionist, scanner

ANARCHIC *adj* anarchistic, disobedient, insurgent, mutinous, nihilistic, seditionary, seditious; **lawless,** disorderly, headless, helmless, illegal, riotous, unattended, unchartered, unregulated; **unruly,** libertine, licentious, pandemoniac, pandemonic, turbulent; **irresponsible,** ruffian, runaway, tearaway, unbitted, unbridled; **arbitrary,** unilateral, unwarranted

ANARCHICALLY *adv* arbitrarily, high-handedly, irresponsibly, lawlessly, out of hand, out of order, seditiously, unwarrantedly, without book

ANARCHISE *v* destabilise, disobey, mutiny, rebel, ride roughshod over the law, run riot, take the law into one's own hands

ANARCHIST *n* destructionist, nihilist; **despiser of the law,** hell's angel, irresponsible, mad mullah, outlaw, revolutionary, ruffian, seditionary, urban guerilla

ANARCHY *n* blackboard jungle, civil disobedience, pandemonium, tumult, turbulence, turmoil; **lawlessness,** brute force, disorderliness, lynch law, misgovernment, misrule, unruliness, Wild West; **irresponsibility,** arbitrariness, irresponsibleness; **anarchism,** nihilism, ruffianism, seditiousness

anarchy *n* → **1** disorder **2** independence **3** liberty

anathema *n* → **1** heresy **2** heretic **3** punishment **4** swearing **5** unpleasant thing

anatomy *n* → **1** analysis **2** body **3** structure

ANCESTRY *n* descent, extraction; **generation,** birth, origin; **genealogy,** family tree, genealogical tree, stemma, tree; **herd-book,** studbook; **pedigree,** blood, heredity, heritance *(Archaic),* inheritance, line, lineage; **pure line,** straight line; **breed,** strain, type; **stock,** root, rootstock, stem, stirps; **branch,** moiety, offshoot, side; **matriline,** distaff side, matriarchy, spear side; **patriline,** patriarchy; **clan,** breed, family, gens, house, kith and kin, nation, race, stock, team *(Obs.),* tribe; **legitimacy; illegitimacy,** bastardy, unlawfulness; **polygenesis,** difference *(Her.).* *See also* GENETICS

ancestry *n* → aristocracy

ANCHOR *n* bower, dead man, dogstick, drag-anchor, kedge anchor, kellick, mudhook, pick *(Colloq.),* sheet anchor, sprag; **hook,** grapnel, grapple, grappler, grappling hook, grappling iron, tenterhook; **clevis,** hame, lunette, ottfur hook

anchor *n* → **1** fortress **2** holder *v* **3** fasten **4** inhabit **5** restrain **6** stop

anchorite *n* → **1** believer **2** solitary

ancient *n* → **1** old people *adj* **2** aged **3** highly regarded **4** old **5** past

ancillary *adj* → **1** additional **2** helpful

AND *conj* along with, as well as, eke *(Archaic),* in addition to, let alone, together with, with; **plus,** beside *(Rare),* besides, not to mention, over and above

and *conj* → on condition that

ane *n* → **1** one *adj* **2** one *pron* **3** one

anecdote *n* → story

anew *adv* → **1** firstly **2** repeatedly

ANGEL *n* archangel, cherub, cherubim, guardian angel, ministering spirit, morning star, pure spirit, seraph, seraphim; **celestial hierarchy,** celestial beings, choir, dominations, dominions, hierarchy, order, powers, princedoms, principalities, thrones, virtues; **angelhood,** divinity

angel *n* → **1** beautiful person **2** financier **3** giver **4** good person **5** helper

ANGER *n* blood and thunder, choler, dudgeon, fury, ill temper, indignation, infuriation, ire, pique, rage, resentment, temper, the Jimmy Brits, the shits, vexation, wrath; **angriness,** crankiness, furiousness, furore, hastiness, incensement, irefulness, lividity, lividness, passion, resentfulness, savageness, savagery, vehemence, wrathfulness; **irascibility,** irascibleness, passionateness, prickliness, shrewishness

ANGER *v* enrage, huff, incense, inflame, infuriate, pique, put someone's back up, rouse, vex; **irritate,** get on someone's goat, give someone the Jimmy Brits, give someone the shits, provoke, shit

anger *n* → **1** displeasure **2** painfulness *v* **3** pain

angle *n* → **1** fishing tackle **2** niche **3** translation **4** trick *v* **5** fish **6** swerve

angora *n* → animal's coat

Angora *n* → cat

ANGRILY *adv* apoplectically, furiously, in a fury, in a huff, in a rage, in high dudgeon, indignantly, infuriately *(Archaic),* irately, irefully, lividly, rampantly, red-facedly, shrewishly, with one's hackles up, wrathfully; **crankily,** hastily, irascibly; **acrimoniously,** rancorously, virulently; **gloweringly,** loweringly, tough; **resentfully,** huffily, sulkily, sullenly, umbrageously; **fiercely,** passionately, savagely, vehemently, warmly; **infuriatingly,** provocatively, provokingly; **invidiously,** odiously

ANGRY *adj* ablaze, blazing, cheesed-off, cross as a cat, cross as a dog, cross as crabs, cross as two sticks, dirty, fit to be tied, full up *(N.Z. Colloq.),* furious, hairy, hopping, hopping mad, hot under the collar, indignant, infuriate *(Archaic),* infuriated, irate, ireful, like a bear with a sore head, livid, mad, mad as a hornet, mad as a maggot, mad as a meataxe, mad with rage, on the warpath, rampant, ranting, red-faced, red-hot, ropeable, shitty-livered, snaky, steamed-up, up in arms, uptight, vexed, wally *(Brit.),* wood *(Obs.),* wrath *(Archaic),* wrathful, wroth, wrought; **fed up,** brassed off, fed up to the back teeth, fed up to the gills, huffy, pissed-off, sick, sick to death; **mean,** apoplectic, black-browed, choleric, cranky, cursed, easily aroused, evil, hasty, irascible, ornery, prickly, quick-tempered, savage, umbrageous *(Rare)*; **glaring,** lowering, wild-eyed

angry *adj* → **1** displeased **2** hot **3** reddish **4** unwholesome

ANGRY ACT *n* flaw *(Obs.),* huff, paddy, paddywhack, pelter, rage, ramp, rampage, tantrum, tear, wax, wobbly *(N.Z.)*; **fireworks,** act, blow-up, explosion, flare, flare-up; **dirty look,** glare, glower, lour; **sulk,** sulks; **diatribe,** rant, yap

ANGRY PERSON *n* angry young man, hellcat, maenad, ranter, shrew, spitfire, thunderbolt, wildcat

anguish *n* → **1** pain **2** unhappiness *v* **3** feel pain **4** grieve **5** pain

angular *adj* → **1** badly-done **2** bent **3** thin

ANIMAL *n* beast, brute, creature, zooid

animal *n* → **1** unkind person *adj* **2** bodily

ANIMAL CALL *n* cry; **talk,** language, utterance; **roar,** bell, bellow, roaring, trumpet; **howl,** caterwaul, hoot, screech, ululation; **growl,** grunt, snarl; **drone,** buzz, hum, whine; **bark,** bay, bow-wow, woof, yap, yip *(U.S.)*; **mew,** miaow, purr; **bray,** heehaw; **bleat,** baa; **whinny,** neigh; **moo,** low; **whimper,** whine. *See also* BIRDCALL

ANIMAL DWELLING *n* doghouse, kennel; **cattery; cowshed,** byre, cowhouse, crib, stall; **stable,** livery stable, loosebox, mews, riding stables, stabling; **pigsty,** piggery, pigpen, sty; **coop,** cage, hutch, terrarium; **beehive,** apiary, hive, vespiary; **dovecot,** henhouse, pigeonhole; **nest,** aerie, aviary, eyrie, hatchery, heronry, nide, nidus, perch, rookery; **ant bed,** ant hill, termitarium; **lair,** den, form, foxhole, home, lodge; **warren,** burrow, crabhole, earth, hole, rabbit-warren, sett, tunnel

ANIMAL-LIKE *adj* beastlike, bestial, brutal, brute, brutish, faunal, zooid, zoological, zoomorphic; **subhuman,** theriomorphic, theroid; **animalcular,** rotiferal; **wild,** ferae naturae *(Law)*, feral, untamed; **mammalian,** mammiferous; **bovine,** canine *(dogs)*, cervine *(deer)*, equine *(horses)*, erinaceous *(hedgehogs)*, feline *(cats)*, hircine *(goats)*, leonine *(lions)*, lupine *(wolves)*, ovine *(sheep)*, phocine *(seals)*, sciurine *(squirrels)*, simian *(apes and monkeys)*, taurine *(bulls)*, ursine *(bears)*, vaccine *(cows)*, vituline *(calves)*

ANIMAL OFFSPRING *n* cub, juvenile, pup, puppy, whelp, wolf cub; **kitten,** kitty, ligon, tigon; **colt,** fawn, filly, foal, yearling; **calf,** bobby calf, heifer, maverick, poddy, slink, staggering bob, weaner, weanling; **lamb,** kid, lambkin, yeanling; **piglet,** piggie, pigling, shoat, sucker, sucking-pig; **joey; chicken,** chick, cygnet, duckling, eaglet, fledgling, gosling, green duck, juvenal, juvenile, nestling, owlet, poult; **tiddler,** alevin, cercaria, codling, fingerling, fry, poddy mullet; **larva,** caseworm, maggot, miracidium, planula, polliwog, tadpole; **pupa,** chrysalid, chrysalis, nymph; **spiderling,** money spider; **dragonet; litter,** drop, farrow, team; **brood,** clutch, hatch, nide; **spawn,** culch, spat

ANIMAL'S COAT *n* coat, fleece, jacket, pelage; **fur,** badger, beaver, blue fox, broadtail, caracul, chinchilla, cony, deerskin, ermine, fisher, fitch, galyak, hamster, kolinsky, lapin, miniver, mink, monkey, muskrat, nutria, pointed fox, puma, sable, seal, skunk, squirrel, vair, wolf, zibeline; **wool,** alpaca, angora, astrakhan, camelhair, cashmere, horsehair, mohair, mother hair, Persian lamb; **crest,** coma, foretop; **bellies,** belly-wool, underfur; **dag,** abb, dagging, daglock, dagwool, tag; **tuft,** fetlock, floccus, flock, switch; **mane,** collar, frill, hackle, torques; **eyeclip,** eyewool, moustache

animate *v* → **1** activate **2** encourage **3** energise **4** enliven **5** move *adj* **6** living

animosity *n* → **1** dislike **2** hate **3** ill will **4** unfriendliness

ankle *n* → leg

annals *n* → **1** magazine **2** narrative **3** record

anneal *v* → **1** heat **2** strengthen

annex *n* → **1** postscript *v* **2** add **3** gain **4** join **5** rob **6** take

annexe *n* → **1** addition **2** building

ANNIHILATE *v* abrogate, annul, disannul, exterminate, extirpate, nullify, wipe out; **expunge,** blank, blot out, void *(Archaic)*, wipe off the map

annihilate *v* → **1** defeat **2** deny **3** destroy **4** massacre

ANNIVERSARY *n* bicentenary, bicentennial *(U.S.)*, biennial, birthday, centenary, decennial, ides, jubilee, millennium, quatercentenary, quincentenary, quindecennial, quinquennial, quotidian *(Archaic)*, sabbatical year *(Rabbinical Law)*, sesquicentenary, tercentenary, tricentennial, triennial

annotate *v* → **1** clarify **2** explain

announce *v* → publicise

ANNOY *v* aggravate, chafe, get across, get in someone's hair, get on one's goat, get on one's nerves, get on one's wick, get to someone, get under one's skin, give someone the pip, give someone the shits, importune *(Obs.)*, irk, nettle, pip, put out, raise a bite, rankle, rub up the wrong way, ruffle; **exasperate,** acerbate, chevy, chivvy, drive someone up the wall, exacerbate, fray, gall, infuriate, madden, piss someone off, rile, roil, sting; **irritate,** antagonise, bug, fret, nark, niggle, offend, play cat and mouse, provoke, try the patience of; **harass,** badger, bait, bedevil, bullyrag, devil, get on someone's back, get on someone's hammer, gig, haggle *(Archaic)*, harry, hassle, haze, keep at, nag, needle, persecute, pester, pick on, plague, rag, rib, stir, tease, torment; **trouble,** bother, fuss, worry

annoy *n* → **1** annoyance *v* **2** damage **3** discontent

ANNOYANCE *n* chafe, exacerbation, exasperation, fret, infuriation, irritation, peeve, trouble, vexation; **annoyingness,** importunacy, importunateness, irksomeness, offensiveness, troublesomeness; **harassment,** bedevilment, persecution, pinpricking, tease; **irritant,** aggravation, annoy *(Archaic)*, pinprick, torment, vexation; **nuisance,** bind, bore, bother, face-ache, menace, pain, pain in the arse, pain in the neck, pest, plague, terror, thorn, thorn in one's flesh, thorn in one's side, trial

ANNOYED *adj* aggravated, bushwhacked, irritated, vexed; **exasperated,** browned off, fed up, fed up to the back teeth, fed up to the gills; **harassed,** hassled, hot and bothered, tormented

ANNOYER *n* aggravator, exasperator, stirrer; **harasser,** baiter, nagger, niggler, persecutor, plaguer, tease, teaser, tormentor, troubler;

trouble, difficulty, problem, the dizzy limit, the last straw, the limit, worry

ANNOYING *adj* abrasive, aggravating, irritating, offensive, plaguy *(Archaic)*, tiresome, trying, vexatious; **troublesome,** bothersome, important *(Obs.)*, importunate, importune, irksome, narky, niggling, pesky *(U.S.)*, pestiferous, pestilent, thorny, troublous *(Archaic)*, worrisome; **exasperating,** galling, infuriating, insupportable, maddening, mother-fucking *(U.S.)*, wicked

annual *n* → **1** cleansing **2** magazine **3** plant

annuity *n* → **1** income **2** insurance

annul *v* → **1** annihilate **2** cancel **3** deny

annunciate *v* → publicise

annunciation *n* → public notice

anodyne *n* → **1** alleviator **2** anaesthetic *adj* **3** alleviant **4** anaesthetic

anoint *v* → **1** coat **2** oil

ANOMALY *n* anomalism *(Obs.)*, discrepancy, irreconcilable, variance; **misfit,** mismatch, mockery, ring-in, square peg in a round hole

anomaly *n* → strangeness

anonymous *adj* → **1** hidden **2** impersonal **3** unknown

another *n* → **1** more **2** similar thing **3** something different *adj* **4** additional

ANSWER *n* acknowledgment, countersign, echo, password, rejoinder, repartee, replication, reply, report, rescript, respondence, response, return; **reaction,** bite, comeback, contradiction, counter charge, counterclaim, defence, retort, riposte; **conditioned response,** conditioned reflex; **responsive singing,** antiphon, antiphony, gradual *(Eccles.)*. *See also* SOLUTION

ANSWER *v* acknowledge, rejoin, reply, respond, return; **retort,** bite back, confute, contradict, counter charge, counterclaim, rebut, repartee *(Obs.)*, riposte; **reduce to silence,** cut the ground from under someone's feet, not leave someone a leg to stand on, silence

answer *n* → **1** reaction *v* **2** be adequate **3** be expedient **4** fit **5** react

answerable *adj* → **1** answering **2** obligated

ANSWERER *n* rebutter, replier, respondent

antagonise *v* → **1** annoy **2** argue **3** counteract

antagonism *n* → **1** dissidence **2** unfriendliness

Antarctic *adj* → cold

ANTECEDENCE *n* anteriority, coming before, lead, precedence, precession, prevenance, priority, right of way; **head start,** advantage, handicap, law *(Sport)*, start

ANTECEDENT *n* archetype, exemplar, model, original, protoplast, prototype; **prefix,** forepart; **leader,** promo, run-in groove, trailer *(Film)*. *See also* FORERUNNER

antedate *v* → **1** be early **2** mistime **3** precede

antediluvian *n* → **1** old people *adj* **2** old **3** past

antenna *n* → **1** aerial **2** feeler

anterior *adj* → **1** bodily **2** front **3** preceding

anteroom *n* → hall

anthem *n* → **1** scripture **2** song *v* **3** sing

anthology *n* → **1** book **2** poetry

anthracite *n* → fuel

anthropoid *adj* → human

ANTHROPOLOGY *n* anthropogenesis, anthropogeography, anthropography, anthropometry, ethnogeny, ethnography, ethnology, palae-ethnology, somatology; **social studies,** demography, social anthropology, social science

antic *n* → **1** act **2** distortion **3** entertainment **4** joke **5** portrait **6** pose *v* **7** joke **8** tomfool *adj* **9** strange

ANTICIPATE *v* look ahead, pre-empt, preconceive, see how the cat will jump, see how the land lies, sniff the morning air; **prepare,** lay in stocks, make allowance for, prepare for; **foresee,** feel in one's bones, forefeel, foreknow, foretaste, prefigure, see one's way ahead; **foreshadow,** adumbrate; **forewarn,** bode *(Archaic)*, forebode, predict, presage, previse

anticipate *v* → **1** expect **2** hope **3** precede **4** prepare

ANTICIPATION *n* aforethought, calculation, forecast, forefeel, foretaste, forethought, hunch, longsightedness, premeditation; **prudence,** forward planning, looking ahead, precaution, preparation, providence *(Rare)*; **foresight,** clairvoyance, divination, ESP, foreknowledge, precognition, prediction, prescience, prevision, second sight; **foreboding,** adumbration, bodement, boding, forewarning, forshadowing, premonition, presage, presentiment

ANTICIPATIVELY *adv* adumbratively, against the time when, anticipatorily, designingly, far-sightedly, foreknowingly, presciently, providently, prudently

ANTICIPATORY *adj* aforethought, precautionary, premeditated; **anticipative,** adumbrative, anticipant of, precognitive; **prudent,** designing, pre-emptory, precautious, prepared, provident, thrifty; **foresighted,** clairvoyant, far-seeing, far-sighted, long-sighted, longheaded, onlooking, prescient, psychic

anticlimax *n* → **1** disenchantment **2** finish

anticlockwise *adj* → spinning

antidote *n* → **1** counterbalance **2** medication

antinomy *n* → incongruity

antipasto *n* → meal

antipathy *n* → **1** dislike **2** repulsion **3** unfriendliness

antipodes *n* → **1** opposite meaning **2** remote place

antiquary *n* → historian

antiquated *adj* → **1** antique **2** disused **3** old

ANTIQUE *adj* antiquarian, classic, obsolete, old-world, olde-worlde, period, veteran, vintage; **outdated,** antiquated, archaic, backward, behind the times, dated, old hat, old-fashioned, old-line *(U.S.)*, out-of-date, outworn, passé; **expired,** elapsed, extinct, lapsed, run out

antique *n* → **1** work of art *adj* **2** old

antiquity *n* → **1** oldness **2** past

antiseptic *n* → **1** cleanser *adj* **2** clean

antisocial *adj* → **1** solitary **2** unsociable

antithesis *n* → 1 contrast 2 difference 3 figure of speech 4 opposite meaning 5 opposite position
antivenene *n* → medication
antler *n* → piercer
antonym *n* → 1 contrast 2 opposite meaning
anus *n* → buttocks
anvil *n* → 1 ear 2 stand
anxiety *n* → 1 enthusiasm 2 fright 3 worry
anxious *adj* → 1 enthusiastic 2 frightened 3 worried
ANY *n* anybody, anyone, anything, what have you, what not, whoever; **everybody,** everyman, everyone, everything; **all and sundry,** every man jack, every Tom Dick and Harry, one and all; **thingummyjig,** sundries, thing, whatnot
any *adj* → 1 general 2 one *pron* 3 one
anybody *n* → any
anyhow *adv* → nevertheless
anyone *n* → any
anything *n* → 1 any 2 matter
anyway *adv* → nevertheless
any way *adv* → how
apart *adj* → 1 excluded 2 separate *adv* 3 particularly
apartheid *n* → 1 exclusion 2 intolerance
apartment *n* → room
APATHETIC *adj* ambitionless, bloodless, dead-and-alive, depressed, depressive, lackadaisical, mopey, mopish, passive, perfunctory, phlegmatic, purposeless, spiritless, unaspiring, viewless; **torpid,** benumbed, comatose, dreamy, dull, inert, languid, lethargic, listless, moony, numb, sluggish, supine; **uninterested,** aloof, disinterested, distanced, impassive, insensible, insusceptible, switched-off, turned off, unaffected, unmoved, unresponsive, unruffled, unsympathetic, untouched, withdrawn; **uncommitted,** apolitical, uninvolved; **indifferent,** detached, easy, half-hearted, half-pie, incurious, irresponsive, lukewarm, uncaring; **nonchalant,** airy, careless, casual, cavalier, easygoing, insouciant, off-hand, pococurante, throwaway, unconcerned
APATHETIC PERSON *n* indifferentist, mope, moper, no-hoper, Norm, pococurante, yawner, zombie; **non-chaser**
APATHY *n* accidie, acedia, depression, mopishness, phlegm *(Obs.)*, purposelessness, spiritlessness; **torpor,** inertia, languidness, lethargy, listlessness, numbness, stupor, torpidity; **indifference,** aloofness, bloodlessness, detachment, disinterest, half-heartedness, impassiveness, impassivity, incuriosity, incuriousness, indifferentism, lack of involvement, lukewarmness, perfunctoriness, unconcern, unconcernedness, uninterestedness; **nonchalance,** carelessness, casualness, easiness, insouciance, jemenfoutisme, pococurantism
apathy *n* → neutrality
ape *n* → 1 imitator *v* 2 imitate
aperitif *n* → a drink
aperture *n* → 1 entrance 2 opening
APEX *n* apogee, apolune, ceiling, critical altitude, upper, vertex, zenith; **summit,** brow, cop *(Obs.)*, crest, crown, head, top; **edge,** brink, verge; **high-water mark,** benchmark *(Survey)*, bush-line, floodmark, timber line, water-level, waterline, watermark. *See also* HEIGHT; MOUNTAIN; TOWER
apex *n* → top
aphasia *n* → psychic disorder
aphorism *n* → proverb
aphrodisiac *n* → 1 sex aid 2 tryst *adj* 3 sexy
apiary *n* → animal dwelling
apiculture *n* → farming
apiece *adv* → 1 each 2 particularly
aplomb *n* → 1 certainty 2 erectness
apocalypse *n* → revealing
apocryphal *adj* → 1 fake 2 false 3 fantastic 4 uncertain
apogee *n* → 1 apex 2 astronomic point 3 top
apologise *v* → 1 atone for 2 be penitent
apology *n* → 1 compensation 2 justification 3 penitence
apostasy *n* → 1 defection 2 unfaithfulness
apostle *n* → 1 enlightener 2 forerunner 3 starter
apostrophe *n* → 1 figure of speech 2 waffle
apothecary *n* → healer
apotheosis *n* → 1 perfect thing 2 worship
appal *v* → 1 displease 2 frighten 3 surprise
apparatus *n* → 1 equipment 2 machine 3 management
apparel *n* → 1 appearance 2 clothes *v* 3 clothe 4 decorate
APPARENT *adj* external, manifest, ostensible, outward, seeming, semblable *(Archaic)*, specious, superficial, surface
apparent *adj* → 1 blatant 2 clear 3 likely 4 obvious 5 visible
APPARENTLY *adv* at first sight, at the first blush, from the look of the thing, manifestly, on the face of it, ostensibly, prima facie, seemingly, superficially, to all appearances, to the eye
apparition *n* → 1 appearance 2 phantom 3 soul
appeal *n* → 1 accusation 2 allure 3 charity 4 entreaty 5 trial *v* 6 lay charges
APPEAR *v* arise, bob up, come, come into view, come to light, come up, crop up, drop in, emerge, figure, front up, gleam, heave in sight, loom, materialise, peep, peer, present, report, rise, shoot *(Bot.)*, show, show a leg, show one's face, show the flag *(Colloq.)*, show through, show up, spring *(Archaic)*, surface, turn up, unroll, uprise *(Archaic)*; **seem,** appear, look, look like, sound
appear *v* → appear
APPEARANCE *n* air, apparel *(Archaic)*, aspect, bearing, cast, clip, colour, complexion, cut of someone's jib, facies *(Ecol.)*, figure, garment, image, light, look, looks, mien, outward, presence; **face,** cheer *(Archaic)*, contour, countenance, facade, features, lineament, physiognomy, profile, visage; **phenomenon,** mode *(Philos.)*, phase; **apparition,**

emergence, emersion, fade-in, forthcoming, loom, manifestation, materialisation

appearance *n* → 1 condition 2 exit 3 phantom 4 presence

APPEARANCES *n* apparentness, colouring, externals, face value, gloss, guise, pretence, seeming, semblance, show, superficiality, superficialness, superficies, surface, surface structure

appease *v* → 1 capitulate 2 make peace 3 mediate 4 moderate 5 satisfy

appellant *n* → 1 asker 2 litigant

appellation *n* → name

append *v* → 1 add 2 hang 3 join

appendix *n* → 1 abdomen 2 book part 3 clarification 4 commentary 5 postscript

appetiser *n* → incentive

appetising *adj* → 1 alluring 2 attractive 3 desirable 4 encouraging

appetite *n* → desire

applaud *v* → approve

APPLAUSE *n* acclaim, bouquet, cheer, clap, curtain call, eclat, hand, handclap, ovation, plaudit, round of applause, salvo, three cheers; **tribute,** compliment, encomium, eulogium, eulogy, hymn, laud, paean, panegyric, toast; **admiring look,** eye-service. *See also* APPROVAL

appliance *n* → 1 machine 2 use

applicable *adj* → 1 apt 2 expedient 3 related

applicant *n* → asker

application *n* → 1 aptness 2 attentiveness 3 entreaty 4 meaning 5 medication 6 operation 7 persistence 8 placement 9 use

applied *adj* → operating

appliqué *n* → 1 lace 2 sewing *v* 3 sew

apply *v* → 1 attempt 2 contact 3 fit 4 join 5 operate 6 place 7 use

appoint *v* → 1 command 2 depute 3 determine 4 elect 5 employ 6 equip

apportion *v* → 1 disperse 2 share out

apposite *adj* → 1 apt 2 related 3 topical

apposition *n* → 1 closeness 2 relation

APPRAISE *v* assess, capitalise, esteem, price, prize, quote, rate, revalue, tag, value; **offer,** bid

appraise *v* → 1 assess 2 examine 3 inquire into

appreciable *adj* → 1 great 2 obvious

appreciate *v* → 1 approve 2 assess 3 become greater 4 be grateful 5 enjoy 6 know 7 perceive

apprehend *v* → 1 arrest 2 capture 3 expect 4 know

apprehensive *adj* → 1 expectant 2 frightened 3 intelligent 4 mental 5 worried

apprentice *n* → 1 learner *v* 2 teach

apprise *v* → inform

approach *n* → 1 access 2 closeness 3 method 4 offer 5 similarity *v* 6 advance 7 be similar 8 come close 9 impend 10 offer

approbation *n* → 1 approval 2 authentication 3 permission 4 tribute

appropriate *v* → 1 rob 2 take *adj* 3 apt 4 conventional 5 expedient 6 particular

APPROVAL *n* a good press, admiration, appreciation, appreciativeness, approbation, endorsement, esteem, opinion, sympathy; **recommendation,** a good word, advocacy, commendation, endorsement, espousal, rave, support, testimonial, wrap-up *(Colloq.)*; **praise,** acclamation, celebration, emblazonment, exaltation, extolment, glory, laudation; **sanction,** acceptance, acceptation, countenance, recognition; **personality cult.** *See also* APPLAUSE

approval *n* → 1 affirmation 2 permission

APPROVE *v* accept, advocate, approbate, bless, countenance, endorse, hand it to, hold a brief for, hold with, recognise, sanction, set one's seal on, sympathise; **acclaim,** bigmouth, carol, celebrate, cry up, emblazon, eulogise, exalt, extol, hail, hymn, laud, magnify *(Archaic)*, panegyrise, plug, polish, praise, rap up; **compliment,** commend, recommend, sing someone's praises, sing the praises of, speak well of; **admire,** appreciate, favour, prize, smile on, take to, think the world of, value; **give full marks,** give points, give someone a good mark, pass, throw a bouquet; **applaud,** clap, huzza *(Archaic)*; **cheer,** barrack for, root for *(U.S.)*; **toast,** bumper, raise one's glass

approve *v* → 1 assent to 2 authenticate 3 display 4 increase 5 test

APPROVED *adj* commended, recommended; **praiseworthy,** admirable, approvable, commendable, exemplary, laudable, prepossessing; **acceptable,** all right, cleared, okay, passed, uncensored; **favourite,** darling, favoured, in favour, in high favour, in someone's good books, popular

APPROVER *n* acclaimer, admirer, amateur *(Obs.)*, applauder, appreciator, caroller, fan, favourer, follower, groupie, supporter, sympathiser; **praiser,** encomiast, eulogiser, eulogist, exalter, lauder, panegyrist, tributary, tributer; **barracker,** cheerer, claque *(Theat.)*, rooter; **recommender,** advocate, advocator, countenancer, extoller, promoter; **following,** fan club

APPROVING *adj* applauding, applausive, approbative, approbatory, commendatory, favourably disposed, lost in admiration, plausive *(Rare)*, recommendatory, shook on; **praising,** acclamatory, complimentary, encomiastic, eulogistic, laudatory, panegyrical, rapt, rave, tributary; **favourable,** acceptant, appreciative, appreciatory, recognitive, recognitory, susceptive, sympathetic, tolerant, uncritical

approximate *v* → 1 be similar 2 come close *adj* 3 close 4 imprecise 5 similar

appurtenance *n* → 1 addition 2 right of way

apricot *n* → 1 orange *adj* 2 orange 3 red

a priori *adj* → true

apron *n* → 1 airport 2 conveyor 3 edge 4 overcoat 5 platform 6 soil 7 stage

apropos *adj* → 1 apt 2 related *adv* 3 aptly

apse *n* → 1 church 2 niche

APT *adj* applicable, apposite, appropriate, fit, german *(Obs.)*, germane, in point, pertinent, relevant, to the point; **up one's street,** congenial, to one's taste, unobjectionable; **fitting,** apropos, becoming, befitting, condign, due, felicitous, just the job, meet *(Archaic)*, perfect, proper, ready-made, right, suitable, toward *(Obs.)*, towardly *(Archaic)*; **compatible,** assorted, coherent, consistent, en rapport, self-consistent, typical

apt *adj* → **1** agreeable **2** intelligent

aptitude *n* → **1** aptness **2** competence **3** intelligence **4** point of view

APTLY *adv* applicably, appositely, appropriately, apropos, felicitously, pertinently, relevantly; **fittingly,** becomingly, befittingly, coherently, condignly, congruously, duly, in order, meetly *(Archaic)*, properly, right, rightly, suitably; **in accordance,** in chime, in compliance, in concert, in keeping, in phase, in register, in step, in tram *(Mech.)*; **adjustably,** reconcilably; **thereunder,** according to, pursuant, pursuantly

APTNESS *n* applicability, applicableness, application, appositeness, appropriateness, aptitude, becomingness, competency *(Law)*, consonance, eligibility, felicitousness, fitness, fittingness, happiness, pertinence, pertinency, relevance, relevancy, suitability; **propriety,** decorum, rightness, suitableness, towardliness, towardness; **horses for courses; compatibility,** compatibleness, reconcilability, reconcilableness, togetherness

aqualung *n* → breathing

aquamarine *n* → **1** blue **2** green

aquaplane *v* → move

aquatic *adj* → sea

aqueduct *n* → **1** bridge **2** channel

aqueous *adj* → **1** liquid **2** rocky

aquiline *adj* → birdlike

arabesque *n* → **1** decoration **2** musical piece

arable *n* → **1** fertile land *adj* **2** fertile

arbiter *n* → **1** judge **2** mediator

arbitrary *adj* → **1** anarchic **2** capricious **3** conservative **4** forceful **5** illogical **6** liberated **7** lucky

arbitrate *v* → **1** assess **2** choose **3** determine **4** mediate

arbitration *n* → **1** judgment **2** mediation

ARBOREAL *adj* arborescent, arborous, silvan, sylvan; **beechen,** cedarn, citrus, olive, palmy, piny, willowy, withy; **arboricultural,** floricultural

arboreal *adj* → resident

arbour *n* → **1** garden **2** shelter

arc *n* → **1** astronomic point **2** curve **3** electricity **4** light *v* **5** electrify

arcade *n* → **1** arch **2** path **3** shop

ARCANE *adj* cabalistic, covert, esoteric, mystic, occult, recondite

arcane *adj* → **1** allusive **2** hidden **3** unclear

ARCANUM *n* esotericism, esotery, invisibility, mystery, mystique, occult

ARCH *n* arching, archlet, archway, extrados, flying buttress, haunch, intrados, ogive, Roman arch, skew arch, squinch; **dome,** arcade, barrel vault, calotte, cloche, cupola, fornix, geodesic dome, hemicycle, hemisphere, hemispheroid, radome, semidome, tholus, vault, vaulting; **beading,** bead, echinus, ovolo, quad, quadrant moulding; **foil,** foliation

archaic *adj* → **1** antique **2** disused **3** old **4** untimely

archangel *n* → angel

Archangel *n* → cat

archbishop *n* → **1** ecclesiastic **2** ruler

archer *n* → soldier

archetype *n* → **1** antecedent **2** model

archipelago *n* → island

architect *n* → **1** builder **2** creator **3** planner

architecture *n* → **1** construction **2** structure

architrave *n* → frame

archives *n* → record

Arctic *adj* → cold

ardent *adj* → **1** desirous **2** emotional **3** enthusiastic **4** glowing **5** hot **6** rash

ardour *n* → **1** desire **2** emotion **3** enthusiasm **4** heat **5** vitality

arduous *adj* → **1** difficult **2** effortful

are *n* → area

AREA *n* circumference, circumscription, compass, extent, spread; **hectare,** acre, are, hide *(Old Eng. Law)*, pole, square; **square measure,** acreage, floor space, floorage. *See also* SPACE

area *n* → **1** course **2** region **3** space **4** subject matter

arena *n* → **1** place of killing **2** sportsground

argent *n* → **1** cash **2** grey **3** white *adj* **4** grey **5** metallic **6** white

argot *n* → **1** language **2** secrecy

arguable *adj* → **1** contentious **2** uncertain

ARGUE *v* altercate, argy-bargy, contend, dispute, have it out, quarrel, row, strive, war; **conflict,** clash, collide; **confront,** antagonise *(U.S.)*, assail, encounter, face, front, frustrate, get on the wrong side of, lead someone a chase, lead someone a dance, meet, oppugn, pit oneself against, subvert, thwart, turn against

argue *v* → **1** assert **2** disagree **3** display **4** persuade **5** reason **6** talk **7** testify **8** theorise

ARGUMENT *n* altercation, argy-bargy, assailment, catfight, clash, collision, combat, confrontation, confrontment, disagreement, dispute, encounter, hassle, imbroglio, miff, quarrel, row, ruckus *(U.S.)*, ruction, run-in, set on, showdown, tangle, vendetta, war, yike; **rebuttal,** con, counterargument, crossing

argument *n* → **1** abridgment **2** disagreement **3** discussion **4** evidence **5** narrative **6** persuasion **7** reasoning

ARGUMENTATIVE *adj* belligerent, contradictious, contradictive, contradictory, contrary, contrasuggestible, contrasuggestive, disputant, disputatious, disputative; **dissenting,** anti, dissentient, dissident, divergent, remonstrant. *See also* CONTENTIOUS

argumentative *adj* → dissident

aria *n* → song

arid *adj* → 1 boring 2 dry 3 infertile

arise *v* → 1 appear 2 ascend 3 erect 4 occur 5 start

ARISTOCRACY *n* ancien régime, daimio, elite, ermine, high society, nobility, patriciate, peerage, purple, ruling class, the haves, top drawer, upper class, upper crust; **gentry,** county, gentlefolk, squattocracy, squirearchy, squiredom; **noble birth,** blue blood, ennoblement, gentility, gentle birth, grandeur, noblesse; **pedigree,** ancestry, descent, durbar, line, lineage, succession, witan; **royalty,** kingliness, majesty, princeliness, queenliness; **lordship,** baronage, barony, dukedom, earldom, emperorship, kingship, ladyship, marquisate, princedom, queenhood, sultanship, thanage, viscountcy. *See also* ARISTOCRAT

ARISTOCRAT *n* blue blood, boyar, Brahman, childe *(Archaic)*, eupatrid, hidalgo, life peer, nob *(Brit.)*, noble, nobleman, patrician, peer, swell *(Brit.)*; **Lord,** archduke, atheling, baron, count, count palatine, daimio, dauphin, donzel *(Archaic)*, duke, earl, emir, grand duke, grandee, jarl, Junker, landgrave, lord, lord temporal, lordling, magnifico, marchese, margrave, marquess, marquis, monseigneur, prince, prince consort, prince imperial, prince regent, prince royal, princeling, rangatira *(N.Z.)*, robber baron, seigneur, sir, sire *(Obs.)*, thane, tsarevitch, viscount; **Lady,** archduchess, baroness, countess, dame, dauphiness, don, donzella *(Archaic)*, dowager, grand duchess, landgravine, life peeress, marchesa, marchioness, margravine, marquise, miladi, milady, noblewoman, peeress, princess, princess royal, sultana, tsarevna, viscountess; **sovereign,** emperor, king, majesty, queen, rajah, rani, rex, sultan, tsar, tsarina; **squire,** armiger, country gentleman *(Brit.)*, laird, landlord, landowner, squatter; **lady-in-waiting,** maid of honour; **dynasty,** noble family. *See also* UPPER CLASS

aristocrat *n* → 1 good thing 2 ruler

ARISTOCRATIC *adj* blue-blooded, highborn, highbred, noble, patrician, pedigreed, thoroughbred, toffee-nosed *(Brit. Colloq.)*, toney, tonky *(N.Z. Colloq.)*, topdrawer, upper, upper-class, well-born; **titled,** archducal, baronial, coroneted, ducal, lordly, seigneurial; **royal,** every inch a king, imperial, kingly, princely, purple, queenly, regal

ARISTOCRATICALLY *adv* imperially, lordly *(Archaic)*, nobly

arithmetic *n* → 1 mathematics 2 textbook *adj* 3 mathematical

ark *n* → 1 container 2 watercraft

arm *n* → 1 addition 2 animal part 3 armed forces 4 authority 5 bay 6 branch 7 committee 8 stream 9 strength 10 support *v* 11 accompany 12 equip 13 militarise 14 prepare 15 strengthen

armada *n* → watercraft

armament *n* → act of war

armature *n* → stand

armchair *adj* → ignorant

ARMED *adj* armoured, capital, heavy-armed, helmeted, mailed, under arms

ARMED FORCES *n* armed services, army, artillery, cavalry, foot, general staff, horse, infantry, light horse, military, musketry *(Obs.)*, rifles, soldiery; **navy,** flotilla, marine, R.A.N., senior service; **airforce,** Kamikaze, R.A.A.F., R.A.F.; **nation in arms,** army of occupation, host *(Archaic)*, land power, Sabaoth, standing army; **unit,** arm, battalion, battery, battle *(Archaic)*, brigade, century, cohort, column, command, contingent, division, force, garrison, legion, maniple, regiment, section; **squad,** cadre, company, element, escadrille *(U.S.)*, group, platoon, squadron, sub-unit, troop; **detachment,** detail, party; **array,** line, square, wedge. *See also* SERVICEMAN; HIGH COMMAND; SOLDIER; COMBAT TROOPS

armistice *n* → 1 mediation 2 peace 3 stoppage

ARMOUR *n* brigandine, chain mail, harness *(Archaic)*, mail, panoply; **shield,** buckler, escutcheon, hielamon *(Aborig.)*, mulga *(Aborig.)*, scutum, targe *(Archaic)*, target; **testudo,** tortoise; **bard,** chamfrain, chanfron; **helmet,** basinet, beaver, burgonet, headpiece, morion; **gauntlet,** basket hilt, coquille *(Fencing)*, glove, palm *(Naut.)*; **breastplate,** box *(Cricket)*, byrnie, codpiece, corslet, cuirass, culet, gorget, habergeon, hauberk, jack, lorica, plastron; **armguard,** bracer *(Archery)*, brassard, palette, rerebrace; **greave,** chausses, cuisse, kneecap, kneepad, kneepiece, pad, tasset; **faceguard,** beaver, eyeshade, goggles, gum-shield, mask, mouthguard, mouthpiece, nasal, nosepiece, visor, vizard *(Obs.)*

armour *n* → 1 defence *v* 2 secure

ARMOURER *n* ballistics expert, bowyer, fletcher

armoury *n* → arsenal

armpit *n* → organic cavity

arms *n* → heraldry

army *n* → 1 armed forces 2 crowd 3 many

aroma *n* → 1 essence 2 smell

around *adv* → 1 closely 2 dispersedly *prep* 3 near

AROUSE *v* actuate, bestir, call forth, goad, instigate, kick up, kindle interest, kittle *(Brit.)*, prompt, provoke, roust, rout out, spur, stir up, tickle, titillate; **incite,** agitate, enkindle, fan, fire, flesh *(Archaic)*, inflame, inspirit, rouse, set on fire, skitch, sool; **stir the possum,** cook up a storm, trail a coat; **goad,** force on, get on someone's back, hound, hurry along, hurry up, hustle, needle, prick, prod, push, scrub *(Horseracing)*, spur, sting, stockwhip

arouse *v* → 1 activate 2 enchant 3 eroticise 4 wake up

arraign *n* → 1 accusation *v* 2 lay charges 3 litigate

ARRANGE *v* fix, manipulate, route, settle, work it; **prearrange,** arrange to meet, ask someone out, invite, make a date, preconcert, prefix *(Rare)*; **rendezvous,** date, tryst

arrange *v* → **1** agree **2** change **3** make do **4** mediate **5** order **6** plan **7** prepare **8** promise

ARRANGED *adj* agreed, decided upon, planned, prearranged, set-up

ARRANGEMENT *n* accord, agreement, composition, deal, pact, pair, set-up, settlement, settling, understanding

arrangement *n* → **1** agreement **2** change **3** contract **4** musical piece **5** order

arrant *adj* → **1** disreputable **2** most **3** thorough **4** travelling **5** unconditional

array *n* → **1** armed forces **2** clothes **3** display **4** many *v* **5** clothe **6** decorate **7** tidy

arrear *n* → rear

ARREST *v* apprehend, bag, bounce, capture, do, give in charge, knock off, lumber, nick, pick up, pinch, pull in, recapture, seize, trap. *See also* IMPRISON

arrest *n* → **1** capture **2** imprisonment **3** inaction **4** stoppage **5** stopper *v* **6** capture **7** obstruct **8** stop

ARRIVAL *n* advent, coming, homecoming, incoming, influx; **disembarkation,** landfall, landing, set-down; **check-in,** registration

ARRIVE *v* bob up, come, fetch up, lob in, roll in, roll up, surface, turn up; **reach,** arrive at, attain, come to, end up at, fetch *(Naut.)*, get to, hit, join, lob at, make, put in at, regain, strike, top; **check in,** register; **pull in,** arrive *(Obs.)*, beach, berth, bring up, cast anchor, come in, drop anchor, land, make land, make landfall, touchdown; **settle on,** light on; **disembark,** alight, debus, detrain, dismount, get down, get off, get out, go ashore, jump ship

arrive *v* → **1** arrive **2** occur **3** succeed

ARRIVER *n* comer, landing party; **new chum,** bine *(W.A. Colloq.)*, black hat *(Archaic)*, blow-in, boat people, immigrant, migrant, new arrival, New Australian, refugee; **immigrant,** Jimmy Grant, pomegranate, pommie; **newcomer,** griffin *(East India)*, stranger

ARROGANCE *n* airs, airs and graces, arrogancy, disdainfulness, haughtiness, hubris, loftiness, pride, self-importance, smugness, stuffiness, superciliousness, toploftiness, uppishness; **disdain,** affectation, hauteur, pomposity, scorn, vainglory; **insolence,** assumption, assurance, hide, impertinence, impudence, nerve, presumption, sauce; **self-assertion,** brass, cheek, conceit, face, front, hide, nerve, pretension, side, swagger, swank, swashbuckling; **insult,** contumely; **snobbery,** elitism, ethnocentrism, inverted snobbery, superiority complex; **dogmatism,** opinionatedness

ARROGANT *adj* assured, autocratic, barefaced, cavalier, full of oneself, high and mighty, high-hat, impertinent, impudent, insolent, loudmouthed, overweening, proud, puffed-up, saucy, smug; **disdainful,** conceited, haughty, highfalutin, hoity-toity, lofty, off-hand, sniffy, supercilious, superior, toffee-nosed *(Brit.)*, too big for one's britches, unashamed; **overconfident,** cockish, cocky, smart-arse; **snobbish,** elitist, ethnocentric; **self-important,** stuffy, toney, tonky *(N.Z.)*, toplofty, uppish, uppity

ARROGANT PERSON *n* assumer, loudmouth, peacock, presumer, swaggerer, upstart; **bully,** bastard from the bush, fascist *(Colloq.)*, hector, pusher, rugger-bugger, swashbuckler, tin god, two-bob boss, upstart; **smart alec,** clever dick, dogmatiser, dogmatist, smart arse; **cock sparrow,** buck, cockalorum, cut-lunch commando, squirt; **snob,** boiled shirt, elitist, his nibs, inverted snob, pannikin snob, patroniser, snoot, snot, snotnose, snotty nose

arrow *n* → **1** indicator **2** piercer **3** signpost

arse *n* → **1** bad person **2** buttocks **3** discourtesy **4** sex object

ARSENAL *n* armory *(U.S.)*, armoury, arms chest, caisson, dump, garderobe *(Archaic)*, gun rack, pile, stack; **guncarriage,** caisson, limber; **magazine,** powder keg; **holster,** pistol-case; **bandolier,** cartridge belt, clip; **scabbard,** sheath; **arrow-case,** quiver; **rifle range,** practice range, rocket range; **bomb bay,** bomb rack, gun emplacement

arsenal *n* → college

arsenic *n* → means of killing

arson *n* → **1** damage **2** firing

art *n* → **1** artistry **2** cunning **3** fine arts **4** representation

artefact *n* → **1** goods **2** tool

artery *n* → blood vessel

artesian bore *n* → borehole

artful *adj* → **1** accomplished **2** cunning **3** opportunist

arthritis *n* → cramp

arthropod *n* → insect

article *n* → **1** deed **2** goods **3** matter **4** moment **5** particulars **6** qualification **7** subject matter **8** word *v* **9** lay charges **10** promise

articulate *n* → **1** insect *v* **2** join **3** speak *adj* **4** clear **5** eloquent **6** spoken

artifice *n* → **1** artistry **2** cunning **3** expedient **4** stratagem

artificial *adj* → **1** affected **2** cunning **3** fake **4** imitative

artillery *n* → armed forces

artisan *n* → **1** craftsman **2** creator **3** labourer **4** seaman

ARTIST *n* depicter, limner, old master; **painter,** aquarellist, colourist, dauber, frescoer, genre painter, landscape painter, marine painter, watercolourist; **illustrator,** caricaturist, commercial artist, copyist, illuminator, vignettist; **designer,** cartoonist, delineator, drafter, draftsman, draughtsman, sign-painter, sign-writer; **drawer,** crayoner, crayonist, pastellist, penciller, sketcher; **black-and-white artist,** monochromist; **bohemian,** dilettante. *See also* CRAFTSMAN; ENGRAVER

artist *n* → **1** actor **2** aesthete **3** expert **4** labourer

ARTISTIC *adj* aesthetic, painterly; **pictorial,** graphic, illustrated, picturesque, vivid; **illustrative,** figurative; **abstract,** non-objective, non-representational, surrealistic; **naturalistic,** impressionist, objective, realist, representational; **formal,** dry; **colouristic; in perspective,** axonometric, cabinet, to scale; **stippled,** daubed, flown, hard-edge, malerisch

ARTISTRY *n* accomplishment, art, artifice *(Obs.)*, craft, delicacy, delicateness, felicity, fineness, finesse, lightness, niceness, power, savoir-faire, subtleness, subtlety; **style,** elegance, grace, handsomeness *(U.S.)*; **technique,** execution, technic; **virtuosity,** bravura, brilliantness, display, fireworks, sparkle, technical skill; **verve,** dash, elan, panache, pizzazz, zest; **know-how,** stock-in-trade, the first string in one's bow

artistry *n* → **1** fine arts **2** good taste

ARTLESS *adj* blue-eyed, childlike, dewy-eyed, dupable, green, gullible, inartificial, ingenuous, innocent, naive, natural, simple, simple-minded, single-hearted, single-minded, trusting, unaffected, uncalculating, undesigning, unguarded, unpretentious, unsophisticated, unsuspecting, unsuspicious, untutored, unvarnished, unworldly, verdant, wide-eyed; **hick,** arcadian, backwoods, provincial, rustic, up-country *(Derog.)*

artless *adj* → **1** ignorant **2** incompetent **3** innocent

ARTLESSNESS *n* childlikeness, dupability, greenness, guilelessness, gullibility, inartificiality, ingenuousness, innocence, lack of sophistication, literality, naivety, naturalness, rusticity, simple heart, simple-mindedness, simplicity, unaffectedness, unpretentiousness, unsophisticatedness, unsophistication, unworldliness, viridity

ARTLESS PERSON *n* babe, dupe, fall guy, gudgeon, gull, ingenue, innocent, lamb, lamb to the slaughter, patsy, primitive, shlemiel, sitting duck, sucker; **hick,** backwoodsman *(U.S.)*, hayseed, rough diamond, rube *(U.S.)*, rustic

art union *n* → gambling

asbestos *n* → building materials

ASCEND *v* arise, levitate, rise, uprise *(Archaic)*, upswing; **gain height,** jump, mount, skyrocket, soar, take off, zoom; **tower,** ramp, rear, rear up, spire, stand up; **surmount,** culminate, top; **climb,** clamber, escalade, scale, shin, shinny, swarm up, walk up, work one's way up; **mount,** back *(Archaic)*, get up, horse, remount; **mountaineer,** back up, herringbone, sidestep, sidle *(N.Z.)*

ascend *v* → tower

ascendant *n* → **1** fortune-telling *adj* **2** ascending **3** influential **4** predominant

ASCENDING *adj* ascendant, assurgent, emergent, orient *(Archaic)*, rising, up; **climbing,** epigeous, positively geotropic, running, scandent; **uplifting,** anabatic; **upward,** heavenward, skyward

ASCENT *n* ascension, assurgency, climb, escalade, escalation, mount, rise, rising, up, uprise *(Archaic)*, uprising, upswing; **upthrust,** upstroke, upthrow; **upsurge,** ridge lift, zoom; **slope,** acclivity, gradient, ramp; **climbing,** alpinism, clambering, layback, mountaineering, rockclimbing

ascent *n* → slope

ascertain *v* → **1** examine **2** test

ascetic *n* → **1** abstainer **2** believer **3** monastic **4** solitary **5** strict person *adj* **6** abstinent **7** monastic **8** solitary **9** strict

ascribe *v* → impute

aseptic *adj* → clean

asexual *adj* → sexual

ash *n* → **1** fire **2** powder **3** remnant

ASHAMED *adj* conscience-smitten, conscience-stricken, contrite, embarrassed, guilt-stricken, penitent, repentant, sorry

ashamed *adj* → **1** meek **2** penitent

ashen *adj* → **1** fiery **2** grey **3** powdery

aside *n* → **1** quiet sound **2** speaking *adv* **3** deflectively **4** sideways

A-side *n* → **1** front **2** recording

asinine *adj* → **1** stubborn **2** stupid

ask *v* → **1** entreat **2** expect **3** insist on **4** necessitate **5** publicise **6** question

askance *adv* → sideways

ASKER *n* adjurer, beseecher, conjurer, impetrator *(Rare)*, implorer, importuner, pleader, postulant, requester, suppliant, supplicant; **applicant,** appealer, appellant, canvasser, imprecator, invoker, petitionary *(Archaic)*, petitioner; **interceder,** intercessor, interpellant, interpellator, lobbyist, urger; **beggar,** beggarman, bludger, cadger, craver, hum, mendicant, panhandler *(U.S. Colloq.)*

askew *adj* → **1** deflective *adv* **2** angularly **3** distortedly **4** sideways

ASLEEP *adj* dead, dead to the world, fast asleep, not awake, out to it, sleeping, sound asleep; **dormant,** dormient; **torpid,** comatose, lethargic, narcoleptic; **sleepy,** heavy with sleep, slumberous, somnolent; **drowsy,** dozy, oscitant, out of it, switched-off; **somnambulant,** somnambulistic

ASLEEP *adv* abed *(Obs.)*, bedward, in the arms of Morpheus; **sleepily,** dozily, drowsily, somnolently; **soporifically,** hypnotically, lethargically, somnolently, soporiferously

asleep *adj* → **1** dead **2** inactive **3** unconscious

a sleep *n* → period

asp *adj* → fluttery

aspect *n* → **1** appearance **2** condition **3** direction **4** face **5** fortune-telling **6** look

asperity *n* → **1** acrimony **2** difficulty **3** misbehaviour **4** misfortune **5** roughness

aspersion *n* → **1** religious ceremony **2** slander **3** wetting

asphalt *n* → **1** paving *v* **2** coat

aspire *v* → desire

ass *n* → **1** fool **2** stupid person **3** transporter

assail *v* → **1** argue **2** attack **3** attempt **4** entreat **5** slander

assassin *n* → **1** destroyer **2** killer

assassinate *v* → kill

assault *n* → **1** attack **2** hitting **3** rape *v* **4** attack **5** be violent **6** rape

assay *n* → **1** analysis **2** attempt **3** investigation **4** listing **5** test *v* **6** attempt **7** examine **8** fight **9** inquire into **10** test

assemblage *n* → **1** combination **2** combine **3** gathering **4** mixture **5** work of art

assemble *v* → **1** combine **2** converge **3** gather

assembly *n* → **1** combine **2** convergence **3** council **4** crowd **5** gathering **6** legislative body **7** machine **8** mixture **9** signal

assent *n* → affirmation

ASSENTING *adj* consenting, signatory; **acquiescent,** agreeable, agreed, compliant, conventional *(Law)*, resigned, willing; **affirmative,** confirmatory, ratifying, recognitive, recognitory. *See also* IN AGREEMENT

ASSENT TO *v* accede to, accept, accord with, acknowledge, admit, agree to, approbate *(Scot. Law)*, be a sport, buy *(Colloq.)*, come to terms with, concede, concur, embrace, fall in with, give one's vote to, give the nod to, go along with, grant, grant consent to, hear, lend oneself to, recognise, say yes to, turn a willing ear to, wear *(Colloq.)*; **confirm,** adopt, affirm, amen, approve, attest, authorise, bear out, corroborate, countersign, endorse, fortify, homologate, ratify, sanction, sign, subscribe to, uphold; **okay,** initial, rubber-stamp, seal; **come to terms with,** acquiesce in, be resigned to, come around to, give in to, have no objection to, lie down under

ASSERT *v* affirm, allege, argue, asseverate, aver, avouch *(Archaic)*, avow, claim, contend, declare, dogmatise, enunciate, insist, maintain, pose, posit, predicate, profess, pronounce, protest, restate, state, submit, swear, vouch, vow; **propose,** advance, move, put forward, suggest; **assert oneself,** be confident, maintain a high profile

ASSERTER *n* affirmant, affirmer, alleger, assurer, claimer, declarer, dogmatiser, dogmatist, enunciator, insister, maintainer, protester, submitter

ASSERTION *n* admission, affirmation, allegation, asseveration, assurance, averment, avouchment, avowal, claim, contention, declaration, dogmatisation, enouncement, enunciation, ipse dixit, offer, pretension, profession, pronouncement, protestation, restatement, statement, submission, vouch *(Obs.)*; **proposition,** predicate, predication, premise; **affidavit,** statutory declaration

ASSERTIVE *adj* assertory, assured, outspoken, positive, strong; **insistent,** categorical, dogmatic, emphatic, peremptory, urgent; **declaratory,** declarative

ASSERTIVENESS *n* peremptoriness, positive thinking; **emphasis,** accent, avowedness, dogmatism, insistence, insistency, stress; **assertiveness training,** positive thinking course, self-development course

ASSESS *v* appraise, appreciate, esteem, estimate, evaluate, gauge, rank, rate, reckon, size up, sum up, valorise, valuate, value, weigh, weigh up; **take stock,** meditate, ponder; **review,** survey; **judge,** adjudicate, arbitrate, criticise, deem, doom, have an eye for, hear, pronounce on, sit in judgment on, try

assess *v* → **1** appraise **2** inquire into **3** measure **4** tax **5** teach

ASSESSMENT *n* appraisal, appreciation, comment, critic *(Obs.)*, criticism, critique, esteem *(Archaic)*, estimate, estimation, evaluation, judgment, marking, measurement *(Survey)*, notice, opinion, rating, report, revaluation, review, reviewal, stocktaking, textual criticism, valorisation, valuation, value

ASSESSOR *n* appraiser, appreciator, estimator, gauger, judge, valuator, valuer, valuer general; **commentator,** critic, reviewer

ASSESSORIAL *adj* critical, estimative, valuational; **judgmental,** moralising, moralistic, sententious; **adjudicative,** arbitral, arbitrational, arbitrative, decretal, decretive, decretory, determinant, determinative, judicative, judicatory, judicial, judiciary

assiduous *adj* → **1** attentive **2** continual **3** friendly **4** persevering

assign *v* → **1** employ **2** give **3** impute **4** particularise **5** share out

ASSIGNATION *n* appointment, blind date, date, double date, engagement, interview, introduction, invitation, meeting, note in one's diary, prearrangement, rendezvous, tryst; **place of assignation,** meeting place, trysting place

assignation *n* → **1** employment **2** imputation **3** love affair **4** sharing out **5** tryst

assignment *n* → **1** agency **2** employment **3** imputation **4** obligation **5** sharing out **6** undertaking **7** work

assimilate *v* → **1** absorb **2** combine **3** eat

assist *v* → **1** be present **2** help **3** partner **4** practise law

assistant *n* → **1** helper **2** inferior **3** partner *adj* **4** helpful **5** inferior

ASSOCIATE *v* bear company, consociate, familiarise *(Obs.)*, forgather with, hobnob, keep company, keep in touch, mingle, pal up with, partner, socialise, stay in touch, take up with, troop with; **rally,** forgather, meet, rendezvous; **club,** band together, cartelise, clique, gang, hang together, hold together, league, squadron; **affiliate,** align, ally, filiate, identify with, nail one's colours to the mast, take sides; **federate,** confederate, federalise, pull together; **unite,** combine, enter into, merge, pool; **organise,** embody, incorporate, institutionalise; **join up,** enlist, sign on, take out membership; **jump on the band wagon,** climb on the band wagon, get with the strength

associate *n* → **1** companion **2** friend **3** helper **4** partner *v* **5** be sociable **6** combine **7** partner **8** relate *adj* **9** accompanying **10** combined **11** inferior

association *n* → **1** combination **2** companionship **3** friendship **4** gathering **5** relation **6** relationship **7** society

assonance *n* → **1** figure of speech **2** rhyme **3** similarity **4** sound

assorted *adj* → **1** apt **2** classificatory **3** mixed
assortment *n* → **1** classification **2** mixture **3** sharing out
assuage *v* → **1** alleviate **2** make peace **3** moderate **4** satisfy
assume *v* → **1** be arrogant **2** believe **3** conjecture **4** take **5** undertake
assurance *n* → **1** arrogance **2** assertion **3** certainty **4** contract **5** insurance **6** surety
assure *v* → **1** encourage **2** persuade
asteroid *n* → heavenly body
astigmatism *n* → faulty sight
ASTONISH *v* amaze, astound, flabbergast, overwhelm, surprise, throw; **dumbfound,** benumb, petrify, stun, stupefy; **awe,** dazzle, take one's breath away; **stagger,** knock someone bandy, make someone sit up and take notice, make someone's hair curl, strike all of a heap, take by surprise
astonish *v* → surprise
ASTONISHED *adj* agog, bug-eyed, goggle-eyed, marvelling, open-eyed, open-mouthed, wondering; **astounded,** aghast, astound *(Archaic),* confounded, dumbfounded, flabbergasted, staggered, stupefied, thunderstruck, unable to believe one's eyes, unexpressive *(Obs.)*; **awe-struck,** overwhelmed, struck dumb, wonderstruck
ASTONISHING *adj* amazing, astounding, remarkable, staggering, stupendous; **awesome,** awe-inspiring, awful, inexpressible, mind-boggling, overwhelming; **wonderful,** extraordinaire, extraordinary, fabulous, fantabulous, fantastic, fazzo, fearful, incredible, insane, marvellous, miraculous, phenomenal, prodigious, wondrous; **superb,** gallant *(Archaic),* massive, singular, splendid, sublime, tremendous
ASTONISHINGLY *adv* amazingly, astoundingly, remarkably, to one's astonishment, wondrous, wondrously; **wonderfully,** awesomely, extraordinarily, fabulously, fantastically, incredibly, inexpressibly, marvellously, miraculously, phenomenally; **sublimely,** dazzlingly, singularly, superbly
ASTONISHMENT *n* amaze *(Archaic),* amazedness, amazement, awe, stupefaction, surprise, wondering, wonderment
astound *v* → **1** astonish **2** surprise *adj* **3** astonished
astral *n* → **1** phantom *adj* **2** ethereal
astray *adj* → **1** false **2** misplaced *adv* **3** deflectively **4** out of place
astringent *n* → **1** drier *adj* **2** contracted **3** drying **4** sour **5** strict **6** unsavoury
astrology *n* → fortune-telling
astronaut *n* → pilot
astronautics *n* → flying
ASTRONOMER *n* astrologer, astrophysicist, lunarian, selenographer, selenologist, stargazer, uranographer, uranographist, uranologer
ASTRONOMIC POINT *n* aberration, annual parallax, diurnal parallax, evection, geocentric parallax, heliocentric parallax, inequality; **brightness,** magnitude; **arc,** azimuth, ecliptic, epicycle, southing; **declination,** celestial latitude, celestial longitude, elongation, emersion, galactic latitude, galactic longitude, latitude, magnetic declination; **degree,** galactic coordinate, trigon, variation; **node,** syzygy; **octant,** opposition, quadrature, quartile, quintile, sextile, trine; **perigee,** pericynthion, perihelion, perilune; **apogee,** aphelion, apocynthion; **precession,** precession of the equinoxes; **solstice,** solstitial point, summer solstice, vertical circle; **equinox,** equinoctial point; **eclipse,** annual eclipse, dichotomy, occultation, total eclipse; **rise,** proper motion, right ascension; **orbit,** apsis, line of apsides, revolution, rotation, synchronous equatorial; **equinoctial,** celestial equator, equinoctial line; **galactic circle,** colure, galactic equator, galactic plane; **tropic,** Tropic of Cancer, Tropic of Capricorn; **pole,** celestial pole, galactic pole, North Pole, South Pole; **zenith,** nadir, radiant, solar apex, vertex; **aclinic line,** magnetic equator
astute *adj* → **1** cunning **2** opportunist **3** wise
asylum *n* → **1** refuge **2** seclusion
AT *prep* before, by, chez, in the teeth of, through, with
atavism *n* → reversion
atheism *n* → irreverence
athlete *n* → **1** sportsman **2** strong person
ATHLETIC *adj* agile, flippant *(Obs.),* nimble; **gymnastic,** aerobic, callisthenic, isometric
athletic *adj* → **1** energetic **2** strong
athletics *n* → exercise
AT ISSUE *adv* before the house, in mind, in question, on the table, under discussion
atlas *n* → **1** diagram **2** list **3** reference book
Atlas *n* → **1** helper **2** mythical being **3** strong person
AT LIBERTY *adv* at large, loose, on the loose, out of the wood
atmosphere *n* → **1** characteristics **2** gas **3** influence **4** sky **5** surroundings
ATMOSPHERIC *adj* aerographic, aerographical, meteoric *(Obs.),* meteorological, stratospheric; **high-pressure,** anticyclonic, hyperbaric; **low-pressure,** cyclonic; **barometric,** barographic
ATMOSPHERIC PRESSURE *n* air-pressure, free air overpressure; **high,** anticyclone; **low,** cyclone, low area; **cold front,** depression; **warm front,** heatwave, warm sector; **occluded front,** occlusion; **eye,** front, ridge, storm centre, trough, vortex, wedge; **convergence,** divergence, frontogenesis, frontolysis
atoll *n* → island
ATOM *n* corpuscle, exotic atom, molecule, nuclide, radionuclide, Rutherford-Bohr atom; **ion,** anion, cation, free radical, negative ion, positive ion, radical, thermion, zwitterion; **atomic structure,** electron orbit, nucleus; **atomic mass,** atomic number, equivalent, isotopic number, mass number, neutron excess, packing fraction, weight; **quantum number,** charm, colour, flavour, isotopic spin, spin, strangeness

atom *n* → small amount

ATOMIC *adj* corpuscular, molecular, nuclear; **intermolecular,** interatomic, intra-atomic, intramolecular, subatomic

atomic *adj* → chain-reacting

ATOMIC BOMB *n* A-bomb, atom bomb, fission bomb, nuclear bomb; **hydrogen bomb,** fusion bomb, H-bomb; **neutron bomb,** clean bomb, clean weapon; **nuclear weapon,** nuclear warhead

atomic energy *n* → energy

ATOMIC RADIATION *n* alpha radiation, beta radiation, cascade shower, colorescence, delta radiation, gamma radiation, rays, re-radiation, secondary emission, soft shower, twenty-one centimetre line; **ray,** alpha ray, beta ray, electron beam, molecular beam; **radioactivity,** alpha decay, artificial radioactivity, beta decay, induced radioactivity, photodisintegration, stimulated emission; **radiation level,** absorbed dose, ambient dose, background count, background radiation, chronic dose, gray count, rad count, rem count, strontium unit; **fallout,** fallout contour, fallout pattern, rainout, yield; **half-life,** becquerel, curie *(Physics)*, roentgen; **X-rays,** roentgen rays, thermal X-rays, X-radiation. *See also* NUCLEAR ENERGY; RADIOACTIVATION; ATOMIC BOMB

atomise *v* → **1** disperse **2** separate

atomiser *n* → disperser

at one *adj* → congruous

ATONE FOR *v* assoil *(Archaic)*, confess, purge, shrive; **reform,** apologise, be on good behaviour, conciliate, heal, live down, make one's peace, pray, propitiate, repair; **excuse,** condone

ATONEMENT *n* expiation, penance, penitence, purgation, purge, shrift *(Archaic)*

atrocious *adj* → **1** bad **2** immoral **3** unkind **4** vulgar

atrocity *n* → **1** bad thing **2** crime **3** evildoing **4** vulgarity

atrophy *n* → **1** contraction **2** deterioration **3** ill health **4** weakness *v* **5** contract **6** deteriorate **7** weaken

AT SEA *adv* overseas, undersea; **offshore,** inshore, outward, seaward, seawards

attach *v* → **1** add **2** capture **3** employ **4** fasten **5** impute **6** join **7** take

attaché *n* → **1** ambassador **2** partner

attaché case *n* → case

ATTACK *n* assailment, assault, attempt on one's life, battery, blow, cannonade, feint, field-gunnery, fire, firing, mining, offence, onset, onslaught, potshot, salvo, shot, volley; **counterattack,** counteroffensive, escalation of violence, retaliation; **foray,** drive, excursion *(Obs.)*, forage, interdiction, offensive, pillage, push, raid, rush, sally, sortie, storm, surprise, thrust; **incursion,** bust, infiltration, ingress, inroad, invasion, irruption; **ambush,** ambuscade, stake-out; **air-raid,** air strike, blitz, blitzkrieg, bombardment, broadside, first strike, plastering, prang, stoush, strafe; **charge,** career *(Obs.)*, course, flèche; **indecent assault,** rape

ATTACK *v* assail, assault, attempt someone's life, beat up, carry the fight, fall on, fall upon, fly at, get, get into, get stuck into, go at, go for, have at *(Archaic)*, hit, hoe into, horsewhip, jump down someone's throat, knuckle, lace into *(Brit.)*, let someone have it, make at, make mincemeat of, mug, pelt, pitch into, prey on, put the boot into, round on, sabre, savage, set about, set on, set upon, sic onto, take the offensive, tear into, turn on, visit, wade into, weigh into, whale into; **counterattack,** retaliate; **strike the first blow,** aggress, draw first blood; **beset,** beleaguer, declare open season on, gang up on, harass, invest, leaguer, mob, press, rabble; **charge,** advance, advance against, advance on, bear down on, erupt, remise *(Fencing)*, run at, rush, sally, tilt; **besiege,** blockade, invade, lay seige to, move in, siege, stake out; **ambush,** ambuscade, bushwhack; **spring,** descend on, jump *(U.S.)*, surprise, swoop on; **depredate,** forage, foray, pillage, plunder, raid. *See also* FIRE ON

ATTACK *interj* banzai, charge, geronimo, go for it, up there Cazaly; **on guard,** have at you

attack *n* → **1** accusation **2** illness **3** reprimand **4** slander *v* **5** attempt **6** be violent **7** impute **8** scold **9** slander **10** wage war

ATTACKER *n* aggressor, assailant, assailer, assaulter, bludgeoner, harasser, hawk; **raider,** air-raider, invader, space invader; **ambusher,** ambuscader; **forager,** forayer, pillager; **front line,** advance party, shock troops, spearhead, storm troops

attain *v* → **1** accomplish **2** arrive **3** gain

ATTEMPT *n* adventure, assay, bid, effort, endeavour, essay, experiment, fetch *(Archaic)*, first-up, go, long shot, offer, shot, speculation, try, try-on, venture; **whack,** burl, crack, fling, fly, pop, run-through, stab, stroke, two bites at the cherry; **striving,** assailment, conation, struggle, trial

ATTEMPT *v* assail, assay, carve out, endeavour, essay, have a lash at it, take on, try; **try for,** aim at, aim for, offer at *(Obs.)*, seek, study, tackle, undertake; **strive for,** attack, exert oneself, grasp, push hard for, put effort into, scrabble for, struggle for, work towards; **audition for,** apply, read for, throw one's hat in the ring, try out for; **venture on,** experiment, gamble, hazard, push one's luck, speculate, take one's chance, tempt fortune, try one's fortune, try one's hand, try one's luck; **try one's hand at,** chance one's arm, give it a bash, give it a buck, give it a go, give it a nudge, give it a whirl, have a bash, have a buck, have a crack, have a go, have a punt, have a smack, make an attempt, take time out to; **keep on trying,** battle on, hammer away at; **go all out,** do one's level best, give it everything one has, go for the doctor, move heaven and earth, put one's best foot forward, shoot one's bolt, sink or swim; **seek**

to, get to grips with, make bold to, settle down to

attempt *v* → **1** allure **2** undertake

attend *v* → **1** be present **2** care for **3** expect **4** help **5** partner **6** result

attendance *n* → **1** care **2** help **3** presence **4** score **5** servant

attendant *n* → **1** helper **2** minder **3** partner **4** result **5** servant *adj* **6** accompanying **7** inferior **8** present **9** resultant

ATTEND TO *v* address oneself to, advert, be all ears, be all eyes, be on the alert, concentrate, consider, dig *(Colloq.)*, focalise, focus, get down to, hang on the lips of, hang upon, have an eye to, heed, keep an eye on, listen, look at, look to, mark, mind, note, reck, regard, see about, sink into, stand by, study, watch; **notice,** animadvert *(Obs.)*, be awake-up, enter into, eye, get with it, observe, remark, sit up and take notice

attention *n* → **1** attentiveness **2** care **3** courtesy **4** help **5** tribute

ATTENTIVE *adj* advertent, alert, alerted, argus-eyed, awake, curious, heedful, interested, mindful, observant, open-eyed, watchful; **aware,** alive to, on the ball, sharp, witting *(Archaic)*; **assiduous,** careful, painful *(Archaic)*, painstaking, sedulous, serious; **fastidious,** finical, finicky; **absorbed,** concerned, deep in, earnest, engrossed, intent, rapt, spellbound, wrapped up in

attentive *adj* → **1** careful **2** courteous **3** hearing

ATTENTIVELY *adv* absorbedly, advertently, alertly, fixedly, heedfully, interestedly, mindfully, on the edge of one's chair, regardfully, with one's ears flapping; **assiduously,** carefully, earnestly, intently; **sharp,** hard

ATTENTIVENESS *n* advertence, advertency, alertness, curiousness, heedfulness, mindfulness, regardfulness, watchfulness; **engrossment,** absorbedness, absorption, fascination, intentness, interestedness; **assiduousness,** application, assiduity, carefulness, sedulity, sedulousness; **fastidiousness,** finicality; **attention,** awareness, engagement, focalisation, heed, interest, note, notice, regard, remark

attenuate *v* → **1** decrease **2** moderate **3** thin **4** weaken *adj* **5** thin

attest *n* → **1** evidence *v* **2** assent to **3** testify

attic *n* → **1** room **2** tower

Attic *adj* → **1** cultivated **2** humorous **3** intelligent **4** simple

attire *n* → **1** clothes *v* **2** clothe

attitude *n* → **1** affectation **2** point of view **3** pose **4** slope

ATTITUDINISE *v* act, affect, emote, feign, go through the motions, peacock, play-act, pose, posture, posturise, prance; **simper,** be affected, mince, prim, smirk; **snivel,** snuffle, turn on the waterworks

attorney *n* → lawyer

attorney-general *n* → **1** lawyer **2** member of parliament

ATTRACT *v* adduce, allure, bring towards, decoy, draw to, engage, gather, lure, magnetise, pull; **gravitate,** cluster

attract *v* → **1** allure **2** be pleasant

ATTRACTION *n* adduction, allurement, appetence, attractiveness, counterattraction, draw, pull; **gravity,** gravitation; **chemical affinity,** chemotaxis, Van der Waals' forces. *See also* MAGNETISM

ATTRACTIVE *adj* adducent, adductive, alluring, appetent, appetising, arresting, seductive; **magnetic,** aeromagnetic, electromagnetic, geomagnetic, ionised, magnetochemical, magnetomotive, magnetostatic, polar, pyromagnetic; **ferromagnetic,** diamagnetic, ferrimagnetic, paramagnetic; **gravitational,** gravitative

ATTRACTOR *n* bait, centre of attraction, decoy, draw, lure, teaser; **magnet,** electromagnet, lodestone, magnetite, permanent magnet; **magnetiser,** keeper

attribute *n* → **1** characteristic **2** essence **3** reputation **4** sign *v* **5** impute

attrition *n* → **1** penitence **2** rubbing **3** truncation **4** war

attune *v* → **1** adjust **2** agree

atypical *adj* → strange

aubergine *adj* → purple

auburn *adj* → brown

auction *n* → **1** selling *v* **2** sell

audacious *adj* → **1** courageous **2** insulting **3** presumptuous **4** rash

AUDACIOUSNESS *n* assuredness, audacity, barefacedness, bumptiousness, effrontery, forwardness, hardihood, presumptuousness, shamelessness; **cockiness,** cockishness, sauciness; **high-handedness,** dictatorialness, domineeringness, high-mindedness, imperiousness, officiousness

audible *adj* → **1** acoustic **2** hearing **3** loud

AUDIBLY *adv* within earshot, within hail

AUDIENCE *n* captive audience, claque, full house, theatre, turnout; **playgoer,** cineaste, cinemagoer, concert-goer, fan, film freak, first-nighter, groundling *(Archaic)*

audience *n* → **1** crowd **2** hearer **3** hearing **4** looker **5** presence

AUDIO *adj* hi-fi, high-fidelity, laser, mono, monophonic, quadraphonic, stereo, stereophonic; **gramophonic,** phonautographic, phonographic; **megaphonic,** microphonic

audiology *n* → hearing

audiovisual *adj* → **1** hearing **2** optical

audit *n* → **1** accounting **2** examination **3** litigation *v* **4** account **5** examine **6** learn

audition *n* → **1** examination **2** hearing **3** sound *v* **4** question **5** stage

AUDITORIUM *n* amphitheatre, circus *(Rom. Antiq.)*, colosseum, house; **theatre,** big top, chamber of horrors, circus, concert-hall, hippodrome, house, music hall, music theatre, nickelodeon *(U.S.)*, odeum, opera house, palace, playhouse, showboat *(U.S.)*, strip joint, theatre in the round, three-ring circus; **picture theatre,** biograph *(Obs.)*, drive-in, drive-it-in, film theatre, fleas-n'-itches

(Colloq.), flicks *(Colloq.)*, hardtop, passion pit *(Colloq.)*, picture house *(Obs.)*, picture palace *(Obs.)*, theatre; **seating**, balcony, box, circle, dress circle, front of house, gallery, loge, lounge, parquet *(U.S.)*, stalls, the gods, upper circle

auditorium *n* → hall

auditory *adj* → hearing

auger *n* → extractor

aught *n* → nothing

augment *v* → increase

augur *n* → **1** predictor *v* **2** predict

august *adj* → **1** enormous **2** important **3** reputable

aunt *n* → relative

aura *n* → **1** characteristics **2** perception **3** surroundings

aural *adj* → **1** characteristic **2** hearing

aurora *n* → light

auspice *n* → omen

auspicious *adj* → **1** favourable **2** fortunate **3** predictive

austere *adj* → **1** abstinent **2** sour **3** strict **4** unsavoury

austral *n* → smallgoods

AUSTRALIA *n* down-under, God's own country, Godzone, Oz, the lucky country; **the mainland**

AUSTRALIAN *n* antipodean, Aussie, Aussielander, dinkum Aussie, dinkydi Aussie, ocker, ockerina, skippy, sullivan; **New Australian,** Balt, black hat *(Obs.)*, new chum, reffo, wog *(Derog.)*; **t'othersider,** Eastern Stater *(W.A.)*, mainlander *(Tas)*; **New South Welshman,** cornstalk; **Victorian,** cabbage-gardener, cabbage-lander, cabbage-patcher, gumsucker, Mexican; **Tasmanian,** apple islander, Derwent duck *(Obs.)*, Derwenter *(Obs.)*, mutton-bird, mutton-bird eater, Tasmaniac, Tassie, Tassielander, Taswegian, Vandemonian *(Obs.)*; **Queenslander,** bananabender, kanakalander *(Obs.)*, sugarlander; **Territorian,** top-ender; **Western Australian,** groper, groperlander, sandgroper, Westralian; **South Australian,** croweater, magpie, wheatlander

autarchy *n* → independence

authentic *adj* → **1** authoritative **2** believable **3** correct **4** faithful **5** honest **6** true

AUTHENTICATE *v* authorise, certify, endorse, notarise, validate; **prove,** approve *(Obs.)*, bear out, confirm, corroborate, demonstrate, document, establish, make good, manifest, re-prove, show, substantiate, sustain, try *(Obs.)*, verify, vouch

authenticate *v* → **1** be true **2** correct

AUTHENTICATION *n* accreditation, approbation *(Obs.)*, certificate *(Law)*, certification, confirmation, jurat *(Law)*, manifestation, probate, probation *(Rare)*, testamur *(Educ.)*, validation, verification, voucher, warrant; **identification,** exequatur, ID, papers; **medical certificate,** aegrotat; **grounds,** corpus delicti *(Law)*, data, document *(Obs.)*, exhibit, gist; **reference,** adduction, authority, chapter and verse, citation, locus classicus

author *n* → **1** creator **2** writer *v* **3** create **4** write

AUTHORIAL *adj* auctorial, subeditorial; **under one's hand,** holographic, manuscript; **clerical,** scribal, secretarial

AUTHORISE *v* accredit, crown, empower, enable, establish, mandate, revest, sanction, seal, swear in, warrant

authorise *v* → **1** assent to **2** authenticate **3** depute **4** justify **5** legalise **6** permit

authoritarian *n* → **1** represser *adj* **2** autocratic **3** commanding **4** repressive

AUTHORITATIVE *adj* commanding, competent, dominant, dominative, imperial, master, predominant, prepotent, sceptred, sovereign, superintendent, supreme; **official,** authentic *(Obs.)*, cathedral, ex-cathedra, ex-officio, oracular

AUTHORITY *n* accreditation, carte blanche, commission, jurisdiction, mandate, officiation, power, prerogative, procuration, roving commission; **authoritativeness,** arbitrament, dominance, dominancy, masterfulness, potence, potency, supremacy, supremeness; **authoritarianism,** absolutism, bumbledom, despotism, divine right of kings, domination, domineeringness, fascism, officialism, peremptoriness, totalitarianism, tyranny; **dominion,** command, commission, condominium, dominium, franchise, imperium, reign, rule, sway; **government,** headship, hegemony, kingship, leadership, lordship, magistracy, masterdom, mastery, seigniory, sovereignty, suzerainty; **rule,** a firm hand, command, governance, law, martial law, say-so, sway; **emblem of authority,** arm, chair, crown, diadem, fasces, mayoral chain, rod, sceptre, throne

authority *n* → **1** authentication **2** expert **3** guide **4** informant **5** justification **6** law **7** power **8** rights **9** specialist

autism *n* → **1** fantasy **2** psychic disorder

autobiography *n* → **1** memory **2** record **3** story

autocracy *n* → **1** nation **2** predominance

AUTOCRATIC *adj* authoritarian, domineering, fascist, feudal, feudalistic, imperious, lordly, masterful, peremptory, totalitarian

autograph *n* → **1** sign **2** title *v* **3** label **4** name

automatic *n* → **1** car **2** gun **3** machine *adj* **4** mechanical **5** unwilling

automation *n* → **1** controlling device **2** mechanisation

automobile *n* → **1** car *adj* **2** moving

automotive *adj* → **1** moving **2** vehicular

autonomous *adj* → independent

autopsy *n* → analysis

autumn *n* → **1** age **2** season *adj* **3** seasonal

auxiliary *n* → **1** helper **2** sailing ship **3** society *adj* **4** additional **5** helpful **6** inferior

avail *n* → usefulness

available *adj* → **1** dishonest **2** useable **3** useful

avalanche *n* → **1** landslide **2** ruin **3** snow *v* **4** fall

avant-garde *n* → **1** innovator *adj* **2** innovative

avarice *n* → 1 desire 2 greed 3 meanness

AVARICIOUS *adj* acquisitive, covetous, extortionate, grasping, greedy, hungry, insatiable, insatiate, rapacious, selfish

avenge *v* → retaliate

AVENGER *n* kadaicha man, nemesis, requiter, revenger, vendettist

avenue *n* → 1 access 2 entrance 3 method 4 road

aver *v* → assert

AVERAGE *n* arithmetic mean, centroid, geometric mean, harmonic mean, indifference point, mean, median, moment, normal, root mean square; **middlings,** intergrade; **golden mean,** compromise, happy medium, middle course

AVERAGE *v* compromise, equalise, even up, iron out differences, split the difference, standardise

average *n* → 1 freight 2 ordinariness *adj* 3 mediocre 4 ordinary

averse *adj* → 1 dissident 2 divergent 3 unwilling

aversion *n* → 1 dislike 2 repulsion

avert *v* → 1 avoid 2 diverge 3 repel

aviary *n* → animal dwelling

aviation *n* → flying

aviator *n* → pilot

avid *adj* → 1 desirous 2 enthusiastic

AVOID *v* avert, back away from, blench from, blink at, dip out on, duck, evade, fight shy of, give a wide berth, jib, miss, not touch with a barge pole, shrink from, shy away from, steer clear of; **bypass,** boycott, cold-shoulder, ditch, eschew, fob off, get off, leave, let sleeping dogs lie, put on one side, shun; **shirk,** bilk, bludge, dingo, dodge, funk, pass the buck, sell the dump *(Colloq.)*, shuffle out of; **equivocate,** avoid the issue, beat about the bush, beg the question, deflect, fence, hedge, hem and haw, parry, prevaricate, procrastinate, quibble, shelve, sidestep, skate over, skate round, stall, temporise

avoid *v* → 1 be neutral 2 cancel 3 deny 4 depart 5 eject 6 empty

AVOIDANCE *n* buck-passing, escapism, evasion, evasiveness, obliqueness, prevention, tokenism; **abstention,** abstinence, eschewal; **act of avoidance,** dodge, duck, escape, flight, flit, shuffle, sidestep

AVOIDER *n* absconder from public labour *(Archaic)*, abstainer, averter, chicaner, deserter, dodger, draft dodger, escaper, escapist, eschewer, evader, shunner, truant; **fleer,** blencher, boggler, ducker, fly-by-night, fugitive, runaway; **shirker,** bilker, bludger, buck-passer, coaster, dingo, hedger, malingerer, quitter, shirk, skulker, slacker; **quibbler,** equivocator, fencer, prevaricator, procrastinator, temporiser

avow *v* → assert

AVOWED *adj* declared, predicate, predicative, professed, sworn

await *v* → expect

AWAKE *adj* wide-awake; **astir,** about, up and about; **wakeful,** insomniac, insomnious, restless, sleepless, watchful *(Archaic)*

awake *v* → 1 encourage 2 know 3 wake up *adj* 4 attentive

awakening *n* → 1 encouragement 2 waking

award *n* → 1 gift 2 judgment *v* 3 determine 4 give

AWARD WINNER *n* diplomate, laureate, licentiate, prizewinner; **medallist,** gold medallist

aware *adj* → 1 attentive 2 knowing 3 perceptive

awash *adj* → 1 flooded 2 wet

AWAY *adv* afield, awa *(Scot.)*, interstate, off *(Naut.)*, o.s., out, overseas; **behind someone's back,** in absentia

away *adj* → 1 absent 2 distant 3 moving *adv* 4 deflectively 5 remotely *interj* 6 piss off

awe *n* → 1 astonishment 2 fright 3 frightfulness 4 high regard *v* 5 astonish 6 command respect 7 frighten

awful *adj* → 1 astonishing 2 bad 3 enormous 4 frightening 5 highly regarded 6 most 7 sombre 8 unpleasant

awkward *adj* → 1 dangerous 2 difficult 3 ill-bred 4 incompetent 5 inconvenient 6 overturned

awl *n* → piercer

A.W.L. *adj* → absent

awning *n* → 1 screen 2 shelter

awry *adj* → 1 false *adv* 2 deflectively 3 distortedly 4 unequally

AXE *n* broadaxe, celt, chopper, cleaver, fasces, hack, hatchet, kelly, meataxe, mogo, palstave, sax, scutch, tomahawk, tommyaxe, tommyhawk, twibill

axe *n* → 1 sword *v* 2 cut 3 decrease 4 dismiss 5 kill

axial *adj* → 1 central 2 long

axiom *n* → 1 conjecture 2 proverb 3 rule 4 truth

axis *n* → 1 centre-line 2 line 3 rod 4 society 5 support

axle *n* → 1 rod 2 support

ay *n* → 1 affirmation *interj* 2 yes

ayatollah *n* → 1 ecclesiastic 2 ruler

azure *n* → 1 blue 2 sky *adj* 3 blue

Bb

babble *n* → **1** nonsense **2** quiet sound **3** speaking *v* **4** reveal **5** speak **6** talk nonsense

babe *n* → **1** artless person **2** ignoramus **3** lover **4** offspring **5** woman

babel *n* → **1** commotion **2** loud sound **3** muddle

baboon *n* → ugly person

baby *n* → **1** alcohol container **2** finished product **3** lover **4** offspring **5** woman *v* **6** be lenient *adj* **7** small **8** youthful

baby-sit *v* → care for

BABY-SITTING *n* child-care, day care

baccarat *n* → gambling

bacchanal *n* → **1** celebration **2** dissipater **3** heavy drinker **4** voluptuousness *adj* **5** celebratory **6** voluptuous

bach *n* → **1** cabin *v* **2** inhabit

bachelor *n* → single person

bacillus *n* → organism

BACK *n* dorsum, paddywhack, small of the back; **spine,** backbone, chine, rachis, spinal column, spinal cord, vertebral column; **hunchback,** dowager's hump, humpback, widow's hump

back *n* → **1** frame **2** rear **3** single person *v* **4** ascend **5** finance **6** gamble **7** go back **8** help **9** swerve *adj* **10** past **11** rear *adv* **12** behind **13** in return **14** in the past

backbone *n* → **1** back **2** characteristics **3** durability

backdrop *n* → stage

backer *n* → **1** financier **2** gambler **3** helper **4** influencer

backfire *n* → **1** explosion *v* **2** explode **3** fail

background *n* → **1** rear **2** surroundings *adj* **3** rear **4** surrounding

backhand *n* → stroke

backlash *n* → **1** dissidence **2** reaction

backlog *n* → **1** accumulation **2** storage

BACK OUT *v* back down, back off, back-pedal, backtrack, chuck it, chuck one's hand in, flunk out, scratch, sling it in, stand down, throw in one's hand; **bale out,** bolt *(U.S.)*, cut one's losses; **withdraw from,** evacuate, give the game away, quit, resign, secede from, surrender, throw in the towel, vacate

back-pedal *v* → **1** back out **2** exercise restraint **3** go back

backroom *adj* → secret

backstage *adj* → **1** hidden **2** rear *adv* **3** behind **4** dramatically **5** in secret

backstop *n* → **1** hinderer **2** protection *v* **3** obstruct

backstroke *n* → **1** reaction **2** stroke **3** swimming

BACK TO BASICS *phr* back to taws, back to the drawing-board, here we go again

backtrack *n* → **1** road *v* **2** back out **3** go back

backup *n* → **1** evidence **2** storage

back up *v* → **1** ascend **2** encourage **3** help **4** meet an obstacle

backward *adj* → **1** antique **2** ignorant **3** late **4** modest **5** overturned **6** rear **7** regressive **8** reticent **9** stupid **10** unwilling

backwards *adv* → behind

backwater *n* → **1** lake **2** seclusion **3** stream *v* **4** go back

back water *v* → swerve

backwoods *n* → **1** remote place **2** the bush *adj* **3** artless **4** ignorant **5** ill-bred **6** remote **7** rural

backyard *n* → **1** field *adj* **2** incompetent **3** unlawful

bacteria *n* → **1** organism **2** plant

BAD *adj* abject, baleful, dismal, egregious, grievous, hopeless, ill, mean, measly, miserable, not much chop, not much cop, paltry, pathetic, pernicious, poor, sad, shameful, sorry, woeful, wretched; **worthless,** base, bodgie, botchy, brum, brummy, bum, cheap, cheapjack, crook, crummy, el cheapo, grotty, inferior, losel *(Archaic)*, low, mean, mongrel, no-good, not worth a pinch of shit, not worth a whoop, onkus, punk, queer, rubbishy, scrubby, scummy, shoddy, sleazy, tacky, tin, tin-pot, unacceptable, unsatisfactory, unworthy, up to putty; **awful,** abominable, abysmal, abyssal, appalling, atrocious, chronic, contemptible, deplorable, despicable, detestable, disastrous, disgraceful, dreadful, enormous, execrable, God-awful, grievous, ignominious, inexcusable, inexpiable, lamentable, monstrous, outrageous, pitiful, rotten, shocking, terrible, unforgivable, ungodly, unholy, unmentionable, unreal, unspeakable, vile; **adverse,** detrimental, dire, direful, hard, impossible, malevolent, malign, opposite *(Obs.)*, portentous, undesirable, unfavourable, unfortunate; **evil,** sinful, wicked; **worst,** of the blackest dye, of the deepest dye; **devilish,** diabolic, diabolical, helluva, infernal; **damned,** cursed, curst, damnable; **squalid,** insalubrious, seamy; **stinking,** cankerous, filthy, foul, lousy, noisome, odious, putrid, R.S., rank, ratshit, rotten, septic, shithouse, shitty

bad *adj* → **1** badly-done **2** deteriorated **3** execratory **4** ill **5** imperfect **6** inconvenient **7** intense **8** penitent **9** unpleasant **10** wrong *adv* **11** badly

BAD DEBT *n* counterfeit notes, debt, forged notes; **dishonoured cheque,** bad cheque, bogus cheque, boomerang, bouncing cheque, floater, rubber cheque; **stop order,** abatement *(Law),* days of grace, moratorium, protest *(Comm.),* stop, stop payment, suspension

badge *n* → **1** emblem **2** label

badger *n* → **1** animal's coat *v* **2** annoy **3** menace

badinage *n* → **1** joke **2** mockery

BADLY *adv* bad, dismally, ill, miserably, shamefully, undesirably, unfortunately, woefully; **awfully,** abominably, abysmally, appallingly, atrociously, damnably, deplorably, despicably, dreadfully, egregiously, execrably, shockingly, terribly, unspeakably

badly *adv* → very

BADLY-BEHAVED *adj* disobedient, ill-behaved, ill-mannered, naughty, pert, perverse, problem, sullen, uncooperative; **rascally,** blackguardly, knavish, pestilent, ratbaggy, roguish, sly; **mischievous,** arch, elfin, elfish, frolicsome, gamin, impish, kittenish, puckish, scampish, tricksy; **disorderly,** destructive, hooligan, larrikinish, rough, rough-and-tumble, rude, undisciplined; **irresponsible,** fly-by-night, improper, wayward, wrong; **uncontrollable,** hyperactive, incorrigible, obstreperous, overactive, rambunctious *(U.S. Colloq.),* restive, restless, unruly

BADLY-DONE *adj* angular, bad, botched, botchy, crappy, faulty, hopeless, ill; **ill-contrived,** ill-chosen, ill-conceived, ill-devised, infelicitous, unhappy, unplanned. *See also* INCOMPETENT

BAD MOOD *n* dismals, fit of depression, fit of the blues, joes, languish *(Obs.),* lousy, low spirits, megrims, moods, mopes, vapours *(Archaic)*; **tears,** waterworks

BAD PERSON *n* bad apple, bad egg, bad hat, bad lot, bad penny, black sheep, bodgie, good-for-nothing, idler, losel *(Archaic),* ne'er-do-well, poor white trash, punk, rag, scum, trash, undesirable, waster, wastrel, whatnot; **bastard,** arse, arsehole, bathplug, bathtub, berk, blister *(Brit.),* bugger, bum, companion *(Obs.),* coyote *(U.S.),* cunt, cunthook *(N.Z.),* cur, deadshit, dog, drop kick *(N.Z.),* dunghill, fucker, hound, mongrel, mother *(U.S.),* mother-fucker *(U.S.),* pimp, rattler, shit, shithead, so-and-so, sod, son of a bitch, stinker, swine, the end, the living end, turd; **louse,** blighter, cad, caitiff *(Archaic),* dastard, dingo, heel, insect, poon, prick, rat, rat-fink, reptile, rotter *(Brit.),* runt, serpent, skulk, skunk, snake, sneak, sneaker, squib, swab, toad, varmint, vermin, viper, wretch; **creep,** creeping Jesus, drip, fink, jerk; **bloodsucker,** bushranger, vampire; **bitch,** cow, fleabag, hag, harpy, hellcat, scold, witch; **fiend,** demon, devil, hellhound, lost soul; **monster,** Frankenstein, ogre, ogress, savage, terror

BAD THING *n* abomination, arsehole, atrocity, bad apple, bad news, bane, bastard, blemish, botch, brummy, bungle, detestation, devil, dirty word, dunghill, fizzer, fucker, horror, mother *(Colloq.),* mother-fucker *(Colloq.),* scandal; **trash,** garbage, goats, mess of pottage, pulp, quickie, rag, rubbish; **the pits,** low tide, the end, the living end; **jonah,** evil omen, evil star, hex, hoodoo, jinx

baffle *n* → **1** obstacle **2** wall *v* **3** confuse **4** hinder **5** puzzle **6** trick

BAG *n* billum, blister pack, carpetbag, carrier bag, carry bag, carryall, cod, dillybag, ditty-bag, duffle bag, garbag, gladbag, grip, gunny, holdall, jiffy bag, kitbag *(Mil.),* musette bag *(U.S.),* paper bag, plastic bag, poke *(Obs.),* seabag, shoulder-bag, string bag, tote bag, workbag; **swag,** bluey, frame pack, haversack, knapsack, matilda, pack, packsack *(U.S.),* rucksack, satchel, scrip *(Archaic)*; **saddlebag,** dosser, pannier; **sack,** cornsack, flourbag, gamebag, mailbag, ragbag, sugarbag; **package,** Christmas stocking, packet, parcel, sachet; **doggie bag,** feedbag, nosebag, tuckerbag, waterbag; **sac,** conceptacle, crop, cupule, cyst, cystoid, utricle, vesica, vesicle; **bladder,** air-chamber, air-cushion, air-sac, balloon, gasbag; **pod,** capsule, peasecod, shell, skin, theca

bag *n* → **1** drug **2** ugly person **3** unpleasant person *v* **4** arrest **5** become greater **6** bulge **7** capture **8** coat **9** disapprove of **10** enclose **11** hang **12** insert **13** kill **14** rob

baggage *n* → **1** disdainer **2** equipment **3** supplies

baggy *adj* → **1** hanging **2** shapeless **3** thick

bail *n* → **1** bar **2** liberation **3** liberty **4** restraints **5** surety *v* **6** restrain **7** transport

bailiff *n* → manager

bain-marie *n* → heater

bait *n* → **1** allure **2** attractor **3** bribe **4** poison **5** stoppage *v* **6** allure **7** annoy **8** poison **9** stop

bake *v* → **1** cook **2** harden **3** heat

baker *n* → cook

balaclava *n* → headgear

balance *n* → **1** account **2** comparison **3** composure **4** congruity **5** equality **6** figure of speech **7** remnant **8** rhetorical device **9** scales **10** steadying *v* **11** account **12** compare **13** counteract **14** dance **15** equal **16** equalise **17** steady **18** vacillate **19** weigh

balance sheet *n* → account

balcony *n* → auditorium

BALD *adj* bald as a bandicoot, baldheaded, balding, baldish, baldpated, eggshell blond, thatchless, tonsured; **hairless,** beardless, clean-shaven, furless, glabrate, glabrous, smooth, smooth-faced; **featherless,** callow, impennate; **depilatory,** exfoliative

bald *adj* → **1** smooth **2** white

bale *n* → **1** accumulation **2** harm **3** misfortune **4** unhappiness **5** vessel *v* **6** gather **7** harvest

baleful *adj* → **1** bad **2** menacing **3** unhappy

BALL *n* bomb *(Geol.),* crystal ball, globe, globoid, moon, orb, sphere, spheroid, toroid, torus; **celestial globe,** celestial sphere; **playing ball,** baseball, basketball, beach ball, billiard ball, bowl, bowling ball, colour, cricket ball, cue ball, eight ball, football, golf ball, medicine ball, pill, ping-pong ball, pioneer ball *(Croquet)*, pushball, rubber ball, shot, six-stitcher, soccer ball, softball, spot-ball *(Billiards)*, squash ball, tennis ball, volleyball; **balloon**

ball *n* → **1** a good time **2** ammunition **3** bulge **4** dance **5** heavenly body **6** party **7** thread *v* **8** have sex **9** round

ballad *n* → **1** poetry **2** song

ballast *n* → **1** building materials **2** steadier *v* **3** steady

ball-bearing *n* → bead

ballerina *n* → dancer

ballet *n* → **1** act **2** dancing

balloon *n* → **1** aircraft **2** bag **3** ball **4** drinking vessel **5** kick **6** written composition *v* **7** bulge **8** fly **9** grow *adj* **10** swollen

ballot *n* → **1** election **2** gambling **3** rights *v* **4** elect **5** gamble

balm *n* → **1** alleviator **2** fragrance **3** medication

balmy *adj* → **1** alleviant **2** climatic **3** fragrant **4** hot **5** moderate

balsa *n* → raft

balsam *n* → **1** alleviator **2** fat **3** medication

bamboo *n* → timber

bamboozle *v* → **1** hide **2** puzzle **3** trick

ban *n* → **1** exclusion **2** industrial action **3** prohibition **4** public notice **5** strike **6** swearing *v* **7** prohibit **8** swear

banal *adj* → **1** boring **2** ordinary

band *n* → **1** belt **2** crowd **3** gathering **4** layer **5** line **6** musical band **7** obligation **8** ring **9** tape *v* **10** gather **11** line

bandage *n* → **1** bond **2** medication **3** tape *v* **4** cover

bandanna *n* → neckwear

bandicoot *v* → dig

bandit *n* → **1** criminal **2** thief

bane *n* → **1** bad thing **2** death **3** destroyer **4** poison

bang *n* → **1** boom **2** drug use **3** excitement **4** explosion **5** hair **6** impact **7** loud sound **8** sexual intercourse **9** vitality *v* **10** be loud **11** boom **12** cut **13** explode **14** have sex **15** hit **16** subtract

bangle *n* → **1** jewellery **2** ring

banish *v* → **1** eject **2** isolate **3** prohibit

banjo *n* → **1** bath **2** cookware **3** digging implement **4** vessel

bank *n* → **1** coastline **2** mariner **3** ridge **4** seaside **5** shallow **6** slope **7** storage **8** treasury *v* **9** account **10** limit **11** place **12** slope **13** store

banker *n* → **1** financier **2** gambler **3** gamesman **4** puller **5** train

banknote *n* → cash

bankrupt *n* → **1** debtor **2** defaulter *v* **3** impoverish **4** take *adj* **5** absent **6** in debt **7** nonpaying **8** poor

banner *n* → **1** flag **2** news item **3** public notice

banns *n* → **1** public notice **2** wedding

banquet *n* → **1** celebration **2** meal *v* **3** eat **4** rejoice

bantam *n* → small person

banter *n* → **1** joke **2** mockery *v* **3** joke **4** mock

baptise *v* → **1** clean **2** initiate **3** name **4** wet

baptism *n* → **1** cleansing **2** religious ceremony **3** wetting

BAR *n* arch bar, bail, capstan bar, crossbar, drawbar, flat, jack, rail, sliprail; **metal bar,** angle iron, channel iron, roll bar, T-bar, U-bolt; **crowbar,** handspike, heaver, jemmy, pinch, pinch-bar, sweep, swipe, tiller, tommy bar

bar *n* → **1** award **2** beam **3** cancellation **4** court of law **5** exclusion **6** fence **7** hindrance **8** island **9** kitchen **10** layer **11** legal profession **12** line **13** metal **14** mineral **15** musical score **16** pressure unit **17** prohibition **18** pub **19** screen **20** shallow **21** shop **22** table *v* **23** boycott **24** come between **25** fasten **26** obstruct **27** prohibit *prep* **28** except **29** less

barb *n* → **1** beard **2** bulge **3** feather **4** neckwear **5** piercer **6** slander *v* **7** sharpen

barbarian *n* → **1** destroyer **2** foreigner **3** ignoramus **4** violent person **5** vulgarian *adj* **6** brutal **7** ignorant **8** ill-bred

barbaric *adj* → **1** brutal **2** ill-bred

barbecue *n* → **1** meal **2** party **3** stand **4** stove *v* **5** cook

barber *n* → **1** hairdresser **2** wind *v* **3** cut **4** rob **5** shear

bard *n* → **1** armour **2** poet **3** singer *v* **4** cook **5** secure

BARE *v* clear out, debark, disfurnish, dismantle, divest, expose, open, uncase, uncover, undrape, unshroud, unswathe, unveil, unwrap; **strip,** clear, deplume, disfurnish, dismantle, undress, unshroud, unswathe; **depilate,** clip, deplume, epilate, fleece, grain, pink, pull, tonsure, unhair; **defoliate,** deflower, denudate, denude, exfoliate, strip; **moult,** exuviate, mew, shed; **clear,** burn off, bush *(Agric.)*, bushwhack *(N.Z.)*, deforest, disafforest, disforest; **pare,** decorticate, excoriate, excorticate, hull, peel, pod, skin, unhusk

BARE *adj* bleak, defoliate, denudate, exposed, hypaethral, leafless, nudicaul, open, uncovered; **featureless,** blank, open; **unpainted,** unvarnished; **nude,** full-frontal, naked, stark, stark-naked, unclad, uncovered; **undressed,** barefaced, barefoot, barefooted, barehanded, bareheaded, barelegged, topless; **revealing,** décolleté, low, low-cut, low-necked, peekaboo

bare *v* → **1** reveal **2** undress *adj* **3** adequate **4** revealed **5** simple **6** smallest **7** smooth

barefaced *adj* → **1** arrogant **2** bare **3** blatant

BARGAIN *n* buy, dicker, go *(U.S.)*, special, steal; **cheapie,** brummy, button, catchpenny, el cheapo, rip; **sale,** garage sale, jumble sale, rummage sale

bargain *n* → **1** buying **2** contract *v* **3** buy **4** offer **5** promise **6** trade

BARGAINER *n* chafferer, shaver

BARGAINING *n* chaffer, haggling

barge *n* → **1** watercraft *v* **2** transport

baritone *n* → **1** brass instrument **2** singer

bark *n* → **1** animal call **2** skin *v* **3** call (of animals) **4** explode **5** menace **6** publicise **7** shout **8** vomit
barley *interj* → stop
barn *n* → **1** stable *v* **2** store
barometer *n* → **1** indicator **2** pressure gauge
baron *n* → **1** aristocrat **2** powerful person **3** wealthy person
baroque *adj* → **1** decorative **2** musical
barque *n* → sailing ship
barrack *v* → **1** inhabit **2** mock
BARRACKS *n* casern, hut, lines, quarters, station; **college,** hall, hall of residence, inn *(Brit.)*; **dormitory,** sleeping quarters; **mess,** long house, pueblo, roundhouse; **selamlik; seraglio,** harem
barrage *n* → **1** defence **2** equal **3** gunfire **4** obstacle *v* **5** wage war
BARREL *n* breaker *(Naut.)*, butt, cask, eighteen, firkin, hogshead, keg, kilderkin, nine, pin, puncheon, quarter cask, scuttlebutt, tierce, tun, water-butt, wood; **vat,** bin, churn, drum, hopper, keeve, kier, lauter tun, tank. *See also* BASIN; BOTTLE; VESSEL
barrel *n* → **1** entertainment **2** feather **3** hat **4** post *v* **5** bowl over **6** insert **7** level
barren *adj* → **1** boring **2** infertile **3** stupid
BARRENLY *adv* aridly, desolately, sterilely; **unproductively,** fruitlessly, in vain, ineffectively, non-productively, unfruitfully, unprofitably, vainly
barricade *n* → **1** embankment **2** fortification **3** obstacle *v* **4** defend **5** obstruct
barrier *n* → **1** exclusion **2** island **3** obstacle
barrister *n* → lawyer
barrow *n* → **1** grave **2** mound **3** shop **4** wagon *v* **5** cut **6** shear
barter *n* → **1** exchange **2** interaction **3** trade *v* **4** exchange **5** trade
base *n* → **1** battleground **2** bottom **3** buttocks **4** essence **5** fortification **6** foundation **7** singer **8** storehouse **9** support *v* **10** support *adj* **11** bad **12** bottom **13** cowardly **14** fundamental **15** ill-bred **16** immoral **17** inferior **18** patriarchal **19** selfish **20** supporting **21** working-class **22** wrong
baseball *n* → ball
basement *n* → **1** bottom **2** rock outcrop **3** room **4** storey **5** support
bash *n* → **1** binge **2** celebration **3** drinking session **4** hit *v* **5** hit
bashful *adj* → **1** modest **2** reticent **3** unwilling
basic *n* → **1** essence *adj* **2** bottom **3** characteristic **4** fundamental **5** important **6** original **7** rocky **8** simple
basilica *n* → church
BASIN *n* baptistery, font, lavabo, lavatory, laver, piscina; **laundry tub,** copper, dolly pot, trough; **bath,** bathtub, footbath, tub; **tank,** boiler, cistern, reservoir, sump, well; **inkwell,** inkhorn; **eyebath,** eyeglass. *See also* VESSEL
basin *n* → **1** bath **2** harbour **3** hollow **4** lake
basis *n* → **1** bottom **2** essence **3** foundation **4** support
bask *v* → **1** be pleased **2** sunbake
BASKET *n* basketry, breadbasket, chip basket, clothes basket, creel, flasket, frail, gondola, hamper, hanaper, kit *(N.Z.)*, linen basket, Maori basket *(N.Z.)*, punnet, scuttle, sewing basket, shopping basket, skep, trug, workbasket; **bassinette,** car-basket, carry basket, carry cot, cradle, crib, Moses basket. *See also* BOX; BAG; CASE
basket *n* → **1** list **2** offspring
basketball *n* → ball
bass *n* → **1** music **2** singer *adj* **3** musical
basset *n* → **1** rock outcrop *v* **2** jut
bassinette *n* → **1** basket **2** bed
bastard *n* → **1** bad person **2** bad thing **3** discourteous person **4** freak **5** man **6** mischief-maker **7** offspring **8** unpleasant person *adj* **9** fake **10** similar **11** strange
bastardise *v* → **1** humble **2** spoil
baste *v* → **1** cook **2** cudgel **3** oil **4** scold **5** wet
bastion *n* → **1** defender **2** fortress **3** helper
bat *n* → **1** binge **2** celebration **3** club **4** drinking session **5** fool **6** hit **7** irritable person *v* **8** flutter **9** hit **10** speed
batch *n* → **1** accumulation **2** amount
BATH *n* basin, bidet, birdbath, bush shower, douche, footbath, hand basin, hipbath, jacuzzi, lavatory, shower, sink, sitz bath, spa, tub, washbasin, washbowl, washtub; **washstand,** commode, vanity unit; **font,** lavabo, laver; **laundry,** laundrette, laundromat, washhouse; **steriliser,** autoclave; **sluice,** banjo, cradle, launder, strake, V-box; **copper,** kier, trough, tub; **carwash; sheep dip,** plunge dip, washpool
bath *n* → **1** basin **2** cleansing **3** heater **4** liquid **5** medication **6** room **7** wetting *v* **8** clean
bathe *n* → **1** journey *v* **2** clean **3** swim **4** wet
bathos *n* → **1** affectation **2** disenchantment **3** figure of speech **4** foolishness **5** unimportance
BATHROOM *n* bagnio, bathhouse, baths, comfort station, facilities, sauna, shower room, steam bath, sudatorium, thermae, toilet facilities, washroom
batik *n* → **1** painting **2** textiles
batman *n* → servant
baton *n* → **1** emblem of office **2** stick
batt *n* → building materials
battalion *n* → **1** armed forces **2** many
batten *n* → brace
batter *n* → **1** slope *v* **2** beat **3** coat **4** slope
battery *n* → **1** accumulation **2** armed forces **3** attack **4** fortification **5** hitting **6** percussion instrument
battle *n* → **1** act of war **2** armed forces **3** fight *v* **4** fight **5** make an effort **6** wage war
BATTLEGROUND *n* Armageddon, cockpit, field, field of battle, fire-zone, trenches; **enfilade,** action stations, echelon, firing line, front, front line, line, line of battle; **minefield; beachhead,** bridgehead; **headquarters,** base, camp, general headquarters, GHQ, HQ, operations room
battlement *n* → fortification
BATTLER *n* grind, ironside, plodder, stayer, sticker, the walking wounded

battler *n* → **1** fighter **2** prostitute **3** striver **4** traveller **5** worker

bauble *n* → **1** stick **2** trinket **3** unimportant thing

baulk *n* → **1** beam **2** cord **3** disenchantment **4** embankment **5** error **6** farmland **7** obstacle **8** shaft *v* **9** be unwilling **10** stop

bawdy *adj* → **1** obscene **2** vulgar

bawl *n* → **1** cry **2** shout *v* **3** grieve **4** publicise **5** shout

BAY *n* bight, embayment, gulf, hole, indentation, ria; **inlet,** arm, armlet, canal, cove, creek, estuary, fiord, firth, flow, frith, lough, tidal inlet; **passage,** sound, strait; **tidal basin,** embouchure, tide-lock. *See also* SEA; LAKE

bay *n* → **1** animal call **2** horse **3** path **4** window *v* **5** call (of animals) *adj* **6** brown

bayonet *n* → **1** sword *v* **2** injure **3** kill

bazaar *n* → **1** selling **2** shop

BE *v* exist, pre-exist; **live,** keep body and soul together, subsist; **occur,** be situated at, happen, lie, take place; **continue,** abide, endure, go on, last, prevail, remain, survive

BE ABSENT *v* be nowhere, exile, flex, flexi, flex off, give something a miss, go bush, miss out on, shoot through; **go missing,** beg off, jig, jig it, jig school, jump bail, play hooky, play the wag, play truant, shoot the moon, truant, wag, wag it

BE ACCUSTOMED TO *v* be always at, be given to, be in the habit of, be used to, be wont to, do regularly, go in for, make a habit of, make a practice of, perform regularly, practise, take to, take up

beach *n* → **1** seaside *v* **2** arrive

beachcomber *n* → **1** gatherer **2** traveller

beach comber *n* → surf

beacon *n* → **1** signal **2** signpost **3** tower **4** warning *v* **5** direct **6** signal

BEAD *n* ball-bearing, bullet, button, gibber, globule, grain, granule, pearl, pellet, pill, pilule, spherule, stone *(Games)*; **nut,** acinus, berry, boll, corn; **bobble,** poi *(N.Z.)*, pompom; **clew; drop,** dewdrop, droplet, gutta; **bubble,** blob

bead *n* → **1** arch **2** bubble **3** bubbling **4** jewellery **5** liquid

BE ADEQUATE *v* be sufficient, cover, last, offset, run to; **suffice,** answer, be enough, do, make do, serve; **qualify,** fill the bill, make the grade, measure up to, pass, pass muster

beagle *n* → **1** hunter **2** spy *v* **3** hunt

beak *n* → **1** bird part **2** judge **3** nose **4** teacher

beaker *n* → drinking vessel

BEAM *n* arch bar, bar, baulk, bellcast batten, bolster, box girder, cleat, crossbar *(Gymnastics)*, crossbeam, crosstree *(Naut.)*, fascine, fish *(Naut.)*, flying shore, gallows top *(Naut.)*, girder, hammerbeam, hydrofoil, I-beam, jack, joist, lintel, manteltree, needle beam, nogging, outrigger, plate, principal, purlin, rafter, rood beam, shore, shoring, sill, sleeper *(Railways)*, splat, straining beam, stretcher, stringer, strut, subprincipal *(Carp.)*, supporter, tie beam, transom, trestletree, trimmer, trussed beam, trussing, upholder

beam *n* → **1** angle **2** buttocks **3** light **4** shaft **5** side **6** signal **7** signpost **8** thickness *v* **9** shine **10** signal **11** telecast

bean *n* → **1** coinage **2** extravagance **3** head

BE ANGRY *v* blow a fuse, blow a gasket, blow one's cool, blow one's top, blow up, boil, boil over, bung on an act, do a slow burn, do one's block, do one's bun, do one's cruet, do one's lolly, do one's nana, do one's nut, do one's quince, do one's scone, flip one's lid, fly off the handle, fly out, foam at the mouth, fume, get off one's bike, get one's back up, get one's dander up, get one's Irish up, get one's monkey up, go bananas, go crook, go hostile *(N.Z.)*, go off one's brain, go off pop, hit the ceiling, hit the roof, let fly, let go, let off steam, let rip, lose one's block, lose one's cool, lose one's temper, lose one's wool, perform, rage, ramp, rampage, rant, rear up, sound off, spit chips, stack on an act, storm, tear one's hair out, throw a fit, throw a willy; **get the shits,** broil, grudge, have a skinful, have the shits; **darken,** glare, glower, lour, sulk; **flare up,** bite, bite back, bridle, bristle, flame, flare out, flash, growl, jangle *(Archaic)*, see red, thunder, yap

beanie *n* → cap

BE ANNOYED *v* be sick of, go off the deep end, have had a bellyful, have had an eyeful, have had it, have the pip, have the shits, have the tomtits

BE APPROVED *v* get the nod, pass muster; **grow on,** be in big with, get in good with, prepossess; **impress,** bring down the house, grab them by the balls, knock their eyes out, lay them in the aisles, take them by storm, wow them

bear *n* → **1** financier **2** mischief-maker *v* **3** be able **4** be fertile **5** display **6** flower **7** give birth **8** invest **9** own **10** persevere **11** support **12** transport **13** use

BEARABLE *adj* endurable, livable, sufferable, supportable, sustainable, swallowable, tolerable

BEARD *n* barb, bumfluff, burnsides *(U.S.)*, down, face fungus, five o'clock shadow, goatee, imperial, Vandyke beard, whiskers, ziff; **moustache,** dundreary, handlebar moustache, lice ladders, mo, mutton-chops, side-whiskers, sideboard, sideburns *(U.S.)*, sidelevers, walrus moustache, whiskers

beard *n* → **1** piercer *v* **2** oppose

bearing *n* → **1** appearance **2** behaviour **3** direction **4** heraldry **5** pose **6** reproduction

BE ARROGANT *v* be too big for one's boots, be up oneself, cavalier, cock *(Obs.)*, flaunt, get a big head, get a swelled head, get on one's high horse, have more front than Mark Foys, have tickets on oneself, lord it over, overween, put on jam, queen it, swagger, swank, swash, swell; **presume,** assume, have a nerve, have oneself on, have the cheek, horn in, perk; **patronise,** high-hat, overbear; **disdain,** cock a snook at, despise, scorn, sneer at; **dogmatise,** lay down the law about; **bully,** bullyrag, domineer, lord it over, overlord

beast *n* → **1** animal **2** dirty person **3** glutton **4** voluptuary **5** vulgarian

Beast *n* → devil

beastly *adj* → **1** unkind **2** unpleasant **3** voluptuous

BEAT *v* batter, belabour, clobber, cob, cream, curry, fib, hammer, lace *(Brit.)*, lam, lambaste, larrup, lather, paste, pelt, plaster, pommel *(U.S.)*, pummel, thrash, towel, trounce, wallop, whale; **beat up,** bash up, beat hell out of, beat the living daylights out of, beat the tripe out of, do for, do over, give someone Bondi *(Obs.)*, give someone Larry Dooley, lam into, lay hands on, tan someone's hide, whale into. *See also* HIT; CUDGEL

beat *n* → **1** boom **2** direction **3** idler **4** job **5** nonconformist **6** poetic rhythm **7** pursuit **8** region **9** rhythm **10** route **11** vibration *v* **12** agitate **13** boom **14** cheat **15** defeat **16** flutter **17** hunt **18** overtake **19** precede **20** set sail **21** shine **22** shower **23** surpass **24** vibrate *adj* **25** losing **26** nonconformist **27** tired

BEAT A PATH *v* pave a way, trail *(U.S.)*; **leave a trail,** lay down a track, track *(U.S.)*; **chart,** navigate, plot, track

BEATEN *adj* battered, creamed, smitten, stricken; **knocked over,** floored, unloaded

beatific *adj* → pleased

beatify *v* → **1** consecrate **2** please **3** worship

beatitude *n* → **1** pleasure **2** reverence

beaut *n* → **1** good thing *adj* **2** good *interj* **3** well done

beauteous *adj* → beautiful

BEAUTIFUL *adj* Adonic, angelic, apollonian, beauteous, comely, dreamy, gorgeous, heavenly, lovely, nymphal, nymphean, ornamental, personable, pulchritudinous, sheen *(Archaic)*, statuesque, stunning; **attractive,** becoming, bonzer, boshter, decorative, easy on the eye, good, jaunty, sightly, smart, soignée, spunky, trig; **good-looking,** brave *(Archaic)*, fine, handsome, proper *(Archaic)*, seemly, well-favoured; **pretty,** blooming, bonny, bright-eyed, dinky, dishy, dollish, fair, mignon, minion, pretty-pretty, prettyish, rosy, rosy-cheeked, ruddy, specious *(Obs.)*; **elegant,** exquisite, polished, refined, silken, thoroughbred; **voluptuous,** bosomy, buxom, callipygian, curvaceous, curvy, long-limbed, pneumatic, sensuous, sexy, shapely, sonsy *(Scot. Irish)*, well-proportioned; **picturesque,** aesthetic, aesthetical, artistic, charming, pleasant; **glorious,** brilliant, flamboyant, grand, grandiose, imperial, lustrous, magnific *(Archaic)*, magnificent, regal, resplendent, splendid, splendorous, stately, sumptuous, superb, triumphant *(Obs.)*; **graceful,** aerial, ethereal, flowing, fluent, gracile, lissom, lithe, supple; **radiant,** blooming, bright, ravishing, splendent; **delicate,** dainty, minikin

beautiful *adj* → **1** perfect **2** pleasant

BEAUTIFUL PERSON *n* Adonis, angel, Aphrodite, Apollo, bathing beauty, bathing belle, beau ideal, beauty, belle, bombshell, corpus delicti, dish, doll, dolly, dolly bird, dream, dreamboat, English rose, eyeful, goddess, good looker, houri, knockout, looker, nymph, peri, phoenix, picture, smasher, spunk, stunner, swan, Venus

BEAUTIFY *v* brave *(Obs.)*, decorate, glamorise, prettify, pretty, refine, set off; **smarten up,** brighten up, chamfer up, slick up *(U.S.)*, tart up, trig up

beautify *v* → decorate

beauty *n* → **1** beautiful person **2** good thing **3** the best **4** woman *interj* **5** well done

beaver *n* → **1** animal's coat **2** armour **3** cap

BE BORED WITH *v* be fed up with, be sick of, be weary of, tire, tire of; **pass the leaden hours,** be in the doldrums, while away the time

BE BUSY *v* burn the candle at both ends, burn the midnight oil, have a number of irons in the fire, have one's hands full, have other fish to fry, not have a moment to call one's own; **be active,** bustle, busy oneself, buzz about, hum, hum with activity, rush, rush around; **gad about,** have one's fling; **be cooking**

BE CALLOUS *v* couldn't care less, give short shrift, have no heart, have no mercy, have no pity, know no mercy, not be moved, stick to the letter of the law, turn a deaf ear; **be ruthless,** give no quarter, have one's pound of flesh; **be insensitive,** have a hide like a rhinocerous, have a thick skin; **harden,** case-harden, deaden, dehumanise, sear

BECAUSE *conj* along of, as, because of, by reason of, for, forwhy *(Archaic or Joc.)*, in the light of, in view of, on account of, owing to, since, sith *(Archaic)*; **for the sake of,** for the love of, in order to; **consequently,** hence, in consequence, so, so as, so that, then, therefore; **thereat,** hereat

BE CAUTIOUS *v* be on the safe side, look twice, mind one's tongue, play safe, take care, take no risks, think twice, tread warily, watch one's step; **feel one's way,** be tentative, tiptoe, tread on eggs, tread softly; **beware,** be on one's guard, guard against, keep a weather eye open, mind, ware *(Archaic)*, watch out; **cover oneself,** insure; **play it cool,** go easy with, let well alone

BE CERTAIN *v* be sure, bet London to a brick, bet your boots; **dare say,** believe, have no doubt; **lay down the law,** dogmatise, know all the answers

BE CHEAP *v* cost little; **slump,** collapse, fall in price

beckon *n* → **1** gesture **2** signpost *v* **3** direct **4** gesture

BE CLOSE *v* appose, border, burn, juxtapose, lie off, neighbour, subjoin

BE COLD *v* do a freeze, do a perish, freeze, go blue with cold, go numb with cold; **chill,** freeze the balls off a brass monkey, frost, glaciate, ice, regelate, rime; **snow,** hail, sleet;

shiver, get goose pimples, shudder, tremble; **become cold,** cloud over, freshen

become *v* → change

BECOME CONFUSED *v* blunder, blush, dither, flap, flounder, fuss, get one's knickers in a knot, get one's knickers in a twist, go off the deep end, lose one's head, not know which way to look, wander

BECOME GREATER *v* accumulate, bank up, gain, gather, grow, regenerate, snowball, thrive; **increase,** advance, appreciate, blow out *(Horseracing)*, boom, develop, gain, harden, jump, lengthen, mount, multiply, proliferate, pullulate, rise, rocket, shoot up, take off, upswing, wax; **intensify,** branch out, concentrate, escalate, fade up *(Television)*, gain strength, make greater, rise; **swell,** bag, belly, blouse out, dilate, fill, fill out, hypertrophy, inflate, intumesce, puff up, stretch, tumefy

BECOME IRRITATED *v* bung it on, bung on an act, chuck a mental, cut off one's nose to spite one's face, frown, get the shits, get up on the wrong side of bed, glower, go to market, look black, lour, pack a shitty, pout, scowl

BECOME KNOWN *v* circulate, get about, get around, get out, percolate, turn out; **dawn on,** dawn upon, sink in, soak in

BECOME SLEEPY *v* begin to nod, one's eyelids become heavy, rub one's eyes, yawn

BECOME UNCONSCIOUS *v* black out, faint, pass out, swoon, swound *(Archaic)*, throw a seven; **conk out,** go out like a light, sleep

becoming *adj* → **1** apt **2** beautiful **3** correct **4** pleasant

BE CONTENT *v* be a box of birds, be in heaven, make no complaint, purr, tread on air, walk on air

BE CONTINGENT ON *v* depend on, hang on, hinge on, rest on

BE CURIOUS *v* dig into, make inquiries, nose about, nose after, nose into, nose out, poke about, poke around, poke one's nose into, pry, root around, rubberneck, stickybeak, wonder

BED *n* bassinette, berth, box bed, bunk, charpoy *(India)*, cot, couch, cradle, day bed, doss, folding bed, four-poster, humidicrib, pad, shakedown, stretcher; **sleeping-bag,** fart sack; **mattress,** air mattress, pallet, palliasse; **sleeping quarters,** crash pad, crew's quarters, dorm, dormer *(Archaic)*, dormitory, doss house, forecastle, glory hole *(Naut.)*; **sleeping car,** campervan, camping body, couchette, overnight caravan, sleeper

bed *n* → **1** bottom **2** garden **3** hotel **4** rock outcrop **5** seaside **6** support *v* **7** farm **8** have sex **9** insert **10** level

BEDCLOTHES *n* bed linen, bed-roll, bedding, nap, pillowcase, pillowslip, sheet, slip; **blanket,** afghan, bunny-rug, electric blanket, kaross, rug, throw *(U.S.)*; **eiderdown,** bedspread, comfort *(U.S.)*, comfortable *(U.S.)*, comforter *(U.S.)*, continental quilt, counterpane, coverlet, doona, duvet, quilt, spread; **swagman's blanket,** bagman's two-up, wagga; **sleeping-bag,** fart sack, fleabag; **saddlecloth,** caparison, housing, trappings

bedding *n* → **1** bedclothes **2** bottom **3** building materials **4** rock outcrop **5** stratification **6** support

BE DEAF *v* have a hearing problem, not hear; **turn a deaf ear,** not listen; **fall on deaf ears; deafen,** split the eardrums

bedeck *v* → **1** decorate **2** show off

bedevil *v* → **1** act unkindly **2** annoy **3** haunt

BE DIFFICULT *v* be no picnic, be uphill, run one hard, try one's patience

BE DISMISSED *v* be given the golden handshake, fall, get one's ticket, get the boot, get the chop, get the sack, get the shunt, get the spear

BE DISSONANT *v* clang, clash, jangle; **blare,** bray; **hoarsen,** crack, croak, snore; **groan,** creak; **grate,** graunch, gride, grind, grit, jar, rasp, saw, scrape, scratch, scroop

bedlam *n* → **1** disorder **2** loud sound **3** psychotherapy

bedpan *n* → **1** toilet **2** vessel

bedraggled *adj* → **1** unkempt **2** untidy

bedridden *adj* → ill

bedrock *n* → **1** bottom **2** important thing **3** rock outcrop **4** support

BEDROOM *n* bedchamber *(Archaic)*, boudoir, bower *(Poetic)*, cabinet, camera, chamber, closet, cubicle, den, dormitory, garderobe *(Archaic)*, pad, passion pit *(Colloq.)*; **cabin,** berth, billet, cabinet, double room, guestroom, roomette *(U.S.)*, single room, sleep-out, sleeper, stateroom; **guardroom,** billet, quarters, rooms, tollbooth

bedspread *n* → bedclothes

bee *n* → gathering

BE EARLY *v* abort, be premature, go off at half-cock, go off half-cocked, miscarry; **take an early mark,** put the clock forward; **antedate; jump the gun,** beat the gun, break, break away, steal a march on

BE EASY *v* be a breeze, be a piece of cake, be no object, be nothing to it

beech *n* → timber

beef *n* → **1** cattle **2** complaint **3** strength

beefy *adj* → **1** fat **2** heavy

beehive *n* → **1** animal dwelling **2** centre of activity **3** container *adj* **4** domed

beeline *n* → direction

BE ENERGETIC *v* brace up, effervesce, feel one's oats, perk up; **bustle,** hustle, make an effort, strive; **get into,** get cracking, get stuck into, hoe into, hop into, put one's shoulder to the wheel, take the bit between one's teeth, warm to

beep *n* → **1** loud sound **2** signal *v* **3** shrill

BEER *n* ale, amber fluid, amber liquid, ball of malt *(Brit.)*, Bishop Barker, bitter *(Brit.)*, bock beer, brown ale, brownie, catch up, chicha, coldie, cruiser, draught beer, fifty-fifty, handle, hops, ice-cold, ketchup, lager, light ale, liquid lunch, lube, malt, malt liquor, mild, mild ale, new beer, nog *(Obs.)*, old, old beer, packaged beer, pale ale *(Brit.)*, paroo sandwich, pilsener, piss, porter, portergaff, poultry lunch *(W.A.)*, rabbit, senator, shandy, shandygaff *(Obs.)*, she-oak *(Obs.)*, shearer's joy, sheepwash, sherbet, shypoo *(W.A.)*, slops, small beer, stout, stringybark, suds, swipes *(Brit.)*, tap, tapping, wassail. *See also* ALCOHOL

beetle *n* → **1** car **2** club *v* **3** hit **4** jut **5** sew *adj* **6** protuberant

BE EXCESSIVE *v* gild the lily, go too far, lay it on, lay it on thick, make a welter of it, overdrive, overshoot the mark, overstep the mark, pile it on, push it; **burn the candle at both ends,** overdo it, overtax oneself

BE EXCITED *v* boil over, cream one's jeans, galumph, go ape over, go wild, hot up, rave, take off, take on, throw a fit, throw a willy; **flutter,** flap, tremble, twitter

BE EXPEDIENT *v* advantage, befit, beseem, suit one's purpose; **fill the bill,** answer, deliver the goods, do, produce results, serve

BE EXPENSIVE *v* be at a premium, be at a price, cost the earth

BE FAITHFUL TO *v* abide by, adhere to, be true to, stand by, stay with, stick by, stick to, stick with, support, uphold; **owe loyalty,** bear allegiance, homage, render; **stick together,** hang together

befall *v* → **1** occur **2** undergo

BE FASHIONABLE *v* be in, be in the swim, be U, be with it, catch on; **dress up,** gussy up, perk up, spruce up; **dandify,** caparison, primp, prink; **set a trend**

BE FASTENED *v* be fixed, fay, tail *(Bldg Trades)*

BE FERTILE *v* bloom, blossom, burgeon, flourish; **produce,** bear, crop, fruit, overbear, overcrop, overproduce, spawn, yield; **abound,** overabound, proliferate, superabound, swarm, teem

BE FEW AND FAR BETWEEN *v* be thin on the ground, be weak in numbers, diminish, run short; **be in the minority,** be too few, be without a quorum

befit *v* → **1** be expedient **2** fit **3** obligate

BEFORE *adv* afore, antecedently, anteriorly, erewhile *(Archaic)*, fore *(Obs.)*, heretofore, previously, prior to; **hereinbefore,** above, thereinbefore, ubi supra; **yesterday,** ult., ultimo, ulto., yesteryear

BEFORE *prep* afore, ere *(Archaic)*, fore *(Obs.)*, or *(Archaic)*

before *adv* → **1** early **2** frontally *prep* **3** at

beforehand *adv* → early

BE FORGETFUL *v* have a head like a sieve

BE FRIENDS *v* associate with, be hand in glove with, be mates with, familiarise *(Obs.)*, fraternise, get along with, get on with, go around with, go out with, go with, hobnob, knock around with, neighbour with, see, stick together, track with; **befriend,** ally, brother, care for, chum up with, fall in with, make friends with, pal, pal up with; **warm to,** click, cotton on to

BE FRIGHTENED *v* be at panic stations, freak out, get cold feet, get the wind up, go off the deep end, have a willy, have kittens, have one's heart in one's boots, have one's heart in one's mouth, have the breeze up, hit the panic button, jump out of one's skin, lose one's nerve, pack death, pack it, pack shit, panic, press the panic button, take a willy, turn to jelly; **fear,** doubt *(Archaic)*, dread, funk, misdoubt *(Archaic)*, misgive, squib; **tremble,** blanch, blench, boggle, cower, quail, shake, shudder, shy, start

befuddle *v* → intoxicate

BEG *v* accost, bite, bludge, cadge, fang, hum, panhandle *(U.S. Colloq.)*, put the acid on, put the fangs into, put the hard word on, put the nips into, sting, touch; **take up a collection,** hold a barrel, hold a benefit, levy, pass round the hat, whip round

BE GENEROUS *v* bestow, do someone proud, do the handsome thing, do the right thing, give carte blanche, give one's all, lavish, shower, spare no expense

beget *v* → **1** cause **2** reproduce

beggar *n* → **1** asker **2** poor person *v* **3** impoverish **4** take

BEGGING *adj* adjuratory, beseeching, impetrative, imploratory, importunate, imprecatory, invocatory, petitionary, precatory, rogatory, suppliant, supplicant, supplicating, supplicatory; **cap in hand,** on bended knees; **intercessional,** intercessory

begin *v* → start

BE GRATEFUL *v* say ta, say thankyou, thank; **appreciate,** bless, praise; **be full of gratitude,** be overwhelmed by someone's generosity; **acknowledge,** acknowledge one's debt to, give credit where credit is due; **thank God,** praise Heaven, thank one's lucky stars; **be grateful for small mercies,** be grateful for what you can get; **accept gratefully,** not look a gift horse in the mouth, receive with open arms

begrudge *v* → **1** be jealous of **2** be miserly **3** be unwilling **4** refuse

BEGUILE *v* bluff, con, delude, wrong-foot; **hook,** catch, catch out, mislead, rope in; **duckshove,** finagle; **outsmart,** circumvent, outfox, outjockey, outmanoeuvre, outwit, pull a fast one, steal a march on, undercut; **machinate,** compass, contrive, engineer, feint, manipulate, mastermind, wangle; **insinuate,** fish, wheedle; **intrigue,** plot, scheme; **know a thing or two,** live by one's wits, never miss a trick, not miss a trick; **cheat,** doublecross; **ambush,** crimp, ensnare, entrap

beguile *v* → **1** allure **2** please

BE GUILTY *v* have a skeleton in the cupboard, have something to hide; **be ashamed,** blush, feel guilty, feel small, hang one's head, hide one's head; **confess,** admit one's guilt, avouch *(Archaic)*, come clean, go to press *(Prison Colloq.)*, own up

BE HAD *v* be sold a pup, bite, fall for, have oneself on

BE HAPPY *v* be full of beans, be in good spirits; **cheer up,** brighten, buck up, ginger up, lighten, liven up, perk up, rise, take heart; **breeze along,** feel one's oats, keep one's chin up, keep one's pecker up, look on the bright side, sparkle, tread on air, walk on air; **make merry,** frolic, kick up one's heels, racket, rollick

BEHAVE *v* acquit oneself, act, bear oneself, behave oneself, carry oneself, comport oneself, conduct oneself, deal, demean oneself, deport oneself, do, do by; **perform,** paddle one's own canoe, play one's part, play the game, shift for oneself; **live,** lead one's life, run one's race; **react,** respond, treat

BEHAVIOUR *n* actions, conduct, conversation *(Archaic)*, course, dealing, form, front, goings-on, manner, manners, mode of conduct, observance, play *(Obs.)*, proceedings, treatment; **behaviour pattern,** collective behaviour, course of action, culture complex, method, modus operandi, path, procedure, response, standards; **custom,** living, mannerism, role, trick, way, way of acting, ways; **bearing,** air, carriage, comportment, countenance *(Obs.)*, demeanour, deportment, mien; **breeding,** finish

behead *v* → **1** cut **2** execute **3** kill

BE HEALTHY *v* be a box of birds, be alive and kicking, feel good; **thrive,** bloom, flourish; **keep fit,** condition, tone up; **recover,** convalesce, feel oneself again, get over, lick one's wounds, pick up, pull round, pull through, rally, recruit, recuperate, rehabilitate, turn the corner

behest *n* → **1** command **2** insistence

BEHIND *adv* after; **backwards,** back, hindwards, rearward, sternwards; **aback,** abaft, aft, astern; **posteriorly,** epaxially, retrorsely; **backstage,** upstage

behind *n* → **1** buttocks **2** rear *adj* **3** nonpaying *adv* **4** after **5** untimely

behold *v* → **1** see *interj* **2** lo

beholden *adj* → **1** grateful **2** obligated

BE HONEST *v* go straight, have clean hands, keep faith, keep one's promise, play fair, play the game, play with a straight bat, turn an honest penny; **call a spade a spade,** lay it on the line, make no bones, nail one's colours to the mast, plump out *(Brit.)*, sound off, speak one's mind, speak out; **confess,** make a clean breast of, own up, put one's cards on the table, reveal all, tell the truth

BE HOT *v* blaze, boil, broil, burn, roast, swelter; **flush,** glow, run a temperature

behove *v* → obligate

BE HUNGRY *v* famish, have a good appetite, have the munchies, raven *(Obs.)*, starve

beige *n* → **1** brown **2** grey *adj* **3** brown **4** grey

BE IGNORANT *v* be none the wiser, have come down in the last shower, have come up by parcel-post, not have a clue, not have an earthly, not have the faintest, not have the foggiest, not know B from a bull's foot, not know someone from Adam; **become ignorant,** lose track

BE ILL *v* ail, have one foot in the grave, sicken; **come down with,** catch, get, go down with, take; **present with,** complain of, suffer from; **relapse; faint,** collapse, lose consciousness, swoon; **waste away,** decay, dwine *(Archaic)*, fall away, invalid, peak, pine

BE IMMORAL *v* err, offend, sin, stray, transgress, trespass; **backslide,** fall, fall from grace, go to the bad, go to the devil, lapse, slip, spoil one's record

BE IMPENITENT *v* be fixed in one's ways, be seared, brazen it out, die game, harden one's heart, have no shame, not give a damn

BE IMPERFECT *v* fall short of perfection, have a fault

BE IMPORTANT *v* carry, import *(Obs.)*, matter, reck *(Archaic)*, signify, tell, weigh; **carry weight,** be in big on, bulk (large); **concern,** affect, interest

BE IMPULSIVE *v* go at something baldheaded, lose one's head, not think twice, take it into one's head; **extemporise,** adlib, improvise; **talk off the top of one's head,** say the first thing that comes into one's mind

BE INACTIVE *v* bide one's time, kill time, not lift a finger, rest on one's laurels, sit, sit tight, sleep, slumber, stagnate, tick over, vegetate, warm a seat, wile away; **become inactive,** cop out, corpse, flag, give up, languish, leave someone to it, rest, slacken, slake, stand, stop, throw in the sponge, throw in the towel, throw it in, wind down; **hibernate,** aestivate, hole up; **sit it out,** leave be, let it be, let sleeping dogs lie, sit on the fence; **hold off,** default, forbear, hold one's peace, pocket *(U.S.)*, refrain, refuse, resist, strike. *See also* IDLE

BE INATTENTIVE *v* be lost in, daydream, dream, have one's head in the clouds, let one's thoughts wander, lose oneself in, moon, muse, nap, nod, sleep, stargaze, switch off, wander; **be distracted,** lose the thread, lose track, pay no attention; **disregard,** blink at, forget, let pass, let slide, miss, overlook, pretermit; **fiddle,** doodle, fool around, play at, toy with; **skim,** pass over, slip, slur over

BE IN DEBT *v* be indebted, be under obligation to pay, have insufficient funds, owe, take the knock *(Horseracing)*; **get into debt,** borrow, dishonour a cheque, incur a debt, overdraw, run up a bill; **go bankrupt,** be gazetted, collapse, crash, go bust, go to the wall

BE INDEPENDENT *v* be one's own boss, be one's own master, be one's own person, call no man master, do one's own thing, fend for oneself, go it alone, go one's own way, paddle one's own canoe, pull oneself up by the bootstraps, shift for oneself; **kick over the traces,** kick against the pricks

BE INDIFFERENT *v* be left cold, blink at, not bat an eye, not care a straw, not give a damn, not give a fuck, not give a hang, not give a shit, not give a stuff, not give a tinker's cuss, not give a tinker's damn, not give a twopenny damn, not give a twopenny dump, shrug off, take for granted; **mope,** dream, moon, switch off

BE INFERIOR *v* be below standard, fall short, not hold a candle to, not measure up, not pass muster, not shape up; **play second fiddle,** bow before, depend, take a back seat

BE INFERTILE *v* go to waste, lie fallow, shrivel, stagnate; **abort,** miscarry, spike

BE INFORMAL *v* let one's hair down, not stand on ceremony, relax, underdress

BEING *n* ens, existence, incidence, life, pre-existence, presence, self-existence, ubiquity; **origin,** category, first principle; **subsistence,** survival, sustentation. *See also* ACTUALITY

being *n* → **1** emotion **2** essence **3** living **4** matter **5** person

BE INNOCENT *v* have a clear conscience, have clean hands, have nothing to hide

BE JEALOUS OF *v* envy; **covet,** crave, eat one's heart out, long for, lust after; **begrudge,** be put out, grudge, have one's nose out of joint, take a jaundiced view, view with a jaundiced eye

belabour *v* → **1** beat **2** make an effort **3** slander

BE LATE *v* miss the boat, miss the bus; **sleep in,** lie over; **delay,** be slow off the mark, dillydally, gain time, play for time, postdate, procrastinate, tarry

belated *adj* → late

belch *n* → **1** burp **2** fire *v* **3** burp

beleaguer *v* → **1** attack **2** wage war

BE LENIENT *v* baby, bear with, fondle *(Obs.)*, go easy on, humour, indulge, mollycoddle; **relent,** come round, give quarter, go soft, take the acid off, take the heat off, yield; **relax,** liberalise, loosen, stretch a point, unbend, unbutton; **dispense,** exempt, indulgence, remit, reprieve

belfry *n* → **1** head **2** mind **3** tower

belie *v* → **1** betray **2** misinterpret **3** slander

BELIEF *n* acceptance, acceptation, assumption, confidence, credence, credit, credulity, credulousness, dependence, faith, fondness *(Archaic)*, presumption, trust, trustfulness, trustingness; **popular belief,** bug *(Colloq.)*, folk myth, folklore, old wives' tale, superstition; **credibility,** accreditation, credential, credibleness, credit; **creed,** articles of faith, canon, catechism, credendum, credo, doctrine, dogma, doxy, faith, gospel, ideology, ism, philosophy, plank *(U.S.)*, platform, standards, teaching, tenet; **misbelief,** miscreance *(Archaic)*, myth. *See also* OPINION

belief *n* → **1** certainty **2** expectation **3** hope **4** religion

BELIEVABLE *adj* authentic, credent *(Obs.)*, credible, fiducial, plausible, plausive *(Obs.)*, swallowable, trustworthy, worthy of belief

BELIEVE *v* accept, assume, credit, deem, hold, imagine, opine, pin one's faith on, presume, profess, put one's trust in, put stock in, swallow, take for, take for granted, take someone at their word, take stock in, think, trow *(Archaic)*, trust, understand; **misbelieve; ascribe to,** accredit with, attribute to

believe *v* → **1** be certain **2** be likely **3** hope

BELIEVER *n* convert, devotee, good liver, initiate, Marian, pietist, puritan, the faithful, votary; **zealot,** Bible Belt, bible-banger, bible-basher, bibliolater, born-again Christian, bush Baptist, fanatic, hot-gospeller, Jesus-freak, Salvationist; **ecstatic,** penitent, spiritualist; **ascetic,** anchorite, contemplative, flagellant, hermit, mystic, stylite, sufi; **pilgrim,** alhaji *(Islam)*, hajji

BELIEVING *adj* bold *(Obs.)*, confident, confiding, credent, credulous, faithful *(Obs.)*, fond *(Archaic)*, superstitious, trustful, trusting, trusty *(Rare)*; **credal,** creedal, doctrinal, ideological, mythical

BE LIFTED *v* scend

BE LIKELY *v* be odds-on favourite, be sure to win, seem probable; **think likely,** believe, count on, dare say, expect, have reason to believe, presume, suppose, take for granted; **seem likely,** bid fair, have a strong probability, imply, lend colour to, point to, promise; **have every chance of winning,** be favoured to win, be the favourite, run a good chance, stand a good chance

BELITTLE *v* debunk, make light of, minify, minimise, set at naught, slight, trivialise, vilipend; **subordinate,** overshadow; **trifle,** coquet, dally

belittle *v* → **1** decrease **2** hold in low regard **3** slander

bell *n* → **1** animal call **2** percussion instrument **3** resonator **4** siren **5** telecommunications *v* **6** be loud **7** call (of animals) **8** shout **9** telephone

belle *n* → **1** beautiful person **2** woman

bellicose *adj* → **1** ferocious **2** warlike

belligerent *n* → **1** fighter *adj* **2** aggressive **3** argumentative **4** unfriendly **5** warlike

bellow *n* → **1** animal call **2** shout *v* **3** be loud **4** call (of animals) **5** shout

belly *n* → **1** abdomen **2** bulge **3** inside *v* **4** become greater **5** bulge **6** shear

BELONG *v* appertain

BE LOUD *v* be enough to wake the dead, be noisy, belt, brawl, broil, clamour, crow, deafen, go hammer and tongs, hoot, racket, roister, rough-house, row, shatter the silence; **shout,** raise the roof, roar, scream blue murder; **vociferate,** ballyhoo, bluster, give tongue, haw-haw, hawk, loudmouth, pipe up, rave, shout down, speak up, stress, talk down, yammer, yap; **bang,** boom, clang, clangour, crash, fulminate, peal, pound, thump, thunder; **resound,** pierce, rattle, ring, volley; **blare,** bell, bellow, bray; **howl,** hoot, shriek, ululate, wail; **blubber,** blub, brattle, snort

BELOVED *adj* darling, dear, honey, lief *(Archaic)*, precious, sweet, well-beloved; **favourite,** blue-eyed, white-haired, white-headed

beloved *n* → lover

BELOW *adv* infra, thereunder, underneath; **low,** down; **basally,** underfoot, underground, ventrally

below *adv* → after

BELT *n* band, belting, cestus, cinch, cincture, girth, strap, surcingle; **ribbon,** aglet, apron-strings, cordon, fillet, string, tie; **lace,** bootlace, latchet *(Archaic)*; **garter,** suspender; **watch-chain,** albert, watch-guard, watchband, watchstrap; **elastic band,** keylock closure, lacker band, rubber band, twist-tie; **octopus strap,** ockie strap, spider; **metal strap,** astrigal

belt *n* → **1** conveyor **2** hit **3** ring **4** tape **5** thinness *v* **6** be loud **7** cudgel **8** enclose **9** hit **10** speed

BELT INTO *v* buckle down to, bury oneself in work, dig into, get cracking at, get into the swim, get into the swing, get stuck into, go all out to, go at something, go at something baldheaded, go in for, go to town, have a go at, lay about oneself mightily, make short work of, make the most of one's time, not let the grass grow under one's feet, peg away at, pull one's finger out, pull one's weight, stick at nothing; **fuss,** carry on, fidget, make a fuss, make a song and dance about, run riot; **activate,** bring on stream, bring into production

BE MAD *v* be a shingle short, have bats in the belfry, have the ha-has, need one's head read, not play with a full deck; **take a fit,** chuck a mental, have a turn, run amuck; **go mad,** crack, get the Darling pea, go haywire, lose one's marbles

BE MEEK *v* bow and scrape, creep, eat crow, eat dirt, eat humble pie, eat one's words, eat out of someone's hand, get off one's high horse, grovel, hide one's head, kiss the dust, know one's place, lick the dust, lose face, not dare to show one's face again, pull in one's horns, sing small, submit; **crawl,** brown-nose, lick someone's arse, lick someone's boots, piss in someone's pocket, pull one's forelock, toady to, touch one's forelock, tug one's forelock; **humble oneself,** condescend, deign, demean oneself, stoop, vouchsafe; **be humbled,** be made to look foolish, receive a snub

BE MISERLY *v* begrudge, dole out, have a death adder in one's pocket, have short arms and long pockets, hold back, pinch, scrimp, skimp, stay at home on a button day, stint, throw money around like a man with no hands, withhold

bemoan *v* → **1** grieve **2** pity

BE MODEST *v* draw in one's horns, hide one's light under a bushel, keep in the background, keep one's distance, not big-note oneself, not give oneself airs, not put on side, sell oneself short, undersell oneself; **blush,** shrink, withdraw

BE MOTIVATED *v* become carried away, become fired with enthusiasm, follow another's lead, obey a call, yield to temptation; **have an axe to grind,** be driven on

bemused *adj* → **1** confused **2** inattentive

bench *n* → **1** court of law **2** judge **3** judgeship **4** religious ministry

bend *n* → **1** curve **2** distortion *v* **3** curve **4** distort **5** fasten **6** swerve

bender *n* → **1** binge **2** drinking session **3** traveller

beneath *prep* → under

benediction *n* → **1** good **2** religious ceremony

benefactor *n* → **1** giver **2** good person **3** helper

beneficial *adj* → **1** advantageous **2** fertile **3** good **4** helpful **5** improving **6** useful

beneficiary *n* → **1** ecclesiastic **2** gainer

benefit *n* → **1** advantage **2** charity **3** entertainment **4** fertility **5** good *v* **6** improve **7** make do **8** take advantage

BE NEGLECTED *v* go by the board, go to rack and ruin, go to waste, lapse; **neglect oneself,** let oneself go, not care how one looks, not take care of oneself, waste away

BE NEUTRAL *v* abstain, abstain from voting, avoid, have no hand in, have nothing to do with, not take sides, pull one's head in, sit on the fence, stand aloof, steer a middle course, take no part, trim one's course; **neutralise,** defuse, depoliticise, keep the peace

benevolent *adj* → **1** good **2** kind **3** unselfish

benighted *adj* → **1** dark **2** ignorant

benign *adj* → **1** fortunate **2** kind **3** pleasant

BENT *adj* antrorse, biflex, crooked, flectional, flexional, flexural, forked; **angular,** angulated, equiangular, isogonic; **acute,** cant, oblique, orthogonal, skew; **perpendicular,** normal, on the beam, square; **angled,** contrary, decussate, inclined, inflexed, jagged, notched, serrated, zigzag

bent *n* → **1** competence **2** curvature **3** desire **4** nonconformist **5** point of view *adj* **6** curved **7** dishonest **8** distorted **9** nonconformist **10** thieving

BE OBVIOUS *v* go without saying, speak for itself, stand to reason, tell its own tale; **be prominent,** be right under one's nose, loom large, stand out, stand out a mile, stare one in the face, stick out, stick out like a sore toe, stick out like dogs' balls; **show up,** keep a high profile, maintain a high profile, shine

BE OF NO REPUTE *v* be at a discount, not be thought much of, stink; **be in disgrace,** be in bad odour with, be in bad with, be in disfavour with, be in dutch with, be in somebody's black books, be in the doghouse, be in wrong with, be on somebody's black list, be persona non grata, be under a cloud, sleep under the house; **fall from grace,** blot one's copybook, come down, fall, go into eclipse, lose ground, stoop

BE OF SERVICE *v* boot *(Obs. Poetic)*, come in handy, come into use, serve, stand in good stead, stead *(Archaic)*, subserve

BE OLD *v* be ancient, have seen its day, have whiskers on it; **age,** fossilise, get on, get on in years, go to seed, run to seed; **stale,** crumble, fade

BE OUT OF LUCK *v* be for it, be in the wars, be up against it, draw the short straw, feel the pinch, go downhill, go through the hoop, go through the mill, hit a bad patch, hit bad times, lead a dog's life, stew in one's own juice; **come to grief,** come a buster, come a cropper, come a stumer, come unstuck, cruel one's pitch, feel the draught, go for a sixer, go for six, slump, take a knock; **cop the lot,** catch a packet, cop a basinful; **ail,** distress

BE PATIENT *v* bide one's time, play a waiting game, sit tight, stand by, sweat it out, wait

BE PATIENT *interj* don't get your knickers in a knot, don't get your knickers in a twist, half a mo, hang on, hold on, hold your horses, hold your water, just a minute, just a tick, simmer down, slow down, steady on, wait a minute

BE PENITENT *v* confess, have learnt one's lesson, mend one's ways, reform, repent, turn over a new leaf; **apologise,** make up, say one is sorry, shake hands; **regret,** cry over spilt milk, deplore, kick oneself, rue, rue the day

BE PERMITTED TO *v* be allowed to, can, may; **get the nod,** clear with, get the Murray cod

BE PLEASANT *v* appeal to, attract, charm, charm the pants off, delight, endear oneself to, please

BE PLEASED *v* congratulate oneself, laugh, purr, rejoice, smile; **have a good time,** enjoy oneself, jet set, kick up one's heels, let one's hair down, live, live it up, rage; **luxuriate,** bask, indulge, wallow

BE PRECISE *v* dot one's i's and cross one's t's, mind one's p's and q's, take care; **get it right,** hit the nail on the head; **elaborate,** emendate, quote chapter and verse, refine; **literalise; formulate,** formularise, formulise; **regulate,** emend, get technical, nick, tram *(Mach.)*; **pinpoint,** bring into focus, define, register *(Print.)*, true

BE PREJUDICED AGAINST *v* have a bias against, have a derry on, have a down on, see one side only; **ossify,** become set in one's ways, congeal *(U.S.)*, fossilise

BE PRESENT *v* assist *(Obs.)*, attend, frequent, front *(Colloq.)*, gatecrash, hang on, lie at, lie in, occupy, sit in on, take one's place; **habituate,** hang about, hang around, haunt, mooch, stick around; **stay,** stick on, stop, tarry

BE PROMISCUOUS *v* go on the streets, prostitute oneself, put out, rig, run around, sleep around, swing, swing the bag, wanton; **philander,** fornicate, sow one's wild oats, wench, whore, womanise; **seduce,** debauch, deflower, ruin; **rape,** force, ravish, violate

BE PUNISHED *v* answer for, catch it, cop it, face the music, get it in the neck, get one's just deserts, get what is coming, take one's medicine, take the rap; **take the high jump,** dance, run the gauntlet, swing

bequeath *v* → give

bequest *n* → **1** getting **2** gift

berate *v* → scold

BE REALISTIC *v* face facts, get wise, have one's feet on the ground, keep one's feet on the ground, know which side one's bread is buttered; **make realistic,** bring to the light of day, deglamourise, demystify, make come true, realise

bereave *v* → take

BEREFT *adj* beggared, deprived, dispossessed, impoverished, pillaged, ravished, stripped, stripped bare

bereft *adj* → **1** absent **2** lost

BE RELIEVED *v* breathe more freely, draw comfort, respire, take a deep breath, take comfort

beret *n* → cap

BE RETICENT *v* clam up, hold aloof, hold off, interiorise, internalise; **underplay,** not give anything away, underact; **suffer in silence,** pocket one's pride, swallow one's pride, swallow one's words; **withhold,** hold back, keep back, keep close, keep dark, keep under one's hat, laugh in one's sleeve, laugh up one's sleeve, reserve, restrain, suppress

BE REVEALED *v* come out in the wash, come to light, leak out, ooze out, see the light of day, transpire

beri-beri *n* → malnutrition

berry *n* → **1** bead **2** fruit **3** knob *v* **4** give birth

berserk *adj* → **1** ferocious **2** mad

berth *n* → **1** bed **2** bedroom **3** employment *v* **4** arrive

beryl *n* → **1** blue **2** green

beseech *v* → entreat

BE SELFISH *v* care about number one, feather one's nest, have an axe to grind, keep an eye to the main chance, not care about anyone else, push one's barrow

beset *v* → attack

beside *adv* → **1** additionally **2** sideways *prep* **3** except **4** near *conj* **5** and

besides *adv* → **1** additionally *prep* **2** except *conj* **3** and

besiege *v* → **1** attack **2** entreat **3** wage war

BE SILENT *v* ace it, ace it up, belt up, can it, cut the cackle, cut the cake, hold one's peace, hold one's tongue, keep one's mouth shut, pipe down, put a cork in it, put a sock in it, rest, shut one's mouth, shut up, stow it; **refuse comment,** button the lip, keep mum, keep one's counsel, stand mute; **lose one's tongue,** save one's breath, waste no words on

BE SIMILAR *v* agree, be all one, be birds of a feather, be in the same boat, be much of a muchness, be nothing in it, be twins, conform, correspond, match, parallel; **approximate,** approach, border on, come close to, remind of, resemble, savour of, smack of, take after

BE SMELLY *v* honk like a gaggle of geese, hum, pong, reek, smell, smell like Dead Horse gully, stink, stink out

BE SOCIABLE *v* accost, bow, gladhand, greet, have the flags out, hello, palm *(Obs.)*, recognise, rub noses *(N.Z.)*, salaam, shake hands with, tin kettle *(N.Z.)*, welcome, wring someone's hand; **meet,** bump into, rencounter, run across, run into, run up against; **introduce,** bring out, present; **associate,** go out, keep company, neighbour with, rub elbows with, rub shoulders with; **ask out,** date; **entertain,** do the honours, give a party, host a party, keep open house, receive, throw a party; **invite,** cultivate, have in, have over; **regale,** dine, do someone proud, serve, sup; **party on,** make whoopee, racket, rage; **socialise,** circulate, come out of one's shell, get about, get around, go around, mix, step out *(U.S.)*, table-hop

besotted *adj* → loving

best *n* → **1** finery **2** show *v* **3** defeat **4** surpass *adj* **5** competent **6** good **7** most **8** superior *adv* **9** superiorly

bestial *adj* → **1** animal-like **2** brutal **3** sexual **4** voluptuous

best man *n* → **1** companion **2** helper **3** wedding

bestow *v* → **1** be generous **2** give **3** place **4** use

BE STRICT *v* bear down on, clamp down on, come down on like a ton of bricks, crack down on, get technical with, give it heaps, give no quarter, rule with a rod of iron, stand no nonsense; **discipline,** gruel, take in hand, tear strips off, tutor, use severely; **harden,** indurate, put one's foot down, stiffen

BE STUPID *v* have come down in the last shower, have kangaroos in the top paddock, have no brains, have slipped one's trolley, have whiteants, not know if it's Bourke Street or Tuesday, not know if it's Pitt Street or Christmas, not know the time of day, not know what day it is, take leave of one's senses

BE SURPLUS *v* go begging, go to waste, overabound, run over, superabound; **overflow,** brim over, burst at the seams, run a bunker, well over

BE SURPRISED *v* hit the ceiling, hit the roof, jump out of one's skin, not know what hit one, sit up, start

bet *n* → **1** gamble *v* **2** be uncertain **3** gamble

betide *v* → occur

BE TIMELY *v* make hay while the sun shines, strike while the iron is hot, take time by the forelock; **catch,** make

BE TIRED *v* droop, faint, feel like a greasespot, languish, sink, stagger; **collapse,** be fagged out, crack up, drop, pack up; **do one's dash,** have shot one's bolt, knock oneself out

betoken *v* → **1** mean **2** signify

BE TRANSPARENT *v* allow light, show through; **make transparent,** clarify, clear

BETRAY *v* collaborate, doublecross, give away, knife in the back, sell down the river, sell out; **dob in,** blow the whistle on, dingo on, dob on, grass on, put in, rat on, scab on, shop, snitch on, turn king's evidence on, weasel; **belie,** fall away from, play fast and loose with, play someone false; **two-time,** cheat on, deceive

betray *v* → **1** disenchant **2** display

BETRAYAL *n* breach of promise, breach of trust, give-away, sell-out; **defection,** collaboration, double-dealing, foul play, high treason, perfidy, treachery, treason; **adultery,** a bit on the side, extramarital sex. *See also* UNFAITHFULNESS

BETRAYER *n* apostate, backstabber, belier, blackleg, changeling *(Archaic)*, Delilah, double-crosser, double-dealer, fairweather friend, fink, grasser, Iscariot, judas, Mata Hari, ratter, recreant, renegade, scab, snake, snake in the grass, snitch, snitcher, stool pigeon, tergiversator, traditor, viper, weasel; **collaborator,** collaborationist, fifth column, fifth columnist, quisling, security risk, silvertail, traitor, traitress, Trojan Horse, welsher; **adulterer,** adulteress, two-timer

betroth *v* → marry

BETROTHED *n* fiancé, fiancée, intended

BE TRUE *v* be a fact, be the case, conform to fact, hold good, hold true, hold water, ring true, stand the test; **prove to be fact,** authenticate, verify

BE TRUTHFUL *v* be in earnest, mean what one says, stick to the facts, tell the truth

better *n* → **1** gambler **2** good thing *v* **3** defeat **4** improve **5** surpass *adj* **6** good **7** healthy **8** improved

BETWEEN *prep* amid, amidst, among, betwixt *(Archaic)*; **'tween,** 'twixt *(Archaic)*

BE UNABLE TO PAY *v* fail, go bankrupt, go bung, go to the wall, take the knock *(Horseracing)*; **postpone payment,** charge, defer payment, put on account, put on the slate; **stop payment,** protest, refuse payment, repudiate, scale down, suspend

BE UNCERTAIN *v* be in a quandary, dither, doubt, flounder, hesitate, lose the scent, lose the trail, misgive, not know which way to turn, vacillate, wonder; **take a chance,** bet, buy a pig in a poke, wager; **hang in the balance,** depend, suspend

BE UNFRIENDLY *v* bear ill will, bear malice, grudge, gun for, have it in for; **quarrel,** come to blows, rencounter; **hound,** oppress, persecute, spite; **snub,** cut someone dead, give someone the deep freeze, give the cold shoulder to, ignore, keep at arm's length, turn one's back on; **ostracise,** boycott, excommunicate, have nothing to do with, send to Coventry, treat as a leper; **alienate,** antagonize, cause bad blood, dissocialise, estrange, rupture, set at odds; **sulk,** have a hate on, have a snout on, have the sulks

BE UNGRATEFUL *v* look a gift-horse in the mouth, take as one's due, take for granted, turn one's nose up; **grumble,** complain, whinge; **omit to thank,** forget to thank; **begrudge a thankyou,** not be beholden to, see no reason to thank; **forget a kindness,** return evil for good

BE UNHAPPY *v* be sad, have a face as long as a fiddle, have a face as long as a wet week, have a lump in the throat, have one's heart in one's boots, sorrow; **droop,** languish, slump; **brood,** chew the rag, moan, mope; **cry,** cry one's eyes out, have a good cry, have a good moan, pipe one's eye *(Brit.)*, snivel, weep; **pine,** eat one's heart out, grieve

BE UNIMPORTANT *v* be no great shakes, be not worth a cracker, be not worth two bob, be nothing to boast about, make no odds, not be a row of beans, not matter a twopenny damn, not matter a twopenny dump; **be all the same,** be neither here nor there; **play second fiddle,** take a back seat

BE UNPALATABLE *v* nauseate, turn, turn one's stomach; **pall,** cloy, lose its appeal, lose its savour

BE UNREADY *v* be caught napping, be caught short, be caught with one's pants down; **go off half-cocked**

BE UNSELFISH *v* be altruistic, be disinterested, bend over backwards, do as you would be done by, go out of one's way, live for others, make a sacrifice, observe the golden rule, put oneself out, sacrifice oneself

BE UNWILLING *v* back off, baulk, baulk at, be disinclined, be reluctant, boggle, boggle at, disincline, fight shy of, have no stomach for, hesitate, jib, jib at, nill *(Archaic)*, not be in the mood for, pussyfoot, scruple, shake one's head, shy away from; **hang back,** drag the chain, not cooperate, not pull one's weight, shirk, slack, slack off; **grudge,** begrudge

bevel *v* → cut

beverage *n* → drink

BE VIOLENT *v* be on the rampage, go on the rampage, lash out, rage, ramp, rampage, rant, swash; **bluster,** roar, storm, thunder; **run wild,** break away, break bounds, run amuck, stampede; **riot,** run riot; **see red,** get up, go beserk; **brutalise,** barbarise, bestialise; **assault,** attack, go bull-headed at, tear into; **manhandle,** bemaul, do violence to, knock about, knock around, tousle; **bully,** bullyrag, chuck one's weight about, give someone the shock treatment, strongarm *(U.S.)*; **violate,** outrage

bevy *n* → **1** gathering **2** many

bewail *v* → grieve

BE WANTING *v* be lacking, not suffice, run dry, run low, run out, run short

BEWARE *interj* action stations, cave *(Brit. Colloq.)*, caveat emptor, look out, watch it, watch out

beware *v* → be cautious

BE WEALTHY *v* be born with a silver spoon in one's mouth, be rolling in it, have a quid, have money to burn; **make money,** clean up, coin; **prosper,** coin it, mint it, strike it rich, thrive; **enrich oneself,** accumulate wealth, aggrandise, batten on, feather one's nest, line one's pocket, stash it away

bewilder *v* → **1** confuse **2** misguide

BE WILLING *v* be disposed, be inclined, be of a mind to, enthuse, have a mind to, have no scruples, lean towards, see fit, think fit; **agree,** acquiesce, concur, give one's consent, go along with, lend a willing ear, make no bones about, turn a willing ear; **volunteer,** offer oneself

BE WISE *v* have a good head on one's shoulders, have a lot of nous, have one's head screwed on the right way

BEWITCH *v* charm, enchant, fascinate *(Obs.)*, mesmerise, spellbind; **cast a spell on,** hex, overlook, point the bone at, put the mozz on, voodoo, witch

bewitch *v* → **1** enchant **2** encourage

BEWITCHER *n* carline *(Scot.)*, charmer, enchanter, enchantress, sorcerer, sorceress, warlock, witch, wizard; **alchemist,** chemist *(Obs.)*, philosopher *(Obs.)*; **witchdoctor,** bone-pointer *(Aborig.)*, fetishist, gulli-gulli man, kadaicha man *(Aborig.)*, koradji, medicine man, voodooist; **miracle-worker,** magus, thaumaturge, theurgist; **conjurer,** magician, prestidigitator

beyond *n* → **1** afterworld *adv* **2** additionally **3** superiorly *prep* **4** outside

bias *n* → **1** distortion **2** inequality **3** intolerance **4** point of view **5** prejudice **6** unfairness *v* **7** persuade

bib *n* → **1** overcoat *v* **2** drink alcohol

bible *n* → breviary

bibliography *n* → **1** list **2** reference book

bicameral *adj* → **1** legislative **2** two

bicentenary *n* → anniversary

bicker *n* → **1** disagreement **2** discussion *v* **3** contest **4** disagree **5** hurry **6** shine **7** talk

BICYCLE *n* bike, BMX, boneshaker, chopper, coaster, cycle, dragster, high-riser, penny-farthing, pushbike, safety bicycle, tandem, treadle, velocipede; **tricycle,** dinky, pedicab, quadricycle, three-wheeler, trike, unicycle; **skateboard,** roller skate, scooter; **motorcycle,** ag-bike, agricultural bike, easy rider, grid, iron horse *(Archaic)*, moped, motor scooter, motorbike, solo, trail bike; **sidecar,** chair *(Colloq.)*, combination

bicycle *v* → drive

bid *n* → **1** attempt **2** cost **3** entreaty **4** gamble **5** offer *v* **6** appraise **7** command **8** gamble **9** offer

bidding *n* → **1** command **2** offering

biddy *n* → **1** old people **2** woman

bide *v* → **1** continue **2** inhabit **3** persevere

bidet *n* → bath

biennial *n* → **1** anniversary **2** plant

bier *n* → coffin

BIG *adj* biggish, bull, decuman, double, family-size, great, large, mickle *(Scot.)*, queen-size, sizeable; **bulky,** cyclopean, elephantine, gross, heavy, massive, massy, megalithic, monumental; **ample,** capacious, expansive, voluminous; **huge,** broad, enormous, jumbo, king, king-size, mammoth, mighty, old-man, titanic; **gigantic,** Brobdingnagian, colossal, Gargantuan, giant, gigantean, gigantesque, immense, monster, monstrous, prodigious, strapping; **extensive,** palatial, spacious, sweeping; **vast,** cosmic, vasty *(Poetic)*; **walloping,** slashing, smacking, swingeing, thumping, whopping

big *adj* → **1** expensive **2** generous **3** great **4** important **5** loud **6** pregnant **7** tasty **8** unselfish *adv* **9** braggingly **10** greatly

bigamy *n* → marriage

bight *n* → **1** bay **2** cord **3** curve *v* **4** fasten

bigot *n* → intolerant person

big top *n* → auditorium

bigwig *n* → important person

bike *n* → **1** bicycle **2** promiscuous person **3** sexual partner
bikini *n* → swimwear
bilateral *adj* → **1** interactive **2** two
bile *n* → irritableness
bilge *n* → **1** bottom **2** dirt **3** nonsense *v* **4** bulge **5** open up
bilious *adj* → **1** irritable **2** nauseous
bilk *n* → **1** dishonesty *v* **2** avoid **3** cheat **4** elude **5** escape **6** fail to pay **7** hinder
BILL *n* blister, demand, dun, final notice, invoice, Jack-n'-Jill; **IOU,** marker; **promissory note,** bill *(Obs.)*, bond, calabash, certificate of deposit, debenture, debenture stock. *See also* DEBT
bill *n* → **1** account **2** accusation **3** bill **4** capital **5** cash **6** insistence **7** law **8** mound **9** public notice **10** spear *v* **11** account **12** insist on **13** kiss **14** list **15** plan **16** publicise
billabong *n* → lake
billet *n* → **1** bedroom **2** employment **3** fuel **4** hotel **5** job **6** record *v* **7** house
billow *n* → **1** bulge **2** surf *v* **3** bulge
billy *n* → **1** cookware **2** sheep
billygoat *n* → **1** incompetent **2** sheep
bin *n* → **1** barrel **2** pocket **3** prison
binary *n* → **1** two *adj* **2** numerical **3** two
bind *n* → **1** adhesive **2** annoyance **3** bond **4** bore **5** musical score **6** restraints **7** soil **8** stroke *v* **9** cover **10** edge **11** fasten **12** harden **13** harvest **14** obligate **15** promise **16** restrain **17** stick together
BINGE *n* bacchanalia, barney, bash, bat, beanfeast, bender, blow-out, bust, debauch, gorge, jag, lost weekend, orgy, saturnalia, splurge, spree, wallow
binge *n* → drinking session
binocular *adj* → optical
BINOMIAL *adj* biquadratic, quadratic, quadric, quintic, trinomial
binomial *n* → **1** name **2** number
biochemistry *n* → biology
biodegradable *adj* → destructive
biography *n* → **1** memory **2** record **3** story
BIOLOGIST *n* bacteriologist, cytologist, ecologist, histologist, microbiologist
biopsy *n* → analysis
bipartite *adj* → **1** halved **2** partial **3** separate
biplane *n* → aeroplane
birch *n* → **1** club **2** stick **3** timber *v* **4** cudgel
bird *n* → **1** aeroplane **2** aim **3** certain thing **4** imprisonment **5** nonconformist **6** period **7** person **8** prison **9** woman *v* **10** hunt
BIRDCALL *n* birdsong, boom, charm, cheep, chirm, chirp, chirr, chirrup, chorus, coo, cuckoo, roll, screech, squawk, toot, trill, tweet, twitter, warble; **cackle,** caw, clack, clang, clink, croak; **song,** note, pipe, piping, woodnote; **dawn chorus,** matin, matin song; **crowing,** cock-a-doodle-doo, cockcrow, gobble, honk, quack, swan song. *See also* ANIMAL CALL
BIRDLIKE *adj* ornithoid; **avian,** avifaunal, ornithic; **winged,** alar, alary, alate, aliform, pennate, volant; **anatine,** anserine *(geese)*, aquiline *(eagles)*, columbine *(doves)*, corvine *(crows)*, gallinaceous *(fowl)*, grallatorial *(wading birds)*, halcyon *(kingfishers)*, hirundine *(swallows)*, larine *(gulls)*, pavonine *(peacocks)*, rasorial *(fowl)*, strigiform *(owls)*, struthious *(ostriches)*, turdine *(thrushes)*, vulturine *(vultures)*
bird's-eye *adj* → multicoloured
biretta *n* → cap
biro *n* → writing materials
BIRTH *n* accouchement, childbed, confinement, delivery, lying-in, time; **child-bearing,** childbirth, parturiency, parturition; **Leboyer birth,** breech birth, breech delivery, caesarean section, homebirth, natural childbirth; **labour,** pains, throes, travail; **false labour,** couvade, pre-labour; **puerperium; abortion,** miscarriage, stillbirth; **delivery room,** labour ward; **farrowing house,** hatchabator, hatchery, nest, rookery, springer paddock, stud-farm
birth *n* → **1** ancestry **2** start
birthday *n* → **1** anniversary **2** festival
birthrate *n* → conception
birthright *n* → rights
biscuit *adj* → brown
bisect *v* → **1** halve **2** separate
BISECTOR *n* diagonal, diameter, divider, dividing line, equator
bisexual *n* → **1** sexual type *adj* **2** opposing **3** sexual
bishop *n* → ecclesiastic
bistro *n* → **1** pub **2** restaurant **3** shop
BIT *n* cut, dab, deal, jot, minim, ounce, peck, pennyworth, piece, pinch, portion, rap, snip, snippet, tittle; **drop,** draught, dreg, dribble, dribs and drabs, drink, droob, sup, thimbleful; **mouthful,** bite, chew, gulp; **block,** cube, nugget, slab; **clod,** clot, divot, divvy, sod, turf. *See also* AMOUNT
bit *n* → **1** coinage **2** information **3** part **4** piercer **5** share **6** small amount **7** woman *v* **8** restrain
bitch *n* → **1** bad person **2** complainer *v* **3** complain **4** spoil
bite *n* → **1** angle **2** answer **3** bit **4** complainer **5** friction **6** hold **7** injury **8** meal **9** part **10** pungency **11** request **12** roughness *v* **13** be angry **14** beg **15** be had **16** discontent **17** eat **18** engrave **19** extort **20** hold **21** injure **22** pain **23** perforate
biting *adj* → **1** disapproving **2** painful **3** sharp
bitter *n* → **1** beer *adj* **2** acrimonious **3** distressing **4** hating **5** painful **6** sharp **7** sour **8** unfriendly **9** unpleasant
bitters *n* → sourness
bittersweet *adj* → **1** pleasant **2** sour
bitumen *n* → paving
bivouac *n* → **1** camp *v* **2** inhabit
bizarre *adj* → **1** nonconformist **2** strange
blab *n* → **1** revelation **2** speaking *v* **3** reveal **4** speak
BLACK *n* blue-black, crow, jet, jet black, raven, sable, sloe; **blackness,** darkness, inkiness, lividness, nigritude, obscurity, pitchiness, sootiness, swarthiness; **nigrescence,**

nigrification; **shading,** shadow; **black and white,** chiaroscuro

BLACK *adj* black as jet, black as pitch, black as the ace of spades, coal-black, dark, dusky, inky, livid, piceous *(Zool.)*, pitch-black, pitchy, raven, sable *(Poetic)*, sombre, swart *(Archaic)*, swarthy; **blackish,** coaly, fuliginous, nigrescent; **blackened,** burnt, corked, japanned, sooty, ustulate; **ebony,** jet, jetty; **black-browed,** black-headed, brunette

black *n* → **1** blackener **2** death **3** grieving **4** single person *v* **5** blacken **6** clean *adj* **7** dark **8** destructive **9** dirty **10** hopeless **11** immoral **12** menacing **13** prohibited **14** sombre **15** unlawful **16** wrong

blackball *n* → **1** boo **2** election **3** prohibiter *v* **4** boycott **5** elect **6** prohibit

blackban *v* → prohibit

black ban *n* → **1** industrial action **2** prohibition **3** strike

blackbird *n* → servant

blackboard *n* → writing materials

BLACKEN *v* black, blot, darken, nigrify, smudge; **black-lead,** charcoal, cork, smoke; **ebonise,** japan

blacken *v* → **1** darken **2** slander **3** swear

BLACKENER *n* animal black, black, blacking, carbon black, ivory black, lampblack, nigrosine; **Indian ink,** japan, kohl, printer's ink

blackguard *n* → **1** discourteous person **2** mischief-maker **3** wrongdoer *v* **4** misbehave **5** slander **6** swear

blackhead *n* → **1** disfigurement **2** sore

black hole *n* → **1** cell **2** room

blackjack *n* → **1** club **2** drinking vessel **3** gambling *v* **4** cudgel **5** force **6** menace

blackleg *n* → **1** betrayer **2** crook

black list *n* → **1** list **2** prohibition

black-list *v* → **1** eject **2** list **3** prohibit

black magic *n* → **1** magic **2** the supernatural

blackmail *n* → **1** embezzlement **2** force **3** menace **4** payment **5** taking *v* **6** bribe **7** extort **8** menace

black-market *adj* → unlawful

blackout *n* → **1** blindness **2** dark **3** disappearance **4** extinguishing **5** forgetting **6** hiding **7** unconsciousness *adj* **8** dark

black out *v* → **1** become unconscious **2** darken **3** extinguish **4** hide **5** keep secret **6** obscure

black sheep *n* → bad person

blacksmith *n* → **1** cook **2** metalworker

blacktracker *n* → pursuer

BLADDER *n* ureter, urethra, vesica, waterworks; **vesicle,** bursa, capsule, cistern, cyst, sinus; **duct,** tube, vas, vessel

bladder *n* → bag

blade *n* → **1** knife **2** man **3** sword **4** thinness

blame *n* → **1** accusation **2** disapproval **3** imputation *v* **4** disapprove of **5** impute

blanch *v* → **1** be frightened **2** cook **3** frighten **4** lose colour **5** separate **6** whiten

bland *adj* → **1** composed **2** insipid **3** pleasant

blandish *v* → **1** flatter **2** persuade

blank *n* → **1** absence **2** centre **3** emptiness **4** gap **5** non-being *v* **6** annihilate **7** remove *adj* **8** absent **9** bare **10** boring **11** colourless **12** confused **13** cursed **14** deficient **15** empty **16** most **17** nonexistent **18** white

blanket *n* → **1** bedclothes **2** cloak *v* **3** cover **4** hide **5** punish **6** set sail *adj* **7** general

blare *n* → **1** boom **2** dissonance **3** loud sound *v* **4** be dissonant **5** be loud **6** call (of animals) **7** publicise **8** ring

blarney *n* → **1** flattery *v* **2** flatter **3** persuade

blasé *adj* → **1** bored **2** composed **3** satisfied

blaspheme *v* → **1** profane **2** swear

blast *n* → **1** explosion **2** loud sound **3** reprimand **4** wind *v* **5** blow **6** contract **7** disease **8** explode **9** scold **10** spoil *interj* **11** God

blast furnace *n* → metalworks

BLATANT *adj* flagrant, glaring, striking; **manifest,** apparent, clear as day, evincible, obvious, patent, unmistakable, visible; **in the limelight,** conspicuous, in the foreground, pronounced; **unconcealed,** barefaced, brazen, flaunting, naked

blatant *adj* → vulgar

blather *n* → **1** nonsense **2** speaking *v* **3** speak **4** talk nonsense

blaze *n* → **1** fire **2** greatness **3** label **4** light **5** multicolour **6** outburst **7** shot *v* **8** be hot **9** blow **10** catch fire **11** cut **12** emblematise **13** label **14** make history **15** publicise **16** shine

blazer *n* → **1** fire **2** jacket

blazon *v* → **1** display **2** emblematise **3** publicise

bleach *n* → **1** decolourant *v* **2** lose colour **3** whiten

bleak *adj* → **1** bare **2** cold **3** hopeless **4** sombre

bleat *n* → **1** animal call **2** complaint *v* **3** call (of animals) **4** complain **5** speak

BLEED *v* haemorrhage; **menstruate,** be leaking, be on the rags, have George visiting, have one's period, have the flags out, see the flowers, see the roses, see the visitors

bleed *n* → **1** bleeding *v* **2** discharge **3** extort **4** extract

BLEEDER *n* haemophiliac

BLEEDING *n* bleed, epistaxis, gush, haemorrhage, nosebleed; **menstruation,** catamenia, flowers, girl's week, menses, menstrual flow, monthly, period, the curse

bleep *n* → **1** signal *v* **2** shrill

blemish *n* → **1** bad thing **2** disfigurement **3** imperfection *v* **4** disfigure **5** uglify

blench *v* → **1** be frightened **2** lose colour **3** whiten

blend *n* → **1** abridgment **2** word *v* **3** combine **4** cook **5** mix

blender *n* → **1** cookware **2** mixer

bless *v* → **1** approve **2** be grateful **3** protect

blessed *adj* → **1** fortunate **2** holy

blessing *n* → **1** good **2** good fortune **3** religious ceremony **4** worship

blight *n* → **1** destroyer **2** deterioration **3** misfortune *v* **4** contract **5** destroy **6** disease **7** spoil

BLIND *v* bedazzle, blear, hoodwink, put another's eyes out, seel *(Archaic)*, throw dust in another's eyes; **be blind,** go blind, lose one's sight; **blindfold,** darken, dazzle, hood

BLIND *adj* amaurotic, blind as a bat, blind as a wombat, blinded, eyeless, moon-blind, sightless, stone-blind, visionless; **temporarily blind,** bedazzled, blind drunk, nyctalopic, snow-blind

blind *n* → **1** darkener **2** drinking session **3** hiding place *v* **4** darken *adj* **5** closed **6** drunk **7** hidden **8** illogical **9** intolerant **10** prejudiced **11** rash **12** stupid **13** unconscious *adv* **14** rashly

blindfold *v* → **1** blind **2** cover *adj* **3** rash

BLINDNESS *n* amaurósis, blackout, moon blindness *(Vet. Sci.)*, retrolental fibroplasia; **temporary blindness,** day blindness, dazzle, flash blindness, hemeralopia, snow blindness. *See also* FAULTY SIGHT

BLIND PERSON *n* four-eyes, myope, protanope, squinter, the blind, tritanope; **boko**

blind spot *n* → **1** ignorance **2** prejudice

blink *n* → **1** light **2** look *v* **3** shine

blinker *n* → indicator

bliss *n* → **1** contentedness **2** heaven **3** pleasure

blister *n* → **1** bad person **2** bill **3** bubble **4** bulge **5** disfigurement **6** legal order **7** sibling *v* **8** bulge **9** insult **10** mock

blithe *adj* → **1** happy **2** joyful

blitz *n* → **1** attack **2** cleansing **3** gunfire *v* **4** fire on **5** wage war

blizzard *n* → **1** snow **2** violent outburst **3** wind

bloat *n* → **1** bulge *v* **2** bulge **3** pride oneself

blob *n* → **1** bead **2** bubble **3** fool **4** liquid

bloc *n* → **1** nation **2** society

block *n* → **1** bit **2** callousness **3** discourager **4** footgear **5** head **6** house **7** information **8** matter **9** model **10** obstacle **11** post **12** sign **13** stocks and shares **14** timepiece **15** yard *v* **16** discourage **17** obstruct **18** shape **19** support

blockade *n* → **1** closure **2** obstacle **3** war *v* **4** attack **5** close **6** come between **7** obstruct **8** wage war

blockbuster *n* → entertainment

blockhouse *n* → **1** fortification **2** fortress **3** house

bloke *n* → man

blond *n* → **1** yellow *adj* **2** white **3** yellow

blood *n* → **1** ancestry **2** character **3** hero **4** immoral person **5** living **6** man *v* **7** initiate

bloodbath *n* → massacre

bloodcurdling *adj* → frightening

bloodhound *n* → **1** hunter **2** searcher

bloodshed *n* → **1** act of war **2** killing

bloodshot *adj* → **1** reddish **2** unwholesome

bloodthirsty *adj* → **1** ferocious **2** murderous **3** warlike

BLOOD VESSEL *n* arteriole, artery, capillary, vein, vena, venule

bloody *v* → **1** redden *adj* **2** cursed **3** disfigured **4** most **5** murderous **6** red **7** stubborn **8** unfair **9** unmanageable *adv* **10** very

bloom *n* → **1** colour **2** glaze **3** health **4** mineral **5** perfection **6** powder *v* **7** be fertile **8** be healthy **9** flower **10** grow **11** prosper

bloomers *n* → underwear

blossom *v* → **1** be fertile **2** flower **3** prosper

blot *n* → **1** buttocks **2** denigration **3** dirt *v* **4** absorb **5** blacken **6** darken **7** depict **8** disgrace **9** dry **10** hide **11** obscure

blotch *n* → **1** dirt **2** disfigurement *v* **3** disfigure

blouse *n* → **1** jacket **2** shirt *v* **3** hang

BLOW *v* blast, blaze *(Obs.)*, bluster, howl, overblow, rage, squall, storm *(U.S.)*

blow *n* → **1** accomplishment **2** attack **3** bragging **4** breathing **5** concert **6** corporal punishment **7** disenchantment **8** hit **9** misfortune **10** rest **11** rock outcrop **12** unpleasant thing **13** walk **14** wind *v* **15** breathe **16** depart **17** eroticise **18** fail **19** hiss **20** report on **21** shape **22** shrill **23** squander

blowhole *n* → opening

blowlamp *n* → heater

blow out *v* → **1** become greater **2** extinguish

blow-out *n* → **1** binge **2** entertainment **3** explosion **4** extravagance **5** meal

blowpipe *n* → **1** gun **2** piping

blow up *v* → **1** air **2** be angry **3** explode **4** increase **5** scold **6** stop

blow-up *n* → **1** angry act **2** explosion **3** irritation **4** photograph

blubber *n* → **1** cry **2** fat *v* **3** be loud **4** grieve **5** speak *adj* **6** increased **7** swollen

bludge *v* → **1** avoid **2** beg **3** borrow **4** idle **5** prostitute oneself

bludgeon *n* → **1** club *v* **2** cudgel **3** force **4** menace

bludge on *v* → take advantage of

BLUE *n* azure, bluebell, caerulean, cerulean, cornflower, forget-me-not, lapis lazuli, sapphire, sky blue; **light blue,** Copenhagen blue, pearl blue, pearl grey, powder blue, Wedgwood blue; **deep blue,** anil, Bristol blue, gentian blue, indigo, perse, royal blue, ultramarine, violet; **navy,** blue-black, navy blue; **electric blue,** peacock blue; **slate,** steel blue; **blue-green,** aqua, aquamarine, beryl, Nile blue, saxe blue, sea, turquoise

BLUE *adj* cold, cyanic, ice-blue, pavonine, sapphirine, woaded; **azure,** azury, cerulean, sky-blue, skyey *(Poetic)*; **bluish,** blue-green, bluey, glaucous; **blue-grey,** cyanotic, livid, slaty

blue *n* → **1** error **2** fight **3** intellectual **4** legal order **5** mister **6** redhead *v* **7** fight **8** squander *adj* **9** cold **10** cooked **11** disfigured **12** dissonant **13** obscene **14** unhappy

bluebell *n* → blue

blue blood *n* → **1** aristocracy **2** aristocrat

blue-collar *adj* → working

BLUENESS *n* bluishness; **lividness,** cyanosis, lividity

BLUE PIGMENT *n* bice, Brunswick blue, cobalt blue, cyanin, indican, indophenol, induline, Prussian blue, smalt, Thenard's blue, true blue, verditer, viridian, woad, zaffre;

washing blue, blue-bag; **blue light,** Bengal light, Bengal match; **blueing**

blueprint *n* → 1 copy 2 diagram 3 photograph *v* 4 copy 5 map

blue-ribbon *adj* → superior

blues *n* → unhappiness

bluestocking *n* → 1 intellectual *adj* 2 intellectual

blue-tongue *n* → 1 farmhand 2 labourer

bluey *n* → 1 bag 2 legal order 3 mister *adj* 4 blue

bluff *n* → 1 bombast 2 display 3 fake 4 mountain 5 stratagem 6 trickery *v* 7 beguile 8 trick *adj* 9 discourteous 10 erect 11 forthright 12 friendly

blunder *n* → 1 bungle 2 error 3 failure *v* 4 become confused 5 bungle 6 err 7 reveal

BLUNT *v* dull, hebetate, obtund, turn

BLUNT *adj* dull, dullish, flat, flat as a tack, obtundent, obtuse, pointless, worn; **rounded,** hebetate *(Bot.)*, obtuse; **club-shaped,** clavate, claviform

blunt *v* → 1 moderate 2 weaken *adj* 3 curvilinear 4 discourteous 5 forthright 6 honest 7 stupid

BLUNTLY *adv* dully, obtusely

blur *n* → 1 imprecision *v* 2 anaesthetise 3 dirty

blurb *n* → public notice

blurt *v* → speak

blush *v* → 1 become confused 2 be guilty 3 be modest 4 redden *adj* 5 red

bluster *n* → 1 bragging 2 loud sound 3 menace 4 violent outburst *v* 5 be loud 6 be violent 7 blow 8 brag 9 menace 10 oppose

boa *n* → neckwear

board *n* → 1 book part 2 coating 3 council 4 court of law 5 edge 6 food 7 hotel 8 legislative body 9 management 10 shaft 11 stable 12 surfboard 13 wrapper *v* 14 contact 15 enter 16 house 17 inhabit

boarder *n* → 1 occupant 2 pupil

boarding school *n* → school

boast *n* → 1 bragging 2 challenge *v* 3 brag 4 pride oneself

boat *n* → 1 vessel 2 watercraft *v* 3 transport

boater *n* → hat

boatswain *n* → seaman

bob *n* → 1 accumulation 2 corporal punishment 3 courtesy 4 float 5 hair 6 hairdressing 7 hitting 8 move 9 pat 10 pendant 11 remnant 12 ringing 13 sledge 14 tangle *v* 15 bow 16 fish 17 float 18 gesture 19 hit 20 lower 21 move

bobby pin *n* → clip

bobsleigh *n* → 1 sledge *v* 2 drive

bode *v* → 1 anticipate 2 predict

bodgie *n* → 1 adolescent 2 bad person 3 faker 4 man 5 name 6 nonconformist *adj* 7 bad 8 fake 9 useless

bodice *n* → 1 jacket 2 underwear

BODILY *adj* animal, corporal, corporeal, fleshly, physical, skeletal, systemic; **anatomical,** audiological, gastrological, ophthalmological, topical; **anterior,** inferior, posterior, sagittal, superior; **organic,** biliary, cardiac, hepatitic, lymphatic, pancreatic, renal, splenetic, thyroid

bodily *adj* → 1 tangible *adv* 2 wholly

BODILY DISCHARGE *n* eccrisis, egestion, excretion; **discharge,** defluxion, flow, gleet, ichor, lochia, matter, maturation, pus, suppuration, swab; **perspiration,** diaphoresis, exudate, exudation, foam, lather, sudor, sweat, transpiration; **menstruation,** catamenia, dysmenorrhoea, friends, George, girls' week, menses, monthly, period, the curse; **gore,** cruor, grume; **excrement,** excreta; **sewage,** effluent, nightsoil, soil. *See also* SECRETION; DEFECATION; URINATION

bodkin *n* → nail

BODY *n* bulk *(Rare)*, carcass *(Joc.)*, corpse *(Obs.)*, corpus, corpus delicti *(joc.)*, corse *(Archaic)*, soma, system, the body beautiful; **anatomy,** physique, vital statistics; **corporality,** corporeality, corporealness, physicality; **physiology,** endocrinology, neuroanatomy, neurology, neurophysiology, organology, otology

body *n* → 1 crowd 2 gathering 3 matter 4 part 5 person 6 solid body 7 taste 8 the dead 9 thickness

bodyguard *n* → 1 defender 2 protector 3 soldier

bog *n* → 1 defecation 2 sludge 3 swamp 4 toilet 5 wetness *v* 6 defecate 7 fall

boggle *n* → 1 bungle 2 fairy 3 fright 4 frightener 5 jumble 6 worry *v* 7 be frightened 8 be unwilling 9 bungle 10 lack courage 11 pretend 12 vacillate 13 worry

bogie *n* → 1 lake 2 wagon 3 wetting

bogus *adj* → fake

bogy *n* → 1 aircraft 2 fairy 3 frightener

bohemian *n* → 1 artist 2 intellectual 3 nonconformist *adj* 4 informal 5 intellectual 6 nonconformist

boil *n* → 1 bulge 2 disfigurement 3 sore 4 turbulence *v* 5 be angry 6 be hot 7 bubble 8 cook 9 feel emotion 10 heat 11 toss

boiler *n* → 1 basin 2 heater 3 woman

boisterous *adj* → 1 liberated 2 noisy 3 violent

bold *n* → 1 letter *adj* 2 believing 3 courageous 4 discourteous 5 nonconformist 6 rash 7 thick 8 visible

bole *n* → soil

bolero *n* → jacket

boll *n* → bead

bollard *n* → 1 ice 2 makefast 3 obstacle 4 post 5 screen

bolshevik *n* → political ideologist

Bolshevik *n* → nonconformist

bolster *n* → 1 beam 2 chisel *v* 3 support

BOLT *n* barrel bolt, cap screw, dzus, explosive bolt, eye bolt, fishbolt, panic bolt, ringbolt; **nut,** butterfly nut, castellated nut, locknut, wing nut; **lock,** ball catch, catch, cylinder lock, dead latch, deadlock, night latch, padlock, safety catch, springlock, steering lock, yale lock; **latch,** hasp; **tumbler,** broach, snib, talon

bolt *n* → **1** escape **2** gun part **3** textiles *v* **4** back out **5** elude **6** escape **7** fasten **8** gorge **9** sew **10** speed

bomb *n* → **1** ball **2** car **3** casualty **4** drug **5** explosive **6** failure **7** rock *v* **8** dive **9** explode **10** fail **11** fire on **12** lose **13** wage war

bombard *n* → **1** gun *v* **2** fire on

BOMBAST *n* bad speaking, balderdash, blah, bluff, boasting, bravado, bunkum *(U.S.)*, fanfaronade, fustian, gasconade, hot air, Johnsonese, rodomontade, wind; **turgidity,** grandiloquence, magniloquence, orotundity, pomposity, pompousness, pretentiousness, sesquipedalianism, swollenness, tumidity; **demagoguery,** demagoguism, demagogy, oratory, rhetoric

bombast *n* → **1** affectedness **2** textiles

BOMBASTIC *adj* all piss'n'wind, circumlocutory, demagogic, fustian, grandiose, infelicitous, inflated, orotund, overblown, pompous, swollen, tub-thumping, tumid, turgid; **affected,** flamboyant, flashy, highfalutin, high-flown, pretentious, stilted; **sententious,** Johnsonian, pedantic, rhetorical

BOMBASTICALLY *adv* loftily, pretentiously, tumidly, turgidly, windily

bomber *n* → **1** aeroplane **2** soldier

bombora *n* → **1** current **2** island **3** shallow

bombshell *n* → **1** beautiful person **2** surpriser

bona fide *adj* → honest

bonanza *n* → **1** abundance **2** good fortune **3** luck **4** wealth

BOND *n* bind, hitch, ligament, link, tie, vinculum; **yoke,** fetter; **bandage,** ligature

bond *n* → **1** adhesive **2** bill **3** capital **4** contract **5** cord **6** funds **7** join **8** obligation **9** order **10** restraints **11** surety *v* **12** lend **13** stick together

bondage *n* → **1** repression **2** restraint **3** sexuality

bond money *n* → **1** funds **2** loan

BONE *n* atomy *(Obs.)*, frame, os, skeleton; **caput,** capitulum, condyle, diaphysis; **joint,** articulation, ball-and-socket joint, diarthrosis, enarthrosis, ginglymus, gomphosis, hinge, pivot joint, symphisis

bone *n* → **1** raw materials *v* **2** cook **3** fertilise **4** kill **5** rob

bonfire *n* → **1** fire **2** signal

bonhomie *n* → sociability

bonnet *n* → cap

bonny *adj* → **1** beautiful **2** good **3** healthy

bonus *n* → **1** addition **2** bribe **3** gift **4** income **5** surplus **6** surpriser *adj* **7** additional **8** surprising

bon voyage *interj* → **1** goodbye **2** hello

bony *adj* → **1** hard **2** knobby **3** thin

bonzer *adj* → **1** beautiful **2** good

BOO *n* brickbat, Bronx cheer, catcall, groan, handclap, hiss, raspberry, slow handclap, the bird, thumbs down; **sneer,** frown, scowl; **demerit,** black mark, blackball

boob *n* → **1** chest **2** error **3** fool **4** prison **5** stupid person *v* **6** err

booby *n* → **1** nonachiever **2** stupid person

booby trap *n* → **1** allure **2** fortification **3** obstacle *v* **4** hinder

BOOK *n* publication, rare book, title, tome, volume; **work,** autonym, classic, magnum opus; **codex,** manuscript, MS, palimpsest; **edition,** casebound, coedition, conflation, hardback, hardcover, limited edition, paperback, three-decker, trade edition, vanity edition, yearly; **first edition,** Aldine, incunabula; **series,** collection, library, set; **bestseller,** potboiler; **reprint,** reissue; **slim volume,** booklet, brochure, chapbook, fascicle, fascicule, fasciculus, pamphlet, part work; **remaindered volume; library book,** floater *(Colloq.)*; **novel; penny dreadful,** dime novel *(U.S.)*, dreadful, shocker, thriller; **pillow book,** curiosa *(U.S.)*, erotica, facetiae, yellowback; **cookery book,** cookbook, recipe book; **storybook,** picture book, pop-up book; **compilation,** anthology, collectanea, festschrift, garland, memoirs, miscellanea, miscellany, omnibus, Parnassus, potpourri, recollections, sketchbook, travels; **notebook,** album, diary

book *n* → **1** accumulation **2** gamble **3** list **4** musical score **5** plan *v* **6** buy **7** entreat **8** hold **9** lay charges **10** list **11** record

BOOKBINDING *n* blocking, border, carpet page, coat of arms, crest, dinkus, doublure, fillet, frontispiece, headpiece, illumination, initial, logo, marbling, panel, rib, tailpiece, tooling, vignette

bookcase *n* → cupboard

booking *n* → **1** contract **2** employment **3** holding

bookish *adj* → intellectual

bookkeeping *n* → accounting

BOOKLOVER *n* bibliomaniac, bibliophile; **book collector,** antiquarian; **librarian,** acquisitions librarian, bibliographer, cataloguer; **bibliomania,** bibliophilism

bookmaker *n* → gambler

BOOK PART *n* binding, board, half-binding, half-leather, rib, thermoplastic binding, three-quarter binding, yapp; **jacket,** cover, wrapper; **page,** bastard title, blocking, centrefold, centrespread, contents page, doublure, endpaper, flyleaf, frontispiece, half-title page, imprint page, leaf, recto, reverso, titlepage, verso; **gathering,** quire, section, signature; **quarto,** eighteenmo, eightvo, elephant, folio, sextodecimo, sixteenmo, thirty-twomo, twenty-fourmo, twentymo, vigesimo, vigesimo-quarto; **addendum,** appendix, colophon, corrigendum, end matter, foreword, index, induction *(Archaic)*, introduction, preface, prelims, subindex

BOOK TRADE *n* proofreading, publishing; **publisher; bookseller,** newsagent; **bookshop,** book store, newsagency, second-hand bookshop; **printer,** book designer, bookbinder, compositor, copytaker, layout artist, proofreader, reader, typesetter

bookworm *n* → **1** intellectual **2** pupil **3** reader

BOOM *n* bang, clank, clonk, clump, knock, thud, thump, wham, whop; **rumble,** growl, grumble, gurgle, thunder; **drumbeat,** beat, drumming, dub, rap, rappel, rataplan, roll, rub-a-dub, ruffle, tap, tapping, tom-tom; **tantara,** blare, honk

BOOM *v* bang, beat, clank, clonk, thud, thump; **rumble,** roll, thunder

boom *n* → **1** birdcall **2** explosion **3** increase **4** obstacle **5** pole *v* **6** become greater **7** be loud **8** explode **9** prosper

boomerang *n* → **1** bad debt **2** loan **3** reaction **4** spear *v* **5** go back **6** react *adj* **7** reactive

boon *n* → **1** good *adj* **2** happy **3** sociable

boor *n* → **1** country dweller **2** discourteous person **3** ignoramus **4** vulgarian

boost *n* → **1** help **2** lifting **3** propellant *v* **4** energise **5** help **6** increase **7** lift

booster *n* → **1** ammunition **2** electric generator **3** energiser **4** helper **5** increaser **6** medication

BOOT *n* Bill Masseys *(N.Z. Colloq.)*, blucher, bovver boot *(Brit. Colloq.)*, buskin, elastic sides, gambado, half-boot, jack boot, riding boot, shoe *(U.S.)*, surgical boot, top-boot, ug boot; **gumboot,** galosh *(Obs.)*, galoshes, gumshoe, overshoes *(U.S.)*, rubbers *(U.S.)*, wellies, wellington boot. *See also* FOOTGEAR

boot *n* → **1** footgear **2** kick **3** medication **4** takings *v* **5** be of service **6** dismiss

booth *n* → **1** compartment **2** election **3** room **4** shelter **5** shop

bootleg *n* → **1** alcohol **2** footgear *adj* **3** secretive

booty *n* → **1** loot **2** profit **3** takings

booze *n* → **1** alcohol **2** drinking session *v* **3** drink alcohol

borax *n* → cleanser

BORDER *v* march upon, skirt, verge on

border *n* → **1** bookbinding **2** edge **3** garden **4** region **5** side **6** surroundings **7** trimming **8** wall *v* **9** be close

borderline *n* → **1** edge **2** uncertain thing *adj* **3** limiting **4** obscene **5** strange **6** uncertain

BORE *n* alf, bromide, drip, fish head, humdrum, pain, pain in the neck, pill, shmo, vegetable, wet blanket; **pedant,** Dryasdust, lugger, sermoniser; **bind,** a big yawn, annoyance, bore, drag, nuisance, yawn; **cliché,** banality, commonplace, platitude; **sermon,** litany; **stodge,** purple prose; **dullsville,** daily grind, grindstone, the nine to five, treadmill, wet weekend; **culture desert**

BORE *v* bore the pants off, irk, leave cold, leave flat, make one yawn, pall on, send one to sleep, tire, try, try one's patience, weary; **be tedious,** cloy, dull, glut, jade, pall, stale; **protract,** do to death, drag out, outstay one's welcome, overdo; **drag on,** jog along, jog on, linger on, wear thin

bore *n* → **1** annoyance **2** bore **3** borehole **4** length **5** opening **6** surf **7** thickness *v* **8** open

BORED *adj* blasé, full of ennui, hipped *(U.S.)*, hippish *(U.S.)*, indifferent, jaded, melancholy, tired of, world-weary; **listless,** lethargic, weary; **fed up,** browned off, cheesed-off, fed up to the back teeth, jack of, pissed-off, sick to death of

BOREDOM *n* discontent, ennui, indifference, languor, lethargy, listlessness, satiety, seven-year itch, taedium vitae, weariness

BOREHOLE *n* artesian bore, artesian well, bore, wellpoint; **funnel,** tundish; **sinkhole,** pothole, sink, swallow-hole

borer *n* → **1** insect **2** opener **3** piercer

BORING *adj* dull, dull as dishwater, featureless; **tedious,** everlasting, stale, unrelieved, weariful, wearing, wearisome; **insipid,** flat, ho-hum, humdrum, incurious, ineffective, institutional, lifeless, pointless, sapless, tame, undramatic, unsatisfying; **pedantic,** dry, pedantical, platitudinous, sententious, sermonic, stodgy, stuffy; **irksome,** bolshie, distasteful, stultifying, tiresome; **slow,** dragging; **commonplace,** banal, clichéd, common, hackneyed, jejune, pedestrian, prosaic, prosy, stupid, trite, uninspired, uninspiring, unreadable, vapid; **monotonous,** monotone, repititious, uniform; **arid,** barren, blank, bovine, desolate, soul-destroying; **drab,** dreary; **leaden,** leady, plodding, ponderous, sodden, soggy; **soulless,** tasteless; **bucolic,** isolated, provincial, small-time

BORINGNESS *n* drabness, dreariness, dullness, pointlessness, stupidness, tedium, wearifulness, wearisomeness; **monotonousness,** everlastingness, humdrum, sameness, uniformity; **insipidity,** insipidness, jejuneness, lifelessness, staleness, sterility, tameness, vapidity, vapidness; **aridity,** aridness, barrenness, blankness, desolation, soullessness, tastelessness; **pedantry,** pedestrianism, prosaicness, prosaism, prosiness, sententiousness, stodginess, stuffiness, unreadability, unreadableness; **leadenness,** ponderosity, ponderousness, sogginess

born *adj* → inborn

borough *n* → **1** city **2** domain **3** electorate

BORROW *v* charter, gear *(Econ.)*, hire, lease, rent; **bludge,** bot, bum, cadge, fang, put in the fangs, put in the hooks, put in the nips, put in the screws, put the acid on, put the bite on, put the fangs into, put the hooks into, put the nips into, scrounge, snip, touch

borrow *v* → **1** be in debt **2** compute **3** take

BORROWER *n* debtor, mortgagor; **lessee,** hirer, renter, sublessee, tenant, under-lessee, undertenant; **leaser,** underletter; **bludger,** bastard from the bush, bloodsucker, bot, bumzack *(W.A.)*, cadger, scrounger

bosom *n* → **1** chest **2** emotion *v* **3** hold **4** kiss *adj* **5** friendly

BOSS *n* baas, boss cocky, boss of the board, bossboy, bwana, cock of the walk, cove *(Archaic)*, employer, foreman, forewoman, ganger, gov. *(Brit.)*, governor, guv, head, head serang, himself *(Colloq.)*, joss, maluka, manager, master, missus, mistress, number one, numero uno, old man, overseer, padrone *(U.S.)*, pannikin boss, sahib, senior, skip *(Sport)*, skipper, straw boss *(U.S.)*, supervisor, the man, top dog, tycoon; **gang boss,** capo, don, gang leader, godfather

boss *n* → 1 bulge 2 manager 3 mister 4 rock outcrop 5 teacher *v* 6 decorate 7 engrave 8 manage

bossy *adj* → 1 knobby 2 presumptuous

bosun *n* → seaman

botany *n* → flora

botch *n* → 1 bad thing 2 bungle 3 failure *v* 4 bungle 5 fail 6 spoil

both *adj* → 1 two *adv* 2 equally

bother *n* → 1 annoyance 2 busyness 3 confusion 4 worry *v* 5 annoy 6 care for 7 confuse 8 worry

bothy *n* → cabin

botte *n* → stroke

BOTTLE *n* aristotle, balthazar, dead marine, demijohn, double magnum, echo, flagon, half-bottle, jeroboam, magnum, methuselah, nebuchadnezzar, pig *(N.Z.)*, plagon, rehoboam, stubby; **flask,** canteen, carafe, costrel, decanter, feeding bottle, fiasco, flasket, glass can, hipflask, phial, water-bottle, water-monkey; **retort,** alembic, matrass, still; **measuring cup,** burette, dispenser, Erlenmeyer flask, graduate *(Rare)*, measuring cylinder, pipette, pycnometer; **vacuum flask,** Dewar flask, thermos; **hot water bottle,** hottie, warming pan; **cylinder,** aerosol container, aqualung, gas cylinder, plenum, pressure pack, soda siphon. *See also* VESSEL; DRINKING VESSEL; BARREL

bottle *n* → 1 toilet 2 vessel *v* 3 bowl over 4 conserve 5 insert

bottle baby *n* → offspring

bottlebrush *n* → washer

bottled gas *n* → fuel

bottle drive *n* → charity

bottle-feed *v* → feed

bottle green *n* → green

bottle-holder *n* → helper

bottleneck *n* → 1 hindrance 2 road 3 thinness *adj* 4 musical

bottle-shaped *adj* → hollow

bottle top *n* → plug

bottle up *v* → restrain

BOTTOM *n* base, bed, bedrock, floor, seat; **foundation,** baseboard, basis, bedding, bottom board, ceiling *(Naut.)*, cordon, deck head, flooring, groundsel *(Obs.)*, groundwork, podium, roadbed, rock, sea-floor, stereobate, sub-base, substratum, substructure, tholobate, understratum; **bottom part,** culet, exergue, foot, footing, heel, heelpiece, predella, skirt, stairfoot, strip footing, tail; **stump,** pedestal, plinth; **underside,** bilge, bulge *(Obs.)*, sole, underbody, undercarriage, underlay, underlayer, underneath, underpart, undersurface; **basement,** downstairs, undercroft, underground; **low level,** base level, baseline, invert, low, low-water mark, nadir, rock bottom

BOTTOM *adj* basal, base, basic, basilar, bottommost, downstairs, ground, lowermost, lowest, nethermost, radical, rock-bottom, stereobatic, sub-basal, submontane, sunken, underfoot, underground, underlaid, undermost; **underlying,** inferior *(Bot.)*, lower, nether, subjacent, under, ventral; **low,** depressed, lowly, prostrate, repent, reptant, surbased

bottom *n* → 1 buttocks 2 essence 3 failure 4 inferiority 5 inside 6 seaside 7 watercraft *v* 8 understand *adj* 9 fundamental

BOTTOMS UP *interj* cheers, chug-a-lug, down the hatch, here's looking at you, here's mud in your eye, here's to you, prost, skol, your health

boudoir *n* → bedroom

bough *n* → means of killing

boulder *n* → rock

boulevard *n* → road

BOUNCE *v* rebound, resile, spring

bounce *n* → 1 bragging 2 dismissal 3 happiness 4 impact 5 jump 6 move 7 pliability *v* 8 arrest 9 brag 10 dismiss 11 eject 12 jump 13 move 14 persuade

bound *n* → 1 jump *v* 2 jump 3 limit *adj* 4 fastened 5 obligated 6 prepared 7 restricted

BOUNDARY *adj* circumferential, circumscriptive, limbic, perimetric, perimetrical; **peripheral,** frontier, outmost, riverside, terminal; **marginal,** limbate, submarginal; **roadside,** wayside; **coastal,** littoral, seaboard, seaside

boundary *n* → 1 frame 2 limit 3 outside *adj* 4 outside

bounteous *adj* → 1 abundant 2 generous

bountiful *adj* → 1 abundant 2 generous

bounty *n* → 1 charity 2 generosity 3 gift 4 income

bouquet *n* → 1 applause 2 plant 3 smell

bourgeois *n* → 1 middle class 2 seller 3 trader *adj* 4 mediocre

bourgeoisie *n* → middle class

bout *n* → 1 fight 2 period

boutique *n* → shop

bovine *n* → 1 cattle *adj* 2 animal-like 3 boring

BOW *v* bend the knee, bob, curtsy, genuflect, kow-tow, make obeisance, salaam

bow *n* → 1 courtesy 2 curve 3 descent 4 front 5 gratefulness 6 greeting 7 knot 8 mariner 9 multicolour 10 pose 11 string instrument 12 tribute 13 worship *v* 14 be sociable 15 curve 16 lower 17 pay homage 18 repose 19 worship *adj* 20 curved

bowel *n* → abdomen

bower *n* → 1 anchor 2 bedroom 3 house 4 room 5 shelter *v* 6 enclose

bowerbird *n* → gatherer

bowl *n* → 1 ball 2 drinking session 3 party 4 tableware 5 throw 6 tobacco *v* 7 move 8 roll 9 speed 10 throw

bowler *n* → 1 hat 2 thrower

BOWL OVER *v* barrel, bottle, bowl down, deck, lay low, skittle; **fell,** flatten, floor, ground, iron out, knock down, knock endways, knock endwise, level, spread-eagle, tackle; **knock out,** concuss, king-hit, lay out, wooden; **overturn,** roll, tip over, tip up

BOX *n* can, carton, crate, packing case, tea-chest; **trunk,** imperial, portmanteau; **hatbox,** bandbox; **casket,** cartouche, chest, coffer; **safe,** moneybox, peter, piggy bank, strongbox, till; **locker,** glove box, glove compartment, medicine box, medicine chest; **letterbox,** ballot-box, mailbox, pillar-box, postbox; **snuffbox,** pillbox; **matchbox,** tinderbox; **window box,** fernery, flowerbox, flowerpot, jardinière, planter box, polyhouse, terrarium; **woodbox,** coalscuttle, hod, woodbin; **lunch box,** canteen, crib-box, crib-tin *(N.Z.)*, tuckerbox; **canister,** breadbin, caddy, firkin, tea caddy; **icebox,** car fridge, chillybin *(N.Z.)*, cool safe, cooler, Coolgardie safe, esky, frig, ice bucket, ice chest, refrigerator, stubby cooler. *See also* CASE; BASKET; BAG

box *n* → **1** armour **2** auditorium **3** cabin **4** cut **5** groin **6** hit **7** mixture **8** room **9** shelter **10** sound system **11** timber *v* **12** enclose **13** hit **14** insert **15** swerve

boxer *n* → **1** gambler **2** hat **3** hitter **4** pugilist

box office *n* → shop

boy *n* → **1** butler **2** children **3** lover **4** man *interj* **5** oh

BOYCOTT *v* bar, blackball, de-list, fence *(Archaic)*, keep out, ward off; **disqualify,** count out, debar, disenfranchise, disfranchise, suspend; **proscribe,** forbid, outlaw, taboo. *See also* ISOLATE; EXCLUDE

boycott *n* → **1** disuse **2** industrial action **3** prohibition *v* **4** avoid **5** be unfriendly **6** disuse **7** prohibit

bra *n* → underwear

BRACE *n* batten, cleat, stair-rod, stretcher, truss; **plate,** chill, cog, fishplate, gang nail, tang

brace *n* → **1** clip **2** holder **3** steadier **4** strengthener **5** support **6** tape **7** two *v* **8** rotate **9** steady **10** strengthen **11** support

bracelet *n* → **1** jewellery **2** restraints **3** ring

BRACHIAL *adj* carpal, clavicular, digital, humeral, index, manual, metacarpal, palmar, scapular; **pedal,** astragalgar, femoral, fibibular, geniculate, patellar, tarsal, tibial

bracket *n* → **1** class **2** concert **3** nose *v* **4** double **5** equalise **6** join **7** support

brackish *adj* → **1** sour **2** unsavoury

BRAG *v* big-mouth, bluster, boast, bounce, brave *(Obs.)*, bull, bulldust, crack up *(Obs.)*, crow, gasconade, pitch a line, puff, rodomontade, shoot a line, shoot off one's mouth, skite, swagger, talk big, trumpet, vapour, vaunt; **ego-trip,** big-note oneself, blow one's own trumpet, exult, glory, glory in, grandstand, sell oneself; **have a swelled head,** have tickets on oneself, think oneself Christmas, think oneself someone, think oneself something

brag *n* → **1** braggart **2** bragging

BRAGGART *n* big noter, big-mouth, bighead, boaster, brag, braggadocio, fanfaron, grandstander, name-dropper, pup, puppy, skite, skiter, vaunter; **blusterer,** blower, bouncer, bull artist, bullshit artist, tinhorn *(U.S.)*; **egoist,** egomaniac, egotist, narcissist

BRAGGART *adj* blustering, boasting, bragging, vainglorious; **boastful,** blustery, spread-eagle *(U.S.)*, swanky, thrasonical; **big-headed,** swelled-headed, swollen headed; **egoistic,** egoistical, egotistic, egotistical, narcissistic

BRAGGARTISM *n* egoism, egomania, egotism, narcissism, vainglory; **boastfulness,** swankiness, vaingloriousness

BRAGGING *n* blustering, boasting, ego-tripping, namedropping, skiting, vapouring; **bluster,** blow, bounce, bravado, puff, self-advertisement, swagger; **braggadocio,** bull, bullshit, fanfaronade, gasconade, jactation, rodomontade; **brag,** boast, ego trip, vaunt

Brahman *n* → **1** aristocrat **2** intellectual

braid *n* → **1** curl **2** hair **3** interlacement **4** string **5** trimming *v* **6** edge **7** interlace **8** twist

brain *n* → **1** head *v* **2** kill

brainstorm *n* → **1** idea **2** madness

brainwash *v* → **1** convert **2** persuade

braise *v* → cook

brake *n* → **1** car **2** restraints **3** steering wheel **4** stopper *v* **5** stop

bran *n* → powder

BRANCH *n* anabranch, arm, embranchment, ramus, side road; **fork,** crotch, crutch, elbow; **radius,** spoke, sprag; **diverter,** divaricator. *See also* DIVERGENCE

branch *n* → **1** ancestry **2** class **3** society **4** stream **5** workplace *v* **6** disperse **7** diverge **8** grow

brand *n* → **1** candle **2** denigration **3** label **4** name **5** sword *v* **6** disgrace **7** fire **8** label

brandish *v* → **1** display **2** flutter

brandy *v* → cook

brash *n* → **1** ice **2** rock *adj* **3** discourteous **4** rash

brass *n* → **1** arrogance **2** brass instrument **3** cash **4** high command **5** important person **6** orange *v* **7** cheat *adj* **8** metallic **9** yellow

brassiere *n* → underwear

BRASS INSTRUMENT *n* brass, brass wind; **trumpet,** Bach trumpet, bugle, clarino, clarion, cornet, flugelhorn, horn, trump *(Poetic)*; **trombone,** sackbut, slush pump; **French horn,** mellophone, Wagner tuba; **tuba,** baritone, bombardon, euphonium, helicon, saxtuba, sousaphone; **cornet,** bass horn, ophicleide, serpent; **saxhorn,** althorn, alto, alto horn, tenor horn, tenor saxhorn; **hand-horn,** alpenhorn, alphorn, coach-horn, shophar; **conch,** murex

brat *n* → children

bravado *n* → **1** bombast **2** bragging

BRAVE *v* bite the bullet, face up to, grasp the nettle, look in the face, outbrave, square up to; **dare,** bell the cat, go through fire and water, venture; **put on a bold front,** crack hardy, crack hearty, keep a stiff upper lip, keep the flag flying, put on a brave face, take it on the chin; **pluck up courage,** take heart

brave *n* → **1** challenge **2** fighter **3** forcer **4** man **5** violent person *v* **6** beautify **7** brag **8** oppose *adj* **9** beautiful **10** courageous **11** good
bravo *n* → **1** hothead **2** killer **3** thief *interj* **4** congratulations **5** cooee **6** well done
bravura *n* → **1** artistry **2** display **3** musical piece **4** show
brawl *n* → **1** fight **2** loud sound *v* **3** be loud **4** fight
brawn *n* → **1** flesh **2** strength
bray *n* → **1** animal call **2** click **3** dissonance *v* **4** be dissonant **5** be loud **6** call (of animals) **7** powder **8** shout
braze *v* → **1** coat **2** work metal
brazen *adj* → **1** blatant **2** discourteous **3** impenitent **4** metallic **5** presumptuous **6** yellow
brazier *n* → **1** craftsman **2** heater **3** rack
breach *n* → **1** crime **2** gap **3** injury **4** opening *v* **5** open **6** separate
bread *n* → **1** cash *v* **2** cook
breadth *n* → **1** fine arts **2** liberty **3** size **4** thickness **5** tolerance
breadwinner *n* → worker
BREAK *n* chink, cleat, cleavage plane, cleft, columnar jointing, crack, crevasse, crevice, cut, divide, fault, fault line, fault plane, fissure, fracture, grain, hair parting, joint, rent, rip, rupture, schism, slip, split, tear, transcrystalline fracture; **divorce,** break-up, bust-up, cut-out, rift; **detachment,** fork, fragment, orphan *(Print.)*, outbuilding, outlier, part, split; **breakaway,** cave
BREAK *v* burst, bust, crack, crash, ding, hole, prang, smash, snap, stave, stave in, tear, wrench; **crush,** chew up, smash
break *n* → **1** amusement **2** change **3** decrease **4** earliness **5** escape **6** failure **7** gap **8** good fortune **9** interruption **10** interval **11** luck **12** musical phrase **13** opening **14** rest **15** small amount **16** stoppage **17** stroke **18** use *v* **19** be early **20** contravene **21** dance **22** defeat **23** demote **24** fluctuate **25** open up **26** ruin **27** separate **28** spoil **29** stop **30** wane
breakage *n* → **1** charge **2** damage
breakaway *n* → **1** break **2** escape **3** escapee **4** gap **5** independent person **6** pole *adj* **7** escaped
break away *v* → **1** be early **2** be violent **3** escape **4** separate
breakdown *n* → **1** analysis **2** destruction **3** illness **4** listing **5** psychic disorder **6** stoppage
break down *v* → **1** cut **2** fail **3** inquire into **4** lose **5** ruin **6** simplify **7** weaken
breaker *n* → **1** barrel **2** surf **3** teacher
breakfast *n* → **1** meal *v* **2** eat
breakneck *adj* → dangerous
breakwater *n* → obstacle
breast *n* → **1** chest **2** emotion **3** mind *v* **4** advance **5** oppose
breath *n* → **1** gas **2** living **3** moment **4** quiet sound **5** rest **6** smell **7** speaking **8** unimportant thing **9** wind
breathalyser *n* → alcotest
BREATHE *v* breathe in, draw breath, inbreathe, inhale, inspire, insufflate, respire, suck the breath, suspire *(Archaic)*; **exhale,** breathe out; **puff,** aspirate, huff, snuffle; **sniff,** snuff, whiff, whiffle; **wheeze,** cough, hiccup, sneeze; **gasp,** blow, breathe hard, breathe heavily, pant
breathe *v* → **1** live **2** rest **3** smell out **4** speak
BREATHING *n* aspiration, expiration, inspiration, insufflation, respiration; **rough breathing,** snoring, spiritus asper, stertor, windedness; **smooth breathing,** spiritus lenis; **artificial respiration,** kiss of life; **inhalation,** draw, puff, toke, whiff; **exhalation,** aspirate, blow, halitus, hiccups, hiss, pant, sibilation, sigh, steam, suspiration; **gasp,** cough, croup, graveyard bark, graveyard cough, rattle, sneeze, sniff, sniffle, snore, snort, snuff, snuffle, sternutation, wheeze; **the breath,** atman, wind; **breathing apparatus,** aqualung, octopus regulator, SCUBA, self-contained underwater breathing apparatus; **oxygen tent,** iron lung, oxygen mask
BREATHLESS *adj* apnoeal, apnoeic, asphyxiated, choked, gasping, panting, puffed, short-winded, smothered, suffocated, winded
breathtaking *adj* → **1** exciting **2** important
breech *n* → **1** buttocks **2** rear *v* **3** cudgel
breeches *n* → trousers
breed *n* → **1** ancestry **2** character **3** class *v* **4** cause **5** create **6** farm **7** flower **8** rear **9** reproduce
BREEDER *n* eugenicist, eugenist, grafter, grower, hybridiser, propagator, stirpiculturist, stockbreeder
breeding *n* → **1** behaviour **2** cause **3** conception **4** courteousness **5** farming **6** good taste **7** radioactivation **8** teaching
BREEDING GROUND *n* incubator, womb; **cradle,** nursery; **hotbed,** fertile soil, good soil, seedbed; **hothouse,** conservatory, garden, glasshouse, greenhouse, terrarium; **auxanometer,** crescograph
breeze *n* → **1** easy thing **2** wind
brethren *n* → partner
BREVIARY *n* antiphonary, bible, catechism, ceremonial, diurnal, family Bible, gradual, hours, hymnal, hymnbook, missal, passional, polyglot, pontifical, prayer book, Psalter, service book, testament, vesperal
BREW *v* malt, rack, still *(Obs.)*, work; **alcoholise,** lace, spike
brew *n* → **1** drink *v* **2** cook **3** create **4** mix **5** occur **6** prepare
BREWER *n* distiller, stiller *(Obs.)*, wet *(U.S.)*; **sly grogger,** bootlegger, moonshiner; **oenologist,** wine-taster, winegrower, winemaker
brewery *n* → pub
briar *n* → tobacco
BRIBABLE *adj* all right *(Colloq.)*, buyable, corrupt, for sale, on the market, purchasable, Tammany-Hall, venal
BRIBE *n* backhander, bonus *(Colloq.)*, boodle *(U.S.)*, consideration, fix, oil, palm oil, sling, sop, under-the-table payment; **hush money,** drugola, inducement allowance, kickback, payola, protection, protection

money, slush fund, subsidisation; **inducement,** bait, douceur, incentive, sweetener

BRIBE *v* blackmail, buy, buy off, cross someone's palm, get at, grease someone's palm, have in one's pay, make it right with, oil, oil someone's palm, pay off, purchase, sling, suborn, subsidise, sweeten, tamper with, throw a sop to

bribe *n* → textiles

BRIBER *n* bagman, bent cop, blackmailer, boodler, crooked politician, embraceor, suborner, subsidiser

BRIBERY *n* corruption, dollar diplomacy, embracery, jobs for the boys, pork *(U.S.)*, pork barrel, protection, protection racket, subornation, watergate

bric-a-brac *n* → trinket

brick *n* → **1** building materials **2** good person **3** imprisonment **4** sound system *v* **5** build

bride *n* → **1** joint **2** spouse **3** string

bridegroom *n* → spouse

bridesmaid *n* → **1** companion **2** helper **3** wedding

BRIDGE *n* Bailey bridge, box-girder bridge, chain-bridge, clapper bridge, drawbridge, floating bridge, flyover *(Brit.)*, humpback bridge, overbridge, overfly, overpass, pivot bridge, span, suspension bridge, swing bridge, toll bridge, transporter bridge, traversing bridge, trestle bridge, truss bridge; **gangplank; crossover,** covered way, covert way, footbridge, pedestrian crossing, scramble crossing, zebra crossing; **conduit,** aqueduct, course, lockage, viaduct; **pass,** access, defile; **tunnel,** corridor, creek *(Obs.)*, crosscut, passage, passageway, shaft; **pontoon,** float; **ford,** stepping stone

bridge *n* → **1** bulge **2** medication **3** path **4** platform **5** support **6** top *v* **7** join **8** traverse

bridle *n* → **1** harness *v* **2** be angry **3** restrain

brief *n* → **1** information **2** message **3** record *v* **4** inform **5** practise law *adj* **6** concise **7** discourteous **8** impermanent **9** short **10** small

briefcase *n* → case

brigade *n* → **1** armed forces **2** crowd

brigand *n* → thief

BRIGHT *adj* aureate, brilliant, effulgent, flashy *(Rare)*, fulgent, gleaming, illustrious *(Obs.)*, irradiate, lambent, lightsome, lively, lucent *(Archaic)*, lucid, radiant, refulgent, relucent, resplendent, sheer *(Obs.)*, shimmery, shining, splendent, splendorous, transparent *(Obs.)*, vivid; **sparkling,** agleam, aglimmer, aglitter, asteriated, aventurine, chatoyant, clinquant, diamanté, glittery, rutilant *(Rare)*, scintillant, scintillating; **glaring,** blinding, garish, glary, lurid; **flashing,** fulgurant, fulgurous, fulminous; **shiny,** ganoid, glare, glassy, glossy, polished, satin, satiny, sheen *(Archaic)*, sheeny, silk, silken, silky, silvery, sleek, slick, waxlike, waxy, wet-look; **lustrous,** iridescent, lustred, nacreous, opalescent, opaline, orient, oriental, pearl, pearly; **clear,** crystal, empyreal, empyrean, glass, mild; **cloudless,** shadeless, shadowless, unshadowed; **sunny,** sun-drenched, sunlit, sunshine, sunshiny; **moonlit,** moonlight, moonshiny, moony, star-studded, starlight, starlit, starry; **lamplit,** lamplight, torchlight, torchlit; **light,** illuminative, photic; **luminous,** fluorescent, irradiant, irradiative, luciferous, luminescent, luminiferous, noctilucent, phosphorescent, photogenic *(Biol.)*, radiative

bright *n* → **1** brightness *adj* **2** beautiful **3** colourful **4** favourable **5** fortunate **6** happy **7** humorous **8** intelligent **9** transparent *adv* **10** beautifully **11** brightly

BRIGHTNESS *n* bright *(Archaic)*, brilliance, brilliantness, dazzle, effulgence, fieriness, fire, flame, flashiness, garishness, glare, glaringness, irradiance, irradiancy, lambency, liveliness, lucence *(Archaic)*, lucency *(Archaic)*, luridness, resplendence, silveriness, splendour, starriness, vividness; **luminescence,** asterism, bioluminescence, chemiluminescence, electroluminescence, fluorescence, luminosity, luminousness, noctilucence, phosphorescence, photoluminescence, radioluminescence, thermoluminescence, triboluminescence; **polish,** burnish, gloss, glossiness, lustrousness, sheen, shine, shininess, sleekness, slickness, varnish; **iridescence,** highlights, lustre, opalescence, orient, pearl, reflet, schiller. *See also* LIGHT

brilliant *n* → **1** jewel **2** jewellery **3** solid *adj* **4** beautiful **5** bright **6** colourful **7** intelligent

brim *n* → **1** edge *v* **2** fill

brindled *adj* → multicoloured

brine *n* → **1** sea **2** sourness *v* **3** conserve **4** sour

bring *v* → **1** cost **2** transport

brink *n* → **1** apex **2** edge

brinkmanship *n* → politics

brisk *adj* → **1** bubbly **2** busy **3** energetic **4** impermanent **5** speedy

brisket *n* → chest

bristle *n* → **1** hair *v* **2** abound **3** be angry

BRITTLE *adj* calcareous, china, crisp, crispy, crispy-crunchy, crunchy, crusty, eggshell, glass, glasslike, glassy, red-short, semivitreous, shivery, splintery, vitreous; **breakable,** brashy, crumbly, fragile, frail, frangible, friable, shatterable, short, tender *(Wool)*

brittle *adj* → irritable

BRITTLENESS *n* crispness, glassiness, vitreosity, vitreousness, vitrification; **breakability,** fragileness, fragility, frailness, frailty, frangibility, tenderness *(Wool)*

broach *n* → **1** abrasive **2** bolt **3** opener **4** rod *v* **5** increase **6** open **7** set sail **8** swerve

broad *n* → **1** lake **2** woman *adj* **3** big **4** general **5** liberated **6** obscene **7** obvious **8** thick **9** thorough **10** vulgar *adv* **11** thoroughly

BROADCAST *adj* beamed, on the air, transmitted

broadcast *n* → **1** publicity **2** telecommunications *v* **3** communicate **4** disperse **5** farm **6** generalise **7** publicise **8** publish **9** telecast *adj* **10** dispersed **11** general *adv* **12** dispersedly

broad-minded *adj* → tolerant

broadsheet *n* → **1** newspaper **2** poetry **3** public notice
broadside *n* → **1** attack **2** gunfire **3** public notice **4** reprimand
brocade *v* → sew
brochure *n* → **1** book **2** public notice
brogue *n* → **1** accent **2** footgear
broil *n* → **1** commotion **2** fight **3** loud sound *v* **4** be angry **5** be hot **6** be loud **7** cook **8** fight **9** heat
broke *adj* → poor
broken *adj* → **1** damaged **2** gaping **3** interrupted **4** irregular **5** non-paying **6** notched **7** obsequious **8** poor **9** separate **10** weak
broker *n* → **1** financier **2** seller **3** trader
brolly *n* → aircraft
bromide *n* → **1** bore **2** photograph **3** proverb
bronco *n* → horse
bronze *n* → **1** buttocks **2** portrait **3** sculpture *v* **4** brown *adj* **5** brown
brooch *n* → jewellery
brood *n* → **1** animal offspring **2** class *v* **3** be unhappy **4** give birth **5** think *adj* **6** pregnant
brook *n* → **1** stream *v* **2** persevere
broom *n* → **1** brush **2** plant *v* **3** clean
BROTHEL *n* bagnio, bawdy house, bordello, cathouse, disorderly house, drum, escort agency, house of ill fame, house of ill repute, knocking shop, massage parlour, stews *(Archaic)*, whorehouse; **red light district**
brothel *n* → untidiness
brother *n* → **1** monastic **2** partner **3** religious follower **4** sibling *v* **5** be friends
brother-in-law *n* → sibling
brouhaha *n* → **1** commotion **2** loud sound
brow *n* → **1** apex **2** edge **3** eye **4** head
browbeat *v* → **1** act unkindly **2** force **3** repress
BROWN *n* beige, dun; **brownness,** rustiness, suntan, tawniness; **brunette,** bitumen blonde, brunet *(Obs.)*; **browning,** tanning; **brown pigment,** bistre, burnt sienna, burnt umber, henna, raw sienna, raw umber, rust, sienna, sinopia, umber; **melanin**
BROWN *v* blanco, bronze, embrown, tan, toast; **rust**
BROWN *adj* brown as a berry, brownish, brunette, nutbrown, spadiceous; **suntanned,** bronzed, sunburned, sunburnt, tanned; **dark brown,** chocolate, cocoa, coffee-coloured, fuscous, mocha, puce, seal brown, sepia, umber, Vandyke brown; **mahogany,** maple, oak, teak, walnut; **light brown,** almond, amber, bisque, camel, khaki, tan; **tawny,** cacky-coloured, cervine, musteline; **buff,** fallow, fawn; **beige,** biscuit, café au lait, caramel, ecru, unbleached; **dun,** drab, fulvous, putty; **snuff-coloured,** nicotine-stained; **reddish-brown,** auburn, bronze, bronzy, cinnamon, copper, coppery, cupreous, ferruginous, foxy, ginger, gingery, hazel, hepatic, liver, rubiginous, russet, rust-coloured, rusty, terracotta, testaceous, titian; **chestnut,** bay, dapple-bay, roan, sorrel
brown *n* → **1** coinage *v* **2** cook
brownie *n* → **1** beer **2** fairy
browse *v* → read
bruise *n* → **1** disfigurement **2** injury *v* **3** injure **4** powder
brunch *n* → **1** meal **2** morning
brunette *n* → **1** brown **2** hair *adj* **3** black **4** brown **5** hairy
brunt *n* → violent outburst
BRUSH *n* banister brush, bootbrush, currycomb, dandy-brush, duster, feather duster, fitch, hairbrush, nailbrush, scrubbing-brush, wire brush; **comb,** bug rake, flea rake, hatchel, heckle; **broom,** besom, Turks' head broom; **carpet-sweeper,** floor polisher, hoover, vacuum cleaner; **mop,** floorcloth, scrim, squeegee; **scraper,** nail-file, strigil; **fibre cleaner,** gin, linter, rippler, scutch
brush *n* → **1** act of war **2** cleansing **3** contact **4** electric circuit **5** fight **6** forest **7** groin **8** the bush **9** touch **10** woman *v* **11** clean **12** contact **13** simplify **14** touch **15** wage war
brusque *adj* → discourteous
BRUTAL *adj* bestial, boarish, brute, bull, bullish, ferocious, hubristic; **barbaric,** barbarian, barbarous, loutish, rude, vandal, vandalic; **ruffianly,** piratical, plug-ugly *(U.S.)*, thuggish, tough. *See also* VIOLENT
brutal *adj* → **1** animal-like **2** callous **3** ill-bred **4** unkind
brute *n* → **1** animal **2** self-seeker **3** shearer **4** unkind person **5** violent person **6** voluptuary **7** vulgarian *adj* **8** animal-like **9** brutal **10** voluptuous
BUBBLE *n* air-bell, bead, bleb *(Rare)*, blob; **blister,** bulla, phlyctena, seed; **artificial horizon; bubble chamber**
BUBBLE *v* boil, burble, effervesce, fizz, fizzle, foam, froth, intumesce, lather, mantle, prickle, sparkle, spume; **gargle,** guggle, gurgle; **ferment,** aerate, carbonate, yeast
bubble *n* → **1** bead **2** delusion **3** embezzlement **4** hiss **5** the intangible **6** trick *v* **7** cheat
bubbler *n* → **1** bubbling **2** spring
BUBBLINESS *n* effervescence, effervescency, foaminess, frothiness, gassiness, life, liveliness, prickle, spumescence, yeastiness; **carbonation,** carbon dioxide, carbonic acid gas, fermentation, zyme *(Obs.)*
BUBBLING *n* burble, burbling, cavitation; **foam,** barm, bead, collar, froth, head *(Alc. Bev.)*, lather, sea-foam, spindrift, spray, spume, suds, surf, yeast; **bubbler,** carbonator, fountain, latherer, soda syphon; **fizzy drink,** bubbly, sherbet; **bubble bath; bubble gum**
BUBBLY *adj* aerated, carbonated, ebullient, effervescent, fizzy, foamy, frothing, frothy, gassy, lathery, spumescent, spumous, spumy, sudsy, with a head on, yeasty; **sparkling,** brisk, lively, petillant, prickly, spritzig; **blistered,** blebby, blistery
bubbly *n* → **1** bubbling **2** wine *adj* **3** aerated
buccaneer *n* → **1** fighter **2** pirate **3** thief *v* **4** rob **5** set sail

buck *n* → **1** affected person **2** arrogant person **3** cash **4** ethnic **5** jump **6** man *v* **7** jump **8** misplace **9** oppose *adj* **10** male
bucket *n* → **1** vessel *v* **2** rain **3** vibrate
buckjump *v* → jump
buckle *n* → **1** button **2** distortion **3** fold *v* **4** distort **5** fight **6** fold
bucolic *n* → **1** country dweller **2** farmer **3** poetry *adj* **4** boring **5** farming **6** poetic **7** rural
bud *n* → **1** adolescent **2** bulge **3** flower **4** sibling **5** start *v* **6** flower
buddy *n* → friend
budge *v* → move
budget *n* → **1** account **2** accumulation **3** case **4** plan *v* **5** account **6** plan
buff *n* → **1** desirer **2** hide **3** hit **4** overcoat **5** skin **6** specialist **7** yellow *v* **8** clean **9** moderate **10** polish *adj* **11** brown **12** yellow
buffalo *n* → **1** cattle *v* **2** confuse
buffer *n* → **1** counterbalance **2** defence **3** fool **4** moderator **5** screen **6** wall
buffoon *n* → **1** butt **2** humorist **3** vulgarian
bug *n* → **1** belief **2** error **3** fairy **4** illness **5** imperfection **6** insect **7** microphone **8** organism *v* **9** annoy **10** displease **11** hear **12** irritate **13** stop
bugbear *n* → **1** fairy **2** frightener
bugger *n* → **1** bad person **2** difficulty **3** man **4** mischief-maker **5** sexual type **6** unpleasant person *v* **7** have sex **8** swear *interj* **9** God
buggy *n* → **1** car **2** carriage *adj* **3** unkempt
bugle *n* → **1** brass instrument **2** nose
BUILD *v* construct, engineer, erect, make, put up, raise; **mason,** brick, carpenter, riprap; **prefabricate,** precast, preform
build *n* → **1** finished product **2** structure *v* **3** lift **4** make
BUILDER *n* architect, checker *(U.S.)*, civil engineer, draughtsman, engineer, erecter, landscape architect, master builder; **mason,** brickie, bricklayer, carpenter, cowan, lather; **rigger,** scaffolder
BUILDING *n* construction, erection, fabric, facility, structure, superstructure, work; **edifice,** complex, dome, megastructure, pile; **outbuilding,** addition, annexe, dependency, extension, finger, outhouse, wing; **substructure,** chassis, foundation, infrastructure, shell, substruction; **framework,** cage, casing, cradling, frame, gantry, roll cage, scaffold, scaffolding, skeleton, truss, trussing, undercarriage; **trellis,** espalier, lattice, pergola
building *n* → **1** construction **2** making
BUILDING MATERIALS *n* bricks and mortar, lath and plaster, wattle and daub; **brick,** adobe, ashlar, cement, concrete, plaster, stone; **mortar,** binder; **roofing,** shingle, slate, thatch, tile; **flooring,** boarding, decking, panelling, paving, planking, studding; **insulation,** asbestos, batt, fibreglass, fireproofing, rockwool; **rubble,** backfill, ballast, bedding, fill, filler, riprap. *See also* TIMBER
building society *n* → lender
build up *v* → **1** increase **2** publicise **3** strengthen
build-up *n* → **1** increase **2** publicity
bulb *n* → **1** lighting **2** plant
BULGE *n* ball, billow, mushroom, pout, swell; **belly,** bay window *(Colloq.)*, beer gut, bloat, potbelly, venter; **hump,** dowager's hump, gibbosity, humpback, hunch, hunchback, widow's hump; **bud,** button, lobation, lobe, lobule, mamilla, nipple, stud, tit, titty; **protuberance,** bridge, cusp, excrescence, outgrowth, shoulder, snout, spine, spur, tenon, tentacle, torus; **crest,** comb; **swelling,** bump, bunion, chondroma, desmoid, goitre, hernia, puff, scrofula, struma, tumescence, tumour, turgescence; **lump,** air-sac, anbury, bedeguar, boss, capped hock, cheloid, condyloma, cyst, diverticulum, fibroid, fibroma, ganglion, keloid, knot, macrocyst, node, nodule, papilla, papilloma, polyp, sebaceous cyst, spavin, tuber, verruca, wart, wen; **blister,** barb, bighead, blain, bleb *(Rare)*, blood blister, bog spavin, boil, bulla, carbuncle, gathering, head, pimple, pock, pustule, tubercle, vesicle; **goose pimples,** heat rash, horripilation; **welt,** wale, weal, wheal. *See also* KNOB
BULGE *v* bag, balloon, belly, bilge, billow, bloat, fill, fill out, heave, mushroom, puff up, swell, tumefy; **hump,** hunch, lump, pod; **butt,** dome, peak, point; **blister,** gather, vesicate, vesiculate; **emboss,** pounce, raise, stud; **knot,** lump; **extrude,** evaginate, herniate. *See also* JUT
bulge *n* → bottom
bulk *n* → **1** body **2** much **3** part **4** size **5** storage **6** thickness *v* **7** weigh *adj* **8** many
bulkhead *n* → **1** door **2** wall
BULL ARTIST *n* babbler, bilge artist, jabberer, joker, magger, magpie, maunderer, patterer, piffler, raver, twaddler, verbalist, yawper
bull-bar *n* → screen
bulldog *n* → **1** gun **2** policeman
bulldoze *v* → **1** force **2** smooth
bulldozer *n* → **1** digging implement **2** forcer **3** smoother
bullet *n* → **1** ammunition **2** bead **3** dismissal **4** recording
bulletin *n* → **1** information **2** magazine **3** message **4** news **5** public notice
bull-headed *adj* → **1** stubborn **2** stupid
bullion *n* → trimming
bullock *n* → cattle
bullocky *n* → **1** swearing **2** transporter **3** traveller *adj* **4** fat **5** strong
bullroarer *n* → **1** idol **2** stick
bullseye *n* → **1** centre **2** circle **3** window
BULLSHIT *interj* all my eye and Betty Martin, apple sauce, arseholes, balls, bull, bullswool, don't make me laugh, eh, fiddle-de-dee, fiddlesticks, get along with you, go on, humph, like fun, my foot, my sainted aunt, oh yeah, pah, phooey, pig's arse, pig's bum, pigs, pigs might fly, pshaw, pull the other one (it has bells), sure, tell that to the horse marines, tell that to the marines, that'll be the day, that's a good one, try another, um, what

bullshit *n* → 1 bragging 2 dung 3 nonsense *v* 4 waffle *interj* 5 God

bully *n* → 1 arrogant person 2 forcer 3 friend 4 lover 5 menacer 6 prostitute 7 violent person *v* 8 act unkindly 9 be arrogant 10 be violent 11 force 12 menace *adj* 13 good 14 happy *interj* 15 well done

bulwark *n* → 1 defence 2 embankment 3 fortification 4 mound 5 protection 6 side *v* 7 defend 8 protect

bum *n* → 1 bad person 2 buttocks 3 idler 4 traveller *v* 5 borrow 6 idle *adj* 7 bad 8 dissonant

bumble *v* → bungle

bump *n* → 1 airflow 2 bulge 3 impact 4 knob *v* 5 collide 6 defeat

bumper *n* → 1 alcohol container 2 fullness 3 giant 4 screen 5 thief 6 throw 7 tobacco *v* 8 approve 9 drink alcohol 10 fill *adj* 11 abundant 12 most

bumper bar *n* → screen

bumpkin *n* → 1 country dweller 2 incompetent 3 pole

bumptious *adj* → presumptuous

bun *n* → hair

bunch *n* → 1 accumulation 2 clique 3 knob *v* 4 gather 5 jut

bundle *n* → 1 accumulation 2 length 3 mixture *v* 4 cover 5 gather 6 kiss

bundy *n* → timepiece

bung *n* → 1 mister 2 plug 3 tap *v* 4 close 5 command 6 position 7 throw *adj* 8 damaged

bungalow *n* → house

BUNGLE *n* boggle, botch, botch-up, clambake *(U.S. Colloq.)*, cock-up, flub, fumble, mistake; **muddle,** dawdling, flounder, potter; **blunder,** a foot in the mouth, fluff, malapropism; **botchery,** piece of incompetence, slopwork; **bad shot,** cow shot, foozle, miscue, misfield *(Cricket)*, mishit

BUNGLE *v* arse up, blow it, boggle, botch, botch up, butcher, cock up, crap up, flub, fluff, foozle, hash, make a hash of, make a mess of, make a poor fist of, maladminister, misconduct, misdo, mishandle, mismanage, muck up, muff; **blunder,** be slipping, bumble, flounder, fumble, get in the road, goof, grope, muddle, put one's foot in it, stumble; **arse about,** arse around, arsehole about, bugger about, bugger around, clown, fool around, muck about, muck around; **dabble,** dawdle, piddle, piss about, piss around, potter, tinker; **be incapacitated,** have two left feet; **jerry-build,** cobble, mullock, slum; **charge at,** charge at like a bull at a gate, go bull-headed at; **fumble,** catch a crab *(Rowing)*, duff *(Sport)*, miscue, misfield *(Cricket)*, mishit, misthrow, pull, slice

bungle *n* → 1 bad thing 2 failure *v* 3 fail 4 spoil

bunion *n* → bulge

bunk *n* → 1 bed 2 nonsense *v* 3 sleep

bunker *n* → 1 hollow 2 obstacle 3 shelter *v* 4 fuel 5 obstruct

bunkum *n* → 1 bombast 2 nonsense

bunny *n* → fool

bunting *n* → 1 decoration 2 flag

bunyip *n* → mythical beast

buoy *n* → 1 float 2 indicator 3 raft *v* 4 embolden 5 help 6 signal

BUOYANT *adj* afloat, floatable, floating, floaty, natant

burble *n* → 1 airflow 2 bubbling 3 quiet sound 4 speaking *v* 5 bubble 6 speak

burden *n* → 1 cost 2 difficulty 3 hindrance 4 imposition 5 insistence 6 music 7 obligation 8 repetition 9 subject matter 10 toil *v* 11 repress 12 weigh

bureau *n* → 1 desk 2 management 3 workplace

bureaucracy *n* → 1 legislation 2 management

BUREAUCRAT *n* administrator, civil servant, legislator, mandarin, official, palatine, public servant

bureaucrat *n* → 1 incompetent 2 manager 3 ruler

burgeon *v* → 1 be fertile 2 flower

burglar *n* → thief

burglary *n* → robbery

burgundy *n* → purple

burial *n* → funeral rites

burl *n* → 1 attempt 2 gamble 3 knob *v* 4 disapprove of 5 mock 6 roll 7 speed

burlesque *n* → 1 comedy 2 drama 3 imitation 4 misrepresentation 5 mockery 6 vulgarism *v* 7 imitate 8 mock *adj* 9 dramatic 10 mocking 11 vulgar

burly *adj* → fat

burn *n* → 1 clearance 2 injury 3 rate 4 stream *v* 5 be close 6 be hot 7 desire 8 feel emotion 9 fire 10 heat 11 kill 12 shine 13 speed 14 wage war

BURNING *n* baking, calcination, carbonisation, decrepitation, firing, flashing, roasting, scorching, singeing, ustulation; **combustion,** ignition, kindling; **pyrography,** branding, cauterisation, cautery, galvanocautery

burnish *n* → 1 brightness *v* 2 illuminate 3 polish

BURN OUT *v* die down, expire

BURP *n* belch, eructation, retch; **fart,** braff, flatulence, flatus, fluff, gas, smelly, wind

BURP *v* belch, eruct, eructate, repeat; **fart,** braff, break wind, drop a bundle, drop one's lunch, fluff, go off, let off, lunch, make a smell, shoot a fairy

burrow *n* → 1 animal dwelling 2 cave 3 shelter *v* 4 dig 5 hollow 6 lie low

bursar *n* → 1 pupil 2 treasury

bursary *n* → 1 allowance 2 storehouse

burst *n* → 1 exit 2 explosion 3 gunfire 4 outburst *v* 5 break 6 expel

BURY *v* coffin, entomb, immure, inhume, inter, inurn, lay to rest, pit, sepulchre, tomb; **lay out,** cere, embalm, mummify, shroud; **lie buried,** lie six feet under, push up daisies

bury *v* → 1 forget 2 hide 3 insert

bus *n* → 1 car 2 truck *v* 3 drive

bush *n* → 1 hair 2 plant 3 woman *v* 4 bare 5 grow *adj* 6 ill-bred

bushed *adj* → 1 confused 2 lost 3 tired

bushfire *n* → fire

bushman *n* → **1** country dweller **2** population **3** woodcutter

bushranger *n* → **1** bad person **2** country dweller **3** criminal **4** thief

bushwalk *v* → travel

bushwhacker *n* → **1** country dweller **2** population **3** woodcutter

BUSILY *adv* hectically; **actively,** energetically, lively, pertly, spiritedly, warmly, with might and main; **sprightly,** bustlingly, dapperly, hurriedly, hurryingly, racily, spryly; **vigorously,** dashingly, dynamically; **restlessly,** exhaustlessly, skittishly, unquietly, unrestingly; **flat out,** at full tilt, flat out like a lizard drinking, full blast, in everything bar a bath, in full swing, in the swim, like a cut snake, like nobody's business, on a hurdy-gurdy, on the hop, on the trot, on the wing, up to one's ears, up to one's elbows, up to one's eyes; **in the press of business,** in medias res, in the middle of things, in the thick of it all; **in action,** in use, on active service, on the job

business *n* → **1** affair **2** defecation **3** gesture **4** job **5** move **6** prostitution **7** trade **8** workplace

businessman *n* → **1** middle class **2** trader

bust *n* → **1** attack **2** binge **3** chest **4** entrance **5** failure **6** indebtedness **7** non-payment **8** portrait **9** robbery **10** sculpture *v* **11** break **12** demote **13** enter **14** rob *adj* **15** damaged **16** in debt **17** ruined

bustle *n* → **1** busyness **2** jumble **3** underwear **4** vitality *v* **5** be busy **6** be energetic

BUSY *adj* active, alive, engaged, hard at work, hearty, hectic, humming, lissom, renascent, smart, warm; **sprightly,** agile, animated, brisk, dapper, fast, full of go, hurried, live, lively, prompt, quick *(Rare)*, racy, spry; **vigorous,** bustling, energetic, go-ahead, jazzy, pert, pushing, red-blooded, slick, spirited, spiritoso, wide-awake; **dashing,** dashy, dynamic, slashing; **tireless,** exhaustless, indefatigable, never-tiring, persevering, sedulous, unresting, unstinting, weariless; **hard-working,** businesslike, industrious, painstaking, practical, pragmatic, unresting, vigilant

busy *adj* → **1** intervenient **2** in use **3** working

BUSYNESS *n* activeness, aliveness, lissomness, pertness, warmness; **activity,** exertion, goings-on, movement at the station, much ado, to-do; **bustle,** coil, hustle, merry-go-round, razzamatazz, razzle-dazzle, rush, song and dance, stir; **much ado about nothing,** all froth and bubble, boondoggle, sound and fury signifying nothing; **burst of activity,** flurry, sally, sprint, spurt, start, tornado; **fuss,** bother, stink

but *n* → **1** qualification *adv* **2** conditionally *prep* **3** except

butane *n* → fuel

butch *n* → **1** man **2** sexual type **3** strong person **4** woman *adj* **5** female **6** male

butcher *n* → **1** alcohol container **2** drinking vessel **3** killer *v* **4** bungle **5** fail **6** massacre

BUTLER *n* maître d'hôtel, major-domo, sewer; **valet,** bearer, body-servant, boots, boy, buttons, cabin boy *(Naut.)*, callboy, fag, garcon, gentleman, gillie, groom, knave, lackey, man, manservant, page, pageboy, valet de chambre, varlet *(Archaic)*; **porter,** bellboy, bellhop, night porter; **flunkey,** chasseur, footboy, footman, yeoman *(Archaic)*; **stableboy,** equerry, groom, horsetailer, ostler, strapper. *See also* SERVANT

butler *n* → supplier

BUTT *n* April fool, Aunt Sally, buffoon, byword, easy prey, fair game, fall guy, figure of fun, guy, laughing stock, object of ridicule, patsy, stooge, zany; **gullible person,** admass, country bumpkin, hick, innocent, innocent abroad, local yokel, rube *(U.S.)*, Simple Simon. *See also* VICTIM

butt *n* → **1** aim **2** amount **3** barrel **4** buttocks **5** extremity **6** joint **7** pat **8** rear **9** remnant **10** tobacco **11** wall *v* **12** bulge **13** contact **14** extinguish **15** join

butter *n* → **1** fat **2** yellow *v* **3** flatter **4** oil

buttercup *n* → yellow

butter-fingers *n* → incompetent

butterfly *n* → **1** gambling **2** swimming

buttermilk *n* → drink

BUTTOCKS *n* acre, arse, backside, base, beam, behind, big A, bot, bottom, breech, bum, butt, can, cheeks, chuff, coit, derrière, ding, dinger, fanny, jacksy *(N.Z.)*, Khyber, nates, posterior, rear, rump, seat, slats, tail; **haunch,** ham, hip, hock, hunkers, loins; **anus,** arsehole, back passage, blot, blurter, breezer, bronze, bronzo, brown-eye, crack, date, freckle, fundament, hole, quoit, ring; **natal cleft**

BUTTON *n* Anzac button, collar stud, cufflink, dome, hook and eye, pearl button, popper, press-stud, snap, snap fastener, stud, tuft; **buckle,** clasp, ouch *(Archaic)*, tache *(Archaic)*; **toggle,** frog; **ring,** woggle; **zipper,** slide fastener, zip, zip-fastener; **buttonhook**

button *n* → **1** bargain **2** bead **3** bulge **4** circle **5** emblem **6** nose *v* **7** contact

buttonhole *n* → **1** fragrance *v* **2** hold **3** open **4** sew **5** stop

buttress *v* → support

buxom *adj* → **1** alluring **2** beautiful **3** fat **4** healthy

BUY *v* acquire, bulk buy, buy into, forestall, get, have, hive off, mail-order, make a purchase, obtain, overbuy, pay for, pre-empt, procure, purchase, take, traffic in, underbuy; **monopolise,** buy out, buy up, corner the market, engross, gridiron *(U.S.)*, peacock; **redeem,** buy back, ransom; **buy on credit,** hire-purchase, lay-by, pay C.O.D., pay cash; **be in the market for; hire,** book, rent; **shop,** bargain, drive a hard bargain, get one's money's worth, go on a shopping spree, go shopping, market, patronise, shop around; **be in the chair,** shout; **buy a pig in a poke**

buy *n* → 1 bargain 2 buying *v* 3 assent to 4 bribe

BUYER *n* consignee, consumer, consumer society, hire purchaser, impulse buyer, peacocker, purchaser, transferee, vendee; **customer,** bargainer, bearer, chap *(Obs.)*, client, haggler, marketer, patron, shopper; **clientele,** carriage trade, clientage; **patronage,** custom

BUYING *n* consumption, mail order, preemption, purchase, retirement *(Comm.)*, shopping, shopping spree; **monopolisation,** coemption, engrossment; **repurchase,** redemption; **hire-purchase,** H.P., lay-away, lay-by; **buy,** a good buy, acquisition, bargain, purchase, short covering

buzz *n* → 1 animal call 2 click 3 drug use 4 excitement 5 news 6 pleasure 7 telecommunications 8 vibration *v* 9 call (of animals) 10 click 11 fly 12 speak 13 telephone 14 vibrate

BY CHANCE *adv* accidentally, adventitiously, arbitrarily, at a venture, at hazard, bechance, casually, coincidentally, desultorily, haphazard, haphazardly, perchance *(Archaic)*, perhaps *(Rare)*, promiscuously, without rhyme or reason; **whatever happens,** in any event; **luckily,** fortuitously, fortunately, providentially; **unluckily,** sadly

bye *n* → unimportant thing

by-election *n* → election

bygone *n* → 1 past *adj* 2 past

by-law *n* → law

bypass *n* → 1 byroad 2 loophole 3 road *v* 4 avoid

by-product *n* → finished product

byre *n* → 1 animal dwelling 2 pen

BYROAD *n* bypass, bypath, bystreet, byway, crossroad, detour, side road, turn-off; **sidetrack,** shunt, siding, tram pinch

bystander *n* → looker

byway *n* → 1 byroad 2 road 3 unimportant thing

byword *n* → 1 butt 2 name 3 proverb 4 slander 5 word

Cc

cab *n* → car
cabal *n* → **1** clique **2** conspiracy **3** secrecy **4** secret society *v* **5** conspire **6** keep secret
cabaret *n* → entertainment
cabbage *n* → cash
CABIN *n* bach *(N.Z.)*, beach hut, box *(Brit.)*, cabana *(U.S.)*, casino, crannog, holiday house, lodge, shooting lodge *(Brit.)*, villa, weekender; **hut,** bothy *(Scot.)*, cabane, caboose, chalet, cot, crib, hutch, rancho, slab hut; **humpy,** goondie, mia-mia, wurley; **lean-to,** skillion; **hovel,** badger-box, hutch, lodge, shack, shanty, shebang, slum, whare *(N.Z.)*; **dump,** den, dogbox *(N.Z. Colloq.)*, doghouse, dugout, hole; **slums,** rabbit-warren, squats, warren. *See also* HOUSE
cabin *n* → **1** bedroom **2** room *v* **3** enclose **4** imprison **5** inhabit
cabinet *n* → **1** bedroom **2** container **3** council **4** cupboard *adj* **5** artistic **6** legislative **7** secret
cable *n* → **1** cord **2** message **3** wire *v* **4** fasten **5** remove **6** send a message
cache *n* → **1** hiding place **2** storage *v* **3** hide
cackle *n* → **1** birdcall **2** mirth **3** talk *v* **4** chirp **5** laugh **6** talk
cacophony *n* → dissonance
cactus *n* → **1** plant **2** the bush *adj* **3** damaged
cad *n* → **1** bad person **2** vulgarian
cadaver *n* → the dead
caddie *n* → servant
caddy *n* → **1** box **2** servant
cadence *n* → **1** finish **2** musical phrase **3** rate **4** speaking
cadet *n* → **1** learner **2** offspring *adj* **3** youthful
cadge *n* → **1** request *v* **2** beg **3** borrow
cadre *n* → **1** armed forces **2** clique **3** teacher **4** workers
caesarean section *n* → birth
cafe *n* → restaurant
café *n* → shop
cafeteria *n* → restaurant
caftan *n* → dress
cage *n* → **1** animal dwelling **2** building **3** cell **4** container **5** prison *v* **6** enclose **7** imprison
cagey *adj* → secretive
caisson *n* → **1** arsenal **2** compartment **3** niche **4** room
cajole *v* → **1** flatter **2** persuade
cake *n* → **1** solid body *v* **2** solidify
calabash *n* → **1** bill **2** drinking vessel **3** plant **4** timber
CALAMITOUS *adj* catastrophic, dire, disastrous, dreadful, evil, ruinous, tragic; **adverse,** difficult, ill, rough, rugged, stiff, thwart, troublesome; **inauspicious,** ill-boding, ill-omened, ill-starred, ominous, sinister, sinistrous, unfavourable; **agonising,** distressful, distressing
calamity *n* → **1** failure **2** misfortune **3** ruin
calcify *v* → harden
calculate *v* → intend
calculating *adj* → **1** cunning **2** opportunist **3** selfish
calculus *n* → mathematics
calendar *n* → **1** list **2** reference book *v* **3** list **4** record
calf *n* → **1** animal offspring **2** hide **3** leg **4** novice
calibrate *v* → **1** graduate **2** measure
calibre *n* → **1** characteristics **2** length **3** order **4** thickness
calico *adj* → multicoloured
caliph *n* → ruler
call *n* → **1** command **2** gamble **3** insistence **4** necessities **5** shout **6** signal **7** talk **8** visit *v* **9** gamble **10** gather **11** name **12** publicise **13** shout **14** speak well **15** telephone **16** visit **17** wake up
CALL ATTENTION TO *v* agitate, engage, enkindle, point out, publicise, ram down someone's throat; **upstage,** do a hollywood, draw attention to oneself, draw the crabs, feature, make a splash; **call after,** catch someone's eye, hello, hist, yoo-hoo
callgirl *n* → prostitute
calligraphy *n* → **1** fine arts **2** writing
calling *n* → **1** command **2** gamble **3** job **4** obligation **5** offering **6** shouting
calliper *v* → measure
callisthenics *n* → exercise
CALL (OF ANIMALS) *v* cry, laugh, sing, speak, talk, whistle; **roar,** bell, bellow, blare, trumpet; **howl,** caterwaul, hoot, screech, ululate, wail; **bark,** bay, bay at the moon, challenge *(Hunting)*, give tongue, growl, grunt, snap, snarl, woof, yap, yelp; **bray,** heehaw; **baa,** bleat; **drone,** buzz, hum, whine; **whinny,** neigh, snicker, whicker; **mew,** miaow, purr; **moo,** low. *See also* CHIRP
CALLOUS *adj* cold-blooded, conscienceless, hard, hard-hearted, hard-nosed, hardened, heartless, indurated, inhumane, inured, loveless, obdurate, rocky, steely, stony, stony-hearted, tough, unfeeling, unsqueamish; **cold-hearted,** bloodless, clinical, cold, frigid, frosty, frozen, icy, marble, marbly, rigid, soulless, uncompassionate, unsympathetic; **ruthless,** harsh, iron-fisted, merciless, pitiless, severe, unpitying; **brutal,** cruel, inhuman; **unrelenting,** implacable, inexorable, in-

flexible, relentless, remorseless; **unmoved,** dry-eyed, impassible, impassive, impervious, passionless, stoic, stoical, tearless, unemotional; **insensitive,** clumsy, heavy-footed, insensible, outspoken, tactless, thick-skinned, unconsidered

callow *adj* → **1** bald **2** ignorant **3** incompetent **4** youthful

callus *n* → **1** thickening *v* **2** harden

calm *n* → **1** composure **2** period of inaction **3** rest *v* **4** inactivate **5** moderate *adj* **6** climatic **7** composed **8** inactive **9** moderate **10** peaceful **11** resting

calorie *n* → energy

calumny *n* → slander

calve *v* → **1** give birth **2** separate

calypso *n* → **1** song *adj* **2** musical

calyx *n* → **1** flower **2** hollow

camaraderie *n* → friendship

camber *n* → **1** curve **2** slope *v* **3** curve

camel *n* → **1** transporter *adj* **2** brown

cameo *n* → **1** abridgment **2** jewel **3** jewellery **4** sculpture **5** written composition

CAMERA *n* box brownie, box camera, camera obscura, continuous strip camera, instamatic, magic eye, miniature camera, polaroid camera, reflex camera, single-lens reflex camera, SLR camera, stop-action camera; **heliograph,** nephograph, photochronograph, spectroheliograph; **optical printer,** sensitometer, vignetter; **projector,** bioscope, magic lantern, viewer

camera *n* → **1** bedroom **2** secret place

camisole *n* → **1** jacket **2** underwear

camouflage *n* → **1** colour **2** disguise *v* **3** hide

CAMP *n* bivouac, bivvy, fly-camp *(N.Z.)*, tentage, transit camp, transit site; **camp site,** camping ground, camping site, caravan park, encampment; **tent,** bell tent, bivvy, canvas, fly; **wigwam,** tepee, tipi, whare *(N.Z.)*, yurt

camp *n* → **1** battleground **2** drama **3** man **4** rest **5** sleep **6** society *v* **7** feminise **8** have sex **9** inhabit **10** rest **11** sleep *adj* **12** male **13** sexual

campaign *n* → **1** act of war **2** undertaking *v* **3** electioneer **4** fight **5** militarise

campus *n* → **1** college **2** field

can *n* → **1** alcohol container **2** box **3** buttocks **4** dismissal **5** drinking vessel **6** toilet *v* **7** be permitted to **8** conserve **9** dismiss **10** disuse **11** know

canal *n* → **1** bay **2** channel **3** furrow **4** line *v* **5** channel

canary *n* → **1** corporal punishment **2** hitting **3** prisoner *adj* **4** yellow

CANCEL *v* abolish, annul, break off, defeat, dele *(Print.)*, delete, derecognise, deregister, dissolve, infirm *(Archaic)*, invalidate, nullify, quash, rescind, scrub, void; **revoke,** abjure, avoid, climb down, countermand, eat one's words, renounce, repudiate, retract, reverse, unsay, unspeak, unswear; **repeal,** abate, abolish, abrogate; **recall,** call back, recede, undo, withdraw

cancel *n* → **1** cancellation **2** exclusion *v* **3** deny **4** exclude

CANCELLATION *n* annulment, cancel, countermand, delenda, deletion, deregistration, dissolution, invalidation, nullification, recision, rescission, reversal, voidance; **revocation,** discontinuance, disuse, recall, repudiation, suspension, undoing, withdrawal; **repeal,** abatement, abolishment, abolition, abrogation, ademption, avoidance, bar, suppression; **renunciation,** abdication, abjuration; **abolitionism**

CANCER *n* growth, Spanish dancer, Jimmy dancer, the big C, tumour; **carcinogenesis,** oncogenesis, sarcomatosis; **cancer form,** adenoma, cancroid, carcinoma, carcinomatosis, encephaloma, enchondroma, endothelioma, epithelioma, fibroid, fibroma, glioma, granuloma, haemangioma, leiomyoma, leukaemia, melanoma, molluscum, myoma, osteoma, rhabdomyoma, sarcoma, scirrhus, scleroma

cancer *n* → destroyer

Cancer *n* → **1** fortune-telling **2** star

candelabrum *n* → **1** candle **2** stand

candid *n* → **1** photograph *adj* **2** clean **3** fair **4** forthright **5** honest **6** truthful **7** white

candidate *n* → **1** desirer **2** politician **3** the chosen

candied *adj* → **1** flattering **2** sweet

CANDLE *n* bougie, dip, taper; **candlestick,** candelabrum, girandole, menorah, pricket; **torch,** brand *(Poetic)*, fire, flambeau, flame, flare, Hawaiian flare, link, luau light

candour *n* → **1** fairness **2** honesty **3** innocence **4** kindness **5** truthfulness

candy *n* → **1** sweetness *v* **2** coat **3** cook

cane *n* → **1** club **2** plug **3** stick *v* **4** cudgel

canine *n* → **1** mouth *adj* **2** animal-like

canister *n* → **1** ammunition **2** box

canker *n* → **1** destroyer **2** deterioration **3** sore *v* **4** destroy **5** spoil

cannabis *n* → marijuana

cannon *n* → **1** gun **2** reaction **3** stroke *v* **4** react

canny *adj* → **1** cautious **2** supernatural **3** wise

canoe *n* → **1** rowing boat *v* **2** transport

canon *n* → **1** belief **2** ecclesiastic **3** example **4** law **5** list **6** monastic **7** religious ceremony **8** repetition **9** rule **10** song

canonise *v* → **1** consecrate **2** worship

canopy *n* → **1** aircraft **2** roof **3** sky *v* **4** cover

cant *n* → **1** fake **2** language **3** move **4** secrecy **5** slope *v* **6** cut **7** lie **8** slope **9** speak **10** throw *adj* **11** bent **12** sloping

cantankerous *adj* → **1** displeased **2** dissident **3** irritable **4** pestering

cantata *n* → song

canteen *n* → **1** bottle **2** box **3** restaurant **4** supplies

canter *n* → **1** rate *v* **2** ride

cantilever *n* → aeroplane

canto *n* → song

canton *n* → **1** administrative area **2** domain **3** part

cantor *n* → **1** religious dignitary **2** singer **3** worshipper

canvas *n* → **1** camp **2** length **3** painting

canvass *n* → **1** electioneering **2** entreaty *v* **3** disapprove of **4** discourse **5** electioneer **6** entreat **7** examine **8** talk

canyon *n* → gap

CAP *n* balmoral, beanie, beaver, beret, billycock *(Colloq.)*, biretta, black cap *(Law)*, bonnet *(Scot.)*, calotte, Cossack hat, coxcomb *(Obs.)*, dunce's cap, fez, fool's cap, forage cap *(Mil.)*, gigglehat *(Mil.)*, glengarry *(Scot.)*, jockey cap, kalpak, kepi, nightcap, sailor hat, shako *(Mil.)*, skullcap, sou'wester *(Naut.)*, tam, tam-o'-shanter, tarboosh, tricorn, tuque, yarmulke, zucchetto *(Rom. Cath. Ch.)*; **bonnet,** blue-bonnet, bluecap, capote, cloche, coif, mob-cap *(Obs.)*; **bathing cap,** shower cap. *See also* HEADGEAR; HAT; HELMET

CAPABILITY *n* ability, capableness, capacity, faculty, power; **effectiveness,** cogency, effectuality, effectualness, efficaciousness, efficacy, forcefulness, forcibility, forcibleness, operation, operativeness, virtuousness *(Archaic)*

CAPABLE *adj* able; **effective,** cogent, effectual, efficacious, forceful, forcible, mean *(Colloq.)*, operative, unstoppable, virtual *(Archaic)*, virtuous *(Archaic)*

capable *adj* → **1** competent **2** intelligent

capacious *adj* → big

capacity *n* → **1** capability **2** competence **3** contents **4** electricity **5** entitlement **6** fullness **7** intelligence **8** mind **9** size

caper *n* → **1** caprice **2** dancing **3** joke **4** jump **5** misdemeanour **6** trick *v* **7** jump

capillary *n* → **1** blood vessel *adj* **2** hairlike

CAPITAL *n* asset backing, authorised capital, capital expenditure, capital stock, circulating capital, corpus, fixed capital, issued capital, paid-up capital, principal, risk capital, shareholders' funds, working capital; **fund,** loan fund, revolving fund; **assets,** current assets, goodwill, intangibles, liquid assets; **bill,** allonge, bank bill, bill of exchange, bill of sale, demand bill, documentary bill, foreign bill, sight bill, Treasury bill *(Brit.)*, Treasury note; **deposit,** fixed deposit, statutory reserve deposit, time deposit; **bank rate,** bond rate, differential rate, dividend rate, interest, rediscount rate; **credit,** credit note, credit rating, credit slip, credit transfer; **charge card,** bank card, credit card, credit plate, plastic, plastic money; **bond,** acceptance, certificate of deposit, security, unsecured note. *See also* STOCKS AND SHARES

capital *n* → **1** city **2** funds **3** letter **4** property **5** top **6** wealth *adj* **7** armed **8** good **9** important **10** murderous

capitalise *v* → **1** account **2** appraise **3** finance

capitalism *n* → economy

CAPITAL PUNISHMENT *n* death penalty, execution, lynching; **electrocution,** electric chair; **fusillade,** firing squad; **hanging,** halter, high jump, long drop; **strangulation,** bowstringing, garrotte; **crucifixion,** impalement; **beheading,** decapitation; **flaying,** cut, hanging drawing and quartering; **burning at the stake,** auto-da-fé, fire, the stake

CAPITULATE *v* back down, bend the knee, buckle under, cave in, cede, condescend *(Obs.)*, defer to, fall, give ground, give in, give way, go under, haul down the flag, knuckle under, lay down one's arms, lose ground, lower the flag, run scared, sag, sky the rag, sky the towel, strike the flag, succumb, surrender, throw in one's hand, throw in the sponge, throw in the towel, throw it in, throw up, yield; **submit,** accede, acquiesce, appease, comply, concede, draw in one's horns, lump it, remit *(Obs.)*, resign oneself, temporise, turn the other cheek

CAPRICE *n* caper, capriccio, dash, megrim *(Archaic)*, prank, vagary; **impulse,** fancy, fantasy, humour, hunch, inspiration, maggot *(Rare)*, notion, spurt of imagination, sudden thought, whim, whimsy; **extemporisation,** ad lib, fantasia, impromptu, improvisation

caprice *n* → **1** indecision **2** misdemeanour **3** musical piece

CAPRICIOUS *adj* artistic, dashing, dashy, fanciful, freakish, giddy, harebrained, hasty, impetuous, impulsive, maggoty *(Rare)*, notional *(Chiefly U.S.)*, promiscuous, reckless, spirited, undisciplined, vagarious, wanton, whimsical; **wilful,** arbitrary, fly-away, headstrong, wayward; **extemporary,** ad hoc, ad lib, extemporal *(Obs.)*, extemporaneous, extempore, impromptu, improvised, spontaneous, unpremeditated

CAPRICIOUSLY *adv* arbitrarily, capriccioso, giddily, impulsively, lightly, like an artist, notionally *(Chiefly U.S.)*, on the spur of the moment, promiscuously, waywardly, whimsically, without a second thought, without arrière-pensée, without rhyme or reason, without thinking; **impetuously,** at the drop of a hat, dashingly, feet first; **extemporaneously,** ad lib, ad libitum, extemporarily, extempore

capsize *v* → overturn

capstan *n* → **1** lift **2** machine **3** puller

capsule *n* → **1** abridgment **2** bag **3** bladder **4** covering **5** fruit **6** medication **7** room

captain *n* → **1** leader **2** pilot **3** ruler **4** seaman *v* **5** have sex

Captain *n* → look

caption *n* → **1** clarification **2** commentary **3** law **4** news item **5** title **6** written composition

captious *adj* → **1** disapproving **2** irritable

captivate *v* → allure

CAPTIVATED *adj* carried away, enthralled, fascinated, much taken by, overcome, seduced, smitten, spellbound, struck by, tempted; **aroused,** horny, lustful, randy, sexually excited

captive *n* → **1** lover **2** prisoner **3** subject *adj* **4** imprisoned **5** loving

captor *n* → **1** gaoler **2** taker

CAPTURE *n* apprehension, arrest, conquest, occupation, seizing, seizure; **pillage,** looting, ravishment, theft; **abduction,** beguilement, enticement

CAPTURE *v* apprehend, arrest, attach *(Obs.)*, carry, conquer, extend *(Obs.)*, get *(Obs.)*, jump *(Draughts)*, possess *(Archaic)*, surprise, swoop down on, take, take by storm, take by surprise, take possession of, take prisoner; **abduct,** abstract, bear off, carry off, convey *(Obs.)*, kidnap, make away with, run away with, spirit away, tear off with; **grab,** bag, catch up, clasp, clutch, collar, fang *(Obs.)*, fist, foot *(Falconry)*, gobble, grip, gripe, help oneself to, hook, jump at, lay by the heels, lay hold of, lay hold on, make a grab for, nab, nail, pocket, pounce on, reach for, scrag, seize, snaffle, snap up, snatch, strip, swoop up, tail, take, take hold of, whisk, wrench, wrest

capture *n* → **1** imprisonment **2** radioactivation *v* **3** arrest

CAR *n* auto *(U.S.)*, automatic, automobile *(U.S.)*, brougham, buggy *(Colloq.)*, bus *(Colloq.)*, courtesy car, demonstrator, electric car, four-door, hatchback, horseless carriage, manual, motor car, plagon wagon *(Derog.)*, rod, steamer, two-door, wheels *(Colloq.)*, Z-car; **runabout,** beetle *(Colloq.)*, bubble car, three-wheeler; **sports car,** fastback, G.T., gran turismo, hardtop, roadster, tourer, two-seater; **convertible,** cabriolet, coupé, landau *(Archaic)*, landaulet *(Obs.)*; **jalopy,** bomb, chaffcutter, crate, crock, flivver, rattletrap, rust bucket, shandrydan, tin lizzie; **limousine,** berline, limmo, phaeton, saloon, saloon car, sedan, touring car, V8, yank tank; **station wagon,** brake, estate car *(Brit.)*, shooting brake *(Brit.)*; **utility,** buckboard, pick-up, tilly, ute, utility truck; **four-wheel drive,** beach buggy, bobcat, dune buggy, four-wheeler, Landrover, off-road vehicle, oversnow vehicle, snowcat, snowmobile; **panel van,** carnal car, fuck truck, shaggin' wagon, sin-bin; **campervan,** camper, kombi; **police car,** black maria, bull car, bun wagon, paddy-wagon, patrol wagon, patrol-car, prowl car *(U.S.)*, squad car, wagon; **racing car,** altered, dragster, go-kart, hot rod, kart, stock car; **taxicab,** cab, hack, jitney *(U.S. Colloq.)*, taxi

car *n* → **1** aircraft **2** carriage **3** train

carafe *n* → bottle

caramel *adj* → brown

carapace *n* → coating

CARAVAN *n* camper, campervan, mobile home, relocatable home, trailer *(U.S.)*; **caravanserai,** serai

caravan *n* → **1** carriage **2** crowd **3** truck *v* **4** inhabit

carbine *n* → gun

carbon dioxide *n* → **1** bubbliness **2** extinguisher

carborundum *n* → smoother

carbuncle *n* → **1** bulge **2** disfigurement **3** sore

carcass *n* → **1** body **2** the dead

card *n* → **1** good person **2** humorist **3** message **4** nonconformist **5** person **6** plan *v* **7** clean **8** compute **9** record **10** sew **11** simplify

cardboard *adj* → ethereal

cardiac *adj* → bodily

cardigan *n* → jacket

cardinal *n* → **1** ecclesiastic *adj* **2** important **3** numerical **4** red

CARE *n* attendance, ministration, tendance, tender loving care, thoughtfulness, TLC; **thought,** attention, deliberation; **carefulness,** attentiveness, deliberativeness, diligence, fussiness, jealousness, mindfulness, solicitousness, vigilance, wariness; **charge,** adoption, care, fosterage, guardianship, keeping, ministry, providence *(Relig.)*, trust, ward; **upbringing,** bringing-up, upkeep

care *n* → **1** care **2** difficulty **3** fright **4** job **5** medical treatment **6** protection **7** work *v* **8** feel emotion

careen *n* → **1** cleansing **2** overturn *v* **3** clean **4** overturn **5** repair

career *n* → **1** attack **2** job **3** rate *v* **4** speed

CARE FOR *v* keep an eye on, minister to, shepherd, take care of, tend; **keep,** look after, save, sit on; **foster,** bring up, fetch up *(U.S.)*, groom, raise, rear; **mind,** attend, baby-sit, sit, take care of, watch; **take pains,** be at pains to, be sure, bother, look out for, look to one's laurels, make sure; **nurse,** fondle, lap, mollycoddle, mother, room in, suckle; **fuss over,** dance attendance on, make a fuss of, wait on hand and foot

CAREFUL *adj* attentive, diligent, heedful, intent, measured, mindful; **ministrant,** clucky, ministrative, regardful, serviceable *(Archaic)*, solicitous, thoughtful; **fussy,** jealous, laboured, old-womanish, overconscientious, pernickety

careful *adj* → **1** attentive **2** cautious **3** mean **4** thrifty

CAREFULLY *adv* attentively, diligently; **solicitously,** on tiptoe, soft, thoughtfully

careless *adj* → **1** apathetic **2** false **3** happy **4** inattentive **5** lucky **6** neglectful

caress *n* → **1** endearments *v* **2** kiss **3** love

caretaker *n* → conservationist

cargo *n* → **1** contents **2** goods

caricature *n* → **1** comedy **2** drawing **3** exaggeration **4** imitation **5** misrepresentation **6** mockery **7** portrait *v* **8** imitate **9** misinterpret **10** portray

carillon *n* → **1** percussion instrument **2** resonator *v* **3** ring

carmine *n* → **1** purple *adj* **2** purple **3** red

carnage *n* → massacre

carnal *adj* → **1** human **2** irreverent **3** sexy **4** voluptuous

carnation *n* → **1** red *adj* **2** red

carnival *n* → **1** amusement **2** amusement park **3** contest **4** festival

carnivore *n* → **1** eater **2** plant

carol *v* → **1** approve **2** rejoice **3** sing

carouse *n* → **1** celebration **2** party *v* **3** drink alcohol **4** overindulge **5** rejoice

carousel *n* → **1** amusement park **2** contest

carp *v* → complain
carpenter *n* → **1** builder **2** joiner *v* **3** build
carpet *n* → **1** coating **2** covering **3** manchester *v* **4** cover **5** lay charges **6** scold
carpetbagger *n* → **1** cunning person **2** extortionist **3** opportunist
CARRIAGE *n* American buggy, barouche, berlin, britzka, brougham, buckboard *(U.S.)*, buggy, cabriolet, calash, car *(Poetic)*, cariole, caroche, carromata, chaise, chariot, coach-and-four, cobb *(Obs.)*, coupé, curricle, diligence, dogcart, drag, droshky, equipage, fiacre, fly, four-in-hand, gharry, gig, hackney, hackney-carriage, hackney-coach, hansom, jaunting car, jingle, landau, phaeton, post-chaise, rig, shay, spider, stage, stagecoach, stanhope, sulky, surrey *(U.S.)*, tally-ho, tandem, tilbury, trap, unicorn, victoria, vis-a-vis, wagonette; **caravan,** covered wagon *(U.S.)*, prairie schooner *(U.S.)*. *See also* WAGON
carriage *n* → **1** behaviour **2** freight **3** pose **4** train **5** transport
carrier *n* → **1** telecommunications station **2** transporter **3** watercraft
carrion *n* → **1** dirtiness *adj* **2** deteriorated
carrot *n* → incentive
carry *n* → **1** length *v* **2** be important **3** capture **4** compute **5** conceive **6** help **7** transport
cart *n* → **1** wagon *v* **2** transport
carte blanche *n* → **1** authority **2** permission
cartel *n* → **1** contract **2** corporation **3** liberty
cartography *n* → representation
carton *n* → box
cartoon *n* → **1** drawing **2** film **3** imitation **4** mockery **5** model **6** portrait *v* **7** portray
cartridge *n* → **1** ammunition **2** case **3** sound system
carve *v* → **1** cut **2** depict **3** portray **4** shape
cascade *n* → **1** lace **2** spring *v* **3** shower
CASE *n* attaché case, beauty case, briefcase, dispatch box, dispatch case, papeterie, portfolio, skippet, sponge bag, vanity case, writing case; **suitcase,** port, valise; **purse,** billfold *(U.S.)*, budget *(Obs.)*, burse, cardcase, handbag, moneybag, notecase, pochette, pocket-book, pouch, reticule, wallet, whippy, willy; **compact,** smelling bottle; **workbox,** ditty-bag, ditty-box, etui, housewife, kit; **sheath,** encasement, holster, quiver, sabretache, scabbard; **magazine,** cartridge, cassette; **specimen case,** solander, vasculum. *See also* BOX; BAG; BASKET
case *n* → **1** condition **2** container **3** covering **4** evidence **5** litigation **6** nonconformist **7** patient **8** plating **9** wrapper *v* **10** enclose **11** investigate **12** look
casement *n* → window
CASH *n* argent *(Obs.)*, big bickies, brass, bread, cabbage, chaff, chips, circulating medium, currency, dibs, dosh, dough, gelt, gold, hard cash, hard-earned, hay, ill-gotten gains, kale *(U.S.)*, l.s.d., legal tender, lolly, loot, lucre, mazuma, mintage, money, moolah, oscar, pelf, ready, shekels, splosh, spon, spondulicks, stuff, tender, wampum *(U.S.)*; **banknote,** bill *(U.S.)*, double-header, greenback *(U.S.)*, money order, note, order, paper, shin plaster *(Obs.)*; **pound,** fiddley, frog, iron man, jim, quid, seine; **dollar,** buck, Oxford, plunk *(U.S.)*, seine, smacker; **folding money,** bankroll, lettuce, paper money, roll, scoop. *See also* COINAGE; FUNDS; ALLOWANCE; TREASURY; CURRENCY
CASH *v* change, collect, draw, draw on, float a loan, go liquid, liquidate, overdraw, raise the wind, realise, run, tap, withdraw from
CASH *adj* financial, fiscal, hip-pocket, monetary, pecuniary; **convertible,** hard, liquid, realisable, utterable; **numismatic,** numismatical, nummary, nummular; **money-minded**
cashier *n* → **1** seller **2** treasury *v* **3** dismiss
cashmere *n* → animal's coat
casing *n* → **1** building **2** covering **3** plating
casino *n* → **1** amusement park **2** cabin **3** gambling hall **4** meeting place
cask *n* → barrel
casket *n* → **1** box **2** coffin *v* **3** enclose
casserole *v* → cook
cassette *n* → **1** case **2** sound system
cassock *n* → **1** jacket **2** uniform
cast *n* → **1** amount **2** appearance **3** character **4** colour **5** copy **6** corporation **7** depth **8** faulty sight **9** length **10** metal **11** model **12** order **13** point of view **14** prediction **15** secretion **16** shape **17** small amount **18** theatrical company **19** throw *v* **20** compute **21** depict **22** distort **23** fish **24** give birth **25** heat **26** plan **27** portray **28** predict **29** separate **30** shape **31** stage **32** throw *adj* **33** drunk **34** fallen **35** lost **36** shaped
castaway *n* → **1** solitary *adj* **2** separate
cast away *v* → **1** refuse **2** repel
caste *n* → **1** class **2** community
castigate *v* → **1** punish **2** scold
cast-iron *adj* → **1** certain **2** durable
castle *n* → **1** fortress **2** house
castor oil *n* → fat
castrate *v* → **1** cut off **2** make infertile
casual *n* → **1** temporary appointment **2** worker *adj* **3** apathetic **4** impermanent **5** inattentive **6** informal **7** irregular **8** lucky **9** neglectful **10** uncertain
CASUALTY *n* the walking wounded, the wounded; **amputee; handicapped person,** cripple, defective, paraplegic, quadriplegic, slow worker; **wreck,** bomb, tin lizzie, write-off
casualty *n* → **1** hospital **2** the dead
CASUISTIC *adj* deceptive, elenctic, illegitimate, Jesuitical, misleading, paralogistic, perverse, sophistic; **quibbling,** fine-spun, inconsequent, over subtle, pettifogging
CAT *n* ballarat, feline, grimalkin, kitten, marmalade cat, mog, moggy, mouser, puss, pussy, tabby, tom, tomcat, tortoiseshell; **Abyssinian,** Angora, Archangel, Burmese, Cheshire, Egyptian, Havana brown, Himalayan, Maltese, Manx, Persian, Russian blue, Siamese, Turkish

cat *n* → **1** club **2** lift **3** lover **4** machine **5** musician **6** raft **7** sailing ship **8** sexual type **9** unkind person *v* **10** cudgel
catabolism *n* → **1** change **2** destruction
cataclysm *n* → **1** change **2** turbulence **3** violent outburst
catacomb *n* → **1** cave **2** grave
catalogue *n* → **1** classification **2** information **3** list **4** reference book *v* **5** inquire into **6** list **7** record
catalyst *n* → **1** causer **2** changer **3** combiner **4** influencer
catamaran *n* → **1** raft **2** sailing ship **3** sledge
catapult *n* → **1** propellant *v* **2** cudgel
cataract *n* → spring
catarrh *n* → cold
catastrophe *n* → **1** finish **2** misfortune **3** ruin **4** turbulence **5** violent outburst
catcall *n* → **1** boo **2** insult *v* **3** disapprove of
catch *n* → **1** amount **2** bolt **3** difficulty **4** holder **5** part **6** song **7** stoppage **8** stratagem **9** takings *v* **10** allure **11** beguile **12** be ill **13** be timely **14** find out **15** gain **16** hear **17** hold **18** surprise **19** trick
CATCH FIRE *v* blaze, burn ahead, deflagrate, go up in smoke, sweal, take fire; **flame,** conflagrate, flare up, flash, spark; **smoke,** smoulder
catechism *n* → **1** belief **2** breviary **3** questioning **4** textbook
categorical *adj* → **1** assertive **2** classificatory **3** unconditional
category *n* → **1** being **2** class
cater *v* → facilitate
caterpillar *n* → puller
caterwaul *n* → **1** animal call *v* **2** call (of animals) **3** shrill
catharsis *n* → **1** cleanser **2** psychotherapy
cathedral *n* → **1** church *adj* **2** authoritative
catholic *adj* → **1** general **2** religious **3** tolerant
catnap *n* → **1** sleep *v* **2** sleep
cat-o'-nine-tails *n* → **1** club **2** cord
CATTLE *n* beef, beef cattle, beefalo, beefer, bobby calf, bovine, buffalo, bull, bullock, catalo, cow, dairy cattle, four-legged kangaroo *(Joc.)*, heifer, kine *(Archaic)*, longhorn, micky, moo-cow, muley, neat *(Obs.)*, ox, poddy, ruminant, Russians, snaily, sook, sookie, springer, steer, vealer
cattle *n* → working class
catwalk *n* → path
caucus *n* → **1** committee **2** legislative body
caulk *v* → fill
CAUSAL *adj* aetiological, determinant, efficient, evocable, occasional; **causative,** ergative, inductive; **provocative,** catalytic, deterministic, evocative, instigative, provoking
CAUSALITY *n* aetiology, determinism, final causes, finalism, teleology
CAUSALLY *adv* aetiologically, causatively
causation *n* → cause
CAUSE *n* causation, determinant, evocation, ground, matter, occasion; **reason,** factor, secret, skill *(Obs.)*, wherefore, why; **engenderment,** beginning, breeding; **catalysis,** induction, precipitation
CAUSE *v* bring about, bring to bear, bring to pass, do, induce, occasion; **produce,** awaken, bring on, catalyse, conduce, evoke, excite, give rise to, incur, inspire, kick up, precipitate, provoke, spark off, waken; **make,** get, have, let; **engender,** be responsible for, beget, breed, bring forth, create, play a part in
cause *n* → litigation
CAUSE DIFFICULTIES *v* complicate, embarrass, entangle, harry, involve, mire, perplex; **mess someone around,** fuck someone about, fuck someone around, lead someone a chase, lead someone a merry dance, make it hot for, mess someone about, put through the hoops, tree
CAUSER *n* evoker, mainspring, pivot, prime mover, primum mobile, principle; **provoker,** begetter, beginner, breeder, engenderer, inducer, inspirer, producer; **catalyst,** casus belli, catalyser, precipitator; **causative,** incentive, instigation, provocative
causeway *n* → **1** path **2** road
caustic *n* → **1** curve **2** destroyer *adj* **3** acrimonious **4** curvilinear **5** fiery **6** heating **7** hot **8** humorous
cauterise *v* → fire
caution *n* → **1** command **2** nonconformist **3** warning *v* **4** warn
CAUTIOUS *adj* canny, careful, chary, circumspect, circumspective, deliberate, discreet, heedful, measured, ware *(Archaic)*, wary; **guarded,** close, conservative, safe, safety-conscious; **prudent,** forethoughtful; **tentative,** gingerly
cavalcade *n* → sequence
cavalier *n* → **1** courteous person **2** fighter **3** rider **4** soldier *v* **5** be arrogant *adj* **6** apathetic **7** arrogant **8** discourteous **9** insulting **10** rash
cavalry *n* → **1** armed forces **2** rider
CAVE *n* cavern, cove, dugout, grot *(Poetic)*, grotto; **chamber,** catacomb, columbarium, hypogeum, tomb; **burrow,** cubbyhole, foxhole, wormhole. *See also* HOLLOW; EXCAVATION
cave *n* → **1** break *interj* **2** beware
cavern *n* → cave
cavil *n* → **1** complaint **2** disagreement **3** sharing out **4** unimportant thing *v* **5** dismiss
cavity *n* → hollow
cease *n* → **1** stoppage *v* **2** die **3** stop
cedar *n* → timber
cede *v* → capitulate
ceiling *n* → **1** apex **2** bottom **3** limit **4** top *adj* **5** top
celebrant *n* → **1** ecclesiastic **2** rejoicer **3** wedding **4** worshipper
celebrate *v* → **1** approve **2** command respect **3** publicise **4** rejoice
CELEBRATION *n* festivities, jollities, revels, silly season; **party,** carouse, chavoo, corroboree, do, hootenanny *(U.S.)*, jamboree, love-in, rage, rave, riot, rort, shindig, shindy, shivaree *(U.S.)*, turn, wayzgoose, wing-ding; **function,** levee, reception; **feasting,** banquet,

beanfeast, beano, bunfight, feast, fete, hangi, junket, love feast, midnight feast, prawn night, umu; **garden party,** annual picnic; **spree,** a night on the tiles, a night on the town, bacchanal, bash, bat, piss-up, stag party. *See also* JOY; FESTIVAL

CELEBRATORY *adj* commemorational, commemorative, commemoratory; **revelling,** bacchanal, bacchanalian, bacchic, convivial, mad, noisemaking, on the loose, on the town, roisterous, rollicking, saturnalian; **triumphant,** exultant, jubilant, jubilatory, triumphal; **congratulatory,** gratulatory

celebrity *n* → famous person

celerity *n* → speed

celestial *adj* → **1** cosmic **2** ghostly **3** heavenly

CELESTIALLY *adv* blissfully, divinely, paradisiacally, supernally

celibacy *n* → **1** abstinence **2** single state

celibate *n* → **1** abstainer *adj* **2** abstinent **3** infertile **4** single

CELL *n* black hole, black peter, calaboose *(U.S.)*, circle, condemned cell, death cell, death row, digger *(N.Z.)*, dummy *(N.Z.)*, dungeon, glasshouse *(Brit.)*, go-slow, oubliette, peter, pound, slot, slough, sweatbox; **penalty box,** sin-bin; **pen,** crib, pound, stabling; **cage,** coop, kennel, Skinner Box; **stocks,** pillory; **black maria,** bun wagon, paddy-wagon, wagon. *See also* PRISON

cell *n* → **1** abbey **2** clique **3** compartment **4** electric generator **5** organism **6** room

cellar *n* → **1** room **2** storey

cellophane *n* → wrapper

CELLULAR *adj* alveolate, amygdaloidal, cellulous, faveolate, geodic, honeycombed, lacunal, lacunar, lacunose, vacuolate; **porous,** poriferous, spongy; **chambered,** ventricular

cellulite *n* → fat

celluloid *n* → **1** entertainment *adj* **2** fake **3** filmic

cellulose *v* → conserve

cement *n* → **1** adhesive **2** building materials **3** paving **4** powder *v* **5** coat **6** stick together

CEMETERY *n* boneyard, burial ground, churchyard, field of Mars, garden of remembrance, God's acre, graveyard, marble orchard, necropolis, potter's field; **crematorium,** cinerarium; **mortuary,** charnel, charnel-house, funeral parlour, morgue. *See also* GRAVE

cenotaph *n* → **1** grave **2** memento

censer *n* → **1** fragrance **2** shrine

censor *n* → **1** disapprover **2** prohibiter **3** psychic disturbance *v* **4** hide **5** prohibit

censure *n* → **1** denigration **2** disapproval *v* **3** disapprove of **4** disgrace

census *n* → **1** computation **2** list **3** record

centaur *n* → mythical beast

centenary *n* → anniversary

CENTRAL *adj* axial, centric, nuclear, nucleate, pivotal, umbilical; **epicentral,** epifocal *(Geol.)*; **centripetal,** centrifugal, focal; **concentric,** homocentric; **intermediate,** intermediary, medium; **middle,** halfway, medial, median, mid, middlemost, midmost, midway; **pivotal,** axial

central *n* → telecommunications

CENTRALISE *v* centre, concentrate, concentre, focalise, focus, middle

centralise *v* → gather

CENTRALLY *adv* axially, centrically, centrifugally, centripetally, focally; **intermediately,** amidships, medially, medianly, midmost; **in midstream,** in medias res, in the middle; **dead-centre,** bang on

CENTRE *n* centrum, core, heart, heartwood, hub, kern, kernel, marrow, nave, node, nucellus, nucleor, nucleus, pith, yolk; **middle,** golden mean, halfway house, hey-diddle-diddle, mean, media, median, midpoint, midriff, midst, midway, waist; **navel,** omphalos, umbilicus; **bullseye,** blank, bull; **centre of gravity,** barycentre, centre of inertia, centre of mass, centroid, dead centre; **centre of buoyancy,** metacentre; **focus,** bunt *(Naut.)*, epicentre *(Geol.)*, eye, fess point *(Her.)*, focal point; **nerve centre,** ganglion, H.Q., headquarters; **storm centre,** eye of the storm

centre *n* → **1** gambler *v* **2** centralise

CENTRE-LINE *n* axis, caudex *(Bot.)*, columella, fulcrum, hinge, newel *(Bldg Trades)*, pivot, polar axis

CENTRE OF ACTIVITY *n* beehive, hive, hive of activity, madding crowd, madhouse, Mecca, thick of things; **peak hour,** rush hour; **period of activity,** session, shift, spell

centrifugal *adj* → **1** central **2** divergent

centrifugal force *n* → energy

centripetal *adj* → **1** central **2** convergent

centripetal force *n* → energy

centurion *n* → soldier

century *n* → **1** armed forces **2** hundred

ceramics *n* → fine arts

cerebellum *n* → head

cerebral *adj* → **1** intellectual **2** mental **3** thinking

ceremonial *n* → **1** breviary **2** custom **3** religious ceremony **4** worship *adj* **5** formal

ceremony *n* → **1** custom **2** formality **3** religious ceremony

cerise *n* → **1** purple *adj* **2** purple **3** red

CERTAIN *adj* apodictic, doubtless, incontrovertible, indubitable, irrefragable, irrefutable, unchallengeable, undeniable, undoubted, unimpeachable, unquestionable, unquestioned; **sure-fire,** dead set, in the bag; **cast-iron,** absolute, perfect *(Obs.)*, unfailing; **unequivocal,** unambiguous, unmistakable; **self-evident,** axiomatic; **inevitable,** bound to happen, unavoidable; **sure,** decided, definite, determinate, positive; **confident,** assured, secure, self-assured, self-confident, self-sufficient; **cocksure,** cool as a cucumber, overconfident; **doctrinaire,** bigoted, dogmatic, opinionated, thetic, unshakeable

certain *adj* → **1** faithful **2** particular **3** serious **4** smallest **5** true

CERTAINLY *adv* abso-bloody-lutely, absolutely, assuredly, beyond a shadow of doubt, beyond question, bound to be, clearly, decidedly, doubtless, doubtlessly, for a certainty, for a monte, for certain, for sure, indubitably, iwis *(Obs.)*, no doubt, rightly, sure as death and taxes, surely, undoubtedly, unimpeachably, unmistakably, unquestionably; **definitely,** by all means, no risk, of course, questionless, sure, without question; **without doubt,** all right, very well; **incontestably,** apodictically, demonstrably, determinately, positively, undeniably; **inevitably,** sure *(U.S.)*, without fail

CERTAIN THING *n* bird *(Horseracing)*, bird in the hand, cert, dead certainty, inevitable, knocktaker, monte, moral, open and shut case, safe bet, sure cop, sure thing; **clincher,** convincer; **dictum,** gospel

CERTAINTY *n* certitude, decidedness, positivism, sureness, surety; **assurance,** aplomb, assuredness, cocksureness, self-assurance, self-confidence, self-sufficiency; **conviction,** belief, confidence, secureness; **doctrinarism,** bigotry, dogmatism; **idée fixe,** obsession

CERTIFICATE *n* birth certificate, death certificate, group certificate, land certificate, lines *(Brit. Colloq.)*, marriage certificate, navicert; **casebook,** bill of health; **licence,** driving licence, learner's permit, miner's right, pass, passport, trading certificate, visa; **ship's papers,** clearance papers, maygo. *See also* RECORD

certificate *n* → authentication

certify *v* → authenticate

certitude *n* → certainty

cervix *n* → groin

cessation *n* → **1** rest **2** stoppage

cesspool *n* → **1** den of vice **2** garbage dump **3** pigsty **4** toilet

chafe *n* → **1** annoyance **2** irritation *v* **3** annoy **4** displease **5** heat **6** irritate **7** pain **8** rub

chaff *n* → **1** cash **2** joke **3** mockery **4** waste *v* **5** joke **6** mock

chagrin *n* → **1** displeasure **2** meekness *v* **3** discontent **4** displease **5** humble **6** irritate

chain *n* → **1** jewellery **2** length **3** mountain **4** restraints **5** sequence **6** series **7** wire *v* **8** restrain

CHAIN-REACTING *adj* multiplicational, subcritical, supercritical; **radioactive,** charged, hot, irradiated, radiogenic, radiological; **fissile,** fertile, fissionable, scissile; **nuclear,** atomic, endoergic, endothermic, exoergic, exothermic, thermonuclear

chain-reaction *n* → radioactivation

chair *n* → **1** authority **2** bicycle **3** educational office **4** leader **5** means of killing *v* **6** glorify

chalet *n* → **1** cabin **2** flat

chalice *n* → **1** drinking vessel **2** shrine

chalk *n* → **1** dye **2** sign **3** white **4** writing materials *v* **5** mark **6** whiten **7** write

CHALLENGE *n* boast, brave *(Archaic)*, cry of defiance, dare, gage, taunt, threat, war cry, whoop; **outcry,** protest

challenge *n* → **1** contest **2** difficulty **3** question *v* **4** call (of animals) **5** contest **6** doubt **7** impute **8** oppose **9** question

chamber *n* → **1** bedroom **2** cave **3** committee **4** compartment **5** council **6** hall **7** legislative body **8** office **9** room **10** toilet **11** treasury *v* **12** enclose

chamberlain *n* → manager

chambermaid *n* → servant

chamber-pot *n* → **1** toilet **2** vessel

champ *n* → **1** winner *v* **2** eat

champagne *n* → **1** wine **2** yellow *adj* **3** yellow

champion *n* → **1** accomplice **2** defender **3** fighter **4** good person **5** helper **6** hero **7** winner *v* **8** help **9** oppose *adj* **10** good

CHAMPIONSHIP *n* ascendancy, mastery

chance *n* → **1** danger **2** fate **3** feasibility **4** luck **5** opportunity **6** uncertain thing *v* **7** risk *adj* **8** lucky

chancel *n* → **1** room **2** shrine

chancellor *n* → **1** judge **2** leader **3** ruler **4** teacher

CHANCE ON *v* fluke, happen on, hit on, hit upon, light on, stumble on; **happen,** fall to one's lot

chandelier *n* → **1** lighting **2** stand

chandler *n* → **1** seller **2** storeman **3** trader

CHANGE *n* alteration, alts and adds, amendment, arrangement, fluctuation, flux, metamorphism, metamorphosis, modification, permutation, perversion, radicalisation, reaction, reformation, rehash, renounce, reorganisation, revisal, revise, revision, sea change, sfumato *(Art)*, shake-up, shift, switch, switch-over, switcheroo, transit, transition, turn, twist, variation, vicissitude; **sudden change,** break, cataclysm, crisis, cut, jump cut, metastasis, revolution; **transformation,** alchemy, bioconversion, conversion, denaturation, denaturisation, differentiation, diversification, endomorphism, fossilisation, heteromorphism, heteromorphy, metaplasm, transfiguration, transfigurement, transmogrification, transmutation, transubstantiation, xenogenesis; **modification,** adaptation, adjustment, dialectic, dissimilation, inflection, modulation, mutation, rectification, saltation; **morphosis,** anabolism, carbonisation, catabolism, cytokinesis, karyokinesis, metabolism, metaplasia, oxidation; **turning point,** climacteric, climacterical, climax, crisis

CHANGE *v* acculturate, affect, alter, amend, catalyse, chequer, counterchange, dissimilate, launder *(Finance)*, leave one's mark on, leaven, make over, manipulate, modify, mutate, permute, pervert, rehash, remodel, revise, revolutionise, touch, twist, vary; **modulate,** adapt, adjust, edit, fair *(Shipbuilding)*, finetune, qualify, recast, reshape, specialise, trim *(Naut.)*; **permutate,** permute, ring the changes; **adapt,** lend oneself to; **differentiate,** diversify, jump, mutate, switch, turn; **grade,** glide, gradate, graduate, melt, range, shade, slide; **change into,** become; **convert,** arrange, colour, deform, metamorphose, radicalise, rectify, transcribe, transfigure, transform, translate, transmogrify, turn; **transmute,**

alchemise, alkalise, denature, elaborate, fossilise, metabolise, transpose *(Obs.)*, transubstantiate

change *n* → 1 coinage 2 information 3 newness 4 outfit 5 ringing 6 something different *v* 7 cash 8 exchange 9 wear

CHANGEABLE *adj* alterable, ambulatory, changeful, mutable, transmutable; **adaptable,** adaptive, elastic, light, mobile, protean, supple, variform, versatile, volatile; **allomorphous,** allomerous, metastable; **unstable,** insecure, instable, rootless, treacherous, unsound, unsteady; **wavering,** fluctuant, fluctuating, roller-coaster, up-and-down, vacillating, vacillatory; **fluky,** variable; **fluidic,** astatic, floating, fluent *(Rare)*, fluid, fluidal, labile, sandy, slippery, unsettled, vagrant; **capricious,** amphibolic, crank, errant, erratic, fickle, flighty, freakish, freaky, Jekyll-and-Hyde, mercurial, slippery, temperamental, variable, varying, wayward, whimsical; **vacillatory,** acrobatic, meandering, uncertain, unsettled, vacillating, wavering; **chameleon-like,** chameleonic, kaleidoscopic, phantasmagorical; **inconstant,** indefinite, indeterminate, movable, vertiginous; **transitory,** caducous, short-life, short-lived

CHANGELESS *adj* invariable, invariant, typecast, unchanging, unfading, unfailing, unflagging, unregenerate; **unchangeable,** immovable, immutable, inadaptable, inalterable, incommutable, indecomposable, indissoluble, irrecoverable, irreducible, unshakeable; **hard-core,** deep-rooted, deep-seated, dyed-in-the-wool; **constant,** endless, enduring, eternal, eterne *(Archaic)*, hard-wearing, indefeasible, indelible, ineffaceable, ineradicable, inerasable, interminable, irremovable, irrepealable, irreversible, lasting, perdurable, perennial, permanent, persistent, quenchless, regular *(Mil.)*, stable, staid *(Rare)*, standing, unending; **fixed,** confirmed, determined, immovable, inexorable, inflexible, infrangible, steadfast; **deathless,** immortal, imperishable, incorruptible, undying

CHANGER *n* alembic, alterant, catalyser, catalyst, catalytic, converter, modifier, modulator, philosopher's stone, transducer, transformer; **adaptor,** adjuster, finetuner; **converter,** alchemist, transmuter; **varier,** amender, manipulator, perverter, reviser, revisionist

CHANGING *adj* heteromorphic, on the turn, transformative, transmutative, variant, vicissitudinary, vicissitudinous, xenogenetic, xenogenic; **adaptive,** acculturative, modificatory; **modulative,** alterant, alterative, amendatory *(U.S.)*, manipulative, manipulatory, revisionary, revisory

CHANNEL *n* aqueduct, canal, conduit, ditch, duct, dyke, irrigator, lane, lead, navigable water, navigation, reach, river, runnel, seaway, ship canal, stream channel, swash, thoroughfare, tideway, trench, trough, wash, watercourse, waterway; **stormwater channel,** floodway, gutter, spillway; **moat,** fosse; **tunnel,** water-tunnel, wind-tunnel; **donga,** dry creek, wadi, winterbourne; **strait,** euripus, gat, neck, sound; **valley,** arroyo, gulch *(U.S.)*, gullet, gully, nullah, pass *(U.S.)*, water-gap

CHANNEL *v* canal; **canalise; pipe,** siphon, spile; **irrigate,** subirrigate; **reticulate,** vein

channel *n* → 1 exit 2 furrow 3 informant 4 method 5 route *v* 6 cut 7 dig 8 direct 9 furrow 10 shear

CHANNELLED *adj* ducted, vascular, veined; **villiform,** funnel-like, gutterlike, pipy, wormlike; **irrigational,** irrigative

chant *n* → 1 song *v* 2 sing

chaos *n* → 1 disorder 2 gap

chapel *n* → 1 church 2 institute 3 room 4 shrine 5 trade union

chaperone *n* → 1 partner *v* 2 accompany 3 partner

chaplain *n* → ecclesiastic

chapter *n* → 1 ecclesiastic 2 number 3 religious ministry 4 society 5 written composition *v* 6 separate

char *n* → 1 cleaner 2 drink 3 fuel 4 servant *v* 5 clean 6 fire

CHARACTER *n* complexion *(Obs.)*, constitution, genius, identity, image, nature, persona, personality, psychology, self; **temperament,** cue *(Archaic)*, disposition, ethos, frame of mind, grain, humour, mind, mood, spirit, temper, tone; **type,** blood, breed, cast, colour, complexion, cut, feather, hue, kidney, make, make-up, manner *(Obs.)*, mien, mould, quality, sort, stamp, style, timber, worth; **grain,** strain, streak, stripe *(U.S.)*, vein; **habit,** idiolect, idiosyncrasy, peculiarity, trait

character *n* → 1 characteristic 2 code 3 essence 4 letter 5 nonconformist 6 person 7 portrait 8 reputation 9 sign 10 writing *v* 11 write

characterise *v* → 1 particularise 2 represent

CHARACTERISTIC *n* attribute, character, difference *(Logic)*, differentia, distinction, distinctive feature, distinguishing feature, essence, flavour, form *(Philos.)*, genius, idiom, idiosyncrasy, individualism, individuality, lineament, mannerism, mark, particularity, parts, peculiarity, personality, singularity, speciality, specific, trait, way

CHARACTERISTIC *adj* attitudinal, complexional, constitutional, dispositional, inherited, invariant, temperamental, typical; **fundamental,** basic, congenital, essential, idiosyncratic, inborn, inbred, inherent, innate, inner, native; **aural,** atmospheric

characteristic *n* → 1 number 2 sign *adj* 3 essential

CHARACTERISTICALLY *adv* at bottom, au fond, idiosyncratically, in character, out of character, temperamentally, to the manner born, typically

CHARACTERISTICS *n* aspects, attributes, endowments, expression, features, inheritance, instincts, physiognomy, properties, qualities, streak, stuff, touch; **soul,** anima, animus, essence, heart, inner man, inner nature, inner woman, inscape, inside; **backbone,** calibre, fibre, mettle, pith, principle, strength; **air,** atmosphere, aura

charade *n* → gesture

charcoal *n* → 1 fire 2 fuel 3 writing materials *v* 4 blacken 5 depict 6 write

CHARGE *n* corkage, cover charge, fixed charge, flag fall, floating charge; **service charge,** breakage, brokerage, cranage, drayage, ferriage, footage *(Mining)*, lockage, quayage; **admission,** admission fee, doormoney, entrance, fare, fee; **gate money,** appearance money, attendance money

CHARGE *v* levy, reverse charges, tax, tithe

charge *n* → 1 accusation 2 act of war 3 a drink 4 attack 5 care 6 command 7 cost 8 dependant 9 electricity 10 excitement 11 explosive 12 guidance 13 heraldry 14 job 15 obligation 16 pleasure 17 religious follower 18 signal 19 work *v* 20 attack 21 be unable to pay 22 command 23 depute 24 electrify 25 emblematise 26 emotionalise 27 fill 28 guide 29 impute 30 lay charges 31 litigate 32 weigh *interj* 33 attack

charger *n* → 1 accuser 2 horse 3 tableware

chariot *n* → 1 carriage *v* 2 drive

charisma *n* → 1 allure 2 influence

CHARITY *n* aid, alms, gate money, relief; **subsidy,** allowance, bounty, expense account, grant, handout, scholarship, studentship, subsidisation; **foreign aid,** economic aid; **benefit,** family allowance, legal aid, meals on wheels, pension, repatriation, social bandaid, social security, social welfare, state aid; **relief work,** casework, social service, social work, welfare work; **appeal,** bottle drive, button day, door knock, drive, flag day, fundraiser, tarpaulin muster, telethon, war effort, whip-around; **fund,** collection plate, community chest *(U.S. Canada)*, kitty, poor box, the tin; **alimony,** keep, maintenance, palimony, supplies *(Obs.)*, support

charity *n* → 1 allowance 2 generosity 3 help 4 love 5 pity

charlatan *n* → faker

charm *n* → 1 allure 2 amulet 3 atom 4 beauty 5 birdcall 6 jewellery 7 magic spell 8 pleasantness 9 poetry *v* 10 allure 11 be pleasant 12 bewitch 13 please 14 protect

chart *n* → 1 diagram 2 list 3 song *v* 4 beat a path 5 map 6 plan

charter *n* → 1 contract 2 law 3 loan 4 power to act 5 record 6 rights *v* 7 borrow

chartreuse *n* → 1 abbey 2 green 3 yellow *adj* 4 yellow

charwoman *n* → 1 cleaner 2 servant

chary *adj* → 1 cautious 2 thrifty

chase *n* → 1 aim 2 furrow 3 nature reserve 4 pursuit 5 racing *v* 6 cut 7 furrow 8 hurry 9 pursue 10 walk

chasm *n* → 1 gap 2 interruption

chassis *n* → 1 building 2 stand

chaste *adj* → 1 abstinent 2 clean 3 modest 4 single

chasten *v* → 1 punish 2 scold

chastise *v* → 1 distil 2 punish 3 restrain 4 scold

chat *n* → 1 dirty person 2 talk 3 untidy person *v* 4 scold 5 talk

chattel *n* → 1 personal property 2 subject

chatter *n* → 1 click 2 nonsense 3 talk *v* 4 click 5 speak 6 talk 7 talk nonsense 8 vibrate 9 worry

chatterbox *n* → talker

chauffeur *n* → driver

chauvinism *n* → 1 enthusiasm 2 intolerance 3 nationalism 4 warmongering

CHEAP *adj* affordable, cheap at the price, dirt-cheap, economic, economical, frugal, inexpensive, low-priced, no-frills, sixpenny; **marked down,** cut-price, cut-rate, depreciated, discounted, half-price, nominal, on special, reduced; **free,** buckshee, complimentary, costless, gratis, gratuitous, honorary, interest-free; **untaxed,** duty-free, scot-free, tax-free; **worthless,** fustian, not worth a bumper, not worth a cracker, not worth a crumpet, unvalued, valueless; **cheap and nasty,** brum, brummy, catchpenny, el cheapo, gimcrack, tawdry, tinhorn *(U.S.)*, tinsel, tinselly, trashy, trumpery; **depreciative,** depreciatory, depressive; **economy-class,** third-class, tourist-class

cheap *adj* → 1 bad 2 easy 3 meek 4 vulgar 5 wrong *adv* 6 cheaply

CHEAPEN *v* beat down, depreciate, depress, devalue, discount, knock down, reduce, undervalue; **underbuy,** buy for a song, go offshore; **undercharge,** underquote; **undercut,** undersell

cheapen *v* → 1 trade 2 vulgarise

CHEAPLY *adv* at a discount, cheap, for a song, for next to nothing, inexpensively, on the cheap; **for free,** for nothing, gratis, gratuitously

CHEAPNESS *n* inexpensiveness; **valuelessness,** worthlessness; **depreciation,** devaluation, price-cutting, undervaluation; **concession,** cut rate, discount, discount rate, trade discount, undercharge; **depression,** recession, slump

CHEAT *v* beat *(U.S.)*, bilk, brass, bubble *(Archaic)*, chisel, clip, cog, con, cozen, cully *(Archaic)*, defraud, diddle, do, do down, do in the eye, do out of, finagle, flim-flam, fob off *(Archaic)*, fudge, gyp, hoozle, hotpoint, jockey, mountebank, nick, overreach, palm, point, quack, ringbolt *(N.Z.)*, rogue, rook, short-change, smuggle, sting, suck in, swindle, swizzle, take down, take the palm, trepan *(Archaic)*, trick out of, work a slanter

cheat *n* → 1 crook 2 cunning person 3 dishonesty 4 embezzlement 5 fake 6 faker 7 trick 8 trickster *v* 9 beguile 10 fail to pay 11 misbehave 12 swindle

check *n* → 1 counterbalance 2 discourager 3 furrow 4 hindrance 5 investigation 6 label 7 losing 8 restraints 9 sign 10 stoppage 11 test *v* 12 correct 13 discourage 14 fit 15 investigate 16 mark 17 oppose 18 restrain

19 stop 20 transport *adj* 21 multicoloured 22 questioning
checkmate *n* → 1 losing *v* 2 defeat
checkpoint *n* → 1 aim 2 indicator
checkup *n* → repair
cheddar *v* → agitate
cheek *n* → 1 arrogance 2 discourtesy 3 face 4 low regard 5 side *v* 6 insult
cheeky *adj* → 1 discourteous 2 insulting
cheep *n* → 1 birdcall *v* 2 chirp
cheer *n* → 1 appearance 2 applause 3 congratulation 4 emotion 5 food 6 happiness 7 help 8 incentive 9 shout *v* 10 approve 11 congratulate 12 encourage 13 feel emotion 14 help 15 shout
cheerful *adj* → 1 happy 2 pleasant
cheery *adj* → happy
cheese *n* → courtesy
chemise *n* → 1 coating 2 dress 3 underwear
chemist *n* → 1 bewitcher 2 healer 3 medication
chemotherapy *n* → medical treatment
CHEQUE *n* bank cheque, bank-draft, banker's draft, blank cheque, certified cheque, counter cheque; **voucher,** coupon, gift token, IOU
chequer *v* → change
cherish *v* → 1 flirt 2 respect
cheroot *n* → tobacco
cherry *n* → 1 abstainer 2 groin *adj* 3 red
cherub *n* → 1 angel 2 good person
CHEST *n* breast, brisket, bust, front, thorax; **torso,** trunk; **rib,** costa, slat; **bosom,** boob, breast, Bristols, bub, bust, charlies, cleavage, dug, fun bags, knockers, norks, tits; **nipple,** areola, diddy, dug, mamilla, pap, teat, tit, titty
chest *n* → box
chestnut *n* → 1 joke *adj* 2 brown
chevron *n* → emblem
chew *n* → 1 bit *v* 2 eat
chiaroscuro *n* → 1 black 2 darkening 3 painting
chic *n* → 1 fashion 2 good taste *adj* 3 fashionable 4 tasteful
chicanery *n* → 1 cunning 2 dishonesty 3 illogicality 4 loophole
chick *n* → 1 animal offspring 2 children 3 woman
chicken *n* → 1 animal offspring 2 children 3 coward *adj* 4 cowardly
chide *v* → scold
chief *n* → 1 cook 2 important person 3 manager 4 ruler *adj* 5 important
chieftain *n* → ruler
chiffonier *n* → cupboard
chignon *n* → hair
CHILD *n* affiliate, descendant, scion, sprig *(Joc.)*, sprout; **son,** daughter; **grandchild,** grand-daughter, grandson, great-grandchild, great-granddaughter, great-grandson; **foster-child,** daughter-in-law, foster-daughter, foster-son, fosterling, godchild, goddaughter, godson, son-in-law, stepchild, stepdaughter, stepson
child *n* → 1 children 2 innocent 3 pupil
childbirth *n* → birth
childish *adj* → 1 foolish 2 youthful
CHILDLESS FEMALE *n* gilt, nullipara, virgin
CHILDREN *n* grandchildren, kiddiewinks, small fry, the young; **child,** ankle-biter, bambino, elf, innocent, joey, junior, kid, kiddie, Little Johnny, little vegemite, littlie, moppet, nipper, piccaninny, slip, sprog, subteen, tiddler, weeny-bopper, youngie; **kindergartener,** preschooler; **prodigy,** child wonder, hopeful, wunderkind; **changeling,** elfchild; **brat,** bantling *(Archaic)*, enfant terrible, jackanapes, little bugger, perisher, pickle, tyke, Young Turk; **urchin,** gamin, latchkey child, ragamuffin, street Arab, waif; **girl,** bint, chick, chicken, girlie, lassie, miss, moppet; **minx,** chit, missy; **tomboy,** gamine, hoyden; **boy,** buster *(U.S.)*, junior, laddie, master, smacker, sonny. *See also* ADOLESCENT; OFFSPRING
chill *n* → 1 brace 2 cold 3 coldness 4 unsociability *v* 5 be cold 6 cool 7 desolate 8 discourage 9 frighten 10 harden *adj* 11 cold 12 distressing 13 unsociable
chime *n* → 1 edge 2 music 3 percussion instrument 4 resonator *v* 5 fit 6 ring
chimera *n* → 1 delusion 2 dream 3 freak
chimney *n* → 1 exit 2 fireplace 3 gap 4 passageway
chin *n* → 1 face *v* 2 speak
china *n* → 1 friend 2 tableware *adj* 3 brittle
chinchilla *n* → animal's coat
chink *n* → 1 break 2 click 3 gap 4 opening *v* 5 fill 6 ring
chintz *n* → manchester
chip *n* → 1 cut 2 jewel 3 part 4 reprimand 5 small amount 6 unimportant thing *v* 7 cook 8 cut 9 depict 10 farm 11 separate
chipboard *n* → timber
chiropractic *n* → healing
chiropractor *n* → healer
CHIRP *v* bill and coo, cheep, chirm, chirrup, coo, cuckoo, peep, pip, squeak, trill, tweet, twitter, warble; **cackle,** caw, clang, gabble, gaggle, gobble, squawk, waul; **crow,** cock-a-doodle-doo, croak, gobble, honk, quack, whoop; **cluck,** chuckle, clack. *See also* CALL (OF ANIMALS)
chirp *n* → birdcall
chirpy *adj* → happy
chirrup *n* → 1 birdcall *v* 2 chirp
CHISEL *n* adze, boaster, bolster, cold chisel, crosscut chisel, drove, firmer chisel, gouge, graver, hack hammer, hardy, icebreaker, leilira, neolith, osteotome, pitching tool, quarrel, set chisel, sett, spud
chisel *v* → 1 cheat 2 cut 3 depict 4 shape
chit *n* → 1 children 2 record
chivalry *n* → 1 courage 2 courtesy
chlorinate *v* → disinfect
chlorine *n* → 1 cleanser 2 decolourant
chloroform *v* → anaesthetise
chlorophyll *n* → 1 colour 2 greenness
chock *n* → 1 obstacle 2 restraints 3 stand *v* 4 obstruct 5 support *adv* 6 almost 7 closely
chocolate *n* → 1 drink *adj* 2 brown

CHOICE *n* alternative, discretion, druthers, elective, first refusal, option, refusal; **preference,** fancy, favourite, predilection; **selection,** adoption, cull, pick; **preselection,** cooption, nomination, preferment, selectness; **free will,** preferentialism, self-determination, voluntariness, will; **smorgasbord,** menu *(Computers)*, variety; **eclecticism**

choice *n* → **1** good thing **2** something different **3** will *adj* **4** chosen **5** good **6** tasteful

choir *n* → **1** angel **2** church **3** crowd **4** room **5** singer *v* **6** sing

choke *n* → **1** steering wheel **2** thinness *v* **3** fill **4** kill **5** obstruct **6** restrain **7** stop **8** suffocate

choker *n* → **1** jewellery **2** neckwear

chook *n* → **1** fool **2** woman

CHOOSE *v* fix on, fix upon, hand-pick, mark out, pick, pick and choose, pick out, pitch on, pitch upon, select, set on, take; **prefer,** fancy, favour, have rather, like best, opt for, plump for, single out; **pick the eyes out of; determine,** arbitrate, decide, resolve; **suit oneself,** work one's will. *See also* ELECT

choose *v* → intend

CHOOSER *n* endorser, nominator, plumper, preferentialist, preferrer, selector; **voter,** ballotter, black-baller, caster, constituent, elector, electoral college *(U.S.)*, electorate, floating voter, quorum, swinging voter; **suffragist,** suffragette; **decider,** determiner, resolver; **eclectic**

chopper *n* → **1** aircraft **2** axe **3** bicycle

choppy *adj* → rough

choral *adj* → musical

chord *n* → **1** line **2** sound **3** thread

chore *n* → **1** difficulty **2** job **3** toil **4** unpleasant thing **5** work

choreography *n* → dancing

chorister *n* → singer

chortle *n* → **1** mirth *v* **2** laugh

chorus *n* → **1** birdcall **2** crowd **3** musical piece **4** repetition **5** singer **6** theatrical company *v* **7** sing

chose *n* → personal property

CHOSEN *adj* choice, elect, favourite, handpicked, pet, picked, select; **eligible,** adoptable, votable

chosen *adj* → superior

chow *n* → food

christen *v* → **1** initiate **2** name

Christian *n* → **1** good person **2** person

Christian name *n* → name

Christmas *n* → holy day

chrome *v* → colour

chromosome *n* → living thing

chronic *adj* → **1** bad **2** eternal **3** unwholesome

chronicle *n* → **1** narrative **2** record *v* **3** narrate **4** record

chronometer *n* → timepiece

chrysalis *n* → animal offspring

chubby *adj* → **1** fat **2** swollen

chuck *n* → **1** lover **2** throw **3** touch **4** vomit *v* **5** do **6** kiss **7** throw **8** touch **9** vomit

chuckle *v* → **1** chirp **2** laugh

chug *n* → hiss

chum *n* → **1** friend **2** remnant

chump *n* → **1** fool **2** head **3** shaft **4** thickening

chunder *n* → **1** vomit *v* **2** vomit

chunk *n* → **1** part **2** thickening

CHURCH *n* fane *(Archaic)*, House of God, kirk *(Scot.)*; **cathedral,** basilica, minster, procathedral, title; **temple,** conventicle, joss house, mosque, naos, pagoda, pantheon, synagogue, tabernacle, ziggurat; **meeting house,** bethel *(U.S.)*, chapel, chapterhouse; **vicarage,** manse, parsonage, presbytery, rectory; **nave,** ambulatory, apse, choir, clerestory, cloister, confessional, decanal, decani, epistle side, gospel side, precinct, retrochoir, rood loft, transept, tribune, triforium; **corona,** Jesse window, tambour; **pulpit,** ambo, lectern, minbar, reading desk, rostrum, tribune; **pew,** faldstool, propitiary, sedile, tribune; **crypt,** Easter sepulchre, sepulchre, undercroft; **steeple,** minaret, spire. *See also* PLACE OF WORSHIP; ABBEY; SHRINE

CHURCH *adj* basilic, synagogical, tabernacular

church *n* → religion

churinga *n* → **1** idol **2** portrait **3** stick

churl *n* → **1** country dweller **2** discourteous person **3** farmer **4** miser **5** vulgarian

churn *n* → **1** barrel *v* **2** agitate **3** toss

CHUTE *n* chinaman, feed, feedpipe, gravity feed; **sluice,** flash, lock, penstock, weir; **race,** flume *(U.S.)*, headrace, leat, millrace, millrun, raceway, sluiceway, spillway, tailrace

chute *n* → **1** aircraft **2** descent **3** exit **4** path **5** slope **6** spring

cicada *n* → insect

cider *n* → drink

cigar *n* → tobacco

cigarette *n* → tobacco

cinch *n* → **1** belt **2** easy thing

cincture *n* → belt

cinder *n* → **1** fire **2** powder

cinema *n* → entertainment

CINEMATISE *v* cinematograph, dissolve, fade, film, flashback, pan, shoot, strip in

cinnamon *adj* → brown

cipher *n* → **1** clarification **2** code **3** disguise **4** letter **5** nonachiever **6** number **7** secrecy **8** unimportant person **9** writing form *v* **10** sound

CIRCLE *n* circumference, cirque *(Phys. Geog.)*, compass *(Obs.)*, epicycle, orbit, radius, roundel, roundlet, spiral; **round,** circuit, gyre *(Poetic)*, lap *(Racing)*, loop, turn; **rim,** felloe, tread; **annual ring,** annulation; **cromlech,** fairy ring; **equator,** celestial equator, ecliptic, equinoctial line, galactic circle, galactic equator, meridian; **disc,** bezant *(Archit.)*, button, coin, plate, slug; **discus,** puck; **bullseye.** *See also* RING; WHEEL; OVAL

circle *n* → **1** auditorium **2** cell **3** idol **4** jewellery **5** light **6** move **7** ring **8** rotation **9** whole *v* **10** rotate **11** surround

circuit *n* → **1** circle **2** edge **3** entertainment **4** move **5** rotation *v* **6** rotate

circuitous *adj* → **1** deflective **2** twisting
CIRCUITOUSNESS *n* anfractuosity, circuity, circularity, circumvolution, convolution, flexuosity, meander, sinuation, sinuosity, sinuousness, tortuosity, tortuousness, wriggle; **intorsion,** circumnutation, koru *(N.Z.)*; **curliness,** crispation, crispness, frizz; **torsion,** wring, writhe; **entwinement,** twine, winding; **volution,** dextrality, verticillation
CIRCULAR *adj* clypeate, cycloid, full, revolving, rounded, spiral, spirelike, spiriferous; **ringed,** annulate, annulose, armillary, circinate *(Bot.)*, hooped, ringleted, torquate; **ringlike,** annular, areolar, areolate, circinate, coronary, coronate, cricoid; **cyclic,** bicyclic, tricyclic
circular *n* → **1** information **2** message **3** public notice *adj* **4** deflective **5** twisting
CIRCULATE *v* coin, counterfeit, forge, issue, mint, monetise, utter; **revalue,** demonetise, devalue
circulate *v* → **1** alternate **2** become known **3** be sociable **4** disperse **5** finance **6** publicise **7** repeat **8** rotate
circulation *n* → **1** flow **2** move **3** rotation **4** score
circumcise *v* → cut
circumference *n* → **1** area **2** circle **3** frame **4** line **5** outside
circumlocution *n* → **1** figure of speech **2** waffle
circumnavigate *v* → rotate
circumscribe *v* → **1** edge **2** enclose **3** imprison **4** limit **5** restrain
circumspect *adj* → cautious
circumstance *n* → **1** condition **2** occurrence **3** particulars **4** unimportant thing *v* **5** inform **6** particularise
circumvent *v* → beguile
circus *n* → **1** auditorium **2** crossway **3** entertainment **4** jewellery **5** ring **6** theatrical company
cirrus *n* → cloud
cistern *n* → **1** basin **2** bladder
citadel *n* → fortress
cite *v* → **1** consult **2** litigate
CITIZEN *n* burgher, townsfolk, townsman, townspeople, townswoman; **cityite,** city slicker, dude *(U.S.)*, suburbanite, townie
citizen *n* → **1** national **2** population
citrus *adj* → arboreal
CITY *n* Babylon, big smoke, burg *(U.S.)*, burgh *(Chiefly Scot.)*, capital, concrete jungle, conurbation, federal capital, free city, megalopolis, metropolis, open city, state capital, system city; **inner city,** business area, business section, central business district, civic centre, downtown, residential district, riverfront, shopping area, the docks, uptown, waterfront, waterfrontage; **suburb,** barrio, borough, built-up area, dormitory, dormitory suburb, faubourg, municipality, parish, precinct *(U.S.)*, subdivision, ward; **suburbia,** commuter belt, exurbia, ribbon development; **slum area,** ruins, shanty-town, skid row, slums, tin pan alley; **native quarter,** chinatown, ghetto, kasbah. *See also* TOWN
city *n* → **1** administrative area **2** nation
civic *adj* → urban
civil *adj* → **1** courteous **2** national
civilian *n* → **1** neutral **2** religious follower
civilisation *n* → **1** good taste **2** teaching
civilise *v* → improve
civilised *adj* → courteous
civility *n* → **1** courtesy **2** good taste **3** high regard
civil liberty *n* → rights
civil war *n* → war
clack *n* → **1** birdcall **2** speaking *v* **3** chirp **4** click **5** speak
claim *n* → **1** assertion **2** entreaty **3** insistence **4** payment **5** request **6** rights *v* **7** assert **8** insist on **9** necessitate **10** pride oneself
clairvoyant *n* → **1** occultist *adj* **2** anticipatory **3** supernatural
clam *n* → **1** clip **2** holder
clamber *v* → ascend
clammy *adj* → **1** cold **2** wet
clamour *n* → **1** commotion **2** insistence **3** loud sound **4** shouting *v* **5** be loud **6** shout
clamp *n* → **1** clip **2** holder **3** press **4** storage *v* **5** fasten **6** hold **7** press **8** support **9** walk
clan *n* → **1** ancestry **2** community **3** relative
clandestine *adj* → secretive
clang *n* → **1** birdcall **2** dissonance **3** loud sound **4** ringing *v* **5** be dissonant **6** be loud **7** chirp **8** ring
clanger *n* → error
clangour *n* → **1** loud sound **2** ringing **3** shouting *v* **4** be loud **5** ring **6** shout
clank *n* → **1** boom *v* **2** boom **3** ring
clannish *adj* → **1** conservative **2** intolerant **3** kindred **4** societal
clap *n* → **1** applause **2** click **3** explosion **4** hit **5** loud sound **6** misfortune *v* **7** approve **8** explode **9** hit
clapper *n* → **1** mouth **2** resonator
claret *adj* → red
CLARIFICATION *n* elucidation, illumination, illustration; **explanation,** appendix, elaboration, exegesis, explication, exposé, exposition, interpretation; **decipherment,** cryptanalysis, decryption, demystification, unravelment; **annotation,** adversaria, apostil, comment, commentary, crib, epexegesis, footnote, gloss, marginalia, note, schedule, scholium; **key,** caption, cipher, legend; **reductionism,** oversimplification
CLARIFY *v* clear, clear up, demystify, elucidate, rationalise, shed light on, speak for itself, speak plainly, throw light on; **explain,** amplify, bring home to, elaborate, explicate, expound, flesh out, illuminate, illumine, illustrate, set out, spell out; **decipher,** decode, decrypt, puzzle out, resolve, see, solve, unravel, unscramble, untangle; **annotate,** comment, interpret
clarify *v* → **1** be transparent **2** explain **3** simplify
clarion *n* → **1** brass instrument **2** shout *adj* **3** shrill

CLARITY *n* clearness, legibility, limpidity, limpidness, lucidity, lucidness, pellucidness, perspicuity, perspicuousness, plainness, preciseness, precision, transparency; **intelligibility,** apprehensibility, cognisability, comprehensibility, comprehensibleness, intelligibleness, interpretability, luminousness

clarity *n* → transparency

clash *n* → **1** act of war **2** argument **3** dissonance **4** impact **5** loud sound *v* **6** argue **7** be dissonant **8** collide

clasp *n* → **1** button **2** endearments **3** hold **4** holder *v* **5** capture **6** fasten **7** hold **8** kiss

CLASS *n* bracket, branch, category, denomination, description, fashion, gender *(Obs.),* genre, group, kidney, kind, persuasion *(Colloq.),* range, set, sort, strain *(Rare),* subcategory, subgroup, subset, subtype, type, variety; **taxon,** alliance, class, family, genus, kingdom, life form, order, phylum, species, strain, subclass, subfamily, subgenus, subkingdom, suborder, subphylum, subspecies, superclass, superfamily, superorder, variety; **tribe,** breed, brood, group, phratry, race, social class, stirps, stock; **rank,** caste, degree, estate, grade, league, place, standard, stratum, stream; **miscellaneous classes,** blood group, Dan *(Judo),* genotype, phenotype, suit *(Cards),* weight *(Boxing).* *See also* CLASSIFICATION

CLASS *v* assort, categorise, classify, code, codify, coordinate, digest, distinguish, distribute, divide, fire-rate, gradate, grade, identify, label, lemmatise, mark, methodise, order, pigeonhole, range, rank, rate, reclassify, schematise, size, sort, staple, stratify, stream, systematise, systemise, zone

class *n* → **1** class **2** community **3** gathering **4** goodness **5** good taste **6** grade **7** lesson **8** similar thing *v* **9** graduate *adj* **10** classificatory **11** good

CLASSER *n* adjuster, categorist, classifier, codifier, digester, grader, identifier, indexer, ranger, ranker, sorter, systematiser, systematist, tabulator; **typologist,** systemiser, taxonomer, taxonomist; **wool classer,** con man, fleece-oh, fleece-picker, fleecy, guesser, piece-picker, stapler, wool sorter

classic *n* → **1** book **2** example **3** perfect thing **4** the best **5** work of art *adj* **6** antique **7** conservative **8** famous **9** model **10** old **11** superior

CLASSIFICATION *n* assortment, categorisation, codification, coordination, dichotomisation, distribution, rating, reclassification, schematisation, systematisation, systematism, systemisation, tabularisation; **typology,** architectonics, systematics, systematology; **miscellaneous classifications,** bulk classing, decimal classification, Dewey decimal classification, multiplication table, nosology, periodic table, petrography, physiography, wool classing; **system,** hierarchy, ladder, method, nomenclature, syntax *(Obs.),* tabulation, taxonomy; **table,** catalogue, code, digest, index, inventory, key, schedule, sequence, subject catalogue, synchronism, timetable. *See also* CLASS

CLASSIFICATORY *adj* categorical, diachronic, hierarchical, Linnean, physiographical, synchronic, systematic, tabular, taxonomic, taxonomical, typological; **classifiable,** classable, identifiable, sortable; **generic,** assorted, class, classified, coordinative, ordinal, phyletic, subgeneric, subordinal, subspecific, typical, varietal

classify *v* → **1** class **2** inquire into **3** keep secret

classy *adj* → **1** superior **2** tasteful

clatter *n* → **1** click **2** commotion *v* **3** click **4** speed **5** talk

clause *n* → deed

claw *n* → **1** animal part **2** arm **3** flower **4** piercer *v* **5** cut **6** rub **7** swerve

clay *n* → **1** raw materials **2** remnant **3** soil *v* **4** coat

CLEAN *v* char, clean out, clean up, cleanse, furbish, mop up, muck out, police *(U.S. Mil.),* polish, scavenge, sponge, spot, spot-clean, spring-clean; **wash,** flush, gargle, kier, shampoo, swill, syringe, wash down, wash out, wash up; **bathe,** bath, lave *(Poetic),* rinse, shower, tub; **sweep,** broom, brush, hoover, mop, swab, swingle, vacuum, vacuum-clean; **scrub,** black, buff, dust, rub, scour; **degrease,** ajax, soap, soft-soap; **comb,** card, hatchel; **launder,** dry-clean; **filter,** cohobate, distil, elutriate, filtrate, refine; **purify,** baptise, heal, lustrate, purge, sanctify; **sluice,** cradle, hush, pan, surface; **scrub a gas,** pickle *(Metall.),* scavenge *(Metall.);* **decarbonise,** decarburise, decoke; **sandblast,** careen, grave *(Naut.),* holystone; **currycomb,** curry; **dag,** chase marguerites, ring *(Agric.).* *See also* DISINFECT

CLEAN *adj* clean as a whistle, dustless, immaculate, spick-and-span, spotless, squeaky-clean, unspotted; **pure,** blameless, candid, chaste, clean, fresh, innocent, irreproachable, lily, pristine, spotless, stainless, uncorrupted, undefiled, unmixed, unsoiled, unstained, unsullied, untainted, virgin, virginal; **uncontaminated,** alembicated, aseptic, axenic, refined, sterile; **sanitary,** antiseptic, hygienic

clean *adj* → **1** abstinent **2** clean **3** competent **4** honest **5** innocent **6** moral **7** perfect **8** thorough **9** wholesome *adv* **10** thoroughly

CLEANER *n* char, charlady, charwoman, cleaner upper *(Colloq. Joc.),* cleaning lady, daily, duster, greasy, old Dutch; **sweeper,** broomie, chimneysweep, street sweeper; **launderer,** drycleaner, laundress, laundryman, laundrywoman, spotter, washerman, washerwoman; **purifier,** clarifier, purger, refiner; **washer,** careener, currier, depurator, scourer; **sanitary inspector,** sanitarian

cleanse *v* → clean

CLEANSER *n* amole, Bob Hope, cold cream, quillai bark, shampoo, soap, soap flakes, soapbark, toiletry, Windsor soap; **detergent,** abluent, abstergent, cleaner, degreaser, detersive, rinser, saddle-soap, sugar soap, washing powder, washing soda; **mouthwash,** gargle, rinse; **purge,** aperient, catharsis, depurative, physic, purgation, purgative; **disinfectant,** antiseptic, argyrol, boric acid, chlorination, chlorine, Dakin's solution, eusol, fumigant, hexachlorophene, hexylresorcinol, Javel water, lysol, orthoboric acid, phenol, silver fluoride, surgical spirit; **cleansing agent,** antifouling, borax, flux, whiting; **sandblast,** holystone, sandsoap; **face-pack,** face mask, facial mask; **purifier,** chlorinator, disinfector, fumigator; **separator,** alembic, distilling apparatus, elutriator, filter, filter bed, filter cloth, filter paper, filter press, filter tip, still

CLEANSING *n* ablutions, annual, bath, bubble bath, douche, footbath, lavage, lavation, pommy wash *(Joc.)*, rinse, rinsing, sauna, shampoo, shower, sitz bath, sluice, splash, sponge, sponge bath, sponge-down, toilet *(Surg.)*, Turkish bath, wash; **quick wash,** a lick and a promise, APC, Mary Pickford in three acts; **scour,** brush, careen, careenage, decarb, decarbonisation, decarburisation, decoke, scrub, ultrasonic cleaning; **housework,** sweep, sweeping, washing-up; **cleaning of clothes,** bull *(Mil.)*, dry-cleaning, shoeshine; **clean-up,** blitz, emu parade, police *(U.S. Mil.)*, spring-clean, spring-cleaning; **washing,** banjoing, box sluicing, surfacing; **purification,** depuration, elutriation, filtration; **sterilisation,** antisepsis, fumigation; **religious cleansing,** ablution, baptism, expurgation, lavabo, lustration, lustrum

CLEANSING *adj* abluent, abstergent, aperient, depurative, detergent, detersive, disinfectant, purgative, purging, saponaceous; **ablutionary,** balneal, cleanly, lavational, sudatory; **self-cleaning,** antifouling, dirt repellant, dust repellant, dustproof; **purificatory,** baptismal, expiatory, lustral, purgatorial, purgatory

CLEAR *adj* apparent, articulate, crystal clear, easily grasped, easy, explicit, fair, legible, limpid, lucid, luculent, obvious, pellucid, perspicuous, plain, precise, readable, straightforward, transparent, unambiguous; **intelligible,** apprehensible, cognisable, cognoscible, comprehendible, comprehensible, decipherable, explainable, explicable, fathomable, graspable, interpretable, knowable, luminous, perceivable, perceptible, recognisable, scrutable

clear *n* → **1** language *v* **2** acquit **3** bare **4** be transparent **5** clarify **6** exit **7** forgive **8** gain **9** jump **10** justify **11** liberate **12** obey **13** pay **14** permit **15** remove **16** simplify *adj* **17** acoustic **18** acquitted **19** bright **20** composed **21** empty **22** innocent **23** obvious **24** perfect **25** thorough **26** transparent **27** unconditional **28** visible *adv* **29** brightly **30** clearly **31** obviously **32** thoroughly **33** unconditionally

CLEARANCE *n* circumdenudation, clearage, defloration, defoliation, deforestation, denudation, disforestation, disfurnishment, excoriation; **burn-off,** burn, burn-back, bushburn *(N.Z.)*; **paring,** decortication, excortication, exfoliation; **clearing,** clears *(N.Z.)*

clearance *n* → **1** acquittal **2** expulsion **3** gap **4** length **5** permission **6** removal

clearing *n* → **1** clearance **2** removal

CLEARLY *adv* articulately, clear, fairly, limpidly, lucidly, luculently, perspicuously, plain, plainly, precisely; **intelligibly,** cognisably, comprehensibly, in plain words, luminously, perceivably, perceptibly, recognisably

cleat *n* → **1** beam **2** brace **3** break *v* **4** support

cleavage *n* → **1** chest **2** gap

cleave *v* → **1** gape **2** hold **3** separate **4** stick together

cleaver *n* → axe

clench *n* → **1** hold **2** press *v* **3** close **4** hold **5** make whole **6** press

clergyman *n* → ecclesiastic

cleric *n* → **1** ecclesiastic *adj* **2** ecclesiastic

clerical *n* → **1** ecclesiastic *adj* **2** authorial **3** ecclesiastic **4** working

clerk *n* → **1** ecclesiastic **2** recorder **3** seller **4** specialist **5** worker **6** writer

clever *adj* → **1** competent **2** cunning **3** humorous **4** intelligent **5** mental

cliché *n* → bore

cliche *n* → conformist behaviour

cliché *n* → **1** figure of speech **2** ordinariness

cliche *n* → proverb

CLICK *n* chink, clink, crack, flick, snap, snick, snip, tick, tick-tock; **clatter,** brattle, chatter, clackety-clack, clop, clutter, death-rattle, pitapat, pitter-patter, rattle, trot-trot; **buzz,** bray, drone, hum, purr, skirr, stertor, whine, whirr, whiz, woof, zoom; **twang,** ping, plonk, plunk, thrum, zing; **clap,** flap, flip-flop, flop, flump, flutter, whack; **footfall,** crunch, footstep, pad, plod, step, tramp, tread

CLICK *v* clip-clop, crunch, smack, snap, snick, tick; **rattle,** brattle, chatter, clack, clatter, clutter, drum, rataplan; **ping,** pink *(Motor Vehicles)*; **flap,** flop; **buzz,** drone, hum, purr, whirr, whiz

click *n* → **1** quiet sound *v* **2** be friends **3** succeed **4** understand

client *n* → **1** buyer **2** dependant

clientele *n* → buyer

clientèle *n* → dependant

cliff *n* → mountain

cliff-hanger *n* → uncertain thing

climate *n* → **1** point of view **2** surroundings **3** weather

CLIMATIC *adj* climatologic, climatological; **fair,** balmy, calm, fair-weather; **intemperate,** dirty, inclement, rough, stormy, tornadic, unsettled; **weathered,** weather-beaten; **weatherwise**

climax *n* → **1** change **2** figure of speech **3** finish **4** good thing **5** important thing **6** sexual intercourse **7** steadiness **8** top *v* **9** finish **10** top

climb *n* → 1 ascent *v* 2 ascend 3 flower 4 improve 5 slope 6 tower

CLIMBER *n* ascender, clamberer, escalader; **mountaineer,** alpinist, cragsman, mountain-climber

clinch *n* → 1 endearments 2 hold *v* 3 accomplish 4 fasten 5 hold 6 make whole

cling *v* → 1 hold 2 stick together

clinic *n* → 1 hospital 2 room

clinical *adj* → 1 callous 2 medical

clink *n* → 1 birdcall 2 click 3 prison 4 quiet sound 5 rhyme *v* 6 ring 7 versify

clinker *n* → 1 holder 2 paving 3 the best *adj* 4 layered

CLIP *n* alligator clip, bicycle clip, binding *(Skiing)*, bulldog clip, clothes peg, crocodile clip, paperclip, peg, staple; **hairclip,** bobby pin, butterfly clip, hair slide, hairgrip, hairpin; **clamp,** agraffe, brace, clam, cramp, head, vice

clip *n* → 1 appearance 2 arsenal 3 embezzlement 4 endearments 5 hairdressing 6 hit 7 holder 8 press 9 rate *v* 10 bare 11 cheat 12 cut 13 hit 14 kiss 15 mispronounce 16 press 17 speed 18 subtract

clipper *n* → 1 sailing ship 2 speedster 3 the best

CLIQUE *n* bunch, coterie, crowd, outfit, smart set; **cult,** push, sect; **cell,** cabal, cadre, inner circle, inside; **connections,** old boy network, old school tie; **salon,** conversazione, reunion

clique *v* → associate

clitoris *n* → groin

CLOAK *n* aba, blanket *(North America)*, burnous, cape, capote, chador *(Islam)*, chrisom *(Obs.)*, chuddar, cope, cowl, dolman, joseph, kaross, korowai *(N.Z.)*, manta, manteau *(Archaic)*, mantelet, mantle, mantua, mat *(N.Z.)*, mozzetta, muffle, opera-cloak, palatine, pall *(Obs.)*, pallium, pelerine, pelisse, plaid, pluvial, poncho, serape, shawl, stole, surplice, tallith, wrap. *See also* OVERCOAT; RAINCOAT

cloak *n* → 1 covering 2 disguise *v* 3 cover 4 hide

clock *n* → 1 hit 2 imprisonment 3 period 4 timepiece 5 trimming *v* 6 hit 7 time

clockwise *adj* → spinning

clockwork *n* → machine

clod *n* → 1 bit 2 fool 3 ignoramus 4 stupid person

clodhopper *n* → 1 footgear 2 ignoramus 3 incompetent

clog *n* → 1 footgear 2 hindrance 3 thickening 4 timber *v* 5 obstruct 6 stick together

cloister *n* → 1 abbey 2 church 3 field 4 path 5 seclusion *v* 6 imprison 7 seclude

clone *n* → 1 copy 2 offspring 3 repetition 4 similar thing *v* 5 reproduce

CLOSE *v* shut, slam; **shutter,** board up; **blockade,** clench, occlude, shut in, shut up, stop down *(Photog.)*, wall in, wall up; **stop,** airproof, bung, cork, obturate, plug, spile, stem, stop up, stopper, stopple *(Archaic)*, top; **seal,** plumb, seel *(Falconry)*, wafer, weather-strip; **gag,** stuff, tampon, wad

CLOSE *adj* approximate, dead *(Golf)*, gimme *(Golf)*, hither, hithermost, hot *(Games)*, near, nearby, nigh, proximate, silly *(Cricket)*, warm *(Colloq.)*; **adjacent,** appositional, approximal, bumper-to-bumper, circumlittoral, close-order, connivent, conterminous, contiguous, end on, immediate, neighbour *(U.S.)*, neighbouring, next, next-door, proximate, ringside, surrounding, vicinal; **approaching,** coming, oncoming; **accessible,** approachable, attainable

close *n* → 1 accomplishment 2 closure 3 field 4 fight 5 finish 6 hold 7 join 8 musical phrase 9 stoppage *v* 10 come close 11 enclose 12 finish 13 make whole 14 obstruct 15 stop *adj* 16 cautious 17 closed 18 enclosed 19 friendly 20 hot 21 imprisoned 22 mean 23 prohibited 24 reticent 25 secret 26 similar 27 sludgy 28 solid 29 thin *adv* 30 closely 31 equally 32 in secret 33 jointly 34 reticently

CLOSED *adj* barred, blind, close, drawn, fast, occluded, occludent, occlusive, shut, unopened; **stopped,** corked, ventless; **impenetrable,** airproof, airtight, gastight, hermetic, hermetically sealed, impermeable, impervious, proof

closed *adj* → 1 inactive 2 prohibited

CLOSELY *adv* a hop step and a jump away, a step away, as near as damn it, as near as makes no difference, at close quarters, at hand, at one's elbow, at one's fingertips, at one's heels, bumper-to-bumper, cheek by jowl, close, eyeball to eyeball, hard by, just round the corner, near at hand, on the back of, on the heels of, on the point of, on the tip of one's tongue, right on top of, to hand, under one's nose, within a hair's breadth, within a stone's throw, within an inch of, within cooee, within earshot, within hearing, within range, within reach, within spitting distance; **together,** adjacently, appositionally, chock, conterminously, contiguously, next-door, nigh; **nearby,** around, by, here, hereabout, hereby *(Archaic)*, hither, in view, near. *See also* ALMOST

CLOSENESS *n* adjacency, contact, contiguousness, immediacy, immediateness, nearness, propinquity, proximity; **close position,** neighbourhood, presence, vicinage, vicinity; **accessibility,** approachability, approachableness, attainability; **approach,** approximation, coming, oncoming; **conjunction,** apposition, cluster, juxtaposition; **a near thing,** close call, dead draw, gimme *(Golf)*, photo finish, squeaker *(Shooting)*; **closest point,** pericynthion, perigee, perilune, periphelion

closet *n* → 1 bedroom 2 compartment 3 cupboard 4 seclusion *v* 5 enclose 6 seclude *adj* 7 secluded 8 secret

CLOSURE *n* blockade, close, obstruction, obturation, occlusion, shut, slam, stop; **im-**

penetrability, impenetrableness, impermeability, impermeableness, imperviousness

closure *n* → **1** enclosure **2** finish **3** stoppage *v* **4** stop

clot *n* → **1** bit **2** fool **3** paste **4** solid body **5** stupid person **6** thickening *v* **7** solidify

cloth *n* → **1** textiles **2** uniform

CLOTHE *v* apparel *(Archaic)*, array, attire, costume, deck out, dress, endue with, equip, frock, garb, habit, invest, rig out, rig up, robe, swaddle, tire *(Archaic)*, tog, tog out, tog up; **style,** tailor, trim *(Obs.)*

clothe *v* → hide

CLOTHED *adj* apparelled, arrayed, done up, dressed, tricked out; **well-dressed,** all done up like a sore toe, all dressed up, dollish, dressed to kill, dressed to the nines, dressed up like a pox doctor's clerk, smart, Sunday-go-to-meeting *(U.S.)*

CLOTHES *n* apparel, array, attire, caparison, cladding *(Obs.)*, clobber, clothing, dress, garb, garment, gear, get-out, get-up, habiliment, habiliments, maternity clothes, menswear, mocker, raiment *(Archaic)*, rig, rig-out, robes, slip-on, things, tire *(Archaic)*, toggery, trappings, trim, vest *(Archaic)*, vesture *(Archaic)*, wardrobe, wear, wearables, wearing apparel; **clothwork,** dart, fly, gore, peplum, tuck. *See also* FINERY; OUTFIT

CLOTHIER *n* cobbler, corsetiere, costumier, couturière, couturier, dresser, dressmaker, equipper, fashion designer, fashioner *(Obs.)*, furrier, glover, haberdasher *(U.S.)*, hatter, hosier, milliner, modiste, outfitter, sewer, slopworker, stylist, tailor; **clothing store,** furriery, haberdashery, hosiery, jeanery, millinery, slopshop

clothing *n* → **1** clothes **2** covering

CLOUD *n* clag, cloudbank, cloudlet, hogsback *(N.Z.)*, low cloud, mare's-tail, rack, rain cloud, sky *(Obs.)*, storm-cloud, thundercloud, woolpack; **cloud-type,** altocumulus, altostratus, cirrocumulus, cirrostratus, cirrus, cu-nim, cumulonimbus, cumulus, cumulus fractus, false cirrus, fractocumulus, fractostratus, funnel cloud, nimbostratus, nimbus *(Obs.)*, orographic clouds, stratocumulus, stratus, stratus fractus; **puff,** scud, whiff; **mist,** brume, gauze, haze; **steam,** effluvium, fumes, vaporescence, vapour, wet steam; **vapour trail,** contrail; **fog,** aerosol *(Physics)*, brume, fogbank, pea soup, pea souper, sea-fog; **smoke,** dust, fug, nuclear cloud, pother, smog, smother, smoulder, smudge

CLOUD *v* becloud, cloud over, overcast, overcloud, shadow; **smoke,** reek; **mist,** fog, gauze; **vaporise,** steam, vapour; **fumigate,** smoke out

cloud *n* → **1** denigration **2** many **3** shade **4** shapelessness *v* **5** darken **6** disgrace **7** make unhappy

cloudburst *n* → **1** rainfall **2** violent outburst

CLOUD STUDY *n* hydrometeorology, nephanalysis, nephology; **isoneph,** nephogram, nephograph, nephoscope

CLOUDY *adj* heavy, nubilous, overcast; **cirrose,** cirrostrative, cumuliform, cumulous, mammatus, stratiform; **cloud-like,** nebulose, nebulous; **sunless,** sullen; **steamy,** vaporescent, vaporific, vaporous, vapour-like, vapouring, vapourish, vapoury; **misty,** gauzelike, hazy; **smoggy,** dusty, fuggy, murky, smudgy, soupy, thick; **foggy,** brumous; **smoky,** fuliginous, fumy

cloudy *adj* → **1** distressing **2** multicoloured **3** opaque **4** shadowy **5** uncertain

clout *n* → **1** corporal punishment **2** hit **3** power *v* **4** hit

cloven *adj* → **1** cut **2** gaping **3** halved **4** separate

clover *n* → a good time

clown *n* → **1** country dweller **2** entertainer **3** humorist **4** incompetent **5** vulgarian *v* **6** bungle **7** perform

cloy *v* → **1** be unpalatable **2** bore **3** oversupply **4** satisfy

CLUB *n* blackjack, bludgeon, cosh, cudgel, donger, knobkerrie, leangle, life-preserver, maul *(Obs.)*, mere, nightstick, nulla-nulla *(Aborig.)*, patu, shillelagh, stave, truncheon, waddy; **staff,** prodder, quarterstaff, rod, shakuhachi, singlestick, stick, taiaha; **whip,** birch, cane, cat, cat-o'-nine-tails, flagellum, lash, rawhide, scourge, strap, switch, whiplash; **flail,** swingle, swipple, thresher; **flyswat,** flapper, swat, swatter; **bat,** battledore, bumble puppy, crosse, racquet, willow; **golf club,** brassy, bulger, cleek, iron, lofting iron, putter; **hammer,** ballpein hammer, claw hammer, club hammer, drop hammer, flatter, fuller, gavel, jackhammer, knapping hammer, lump hammer, mallet, maul, plexor, sledge-hammer, steam hammer, tilt hammer, trip hammer, water-hammer; **ram,** battering ram, beetle, pile-driver, pounder, rammer

club *n* → **1** extremity **2** living room **3** society **4** stick *v* **5** associate **6** combine **7** cudgel **8** kill

cluck *v* → chirp

clue *n* → **1** evidence **2** explanation **3** information **4** signal

clump *n* → **1** accumulation **2** boom **3** hit **4** organism *v* **5** gather **6** hit **7** jut **8** walk

clumsy *adj* → **1** callous **2** incompetent **3** inconvenient **4** ugly

cluster *n* → **1** accumulation **2** closeness **3** emblem **4** solid body *v* **5** attract **6** gather **7** solidify

clutch *n* → **1** accumulation **2** animal offspring **3** hold **4** steering wheel *v* **5** capture **6** give birth **7** hold

clutter *n* → **1** click **2** jumble **3** muddle *v* **4** click **5** mispronounce **6** untidy

coach *n* → **1** teacher **2** train **3** truck *v* **4** teach

coagulate *v* → solidify

coal *n* → **1** fire **2** fuel *v* **3** fuel

coalesce *v* → combine

coalition *n* → **1** alliance **2** combination **3** society *adj* **4** combined **5** cooperative **6** societal

coarse *adj* → **1** discourteous **2** execratory **3** obscene **4** rough **5** ugly **6** unsavoury **7** vulgar

coast *n* → **1** coastline **2** edge **3** seaside *v* **4** descend **5** glide **6** go slowly **7** move

coaster *n* → **1** a drink **2** amusement park **3** avoider **4** bicycle **5** sledge **6** stand **7** traveller **8** watercraft

coastguard *n* → **1** police **2** protector

COASTLINE *n* bank, coast, littoral, rivage *(Archaic)*, seafront, seashore, seaside, shore, the coast; **waterfront,** lakefront, ocean beach, riverfront, shoreline, strand, strandline, waterside; **continental shelf,** embayment

COAT *v* anoint, bedaub, besmear, flock, lather, powder, smear, spread, wipe *(Plumbing)*; **batter,** breadcrumb, candy, frost, glair, glaze, ice; **paint,** calcimine, clobber, distemper, duco, japan, kalsomine, lacquer, prime, shellac, undercoat, varnish, whitewash; **plate,** anodise, braze, copper, electroplate, ferrotype, foil, galvanise, nickel, nickelplate, oxidise, platinise, sherardise, silverplate, sputter *(Physics)*, tin, veneer, zinc; **gild,** foliate, overgild; **bituminise,** asphalt, pave, seal, tarmac, underseal; **cement-render,** bag, cement, clay, daub, flush, impaste, paper, parget, paste, pay, plaster, puddle, putty, render, roughcast. *See also* COVER

coat *n* → **1** animal's coat **2** coating **3** covering **4** jacket *v* **5** cook **6** smooth

COATING *n* backing, carapace, cladding, coat, collodion, colouring, covering, deposit, double glazing, frost, glaze ice, impasto, integument, macadamisation, mother-of-pearl, nacre, petrifying liquid, plating, pricking coat, respray, rind, sheathing, sheet, shell, shield, shingle, silver frost, skin, slate, stucco, test, tile, top dressing, veneering, wash, washing; **facing,** chemise, crib, cribbing, fireback, leaf, liner, lining, overlay, revetment, veneer; **panel,** board, flag, foil, lath, plank, plate, shale, shaving, slab, slat, strip, wafer; **sheeting,** aponeurosis, carpet, dust sheet, endoperidium, endopleura, endothelium, epidermis, epithelium, exoperidium, membrane, mesothelium, peridium, skin, squama, tissue; **stripe,** section, vitta, zone; **shoe lining,** heeltap, insole, lift, sole, welt; **underlay,** underfelt

coax *v* → **1** kiss **2** persuade

cob *n* → **1** horse **2** irritation *v* **3** beat

cobber *n* → **1** friend **2** mister

cobbler *n* → **1** clothier **2** incompetent **3** repairer **4** sheep **5** worker

cobblestone *n* → **1** paving **2** rock

cobweb *n* → thread

cock *n* → **1** groin **2** gun part **3** indicator **4** leader **5** piercer **6** tap *v* **7** be arrogant **8** prepare

cockatoo *n* → **1** farmer **2** gambler **3** prisoner **4** warner

cockeyed *adj* → **1** drunk **2** nonsensical

cockle *n* → **1** fold **2** heater **3** watercraft *v* **4** furrow

cockney *n* → accent

cockpit *n* → **1** battleground **2** niche **3** room **4** sportsground

cocksure *adj* → **1** certain **2** safe

cocky *n* → **1** farmer *v* **2** farm *adj* **3** arrogant

cocoa *n* → **1** drink *adj* **2** brown

cocoon *v* → **1** cover **2** secure

coda *n* → **1** finish **2** musical phrase

coddle *v* → cook

CODE *n* arcanum, character *(Obs.)*, cipher, cryptograph, enigma, morse code, riddle, secret; **gabble,** double-dutch, gibberish, splutter

code *n* → **1** classification **2** communication **3** disguise **4** language **5** law **6** rule **7** secrecy *v* **8** class **9** codify

codger *n* → **1** man **2** miser

codicil *n* → **1** postscript **2** qualification

CODIFY *v* code, conventionalise, institutionalise, prescribe, ritualise, subsume

codify *v* → **1** class **2** inquire into **3** legalise **4** order

coeducation *n* → education

coefficient *n* → **1** number *adj* **2** cooperative

coerce *v* → force

coeval *adj* → simultaneous

coexist *v* → compromise

coffee *n* → drink

coffer *n* → box

COFFIN *n* casket, cist, columbarium, ossuary, sarcophagus, urn; **bier,** catafalque, hearse, pall

coffin *v* → bury

cog *n* → **1** brace **2** inferior **3** knob *v* **4** cheat

cogent *adj* → **1** capable **2** logical

cogitate *v* → **1** devise **2** plan **3** think

cognate *n* → **1** relative *adj* **2** kindred **3** similar

cognisance *n* → **1** emblem **2** understanding

cognition *n* → **1** knowledge **2** understanding

cohabit *v* → **1** have sex **2** inhabit **3** marry

cohere *v* → **1** fit **2** relate **3** solidify **4** stick together

coherent *adj* → **1** apt **2** logical **3** sticky

cohesion *n* → **1** solidity **2** stickiness

cohort *n* → **1** armed forces **2** crowd **3** gathering

coiffure *n* → hairdressing

coil *n* → **1** busyness **2** difficulty **3** twist *v* **4** twist

coin *n* → **1** circle **2** coinage *v* **3** be wealthy **4** circulate **5** create **6** fantasise **7** work metal

COINAGE *n* change, cobar, Kembla, loose change, rouleau, shrapnel, silver, small change, specie; **coin,** bean, billon, bit *(Obs.)*, brown *(Obs.)*, copper, mite, picayune *(U.S.)*; **numismatics,** coin collector, numismatologist, numismatology; **counterfeit coin,** grey, jack, nob, rap, slug. *See also* CASH

coincide *v* → fit

coincidence *n* → **1** conformity **2** congruity **3** luck

coitus *n* → sexual intercourse

coke *n* → **1** drink **2** fuel *v* **3** fuel

cola *n* → drink
COLD *n* chill, coryza, flu, grippe, rheum, the dog's disease, the sniffles, the snuffles, URTI; **cold symptom,** catarrh, cough, hacking cough, rhonchus, sneezing, the bot, tussis, wheeziness; **septic throat,** adenoids, laryngitis, pharyngitis, quinsy, relaxed throat, rhinitis, sinusitis, strep throat, tonsillitis, tracheitis, uvulitis; **ear infection,** glue ear, labyrinthitis, Ménière's syndrome, otalgia, otitis, tinnitus, tympanitis, utriculitis
COLD *adj* Antarctic, Arctic, freezing, frigid, frigorific, frosty, glacial, hyperborean, ice-cold, icy, nipping, perishing; **stone-cold,** marble; **cool,** coldish, coolish, fresh, nippy, sharp; **chilled,** agued, algid, clammy, hypothermal, shivering, trembly; **blue,** frostbitten; **wintry,** bleak, brumal, chill, chilly, cold as a nun's tits, raw, winter; **snowy,** niveous, white; **sleety,** slushy; **frosted,** frostlike, frosty, hoar, iced, rimy; **frozen,** gelid, glacé *(U.S.)*, icicled; **glacial,** englacial, glaciered, glaciological, subglacial, superglacial
cold *n* → **1** coldness *adj* **2** blue **3** callous **4** dead **5** distant **6** unready **7** unsociable
cold-blooded *adj* → **1** callous **2** unkind
COLDLY *adv* bleakly, fresh, freshly, wintrily; **icily,** chillily, chillingly, frigidly, frostily, gelidly, glacially; **tremblingly,** aguishly
COLDNESS *n* bleakness, cold, coolness, wintriness; **chilliness,** chillness, nip, nippiness, sharpness; **frozenness,** clamminess, frigidity, frostiness, gelation, gelidity, gelidness, glaciation, iciness, regelation; **chill,** ague, algidity, algor, rigour; **shiver,** shudder, tremble, tremor; **goose pimples,** cold shivers, goose bumps, horripilation, the shivers; **frostbite,** chillblains; **cold snap,** brass monkey weather, cold change, cold front, cold wave, perisher; **winter,** the big freeze, the dead, the dead of winter; **ice age,** glacial epoch
cold shoulder *n* → repulsion
cold-shoulder *v* → **1** avoid **2** isolate
cold sore *n* → sore
cold war *n* → politics
colic *n* → **1** ache **2** nausea
collaborate *v* → **1** betray **2** cooperate **3** help
collage *n* → **1** mixture **2** work of art
COLLAPSE *v* be history, bite the dust, come undone, come unstuck, crash, crumple, fall, give way, go by the board, go for a burton *(Naut.)*, go phut, go to the dogs, go under, go up in smoke, have had it, have had the dick, have had the sword, perish; **disintegrate,** dissipate, dissolve
collapse *n* → **1** failure **2** psychic disorder **3** ruin **4** tiredness *v* **5** be cheap **6** be ill **7** be in debt **8** be tired **9** fail **10** fall **11** lose **12** weaken
collar *n* → **1** animal's coat **2** bubbling **3** edge **4** emblem **5** jewellery **6** neckwear **7** ring *v* **8** capture **9** control **10** cook **11** hold **12** restrain
collate *v* → **1** compare **2** tidy
collateral *n* → **1** relative **2** surety *adj* **3** accompanying **4** genetic **5** kindred **6** side
collation *n* → **1** comparison **2** meal **3** order
colleague *n* → **1** companion **2** partner **3** workers
collect *n* → **1** gamble **2** religious ceremony *v* **3** cash **4** gain **5** gather **6** get **7** reason **8** transport *adj* **9** payable
collection *n* → **1** accumulation **2** allowance **3** book **4** getting **5** mixture **6** transport **7** work of art
collective *n* → **1** accumulation **2** combine **3** community *adj* **4** accumulative **5** combinative **6** general **7** societal
COLLECTIVELY *adv* associatively, communally, mutually, shoulder to shoulder, together, unitedly; **federally,** corporately; **clannishly,** cliquishly, fraternally, tribally
COLLEGE *n* Academe, academy, athenaeum, college of advanced education, institute, institution, lyceum, poly, polytechnic *(Brit. U.S.)*, seminary, teacher's college, university college; **university,** campus, Ivy League, open university, state university *(U.S.)*, the shop, varsity; **technical college,** tech, trade school, training college, training school, vocational school, W.E.A.; **evening college,** mechanics' hall, mechanics' institute, night school, school of arts; **business college,** commercial college; **agricultural college,** agricultural high school; **naval college,** arsenal, military college, training ship; **conservatorium,** conservatoire; **teaching hospital,** medical school. *See also* SCHOOL
college *n* → **1** barracks **2** gathering **3** institute **4** prison
COLLIDE *v* clash, connect, crash, fall foul of each other, hurtle *(Rare)*, impact, impinge, jostle, smash together; **bump,** barge into, cannon into, foul, knock, push; **crash,** crack up, pile up, prang, smash, stack
collide *v* → argue
collier *n* → **1** digger **2** transporter **3** watercraft
colliery *n* → factory
collision *n* → **1** argument **2** convergence **3** impact
colloquial *adj* → **1** figurative **2** informal
collusion *n* → **1** conspiracy **2** crime **3** secrecy
cologne *n* → fragrance
colon *n* → abdomen
colonial *adj* → crowded
colonnade *n* → path
colony *n* → **1** community **2** dwelling **3** gathering **4** nation **5** organism **6** region
coloratura *n* → singer
colossal *adj* → **1** big **2** enormous **3** important **4** tall
colossus *n* → **1** giant **2** tall person
COLOUR *n* complementary colour, primary colour, prismatic colours, secondary colour, tertiary colour; **hue,** cast, grain *(Obs.)*, nuance, patina, taint *(Obs.)*, tainture *(Obs.)*, tinct *(Obs.)*, tinge, tint, undertint, undertone; **spectrum,** palette, prism, rainbow; **areola,** areolation, sunbow, sundog; **colour-scheme,** colour coordination, decorator colours,

fashionable colours; **colours,** military colours, national colours, racing colours, strip, team colours; **complexion,** bloom, rubicundity, skin colour; **skin pigmentation,** chloasma, freckle, melanin, melanism; **chromophore,** chlorophyll, chromatoplasm, chromogen, chromoplasm, chromoplast, chromoprotein, haemoglobin; **camouflage,** countershading, protective colouring; **colouring,** colouration, pigmentation; **colour quality,** chroma, gradation, intensity, purity, saturation, tone, value. *See also* DYE

COLOUR *v* chrome, counterstain, distemper, dye, ink, mordant, ochre, overdye, paint, pencil, reddle, stain, umber; **tint,** sickly *(Obs.),* taint *(Obs.),* tinct *(Obs.),* tincture, tinge, wash; **brighten,** highlight, tone up; **tone,** tone down

colour *n* → **1** appearance **2** atom **3** ball **4** character **5** entitlement **6** jewel **7** justification **8** mineral **9** redness *v* **10** change **11** depict **12** redden

colour-blindness *n* → faulty sight

COLOURED *adj* florid, high-coloured, hued, roseate, rosy, rubicund, self-coloured; **dyed,** double-dyed, fumed, piece-dyed, tinct *(Poetic)*; **mordant,** sunfast; **colourable,** stainable

COLOURFUL *adj* deep, glowing, iridescent, purple, rich, saturated, strong; **bright,** brilliant, colouristic, fiery, gay, hot, jazzy, live, lively, psychedelic, snazzy, technicolour, vivid; **gaudy,** garish, glaring, loud, lurid

COLOURIST *n* brightener, chromolithographer, colourer, dyer, painter, seagull *(Colloq.),* stainer, tinter, toner

COLOURLESS *adj* achromatic, achromatous, achromic, untinged; **neutral,** delicate, light, mousy, pastel, thin; **black-and-white,** sepia; **anaemic,** green, mealy, pallid, pasty, pasty-faced, sallow, sallowish, sick, sickly, wan, wannish, washed-out, wheyfaced, white, white-faced, white-livered; **cadaverous,** bloodless, ghastly, ghostlike, lurid; **pale,** ashy, blank, palish; **dull,** dullish, muddy, old, sad, sober, sombre, subdued; **watery,** wheyish, wheylike; **bleached,** etiolated, faded

COLOURLESSNESS *n* achromatism, lack of colour; **fading,** blanching, decolouration, discolouration, etiolation, tarnish; **paleness,** delicateness, lightness, thinness, whiteness; **dullness,** soberness, sobriety, sombreness; **pallor,** anaemia, bloodlessness, cadaverousness, ghastliness, mealiness, pallidness, pastiness, sallowness, sickliness, wanness; **albinism,** alphosis

colt *n* → **1** adolescent **2** animal offspring **3** cord **4** man

Colt *n* → gun

column *n* → **1** armed forces **2** news item **3** post **4** printwork **5** rock outcrop **6** sequence **7** series **8** tower **9** watercraft

columnist *n* → **1** journalist **2** writer

coma *n* → **1** animal's coat **2** meteor **3** reflection **4** sleeping **5** unconsciousness

comb *n* → **1** bird part **2** brush **3** bulge **4** smoother **5** surf *v* **6** clean **7** search **8** sew **9** simplify **10** smooth

combat *n* → **1** act of war **2** argument **3** fight *v* **4** fight **5** wage war

COMBAT TROOPS *n* cannon fodder, field army, firing line, front line, ranks, troops; **task force,** advance *(U.S.),* advance guard, chasseur, flying column, sally, sortie, spearhead, van, vanguard; **outpost,** flank, post *(U.S.),* rear, rearguard, screen, wing; **storm troops,** commando, paras, paratroops, perdu *(Obs.),* shock troops, SS; **guerilla,** ambusher, freedom fighter, irregular, partisan, skirmisher, terrorist, urban guerrilla; **fighter pilot,** ace, aircraftman, aircraftwoman, airman. *See also* SOLDIER; SERVICEMAN; ARMED FORCES

COMBINATION *n* addition, aggregation, amalgamation, assemblage, association, coalescence, coalition, commixture, composition, confection, conglomeration, conjunction, conjuncture *(Obs.),* consolidation, coordination, flux, fusion, incorporation, interfusion, intermingling, interweaving, mergence, mixture, polysynthesism, summation, symbiosis, synergism, synergy, synthesisation, synthesism, synthetisation, totalisation, unification, union, unity, zygosis; **desegregation,** assimilation, integration

combination *n* → **1** bicycle **2** combine **3** hit **4** joining **5** order **6** society

COMBINATIVE *adj* aggregative, amalgamative, collective, combinational, conjunctional, conjunctive, federative, integrative; **connective,** copulative, syndetic

COMBINE *n* aggregate, amalgam, assemblage, assembly, collective, combination, compound, condensate, consolidation, ensemble, fusion, melting pot, merger, mix, synthesis, system, tie, union, web

COMBINE *v* associate, club, commingle, compound, confect *(Obs.),* conjoin, consolidate, decompound, merge, organise, synergise, unify; **synthesise,** assemble, compose, make, synthetise; **blend,** commix, fuse, incorporate, interfile, interfuse, mix, temper *(Archaic)*; **amalgamate,** coalesce, compact, conflate, conglomerate, consolidate, coordinate, hang together, join; **desegregate,** assimilate, integrate

combine *n* → **1** alliance **2** corporation *v* **3** associate **4** cooperate

COMBINED *adj* allied, associate, associated, coalescent, confederate, conjoint, coordinate, joint, synthetic, tight-knit, unified, unsegregated; **composite,** aggregate, coalition, complex, compound

COMBUSTIBILITY *n* combustibleness, flammability, ignitability, inflammability, inflammableness

combustible *n* → **1** fuel **2** lighter *adj* **3** excited **4** fiery

combustion *n* → **1** burning **2** excitement **3** firing

come *n* → 1 reproductive agent *v* 2 appear 3 arrive 4 eroticise 5 excrete 6 finish 7 perform 8 start

comeback *n* → answer

come back *v* → remind

COME BETWEEN *v* intercept, interlope, interpose, intervene, punctuate; **partition,** bar, blockade, cordon off, curtain off, obstruct, rope off; **intercept,** cut off, occult

COME CLOSE *v* approach, bear down, close, close in, close with, come near, confront, congress *(Rare)*, draw near, draw on, gain on, lay aboard *(Naut.)*, near, overtake, reach, rise *(Naut.)*, sap *(Fort.)*, shave, trench on, verge, walk up; **approximate,** be in the neighbourhood of, be in the vicinity of, be on the point of, border on

comedian *n* → humorist

COMEDY *n* comic opera, farce, high comedy, sitcom, situation comedy, sketch, skit; **burlesque,** antimasque, buffoonery, caricature, clownery, commedia dell'arte, harlequinade, low comedy, mime, parody, slapstick; **practical joking,** prankery; **black comedy,** gallows humour, graveyard humour, sly humour, tragicomedy; **sarcasm,** irony, lampoon, lampoonery, satire. *See also* HUMOUR; JOKE

comedy *n* → 1 drama 2 humour

comely *adj* → 1 beautiful 2 pleasant

comestible *n* → food

comet *n* → meteor

COME TO ONE'S SENSES *v* cease to be irrational, have all one's marbles

comfort *n* → 1 alleviator 2 bedclothes 3 contentedness 4 easiness 5 help 6 pleasure 7 satisfaction *v* 8 alleviate 9 ease 10 help

comfortable *n* → 1 bedclothes *adj* 2 alleviant 3 content 4 easy 5 happy 6 helpful 7 satisfied

comic *n* → 1 humorist 2 newspaper 3 portrait *adj* 4 dramatic 5 humorous

comical *adj* → 1 dramatic 2 humorous

comic strip *n* → 1 joke 2 portrait

coming *n* → 1 arrival 2 closeness *adj* 3 advanced 4 close

COMING AFTER *n* consecutiveness, posteriority, postposition, subsequence, successiveness; **consequentiality,** consequentialness; **supersedure,** follow, supersession, supervenience, supervention; **consequence,** after-effect, corollary, flow-on, result, resultant, secondary, sequel, sequent

COMMAND *n* adjuration, behest, bidding, call, calling, caution, charge, commission, demand, dictate, enjoinment, hest *(Archaic)*, imperative, injunction, instruction, order, order of the day, placet, prescript, prescription, request, requisition, rubric, sanction, say-so, testament, threat, ultimatum, will, word, word of command; **decree,** act, appointment, brevet, bull, commandment *(Obs.)*, decretal, dictum, directive, dispensation, edict, fiat, instruction, law, mandate, mitzvah, ordinance, precept, prescript, regulation, rescript, rule, ukase; **countermand,** caveat, recall, revocation. *See also* LEGAL ORDER

COMMAND *v* acquisition, adjure, appoint, bid, bung, call upon, charge, commission, conjure, demand, dictate, direct, enjoin, give orders, give the command, insist on, instruct, order, prescribe, require, send for, tell; **summon,** commit, remand, subpoena; **decree,** appoint, enact, legislate, ordain, set

command *n* → 1 advantage 2 armed forces 3 authority 4 insistence 5 operator 6 view *v* 7 entreat 8 impose 9 look 10 operate 11 own 12 predominate 13 tower

commandant *n* → high command

commandeer *v* → 1 impose 2 take

commander *n* → seaman

COMMANDING *adj* adjuratory, authoritative, decisive, decretal, decretive, decretory, edictal, imperatival, imperative, injunctive, instructional, mandatory, official, preceptive, prescriptive; **jussive; dictatorial,** authoritarian, imperious, in command, masterful, peremptory

COMMANDINGLY *adv* at the stroke of a pen, imperatively, officially, preceptively, prescriptively

commandment *n* → command

commando *n* → combat troops

COMMAND RESPECT *v* awe, dazzle, impress, inspire respect, overawe; **sanctify,** consecrate, enshrine; **stand on one's dignity,** observe due decorum, stand on ceremony; **commemorate,** celebrate, do honour to, observe, remember

COMMEMORATE *v* immortalise, memorialise, monumentalise, preserve

commemorate *v* → 1 command respect 2 rejoice

COMMEMORATION *n* ceremonial parade, fly-past, honour board, honour book, honour guard, honour roll, march-past, procession; **commemorative,** memorial, retrospective, war memorial; **honour,** decoration, honourable mention, honours list, knighthood, medal, wreath. *See also* TRIBUTE

COMMEMORATIVE *adj* commemorational, commemoratory, epitaphic, memorial

commence *v* → start

commend *v* → 1 approve 2 guide

commensurate *adj* → 1 equal 2 related

comment *n* → 1 assessment 2 clarification 3 commentary 4 speaking 5 written composition *v* 6 clarify 7 discourse 8 explain 9 speak

COMMENTARY *n* comment, criticism, critique, discussion, editorial, press, review; **caption,** inscription, legend; **footnote,** adversaria, annotation, appendix, critical apparatus, excursus, gloss, glossary, marginalia, notes, scholium

commentary *n* → 1 clarification 2 record

commentator *n* → 1 assessor 2 essayist 3 interpreter

commerce *n* → 1 communication 2 sexual intercourse 3 sociability 4 talk 5 trade

commercial *n* → 1 incentive 2 public notice *adj* 3 mixed 4 popular 5 trading 6 vulgar

COMMERCIALLY *adv* on the market, retail, wholesale; **by auction,** by mail order, door-to-door, over the counter

commercial traveller *n* → 1 encourager 2 seller

commiserate *v* → pity

commissar *n* → 1 manager 2 ruler

commission *n* → 1 agency 2 authority 3 command 4 committee 5 cost 6 employment 7 job 8 legislative body 9 management 10 obligation 11 operator 12 payment 13 profit 14 undertaking 15 work *v* 16 command 17 depute 18 employ 19 entreat

commissionaire *n* → 1 enterer 2 messenger

commissioner *n* → 1 ambassador 2 manager

commit *v* → 1 command 2 give 3 involve 4 promise

COMMITTEE *n* caucus, comitia, commission, panel, quango, shop committee, vigilance committee, works council; **conference,** colloquium, convention, round table, summit, symposium, think-tank, workshop; **forum,** chamber, court, curia, diet, duma, General Assembly, moot, parliament; **quorum,** plenum; **faction,** arm, left wing, right wing, the Opposition; **conclave,** conventicle; **gang,** camorra, Mafia, tong; **picket line,** line-up

committee *n* → 1 council 2 protector 3 questioner

commode *n* → 1 bath 2 headgear 3 toilet

commodious *adj* → 1 expedient 2 spacious

commodity *n* → 1 goods 2 supplies

commodore *n* → seaman

common *n* → 1 field 2 religious ceremony 3 the public 4 working class *adj* 5 boring 6 customary 7 frequent 8 general 9 inferior 10 liberated 11 mediocre 12 ordinary 13 public 14 related 15 shared 16 societal 17 ugly 18 vulgar

common law *n* → law

commonplace *n* → 1 bore 2 ordinariness 3 proverb *adj* 4 boring 5 conventional 6 customary 7 mediocre 8 ordinary 9 simple

commonsense *n* → 1 realism 2 wisdom

common sense *n* → logic

commonweal *n* → 1 good 2 nation 3 the public

commonwealth *n* → 1 administrative area 2 good 3 nation 4 society 5 the public

Commonwealth *n* → nation

COMMOTION *n* bobberie, bovver *(Brit. Colloq.)*, breach of the peace, brouhaha, bunfight, bust-up, clamour, clatter, corroboree, distraction, disturbance, hoo-ha, hubble-bubble, hurly-burly, pandemonium, pell-mell, squall, tempest, three-ring circus; **riot,** broil, merry hell, outbreak, race riot, rout, rumpus, scrimmage, sedition *(Archaic)*, trouble, tumult, uproar; **hullabaloo,** bobsydie, fuss, hubbub, pother, rhubarb, to-do; **free-for-all,** dust, dust-up, fracas; **jungle,** no-man's-land, wilderness; **babel,** bear garden, bloodhouse; **troubled waters**

commotion *n* → turbulence

communal *adj* → 1 public 2 societal

commune *n* → 1 community 2 dwelling 3 talk *v* 4 talk

COMMUNICATE *v* broadcast, convey, disseminate, get across, give, impart, pass on, project, put across, put over, relay, rumour, transmit; **link up with,** be in touch with, converse with, get in touch with, get on to, intercommunicate, keep in touch with, liaise with, look up, normalise relations with, stay in touch with, telephone; **contact,** connect with, get, get through to, make contact with, raise; **signal,** flag, tick-tack *(Horseracing)*, wave to

communicate *v* → inform

COMMUNICATION *n* commerce, communion, congress, connection, contact, converse, dialogue, fellowship, impartation, impartment, information transmission, intelligence *(Obs.)*, interchange, intercommunication, intercommunion, intercourse, liaison, propagation, transmittal, transmittance; **nonverbal communication,** body language, semaphore, sign language, signalling, tick-tack; **code,** cryptosystem; **telepathy,** thought transference, thought-reading; **afflatus,** afflation, gift of tongues

communication *n* → 1 dissemination 2 joining 3 message 4 revealing

communion *n* → 1 communication 2 crowd 3 interaction 4 reverence 5 talk

Communion *n* → religious ceremony

communiqué *n* → 1 information 2 news

communism *n* → 1 economy 2 sharing out

COMMUNITY *n* hamlet, kraal, street, town; **clan,** colony, house, people, primary group, race, rod; **commune,** ashram, collective, cooperative, kibbutz, kolkhoz; **class,** caste, order, stratum; **social system,** matriarchate, matriarchy, patriarchate, patriarchy

community *n* → 1 gathering 2 similar thing 3 the public

commute *v* → 1 interact 2 travel

compact *n* → 1 case 2 contract *v* 3 combine 4 harden 5 join 6 steady *adj* 7 concise 8 made 9 small

COMPANION *n* associate, beau, bedfellow, collaborator, colleague, commensal, compeer, comrade, consort *(Obs.)*, fellow traveller, helpmate, helpmeet *(Archaic)*, partner, running mate *(U.S.)*; **follower,** camp follower, hanger-on, inseparable, satellite, shadow; **bridesmaid,** best man, maid of honour, matron of honour, paranymph; **accompanist,** backing group, backing musician

companion *n* → 1 bad person 2 friend 3 helper 4 reference book *v* 5 accompany

companionable *adj* → sociable

COMPANIONSHIP *n* coexistence, commensalism, commensality, comradeship, partnership, presence, togetherness; **accompaniment,** backing, obbligato, support, vamp; **company,** association, concomitance, conjunction

company *n* → 1 armed forces 2 companionship 3 corporation 4 crowd 5 gathering 6 mariner 7 sociability *v* 8 accompany 9 partner

COMPARABLE *adj* analogous, assimilable; **comparative,** allegorical, collative, parallel, relative, typological; **contrastable,** compared with, contrasted with, contrastive, contrasty
comparable *adj* → **1** equal **2** similar
COMPARABLY *adv* by analogy, comparatively, in proportion, relatively
comparative *adj* → comparable
COMPARE *v* balance, cf., collate, confer *(Obs.)*, draw a parallel, liken, resemble *(Archaic)*, weigh up
compare *n* → **1** comparison *v* **2** equal
COMPARER *n* collator, comparator, measurer, standardiser, typologist
COMPARISON *n* allegory, analogy, balance, collation, compare, likening, parallel, proportion *(Archaic)*, simile, similitude
COMPARTMENT *n* booth, caisson, cell, chamber, closet, crib; **niche,** cranny, cubbyhole, nook, pigeonhole
compartment *n* → **1** part **2** room *v* **3** separate
compass *n* → **1** area **2** circle **3** direction finder **4** edge **5** rotation **6** space *v* **7** accomplish **8** beguile **9** learn **10** plan **11** surround
compassion *n* → **1** lenience **2** pity *v* **3** pity
compatible *adj* → **1** apt **2** friendly **3** in agreement **4** pleasant
compatriot *n* → **1** national **2** partner
compel *v* → **1** force **2** repress
compelling *adj* → highly regarded
compendium *n* → abridgment
COMPENSATE *v* expiate, indemnify, make amends, make good, overcompensate, pay back, ransom, recompense, redeem, render, render back, repay, requite, restitute, satisfy, square off with; **offset,** allow for, countervail, cover; **recoup,** catch up on, get back, recover, replevy, retrieve; **reward,** guerdon, reimburse, remit, remunerate, replace, restore, return, revest
COMPENSATION *n* amends, apology, guerdon *(Poetic)*, indemnity, recession, redress, reparation, requital, requitement, restitution, restoration, satisfaction; **recoupment,** poundbreach, recaption, recoup, recovery, replevin, resumption, retrieval; **remuneration,** attachment, golden handshake, meed *(Archaic)*, offset, pay-off, payment, refund, reimbursement, repayment, return, reward, salvage; **damages,** blood money, distrainment, hoot *(N.Z.)*, indemnification, recompense, square-off; **penalty rate,** allowance, climatic allowance, compo, dirt money, disability allowance, district allowance, isolation allowance, shift allowance, subsistence allowance, time allowance, tool allowance, workers' compensation
COMPENSATORY *adj* apologetic, conciliatory, offset, propitiatory, reparative, restoring; **redemptive,** expiatory, Lenten, lustral, piacular, purgatorial, purgatory, redemptory; **penitent,** reformed, repentant
compere *v* → perform
compete *v* → contest
COMPETENCE *n* accomplishment, capableness, competency, completeness *(Archaic)*, efficiency, goodness, handiness, nimbleness, proficiency, resourcefulness, skilfulness, skill, workmanship; **adeptness,** adroitness, craft, craftiness, cunning, cunningness, deftness, dexterity, dexterousness, facility, featliness *(Archaic)*; **expertise,** address, craftsmanship, expertness, masterfulness, masterliness, mastery, professionalism, science; **ability,** capability, control, endowment, flair, grasp, grip, knowledge, prowess, talent, verve *(Rare)*; **aptitude,** bent, faculty, flair, forte, genius, gift, innate ability, knack, metier, sense, strong point, talent, the right stuff, the stuff; **skills,** abilities, capabilities, capacity, cleverness, colonial experience, creativity, giftedness, powers; **versatility,** enterprise, resource, versatileness; **dexterity,** ambidexterity, ambidextrousness, dexterousness; **athleticism,** ball sense, gross motor skills, suppleness, surefootedness
COMPETENT *adj* able, adept, adroit, capable, clean, complete *(Archaic)*, efficient, expert, extraordinaire, fully-fledged, good, good at, practical, proficient, resourceful, skilful, skilled, sure, together, workmanlike; **dexterous,** crafty *(Archaic)*, deft, feat *(Archaic)*, fit, habile, handy, nimble, quaint *(Archaic)*, smart, sure-footed, wristy; **cunning,** curious *(Archaic)*, daedal *(Poetic)*, neat, slick; **versatile,** all-round, ambidexter *(Archaic)*, ambidextrous; **clever,** gifted, heaven-born, peart, talented; **best,** gun, top. *See also* ACCOMPLISHED
competent *adj* → **1** adequate **2** authoritative
competition *n* → contest
COMPETITIVE *adj* agonistic, combatant, combative, conflictive, dog-eat-dog, emulative, emulous, gladiatorial, vying; **hand-to-hand,** fistic, stand-up; **knockout,** elimination, sudden-death
COMPETITIVELY *adv* agonistically, combatively, vyingly; **hand to hand**
COMPETITIVENESS *n* combativeness, emulation, keenness, rivalry
COMPETITOR *n* adversary, backmarker, challenger, combatant, combater, concurrent *(Rare)*, contender, contestant, contester, dragracer, dueller, duellist, emulator, entrant, entry, field, logomachist, principal, racer, rival, selection, starter, striver, struggler, tourneyer, vendettist; **finalist,** quarterfinalist, semifinalist; **dark horse,** also-ran, front-runner, hotpot, outsider, roughie, runner-up, skinner
COMPLAIN *v* belly-ache, bitch, bitch and bind, bleat, carp, chew the rag, croak, fratch, fret, fuss, gripe, grizzle, grouch, grouse, growl, grumble, moan, murmur, mutter, plain *(Archaic)*, repine, scream blue murder, seethe, squawk, squeal, whine, whinge, yammer; **be discontented,** feel blue, feel sad, get upset, take in bad part, take on
complain *v* → be ungrateful
COMPLAINER *n* bitch, bite *(N.Z.)*, bleater, carper, fault-finder, fuss-budget *(U.S.)* fusspot, griper, grizzleguts, grouch, grouser,

growler, grumblebum, grumbler, grump, lemon, malcontent, miseryguts, moaner, mopoke, murmurer, mutterer, nark, sorehead, squawker, squealer, whiner, whingeing Pom, whinger, yammerer

COMPLAINT *n* beef, belly-ache, bleat, cavil, chip on the shoulder, dissent, gravamen, grievance, gripe, grouse, grumble, kick, lamentation, moan, murmur, peeve, plaint, regret, repining, squawk, squeal, whine, whinge, yammer

complaint *n* → **1** accusation **2** illness

complaisant *adj* → **1** agreeable **2** lenient

complement *n* → **1** amount **2** mariner **3** whole **4** word *v* **5** make whole

complete *v* → **1** accomplish **2** finish **3** make whole **4** perfect *adj* **5** competent **6** finished **7** perfect **8** unconditional **9** whole

COMPLEX *adj* complicate, complicated, higher *(Biol.)*, involved, sophisticated; **intricate,** convolute, curious *(Obs.)*, elaborate, Gordian, involute, involutional, labyrinthine, perplexing, reticular, winding; **compound,** composite, decompound; **overelaborate,** fussy, Heath Robinson, overproduced *(Music)*, overworked, overwrought; **elaborated,** developed, elaborative. *See also* TANGLED

complex *n* → **1** building **2** psychic disturbance **3** tangle *adj* **4** combined **5** mixed

complexion *n* → **1** appearance **2** character **3** colour

COMPLEXITY *n* complexness, complicacy, complicatedness, complicity, convolution, fussiness, intricacy, intricateness, involution, knottiness, overelaborateness, overelaboration, perplexity, sophistication, winding; **inextricability,** inextricableness; **compositeness,** composition, multifariousness; **maziness,** mazement, tortuousness; **complication,** embellishment, embranglement, enmeshment, entanglement. *See also* TANGLE

compliance *n* → **1** acquiescence **2** agreement **3** obedience

COMPLICATE *v* develop, elaborate, embarrass, embellish, involve, overelaborate, overwork, thicken; **confound,** confuse, perplex

complicate *v* → **1** cause difficulties *adj* **2** complex **3** folded

complicated *adj* → **1** complex **2** difficult

complicity *n* → **1** complexity **2** guilt **3** help **4** participation

compliment *n* → **1** applause **2** congratulation **3** flattery **4** gift **5** greeting *v* **6** approve **7** congratulate

complimentary *adj* → **1** approving **2** cheap **3** flattering **4** unpaid

comply *v* → **1** capitulate **2** conform **3** obey

compo *n* → **1** adhesive **2** compensation

component *n* → **1** part *adj* **2** constituent

compose *v* → **1** combine **2** create **3** make **4** mediate **5** order **6** print **7** write

COMPOSED *adj* controlled, cool, coolheaded, dégagé, deliberate, detached, imperturbable, level-headed, poised, self-composed, self-contained, self-possessed, stable, steady, take-it-or-leave-it, unflappable, unfussed, unhurried, unruffled; **placid,** ataractic, bland, calm, clear, equal *(Archaic)*, even, impassionate *(Rare)*, level, secure, sedate, subdued, tranquil, tranquillo *(Music)*, undisturbed, untouched; **easygoing,** balanced, easy, equable, even-minded, even-tempered, lackadaisical, lenient, mild, philosophical; **impassive,** dead-pan, inscrutable; **phlegmatic,** dull, fireless, flat, passive, phlegmy, spiritless, stoic, stolid, torpid, unemotional, unfired, unimpassioned; **blasé,** jaded, smooth, sophisticated, suave, unblinking, world-weary; **reposeful,** docile, easeful, sedative

composed *adj* → resting

COMPOSE ONESELF *v* calm down, recover oneself, relax, simmer down, unbend, unwind; **keep calm,** get a hold of oneself, get the better of one's feelings, get the better of oneself, hold on, keep one's hair on, keep one's shirt on, keep one's temper; **be indifferent,** not bat an eyelid, not turn a hair, play it cool; **be unenthused,** be left cold, keep one's cool, not go nap on; **endure,** be patient, submit

composite *n* → **1** plant **2** tangle *adj* **3** combined **4** complex **5** mixed

composition *n* → **1** arrangement **2** combination **3** complexity **4** creation **5** making **6** musical piece **7** order **8** payment **9** printing **10** structure

compositor *n* → book trade

compost *v* → fertilise

COMPOSURE *n* balance, cool *(Colloq.)*, coolness, equanimity, equilibrium, even-mindedness, level-headedness, levelness, poise, sangfroid, savoir-faire, self-possession, steadiness, unflappableness; **imperturbability,** blandness, equability, equableness, imperturbableness, stoicism, stolidity, stolidness; **ease,** confidence, easefulness, repose, reposefulness, secureness, security; **calmness,** ataraxia, calm, imperturbation, placidity, placidness, sedateness, tranquillity, tranquilness; **restraint,** control, docility, self-control, temperance; **mildness,** clemency, lenience, leniency, lenity; **patience,** submission; **detachment,** dispassionateness, impassiveness, impassivity, indifference, nonchalance, uninvolvement

composure *n* → rest

comprehend *v* → **1** include **2** know **3** understand

comprehensive *adj* → **1** general **2** inclusive **3** thorough

compress *n* → **1** medication *v* **2** press

compression *n* → abridgment

comprise *v* → include

COMPROMISE *v* coexist, come to terms, compound, live and let live, meet halfway, split the difference, strike a bargain; **go with the fashion,** bend with the breeze, jump on the band wagon, swim with the stream

compromise *n* → **1** adjustment **2** average **3** mediation **4** pacification **5** peace *v* **6** average **7** endanger **8** involve **9** make peace **10** mediate **11** reveal

comptroller *n* → **1** accountant **2** manager

compulsion *n* → **1** desire **2** forcefulness **3** necessity **4** obedience **5** psychic disturbance **6** unwillingness

compulsive *adj* → **1** forceful **2** overindulgent **3** psychologically disturbed **4** unwilling

compulsory *adj* → forced

compunction *n* → penitence

COMPUTATION *n* calculation, compute, figure work, figures, numeration, reckoning, workings; **count,** aggregate, headcount, recount, sum, summation, tale *(Archaic)*, tally, tot, total; **estimate,** approximation, cast-off *(Print.)*, guess, guesstimate; **demography,** capitation, census, demographics

COMPUTE *v* cast up, figure, find, reckon, recount, work out; **count,** add up, card *(Golf)*, cash up, cast, differentiate, enumerate, number, numerate, re-count, reach, sum, sum up, tally, tell, tell off, tot up, total; **divide,** add, cube, factorise, integrate, multiply, permute, quantise *(Physics)*, raise, rationalise, reduce, square, subtract, transpose; **borrow,** carry, dot and carry one *(Colloq.)*; **estimate,** guesstimate, make

compute *n* → computation

COMPUTER *n* analog computer, artificial intelligence, control computer, data-handling system, digital computer, digital controller, electronic computer, macrocomputer, mainframe computer, microcomputer, PC, personal computer, processor, supercomputer, synchronous computer, Turing Machine, word processor; **adding machine,** cash register, comptometer, tab, tabulator, taximeter, totalisator, totaliser *(U.S.)*; **slide rule,** difference engine, ready reckoner; **abacus,** cuisenaire rods, Napier's bones (rods), quipu

computer *n* → mathematician

COMPUTER CONTROLS *n* cursor box, joystick, light-pen, mouse

COMPUTER PROGRAMMER *n* liveware, logical designer, operator, programmer, systems analyst, systems engineer

COMPUTER RECORD *n* core memory, core store, counter, disc file, disc storage, file, hard copy, location, memory, memory bank, record, register, registration, store, working memory

COMPUTING *n* ADP, automatic data processing, batch processing, data capture, data processing, data retrieval, electronic data processing, number crunching *(Colloq.)*, systems analysis, systems engineering

comrade *n* → **1** companion **2** friend **3** mister **4** partner **5** political ideologist

CONATIVE *adj* appetent, appetitive, orectic

concave *v* → **1** hollow *adj* **2** curved **3** hollow

conceal *v* → hide

concede *v* → **1** assent to **2** capitulate **3** give

conceit *n* → **1** arrogance **2** figure of speech **3** idea **4** image **5** pride **6** reputation *v* **7** devise **8** flatter

conceited *adj* → **1** arrogant **2** intelligent **3** proud

CONCEIVE *v* fall, teem *(Obs.)*; **be pregnant,** be with child, carry, expect, gestate, have a bun in the oven; **make pregnant,** duff *(Colloq.)*, get with child, impregnate, inseminate, knock up *(Colloq.)*, pot; **be at stud,** service, stand; **rut,** be on heat

conceive *v* → **1** create **2** devise

concentrate *v* → **1** attend to **2** become greater **3** centralise **4** converge **5** solidify **6** think *adj* **7** increased

concentric *adj* → central

concept *n* → **1** idea **2** the intangible

CONCEPTION *n* fecundation, impregnation; **polyembryony,** superfecundation, superfetation, twinning; **fertilisation,** artificial insemination, cross-fertilisation, crosspollination, in-vitro fertilisation, insemination, IVF, pollination, self-fertilisation, self-pollination; **breeding,** artificial selection, crossing, dysgenics, engraftation, engraftment, eugenics, fancy, genetic engineering, grafting, hybridisation, hybridism, interbreeding, intercross, layering, mongrelisation, natural selection, outbreeding, outcrossing, propagation, selection, stirpiculture, thremmatology; **seedbed; birthrate,** hatchability. *See also* PREGNANCY; BIRTH; REPRODUCTION

conception *n* → **1** creation **2** idea **3** opinion **4** plan **5** start **6** the intangible

concern *n* → **1** affair **2** eye-catcher **3** fright **4** importance **5** job **6** trade *v* **7** be important **8** involve **9** relate

CONCERNING *prep* about, after, anent *(Scot.)*, apropos of, as for, as regards, as to, in point of, in respect, of, on, regarding, respecting, touching on, towards, vis-a-vis, with reference to, with regard to, with respect to

CONCERT *n* chamber concert, gig, prom concert, recital, soirée, subscription concert; **eisteddfod,** festival; **musicale,** blow, community singing, jam, jam session, rockfest, sing-sing, singsong; **serenade,** shivaree *(U.S.)*; **item,** bracket, number

concert *n* → **1** agreement *v* **2** agree **3** plan

concerted *adj* → planned

concertina *v* → fold

concession *n* → cheapness

conch *n* → **1** brass instrument **2** niche **3** peacemaker

conciliate *v* → **1** atone for **2** mediate

CONCISE *adj* brief, compact, compressed, exact, laconic, precise, short, short-spoken, short-winded, succinct; **abbreviated,** abridged, condensed, elliptical, potted, telescoped; **abstractive,** compendious, epitomic, epitomical, summarised, synoptic; **epigrammatic,** crisp, pithy, pointed, pregnant, sententious, straight, terse, trenchant

CONCISELY *adv* briefly, compendiously, laconically, summarily, synoptically; **in brief,** in a few words, in a nutshell, in a word, in fine, in short; **epigrammatically,** crisply, directly, elliptically, pithily, shortly, straight out, straightly, tersely, to the point, trenchantly

conclave *n* → 1 committee 2 legislative body 3 secret place

conclude *v* → 1 accomplish 2 determine 3 enclose 4 finish 5 reason 6 solve

concoct *v* → 1 create 2 fantasise 3 plan 4 prepare

concomitant *adj* → simultaneous

concord *n* → 1 agreement 2 contract 3 peace

concourse *n* → convergence

concrete *n* → 1 adhesive 2 building materials 3 matter 4 paving 5 solid body *v* 6 harden 7 solidify *adj* 8 hard 9 real 10 solid 11 tangible

concubine *n* → 1 servant 2 sexual partner 3 spouse

concur *v* → 1 assent to 2 be willing 3 cooperate 4 fit

concurrent *n* → 1 competitor *adj* 2 congruous 3 cooperative 4 equal 5 simultaneous

concussion *n* → 1 impact 2 unconsciousness 3 vibration

condemn *v* → 1 disapprove of 2 disuse 3 involve 4 punish

condensation *n* → 1 abridgment 2 solidity

condense *v* → 1 abbreviate 2 harden 3 solidify

condescend *v* → 1 be meek 2 capitulate 3 pride oneself

CONDITION *n* affection *(Archaic)*, fettle, kilter, shape, state, state of repair, strain, temper, trim *(Naut.)*; **situation,** case, clinical picture, conjuncture, fare *(Archaic)*, lot, pass, pickle, place, plight, position, posture, predicament; **phase,** appearance, aspect, facies, phasis; **dimension,** plane; **status,** estate, footing, place, quality, rank, situation, standing, station, status quo; **circumstance,** circs, how it is, how things stand, terms, the state of affairs, the state of play, the state of the nation, the way of it; **mode,** feel *(Music)*, modality, phase, phasis, state, way

condition *n* → 1 deed 2 health 3 qualification *v* 4 be healthy 5 habituate 6 persuade 7 qualify

CONDITIONAL *adj* contingent, dependent, eventual, hypothetical, interlocutory *(Law)*, nisi, provisional, provisory

conditional *adj* → uncertain

CONDITIONALLY *adv* provisionally, qualifiedly; **but,** however, though

condole *v* → pity

condom *n* → contraception

condominium *n* → 1 authority 2 nation

condone *v* → 1 atone for 2 forgive

conduct *n* → 1 behaviour 2 management *v* 3 accompany 4 electrify 5 manage

CONDUCTOR *n* bandmaster, choirmaster, choragus, kapellmeister, maestro, timekeeper; **leader,** band leader, concertmaster, first violinist, principal; **pipe major,** drum-major, trumpet-major

conductor *n* → 1 driver 2 leader

conduit *n* → 1 bridge 2 channel 3 dam 4 spring

cone *n* → 1 mountain 2 signal 3 solid 4 tableware

confection *n* → 1 combination 2 medication

confederacy *n* → 1 alliance 2 society

confederate *n* → 1 accomplice 2 cooperator *v* 3 associate 4 cooperate *adj* 5 combined 6 cooperative

confer *v* → 1 compare 2 give 3 talk

conference *n* → 1 committee 2 corporation 3 council 4 discussion

CONFESS *v* acknowledge, admit, betray oneself, break cover, come clean, come one's guts, get something off one's chest, make a clean breast of, out with, own up, shrive, spit it out, unbosom oneself, unburden oneself, wash one's dirty linen in public; **declare one's hand,** give oneself away, give the game away, give the show away, have egg on one's face, lay one's cards on the table, put one's foot in one's mouth, show one's true colours, wear one's heart on one's sleeve; **express,** come out on, declare, indicate, intimate. *See also* REVEAL

confess *v* → 1 atone for 2 be guilty 3 be honest 4 be penitent

confessor *n* → 1 ecclesiastic 2 guide 3 revealer

confidant *n* → 1 friend 2 guide

confidence *n* → 1 belief 2 certainty 3 composure 4 hope 5 secrecy 6 secret

confidence trick *n* → 1 embezzlement 2 trick

confident *adj* → 1 believing 2 certain 3 hopeful 4 rash

confidential *adj* → 1 hidden 2 secret

configuration *n* → 1 order 2 positioning

confine *v* → 1 enclose 2 imprison 3 restrict 4 thin

confirm *v* → 1 assent to 2 authenticate 3 strengthen

confiscate *v* → take

conflagration *n* → 1 fire 2 ruin

conflict *n* → 1 contest 2 disagreement 3 dissidence 4 impact *v* 5 argue 6 disagree 7 fight

CONFORM *v* accommodate, act one's age, adapt oneself, agree, be guided by, be one's age, behave properly, bend with the breeze, comply, do as others do, fall into line, follow, follow the beaten track, follow the precedents, go by the book, keep up appearances, obey, observe conventions, observe proprieties, observe the rules, play the game, quadrate, run with the herd, run with the mob, swim with the tide, toe the line

conform *v* → 1 be similar 2 fit

conformation *n* → 1 adjustment 2 conformity 3 equality 4 order

CONFORMER *n* Babbitt, capitalist roader, classicist, conformist, conservative, conventionalist, dag *(Colloq.)*, formalist, observer of conventions, reactionary, right wing, right winger, schoolmarm, silvertail, stick-in-the-mud, stickler, straight, suburbanite, suburbia, WASP; **normaliser,** adjuster, aligner, regulator, styliser; **yes-man,** company man, party man

CONFORMIST BEHAVIOUR *n* a matter of form, accepted behaviour, convention, conventionalism, custom, form, formality, good form, orthodoxy, usage; **stereotype,** cliche, set piece, type *(Biol.)*, type genus, yardstick; **clannishness,** desire to conform, herd instinct; **conservatism,** Babbittry, conservativeness, conventionality, reaction, WASPishness

CONFORMITY *n* agreement, assimilation, coincidence, conformability, conformableness, conformation, correspondence, straightness, uniformity, uniformness; **conformance,** abidance, appropriateness, felicitousness, good form, observance, order, propriety; **typicalness,** commonness, normalcy, normality, ordinariness, regularity, the ordinary; **rightness,** fitness, legitimacy, legitimateness; **classicism,** academicism, classicalism, classicality, formalism; **adaptation,** adjustment

confound *v* → **1** complicate **2** confuse **3** disagree **4** disprove **5** humble **6** squander **7** swear

confront *v* → **1** argue **2** come close **3** invert

CONFUSE *v* amaze *(Obs.)*, baffle, becloud, bedazzle, befog, bewilder, bother, bowl over, buffalo, confound, daze, dazzle, discombobulate *(Colloq.)*, discomfit, discompose, disconcert, discountenance, disorientate, distract, disturb, dizzy, faze, floor, flummox, flurry, fluster, flutter, fog, hobble, maze *(Archaic)*, muddle, mystify, nonplus, obfuscate, perplex, perturb, puddle, puzzle, rattle, shake up, stick, stumble, stump, stun, throw

confuse *v* → **1** complicate **2** humble **3** misguide **4** puzzle **5** untidy

CONFUSED *adj* adrift *(Colloq.)*, aflutter, at a loss, at one's wits end, at sea, bemused, bewildered, boxed, bushed, confounded, disconcerted, distracted, distrait, distraught, fluttery, mixed-up, muddled, perplexed, up a gumtree, up the wall; **muddle-headed,** dithering, dithery, dizzy, unbalanced; **blank,** in limbo, lost

CONFUSING *adj* bewildering, clear as mud, distracting, distractive, perplexing; **mazelike,** labyrinthine, mazy

CONFUSINGLY *adv* bewilderingly, blunderingly, discomposingly, disconcertingly, disturbingly, perplexingly

CONFUSION *n* amazement *(Obs.)*, bamboozlement, bedevilment, bewilderment, daze, discomfiture, discomposure, disconcertedness, disconcertion, disconcertment, dismay, disorientation, distraction, dizziness, embarrassment, fog, mazement *(Archaic)*, muddle-headedness, muzziness, mystification, nonplus, obfuscation, perplexity, perturbation, wilderment *(Archaic)*, wooziness; **dither,** bother, flap, flat spin, flurry, fluster, flustration, flutter, fuss, ruffle, spin, tail spin, tizz, tizzy

confute *v* → **1** answer **2** defeat **3** disprove

congeal *v* → **1** be prejudiced against **2** solidify

congenial *adj* → **1** apt **2** in agreement

congenital *adj* → **1** characteristic **2** inborn **3** pregnant

congest *v* → **1** abound **2** gather **3** obstruct **4** oversupply

conglomerate *n* → **1** accumulation **2** solid body *v* **3** combine **4** gather **5** mix **6** solidify *adj* **7** accumulative **8** mixed **9** rocky **10** round

CONGRATULATE *v* cheer, compliment, drink to, felicitate, gratulate *(Archaic)*, pat on the back; **wish someone joy,** wish happy returns; **show one's respect,** dip one's lid, shake someone's hand; **honour,** duchess, fête, lionise, make much of; **congratulate oneself,** thank one's lucky stars, thank one's stars

congratulate *v* → **1** pay homage **2** rejoice

CONGRATULATION *n* compliment, compliments, compliments of the season, congratulations, felicitation; **best wishes,** good wishes, happy returns, regards; **toast,** a pat on the back, cheer, handshake, health, salute, salvo

CONGRATULATIONS *interj* congrats; **bravo,** cheers, hooray

CONGRATULATORY *adj* congratulant, gratulatory, well-wishing

congregate *v* → **1** gather *adj* **2** accumulative

congregation *n* → **1** crowd **2** gathering **3** monasticism **4** religious follower **5** worshipper

congress *n* → **1** communication **2** convergence **3** council **4** discussion **5** legislative body **6** sexual intercourse *v* **7** come close

congruent *adj* → congruous

CONGRUITY *n* accord *(Archaic)*, accordance, affinity, agreement, coherence, concurrence, concurrency, conformableness, conformance, conformity, congruence, congruousness, consentaneity, consentaneousness, consistency, consonance, correspondence, fit; **harmony,** accord, balance, concinnity, congeniality, harmoniousness, harmonisation, sympathy, syntonisation, syntony; **unity,** oneness, unison; **equivalence,** coincidence, commensurability, correspondence, parallelism, parity, sameness; **homology,** homonymy, homophony, isomerism, synonymity, synonymousness

CONGRUOUS *adj* accordable, accordant, agreeing, answerable to, commeasurable, concurrent, conformable, consentaneous, consistent, consonant, corroborant, felicitous, happy, natural, pursuant to, sympathetic; **harmonious,** at one, cosmic, harmonic, homophonic, homophonous, one, true, unisonous; **equivalent,** actinomeric, correspondent, homologous, isomeric, parallel, same, synonymous; **congruent,** coincident, coincidental

CONGRUOUSLY *adv* accordantly, accordingly, answerably, compatibly, concurrently, conformably, congenially, consentaneously, consistently, consonantly, happily, harmoniously, sympathetically, sympathisingly, thereafter *(Obs.)*, unobjectionably;

correspondingly, coincidentally, coincidently, commensurably, correspondently; **equivalently,** just the same, the same, typically, uniformly
conifer *n* → plant
CONJECTURAL *adj* abstract, academic, baseless, doctrinaire, hypothetical, notional, speculative, theoretical; **supposed,** assumptive, axiomatic, ballpark, estimated, presumptive, putative, quasi, reputed, so-called, suppositional, suppositious, supposititious, suppositive; **conjecturable,** assumable, guessable, supposable, surmisable; **assumed,** conjectured, given, mooted, postulated, presumed
CONJECTURE *n* aim *(Obs.)*, bush reckoning, extrapolation, forecast, guess, guesstimate, guesswork, hunch, inkling, intuition, shot, shot in the dark, surmisal, surmise, suspicion; **theory,** abstraction, ideology, ism, philosophy, principle, school of thought, view; **assumption,** axiom, hypothesis, postulate, postulation, premise, presumption, presupposition, presurmise, proposition, speculation, supposal, supposition
CONJECTURE *v* expect *(Colloq.)*, extrapolate, guess, guesstimate, imagine, smell a rat, suppose, surmise, suspect, trow *(Archaic)*; **assume,** give, posit, postulate, presume, presuppose
conjecture *n* → uncertain thing
conjoin *v* → **1** combine **2** join
conjugal *adj* → marital
conjugate *v* → **1** join **2** marry *adj* **3** two
conjunction *n* → **1** closeness **2** combination **3** companionship **4** joining **5** oneness **6** word
conjunctivitis *n* → faulty sight
conjure *v* → **1** command **2** conspire **3** entreat
conk *n* → **1** hit **2** nose *v* **3** hit
connect *v* → **1** collide **2** electrify **3** join **4** relate
CONNECTING *adj* conjugative, conjunctional, conjunctive, connective, copulative, intercommunicative, syndetic; **unitive,** integrative
connection *n* → **1** communication **2** join **3** relation **4** relationship **5** relative **6** religion **7** sexual intercourse
connive *v* → **1** cooperate **2** make do
connoisseur *n* → **1** aesthete **2** discriminator **3** intellectual **4** specialist
connote *v* → **1** imply **2** mean **3** signify
connubial *adj* → marital
conquer *v* → **1** capture **2** defeat
conquest *n* → **1** capture **2** losing **3** repression **4** success
consanguineous *adj* → **1** kindred **2** similar
conscience *n* → **1** dutifulness **2** moral sense **3** perception
conscientious *adj* → dutiful
conscious *adj* → **1** mental **2** perceptive **3** willing
conscript *n* → **1** serviceman *v* **2** force **3** militarise *adj* **4** forced
CONSECRATE *v* dedicate, hallow, sanctify; **saint,** beatify, canonise
consecrate *v* → command respect
consecutive *adj* → **1** following **2** resultant **3** sequential
consensus *n* → **1** agreement **2** cooperation
consent *n* → **1** affirmation **2** agreement **3** permission *v* **4** agree
consequence *n* → **1** coming after **2** importance **3** reputation **4** result
CONSERVATION *n* conservancy, environmentalism; **green ban; preservation,** bottling, canning, cold storage, dehydration, desiccation, ensilage, freeze-drying, hydrocooling, pickling, refrigeration; **insulation,** insulator, lagging, mineral wool, rock-wool; **proofing,** fireproofing, resist, waterproofing; **embalmment,** mummification, taxidermy
CONSERVATIONIST *n* environmentalist, greenie, preservationist; **caretaker,** aquarist, archivist, conservator, curator, gamekeeper, guard, guardian, keeper, nightwatchman, warden, watchman; **preserver,** embalmer, salter, taxidermist
CONSERVATIVE *adj* Biedermeier, blue-rinse, daggy, reactionary, straight, straight-arrow, suburban, twin-set and pearls, uptight, WASP; **clannish,** closely adhering, loyal; **right-wing,** arbitrary, overbearing, procrustean, right; **orthodox,** canonical, classic, classical, conformist, fundamentalist, law-abiding, strict
conservative *n* → **1** conformer **2** political ideologist *adj* **3** cautious **4** intolerant
conservatorium *n* → college
conservatory *n* → **1** breeding ground **2** garden **3** living room
CONSERVE *v* keep, preserve, put up, salt away, salt down; **refrigerate,** bottle, brine, can, corn, cure, dehydrate, desiccate, dry, ensile, freeze-dry, jerk, kipper, lyophilise, pickle, pot, salt, silo, smoke, tin; **proof,** fireproof, prove, rainproof, showerproof, waterproof; **plate,** cellulose, underseal; **embalm,** fix *(Microscopy)*, mummify, stuff
conserve *v* → cook
consider *v* → **1** attend to **2** intend **3** think
considerable *adj* → **1** great **2** important **3** many **4** reputable
considerate *adj* → **1** kind **2** thinking
consideration *n* → **1** bribe **2** deed **3** gift **4** high regard **5** importance **6** incentive **7** kindness **8** reputation
consign *v* → **1** give **2** label **3** send a message **4** transport
consignment *n* → giving
consistency *n* → **1** congruity **2** texture
consistent *adj* → **1** apt **2** congruous **3** hard **4** persevering **5** steady **6** sticky
console *v* → ease
consolidate *v* → **1** combine **2** harden **3** strengthen *adj* **4** solid
consonance *n* → **1** agreement **2** aptness **3** congruity **4** music **5** sound
consonant *n* → **1** letter *adj* **2** congruous **3** musical

consort *n* → **1** companion **2** crowd **3** singer **4** spouse **5** watercraft *v* **6** accompany **7** fit **8** partner **9** sing

consortium *n* → corporation

conspicuous *adj* → **1** blatant **2** important **3** interesting **4** obvious **5** visible

CONSPIRACY *n* cabal, collusion, complot, conjuration *(Obs.)*, countermine, counterplot, frame, frame-up, intrigue, machinations, plant, plot, practices *(Archaic)*, ready. *See also* PLAN

conspiracy *n* → secrecy

CONSPIRE *v* cabal, complot, conjure *(Obs.)*, contrive, counterplot, intrigue *(Obs.)*, lay heads together, lay plans, machinate, plot, practise *(Archaic)*, put heads together, scheme, work one's nut. *See also* PLAN

conspire *v* → cooperate

constable *n* → **1** high command **2** policeman **3** ruler

constant *n* → **1** number *adj* **2** changeless **3** continual **4** eternal **5** faithful **6** homogeneous **7** serious

constellation *n* → **1** fortune-telling **2** gathering

consternation *n* → **1** fright **2** worry

constituency *n* → **1** administrative area **2** domain **3** electorate

CONSTITUENT *adj* cantonal, component, elemental, elementary, fractional, integral, integrant

constituent *n* → **1** chooser **2** electorate **3** part

constitute *v* → **1** create **2** employ **3** make

constitution *n* → **1** character **2** creation **3** custom **4** essence **5** health **6** making **7** rule **8** structure

constrain *v* → **1** force **2** restrain

constraint *n* → **1** forcefulness **2** imprisonment **3** modesty **4** restraints

constrict *v* → **1** contract **2** press **3** restrict **4** thin

construct *n* → **1** finished product **2** idea *v* **3** build **4** make

CONSTRUCTION *n* building, civil engineering, prefabrication, public works, reconstruction, restoration; **architecture,** architectonics, draughtsmanship, landscape architecture, tectonics; **bricklaying,** indenting, infilling, masonry, rubblework, stonework, toothing; **carpentry,** post-and-beam construction, timber-framing

construction *n* → **1** building **2** essence **3** evidence **4** finished product **5** making **6** translation

constructive *adj* → **1** creative **2** structural

construe *n* → **1** translation *v* **2** explain

consul *n* → **1** ambassador **2** ruler

CONSULT *v* cite, refer to; **wise up on,** gen up on, get a line on, get the good guts on, scout, scout out

consult *v* → entreat

consultant *n* → **1** guide **2** healer **3** informant **4** specialist

consultation *n* → **1** discussion **2** gambling **3** guidance

consume *v* → **1** absorb **2** destroy **3** engross **4** squander **5** use up

consumer *n* → **1** absorber **2** buyer **3** user

consummate *v* → **1** accomplish **2** finish **3** make whole **4** perfect *adj* **5** most **6** perfect **7** whole

consumption *n* → **1** absorption **2** buying **3** destruction **4** ill health **5** use

CONTACT *n* attaint *(Obs.)*, brush, contingence, dab, graze, interface, kiss, osculation, taction *(Obs.)*, tag, touch; **junction,** abutment, abuttal; **meeting,** link-up, occlusion; **meshing; contiguity,** contiguousness, tangency

CONTACT *v* apply, hit, join, make contact, meet, touch; **abut,** adjoin, border on, impinge, juxtapose, subjoin; **intertwine,** be in mesh, dovetail, fay, mesh, tooth, twist; **hit,** alight upon, chance upon; **brush,** button *(Fencing)*, dab, graze, kiss, nose, nuzzle, tongue; **join,** be tangent to, board, butt, link up, occlude, touch

contact *n* → **1** closeness **2** communication **3** friend **4** joining **5** touch *v* **6** communicate **7** join

CONTACTING *adj* adjoining, valvate; **contiguous,** conterminous, impingent, meeting, osculatory, striking, tangent, tangential, touching

contain *v* → **1** include **2** limit **3** restrain **4** restrict

CONTAINER *n* case, frame, holder, receiver, receptacle; **cover,** enclosure, wrapper; **cupboard,** cabinet, dresser, filing cabinet, locker, press, wardrobe; **reliquary,** ark, burse, chrismatory, cist, monstrance, phylactery, pyx, pyxis, shrine, tabernacle; **cage,** beehive, coop, enclosure, fishbowl, goldfish-bowl, hutch, pen, skep. *See also* BASKET; BOX; CASE; BAG; BASIN; BARREL; VESSEL; BOTTLE

contaminate *v* → **1** dirty **2** err **3** mix **4** poison **5** spoil

contemplate *v* → **1** expect **2** hope **3** intend **4** look **5** think **6** worship

contemplative *n* → **1** believer *adj* **2** reverent **3** thinking

contemporaneous *adj* → simultaneous

contemporary *adj* → **1** current **2** innovative **3** real **4** simultaneous

contempt *n* → **1** disapproval **2** disobedience **3** disrepute **4** low regard

contemptible *adj* → **1** bad **2** hateful **3** wrong

contemptuous *adj* → **1** disapproving **2** discourteous **3** disdainful **4** slanderous

contend *v* → **1** argue **2** assert **3** contest **4** reason

CONTENT *adj* contented, easy, satisfied; **comfortable,** comfy, cottonwool, dégagé, satisfactory, snug, well-off, well-to-do; **complacent,** relaxed, self-complacent, self-content, self-satisfied, sitting pretty; **happy,** eudemonic, felicific, happy as a lark, happy as Larry, joyful

content *n* → **1** contentedness **2** contents **3** essence **4** meaning **5** satisfaction *v* **6** satisfy *adj* **7** agreeable **8** satisfied

contented *adj* → **1** content **2** satisfied

CONTENTEDLY *adv* at home, at one's ease, comfortably, in one's element; **complacently,** self-complacently

CONTENTEDNESS *n* content, contentment, peace of mind; **comfortableness,** featherbed, heavenliness; **comfort,** cottonwool, ease, weal *(Archaic)*; **happiness,** bliss, blissfulness, eudemonia, felicity, glory, honeymoon, seventh heaven; **complacency,** gratification, satisfaction, self-satisfaction

contention *n* → **1** assertion **2** contest **3** disagreement **4** dissidence **5** incongruity

CONTENTIOUS *adj* conflictive, controversial, dissentious, divisive, eristic; **at variance,** inconsonant; **arguable,** contestable, contradictable, disputable, exceptionable. *See also* ARGUMENTATIVE

CONTENTIOUSNESS *n* argumentativeness, contrariness, disputatiousness, divisiveness, negativeness, negativity, pettifoggery; **discord,** disunion, disunity

CONTENTS *n* cargo, content, fraught *(Obs.)*, freight, lading, load, pack, payload, wealth; **capacity,** capaciousness, cubature, mass, tonnage, volume

CONTEST *n* agony *(Rare)*, comp, competition, concurrence *(Rare)*, conflict, confliction, contention, contestation, engagement, game, infighting, match, prize *(Archaic)*, stakes *(Joc.)*, struggle, toil *(Archaic)*, trial, tug of war, war; **tournament,** carnival, challenge, grudge match, local derby, meet, meeting; **boxing match,** arm-wrestling, duello, prize fight, sciamachy, spar; **bullfighting,** cockfighting, main, tauromachy; **rodeo,** buckjumping, bulldogging, camp draft, carousel, gymkhana; **jousts,** lists, pool *(Fencing)*, tilting, tournament *(Hist.)*, tourney *(Archaic)*; **panel game,** game show, quiz, spelling bee; **boatrace,** stew; **miscellaneous contest,** eisteddfod, roller derby, sheepdog trial, shoot, shooting match, spider *(Bowling)*, surf carnival, woodchop; **championship,** cup, cup final, cup tie, decider, final, finals, grand final, match-of-the-day, open, preliminary final, premiership, quarterfinal, replay, run-off, semi, semifinal, test, test match, tie breaker. *See also* FIGHT; RACE

CONTEST *v* compete, contend, emulate, play, race, rival, run, run close, run hard, strive, try out, vie; **challenge,** draw, throw down the gauntlet, throw down the glove; **enter the lists,** take up the cudgels, take up the gauntlet, take up the glove, throw one's hat into the ring; **walk over,** run rings round; **bandy words,** argy-bargy, bicker, chaffer, chop *(Obs.)*, debate *(Archaic)*, haggle, have words, jangle *(Archaic)*, join issue, make the fur fly, row, squabble, tiff, wrangle. *See also* FIGHT

contest *n* → **1** act of war **2** disagreement *v* **3** disagree **4** wage war

contestant *n* → **1** competitor **2** fighter

context *n* → surroundings

contiguous *adj* → **1** close **2** contacting

continence *n* → abstinence

continent *n* → **1** land *adj* **2** abstinent

contingent *n* → **1** armed forces **2** dependant **3** occurrence **4** part **5** uncertain thing *adj* **6** conditional **7** dependent **8** feasible **9** uncertain

CONTINUAL *adj* abiding, constant, continuative, continuous, enduring, lasting, ongoing, persistent, standing; **everlasting,** ceaseless, continuing, endless, incessant, non-stop, perennial, perpetual, round-the-clock, unceasing, unending, uninterrupted, unrelenting, unrelieved, year-round; **assiduous,** unfailing, unflagging, unremitting, unresting, unwearied; **extended,** continued, drawn-out, interminable, long-term, long-standing, prolonged, protracted, protractive; **continuable,** maintainable, retainable, sustainable

continual *adj* → **1** frequent **2** repetitive

CONTINUALLY *adv* all along, constantly, continuatively, continuously, incessantly, momently, non-stop, persistently, sempre *(Music)*; **unremittingly,** abidingly, assiduously, at a run, ceaselessly, on end, unceasingly, unfailingly, unflaggingly, unrelentingly, unrelievedly, unrestingly, unswervingly, unweariedly; **always,** alway *(Archaic)*, e'er *(Poetic)*, ever, still *(Poetic)*, yet; **successively,** consecutively, in succession, one after another, sequentially, serially, seriately, seriatim; **unbrokenly,** flowingly, on, solidly, steadily, straight, uninterruptedly; **forever,** day in day out, endlessly, ever and again, ever and anon, everlastingly, evermore, on and on, perennially, perpetually, week in week out, without a break, year in year out

CONTINUATION *n* abidance, abidingness, continuance, continuativeness, continuity, continuousness, duration, long standing, maintenance, progress, progression, subsistence, sustainment; **protraction,** prolongation, prolongment; **incessantness,** endlessness, incessancy, uninterruptedness, unremittingness; **successiveness,** consecutiveness, perseverence, seriation; **unbrokenness,** solidity, solidness

CONTINUE *v* endure, flow, go on, keep the ball rolling, keep up, kick on, last, proceed, push on, soldier on, survive, wear, weather; **attacca,** segue *(Music)*; **abide,** bide *(Archaic)*, dwell, remain, rest, stay; **persist,** hold on, hold out, keep going, persevere, sit out, stick around, stick on

continue *v* → **1** advance **2** be **3** defer **4** extend

continuity *n* → **1** continuation **2** frequency **3** narrative **4** sequence

continuous *adj* → continual

continuum *n* → **1** number **2** series **3** space **4** whole

contort *v* → **1** distort **2** uglify

contour *n* → **1** appearance **2** edge **3** line *v* **4** edge **5** map

contraband *n* → 1 prohibition *adj* 2 prohibited 3 unlawful

CONTRACEPTION *n* birth control, family planning; **rhythm method,** safe period, Vatican roulette; **sterilisation,** castration, tubal ligation, vasectomy; **abortion,** aborticide, D and C, dilation and curettage, embryectomy, vacuum aspiration; **contraceptive,** cap, combination pill, condom, contraceptive sheath, copper 7, diaphragm, durex *(Brit.)*, Dutch cap, French letter, Frenchy, frog, I.U.D., intra-uterine device, loop, minipill, once a month pill, pessary, preventive, prophylactic, raincoat, rubber *(U.S.)*, sequential pill, sheath, skin, spermicide, the pill; **abortifacient,** morning-after pill

CONTRACT *n* agreement, arrangement, bargain, bond, compact, convention, covenant, deal, dicker, gentlemen's agreement, mise, settlement, testament, truck, understanding; **promise,** assurance, commitment, engagement, gage, guarantee, guaranty, Hippocratic oath, homage, insurance, oath, obligation, parole, pledge, sacrament, simple vow, swear, troth *(Archaic)*, undertaking, vote *(Obs.)*, vow, wager *(Archaic)*, warranty, word of honour; **pact,** concord, concordat, entente, league, protocol, treaty, truce; **bond,** cartel, charter; **booking,** gig, pre-engagement; **type of contract,** affreightment *(Comm.)*, aleatory contract, assumpsit, binder, bottomry *(Marine Law)*, carryover, collateral agreement, collective agreement, consent agreement, futures contract, immoral contract, implied contract, knock-for-knock agreement *(Insurance)*, lend-lease, mandate *(Roman and Civil Law)*, nudum pactum, quasi contract, quit claim deed, restrictive covenant, social contract, subcontract, sweetheart deal, turnkey contract, wagering contract. *See also* DEED

CONTRACT *v* astringe, constrict, constringe; **shrink,** atrophy, blast, blight, draw in, dwindle, retract, shrivel, waste, wither, wizen; **crumple,** corrugate, crush, rumple, wrinkle; **take in,** pleat, tuck

contract *n* → 1 gamble 2 obligation 3 wedding *v* 4 decrease 5 promise

CONTRACTED *adj* constricted, cramped, straitlaced *(Archaic)*, tense; **withered,** atrophied, blasted, marasmic, shrivelled, shrunken, stunted, tabescent, tabetic, tabid, wasted, wizened; **retractive,** astringent, constrictive, constringent, contractile, contractive, retractile; **spasmodic,** spastic; **systolic,** systaltic; **retractable,** contractible, foldaway

CONTRACTION *n* constriction, gather, intake, retraction, shrink, shrinkage; **spasm,** peristalsis, plasmolysis, systole, tetanus, vaginismus, vasoconstriction; **atrophy,** marasmus, tabefaction, wasting; **astringency,** constringency; **contractedness,** contractibility, contractibleness, contractility, contractiveness, retractility

CONTRACTOR *n* agent of necessity, arranger, bargainer, binder, covenantor, engager, indenter, obligor *(Law)*, subcontractor, undertaker; **promiser,** pledger, swearer, vower

contractor *n* → agent

contradict *v* → 1 answer 2 deny 3 disagree

contralto *n* → singer

contraption *n* → machine

contrary *n* → 1 contrast 2 opposite meaning *adj* 3 argumentative 4 bent 5 disobedient 6 dissident 7 opposing 8 opposite

CONTRAST *n* antithesis, contradiction, contrariety, discrepancy, disparity, dissimilarity, inversion, oppositeness; **contrary,** antonym, counterpart, foil, opposite, opposite pole, reverse, the other side

CONTRAST *v* invert, oppose, reverse, set against

contrast *n* → 1 difference *v* 2 differ

CONTRAVENE *v* break, infract, infringe; **offend; racketeer,** traffic; **trespass,** encroach

contribute *v* → 1 cooperate 2 give 3 pay 4 write

contrite *adj* → 1 ashamed 2 penitent

contrition *n* → 1 guilt 2 penitence

contrivance *n* → 1 expedient 2 finished product 3 machine 4 making 5 stratagem

contrive *v* → 1 beguile 2 conspire 3 create 4 make do 5 plan

CONTROL *v* curb, damp, govern, keep in check, keep under control, manage, monitor, regulate, restrain, size *(Obs.)*; **monopolise,** collar, corner the market, engross, rort, take over

control *n* → 1 competence 2 composure 3 operation 4 restraint *v* 5 manage 6 restrain 7 test

CONTROLLED *adj* automated, computer-controlled, monitored, regulated

CONTROLLING *adj* checking, dedicated *(Computers)*, governing, regulating, regulative, regulatory

CONTROLLING DEVICE *n* checker, controller, curb, damper, dedicated computer, governor, guide, monitor, regulator, rein, the controls; **automatic control,** auto, automation, computer control, process control, remote control, servocontrol

controversy *n* → 1 disagreement 2 discussion 3 subject matter

contumely *n* → 1 arrogance 2 disapproval 3 low regard

contuse *v* → injure

contusion *n* → 1 injury 2 sore

conundrum *n* → puzzle

convalesce *v* → be healthy

convection *n* → 1 flow 2 heat transfer 3 wind

convene *v* → 1 gather 2 litigate

convenience *n* → 1 expedient 2 facilitation 3 toilet

convenient *adj* → 1 easy 2 expedient

convent *n* → 1 abbey 2 school 3 seclusion

convention *n* → 1 committee 2 conformist behaviour 3 contract 4 custom 5 rule

CONVENTIONAL *adj* academic, accepted, appropriate, common-or-garden, customary, decorous, felicitous, habitual, prosaic, set, usual; **commonplace,** copybook, household, normal, ordinary, ready-made, stereotyped, unexceptional, unremarkable; **typical,** entopic, in character, stereotypic, stereotypical, true *(Biol.)*; **conformable,** acquiescent, adjustable, agreeable, assimilative, assimilatory, complacent, pliable

conventional *adj* → **1** assenting **2** customary **3** mediocre

CONVENTIONALLY *adv* appropriately, as a matter of course, as a matter of form, in line, in step, pro forma, rightly, true; **conservatively,** classically, formally, straightly; **orthodoxly,** according to, by rule, conformably, in accordance with, in conformity with, in keeping with, strictly; **commonly,** as usual, in the natural order of things, invariably, normally, ordinarily, regularly, typically, unexceptionally, uniformly, unremarkably

CONVERGE *v* be on a collision course with, come together, come up to, cut off, focus, intercept, join, unite, unite with; **meet,** bump into, collide with, come across, come upon, encounter, fall in with, meet up with; **concentrate,** assemble, bring together, gather together

CONVERGENCE *n* accession, afflux, assembly, coming together, concentration, concourse, confluence, conflux, congress, encounter, flection, flexion, flocking together, huddling together, junction; **meeting,** collision, encounter

CONVERGENT *adj* asymptotic, asymptotical, flexional, synclinal; **confluent,** centring, centripetal, cusped, cuspidal, cuspidate

conversant *adj* → knowledgeable

conversation *n* → **1** behaviour **2** friendship **3** talk

converse *n* → **1** communication **2** opposite meaning **3** talk *v* **4** talk *adj* **5** opposing **6** overturned

CONVERT *v* bring over, bring round, episcopise, reclaim, reform, regenerate; **teach,** brainwash, evangelise, missionise, proselytise; **corrupt,** heathenise, paganise

convert *n* → **1** believer **2** defector *v* **3** change **4** defect **5** electrify **6** take

convertible *n* → **1** car *adj* **2** buyable **3** cash **4** useful **5** variable **6** vehicular

convex *adj* → curved

convey *v* → **1** capture **2** communicate **3** inform **4** rob **5** transport

conveyance *n* → **1** dissemination **2** transport

CONVEYOR *n* apron, beef chain, belt, chainpump, conveyor belt, ship-loader, the chain *(Butchering)*; **escalator,** moving pathway, moving staircase, travelator; **lift,** dumb waiter, elevator, goods lift, service lift

conveyor belt *n* → conveyor

convict *n* → **1** criminal **2** prisoner

conviction *n* → **1** certainty **2** opinion

convince *v* → persuade

convivial *adj* → **1** celebratory **2** happy **3** sociable

convoke *v* → gather

convolution *n* → **1** circuitousness **2** complexity **3** distortion **4** head **5** spiral **6** twist

convoy *n* → **1** protection **2** protector **3** truck **4** watercraft *v* **5** accompany

convulse *v* → **1** laugh **2** toss

coo *n* → **1** birdcall *v* **2** chirp **3** kiss *interj* **4** oh

COOEE *interj* ahoy, halloo, hallow, ho, hoy, yo-ho, yoo-hoo; **oyez,** hear ye; **hurray,** banzai *(Japan)*, bravo, hosanna, huzza, tiger *(U.S.)*; **carn,** have a go; **tally-ho,** tantivy, view halloo, yoicks

cooee *n* → **1** shout *v* **2** shout *interj* **3** hey

COOK *n* baker, chief, confectioner, doctor *(Naut.)*, kitchen hand, pastry-cook, restaurateur; **bush cook,** babbler, baitlayer, blacksmith, crippen, doughpuncher, greasy, gutstarver, poisoner, Sally Thompson, water burner

COOK *v* fix, get, microwave, pan *(U.S.)*, pick, precook, prepare; **grill,** barbecue, broil, carbonado, griddle, toast; **bake,** plank *(U.S.)*, roast, shirr; **fry,** brown, deep-fry, French-fry, frizzle, pan fry, parch, sauté, scramble, sear, shallow-fry, stir-fry; **boil,** coddle, hard-boil, parboil, poach, simmer; **braise,** casserole, fricassee, ragout, scallop, stew; **blanch,** scald; **steep,** brew, draw, infuse, percolate, seethe *(Obs.)*; **dredge,** bread, breadcrumb, coat, crumb, egg, flour; **mince,** bone, chip, chop, dice, filet, fillet, spatchcock, spitchcock; **tenderise,** hang, macerate, marinate, soak; **crackle,** decrepitate; **strain,** tammy; **season,** flavour, pepper, spice; **curry,** devil, korma; **preserve,** brandy, brew, corn, jug, kipper, pickle, pot, salt, smoke, souse; **garnish,** dress, sauce, stuff; **baste,** bard, lard; **make tea,** boil the billy; **truss,** collar; **cream,** blend, puree, whip, whisk; **candy,** caramelise, conserve *(Obs.)*, crystallise, sugar, thread; **prove,** raise, shorten; **deglaze**

cook *n* → **1** look *v* **2** fake **3** heat **4** spoil

COOKERY *n* catering, cooking, cordon bleu cookery, cuisine, domestic science, gastrology, haute cuisine, nouvelle cuisine; **baking,** boiling, broiling, grilling, infusion, marination, red cooking, roasting, simmering, stewing, toasting; **peeling,** KP *(U.S.)*, paring, spud-bashing; **cookbook,** cookery book, recipe book; **recipe,** receipt

COOL *v* air-condition, air-cool, fan, water-cool; **refrigerate,** chill, ice, supercool; **freeze,** deep freeze, quick-freeze, snap-freeze

cool *n* → **1** composure *adj* **2** cold **3** composed **4** fashionable **5** good **6** moderate **7** musical **8** unconditional **9** unsociable

COOLED *adj* chilled, iced; **refrigerative,** refrigerant, thermolytic; **air-conditioned,** air-cooled, water-cooled; **frozen,** frappé, quick-frozen, snap-frozen

COOLER *n* coolant, cooling tower, radiator, ultracooler *(Winemaking)*, water-cooler, water-jacket; **refrigerator,** creamer, crisper, fridge, frost-free refrigerator, reefer; **freezer,** chiller, deep freeze, freezing chamber, ice chest, ice machine, icebox; **Coolgardie safe,** bush refrigerator, cool safe; **ice bucket,**

chillybin, esky, wine-cooler; **freezing works,** icehouse; **freezing mixture,** carbon dioxide snow, cryogen, cryohydrate, isobutane, rhigolene; **ice-cubes,** iceblocks, rocks; **air-conditioner,** fan

coolie *n* → labourer

COOLING *n* cold storage, cryonics, refrigeration, thermolysis, ventilation; **air-conditioning,** regenerative cooling; **cryogenics**

coop *n* → **1** animal dwelling **2** cell **3** container **4** prison *v* **5** imprison

co-op *n* → **1** corporation **2** shop

COOPERATE *v* club together, collaborate, combine, confederate, coordinate, go hand in hand, pull together, synergise, team up, unite, work as a team, work together; **conspire,** connive, plot, tick-tack with; **participate,** club in, contribute, pitch in; **concur,** go along with, help, play ball, string along with

COOPERATION *n* consensus, cooperativeness, give-and-take, helpfulness, reciprocity; **team spirit,** clannishness, esprit de corps, fellowship, party spirit, solidarity, unitedness; **collaboration,** combined operation, concurrence, concurrency, connivance, coordination, joint effort, participation, synergism, synergy, teamwork, working together

COOPERATIVE *adj* coefficient, collaborative, concurrent, coordinative, solidary, synergetic, synergic, synergistic; **allied,** coalition, cobelligerent, confederate, confederative, united, unitive

cooperative *n* → **1** community *adj* **2** helpful **3** societal

COOPERATIVELY *adv* collaboratively, concurrently, coordinately, hand-in-glove, in cahoots, in league; **unitedly,** jointly, together

COOPERATOR *n* collaborator, cooperationist, coworker, fellow worker, participant, participator, partner; **ally,** cobelligerent, confederate; **conspirator,** accessory, accessory after the fact, accessory before the fact, accomplice, conniver, plotter; **coordinator,** combiner, organiser, uniter

coopt *v* → elect

coordinate *v* → **1** class **2** combine **3** cooperate **4** order *adj* **5** combined **6** equal

coot *n* → **1** fool **2** man

cop *n* → **1** apex **2** imprisonment **3** payment **4** policeman **5** thread **6** top *v* **7** get **8** persevere **9** rob

cope *n* → **1** cloak **2** sky **3** top **4** uniform *v* **5** cover

COPIED *adj* duplicate, duplicative, ectypal, facsimile, reproductive; **transcriptive,** word for word

COPIER *n* imitator, reproducer; **transcriber,** copyist, exemplifier *(Law)*; **manifolder,** cyclostyle, diagraph, electrotyper, fordigraph, gestetner, hectograph, mimeograph, pantograph, photocopier, polygraph, tracer

copious *adj* → **1** abundant **2** fertile **3** great **4** many

cop out *v* → **1** be inactive **2** fail

cop-out *n* → means of escape

copper *n* → **1** basin **2** bath **3** coinage **4** orange **5** policeman *v* **6** coat *adj* **7** brown **8** metallic

copperplate *n* → **1** writing *adj* **2** perfect

coppice *n* → **1** forest *v* **2** cut

copse *n* → forest

copula *n* → join

copulate *v* → **1** have sex **2** join *adj* **3** joined

COPY *n* blind copy, clone, ditto, double, dubbing, dummy, duplicate, ectype, facsimile, fax, match, model, moulding, repeat, replica, reproduction; **counterfeit,** forgery, semblance; **tracing,** transfer; **transcript,** engrossment, estreat, exemplification *(Law)*, fair copy, transcription, typescript; **carbon copy,** flimsy, manifold; **plate,** electro, electrotype, offset, zincograph; **photocopy,** autotype, blueprint, gestetner, microcopy, photostat, xerograph, xerox, zincograph; **offprint,** decal, galley, galley proof, print, proof; **woodblock,** intaglio, wood engraving, woodcut; **cast,** death mask, mould, squeeze; **magnification,** reduction

COPY *v* ditto, dub, duplicate, facsimile, imitate, match, replicate, reproduce, simulate; **transcribe,** engross, estreat, exemplify *(Law)*, take down word for word; **trace,** calk, cyclostyle, generate *(Maths)*, prick; **mould,** squeeze; **photostat,** autotype, blueprint, decal, electrotype, fordigraph, gestetner, hectograph, manifold, mimeograph, offprint, roneo, xerox

copy *n* → **1** imitation **2** model **3** portrait **4** repetition *v* **5** follow **6** imitate

COPYING *n* duplication, repetition, replication, reproduction, transcription; **reprography,** autography, autotypy, decal, decalcomania, intaglio, zincography

copyright *n* → **1** intellectual property **2** ownership

copywriter *n* → **1** publicist **2** writer

coquette *n* → flirt

coral *n* → **1** orange *adj* **2** red

CORD *n* bond, cable, cablet, line, rope; **leash,** lariat *(U.S.)*, lashing, lasso *(Agric.)*, lead, leading rein, leg rope, lune, lunge, lunging rein, tether; **towrope,** guide rope, lifeline, tow, towline; **tightrope,** highwire, slackwire; **whip,** cat-o'-nine-tails, knout, lash, quirt *(U.S.)*, rawhide, rope's end, sjambok, stockwhip, tawse *(Scot.)*; **rigging,** bight, boltrope, brail, breeching, buntline, cable, cablet, clew line, colt, cordage, downhaul, earing, gantline, grabrope, guestrope, halliard, halyard, handy billy, hawser, inhaul, jackstay, knife lanyard, lanyard, lashing, messenger, monkey rope, outhaul, painter, pendant, preventer, ratline, reef point, sennit, sheet, shroud, slings, spring, standing rigging, stay, stirrup, stop, stopper, sweep, swifter, tack, tackle, traveller, triatic stay, tripping line, vang, warp; **miscellaneous cords,** baulk, bellpull, chalk-line *(Building Trades)*, clothes line, creance, dragline, dragrope, footrope, guide rope, heddle, marline, match, mooring, ripcord, sashcord, skipping-rope, stringline, surf-line, tagrope, topping lift, trail rope, trip-wire, wick. *See also* STRING; TAPE; THREAD; WIRE

CORD *v* rope, string, wire; **fibrillate,** rove, sleave; **tie,** lace; **thread,** interweave, thrum; **rein in,** lasso, rope in; **spin,** strand, wiredraw

cord *n* → **1** wire *v* **2** fasten **3** restrain

CORDED *adj* corduroy, funicular, ropy, stringed; **right-handed,** cable-laid, hawser-laid, shroud-laid, twice-laid; **stringy,** desmoid, sinewy, wiry; **fibrous,** fibred, fibriform, fibrillar, fibrilliform, fibrillose, fibroid, filamentary, filamentous, filar, filiform, filose, piled, piliform, tendrillar, tentacular, threadlike, thready, unifilar, wirewove; **silky,** byssaceous, cobwebbed, cobwebby, silk

corded *adj* → **1** fastened **2** restricted

cordial *n* → **1** alcohol **2** drink *adj* **3** friendly **4** happy **5** sociable

cordon *n* → **1** belt **2** bottom **3** emblem **4** frame **5** string **6** trimming *v* **7** edge

corduroy *adj* → **1** corded **2** corrugated

core *n* → **1** centre **2** extract **3** inside **4** model **5** opening *v* **6** extract **7** subtract

cork *n* → **1** indicator **2** plug *v* **3** blacken **4** close

corkage *n* → **1** charge **2** cost

corkscrew *n* → **1** extractor *v* **2** rotate **3** twist *adj* **4** twisted

cormorant *n* → glutton

corn *n* → **1** bead **2** disfigurement **3** powder *v* **4** conserve **5** cook **6** powder

corner *n* → **1** dilemma **2** economy **3** ownership **4** region **5** seclusion **6** secret place *v* **7** drive **8** imprison **9** own **10** swerve **11** turn

cornet *n* → **1** brass instrument **2** headgear **3** soldier **4** tableware

cornice *n* → ice

cornucopia *n* → **1** abundance **2** fertility **3** storage **4** tableware

corny *adj* → emotional

corollary *n* → **1** coming after **2** postscript

corona *n* → **1** church **2** electricity **3** flower **4** light **5** lighting **6** ring **7** sun

coronary *adj* → circular

coronation *n* → employment

coroner *n* → judge

coronet *n* → **1** emblem of office **2** jewellery **3** ring

corporal *adj* → **1** bodily **2** tangible

CORPORAL PUNISHMENT *n* flogging, lashing, strapping, the cuts, whipping; **beating,** bastinado, belting, doing, drubbing, flagellation, fustigation *(Archaic)*, hiding, running the gauntlet, scourging, thrashing, trouncing, walloping; **Botany Bay dozen,** bob, bull, canary, tester; **blow,** buffet, clout, cuff, domino *(Obs.)*, pandy, stripe, stroke; **smack,** blanketing, box on the ear, dusting, going-over, paddle, paddywhack, rap over the knuckles, slap, spank, spanking, wallop; **torture,** breaking on the wheel, Chinese burn, Chinese water torture, excruciation, sensory deprivation, strappado, third degree, torment *(Obs.)*

corporate *adj* → societal

CORPORATION *n* body corporate, business house, enterprise, no-liability company, unincorporated association, unlimited company; **establishment,** aunty, organisation; **cartel,** combine, conference *(Shipping)*, consortium, monopoly, pool, ring, syndicate; **trading bloc,** co-op, common market, EEC, farmers' cooperative, OPEC; **company,** cast, firm, line-up, outfit; **partnership,** duumvirate, group practice, triumverate; **team,** rink, side

corporation *n* → **1** abdomen **2** legislative body

corporeal *adj* → **1** bodily **2** tangible

corps *n* → **1** crowd **2** the dead

corpse *n* → **1** body **2** the dead *v* **3** be inactive

corpus *n* → **1** body **2** capital **3** record **4** whole

corpuscle *n* → **1** atom **2** organism

CORRECT *v* blue-pencil, copyedit, crosscheck, edit, emend, proofread, red-pencil, revise, subedit; **rectify,** amend, disabuse, edify, expurgate, set to rights, straighten; **check,** authenticate

CORRECT *adj* exact, just, lawful, right as rain, unerring, unimpeachable; **authorised,** canonical, orthodox, recognised; **true,** authentic, factual, fiducial, genuine, historical, infallible, real, ridge, ridgy-didge, sooth *(Archaic)*, veracious, veritable, very; **right,** becoming, comme il faut, decent, decorous, fair and above board, family *(Films Television)*, fitting, incorrupt, irreproachable, just, moral, principled, proper, reproachless, right-minded, righteous, rightful, savoury, scrupulous, seemly, squeaky-clean, straight, true, unspotted, up to the mark, upright, viceless, virtuous

correct *v* → **1** adjust **2** punish *adj* **3** formal **4** precise **5** true

CORRECTION *n* emendation, proofreading, recension, redaction, revision; **rectification,** amendment, edification, reform, reformation

CORRECTIVE *adj* amendatory *(U.S.)*, rectifying, reformational, reformative, reformatory

CORRECTLY *adv* aright, by the book, exactly, orthodoxly, scrupulously, unerringly; **rightly,** by right, fairly, incorruptly, irreproachably, lawfully, morally, righteously, straight, truly, unimpeachably, uprightly, virtuously; **decorously,** decently, in reason, properly, seemly, within bounds, within reason

CORRECTNESS *n* becomingness, decency, decentness, decorousness, decorum, irreproachability, irreproachableness, propriety, right-mindedness, savouriness, seemliness, the conventionalities, the conventions, the thing; **right,** ethicalness, justness, morality, principle, rectitude, righteousness, rightness, the straight and narrow, virtue, virtuousness, welldoing; **straightness,** a step in the right direction, lawfulness, orthodoxy, scrupulosity, the right track, the ticket, trueness, unerringness

CORRECTOR *n* book editor, checker, copyeditor, emendator, proofreader, redactor, reviser, subeditor; **righter of wrongs,** amender, edifier, rectifier
correlate *v* → **1** interact **2** relate *adj* **3** related
correlation *n* → **1** interaction **2** relation **3** relationship
correspond *v* → **1** be similar **2** fit **3** interact **4** send a message
correspondence *n* → **1** conformity **2** congruity **3** equality **4** interaction **5** message **6** relation **7** similarity
CORRESPONDENT *n* addressee, consignee, epistler, letter writer, penfriend
correspondent *n* → **1** equivalent **2** journalist *adj* **3** congruous **4** related **5** similar
corridor *n* → **1** bridge **2** hall **3** path **4** region
corroborate *v* → **1** assent to **2** authenticate
corroboree *n* → **1** celebration **2** commotion **3** gathering **4** religious ceremony
corrode *v* → deteriorate
corrugate *v* → **1** contract **2** fold
CORRUGATED *adj* carinal, carinate, corduroy, knurled, ribbed, striate, strigose
corrupt *v* → **1** convert **2** dirty **3** ill-treat **4** spoil **5** wrong *adj* **6** bribable **7** deteriorated **8** dishonest **9** immoral
corsage *n* → plant
corset *n* → underwear
cortege *n* → **1** sequence **2** servant
cortex *n* → **1** head **2** skin
coruscate *v* → shine
cosh *n* → **1** club *v* **2** cudgel
COSMETICS *n* beauty spot, blusher, court plaster, eye shadow, eyeliner, face powder, foundation, foundation cream, greasepaint, highlighter, kohl, liner, lippie, lipstick, mascara, nail polish, nail varnish, pancake, pencil, rouge, vanishing cream; **make-up,** face, face paint, war paint
COSMIC *adj* cosmical, galactic, macrocosmic, universal; **heavenly,** celestial, empyreal, firmamental, sphery, superlunary, supernal, superterrestrial, uranian, uranic; **extragalactic,** intergalactic, interlunar, interplanetary, intersidereal, interstellar; **ethereal,** skyey *(Poetic)*
cosmic *adj* → **1** big **2** congruous **3** eternal **4** ordered **5** tangible
cosmonaut *n* → pilot
cosmopolitan *adj* → **1** dispersed **2** general **3** tolerant **4** urban
cosmos *n* → **1** matter **2** sky
cosset *n* → sheep
cossie *n* → swimwear
COST *n* charge, damage, differential rate, expenditure, expense, price, rate, score; **cost price,** floor price, net price, trade price, wholesale price; **unit cost,** cost unit, operating cost, unit price; **market price,** going price, market, retail price, spot price; **asking price,** knockdown price, reserve price, upset price; **offer,** ante, bid, nearest offer, o.n.o.; **admission,** entrance fee, footing, gate, gate money, gate-takings; **overheads,** burden, oncost, outlay; **production cost,** prime cost; **corkage,** service charge; **commission,** bank charge, cut, percentage; **fee,** contract sum, cost-plus, honorarium, most common fee *(Med.)*, refresher, transfer fee *(Football)*, tuition, tutorage; **brassage,** seigniorage. *See also* FREIGHT; VALUE
COST *v* bring, fetch, sell for, set one back; **be worth,** close at *(Stock Exchange)*; **amount to,** add up to, come to, run to; **valorise,** bull, fix a price, set; **change in value,** down-value, fall, rise, transvalue, upvalue
cost *n* → **1** payment *v* **2** predict
costly *adj* → **1** expensive **2** extravagant
COSTUME *n* cap and bells, domino, drag, fancy dress, masquerade, motley
costume *n* → **1** swimwear *v* **2** clothe
cosy *adj* → pleasant
cot *n* → **1** bed **2** cabin **3** refuge
cote *n* → shelter
coterie *n* → clique
cottage *n* → house
cotton *v* → **1** agree **2** prosper
cottonwool *n* → **1** contentedness *adj* **2** content
COUCH *n* banana bed, banana chair, canapé, chaise longue, chesterfield, cuddle seat, davenport *(U.S.)*, day bed, divan, fauteuil, lounge, lounge suite, night-and-day, ottoman, settee, settle, sofa, sofa-bed, studio couch. *See also* CHAIR; BED
couch *n* → **1** bed **2** beds **3** paint *v* **4** lie low **5** repose **6** rest
cough *n* → **1** breathing **2** cold *v* **3** breathe
COUNCIL *n* divan, junta, politburo, presidium, soviet, zemstvo; **board,** board of reference, directorate, syndicate; **forum,** discussion group, panel, round table, workshop; **parliament,** agora, assembly, chamber, congress, diet, gemot, house, House of Assembly, senate; **cabinet,** camarilla, council of war, court, genro, Privy Council, shadow cabinet; **committee,** select committee, sessional committee, standing committee, steering committee, subcommittee; **consistory,** conference, convocation, ecumenical council, parish council, presbytery, Sanhedrin, synod, Vatican Council, vestry
counsel *n* → **1** guidance **2** lawyer **3** plan **4** wisdom *v* **5** guide
count *n* → **1** accusation **2** aristocrat **3** computation **4** score *v* **5** compute **6** publicise
countenance *n* → **1** appearance **2** approval **3** behaviour **4** face *v* **5** approve **6** permit
COUNTERACT *v* antagonise *(Physiol.)*, counter, countercheck, countermand, countervail, counterwork, frustrate, neutralise, overturn, remedy, slap down, undo; **balance,** counterpoise, counterweigh, equiponderate, match, offset, write off
COUNTERACTING *adj* antidotal, counterrevolutionary, counteractive, diriment, remedial, rescissory, revocatory
COUNTERACTION *n* counter, counterreformation, counter-revolution *(Politics)*, counterattack, counterblast, countercheck, counterclaim, countermove,

counterpressure, neutralisation, reaction, recoil, retroaction

COUNTERBALANCE *n* balancer, check, counterpoise, counterweight, counterwork, equilibrant, offset, tare *(Chem.)*; **antidote,** antacid, antalkali, buffer, counterirritant, counterpoison, neutraliser

counterfeit *n* → **1** copy **2** imitation **3** portrait *v* **4** circulate **5** imitate **6** trick *adj* **7** fake **8** imitative

countermand *n* → **1** cancellation **2** command **3** denial *v* **4** cancel **5** counteract

counterpane *n* → bedclothes

counterpart *n* → **1** contrast **2** similar thing

counterproductive *adj* → infertile

countersign *n* → **1** answer **2** signal *v* **3** assent to **4** label

countess *n* → aristocrat

country *n* → **1** land **2** nation **3** region **4** the public *adj* **5** farming **6** ill-bred **7** national **8** rural

COUNTRY DWELLER *n* back-countryman, bushman, bushranger, bushwhacker, country cousin, countryman, countrywoman, plainsman, provincial, ruralist, rustic, villager, wench; **peasant,** bogtrotter, boor, bumpkin, bushie, churl, clown, hayseed, hillbilly, muzhik, ploughboy, ploughman, yeoman *(Brit.)*; **country people,** country folk, peasantry; **bucolic,** swain *(Poetic)*

county *n* → **1** administrative area **2** aristocracy **3** domain *adj* **4** legislative **5** regional

coup *n* → accomplishment

coup d'état *n* → revolution

couple *n* → **1** lover **2** shaft **3** spouse **4** two *v* **5** double **6** have sex **7** join

couplet *n* → two

coupon *n* → cheque

COURAGE *n* braveness, bravery, courageousness, crest, fortitude, guts, prowess, valiance, valiantness, valorousness, valour; **daring,** adventurousness, daringness, derring-do, emprise *(Archaic)*, enterprise, liveliness, venturesomeness, venturousness; **heroism,** chivalrousness, chivalry, gallantness, gallantry, knight-errantry; **boldness,** audaciousness, audacity, chutzpah, gall, moxie *(U.S.)*, nerve; **fearlessness,** dauntlessness, doughtiness, great-heartedness, intrepidity, stoutness; **hardiness,** game, gameness, gaminess, grit, hardihood, pluck, pluckiness; **spirit,** heart, mettle, spiritedness, sportsmanship, spunk, spunkiness, stomach *(Obs.)*; **undauntedness,** heart of oak, unshrinkingness; **stalwartness,** manliness, Spartanism, virtue *(Obs.)*; **pot-valiance,** Dutch courage

courage *n* → emotion

COURAGEOUS *adj* brave, mentioned in dispatches, proud *(Obs.)*, valiant, valorous; **daring,** adventuresome, adventurous, venturesome, venturous; **heroic,** chivalric, chivalrous, epic, gallant, herculean, lion-hearted; **bold,** audacious, defiant, nervy; **fearless,** dauntless, doughty, great-hearted, inapprehensive, indomitable, intrepid, stout, stout-hearted; **hardy,** game, game as a pissant, game as Ned Kelly, gamy, gritty, plucky, pretty *(Scot. Archaic)*; **spirited,** full of fight, high-spirited, mettled, mettlesome, spunky; **undaunted,** fortitudinous, unblinking, unflinching, unshrinking; **stalwart,** gutsy, manly, Spartan, strong; **pot-valiant**

courier *n* → **1** informant **2** messenger **3** trader **4** transporter

COURSE *n* correspondence course, extension course, external course, in-service course, internship, novitiate, postgraduate course, refresher course, sandwich course; **introductory course,** ABC's, elementary course, elements, initiation, isagogics, propaedeutics, rudiments, three R's; **curriculum,** program, syllabus; **discipline,** area, elective, field, honours, major, minor *(U.S.)*, speciality, study; **arts,** classics, humanities, liberal arts, manual arts, quadrivium, the sciences, trivium. *See also* LESSON; LEARNING

course *n* → **1** advance **2** attack **3** behaviour **4** bridge **5** direction **6** hunting **7** layer **8** meal **9** method **10** move **11** path **12** point of view **13** race **14** regularity **15** route **16** sequence *v* **17** flow **18** head for **19** hunt **20** pursue

court *n* → **1** committee **2** council **3** court of law **4** field **5** house **6** judge **7** tribute *v* **8** allure **9** desire **10** entreat **11** flirt

COURTEOUS *adj* attentive, chivalric, chivalrous, civil, debonair, decent, decorous, diplomatic, fair, fair-spoken, gallant, gracious, polite, proper; **well-mannered,** civilised, couth, cultivated, mannered, mannerly, refined, tasteful, well brought up, well-behaved, well-bred, well-educated, well-spoken, well-tried; **gentlemanlike,** gentlemanly; **ladylike,** gentlewomanly, lady; **genteel,** euphemistic, euphemistical, gentle *(Archaic)*, mild *(Obs.)*, soft-spoken; **suave,** polished, sleek, slick, smooth, smooth-spoken, sophisticated, urbane

courteous *adj* → pleasant

COURTEOUSNESS *n* decorousness, diplomacy, gentility, gentleness *(Archaic)*, graciosity, graciousness, hypocorism, mannerliness, mildness, politeness, politesse; **attentiveness,** chivalrousness, debonairness, decentness, errantry, gallantness; **suaveness,** breeding, decorum, sleekness, slickness, suavity, urbaneness, urbanity

COURTEOUS PERSON *n* cavalier, chevalier, diplomatist, gentleman, gentlewoman, lady

courtesan *n* → prostitute

COURTESY *n* civility, comity, complacency *(Obs.)*, decency, good manners, manners, respect; **chivalry,** gallantry; **attentions,** attention, complacency *(Obs.)*, devoir, devoirs; **deference,** regard; **curtsy,** bob, bow, cheese *(Obs.)*, kow-tow, salaam; **salutation,** greetings, red carpet, respects, salute, welcome; **suavities,** urbanities

courtesy *n* → **1** high regard **2** permission

courtier *n* → flatterer

courtly *adj* → **1** flattering **2** formal *adv* **3** formally

court martial *n* → **1** court of law **2** trial

COURT OF LAW *n* assizes *(Brit.)*, bar, bench, board, board of enquiry, closed court, court, divan, durbar *(Indian)*, forum, inquest, judicatory, law court, open court, tribunal; **arbitration court,** Chancery *(Brit.)*, common court, Conciliation and Arbitration Commission, coroner's court, County Court, court leet *(Obs.)*, court martial, Court of Appeal, Court of Common Pleas *(Brit.)*, Court of Disputed Returns, Court of Petty Sessions, Court of Quarter Sessions, court of record, crown court *(Brit.)*, District Court, drumhead court martial, Exchequer, Family Court, high court, High Court of Australia, High Court of Justice *(Brit.)*, higher court, industrial court, inferior court, juvenile court, leet *(Obs.)*, Magistrate's Court, moot *(Obs.)*, moot court, oyer and terminer, police court, probate court, quarter sessions, sessions, Star Chamber, superior court, Supreme Court; **courthouse,** cells, courtroom, dock, judge's chambers, jury-box, witness box

COURT SESSION *n* high jump *(Colloq.)*, oyer *(Obs. Brit.)*, session, sitting, woodpeckers' day *(Prison Colloq.)*

courtship *n* → flirtation

courtyard *n* → field

cousin *n* → relative

couturier *n* → clothier

cove *n* → **1** bay **2** boss **3** cave **4** farmer **5** man

coven *n* → worshipper

covenant *n* → **1** agreement **2** contract **3** religion **4** restraining order *v* **5** promise

COVER *v* face, invest, pall, throw something over, web; **shroud,** drape; **jacket,** blanket, caparison, cloak, cushion, mantle, trap *(Obs.)*, tuck, vest; **mask,** blindfold, cowl, hood; **swathe,** bandage, cocoon, enfold, enswathe, enwrap, insulate, involve, muffle, smother, swaddle; **wrap,** bundle, gift-wrap, pack, package; **bind,** fother *(Naut.)*, parcel, serve *(Naut.)*, whip; **overlay,** bespread, carpet, litter, perfuse; **line,** brattice, face, fettle, resurface, revet; **upholster,** overstuff *(Furnit.)*, trim; **roof,** canopy, cope, embower, plash, rafter, shade, shingle, thatch, tile; **grass,** loam, sod, sward, top, top-dress, topsoil, turf. *See also* COAT

cover *n* → **1** book part **2** container **3** covering **4** disguise **5** protection **6** refuge **7** surety *v* **8** be adequate **9** compensate **10** darken **11** flood **12** give birth **13** hide **14** include **15** publish **16** secure

cover charge *n* → charge

COVERED *adj* covert; **hooded,** cowled, cucullate, veiled; **tegminal,** tegumental; **jacketed,** armour-plated, ermined, ironclad, loricate, panoplied. *See also* COATED

COVERING *n* carpet, cladding, cloak, clothing, cover, covert, gilding, housing, involucre, mantle, overlay, pall, panoply, sheet, shroud, skin, tegmen, tegument, umbrella, veil; **sheath,** case, casing, casing shoe, jacket, scabbard, sheathing; **capsule,** husk, integument, pod, rind, seed capsule, seed vessel, shell; **hatch,** booby hatch *(Naut.)*, calash, grate, lid, shutter; **coating,** coat, crust, encrustation, film, plaque *(Dentistry)*, scale, skin; **icing,** spread, topping; **scum,** dusting, fur, fuzz, fuzziness, head *(Winemaking)*, scurf; **antimacassar,** facings, lambrequin *(Armour)*, loose cover, pall, pallium, pillow sham, runner, shower, slip cover, throwover, tidy *(U.S.)*, trim; **placemat,** damask, duchesse set, tablecloth; **drapery,** dossal *(Archaic)*, dosser, frontal, frontlet, lambrequin, scrim; **cover glass,** bell glass, bell jar, cloche, crystal, watch-glass; **tea-cosy,** eggcosy

coverlet *n* → bedclothes

cover note *n* → insurance

covert *n* → **1** covering **2** hiding place **3** refuge *adj* **4** arcane **5** covered **6** hidden

covet *v* → **1** be jealous of **2** desire

covey *n* → gathering

cow *n* → **1** bad person **2** cattle **3** irritable person **4** ugly person *v* **5** menace

COWARD *n* chicken, chocolate soldier, cowardy custard, craven, creamer, cry-baby, dastard, dingo, faint-heart, fraidy-cat, funk, gutless wonder, milksop, nervous Nellie, niddering *(Archaic)*, poltroon, poofter, recreant, scaredy-cat, sheep, sissy, skulk, skulker, softie, sook, sop, squib, weakie, wheyface, wimp, yellow streak, yellow-belly

coward *adj* → cowardly

COWARDICE *n* baseness, cowardliness, cravenness, dastardliness, faint-heartedness, fearfulness, nervelessness, poltroonery, pusillanimity, recreance, spinelessness

COWARDLY *adj* base, chicken, chicken-hearted, coward, craven, dastard, dastardly, faint, faint-hearted, fearful, fearsome, frightened, gritless, gun-shy, gutless, lily-livered, mealy-mouthed, milky, nerveless, niddering *(Archaic)*, piss-weak, poor, poor-spirited, pusillanimous, recreant, sooky, spineless, spiritless, tame, terrified, timid, unheroic, unknightly, unmanly, white-livered, yellow, yellow-bellied

cowboy *n* → farmhand

cower *v* → **1** be frightened **2** lack courage

cowl *n* → **1** cloak **2** headgear **3** screen *v* **4** cover

cowlick *n* → hair

cox *n* → **1** seaman **2** steerer *v* **3** direct

coxcomb *n* → **1** affected person **2** cap

coxswain *n* → **1** seaman **2** steerer

coyote *n* → bad person

cozen *v* → cheat

crab *n* → **1** puller *v* **2** fish **3** flank **4** fly **5** spoil

crack *n* → **1** attempt **2** break **3** buttocks **4** click **5** dissonance **6** expert **7** explosion **8** gap **9** groin **10** hit **11** joke **12** madness **13** mockery **14** moment **15** opening **16** prostitute **17** robbery **18** specialist *v* **19** be dissonant **20** be mad **21** break **22** explode **23** fail **24** gape **25** perforate **26** separate **27** solve **28** succeed *adj* **29** superior

cracker *n* → **1** good thing **2** poor person **3** the best

CRACKLE *n* crackling, crepitation, decrepitation, rattle; **sputter,** fizz, fizzing, hizz, snort

CRACKLE *v* crepitate, decrepitate, fizz, fizzle, spatter, splutter, sputter

crackle *n* → **1** interlacement *v* **2** cook

crackling *n* → crackle

CRACKLY *adj* fizzy, snappy, sputtering, sulphury

crackpot *n* → **1** mad person *adj* **2** mad

cradle *n* → **1** basket **2** bath **3** bed **4** beds **5** breeding ground **6** knife **7** platform **8** vessel *v* **9** clean **10** hold

craft *n* → **1** aircraft **2** artistry **3** competence **4** cunning **5** fine arts **6** institute **7** job **8** stratagem **9** trickery **10** watercraft

CRAFTSMAN *n* artisan *(Obs.)*, handicraftsman, mosaicist, technician; **woodworker,** ebonist, woodcraftsman; **sculptor,** carver, modeller, sculptress; **potter,** ceramist; **metalworker,** brazier, goldsmith, silversmith; **jeweller,** lapidary; **enameller,** enamellist; **photographer,** retoucher. *See also* ARTIST; ENGRAVER

crafty *adj* → **1** competent **2** cunning **3** deceitful **4** opportunist

crag *n* → **1** mountain **2** rough

cram *n* → **1** fullness **2** learning *v* **3** fill **4** gorge **5** oversupply **6** study **7** teach

CRAMP *n* charley horse *(U.S.)*, cork knee (leg), coxalgia, sprain, stiffness, stitch, strain, subluxation, tic, writer's cramp; **slipped disc,** spondylitis, spondylolisthesis; **rheumatism,** ankylosis, arthritis, bursitis, gout, housemaid's knee, lumbago, osteoarthritis, podagra, rheumatoid arthritis, synovitis, tennis elbow, tenosynovitis, tophus; **fibrositis,** tenonitis; **repetition strain injury,** carpal tunnel syndrome, repetitive strain injury, RSI

cramp *n* → **1** clip **2** holder **3** press **4** restraints *v* **5** hinder **6** hold **7** imprison **8** restrict

crane *n* → **1** lift *v* **2** extend

cranium *n* → head

crank *n* → **1** figure of speech **2** nonconformist *v* **3** initiate *adj* **4** changeable **5** nonconformist

crankshaft *n* → rod

cranky *adj* → **1** angry **2** irritable **3** nonconformist

cranny *n* → **1** compartment **2** opening

crap *n* → **1** defecation **2** nonsense *v* **3** defecate **4** talk nonsense *interj* **5** God

craps *n* → gambling

crash *n* → **1** defecation **2** explosion **3** failure **4** fall **5** impact **6** loud sound **7** ruin *v* **8** be in debt **9** be loud **10** break **11** collapse **12** collide **13** defecate **14** descend **15** enter **16** explode **17** fail **18** separate **19** sleep *adj* **20** increased

crass *adj* → **1** stupid **2** thick **3** vulgar

crate *n* → **1** box **2** car *v* **3** enclose

crater *n* → **1** hollow **2** moon **3** tableware *v* **4** dig **5** hollow

cravat *n* → neckwear

crave *v* → **1** be jealous of **2** desire **3** entreat **4** necessitate

craven *n* → **1** coward *adj* **2** cowardly

crawl *n* → **1** swimming *v* **2** be meek **3** go slowly

CRAWLER *n* arse-licker, brown-nose, bumboy, creeping Jesus, fawner, flunkey, groveller, lackey, lickspittle *(Brit.)*, spaniel, sponger, sycophant, toady; **doormat,** earthworm, groveller, the muck of the earth, worm

crayon *n* → **1** dye **2** writing materials *v* **3** depict

craze *n* → **1** enthusiasm **2** fashion **3** gap **4** interlacement **5** madness **6** psychic disorder **7** psychic disturbance *v* **8** cross **9** madden

crazy *adj* → **1** excited **2** inappropriate **3** mad **4** nonconformist **5** rash **6** strange

creak *n* → **1** dissonance *v* **2** be dissonant **3** shrill

cream *n* → **1** white **2** yellow *v* **3** agitate **4** beat **5** cook **6** separate *adj* **7** sweet **8** white **9** yellow

creamy *adj* → **1** smooth **2** soft **3** tasty **4** white **5** yellow

crease *n* → **1** fold **2** sword *v* **3** fold **4** furrow **5** hit

CREATE *v* author, bring into being, call into being, compose, conceive, father, form, give rise to; **concoct,** brew, contrive, cook up, make up, throw together; **invent,** coin, compose, extemporise, fabricate, forge, improvise, innovate, mint, originate, toss, turn; **develop,** be responsible for, beat out, bring about, contrive, design, devise, engineer, evolve, excogitate, formulate, frame, incubate, stage, think out, think up; **establish,** constitute, found, inaugurate, institute, institutionalise, open the door to, plant, set up, stablish *(Archaic)*; **breed,** bring forth, engender, generate, germinate, ingenerate *(Archaic)*, procreate; **re-create,** re-form, recast, reconstitute, regenerate. *See also* MAKE

create *v* → **1** cause **2** disorder **3** initiate

CREATION *n* coinage, composition, conception, cross-fertilisation, design, devisal, excogitation, fabrication, generation, genesis, innovation, invention, origin, origination, procreation, production, reproduction; **spontaneous generation,** abiogenesis, autogenesis, autogeny, continuous creation, parthenogenesis; **improvisation,** extemporisation; **establishment,** constitution, engenderment, institution; **re-creation,** destructive distillation, recast, reconstitution, reconstruction, regeneracy, regeneration. *See also* MAKING

creation *n* → **1** finery **2** finished product **3** living **4** matter **5** sky **6** work of art

CREATIVE *adj* excogitive, generative, groundbreaking, innovational, innovative, innovatory, inventive, omnific, original, originative, Promethean; **seminal,** primordial, procreative, productive; **industrial,** factorial, factory-like, handcrafted, handmade; **constructive,** formative, tectonic; **creational,** authorial, conceptional, genetic, institutive, parturient

creative *adj* → new

CREATIVITY *n* creativeness, formativeness, innovation, inventiveness, originality, parturiency, productivity; **workmanship,** craftsmanship, fashion *(Obs.)*, handicraft; **authorship,** creatorship

CREATOR *n* architect, author, authoress, coiner, composer, conceiver, constituter, designer, deviser, engenderer, excogitator, fabricator, framer, generator, hatcher, inventor, original *(Archaic)*, originator, procreator, source; **maker,** artificer, artisan, builder, constituter, constructor, contriver, craftsman, developer, erecter, fabricant, fabricator, former, framer, manufacturer, producer, smith, wright; **innovator,** idea-monger, innovationist, mastermind; **founder,** establisher, father, first cause, fons et origo, fountainhead, institutor, mainspring, mother, parent, prime mover; **improviser,** extemporiser, improvisator

creature *n* → **1** animal **2** person **3** subject

creche *n* → **1** hotel **2** nursery **3** school

credence *n* → **1** belief **2** cupboard **3** shrine

credential *n* → belief

credible *adj* → **1** believable **2** feasible **3** likely

credit *n* → **1** account **2** belief **3** capital **4** debt **5** funds **6** gratefulness **7** reputation *v* **8** account **9** believe

credit card *n* → capital

creditor *n* → lender

credulous *adj* → believing

creed *n* → belief

creek *n* → **1** bay **2** bridge **3** stream

creep *n* → **1** bad person **2** distortion *v* **3** be meek **4** flower

creeper *n* → **1** piercer **2** plant

cremate *v* → fire

crematorium *n* → **1** cemetery **2** fireplace

creole *n* → language

Creole *n* → foreigner

crepe *n* → funeral rites

crescendo *n* → **1** increase **2** loudness *adj* **3** increasing **4** loud

CRESCENT *n* half-moon, lune, lunette, lunula, meniscus, semicircle

crescent *n* → **1** moon **2** percussion instrument *adj* **3** curved **4** growing **5** increasing

crest *n* → **1** animal's coat **2** apex **3** bird part **4** bookbinding **5** bulge **6** courage **7** feather **8** heraldry **9** pride **10** top **11** trimming *v* **12** top

crestfallen *adj* → **1** meek **2** unhappy

cretin *n* → **1** fool **2** stupid person

crevasse *n* → **1** break **2** gap *v* **3** open up **4** separate

crevice *n* → **1** break **2** gap **3** passageway

crew *n* → **1** gathering **2** mariner **3** pilot **4** workers

crew cut *n* → hairdressing

crib *n* → **1** animal dwelling **2** basket **3** cabin **4** cell **5** clarification **6** coating **7** compartment **8** explanation **9** meal **10** restraints **11** robbery **12** room *v* **13** restrain

cribbage *n* → gambling

cricket *n* → fair go

CRIME *n* capital crime, felony, inside job, malfeasance, malversation, misdeed, misprision, racket; **crime wave; extortion,** collusion, collusiveness, fraud, protection racket, solicitation; **infringement,** breach, contravention, dereliction, encroachment, infraction, misdemeanour, offence, transgression, trespass; **wrong,** injury, injustice, offence, tort; **atrocity,** malpractice, outrage, war crime. *See also* UNLAWFULNESS

crime *n* → **1** dishonesty **2** evildoing **3** wrong

CRIMINAL *n* accessory, bandit, bushranger, conman, crim, crook, demon, desperado, felon, gangster, gunnie, hood, hoodlum, outlaw, principal, punk, standover man, torch; **law-breaker,** contravener, encroacher, infractor, malfeasant, offender, trespasser; **convict,** hardnose, incorrigible *(Obs.)*, lag, old chum, old hand, prisoner of the crown, recidivist; **racketeer,** black marketeer, colluder, mobster *(U.S.)*; **Mafia,** Cosa Nostra, crime ring, family *(U.S.)*, Honourable Society; **underworld,** gangland

criminal *n* → **1** prisoner **2** wrongdoer *adj* **3** guilty **4** unlawful **5** wrong

crimp *n* → **1** curl **2** fold *v* **3** beguile **4** cut **5** fold **6** rob **7** twist

crimson *n* → **1** red *v* **2** redden *adj* **3** murderous **4** red

crinkle *n* → **1** fold **2** hiss **3** twist *v* **4** fold **5** hiss **6** twist

crinoline *n* → underwear

cripple *n* → **1** casualty *v* **2** hinder **3** injure

crisis *n* → **1** change **2** crucial moment **3** important thing

crisp *v* → **1** twist *adj* **2** brittle **3** concise **4** energetic **5** twisting

crisscross *n* → **1** interlacement *v* **2** cross *adj* **3** crossed *adv* **4** crosswise

criterion *n* → **1** rule **2** tester

critic *n* → **1** aesthete **2** assessment **3** assessor **4** disapprover **5** essayist **6** interpreter **7** questioner

critical *adj* → **1** assessorial **2** dangerous **3** disapproving **4** discursive **5** important **6** sloping **7** steady **8** timely

criticise *v* → **1** assess **2** disapprove of **3** discourse

criticism *n* → **1** analysis **2** assessment **3** commentary **4** disapproval **5** guidance **6** investigation **7** slander

critique *n* → **1** analysis **2** assessment **3** commentary

croak *n* → **1** birdcall **2** dissonance *v* **3** be dissonant **4** chirp **5** complain **6** die **7** kill **8** speak

crochet *n* → **1** sewing *v* **2** sew

crock *n* → **1** car **2** sheep **3** vessel

crockery *n* → tableware

crocodile *n* → affected person

crocus *n* → **1** powder **2** yellow

crone *n* → **1** old people **2** woman

crony *n* → friend

CROOK *n* adventurer, adventuress, corrupter, dodger, fake, faker, fraud, judas, knave, racketeer, rascal, ratbag, rogue, shark, twister, wangler, wrong 'un; **swindler,** ambidexter *(Archaic)*, bilker, chicaner, double-dealer, front man, pettifogger, sharp dealer, shicer, shyster, twicer; **cheat,** blackleg, cardsharper, cheater, gypper, gypster, kite, palmer, rook, sharp, sharper, short-changer, spieler; **self-seeker,** company politician, sycophant; **corrupt official,** bent cop, dishonest politician, jobber, security risk

crook *n* → **1** criminal **2** curve *v* **3** curve *adj* **4** bad **5** difficult **6** ill

crooked *adj* → **1** bent **2** curved **3** disfigured **4** dishonest **5** distorted **6** thieving **7** ugly **8** unlawful

croon *n* → **1** cry **2** quiet sound *v* **3** grieve **4** sing

crop *n* → **1** accumulation **2** bag **3** cut **4** finished product **5** hairdressing **6** hide **7** label **8** propellant *v* **9** be fertile **10** cut **11** harvest **12** shorten **13** smooth **14** take

cropper *n* → **1** failure **2** fall **3** farmer **4** smoother

croquet *n* → impact

CROSS *n* ankh, crosslet *(Heraldry)*, crux ansata, flyfot, swastika, tau cross, tee; **crucifix,** Celtic cross, Greek cross, Holy Rood, Jerusalem cross, Maltese cross, papal cross, Saint Andrew's Cross, Saint George's Cross, Saint Patrick's Cross, tree *(Eccles. Archaic)*; **decussation,** chiasm, chiasma, X-shape

CROSS *v* cross, cut, decussate, gauntlet *(Railways)*, intersect, overlap, traverse; **crisscross,** craze; **bestraddle,** bestride, overstride

crossbones *n* → death

CROSSED *adj* crisscross, cross-grained, cross-legged; **netlike,** arachnoid, clathrate, crazed, cross-grained, mesh, meshy, net, reticulate

cross-examine *v* → question

cross-fire *n* → discussion

CROSSING *n* intersection, junction, overlapping

CROSSING *adj* equitant, overlapping; **intersectional,** secant; **transversal,** athwart, cross, jessant *(Heraldry)*, thwart, transverse, traverse; **cruciform,** chiasmal, chiasmic, crucial, cruciate, decussate, tee-shaped, X-shaped

crossing *n* → **1** argument **2** conception **3** obstructiveness **4** stocks and shares

CROSSPIECE *n* buttock line *(Naut.)*, crossbar, crossbeam, crosstree, thwart, transversal, transverse, traverse

cross-reference *n* → written composition

cross-section *n* → **1** cut **2** diagram **3** part *v* **4** cut

CROSSWAY *n* circus *(Brit.)*, cross-street, crossroad, level crossing, roundabout, traffic circle

CROSSWISE *adv* crisscross, fesswise *(Heraldry)*; **transversally,** on the cross, transversely, traverse *(Obs.)*; **cruciformly,** crucially, decussately

crotch *n* → **1** branch **2** groin

crotchet *n* → **1** curve **2** image

crotchety *adj* → **1** curved **2** irritable

crouch *v* → **1** lower **2** repose

croup *n* → breathing

croupier *n* → **1** gambler **2** helper

crow *n* → **1** black **2** farmhand **3** machine *v* **4** be loud **5** brag **6** chirp **7** rejoice **8** shout

crowbar *n* → **1** bar **2** machine

CROWD *n* army, cohort, galaxy, host; **band,** caravan, choir, chorus, company, consort *(Obs.)*, flock *(Rare)*, rout *(Archaic)*, squad, tribe, troop *(Rare)*, troupe; **corps,** body, brigade, phalanx, regiment; **meeting,** assembly, jamboree, mass meeting, muster, parade, rally, unlawful assembly; **congregation,** communion, ecclesia, parish council, vestry; **reception,** audience, durbar, levee

crowd *n* → **1** clique **2** gathering **3** many **4** working class *v* **5** abound **6** advance **7** fill **8** gather **9** thrust

CROWDED *adj* mobbish, multitudinous *(Poetic)*, serried, thronged; **congregational,** colonial, convocational

crown *n* → **1** apex **2** authority **3** bird part **4** emblem of office **5** head **6** headgear **7** jewellery **8** medication **9** ring **10** stem **11** top *v* **12** accomplish **13** authorise **14** employ **15** hit **16** top **17** tower

crucial *adj* → **1** crossing **2** difficult **3** essential **4** necessary **5** timely

CRUCIAL MOMENT *n* appropriate moment, climacteric, crisis, high time, moment of truth, one's hour, psychological moment, the fullness of time, tide *(Archaic)*, turning point, watershed; **deadline,** crunch *(Colloq.)*, crux, eleventh hour, last minute, term day; **time,** day, hour, minute, moment, opportunity, turn

crucible *n* → test

crucifix *n* → cross

crucify *v* → **1** execute **2** pain

crude *adj* → **1** discourteous **2** raw **3** ugly **4** vulgar

cruel *v* → **1** spoil *adj* **2** callous **3** painful **4** strict **5** unkind

cruet *n* → head

cruise *v* → **1** move **2** set sail

cruiser *n* → **1** alcohol container **2** beer **3** drinking vessel **4** motor vessel **5** watercraft

crumb *n* → **1** part **2** small amount *v* **3** cook

crumble *v* → **1** be old **2** powder **3** separate **4** wane

crummy *adj* → bad

crumpet *n* → **1** head **2** sex object

crumple *n* → **1** fold *v* **2** collapse **3** contract **4** fold **5** furrow

crunch *n* → **1** click **2** crucial moment **3** ruin *v* **4** click **5** powder

crusade *n* → **1** act of war **2** electioneering **3** undertaking **4** war *v* **5** electioneer **6** militarise

crush *n* → **1** drink **2** extract **3** gathering **4** love **5** path **6** pen **7** press *v* **8** break **9** contract **10** extract **11** humble **12** powder **13** press **14** repress

crust *n* → **1** covering **2** discourtesy **3** glaze **4** income **5** land **6** outside **7** remnant *v* **8** accuse **9** harden

crusty *adj* → **1** brittle **2** discourteous **3** irritable **4** layered **5** outside **6** skin

crutch *n* → **1** branch **2** help **3** medication **4** stand **5** stick **6** support *v* **7** shear **8** support

crux *n* → **1** crucial moment **2** difficulty **3** essence

CRY *n* bawl, blubber, boohoo, howl, snivel, sob, wail, weep, whimper, whine; **keen,** croon *(Scot. Irish)*, ululation; **groan,** sigh

cry *n* → **1** act of war **2** animal call **3** hunter **4** public notice **5** shout **6** shouting **7** word *v* **8** be unhappy **9** call (of animals) **10** grieve

crypt *n* → **1** church **2** grave **3** indentation **4** room

cryptic *adj* → **1** hidden **2** imprecise **3** supernatural **4** uncertain **5** unclear

crystal *n* → **1** chemical agent **2** covering **3** electrical device **4** fortune-telling **5** matter **6** solid **7** sound system **8** telecommunications station **9** transparent substance *adj* **10** bright **11** transparent

crystallise *v* → **1** cook **2** harden **3** materialise **4** take shape

cub *n* → **1** adolescent **2** animal offspring **3** incompetent **4** man

cube *n* → **1** bit **2** number **3** solid *v* **4** compute **5** measure

cubicle *n* → **1** bedroom **2** room

cuckold *v* → have sex

cuckoo *n* → **1** birdcall **2** fool **3** foreigner **4** stupid person *v* **5** chirp **6** repeat *adj* **7** foolish **8** mad

cuddle *n* → **1** endearments **2** hold *v* **3** hold **4** kiss **5** love

CUDGEL *v* baste, bastinado, drub, fustigate *(Archaic)*, pistol-whip; **bludgeon,** blackjack, club, cosh, sledge, sledge-hammer, truncheon, waddy; **belt,** cane, ferule, pandy *(Scot.)*, strap, welt; **whip,** birch, breech *(Archaic)*, cat, cowhide *(U.S.)*, cut, flagellate, flail, flog, horse *(Obs.)*, horsewhip, knout, lash, leather, scourge, scratch, see (someone's) backbone, slash, swinge *(Archaic)*, swish, switch, taw *(Obs.)*, thresh; **pelt,** catapult, lapidate, pebble, pellet, pip. *See also* HIT; BEAT

cudgel *n* → club

cue *n* → **1** character **2** hair **3** reminder **4** signal **5** stick *v* **6** gesture **7** remind

cuff *n* → **1** corporal punishment **2** fold **3** glove **4** hit *v* **5** hit

cuisine *n* → **1** cookery **2** kitchen

cul-de-sac *n* → **1** finish **2** hindrance **3** road

cull *n* → **1** choice *v* **2** exclude **3** separate **4** take

culminate *v* → **1** accomplish **2** ascend **3** top

culottes *n* → dress

cult *n* → **1** clique **2** fashion

CULTISM *n* cargo cult, dendrolatry, divinisation, druidism, fertility cult, fetishism, firewalking, heliolatry, hero-worship *(Antiq.)*, idolism, Magianism, paganism, phallicism, ritualism, shamanism, sun-dance, sun-worship; **Satanism,** black mass, demonism, demonolatry, diabolism; **snake-worship,** ophiolatry, zombiism; **zoolatry,** animal worship; **Rastafarianism**

cultivate *v* → **1** be sociable **2** farm **3** flower **4** help **5** improve **6** study **7** teach **8** welcome

CULTIVATED *adj* a cut above, appreciative, Attic, cultured, discriminating, educated, fine, polished, polite, refined, seemly, well-bred; **aesthetic,** aesthetical, delicate, exquisite, pretty *(Archaic)*, rarefactive, sensitive

culture *n* → **1** custom **2** discrimination **3** farming **4** finished product **5** good taste **6** learning **7** organism **8** period

cultured *adj* → **1** cultivated **2** discriminating **3** educated

culvert *n* → drain

cumbersome *adj* → **1** difficult **2** heavy **3** hindering

cumulative *adj* → **1** accumulative **2** growing **3** increasing

cumulus *n* → **1** accumulation **2** cloud

cuneiform *n* → letter

cunnilingus *n* → sexual intercourse

CUNNING *n* art, artifice, chicanery, craft, double-dealing, finesse, gimmickry, guile, guilefulness, hanky-panky, Jesuitism, Jesuitry, Machiavellianism, Machiavellism, nimbleness, sharp practice, subtleness, subtlety, supersubtlety, trickery; **machination,** engineering, enginery, insinuation, manipulation, politicking; **politics,** fancy footwork, intrigue, manoeuvring, strategy; **craftiness,** archness, cleverness, deviousness, diabolicalness, insidiousness, shiftiness, slyness, trickiness, trickishness, tricksiness, wiliness, wryness; **astuteness,** cuteness, knowingness, sharpness, shrewdness

CUNNING *adj* calculating, diabolic, diabolical, guileful, insidious, insinuative, Machiavellian, mephistophelian, subtle, supersubtle, wily; **crafty,** artful, artificial *(Obs.)*, carney, clever, cute, daedal *(Poetic)*, deep, deep-laid, devious, dodgy, hard-headed, Jesuitical, nimble, serpentine, slim *(Obs.)*, smart, wry; **astute,** all there, fly *(Colloq.)*, foxy, sharp, shrewd; **underhand,** arch, leery, shifty, sleeky, slick, sly, spivvy, weaselly; **trick,** catchy, gimmicky, rorty, trickish, tricksy, tricky; **diversionary,** distracting, feinting; **politic,** manipulative, strategic

cunning *n* → **1** competence **2** opportunism **3** trickery *adj* **4** competent **5** opportunist

CUNNING PERSON *n* artful dodger, bag of tricks, dodger, Jesuit, shrewdie, wangler; **con man,** bluffer, con woman, entrapper, faker, fraud, rorter, spiv; **machinator,** carpetbagger *(U.S.)*, downy bird, insinuator, political animal, shaver; **fox,** duckshover, finagler, gamesman, serpent, slyboots, trepan *(Archaic)*, trepanner, tricker, trickster, weasel; **cheat,** cardsharp, double-dealer, sharper; **intriguer,** plotter, politician, schemer

cup *n* → **1** contest **2** drinking vessel **3** hollow **4** medication **5** underwear

CUPBOARD *n* almery *(Archaic)*, ambry *(Archaic)*, armoire, base unit, bookcase, cabinet, cellaret, chiffonier, china cabinet, closet, cocktail cabinet, corner cabinet, display unit, filing cabinet, glory hole, hutch, kitchen cupboard, larder, linen closet, linen cupboard, locker, medicine cabinet, pantry, press, safe, wall unit, Welsh dresser; **sideboard,** buffet, credence, credenza, dresser; **wardrobe,** built-in wardrobe, clothes cupboard, clothes press, garderrobe *(Archaic)*, lowboy, robe, tallboy, walk-in wardrobe; **chest of drawers,** chiffonier, dressing-table, glory box, hope chest

cupboard *n* → **1** container **2** shelf

cupidity *n* → **1** desire **2** greed

cupola *n* → **1** arch **2** heater **3** roof **4** tower

cur *n* → bad person

curate *n* → **1** ecclesiastic **2** religious dignitary

curative *n* → **1** medication *adj* **2** medicinal

curator *n* → **1** conservationist **2** manager **3** protector

curb *n* → **1** controlling device **2** restraints *v* **3** control **4** restrain

curd *n* → **1** solid body *v* **2** solidify

curdle *v* → solidify

curé *n* → ecclesiastic

cure *n* → **1** medication **2** recovery *v* **3** conserve **4** heat **5** medicate **6** practise medicine

curette *v* → medicate

curfew *n* → **1** evening **2** restraint **3** timepiece **4** warning

curio *n* → morbid curiosity

CURIOSITY *n* curiousness, inquisitiveness, nosiness

CURIOUS *adj* agog, inquiring, questioning; **inquisitive,** nosy, prying, rubberneck

curious *adj* → **1** attentive **2** competent **3** complex **4** intervenient **5** obscene **6** questioning

CURL *n* braid, crimp, crimps, frizz, frizzle, ringlet; **permanent wave,** cold wave, marcel; **curler,** braider, crimper, crisper, frizzler

curl *n* → **1** curvature **2** hair **3** spiral **4** twist *v* **5** curve **6** react **7** twist

CURRENCY *n* exchange, floating currency, foreign currency, foreign exchange, forward exchange, fractional currency, managed currency; **standard,** bimetallism, gold bullion standard, gold standard, gold-exchange standard, monometallism, silver standard, symmetallism; **sterling,** decimal currency, Eurodollars, gold reserve, petrodollars; **mintage,** monetisation. *See also* CASH; COINAGE

currency *n* → **1** cash **2** temporariness *adj* **3** resident

CURRENT *n* backwash, bombora, countercurrent, cross-current, drift, ebb and flow, flood, flux, overfall, rip, tidal current, tide-rip, underset, undertow; **tide,** dodge tide, ebb tide, flood tide, half-tide, high tide, lee tide, low tide, low water, neap, neap tide, rip-tide, spring tide; **flash flood,** eustatic movement, freshet, stormwater, tidal wave; **surge,** disemboguement, ground swell, surf, wash; **race,** millrace, millrun, tide-race, tideway; **eddy,** maelstrom, vortex, whirlpool. *See also* FLOW; STREAM; SPRING

CURRENT *adj* live *(Broadcasting)*, now happening, passing, present, running; **immediate,** instant, latest; **existing,** actual; **contemporary,** current, living, modern-day, present-day, rife; **modern,** in fashion, up-to-date, up-to-the-minute, up-to-the-moment, with-it

current *n* → **1** airflow **2** direction **3** point of view **4** wind *adj* **5** current **6** general **7** innovative **8** real **9** revealed

curriculum *n* → course

CURRIER *n* fellmonger, flesher, skinner

CURRIERY *n* skinnery, tannery

curry *v* → **1** beat **2** clean **3** cook **4** prepare

curse *n* → **1** misfortune **2** swearing *v* **3** swear

CURSED *adj* accursed, b., bally, blamed *(U.S.)*, blank *(euph.)*, blankety, blasted, bleeding, bloody, blooming *(euph.)*, buggered, confounded, cussed, damned, darned, doggone *(U.S.)*, dratted, f'ing, flaming, frigging, fucking, plurry

cursive *n* → writing

cursory *adj* → **1** impermanent **2** inattentive **3** smallest

curt *adj* → discourteous

curtail *v* → **1** cut **2** shorten **3** subtract

curtain *n* → **1** finish **2** manchester **3** stage **4** wall *v* **5** hide

curtsy *n* → **1** courtesy **2** pose **3** tribute *v* **4** bow **5** lower **6** repose

CURVATURE *n* arcuation, bent, concaveness, concavity, convexity, convexness, curvedness, spiling; **curling,** assurgency, curl, flexure, incurvation, incurvature, resupination, retroflexion; **waviness,** damascene, damask, sinuosity

curvature *n* → hollow

CURVATURE OF THE SPINE *n* crouchback *(Archaic)*, gibbousness, hunchback, kyphosis, roach back, scoliosis, stoop, sway-back

CURVE *n* arc, bow, camber, crispation, roll, scallop, sinus, undulation, wave; **arithmetic curve,** cardioid, catenary, cissoid, conchoid, conic section, cycloid, envelope *(Geom.)*, epicycloid, folium, geodesic line, gradient *(Physics)*, hyperbola, hypocycloid, locus, parabola, quadrant, rhumb, segment, sine wave, sinusoid, synergic curve, trajectory, trochoid; **caustic,** catacaustic, diacaustic; **figure 8,** lemniscate; **bend,** bight, flexure, gooseneck, heel *(Golf)*, inflection, inturn, offset, ogee, quirk, S-bend, sheer, sigmoid flexure, swan neck, turn, twist; **loop,** hank, picot; **horseshoe,** U-bolt; **hook,** crook, crotchet, falx, fleshhook, sickle, uncinus, uncus

CURVE *v* arch, bend, bow, camber, curl, flex, hog, incurve, loop, overarch, sag, stoop, sweep, turn; **recurve,** retroflect; **hook,** crook, incurvate; **wave,** scallop, undulate

curve *n* → line

CURVED *adj* bent, bow, bowed, bowlike, cambered, incurvate, loopy, saddle-backed, sigmoid; **U-shaped,** horseshoe; **hooked,** crooked, crotchety, falcate, falciform, hamate, hooky, quirky, scorpioid, unciform, uncinate; **convex,** biconcave, biconvex, concave, lenticular; **crescent,** horned, lunar, lunarian, lunate, lunular, lunulate, meniscoid, semilunar; **heart-shaped,** bell-shaped, cordate, flabellate, pear-shaped; **semicircular,** hemicyclic, semielliptical

CURVEDLY *adv* fully, wavily; **convexly,** archwise, concavely

CURVILINEAR *adj* conchoidal, epicycloidal, hypocycloidal; **geodesic,** caustic, geodetic, toric, toroidal; **wavy,** damascene, gyrose, repand, undulative, undulatory, wavelike; **parabolic,** catenarian, catenary, hyperbolic, paraboloidal, sinusoidal, trochoidal; **blunt,** lobate, obtuse; **recurvate,** assurgent, resupinate, retroflex, retroussé, revolute, tip-tilted, turned up

cushion *n* → **1** frame **2** moderator **3** wall *v* **4** cover **5** ease **6** hide **7** moderate **8** soften **9** support

cusp *n* → **1** bulge **2** fortune-telling **3** join **4** point of convergence **5** sharp point

custodian *n* → protector

custody *n* → **1** imprisonment **2** protection **3** restraint

CUSTOM *n* common practice, constitution, consuetude, convention, established custom, habit, habitude, institute, institution, matter of course, practice, praxis, second nature, usage, usance *(Obs.)*, usual practice, wont; **routine,** beaten track, daily grind, daily round, groove, rut, the ordinary, the usual; **protocol,** etiquette, good form, manners, the done thing; **mores,** the conventionalities, the proprieties, ways; **tradition,** culture, culture complex *(Sociol.)*, folklore, folkways, survival, unwritten law, way of our forebears; **procedure,** manner, mode, way, way of doing things; **ceremony,** ceremonial, observance, rite, rite of passage, ritual

custom *n* → **1** behaviour **2** buyer **3** conformist behaviour **4** method **5** rule **6** tax

CUSTOMARILY *adv* as a rule, generally, in general, ordinarily, regularly, usually; **habitually,** by force of habit, by habit, inveterately, wontedly; **as usual,** according to habit, as can be expected

CUSTOMARY *adj* accustomed, consuetudinary, habitual, habitudinal, usual, wonted *(Archaic)*; **traditional,** accepted, conventional, time-honoured, traditive; **approved,** de rigueur, established, recognised, settled; **regular,** common, commonplace, general, normal, ordinary, stock; **stereotyped,** clichéd, hackneyed, trite, unoriginal; **rooted in tradition,** folkloristic, passed on by word of mouth, unwritten

customary *adj* → conventional

customer *n* → **1** buyer **2** person

custom-made *adj* → **1** made **2** particular

customs duties *n* → tax

CUT *n* gash, incision, kerf, laceration, lancination, score, scotch, slash, slit, snick, snip, stab, tear; **notch,** box, chip, cleft, crenature, crop, dap, gain, hack, incisure, indent, indentation, nock, undercut; **scarification,** chatter marks, graze, scoring; **cross-section,** crosscut, exsection, microtomy, section, transection; **haircut,** Dad'n'Dave, shave; **shear,** long blow, second cut

CUT *v* bite into, chine, gash, gride, heckle, knife, lance, prick, scissor, scotch, shear *(Archaic)*, slit, snip, tool, trench *(Obs.)*, vivisect; **sliver,** dice, flitch, hash, mince, ribbon; **axe,** adze, chip, chop, swing kelly, tomahawk; **fell,** clear-cut, clear-fell, coppice, hew, knock down *(N.Z.)*, log, poll, pollard; **scratch,** carbonado, claw, crimp, graze, hack, hackle, overscore, raze *(Obs.)*, scarify, score, scribe; **ringbark,** girdle; **notch,** blaze, chase, crenel, crenellate, gain, indent, jag, nick, nock, pink, serrate, snick, trench, undercut; **slice,** cross-section, crosscut, section, skive, thickness, transect; **saw,** break down, crosscut, lumber, quartersaw, rip, stave, whipsaw; **carve,** chisel, engrave, etch, gouge, grave *(Archaic)*, incise, rough-hew, whittle; **thread,** die, rifle, tap; **mutilate,** give someone a facial, grangerise, lacerate, mangle, rip, slash; **barber,** cut, poll, scalp, shingle; **mow,** head, make hay, reap, scythe; **shear,** barrow, channel, dag, razor, shave, undress; **clip,** abscind, bang, bobtail, crop, curtail, cut short, disbranch, guillotine, hog, pinch, poll, prune, sever, trim; **whittle,** edge, snig; **cut out,** excide, excise, exscind, exsect; **bevel,** cant, chamfer, countersink, facet, rake; **circumcise,** decerebrate, resect; **behead,** decapitate

CUT *adj* cleft, cloven, incised; **clipped,** trimmed; **diced,** brunoise, fine-cut, julienne; **carved,** carven *(Poetic)*, chiselled, engraved, graven, step-cut, table-cut; **clear-cut,** clear-felled

cut *n* → **1** bit **2** break **3** capital punishment **4** change **5** character **6** cost **7** decrease **8** exclusion **9** fashion **10** furrow **11** gap **12** hairdressing **13** hit **14** part **15** recording **16** repulsion **17** share **18** stroke *v* **19** abstain **20** act unkindly **21** cross **22** cudgel **23** cut **24** decrease **25** deflect **26** depart **27** dig **28** displease **29** do **30** engrave **31** escape **32** exclude **33** harvest **34** interrupt **35** level **36** medicate **37** repel **38** separate **39** shape **40** shear **41** shorten **42** stop **43** subtract *adj* **44** decorative **45** decreased **46** drunk **47** mixed **48** separate

cute *adj* → **1** cunning **2** pleasant

cuticle *n* → skin

cutlass *n* → sword

CUT OFF *v* amputate, decapitate, dehorn, head, mutilate, pinion, poll, tail; **disembowel,** eviscerate, exenterate, gut; **epilate,** depilate, shave; **sterilise,** alter, castrate, de-sex, deknacker, do, doctor, emasculate, geld, mark, spay, unman. *See also* SUBTRACT

CUTTER *n* cheese-cutter, cigar-cutter, glass-cutter, guillotine, microtome; **cutting machine,** burr, capstan lathe, chaser, chipper, decapitator, dicer, die, lathe, machine tool, milling machine, mincer, scarificator, scarifier, scorer, skiver, tap; **mower,** header, lawn-mower, mowing machine, reaper, reaping machine, slasher. *See also* AXE; KNIFE; SAW; SCISSORS; CHISEL

cutter *n* → **1** sailing ship **2** watercraft

cutthroat *n* → **1** killer **2** knife *adj* **3** murderous **4** unkind

CUTTING *n* bushing, clipping, mowing, pruning, rod pruning, xylotomy; **severance,** curtailment, decapitation, decerebration, dissection, disseverance, disseveration, disseverment; **carving,** engraving, rifling, tapping, trepanation, turnery, whittling; **surgery,** abscission, amputation, circumcision, excision, microsurgery, necrotomy, nephrotomy, vivisection; **timber-getting,** bush bashing, bush-falling, clear-felling, logging, lumbering

CUTTING *adj* slashing; **jagged,** jaggy, lacerate, lacerated, laciniate, retuse; **scissile,** cleavable, dissectible, fellable, lacerable, sectile, severable

cutting *n* → **1** excavation **2** remnant *adj* **3** sharp **4** strict **5** unkind

CUTTINGLY *adv* incisively, keenly, sharply

cyanide *n* → **1** means of killing *v* **2** poison

cyclamate *n* → sweetness

cycle *n* → **1** bicycle **2** musical piece **3** operation **4** period **5** rotation **6** sequence **7** story **8** whole *v* **9** alternate **10** drive

cyclone *n* → **1** atmospheric pressure **2** spin **3** violent outburst **4** wind

cygnet *n* → animal offspring

cylinder *n* → **1** bottle **2** press **3** solid

cynic *n* → **1** disapprover **2** mocker *adj* **3** disdainful

cynosure *n* → **1** allure **2** eye-catcher

cypher *n* → language

cypress *n* → timber

cyst *n* → **1** bag **2** bladder **3** bulge **4** disfigurement

czar *n* → ruler

Dd

dab *n* → 1 bit 2 contact 3 expert 4 pat 5 small amount *v* 6 contact 7 hit

dabble *v* → 1 amuse oneself 2 bungle 3 wet

dad *n* → parent

daddy-long-legs *n* → insect

daffodil *n* → yellow

daft *adj* → 1 foolish 2 mad

dag *n* → 1 animal's coat 2 conformer 3 dirt 4 dirty person 5 fool 6 humorist 7 nonconformist 8 untidy person *v* 9 clean 10 cut 11 flatter 12 shear

dagger *n* → 1 knife 2 separator 3 shearer 4 sword *v* 5 mark

dago *n* → foreigner

DAILY *adj* diurnal, quotidian; **dawn,** auroral; **morning,** antemeridian, breakfast-time, forenoon, matin, matutinal, midmorning; **midday,** lunchtime, meridian, noonday; **afternoon,** postmeridian

DAILY *adv* all day, diurnally, morning noon and night, overday; **a.m.,** ante meridiem; **p.m.,** post meridiem

daily *n* → 1 cleaner 2 newspaper 3 servant

dainty *n* → 1 food *adj* 2 beautiful 3 delicious 4 small

dairy *n* → 1 farm 2 kitchen 3 shop

dais *n* → platform

daisy *n* → 1 good thing 2 plant *adj* 3 good

dale *n* → 1 gap 2 hollow

dally *v* → 1 amuse oneself 2 belittle 3 flirt 4 go slowly 5 idle

DAM *n* conduit, floodgate, gate, levee, lock, lock-gate, penstock, retaining wall, revetment, sluice, sluicegate, spillway, tide-gate, water-gate, weir

dam *n* → 1 lake 2 obstacle *v* 3 obstruct

DAMAGE *n* defacement, disablement, disfeaturement, disfigurement, ill-treatment, molestation; **wounding,** concision, forging *(Horseracing),* maiming, mutilation; **wreckage,** arson, breakage, ruination, sabotage, vandalism, wreck; **wear,** wear and tear; **disrepair,** brokenness, disruption, rack and ruin, ruin, ruination, unsoundness; **shabbiness,** dilapidation, raggedness, seediness, worminess, wornness. *See also* HARM; INJURY

DAMAGE *v* annoy, damnify, grangerise, hack, ill-treat, ill-use, impair, mar, pinch, play hell with, play the devil with, prejudice, scathe *(Archaic),* vandalise, vex *(Archaic),* wrong; **devastate,** eat, ravage, smite; **undermine,** put the skids under, sabotage, white-ant. *See also* INJURE; BREAK; SPOIL

damage *n* → 1 cost 2 harm

DAMAGED *adj* broken, buggered, bung, bust, busted, cactus, clapped-out, cracked, defective, disrupt, disserviceable, foxy, fucked, impaired, in dock, kaput, no good to Gundy, on the blink, on the fritz, on the skids, on the turn, out of joint, out of order, pakaru *(N.Z.),* R.S., ratshit, ruined, worn-out; **unsound,** affected, sick, stricken, unhealthy. *See also* INJURED; DILAPIDATED

damask *n* → 1 covering 2 curvature *v* 3 sew *adj* 4 red

dame *n* → 1 actor 2 aristocrat 3 Ms 4 old people 5 ruler 6 teacher 7 woman

damn *v* → 1 disapprove of 2 punish 3 slander 4 swear *interj* 5 God

damp *n* → 1 discourager 2 gas 3 hindrance 4 poison 5 unhappiness 6 wetness *v* 7 control 8 decrease 9 discourage 10 hinder 11 quieten 12 wet *adj* 13 unhappy 14 wet

damper *n* → 1 controlling device 2 discourager 3 hinderer 4 moderator 5 quietener 6 sobersides

damsel *n* → 1 adolescent 2 woman

DANCE *n* ball, fandango, formal, knees-up, prom *(U.S.),* ridotto; **barn-dance,** b. and s., country dance, hoedown, hop, moondance, square dance, woolshed hop; **breakdance,** rapdance; **routine,** phrase, set

DANCE *v* cut a rug *(U.S. Colloq.),* dance the night away, frisk, have a bop, hoof it, hop, jig, prance, shuffle, tread, trip, trip the light fantastic; **jive,** bop, bump and grind, frug, jazz, jitterbug, rock, shimmy, stomp, twist; **foxtrot,** cakewalk, dosido, mambo, polka, square-dance, tango, twostep, waltz; **pirouette,** balance, chassé, glissade, promenade, set; **breakdance,** break, rapdance, rap; **choreograph**

dance *n* → 1 party *v* 2 be punished 3 jump

DANCE HALL *n* ballroom, disco, discotheque, palais de danse

DANCER *n* belly dancer, breakdancer, frisker, glider, go-go girl, hoofer *(U.S.),* jitterbug, prancer, rapdancer, rope-dancer, shuffler, square-dancer, stripper, tangoist, tap-dancer, terpsichorean, wiredancer; **ballet-dancer,** ballerina, corps de ballet, coryphée, danseur, danseuse, figurant, figurante; **partner,** gigolo, taxi dancer *(U.S.)*; **choreographer,** choreologist, dance arranger

DANCING *n* ballet, ballroom dancing, belly dancing, breaking, breakdancing, disco dancing, eurhythmics, exhibition dancing, flamenco, jazz dance, light fantastic, modern dance, nautch *(India),* rapdancing, rapping, street dancing, tap dancing, wiredancing; **folk dancing,** bush dancing, clogdancing, morris dancing, square dancing; **caper,** frisk, gambol, leap, saltation, skip; **choreography,** choreology

dandruff *n* → dirt

dandy *n* → **1** affected person **2** fashionable person **3** good thing **4** man **5** sailing ship *adj* **6** affected **7** fashionable **8** good

DANGER *n* a matter of life and death, jeopardy, peril; **risk,** adventure *(Obs.)*, chance, venture *(Archaic)*; **threat,** dynamite, menace, shadow, sword of Damocles; **hazard,** a trap for young players, awkwardness, hot seat, hot spot, pit, pitfall, predicament, three-day night; **trap,** black spot *(Brit.)*, deathtrap, fire hazard, fire risk, firetrap, snorter, vigia; **minefield,** no-man's-land

danger *n* → power

DANGEROUS *adj* critical, forbidding, parlous, perilous, precarious, touch-and-go, unhealthy, unsafe; **risky,** awkward, chancy, dicey, equilibristic, hard-hat, hazardous, kittle *(Brit.)*, touchy, tropical *(Colloq.)*, unreliable, venturesome; **ominous,** imminent, malignant, menacing, serious, threatening; **suicidal,** breakneck, desperate, Kamikaze

DANGEROUSNESS *n* chanciness, criticalness, desperateness, forbiddingness, imperilment, ominousness, perilousness, precariousness, seriousness, venturesomeness; **endangerment,** imperilment, obnoxiousness; **weak spot,** Achilles heel, chink in one's armour, hazardousness, incertitude, insecurity, soft underbelly

dangle *n* → **1** hanging **2** pendant *v* **3** accompany **4** display **5** hang **6** kill

dank *adj* → wet

dapper *adj* → **1** busy **2** fashionable **3** small **4** tasteful

dare *n* → **1** challenge *v* **2** brave **3** oppose **4** risk

daredevil *n* → **1** good person **2** hero **3** hothead *adj* **4** rash

daring *n* → **1** courage *adj* **2** courageous **3** obscene

DARK *n* moonset, night, the dead of night; **nightfall,** crepuscule, dusk, evening, gloaming, half-light, sundown, sunset, twilight; **eclipse,** annular eclipse, lunar eclipse, solar eclipse, total eclipse; **blackout,** brownout, dim-out *(U.S.)*, lights out, outage

DARK *adj* aphotic, benighted, cimmerian, darkling *(Poetic)*, darksome *(Poetic)*, lightless, midnight, obscurant, obscure, pitch-dark, rayless, starless, stygian, thick; **dark-coloured,** black, blackish, dusky, grey, infuscate *(Entomol.)*, pitchy, sable *(Poetic)*, sooty, swart, swarthy; **ecliptic,** blackout, blinding, ecliptical, opaque, umbral. *See also* SHADOWY

dark *n* → **1** evening **2** secrecy *v* **3** darken *adj* **4** black **5** distressing **6** hidden **7** ignorant **8** immoral **9** reticent **10** silent **11** unclear

DARKEN *v* blacken, dark *(Obs.)*, embrown, opaque; **become dark,** darkle, dim, dusk, fade, fog, grow dark, lour; **obscure,** adumbrate, becloud, blind, blot, cloud, cover, eclipse, obfuscate, overcast, overcloud, overshade, overshadow; **black out,** brown out, turn down the lights, turn out the lights; **shade,** crosshatch, hatch, shadow, silhouette

DARKENER *n* blackener, dimmer, eclipser, fader, opaque; **blind,** blinder, holland blind, jalousie, shade, venetian, venetian blind; **sunglasses,** dark glasses, polaroids, shades

DARKENING *n* obfuscation, obscuration, occultation, overshadowing, shadowing; **shading,** chiaroscuro *(Painting)*, crosshatching, hatching

dark horse *n* → **1** competitor **2** surpriser **3** unknown

DARKLY *adv* blackly, greyly; **in the dark,** darkling *(Poetic)*, in the shadows; **ecliptically,** blindingly; **dimly,** duskily; **murkily,** cloudily, foggily, loweringly, smokily; **obscurely,** opaquely

darkroom *n* → room

darling *n* → **1** friend **2** lover *adj* **3** approved **4** beloved

darn *n* → **1** repair *v* **2** repair **3** sew **4** swear *interj* **5** God

dart *n* → **1** clothes **2** plan **3** rate **4** spear **5** tobacco *v* **6** speed **7** throw

dash *n* → **1** artistry **2** caprice **3** discourager **4** hindrance **5** line **6** race **7** small amount **8** splash **9** sprightliness **10** vitality **11** wetting *v* **12** hinder **13** hit **14** humble **15** hurry **16** make unhappy **17** mix **18** separate **19** throw **20** wet *interj* **21** God

dashing *adj* → **1** busy **2** capricious **3** fashionable **4** spectacular

dastard *n* → **1** bad person **2** coward *adj* **3** cowardly

data *n* → **1** authentication **2** information

database *n* → information

date *n* → **1** assignation **2** buttocks **3** groin **4** love affair **5** time *v* **6** arrange **7** be sociable **8** flirt **9** time

datum *n* → information

daub *n* → **1** paint *v* **2** coat **3** depict **4** dirty

daughter *n* → **1** child **2** offspring

daughter-in-law *n* → child

daunt *v* → **1** discourage **2** frighten

dawdle *v* → **1** bungle **2** go slowly **3** idle

dawn *n* → **1** light **2** morning **3** start *v* **4** start *adj* **5** daily

day *n* → **1** crucial moment **2** light **3** period

daybreak *n* → **1** light **2** morning

daydream *n* → **1** delusion **2** dream *v* **3** be inattentive **4** delude oneself **5** fantasise

DAYDREAMER *n* doodler, stargazer, woolgatherer

daze *n* → **1** confusion **2** unconsciousness *v* **3** anaesthetise **4** confuse

dazzle *n* → **1** blindness **2** brightness **3** reputability *v* **4** astonish **5** blind **6** command respect **7** confuse

deacon *n* → preacher

DEAD *adj* breathless *(Archaic)*, cold, dead as a dodo, dead as a doornail, deceased, defunct, departed, done for, exanimate, fallen, gone, inanimate, lifeless, no more, parted *(Archaic)*, stillborn, stone-cold, stone-dead; **deceased,** lamented, late, mourned, regretted, sainted; **asleep,** at rest; **mortal,** ephemeral, perishable, short-lived, transitory; **doomed,** condemned to death, done for, fey; **dying,** far gone, moribund, sick unto death; **drowned,** asphyxiate, frozen, strangled, suffocated; **extinct,** defunct, moribund

dead *adj* → **1** asleep **2** close **3** disused **4** dull **5** empty **6** extinguished **7** hidden **8** inactive **9** infertile **10** insensible **11** insipid **12** invisible **13** quiet **14** tired **15** whole *adv* **16** precisely **17** wholly

deaden *v* → **1** anaesthetise **2** be callous **3** die **4** dull **5** moderate **6** quieten **7** silence **8** weaken

deadline *n* → **1** crucial moment **2** limit

deadlock *n* → **1** bolt **2** hindrance **3** stoppage *v* **4** stop

DEADLY *adj* deathful, deathly, fatal, fateful, feral *(Archaic)*, lethal, malignant, mortal, sublethal, terminal

deadly *adj* → **1** excessive **2** killing *adv* **3** excessively

dead-pan *adj* → composed

DEAF *adj* deaf and dumb, deaf as a doorpost, deaf as a post, deaf-mute, hard of hearing, stone-deaf, tone-deaf; **deafened,** unable to hear; **deaf to,** not listening, unhearing

DEAFNESS *n* anacusis, deaf-mutism, faulty hearing, tone-deafness; **deaf person,** deaf-mute

deal *n* → **1** arrangement **2** bit **3** contract **4** drug **5** shaft **6** share **7** sharing out *v* **8** behave **9** share out **10** trade

DEAL FAIRLY *v* deal honestly, do justice to, right, see that justice is done; **give someone a go,** give a person his due, give someone a break, give someone a fair go, give the devil his due; **play the game,** be a sport

dean *n* → **1** ecclesiastic **2** leader **3** teacher

dear *n* → **1** lover *adj* **2** beloved **3** difficult **4** excessive **5** expensive **6** highly regarded *interj* **7** oh

dearth *n* → insufficiency

DEATH *n* biolysis, curtains, decease, demise *(Obs.)*, depart *(Obs.)*, departure *(Archaic)*, dissolution, dying, end, ending, expiration *(Obs.)*, great divide, megadeath, mort *(Obs.)*, one's hour, parting, release, sticky end, supreme sacrifice, time, utterance *(Obs.)*; **lifelessness,** cadaverousness, coldness, deadness, defunctness, exanimation, inanimateness, moribundity, mortification, rigor mortis; **asphyxiation,** brain death, cot death, crucifixion, euthanasia, famishment, martyrdom, natural death, race suicide, starvation, stillbirth, strangulation, sudden-death syndrome, suicide; **doom,** bane, fate, Götterdämmerung, sentence of death; **Death,** the grim reaper; **death's-head,** black, crossbones, marrowbones, skull and crossbones; **dance of death,** danse macabre; **deathwatch,** death bell, death knell, passing bell, wake; **death throes,** death-rattle, deathbed, dying day, last agony, last gasp (breath), last hour, last words, swan song; **death-wish,** thanatophobia, thanatopsis; **necromania,** necrophilia, necrophilism, necrophobia

death *n* → destruction

Death *n* → **1** death **2** devil

death adder *n* → miser

DEATHLIKE *adj* biolytic, deathful, deathly, funeral, ghastly, macabre; **corpselike,** cadaveric, cadaverous; **posthumous,** defunctive, post-mortem, post-obit

debacle *n* → **1** flow **2** misfortune **3** nonachiever **4** ruin

debar *v* → **1** boycott **2** prohibit

debase *v* → **1** demote **2** mix

debate *n* → **1** discussion **2** fight **3** reasoning *v* **4** contest **5** reason **6** talk

debauch *n* → **1** binge **2** immorality *v* **3** be promiscuous **4** misguide **5** overindulge **6** wrong

debenture *n* → bill

debilitate *v* → weaken

debility *n* → **1** powerlessness **2** weakness

debit *n* → **1** account **2** debt *v* **3** account

debonair *adj* → **1** courteous **2** happy

debris *n* → **1** remnant **2** rock **3** waste

DEBT *n* a dead horse, a dog tied up, bad debt, book debt, debit, debt of honour, deficit, funded debt, interminable debt, national debt, outstanding account, set-off *(Finance)*; **liability,** charges, current liabilities, dues, fixed liability, insury, interest; **credit,** advance, house loan, mortgage, overdraft, personal loan, second mortgage; **hire-purchase,** H.P., lay-by, never-never. *See also* BILL

debt *n* → **1** bad debt **2** evildoing

DEBTOR *n* arrestee, bankrupt, borrower, contributory, defaulter, garnishee, mortgagee

debunk *v* → **1** belittle **2** disgrace **3** mock

debut *n* → **1** greeting **2** performance **3** start

debutante *n* → **1** adolescent **2** starter

decadence *n* → **1** descent **2** deterioration

decagon *n* → plane figure

decamp *v* → **1** abandon **2** depart

decant *v* → flow

decanter *n* → bottle

decapitate *v* → **1** cut **2** cut off **3** kill

decay *n* → **1** deterioration **2** ill health **3** illness **4** powerlessness **5** weakness *v* **6** be ill **7** deteriorate **8** wane

decease *n* → **1** death *v* **2** die

deceit *n* → **1** fake **2** trickery

DECEITFUL *adj* crafty, deceptive, delusive, devious, dishonest, dissimulative, double, double-faced, double-tongued, fast, fraudulent, hollow, insidious, Janus-faced, lying, mendacious, misleading, mythomaniac, tortuous, two-faced, untruthful; **hypocritical,** pharasaical, sanctimonious; **plausible,** disingenuous, evasive, fast-talking, insincere, smooth, tricksy; **unfaithful,** double-dealing, perfidious, two-timing; **perjured,** forsworn

deceive *v* → **1** betray **2** misguide **3** swindle **4** trick

decent *adj* → 1 adequate 2 correct 3 courteous 4 good 5 highly regarded 6 kind 7 modest 8 moral

decentralise *v* → disperse

deception *n* → 1 fake 2 trickery

decide *v* → 1 choose 2 determine 3 influence 4 mediate

decided *adj* → 1 certain 2 serious

deciduous *adj* → 1 fallen 2 impermanent

decimal *adj* → numerical

decimal fraction *n* → number

decimal number *n* → number

decimal point *n* → number

decimate *v* → 1 destroy 2 massacre 3 subtract 4 victimise

decipher *v* → 1 clarify 2 translate

decision *n* → 1 judgment 2 wilfulness

decisive *adj* → 1 commanding 2 influential 3 serious

DECISIVELY *adv* earnestly, in earnest, resolvedly, seriously, stably, steadfastly, steadily; **resolutely,** immovably, risoluto *(Music),* single-mindedly, unbendingly, uncompromisingly; **wilfully,** wantonly

deck *n* → 1 drug 2 floor *v* 3 bowl over 4 decorate 5 lower

declaim *v* → speak well

declare *v* → 1 assert 2 confess 3 pay 4 publicise 5 stop

declension *n* → 1 deflection 2 descent 3 deterioration 4 refusal 5 slope

decline *n* → 1 decrease 2 deterioration 3 evening *v* 4 age 5 deteriorate 6 finish 7 refuse 8 slope 9 wane

declivity *n* → slope

decode *v* → 1 clarify 2 translate

DECOLOURANT *n* blancher, bleacher, decolouriser, diluter; **bleach,** chlorine, hydrogen peroxide, oxalic acid

decompose *v* → 1 deteriorate 2 separate

decor *n* → 1 decoration 2 stage

DECORATE *v* adorn, beautify, boss, embellish, enrich, frost, furbish, garnish, mould, ornament, titivate; **array,** apparel *(Archaic),* bedeck, bedight *(Archaic),* bedizen, bespangle, deck, dight *(Archaic),* dress up, prank, preen, primp, tire *(Archaic),* trim; **bejewel,** bespangle, powder, set, stud; **overelaborate,** pansy up, tart up; **pattern,** detail, dice, figure, trace, vermiculate, wreathe; **festoon,** dress ship, flag; **pink,** engrail

decorate *v* → 1 beautify 2 depict

DECORATION *n* adornment, beautification, bedecking, blazonry, decor, embellishment, embossment, encrustation, enrichment, figure, frost, frostwork, garnish, garnishment, garniture, moiré, motif, openwork, ornament, ornamentation, pattern, pride *(Archaic);* **figuration,** arabesque, cuspidation, foliation, gammadion, toreutics, vermiculation; **decorativeness,** ornamentality; **floridness,** floridity, overelaborateness, overelaboration; **interior decoration,** paperhanging; **bunting,** Christmas tree, festoonery, paperchain, streamer; **pokerwork,** pyrography; **scroll,** curlicue, flourish, quirk, volute; **fretwork,** fret, meander, scrollwork; **iron lace; centrepiece,** epergne; **figurehead,** fiddlehead

DECORATIVE *adj* Christmassy, dressy, elaborate, embroidered, fancy, fine, frosted, highly-wrought, non-functional, ornamental, rich, worked, wrought; **florid,** alhambresque, baroque, clinquant, luxuriant, ornate, overelaborate, overwrought, plateresque, rococo, trumpery; **bannered,** beribboned, cockaded; **annular,** floriated, foliate, foliated, geometric, multifoil, runic; **enamelled,** champlevé, cloissoné; **gilt,** chryselephantine, gilded, gilt-edged, ormolu; **cut,** engraved, glyptic, incised, step-cut, toreutic, trap-cut; **fluted,** repoussé; **inlaid,** inwrought

decorum *n* → 1 aptness 2 correctness 3 courteousness 4 dutifulness 5 modesty

decoy *n* → 1 attractor *v* 2 attract

DECREASE *n* abatement, contraction, damping, decrement, depletion, detumescence, diminution, lessening, maceration, miniaturisation, minimisation, reduction, shrinkage, shrinking, taper; **depreciation,** break, cut, deflation, devaluation, discount, disinflation, drop, markdown, sag, subtraction; **mitigation,** alleviation, attenuation, extenuation; **decline,** downswing, downturn, ebb, fall, subsidence, wane; **abridgment,** abbreviation, curtailment; **cutback,** depression, recession, redundancy, retrenchment, short-time, the axe

DECREASE *v* abate, bate, diminish, lessen, lower, miniaturise, minify, minimise, reduce; **depreciate,** belittle, bring down, deflate, degrade, derogate, devalue, discount, downvalue, downgrade, hammer, laugh away, laugh off, lower, make little of, mark down, play down, pooh-pooh, pull down, sink; **mitigate,** allay, alleviate, ease, extenuate, moderate; **weaken,** attenuate, damp, depress, dilute, relax, slack, underdamp *(Physics);* **shorten,** abridge, axe, cut, precis; **cut back,** downsize, draw one's horns in, pare, prune, pull one's horns in, retrench, scale down, scant, slash, step down, taper, whittle, whittle down, wind down; **shrink,** contract, sanforise *(Textiles).* *See also* WANE

decrease *v* → subtract

DECREASED *adj* diminished, less, lesser, miniature, miniaturised, under; **reduced,** abridged, censored, cut, expurgated, watered-down

DECREASING *adj* decrescent, detumescent, dwindling, reducing, waning; **depreciative,** deflationary, depreciatory; **mitigatory,** alleviant, alleviative, extenuatory, mitigative

DECREASINGLY *adv* diminishingly; **less,** at a discount, down, off, under; **on the wane,** at low ebb, decrescendo, in decline, less and less

decree *n* → 1 command 2 insistence 3 judgment 4 law 5 public notice *v* 6 command 7 determine 8 publicise

decrepit *adj* → 1 aged 2 old 3 powerless 4 weak

decry *v* → slander

dedicate *v* → **1** consecrate **2** give

deduce *v* → **1** reason **2** solve

deduct *v* → subtract

DEED *n* articles, escrow, guarantee, indent, indenture, instrument, memorandum, memorandum of association, specialty *(Law)*, statute, submission *(Law)*, trust deed, written contract; **article,** clause, condition, condition precedent, condition subsequent, consideration *(Law)*, provision, small print, stipulation; **escalation clause,** escalator clause, exclusion clause *(Insurance)*, habendum, reddendum, roll-over provision, wet-weather clause. *See also* CONTRACT

deed *n* → **1** accomplishment **2** action

deem *v* → **1** assess **2** believe

DEEP *adj* abysmal, abyssal, bottomless, cavernous, profound, unsounded, yawning

deep *adj* → **1** colourful **2** cunning **3** distant **4** emotional **5** loud **6** sombre **7** thick **8** unclear **9** wise

DEEPLY *adv* profoundly

deface *v* → **1** destroy **2** disfigure **3** injure **4** uglify

de facto *n* → **1** lover **2** spouse *adj* **3** real *adv* **4** in fact

defame *v* → **1** disgrace **2** slander

default *n* → **1** absence **2** deficiency **3** inaction **4** indebtedness **5** neglectfulness **6** nonpayment *v* **7** be inactive **8** fail **9** fail to pay **10** neglect

DEFAULTER *n* absconder, bankrupt, bilker, dishonourer, fly-by-night, insolvent, scaler, stag *(Stock Exchange)*, welsher, wife starver

DEFEAT *v* afflict *(Obs.)*, annihilate, break, come all over, conquer, dish up, do for, go through like a dose of salts, go through like a packet of salts, overcome, overmaster, overthrow, overturn, overwhelm, piss all over, piss over, prostrate, rout, shit all over, slaughter, subdue, subjugate, take by storm, tame, triumph over, whelm *(Archaic)*; **beat,** beat the stuffing out of, beat the tripe out of, clobber, do like a dinner, down, drub, fight down, floor, give someone Bondi *(Obs.)*, knock into a cocked hat, knock someone bandy, knock the bejesus out of, knock the bottom out of, knock the stuffing out of, pulverise, punish, thrash, towel, trim *(U.S. Colloq.)*, trounce, wallop, whop; **checkmate,** confute, euchre, master, mate, outargue, outplay, outstare, shoot down, stump, whipsaw *(U.S.)*; **stop,** foil *(Archaic)*, ignore *(U.S. Law)*, upset; **best,** better, bowl over, bump, dismiss, donkey-lick, get ahead of, get the best of, get the drop on, have the best of, have the drop on, knock off, knock spots off, lick, outbox, peg *(Baseball)*, polish off, roll, shout down, skunk *(U.S. Colloq.)*, whip *(U.S. Colloq.)*, whitewash, wipe the floor with, worst

defeat *n* → **1** hindrance **2** losing **3** ruin *v* **4** cancel **5** surpass

DEFECATE *v* bog, cack, choke a darkie, crap, crash, do a job, drop a darkie, evacuate, lay an egg, loosen, move the bowels, open the bowels, pass, pass excrement, see a man about a dog, see a man about a job, shit; **go to the toilet,** be caught short, kangaroo, spend a penny, visit aunty, visit Mary

DEFECATION *n* big jobs, bog, business, crash, Edgar Britt, evacuation, jobbies, movement, number two, passage, shit; **faeces,** blind mullet, business, cack, crap, darkie, egesta, faecal pellets, gruff nuts, Henry the Third, meconium, motion, ordure, poo, poop, Richard the Third, scat, shit, stool, turd, weenies; **scatology,** coprology. *See also* DUNG

DEFECT *v* change one's allegiance, change one's mind, change one's spots, change one's tune, do an about-face, go back on one's word, renege, sing a different tune, sing another tune, tergiversate, unthink, unwill; **see the light,** change one's ways, convert, go over, go straight, mend one's ways, regenerate, repent, turn, turn over a new leaf; **apostatise,** fall away, renegade, throw over; **err,** fall from grace, fall into evil ways, go to the bad, turn away from God

defect *n* → **1** deficiency **2** disfigurement **3** imperfection **4** insufficiency

DEFECTION *n* about-face, apostasy, backsliding, change of allegiance, changeover, desertion, renunciation, secession, transfer *(Football)*, treason, turnabout; **conversion,** proselytism, rebirth, redemption, reformation, regeneracy, regeneration, renascence; **rehabilitation,** re-education, reconditioning, repatriation; **brainwashing,** alienation, indoctrination

DEFECTOR *n* apostate, deserter, renegade, reneger, transfer *(Football)*, turncoat; **tergiversator,** acrobat, tergiversant; **convert,** born-again, catechumen, changed person, disciple, neophyte, new man, new woman, novice, proselyte; **degenerate,** sinner

DEFENCE *n* resistance, security, self-defence, self-preservation, self-protection; **protection,** armour, buffer, bulwark, safeguard, shield; **civil defence,** national service; **defence policy,** Fortress Australia, forward defence, scorched earth policy; **air cover,** air picket, umbrella; **barrage,** balloon barrage, flak, screen, smokescreen; **early warning system,** dumaresq, radar

defence *n* → **1** answer **2** justification **3** oration **4** protection

DEFEND *v* fence, fend *(Archaic)*, forfend, stand up for, take someone's part; **entrench,** dig in, retrench, sap, trench; **barricade,** bulwark, crenellate, embattle *(Archaic)*, fortress *(Rare)*, garrison, palisade, rampart, rearm, stockade; **repel,** ward off; **be on the defensive,** man, steel oneself

defend *v* → **1** help **2** practise law **3** protect

defendant *n* → **1** accused **2** litigant

DEFENDER *n* bastion, champion, crusader, protector; **sentry,** bodyguard, coast-watcher, lifeguard, sentinel; **army reserve,** Dad's army, Home Guard; **deliverer,** rescuer, saviour

DEFER *v* adjourn, carry over, continue *(Law)*, count out *(Brit.)*, enlarge *(Law)*, hold over, postpone, prorogue, put off, put over *(U.S.)*, remit, sleep on it, suspend, wait *(Colloq.)*; **retard,** hold up, leg-rope

deference *n* → **1** courtesy **2** obedience **3** obsequiousness **4** tribute

DEFERMENT *n* abeyance, adjournment, continuance *(Law)*, deferral, postponement, raincheck, respite

defiance *n* → **1** dissidence **2** menace

DEFIANTLY *adv* antagonistically, eyeball to eyeball, in someone's teeth, in the teeth of the wind, insurrectionally, obstructively, perversely, rebelliously, resistently, tauntingly; **combatively,** militantly; **controversially,** argumentatively, cantankerously, contentiously, disputatiously, divisively, protestingly, quarrelsomely; **contrariwise,** au contraire, by contraries, con, contrarily, crosswise *(U.S.)*, incompatibly; **unyieldingly,** implacably, irreconcilably, persistently, unshrinkingly

DEFICIENCY *n* default, defect, deficit, depletion, insufficiency, lack, missing link, need, omission, requirement, shortage, shortcoming, shortfall, want, wantage; **incompleteness,** incompletion, incomprehensiveness; **perfunctoriness,** paucity, scrappiness, sketchiness, superficiality

deficiency *n* → insufficiency

DEFICIENT *adj* half-and-half, in short supply, insufficient, meagre, out of, rationed, short, short of, strapped for, wanting; **incomplete,** bitty, fragmental, fragmentary, imperfect, incomprehensive, on the anvil, perfunctory, scant, scrappy, sketchy, superficial, touch-and-go; **unfinished,** cut short, partial, truncated, uncompleted; **unaccomplished,** blank, unbegun, undone, unexecuted, unfinalised, unrealised; **rudimentary,** abortive

deficit *n* → **1** debt **2** deficiency **3** insufficiency

defile *n* → **1** access **2** bridge **3** gap *v* **4** dirty **5** disgrace **6** line **7** profane **8** rape **9** walk

define *v* → **1** be precise **2** explain **3** limit **4** particularise **5** shape

definite *adj* → **1** certain **2** limiting **3** particular **4** precise **5** true

definition *n* → **1** meaning **2** precision

definitive *n* → **1** word *adj* **2** unconditional

deflate *v* → **1** decrease **2** expel

DEFLECT *v* deviate, perturb *(Astron.)*; **reflect,** backscatter, refract; **hook,** cut, edge, seam, slice, swing; **deviate,** depart from, digress, divagate, diverge, fly off at a tangent, pull over, sheer, shunt, sidetrack, turn off; **sidle,** move aside, oblique *(Mil.)*

deflect *v* → avoid

DEFLECTION *n* aberration, declension, departure, deviation, digression, divergence, excursion, perturbation *(Astron.)*, variation *(Astron.)*; **reflection,** backscatter *(Physics)*, refraction, refringence; **diversion,** circumvention, circumvolution, divagation, indirection

DEFLECTIVE *adj* aberrant, aberrational, deviating, divergent, inflective, sideward, sideways, tangential, transverse, veering; **refractive,** reflectional, refractional, refringent; **indirect,** anfractuous, circuitous, circular, circumventive, devious, diversionary, doglegged, errant, erratic, roundabout, sinuous, tortuous, twisting, winding, wry; **off-course,** askew, oblique, sharp, skew, squiffy, straggly, wide

DEFLECTIVELY *adv* across, aside, athwart, athwartships, away, collaterally, divergently, obliquely, off, sidelong, sideward, sidewards, sideways, transversely; **astray,** afield, agley *(Scot.)*, awry, indirectly, off the track, off to billyo, off to buggery, wide, wide of the mark, wild; **circuitously,** circularly, deviously, eccentrically, round, tortuously, wryly

defoliate *v* → **1** bare *adj* **2** bare

deform *v* → **1** change **2** disfigure **3** distort **4** injure **5** uglify

defraud *v* → **1** cheat **2** fail to pay

defray *v* → pay

defrost *v* → heat

deft *adj* → competent

defunct *adj* → **1** dead **2** disused

defuse *v* → **1** be neutral **2** extinguish **3** make peace **4** moderate

defy *v* → oppose

degenerate *n* → **1** defector *v* **2** deteriorate **3** go back *adj* **4** deteriorated **5** immoral **6** unwholesome

degrade *v* → **1** decrease **2** demote **3** disgrace **4** materialise **5** rub **6** simplify

degree *n* → **1** astronomic point **2** class **3** gradation **4** length

dehydrate *v* → **1** conserve **2** dry

deify *v* → worship

deign *v* → be meek

deity *n* → god

deject *v* → make unhappy

delay *n* → **1** inaction **2** lateness **3** slowness *v* **4** be late **5** go slowly **6** idle

delectable *adj* → **1** alluring **2** pleasant

DELEGATE *n* delo *(Colloq.)*, emissary, envoy, go-between, intermediatory, mediator, middle man, negotiator, plenipotentiary, proxy; **delegation,** deputation, mission. *See also* AGENT; AMBASSADOR

delegate *n* → **1** trade unionist *v* **2** depute **3** give

delegation *n* → **1** delegate **2** employment

delete *v* → **1** cancel **2** exclude

deleterious *adj* → **1** harmful **2** unwholesome

deliberate *v* → **1** think *adj* **2** cautious **3** composed **4** opportunist **5** slow **6** willing

delicacy *n* → **1** artistry **2** beauty **3** food **4** good taste **5** ill health

delicate *adj* → **1** beautiful **2** colourless **3** cultivated **4** delicious **5** discriminating **6** emotional **7** ethereal **8** light **9** small **10** soft **11** tasty **12** weak

delicatessen *n* → shop

DELICIOUS *adj* ambrosial, ambrosian, delish, epicurean, fit for the gods, goluptious, luscious, more-ish, mouth-watering, nice, nummy, scrumptious, succulent, yum, yummy; **delicate,** dainty; **savoury,** appetizing, flavoursome, palatable, sapid, savorous *(U.S.)*, tangy, tasty, tempting, toothsome, zesty

delicious *adj* → **1** fragrant **2** pleasant **3** tasty

delight *n* → **1** pleasure *v* **2** be pleasant **3** please

delineate *v* → **1** narrate **2** portray

delinquent *n* → **1** disobeyer **2** mischief-maker *adj* **3** disobedient **4** guilty **5** neglectful **6** wrong

delirious *adj* → **1** excited **2** feverish

delirium *n* → **1** excitement **2** madness

deliver *v* → **1** give **2** give birth **3** liberate **4** speak **5** throw **6** transport

delta *n* → land

delude *v* → **1** beguile **2** trick

DELUDE ONESELF *v* deceive oneself, have oneself on, labour under a false impression, misapprehend, wank; **dream,** daydream, feign, imagine, make as if, make as though, make believe, pretend; **hallucinate,** flashback, hear things, see pink elephants, see things

deluge *n* → **1** flood **2** rainfall **3** surplus *v* **4** flood **5** flow **6** oversupply **7** rain

DELUSION *n* error, false impression, misconception, superstition, warped notion; **illusion,** bubble, dream, figment, fixed idea, hallucination, mirage, myth, reverie; **daydream,** chimera, idle fancy, imagining, make-believe, phantasm, phantasmagoria, play-acting, vision; **dream world,** castle in the air, cloud-cuckoo-land, cloudland, dreamland, fool's paradise, pie in the sky; **will-o'-the-wisp,** ignis fatuus. *See also* ILLUSION

delusion *n* → **1** psychic disturbance **2** trickery

DELUSIVE *adj* airy, dreamlike, dreamy, fatuous, illusional, illusionary, illusive, illusory, quixotic, spurious, unreal; **delusional,** barmecidal, chimerical, feigned, fictitious, imaginary, imagined, make-believe, phantasmagorical, phantasmal, visional, visionary; **phantom,** apparitional, ghostly, shadowy, spectral; **hallucinatory,** psychedelic, spaced, spaced-out, spacey, transcendental

deluxe *adj* → **1** good **2** superior **3** tasteful

delve *v* → **1** dig **2** farm **3** slope

demagogue *n* → **1** haranguer **2** orator

demand *n* → **1** bill **2** command **3** desire **4** imposition **5** insistence **6** question **7** request *v* **8** command **9** impose **10** insist on **11** necessitate **12** question

demarcation *n* → limit

demean *v* → slander

demeanour *n* → behaviour

demented *adj* → mad

demerit *n* → **1** boo **2** evildoing

demise *n* → **1** death *v* **2** lend

democracy *n* → **1** equality **2** nation **3** the public

DEMOCRATISE *v* communise, give to the people, socialise; **popularise,** vernacularise, vulgarise

DEMOGRAPHY *n* demographics, ekistics; **demographer,** demographist, town planner

demography *n* → **1** anthropology **2** computation

demolish *v* → **1** destroy **2** disprove **3** eat

demonstrate *v* → **1** authenticate **2** display **3** fire on **4** teach

demonstration *n* → **1** display **2** evidence **3** show

demonstrative *adj* → **1** displayed **2** emotional

demoralise *v* → **1** desolate **2** discourage **3** frighten **4** misguide **5** weaken

DEMOTE *v* abase, break, bust, debase, declass, degrade, disrate, relegate, shaft

DEMOTION *n* abasement, debasement, degradation, relegation

demur *n* → **1** disagreement **2** slowness *v* **3** disagree **4** go slowly

demure *adj* → **1** modest **2** sombre

den *n* → **1** animal dwelling **2** bedroom **3** cabin **4** hiding place **5** room **6** shelter

DENIAL *n* apophasis *(Rhet.)*, contradiction, disclaimer, nay, negative, non est factum, rebuttal, traverse *(Law)*; **repudiation,** disaffirmance, disaffirmation, disavowal, disclamation, disownment, negation, palinode, recarnation, renouncement, renunciation, retraction; **nullification,** abolishment, abolition, abrogation, annulment, avoidance *(Law)*, cancellation, cassation, countermand, disaffirmance, discharge *(Law)*, frustration, repeal, rescission, revocation, self-contradiction, voidance

denial *n* → **1** abstinence **2** disagreement **3** doubt **4** justification **5** refusal

denigrate *v* → **1** disgrace **2** slander

DENIGRATION *n* disparagement, stigmatisation, vilification; **reproach,** censure, derogation; **defilement,** corruption, pollution; **taint,** attaint *(Obs.)*, blot, brand, cloud, slur, smear, smirch, stain, stigma; **skeleton in the cupboard,** badge of infamy, blot on the escutcheon, dirty linen, family skeleton, mark of Cain

DENIGRATOR *n* stigmatiser; **disgracer,** defiler, dishonourer, low joint; **scandal sheet,** gutter press, rag, yellow press

denizen *n* → **1** foreigner **2** inhabitant

DEN OF VICE *n* cesspool, cloaca, den of iniquity, sewer, sink; **Babylon,** cities of the plain, iron age, Sodom and Gomorrah

denomination *n* → **1** class **2** gradation **3** name **4** religion

denominator *n* → number

denote *v* → **1** mean **2** name **3** signify

denounce *v* → **1** accuse **2** scold

dense *adj* → **1** hard **2** intense **3** opaque **4** pressed **5** solid **6** stupid **7** thick

density *n* → **1** opacity **2** solidity **3** stupidity

dent *n* → **1** indentation **2** knob *v* **3** hollow

dental *adj* → medical

dentist *n* → healer

dentistry *n* → healing

dentition *n* → mouth

denture *n* → mouth

denude *v* → **1** bare **2** rub

denunciation *n* → 1 accusation 2 disapproval 3 warning

DENY *v* contradict, controvert, disaffirm, gainsay, give the lie to, negate, negative, rebut, traverse *(Law)*; **repudiate,** abjure, disavow, disclaim, disown, forswear, recant, renege *(Archaic)*, renounce, retract; **annul,** annihilate, avoid *(Law)*, cancel, derecognise, disaffirm *(Law)*, dissolve, do away with *(Colloq.)*, invalidate, nullify *(Law)*, repeal, rescind, set aside, think better of, vacate, void

deny *v* → 1 doubt 2 refuse

DENYING *adj* abjuratory, adversative, contradictious, contradictive, contradictory, negative, negatory, repudiative

deodorant *n* → 1 odourlessness *adj* 2 odourless

DEODORISE *v* freshen the air; **ventilate,** air a room

DEPART *v* alley, avoid *(Obs.)*, beat a retreat, beat it, blow, buzz along, buzz off, chuff off, clear out, disappear, eloign, evacuate, exit, flit *(Obs.)*, get along, get away, get lost, get nicked, go, go away, go bush, go off, hook it, hop, hop it, leave, lob off, make off, mooch off, move, move out, nick out, part, pull out, push along, push off, quit, remove oneself, retire, retreat, shove off, shuffle off, take an early mark, tie a knot in one's bluey, tootle off, void *(Archaic)*; **set off,** blast off, cast off, get under way, hit the road, make sail, put forth, put off *(Naut.)*, put out *(Naut.)*, put to sea, sail, sally forth, set forth, set out, set sail, shake the dust from one's feet, sling one's hook, step out, take off, take to the road, take wing, weigh anchor; **embark,** embus, entrain, go on board; **storm out,** bounce out, flounce out, vote with one's feet, walk out; **break camp,** check out, decamp, make tracks, pull up stakes, saddle up; **run off,** arsehole off, beat a hasty retreat, bugger off, cut, cut and run, flee, fuck off, hightail, light out, micky quick, nip, piss off, pop off, rack off, run out, scat, scram, shoot off, shoot through like a Bondi tram, skedaddle, skiddoo, split, strike, take a powder, take flight, take to flight, take to one's heels, tear, turn tail, vamoose, zot; **abscond,** absent oneself, blow through, decamp, desert, do a bunk, do a getaway, do a moonlight flit, do a sneak, get off, go A.W.O.L., leave in the lurch, make oneself scarce, nick off, play truant, run away, run off, run out on, scarper, shoot the moon, shoot through, skip, slope off, take French leave, take to the bush, take to the hills; **withdraw from,** abandon, evacuate, leave, pull back from, quit, vacate; **withdraw,** bow out, fall back, fall off, go down *(Brit. Educ.)*, make an exit, retire *(Sport)*, take one's leave; **emigrate,** migrate, transmigrate

depart *n* → 1 death *v* 2 die 3 exit

department *n* → 1 administrative area 2 domain 3 job 4 part 5 teacher

department store *n* → shop

DEPARTURE *n* debarkation, embarkation, emigration, exodus, going, issue; **withdrawal,** decampment, exit, pullout, retirement, walkout; **take-off,** blast-off, lift-off, sailing, start; **moonlight flit,** French leave, moonlight flitting, skedaddle *(U.S. Colloq.)*; **dismissal,** congé, congee *(Obs.)*, nunc dimittis, retrenchment; **early mark,** early minutes, nick

depend *v* → 1 be inferior 2 be uncertain 3 hang

DEPENDANT *n* camp-follower, client, clientèle, hanger-on, parasite, satellite; **ward,** charge, foster-child, mother's boy, protégé; **vassal,** feudatory, henchman, liegeman; **pensioner; contingent,** appendant *(Law)*, contingency

DEPENDENCE *n* clientship, dependency, entrustment, reliance; **guardianship,** tutelage, wardship

DEPENDENT *adj* at the mercy of, in chancery, in the hands of, parasitic, reliant, semiparasitic, tied to the apron-strings; **contingent,** appendant

dependent *adj* → 1 conditional 2 hanging

DEPEND ON *v* hang on, hinge on, turn on; **bank on,** bargain on, figure on, lean on, pend *(Obs.)*, reckon, rely on, repose; **live for,** hope *(Archaic)*, swear by, trust to

DEPICT *v* depicture, limn, portray, represent; **draw,** design, draft, illustrate, outline, profile, sketch; **paint,** blot, colour, daub, illuminate, scumble, tint, touch up; **pencil,** charcoal, crayon, crosshatch, hachure, hatch, ink, shade, shadow *(Obs.)*, stipple; **glaze,** decorate; **model,** cast, mould; **sculpt,** carve, chip, chisel, sculpture; **fecit,** sculpsit

depict *v* → 1 narrate 2 portray 3 write

DEPICTIVE *adj* delineative, descriptive, imitative, pictorial; **graphic,** diagrammatic; **cartographic,** cartographical, cosmographic, cosmographical

DEPILATION *n* deplumation, ecdysis *(Zool.)*, epilation, exuviation, moulting

depilatory *adj* → bald

deplorable *adj* → bad

deplore *v* → 1 be penitent 2 grieve

deploy *v* → 1 disperse 2 position 3 use 4 wage war

deport *v* → eject

deportment *n* → 1 behaviour 2 pose

depose *v* → 1 dismiss 2 testify

deposit *n* → 1 accumulation 2 capital 3 coating 4 mineral 5 placement 6 remnant 7 soil 8 surety *v* 9 lower 10 pay 11 place

depot *n* → 1 shelter 2 storage

depraved *adj* → 1 immoral 2 wrong

deprecate *v* → disapprove of

depreciate *v* → 1 cheapen 2 decrease 3 hold in low regard 4 slander 5 wane

depreciation *n* → 1 cheapness 2 decrease 3 disapproval

depredation *n* → 1 destruction 2 robbery

depress *v* → 1 cheapen 2 decrease 3 hollow 4 make unhappy 5 press 6 sound

depression *n* → 1 apathy 2 atmospheric pressure 3 cheapness 4 decrease 5 despair 6 hollow 7 inaction 8 indentation 9 unhappiness

deprive *v* → **1** dismiss **2** refuse **3** take

DEPTH *n* deepness, lowness, profoundness, profundity; **depths,** abysm, abyss, gulf, profound; **sounding,** bathometry, cast, echo sounding, plumbing; **bathometer,** echo sounder, flashboard, lead line; **mark,** isobath

depth *n* → **1** gap **2** sombreness **3** thickness

deputation *n* → **1** delegate **2** employment

DEPUTE *v* accredit, appoint, authorise, charge, commission, commit into the hands of, commit into the keeping of, delegate, employ, empower, entrust with, hire, name, nominate, place in charge

deputy *n* → **1** agent **2** helper **3** member of parliament **4** religious dignitary *adj* **5** agential

derange *v* → **1** madden **2** untidy

derby *n* → hat

derelict *n* → **1** poor person **2** unfortunate **3** untidy person *adj* **4** abandoned **5** disused **6** neglected **7** neglectful **8** vulnerable

dereliction *n* → **1** abandonment **2** crime **3** drying **4** misbehaviour **5** neglectfulness

deride *v* → mock

derision *n* → mockery

derive *v* → **1** extract **2** inquire into **3** reason

DERIVE FROM *v* come from, grow out of, hail from, originate in, stem from

dermatitis *n* → sore

derogatory *adj* → **1** disapproving **2** disdainful **3** slanderous

derrick *n* → lift

dervish *n* → monastic

descant *n* → **1** song *v* **2** discourse **3** sing **4** waffle

DESCEND *v* coast, drop, glissade, go down, lapse, set, slip down; **free-fall,** bale out, jump, parachute; **abseil,** climb down, rappel; **land,** bellyland, crash, ditch, flop, put down, touch down

descend *v* → slope

DESCENDANT *n* chip off the old block, heir, heritor *(Archaic),* heritress, inheritor, inheritress, inheritrix; **offshoot,** root, scion; **full blood,** purebred; **half-blood,** bronzewing *(N.T. W.A.),* half-breed, half-caste, ladino, métis, métisse, mestiza, mestizo, mulatto, muleteer, mustee, octoroon, quadroon, quartes caste; **hybrid,** crossbred, crossover, mongrel, top cross; **throwback,** atavist, reverter

descendant *n* → **1** child **2** offspring **3** successor

DESCENT *n* decadence, declension, declination, down, downswing, downwardness, drop, dropping, gravitation; **landing,** bellylanding, crash-landing, dead-stick landing, instrument landing, soft landing, three-point landing, touchdown; **slide,** chute, ramp, slippery dip; **abseil,** rappel; **bow,** droop, sag, stoop; **prolapse,** lapse

descent *n* → **1** ancestry **2** aristocracy **3** slope

describe *v* → narrate

description *n* → **1** class **2** narrative

desecrate *v* → profane

desert *n* → **1** dryness **2** wasteland *v* **3** abandon **4** depart *adj* **5** infertile

DESERVE *v* be entitled to, merit, rate; **be hoist with one's own petard,** have it coming to one, reap the whirlwind, serve one right; **be right,** be only natural justice

desiccate *v* → **1** conserve **2** dry

design *n* → **1** creation **2** diagram **3** drawing **4** expedient **5** model **6** plan **7** shape *v* **8** create **9** depict **10** plan **11** shape **12** signify

designate *v* → **1** label **2** mean **3** name **4** particularise *adj* **5** employed

DESIRABLE *adj* appetising, covetable, eligible, enviable, in demand, inviting, mouthwatering, popular, preferable, succulent, tantalising, top

desirable *n* → **1** allurer *adj* **2** advantageous **3** alluring **4** expedient **5** good

DESIRE *n* achage, ache, affectation *(Obs.),* appetence, appetite, craving, demand, eagerness, famishment, hunger, hungriness, keenness, longing, mania, need, passion, pine *(Obs. Archaic),* rage, thirst, thirstiness, will, yearning; **ardour,** ardency, concupiscence, fire, flame, libido, lust, passion, passionateness; **obsession,** compulsion, insane desire; **desires,** sighs, wishes; **wish,** conation, desideration, fancy, hankering, itch, mind, urge, velleity, volition, want, whim, whimsy, willingness, yen; **partiality,** bent, inclination, leaning, penchant, prediliction, propensity; **aspiration,** ambition, ambitiousness, arrivisme, zeal; **languishing,** nostalgia, wistfulness; **fondness,** liking, love, relish, stomach, taste; **avarice,** acquisitiveness, avariciousness, avidity, covetousness, cupidity, graspingness, greed, greediness, insatiability, insatiableness, insatiateness, mammonism, rapaciousness, rapacity, selfishness, voracity; **gluttony,** bulimia, edacity, gluttonousness, sitomania

DESIRE *v* admire *(U.S.),* be all for something, be hell-bent on, covet, crave, desiderate, hanker after, hunger after, hunger for, long for, wish for, yearn for; **seek,** court, make eyes at, make sheep's eyes at, moon over, solicit, woo; **wish,** be inclined towards, care for, fancy, feel like, have a heart to, have a mind to, incline towards, intend, like, list *(Archaic),* need, require, take a fancy to, take to, want, will, would be glad to; **languish,** ache for, pant, pine for, sigh for, starve for, thirst for; **have high ambitions,** aim high, ambition *(Obs.),* aspire, raise one's sights, set one's cap at, want the earth; **run after,** die for, do one's balls on, gasp after, gasp for, give one's eyeteeth for, have eyes only for, itch for, lust after, pant after, run mad after, scream for, set one's hat at, set one's heart on, slaver over, yen for; **flame,** burn, fire, rage; **offer oneself,** be in for, throw one's hat in the ring

desire *n* → **1** will **2** willingness *v* **3** entreat **4** intend

DESIRER *n* coveter, hankerer, mammonist, mammonite, thirster, votary, wanter, wisher;

lover, admirer, buff, devotee, enthusiast, votary; **languisher,** sigher; **glutton,** greedy-guts, trencherman; **social climber,** arriviste, careerist, company man, company woman, go-getter, pothunter; **aspirer,** aspirant, candidate, intender, seeker

DESIROUS *adj* desiderative, disposed, fain, inclined, partial, solicitous, volitional, volitionary, volitive, willing, wishful, would-be; **eager,** agog, all agog, breathless, impatient, keen; **ardent,** athirst, avid, fervent, libidinal, on fire, passionate; **mad for,** dying to, fixated on, keen on, longing for, nuts, nutty over, partial to, queer for, set on; **aspiring,** ambitious, aspirant *(Rare)*; **longing,** languishing, nostalgic, sentimental, wistful, yearning; **lustful,** aroused, concupiscent, libidinous, lickerish, lusty *(Archaic)*, on heat, randy, ruttish *(Obs.)*, toey; **votive**

desist *v* → stop

DESK *n* bureau, davenport, escritoire, roll-top desk, secretaire, secretary, worktable, writing desk, writing table. *See also* TABLE

desk *n* → part

DESOLATE *v* cast down, chill, demoralise, drive to despair, leave no hope

desolate *v* → **1** abandon **2** destroy *adj* **3** abandoned **4** boring **5** despairing **6** grieving **7** hopeless **8** infertile **9** secluded

DESPAIR *n* demoralisation, desolateness, desolation, desperateness, desperation, hopelessness, inconsolability, inconsolableness; **pessimism,** defeatism; **melancholy,** depression, despond *(Archaic)*, despondency, oppression. *See also* HOPELESSNESS

DESPAIR *v* buckle under, despond, drop one's bundle, give it away, give up, give up the ghost, go to the pack, lose heart, lose hope; **be pessimistic,** look on the worst side; **write off,** hope for nothing more from

DESPAIRING *adj* broken-down, desolate, desperate, inconsolable, past hope or caring; **pessimistic,** dyspeptic; **melancholy,** byronic, depressed, melancholic, world-weary

desperado *n* → **1** criminal **2** hothead

desperate *adj* → **1** dangerous **2** despairing **3** hopeless **4** rash **5** striving

despicable *adj* → bad

despise *v* → **1** be arrogant **2** hold in low regard

despite *n* → **1** hate **2** ill will **3** low regard *prep* **4** notwithstanding

despoil *v* → rob

despondent *adj* → unhappy

despot *n* → **1** forcer **2** represser **3** ruler

dessert *n* → meal

destination *n* → **1** aim **2** finish

destine *v* → **1** intend **2** ordain

destiny *n* → **1** expected thing **2** fate **3** omen

destitute *adj* → **1** abandoned **2** poor

DESTROY *v* annihilate, decimate, demolish, destruct, finish off, hit for six, make mincemeat of, make short work of, pull down, pulverise, ride down, slay *(Archaic)*, smash, smite, spiflicate, take out, tear down, wipe out, wipe the floor with, zap; **ravage,** desolate, devastate, eat, lay waste to, rape, waste; **eradicate,** deracinate, exterminate, extirpate, get rid of, outroot, root up; **erase,** blot out, efface, expunge; **abolish,** do away with, liquidate, make away with, unmake; **overthrow,** bring down, do for, fordo *(Archaic)*, subvert, undo; **deface,** depredate, undermine, vandalise; **consume,** gut, incinerate, put to the torch, raze; **poison,** blight, canker. *See also* RUIN

destroy *v* → kill

DESTROYER *n* abolisher, annihilationist, annihilator, decimator, demolisher, exterminator, extirpator, juggernaut, pulveriser, razer, unmaker; **desolator,** barbarian, depredator, havocker, Hun, ravager, ruiner, Visigoth, waster, wrecker; **scourge,** destructor, poison, the sword, thunderbolt; **bane,** blight, cancer, canker, devil, mould, must; **defacer,** hoodlum, vandal; **arsonist,** fire-raiser, firebug, incendiary, pyromaniac; **destructive agent,** acid, autolysin *(Biochem.)*, caustic, cautery, corrosive; **eraser,** effacer, eradicator, expunger; **nihilist,** anarchist, assassin, iconoclast, subversive, subverter

destroyer *n* → watercraft

DESTRUCTION *n* abolishment, abolition, annihilation, consumption, death, decimation, decomposition, demolition, dissimilation *(Biol.)*, extinction, liquidation, pulverisation; **desolation,** depredation, devastation, havoc, ravage, ruin; **disintegration,** breakdown, dissipation, dissolution; **eradication,** deracination, extermination, extirpation; **erasure,** defacement, effacement, erasion, expunction, obliteration; **chemical breakdown,** autolysis, biodegradation, biolysis, catabolism, electrolysis, lysis, radiolysis; **destructiveness,** destructivity; **perniciousness,** fatalness, fellness; **vandalism,** hoodlumism. *See also* RUIN

destruction *n* → non-being

DESTRUCTIVE *adj* depredatory, despoiling, devastating, ruinous, vandal, vandalic, wasting; **annihilative,** abolitionary, eradicative, exterminatory, extirpative, obliterative; **catabolic,** biodegradable, biolytic; **apocalyptic,** black, holocaustic; **pernicious,** baneful, cancerous, cankerous, consumptive, gnawing, pestiferous, poisonous

desultory *adj* → **1** disorderly **2** interrupted **3** irregular **4** lucky

detach *v* → separate

detachment *n* → **1** apathy **2** armed forces **3** break **4** composure **5** neutrality

detail *n* → **1** armed forces **2** employment **3** part **4** particulars **5** record *v* **6** decorate **7** employ **8** improve **9** particularise **10** share out

detain *v* → **1** hold **2** imprison **3** restrain

detect *v* → **1** find **2** see

detective *n* → **1** policeman **2** searcher

détente *n* → **1** agreement **2** pacification

detention *n* → **1** imprisonment **2** restraint

deter *v* → discourage

detergent *n* → 1 cleanser *adj* 2 cleansing

DETERIORATE *v* decline, degenerate, dilapidate, disintegrate, get worse, go backwards, go downhill, go from bad to worse, go to pot, go to seed, go to the pack, pejorate, retrograde, retrogress, sicken, sink, slide, slip, wear out, worsen; **wear,** eat, erode, fray, frazzle, fret, ravel, scab, scuff, weather; **decay,** age, atrophy, caseate, shrivel, wither; **rot,** decompose, fester, go bad, go off, perish, putrefy, turn; **rust,** corrode, oxidise

DETERIORATED *adj* atrophic, atrophied, decadent, degenerate, degenerative, retrograde, retrogressive, wasted; **rotten,** acetified, adulterate, bad, cankerous, carrion, corrupt, decadent, high, off, pricked, putrescent, putrid, putrilaginous, spoiled, tainted, vitiated; **flyblown,** blown, fly-struck, maggoty, vermiculate, worm-eaten, wormy; **rusty,** corroded, eroded, worn away; **decayed,** carious

DETERIORATING *adj* declining, failing, flagging, getting worse, in decline, no better, on the decline, on the downward path, sinking, slipping, wilting, worse

DETERIORATION *n* debasement, declension, declination *(U.S.)*, decline, degeneracy, degenerateness, degeneration, impair *(Archaic)*, impairment, involution, pejoration, retrogradation, retrogression; **contamination,** adulteration, bastardisation, contagion, corruption, rancidity, sophistication, spoilage, taint, tarnish, vitiation; **rottenness,** corruptness, putrefaction, putrescence, putridity, putridness, putrilage, rot; **decay,** atrophy, decadence, decomposition, disintegration, waste, wasting; **rustiness,** corrosion, corrosion fatigue, erosion; **rot,** blight, canker, dry rot, pest, wet rot; **rust,** corrosion; **bottle sickness,** casse

DETERIORATIVE *adj* contaminative, corrosive, corruptive, degenerative

determination *n* → 1 judgment 2 solution 3 wilfulness

DETERMINE *v* adjudge, appoint, arbitrate, award, bring in a verdict, conclude, decide, decree, dispose, find *(Law)*, judge, pass judgment on, resolve, rule, sentence, will

determine *v* → 1 choose 2 influence 3 particularise 4 position

determined *adj* → 1 changeless 2 persevering 3 serious 4 stubborn

deterrent *n* → 1 discourager 2 warning *adj* 3 discouraging

detest *v* → 1 dislike 2 hate

detonate *v* → explode

detour *n* → 1 byroad 2 road *v* 3 diverge

detract *v* → subtract

detriment *n* → harm

detritus *n* → powder

deuce *n* → 1 devil 2 equal 3 two

devalue *v* → 1 cheapen 2 circulate 3 decrease

devastate *v* → 1 damage 2 destroy

develop *v* → 1 become greater 2 complicate 3 create 4 evolve 5 grow 6 improve 7 increase 8 photograph 9 shape

deviant *n* → 1 nonconformist 2 strange person *adj* 3 nonconformist 4 strange

deviate *n* → 1 nonconformist *v* 2 deflect

device *n* → 1 machine 2 method 3 plan 4 proverb

DEVIL *n* Antichrist, Beast, Beelzebub, cloven hoof, deuce, dragon, fiend, Lucifer, mischief *(Obs.)*, Old Nick, Prince of Darkness, Satan, serpent, the Adversary, the evil one, the Tempter; **demon,** archenemy, belial, cacodaemon, daemon, Davy Jones, debil-debil *(Aborig.)*, deil *(Scot.)*, fiend, Flibbertigibbet, ghoul, hellhound; **vampire,** ghoul, incubus, mare *(Obs.)*, nightmare, succubus, therianthrope; **werewolf,** loup-garou, lycanthrope; **devilishness,** Death, diabolicalness, diabolism, fiendishness, ghoulishness, lycanthropy, vampirism

devil *n* → 1 bad person 2 bad thing 3 destroyer 4 heater 5 immoral person 6 messenger 7 writer *v* 8 annoy 9 cook 10 work

DEVILISH *adj* cloven-footed, cloven-hoofed, daemonic, demiurgeous, demiurgic, demoniac, demonian, demonic, diabolic, diabolical, evil-eyed, fiendish, satanic

devious *adj* → 1 cunning 2 deceitful 3 deflective 4 opportunist 5 remote

DEVISE *v* cogitate, conceit *(Obs.)*, conceive, dream up, glimpse, ideate, image, imagine, reckon, suppose, think, visualise; **occur to one,** come to one, cross one's mind, dawn on, dawn upon, pop into one's mind

devise *n* → 1 getting 2 gift *v* 3 create 4 give 5 plan

devoid *adj* → empty

devolution *n* → reversion

devolve *v* → 1 obligate 2 roll

devotee *n* → 1 believer 2 desirer 3 enthusiast 4 worshipper

devotion *n* → 1 enthusiasm 2 faithfulness 3 friendship 4 high regard 5 love 6 reverence

devour *v* → 1 absorb 2 engross 3 gorge

devout *adj* → 1 friendly 2 reverent

dew *n* → 1 liquid *v* 2 wet

dexterity *n* → 1 competence 2 right

diabolic *adj* → 1 bad 2 cunning 3 devilish 4 difficult 5 immoral

diadem *n* → 1 authority 2 emblem of office 3 jewellery

diagnosis *n* → 1 analysis 2 investigation 3 judgment

diagonal *n* → bisector

DIAGRAM *n* atlas, carte *(Obs.)*, chart, delineation, figure, graph, histogram, map, plat *(U.S.)*, plot *(U.S.)*, schema, schematic, spectrum; **blueprint,** cross-section, delineator *(Sewing)*, design, draft, draught, drawing, elevation, green paper *(Brit.)*, ground plan, illustration, layout, lines, outline, pattern, plan, profile, rough draft, section, skeleton, sketch; **formula,** prescription, receipt, recipe, scrip; **map projection,** azimuthal projection, conic projection, conical projection, cylindrical projection, Mercator's projection, trimetric projection, zenithal projection

diagram *v* → map

dialect *n* → **1** accent **2** language
dialectic *n* → **1** change **2** questioning **3** reasoning
dialogue *n* → **1** communication **2** questioning **3** talk *v* **4** talk
diameter *n* → **1** bisector **2** line **3** thickness
diametrical *adj* → whole
diamond *n* → jewel
diaphanous *adj* → transparent
diaphragm *n* → **1** contraception **2** wall
DIARRHOEA *n* Bali belly, dysentery, Edgar Britts, incontinence, Jimmy Brits, Montezuma's revenge, runs, scouring, scours, shits, squitters, tomtits, trots
diarrhoea *n* → nausea
DIARY *n* black book, casebook, commonplace book, daybook, diurnal *(Archaic)*, flightlog, journal, log, tickler *(U.S.)*, workbook; **album,** scrapbook, skitebook. *See also* RECORD
diary *n* → book
diatribe *n* → **1** angry act **2** harangue **3** reprimand
dice *n* → **1** gambling **2** solid *v* **3** cook **4** cut **5** decorate **6** gamble
dichotomy *n* → astronomic point
dick *n* → **1** fool **2** groin **3** searcher **4** stupid person **5** vulgarian
dictate *n* → **1** command **2** rule *v* **3** command **4** speak
dictator *n* → **1** forcer **2** powerful person **3** ruler
dictatorial *adj* → **1** commanding **2** forceful **3** powerful **4** presumptuous
diction *n* → speaking
dictionary *n* → **1** list **2** reference book
dictum *n* → **1** certain thing **2** command **3** proverb **4** public notice
did *n* → toilet
didactic *adj* → **1** dramatic **2** teaching
diddle *v* → cheat
DIE *v* be carried out feet first, be gathered to one's fathers, breathe one's last, buy it, cark, cark it, cash in, cash in one's chips, cease *(Obs.)*, conk out, croak, deaden, decease, depart, die off, die on someone, do a perish, exit, expire, finish *(Obs.)*, flit *(Obs.)*, give up the ghost, go, go the way of all flesh, go to one's account, go west, kick off *(U.S. Colloq.)*, kick the bucket, part, pass, pass away, pass in one's marble, pass on, peg out, perish, pop off, predecease, snuff it, starve *(Obs.)*, succumb, throw a seven, toss in the alley, turn up one's toes; **fall,** bite the dust, drop, kiss the dust, lick the dust; **asphyxiate,** catch one's death, drown, famish *(Archaic)*, feed the fishes, freeze, starve, suffocate, swing, walk the plank; **commit suicide,** die a martyr's death, die for the cause, kill oneself; **die down,** die back, die off, fade, fade away, fade out, fail away, miff *(Bot.)*, wither, wither away; **receive one's death warrant,** die the death; **have had it,** be a goner, be as good as dead, be at death's door, be written off; **be dead,** be dead and buried, be dead and gone, be history, be no more, lie six feet under, push up daisies; **sleep,** lie in state, repose, rest
die *n* → **1** cutter **2** labeller **3** model **4** post **5** shape *v* **6** cut **7** fail **8** finish **9** shape **10** weaken
diehard *adj* → stubborn
die-hard *n* → strict person
diesel *n* → **1** fuel **2** train
diet *n* → **1** committee **2** council **3** fast **4** food *v* **5** abstain **6** eat **7** thin
DIFFER *v* bear no resemblance, disagree, diverge, divide, go different ways, speak a different language, vary; **contrast,** foil, mismatch; **discriminate,** separate the men from the boys, separate the sheep from the goats, sort, tell one from the other; **cause to differ,** modify, rearrange
differ *v* → disagree
DIFFERENCE *n* antithesis, diff, discord, dissemblance *(Archaic)*, dissimilarity, dissimilitude, dissonance, distinctness, inequality, shade of difference; **contrast,** contradistinction, foil; **disparity,** a fine distinction, a nice distinction, deviation, discrepancy, distance between, distinction, divergence, error, gap, generation gap, interval, variance; **spectrum,** cline, range; **heterogeneity,** diverseness, diversity, variety, variousness; **disparateness,** incommensurability, incommensurableness, incomparability, incomparableness, incompatibility, nonconformity, otherness, unlikeness, variation, variedness; **asymmetry,** dissymmetry
difference *n* → **1** ancestry **2** characteristic **3** disagreement **4** discrimination *v* **5** discriminate
DIFFERENT *adj* aliunde, as like as chalk and cheese, cast in a different mould, contradistinctive, discrepant, disparate, dissimilar, divergent, foreign, heterologous, incommensurable, incomparable, other, otherwise, poles apart, removed, unequal, unlike; **heterogeneous,** all kinds of, all manner of, diverse, diversified, manifold, of all kinds, polytypic, varied, various; **distinct,** disjointed, disjunct, distinctive, separate, unconnected, unrelated; **asymmetric,** asymmetrical, dissymetric, dissymmetrical; **contrastive,** contrastable, contrasting, contrasty, distinguishable; **modified,** altered, varied; **mismatching,** clashing, discordant, dissociable, dissonant, incongruous, inconsistent, non-congruent
different *adj* → **1** particular **2** strange
differential *adj* → numerical
differentiate *v* → **1** change **2** compute **3** discriminate **4** particularise
DIFFICULT *adj* awkward, complicated, cow of a, crook, crucial, curly, devil of a, diabolic, diabolical, dilemmatic, fiddly, hard, hell of a, helluva, intricate, knotty, nodal, tough; **painful,** distressful, distressing, trying; **arduous,** backbreaking, formidable, herculean, laborious, stiff, uphill; **burdensome,** bothersome, cumbersome, cumbrous, dear *(Archaic)*, grievous, heavy, onerous, op-

pressive, troublesome, weighty; **harsh,** rugged, scabrous, severe; **hairy,** dicky, dodgy, icky, kittle, spooky *(Surfing)*, sticky, ticklish, tight; **challenging,** demanding, formidable, graunchy *(N.Z.)*; **prickly,** spiny, thorny

difficult *adj* → **1** calamitous **2** hindering **3** stubborn **4** teaching **5** unclear **6** unwilling

DIFFICULTY *n* awkwardness, complexity, perplexity, thorniness; **arduousness,** onerousness, painfulness, toughness; **refractoriness,** bloody-mindedness, intractability, intractableness, prickliness; **a difficulty,** catch, coil, complication, entanglement, fun and games, matter, nigger in the woodpile, node, rub, stick *(Obs.)*, trouble; **problem,** bugger, crux, facer, fair cow, headache, knot, stymie, the devil to pay, tickler; **task,** an uphill battle, backbreaker, challenge, chore, hard nut to crack, job, long haul, murder, snorter, stinker, struggle, tall order, the devil's own job; **burden,** care, cumber *(Archaic)*, weight; **teething troubles,** growing pains; **hardship,** asperity, rigour. *See also* DILEMMA

diffident *adj* → **1** doubting **2** modest

diffraction *n* → **1** acoustics **2** reflection

diffuse *v* → **1** disperse *adj* **2** dispersed **3** verbose

DIG *v* delve *(Archaic)*, ditch, dredge, fossick out, gouge, plough, shovel, spade, spud, unearth; **mine,** cut, drive, excavate, open-cut, pan, quarry, sink, stope, surface; **tunnel,** channel, sap; **root up,** bandicoot, burrow, grub, scratch out, undermine; **crater,** cave in, dibble, dish, hole, pit, scoop

dig *n* → **1** inspection **2** mister **3** mockery **4** pat *v* **5** attend to **6** enjoy **7** farm **8** investigate

digest *n* → **1** abridgment **2** classification **3** reference book *v* **4** abbreviate **5** absorb **6** class **7** eat **8** inquire into **9** know **10** learn **11** persevere

DIGGER *n* bogger, boodler, burrower, fossicker, harrower, shoveller; **miner,** alluvial miner, black-sander *(N.Z.)*, coalminer, collier, Cousin Jack, gold-digger, goldfielder, goldminer, gouger, grass captain, gravedigger, gum-digger, mineworker, opal miner, pitman, pitworker, reefer, sand miner, tributer; **excavator,** bore sinker, ditcher, navvy, sapper, tank sinker, tunneller

digger *n* → **1** cell **2** friend **3** mister **4** soldier

DIGGING *n* banjoing, shovelling; **mining,** blacksanding, coalmining, drift mining, fossicking, longwall mining; **excavation,** shallow sinking, stoping, wet sinking; **gold-digging,** goldmining; **gum-digging**

DIGGING *adj* burrowing, fossorial; **mining,** coalmining

DIGGING IMPLEMENT *n* banjo *(Colloq.)*, bogger, digging stick *(Aborig.)*, mattock, pick, pickaxe, scoop, shovel, spade, spud, trowel; **hoe,** dutch hoe, grub hoe, rotary hoe; **mechanical shovel,** steam shovel, tractor shovel; **dredge,** dredger, dredging machine; **grader,** bulldozer, calfdozer, dozer; **plough,** chain harrow, chisel-plough, disc harrow, disc plough, gang plough, harrow, rotary plough, seed drill, stump-jump plough; **excavator,** backhoe, drott; **jackhammer,** post-hole digger

DIGGINGS *n* coalface, workings; **mine,** chalkpit, coal pit, open cut, pit, quarry; **reef,** alluvial, lode, mullocky reef, vein; **face,** prospect, workface; **trench,** cross-drive, crosscut, entrenchment, retrenchment, sap, tunnel; **pit,** downcast, downcast shaft, mineshaft, stope, well; **dump,** leavings, mullock, slagheap, spoil, tailings

digit *n* → **1** length **2** number

digital *adj* → **1** brachial **2** numerical

dignified *adj* → **1** formal **2** reputable

dignify *v* → glorify

dignitary *n* → **1** important person **2** manager

dignity *n* → **1** formality **2** mister **3** reputability

digress *v* → **1** deflect **2** waffle

DILAPIDATED *adj* attrite *(Obs.)*, beat-up, broken-down, dog-eared, down at heel, flea-bitten, hairy *(N.Z.)*, moth-eaten, old, out at elbows, ragged, ramshackle, ratty, rusty, scrubby, second-hand, seedy, shabby, shopsoiled, tacky, the worse for wear, third-hand, timeworn, toilworn, tumbledown, used, weather-beaten, weathered, weatherworn, well-worn, worn. *See also* DAMAGED

dilate *v* → become greater

dilatory *adj* → **1** late **2** slow

DILEMMA *n* blind alley, catch 22, double bind, impasse, nonplus, predicament, quandary, vicious circle; **fix,** corner, hole, hot water, pickle, quagmire, spot, squeeze, straits; **sticky wicket,** death seat *(Horseracing)*, hot seat, tight corner, tight spot; **mess,** can of worms, fine kettle of fish, hobble, hot potato, how-do-you-do, nodus, pretty kettle of fish, rat-trap, scrape. *See also* DIFFICULTY

dilemma *n* → uncertain thing

dilettante *n* → **1** artist **2** gamesman **3** novice **4** unimportant person

diligent *adj* → **1** careful **2** effortful **3** patient **4** persevering

dill *n* → **1** fool **2** incompetent **3** stupid person

dillybag *n* → bag

dilute *v* → **1** decrease **2** lose colour

dimension *n* → condition

diminish *v* → **1** be few and far between **2** decrease **3** slander **4** subtract

diminutive *n* → **1** small thing *adj* **2** small

dimple *n* → **1** indentation *v* **2** hollow

dimwit *n* → stupid person

din *n* → loud sound

dine *v* → **1** be sociable **2** eat

ding *n* → **1** buttocks **2** disagreement **3** fight **4** groin **5** impact **6** indentation **7** party **8** ringing *v* **9** break **10** eject **11** hit **12** repeat **13** ring

dinghy *n* → rowing boat

dingo *n* → **1** avoider **2** bad person **3** coward *v* **4** avoid **5** lack courage

dingy *adj* → **1** dirty **2** dull **3** shadowy **4** ugly

dinkum *n* → **1** good thing **2** the best *adj* **3** honest **4** true *interj* **5** honestly

dinner *n* → meal

dint *n* → **1** hit **2** indentation

diocese *n* → domain

diphthong *n* → letter

diplomacy *n* → **1** courteousness **2** mediation **3** politics

dipper *n* → **1** diver **2** vessel

dipsomania *n* → drunkenness

dire *adj* → **1** bad **2** calamitous **3** frightening **4** unpleasant

DIRECT *v* aim, channel, cox, helm, lay, level, luff, steer, up *(Naut. Colloq.)*; **guide,** beacon, beckon, home, lead, motion, pilot, point, sign *(Obs.)*, talk down; **orientate,** point towards, range, redirect, set, sight, train, traverse; **lie,** face, give on to, look out on, present, tail

DIRECT *adj* on the beam, one-way, point-blank, rectilinear, straight, straightaway *(U.S.)*, straightforward, true, unerring

direct *v* → **1** command **2** inform **3** manage **4** mark **5** send a message **6** stage *adj* **7** forthright **8** genetic **9** sequential **10** simple **11** straight

DIRECTION *n* aim, alignment, azimuth, bearing, beat, beeline, course, current, drift, eye *(Naut.)*, fly *(U.S.)*, heading, line, line of sight, loxodromic curve, magnetic bearing, orbit, orientation, path, rhumb, rhumb line, set, stream, streamline, streamline flow, stretch, sweep, tack, track, trajectory, trend, way; **aspect,** bearings, kiblah *(Islam)*, lie, sense *(Maths)*

direction *n* → **1** dissemination **2** guidance **3** management **4** musical score **5** point of view **6** teaching

DIRECTIONAL *adj* omnidirectional, omnirange, unidirectional, vaned; **steerable,** dirigible; **geotropic,** apogeotropic, chemotropic, heliotropic, negatively geotropic, positively geotropic, transversely geotropic

directive *n* → **1** command *adj* **2** guide **3** informative

DIRECTLY *adv* point-blank, straight, unerringly

directly *adv* → **1** concisely **2** hurriedly **3** now **4** straight

director *n* → **1** guide **2** manager **3** ruler

directory *n* → **1** list **2** reference book *adj* **3** informative

dirge *n* → **1** funeral rites **2** grieving **3** poetry **4** song

dirigible *n* → **1** aircraft *adj* **2** directional

DIRT *n* filth, grime, grot, mess, soil, toe jam; **smudge,** blot, blotch, greasespot, pick, smirch, smut, smutch, stain, sully *(Obs.)*; **dust,** cinders, cobwebs, fallout, soot; **waste,** putrilage, sewage, sullage; **swill,** bilge, drainage, effluent, rinsings, slops, slush, wash; **muck,** cack, grease, scum, scunge, skim *(Obs.)*, slime, slush; **dandruff,** scurf; **mould,** fungus, mildew, must, rot; **sweepings,** garbage, refuse; **dag,** daglock, dagwool; **flytrap,** Afghan flytrap, Australian flytrap, Bedourie flytrap, Boulia flytrap

dirt *n* → **1** news **2** slander **3** soil **4** swearing **5** talk

DIRTINESS *n* feculence, filthiness, foulness, nastiness; **grubbiness,** griminess, miriness, muckiness, muddiness, sliminess, sloppiness; **impurity,** impureness, insanitariness, insanitation, uncleanliness, verminousness; **dustiness,** sootiness; **smeariness,** greasiness, smudginess, stickiness; **mouldiness,** mucidness, mustiness; **pollution,** carrion, contamination, corruption, defilement, putrefaction, putrescence, putridity, putridness, stagnancy, stagnation; **squalor,** dinginess, sleaziness, sordidness, squalidity, squalidness; **messiness,** frowziness, lousiness, manginess, scruffiness, slovenliness, untidiness; **piggishness,** hoggishness, piggery

DIRTY *v* befoul, begrime, besmirch, defile, foul, grime, smirch, soil; **smear,** bedaub, besmear, blur, clart *(Scot.)*, daub, slime, slur *(Obs.)*, smudge, smut, smutch, spot, thumb; **contaminate,** corrupt, desterilise, flyblow, infect, maculate, pollute, sully, taint; **mire,** bemire, bespatter, muddy, puddle, splash; **mess up,** muck, untidy

DIRTY *adj* black, dingy, dusty, grimy, grotty, scungy, smoky, smutty, sooty, thick with dust, unswept; **unclean,** impure, insalubrious, insanitary, maculate, polluted, uncleanly; **smeary,** cacky, clarty, greasy, miry, muddy, smudgy, smutchy; **grubby,** shopsoiled; **messy,** trashy *(U.S.)*, untidy; **foul,** feculent, filthy, mucky, nasty, offensive; **stagnant,** festering, septic; **rotting,** maggoty, tainted, verminous; **slimy,** mucid, sloppy, slushy. *See also* UNKEMPT

dirty *adj* → **1** angry **2** climatic **3** dull **4** obscene **5** shadowy **6** sickening **7** unfair **8** violent

DIRTY PERSON *n* chat *(Colloq.)*, dag, draggletail, mucker, scruff, scunge, sloven, slut, warb; **polluter,** corrupter, defiler, pollutant; **guttersnipe,** mudlark, street Arab; **pig,** beast, hog, wallower; **litterbug,** litterer

disability *n* → **1** incompetence **2** injury **3** prohibition **4** weakling

disable *v* → **1** injure **2** prohibit **3** weaken

disadvantage *n* → **1** harm **2** inconvenience **3** uselessness *v* **4** incommode

disaffect *v* → provoke hatred

DISAGREE *v* conflict, differ, diverge; **argue,** argue the toss, argufy, argy-bargy, bicker, contest, cook up a storm, disagree, dispute, fall out, have words, pettifog, stickle, wrangle; **object to,** buck at, cavil at, confound, contradict, controvert, disagree with, except against, pay out, protest against, reluct to *(Archaic)*, remonstrate, take exception to, take issue with; **dissent,** demur, shake one's head, stir the possum

disagree *v* → **1** differ **2** disagree

disagreeable *adj* → unpleasant

DISAGREEMENT *n* argument, argy-bargy, bicker, bust-up, conflict, contention, contest, controversy, difference, ding, disputation, dispute, dissension, distance *(Obs.)*, division, set-to, strife, unpleasantness, upset, variance, words, wrangle; **objection,** cavil, contradiction, contrasuggestion, demur, demurral, difficulty, point of order; **denial,** denegation, disallowance, nay, negative, no; **dissent,** dissentience, dissidence; **protest,** remonstrance, remonstration

disallow *v* → **1** prohibit **2** refuse

DISAPPEAR *v* dematerialise, disperse, dissolve, drop *(Naut.)*, evanesce, evanish *(Archaic)*, evaporate, fade, fleet *(Archaic)*, immerge *(Rare)*, leave no trace, melt, peter out, vanish; **melt into thin air,** become lost to sight, become lost to view, do a vanishing trick, go into smoke, pass out of sight, take a powder

disappear *v* → depart

DISAPPEARANCE *n* blackout, dematerialisation, departure, dispersion, evanescence, evaporation, fade-out, fading, passing, vanishing; **eclipse,** occultation, total eclipse; **vanishing point**

DISAPPEARING *adj* evanescent, evaporating, fading, vanishing; **dispersive,** evaporative

disappoint *v* → disenchant

DISAPPROVAL *n* disapprobation, discountenance, disfavour, dislike, odium; **censure,** abuse, blame, commination, condemnation, criticism, denunciation, detraction, flak, invective, obloquy, rebuff, vitriol, vituperation; **remonstration,** admonition, execration, expostulation, protestation, remonstrance; **chastisement,** castigation, objurgation, reprehension, reprobation, reproval; **denunciation,** condemnation, crimination, damnation, denouncement, fulmination; **criticism,** animadversion, depreciation, dispraise, reflection, stricture; **contempt,** contumely, disparagement, scorn; **fault-finding,** captiousness, censoriousness, nitpicking, quibbling; **self-criticism,** self-abuse, self-reproach. *See also* REPRIMAND; BOO

disapprove *v* → refuse

DISAPPROVE OF *v* be unimpressed, deprecate, discommend, discountenance, frown on, frown upon, look down on, object to, take a dim view of, take exception to; **censure,** animadvert on, blame, condemn, criminate, damn, fault, pick to pieces, tax; **criticise,** bag, canvass *(Obs.)*, knock, monster, pan, pooh-pooh, roast, scarify, scathe, scorch, score *(U.S.)*, slam, slate, tear strips off, vituperate; **boo,** burl, catcall, hiss, slow clap. *See also* SCOLD

DISAPPROVER *n* booer, deprecator, hisser; **censurer,** carper, caviller, censor, complainer, critic, criticiser, cynic, Dutch uncle, fault-finder, hypercritic, knocker, niggler, nitpicker, quibbler, whingeing Pom *(Derog.)*, whinger; **denouncer,** condemner, denunciator, jeremiah, vituperator; **scolder,** admonisher, chider, rebuker, reproacher, reprover, scold, upbraider; **chastiser,** castigator, chastener; **protester,** expostulator, objector, remonstrant, remonstrator

DISAPPROVING *adj* admonitory, monitory, remonstrant, remonstrative, reproving, scolding; **censorial,** censorious, critical, hypercritical, overcritical; **fault-finding,** captious, derogatory, nitpicking, picky, quibbling, snide; **deprecatory,** contemptuous, contumelious, despiteous *(Archaic)*, insinuating, pejorative, sarcastic; **denunciatory,** comminatory; **disapprobative,** disapprobatory, dyslogistic, opprobrious; **condemnatory,** damnatory, damning, objurgatory, reprehensive, reprobative, uncharitable, upbraiding, vituperative; **scathing,** biting, blistering, blistery, scorching, slashing, withering

disarm *v* → make peace

disarray *n* → **1** disorder *v* **2** untidy **3** wear

disaster *n* → **1** failure **2** misfortune **3** nonachiever **4** ruin

disavow *v* → deny

disband *v* → **1** disperse **2** separate

disbar *v* → **1** dismiss **2** eject **3** prohibit

disburse *v* → pay

disc *n* → **1** circle **2** flower **3** recording *v* **4** farm

DISCARD *n* cast-off, jetsam, jettison, slough; **reject,** rejectamenta, throw-out, throwaway; **has-been,** heap, hulk, junk; **retired list,** scrap heap, slab-heap *(N.Z. Colloq.)*; **leftover,** cotton waste, dead letter, discontinued line, remainders, remnant, scrap, scrap iron, scrap metal, waste; **hand-me-down,** reach-me-down

discard *n* → **1** rejection *v* **2** abandon **3** disuse **4** refuse

discern *v* → **1** discriminate **2** see

DISCHARGE *v* bleed, drain, draw, drip, effuse, emanate, emit, exhaust, exude, flow out, froth, give off, issue, leak, let out, ooze, outflow, outpour, run, seep, spill, spout, teem, vent, weep, well

discharge *n* → **1** accomplishment **2** acquittal **3** bodily discharge **4** denial **5** dismissal **6** dutifulness **7** electricity **8** exit **9** explosion **10** expulsion **11** finished product **12** liberation **13** payment **14** record **15** shot *v* **16** accomplish **17** acquit **18** dismiss **19** electrify **20** excrete **21** expel **22** explode **23** liberate **24** pay **25** transport

disciple *n* → **1** defector **2** learner **3** religious follower

disciplinarian *n* → **1** strict person **2** teacher

discipline *n* → **1** course **2** monasticism **3** punishment **4** rule **5** sexuality *v* **6** be strict **7** punish **8** rear

disclaim *v* → **1** abandon **2** deny

disclose *v* → reveal

disco *n* → dance hall

discolour *v* → **1** disfigure **2** dull **3** lose colour

discomfit *v* → **1** confuse **2** hinder

discomfort *n* → **1** displeasure **2** illness **3** pain **4** unpleasantness *v* **5** discontent

disconcert *v* → confuse

disconsolate *adj* → unhappy

DISCONTENT *v* annoy, bite, chagrin, discomfort, disgruntle, dissatisfy, irritate, nag, nark, put out, put out of countenance, roil, worry

discontent *n* → 1 boredom 2 discontentedness *adj* 3 discontented

DISCONTENTED *adj* aggrieved, browned off, cast down, discontent, disgruntled, dissatisfied, fretful, fretting and fuming, ill-conditioned, malcontent, moody, never satisfied, not happy, out of humour, pissed-off, querulous, restless, seething, shitty, shitty-livered, sore, soured, troubled, uneasy, ungruntled *(Joc.)*, weary, wry; **grouchy**, bleating, carping, griping, grumbling, grumpy, moaning, murmuring, murmurous, narky, sulky, whingeing

DISCONTENTEDNESS *n* cold comfort, disappointment, discontent, discontentment, dissatisfaction, distemper, ennui, hatred, heartburning, moods, restlessness, seven-year itch *(Colloq.)*, unrest, verjuice; **grumpiness**, bitchery, disgruntlement, fretfulness, grouchiness, grumbles, murmuring, querulousness, s.o.l., shit on liver, sourness

discontinue *v* → 1 abandon 2 disuse 3 stop

discord *n* → 1 contentiousness 2 difference 3 disorder 4 dissonance 5 fight 6 incongruity

discotheque *n* → dance hall

discount *n* → 1 cheapness 2 decrease *v* 3 cheapen 4 decrease 5 forgive 6 sell 7 subtract

DISCOURAGE *v* beat the stuffing out of, daunt, demoralise, disenchant, dishearten, disillusion, get someone down, knock the stuffing out of, slap down; **dissuade**, advise against, block, check, chill, damp, dampen, demotivate, deter, put a damper on, put off, quench someone's enthusiasm, restrain, talk out of, throw cold water on, wet-blanket; **remonstrate**, expostulate, protest; **stop**, frustrate, thwart

discourage *v* → 1 frighten 2 hinder

DISCOURAGEMENT *n* demoralisation, determent, deterrence, disenchantment, disheartenment, dispiritedness, dissuasion; **remonstrance**, expostulation, protest, warning

DISCOURAGER *n* block, check, damp, dampener, damper, dash, demoraliser, deterrent, disincentive, dissuader, obstacle, restraint, stop; **remonstrant**, expostulator, protestor; **killjoy**, spoilsport, wet blanket, wowser

DISCOURAGING *adj* deterrent, dispiriting, dissuasive, off-putting, soul-destroying; **remonstrative**, expostulatory, warning; **forbidding**, prohibitive

DISCOURSE *v* canvass, comment, criticise, descant, discuss, dissert *(Obs.)*, dissertate, lucubrate, pamphleteer, review, treat, write about, write up

discourse *n* → 1 oration 2 talk *v* 3 sing 4 talk

DISCOURTEOUS *adj* badly behaved, disobliging, hoyden, hoydenish, ignorant *(Colloq.)*, ill-bred, ill-mannered, impolite, inurbane, mannerless, rude, tactless, uncivil, uncourtly, ungentlemanly, ungracious, unhandsome, unknightly, unladylike, unmannered, unmannerly; **brusque**, abrupt, bluff, blunt, brief, curt, short, short-spoken, terse; **insolent**, abusive, bold, bold-faced, brash, brassy, brazen, brazen-faced, cheeky, forward, fresh, impertinent, impudent, insulting, pert, sassy, saucy; **coarse**, coarse-grained, common as muck, crude, dead common, foul-mouthed, improper, rough, uncivilised, uncouth, unmannerly, unpolished, vulgar; **haughty**, cavalier, contemptuous, contumelious, disdainful, inconsiderate, offhand, overbearing, presumptuous, snubby, supercilious; **surly**, bearish, boorish, churlish, crusty, gruff, ill-conditioned, immodest

discourteous *adj* → insulting

DISCOURTEOUS PERSON *n* bastard, blackguard, boor, bull in a china shop, churl, Goth, gremmie, ocker, roughie, vulgarian, yahoo; **minx**, fishwife, hoyden, quean, tactless Tilly; **insulter**, knocker, snubber

DISCOURTESY *n* bad form, bad manners, conduct unbecoming, discourteousness, disobligingness, disrespect, ill-breeding, impoliteness, incivility, inurbanity, rudeness, solecism, tactlessness, ungraciousness, unhandsomeness, unknightliness, unmannerliness; **brusqueness**, abruptness, bluffness, bluntness, briefness, brusquerie, curtness, shortness, terseness; **impudence**, arse, brassiness, brazenness, cheek, chutzpah, crust, dumb insolence, forwardness, freshness, gall, hide, impertinence, sauce, sauciness, temerity; **coarseness**, bastardry, boorishness, crudeness, crudity, immodesty, improperness, impropriety, savageness, vulgarity; **surliness**, bearishness, churlishness, crustiness, grouchiness, moroseness

discover *v* → 1 find 2 reveal

discredit *n* → 1 disrepute 2 doubt *v* 3 disgrace 4 doubt

discreet *adj* → 1 cautious 2 discriminating 3 restricted

discrepancy *n* → 1 anomaly 2 contrast 3 difference

discrete *adj* → 1 interrupted 2 separate

discretion *n* → 1 choice 2 discrimination 3 independence

DISCRIMINATE *v* have an ear for, have an eye for, know, know chalk from cheese, know the difference; **discern**, contradistinguish, difference, differentiate, distinguish, distinguish between, distinguish from, pick out, resolve *(Optics)*, secern, separate the sheep from the goats, tell, winnow; **split hairs**, fine-draw, refine

discriminate *v* → 1 act unfairly 2 differ *adj* 3 discriminating

DISCRIMINATING *adj* clear-eyed, clear-headed, clear-sighted, discriminate, discriminative, penetrating, perspicacious, sagacious; **subtle**, fine, fine-drawn, fine-spun, hairsplitting, nice, overcritical; **discerning**, cultured, delicate, fastidious, nice, refined, selective; **discreet**, judicious, tactful; **discretional**, discretionary, judicial

discriminating *adj* → cultivated

DISCRIMINATION *n* difference, differentiation, distinction, hairsplitting, selectivity; **discernment,** culture, delicateness, discretion, finesse, refinement, tact, taste; **perspicacity,** clear-headedness, clear-sightedness, insight, penetration, sagaciousness, sagacity

DISCRIMINATOR *n* differentiator, discerner, distinguisher, hairsplitter; **connoisseur,** aesthete, cognoscente

DISCURSIVE *adj* critical, disquisitional, dissertational, dissertative, expository

discursive *adj* → **1** logical **2** verbose

discus *n* → circle

discuss *v* → **1** discourse **2** talk **3** test

DISCUSSION *n* argumentation, consultation, controversy, cross-fire, cross-talk, debate, dialogism, disputation *(Obs.)*, korero *(N.Z.)*; **argument,** argy-bargy, bicker, polemic, words; **conference,** colloquium, colloquy, congress, gabfest, negotiation, palaver, parlance *(Archaic)*, parley, pourparler, powwow, seminar, symposiac, symposium, teach-in, workshop. *See also* TALK

disdain *n* → **1** arrogance **2** low regard *v* **3** be arrogant **4** hold in low regard

DISDAINER *n* contemnor, despiser, scorner, sneerer, snubber, spurner; **dishonourer,** profaner, violator; **insolent,** baggage, minx, missy

DISDAINFUL *adj* coy *(Obs.)*, cynic, cynical, scornful, sneering; **derogatory,** derogative, disparaging, slighting, snide; **contemptuous,** contumelious, supercilious; **pejorative,** depreciative; **disrespectful,** impious, irreverent

DISEASE *v* disorder, distemper, fever, infect, inflame; **blast,** blight; **paralyse,** palsy

disease *n* → illness

dis-ease *n* → fright

disembark *v* → **1** arrive **2** dismount

disembowel *v* → cut off

DISENCHANT *v* betray, betray one's hopes, dash one's hopes, disappoint, disillusion, dismay, mock one's hopes; **frustrate,** foil, tantalise, thwart; **be a disappointment to,** be less than one's hopes, fall short of the goal, not come up to expectations, not come up to scratch

disenchant *v* → discourage

DISENCHANTED *adj* baffled, disappointed, foiled, frustrated, let down, rooted *(Colloq.)*, stuffed *(Colloq.)*, thwarted

DISENCHANTMENT *n* disillusion, disillusionment, dismay, frustration, tantalisation; **anticlimax,** bathos, baulk, blow, bummer, comedown, disappointment, fizzer, foozle, hitch, letdown, mare's-nest, sell *(Colloq.)*, setback, swiz

disengage *v* → **1** liberate **2** separate

disentangle *v* → simplify

disfavour *n* → **1** disapproval **2** displeasure **3** disrepute

DISFIGURE *v* deface, deform, mar, misshape, mutilate; **blemish,** blotch, discolour, distain, ensanguine, imbrue, imbue, splotch, stain; **scar,** pit, scratch; **freckle,** maculate, speckle, spot

disfigure *v* → **1** injure **2** uglify

DISFIGURED *adj* crooked, deformed, misshapen; **bruised,** black-and-blue, blebby, blistery, blue, ecchymosed, ecchymotic; **bloody,** blood-spattered, bloodstained, gory, sanguinary; **splotchy,** blotchy, blurry, patchy, scabby, smeary; **freckled,** freckly, macular, maculate, naevoid, spotted; **pimply,** acned, pimpled, spotty; **scarred,** cheloidal, cicatrised, keloidal, pockmarked, pocky, scarified

DISFIGUREMENT *n* beauty spot, birthmark, blemish, defect, deformity, fault, flaw, imperfection, lentigo, macula, mole, mutilation, naevus, stigma, strawberry mark, tarnish; **discolouration,** imbruement, imbuement, patchiness, scratchiness, spottiness; **pimple,** acne, blackhead, comedo, hic *(U.S.)*, milium, zit; **sore,** bleb *(Rare)*, blister, blood blister, bloodstain, bruise, ecchymosis, granulation, granulation tissue, phlyctena, proud flesh; **scar,** cheloid, cicatrix, keloid, pit, pock, pockmark, scratch; **wart,** boil, carbuncle, corn, cyst, furuncle, sty, verruca, wen; **wale,** weal, welt; **freckle,** blotch, do[t], fleck, maculation, speckle, spot

disfranchise *v* → boycott

disgorge *v* → expel

DISGRACE *v* attaint, bring shame upon, degrade, dishonour; **shame,** derogate from, expose, humiliate, pillory, reproach, show up; **defame,** brand, discredit, disparage, drag through the mire, stigmatise, vilify; **defile,** blot, cloud, denigrate, foul, smear, smirch, stain, sully, taint, tarnish; **detract from,** cast a slur on, censure, cut down to size, debunk, put to shame, throw dishonour upon; **have a low opinion of,** see in a bad light, view unfavourably

disgrace *n* → disrepute

disgruntle *v* → discontent

DISGUISE *n* cache-sexe, cloak, domino, false face, fig leaf, G-string, incognito, loup, mask, veil, visor; **camouflage,** cover, disguise, in[k] *(Ichthyol)*, protective colouring; **masquerade,** fancy dress party, masked ball; **alias,** alter ego, nom de plume, pen-name, persona, pseudonym; **pretext,** dissemblance *(Archaic)*, dissimulation, double bluff, stalking-horse; **enigma,** riddle; **cryptography,** cipher, code, cryptochannel, cryptogram, cryptograph, cryptology, invisible ink, microdot, palimpsest

disguise *n* → **1** disguise **2** portrait *v* **3** hide

disgust *n* → **1** hate *v* **2** displease **3** provoke hatred

dish *n* → **1** allurer **2** beautiful person **3** hollow **4** meal **5** tableware *v* **6** abandon **7** dig **8** hinder **9** hollow

disharmony *n* → incongruity

dishearten *v* → **1** discourage **2** frighten

dishevelled *adj* → untidy

DISHONEST *adj* ambidextrous *(Archaic)*, cronk, crooked, cross, double-dealing, knav ish, lurky, pettifogging, racketeering, rascally, roguish, rorty, shady, shifty, shonkie, slippery, two-faced, unjust *(Archaic)*; **corrupt,** available, bent, in it up to the hilt, open to bribery, Tammany-Hall, venal; **fraudulent,** fixed, set-up

dishonest *adj* → deceitful

DISHONESTLY *adv* cheatingly, corruptly, crookedly, fraudulently, knavishly, on the cross, on the fiddle, shadily, shiftily

DISHONESTY *n* crookedness, fraudulence, fraudulency, improbity, knavery, knavishness, rascality, roguery, shiftiness, trickery; **insincerity,** faithlessness, prevarication, unjustness *(Archaic)*; **corruption,** corruptibility, corruptibleness, corruptness, graft, jobbery, jobs for the boys, kick back, malversation, nepotism, payola, pork-barrelling, racketeering, venality; **cheating,** ambidexterity *(Archaic)*, barratry, cardsharping, champerty *(Law)*, chicane, chicanery, double-dealing, double dipping, jiggery-pokery, pettifoggery, rookery, sharp practice, shifty business, skin game; **swindle,** bilk, cheat, dodge, fix, fraud, funny business, gerrymander, gyp, lurk, medifraud, racket, ramp, skulduggery, subreption, tax lurk, wangle, wile; **crime,** foul play, lawlessness, theft

dishonour *n* → **1** disrepute **2** low regard **3** non-payment *v* **4** disgrace

disillusion *n* → **1** disenchantment *v* **2** discourage **3** disenchant

DISINFECT *v* antisepticise, chlorinate, dip *(Agric.)*, fog, fumigate, sanitise, smoke, sterilise; **depurate,** deterge, douche, physic. *See also* CLEAN

disinfectant *n* → **1** cleanser *adj* **2** cleansing

disinherit *v* → **1** isolate **2** take

disintegrate *v* → **1** collapse **2** deteriorate **3** liquefy **4** powder **5** separate **6** simplify **7** weaken

disinterested *adj* → **1** apathetic **2** fair **3** honest **4** neutral **5** unselfish

disjoint *v* → **1** disorder **2** misplace **3** separate

disjointed *adj* → **1** different **2** disorderly **3** illogical **4** inarticulate **5** partial **6** separate

DISLIKE *n* abhorrence, abomination, antipathy, averseness, aversion, detestation, disrelish, distaste, hatred, loathing, odium, repugnance, scunner; **opposition,** animosity, recalcitration, resistance

DISLIKE *v* abhor, abominate, detest, distaste *(Archaic)*, hate, have had, have no stomach for, have no use for, loathe, mind, object to, take a dislike to; **frown,** curl one's lip, make a face, pout, scowl; **fret and fume,** be on pins and needles, be put out, have a bad time of it; **put up with,** bear with, endure, hack, suffer

dislike *n* → **1** disapproval **2** hate **3** repulsion

dislocate *v* → **1** disorder **2** misplace

dislodge *v* → misplace

disloyal *adj* → **1** unfaithful **2** unfriendly

dismal *adj* → **1** bad **2** distressing **3** shadowy **4** sombre

dismantle *v* → **1** bare **2** separate

dismay *n* → **1** confusion **2** disenchantment **3** fright *v* **4** disenchant **5** frighten

dismember *v* → separate

DISMISS *v* amove *(Law)*, arsehole, axe, boot, bounce, can *(U.S.)*, cavil *(Mining)*, chop, disbar, disbench, displace, drop, eject, fire, give someone notice, hunt, kick out, lay off, put out to grass, recall, relieve, remove, retrench, sack, shelve, stand down, strike off, unmake; **discharge,** board out, cashier, decommission, demob, demobilise, drum out, muster out *(U.S.)*, pay off, pension off; **defrock,** deprive, disfrock, disordain, disrobe, unfrock; **suspend,** stand off; **depose,** deplume, dethrone, disseat, oust, overthrow, put the skids under, uncrown, unseat

dismiss *v* → **1** abandon **2** defeat **3** eject **4** forgive **5** repel

DISMISSAL *n* cavil-out *(Mining)*, discharge, lay-off, lockout, loss of employment, retrenchment, stand-down; **the axe,** bounce *(U.S. Colloq.)*, bullet, bum's rush, can *(U.S. Colloq.)*, chop, D.C.M., demission *(Rare)*, heave-ho, marching orders, notice, order of the boot, push, spear, the chuck, the sack, walking papers, walking ticket; **deposal,** comedown, deplumation, deposition, dethronement, disrobement, downfall, overthrow, removal; **resignation,** abdication, demission, retirement, spill *(Politics)*

DISMISSED *adj* axed, retrenched, sacked, time-expired, unemployed; **raddle-marked,** for the chop, on the skids

DISMOUNT *v* get down, get off; **alight,** disembark, land, light, perch, settle

dismount *v* → **1** arrive **2** separate

DISOBEDIENCE *n* civil disobedience, contempt, disturbance, filibusterism, non-compliance, non-cooperation, non-observance, passive resistance, rebeldom, transgression, violation; **delinquency,** contumaciousness, contumacy, disrespect, fractiousness, mutinousness, naughtiness, unruliness; **rebelliousness,** incompliancy, insubordination, recalcitrance, recalcitrancy, recalcitration, recreance, recreancy; **incorrigibleness,** frowardness, incorrigibility, indocility, perverseness, perversity, refractoriness, ungovernableness

DISOBEDIENT *adj* incompliant, non-compliant, transgressive; **disorderly,** anarchistic, insurgent, lawless, riotous; **rebellious,** contrary, contumacious, froward, indocile, insubordinate, mutinous, perverse, recalcitrant, recreant, seditious, treasonable, treasonous, violative *(U.S.)*, wilful; **delinquent,** naughty, rebel, urchin; **incorrigible,** fractious, rambunctious *(U.S.)*, refractory, unbroken, undisciplined, ungovernable, unmanageable, unruly; **illegal,** foul *(Sport)*

DISOBEY *v* drag one's feet, foul *(Sport)*, infringe, mutiny, rebel, recalcitrate, transgress, violate; **take the law into one's own hands,** go under someone's neck, kick over the traces, run riot

disobey *v* → anarchise

DISOBEYER *n* infringer, insubordinate, looter, non-complier, outlaw, rioter, traitor, violator; **rebel,** anarchist, dissenter, dissident, diversionist, insurgent, mutineer, recalcitrant, recreant, transgressor, urban guerilla; **delinquent,** hellion, juvenile delinquent, spiv, tear-arse, tearaway, urchin, wide boy *(Brit.)*

DISORDER *n* anarchy, bedlam, bouleversement, chaos, confusion, discord, distemper, fuddle, moil, snafu *(U.S.)*, turmoil; **untidiness,** confusedness, derangement, disarrangement, disarray, dislocation, disorderliness, disorganisation, entanglement, labyrinth, messiness, misarrangement, sprawl, tangle, topsy-turviness, twine; **riotousness,** rampageousness, rowdiness, rowdyism, tumultuousness, uproariousness. *See also* COMMOTION

DISORDER *v* addle, balls up, box up, disjoint, dislocate, disorganise, disrupt, disturb, foul up, frig up, make a box of, mess up, mix up, muss up *(U.S.)*, scamp, snafu *(U.S.)*, tumble, upset; **raise Cain,** create, cry blue murder, make a song and dance about, rabble, raise hell, raise the dust, scream blue murder, whoop it up, whoop things up

disorder *n* → **1** illness **2** misdemeanour **3** muddle **4** tangle *v* **5** disease **6** tangle

DISORDERLY *adj* chaotic, deranged, disordered, haywire, higgledy-piggledy, hugger-mugger, messy, out of joint, snafu *(U.S.)*, sprawly, topsy-turvy, upside down; **unorganised,** desultory, immethodical, random, unbusinesslike, unclassified, undisciplined, unjustified *(Print.)*, unmethodical, unstructured, unsystematic; **disorganised,** disjointed, dislocated, fragmented, incoherent; **unsettled,** disturbed, troublous *(Archaic)*; **riotous,** harum-scarum, pandemoniac, pandemonic, rampageous, rowdy, rowdyish, tumultuary, tumultuous, turbulent, uproarious, wild

disorganise *v* → disorder

disorientate *v* → confuse

disown *v* → **1** abandon **2** deny **3** refuse

disparage *v* → **1** disgrace **2** slander

disparate *adj* → **1** different **2** unequal

dispassionate *adj* → fair

dispatch *n* → **1** accomplishment **2** information **3** killing **4** means of killing **5** message **6** news **7** speed **8** transport *v* **9** accomplish **10** hurry **11** kill **12** transport

dispel *v* → **1** disperse **2** repel

dispensable *adj* → unimportant

dispensary *n* → medication

dispensation *n* → **1** command **2** disuse **3** lenience **4** management **5** order **6** permission **7** sharing out

dispense *v* → **1** be lenient **2** give **3** medicate **4** share out

DISPERSE *v* put to flight, rout, scatter, scatter to the winds, stampede; **deploy,** decentralise, diversify, farm out; **demobilise,** cast adrift, cast out, disband; **dissipate,** dispel, dissolve; **fan out,** branch, divaricate, radiate, ramify, spread, spread like wildfire, straggle; **diffuse,** circumfuse, effuse, pervade, thin; **strew,** bestrew, intersperse, sift, spill, string out; **disseminate,** apportion, broadcast, circularise, circulate, deal out, distribute, dole out, pass out, retail, seed, sow; **spread out,** make hay, ted; **sprinkle,** bespatter, besprinkle, dot, patter, sparge *(Rare)*, spot, spray; **atomise,** aerate, nebulise, spray; **dust,** powder, sand; **spatter,** flash *(Obs.)*, slosh, splash; **sputter,** spit, splutter

disperse *v* → **1** disappear **2** liquefy **3** separate

DISPERSED *adj* broadcast, cosmopolitan, diffuse, dissipated, far-flung, pervasive, scattered, widespread; **besprinkled,** besprent *(Poetic)*, bestrewn; **sparse,** isolated, sporadic; **diffused,** branching, extended, ramiform

DISPERSEDLY *adv* abroad, around, broadcast, diffusely, diffusively, dissipatedly, flaringly, here and there, passim, sporadically; **scatteringly,** spatteringly; **pervasively,** contagiously

DISPERSER *n* stampeder, tedder; **scatterer,** diffuser, disseminator, dotter, duster, sifter; **dispeller,** nebuliser; **distributor,** broadcaster, circulariser; **sprinkler,** aerator, aerosol, aspergillum, aspersorium, atomiser, knapsack spray, scent spray, sparge pipe, sparger *(Rare)*

dispirit *v* → frighten

displace *v* → **1** dismiss **2** eject **3** misplace

DISPLAY *n* array, demo, demonstration, exhibition, expo, exposition, fair, panoply, show; **presentation,** exposure, manifestation, presentment, production, re-presentation, rendition, showing, unfoldment; **spectacle,** pageantry, phantasmagoria, pomp and circumstance, riot, splash, splurge, sunburst; **preview,** sneak preview, view; **ostentation,** bluff, bravura, colouring, exhibitionism, pyrotechnics, showmanship, trim *(U.S.)*, window-dressing

DISPLAY *v* approve *(Obs.)*, bring forward, demonstrate, exhibit, present, troop; **expose,** argue, bear, betray, bring to light, evidence, evince, lay bare, point up, release, reveal, uncover; **spotlight,** highlight, illuminate; **manifest,** act out, express, indicate, turn on, vent; **lay out,** hang out, hold up, produce, spread out, trot out, unfold, unroll; **parade,** make perform, put through one's paces, show off to its best advantage; **show,** blazon, brandish, dangle, flaunt, flourish, maintain a high profile, parade, shew *(Archaic)*, sport, wear; **show off,** make a spectacle, promenade, steal the limelight

display *n* → **1** artistry **2** show *v* **3** reveal **4** show off

DISPLAY CASE *n* display window, gallery, goldfish-bowl, museum, open book, shopwindow, showcase, showroom

DISPLAYED *adj* arrayed, open, public; **exhibitive,** demonstrational, demonstrative, exhibitory, presentational

DISPLAYER *n* demonstrationist, demonstrator, exhibitor, manifestant, presenter, unfolder, window-dresser; **showman**, blazoner, exhibitionist, limelighter, pyrotechnist

DISPLEASE *v* bug, cause pain, cause trouble, chagrin, cut, displeasure *(Archaic)*, dissatisfy, hurt, make life unpleasant, open Pandora's box, stir up a hornet's nest, upset, vex, wound; **sicken**, disgust, nauseate, offend, rankle, repel, revolt, set the teeth on edge, turn off, turn the stomach; **horrify**, appal, chill the spine, freeze the blood, frighten, give the heebie-jeebies, make one's hair stand on end, make the flesh creep; **grate**, be no picnic, chafe, jar, rub up the wrong way, sadden, trouble

DISPLEASED *adj* angry, black-browed, browned off, cut up, dissatisfied, ill-at-ease, indignant, jack of, miffed, narked, offended, out of humour, pissed-off, put out, resentful, sore, umbrageous *(Rare)*, vexed, whingeing, wry; **hard to please**, cantankerous, discontented, perverse

DISPLEASURE *n* anger, chagrin, disfavour, dissatisfaction, indignation, miff, umbrage, vexation, vexedness; **discomposure**, discomfort, embarrassment, inquietude, malaise, mortification, uneasiness; **an awkward moment**, a bad patch, a moment's uneasiness, a sticky moment, a trouble spot, mauvais quart d'heure

disposal *n* → **1** order **2** selling

dispose *v* → **1** determine **2** position **3** tidy

disposition *n* → **1** character **2** order **3** point of view

dispossess *v* → **1** refuse **2** take

DISPROOF *n* confutation, counterevidence, disproval, elenchus *(Logic)*, falsification, ignoratio elenchi *(Logic)*, invalidation, rebuttal *(Law)*, refutation

DISPROVE *v* confound, confute, cut the ground from under someone's feet, demolish, give the lie to, invalidate, knock the bottom out of, make a liar of, prove wrong, rebut, refute, reprove *(Obs.)*; **tell another story**

DISPUTANT *n* arguer, bickerer, contester, controversialist, disputer, eristic, pettifogger, stirrer, wrangler; **dissenter**, anti, contradictor, controverter, demurrer, denier, dissentient, dissident, maverick, objector, protestant, protester, remonstrant, remonstrator

dispute *n* → **1** argument **2** disagreement **3** fight **4** litigation *v* **5** argue **6** disagree

disqualify *v* → **1** boycott **2** prohibit

disquiet *n* → **1** fright **2** worry *v* **3** alarm

disregard *n* → **1** inattentiveness **2** low regard **3** neglectfulness *v* **4** be inattentive **5** forgive **6** hold in low regard **7** neglect

disrepair *n* → damage

DISREPUTABLE *adj* disrespectable, doubtful, odious, questionable, shady; **disgraceful**, damnable, dishonourable, illaudable, opprobrious; **discreditable**, compromising, damaging, invidious; **degrading**, demeaning, lowering; **ignoble**, ignominious, inglorious, shameful; **scandalous**, arrant, famous *(Obs.)*, flagrant, glaring, ill-famed, infamous, notorious, outrageous; **blameworthy**, exceptionable, inexcusable, inexpiable; **reproachable**, censurable, criticisable, rebukeable; **of doubtful reputation**, questionable, suspect, suspicious, suss; **disgraced**, discredited, fallen, honourless; **humbled**, cut down to size, debunked; **nameless**, characterless, obscure; **unsung**

DISREPUTE *n* attainder *(Obs.)*, bad odour, contempt, disesteem, disfavour, disreputability, disreputation *(Archaic)*, disrespect, disrespectability; **bad reputation**, bad name, doubtful character, past, shady reputation; **dishonour**, discredit, humiliation, indignity, insult; **disgrace**, crying shame, ignominy, obloquy, odium, opprobrium, shame; **scandal**, stink, watergate; **notoriety**, ill fame, infamy, notoriousness; **anonymity**, obscurity

disrespect *n* → **1** discourtesy **2** disobedience **3** disrepute **4** low regard **5** misbehaviour *v* **6** hold in low regard

disrupt *v* → **1** disorder **2** separate *adj* **3** damaged **4** separate

dissatisfy *v* → **1** discontent **2** displease

dissect *v* → **1** inquire into **2** investigate **3** separate

dissemble *v* → **1** hide **2** pretend

disseminate *v* → **1** communicate **2** disperse

DISSEMINATION *n* circularisation, communication, conveyance, notification, transmission; **briefing**, direction, exposition, instruction, showing; **debriefing**, feedback, interrogation; **propagandism**, indoctrination, proselytism

dissension *n* → **1** disagreement **2** dissidence

dissent *n* → **1** complaint **2** disagreement **3** heresy *v* **4** disagree

disservice *n* → **1** harm **2** uselessness

DISSIDENCE *n* conflict, confliction, contention, dissension, disunion, disunity, division; **resistance**, adverseness, antagonism, confrontation, contrariness, defiance, obstruction, obstructiveness, opponency, opposition, oppugnancy, rebelliousness, resistivity; **insurgence**, direct action, insurgency, insurrection, insurrectionism, sabotage, sedition; **passivism**, civil disobedience, noncooperation, passive resistance; **recalcitrance**, obstructionism, recusancy, renitency, stand; **counterinsurgency**, backlash, counterplot

DISSIDENT *n* irreconcilable, noncooperator, objector, obstructer, obstructionist, opposer, oppositionist, oppugner, protester, resistant, resister, thwarter, withstander, Young Turk; **rebel**, guerilla, hostile, insurgent, insurrectionary, insurrectionist, maquis, opposite *(Rare)*, saboteur, terrorist, underground, urban guerilla; **challenger**, darer, defier, pebble *(Colloq.)*, taunter; **antagonist**, adversary, assailant, assailer, combatant, combater, confrontationist, confronter, contender, enemy, foe, opponent, quarreller, splinter group; **arguer**, anti, con, contravener, controversialist, devil's advocate, disputer, eristic, gainsayer, rebutter

DISSIDENT *adj* antagonistic, anti, defiant, offside, opponent, opposing, oppositional, oppugnant, rival; **resistant,** averse, combative, defiant, defying, insolent, insurgent, insurrectional, insurrectionary, militant, noncooperative, rebellious, reluctant *(Rare),* resistive, up in arms; **argumentative,** altercative, cantankerous, conflictive, confrontationist, contentious, contrary, crossgrained, disputatious, disputative, dissentious, incompliant, peevish *(Obs.),* perverse, quarrelsome, stroppy; **obstructive,** aversive, obscurant, obscurantist; **incompatible,** alien, at loggerheads, at odds, irreconcilable, opposed; **unyielding,** adamant, firm of purpose, implacable, indomitable, persistent, recalcitrant, renitent, unshrinking

dissident *n* → 1 disobeyer 2 disputant *adj* 3 argumentative

dissimilar *adj* → different

dissipate *v* → 1 collapse 2 disperse 3 overindulge 4 squander

DISSIPATER *n* bacchanal, bacchant, Corinthian, goliard, good timer, indulger, profligate, rioter, rip, surfeiter, wallower; **rake,** debauchee, debaucher, libertine, rakehell, roué, swinger *(Obs.)*

dissociate *v* → 1 separate 2 simplify

dissolute *adj* → overindulgent

dissolve *v* → 1 cancel 2 cinematise 3 collapse 4 deny 5 disappear 6 disperse 7 finish 8 liquefy 9 separate

DISSONANCE *n* atonalism, atonality, cacophony, discord, discordance, inharmoniousness, wolf, wolf note; **cross-relation,** consecutive fifths, false relation, suspension; **unmusicalness,** tonelessness; **harshness,** roughness; **hoarseness,** frog in the throat, graininess, gutturalness, raggedness; **raucousness,** brassiness, raucity, stridency; **clang,** clash, jangle; **blare,** bray, stridor; **croak,** crack, goose, guttural, roup, snore; **groan,** creak; **rasp,** grate, gride, grind, jar, scraping, scratch, scroop, skirr

dissonance *n* → difference

DISSONANT *adj* cacophonous, discordant, inharmonious; **atonal,** ajar, anharmonic, inharmonic, non-harmonic; **out of tune,** blue, bum, flat, off key, off pitch, sharp; **unmusical,** tuneless; **harsh,** grating, grinding, rasping, rough, rude, rugged; **hoarse,** cracked, croaky, grainy, gravelly, gritty, ragged, roupy; **creaky,** scrannel *(Archaic),* squeaky; **raucous,** brassy, strident

dissuade *v* → discourage

DISSYMETRIC *adj* dissymmetrical; **pinnate,** distichous, imparipinnate, pinnatifid, pinnatilobate, pinnatisect

distance *n* → 1 advance 2 disagreement 3 length 4 solitude 5 unrelatedness 6 unsociability *v* 7 succeed

DISTANT *adj* advanced, deep, far, far-off, faraway, farther, further, high, long *(Cricket),* offshore; **away,** aloof *(Archaic),* cold *(Games),* distal, removed, terminal, wide; **furthermost,** apogean, endmost, extreme, farthermost, farthest, furthest, outermost, solstitial, ultimate, utmost, uttermost; **long-distance,** cross-country, langlauf, long-range, marathon; **yonder,** thither, yon *(Archaic),* yond *(Archaic).* *See also* REMOTE

distant *adj* → 1 quiet 2 secluded 3 unsociable

distemper *n* → 1 discontentedness 2 disorder 3 dye 4 illness 5 irritableness 6 paint *v* 7 coat 8 colour 9 disease

distend *v* → 1 exaggerate 2 grow

DISTIL *v* boil down, chastise *(Archaic),* decoct, distill, isolate, smelt, still *(Obs.)*

distil *v* → 1 clean 2 separate

DISTILLED *adj* alembicated, distillable, distillatory

DISTILLERY *n* alembic, distillation column, pot still, smelter, smeltery

distinct *adj* → 1 acoustic 2 different 3 loud 4 obvious 5 separate

DISTINCTION *n* nicety, nuance, quiddity, quillet *(Archaic),* subtlety

distinction *n* → 1 characteristic 2 difference 3 discrimination 4 importance 5 reputation 6 superiority

distinguish *v* → 1 award 2 class 3 discriminate 4 glorify 5 particularise 6 see

DISTORT *v* deform, misshape, put out of shape; **contort,** bend, buckle, cast, convolute, overdraw, strain, torture, twist, warp, wrench, wrest, wrick, wring, writhe

distort *v* → 1 lie 2 misinterpret 3 uglify

DISTORTED *adj* anamorphic, anamorphous, axonometric, bent, buckled, contorted, convoluted, convulsed, perverted; **deformed,** crooked, diastrophic *(Geol.),* disfigured, epeirogenic, grotesque, miscreate *(Archaic),* miscreated, misshapen; **warped,** kinky, twisted, wry

DISTORTEDLY *adv* convolutely, crookedly, deformedly, misshapenly, pervertedly; **askew,** awry, out of shape, skew-whiff

DISTORTION *n* abnormity, crookedness, deformity, disfigurement, distortedness, malformation, misshapenness; **warp,** bend, bias, buckle, convolution, kink, knar *(Bot.),* screw, strain, stress, twist, wrench, wrest, writhe; **deformation,** anamorphosis, antic *(Archaic),* creep *(Engineering),* diastrophism, set, shear, strain, upheaval, uplift, upthrust; **facial distortion,** grimace, grin, snarl; **contortion,** convulsion, rictus, spasm

DISTORTIONAL *adj* contortional, convulsionary, convulsive

distract *v* → 1 amuse 2 confuse

distraught *adj* → 1 confused 2 mad

distress *n* → 1 pain 2 poverty 3 taking 4 unfortunateness 5 unhappiness 6 worry *v* 7 alarm 8 be out of luck 9 force 10 make unhappy 11 pain

DISTRESSING *adj* bitter, grievous, harrowing, heartbreaking, hurtful, lamentable, pathetic, poignant, pungent, ruthful *(Archaic),* upsetting; **dismal,** cheerless, chill, cloudy, dark, depressive, dreary, gloomy, joyless murky, oppressive, sepulchral, sunless; **mournful,** elegiac, epicedial, epicedian, funereal, lugubrious, plaintive, sorrowful, tragic

distribute *v* → **1** class **2** disperse **3** share out **4** tidy

district *n* → **1** domain **2** region

distrust *n* → **1** doubt *v* **2** doubt

disturb *v* → **1** agitate **2** confuse **3** disorder **4** hinder **5** interrupt

DISUSE *n* desuetude, dispensation; **boycott,** discontinuance, discontinuation, rejection; **obsolescence,** defunctness, retirement, supersedure, supersession; **planned obsolescence,** throwaway society; **lack of use,** suspension, virginity; **lack of practice,** rustiness

DISUSE *v* decommission, de-emphasise, lay aside, mothball, retire, set aside; **discard,** can, condemn, ditch, dump, give the sword, have no use for, reject, scrap, throw away, throw out; **jettison,** throw overboard; **dispense with,** boycott, discontinue, leave off, pension off, put out to grass, superannuate; **outgrow,** cast off, doff, shed; **leave unused,** do without, hold, hold in abeyance, reserve, save, shepherd, spare

disuse *n* → cancellation

DISUSED *adj* derelict, scrap, waste; **obsolete,** antiquated, archaic, dead, discredited, extinct, obsolescent, out-of-date; **discarded,** cast-off, outgrown, outworn; **out of use,** defunct, in mothballs, laid up, out of commission; **superannuated,** on the shelf, retired, written off; **rusty,** out of practice, out of the habit

ditch *n* → **1** channel **2** drain **3** fortification **4** furrow **5** limit **6** sea *v* **7** abandon **8** avoid **9** descend **10** dig **11** disuse **12** furrow **13** lower **14** repel

dither *n* → **1** confusion **2** excitement **3** vibration **4** worry *v* **5** become confused **6** be uncertain **7** vibrate

ditto *n* → **1** copy **2** repetition *v* **3** copy **4** repeat *adv* **5** repeatedly

ditty *n* → **1** poetry **2** song

diurnal *n* → **1** breviary **2** diary *adj* **3** daily

divan *n* → **1** couch **2** council **3** court of law **4** hall **5** living room **6** poetry

DIVE *n* bellybuster, bellyflop, bellywhacker *(Vic.)*, gainer, header, immersion, jackknife dive, plunge, swallow dive, tuck; **dip,** duck, souse; **swoop,** pounce, stoop; **power-dive,** crash dive *(Aeron.)*, tail spin; **skydiving,** freefalling

DIVE *v* bellyflop, bomb, dive-bomb, go down like a stone, honey-pot, plummet, plunge, sound, submerge, take a header; **dip,** duck, dunk, immerse, souse; **swoop,** pounce, stoop; **bail out,** free-fall, jump; **nosedive,** crash-dive, power-dive, skydive

dive *n* → **1** fall **2** kitchen *v* **3** fly **4** speed

DIVER *n* frogman, skindiver; **dipper,** ducker, dunker; **skydiver,** freefaller

DIVERGE *v* bifurcate, branch, divaricate, divide, fork, furcate, gape, move apart, ramify, splay, trifurcate; **divert,** avert, detour, fly off, fly off at a tangent, haul off; **radiate,** branch out, branch out in all directions, eradiate, scatter, spread; **abduce,** abduct

diverge *v* → **1** deflect **2** differ **3** disagree **4** waffle

DIVERGENCE *n* arborisation, bifurcation, branching, divarication, embranchment, furcation, moving apart, radiation, ramification, separation, trifurcation. *See also* BRANCH

DIVERGENT *adj* bifurcate, crotched, divaricate, furcate, splay, trifurcate; **radial,** abducent, averse, centrifugal, radiate; **branching,** arterial, brachiate, branchy, enate, ramiform, ramose, ramous, ramulose

diverse *adj* → **1** different **2** mixed

DIVERSELY *adv* diffusely, heterogeneously, miscellaneously, multifariously; **pell-mell,** indiscriminately

diversion *n* → **1** amusement **2** deflection **3** stratagem

DIVERT *v* canalise, flume *(U.S.)*, head off, inflect, switch

divert *v* → **1** amuse **2** diverge **3** please

divest *v* → **1** bare **2** refuse **3** take **4** undress

divide *n* → **1** break **2** sharing out *v* **3** class **4** compute **5** differ **6** diverge **7** elect **8** graduate **9** separate **10** share out

dividend *n* → **1** part **2** profit **3** share

divine *n* → **1** ecclesiastic *v* **2** predict *adj* **3** good **4** heavenly **5** religious **6** superior

divinity *n* → **1** angel **2** god **3** religion **4** superiority

division *n* → **1** administrative area **2** armed forces **3** disagreement **4** dissidence **5** domain **6** election **7** half **8** mathematical operation **9** parliamentary procedure **10** part **11** sharing out **12** train

divisive *adj* → contentious

divisor *n* → number

DIVORCE *n* annulment, divorcement, family break-up, legal separation, separation; **maintenance,** alimony, support, visiting rights; **nullity of marriage,** discretion statement

divorce *n* → **1** break *v* **2** separate

dizzy *v* → **1** confuse **2** spin *adj* **3** confused **4** foolish **5** neglectful **6** stupid

DO *v* chuck, cut, effect, engineer, execute, exercise, follow out, fulfil, get round to, perform, perpetrate, transact, wreak; **act,** do one's stuff, do one's thing, function, functionalise, run; **proceed,** go on, keep one's hand in, practise, take steps; **engage in,** deal with, play, wage; **get stuck into,** get one's teeth into, whale into; **take the bull by the horns,** have the courage of one's convictions, put one's shoulder to the wheel, rush one's fences, sail in, take the plunge

dob *v* → hit

docile *adj* → **1** composed **2** obedient

dock *n* → **1** court of law **2** harbour **3** prison *v* **4** subtract

docket *n* → **1** agenda **2** label **3** record *v* **4** list

doctor *n* → **1** cook **2** expert **3** healer **4** intellectual **5** wind **6** wise person *v* **7** cut off **8** fake **9** medicate **10** mix **11** practise medicine **12** repair

Doctor *n* → mister
doctrine *n* → belief
document *n* → **1** authentication **2** information **3** record **4** written composition *v* **5** authenticate
documentary *n* → **1** film *adj* **2** informative **3** testimonial
dodder *v* → vibrate
dodge *n* → **1** avoidance **2** dishonesty **3** expedient **4** ringing **5** stratagem *v* **6** avoid
DO EASILY *v* breeze through, do on one's ear, drive a coach and four through, glide through, iron out, lope through, make nothing of, make short work of, rest, romp, romp in, skate, step into, walk over, waltz; **win hands down,** romp home, shit it in, walk the course, win at a canter; **have it easy,** be on a soda, cop it sweet, have it made, live the life of Riley
DOER *n* actor, engager, executant, executioner, executor, executrix, exerciser, performer, perpetrator, practitioner, transactor; **initiator,** activist, actuator, animator, arouser, initiatress, initiatrix, provocative, provoker, stirrer, wakener; **agent,** agency, applier, fulfiller, wreaker; **pragmatist**
doff *v* → **1** disuse **2** repel
dog *n* → **1** bad person **2** informant **3** man **4** stand *v* **5** pursue
dogged *adj* → **1** persevering **2** stubborn
doggerel *n* → poetry
dogma *n* → belief
dogmatic *adj* → **1** assertive **2** certain **3** intolerant **4** presumptuous
DOING *n* engagement, execution, exercise, initiative, perpetration, play, pursuance
doldrums *n* → weather
dole *n* → **1** fate **2** grieving **3** income **4** share **5** unhappiness
doll *n* → **1** beautiful person **2** portrait **3** woman
dollar *n* → cash
dollop *n* → part
dolly *n* → **1** beautiful person **2** powderer **3** stick **4** wagon *v* **5** fake **6** powder **7** shape
dolphin *n* → makefast
dolt *n* → **1** fool **2** stupid person
DOMAIN *n* demesne, estate, grounds, realm; **kingdom,** archduchy, archdukedom, barony, duchy, dukedom, empery, grand duchy, margravate, marquisate, palatinate, princedom, regency, vicegerency, viceroyalty, viscounty; **emirate,** khanate, sheikhdom, sultanate; **district,** arrondissement, barrio, borough *(U.S.)*, canton, county *(Brit.)*, deme, department, division, eparchy, hundred, local government area, municipal district *(Tas.)*, municipality, nomarchy, nome, precinct *(U.S.)*, prefecture, province, riding, shire, state, territory, ward; **electorate,** constituency *(Brit.)*; **jurisdiction,** judicature, magistracy, verge; **church land,** glebe, glebe land, prebend; **parish,** mission, vicariate; **diocese,** archbishopric, archdeaconry, archdiocese, bishopric, eparchy, see
domain *n* → **1** job **2** number **3** ownership **4** power **5** real estate **6** subject matter
dome *n* → **1** arch **2** building **3** button **4** head **5** roof **6** tower *v* **7** bulge
DOMED *adj* arched, arcuate, arcuated, beehive, round, testudinate, vaulted, vaultlike, wagon-headed; **hemispherical,** hemispheroidal
DOMESTIC *adj* domiciliary, home, house, household; **residential,** tenemental, tenementary; **homey,** domestic, homely; **manorial,** seignorial *(Archaic)*
domestic *n* → **1** fight **2** servant *adj* **3** domestic **4** inside **5** national **6** resident
DOMESTICITY *n* domestication, domiciliation, homeliness; **domestic life,** domesticities, home life
domicile *n* → **1** dwelling *v* **2** house
dominant *adj* → **1** authoritative **2** important **3** most
dominate *v* → tower
domineer *v* → **1** be arrogant **2** impose **3** manage **4** repress **5** tower
dominion *n* → **1** authority **2** influence **3** nation **4** power
domino *n* → **1** corporal punishment **2** costume **3** disguise
don *n* → **1** aristocrat **2** boss **3** intellectual **4** teacher *v* **5** wear
Don *n* → mister
donate *v* → give
DONE *adj* accomplished, all over bar the shouting, finished, in the can, over the hump, well-done, wrapped up
done *adj* → **1** finished **2** useless
donkey *n* → **1** fool **2** heater **3** stubborn person **4** stupid person **5** transport **6** transporter *v* **7** transport
donor *n* → giver
doodle *v* → **1** be inattentive **2** write
doom *n* → **1** death **2** fate **3** judgment **4** punishment **5** ruin *v* **6** assess **7** ordain
DO ONE'S DUTY *v* acquit oneself well, act honourably, answer the call of duty, avenge someone's honour, be at one's post, comport oneself well, discharge a duty, fulfil an obligation, pay off a score, perform a duty, satisfy, serve, settle a score, supererogate; **be responsible,** carry the can, have broad shoulders, have the ball in one's court, have the matter rest on one's shoulders, take it upon oneself
DOOR *n* back door, bulkhead, deadlight, Dutch door, fly, folding doors, French doors, French window, jib door, louvre, paddle, port, portal, portcullis, postern, screen door, shutter, stable door, stern door, stop door, storm door *(U.S.)*, swing door, trap, trapdoor, wing; **gate,** Bogan gate, boom gate, drafting gate, drop-rail, floodgate, headgate, hurdle gate, lock-gate, swing gate, taranaki gate *(N.Z.)*, tollgate, water-gate, wicket
door *n* → entrance
dope *n* → **1** drug **2** fool **3** information **4** marijuana **5** paint **6** paste **7** stupid person *v* **8** anaesthetise

dormant *adj* → **1** asleep **2** inactive

dormitory *n* → **1** barracks **2** bed **3** bedroom **4** city

dose *n* → **1** amount **2** illness **3** medication **4** unpleasant thing *v* **5** medicate

doss *n* → bed

dossier *n* → information

dot *n* → **1** disfigurement **2** groin **3** musical score **4** property **5** sign **6** small amount *v* **7** disperse **8** hit **9** mark

dotty *adj* → **1** mad **2** weak

DOUBLE *v* duplicate, geminate, redouble; **couple,** bracket, match, pair, twin

double *n* → **1** actor **2** copy **3** gamble **4** gun **5** similar thing **6** stratagem **7** transport *v* **8** increase **9** speed **10** transport *adj* **11** big **12** deceitful **13** folded **14** two *adv* **15** in twos

doublecross *v* → **1** beguile **2** betray

DOUBT *n* credibility gap, distrust, distrustfulness, misdoubt, misgiving, mistrust, mistrustfulness, scepticalness, suspicion, uncertainty; **disbelief,** denial, discredit, incredulity, incredulousness, unbelief, unbelievingness; **scepticism,** agnosticism, nihilism, pyrrhonism

DOUBT *v* call into question, deny, disbelieve, entertain doubts, harbour suspicions, have one's doubts, question, smell a rat, suspect, take with a grain of salt; **disbelieve,** discredit, distrust, misbelieve *(Obs.)*, mistrust; **bring into question,** cause uncertainty, challenge, query, raise doubts

doubt *n* → **1** fright **2** uncertainty *v* **3** be frightened **4** be uncertain

DOUBTER *n* agnostic, denier, disbeliever, distruster, doubting Thomas, infidel, mistruster, nihilist, nullifidian, sceptic, unbeliever

doubtful *adj* → **1** disreputable **2** doubting **3** indecisive **4** uncertain

DOUBTING *adj* agnostic, diffident *(Rare)*, disbelieving, distrustful, doubtful, inconvinceable, incredulous, mistrustful, sceptical, suspicious of, unbelieving

douche *n* → **1** bath **2** cleansing *v* **3** disinfect

dough *n* → **1** cash **2** pulp

dour *adj* → **1** sombre **2** strict

douse *v* → **1** extinguish **2** lower **3** wet

dove *n* → **1** good person **2** innocent **3** pacification **4** peacemaker

dovetail *v* → **1** contact **2** fit **3** join

dowager *n* → **1** aristocrat **2** single person **3** woman

dowdy *n* → **1** ugly person **2** untidy person *adj* **3** ugly **4** vulgar

dowel *n* → nail

down *n* → **1** beard **2** descent **3** feather **4** grassland **5** mound *v* **6** absorb **7** defeat **8** drink **9** eat **10** lower **11** repress *adj* **12** ill **13** inactive **14** losing **15** unhappy *adv* **16** below **17** decreasingly **18** inactively

downcast *n* → **1** diggings *adj* **2** fallen **3** unhappy

downfall *n* → **1** dismissal **2** failure **3** losing **4** ruin

downgrade *n* → **1** slope *v* **2** decrease **3** slander *adj* **4** fallen

downpour *n* → rainfall

downright *adj* → **1** forthright **2** honest **3** most **4** truthful **5** unconditional *adv* **6** greatly **7** simply **8** wholly

Down's syndrome *n* → psychic disorder

downstairs *n* → **1** bottom *adj* **2** bottom

down-to-earth *adj* → realistic

downtown *n* → **1** city *adj* **2** urban

downtrodden *adj* → **1** obsequious **2** repressed **3** victimised

downward *adj* → fallen

dowry *n* → **1** gift **2** property **3** wedding

doyen *n* → old people

doze *n* → **1** sleep *v* **2** sleep

drab *n* → **1** grey **2** prostitute *adj* **3** boring **4** brown **5** dull **6** grey

draconian *adj* → strict

draft *n* → **1** diagram **2** drawing **3** forcefulness **4** military service **5** serviceman **6** written composition *v* **7** depict **8** force **9** map **10** separate **11** write

drag *n* → **1** bore **2** carriage **3** costume **4** friction **5** hindrance **6** imprisonment **7** pull **8** race **9** road **10** smell **11** tobacco *v* **12** go slowly **13** hang **14** pull

drag-net *n* → interlacement

dragon *n* → **1** devil **2** groin **3** mythical beast **4** violent person

drag on *v* → bore

dragoon *n* → **1** soldier *v* **2** force

DRAIN *n* culvert, ditch, downcomer, downpipe, drainpipe, gutter, ponding board, sewer, spitter, spreader, watertable; **wastepipe,** gully trap, S-trap, soil pipe, stench trap; **spout,** gargoyle, spile *(U.S.)*, waterspout

drain *n* → **1** electricity **2** exit *v* **3** discharge **4** drink **5** dry **6** empty **7** extract **8** flow

drainage *n* → **1** dirt **2** drying **3** exit **4** expulsion **5** extraction **6** removal

dram *n* → a drink

DRAMA *n* closet drama, conversation piece, costume drama, costume piece, epic, experimental theatre, Grand Guignol, history, kitchen-sink drama, mask, masque, melodrama, miracle play, monodrama, morality play, music drama, mystery play, panto *(Colloq.)*, pantomime, passion play, piece, play, playlet, poetic drama, problem play, Punch and Judy show, puppet play, sequel, shadow play, tetralogy *(Class. Antiq.)*, trilogy, work; **No,** kabuki, Noh, tamasha, wayang; **tragedy,** buskin, tragicomedy; **comedy,** bedroom comedy, black comedy, burlesque, camp, comedy of ideas, comedy of manners, commedia dell'arte, farce, high camp, high comedy, interlude, low comedy, musical comedy, sitcom, situation comedy, slapstick, theatre of the absurd, tragicomedy

DRAMATIC *adj* dramaturgic, dramaturgical, Grand Guignol, heavy, Thespian, tragic, tragicomic; **comic,** burlesque, clownish, comical *(Obs.)*, custard-pie, farcical, hammy, harlequinesque, pantomimic, slapstick, variety, vaudevillian; **didactic,** agitprop; **theat-**

rical, histrionic, make-believe, scenic, stagy; **choric,** stichomythic; **solo,** monologic, one-man, one-woman

dramatic *adj* → affected

DRAMATICALLY *adv* acrobatically, cinematically, clownishly, farcically, histrionically, scenically, stagily, theatrically, tragically; **backstage,** behind the scenes, downstage, in the limelight, in the spotlight, in the wings, offstage, on the boards, on the stage, onstage, upstage

dramatise *v* → **1** act pretentiously **2** excite **3** stage

drape *n* → **1** hanging **2** manchester *v* **3** cover **4** fold

drastic *adj* → violent

draught *n* → **1** amount **2** bit **3** diagram **4** drink **5** extraction **6** medication **7** pulling **8** wind

draughtsman *n* → **1** artist **2** builder **3** planner

draw *n* → **1** allure **2** attraction **3** attractor **4** breathing **5** equal **6** length **7** pull *v* **8** cash **9** contest **10** cook **11** depict **12** discharge **13** equal **14** extract **15** fill **16** portray **17** position **18** pull

drawback *n* → **1** hindrance **2** inconvenience **3** payment **4** tobacco

drawbridge *n* → **1** bridge **2** path

drawer *n* → **1** artist **2** extractor **3** waiter

DRAWING *n* drafting, sketching, technical drawing; **sketch,** line drawing, outline, perspective; **draft,** cartoon, graffiti, rough, sinopia, thumbnail sketch, vignette, visual; **caricature,** strip cartoon; **pattern,** blot drawing, design; **shading,** crosshatching, hachure, hatching, shadow

drawing *n* → **1** diagram **2** portrait **3** pulling

drawing-pin *n* → nail

drawing room *n* → living room

drawl *n* → **1** accent *v* **2** speak

drawn *adj* → **1** closed **2** equal **3** worried

dray *n* → **1** wagon *v* **2** transport

dread *n* → **1** fright **2** high regard *v* **3** be frightened **4** respect *adj* **5** frightening **6** highly regarded

DREADFUL *adj* crushing, demoralising, frightening, horrible, horrid, terrifying, traumatic; **gruesome,** appalling, creepy, frightful, ghastly, ghoulish, grim, grisly, horrendous, horrific, macabre, monstrous, nightmarish, shocking. *See also* UNPLEASANT; UNBEARABLE; SICKENING; PESTERING

dreadful *n* → **1** book **2** magazine *adj* **3** bad **4** calamitous **5** frightening **6** highly regarded **7** ugly

DREAM *n* chimera, hallucination, mirage, nightmare, phantasm, phantasmagoria; **daydream,** pipedream, romantics, stardust; **utopia,** cloud-cuckoo-land, fairyland, pie in the sky, pious hope, wonderland

dream *n* → **1** beautiful person **2** delusion **3** example **4** expected thing **5** hope **6** period **7** sleeping *v* **8** be inattentive **9** be indifferent **10** delude oneself **11** fantasise **12** hope **13** sleep

Dreamtime *n* → **1** afterworld **2** past **3** start

dreamy *adj* → **1** apathetic **2** beautiful **3** delusive **4** good **5** imprecise **6** inattentive **7** quiet

dreary *adj* → **1** boring **2** distressing **3** dull **4** unhappy

dredge *n* → **1** digging implement *v* **2** cook **3** dig **4** extract

dregs *n* → **1** remnant **2** waste

drench *n* → **1** drink **2** medication **3** wetness **4** wetting *v* **5** medicate **6** wet

DRESS *n* caftan, chemise, cheongsam, dirndl, Dolly Varden, evening gown, exclusive, frock, gown, halter-neck, hostess gown, jumper *(U.S.)*, kimono, mantua, maternity dress, Mother Hubbard, muu-muu, pinafore frock, polonaise, Princess line, robe, sack, sheath, shift, shirtmaker, stole *(Archaic)*, suit, sundress, tea-gown, topless, tunic, wedding dress; **wraparound,** haik, ihram *(Islam)*, lava-lava, pareu, sari *(India)*, sarong *(S.E. Asia)*; **skirt,** culottes, filibeg *(Scot.)*, hobble skirt, hoop, hoop skirt, hula skirt, kilt, kirtle, maxi, maxiskirt, midi, mini, miniskirt, overskirt, peg top, piupiu *(N.Z.)*, tutu; **tunic,** gym-tunic. *See also* OUTFIT

dress *n* → **1** clothes **2** equipment **3** formal dress *v* **4** clothe **5** cook **6** fertilise **7** prepare **8** tidy *adj* **9** formal

dress circle *n* → auditorium

dresser *n* → **1** clothier **2** container **3** cupboard **4** decorator **5** healer

dressing *n* → medication

dressing-table *n* → cupboard

DRESSMAKING *n* corsetry, rag trade *(Colloq.)*, tailoring

dressy *adj* → **1** decorative **2** tasteful

dribble *n* → **1** bit **2** flow **3** impact **4** small amount *v* **5** flow

dried *adj* → dry

DRIER *n* blow-drier, clothes drier, fugal, hair drier, mangle, spin-drier, tumble-drier, tumbler, whizzer, wringer; **clothes hoist,** clothes horse, clothes line; **dehumidifier,** air conditioner, evaporator, exsiccator; **desiccant,** desiccator, siccative; **drainer,** draining-board; **wiper,** squeegee, windscreen-wiper; **towel,** bath sheet, bath towel, beach towel, handtowel, paper towel, tea-cloth, tea-towel; **blotter,** pounce; **astringent,** antiperspirant

drift *n* → **1** accumulation **2** current **3** direction **4** length **5** meaning **6** move **7** passageway **8** point of view **9** soil **10** thrust *v* **11** farm **12** swim

driftwood *n* → timber

drill *n* → **1** formality **2** furrow **3** inserter **4** lesson **5** opener **6** piercer **7** preparation *v* **8** hollow **9** open **10** prepare **11** study **12** teach

DRINK *n* amrita, beverage, dishwater, draught, drench *(Obs.)*, drinkables, drinking water, eye-opener, heart-starter, nectar, potables, tap *(Archaic)*, wash; **tea,** billy tea, black tea, brew, bush tea, chai, char, cuppa, Darjeeling, green tea, gunpowder, hyson, Jack the Painter, oolong, orange pekoe, Paraguay tea, pekoe, post-and-rail tea, saloop, tisane; **coffee,** café au lait, cappuccino, coffee royal, congou, drip coffee, espresso, flat white, Irish coffee, long black, milk coffee, mocha, plunger coffee, short black, vienna; **soft drink,** barley water, chalybeate, cider, cider-cup, coke, cola, cordial, creaming soda, crush, dry, fizz, fruit cup, ginger ale, ginger beer, hydromel, ice-cream soda, julep, lemon squash, lemonade, lolly water, mead *(U.S.)*, mineral water, orangeade, orgeat, pop, ptisan, punch, root beer *(U.S.)*, sarsaparilla *(U.S.)*, seltzer, soda, soda-water, spa water, spider, squash, tonic, tonic water, vichy water; **milk,** buttermilk, colostrum, cow juice, malted milk, milkshake, polymilk, shake, skim milk, the bottle, thick shake, whey, whole milk; **eggflip,** flip, Murrumbidgee oyster, prairie oyster; **guarana; cocoa,** chocolate

DRINK *v* bend one's elbow, down, drain, imbibe, quaff, raise one's elbow, refresh oneself with, sip, slurp, suck, swallow, swig, swill, toss off

drink *n* → **1** alcohol **2** bit *v* **3** absorb

DRINK ALCOHOL *v* bib *(Obs.)*, get a drink across one's chest, imbibe, lush, soak up, sock away, stop one, swig, tip the little finger, tipple, wet one's whistle; **drink heavily,** bash the turps, be on the bottle, bend the elbow, booze, carouse, drink like a fish, get into it, give it a bash, go on the scoot, go on the squiff, go on the stun, go on the tank, grog on, hit the booze, hit the bottle, indulge, iron oneself out, lay into it, mix one's drinks, nudge the bottle, piss on, souse, tank up, tope, turn to drink, write oneself off; **shout,** be in the chair, carry the mail, sneeze, splice the mainbrace, stand one's hand; **toast,** bumper

DRINKING SESSION *n* bacchanalia, barney, bash, bat, beer-up, bender, binge, blind, blinder, boatrace, booze, booze-up, boozeroo *(N.Z.)*, compotation, grog-on, grog-up, happy hour, jag, jamberoo, lush, piss-up, pub crawl, rort, scatter, six o'clock swill, soak, spree; **cocktail party,** bowl, drinks, wine-tasting, winebibbing

DRINKING VESSEL *n* beaker, blackjack, calix, can, cannikin, chalice *(Poetic)*, ciborium, coffee cup, cup, cylix, demitasse, goblet, grace-cup, grail, loving-cup, mug, pannikin, pint-pot, pottle, quart pot, rhyton, rummer, scyphus, skin, stein, stoup *(Scot. Archaic)*, tallboy, tankard, taster, teacup, toby jug; **drinking glass,** balloon, beer glass, bobby *(W.A.)*, brandy balloon, butcher, champagne flute, cruiser, handle, Lady Blamey, lady's waist, long-sleever, middy, pony, pot, schooner, snifter, tumbler, vegemite jar, wineglass; **glassware,** stemware; **gourd,** calabash, horn, wineskin; **can,** ring-pull can, tin, tin can, tinnie, tinny, tube

drip *n* → **1** bad person **2** bore **3** flow **4** fool **5** liquid **6** splash *v* **7** discharge **8** flow

dripping *n* → **1** fat **2** flow

DRIVE *v* corner, fang, guttercrawl, motor, ride, scramble *(Racing)*, tool, tootle; **taxi,** bus, jitney, post, stage, train, tram; **cycle,** bicycle, scooter; **sledge,** bobsled, bobsleigh, skibob, sled, sleigh; **chariot,** gig; **hitch,** bum a ride, hitchhike, jump the rattler, ringbolt *(N.Z. Colloq.)*, scale, stow away

drive *n* → **1** access **2** attack **3** charity **4** effort **5** excavation **6** journey **7** motive **8** psyche **9** stroke **10** thrust **11** vitality *v* **12** dig **13** force **14** hollow **15** hunt **16** manage **17** operate **18** thrust **19** tire

drive-in *n* → auditorium

drivel *n* → **1** nonsense **2** speaking *v* **3** excrete **4** speak

DRIVER *n* cabbie, chauffeur, chauffeuse, defensive driver, hackie, motorist, road rider, road-hog, Sunday driver, syce, taxi-driver, wheelman; **motorcyclist,** biker, bikie, hell's angel, milk bar cowboy; **bicyclist,** cyclist, wheelman; **engine-driver,** engineer *(U.S.)*, engineman, gripman, shunter; **charioteer,** carter, coachman, wagoner, whip; **conductor,** busman, connie, motorman, ticket inspector, trammie

driver *n* → **1** leader **2** steerer **3** transporter

driving *adj* → **1** energetic **2** forceful **3** rhythmical **4** violent

drizzle *n* → **1** rainfall *v* **2** rain

droll *adj* → humorous

drone *n* → **1** accent **2** animal call **3** click **4** idler **5** music *v* **6** call (of animals) **7** click **8** speak

drool *v* → expect

droop *n* → **1** descent **2** hanging **3** pose **4** weakness *v* **5** be tired **6** be unhappy **7** fall **8** hang **9** weaken

drop *n* → **1** a drink **2** animal offspring **3** bead **4** bit **5** decrease **6** descent **7** jewellery **8** length **9** liquid **10** means of killing **11** opening **12** pendant **13** slope **14** small amount **15** wall *v* **16** abandon **17** be tired **18** descend **19** die **20** disappear **21** dismiss **22** exclude **23** finish **24** give birth **25** lower **26** quieten **27** report on **28** speak **29** stop **30** take drugs **31** transport **32** wane **33** wet

drop-out *n* → **1** nonconformist **2** photograph

droppings *n* → dung

dross *n* → **1** remnant **2** waste

drought *n* → dryness

drove *n* → **1** chisel **2** gathering **3** road **4** smoother *v* **5** farm **6** smooth

drover *n* → **1** farmhand **2** traveller

drown *v* → **1** die **2** fill **3** flood **4** kill **5** quieten **6** suffocate

drowse *n* → **1** sleepiness *v* **2** idle **3** sleep

drub *n* → **1** hit *v* **2** cudgel **3** defeat

drudge *n* → **1** worker *v* **2** make an effort

drudgery *n* → toil

DRUG *n* addictive drug, Bob Hope, bomb, dope, drug of dependence, gear; **narcotic,** hard stuff, junk; **tranquilliser,** stopper, stupefacient, stupefier; **hallucinogen,** mind-altering drug, psychedelic, psychoactive drug, psychochemical; **deal,** bag, deck, packet. *See also* NARCOTIC; MARIJUANA; STIMULANT; HALLUCINOGEN

drug *n* → **1** medication **2** surplus *v* **3** anaesthetise **4** oversupply **5** poison

DRUG ADDICTION *n* habit, monkey on one's back; **narcotism,** cocainism, morphinism, opiumism; **withdrawal,** cold-turkey, drying-out, methadone treatment

DRUG DEALER *n* dealer, dope-pedlar, doper, greengrocer, pusher, trafficker; **opium den**

DRUG EQUIPMENT *n* bong, chillum, hookah, hubble-bubble, water pipe; **hypodermic,** fit, hype, outfit, pick, works

DRUGGED *adj* blocked, bombed, dopey, loaded, mandied, off one's face, poppied, ripped, smacked-out, smashed, stoked, stoned; **high,** high as a kite, on a high, spaced, spaced-out, spacey

DRUG USE *n* bang, fix, hit, skinpop, trip; **high,** buzz; **overdose,** narcosis, OD, stupor

DRUG USER *n* acidhead, dope fiend, doper, glue-sniffer, head, hophead, hound *(U.S.)*, hype, mainliner, pothead, shithead, snowbird; **addict,** druggie, junkie, smackhead

drum *n* → **1** barrel **2** brothel **3** information **4** percussion instrument **5** support *v* **6** click **7** hit **8** repeat

DRUNK *adj* all-overish *(Obs.)*, blasted, blind, blithered, blotto, blued, canned, cast *(N.Z.)*, chocker, cockeyed, corked, cut, drunken, full, groggy, half-seas-over, high, high as a kite, in one's cups, inebriated, inked, intoxicated, jagged, lit, lit up, lushy, molo, pickled, pie-eyed, pinko, pissed, pissy, plastered, potted, primed, ripe, rolling, screwed, shickered, slewed, sloshed, sozzled, spiflicated, spliced, stewed, stiff, stinking, stinko, stoked, stonkered, stung, tanked, the worse for wear, three sheets in the wind, tight, tired and emotional, under the weather, well-oiled, winy; **dead drunk,** dead to the world, drunk as a lord, drunk as a pissant, drunk as Chloe, far gone, flakers, fuddled, full as a boot, full as a bull, full as a fart, full as a goog, full as a state school, full as a tick, loaded, non compos, off one's face, out to it, paralytic, ripped, rotten, smashed, stoned, unable to scratch oneself, unconscious, under the table; **tipsy,** elevated, maudlin, merry, muzzy, squiffy, tiddly, woozy; **alcoholic,** bacchanalian, bacchic, beery, bibulous, boozy, dipso, dipsomaniacal, in the grip of the grape, sottish; **hungover,** gone to Gowings, morning-after

drunk *n* → heavy drinker

DRUNKENLY *adv* bibulously, groggily, maudlinly, merrily, sottishly, tipsily, woozily; **intoxicatingly,** headily; **on the booze,** on the ran-tan, on the shicker, on the tank, on the turps

DRUNKENNESS *n* bacchanalianism, bibulousness, ebriety, fuddle, inebriation, inebriety, insobriety, intoxication, sottishness, tightness, tipsiness, wooziness; **alcoholism,** blue devils, d.t.'s, delirium tremens, dipsomania, heebie-jeebies, horrors, Joe Blakes, pink elephants *(Obs.)*, the dingbats, the shakes; **hangover,** a head, a terrible head, morning after

DRY *v* air-dry, blow-dry, drip-dry, kiln-dry, rough-dry, spin-dry, sun, ted, win *(Scot.)*; **wipe,** absorb, blot, mop, rub, sponge, squeegee, swab, towel; **drain; desiccate,** dehumidify, dehydrate, evaporate, exsiccate, mummify, season, torrefy, weather; **parch,** sear, shrivel, wither, wizen

DRY *adj* bone-dry, dry as a bird's arse, dry as a nun's cunt, dry as a nun's nasty, dry as a sunstruck bone, dry as the Nullarbor, fair, fine, high and dry, rough-dry, thirsty, tinderlike; **desiccated,** anhydrous, dried; **arid,** cloudless, dewless, droughty, floodless, fountainless, hazed-off, rainless, semiarid, subarid, sun-dried, sunbaked, torrid, waterless, xeric; **withered,** marcescent, sapless, sere, wizened; **waterproof,** coated, dampproof, showerproof, staunch, water-repellent, water-resistant, watertight; **xerophilous,** xerophytic

dry *n* → **1** drink **2** economics **3** prohibiter *v* **4** conserve *adj* **5** absent **6** abstinent **7** artistic **8** boring **9** humorous **10** infertile **11** sour **12** thirsty **13** winy

dry-clean *v* → clean

DRYING *n* airing, dehumidification, dehydration, desiccation, evaporation, exsiccation, torrefaction, ustulation; **drainage,** dereliction *(Law)*; **marcescence**

DRYING *adj* desiccant, desiccative, evaporative, exsiccative, parching, siccative, subastringent; **astringent,** styptic

DRYNESS *n* aridity, aridness, drought, semiaridity, the dry, torridity, torridness; **astringency,** stypticity; **watertightness; desert,** dead centre, dead heart, erg *(Geog.)*, rain shadow

dual *adj* → two

dub *n* → **1** boom *v* **2** copy **3** hit **4** name **5** perforate **6** polish **7** substitute

dubious *adj* → uncertain

duchess *n* → **1** show-off *v* **2** congratulate **3** flatter

duck *n* → **1** avoidance **2** dive **3** lover **4** nothing **5** vehicle **6** wetting *v* **7** avoid **8** dive **9** lower **10** punish **11** wet

duckling *n* → animal offspring

duct *n* → **1** bladder **2** channel

ductile *adj* → **1** metallurgic **2** obsequious **3** pliable **4** soft

dud *n* → **1** ineffectual person **2** nonachiever *adj* **3** useless

dudgeon *n* → anger

due *adj* → **1** apt **2** owing **3** payable **4** unpaid *adv* **5** adequately **6** straight

duel *n* → **1** fight *v* **2** fight

duff *n* → **1** soil *v* **2** bungle **3** conceive **4** rob

duffer *n* → **1** incompetent **2** stupid person **3** thief **4** wasteland

dug *n* → chest

dugout *n* → **1** cabin **2** cave **3** rowing boat

dug-out *n* → fortification

duke *n* → aristocrat

dulcet *adj* → 1 fragrant 2 pleasant 3 sweet

DULL *v* bedim *(Poetic)*, faint *(Rare)*, soften, take the shine out of; **matt**, deaden, fade, opaque; **tarnish**, discolour, muddy

DULL *adj* drab, dreary, faded, lacklustre, old, sad, toneless; **pale**, fishy, muted, soft, washed-out; **dingy**, dirty, gloomy, muddy, muggy, murky; **dim**, dusky, faint, obscure; **unreflecting**, antidazzle, antiglare, dead, dun, flat, glossless, leaden, lustreless, matt, matte, matted

dull *v* → 1 anaesthetise 2 blunt 3 bore 4 lose colour 5 moderate 6 quieten *adj* 7 apathetic 8 blunt 9 boring 10 colourless 11 composed 12 inactive 13 insensible 14 moderate 15 quiet 16 shadowy 17 stupid 18 tired

duly *adv* → aptly

dumb *adj* → 1 absent 2 inarticulate 3 reticent 4 silent 5 stupid

dumbbell *n* → 1 fool 2 stupid person

dumbfound *v* → astonish

dummy *n* → 1 cell 2 copy 3 fool 4 gamesman 5 model 6 portrait 7 printwork 8 room 9 stupid person 10 tram *adj* 11 fake 12 imitative 13 inactive

dump *n* → 1 arsenal 2 cabin 3 diggings 4 garbage dump 5 poorhouse 6 remnant 7 seclusion 8 storage 9 untidiness *v* 10 disuse 11 expel 12 lower 13 sell 14 store 15 throw 16 transport

dun *n* → 1 bill 2 brown 3 grey 4 insistence *v* 5 entreat 6 insist on *adj* 7 brown 8 dull 9 grey

dunce *n* → 1 incompetent 2 stupid person

dune *n* → mound

DUNG *n* bullshit, coprolite, cow cake, cow pat, droppings, dunghill, manure, meadow cake, mess, muck, taranaki topdressing *(N.Z.)*. *See also* DEFECATION

dungeon *n* → cell

dunk *v* → dive

dunny *n* → toilet

duodenum *n* → abdomen

dupe *n* → 1 artless person 2 victim *v* 3 trick

duple *adj* → two

duplex *n* → 1 house *adj* 2 two

duplicate *n* → 1 copy 2 imitation 3 repetition *v* 4 copy 5 double 6 imitate 7 reproduce *adj* 8 copied 9 two

duplicity *n* → 1 fakery 2 trickery

DURABILITY *n* durableness, serviceability, serviceableness; **fortitude**, backbone, doughtiness, hardiness, manliness, marrow, nerve, stalwartness, staunchness; **stamina**, inexhaustibility, relentlessness, staying power, tenacity, tirelessness; **indestructibility**, imperishability, impregnability, inexpugnability, inexpugnableness, invincibility, inviolability

DURABLE *adj* fortified, hard-wearing, heavy-duty, knockabout, serviceable, tough; **sturdy**, cast-iron, iron, steel, steely; **indestructible**, imperishable, impregnable, indomitable, inexpugnable, inextinguishable, invincible, inviolable; **tempered**, case-hardened, post-tensioned, pre-tensioned, thermotensile

DURATION *n* length, standing; **life span**, generation, life, lifetime, one's born days, run time, shelf life, short life, time limit; **aeon**, ages, donkey's years, eternity, yonks

duration *n* → continuation

duress *n* → 1 forcefulness 2 imprisonment

DURING *prep* round, since, through, throughout, under

dusk *n* → 1 dark 2 evening *v* 3 darken *adj* 4 shadowy

dusky *adj* → 1 black 2 dark 3 dull

dust *n* → 1 cloud 2 commotion 3 dirt 4 mineral 5 powder 6 remnant *v* 7 clean 8 disperse

DUTIFUL *adj* civic-minded, conscientious, observant, religious, supererogatory

DUTIFULLY *adv* conscientiously, observantly, responsibly; **on duty**, on the spot; **by reason of obligation**, of necessity, perforce

DUTIFULNESS *n* religiousness, responsibleness; **conscientiousness**, conscience, morality, morals, sense of fitness, sense of right and wrong, still small voice within, voice of conscience; **loyalty**, allegiance, fealty; **propriety**, conduct becoming, decorum, discharge, fitness, fulfilment, observance, proper behaviour, seemliness, the proper thing, the right thing

duty *n* → 1 job 2 obedience 3 obligation 4 tax 5 tribute 6 value 7 work

dwarf *n* → 1 fairy 2 short person 3 small person

dwell *n* → 1 interval *v* 2 continue 3 inhabit

DWELLING *n* abode, accommodation, address, domicile, dwelling house, dwelling place, establishment, habitation, hang-out, harbour, hermitage, home, home away from home, joint, kipsie, mansion *(Archaic)*, pad, pied-à-terre, place, residence, roof over one's head, shelter, shovel, squat, tabernacle *(Archaic)*, tenement; **habitat**, element, home ground, home range, medium, microhabitat, province, purlieu, range, sphere, zone; **residency**, consulate, Government house, prefecture; **fireside**, hearth, roof; **settlement**, colony, commune, plantation *(Hist.)*; **reservation**, Aboriginal reserve, Indian reservation, pa *(N.Z.)*, reserve; **retirement village**, halfway house, receiving home, rest home, sheltered housing; **foster home**, orphanage; **outstation**, country camp, outpost. *See also* BARRACKS; FLATS; HOUSE; CABIN; CARAVAN; CAMP; HOTEL

dwindle *v* → 1 contract 2 wane

DYE *n* azo dye, chromogen, colorant, colour fast, dyestuff, ink, lake, mordant, natural dye, opaque, pigment, reactive dye, rinse, tincture *(Obs.)*, vat dye, wash; **counterstain**, stain; **paint**, acrylic colour, body colour, colourwash, distemper, gouache, oil colour, oils, polymer colour, primer, scumble, tempera, undercoat, underglaze, watercolour; **make-up**, blusher, eyeliner, eye shadow, greasepaint, lipgloss, lipstick, mascara, rouge, war paint; **pencil**, chalk, crayon, felt pen, texta. *See also* COLOUR

dye *v* → colour

dying *n* → **1** death *adj* **2** dead **3** finished
dyke *n* → **1** channel **2** embankment **3** fortification **4** furrow **5** obstacle **6** road **7** rock outcrop **8** sexual type **9** toilet **10** woman *v* **11** furrow
dynamic *adj* → **1** busy **2** energetic **3** moving
dynamics *n* → **1** energy **2** movement
dynamism *n* → vitality
dynamite *n* → **1** ammunition **2** danger **3** explosive **4** the best *v* **5** explode **6** separate
dynamo *n* → powerful person
dynasty *n* → aristocrat
dyne *n* → energy
dysentery *n* → **1** diarrhoea **2** nausea
dyslexia *n* → psychic disorder
dyspepsia *n* → nausea

Ee

EACH *adv* a pop, apiece, individually, one at a time, one by one, per capita, respectively, singly

each *adj* → **1** particular *adv* **2** particularly *pron* **3** one

eager *adj* → **1** desirous **2** enthusiastic

eaglet *n* → animal offspring

earl *n* → aristocrat

EARLY *adj* earliest, first, premier; **earlier,** elder, former, olden, youthful; **premature,** abortive, immature, premmie, previous, rathe, slink, unripe, untimely; **forward,** precocious; **seasonable,** timely *(Rare)*

EARLY *adv* at crack of dawn, at first crack, at sparrow fart, before time, bright and early, early on, first thing, in the wee small hours; **earlier,** before, sooner; **beforehand,** ahead of time, in advance; **timely,** betimes, in good season, in time; **prematurely,** precociously, rathe *(Archaic)*

early *adj* → **1** original **2** past **3** preceding **4** untimely *adv* **5** in the past

earmark *n* → **1** label *v* **2** label

earn *n* → **1** loot *v* **2** gain

earnest *n* → **1** surety *adj* **2** attentive **3** emotional **4** honest **5** important **6** serious

earnings *n* → **1** income **2** profit

earphone *n* → radio

earring *n* → **1** jewellery **2** ring

earshot *n* → hearing

earth *n* → **1** animal dwelling **2** chemical element **3** land **4** remnant **5** shelter **6** soil *v* **7** electrify

Earth *n* → heavenly body

earthquake *n* → vibration

earthworm *n* → **1** crawler **2** insect

earthy *adj* → **1** land **2** obscene **3** pungent **4** realistic **5** sexy **6** voluptuous **7** vulgar

EASE *v* alleviate, comfort, console, cushion, facilitate *(Archaic)*, lighten, mitigate, relieve, soften, soothe, spare, sugar the pill, temper

ease *n* → **1** alleviation **2** composure **3** contentedness **4** informality **5** pleasure **6** rest *v* **7** alleviate **8** decrease **9** facilitate **10** rest **11** soften

easel *n* → **1** painting **2** stand

easement *n* → **1** facilitation **2** ownership **3** right of way **4** use

EASILY *adv* comfortably, conveniently, easy, effortlessly, facilely, familiarly, flowingly, fluently, freely, hand over fist, home on the pig's back, lightly, like a bird, painlessly, readily, smooth, smoothly, well; **snugly,** cheaply, comfortably, comfortingly, glidingly, on a plate, on a platter, on easy street, snug, soothingly

Easter *n* → holy day

EASY *adj* cinchy, comfortable, easy as falling off a log, easy as pie, effortless, facile, familiar, fatty, jammy, light, like shooting fish in a barrel, like taking candy from a baby, painless, right, sweet, undemanding, unexacting; **simple,** cheap, convenient, fair, flat *(Racing)*, foolproof, free, intelligible, knotless, runaway, smooth, uncomplicated; **manageable,** do-it-yourself, manoeuvrable, tractable, wieldy; **convenient,** handy, ready; **facile,** flowing, fluent, glib, light

easy *v* → **1** inactivate *adj* **2** alleviant **3** apathetic **4** clear **5** composed **6** content **7** inactive **8** influenced **9** informal **10** lenient **11** many **12** promiscuous *adv* **13** easily

EASY THING *n* a sweet cop, armchair ride, breeze, child's play, cinch, fat *(Print.)*, gift, loaf, picnic, piece of cake, piece of piss, pushover, sitter, sitting duck, snack, snap, walkaway, walkover; **plain sailing,** highroad, line of least resistance, primrose path, romp, set-up, soda; **head start,** walk-up start

EAT *v* bog in, demolish, dig in, down, eat like a horse, engorge, get into, get outside of, get stuck into, gobble, gollop, gorge, grub, gulp, hoe in, hoe into, ingest, ingurgitate, knock back, knock off, live on, nosh, overeat, pick, pick at, put away, refresh oneself with, scoff, sink, slurp, stodge, swallow, take, taste, toss off, tuck in, wash down, wolf; **chew,** bite, champ, chomp, masticate, mumble, munch, nibble; **diet,** be on a diet; **dine,** banquet, break bread, breakfast, dine out, eat out, feast, junket, lunch, mess, put on the feedbag, sup, tiffin *(India)*, wine and dine; **flash one's dover; digest,** absorb *(Obs.)*, assimilate, keep down, stomach; **predigest,** peptonise

eat *v* → **1** absorb **2** alarm **3** damage **4** destroy **5** deteriorate **6** have sex **7** taste

EATING *n* assimilation, deglutition, digestion, engorgement, eupepsia, feasting, gastronomy, ingestion, ingurgitation, mastication, monophagia, monophagy, omnivorousness, omophagia, polyphagia; **cannibalism,** anthropophagy; **geophagy,** geophagism; **swallow,** bolus, gulp

eavesdrop *v* → hear

ebb *n* → **1** decrease *v* **2** flow **3** go back **4** wane

ebony *n* → **1** timber. *adj* **2** black

ebullient *adj* → **1** bubbly **2** energetic **3** enthusiastic **4** excited **5** turbulent

eccentric *n* → **1** nonconformist **2** strange person *adj* **3** misplaced **4** nonconformist **5** strange

ECCLESIASTIC *n* Amen snorter, beneficiary, bush brother, chaplain, churchman, clergyman, cleric, clerical, clerk, confessor, curate *(Archaic)*, curé, dominie, ecclesiast *(Archaic)*, incumbent, josser, kirkman *(Scot.)*, man of God, man of the cloth, minister, Monsignor, padre, parish priest, parson, pastor, prebendary, presbyter, priest, priestess, rector, residentiary, Reverence, reverend, shepherd, sin-shifter, sky pilot, vicar, vicar-general; **divine,** Doctor of the Church, evangelist, father, lawyer, rabbi, rabbin, rabbinate, seminarian, seminarist; **sanctifier,** anointer, baptiser, celebrant, consecrator, insufflator, mystagogue, officiant, officiator, ordainer, seculariser; **dean,** archpriest, canon, capitular, capitulary, chapter, prebendary, subdean, vicar forane; **bishop,** diocesan, patriarch, pontiff, prelate, suffragan; **Chief Rabbi,** high priest, rabbi, rabbin, rabbinate; **ayatollah,** high priest, imam, imaum, mullah; **archbishop,** Abba, archdeacon, eparch *(Greek Orthodox)*, Evangelist *(Mormon)*, exarch *(Eastern)*, ordinary, primate, provincial, vicar apostolic; **cardinal,** cardinalate, ecclesiarch, Eminence, hat, prince, red hat; **pope,** ecumenical patriarch, Holy Father, patriarch, Patriarch of Rome, pontiff, primate, vicar; **the clergy,** the cloth, the pulpit. *See also* PREACHER; RELIGIOUS DIGNITARY; MONASTIC

ECCLESIASTIC *adj* ecclesiastical, hierarchal, priest-ridden *(Derog.)*; **missionary,** evangelical, evangelistic, revivalist; **clerical,** Aaronic, churchmanly, cleric, hieratic, ministerial, pastoral, presbyteral, priestly, rabbinical, rectorial, reverend, sacerdotal, secular, vicarial, vicarly; **synodal,** capitular, capitulary, consistorial, consistorian; **diaconal,** archidiaconal, decanal, neophytic, proctorial, subdiaconal; **episcopal,** archiepiscopal, metropolitan, prelatic, primatial, suffragan; **papal,** apostolic, curial, legatine, pontifical, primatial, suburbicarian

ecclesiastical *adj* → **1** ecclesiastic **2** religious

echelon *n* → **1** battleground **2** order

Echidna *n* → mythical beast

echo *n* → **1** alcohol container **2** answer **3** bottle **4** imitation **5** reaction **6** resonance *v* **7** imitate **8** repeat **9** resonate

eclectic *n* → **1** chooser *adj* **2** mixed **3** optional

eclipse *n* → **1** astronomic point **2** dark **3** disappearance **4** extinguishing **5** invisibility *v* **6** darken **7** surpass

ecology *n* → nature

economical *adj* → **1** cheap **2** thrifty

ECONOMICS *n* classical economics, demand-side economics, econometrics, macro-economics, micro-economics, monetarism, motivational research, political economy, supply-side economics; **economist,** cambist, chartist, dry, econometrician, free-trader, Keynesian, Marxist, monetarist, physiocrat, wet

economise *v* → **1** manage **2** save

ECONOMY *n* cash economy, demand economy, market economy; **free trade,** free enterprise, mercantile system; **monopoly,** corner, duopsony, monopsony, oligopoly, oligopsony; **private enterprise,** capitalism; **planned economy,** communism, socialism; **mixed economy,** welfare state

economy *n* → **1** management **2** systematisation **3** thrift

ecstasy *n* → **1** emotion **2** excitement **3** pleasure **4** reverence

ecumenical *adj* → general

eczema *n* → sore

eddy *n* → **1** current **2** spin *v* **3** flow **4** spin

EDGE *n* brim, brink, brow, limbus; **outline,** contour, profile; **border,** board, fringe, headland *(Agric.)*, margin, rand, skirt, verge; **ambit,** bounds, bourn, circuit, circumscription, compass, confines, girdle; **rim,** chime, collar, flange, gunwale, lip, rail *(Surfing)*; **ledge,** eave; **hem,** apron, basque, flounce, frill, fringe, furbelow, orphrey, ruffle, selvedge, thrum, valance; **frontier,** borderline, bounds, coast *(Obs.)*, march, outskirts, precincts. *See also* LIMIT; KERBING; COASTLINE; FRAME

EDGE *v* engrail, fringe, mill, rim; **bind,** braid, hem, list, twine; **frame,** cordon, hedge in, margin, marginate, mat; **outline,** circumscribe, contour

edge *n* → **1** advantage **2** apex **3** knife **4** pungency **5** side **6** stroke *v* **7** cut **8** deflect **9** sharpen **10** thrust

edgy *adj* → worried

edict *n* → **1** command **2** imposition **3** law **4** public notice

edifice *n* → building

edify *v* → **1** correct **2** improve **3** teach

edit *v* → **1** change **2** correct **3** explain **4** publish

edition *n* → book

editorial *n* → **1** commentary **2** news item **3** opinion *adj* **4** interpretive

educate *v* → teach

EDUCATED *adj* academic, antiquarian, book-learned, cultivated, cultured, erudite, learned, lettered, literate, owlish, pedantic, pseudolearned, scholarly, scholastic, self-educated, self-taught, studied *(Rare)*, studious, well-educated; **practised,** full-fledged, schooled, well-grounded, well-versed; **informed,** abreast of, au courant, briefed, enlightened, posted, primed, up on, up-to-date

EDUCATION *n* adult education, coeducation, continuing education, day classes, evening classes, further education, higher education, physical education, physical training, primary education, re-education, schooling, secondary education, self-education, sex education, special education, technical education, tertiary education, three R's, vocational training. *See also* TEACHING

EDUCATIONAL *adj* edifying, educative, educatory, instructive

EDUCATIONAL OFFICE *n* chair, deanship, headmastership, lectureship, position, proctorship, professoriate, professorship; **tutorship,** instructorship, supervisorship

eerie *adj* → **1** frightening **2** strange **3** supernatural

efface *v* → **1** destroy **2** hide

effect *n* → **1** accomplishment **2** influence **3** meaning **4** power **5** result **6** stage **7** trick *v* **8** accomplish **9** do **10** make

effective *n* → **1** serviceman *adj* **2** capable **3** operating **4** useable

effectual *adj* → **1** adequate **2** capable **3** operating

effeminate *n* → **1** sexual type *adj* **2** female **3** male **4** weak

effervesce *v* → **1** be energetic **2** bubble **3** hiss

effete *adj* → **1** infertile **2** useless **3** weak

efficacy *n* → capability

efficient *adj* → **1** causal **2** competent **3** operating

effigy *n* → **1** imitation **2** portrait

effluent *n* → **1** bodily discharge **2** dirt **3** exit **4** stream **5** waste *adj* **6** emergent **7** flowing

EFFORT *n* diligence, exertion, industriousness, industry, labour, lucubration, work; **drive,** conatus, endeavour, nisus, push, striving; **strain,** overexertion, overwork, stress *(Rare)*, travail, trouble; **muscle,** elbow grease, sweat of one's brow

effort *n* → **1** accomplishment **2** attempt **3** energy

EFFORTFUL *adj* arduous, backbreaking, burdensome, exertive, hard, heavy, herculean, laborious, labour-intensive, laboured, operose, strenuous, sweaty, toilful, toilsome, uphill, wearisome, weary; **industrious,** energetic, hard at it, hard-working, notable *(Archaic)*; **thorough,** diligent, painstaking, sedulous

effrontery *n* → **1** audaciousness **2** low regard

effusive *adj* → **1** emergent **2** emotional

e.g. *adv* → particularly

egalitarian *adj* → **1** equal **2** fair

egg *n* → **1** oval *v* **2** cook

ego *n* → psyche

egotism *n* → **1** braggartism **2** selfishness

egregious *adj* → **1** bad **2** important

egress *n* → **1** exit **2** liberty

egret *n* → feather

eiderdown *n* → **1** bedclothes **2** feather

eight *n* → **1** mariner **2** rowing boat

eighteen *n* → **1** alcohol container **2** sportsman

eisteddfod *n* → **1** concert **2** contest

either *adv* → additionally

ejaculate *v* → **1** eroticise **2** excrete **3** expel **4** speak

EJECT *v* avoid *(Obs.)*, boot out, bounce, chuck out, clean out, clear out, defenestrate, ding, fling out, jettison, kick out, oust, out, reject, rout, shoo, show one the door, throw out, turf out; **evict,** displace, turn out, turn out of house and home; **banish,** deport, exile, extradite, transport; **disbar,** black-list, dismiss, drum out, exclude, send down, strike off. *See also* EXPEL

eject *v* → dismiss

eke *v* → **1** increase *adv* **2** additionally *conj* **3** and

elaborate *v* → **1** be precise **2** change **3** clarify **4** complicate **5** improve **6** make an effort **7** particularise *adj* **8** complex **9** decorative **10** precise

elan *n* → **1** artistry **2** emotion **3** vitality

ELASTIC *n* elastic band, lacker band, rubber band; **spring,** cee-spring, leaf spring, mainspring, spring-loading, springboard, torsion bar, valve spring

elastic *n* → **1** lace *adj* **2** changeable **3** lenient **4** pliable

elate *v* → **1** make happy *adj* **2** happy **3** joyful

elbow *n* → **1** arm **2** branch *v* **3** thrust

elder *n* → **1** old people **2** religious dignitary **3** ruler **4** wise person *adj* **5** aged **6** early

elderly *adj* → aged

eldest *adj* → aged

ELECT *v* put in, return, vote into office; **vote,** ballot, blackball, cast a vote, coopt, divide *(Parl. Proc.)*, go to the polls; **appoint,** adopt, affect, ordain *(Obs.)*, preselect. *See also* CHOOSE

elect *n* → **1** eternity **2** religious follower *v* **3** eternalise *adj* **4** chosen **5** employed **6** eternal **7** good **8** superior

ELECTION *n* by-election, general election, hustings, plebiscite, poll, presidential primary *(U.S.)*, primary *(U.S.)*, referendum, tanistry *(Hist.)*; **vote,** acclaim, ballot, blackball, division *(Parl. Proc.)*, show of hands, voice; **kind of vote,** absence vote, card-vote, casting vote, compulsory voting, conscience vote, cumulative voting, deliberative vote, donkey vote, exhaustive ballot, first-past-the-post voting, free vote, free vote, postal vote, preferential voting, second ballot, secret ballot; **suffrage,** franchise; **polling booth,** ballot-box, ballot-paper, booth, voting machine *(U.S.)*, voting paper; **psephology,** psephologist

election *n* → eternity

ELECTIONEER *v* barnstorm, campaign, canvass, crusade, go on the stump *(U.S.)*, meet the people, press flesh, stump *(U.S.)*; **run for parliament,** stand; **hold an election,** dissolve parliament, go to the country, go to the people, go to the polls, prorogue parliament

ELECTIONEERING *n* agitprop, canvass, crusade, party political broadcast, party political speech, stump oratory, television debate, whistlestop *(U.S.)*; **dirty tricks,** gerrymander, pork-barrelling, smear campaign; **redistribution**

elective *n* → **1** choice **2** course *adj* **3** optional

elector *n* → **1** chooser **2** electorate **3** ruler

ELECTORATE *n* borough *(Brit.)*, congressional district *(U.S.)*, constituency *(Brit.)*, country seat, rotten borough *(Brit. Hist.)*, seat, swinging seat; **voter,** abstainer, constituent, elector, electoral college, floating vote, floating voter, mandator, swinging voter; **right to vote,** franchise, isonomy, suffrage, universal suffrage

electorate *n* → 1 administrative area 2 chooser 3 domain

ELECTRICIAN *n* auto-electrician, electrical engineer, sparks, wirer

ELECTRICITY *n* juice, power, supply; **faradism,** galvanism, hydro-electricity, magneto-electricity, piezoelectricity, pyroelectricity, static electricity, thermoelectricity, triboelectricity, voltaism; **electric current,** alternating current, amperage, charge, current density, direct current, eddy current, Foucault current, grid current, impulse, ripple current, thermionic current; **spark,** arc, carbon arc; **voltage,** electric potential, electromotive force, grid bias, potential, potential difference, tension; **capacitance,** absolute permittivity, admittance, capacity, commutation, conductance, dielectric strength, elastance, electric field strength, flux, impedance, inductance, induction, load, power factor, reactance, relative permittivity, resistance, resistivity, superconductivity, susceptance, susceptibility, wattage; **static,** atmospherics, interference; **discharge,** brush discharge, corona, disruptive discharge, drain, flashover, gas discharge, glow discharge, leakage current, shot noise

ELECTRIFY *v* charge, electrolyse, excite, galvanise, power, shock; **transistorise; earth,** ground, neutralise; **spark,** arc, discharge, flashover, strike an arc; **conduct,** commutate, convert; **connect,** patch

electrify *v* → excite

electrocute *v* → 1 execute 2 kill

electrolysis *n* → 1 destruction 2 medical treatment

elegant *adj* → 1 beautiful 2 good 3 tasteful

elegy *n* → 1 funeral rites 2 grieving 3 poetry 4 song

element *n* → 1 armed forces 2 dwelling 3 part 4 particulars 5 person 6 stove 7 surroundings 8 word

elemental *adj* → 1 airy 2 constituent 3 fundamental 4 powerful 5 simple

elementary *adj* → 1 airy 2 constituent 3 fundamental 4 original 5 simple

elephant *n* → book part

elevate *v* → 1 lift 2 make happy 3 promote 4 raise up

elevation *n* → 1 diagram 2 height 3 lifting

ELEVATOR *n* dumb waiter, escalator, heightener, lift

elevator *n* → 1 conveyor 2 lift 3 steering wheel 4 storehouse 5 tower

eleven *n* → sportsman

elf *n* → 1 children 2 fairy 3 mischief-maker 4 small person

elicit *v* → find

eligible *adj* → 1 chosen 2 desirable

eliminate *v* → 1 exclude 2 expel

elision *n* → 1 abridgment 2 exclusion

elite *n* → aristocracy

elixir *n* → 1 essence 2 medication

ellipse *n* → oval

ellipsis *n* → 1 abridgment 2 exclusion

elm *n* → timber

elongate *v* → 1 extend *adj* 2 long

elope *v* → 1 escape 2 marry

ELOQUENCE *n* articulateness, fluency, gift of the gab, good speaking, oratory; **rhetoric,** floridness, floweriness, grandiloquence, loftiness, magniloquence, orotundity, picturesqueness, word-painting; **wit,** Atticism, esprit, pungency, repartee, spice

ELOQUENT *adj* articulate, epideictic, epidictic, magniloquent, picturesque, silver, silver-tongued, slick, smart, smooth, smooth-spoken; **rhetorical,** apostrophic, cadenced, declamatory, florid, flowery, flowing, grandiloquent, grandiose, heroic, high-flown, high-sounding, homiletic, Johnsonian, lofty, oratorical, polemic, polemical, purple, recitative, sermonic, sonorous, swelling

else *adv* → additionally

elucidate *v* → 1 clarify 2 explain

ELUDE *v* get away from, shake, shake off; **flee,** abscond, bilk, blow through, bolt, do a bunk, escape, flit, fly, run, take flight, take to flight, turn tail

elude *v* → 1 escape 2 puzzle

ELUSIVE *adj* escapist, evasive, slippery; **fugitive,** fly-by-night, runaway; **aloof,** noncommittal, unforthcoming; **oblique,** equivocal, equivocating, prevaricating, quibbling

elusive *adj* → 1 escaped 2 unavailable 3 unclear

emanate *v* → 1 discharge 2 result

emancipate *v* → liberate

emancipist *n* → 1 liberator 2 prisoner

emasculate *v* → 1 cut off 2 feminise *adj* 3 female

embalm *v* → 1 bury 2 conserve 3 memorise

EMBANKMENT *n* baulk, dyke, floodbank, floodgate *(N.Z.)*, levee, mound, retaining wall, revetment; **rampart,** barricade, berm, bulwark, parapet, stockade, vallation

embankment *n* → 1 fortification 2 mound 3 obstacle 4 ridge 5 support

embargo *n* → 1 prohibition 2 restraining order *v* 3 prohibit 4 restrict

embark *v* → 1 depart 2 enter 3 invest 4 undertake

embarrass *v* → 1 cause difficulties 2 complicate 3 hinder 4 incommode

embassy *n* → agency

embed *v* → 1 insert 2 interiorise

embellish *v* → 1 complicate 2 decorate

ember *n* → fire

EMBEZZLEMENT *n* defalcation, misappropriation, peculation; **fraud,** blackmail, bubble, cheat *(Law)*, clip, confidence trick, do, false pretences, fraudulent speculation, licence to print money, plant, rip-off, set-up, skin game, swindle; **plagiarism,** cribbing

embitter *v* → provoke hatred

EMBLEM *n* caduceus, image, status symbol, symbol, totem; **badge,** armband, brassard, button, chevron, cluster *(U.S. Army)*, cockade, cockleshell *(Hist.)*, cognisance *(Her.)*, collar, cordon, cordon bleu, facings, favour, flash, gong, gorget, hatband, love knot, medal, medallion, patch, pip, plaque, ribbon, shoulder-flash, spur, star, stripe, truelove knot, weeper; **seal,** broad seal, bull, bulla, cachet, chop *(India)*, colophon, common seal, great seal, hallmark, impress, imprint, seal of office, seal of state, sigil, signet, trademark; **insignia,** badges of honour, badges of office, colours, racing stripes, seals of office, the seals

emblem *n* → sign

EMBLEMATISE *v* hallmark, seal, signet; **blazon,** blaze, charge, emblazon, marshal, quarter, unpale

EMBLEMATIST *n* armorist, blazoner

EMBLEM OF OFFICE *n* ; **crown** coronal, coronet, diadem; **badge of sovereignty,** globe *(Hist.)*, orb, sceptre, sword of state; **badge of authority,** baton, Black Rod, crosier, gavel, mace, mark of office, pastoral, rod, staff, truncheon, verge, wand, warder; **regalia,** hood *(Educ.)*, livery, pontificals, regimentals, robes of office, trappings of power, uniform, vestments

embody *v* → **1** associate **2** materialise

EMBOLDEN *v* buoy, encourage, hearten, inspire, inspirit, nerve, psych up

emboss *v* → **1** bulge **2** engrave **3** sew

embrace *n* → **1** endearments **2** friendship **3** hold *v* **4** absorb **5** assent to **6** hold **7** include **8** kiss **9** look **10** love **11** surround

embroider *v* → **1** exaggerate **2** sew

embroil *v* → **1** muddle **2** untidy

embryo *n* → **1** start *adj* **2** original **3** prototypal

emend *v* → **1** be precise **2** correct

emerald *n* → green

emerge *v* → **1** appear **2** exit

EMERGENT *adj* effluent, effusive, emanating, emanative, emanatory, emerging, excurrent, exoreic, forthcoming, issuant *(Rare)*, issuing, jessant *(Heraldry)*, outflowing, outgoing, outpouring; **eruptive,** effusive, expulsive

emergent *adj* → **1** ascending **2** new **3** occurrent

emetic *n* → expeller

emigrate *v* → **1** depart **2** exit **3** travel

eminent *adj* → **1** enormous **2** important **3** predominant **4** protuberant **5** reputable **6** tall

emissary *n* → delegate

emission *n* → **1** exit **2** expulsion **3** finished product

emit *v* → **1** discharge **2** expel **3** speak

emollient *n* → **1** medication *adj* **2** alleviant **3** soft

emolument *n* → income

EMOTION *n* affect *(Psychol.)*, affection, feeling, feelings, mood, pulse, sensation, sentiment, thing, tune *(Obs.)*, vibes, vibrations; **spirits,** cheer, courage *(Obs.)*, morale, temper; **heart,** being, bosom, breast, heart of hearts, heartstrings, mind, soul, spirit; **fervour,** ardency, ardour, elan, enthusiasm, fervency, ferventness, fervidness, fieriness, fire, flame, franticness, glow, heat, histrionics, impassionedness, melodrama, passion, passionateness, perfervour, rage, tear, torridity, torridness, vehemence, warmth; **ecstasy,** paroxysm, spasm, throe, transport

EMOTIONAL *adj* affective, feeling, passional, temperamental; **fervent,** ardent, churned up, enthusiastic, fervid, feverish, fiery, flaming, high-pitched, hot, impassionate *(Rare)*, impassioned, intense, passionate, perfervid, torrid, vehement, warm-blooded; **heartfelt,** close to one's heart, deep, earnest, gut, heart-whole, infelt, profound, sincere; **effusive,** demonstrative, gushy; **ecstatic,** beside oneself, lyrical, rapt, rhapsodical; **sensitive,** delicate, hypersensitive, miffy, moody, passible, prickly, sensible *(Obs.)*, sentient, supersensitive, susceptible, susceptive, thin-skinned, touchy; **sympathetic,** empathetic, empathic, responsive, understanding, warm; **sentimental,** bathetic, corny, gooey, icky, maudlin, mawkish, Mills-and-Boon, mushy, novelettish, romantic, rosewater, sloppy, soft, soppy, soulful, soupy, syrupy; **theatrical,** histrionic, melodramatic

emotional *adj* → illogical

EMOTIONALISE *v* charge, get up a feeling, supercharge; **affect,** get to, move, stir; **impassion,** fire, inflame, kindle, set fire to, set on fire; **ravish,** rock, smite, transport

EMOTIONALIST *n* drama queen, dramatiser, prima donna, sob-sister, tinderbox; **romantic,** sentimentalist

EMOTIONALLY *adv* affetuoso, animato, con anima, con espressione, demonstratively, effusively, feelingly, sympathetically, sympathisingly, warmly; **emotively,** affectingly, affectively, movingly, poignantly, pungently, touchingly; **fervently,** appassionato, ardently, con fuoco, enthusiastically, fervidly, fierily, glowingly, impassionedly, passionately, torridly, vehemently; **sensitively,** delicately; **deeply,** earnestly, from the bottom of one's heart, heart and soul, inly *(Archaic)*, intensely, sincerely, with all one's heart; **sentimentally,** languishingly, mawkishly, melodramatically, sloppily, soppily, soulfully; **ecstatically,** rhapsodically

EMOTIVE *adj* affecting, heart-warming, moving, pathetic, poignant, pungent, rousing, stirring, touching

empathy *n* → **1** agreement **2** pity

emperor *n* → **1** aristocrat **2** ruler

emphasis *n* → **1** assertiveness **2** importance **3** repetition **4** speaking

EMPHASISE *v* accent *(U.S.)*, accentuate, boot home, labour, make a point of, make a thing of, press, stress, underline; **bring to the fore,** enhance, give weight to, highlight, put on the map; **magnify,** fete, glorify, lift

empire *n* → **1** nation **2** power

EMPIRICAL *adj* a posteriori, empiric, experimental, hypothetical, provisional; **tentative,** speculative

empirical *adj* → occurrent

EMPIRICISM *n* empirical formula, experimentalism, experimentation, tentation, trial and error, verification

EMPLOY *v* accredit, appoint, assign, commission, constitute, empanel, engage, entrust, give power of attorney, hire, make, name, nominate, panel, place, postulate *(Eccles.)*, seat, set in place over, slate, take on; **invest,** crown, enthrone, incardinate, mitre, ordain; **install,** inaugurate, induct, institute; **assign,** attach, depute, detail, tell off; **dob in for,** nobble with, put in; **reinstate,** revest

employ *v* → **1** depute **2** use

EMPLOYED *adj* actively employed, appointed, designate, elect, in a job, investitive, nominative, working

employee *n* → worker

employer *n* → **1** boss **2** manager **3** middle class

EMPLOYMENT *n* admission, appointment, assignation, assignment, body hire, designation, empanelment, entrustment, nomination, placement, reinstatement, secondment; **overemployment,** featherbedding; **investiture,** coronation, enthronement, incardination, investment, ordainment, ordination, provision *(Eccles.)*; **commission,** berth, billet, booking, brevet, detail *(Mil.)*, errand, hat, incumbency, office, place, post, vacancy; **delegation,** deputation, procuration; **divine appointment,** the call, vocation

EMPLOYMENT OFFICE *n* employment service, labour exchange

emporium *n* → shop

empower *v* → **1** authorise **2** depute **3** permit

empress *n* → ruler

EMPTINESS *n* inanition, inanity, vacancy, vacuity, vacuousness; **emptying,** evacuation, vacation; **vacuum,** inane, void; **blank,** blank space, clean slate, tabula rasa, white, white line, white space; **empty bottle,** dead marine, empty

EMPTY *v* avoid *(Obs.)*, evacuate, turn out, vacate, void; **drain,** exhaust, use up

EMPTY *adj* a skinner, dead, exhausted, finished, inane, vacuous, vacuum, void; **vacant,** deserted, devoid, uninhabited, unoccupied; **blank,** clear, white; **unladen,** empty-handed

empty *n* → **1** emptiness *adj* **2** foolish **3** hungry **4** stupid **5** useless **6** verbose

emu *n* → gatherer

emulate *v* → **1** contest **2** imitate

emulsion *n* → liquid

enable *v* → **1** authorise **2** facilitate **3** make possible

enact *v* → **1** command **2** legalise

enamel *n* → **1** jewellery **2** plating

encapsulate *v* → **1** abbreviate **2** insert

ENCHANT *v* appeal to, appetise, arouse, bewitch, bowl someone over, create desire, engage, enrapture, enthral, excite desire, fetch *(Colloq.)*, have a way with one, knock one's eye out, knock sideways, make one's mouth water, ravish, stimulate, take one's fancy, tempt, turn one's head

enchant *v* → **1** bewitch **2** encourage **3** please

enclave *n* → region

ENCLOSE *v* box in, brick up, cabin, close, close in, conclude *(Obs.)*, coop up, kernel, pinch, shut in, smother, surround; **envelop,** do up, enswathe, enwrap, wrap up; **encase,** bag, box, cage, case, casket *(Obs.)*, crate, enshrine, mew, pocket, sack, saggar, shrine; **sheathe,** insheathe; **encircle,** belt, circumscribe, embay, gird, girdle, orb *(Poetic)*, ring, surround; **wall in,** bower, chamber, closet, confine, embank, embower, enwall, fence in, hedge, immure, impale *(Rare)*, imprison, incarcerate, lock off, pale; **pen,** corral, fold, impark, impound, paddock, pinfold, pound, sty

enclose *v* → **1** insert **2** surround

ENCLOSED *adj* boxed in, circumscribed, cleidoic, cloistered, close, confined, encased, enveloped, fenced-in, included, landlocked, shut-in, snowbound; **encircled,** ringed, succinct *(Archaic)*, surrounded; **close,** claustrophobic, smothery, without room to swing a cat

ENCLOSURE *n* approvement *(Law)*, circumscription, closure *(Obs.)*, encirclement, encompassment, entrapment, inning, purpresture, subdivision, surrounding; **envelopment,** boxing, encapsulation, encasement, enshrinement, enswathement, packaging; **incarceration,** confinement, immurement, impoundage, impoundment, poundage; **surround,** frame, gobo

encompass *v* → **1** surpass **2** surround

encore *n* → **1** repetition **2** shout *v* **3** repeat **4** shout *interj* **5** well done

encounter *n* → **1** argument **2** convergence **3** fight *v* **4** argue **5** converge **6** fight **7** undergo

ENCOURAGE *v* abet, entice, excite, heart *(Archaic)*, hype up, impel, importune *(Obs.)*, induce, motivate, motive, move, press, provide an example, put someone up to, set an example, stimulate, urge, work up; **inspire,** animate, awake, inform; **influence,** impress, lead by the nose, persuade, play upon another's feelings, prevail upon, sway, talk over, turn someone's head, weigh heavily with; **seduce,** bewitch, enchant, entrance, lead astray; **cheer,** barrack for, egg on, spirit, whoop; **promote,** advertise, drum up trade, sell, spiel, spruik; **recommend,** advocate, suggest; **nurture,** foster, nourish; **back up,** assure, support

encourage *v* → **1** embolden **2** help

ENCOURAGEMENT *n* abetment, exhortation, moral support; **motivation,** actuation, impulsion, incitation, incitement, inducement, induction *(Physiol.)*, influence, provocation, provocativeness, stimulation; **inspiration,** afflatus, awakening, soul; **enticement,** bewitchment, enchantment, seduction, temptation; **agitation,** activism, barratry, consciousness raising, incendiarism, inflammation, revolutionary activity, sedition, seditiousness, stirring

ENCOURAGER *n* abetter, patron, supporter; **motivator,** ampster, lobbyist, promoter, ring leader, urger; **inspirer,** actuator, animator, impeller; **barracker,** cheer squad, cheerer, cheerleader, flagwaver, rooter; **agitator,** actionist, activist, agent provocateur, enkindler, firebrand, incendiary, inciter, inflamer, provoker, rouser, seditionary, shit-stirrer, spurrer, stirrer, Yarra banker *(Vic.)*; **promoter,** advertiser, advertising agency, commercial traveller, drummer, salesperson, spruiker; **fosterer,** kindler, nourisher; **enticer,** blandisher, coaxer, enchantress, seducer, siren, tempter, wheedler

ENCOURAGING *adj* hortatory, incentive, inductive, motivational, motive, moving, stimulant, stimulative, tonic, touching; **inviting,** appetising, entrancing, inspirational, irresistible, piquant, provocative, provoking, rousing, seductive, stimulating, stirring, tempting, titillative; **impellent,** impulsive; **incendiary,** barratrous, inflammatory, seditionary, seditious

encroach *v* → **1** advance **2** contravene **3** enter **4** impose

encumber *v* → **1** hinder **2** weigh

encyclopaedia *n* → reference book

end *n* → **1** aim **2** death **3** extremity **4** finish **5** frame **6** remnant **7** remote place **8** result *v* **9** finish **10** result **11** stop

ENDANGER *v* compromise, entrap, expose, imperil, jeopardise, peril, put the skids under; **menace,** bode ill, threaten

ENDEARMENTS *n* addresses, assiduities, attentions, blandishments, compliments; **amorous glances,** ogle, sheep's eyes; **kiss,** buss, osculation, pash, peck, smack, smacker; **embrace,** caress, clasp, clinch, clip *(Archaic)*, cuddle, hug, snuggle, squeeze, stroke; **petting,** fondling, necking, smooching, smoodging, spooning; **hanky-panky,** fun and games, slap-and-tickle, sport *(Obs.)*

endeavour *n* → **1** attempt **2** effort *v* **3** attempt

endemic *adj* → unwholesome

endless *adj* → **1** changeless **2** continual **3** eternal **4** infinite

ENDMAN *n* lanterne rouge, tail ender; **bell sheep,** cut-out

ENDMOST *adj* distal, furthermost, hindmost, rearmost

endorse *v* → **1** approve **2** assent to **3** authenticate **4** name

endow *v* → **1** equip **2** give

endurance *n* → **1** patience **2** persistence

endure *v* → **1** be **2** compose oneself **3** continue **4** dislike **5** eternalise **6** live **7** persevere **8** persist **9** support **10** undergo

enema *n* → insert

ENEMY *n* adversary, archenemy, foe, ill-wisher, public enemy; **antagonist,** opponent, opposite side, rival, the other side; **firebrand,** fighting cock, troublemaker; **snake,** snake in the grass, traitor; **snubber,** xenophobe; **persona non grata,** bête noir

enemy *n* → **1** dissident **2** hater

ENERGETIC *adj* aggressive, driving, dynamic, forceful, high-powered, high-pressure, impetuous, intense, motivated; **tireless,** unwearied, weariless; **vigorous,** active, athletic, quick *(Rare)*, sinewy, spirited, virile; **lively,** bouncing, ebullient, effervescent, flush, fresh, live, lusty, oomphy, peppy, proud *(Poetic)*, rompish, sappy, spritely, swinging, vibrant, vital, vivacious, vivid; **alive,** alive and kicking, full of beans, full of piss and vinegar; **spirited,** animated, ding-dong, rousing, spanking, warm; **jazzy,** jazzed up, racy, souped-up; **invigorating,** bracing, brisk, crisp, invigorative

ENERGETICALLY *adv* aggressively, briskly, bustlingly, strenuously, tirelessly, unweariedly, vigorously; **full pelt,** amain *(Archaic)*, animatedly, forcefully, impetuously, impulsively, like billyo, madly, violently, with a vengeance; **spiritedly,** con forza, forzando, sforzando, sforzato; **vibrantly,** ebulliently, effervescently, invigoratingly, lively, vivaciously, warmly

ENERGISE *v* activate, animate, boost, brisk up, enliven, exhilarate, flush, ginger up, innerve, invigorate, jazz up, pep up, quicken, sauce, soup up, stimulate, vitalise, vivify, zest

ENERGY *n* action, conatus, effort, force, impetus, impulse, motive power, motivity, power, stress, thrust, torque, vis viva; **atomic energy,** atomic power, binding energy, electric power, enthalpy, entropy, fusion energy, hydraulic power, hydro-electric power, internal energy, kinetic energy, momentum, nuclear energy, potential energy, shear stress, sun-power, waterpower, wattage, windpower, zero point energy; **quantum,** phonon, photon; **force,** centrifugal force, centripetal force, electrokinetic potential, electromotive force, magnetomotive force, solar energy, zetapotential; **erg,** British thermal unit, calorie, joule, kilojoule, kilowatt-hour; **dyne,** newton, pound-force, poundal; **energetics,** biodynamics, dynamics, geodynamics, hydrodynamics, hydromechanics, physics; **watt,** horsepower, joules per second. *See also* VITALITY

energy *n* → **1** power **2** sprightliness

enervate *v* → **1** weaken *adj* **2** powerless **3** weak

ENERVATING *adj* castrating, enervative, exhausting, exhaustive, gorgonian

enfold *v* → **1** cover **2** fold **3** kiss **4** surround

enforce *v* → force

engage *v* → **1** attract **2** call attention to **3** employ **4** enchant **5** fasten **6** join **7** marry **8** promise

engaging *adj* → **1** alluring **2** pleasant

engender *v* → **1** cause **2** create **3** reproduce

engine *n* → **1** machine **2** train

engineer *n* → **1** builder **2** driver **3** expert **4** manager **5** soldier *v* **6** beguile **7** build **8** create **9** do **10** plan

ENGRAVE *v* cut, grave, incise, scrimshaw; **print,** aquatint, lithograph, mezzotint, photolithograph, silk-screen print; **emboss,** boss, snarl; **etch,** bite; **impress,** stamp

engrave *v* → **1** cut **2** furrow **3** portray **4** print

ENGRAVER *n* burinist, cerographist, chalcographer, chaser, embosser, graver *(Archaic)*, pyrographer, tattooer, wood engraver, woodcutter, xylographer; **etcher,** lithographer, printer, tinter. *See also* ARTIST; CRAFTSMAN

ENGRAVING *n* cerography, chalcography, glyptography, pyrography, toreutics, woodcutting, xylography; **print,** aquatint, block print, cerograph, chromolithograph, halftone, line engraving, linocut, lithograph, mezzotint, oleograph, photolithograph, rubbing, silk-screen print, woodcut, wood engraving, xylograph; **printing,** die-sinking, die-stamping, etching, intaglio, lithography, metallography, oleography, photolithography; **plate,** remargue; **artist's proof,** proof

ENGROSS *v* absorb, amuse *(Obs.)*, consume, devour, enwrap, fascinate, grip, hold the stage, interest, intrigue, involve, occupy, spellbind

engross *v* → **1** buy **2** control **3** copy **4** own

engulf *v* → **1** absorb **2** flood

enhance *v* → **1** emphasise **2** improve **3** increase

enigma *n* → **1** code **2** disguise **3** uncertain thing

ENJOY *v* admire, appreciate, fancy, relish, savour, taste *(Archaic)*; **like,** care for, delight in, dig, get a kick out of, have a soft spot for something, love, take a fancy to, take pleasure in, take to, welcome; **revel in,** feast on, groove on; **go into ecstasies,** be crazy about, be mad about, blow one's mind, drool over, rave, swoon, trip

enjoy *v* → **1** have sex **2** own **3** use

ENJOYER *n* delighter, reveller; **indulger,** feaster, sybarite, voluptuary; **bon vivant,** bon viveur, epicure, epicurean, gourmand, hedonist, high-stepper, jetsetter, worldling; **jet set,** beau monde, beautiful people; **admirer,** appreciator, fancier, lover

enlarge *v* → **1** add **2** defer **3** grow **4** increase **5** photograph

ENLARGEMENT *n* dilation, elongation, erection, excrescence, growth, hypertrophy, stretch, swell, swelling, tumidity; **inflatedness,** dilatancy, erectility, excrescency, pulse, swollenness

enlighten *v* → **1** inform **2** reveal **3** teach

ENLIGHTENER *n* civiliser, demonstrator, initiator, refiner, torchbearer; **apostle,** evangelist, missionary, preacher, prophet; **adviser,** careers adviser, counsellor; **guru,** maharishi, sage, swami; **indoctrinator,** implanter, inculcator, promulgator, propagandist, publicist. *See also* TEACHER

enlist *v* → **1** associate **2** join up **3** militarise

ENLIVEN *v* animate, breathe life into, inspire, inspirit, jazz, jazz up, liven, liven up, pep, pep up, put new life into, vitalise, vivify, zap up

enmity *n* → **1** hate **2** ill will **3** unfriendliness

ennui *n* → **1** boredom **2** discontentedness

ENORMOUS *adj* astronomical, colossal, cyclopean, elephantine, giant, gigantean, gigantesque, gigantic, herculean, huge, immense, mammoth, mountain, mountainous, overblown, overgrown, prodigious, titanic, towering, tremendous, vast, vasty *(Poetic)*; **bulky,** ample, full, massive, massy, monumental, portly, solid, voluminous; **grandiose,** august, distinguished, eminent, grand, great, Homeric, lordly, majestic, noble, princely, proud, regal; **awesome,** awe-inspiring, awful, fabulous, ineffable, mind-boggling, overwhelming, phenomenal, portentous, stupendous, terrible

enormous *adj* → **1** bad **2** big **3** immoral

enough *n* → **1** adequacy *adj* **2** adequate *interj* **3** stop

enquire *v* → question

enrage *v* → anger

enrich *v* → **1** decorate **2** fertilise **3** improve **4** increase

enrol *v* → **1** insert **2** list **3** record

en route *adv* → forward

ensconce *v* → **1** hide **2** shelter

ensemble *n* → **1** beds **2** combine **3** inferior **4** music **5** musicianship **6** outfit **7** result **8** theatrical company **9** whole *adv* **10** simultaneously

ensign *n* → **1** flag **2** seaman **3** sign **4** soldier

ensue *v* → **1** follow **2** result

entail *n* → **1** getting **2** real estate *v* **3** include

entangle *v* → **1** cause difficulties **2** interlace **3** involve **4** muddle **5** tangle

entente *n* → **1** contract **2** friendship

ENTER *v* bounce into, come in, get in, get inside, get into, go into, hop in, immigrate, jump in, re-enter, set foot in, step in; **board,** embark, embus, emplane, enplane, entrain; **encroach,** barge in, break in, break into, bust, butt in, crash, gatecrash, infiltrate, invade, push in, trespass

enter *v* → **1** account **2** insert **3** participate **4** record **5** take

ENTERER *n* arrival, comer, entrant, immigrant, import, incomer, invitee; **invader,** encroacher, forcer, gatecrasher, interloper, intruder, trespasser; **doorkeeper,** commissionaire, concierge, doorman

ENTERING *adj* immigrant, incoming, ingoing, ingressive, inpouring, inrushing, invasive, inward; **embarking,** embussing

enterprise *n* → **1** competence **2** corporation **3** courage **4** hope **5** undertaking **6** vitality

ENTERPRISING *adj* adventurous, venturesome

entertain *v* → **1** be sociable **2** welcome

ENTERTAINING *adj* absorbing, amusing, engrossing, riveting

ENTERTAINMENT *n* attraction, divertissement, night-life, performing arts, regalement, show business, vaudeville; **an evening out,** a night on the town, blow-out, rage; **show,** antic, blockbuster, circus, cirque, exhibition, extravaganza, fantoccini, festival, fluxus, follies, happening, harlequinade, ice show, lightshow, pageant, phantasmagoria, pyrotechnics, son et lumière, spectacle, spectacular, street theatre, three-ring circus, variety show, vaudeville; **cinema,** bioscope *(S. African)*, celluloid, circuit, the cinema, the movies, the pictures, the silver screen; **cabaret,** floor show, revue; **road show,** sideshow; **benefit,** barrel, bespeak *(Obs.)*

enthral *v* → 1 enchant 2 repress

ENTHUSE *v* fanaticise, fire, pique, switch on, warm, whet; **be eager,** be pie on *(N.Z.)*, be sold on, be spoiling for, beat the gun, champ at the bit, fall over oneself, go to town about, jump the gun, rave, take fire, warm to, wax lyrical

ENTHUSIASM *n* anxiety, anxiousness, ardency, ardour, avidity, eagerness, ebullience, ebulliency, fire, flame, forwardness, furore, get-up-and-go, greediness, gusto, heart, heartiness, keenness, party spirit, pizzazz, rage, second wind, sharpness, vehemence, warmness, warmth, zeal, zealousness, zest, zestfulness, zing, zip; **devotion,** craze, dedication, devotedness, devotement, passion; **fanaticism,** chauvinism, desperation *(Colloq.)*, monomania, rabidity, rabidness, radicalness, voraciousness, voracity, zealotry

enthusiasm *n* → 1 emotion 2 reverence 3 willingness

ENTHUSIAST *n* a beggar for, a nut about, aficionado, a glutton for, a great one for, boffin, devotee, eager beaver, fan, fancier, freak, high-flier, votaress, votary; **fanatic,** chauvinist, energumen, lunatic fringe, mad mullah, radical, tub-thumper, zealot

ENTHUSIASTIC *adj* ablaze, afire, aflame, agog, anxious, ardent, athirst, avid, eager, ebullient, fain *(Archaic)*, forward, greedy, hearty, hipped *(U.S. Colloq.)*, keen, on fire, raring, red-hot, sharp, sharp-set, toey, vehement, vital, warm, willing, wrapped, young-eyed, zealous, zestful, zesty, zingy; **extravagant,** gung ho, high-flown, high-flying, keen as mustard, on edge, voracious, wild *(Colloq.)*; **fanatical,** chauvinist, chauvinistic, fanatic, mad, overzealous, rabid

entice *v* → 1 allure 2 encourage

entire *n* → 1 whole *adj* 2 perfect 3 sequential 4 simple 5 whole

entitle *v* → 1 have the right 2 name

ENTITLEMENT *n* capacity, colour, competence, droit, jus, majority, power, right, title

entity *n* → 1 actuality 2 essence

entourage *n* → 1 servant 2 surroundings

entrails *n* → 1 abdomen 2 inside

ENTRANCE *n* adit, aperture, archway, avenue *(Brit.)*, conning tower, doorway, entry, entryway, foyer, gateway, gorge, hall, hallway, hatchway, ingress, inlet, intake, introitus, loading bay, opening, passage, passageway, platform, porch, port, port of entry, porte-cochère, portico, vestibule; **door,** cat door, gate, hatch, lichgate, pearly gates, portal, postern, revolving door, stable door, stile, tollgate, trapdoor, turnstile, wicket; **access,** admission, admittance, embarkation, entrée, open door, re-entrance, re-entry; **encroachment,** break-in, breaking and entering, bust, inflow, influx, inroad, invasion, trespass

entrance *n* → 1 access 2 charge 3 liberty *v* 4 encourage 5 please

entrant *n* → 1 competitor 2 enterer 3 member

ENTREAT *v* adjure, ask a boon, assail, beseech, impetrate, implore, importune, intreat *(Archaic)*, obsecrate, obtest, plead, pray, supplicate; **petition,** address, appeal to, apply to, go cap in hand to, go on bended knees to, have recourse to, re-petition, recur to *(Rare)*, turn to; **apply for,** bid for, make a bid, make an approach, move for, put in for; **desire,** crave *(Obs.)*, cry for, whistle for; **request,** ask, court, invite, pop the question, solicit, woo; **invoke,** call on, command, conjure, imprecate, require; **intercede,** interpellate, intervene; **bespeak,** book, commission; **lobby,** besiege, dun, ply, press, urge; **canvass,** ask around, consult, enquire of

ENTREATY *n* adjuration, assailment, begging, canvass, conjuration *(Archaic)*, impetration *(Rare)*, imploration, obsecration, pleading, solicitation, suppliance, treaty *(Obs.)*, urging; **plea,** appeal, epiclesis *(Liturgy)*, importunities, imprecation, invocation, prayer, supplication; **petition,** application, bid, claim, motion, postulate, postulation, proposal, round robin, suggestion, suit; **intercession,** interpellation; **invitation,** invite *(Colloq.)*, solicitation

entrée *n* → entrance

entree *n* → 1 liberty 2 meal

entrepreneur *n* → 1 manager 2 trader

entrust *v* → 1 employ 2 give

entry *n* → 1 account 2 competitor 3 entrance 4 liberty 5 record 6 taking

enumerate *v* → 1 compute 2 list

enunciate *v* → 1 assert 2 publicise 3 speak

envelop *v* → 1 enclose 2 hide

envelope *n* → 1 curve 2 wrapper

enviable *adj* → desirable

envious *adj* → jealous

environment *n* → surroundings

environs *n* → surroundings

envisage *v* → 1 see 2 think

envoy *n* → 1 delegate 2 finish 3 messenger 4 postscript

envy *n* → 1 jealousy *v* 2 be jealous of

epaulet *n* → trimming

EPHEMERAL *n* ephemera, ephemeron; **nine day wonder,** flash in the pan, one-hit wonder, puppy love; **flash,** flicker, pulse, spurt, vapour *(Archaic)*

ephemeral *n* → 1 plant *adj* 2 dead 3 impermanent

epic *n* → 1 drama 2 heroic story 3 poetry 4 story *adj* 5 courageous 6 famous 7 poetic

epicene *n* → 1 sexual type *adj* 2 sexual

epicure *n* → 1 aesthete 2 enjoyer 3 glutton 4 voluptuary

epidemic *n* → **1** flood **2** illness *adj* **3** flooding **4** unwholesome
epidermis *n* → **1** coating **2** outside **3** skin
epigram *n* → **1** abridgment **2** joke **3** poetry **4** proverb
epilepsy *n* → unconsciousness
epilogue *n* → **1** act **2** finish **3** postscript
episode *n* → **1** act **2** interruption **3** interval **4** musical phrase **5** occurrence **6** period **7** story **8** waffle
EPISTEMOLOGICAL *adj* encyclopaedic, epistemic, pantologic, pantological, philosophical, polyhistoric; **scientific,** polytechnic, technical, technological
epistemology *n* → knowledge
epistle *n* → message
Epistle *n* → religious ceremony
epitaph *n* → **1** abridgment **2** funeral rites **3** memento
epithet *n* → **1** name **2** slander **3** swearing **4** word
epitome *n* → **1** abridgment **2** essence **3** translation
epoch *n* → **1** length **2** moment **3** period **4** start
equable *adj* → **1** composed **2** fair
EQUAL *n* coequal, compeer, equivalent, fellow, match, parallel, peer, vis-a-vis; **dead heat,** barrage, deuce, draw, Mexican standoff, tie; **break-even,** margin *(Econ.)*
EQUAL *v* compeer *(Archaic)*; **be evens,** balance, draw, poise, tie; **amount to,** add up to, come up to; **democratise,** level; **match,** be up with, get the measure of someone, go all the way with, measure up to, rival, run abreast, see *(Cards)*; **compare,** amount to the same thing, parallel
EQUAL *adj* equational, level; **even,** commeasurable, commensurate, fifty-fifty, half-and-half, isometric, par, proportionate; **equivalent,** enharmonic, equipollent, fellow, like, matchable, one-to-one, same; **level-pegging,** drawn, equalised, level, quits, tied; **ambidextrous,** two-handed; **coequal,** assessorial, comparable, concurrent, coordinate; **democratic,** egalitarian, equalitarian, isonomic; **as good as,** tantamount; **equidistant,** coextensive; **equipotent,** equimolecular, equinoctial, equipollent, equiponderant, equipotential; **symmetric,** balanced, bisymmetrical, isodiametric, isogonic, spheral, symmetrical; **equilateral,** equiangular, isosceles, square; **isostatic,** isenthalpic, isentropic, isoclinal, isodimorphous, isodynamic, isomerous, isotropic
equal *n* → **1** similar thing *adj* **2** composed **3** fair **4** level
EQUALISE *v* balance, bracket, equate, equilibrate, even out, level out, match, symmetrise; **break even,** break square; **coextend,** commeasure; **counterbalance,** counterpoise, counterweigh
EQUALITY *n* balance, commensuration, comparableness, evenness, levelness, parity, sameness; **symmetry,** bisymmetry, conformation, evenness, parallelism, regularity, symmetricalness; **equilibrium,** equilibration, equipoise, equiponderance, isostasy, poise; **counterweight,** balance, counterpoise; **egalitarianism,** democracy, equalitarianism, isonomy; **equalisation,** equation; **equivalence,** closeness, coextension, correspondence, equidistance, equipollence, equipollency, isometry, par; **coequality,** coordinateness, coordination, parity; **isomorphism,** isodimorphism
EQUALLY *adv* alike, both, correspondingly, identically, level, levelly, proportionately; **democratically; fifty-fifty,** ana *(Med.)*, close, commensurately, evenly, evens, half-and-half, isometrically; **abreast,** even stevens, neck and neck, nip and tuck *(U.S.)*, pari passu; **equivalently,** enharmonically; **equidistantly,** coextensively; **equilaterally,** bisymmetrically, isostatically, symmetrically; **comparably,** coequally, comparatively, coordinately
equanimity *n* → composure
equate *v* → equalise
equation *n* → equality
equator *n* → **1** bisector **2** circle **3** limit **4** line
equestrian *n* → rider
equilateral *adj* → equal
equilibrium *n* → **1** composure **2** equality **3** rest
equine *adj* → animal-like
equinox *n* → **1** astronomic point **2** season
EQUIP *v* accommodate, accoutre, appoint, arm, dight *(Archaic)*, fit, fit out, fit up, fix, fix up, furnish, gear, grubstake, implement, kit *(Mil.)*, outfit, refit, rig out *(Naut.)*, rig up, set up, turn out; **endow,** keep in, maintain, support, sustain
equip *v* → **1** clothe **2** prepare
EQUIPMENT *n* accessories, accessory, accoutrements, apparatus, appointments, appurtenances, baggage *(Mil.)*, equipage, gear, kit, manavelins *(Naut.)*, munitions, necessaries, outfit, paraphernalia, tackle, tackling, the necessary, turnout; **personal effects,** dunnage, luggage, stuff, swag, things; **fittings,** caparison, covering, dress, garnish, garnishment, garniture, harness, ornament *(Eccles.)*, rig, rigging, trappings, trim *(Motor Vehicles)*; **replacement part,** doover, spare, thingummubob, thingummujig
equipment *n* → **1** knowledge **2** machine **3** personal property **4** supplies
EQUIPPED *adj* fitted, fitted out, full-rigged, good for, ready, rigged out, right, supplied, trim *(Obs.)*, well appointed, well-found
equitable *adj* → fair
equity *n* → law
EQUIVALENT *n* actinomere, antimere, coequal, compeer, correspondent, fellow, homograph, homologue, homonym, homophone, isologue, isomer, match, parallel, peer, synonym
equivalent *n* → **1** atom **2** equal *adj* **3** congruous **4** equal **5** meaningful
equivocal *adj* → **1** elusive **2** imprecise **3** uncertain
equivocate *v* → **1** avoid **2** lie **3** trick

EQUIVOCATOR *n* prevaricator, procrastinator, temporiser; **waverer,** weathercock, wobbler; **abstainer,** fence-sitter, trimmer

era *n* → period

eradicate *v* → **1** destroy **2** extract

erase *v* → **1** destroy **2** hide **3** remove

ERECT *v* pitch, plumb, raise, raise up, right, set up, up-end, upraise, uprear; **cock up,** prick up, prickle, rear, rear up, sit up, uprise *(Archaic)*; **stand,** hold up, keep one's feet, stand up; **arise,** get to one's feet, rise, rise up

ERECT *adj* columnar, columned, rampant, ramping, stand-up, standing, standing up, steady, straight, straight up, tower-like, up, upright, upstanding; **vertical,** bluff, normal *(Maths)*, orthogonal, perpendicular, plumb, square

erect *v* → **1** build **2** lift **3** make **4** operate **5** raise up *adj* **6** hard **7** increased **8** protuberant **9** risen **10** straight

ERECTLY *adv* at right angles, bolt upright, on end, on hind legs, topside up, up, upright, uprightly; **perpendicularly,** plumb, vertically

ERECTNESS *n* straightness, uprightness; **perpendicularity,** aplomb, orthogonality, plumbness, right-angledness, verticality, verticalness; **perpendicular,** altitude, apothem, plumb, vertical; **plumbline,** plumb-bob, plumb-rule, plummet

erg *n* → **1** dryness **2** energy

ermine *n* → **1** animal's coat **2** aristocracy

erode *v* → **1** deteriorate **2** rub

erogenous *adj* → sexy

erosion *n* → **1** deterioration **2** rubbing

erotic *n* → **1** poetry **2** sexual partner **3** voluptuary *adj* **4** loving **5** obscene **6** sexy **7** voluptuous

EROTICISE *v* arouse, bring off, bring on, excite, feel someone up, finger up, fumble, go the grope, grope, pet, play stink finger, titillate, turn on; **have an erection,** crack a fat, get a hard on, put lead in one's pencil; **orgasm,** blow, come, cream one's jeans, ejaculate, shoot one's bolt, toss off; **practise coitus interruptus,** get off at Redfern; **masturbate,** flip oneself off, frig, jerk off, pull oneself off, toss off, wank, whack off. *See also* HAVE SEX

ERR *v* back the wrong horse, bark up the wrong tree, blunder, boob, contaminate, fall in, fault, get one's lines crossed, get the wrong end of the stick, goof, lapse, make a boo-boo, misapply, miscount, misdo, mismeasure, misplace, mispronounce, misstate, slip, stumble, trip up; **misconceive,** get someone wrong, misconstrue, mistake

err *v* → **1** be immoral **2** defect **3** wrong

errand *n* → **1** agency **2** aim **3** employment **4** job **5** work

errant *adj* → **1** changeable **2** deflective **3** indecisive **4** travelling

erratic *n* → **1** fish out of water **2** nonconformist **3** rock *adj* **4** changeable **5** deflective **6** irregular **7** misplaced **8** nonconformist **9** strange

erratum *n* → error

erroneous *adj* → **1** false **2** illogical

ERROR *n* bad idea, balls-up, baulk, bloomer, blooper, blue, blunder, boner, boo-boo, boob, boss-shot, bug, clanger, fault, faux paus, fluff, foot-fault, Freudian slip, fuck-up, gaffe, GIGO, howler, inaccuracy, lapse, malapropism, misapplication, misapprehension, miscalculation, misconception, miscount, misjudgment, mismeasurement, mismove, misplacement, mispronunciation, mistake, oversight, parapraxis, slip, slip of the tongue, slip-up, solecism, stumble, trip, wrong foot; **comedy of errors,** farce; **clerical error,** author's error, contamination, corrigendum, erratum, haplography, literal *(Print.)*, misprint, offset, out *(Print.)*, printer's error, set-off, strike-through, typo; **false alarm.** *See also* FALSITY

error *n* → **1** delusion **2** difference **3** failure **4** grammatical error **5** illogicality **6** misjudgment **7** wrong

erstwhile *adj* → **1** past *adv* **2** in the past

erudite *adj* → **1** educated **2** knowledgeable

erudition *n* → learning

erupt *v* → **1** attack **2** exit **3** expel

escalate *v* → **1** become greater **2** increase

escalator *n* → **1** conveyor **2** elevator **3** stairs

escapade *n* → **1** escape **2** misdemeanour

ESCAPE *n* elusion, escapade, escapement *(Archaic)*, evasion, lam *(U.S.)*, runaway, scape *(Archaic)*; **moonlight flit,** disappearing trick, elopement, flit, slip, truancy; **breakout,** gaolbreak, getaway; **breakaway,** bolt, break, gambado, stampede; **close shave,** close call, close thing, narrow escape, near miss, near thing, squeak. *See also* MEANS OF ESCAPE

ESCAPE *v* break out, cut, cut and run, do a get, do a getaway, extricate oneself, flee, hit the toe *(Prison)*, lam *(U.S.)*, make a getaway, show a clean pair of heels, take it on the lam, turn tail; **bolt,** break away, stampede; **skip,** abscond, do a moonlight flit, elope, flit, fly the gap, get away, jump, run away, shoot the moon; **give someone the slip,** bilk, elude, shake, shake off, throw off; **slip through one's fingers,** get away, slip the collar; **scrape through,** get away with it, save one's bacon, save one's skin, survive; **get out from under,** do a fade, fade out; **get off,** secure an acquittal

escape *n* → **1** avoidance **2** exit *v* **3** elude **4** exit

ESCAPED *adj* at large, free, off the hook, on the lam, on the run, runaway; **fugitive,** truant; **elusive,** slippery; **breakaway,** ladino

ESCAPEE *n* absconder from public labour, absconder into the woods, absentee, absentee into the woods, absentee without leave, escaper, fleer, prison-breaker; **runaway,** bolter, breakaway, ladino, stampeder; **truant,** eloper; **dodger,** absconder, bilker, eluder; **fugitive,** boat people, reffo, refugee; **escapologist,** Houdini

escarpment *n* → **1** fortification **2** mountain

eschew *v* → **1** abstain **2** avoid

escort *n* → 1 protection 2 protector *v* 3 accompany
escutcheon *n* → 1 armour 2 label
esoteric *adj* → 1 allusive 2 arcane 3 known 4 strange 5 supernatural 6 unclear
espionage *n* → investigation
esplanade *n* → 1 field 2 road
espouse *v* → marry
esquire *n* → mister
essay *n* → 1 abridgment 2 attempt *v* 3 attempt 4 test
ESSAYIST *n* belletrist, editor, expositor, leader writer, monographer, pamphleteer; **critic,** commentator, editorialist, reviewer, scholiast
ESSENCE *n* basic, deep structure, fundamental, hypostasis, point, quick, the name of the game; **basis,** accidence, base, bottom, elements, first principle, root; **skeleton,** alphabet, constitution, construction, contexture, grammar, matrix; **grassroots,** brass tacks, nuts and bolts; **nitty-gritty,** crux, gist, juice, marrow, nub, pith, point, stuff; **spirit,** ABC, flavour, gist, meaning, sum, the long and the short of; **substance,** content, hard core, meat, substratum; **epitome,** abstract, being, dharma, elixir, entity, form, inscape, quiddity, quintessence, soul, type, vitals; **nature,** aroma, character, inbeing, inside, noumenon, principle, quality; **soul,** ambience, personality; **attribute,** property, quality; **extract,** boil-down, decoction, distillation, distillment, spirit
essence *n* → 1 characteristic 2 characteristics 3 extract 4 fragrance
ESSENTIAL *adj* constitutional, constitutive, crucial, formal, intimate, intrinsic, qualitative, quintessential, resident, substantial, substantival, substantive, true, veritable, very; **epitomic,** epitomical; **typical,** characteristic
essential *n* → 1 necessities *adj* 2 characteristic 3 fundamental 4 important 5 necessary
ESSENTIALLY *adv* constitutively, in substance, intimately, intrinsically, per se, qualitatively, subjectively, substantially, substantively; **veritably,** vitally; **inherently,** congenitally, connately, connaturally, immanently, innately, radically; **naturally,** by nature, in rerum natura, indigenously; **typically,** characteristically; **basically,** at bottom, at heart, basally, fundamentally, in essence, originally, primarily, ultimately; **elementarily,** elementally, hypostatically
establish *v* → 1 authenticate 2 authorise 3 create 4 initiate 5 position
establishment *n* → 1 corporation 2 creation 3 dwelling 4 factory 5 habitation 6 income 7 positioning 8 religion 9 shop 10 start
estate *n* → 1 class 2 condition 3 domain 4 farm 5 good fortune 6 house 7 ownership 8 property
esteem *n* → 1 approval 2 assessment 3 high regard 4 reputation *v* 5 appraise 6 assess 7 respect
estimable *adj* → 1 highly regarded 2 reputable
estimate *n* → 1 assessment 2 computation 3 opinion 4 prediction 5 value *v* 6 assess 7 compute 8 predict
estrange *v* → 1 be unfriendly 2 provoke hatred
estuary *n* → 1 bay 2 stream
et cetera *adv* → additionally
etch *v* → 1 cut 2 engrave 3 furrow 4 portray
ETERNAL *adj* aeonian, coeternal, cosmic, eterne *(Archaic)*, sempiternal *(Archaic)*; **endless,** ceaseless, chronic, constant, incessant, interminable, lasting, never-ending, perpetual, unending; **permanent,** amaranthine, everlasting, imperishable, perdurable, perennial, unfading; **immortal,** ageless, dateless, deathless, elect *(Theol.)*, evergreen, timeless, undying
eternal *n* → 1 eternity 2 infinity *adj* 3 changeless
ETERNALISE *v* eternise, perpetuate; **immortalise,** elect *(Theol.)*; **last,** endure, go on and on, have no end, outlast
ETERNALLY *adv* coeternally, everlastingly, immortally, lastingly, perdurably, perennially, perpetually, unfailingly; **endlessly,** ceaselessly, constantly, interminably, timelessly, undyingly, week in week out, without cease; **permanently,** alway *(Archaic)*, always, aye, e'er, evermore, for ever, for ever and a day, for good, for good and all, for the duration, forever, forevermore, from age to age, from go to whoa, in perpetuity, in perpetuum, till the cows come home, till the end of time, without term, world without end
ETERNITY *n* coeternity, everlasting, sempiternity *(Archaic)*, time immemorial, time out of mind; **immortality,** amrita, athanasia, deathlessness; **immortal,** elect *(Theol.)*; **everlasting,** amaranth, eternal, perpetual motion, perpetuity, perpetuo moto; **permanence,** endlessness, eternalness, everlastingness, lastingness, perpetuality, timelessness; **perpetuation,** election *(Theol.)*, immortalisation, perpetuance
eternity *n* → 1 duration 2 infinity
ether *n* → 1 air 2 anaesthetic 3 sky
ETHEREAL *adj* aerial, airy, airy-fairy, astral, nebulous, shadowy, shady, vaporous; **evanescent,** fleeting, fugitive, transient, transitory; **ghostly,** spectral, wraithlike; **flimsy,** cardboard, insubstantial, paper, slight, tenuous, thin; **delicate,** gossamer. *See also* INTANGIBLE
ethereal *adj* → 1 airy 2 beautiful 3 cosmic 4 light
ETHEREALISE *v* dematerialise, immaterialise, spiritualise, thin, vaporise; **idealise,** abstract, internalise, transcend
ethical *adj* → 1 medicinal 2 moral
ethics *n* → 1 morality 2 rule
ethnic *n* → 1 foreigner 2 population *adj* 3 foreign 4 human 5 resident
ethos *n* → character
etiquette *n* → 1 custom 2 formality

eucharist *n* → gratefulness
Eucharist *n* → religious ceremony
euchre *v* → 1 defeat 2 surpass
eulogy *n* → 1 applause 2 flattery 3 oration
eunuch *n* → man
euphemism *n* → 1 figure of speech 2 toilet 3 word
euphonium *n* → brass instrument
euphoria *n* → pleasure
euthanasia *n* → 1 death 2 killing
evacuate *v* → 1 back out 2 defecate 3 depart 4 empty 5 expel
evade *v* → 1 avoid 2 neglect 3 vacillate
evaluate *v* → 1 assess 2 examine 3 measure 4 test
evangelist *n* → 1 ecclesiastic 2 enlightener 3 preacher 4 religious follower 5 religious person
Evangelist *n* → ecclesiastic
evaporate *v* → 1 disappear 2 dry
evasion *n* → 1 avoidance 2 escape 3 indecision 4 lie 5 neglectfulness 6 non-payment 7 stratagem 8 war
eve *n* → evening
even *n* → 1 evening *v* 2 level 3 smooth *adj* 4 composed 5 equal 6 fair 7 homogeneous 8 level 9 moderate 10 numerical 11 precise 12 regular 13 smooth 14 steady 15 straight *adv* 16 additionally 17 fairly 18 fully 19 precisely 20 smoothly 21 steadily *conj* 22 still
EVENING *n* curfew, e'en *(Poetic)*, eve *(Archaic)*, even *(Archaic)*, eventide, vesper; **sunset,** dark, decline, evenfall *(Archaic)*, fall of evening, nightfall, sundown; **twilight,** candlelight, dusk, gloaming *(Poetic)*, night, shades, shadows; **dinnertime,** bedtime, suppertime, teatime; **Evensong,** vespers *(Eccles.)*, vigil *(Eccles.)*. *See also* NIGHT
evening *n* → 1 dark 2 finish *adj* 3 nightly
event *n* → 1 occurrence 2 result
eventual *adj* → 1 conditional 2 final 3 future
eventuality *n* → feasibility
ever *adv* → continually
evergreen *n* → 1 adolescent 2 plant *adj* 3 eternal 4 youthful
everlasting *n* → 1 eternity *adj* 2 boring 3 continual 4 eternal
every *adj* → general
everybody *n* → any
everyday *adj* → 1 ordinary 2 simple
everyone *n* → 1 any 2 the public
everything *n* → 1 any 2 important thing
evict *v* → eject
EVIDENCE *n* ammunition *(Colloq.)*, backup, circumstantial evidence, clue, corroborant, corroboration, cumulative evidence, direct evidence, documentation, goods *(Colloq.)*, indirect evidence, king's evidence, matter *(Law)*, prima-facie evidence, probable cause, proof, queen's evidence, state's evidence *(U.S.)*, title; **testimony,** alibi, appearances, attest *(Archaic)*, attestation, citation, deposition, statement, testimonial, witness; **conclusive evidence,** apodixis; **argument,** allegation, case, con, construction *(Geom.)*, demonstration, presumption, pro, proof, substantiation, the proof of the pudding; **swearing on oath,** affidavit, affirmation, avouchment, sustainment, sworn statement, testification *(Law)*, verification, vouch *(Obs.)*
EVIDENCE *v* evince, go to show, show, speak for itself, speak volumes, tell its own tale
evidence *n* → 1 sign *v* 2 display
evident *adj* → 1 obvious 2 visible
evil *n* → 1 evildoing 2 harm 3 illness 4 misfortune 5 wrongfulness *adj* 6 angry 7 bad 8 calamitous 9 harmful 10 immoral 11 wrong
EVILDOING *n* abomination, atrocity, crime, evil, infamous conduct, malefaction, seduction, villainy; **sin,** cardinal sin, deadly sin, debt, ill, original sin, trespass, wrong, wrongdoing; **fault,** demerit, foible, peccadillo, venial sin; **fall,** lapse; **debauchment,** depravation. *See also* IMMORALITY
evince *v* → 1 display 2 evidence
evoke *v* → 1 cause 2 remind
EVOLUTION *n* coevolution, development, emergent evolution, evolvement, intergradation, natural selection, phylogeny, progress *(Biol.)*, sexual selection, speciation, survival of the fittest; **convergent evolution,** adaptation, convergence, naturalisation; **accommodation,** acculturation; **anthropogenesis,** cainogenesis, cytogenesis, monogenesis, orthogenesis, palingenesis, phytogenesis *(Bot.)*; **genetics,** cytogenetics, physical anthropology; **Darwinism,** Lamarckism, Neo-Darwinism, Neo-Lamarckism, transformism; **adaptiveness,** accommodativeness, struggle for existence
evolution *n* → 1 gaseousness 2 mathematical operation 3 movement 4 result
EVOLUTIONARY *adj* anthropogenic, cainogenetic, monogenetic, orthogenetic, palingenetic, phylogenetic, phylogenic, phytogenetic, phytogenetical; **mutant,** mutational, mutative; **evolutionistic,** Darwinian, Darwinist
EVOLUTIONIST *n* Darwinian, Darwinist, transformist
EVOLVE *v* coevolve, develop, intergrade; **adapt,** accord, acculturate, naturalise
evolve *v* → 1 create 2 improve
ewe *n* → sheep
ewer *n* → vessel
exacerbate *v* → 1 annoy 2 increase
exact *v* → 1 extort 2 force 3 impose 4 insist on *adj* 5 concise 6 correct 7 precise
exacting *adj* → 1 insistent 2 strict
EXAGGERATE *v* amplify, bull, bulldust, distend, embroider, hyperbolise, magnify, make a mountain out of a molehill, melodramatise, out-Herod Herod, puff up, sound off, stack it on, theatricalise, wiredraw; **overstate,** lay it on, lay it on thick, overwrite, pile on the agony, turn on the agony; **make a good story,** draw a long bow, imagine, pitch a tale, pull a long bow, romance, spin a yarn, tell stories; **overplay,** make too much of, overact, overcharge, overdo, overdraw, overkill, overshoot the mark
exaggerate *v* → 1 increase 2 lie

EXAGGERATED *adj* exaggerative, extravagant, high-flown, high-flying, highly coloured, histrionic, hyperbolic, magniloquent, outré, overdone, overstated, strained, tall

EXAGGERATION *n* embroidery *(Colloq.)*, enlargement, extravagance, hyperbole, hyperbolism, overkill, overstatement, puff, wiredrawing; **much ado about nothing,** all piss and wind, storm in a teacup; **tall story,** flight of fancy, lulu, purple passage, traveller's tale; **caricature,** parody; **theatricality,** heroics, histrionics, melodrama, melodramatics, play-acting, theatricalism, theatricalness

EXAGGERATOR *n* boomerang bender, bull artist, bullshit artist, embroiderer, romancer, storyteller, wiredrawer

exalt *v* → **1** approve **2** glorify **3** lift **4** promote **5** rejoice **6** worship

EXAMINATION *n* audition, baccalaureate, eleven-plus *(Brit.)*, exam, examen *(Eccles.)*, finals, matriculation, open-book examination, oral examination, paper, post, supplementary, test, test paper, tripos, viva, viva voce; **trial,** tryout; **driving test,** road test; **audit,** means test. *See also* INVESTIGATION; INSPECTION

examination *n* → investigation

EXAMINE *v* analyse, canvass, explore; **test,** ascertain, assay, prove, put to the proof, reexamine, take, try, try out, verify; **study,** audit, monitor, scan, scrutineer, scrutinise, vet; **inspect,** appraise, evaluate, overhaul, review; **diagnose,** auscultate, palpate, sound, X-ray. *See also* INVESTIGATE

examine *v* → **1** inquire into **2** question **3** teach

EXAMPLE *n* etymon, exemplification, exemplum, instance, paradigm, pattern, praxis, precedent; **specimen,** piece, sample, sort, type, type genus, type specimen; **pacesetter,** fugleman, pacemaker; **paragon,** classic, exemplar, mirror; **ideal,** beau ideal, dream, ego ideal, idea, picture, the abstract; **standard,** canon, classic, measure, norm

example *n* → **1** part **2** warning

exasperate *v* → annoy

excavate *v* → **1** dig **2** hollow

EXCAVATION *n* bal, coal pit, cutting, goaf, gob, gullet, gum-hole *(N.Z.)*, gunny, mine, mineshaft, pit, quarry, salt mine, saltpit, sawpit, stope, trench; **well,** oilwell, step-out well; **shaft,** drive, moulin, winze. *See also* HOLLOW; CAVE

exceed *v* → surpass

EXCEL *v* be good value, be great at, be no slouch at, be pie on *(N.Z.)*, be worth one's salt, come into one's own, have a way with, have the game sewn up, have the knack, have what it takes, know a thing or two, know how many beans make five, know one's onions, know what's what, make a good fist of, not put a foot wrong, pull off a hat-trick, rise to the occasion, shine at, sparkle; **master,** get on top of, learn, perfect; **be one's strong suit,** be in one's bailiwick, be up one's alley

excel *v* → surpass

excellence *n* → **1** goodness **2** superiority

excellent *adj* → **1** good **2** superior

EXCEPT *prep* apart from, bar, barring, bating *(Archaic)*, beside, besides, but, ex *(Finance)*, excepting, outside, save, with the exception of

except *v* → **1** exclude *prep* **2** less *conj* **3** on condition that

exception *n* → **1** exclusion **2** nonconformist **3** strangeness

exceptional *adj* → **1** good **2** nonconformist

excerpt *n* → written composition

excess *n* → **1** extravagance **2** overindulgence **3** surplus *adj* **4** surplus

EXCESSIVE *adj* dear, exceeding, exorbitant, overmuch, stiff; **immoderate,** all-fired *(U.S.)*, deadly, devilish, extravagant, extreme, fearful, inordinate, obsessive, over-the-top, overweening, overwhelming, radical, unconscionable, undue; **too much,** cloying, de trop, satiating, syrupy, too-too

EXCESSIVELY *adv* a fair treat, beyond measure, deadly, devilish, devilishly, exceedingly, exorbitantly, extravagantly, fearfully, immoderately, inordinately, overly, overweeningly, overwhelmingly, unconscionably, unduly, unnecessarily; **superfluously,** redundantly, superabundantly; **extra,** by half, over, over and above; **too much,** a bit thick, ad nauseam, over the fence, over the odds, overmuch, tanto, to a fault, to the skies, too, troppo

EXCESSIVENESS *n* exorbitance, extremism, immoderateness, immoderation, inordinacy, inordinateness, intemperance, lavishness, unconscionableness; **extravagance,** conspicuous consumption, costliness *(Archaic)*, extravagancy, extravagantness, prodigality, profligacy, recklessness; **overabundance,** ebullience, ebulliency, embarrassment, luxuriousness, overmuchness, overproduction, superabundance; **superfluousness,** redundancy; **congestion,** engorgement, fullness, overcrowding, overpopulation

EXCHANGE *n* barter, commutation, interchange, intermigration, metathesis, passage, reciprocation, traffic, transposition; **substitution,** grafting, metasomatism, novation, shift, subrogation, succession *(Ecol.)*, surrogation, transformation; **swap,** dicker, fungible, quid pro quo, trade, trade-in, valuable consideration. *See also* SUBSTITUTE

EXCHANGE *v* change, counterchange, swap, switch, trade, transpose; **interchange,** alternate, change places, compare notes, pass, reciprocate; **barter,** chop *(Obs.)*, dicker, trade. *See also* SUBSTITUTE

exchange *n* → **1** currency **2** interaction **3** medical treatment **4** shop **5** telecommunications **6** trade *v* **7** interact

exchequer *n* → **1** funds **2** storehouse **3** treasury

Exchequer *n* → court of law

excise *n* → **1** tax *v* **2** cut **3** extract **4** medicate **5** remove **6** subtract **7** tax

EXCITABLE *adj* feisty *(U.S.)*, nervous, skittish, volitant; **restless**, excited, exhaustless, unquiet, unresting; **hyperactive**, always on the go, overactive

EXCITE *v* agitate, electrify, exhilarate, thrill; **overexcite**, frenzy, hype up, whip up, wind up, work up; **turn on**, intoxicate, send; **sensationalise**, dramatise

excite *v* → **1** activate **2** cause **3** electrify **4** encourage **5** eroticise

EXCITED *adj* above oneself, agog, ebullient, exalted, feverish, feverous, frisky, gone *(Colloq.)*, hectic, hyped-up, intoxicated, keyed up, on tenterhooks, red-hot; **agitated**, dithering, dithery, fluttery, jumpy, overwrought, tremulous, twittery, uncool, wrought-up; **frenzied**, crazy, delirious, hysterical, mad, maenadic, off one's head, phrenetic, wild; **hot-blooded**, passionate, rackety; **excitable**, combustible, combustive, feisty *(U.S.)*, inflammable, nervy, overexcitable, toey

EXCITEMENT *n* agitation, ecstasy, excitation, exhilaration, fever, feverishness, orgasm, tension, thrillingness, wildness; **frenzy**, agony, conniptions, delirium, hysteria, hysterics, nympholepsy, overexcitement, pink fit, spin, state, stir; **fluster**, ado, dither, flurry, flustration, flutter, fuss, twitter; **sensationalism**, luridness, sensuism, titillation; **thrill**, bang, buzz, charge, frisson, kick; **furore**, boil-up, combustion, ferment, scene, sensation, three-day night; **much ado about nothing**, a storm in a teacup; **boiling point**, fever pitch, white heat

EXCITING *adj* awe-inspiring, breathtaking, excitative, exhilarating, exhilarative, hairy *(Colloq.)*, heady, intoxicative, lively, mind-bending, mind-blowing, nail-biting, thrilling, vibrant; **sensational**, lurid

exclaim *v* → **1** shout **2** speak

exclamation mark *n* → warning

EXCLUDE *v* except, include out, leave off, leave out, omit, overleap, preclude, skip; **eliminate**, cancel, cut, dele, delete, drop, rule out, sink; **get rid of**, cull, cut out, give the boot, off-load, weed out, winnow. *See also* ISOLATE; BOYCOTT

exclude *v* → **1** eject **2** prohibit

EXCLUDED *adj* apart, beyond the pale, fringe, inadmissable, not included, out of court; **culled**, cast for age *(Agric.)*, separated; **exiled**, expatriate, in exile, ostracised, outcast

EXCLUSION *n* elimination, exception, omission, ostracism, reservation, shut-out; **segregation**, apartheid, colour-bar, exclusionism, white Australia policy; **disqualification**, ban, debarment, disenfranchisement, disinheritance, excommunication, forbiddance, order of the boot, preclusion, reprobation; **bar**, barrier, no-go area, taboo; **exile**, banishment, estrangement, riddance, sequestration; **isolation**, aloneness; **deletion**, cancel *(Print.)*, cancellation, cut, dele, delenda, elision, ellipsis

EXCLUSIVE *adj* exclusory, preclusive, segregated, segregative; **restricted**, off-limits; **eliminative**, elimination, eliminatory, exceptive, knockout, omissive

exclusive *n* → **1** dress **2** news item *adj* **3** fashionable **4** one **5** own **6** unsociable

excommunicate *v* → **1** be unfriendly **2** isolate **3** profane **4** punish *adj* **5** heretical **6** punished

excrement *n* → bodily discharge

excrescence *n* → **1** bulge **2** enlargement

EXCRETE *v* exude; **perspire**, feel like a greasespot, foam, lather, sweat, swelter, transpire; **slaver**, drivel, expectorate, gob, golly, hawk, hoick, salivate, slag, slobber, snivel, spit, water; **ejaculate**, come, drop a load, dump a load, get one's rocks off, shoot one's bolt, toss off; **discharge**, matter, maturate, run, suppurate, weep; **menstruate**, be on the rags, flood, have the flags out, have the painters in, see the flowers, see the roses, see the visitors; **purge**, go through like a dose of salts, physic, scour; **secrete**; **lactate**, express milk, give milk. *See also* DEFECATE; URINATE

excrete *v* → expel

excruciating *adj* → painful

excursion *n* → **1** attack **2** deflection **3** journey

excuse *n* → **1** justification **2** penitence *v* **3** acquit **4** atone for **5** forgive **6** justify

execrable *adj* → **1** bad **2** hateful **3** unpleasant

EXECRATORY *adj* abusive, anathematic, blasphemous, damnatory, execrative, foul, foul-mouthed, hard-mouthed, imprecatory, maledictory; **coarse**, bad, foul, strong, unparliamentary

EXECUTE *v* lynch, point the bone at; **electrocute**, gas; **hang**, gibbet, halter, stretch, string up, supercollate, turn off *(Obs.)*; **garrotte**, bow-string, strangle; **crucify**, impale; **behead**, guillotine, send to the scaffold; **hang draw and quarter**, flay, quarter

execute *v* → **1** accomplish **2** do **3** kill

executive *n* → **1** legislative body **2** manager *adj* **3** managerial

executor *n* → **1** agent **2** doer **3** manager

exegesis *n* → **1** clarification **2** explanation **3** teaching

exemplary *adj* → **1** approved **2** model **3** warning

exemplify *v* → **1** copy **2** explain

exempt *v* → **1** be lenient **2** liberate

exequies *n* → **1** funeral rites **2** grieving

EXERCISE *n* constitutional; daily dozen, exercitation, pacework, practice, sweat, work-out; **physical education**, acrobatics, aerobics, athletics, body building, calisthenics, exercises, gymnastics, isometrics, P.E., P.T., phys. ed., physical jerks, physical training, sport, weightlifting, yoga; **knee-bend**, forward roll, half lever, handspring, handstand, hang, heave, lunge, neck roll, press-up, push-up, scissors, somersault, split, turn

exercise *n* → **1** doing **2** lesson **3** operation **4** reasoning **5** use *v* **6** alarm **7** do **8** operate **9** use

EXERCISE RESTRAINT *v* back-pedal, be moderate, mince one's words, soft-pedal, take the middle road, trim

exert *v* → use

exhale *v* → breathe

exhaust *n* → **1** exit **2** gas *v* **3** discharge **4** empty **5** extract **6** make infertile **7** tire **8** use up

exhaustive *adj* → **1** enervating **2** thorough **3** tiring **4** weak

exhibit *n* → **1** authentication *v* **2** display **3** testify

exhibitionism *n* → **1** display **2** sexuality

exhilarate *v* → **1** energise **2** excite **3** make happy

exhort *v* → **1** guide **2** warn

EXHUMATION *n* body-snatching, disentombment, disinterment

EXHUME *v* disentomb, disinter

exhume *v* → remove

exigency *n* → necessities

exile *n* → **1** absence **2** absentee **3** exclusion **4** exit **5** expulsion **6** outsider **7** punishment *v* **8** be absent **9** eject **10** isolate **11** repel **12** separate

exist *v* → **1** be **2** live

existentialism *n* → liberalism

EXIT *n* débouché, debouch *(Fort.)*, egress, mouth *(Phys. Geog.)*, outfall, outlet, solfatara, way out; **emergence,** appearance, coming out, debouchment, surfacing; **outflow,** burst, discharge, drainage, effluent, efflux, effluxion, effusion, emanation, emission, eruption, exudation, flash, issuance, issue, leak, leakage, outbreak, outburst, outpour, runoff, seep, seepage; **emigration,** brain drain, exile; **vent,** channel, chimney, chimneystack, chute, drain, exhaust, exhaust pipe, nozzle, opening, orifice, snout, spout, stovepipe, tap, taphole, venturi *(Naut.)*, vomitory, zoomie; **egression,** departure, escape, escapement *(Archaic)*, exodus, outgo, outgoing; **sally,** sortie

EXIT *v* clear *(Shipping)*, depart, emigrate, export, go forth, go out, hop it, issue forth, outfly *(Poetic)*, sally, sortie *(Mil.)*, spring forth, spring out; **emerge,** come forth, come out, debouch; **erupt,** break out, burst forth, burst out, escape

exit *n* → **1** access **2** departure *v* **3** depart **4** die *interj* **5** piss off

exodus *n* → **1** departure **2** exit **3** foreigner

exonerate *v* → **1** acquit **2** forgive **3** justify **4** liberate

exorbitant *adj* → **1** excessive **2** expensive

exotic *n* → **1** foreigner *adj* **2** foreign **3** strange

expand *v* → **1** grow **2** increase **3** open up **4** waffle

expanse *n* → **1** length **2** space **3** thickness

expansion *n* → **1** increase **2** length **3** waffle

expansive *adj* → **1** big **2** increasing **3** liberated **4** long **5** psychologically disturbed **6** sociable **7** spacious **8** thick

expatiate *v* → waffle

expatriate *n* → **1** outsider *v* **2** isolate *adj* **3** excluded

EXPECT *v* anticipate, ask, bargain for, contemplate, count upon, envision, foresee, have in store, look for, look to, prepare for, suppose, think, think likely; **plan against,** forestall, prevent *(Obs.)*, take precautions; **await,** attend, cool one's heels, drool, hold one's breath, kick one's heels, lie in wait, listen for, mark time, tarry *(Archaic)*, wait for, watch for, watch out for; **apprehend,** bide one's time, contemplate, sweat on; **hope for,** look forward to, look to, pitch one's hopes at, promise oneself

expect *v* → **1** be likely **2** conceive **3** conjecture **4** hope

EXPECTANT *adj* anticipant of, hopeful, tiptoe, tiptoe with excitement; **clockwatching,** anticipating, looking forward to; **anticipatory,** anticipative, expectative, prevenient; **apprehensive,** fearful, threatened

EXPECTANTLY *adv* agog, anticipatively, anticipatorily, apprehensively, in expectation of, on tenterhooks, on tiptoe, prospectively; **on the horizon,** almost upon us, in the pipeline, in view, just around the corner

EXPECTATION *n* anticipation, breathless expectation, clockwatching, eager anticipation, expectance, expectancy, foresight, wait, waiting; **hope,** belief, good faith, optimism; **apprehension,** apprehensiveness, curiosity, suspense; **prevenience,** prevenance

EXPECTED *adj* anticipated, future, imminent, impending, pending, prospective; **foreseen,** long expected, Messianic, prophesied; **favourite,** deemed most likely to succeed, fancied, kindly *(Mining)*

EXPECTED THING *n* consummation greatly to be desired, contingency, destiny, future, presumption, prospect, sanguine hope, the goods *(Colloq.)*; **dream,** thought, view; **foretaste,** prelibation; **time bomb,** pregnant situation; **expected person,** comer *(Colloq.)*, great white hope, hopeful, Messiah; **fancy,** favourite *(Sport)*

expectorate *v* → excrete

EXPEDIENCE *n* advantageousness, advisability, appropriateness, desirability, expediency, suitability; **resourcefulness,** extemporaneousness, extemporariness, extemporisation, pragmatism, utilitarianism; **fitness,** commodiousness, judiciousness, propriety, towardliness, towardness

EXPEDIENT *n* ad hoc decision, cards to play, gambit, means, means to an end, method, nostrum, plan, plot, policy, recourse, remedy, resort, resource, scheme, stepping stone, stock-in-trade, strategem, strings to one's bow, wherewithal; **convenience,** accommodation, advantage; **contrivance,** artifice, connivance, design, dodge, fiddle, gimmick, knack, loophole, shift, trick, waiting game, wangle; **makeshift,** bandaid solution, improvisation, jury mast, jury rig, locum tenens, remount, stopgap, substitute, temporary expedience; **last resort,** insurance, sheet anchor

EXPEDIENT *adj* advantageous, advisable, conducive to advantage, desirable, expediential, handy, opportune, profitable, timely, worth one's while; **appropriate,** applicable, befitting, fit, meet *(Archaic)*, proper, ripe, suitable, towardly *(Archaic)*; **politic,** deliberative, judicious; **workable,** practical, useful, utilitarian, utility; **convenient,** commodious, satisfactory; **improvised,** ad hoc, extemporal *(Archaic)*, extemporaneous, extemporary, extempore, improvisatory, jury *(Naut.)*, makeshift, stopgap

expedient *n* → **1** method *adj* **2** operating

EXPEDIENTLY *adv* advantageously, advisably, desirably; **by means of,** through the means of, with the aid of; **conveniently,** appropriately, at the last moment, commodiously, in the nick of time; **to advantage,** just as well; **extemporarily,** extemporaneously, resourcefully; **in cold blood,** deliberatively, politicly, with an eye to the main chance

expedite *v* → **1** accomplish **2** hurry **3** publicise *adj* **4** prepared

expedition *n* → **1** act of war **2** journey **3** speed

EXPEL *v* disgorge, dump, egest, ejaculate, eliminate, evacuate, express, extrude, pump out, spout, vent, void; **emit,** give off, give out, radiate, reek, send off, send out, spit, sputter, utter *(Rare)*; **deflate,** degas, degasify; **erupt,** burst, effuse, extravasate, regorge; **discharge,** excrete, exude, flux *(Obs.)*, pour out, suppurate. *See also* EJECT

expel *v* → prohibit

EXPELLER *n* eliminator, evacuator, vomiter; **expellant,** aperient, cathartic, emetic; **ejector,** banisher, bouncer, chucker-out, evictor

expend *v* → **1** pay **2** use up

expendable *adj* → **1** payable **2** unimportant **3** useable

expenditure *n* → **1** allowance **2** cost **3** payment **4** use

expense *n* → **1** cost **2** payment

EXPENSIVE *adj* a bit hot, dear, high-priced, pricey; **prohibitive,** beyond one's means; **extravagant,** big, excessive, exorbitant, extortionate, high, inflated, inflationary, steep; **valuable,** costly, precious, rich; **priceless,** beyond price, invaluable, unpriced *(Poetic)*, unvalued *(Obs.)*; **sumptuous,** plush, plushy, ritzy, swanky

experience *n* → **1** knowledge **2** occurrence **3** perception *v* **4** feel emotion **5** learn **6** perceive **7** undergo

experienced *adj* → **1** accomplished **2** knowledgeable

experiment *n* → **1** attempt **2** investigation **3** test *v* **4** attempt **5** investigate **6** test

EXPERT *n* dab, dab hand, dead hand, gun, hot-shot, jack-of-all-trades, old chum, old hand, old stager, right-hand man, ringer; **master,** adept, artist, authority, craftsman, doctor *(Colloq.)*, engineer, master hand, master workman, master-craftsman, past master, professional, proficient, rattler *(Colloq.)*, specialist; **virtuoso,** ace, crack, giant, hepcat, high priest, king, maestro, old master, the greatest, thoroughbred, whiz, wizard; **talent,** enfant terrible, good material, prodigy, whiz kid, wunderkind; **all-rounder,** ambidexter, renaissance man, universal genius

expert *n* → **1** shearer **2** specialist **3** wise person *adj* **4** competent **5** knowledgeable

expertise *n* → **1** competence **2** knowledge

expiate *v* → compensate

expire *v* → **1** burn out **2** die **3** finish

EXPLAIN *v* clarify, define, elucidate, explicate, expound, shed light on, throw light on, unfold; **interpret,** construe, deconstruct, make of, read, read between the lines, take, understand; **comment,** commentate, editorialise; **illustrate,** exemplify; **annotate,** edit, gloss, margin, pave

explain *v* → **1** clarify **2** justify **3** solve

EXPLANATION *n* anagoge, clarification, eisegesis, elucidation, exegesis, explication, illumination, interpretation; **illustration,** exemplification; **exegetics,** deconstruction, diagnostics, euhemerism, hermeneutics, higher criticism, oneirocriticism, oneirology, semiotics, solarism, symbology; **key,** clue, crib, solution

explanation *n* → **1** clarification **2** solution **3** teaching

EXPLANATORY *adj* declarative, declaratory, elucidative, elucidatory, explicative, exponential, expository, illuminating, illuminative, illustrational, illustrative, interpretational, interpretive; **annotative,** commentarial, epexegetic, exegetic, glossarial, scholiastic

expletive *n* → **1** language **2** word

explicable *adj* → clear

explicate *v* → **1** clarify **2** explain

explicit *adj* → **1** clear **2** meaningful **3** precise

EXPLODE *v* backfire, burst asunder, burst on the ear, fly off, fulminate, go off, implode, pop, selfdestruct; **set off,** blast, blow up, bomb, destruct *(Mil.)*, detonate, discharge, dynamite, fire, let off, shoot *(Mining)*, spring, squib, torpedo *(U.S.)*; **bang,** bark, boom, clap, crack, crash, peal, pound, slam, thump, thunder

explode *v* → separate

exploit *n* → **1** accomplishment **2** action *v* **3** use

explore *v* → **1** examine **2** investigate **3** pursue **4** search

EXPLOSION *n* blast, blow-out, blow-up, destruct, dissilience, eruption, fulmination, implosion; **report,** airburst, backfire, burst, fire, gunfire; **discharge,** detonation, salvo, volley; **outburst,** storm, tornado; **explosive power,** brisance, explosiveness, groundshock effect, megaton; **bang,** boom, clap, crack, crash, crump, peal, pop, pound, slam, slap, smash, thump, thunder, whiz-bang

explosion *n* → **1** angry act **2** firing **3** loud sound

EXPLOSIVE *n* charge, destruct system, shot *(Mining)*; **detonator,** cap, gunlock, igniter, matchlock, percussion cap, primer, selfdestruct, squib; **explosive device,** bomb, infernal machine, mine, shell, smokebomb, star shell, time bomb; **high explosive,** amatol, ammonal, atomic explosives, cheddite, cordite, cyclonite, cydonite, dynamite, gelignite, guncotton, gunpowder, hexogen, jelly, lycopodium, lyddite, maximite, melinite, mercury fulminate, nitro, nitroglycerine, nuclear explosives, picric acid, plastic, plastic explosive, smokeless powder, T.N.T., tonite, trinitrotoluene; **low explosive,** fulminating compound, fulminating powder, propellant; **wick,** fuse, touchpaper, train, trip-wire

EXPLOSIVE *adj* dissilient, dynamitic, fulminatory, live, pyrotechnic, selfdestruct *(Mil.)*

explosive *n* → ammunition

exponent *n* → **1** interpreter **2** number

export *n* → **1** trade *v* **2** exit **3** trade *adj* **4** superior

exposé *n* → **1** clarification **2** revelation

expose *v* → **1** abandon **2** air **3** bare **4** disgrace **5** display **6** endanger **7** find out **8** photograph **9** report on **10** reveal

exposition *n* → **1** clarification **2** display **3** dissemination

expostulate *v* → **1** discourage **2** guide

expound *v* → **1** clarify **2** explain

express *n* → **1** message **2** messenger **3** speedster **4** transport *v* **5** confess **6** display **7** expel **8** extract **9** hurry **10** mean **11** press **12** represent **13** speak **14** transport **15** write *adj* **16** precise **17** speedy *adv* **18** hurriedly

expression *n* → **1** characteristics **2** extraction **3** figure of speech **4** number **5** pressing **6** representation **7** speaking **8** word **9** writing

expropriate *v* → take

EXPULSION *n* clearance, dehiscence, disgorgement, ejaculation, elimination, evacuation, extrusion, voidance; **eruption,** drainage, effusion, excretion, extravasation, flux, precipitation, suppuration; **discharge,** emission, eradiation, radiation; **regurgitation,** emesis, hurl, hyperemesis, vomiturition; **deflation,** degasification; **ejection,** defenestration, displacement, ejectment, eviction; **banishment,** deportation, exile, extradition, transportation; **disbarment,** dismissal, disqualification, exclusion, ouster

expunge *v* → **1** annihilate **2** destroy

expurgate *v* → **1** correct **2** regularise

exquisite *n* → **1** affected person *adj* **2** beautiful **3** cultivated **4** good **5** intense **6** perceptive **7** tasteful

extant *adj* → **1** protuberant **2** real

extempore *adj* → **1** capricious **2** expedient *adv* **3** capriciously **4** momentarily

EXTEND *v* coextend, continue, cross, go, reach, run, span, spread, track *(U.S. Railways)*; **stretch out,** crane, outstretch; **lengthen,** draw out, drop the hem of, elongate, stretch, wiredraw

extend *v* → **1** capture **2** give **3** grow **4** increase **5** jut **6** offer **7** straighten

extension *n* → **1** addition **2** building **3** increase **4** length **5** meaning **6** telecommunications

extensive *adj* → **1** big **2** thick **3** thorough

extent *n* → **1** area **2** length **3** region **4** size **5** thickness

extenuate *v* → **1** decrease **2** forgive **3** justify **4** thin

exterior *n* → **1** outside *adj* **2** outside

exterminate *v* → **1** annihilate **2** destroy **3** massacre

external *n* → **1** outside *adj* **2** apparent **3** foreign **4** outside **5** tangible

extinct *adj* → **1** antique **2** dead **3** disused **4** extinguished **5** nonexistent **6** old

EXTINGUISH *v* bank down, blow out, damp down, douse, puff out, quench, rake out, smother, snuff out; **butt,** stub out; **put out,** defuse, switch off, turn out; **black out,** brown out

extinguish *v* → **1** pay **2** surpass

EXTINGUISHED *adj* dead, extinct, quenched, spent

EXTINGUISHER *n* douser, quencher; **sprinkler system,** fire hydrant, fire-engine, fireplug *(U.S.)*; **fire-extinguisher,** BCF, carbon dioxide, carbon tetrachloride, carbonic acid gas, foam, sand, sand, soda-acid, water

EXTINGUISHING *n* eclipse, extinction, extinguishment; **blackout,** brownout, darkness, lights out

extirpate *v* → **1** annihilate **2** destroy **3** remove **4** subtract

extol *v* → **1** approve **2** glorify **3** worship

EXTORT *v* blackmail, exact, force, garnish *(Brit.)*; **bludge off,** bite, bleed, bleed dry, cadge from, eat out of house and home, put the nips in, put the screws on, rack-rent, screw, shake, sweat

EXTORTIONIST *n* blackmailer, extorter, extortioner, grafter *(U.S.)*, rack-renter, Shylock, usurer; **swindler,** card sharp, card sharper, carpetbagger, hawk, kite, Ned Kelly, profiteer, sharper, thief; **vulture,** bloodsucker, vampire, wolf; **parasite,** bludger, leech, sponge, ten-per-center

EXTRACT *n* core, crush, decoction, educt, essence, extractive, infusion

EXTRACT *v* draw, draw out, epilate, eradicate, exhaust, extricate, pluck, pluck out, pull out, remove, root out, take out, weed out, withdraw; **cut out,** core, excise, exsect, rip out, tear out; **dig out,** dredge, mine, pull up, root up, unroot; **drain,** bleed, crush, decoct, exhaust, express, filter, filtrate, juice, milk, press, press out, pump, pump out, sluice, squeeze, squeeze out, start, suck, tap, wring from; **derive,** aspirate, render *(Cookery)*, seethe *(Obs.)*, soak, sublimate, sublime

extract *n* → **1** essence **2** written composition *v* **3** separate **4** solve

EXTRACTION *n* epilation, eradication, exsection, extrication, removal, taking out, withdrawal; **pull,** tug, wrench; **drainage,** bleeding, decoction, draught, evulsion, expression, filtration, sublimation, suction, tapping

EXTRACTOR *n* drawer *(Archaic)*, gouger, sucker; **auger,** corer, corkscrew, deriver, pigs'-feet *(Railways)*, wimble; **forceps,** pincers, pliers, tweezers; **pump,** stomach pump, vacuum pump, worm pump; **drainer,** crusher, filter, filterer, juicer, milker, milking machine, mill, squeezer, sweatbox, tapper, trocar *(Surg.)*; **bloodsucker,** leech, phlebotomist

extraneous *adj* → **1** foreign **2** outside

extraordinary *adj* → **1** astonishing **2** nonconformist **3** strange

extrapolate *v* → conjecture

EXTRAVAGANCE *n* a taste for luxury, champagne taste, conspicuous consumption, extravagant desire, extravagantness; **prodigality,** excess, profuseness, profusion, superfluity; **wastefulness,** dissipation, profligacy, profligateness, squander, thriftlessness, unthriftiness, wantonness, waste; **splurge,** bean, beanfeast, blow-out, jag, midnight feast, spree

EXTRAVAGANT *adj* costly *(Archaic)*, dissipative, lavish, prodigal, profuse, superfluous *(Obs.)*; **wasteful,** improvident, pound-foolish, profligate, thriftless, uneconomical, wanton

extravagant *adj* → **1** enthusiastic **2** exaggerated **3** excessive **4** expensive **5** nonsensical **6** showy **7** travelling

extravaganza *n* → entertainment

extreme *n* → **1** finish **2** much *adj* **3** distant **4** excessive **5** final **6** limiting **7** most **8** thorough

EXTREMITY *n* butt, club, end, finial, foot, heelpiece, pole, tag, tail, tail end, tailpiece, termination, tip, toe

extremity *n* → **1** limb **2** much

extricate *v* → **1** extract **2** liberate

extrude *v* → **1** bulge **2** expel **3** press

exuberant *adj* → **1** happy **2** joyful

exude *v* → **1** discharge **2** excrete **3** expel

exult *v* → **1** brag **2** jump **3** rejoice

EYE *n* eyeball, lamps, orb *(Poetic)*, peepers, white, winker; **eyelid,** lid; **pupil,** apple of the eye, iris, retina, yellow spot; **lash,** brow, eyebrow; **eye socket,** eyehole, orbit

eye *n* → **1** atmospheric pressure **2** centre **3** direction **4** look *v* **5** attend to **6** look **7** open

eyeball *n* → **1** eye *v* **2** look

eyebrow *n* → **1** eye **2** hair

EYE-CATCHER *n* centre of attraction, concern, cynosure, fascinator, focal point, focus of attention, lodestar, spellbinder

eyelash *n* → hair

eyelid *n* → eye

eyesore *n* → ugly person

eyetooth *n* → mouth

eyrie *n* → **1** animal dwelling **2** tower

Ff

fable *n* → **1** figure of speech **2** lie **3** narrative **4** nonsense **5** representation **6** story *v* **7** lie **8** narrate

fabric *n* → **1** building **2** textiles **3** texture

fabricate *v* → **1** create **2** fantasise **3** lie **4** make

fabulous *adj* → **1** astonishing **2** enormous **3** fake **4** famous **5** fantastic **6** good

facade *n* → **1** appearance **2** front **3** outside

FACE *n* aspect, countenance, dial, features, metope, moosh, mug, pan, phiz, physiognomy, puss, visage; **jowl,** cheek, dewlap; **jaw,** chin, chops, point *(Boxing),* underjaw. *See also* HEAD; EYE; NOSE; EAR; MOUTH

face *n* → **1** appearance **2** arrogance **3** cosmetics **4** diggings **5** famous person **6** front **7** important thing **8** outside **9** reputation **10** sign *v* **11** argue **12** cover **13** direct **14** front **15** invert **16** oppose **17** smooth **18** swerve

facet *v* → cut

facetious *adj* → humorous

facile *adj* → **1** easy **2** influenced **3** liberated **4** stupid

FACILITATE *v* cater, disencumber, ease, enable, frank, grease, make way for, speed

facilitate *v* → **1** ease **2** help **3** improve

FACILITATION *n* convenience, easement, easer, simplification, stepping stone

facility *n* → **1** agreement **2** building **3** competence **4** help

facsimile *n* → **1** copy **2** imitation **3** photograph **4** portrait *v* **5** copy *adj* **6** copied

fact *n* → **1** actuality **2** honesty **3** truth

faction *n* → committee

factitious *adj* → affected

factor *n* → **1** cause **2** manager **3** number

factorial *n* → **1** number *adj* **2** creative

FACTORY *n* assembly line, establishment, hong, industrial estate, industrial park, manufactory *(Archaic),* sheltered workshop, shop, stable, trading estate, workshop; **foundry,** grindery, ironworks, machine shop, smelter, smeltery, steelworks, wireworks, works; **smithery,** blacksmith's shop, forge, smithy, stithy; **yard,** brickfield, brickyard, dockyard, freight terminal, goods yard, shipyard; **saltworks,** salina, saltern; **plant,** gasworks, installation, pilot plant, refinery, station; **sweatshop,** female factory *(Convict),* salt mines, workhouse; **meatworks,** boiling-down works, freezing works, knackery, slaughterhouse; **mine,** colliery, pithead, stall

factory *n* → prison

faculty *n* → **1** capability **2** competence **3** institute **4** permission **5** specialist **6** teacher

fad *n* → fashion

fade *v* → **1** be old **2** cinematise **3** darken **4** die **5** disappear **6** dull **7** graduate **8** lose colour **9** quieten **10** swerve **11** weaken

faeces *n* → defecation

fag *n* → **1** butler **2** remnant **3** sexual type **4** tobacco **5** toil *v* **6** tire **7** work

faggot *n* → **1** accumulation **2** fuel **3** man **4** sexual type

FAIL *v* bomb, die, die in the hole, die standing up, die the death, fall flat, fall short, fall through, give way, lapse, melt *(Archaic),* miss the boat, miss the bus, not come up to scratch, not make the grade, not suffice, slump, wither on the vine; **collapse,** backfire, break down, clap out, come undone, crack, crack up, crash, end up in smoke, fall down, fizzle, flop, fold, fold up, go down like a lead balloon, go up in smoke, miscarry, misfire, nosedive; **come unstuck,** bomb, bomb out, come a buster, come a cropper, come a gutser, come to grief, do no good, draw a blank, fall flat on one's face, get nowhere, go to the devil, go to the wall, go under, have had it, have had one's chips, lay an egg, lose out on, not be able to take a trick, not get to first base; **miss,** go wide; **bungle,** abort, arse up, balls up, blow, botch, butcher, cock up, dig one's own grave, dud up, foozle, foul up, mess about, muck up, muff, mull, scupper *(Brit. Colloq.),* trip up; **make a blue,** flunk, make a false step, strike out; **underachieve,** run dead *(Horseracing);* **lose,** be among the also-rans, be bested, bite the dust, come off second best, get left behind, lose out, take a beating; **give in,** admit defeat, cop out, crap out, default, dip out, give it best, give way, go back on, let someone down, mess someone about, put up the shutters

fail *n* → **1** failure *v* **2** be unable to pay **3** fall short **4** lose **5** weaken

FAILED *adj* done like a dinner, gone to Gowings, manqué, ruined, washed-up; **unsuccessful,** ineffective, ineffectual, lost, stickit *(Scot.),* unplaced; **losing,** no-win, self-defeating; **unaccomplished,** abortive, stillborn

failing *n* → **1** failure **2** imperfection **3** weakling *adj* **4** aged **5** deteriorating *prep* **6** less

FAIL TO PAY *v* break an agreement, default, dishonour a cheque, do a moonlight flit, freeload, nullify an agreement, scarper, shoot through, welsh; **defraud,** bilk, cheat, swindle

FAILURE *n* abort, abortion, bomb, calamity, damp squib, disaster, fiasco, fizz, fizzle, fizzler, flop, forlorn hope, frost, lemon, misfire, muff, squib, turkey, wash-out, wipe-out, write-off; **fail,** flunk, plough *(Brit. Colloq.);*

fall, cropper, downfall, failing, lapse, nosedive; **collapse,** bust-up, crack-up, crash, slump, smash; **loss,** a dead loss, blue duck *(Mil.)*, bottom, bummer, bust, naught, no-no; **bungle,** balls-up, blunder, botch, cock-up, error, foozle, hash, miscarriage, muck-up, muddle, slip, slip-up, stuff-up; **miss,** break *(Tenpin Bowling)*, fault, near miss, rabbit *(Cricket)*, strike *(Baseball)*; **unsuccessfulness,** abortiveness

failure *n* → **1** nonachiever **2** non-payment **3** weakling

faint *n* → **1** unconsciousness *v* **2** become unconscious **3** be ill **4** be tired **5** dull **6** weaken *adj* **7** cowardly **8** dull **9** feverish **10** imprecise **11** invisible **12** quiet **13** weak

FAIR *adj* candid, disinterested, dispassionate, fair-minded, impartial, objective, uninterested; **egalitarian,** democratic, equalitarian; **even-handed,** equable, equal *(Archaic)*, equitable, even, fair and square; **sporting,** sportsmanlike; **just,** conscionable, honest, morally right, reasonable, right, rightful, square; **deserved,** as it should be, fit, fitting, justifiable, lawful, legitimate, well-earned

fair *n* → **1** amusement park **2** display **3** festival **4** lover **5** shop **6** woman *v* **7** change **8** improve *adj* **9** adequate **10** beautiful **11** clear **12** climatic **13** courteous **14** dry **15** easy **16** favourable **17** honest **18** hot **19** mediocre **20** perfect **21** smooth **22** white **23** windy *adv* **24** fairly **25** wholly

FAIR GO *n* fair buck *(N.Z.)*, fair do *(N.Z.)*; **fair play,** cricket, good sportsmanship, Marquis of Queensbury rules, square deal

FAIR GO *interj* fair buck *(N.Z.)*, fair crack of the whip, fair do *(N.Z.)*, fair shake of the dice, fair suck of the sauce bottle, fair suck of the sav, fair's fair

FAIRLY *adv* candidly, fair, fair and square, justly, on the square, sportingly, square; **impartially,** dispassionately, equably, equitably, even, objectively, without fear or favour, without prejudice, without regard to person; **rightfully,** by rights, in justice

fairly *adv* → **1** clearly **2** correctly **3** courteously **4** honestly **5** wholly

fairway *n* → access

FAIRY *n* banshee *(Scot. Irish)*, brownie, elf, elfin, faerie *(Archaic)*, leprechaun, little people, pixie, pixy, sandman, sprite, tooth fairy, urchin *(Archaic)*; **imp,** bug, devilkin, eudemon, gremlin, hob, hobgoblin, kobold *(German)*, puck, siren, sprite, sylph, sylphid; **ogre,** dwarf, hag, monopode, pygmy, troll, witch; **bogyman,** boggle, bogle, bogy, boogieman, bugaboo, bugbear *(Obs.)*, Jack Frost; **Santa Claus,** Father Christmas, Kris Kringle, Saint Nicholas, Saint Nick, Santa. *See also* MYTHICAL BEING

fairy *n* → **1** sexual type *adj* **2** ghostly

faith *n* → **1** belief **2** hope **3** obligation **4** religion **5** reverence

FAITHFUL *adj* leal *(Scot. Archaic)*, liege, loyal, single-hearted, true, true-blue, true-hearted, white *(Brit. Colloq.)*; **honourable,** as good as one's word, good, straight, trustworthy; **dutiful,** allegiant, duteous, wedded; **reliable,** dedicated, dependable, devoted, trusty, unfailing; **resolute,** certain, constant, fixed, set, staunch, steadfast, strong, sure, unwavering; **authentic,** genuine

faithful *adj* → **1** believing **2** obedient **3** reverent

FAITHFULNESS *n* allegiance, devotedness, fealty *(Archaic)*, fidelity, loyalism, loyalty, troth *(Archaic)*, truth *(Archaic)*; **integrity,** bona fides, dependability, good faith, honour, probity, sincerity, true-heartedness, trustworthiness; **authenticity,** certainty, genuineness; **dutifulness,** devotion, duteousness, sense of responsibility, supererogation; **reliability,** adherence, adhesion, constancy, resolution, staunchness, steadfastness, strength

FAKE *n* act, bluff, cheat, deceit, deception, dissimulation, fraud, impersonation, imposture, pretence, sham; **frame-up,** put-up job, verbal; **hypocrisy,** cant, humbug, tokenism; **cupboard love,** crocodile tears, Judas kiss

FAKE *v* cook, doctor, falsify, fiddle, juggle, rig, trump up, twist; **frame,** bear false witness against, dolly, set up, verbal

FAKE *adj* bastard, bastardly *(Obs.)*, bodgie, bogus, counterfeit, done with mirrors, dummy, persuado, phoney, pinchbeck, pseudo, sham, simular, simulate *(Archaic)*, suppositious, supposititious, suppositive, unauthentic; **artificial,** celluloid, cheesy, ersatz, imitation, plastic; **pretended,** assumed, feigned, imposturous, ostensible, ostensive, professed, so-called, soi-disant, would-be; **meretricious,** flash, painted; **false,** adulterine, adulterous *(Obs.)*, fictitious, made out of whole cloth *(U.S.)*, spurious, untrue; **apocryphal,** fabulous, fairytale, mythical

fake *n* → **1** crook **2** stratagem *v* **3** trick

FAKER *n* bodgie, cheat, dissembler, dissimulator, four-flusher, fraud, front man, impersonator, impostor, malingerer, persuado, phoney, pretender, pseud, pseudo, ringer, shammer, whited sepulchre, wolf in sheep's clothing; **charlatan,** empiric *(Obs.)*, mountebank, quack, quacksalver *(Archaic)*; **hypocrite,** boggler, equivocator, humbug, prevaricator

FALL *n* crash, cropper, dive, flop, flump, plop, plump, plumper, pratfall *(U.S.)*, precipitation, prostration, purler, slip *(Geol.)*, slump, stumble, trip, tumble, whop, wipe-out *(Surfing)*; **pounce,** downrush, swoop; **free fall,** flat spin, jump, nosedive, sideslip, skydiving

FALL *v* bite the dust, come a cropper, come a gutser, crash-land, fall off, flop, flump, go for a sixer, go for six, hit the deck, keel over, knuckle over, lose one's balance, measure one's length, overbalance, pitch, slip, stumble, take a toss, take a dive, topple, trip, tumble; **plump,** plunk, whop; **collapse,** avalanche, cave in, subside; **slump,** droop, prolapse, sag; **sink,** bog, founder, settle, swamp, touch bottom; **scuttle,** send to the bottom, sink, torpedo

fall *n* → **1** decrease **2** evildoing **3** failure **4** hairpiece **5** hanging **6** ruin **7** season **8** slope *v* **9** be dismissed **10** be immoral **11** be of no repute **12** capitulate **13** collapse **14** conceive **15** cost **16** die **17** hang **18** occur **19** slope **20** wane

fallacy *n* → illogicality

FALLEN *adj* bowed, cast *(Agric.)*, downcast, droopy, sunken; **descending,** cataclinal, declivitous, descendent, downgrade, downhill, downward, katabatic; **deciduous,** caducous

fallible *adj* → **1** false **2** uncertain

FALL INTO DISUSE *v* antiquate, archaise, be superseded, give place, lapse, not catch on, rust; **go by the board,** go begging, go to waste, waste

fallow *n* → **1** farmland **2** rest *v* **3** farm **4** rest *adj* **5** brown **6** infertile **7** resting **8** yellow

FALL SHORT *v* fail, run short, ullage; **lack,** need, want; **be lacking,** be badly off for, be light on, be short of

FALSE *adj* apocryphal, erroneous, fallacious, inaccurate, incorrect, misleading, mistaken, off the beam, out, unfactual, unhistorical, untrue, wide of the mark, wrong; **astray,** awry, misapprehensive, off to billyo, on the wrong tack, up a gumtree, up the booay, up the pole; **deceptive,** hallucinatory, illusory; **fallible,** careless, erring; **misguided,** perverse, wrong-headed; **subjective**

false *adj* → **1** fake **2** illogical **3** unfaithful

falsehood *n* → **1** lie **2** misrepresentation

falsetto *n* → **1** singer *adj* **2** musical **3** shrill

falsify *v* → **1** fake **2** misinterpret

falter *v* → **1** mispronounce **2** weaken

fame *n* → **1** reputation *v* **2** glorify

familiar *n* → **1** friend **2** phantom *adj* **3** easy **4** friendly **5** insulting **6** kindred **7** knowledgeable **8** known **9** presumptuous

family *n* → **1** ancestry **2** class **3** criminal **4** language **5** occupant **6** offspring **7** relative **8** similar thing *adj* **9** correct **10** kindred

famished *adj* → hungry

FAMOUS *adj* epic, front-line, mentionable, notable, noted, noteworthy, notorious, of note, renowned; **well-known,** fashionable, hit, popular, well-established; **legendary,** deathless, fabled, fabulous, immortal, imperishable, never-fading, proverbial; **classic,** classical, historic, time-honoured

famous *adj* → **1** disreputable **2** good **3** known

FAMOUS PERSON *n* celebrity, face, figure, first fiddle, heavy, heavyweight, hero, household name, identity, leading light, lion, luminary, magnate, notable, personage, personality, public figure, somebody, star, talk of the town, tall poppy, toast of the town, V.I.P., visiting fireman, worthy

fan *n* → **1** airway **2** approver **3** audience **4** cooler **5** enthusiast **6** helper *v* **7** arouse **8** cool **9** harvest

fanatic *n* → **1** believer **2** enthusiast **3** worshipper *adj* **4** enthusiastic

fanciful *adj* → **1** capricious **2** illogical **3** strange **4** unrealistic

fancy *n* → **1** caprice **2** choice **3** conception **4** desire **5** expected thing **6** fantasy **7** good taste **8** hope **9** pleasure *v* **10** choose **11** desire **12** enjoy *adj* **13** decorative **14** fantastic **15** tasteful *interj* **16** how about that

fanfare *n* → **1** musical piece **2** show

fang *n* → **1** groin **2** journey **3** knob **4** mouth **5** rate *v* **6** beg **7** borrow **8** capture **9** drive **10** speed

fanlight *n* → window

FANTASISE *v* be away with the fairies, build castles in the air, daydream, dream, dream dreams, goof off, have visions, hear voices, live in a fantasy land, romance, romanticise, stargaze, tilt at windmills; **pretend,** make-believe; **imagine,** conjure up, ideate, invent; **envision,** image, picture, project, visualise; **concoct,** coin, fabricate, hatch, improvise

FANTASISER *n* daydreamer, Don Quixote, dreamer, fabler, fabulist, idealist, imaginer, improviser, poet, romancer, stargazer, storyteller, surrealist, Walter Mitty, woolgatherer

FANTASTIC *adj* apocryphal, chimerical, fabled, fabulous, fancied, fictional, fictitious, ideational, imaginary, imaginational, legendary, made-up, metaphysical *(Archaic)*, mythic, mythological, poetic, storybook; **surreal,** phantasmal, phantom, surrealist, surrealistic, transcendental; **imaginative,** daedal *(Poetic)*, fancy, improvisatorial, improvisatory, ingenious

fantastic *adj* → **1** astonishing **2** good **3** illogical **4** most **5** nonsensical **6** strange

FANTASY *n* fancifulness, fancy, imagery *(Psychol.)*, imagination, imaginativeness, improvisation, ingeniousness, ingenuity, mind's eye; **imaginariness,** apocryphalness, fabulousness, fictitiousness, idealness, unreality, vaporosity, vaporousness; **idealism,** escapism, romanticism, surrealism, vision, visionariness; **stargazing,** wool-gathering; **autism,** introversion, schizophrenia, withdrawal *(Psychol.)*

fantasy *n* → caprice

far *adj* → **1** distant *adv* **2** greatly **3** remotely **4** then

faraway *adj* → **1** distant **2** imprecise

far away *adv* → remotely

farce *n* → **1** comedy **2** drama **3** error *v* **4** joke

fare *n* → **1** charge **2** condition **3** food **4** passenger *v* **5** occur **6** travel **7** undergo

FAREWELL *n* adieu, godspeed, goodbye, goodnight, send-off, valedictory; **parting,** leave, leave-taking, parting of the ways, valediction

FAREWELL *v* bundle off, ring out, see off, see out, see to the door, send off

farewell *interj* → goodbye

FARM *n* bush farm *(N.Z.)*, croft *(Scot.)*, estate, free selection, hobby farm, homestead selection, plantation, property, selection, smallholding, stud-farm, vinery, vineyard; **farmhouse,** farmstead, grange, hacienda, homestead; **collective farm,** cooperative farm, kibbutz, kolkhoz; **station,** back-station, cattle-run, dude ranch *(U.S.)*, estancia, out-station, ranch, rancho, sheep station, sheep-run, spread *(U.S.)*, stock farm; **dairy farm,** creamery, dairy, herringbone dairy; **oyster-farm,** trout-farm, turtle-farm

FARM *v* be on the land, cocky, cowbang, cowspank, ranch; **drove,** drift, herd, hoozle, hunt away, jackeroo, muster, stockkeep, tail, wrangle *(U.S.)*; **graze,** agist, block-graze, crash-graze, creep-graze, fatten, feed, open-graze, pasture, range, run; **breed,** grow, lamb down, overstock, stock; **milk,** strip; **cultivate,** bring in *(N.Z.)*, grow, husband *(Obs.)*, improve, subdue; **plough,** chip, chisel-plough, delve, dibble, dig, disc, grub, harrow, hoe, labour *(Archaic or Poetic)*, rake, scarify, stub, stump, till; **fallow,** rest; **plant,** bed, heel in, implant, pot, prick out, slip, transplant, vernalise; **sow,** broadcast, checkrow *(U.S.)*, seed, sod-seed, stratify; **afforest,** forest. *See also* HARVEST

farm *n* → **1** house **2** income **3** loan **4** tax

FARMER *n* boss cocky, husbandman, landsman, pastoralist, primary producer, ruralist, the man on the land; **small farmer,** agistor, blocker, blockie, bush-farmer, cockatoo, cocky, cove, crofter *(Scot.)*, dungaree settler, free selector, selector, stringy-bark cockatoo, wheat-cocky; **stockbreeder,** breeder, cutter-out, stirpiculturist, stock farmer, stock raiser; **dairy farmer,** cow-cocky, cowbanger, cowspanker, herd tester; **grazier,** cattleman, rancher, ranchero, run-holder, sheepman, station-owner, stockholder, stockkeeper, stockman *(U.S.)*, woolgrower; **apiarist,** apiculturist, beekeeper, sericulturist; **planter,** cane-cocky, canefarmer, canegrower, sugar farmer, tea planter; **winegrower,** blocker *(S.A.)*, oenologist, vigneron, vinedresser, vineyardist, viniculturist, viticulturer, viticulturist; **orchardist,** fruit-grower, fruiter, pomiculturist, pomologist; **hobby farmer,** Collins Street cocky, Piccadilly bushman *(Brit.)*, Pitt Street farmer, Queen Street bushie; **tenant farmer,** cropper, sharecropper *(U.S.)*, sharefarmer, sharemilker *(N.Z.)*; **farm manager,** overseer, station manager; **peasant,** bucolic, bushie, carl *(Archaic)*, churl, cottager, cottar, cottier, hick, redneck *(U.S.)*, ryot; **stock and station agent,** stock agent; **agriculturalist,** agriculturist, agrobiologist, agronomist, forester

FARMHAND *n* blue-tongue, help, jackeroo, jillaroo, knockabout, leatherneck, loppy, narangy, rouseabout, rouser, station hand, wood-and-water joey; **stockman,** buckaroo, cow hand, cowboy, cowgirl, cowpuncher *(U.S.)*, drover, gaucho, musterer, nutter, ringer, stock-driver *(N.Z.)*, stockrider, tailer, tailer-up, vaquero *(U.S.)*; **boundary rider,** jerker, lizard; **shepherd,** cowherd, crawler, dog driver, goatherd, gooseherd, herder, herdsman, monkey dodger, motherer, shepherdess, snail, swanherd, swineherd, wrangler *(U.S.)*; **dairyman,** cowman, dairymaid *(Archaic)*, dairywoman, milkmaid; **tiller,** ploughboy, plougher, ploughman; **reaper,** canecutter, cocksfooter *(N.Z.)*, emubobber, gleaner, harvester, harvestman, thresher; **haymaker,** crow *(N.Z.)*, tedder, windrower; **picker,** hop-picker, vintager

FARMING *n* agrarianism, agribusiness, agriculture, cultivation, husbandry, pastoralism, primary industry, ruralism; **agronomy,** agrobiology, agrology, agronomics, chemurgy, geoponics, pedology, soil mechanics, soil science; **mixed farming,** bush-farming, market gardening, subsistence farming; **stock farming,** agistment, animal husbandry, breeding, custom feeding, stock raising, wool-growing; **dairy farming,** cow-cockying, dairying, herd testing, sharemilking; **forestry,** afforestation, arboriculture, forestation, reforestation, silviculture; **viticulture,** oenology, viniculture, winegrowing; **apiculture,** sericulture; **marine farming,** aquiculture, mariculture; **organic farming,** biological control, companion planting, hydroponics, permaculture, tank farming; **ploughing,** contour ploughing, culture; **clean cultivation,** crop rotation, dry farming, extensive cultivation, intensive cultivation, ley farming, monoculture, multiple cropping, strip cropping; **harvesting,** cocksfooting *(N.Z.)*, harvest home, haymaking, inning, mowing, reaping; **grazing,** crash-grazing, intensive stocking, rotational grazing, set stocking, strategic grazing, strip grazing, zero grazing; **muster,** bangtail muster, round-up, yarding; **drenching,** dipping, mulesing

FARMING *adj* agrarian, agrestic, bucolic, country, georgic, pastoral, peasant, rural, rustic, villatic; **agricultural,** agrobiologic, agrologic, agrological, agronomic, agronomical, geoponic, hydroponic; **farmyard,** free-range, open-range, organic; **arboricultural,** silvicultural; **vinicultural,** oenological, viticultural; **apicultural,** apiarian, sericultural

FARMLAND *n* baulk, downland, fallow, field, glebe *(Poetic)*, infield, lea *(Archaic)*, ley, mead *(Poetic)*, meadow *(Brit.)*, paddock, swidden, turbary, water-meadow; **back paddock,** back country, back run, outfield; **tillage,** cornfield, cultivation paddock, hayfield, paddy, plough, tilth; **wheat-belt,** rice bowl; **pasture,** artificial grass, grass, improved pasture, pasturage, run-off *(N.Z.)*; **grazing land,** long paddock, sheepwalk *(Brit.)*, springer paddock, stock run; **farmyard,** barnyard, feedlot, home paddock, resting paddock, stockyard

fart *n* → **1** burp **2** fool **3** incompetent *v* **4** burp

farther *adj* → **1** distant *adv* **2** additionally

farthest *adj* → **1** distant **2** long

fascinate *v* → **1** allure **2** bewitch **3** engross

fascism *n* → authority

FASHION *n* craze, cult, fad, fangle *(Obs.)*, rage, the going thing, the last word, the latest, the new look, the thing, vogue; **style,** cut, guise, tone, trend; **haute couture,** bon ton; **fashionableness,** chic, coolness, dressiness, exclusiveness, faddishness, height of fashion, modishness, smartness, stylishness, trendiness, up-to-dateness; **dapperness,** jauntiness, nattiness, rakishness, sauciness, snappiness, sportiness, spruceness, swank, swankiness; **cultism,** dandyism, faddism, trendyism; **titivation,** dandification

fashion *n* → **1** class **2** creativity **3** making **4** shape *v* **5** make **6** shape *adj* **7** fashionable

FASHIONABLE *adj* all the go, all the rage, in, in vogue, up-to-date, up-to-the-minute, with-it; **dapper,** all gussied up, dandy, dandyish, dressed to the nines, snappy, spiffy, sporty, spruce, swanky; **chic,** cool, dashing, dashy, exclusive, faddish, faddy, fashion, gear *(Brit.)*, high-stepping, hot, jaunty, mod, modish, natty, newfangled, rakish, saucy, smart, snazzy, stylish, supercool, swell, swish, swishy; **trendy,** ultrafashionable

FASHIONABLE PERSON *n* cultist, faddist, teeny-bopper, trendsetter, trendy; **beau monde,** grand monde, haut monde, the scene; **high society,** beautiful people, glitterati, jet set, smart set; **socialite,** jetsetter; **dandy,** ball of style, fop, gallant, gilded youth, high-stepper, jack-a-dandy, prinker, swell, titivator

FASHIONABLY *adv* à la mode, exclusively, modishly, on the scene, stylishly, stylistically; **dapperly,** dashingly, jauntily, nattily, rakishly, saucily, snappily, sprucely, swankily

FAST *n* hunger strike; **diet,** bread and water, iron rations, short commons, starvation diet; **fast day,** Advent, Asalahabuja, Friday, Lent, Ramadan, Yom Kippur. *See also* ABSTINENCE

fast *n* → **1** holy day *v* **2** abstain *adj* **3** busy **4** closed **5** deceitful **6** fastened **7** imprisoned **8** promiscuous **9** restricted **10** speedy **11** steady **12** sticky **13** untimely *adv* **14** speedily **15** steadily

FASTEN *v* affix, attach, fix, lace, secure, stick; **infix,** engage *(Archaic)*, house, joggle, mortice, seat; **hang,** hook up, suspend; **bind,** bend, bight, colligate, knot, strap, tie, withe, wrap, wrap up; **do up,** belt up, button up, zip up; **lash,** bowse, cable, cord, frap, gammon *(Naut.)*, gripe *(Naut.)*, lace, reeve, rope, seize *(Naut.)*; **nail,** bolt, rivet, screw, skew *(Carp.)*, tack; **clamp,** clasp, clinch, grasp, grip; **stitch,** side-stitch, staple; **make fast,** anchor, moor, tie up; **tether,** enchain, hobble, hopple, leash, picket, shackle, stake; **lock,** bar, double-lock

fasten *v* → join

FASTENED *adj* engaged, fast, firm, fixed, iron, secure; **bound,** bandaged, corded, fasciate, lashed, tied; **at anchor,** girt

FASTENER *n* bonder, locker, securer; **binder,** bracer, lasher, tier, trusser; **nailer,** pinner, riveter; **grasper,** clasper, clincher, gripper, hooker; **hitcher,** hobbler, shackler

fastidious *adj* → **1** attentive **2** discriminating **3** precise

FAT *n* adipose, animal fat, blubber, cellulite, sebum, suet, tallow, yolk; **edible oil,** blown oil, butter, butterfat, castor oil, cooking oil, cottonseed oil, dripping, fat, ghee, gingili, grease, lard, marg, margarine, nut oil, oleo oil, olive oil, palm oil, safflower oil, sesame oil, soya bean oil, sweet oil *(U.S.)*, vegetable butter, vegetable oil; **fuel oil,** black gold, derv *(Brit.)*, diesel oil, dieseline, distillate, gas oil, mineral oil, petroleum, rock-oil, shale oil, train oil; **ointment,** anointment, balsam, lanolin, petrolatum, petroleum jelly, retinol, salve, unction, unguent, vaseline, wool fat; **essential oil,** bergamot, cajuput oil, cineol, eucalyptol, eucalyptus oil, eugenol, neroli oil, peppermint, sassafras oil, wintergreen, ylang-ylang; **cosmetic oil,** almond oil, brilliantine, coconut oil, face cream, hair oil, hand cream, hand lotion, lotion, Macassar oil; **lubricant,** antifriction, axle-grease, coolant, cyclopentane, grease; **wax,** cerumen, earwax, spermaceti; **miscellaneous oil,** bone oil, chrism, drying oil, fish oil, linseed oil, mustard oil, neat's-foot oil, rapeseed oil, sperm oil, stand oil, tung-oil, turpentine, vegetable tallow, wood pitch, wood tar; **lubrication,** force-feed, lube

FAT *adj* adipose, beefy, bloated, burly, chubby, corpulent, fleshy, gross, hulking, meaty, obese, overweight, plump, portly, pursy, roly-poly, rotund, stout, tubby; **pot-bellied,** abdominous, paunchy; **buxom,** bosomy, busty, chesty, deep-bosomed, junoesque, pneumatic, stacked, Wagnerian, well-stacked, well-upholstered; **squat,** bullocky, dumpty, dumpy, endomorphic, hefty, hippy, hunky, pudgy, pyknic, squab, squabby, squatty, stocky, thickset, well-built; **steatopygous,** steatopygic; **outsize,** overgrown, oversize, oversized

fat *n* → **1** easy thing **2** fat **3** flesh **4** groin **5** marble *adj* **6** abundant **7** fertile **8** oily **9** thick

fatal *adj* → **1** deadly **2** hopeless **3** important **4** inevitable **5** killing **6** predictive

fatalism *n* → inevitability

fatality *n* → **1** fate **2** inevitability **3** ruin **4** the dead

FATE *n* chance, destiny, Fates, Fortune, karma, kismet, luck, providence, the inevitable, Weird Sisters, wheel of Fortune; **destiny,** appanage, dole *(Archaic)*, doom, fatality, foredoom, fortune, fortunes, lot, star, sticky end; **predestination,** foreordainment, foreordination, predetermination, preordainment, preordination. *See also* INEVITABILITY

fate *n* → **1** death **2** omen **3** ruin

fateful *adj* → **1** deadly **2** important **3** predictive

father *n* → **1** creator **2** ecclesiastic **3** leader **4** old people **5** parent **6** protector *v* **7** create **8** reproduce

Father Christmas *n* → fairy

father-in-law *n* → parent

fathom *n* → **1** length *v* **2** measure **3** understand

fatigue *n* → **1** tiredness **2** toil **3** weakness **4** work *v* **5** tire

fatten *v* → **1** farm **2** fertilise **3** gamble

fatuous *adj* → **1** delusive **2** foolish **3** stupid

fault *n* → **1** break **2** disfigurement **3** error **4** evildoing **5** failure **6** guilt **7** imperfection **8** interruption **9** wrong *v* **10** disapprove of **11** err **12** separate

faulty *adj* → **1** badly-done **2** guilty **3** imperfect **4** incorrect **5** interrupted

FAULTY SIGHT *n* ametropia, aniseikonia, anisometropia, astigmatism, cataracts, detached retina, diplopia, double image, eye defect, miosis, muscae volitantes, mydriasis, nebula, nystagmus, presbyopia, retinitis, scleritis, sclerotitis, scotoma; **short-sightedness,** myopia, nearsightedness; **long-sightedness,** hypermetropia, hyperopia; **dimness,** amblyopia, blear, dimness of vision, purblindness, tunnel vision; **night blindness,** nyctalopia; **ophthalmia,** conjunctivitis, ophthalmitis, pinkeye, sandy blight, trachoma; **cross-eye,** cast, cockeye, squint, strabismus, walleye; **colour-blindness,** blue-blindness, daltonism, dichromatism, dichromic vision, monochromasia, protanopia, red-blindness, tritanopia. *See also* BLINDNESS

fauna *n* → reference book

favour *n* → **1** advantage **2** emblem **3** generosity **4** gift **5** good **6** help **7** message *v* **8** act unfairly **9** approve **10** choose **11** help

FAVOURABLE *adj* auspicious, bright, encouraging, fair, favonian, golden, hopeful, likely, promising, propitious, roseate, rosy, toward *(Obs.)*, towardly *(Archaic)*

favourable *adj* → **1** approving **2** helpful

FAVOURABLENESS *n* rosiness, towardliness, towardness; **promise,** favourable auspices, good omen, likelihood *(Archaic)*; **prospects,** expectations

favourite *n* → **1** choice **2** expected thing **3** friend **4** hope **5** likelihood **6** lover *adj* **7** approved **8** beloved **9** chosen **10** expected

favouritism *n* → **1** help **2** unfairness

fawn *n* → **1** animal offspring *v* **2** flatter **3** give birth **4** grovel *adj* **5** brown

fear *n* → **1** fright **2** high regard *v* **3** be frightened **4** frighten **5** respect

fearsome *adj* → **1** cowardly **2** frightening

FEASIBILITY *n* conceivability, conceivableness, feasibleness, practicability, practicalness, viability, workability, workableness; **possibility,** chance, contingency, eventuality, fighting chance, gamble, half chance, happenstance, liability, likelihood, off-chance; **accessibility,** attainability

FEASIBLE *adj* accessible, accomplishable, achievable, actable, executable, performable, practicable, superable, sustainable, viable, within reach, within the bounds of possibility, workable; **possible,** believable, conceivable, contingent, credible, imaginable, liable, on the cards, open, open-ended, potential

feast *n* → **1** a good time **2** celebration **3** festival **4** meal *v* **5** eat **6** rejoice

feat *n* → **1** accomplishment **2** action *adj* **3** competent **4** tidy

FEATHER *n* aftershaft, alula, auricular, axillary, coverts, filoplume, flight feather, hackle, penna, pin-feather, pinion, pinna, plume, plumelet, plumule, primary, rectrix, remex, secondary, sickle feather, tertial, tertiary, vibrissa; **quill,** barb *(Obs.)*, barbicel, barbule, barrel, calamus, flue, herl, pinnula, rachis, shaft; **marabou,** osprey, ostrich feather, peacock feather; **plumage,** feathering; **contour feathers,** aigrette, barb, crest, crissum, ducktail, egret, flag, hackle, moustache, muff, topknot, torques, web, wing-coverts; **down,** eiderdown, floccus, swan's-down; **plume,** fletching, flight, panache, wing

FEATHER *v* fledge, fluff, plume, preen, ruffle; **fletch,** flight, tuft

feather *n* → **1** character **2** hair **3** small person *v* **4** injure **5** stop

FEATHERY *adj* downy, fledgy *(Rare)*, plumy; **plumate,** crested, cristate, plumose; **feathered,** pennate; **feather-like,** pinnal, pinnate, plumelike

feature *n* → **1** film **2** telecommunications *v* **3** call attention to **4** publish **5** signify

feckless *adj* → weak

fecund *adj* → fertile

federal *adj* → **1** legislative **2** societal

Federal *n* → soldier

federate *v* → associate

fee *n* → **1** charge **2** cost **3** income **4** ownership

feeble *adj* → **1** ill **2** powerless **3** weak

FEED *v* bottle-feed, breastfeed, drip-feed *(Med.)*, foster *(Obs.)*, grub, nourish, nurse, nurture, regale, spoon-feed, suckle, victual *(Archaic)*; **keep a good table; serve,** dish up

feed *n* → **1** actor **2** chute **3** fuel **4** meal *v* **5** farm **6** help **7** satisfy **8** supply

feedback *n* → **1** dissemination **2** reaction *adj* **3** reactive

feel *n* → **1** condition **2** perception **3** sexual intercourse **4** touch *v* **5** perceive **6** touch

FEEL EMOTION *v* be overcome, care, cheer *(Obs.)*, experience, mind, take to heart; **sympathise,** feel for, know what it is to, respond; **sentimentalise,** gush, slobber, slop over; **theatricalise,** bung it on, emote, ham it up, melodramatise, stack it on; **burn,** boil, fire, flame, glow, rage, seethe, smoulder, tear one's hair out; **thrill,** throb, vibrate

FEELER *n* antenna, finger, hand, palp, paw, tentacle

feeler *n* → **1** offer **2** question

feeling *n* → **1** emotion **2** fine arts **3** idea **4** musicianship **5** perception **6** pity **7** touch *adj* **8** emotional **9** perceptive **10** pitying

FEEL PAIN *v* agonise, anguish, burn one's fingers, suffer; **travail,** be on the rack, do a perish, have a bad time of it, have got 'em bad; **flinch,** start, twitch, wince; **writhe,** squirm

feign *v* → **1** attitudinise **2** delude oneself **3** imitate **4** pretend

feint *n* → **1** attack **2** stratagem **3** trick *v* **4** beguile **5** fire on **6** trick

felicity *n* → **1** artistry **2** contentedness **3** joy

feline *n* → **1** cat *adj* **2** animal-like **3** unfaithful

fell *n* → **1** hide *v* **2** bowl over **3** cut **4** level **5** lower *adj* **6** unkind

fellow *n* → **1** equal **2** equivalent **3** friend **4** intellectual **5** man **6** partner **7** person **8** pupil **9** similar thing **10** two *adj* **11** equal

felon *n* → **1** criminal **2** illness

felony *n* → **1** crime **2** wrong

felt *v* → **1** sew *adj* **2** tactile

FEMALE *adj* gynaecomorphous, negative, yin; **feminine,** distaff, gentlewomanly, lady, ladylike, muliebral *(Rare),* petticoat, spindle *(U.S.),* womanlike, womanly; **matronly,** housewifely, matronal; **old-womanish,** anile, spinsterish; **girlish,** girly-girly, maidenly; **amazonian,** butch, mannish, viraginous; **tomboyish,** hoydenish; **effeminate,** emasculate, female *(Obs.),* old-womanish, pooncey, queeny, sawney, unmanly, womanish

female *n* → **1** sex **2** woman *adj* **3** female **4** sexual **5** weak

feminine *adj* → **1** female **2** weak

FEMINISE *v* effeminise, emasculate, emolliate, woman *(Obs.),* womanise; **camp it up,** camp, pansy, ponce, queen it up

fence *n* → **1** obstacle **2** seller **3** thief *v* **4** avoid **5** boycott **6** defend **7** jump

fencing *n* → loophole

fend *v* → defend

fender *n* → **1** screen **2** wall

feral *adj* → **1** animal-like **2** deadly **3** hopeless **4** natural

ferment *n* → **1** excitement **2** perception **3** turbulence *v* **4** agitate **5** bubble

fermentation *n* → bubbliness

fern *n* → plant

FEROCIOUS *adj* aggressive, aggro, bellicose, savage, truculent; **maenadic,** shrewish, termagant; **fierce,** furious, grim, hot, mad, rabid, rampant, red-hot, vehement; **bloodthirsty,** sanguinary, sanguine; **berserk,** paroxysmal. *See also* VIOLENT

ferocious *adj* → brutal

ferret *n* → **1** groin **2** nonachiever **3** tape *v* **4** hunt

ferrous *adj* → metallic

ferry *n* → **1** motor vessel *v* **2** transport

FERTILE *adj* eutrophic, fat, fecund, fructuous, fruitful, hearty, lush, luxuriant, pinguid, productive, rich; **abundant,** copious, generous, overabundant, plenteous, polycarpic *(Bot.),* pregnant, prodigal, profuse, prolific, rampant, superabundant, teeming, wealthy; **arable,** farmable; **profitable,** beneficial, useful, worthwhile

fertile *adj* → chain-reacting

FERTILE LAND *n* arable, farmland, kindly ground, land of milk and honey, oasis, water-meadow; **topsoil,** humus, leaf mould, litter, potting mixture

FERTILISATION *n* enrichment, fecundation, green revolution, impregnation; **fruition,** emblements, fructification, fruitage, output, pullulation, vintage

FERTILISE *v* enrich, fatten, fructify, improve; **manure,** bone, compost, dress, inoculate, lime, marl, mulch, nitrify, side-dress, super, top, top-dress

fertilise *v* → **1** flower **2** reproduce

FERTILITY *n* arability, fatness, fecundity, fructuousness, fruitfulness, heartiness, luxuriance, pinguidity, productivity; **lushness,** richness, verdancy, verdure; **abundance,** cornucopia, foison *(Archaic),* overabundance, plenty, prolificacy, prolificness, rampancy, superabundance; **teeming womb,** teeming loins; **profitableness,** benefit, usefulness, utility

fervent *adj* → **1** desirous **2** emotional **3** hot

fervour *n* → **1** emotion **2** heat

fester *n* → **1** sore *v* **2** deteriorate **3** pain

FESTIVAL *n* bangtail muster, carnival, fair, festa, festivity, fete, fete day, fiesta, gala, holiday, kermis, mardi gras, pageant, potlatch, Royal Show, saturnalia, show, Venetian carnival; **jubilee,** birthday, commemoration, commemorative, encaenia, feast, name-day, red-letter day, wedding anniversary; **holy day,** feast-day, high day; **harvest festival,** harvest home. *See also* JOY; CELEBRATION

festival *n* → **1** concert **2** entertainment **3** holy day *adj* **4** festive

FESTIVE *adj* carnie, festal, festival, holiday, merrymaking

festivity *n* → **1** festival **2** happiness **3** party **4** pleasure

festoon *v* → decorate

fetch *n* → **1** attempt **2** length **3** trick *v* **4** arrive **5** cost **6** enchant **7** gain **8** head for **9** initiate **10** transport

fetching *adj* → alluring

fete *n* → **1** celebration **2** festival **3** holiday **4** holy day **5** selling

fête *v* → congratulate

fete *v* → **1** emphasise **2** rejoice

fetid *adj* → **1** smelly **2** unsavoury

fetish *n* → **1** idol **2** magic spell **3** psychic disturbance

fetlock *n* → animal's coat

fetter *n* → **1** bond *v* **2** imprison **3** restrain

fettle *n* → **1** condition *v* **2** cover **3** smooth **4** tidy

feud *n* → **1** fight **2** ownership *v* **3** fight

feudal *adj* → autocratic

FEVER *n* ague, calenture, febricity, febricula, feverishness, fire, flush, hectic, hyperpyrexia, pyrexia; **shaking,** algor, rigour

fever *n* → **1** excitement **2** worry *v* **3** disease

FEVERISH *adj* agued, aguish, febriferous, febrific, febrile, feverous; **delirious; faint,** giddy, gone, swimming; **unconscious,** comatose

FEW *adj* hardly any, infrequent, not many, rare, rare as hen's teeth, scarce as hen's teeth, several; **scant,** exiguous, light, little, low-density, scanty, scattered, skimpy, small, sparse, thin; **scarce,** diminished, reduced, tight

few *adj* → rare

fey *adj* → **1** dead **2** inevitable **3** strange

fiancée *n* → betrothed

fiasco *n* → **1** bottle **2** failure

fib *n* → **1** lie *v* **2** beat **3** lie

fibre *n* → **1** characteristics **2** raw materials **3** thread

fibreglass *n* → building materials

fibula *n* → jewellery

fickle *adj* → **1** changeable **2** indecisive

fiction *n* → **1** image **2** lie **3** story

fid *n* → rod

fiddle *n* → **1** expedient **2** restraints **3** steadier **4** string instrument **5** trick *v* **6** be inattentive **7** fake

fiddly *adj* → difficult

fidelity *n* → **1** faithfulness **2** precision

fidget *n* → **1** worrier *v* **2** belt into **3** worry

FIELD *n* approvement, back run, close, common *(Brit.)*, cornfield, granary, gumfield, mead *(Poetic)*, meadow, outfield, outland *(Obs.)*, paddock, sheepwalk *(Brit.)*, stock run; **saddling paddock,** birdcage, enclosure, home paddock, paddock; **farmyard,** barnyard; **schoolyard,** campus, playground, quad, quadrangle; **park,** parkland, pleasance, preserve, reserve; **meeting place,** agora, forum; **square,** esplanade, piazza, place, plaza, walk; **courtyard,** atrium, backyard, cloister, cloister-garth, close, cortile, court, forecourt *(Brit.)*, frontage, garden, garth *(Archaic)*, lawn *(Archaic)*, parvis, yard; **patio,** terrace

field *n* → **1** battleground **2** competitor **3** course **4** farmland **5** hunter **6** information **7** job **8** number **9** subject matter *adj* **10** outside

fiend *n* → **1** bad person **2** devil

fierce *adj* → **1** acrimonious **2** ferocious **3** strict **4** unkind

FIERY *adj* alight, conflagrant, flagrant *(Rare)*, flaming, flamy, flaring, on fire; **fireable,** combustible, combustive, flammable, ignescent, ignitable, inflammable, piceous, touchy; **incendiary,** calcinatory, caustic, igneous, inflammatory; **burnt,** ashen, ashy, charred, charry, sooty

fiery *adj* → **1** colourful **2** emotional **3** hot **4** irritable **5** pungent

fiesta *n* → festival

fife *n* → wind instrument

fifteen *n* → sportsman

fifty-fifty *n* → **1** beer *adj* **2** equal **3** mediocre **4** mixed *adv* **5** equally

FIGHT *n* barney, battle, blue, boil-up, bout, box-on, broil, brush, chance-medley, close, combat, ding, ding-dong, dogfight, domestic *(Colloq.)*, dust-up, encounter, go-in, grapple, lash *(Obs.)*, mayhem, mix-up, passage, pillow-fight, punch-up, rencounter, roughhouse, rough-up, rumble, running battle, scrape, scrimmage, scuffle, set-to, skirmish, spat, tug, tug of war, turn-in, turn-up, tussle, wrestle, yike; **dispute,** altercation, argy-bargy, cut and thrust, debate, disagreement, discord, friction, fuss, high words, jangle, jar, kafuffle, logomachy, Mexican stand-off, misunderstanding, quarrel, ruckus, run-in, slanging match, splutter, squabble, war of nerves, words, wrangle; **free fight,** affray, battle royal, boilover, brawl, donny *(N.Z.)*, donnybrook, fray, free-for-all, gang-fight, melee, pitched battle, shebang *(N.Z.)*; **feud,** blood feud, gang warfare, vendetta; **duel,** affaire d'honneur, gunfight *(U.S.)*, shoot-out *(U.S.)*. *See also* CONTEST

FIGHT *v* barney, blue, box on, brawl, broil, buffet, come to blows, fight like Kilkenny cats, fisticuff, go the knuckle, mix it, roughhouse, rumble, scrap, skirmish, spar, spat, thump; **wrestle,** buckle, grapple, scuffle, struggle, tussle; **set to,** assay, close with, combat, cross swords, draw first blood, encounter, join, meet, take arms, take on; **duel,** have someone on, joust, tilt, tourney *(Archaic)*, undertake *(Obs.)*. *See also* CONTEST; **campaign,** battle, conflict, feud, fight it out, wage war

fight *n* → **1** act of war **2** warmongering *v* **3** wage war

FIGHTER *n* battler, combatant, combater, contender, contestant, striver, struggler, tussler; **aggressor,** assailant, belligerent, feudist, fire-eater, swashbuckler; **knight,** banneret, cavalier, chevalier, jouster, knight-errant, paladin, samurai, shogun *(Jap.)*, tilter, younker *(Obs.)*; **warrior,** amazon, baresark, berserker, brave, champion, ghazi *(Islam.)*, hero, Hun, valkyrie; **fighting drunk,** fighting cock; **bullfighter,** matador, picador, toreador, torero; **swordsman,** backswordsman, duellist, épéeist, fencer, foilsman, gladiator, sabreur, sword; **gunfighter,** firelock, firer, franc-tireur, gun, gunman, gunner, gunslinger *(U.S.)*, marksman, markswoman, sharpshooter, shooter, sniper; **militarist,** chauvinist, hawk, jingoist, militant, war lord, warmonger; **mercenary,** auxiliaries, condottiere, foreign legion, freelance, hired gun, hireling, landsknecht, lansquenet, legionnaire, professional soldier, soldier of fortune; **adventurer,** buccaneer, filibuster, freebooter. *See also* PUGILIST; ARMED FORCES; SERVICEMAN; SOLDIER; HIGH COMMAND; COMBAT TROOPS

fighter *n* → **1** aeroplane **2** warmonger

figment *n* → **1** delusion **2** the intangible

FIGURATIVE *adj* allusive *(Obs.)*, figural, figured, metaphoric, metaphorical, tropical, tropologic; **allegorical,** allegoristic, anagogical, archetypal, symbolic; **rhetoric,** euphuistic, hyperbolic; **idiomatic,** clichéd, colloquial; **ironic,** sardonic; **punning,** paronomastic; **antithetic,** climactic, inverted; **euphemistic,** hypocoristic, pantagruelian; **alliterative,** assonant, metrical, onomatopoeic, rhyming, rhythmic, rhythmical; **metonymical,** synecdochic

figurative *adj* → **1** artistic **2** indicative

figure *n* → **1** appearance **2** decoration **3** diagram **4** famous person **5** figure of speech

6 musical phrase **7** number **8** painting **9** shape **10** sign *v* **11** appear **12** compute **13** decorate **14** reason **15** represent **16** shape

figurehead *n* → **1** decoration **2** unimportant person

FIGURE OF SPEECH *n* allusion *(Obs.)*, asyndeton, calque, enallage, figuration, figure, hendiadys, kenning, metaphor, mixed metaphor, onomatopoeia, polysyndeton, rhetorical device, rhetorical question, simile, syllepsis, tmesis, trope, zeugma; **allegory,** anagoge, apologia, apologue, cautionary tale, exemplum, fable, old wives' tale, parable, proverb, satire, sermon; **idiom,** Americanism, Australianism, colloquialism, expression, idiotism *(Obs.)*, mot juste, phrase; **conceit,** catachresis, circumlocution, cliché, crank, malapropism, pleonasm, solecism, tautology; **imagery,** image, symbolism; **irony,** antiphrasis, bathos, dramatic irony; **play on words,** double entendre, equivoque, paronomasia, pun, quibble *(Archaic)*, riddle; **alliteration,** acrostic, anadiplosis, assonance, balance, gemination, hypallage, metanalysis, metathesis, metre, palindrome, parallelism, parenthesis, poetry, repetition, rhyme, rhythm, spoonerism; **antithesis,** anacoluthon, chiasmus, climax, euphuism, hysteron proteron, inversion, litotes, oxymoron; **allusion,** dysphemism, epexegesis, euphemism, hyperbole, hyperbolism, hypocorism, paralipsis; **metonymy,** metonym, synecdoche; **personification,** antonomasia, apostrophe, prosopopoeia

figurine *n* → **1** portrait **2** sculpture

filament *n* → **1** electric circuit **2** flower **3** hair **4** thread

filch *v* → rob

file *n* → **1** computer record **2** information **3** line **4** list **5** powderer **6** record **7** series **8** smoother *v* **9** inquire into **10** insert **11** powder **12** record **13** smooth **14** tidy

filibuster *n* → **1** fighter **2** hindrance **3** thief *v* **4** hinder

filigree *n* → jewellery

FILL *v* brim, bumper, charge, draw, fill up, run; **refill,** replenish, top up; **pack,** freight, lade, load, stow, supply; **occupy,** preoccupy; **fill in,** backfill, caulk *(Naut.)*, chink *(U.S.)*, chinse *(Naut.)*, grout, loam, pad, plaster, point *(Building)*, pug, shim, silt; **plug,** stop, stopper, tamp, wedge; **overfill,** drown, saturate, swamp; **cram,** choke, engorge, glut, jam, line, pack, stuff; **overrun,** crowd, throng

fill *n* → **1** building materials **2** musical phrase **3** satisfaction *v* **4** become greater **5** bulge **6** have a job **7** make whole **8** satisfy **9** supply

FILLER *n* packer, padder; **filling,** backfill, grout, packing, padding, sand fill, shim, washer; **occupant,** occupier, preoccupant, preoccupier

fillet *n* → **1** belt **2** bookbinding **3** headband **4** string **5** thinness *v* **6** cook

filling *n* → **1** filler **2** medication

filly *n* → **1** adolescent **2** animal offspring **3** woman

FILM *n* art film, B-grade film, bioscope *(Obs.)*, blue movie, cinéma-vérité, cinefilm, doco, documentary, double bill, double-feature, feature, films, flicks, footage, horror film, magazine, motion picture, movie, moving picture *(U.S.)*, mute negative, mute print, new wave, newsreel, nouvelle vague, peepshow, photoplay *(Obs.)*, picture, picture show, porno movie, reduction print, remake, rough cut, semidocumentary, silent film, skin flick, talkie, talking picture *(Obs.)*, telemovie, underground movie, video, video clip; **horse opera,** meat-pie western, spaghetti western; **short,** trailer, travelogue; **cartoon,** animated cartoon; **cinemascope,** cinematography, cinerama, computer animation, technicolour, vista-vision

film *n* → **1** covering **2** fluff **3** glaze **4** skin *v* **5** cinematise **6** photograph

FILM CREW *n* best boy, camera crew, cameraman, cinematographer, clapper loader, clapper preparer, continuity girl, floor manager, focus puller, gaffer, gofer, sound mixer

FILMIC *adj* celluloid, cinematic, cinematographic, filmable; **all-star,** star-studded; **movie-minded,** star struck; **slow-motion,** split-screen, wide-screen

filter *n* → **1** cleanser **2** extractor **3** tobacco *v* **4** clean **5** extract

filth *n* → **1** dirt **2** police **3** pornography **4** swearing

filthy *adj* → **1** bad **2** dirty **3** immoral **4** obscene **5** sickening

FINAL *adj* back-end, climactic, eventual, extreme, last, lattermost, net, nth, supreme, terminal, ultimate; **latter,** afternoon, last-minute

final *n* → **1** contest **2** finish **3** newspaper

finale *n* → **1** finish **2** musical piece

FINALLY *adv* at last, at long last, eventually, in the long run, terminally, ultimately; **terminably,** definitively, once and for all, terminatively; **right through,** al fine, to the bitter end; **last,** lastly, latterly

FINANCE *v* back, bankroll, capitalise, fund, overcapitalise, put money into, underwrite; **float,** circulate, utter; **freeze,** tie up

finance *v* → **1** help **2** lend

FINANCIER *n* angel, backer, banker, gnome, merchant banker; **speculator,** arbitrager, bear, bull, investor, operator, piker, plunger, stag; **broker,** bucket shop, cambist, discount broker, jobber, kerb broker, share-pusher, sharebroker, stockbroker, stockjobber; **shareholder,** bondholder, stockholder

FIND *v* detect, discover, locate, trace, track down; **perceive,** descry, recognise, see, see through, spot; **light on,** alight on, alight upon, come by, come on, come upon, fall on, hit on, lob onto, pick up, stumble on; **strike,** be on a streak, hit upon; **unearth,** bring to light, dig out, dig up, elicit, ferret out, nose into, rummage out, rummage up, smell out, turn up, unkennel, worm out; **scent,** follow one's nose, get wind of, nose about, smell a rat

find *n* → **1** finding *v* **2** compute **3** determine **4** solve **5** supply **6** use

FINDABLE *adj* ascertainable, detectable, discoverable; **on the right track,** getting warm, on the scent, warm

FINDING *n* detection, discovery, exploration; **accidental discovery,** serendipity; **detective instinct,** nose; **find,** strike *(Mining),* treasure-trove, turn-up; **exposure,** a fair cop, revelation

FIND OUT *v* get on to, glean, realize, tumble to; **catch,** catch out, expose, find someone out, rumble, show up, spring, surprise, take by surprise

fine *n* → **1** finish **2** powder **3** punishment *v* **4** improve **5** punish **6** thin *adj* **7** accomplished **8** affected **9** beautiful **10** cultivated **11** decorative **12** discriminating **13** dry **14** good **15** healthy **16** hot **17** light **18** perfect **19** powdered **20** precise **21** sharp **22** tasteful **23** thin *adv* **24** well

FINE ARTS *n* art, graphic arts, plastic arts, visual arts; **depiction,** abstraction, illustration, representation, scenography *(Obs.)*; **artistry,** brushwork, craft, craftsmanship, draughtsmanship, feeling, touch; **art form,** calligraphy, ceramics, commercial art, computer art, embroidery, enamelling, engraving, folk art, graphics, illumination, intarsia, marquetry, mosaic, ordonnance, origami, painting, primitive art, printing, sculpture, serigraphy, tapestry, tessellation, weaving; **style,** breadth, form, idiom, tonality, tone; **technography,** art history. *See also* WORK OF ART; PAINTING; SCULPTURE; CERAMICS; DRAWING

FINERY *n* best, best bib and tucker, creation, evening dress, fallal, fallalery, formal dress, formals, frippery, full dress, gala outfit, glad rags, going-away outfit, Sunday best, tails, white tie

finery *n* → **1** good taste **2** metalworks **3** show

finesse *n* → **1** artistry **2** cunning **3** discrimination **4** goodness **5** good taste **6** trick

finger *n* → **1** building **2** feeler **3** glove **4** knob **5** length **6** part *v* **7** accuse **8** make music **9** rob **10** touch

fingerprint *n* → **1** sign *v* **2** label

finicky *adj* → attentive

FINISH *n* anticlimax, bitter end, catastrophe, climax, close, conclusion, consummation, dead finish, denouement, end, end point, ending, eventuation, expiry, finale, finals, grandstand finish, omega; **coda,** cadence, codetta, fine, stretta, tag; **epilogue,** amen, desinence, envoy, finis, punch line, ultimatum; **coup de grâce,** burn out, death knell, death-knock, expiration, quietus, tag end, the last straw; **last,** dernier cri, extreme *(Obs.),* final, last word, point *(Obs.),* term *(Archaic)*; **ending,** endgame, wind-up; **termination,** abruption, closure, closure motion, cut-off, discontinuance, finalisation, winding-up; **finality,** definitiveness, terminability, terminableness, ultimateness; **goal,** tape, ultimate, winning post, wire; **home straight,** home stretch, run-in; **terminus,** cul-de-sac, dead-end, railhead; **terminal,** destination; **closing time,** afternoon, curtain, evening, full-time, knock-off time, muck-up day, no-side, period, stumps, sunset, time; **settlement,** settling, upshot

FINISH *v* abolish, be in at the death, be on the home straight, be on the home stretch, close, complete, conclude, consummate, end, finalise, have done with, muddle through, perfect, play out, polish off, put the lid on, see the back of, settle, sew up, wind up, wrap up; **terminate,** break off, chop off, dissolve, draw stumps, drop, phase out, ring down the curtain on, rule off; **be ancient history,** be a closed book, be done with; **climax,** come, eventuate; **expire,** be all over with, be all up with, be curtains for, come to a sticky end, decline, die, drop, end, pass away, surcease *(Archaic),* wane; **give out,** go out

finish *n* → **1** accomplishment **2** behaviour **3** glaze **4** goodness **5** good taste **6** taste **7** texture *v* **8** accomplish **9** die **10** make whole

FINISHED *adj* all over, all over bar the shouting, complete, completed, completive, done, made-up, over, washed up, winding-up, wound up; **moribund,** ante-mortem, dead-end, dying, extinguishable, extirpative, terminational, terminative

FINISHED PRODUCT *n* build, construct, construction, contrivance, fabrication, facture, form, handiwork, invention, job, make, making, manufacture, output, outturn, production, stuff, throughput, work; **creation,** baby, brainchild; **by-product,** breakdown product, catabolite, daughter product, end product, spin-off; **yield,** crop, culture, first fruits, fructification, fruit, fruitage, growth, harvest, produce, product; **derivate,** derivation, derivative; **discharge,** emanation, emission

finite *adj* → limiting

FINITENESS *n* definability, definiteness, delimitation, finitude; **margination,** engrailment

fink *n* → **1** bad person **2** betrayer

fiord *n* → bay

fir *n* → timber

FIRE *n* blaze, conflagration, deflagration, flames, flare-up, phlegethon; **open fire,** balefire *(Archaic),* bonfire, camp fire, pyre, watch-fire; **bushfire,** back-burn, blazer, burnback, bush-burn *(N.Z.),* grassfire, red steer, regeneration burn; **volcano,** fumarole, hellfire, hot spot, mantle plume, solfatara; **flare,** flash, gleam, glint, glow, sparkle; **ember,** coal *(Obs.),* spark; **ash,** ashes, charcoal, cinder, soot; **smoke,** belch, smother, smoulder; **fieriness,** inflammation

FIRE *v* emblaze *(Archaic),* enkindle, ignite, kindle, light, set fire to, set on fire; **incinerate,** burn in effigy, cremate, gut; **burn,** calcinate, carbonise, char; **roast,** scald, scorch, sear, singe, sizzle, toast; **cauterise,** brand, burn in; **burn off,** back-burn; **burn at the stake,** self-immolate

fire *n* → **1** attack **2** brightness **3** candle **4** capital punishment **5** desire **6** emotion **7** enthusiasm **8** explosion **9** fever **10** lightning **11** misfortune **12** shot *v* **13** arouse **14** desire **15** dismiss **16** emotionalise **17** enthuse **18** explode **19** feel emotion **20** fuel **21** heat

firearm *n* → gun

firebreak *n* → screen

FIREFIGHTER *n* bush brigade, fire brigade, fireman; **fire station,** firehouse *(U.S.)*

fireman *n* → firefighter

FIRE ON *v* open up, pepper, shoot, snipe at; **bomb,** bombard, lay an egg, plaster, prang, saturate; **strafe,** pelt, shell, storm; **fusillade,** cannonade, enfilade; **feint,** demonstrate *(Mil.)*; **raid,** air-raid, blitz. *See also* ATTACK

FIREPLACE *n* chimney, chimney corner, grate, hearth; **incinerator,** crematorium, crematory, furnace

fireplace *n* → heater

FIRER *n* enkindler, igniter, inflamer, kindler; **burner,** cremationist, cremator; **firebug,** arsonist, fire-raiser, incendiary

FIRING *n* auto-ignition, ignition, kindling, lighting; **combustion,** afterburning, detonation, explosion, flashback, spontaneous combustion; **burning,** auto-da-fé, cremation, incineration, the stake; **carbonization,** calcination; **arson,** black lightning, fire-raising, incendiarism, jewish lightning, pyromania

firing squad *n* → **1** capital punishment **2** killer **3** punisher

firm *n* → **1** corporation **2** healer *v* **3** harden **4** steady *adj* **5** fastened **6** hard **7** joined **8** persevering **9** serious **10** steady **11** strict *adv* **12** perseveringly **13** steadily

firmament *n* → sky

FIRST *adv* ahead, ahead of time, first-up, firstly, foremost, in advance, primarily, up front; **introductorily,** prefatorily, preliminarily, prelusively

first *n* → **1** starter **2** successfulness *adj* **3** advanced **4** early **5** important **6** new **7** original **8** prototypal **9** superior *adv* **10** firstly **11** optionally

first aid *n* → medical treatment

FIRSTLY *adv* basically, first, for starters, fundamentally, imprimis, initially, to begin with; **originally,** ab initio, ab origine, ab ovo, anew, at first, at the first, da capo, de novo, first-up, from scratch, from the first, from the top, from the word go, in limine, in the bud, in the egg; **primevally,** primitively, primordially

fiscal *n* → **1** lawyer *adj* **2** cash

FISH *n* food fish, free-swimmer, freshwater fish, ichthyoid, mouth-breeder, Pisces, saltwater fish; **benthos,** groundling, nekton, plankton; **tiddler,** fingerling; **shoal,** school

FISH *v* angle, bob, cast, dap, dib, fly-fish, gaff, gig, guddle, land, leister, net, play, rock-hop, seine, skitter, spin, spoon, strike, trawl, troll, whale, whip; **crab,** prawn, seal, shrimp, turtle

fish *n* → **1** beam *v* **2** beguile

Fish *n* → train

FISHERMAN *n* angler, crabber, fisher, fly-fisher, prawner, prawnie, rock-hopper, sealer, shrimper, spearfisherman, striker, trammeller, trawler, troller, whaleman, whaler

fisherman *n* → watercraft

FISHING *n* angling, bay whaling, fly-fishing, ledger-baiting, ledgering, sealery *(Archaic)*, shark meshing, shore whaling, spinning, whaling. *See also* PURSUIT

FISH OUT OF WATER *n* erratic, horse marine *(U.S.)*, misfit, square peg in a round hole

FISHY *adj* elasmobranch, finned, finny, fishlike, ichthyic, ichthyoid, piscine

fishy *adj* → **1** dull **2** unlikely

fission *n* → **1** radioactivation **2** reproduction

fissure *n* → **1** break **2** gap **3** head **4** inside **5** opening *v* **6** open up **7** separate

fist *n* → **1** writing *v* **2** capture **3** hit

FIT *v* assort, comport with, consist with, get along, go with *(Colloq.)*, interlock, intermesh, match, mate, satisfy, suit; **agree,** answer, check, coincide, concur, conform, match, parallel; **add up,** cohere, commeasure, hang together *(Colloq.)*, square, tally; **apply,** pertain; **correspond,** accord, chime, concur, consort, dovetail, go hand in hand, go with, harmonise, key in, live up to, match, sympathise, tone in; **befit,** be cut out for, be one's cup of tea *(Colloq.)*, belong to, beseem, fit the bill, suit

fit *n* → **1** congruity **2** drug equipment **3** madness **4** poetry **5** story **6** unconsciousness *v* **7** accuse **8** equip **9** join **10** litigate **11** prepare **12** regularise *adj* **13** apt **14** competent **15** expedient **16** fair **17** healthy **18** prepared

fitful *adj* → **1** interrupted **2** irregular

fix *n* → **1** bribe **2** dilemma **3** dishonesty **4** drug use **5** positioning *v* **6** arrange **7** conserve **8** cook **9** equip **10** fasten **11** harden **12** make infertile **13** materialise **14** order **15** photograph **16** repair **17** steady **18** stick together **19** swindle **20** undertake

fixation *n* → **1** changelessness **2** psychic disturbance **3** steadying **4** stickiness

fixture *n* → **1** personal property **2** steadiness

fizz *n* → **1** crackle **2** drink **3** failure **4** hiss **5** wine *v* **6** bubble **7** crackle **8** hiss

fizzle *n* → **1** failure **2** hiss *v* **3** bubble **4** crackle **5** fail **6** hiss

flabbergast *v* → astonish

flabby *adj* → **1** hanging **2** weak

flaccid *adj* → **1** hanging **2** weak

FLAG *n* banderol, banner, bannerette, burgee, dogvane, ensign, fanion, gonfalon, guidon, hoist, jack, labarum, pennant, pennon, standard, streamer, vexillum; **colours,** bunting, flying colours, racing colours; **flogger**

flag *n* → **1** animal part **2** coating **3** feather **4** shirt **5** watercraft *v* **6** be inactive **7** communicate **8** decorate **9** hang **10** signal **11** weaken

flagellate *v* → cudgel

flagon *n* → bottle

flagrant *adj* → **1** blatant **2** disreputable **3** fiery **4** glowing **5** most **6** obvious
flagship *n* → watercraft
flail *n* → **1** club **2** spear *v* **3** cudgel **4** harvest
flair *n* → **1** competence **2** smell
flak *n* → **1** defence **2** disapproval **3** gunfire
flake *n* → **1** layer **2** part **3** twist *v* **4** separate **5** sleep
FLAKY *adj* exfoliative, flocculent, foliaceous, foliated, imbricate, imbricated, imbricative, lamellar, lamellate, laminable, laminar, scalelike
flamboyant *adj* → **1** beautiful **2** bombastic **3** showy
flame *n* → **1** brightness **2** candle **3** desire **4** emotion **5** enthusiasm **6** lover *v* **7** be angry **8** catch fire **9** desire **10** feel emotion **11** shine
flamingo *adj* → red
flammable *adj* → fiery
flange *n* → **1** edge **2** knob *v* **3** jut
FLANK *v* come alongside, crab *(Aeron.)*, go alongside, juxtapose, lap *(Obs.)*, outflank, outskirt, sidle, skirt
flank *n* → **1** combat troops **2** side
flannel *n* → **1** flattery **2** washer *v* **3** rub
flap *n* → **1** addition **2** click **3** confusion **4** hit **5** move **6** pendant **7** worry *v* **8** become confused **9** be excited **10** click **11** flutter **12** hit **13** worry
flare *n* → **1** angry act **2** candle **3** fire **4** light **5** signal *v* **6** shine **7** signal
flash *n* → **1** chute **2** emblem **3** ephemeral **4** exit **5** fire **6** jewel **7** language **8** light **9** lighting **10** moment **11** news item **12** show **13** signal *v* **14** be angry **15** catch fire **16** disperse **17** increase **18** shine **19** show off **20** speed **21** undress *adj* **22** fake **23** showy
flashback *n* → **1** firing **2** memory **3** nostalgia *v* **4** cinematise **5** delude oneself **6** remember
flask *n* → bottle
flat *n* → **1** bar **2** footgear **3** honest person **4** level **5** policeman **6** racecourse **7** shallow **8** stage **9** storey **10** swamp **11** tobacco *v* **12** inhabit *adj* **13** blunt **14** boring **15** composed **16** dissonant **17** dull **18** easy **19** honest **20** inactive **21** insipid **22** level **23** shallow **24** smooth **25** unconditional *adv* **26** precisely **27** unconditionally
flathead *n* → **1** fool **2** stupid person
FLATTER *v* brown-nose, buddy-buddy, butter, butter up, carney, eulogise, fawn, flannel up *(Brit.)*, lay it on thick, make much of, oil, overpraise, praise to the skies, puff, smarm, smoodge, speak someone fair, throw a bouquet; **behave sycophantically,** chum up to, dag *(Horseracing)*, get gravel rash, jolly along, lick another's arse, make up to, pander to, pee in someone's pocket, play up to, slime, suck up to, toady; **cajole,** blandish, blarney, get round, palaver, sweet-talk, wheedle; **hero-worship,** adulate, conceit *(Obs.)*; **curry favour,** duchess, make one's alley good, soap up, soft-soap; **be up each other,** be up one another
flatter *n* → **1** club **2** leveller *v* **3** misinterpret
FLATTERER *n* adulater, arse-licker, bootlicker, brown-nose, courtier, crawler, encomiast, eulogist, fawner, flunkey, greaser, greasespot, member of a claque, pickthank, reptile, respecter of persons, satellite, smoodger, sycophant, toady; **wheedler,** blandisher, cajoler, carney, smooth talker, soft-soaper, sweet-talker; **self-flatterer,** mutual-admiration society
FLATTERING *adj* adulatory, complimentary, courtly, ingratiating, mealy-mouthed, obsequious; **sycophantic,** buddy-buddy, fawning, flunkeyish, fulsome, reptilean, servile, smarmy, smooth-faced, smooth-tongued, subservient, toadyish; **unctuous,** buttery, candied, honeyed, oily, soapy, soft
FLATTERY *n* adulation, blandishment, blandishments, compliment, flummery, gloze *(Rare)*, oil; **sweet talk,** blarney, flannel *(Brit.)*, honeyed words, jolly, palaver, soft soap, syrup; **panegyric,** encomium, eulogy, paean of praise; **ingratiation,** cajolement, cajolery, insinuation; **sycophancy,** fawning, flunkeydom, flunkeyism, obsequiousness, oiliness, puffery, smarm, smoodging, toadyism, unctuousness; **hero-worship,** personality cult
flaunt *n* → **1** show *v* **2** be arrogant **3** display **4** show off
flavour *n* → **1** atom **2** characteristic **3** essence **4** taste *v* **5** cook **6** taste
flaw *n* → **1** angry act **2** disfigurement **3** illogicality **4** imperfection **5** outburst **6** wind
flaxen *adj* → yellow
flay *v* → **1** execute **2** scold
fleck *n* → **1** disfigurement **2** small amount
fledgling *n* → **1** adolescent **2** animal offspring *adj* **3** new
flee *v* → **1** depart **2** elude **3** escape
fleece *n* → **1** animal's coat **2** textiles *v* **3** bare **4** swindle **5** take
fleet *n* → **1** many **2** watercraft *v* **3** disappear **4** flow **5** speed **6** swerve **7** swim *adj* **8** speedy
fleeting *adj* → **1** ethereal **2** impermanent
flesh *n* → **1** humanity **2** red **3** relative **4** size *v* **5** arouse
flex *n* → **1** wire *v* **2** be absent **3** curve **4** rest
flexible *adj* → **1** obsequious **2** pliable **3** soft **4** useful **5** variable
flexitime *n* → time
flick *n* → **1** click **2** hit **3** pat **4** touch *v* **5** flutter **6** hit **7** thrust
flicker *n* → **1** ephemeral **2** flutter **3** light *v* **4** flutter **5** shine
FLIGHT *n* air alert *(Mil.)*, air cover, air picket, airflight, charter flight, contact flight, flip, fly, hop *(Colloq.)*, joy-flight, milk run, overflight, paradrop, solo, sortie; **fly-past,** flying circus; **formation,** escadrille *(U.S. Mil.)*, flight, flying squad, squadron, stack, wing
flighty *adj* → **1** changeable **2** foolish **3** indecisive **4** speedy
flimsy *n* → **1** copy *adj* **2** ethereal **3** illogical **4** light
flinch *v* → **1** feel pain **2** go back **3** lack courage

fling *n* → **1** attempt **2** liberty **3** slander **4** throw *v* **5** throw

flint *n* → lighter

flip *n* → **1** drink **2** flight **3** pat **4** roll *v* **5** move **6** rotate **7** throw *adj* **8** happy **9** insulting

flippant *adj* → **1** athletic **2** happy **3** insulting **4** pliable

flipper *n* → **1** arm **2** throw

FLIRT *n* beau, dallier, Don Juan, flirter, ladies' man, masher, ogler, philanderer, rake, seducer; **coquette,** cockteaser, light o' love, minx, seductress, tease, teaser; **toy,** plaything; **caresser,** dandler, fondler, kisser, smoocher, smoodger; **wooer,** admirer, gallant, lover, serenader, suer, suitor, swain

FLIRT *v* coquet, dally, fool around, gallivant, play footsies, play the field, play tootsy, tease; **flirt with,** do a line with, do a mash with *(Obs.)*, lead on, mash *(Obs.)*, throw oneself at, toy with, vamp; **give someone the glad eye,** bat one's eyelids at, make a pass at, make eyes at, ogle, perv on; **proposition,** chat up, crack onto, do a line for, get off with, put the hard word on, seduce; **take out,** date, go steady, see, walk out with; **have an affair,** philander, play around, play up; **court,** address, pay court to, pursue, set one's cap at, spark *(U.S.)*, sue *(Archaic)*, woo; **love,** be in love with, care for, cherish, conceive a passion for, develop feelings for, die for, fall in love with, have a crush on, have eyes only for, look sweetly on; **have an understanding with,** plight one's troth to

flirt *n* → **1** throw *v* **2** thrust

FLIRTATION *n* amour, billing and cooing, coquetry, dalliance, seduction; **courtship,** courting, courtly attention, courtly love, gallantry, lovemaking *(Archaic)*, serenading, suit, wooing; **affair,** love affair, romance

FLIRTATIOUS *adj* coquet, coquettish; **romantic,** gallant, swainish; **amorous,** amatory, love-sick, lovelorn, sighing, sighing like a furnace, smitten, smitten by another's charms, spoony; **kissable,** embraceable, lovable, osculant

flit *n* → **1** avoidance **2** escape **3** sexual type *v* **4** depart **5** die **6** elude **7** escape **8** fly **9** speed **10** take

FLOAT *n* bob *(Angling)*, bobber, buoy, buoyage, floater, rubber ring, torpedo tube; **raft,** floating island, flotsam, pontoon, spar buoy

FLOAT *v* bob, hover, levitate, swim, waft

float *n* → **1** bridge **2** fishing tackle **3** funds **4** leveller **5** propellant **6** raft **7** smoother **8** support **9** wagon **10** weave *v* **11** finance **12** hang **13** initiate **14** level **15** operate **16** smooth **17** swim **18** wet

floating *adj* → **1** buoyant **2** changeable **3** hanging **4** nautical **5** owing

flock *n* → **1** animal's coat **2** crowd **3** gathering **4** many **5** powder **6** religious follower **7** textiles *v* **8** abound **9** coat **10** gather

floe *n* → ice

flog *v* → **1** cudgel **2** rob **3** sell

FLOOD *n* deluge, inundation; **overflow,** overgrowth, overrun, profusion, smother; **spread,** pervasion, suffusion; **pervasiveness; epidemic,** eruption, outbreak, plague; **infestation,** invasion

FLOOD *v* deluge, drown, engulf, inundate, overwhelm, poop *(Naut.)*, swamp, whelm *(Archaic)*; **overflow,** boil over, brim over, pour out, pour over, run over, spill, spill out, spill over, well over; **overrun,** cover, overgrow, overspread, run riot, smother; **spread,** ramble, run on, sprawl, spread out, swarm, trail; **pervade,** spread like wildfire, spread through, suffuse; **permeate,** metastasise, perfuse; **infest,** plague, swarm

flood *n* → **1** abundance **2** current **3** much **4** surplus *v* **5** advance **6** excrete **7** flow **8** oversupply **9** wet

FLOODED *adj* awash, inundated, overrun

FLOODING *adj* diluvial, torrential; **diffused,** outspread, widespread; **rambling,** sprawling, trailing; **pervasive,** suffusive; **epidemic,** epidemical, rife

FLOOR *n* deck, decking, flooring, promenade deck; **landing,** fly gallery *(Theat.)*, flyfloor *(Theat.)*

floor *n* → **1** bottom **2** land **3** layer **4** room **5** storey *v* **6** bowl over **7** confuse **8** defeat **9** level

flop *n* → **1** click **2** failure **3** fall **4** nonachiever **5** performance *v* **6** click **7** descend **8** fail **9** fall **10** throw

FLORAL *adj* flowery; **botanical,** vegetable, vegetal, vegetational, vegetative; **abloom,** blooming, bloomy, blossomy, efflorescent, florescent, florid *(Archaic)*, flowered, full-blown; **green,** grassy, lush, turfy, verdant, verdurous; **leafy,** foliaceous, foliaged, foliar, foliate, foliated, foliose, frondescent, in leaf, leaved; **viny,** ivied, twining; **tufty,** caespitose, stubbled, stubbly; **herbaceous,** herbal, herby; **shrubby,** broomy, scrubby, shrub-like, stumpy; **ferny,** rushy; **brambly,** branchy, brushy, furzy; **bushy,** arboreous, bosky, forest-like, forested, wooded, woodsy, woody; **frutescent,** fruticose

florid *adj* → **1** coloured **2** decorative **3** eloquent **4** floral **5** musical **6** reddish **7** showy

floss *n* → **1** fluff **2** thread

flotation *n* → lightness

flotilla *n* → **1** armed forces **2** watercraft

flounce *n* → **1** edge **2** fold **3** scowl **4** trimming *v* **5** show off

flounder *n* → **1** bungle *v* **2** become confused **3** be uncertain **4** bungle

flour *n* → **1** powder **2** white *v* **3** cook

flourish *n* → **1** decoration **2** health **3** musical piece **4** show *v* **5** be fertile **6** be healthy **7** display **8** flower **9** flutter **10** make music **11** prosper **12** show off

flout *n* → **1** insult **2** mockery **3** slander *v* **4** hold in low regard **5** mock

FLOW *n* eruption, flowage, fluency, flux, fluxion *(Obs.)*, gurgitation, primary flow, run-off, turbulent flow, wash; **torrent,** debacle, flush, gush, gust, jet, onrush, spate, spurt, staunch, surge, uprush, upsurge, upsurgeance; **effluence,** efflux, exosmosis, issue; **influx,** affluence, afflux, endosmosis, incursion, inflow, inrush, inrushing, inset; **circulation,** capillarity, capillary action, convection, osmosis; **dribble,** drip, dripping, dropping, seep *(U.S.)*, spray, sprinkle, trickle; **pour,** decantation; **ash flow,** coulee, earthflow, lava flow, mudflow. *See also* CURRENT; STREAM; SPRING

FLOW *v* course, eddy, fleet *(Archaic)*, flux, gutter, run, stream, swirl; **swell,** issue, run a banker, upsurge, well; **wash,** lap, lave, splash, swash; **flood,** deluge, inundate, overflow, overspill; **spurt,** gush, jet, spout, squirt; **flush,** disembogue, sluice, wash out; **ooze,** meander, wind; **set,** ebb, make; **dribble,** drip, seep, trickle; **strain,** drain, percolate, perk; **pour,** decant, spill

flow *n* → **1** advance **2** amount **3** bay **4** bodily discharge **5** stream **6** swamp *v* **7** continue **8** hang

FLOWER *n* bud, floret, ray; **flower organ,** androecium, anther, bud, calycle, calyptra, calyx, carpel, carpogonium, carpophore, claw, connective, corolla, corona, disc, endothecium, filament, floral envelope, flower bud, footstalk, foramen, galea, gynoecium, gynophore, hypanthium, integument, labellum, labium, limb, lip, lodicule, nectary, operculum, ovary, ovule, palea, pedicel, perianth, petal, phalanx, pistil, pistillode, placenta, podium, pollen, pollen tube, receptacle, rictus, rostellum, sepal, spur, stamen, staminode, standard, stigma, stipe, style, stylopodium, tepal, torus, tube, unguis, valve, wing; **inflorescence,** anthodium, capitulum, catkin, cincinnus, corymb, cupule, dichasium, head, locusta, monochasium, panicle, raceme, spike, thyrsus, umbel, umbellule

FLOWER *v* bloom, blossom, bud, burgeon, foliate, fungate, gemmate, ratoon, spindle *(U.S. Obs.)*, tassel; **bear,** fruit; **germinate,** rise, root, shoot, spring, sprout, stool, strike, strike root, take, take root, tiller; **breed,** multiply, proliferate, pullulate, reproduce, teem; **cultivate,** fertilise, force, revegetate, scarify; **ripen,** flourish, hay off, run riot, thrive, wax; **climb,** creep, ramble, run, spindle *(U.S. Obs.)*, twine. *See also* GROW

flower *n* → **1** good thing *v* **2** age **3** make whole

flowery *adj* → **1** eloquent **2** floral

FLOWING *adj* affluent, fluent, fluxional, fluxionary, inrushing, mobile, osmotic, profluent; **effluent,** exosmic, exosmotic; **influent,** endoreic, endosmotic, incurrent

flown *adj* → **1** artistic **2** surplus

flu *n* → cold

FLUCTUATE *v* break, flutter, intermit, stutter; **jerk,** break step, joggle, jolt, snatch *(Rowing)*

fluctuate *v* → **1** flutter **2** vacillate

flue *n* → **1** feather **2** hair **3** passageway **4** piercer

fluent *adj* → **1** beautiful **2** changeable **3** easy **4** flowing **5** liquid **6** smooth

FLUFF *n* film, floss, foam, fuzz, gauze, thistledown

fluff *n* → **1** bungle **2** burp **3** error **4** hair *v* **5** bungle **6** burp **7** feather

fluid *n* → **1** gas **2** liquid *adj* **3** changeable **4** gaseous **5** liquid

fluke *n* → **1** luck **2** piercer *v* **3** chance on

flunk *n* → **1** failure *v* **2** fail

flunkey *n* → **1** butler **2** crawler **3** flatterer **4** incompetent **5** subject

fluorescence *n* → brightness

flurry *n* → **1** busyness **2** confusion **3** excitement **4** rainfall **5** snow **6** turbulence **7** wind **8** worry *v* **9** confuse **10** worry

flush *n* → **1** fever **2** flow **3** outburst **4** redness **5** stream *v* **6** be hot **7** clean **8** coat **9** energise **10** flow **11** level **12** redden *adj* **13** energetic **14** level **15** precise **16** surplus **17** wealthy *adv* **18** precisely

fluster *n* → **1** confusion **2** excitement **3** worry *v* **4** confuse **5** worry

flute *n* → **1** furrow **2** passageway **3** subject matter **4** wind instrument *v* **5** furrow **6** make music **7** shrill

FLUTTER *n* flicker, fluctuation, nutation, seesaw, shake, sway, swing, teeter, totter, undulation, waddle, wag, waggle, wave, wiggle. *See also* VIBRATION

FLUTTER *v* bat, beat, flick, flicker, flitter, quiver; **vibrate,** fluctuate, hunt *(Mach.)*, librate, oscillate, reciprocate, shuttle, shuttlecock, vacillate, waver; **roll,** seesaw, sway, swing, teeter, toss, totter, waddle, waggle, weave, wriggle; **wave,** brandish, flap, flourish, wag, wigwag

flutter *n* → **1** click **2** confusion **3** excitement **4** gamble **5** perception **6** worry *v* **7** be excited **8** confuse **9** fluctuate **10** fly **11** move **12** toss **13** worry

FLUTTERINGLY *adv* atremble, pantingly, tremulously, waveringly; **resonantly,** thrillingly, throbbingly; **shakily,** totteringly, waddlingly, wobblingly; **swayingly,** back and forth, backwards and forwards, flip-flop, pendulously, to and fro

FLUTTERY *adj* aflutter, asp *(Archaic)*, aspen, fly-away, palpitant, pulsatile, quavery, quivering, quivery, shivery, trembly, tremulant, tremulous, vibrant, vibratile, vibrative, vibratory, wavering; **resonant,** thrilling

flux *n* → **1** advance **2** change **3** cleanser **4** combination **5** current **6** electricity **7** expulsion **8** flow **9** liquidity *v* **10** expel **11** flow **12** liquefy

FLY *v* be wafted, flit, flutter, hover, swarm, wing, wing one's way, winnow; **take off,** lift off, take wing; **glide,** hang-glide, plane, sailplane, soar, volplane; **parachute,** balloon, hot-air balloon; **pilot,** navigate; **loop,** buzz, crab, dive, fishtail, flatten, hedgehop, loop the loop, power-dive, pull out, roll, sideslip, trim, undershoot, whipstall; **swoop,** souse

fly *n* → **1** attempt **2** camp **3** carriage **4** clothes **5** direction **6** door **7** flight **8** roof *v* **9** elude **10** hang **11** lift **12** speed **13** transport *adj* **14** cunning **15** intelligent

flyer *n* → public notice

FLYING *n* aviation, volitation; **gliding,** aerodonetics, aerostation, ballooning, hang-gliding, parachuting, paraflying, soaring; **aerobatics,** hedgehopping, skywriting; **take-off,** landing, lift-off, souse, stoop; **aero tow,** auto tow; **navigation,** area navigation, instrument flying, instrument landing; **aeronautics,** aerostatics; **airmanship,** airmindedness; **space travel,** astronautics, bioastronautics, cosmonautics, moonshot, walk in space

FLYING *adj* aerial, airborne, airworthy, volant *(Heraldry),* volitant, volitational, winged; **aerobatic,** hedgehopping; **aerostatic,** heavier-than-air, lighter-than-air; **aeronautic,** aero, aeromarine; **astronautic,** aerospace, cosmonautic

flying saucer *n* → aircraft

foal *n* → **1** animal offspring *v* **2** give birth

foam *n* → **1** bodily discharge **2** bubbling **3** extinguisher **4** fluff *v* **5** bubble **6** excrete

fob *n* → pocket

focus *n* → **1** centre **2** foundation **3** length **4** point of convergence **5** reflection *v* **6** attend to **7** centralise **8** converge

foe *n* → **1** dissident **2** enemy

fog *n* → **1** cloud **2** confusion **3** imprecision **4** shade *v* **5** cloud **6** confuse **7** darken **8** disinfect **9** medicate **10** obscure **11** photograph

fogy *n* → intolerant person

foible *n* → **1** evildoing **2** sword **3** weakling

foil *n* → **1** actor **2** arch **3** coating **4** contrast **5** difference **6** losing **7** metal **8** sword *v* **9** coat **10** defeat **11** differ **12** disenchant **13** hinder **14** stop

FOLD *n* buckle, cockle, crease, crimp, crumple, dog-ear, press *(Obs.),* ruga, rumple; **wrinkle,** crinkle, crow's-foot, laugh-line, laughter-line, line, pucker, rugosity; **pleat,** box pleat, knife pleat, pintuck, plait, ruche, tuck; **turn-up,** cuff, hem, lap, lapel, lappet; **frill,** flounce, gathering, gathers, ruff, ruffle, shirr, shirring

FOLD *v* crease, crumple, dog-ear; **wrinkle,** crinkle, furrow, knit, line, pucker, purse, shrivel; **corrugate,** concertina, knurl, ridge, rumple; **buckle,** double up, jackknife; **pleat,** kilt, pintuck, tuck; **lap,** enfold, hem, imply *(Obs.),* interfold, reflex, turn back, turn down, turn up, wrap; **frill,** crimp, crimple, drape, gather, gauge, goffer, ruck, shirr

fold *n* → **1** pen **2** religious follower *v* **3** enclose **4** fail **5** hold **6** mix **7** roll up

FOLDED *adj* complicate *(Bot.),* conduplicate, dog-eared, double, replicate, turn-up, turn-down; **crinkly,** rugate, rugged, rugose, wrinkly; **frilly,** crimpy, puckery, ruffed; **pleated,** accordion-pleated, box-pleated, kilted, plicate

folder *n* → **1** holder **2** wrapper

FOLDING *n* enfoldment, invagination, plication; **paper folding,** origami

folio *n* → **1** account **2** book part *v* **3** number

folk *n* → **1** humanity **2** working class *adj* **3** public

folklore *n* → **1** belief **2** custom **3** knowledge

follicle *n* → fruit

FOLLOW *v* come after, ensue, result, succeed, supervene, supervene on; **supersede,** supplant; **follow in someone's footsteps,** copy, follow suit

follow *n* → **1** coming after **2** stroke *v* **3** accompany **4** advance **5** conform **6** have a job **7** head for **8** imitate **9** obey **10** partner **11** result **12** understand

follower *n* → **1** accomplice **2** approver **3** companion **4** imitator **5** learner **6** lover **7** obeyer **8** religious follower **9** servant **10** successor

FOLLOWING *adj* in tow, incoming, proximate; **next,** immediate, junior, second, second-best; **consecutive,** alternate, continued, progressive, sequacious *(Archaic),* sequent, sequential, subsequent, succeeding, successional, successive; **consequent,** consequential, ex post facto, resultant, supervenient; **after,** later, latter, posterior, postposed, postpositive, ulterior

folly *n* → **1** foolery **2** foolishness **3** incompetence **4** stupidity

foment *v* → **1** help **2** wet

fond *n* → **1** storage *adj* **2** believing **3** foolish **4** illogical **5** loving

fondle *v* → **1** be lenient **2** care for **3** kiss **4** love

font *n* → **1** basin **2** bath **3** shrine **4** spring

FOOD *n* aliment, ambrosia *(Class Mythol.),* blotting paper *(Colloq.),* board, bush tucker, cate *(Archaic),* cheer, chow, chow-chow, comestible, commons *(Brit.),* compo rations *(Mil.),* consumable, convenience food, dainty, delicacy, dodger, drip-feed *(Med.),* eatables, eats, edibles, esculent, fare, fast food, finger food, foodstuff, forage, good cheer, goodies, grub, hangi *(N.Z.),* health food, junk food, kosher, lazy ration *(Convict),* macronutrient, manna, meat *(Archaic),* mess, munga *(Mil. Colloq.),* num-num, num-nums, nutrient, nutriment, nyum-nyum, pabulum, pig-swill *(Colloq.),* pig-tucker *(N.Z. Colloq.),* potluck, provender, provisions, roughage, scoff, scouse *(Naut.),* scran, slipslop, slops, solids, staple diet, stodge, sustenance, table, tack, trencher *(Archaic),* tuck *(Brit.),* tucker, viand, viands, victual *(Archaic),* victuals, wholefood; **nourishment,** alimentation, diet, food value, nutrition, nutritiveness, survival level feeding, sustentation; **dietetics.** *See also* MEAL

FOOL *n* ass, automaton, bat, berk, Billy Muggins, blob, blockhead, boob, boofhead, buffer, bull head, bullet head, bunny, charlie, chinless wonder, chook, chucklehead, chump, clod, clodpate, clodpoll, clot, coot, cough drop, cretin, cuckoo, cully, dag, deadshit, dick, dickhead, dill, dillpot, ding-a-ling, dodo, dolt, donkey, dope, drip, driveller, drongo, drube, dullard, dumb Dora, dumbbell, dumbcluck, dumdum, dummy, dunderhead, fart, fathead, flathead, foolish virgin, Fred Nerk, fuckwit, galah, galoot, gawk, gazob, gig, gimp, git *(Brit.),* goat, goof, goon, goose, great ape, gup *(Aborig.),* half-axe, hen, hoon, idiot, imbecile, imbo, jackass, jay, jerk, jerk-off, joe, juggins, knucklehead, lamebrain, lardhead, lemon, log, log of wood, loggerhead, loghead, lolly, loop, lunkhead *(U.S.)*, meat-head, melon, melonhead, muddle-head, mug, mug alec, muggins, mutton-head, nerd, nig-nog, nincompoop, ning-nong, ninny, nit, nitwit, noddy, nong, noodle, numbskull, nut, nut case, nutter, old woman, pea eater, pinhead, poon, popinjay, possum, pudding, pudding head, quoit, rabbit, sap, saphead, schmuck, shlemiel, shmo, silly, silly-billy, simple, simpleton, spoony, thickhead, tomfool, tonk, turkey, twaddler, twerp, twit, wally *(Brit.)*, whacker, wild goose, woodenhead; **birdbrain,** featherbrain, featherhead, flibbertigibbet, rattlebrain, scatterbrain, whirligig

fool *n* → **1** incompetent **2** stupid person *v* **3** joke **4** misguide **5** trick

FOOLERY *n* apery, baboonery, bêtise, buffoonery, carryings-on, chenanigans, fandangle, folly, funny business, stuff and nonsense, three-ring circus, tomfoolery

foolhardy *adj* → rash

FOOLISH *adj* anserine, apish, baboonish, buffoonish, childish, clottish, empty, fatuous, footling, frivolous, idiotic, inane, light, light-headed, mad, moony, puerile, senseless, shallow, silly, Uncle Willy, vain *(Archaic)*, witless; **featherbrained,** batty, chuckle-headed, cuckoo, daffy, daft, dilly, dippy, dizzy, empty-headed, featherheaded, flighty, giddy, giggly, goofy, headless, hoity-toity, insipient, loony, luny, mad as a two-bob watch, mental, mug, nitty, nutty, nutty as a fruitcake, off one's nut, old-womanish, potty, sapheaded, sappy, scatterbrained, scatty, silly as a two-bob watch, silly as a wet hen, sonky, spoony, twitty, wacky; **ludicrous,** absurd, bathetic, farcical, imbecile, imbecilic, impertinent, nonsensical, preposterous, ridiculous, tomfool, unearthly, zany; **imprudent,** ill-advised, impolitic, unguarded, unwary, wild; **infatuated,** fond *(Archaic)*, infatuate, sloppy, spoony

foolish *adj* → **1** incompetent **2** nonsensical **3** stupid **4** unimportant

FOOLISHNESS *n* asininity, childishness, chuckleheadedness, daftness, dizziness, fatuity, fatuousness, flightiness, folly, frivolousness, goofiness, idiocy, imbecility, juvenileness, light-headedness, looniness, lunacy, madness, midsummer madness, nonsense, preposterousness, puerility, senselessness, silliness, stupidness, unwariness, witlessness; **ludicrousness,** absurdity, absurdness, bathos, ridiculousness; **infatuation,** dotage, sloppiness

fool's cap *n* → cap

foot *n* → **1** account **2** armed forces **3** bottom **4** extremity **5** leg **6** length **7** remnant *v* **8** capture **9** kick **10** walk

football *n* → **1** ball **2** medication

FOOTGEAR *n* footwear; **shoe,** balmoral, block, blocked shoe, boot, brogan, brogue, brothel creepers, chopin, clodhopper, court shoe, desert boot, flat, flattie, gillie, kadaicha shoes, loafers, moccasin, Oxford, point shoe, pump, winklepicker; **clog,** patten, sabot, wooden shoe; **spats,** puttee, spatterdashes; **shoe part,** bootleg *(U.S.)*, counter, half-sole, heel, heelpiece, heeltap, insole, platform, rand, sole, stiletto heel, tongue, upper, vamp, wedge heel; **sandshoe,** plimsoll *(Brit.)*, runner, sneaker, tennis shoe; **spikes,** running spikes, sprigs, track shoe; **roller skate,** ice skate; **snowshoe,** racquet. *See also* BOOT; SANDAL; SOCK

footing *n* → **1** bottom **2** condition **3** cost **4** grade **5** reputation **6** steadiness **7** support **8** walking

footlights *n* → **1** lighting **2** stage

footman *n* → **1** butler **2** soldier

footnote *n* → **1** clarification **2** commentary **3** postscript **4** written composition *v* **5** add

footstep *n* → **1** click **2** length **3** sign **4** stairs

fop *n* → **1** affected person **2** fashionable person

forage *n* → **1** attack **2** food *v* **3** attack **4** pursue

foray *n* → **1** attack *v* **2** attack **3** pursue

forbear *v* → **1** abstain **2** be inactive **3** persevere

forbid *v* → **1** boycott **2** hinder **3** prohibit

forbidding *adj* → **1** dangerous **2** discouraging **3** frightening **4** unpleasant **5** unsociable

FORCE *n* brute force, muscle, power, pressure, strength, the sword; **force majeure,** vis major; **threat,** blackmail, Hobson's choice; **enforcement,** exaction, penalty, sanction

FORCE *v* coerce, compel, constrain, distress *(Archaic)*, dragoon, drive, frogmarch, juggernaut, lead by the nose, make, press, railroad *(U.S.)*, screw; **intimidate,** give the third degree, lean on, put the heat on, put the screws on, slap down, terrorise; **bully,** blackjack, bludgeon, browbeat, bulldoze, bullyrag, squeeze *(Colloq.)*, steamroll, steamroller, throw one's weight around, tyrannise; **conscript,** conscribe, draft, impress; **enforce,** exact; **force someone's hand,** rush; **insist on,** not take no for an answer, ram down someone's throat; **override,** pull rank on

force *n* → **1** armed forces **2** energy **3** importance **4** influence **5** meaning **6** operator **7** police **8** power **9** strength **10** violent outburst *v* **11** be promiscuous **12** extort **13** flower **14** impose **15** open **16** operate

FORCED *adj* coerced, compelled, constrained, enforced, hard-pressed; **compulsory,** necessary, required; **coercible,** compellable, constrainable, exactable; **conscript,** conscripted, press-ganged

FORCEFUL *adj* driving, forcible, powerful, punchy, strong, strong-willed, swingeing *(Colloq.)*; **sledge-hammer,** steamroller; **tyrannical,** arbitrary, despotic, dictatorial, Nazi; **intimidating,** bullying, coactive, coercive, compulsive, heavy, impellent, jack-booted, overbearing, terrorist

FORCEFULNESS *n* powerfulness; **compulsion,** coaction, coercion, constraint, duress, rape; **conscription,** draft, impress *(Obs.)*, impressment, press; **tyranny,** arbitrariness, despotism, Nazism, tyrannicalness; **intimidation,** bullying, terrorisation; **forcedness,** compulsoriness

forceps *n* → **1** extractor **2** holder

FORCER *n* coercer, compeller, constrainer, enforcer, exacter, impeller; **drafter,** press-gang; **tyrant,** despot, dictator, dictatrix, tyranniser; **bully,** bludgeoner, brave *(Obs.)*, browbeater, bruiser, bulldozer *(Colloq.)*, hector, intimidator, Nazi, standover man, steamroller, terroriser

forcible *adj* → **1** capable **2** forceful **3** violent

ford *n* → **1** bridge **2** shallow *v* **3** traverse

forebode *v* → **1** anticipate **2** predict

forecast *n* → **1** anticipation **2** conjecture **3** prediction *v* **4** plan **5** predict

forecastle *n* → **1** bed **2** front

foreclose *v* → **1** hinder **2** insist on **3** isolate

forefather *n* → forerunner

forego *v* → precede

forehand *n* → **1** right *adj* **2** prototypal **3** right

forehead *n* → head

FOREIGN *adj* alien, imported, irregular, non-resident, outlandish *(Archaic)*, strange *(Archaic)*, unacclimatised, unassimilated; **ethnic,** extraterritorial, peregrine; **gentile,** barbarous, pagan, paganish, tramontane, uncircumcised; **exotic,** adventive, unfamiliar; **extraneous,** adventitious, stray; **external,** ecdemic, heterogenous, outside; **uninvited,** excluded, intrusive

foreign *adj* → **1** different **2** unrelated

FOREIGNER *n* alien, denizen, non-resident, outlander, outsider, stranger *(Archaic)*, unco *(Scot. Obs.)*; **gentile,** barbarian, pagan, tramontane, uncircumcision *(Rare)*; **ethnic,** Arab, bohunk *(U.S.)*, continental, Creole *(U.S.)*, dago, ethno, gook *(U.S.)*, gringo, hollow log, hunky *(U.S.)*, spic, wog, wop; **refugee,** boat people, D.P., displaced person, reffo; **foreign population,** minority, outgroup; **diaspora,** exodus; **stray,** adventive, cuckoo, irregular, straggler *(Agric.)*; **curiosity,** exotic; **foreign body,** inclusion, xenolith; **intruder,** a grape on the business, gatecrasher, interloper, stowaway, trespasser, uninvited guest

FOREIGNNESS *n* adventitiousness, alienage, alienism, exoticism, extraneousness, foreignism *(U.S.)*, outlandishness, strangeness; **alienation,** estrangement, exclusion; **migration,** emigration, immigration, transportation; **non-residency**

forelock *n* → **1** hair **2** nail

foreman *n* → **1** boss **2** jury **3** manager

forensic *adj* → lawful

FORERUNNER *n* anticipator, apostle, early bird, forefather, foregoer, harbinger, herald, introducer, leader, outrider, outrunner, pioneer, precursor, predecessor, prophet, spearhead, trailblazer, usher *(Archaic)*, van, vanguard. *See also* ANTECEDENT

foresee *v* → **1** anticipate **2** expect **3** predic **4** prepare

foreshore *n* → seaside

foresight *n* → **1** anticipation **2** expectatio **3** hope

foreskin *n* → groin

FOREST *n* greenwood, jungle, rainfores sclerophyll forest, taiga, woodland, woods **scrub,** boscage, bosket, brush, brushwood canebrake *(U.S.)*, chaparral *(U.S.)*, coppice copse, grove, hurst, spinney *(Brit.)*, thicke wallum; **undergrowth,** underbrush understorey, underwood

forest *n* → **1** accumulation **2** many *v* **3** farm

forestall *v* → **1** buy **2** expect **3** hinder

forever *adv* → **1** continually **2** eternally

for ever *adv* → eternally

foreword *n* → **1** book part **2** introduction

forfeit *n* → **1** punishment *adj* **2** lost

forge *n* → **1** factory *v* **2** circulate **3** creat **4** imitate **5** make **6** shape

FORGET *v* clean forget, disremember, hav no recollection of, let in one ear and out th other, misremember; **consign to oblivion,** blo out, bury, live down, repress, unlearn; **be o the tip of one's tongue,** be almost there; **go ou of one's head,** fly out of one's mind, slip one' mind

forget *v* → **1** be inattentive **2** neglect

FORGETFUL *adj* absent, absent-minded, i retentive, oblivious, preoccupied, woolly minded; **amnesic,** amnesiac, amnestic forgetful-making *(Poetic)*, nepenthean; **for gotten,** out of mind, sunk in oblivion

FORGETFULNESS *n* lotus land, oblivion silence; **omission,** oversight, slip of the mem ory, slip of the mind

FORGETTER *n* absent-minded professo amnesiac, lotus-eater; **nepenthe,** lotus

FORGETTING *n* blackout, memory lapse mental block, overlooking, total blank **absent-mindedness,** absence of mind, absent ness, forgetfulness, irretentiveness obliviousness, obliviscence, preoccupation **amnesia,** anomia, fugue

FORGIVABLE *adj* absolvable, atonable, ex cusable, expiable, pardonable, remittable venial

FORGIVE *v* condone, discount, dismiss, dis regard, extenuate, let bygones be bygones overlook, pass over, think no more of; **par don,** absolve, amnesty, assoil *(Law Archaic)* excuse, justify, shrive; **spare,** acquit, clear exculpate, exonerate, have a heart, release remit, reprieve

forgive *v* → acquit

FORGIVER *n* absolvent, condoner, excuser pardoner, redeemer, sparer

FORGIVING *n* absolute pardon, amnesty conditional pardon, exemption, indemnity pardon, reprieve; **exoneration,** acquittal condonation, exculpation, excusal, justifica tion, vindication; **forgiveness,** grace; **absolu tion,** jubilee *(Rom. Cath. Ch.)*, plenary indul gence *(Rom. Cath. Ch.)*, remission *(Law)* shrift *(Archaic)*

FORGIVING *adj* absolutory; **magnanimous,** graceful, placable

FORGIVINGLY *adv* gracefully, magnanimously, placably

FORGIVINGNESS *n* forbearance, forgiveness, magnanimity, magnanimousness, placability, placableness

forgo *v* → **1** abandon **2** abstain **3** neglect

forgotten *adj* → forgetful

fork *n* → **1** bend **2** branch **3** break **4** groin **5** piercer *v* **6** diverge **7** lift **8** separate

forlorn *adj* → **1** abandoned **2** unhappy

form *n* → **1** animal dwelling **2** behaviour **3** characteristic **4** conformist behaviour **5** essence **6** fine arts **7** finished product **8** formality **9** health **10** idea **11** model **12** number **13** order **14** record **15** reputation **16** shape *v* **17** create **18** make **19** order **20** shape

FORMAL *adj* ceremonial, ceremonious, courtly, dignified, official, public, ritual, ritualistic, solemn, state, stately; **precise,** correct, starchy, stickling; **reserved,** frigid, icy, perfunctory, stiff, stilted, undemonstrative, uneasy; **dress,** full-dress, Sunday-go-to-meeting *(U.S.)*

formal *n* → **1** dance *adj* **2** artistic **3** essential

FORMAL DRESS *n* academic dress, academicals, ball dress, best bib and tucker, black tie, class A's *(U.S.)*, court dress, dinner jacket, dinner suit, dress, dress coat, dress suit, evening dress, formals, number ones *(Navy)*, regalia, Sunday best, tails, uniform, white tie

FORMALISE *v* ceremonialise, officialise, solemnify, solemnise; **stand on ceremony,** observe protocol

FORMALITY *n* ceremoniousness, ceremony, dignity, pomp and circumstance, solemness, state, stateliness; **etiquette,** form, protocol; **spit and polish,** drill; **preciseness,** correctness, gentility, precision, punctilio, punctiliousness, savoir-faire, savoir-vivre; **refinement,** niceness; **reservedness,** frigidity, frigidness, ice, iciness, perfunctoriness, reserve; **stiffness,** starch, starchiness, stiltedness, undemonstrativeness

FORMALLY *adv* ceremonially, ceremoniously, courtly, precisely, reservedly, solemnly, starchily, stiffly, stiltedly, with colours, with colours flying; **perfunctorily,** by the book, frigidly, icily, pro forma, undemonstratively

FORMAL OCCASION *n* formal function, observance, rite, ritual, solemnities, solemnity; **formalisation,** solemnification, solemnisation

format *n* → plan

formation *n* → **1** flight **2** making **3** structure

formative *n* → **1** word part *adj* **2** creative

former *n* → **1** creator *adj* **2** early **3** old **4** past **5** preceding

formidable *adj* → **1** difficult **2** frightening

formula *n* → **1** diagram **2** number **3** rule

formulate *v* → **1** abbreviate **2** be precise **3** create **4** legalise **5** shape

fornicate *v* → **1** be promiscuous **2** have sex

fornication *n* → sexual intercourse

forsake *v* → abandon

fort *n* → fortress

forth *adv* → **1** forward **2** in the future **3** remotely

forthcoming *n* → **1** appearance *adj* **2** emergent **3** prepared

FORTHRIGHT *adj* aboveboard, bluff, blunt, candid, direct, downright, extroverted, foursquare, frank, genuine, guileless, honest, literal, matter-of-fact, open, open as the day, plain, plain-dealing, plain-spoken, sincere, straightforward, up-front

forthright *adv* → **1** hurriedly **2** momentarily

forthwith *adv* → **1** hurriedly **2** momentarily

FORTIFICATION *n* fieldwork, flanker, flèche, gabionade, lunette, muniment; **parapet,** bailey *(Archaic)*, barbican, bulwark, rampart, redan, walls; **barricade,** parallel, salient, traverse; **battlement,** battery, blockhouse, crenellation, embrasure, emplacement, pillbox; **stockade,** abatis, air base, base, fastness, fraise, palisade; **stake,** barbwire, caltrop, gabion, spike; **movable shelter,** manta, mantelet, testudo, tortoise; **earthwork,** breastwork, contravallation, counterscarp, embankment, entrenchment, entrenchments, escarp, escarpment, glacis, mound, outwork, parados, ravelin, redoubt, retrenchment, scarp, sconce, vallum, works; **trench,** ditch, dug-out, dyke, enfilade, fosse, foxhole, moat, trenches; **trap,** booby trap. *See also* FORTRESS

fortify *v* → **1** assent to **2** strengthen

fortitude *n* → **1** courage **2** durability **3** patience

FORTRESS *n* acropolis, bastille, castle, citadel, donjon, fastness, fort, fortalice, fortifications, garrison, hold *(Archaic)*, keep, kremlin, Martello tower, peel, presidio, quadrilateral, stronghold, tower; **blockhouse,** gatehouse, watch-house, watchtower; **garrison town,** burg; **defensive position,** anchor, approaches, bastion, bridgehead, outpost. *See also* FORTIFICATION

fortress *v* → defend

fortuitous *adj* → lucky

FORTUNATE *adj* gracious *(Obs.)*, happy, heaven-sent, lucky, providential; **prosperous,** blooming, booming, flourishing, made, palmy, roseate, rosy, Saturnian, thriving, up-and-coming; **auspicious,** benign, benignant, blessed, blest, bright, promising, propitious

fortunate *adj* → lucky

FORTUNATELY *adv* auspiciously, beneficially, blessedly, for the best, happily, luckily, propitiously, providentially, rosily; **prosperously,** flourishingly, swimmingly, thrivingly

fortune *n* → **1** fate **2** luck **3** omen **4** wealth

Fortune *n* → fate

FORTUNE-TELLER *n* astrologer, ballgazer, chiromancer, crystal-gazer, futurologist, numerologist, palmist, rhabdomantist, stargazer, water diviner. *See also* PREDICTOR

FORTUNE-TELLING *n* astrology, augurship, augury, ballgazing, chirognomy, crystal-gazing, divination, divining, foretelling, futurology, hand-reading, metagnomy, palmistry, prefiguration, prefigurement, prognostication, soothsaying, vaticination; **crystal ball,** crystal, fortune cookie; **horoscope,** ascendant, aspect, constellation, cusp, house, midheaven, planet, sign, star; **signs of the zodiac,** Aquarius *(water-bearer)*, Aries *(Ram)*, Cancer *(Crab)*, Capricorn *(Goat)*, Gemini *(Twins)*, Leo *(Lion)*, Libra *(Scales)*, Pisces *(Fish)*, Sagittarius *(Archer)*, Scorpio *(Scorpion)*, Taurus *(Bull)*, Virgo *(Virgin)*; **palmistry,** fate line, head line, heart line, lifeline, line of happiness, line of health, line,of wealth, mount, mount of the moon, mount of Venus, rascette, simian line; **tarot cards,** Judgment, lesser arcanum, major arcanum, minor arcanum, the Fool, the Hanged Man, the Moon, the wheel of Fortune, triumph card, trump; **tarot suits,** cups, pentacles, swords, wands. *See also* PREDICTION

forty *n* → thief

forum *n* → 1 committee 2 council 3 court of law 4 field

FORWARD *adv* ahead, forwards, in advance, in the forefront, in the lead, on, on ahead; **onward,** along, en route, forth, onwards

forward *v* → 1 prepare 2 transport *adj* 3 advanced 4 discourteous 5 early 6 enthusiastic 7 front 8 future 9 happy 10 presumptuous *adv* 11 frontally

fossick *v* → 1 pursue 2 search

FOSSIL *n* eolith, neolith, petrified forest, relics, reliquiae, remains, ruins, stone-lily, vestige

fossil *n* → 1 old people 2 rock *adj* 3 old 4 past

foster *v* → 1 care for 2 encourage 3 feed 4 help

foul *n* → 1 impact *v* 2 collide 3 dirty 4 disgrace 5 disobey 6 obstruct 7 tangle *adj* 8 bad 9 dirty 10 disobedient 11 execratory 12 immoral 13 mixed 14 obscene 15 opposite 16 sickening 17 tangled 18 ugly 19 unfair 20 violent 21 wrong *adv* 22 unfairly

found *v* → 1 create 2 heat 3 initiate 4 shape 5 underlie

FOUNDATION *n* base, basics, basis, first principles, groundwork, principle, rudiments; **spadework,** preparation; **initiative,** lead; **root,** grassroots, radix *(Maths)*; **baseline,** datum level, datum plane, datum point, focus

foundation *n* → 1 bottom 2 building 3 cosmetics 4 gift 5 preparation 6 society 7 support *adj* 8 original 9 supporting

founder *n* → 1 creator 2 metalworker 3 starter *v* 4 fall

foundry *n* → 1 factory 2 metalworks

fount *n* → 1 spring 2 start

fountain *n* → 1 bubbling 2 spring 3 start

fountain pen *n* → writing materials

FOUR *n* quartet, quaternary, quaternion, tetrad, tetralogy; **quadruplet,** quad, quadruplicate; **quadruple,** quadrivalency, quadruplication; **quarter,** fourth, quartering, quartern *(Obs.)*

four *n* → mariner

fowl *v* → hunt

fox *n* → 1 cunning person *v* 2 intoxicate 3 repair 4 trick

foyer *n* → 1 entrance 2 hall

fracas *n* → 1 commotion 2 tangle

fraction *n* → 1 number 2 part 3 religious ceremony 4 share *v* 5 separate

fractious *adj* → 1 disobedient 2 irritable

fracture *n* → 1 break 2 gap 3 injury *v* 4 separate

fragile *adj* → brittle

fragment *n* → 1 break 2 part

FRAGRANCE *n* aromaticity, balminess, deliciousness, odoriferousness, odorousness, perfumery, redolence, savour, savouriness, spice *(Poetic)*, spicery, spiciness, sweet, sweetness, tang; **perfume,** aromatic, balm, bath cube, bath salts, essence, essential oil, incense, joss stick, scent; **cologne,** bay rum, eau de Cologne, lavender water, pomade, rosewater, toilet water; **pomander,** lavender bag, potpourri, pouncet box, sachet; **buttonhole,** nosegay, spray; **censer,** thurible; **breath-sweetener,** pastille

FRAGRANT *adj* aromatic, balmy, dulcet *(Archaic)*, odoriferous, redolent, sweet, sweet-scented; **savoury,** ambrosial, ambrosian, delicious, flavorous; **spicy,** aloetic, balsamaceous, balsamic, moschate, musky; **strong,** fruity, heady, rich; **garlicky,** alliaceous

fragrant *adj* → pleasant

frail *n* → 1 amount 2 basket *adj* 3 brittle 4 immoral 5 weak

FRAME *n* annulet, architrave, archivolt, cased frame, epistyle, framing, lipping, moulding, ovolo, reeding, skirting board, washboard; **edging,** beading, bias binding, binding, braiding, gimp, list, piping, purfling, skirting, welting; **surround,** back, gutter *(Print)*, mat, passe-partout; **circumference,** boundary, cordon, cushion *(Billiards)*, perimeter, periphery, railing, ropes; **end,** beam-ends, head. *See also* EDGE

frame *n* → 1 bone 2 building 3 conspiracy 4 container 5 enclosure 6 photograph 7 stand 8 structure *v* 9 accuse 10 create 11 edge 12 fake 13 make 14 plan 15 shape 16 support

framework *n* → building

franchise *n* → 1 authority 2 election 3 electorate 4 liberty 5 rights

frank *n* → 1 label *v* 2 facilitate 3 label 4 liberate 5 transport *adj* 6 forthright 7 honest 8 truthful

frantic *adj* → 1 mad 2 worried

fraternal *adj* → 1 friendly 2 societal

fraternise *v* → be friends

fraternity *n* → 1 friendship 2 institute 3 kinship

fraud *n* → 1 crime 2 crook 3 cunning person 4 dishonesty 5 embezzlement 6 fake 7 faker

fraught *adj* → 1 full 2 worried

fray *n* → 1 act of war 2 fight 3 fright *v* 4 annoy 5 deteriorate 6 rub

FREAK *n* chimera, grotesquerie, irregularity, monstrosity, neither fish flesh fowl nor good red herring, one of a kind, quip, rogue *(Biol.)*, sport *(Biol.)*, tertium quid, vagary, wonder; **rarity,** bastard, exotica, irregular, lusus naturae, odd, oncer, sight, unco *(Scot.)*. *See also* STRANGENESS

freak *n* → **1** enthusiast **2** nonconformist *v* **3** frighten *adj* **4** strange

freckle *n* → **1** buttocks **2** colour **3** disfigurement *v* **4** disfigure

free *v* → **1** alleviate **2** liberate *adj* **3** cheap **4** easy **5** escaped **6** generous **7** independent **8** liberated **9** promiscuous **10** separate **11** unpaid **12** unused **13** windy *adv* **14** freely

freedom *n* → **1** independence **2** liberty **3** rights

freehold *n* → **1** ownership **2** real estate *adj* **3** liberated

freelance *n* → **1** fighter **2** independent person **3** member of parliament **4** worker *v* **5** work *adj* **6** self-sufficient

FREELY *adv* free, imprescriptibly, liberally, like water, open-handedly; **unconditionally,** by the run *(Naut.)*, unboundedly, unlimitedly; **unreservedly,** anarchically, boisterously, incontinently, inordinately, intemperately, outright, outspokenly, spontaneously, unashamedly, unbiasedly, unconventionally, wantonly, wildly

freeway *n* → road

free will *n* → **1** choice **2** independence **3** will **4** willingness

free-will *adj* → willing

freeze *n* → **1** season **2** snow **3** stoppage *v* **4** anaesthetise **5** be cold **6** cool **7** die **8** finance **9** harden **10** stop

FREIGHT *n* airfreight, carriage, cartage, expressage, freightage, haulage, pipage, portage, porterage, postage, towage, trackage *(U.S.)*, truckage, wagonage *(Archaic)*, waterage; **storage,** cellarage, poundage, stowage, tankage, yardage; **dockage,** anchorage, average, demurrage, dock-dues, ground, groundage, keelage, metage, pilotage, tonnage, wharfage. *See also* COST

freight *n* → **1** goods *v* **2** fill **3** transport

French horn *n* → brass instrument

French letter *n* → contraception

frenetic *adj* → **1** mad **2** worried

frenzy *n* → **1** excitement **2** madness **3** psychic disturbance *v* **4** excite **5** madden

FREQUENCY *n* commonness, continuity, relative frequency; **hertz,** cps, cycles per second, Hz, kHz, kilohertz, megahertz, MHz

frequency *n* → **1** regularity **2** urination

FREQUENT *adj* common, continual, ever-recurring, habitual, incessant, non-stop, often *(Archaic)*, recurrent, recurring, repeated, repetitional, rife; **repetitive,** cyclic, harping, iterative, nagging, stuck in a groove, tautological; **worn-out,** cliché-ridden, clichéd, old, stale, well-worn; **monotonous,** singsong; **multitudinous,** a dime a dozen, all over the place, thick on the ground; **regular** drumming, rhythmical

frequent *v* → **1** be present **2** visit

FREQUENTLY *adv* continually, many a time, oft *(Poetic)*, often, oftentimes *(Archaic)*, recurrently, regularly, time after time

fresco *n* → painting

fresh *n* → **1** stream *adj* **2** additional **3** clean **4** cold **5** discourteous **6** energetic **7** healthy **8** ignorant **9** living **10** memorable **11** new **12** tasty **13** youthful *adv* **14** coldly **15** newly

fret *n* → **1** annoyance **2** decoration **3** irritation **4** rubbing *v* **5** annoy **6** complain **7** deteriorate **8** irritate **9** pain **10** rub **11** toss **12** worry

fretwork *n* → decoration

friable *adj* → **1** brittle **2** soft

friar *n* → monastic

FRICTION *n* bite, traction; **drag,** pressure drag, profile drag, skin friction drag, windage; **aerodynamics,** tribology

friction *n* → fight

fridge *n* → **1** cooler **2** sexual partner

FRIEND *n* ally, amigo, buddy, buddy-buddy, bully *(Obs.)*, butty *(Brit.)*, china, chum, cobber, comate, companion, comrade, crony, digger, ehoa *(N.Z.)*, fellow, gossip *(Archaic)*, hearty, hetaerist, mate, mucker *(Brit.)*, neighbour, pal, pard *(U.S.)*, pardner *(U.S.)*, partner, sidekick, sparring partner, yokefellow; **acquaintance,** associate, contact, contact man, familiar, fraterniser, penfriend; **intimate,** best friend, blood brother, bosom friend, cater-cousin *(Archaic)*, close friend, confidant, kith and kin, soul mate; **favourite,** minion, pet; **inseparables,** alter ego, birds of a feather, shadow; **sweetheart,** darling, love, lover; **girlfriend,** bovver boot *(Brit. Colloq.)*, clinah *(Obs.)*, moll, sheila; **boyfriend,** man

friend *n* → helper

FRIENDLINESS *n* affability, affableness, amiability, amiableness, amicability, amicableness, amity; **cordiality,** approachability, approachableness, heartiness, hospitality; **warmth,** soft spot, warm-heartedness

FRIENDLY *adj* affable, amiable, amicable; **chummy,** brotherly, fraternal, matey, neighbourly, on good terms, pally; **warm-hearted,** approachable, folksy *(U.S.)*, homey, openhearted, outgoing; **welcoming,** cordial, genial, hospitable, warm; **hail-fellow-well-met,** backslapping, bluff, hearty; **acquainted,** familiar; **intimate,** bosom, close, incestuous, inseparable, involved, thick, thick as thieves, well in with; **devoted,** assiduous, devout, staunch; **compatible,** after one's own heart, hetaeristic, platonic, simpatico, sympathetic

FRIENDLY *adv* affably, amiably, amicably, friendlily, heartily, warm-heartedly, warmly, with open arms; **devotedly,** assiduously, devoutly; **intimately,** familiarly, fraternally, hetaeristically

friendly *adj* → **1** kind **2** sports

FRIENDSHIP *n* backslapping, brotherhood, brotherliness, camaraderie, companionship, comradeship, fellowship, fraternalism, fraternity, hetaerism, mateship, mateyness, neighbourhood *(Archaic)*, neighbourliness, sodality; **goodwill,** fellow feeling, regard, solidarity, sympathy; **intimacy,** closeness, devotion, familiarisation, familiarity, intimateness, involvement, togetherness; **understanding,** entente; **fraternisation,** acquaintance, acquaintanceship, association, consociation, conversation, society; **greetings,** ingratiation, open arms, welcome; **attentions,** assiduities, embrace, endearment, handclasp, handshake, hug, kiss, squeeze

frieze *n* → **1** layer **2** painting

frigate *n* → watercraft

FRIGHT *n* affright *(Archaic)*, alarm, amazement *(Obs.)*, awe, blue funk, boggle, consternation, dismay, doubt *(Obs.)*, fear, fray *(Archaic)*, funk, heebie-jeebies, horror, horrors, jumpiness, panic, phobia *(Psychol.)*, scare, superstition, terror, the creeps, the jitters, willies; **apprehension,** alarm, alarum *(Archaic)*, angst, anxiety, anxiousness, apprehensiveness, care, concern, concernment, dis-ease, disquiet, disquietude, dread, misgiving, nervousness, qualm, trepidation, worriment; **timidity,** diffidence, shyness, timidness, timorousness, tremulousness; **tremble,** cold shivers, cold sweat, horripilation, shudder, start, tremor, turn *(Colloq.)*

fright *n* → **1** ugly person *v* **2** frighten

FRIGHTEN *v* affray *(Archaic)*, affright *(Archaic)*, alarm, appal, awe, blanch, consternate, curdle the blood, fear *(Archaic)*, freak, fright *(Poetic)*, horrify, make one's flesh creep, make one's hair stand on end, petrify, put the breeze up, put the wind up, scare, scare the living daylights out of, strike fear into, terrify, terrorise, turn one's bowels to water; **daunt,** chill, demoralise, discourage, dishearten, dismay, dispirit

FRIGHTENED *adj* afraid, aghast, alarmed, awe-struck, green at the gills, horror-stricken, horror-struck, out of one's wits, panic, panic-stricken, panicky, petrified, scared, scared stiff, shit-scared, spooked, terror-stricken, terror-struck, trembly, tremulant, tremulous, white, white at the gills; **timorous,** afeard *(Archaic)*, anxious, apprehensive, dispirited, fearful, gun-shy, haunted, jittery, jumpy, nervous, pavid, phobic, shy, superstitious, timid, toey, windy, worried, worrisome

FRIGHTENED PERSON *n* blencher, milquetoast *(U.S.)*, panic merchant, shyer

FRIGHTENER *n* alarmist, boggle, bogle, bogy, bogyman, boogieman, bugaboo, bugbear, chamber of horrors, demoraliser, discourager, gorgon, gorgonian, hair-raiser, hobgoblin, holy terror, horror, intimidator, scarecrow, scaremonger, scarer, spinechiller, startler, taipo *(N.Z.)*, terrifier, terror, terroriser, thunderbolt

FRIGHTENING *adj* appalling, awe-inspiring, awesome, awful, bloodcurdling, crawly, creepy, creepy-crawly, Dantean, Dantesque, dire, direful, dread, dreadful, eerie, fearful, fearsome, forbidding, formidable, frightful, grim, grisly, hair-raising, hairy *(Colloq.)*, horrendous, horrible, horrid, horrific, nerve-racking, nightmarish, redoubtable, redoubted, scary, spinechilling, terrible, terrific

frightful *adj* → **1** dreadful **2** frightening **3** intense **4** ugly

frigid *adj* → **1** callous **2** cold **3** formal **4** unsociable

frill *n* → **1** affectation **2** animal's coat **3** edge **4** fold **5** trimming *v* **6** fold **7** remove

fringe *n* → **1** edge **2** hair **3** reflection **4** trimming *v* **5** edge *adj* **6** excluded

frisk *n* → **1** dancing **2** inspection **3** jump *v* **4** amuse oneself **5** dance **6** jump **7** rob **8** search

frisky *adj* → **1** amused **2** excited

fritter *n* → **1** part *v* **2** separate **3** squander

frivolous *adj* → **1** foolish **2** happy **3** illogical **4** stupid **5** unimportant

frizz *n* → **1** circuitousness **2** curl **3** hair **4** hairdressing *v* **5** twist

frizzle *n* → **1** curl *v* **2** cook **3** hiss **4** twist

frock *n* → **1** dress **2** overcoat **3** uniform *v* **4** clothe

frog *n* → **1** button **2** cash **3** contraception **4** quietness **5** stand *v* **6** hunt

frogman *n* → diver

frolic *n* → **1** amusement *v* **2** amuse oneself **3** be happy *adj* **4** happy

FRONT *n* A-side, face, fore edge, obverse; **head,** lead, top; **forefront,** firing line, fore, foreside; **anteriority,** forwardness; **facade,** facing, front, frontage, frontispiece *(Archit.)*, heading; **bow,** bowsprit, cutwater, forecastle, hawse, head, prow

FRONT *v* affront *(Archaic)*, face

FRONT *adj* anterior, frontal; **forward,** fore; **head,** head-on, headmost; **obverse,** facing-out, right

front *n* → **1** advance **2** arrogance **3** atmospheric pressure **4** battleground **5** behaviour **6** chest **7** front **8** important thing **9** neckwear **10** outside **11** road **12** society *v* **13** argue **14** be present

FRONTALLY *adv* anteriorly, forwardly; **forward,** afore, ahead, before, fore, forwards, frontwards, in advance, to the fore; **headfirst,** down by the head, head-on, headlong

frontier *n* → **1** edge **2** region **3** wall *adj* **4** boundary

frost *n* → **1** coating **2** decoration **3** failure **4** snow **5** trick *v* **6** be cold **7** coat **8** decorate

frostbite *n* → coldness

froth *n* → **1** bubbling *v* **2** bubble **3** discharge

frown *n* → **1** boo **2** scowl *v* **3** become irritated **4** dislike

frozen *adj* → **1** callous **2** cold **3** cooled **4** dead **5** injured **6** preserved **7** unsociable

frugal *adj* → **1** abstinent **2** cheap **3** thrifty

fruit *n* → **1** finished product **2** sexual type *v* **3** be fertile **4** flower **5** give birth

fruition *n* → **1** accomplishment **2** fertilisation

fruity *adj* → **1** fragrant **2** obscene **3** resonant **4** sexual **5** sexy **6** tasty

frump *n* → ugly person

frustrate *v* → **1** argue **2** counteract **3** discourage **4** disenchant **5** hinder

fry *n* → **1** animal offspring **2** party *v* **3** cook

udge *n* → **1** nonsense **2** substitute *v* **3** cheat **4** pretend **5** talk nonsense

FUEL *n* combustible, feed, juice; **fueling,** bunkering, fuel-injection, priming; **woodheap,** pyre, woodpile; **firewood,** billet, brushwood, faggot, greasebush, greasewood, log, mallee roots, ovenwood, torchwood, yarran; **kindling,** briquette, firelighter, firing, morning sticks, mornings wood, tinder; **wick,** mantle, touchpaper; **coal,** anthracite, brown coal, coking coal, culm, lignite, wood coal; **coke,** char, charcoal; **peat,** turf; **gas,** bottled gas, coal gas, liquefied petroleum gas (L.P.G.), producer gas, town gas; **fossil fuel,** benzine *(U.S.)*, carburant, derv *(Brit.)*, diesel, diesel oil, dieseline, gas *(U.S.)*, gasoline *(U.S.)*, naphtha *(Obs.)*, oil, petrol, petroleum, standard, super; **kerosene,** avgas, kero, paraffin *(Brit.)*; **propellant,** acetylene, borane, butane, carbinol, ethine, ethyl, grain *(Aerospace)*, heptane, isobutane, lead tetraethyl, liquid oxygen, lox, pentaborane, propane, solid propellant; **incendiary,** fireball, Greek fire, napalm, wildfire; **nuclear fuel,** pile, rod, uranium

FUEL *v* bunker, coal, coke, refuel, tank up; **fire,** feed the flames, lay a fire, prime, stoke, underfeed

fugitive *n* → **1** avoider **2** escapee *adj* **3** elusive **4** escaped **5** ethereal **6** impermanent

fugue *n* → **1** forgetting **2** psychic disorder **3** repetition

fulcrum *n* → **1** centre-line **2** support

fulfil *v* → **1** accomplish **2** do **3** make whole **4** obey **5** satisfy

FULL *adj* chock-a-block, chock-full, chocker, choke-full, cram-full, crammed, full up, jam-packed, jammed, replete, stopped; **brimful,** brimming, topped up, well filled; **loaded,** charged, fraught, laden; **bulging,** big with, pregnant with; **occupied,** preoccupied; **overfull,** at saturation point, drowned, overflowing, rolling in, saturate *(Poetic)*, saturated, slopping, swamped; **crowded,** packed, plethoric, solid, tight; **bursting at the seams,** gorged, sated

full *v* → **1** solidify *adj* **2** circular **3** drunk **4** enormous **5** loud **6** thick **7** whole *adv* **8** precisely **9** very

FULLNESS *n* capacity, impletion, maximum, one's fill, plenitude, satiety, saturation; **plenty,** abundance, full and plenty, plentifulness; **tightness,** cram, engorgement, saturation point; **replenishment,** completion, fill-up, refill; **occupancy,** occupation, preoccupancy; **cupful,** bumper

full stop *n* → stoppage

FULLY *adv* even, quite; **plenty,** solidly

fulminate *v* → **1** be loud **2** explode **3** menace

fulsome *adj* → **1** abundant **2** flattering **3** sickening **4** vulgar

fumble *n* → **1** bungle **2** sexual intercourse *v* **3** bungle **4** eroticise **5** mispronounce

fume *n* → **1** smell *v* **2** be angry

fumigate *v* → **1** cloud **2** disinfect

fun *n* → **1** amusement **2** humour *v* **3** joke *adj* **4** amusing **5** humorous

function *n* → **1** action **2** celebration **3** obligation **4** operation **5** usefulness *v* **6** do **7** operate

fund *n* → **1** capital **2** charity **3** funds **4** storage *v* **5** finance **6** lend

FUNDAMENTAL *adj* au fond, basal, base, basic, basilar, bottom, deep down, essential, key, material, original, radical, ultimate, underlying, vital; **primary,** prime; **elementary,** elemental, hypostatic, raw, simple, skeleton; **substantial,** meaty

fundamental *n* → **1** essence *adj* **2** characteristic **3** important **4** original **5** simple

FUNDS *n* assets, bread and butter, capital, credit, cunning kick, exchequer, fast buck, finances, float, fund, income, liquid assets, liquidity, money in hand, petty cash, pocket, purse, quick assets, resources, revenue, royalty, savings, slush fund, slush money, supply *(Govt.)*; **kitty,** jackpot, pool, stakes; **bond,** bond money; **funny money,** mickey mouse money. *See also* ALLOWANCE; TREASURY

funeral *n* → **1** funeral rites *adj* **2** deathlike

FUNERAL RITES *n* exequies, funeral, obsequies, office *(Eccles.)*; **burial,** committal, entombment, immurement, inhumation, interment, intombment, inurnment, sepulture; **cremation,** incineration; **embalment,** mummification; **requiem,** dead march, dirge, knell, last post, requiem mass, resquiescat, resquiescent in pace, taps, threnody; **obituary,** elegy, epitaph, funeral oration, in memoriam, R.I.P.; **lamentation,** vigil, wake; **mourning,** crepe, widow's weeds; **funeral pyre,** balefire *(Archaic)*, pile; **shroud,** cerecloth, cerements, graveclothes, winding sheet. *See also* GRAVE; CEMETERY

FUNEREAL *adj* funerary; **obituary,** elegiac, obsequial, threnodial, threnodic; **sepulchral,** cinerary, crematory, cryptal, mausolean, mortuary, tomblike

fungus *n* → **1** dirt **2** growth **3** plant

funicular railway *n* → railway

funk *n* → **1** coward **2** fright **3** stench **4** worry *v* **5** avoid **6** be frightened **7** lack courage **8** worry

funnel *n* → **1** borehole **2** hollow **3** passageway

funny *n* → **1** joke *adj* **2** humorous **3** strange

fur *n* → **1** animal's coat **2** covering **3** hide **4** remnant **5** skin

furbish *v* → **1** clean **2** decorate **3** polish **4** prepare

furious *adj* → **1** angry **2** ferocious **3** speedy **4** violent

furlong *n* → length

furlough *n* → **1** absence **2** holiday

furnace *n* → **1** fireplace **2** heater **3** metalworks

furnish *v* → **1** equip **2** prepare **3** supply

FURNITURE *n* accoutrements, appointments, appurtenances, fittings, fixtures, furnishings, furnishments *(Archaic)*

furore *n* → **1** anger **2** enthusiasm **3** excitement **4** muddle

furphy *n* → **1** misguidance **2** talk

FURROW *n* cannelure, channel, chase, check *(Masonry)*, croze, dap, drill, fillister, flute *(Archit.)*, glyph, gouge, groove, nick, notch, rabbet, rebate, recess, rifle, rut, scarf, seam, stria, sulcus, vallecula, wrinkle; **ditch,** canal, costean, coulisse, cut, dyke, entrenchments, gutter, keyway, moat, rill *(Astron.)*, rubble drain, sap *(Fortifications)*, slit trench, slot, sondage, trench, trough; **scratch,** microgroove, run-in groove, scarification, score; **milling,** broom finish, chatter marks, fluting, rifling, ruttiness, striation, sulcation

FURROW *v* chamfer, channel, flute, groove, mill, nick, rabbet, rebate, rifle, rout, rut, striate, trepan; **crease,** cockle, crumple, ripple, seam, wrinkle; **ditch,** costean, dyke, sap *(Fortifications)*, trench; **engrave,** chase, etch; **plough,** till; **scratch,** overscore, scarify, score

furrow *n* → **1** indentation **2** passageway *v* **3** fold

FURROWED *adj* fluted, glyphic, grooved, milled, ripply, rutty, scrobiculate, seamed, striate, sulcate, vallecular, valleculate, wrinkly

further *v* → **1** help *adj* **2** additional **3** distant *adv* **4** additionally

furtive *adj* → secretive

fury *n* → **1** anger **2** violent outburst **3** violent person

fuse *n* → **1** electric circuit **2** explosive **3** lighter *v* **4** combine **5** join **6** liquefy **7** mix **8** stick together

fusillade *n* → **1** capital punishment **2** gunfire **3** shot *v* **4** fire on

fusion *n* → **1** amalgamation **2** combination **3** combine **4** joining **5** liquefaction **6** mixture **7** radioactivation **8** stickiness

fuss *n* → **1** busyness **2** commotion **3** confusion **4** excitement **5** fight **6** turbulence **7** worry *v* **8** annoy **9** become confused **10** belt into **11** complain **12** worry

fussy *adj* → **1** careful **2** complex

fusty *adj* → **1** old **2** smelly **3** untimely

futile *adj* → **1** inappropriate **2** nonsensical **3** unavailable **4** unimportant **5** useless

FUTURE *n* afterlife, coming ages, futurity, hereafter, time to come; **tomorrow,** morrow *(Archaic)*, tonight; **mañana,** doomsday, judgment day, millenium, Pancake Day, the by and by, the sweet by and by; **imminence,** impendence, impendency

FUTURE *adj* after, eventual, to-be, unborn; **forward,** long-range, prospective; **futuristic,** space-age, twenty-first century; **imminent,** close at hand, impendent, impending, in the offing, in view, near, nearly upon one, nigh, pendent, pending, toward *(Obs.)*

future *n* → **1** expected thing *adj* **2** expected

futuristic *adj* → **1** future **2** innovative

fuzz *n* → **1** covering **2** fluff **3** hair **4** police

Gg

gaberdine *n* → overcoat
gadget *n* → tool
gaffe *n* → error
gag *n* → **1** joke **2** restraining order **3** stoppage *v* **4** close **5** joke **6** restrain **7** silence **8** stop **9** trick
gage *n* → **1** challenge **2** contract **3** surety *v* **4** gamble
gaggle *n* → **1** gathering *v* **2** chirp
gaiety *n* → **1** happiness **2** joy
GAIN *v* achieve, acquire, acquisition, annex, attain, bring home, catch, clear, collect, fetch, gather, get, get hold of, land, lay one's hands on, obtain, procure, realise, receive, recover *(Law)*, secure, take out, take over, win, wrest; **reach,** accede to, attain to, get to; **earn,** gross, net
gain *n* → **1** cut **2** increase **3** profit *v* **4** become greater **5** cut **6** get **7** succeed
GAINER *n* abandonee, accepter, alienee, appointee, assignee, concessionaire, concessionary, conferee, consignee, dole bludger, doley, donee, earner, endorsee, grantee, presentee, receiver, recipient; **heir,** assigns *(Law)*, beneficiary, coheir, coheiress, coinheritor, devisee, distaff, heir apparent, heir-at-law, heiress, heres, heritor *(Archaic)*, heritress, inheritor, inheritress, inheritrix, jointress, legatee; **insured,** assured *(Insurance)*, cestui que trust
gainsay *v* → deny
gait *n* → **1** move **2** walking
gaiter *n* → sock
gala *n* → **1** festival *adj* **2** spectacular
galah *n* → **1** fool **2** stupid person
galaxy *n* → crowd
gale *n* → **1** violent outburst **2** wind
gallant *n* → **1** fashionable person **2** flirt **3** hero **4** lover *adj* **5** astonishing **6** courageous **7** courteous **8** flirtatious
galleon *n* → sailing ship
gallery *n* → **1** auditorium **2** display case **3** kitchen **4** living room **5** path **6** room
galley *n* → **1** copy **2** kitchen **3** rowing boat
galling *adj* → annoying
gallivant *v* → **1** flirt **2** travel
gallop *n* → **1** path **2** rate *v* **3** ride **4** speed
gallows *n* → means of killing
gallup poll *n* → investigation
galore *adv* → greatly
galoshes *n* → boot
galvanise *v* → **1** activate **2** coat **3** electrify
gambit *n* → expedient
GAMBLE *n* a pig in a poke, act of faith, adventure, bid, burl, flutter, leap in the dark, punt, Russian roulette, spec, speculation, venture; **bet,** aleatory contract, all-in bet, collect, daily double, double, double or quits, doubles, each-way bet, forecast quinella, jackpot tote, martingale, overround system, parlay, parimutuel *(U.S.)*, quadrella, quinella, saver, side bet, skinner, stakes, straight-out bet, triella, trifecta, wager; **bid,** call, calling, contract, declaration, jump bid, psychic bid; **record of bets,** book; **the luck of the draw,** the toss of the coin
GAMBLE *v* ballot, chance it, chance one's arm, dice, game, have a flutter, play, play the market, speculate, take a punt on, take risks, throw dice, try one's luck; **bet,** gage *(Archaic)*, get set, hazard, lay, plunge, punt, put, roll, stake; **play two-up,** head 'em; **take bets,** field a book, frame a book, make a book, run a book, tout; **bid,** call, go, outbid, overbid; **raise,** fatten *(Poker)*, jump *(Contract Bridge)*, sweeten *(Poker)*; **bid on,** back; **hedge,** lay off; **stake,** ante, vie *(Obs.)*, wage *(Obs.)*, wager; **bet each way,** be on the grouter, bet all-up, bet double or quits, bet evens, come in on the grouter, crush the price, go for broke, go for the doctor, parlay, play for dibs, put one's shirt on, stay; **toss,** come in, head them, mick, ned them, nut them, one them, skull them; **win,** be in the black, be on a good thing, be on a winning streak, whipsaw; **be at stake,** be in hazard
gamble *n* → **1** feasibility **2** unknown *v* **3** attempt **4** hope **5** risk
GAMBLER *n* better, bettor, bidder, crapshooter *(U.S.)*, dicer, gamester, hazarder, hippomaniac, player, punter, sidebetter, sport, stool pigeon, wagerer; **bookmaker,** bagman, bagswinger, balancer, bester, bookie, commission agent *(Brit.)*, fielder, geno *(Horseracing Colloq.)*, Ikey Mo, rails bookmaker, SP bookmaker, tick-tack man, turf accountant *(Brit.)*; **banker,** monte, ombre; **backer,** plunger, turfman; **alley loafer,** welsher; **bagboy,** bookie's runner, boxer, croupier, crusher *(Horseracing)*, ringkeeper, stakeholder; **two-up player,** alley clerk, boxer, centre, centre-man, cockatoo, headie, ringie, spinner, tailie, tosser; **adventurer,** adventuress, gentleman of fortune, land shark, landjobber, speculator
GAMBLING *n* bookmaking, fan-tan, gaming, hippomania; **bingo,** housie-housie, hoy, lotto, tombola; **card game,** baccarat, blackjack, chemin de fer, chemmy, cooncan, cribbage, faro, poker, pontoon, rouge et noir, rummy, stud game, stud poker, trente et

quarante, twenty-one, vingt-et-un; **dice,** craps, dicing, hazard, poker dice, thimblerig; **two-up,** swy, toss, toss-up; **chocolate wheel,** roulette; **lottery,** art union, ballot, Calcutta, consultation *(Colloq.)*, football pools, grab bag, lot, lucky dip, pakapoo, policy *(U.S.)*, pools, raffle, sweep, sweepstake, Tambaroora muster, the casket, the Golden casket; **odds,** even money, evens, long odds, long shot, pot, quotation, short odds, starting price, toss-up; **ambs-ace,** butterfly, crabs, doublets, floater, showdown, sixer, tern

GAMBLING *adj* hippomanic, sporting, turfy *(Horseracing)*

GAMBLING HALL *n* casino, disorderly house, gaming house, hell *(Brit.)*, poolroom; **two-up school,** alley, betting ring, outer; **betting shop,** betting ring, lucky shop, pub TAB, ring, TAB, the machine *(N.Z. Horseracing)*, totalisator, Totalisator Agency Board

gambol *n* → **1** dancing **2** jump *v* **3** amuse oneself **4** jump

game *n* → **1** amusement **2** contest **3** courage **4** job **5** stratagem *v* **6** gamble *adj* **7** courageous **8** injured

GAMESMAN *n* player; **enjoyer,** dabbler, dilettante; **frolicker,** larker, reveller; **card-player,** banker, dealer, discarder, dummy, elder hand, hand, lone hand, maker, pairs, pone

gammon *n* → **1** nonsense *v* **2** fasten **3** talk nonsense **4** trick

gamut *n* → whole

gamy *adj* → **1** courageous **2** pungent **3** unsavoury

gander *n* → look

gang *n* → **1** committee **2** gathering **3** workers *v* **4** associate **5** travel

gangling *adj* → **1** long **2** thin

gangplank *n* → **1** bridge **2** shaft

gangster *n* → **1** criminal **2** killer **3** strong person

gangway *n* → **1** path **2** shaft **3** slope

gantry *n* → building

gaol *n* → **1** prison *v* **2** imprison

GAOLER *n* cerberus, deathwatch, four-by-two, guard, guarder, guardsman, kangaroo, mod squad, provost *(Obs.)*, screw, trump, turnkey, warden, warder, wardress; **incarcerator,** confiner, detainer, securer; **trusty,** farm constable; **apprehender,** captor, capturer

GAP *n* areola, blank, break, clearance, gape, hiatus, interspace, interstice, interval, lacuna, opening, space, vacancy, void; **split,** rent, slit, tear, vent; **air-gap,** crenel, intercolumniation, shake, spirket; **crack,** breach, chap, chimney, chink, cleavage, cleft, craze, crevice, cut, fissure, fracture, gash, mofette, rift, sand-crack; **chasm,** abysm *(Poetic)*, abyss, breakaway, canyon, chaos *(Obs.)*, chine *(Brit.)*, coomb, crevasse, dale, defile, dell, depth, dingle, gate, glen, gorge, graben, grike, gulch, gulf, gully, gut, hanging valley, pass, profundity, ravine, vale, valley, water-gap, wind-gap, yawn

gap *n* → **1** difference **2** interruption **3** interval **4** length **5** opening *v* **6** gape **7** open

GAPE *v* open, yawn; **space,** gap, interspace, separate, set apart, space out, spread out; **split,** cleave, crack, part

gape *n* → **1** gap **2** look **3** opening **4** openness *v* **5** diverge **6** look **7** open up **8** wonder

GAPING *adj* agape, ajar, broken, dehiscent, open, yawning; **spaced,** areolar, areolate, effuse, gappy, hiatal; **cleft,** cloven, cracked, dissected, parted, rent, slit, split; **interspatial,** interstitial

garage *n* → **1** shelter *v* **2** shelter **3** store

garb *n* → **1** clothes *v* **2** clothe

garbage *n* → **1** bad thing **2** dirt **3** illogicality **4** nonsense **5** waffle **6** waste

GARBAGE DUMP *n* dump, junk-heap, junkyard, midden, slagheap, tip; **rubbish tin,** ash can *(U.S.)*, dirt box, dustbin, garbage tin, kitchen tidy, litter bin, trash can *(U.S.)*, w.p.b., w.p.b. file, wastebasket, wastepaper basket; **cesspit,** cess, cesspool, grease trap

garble *n* → **1** misrepresentation *v* **2** lie **3** misinterpret **4** talk nonsense

GARDEN *n* garth *(Archaic)*, knot garden, roof garden, rooftop garden; **bed,** border, flowerbed, hotbed, rockery, seedbed; **plot,** patch, plat; **market garden,** allotment, kitchen garden, vegetable garden; **nursery,** bush house, conservatory, fernery, garden centre, glasshouse, grapery, greenery, greenhouse, hothouse, rosary, shrubbery; **green,** lawn, nature strip; **orchard,** arboretum, arbour *(Obs.)*, orangery, pinery; **park,** botanical garden, parterre, wilderness, wintergarden

garden *n* → **1** breeding ground **2** field *v* **3** level

GARDENER *n* arborist, landscape gardener, nurseryman, rosarian, topiarist; **market gardener,** cabbage-gardener, trucker *(U.S.)*; **groundsman,** greenkeeper, hedger

GARDENING *n* carpet bedding, espalier, horticulture, landscape gardening, pomiculture, pomology, topiary, trucking *(U.S.)*

gargle *n* → **1** a drink **2** cleanser *v* **3** bubble **4** clean

gargoyle *n* → **1** drain **2** knob **3** portrait

garish *adj* → **1** bright **2** colourful **3** showy **4** ugly **5** vulgar

garland *n* → **1** book **2** ring

garment *n* → **1** appearance **2** clothes

garnet *n* → **1** machine **2** puller *v* **3** sew *adj* **4** red

garnish *n* → **1** decoration **2** equipment *v* **3** cook **4** decorate **5** extort **6** warn

garret *n* → **1** room **2** tower

garrison *n* → **1** armed forces **2** fortress **3** house *v* **4** defend

garrotte *n* → **1** capital punishment **2** killing *v* **3** execute **4** kill

garrulous *adj* → **1** talkative **2** verbose

garter *n* → belt

GAS *n* ablative, aerosol, coal gas, detonating gas, electrolytic gas, flue gas, fluid, marsh gas, methane, natural gas, plasma, sewer gas, tear gas, town gas, water gas; **vapour,** breath

(Obs.), fumes, live steam, saturated vapour, steam, water-vapour; **smoke,** reek; **air,** atmosphere, exhalation, wind; **damp,** afterdamp, blackdamp, choke damp, firedamp, whitedamp; **effluvium,** eduction, emanon, exhaust, mofette; **choof,** chuff, huff, puff; **inert gas,** noble gas, rare gas; **ideal gas,** perfect gas, permanent gas; **fireball,** chromosphere, photosphere, prominence; **vapour trail,** condensation trail

gas *n* → 1 air 2 ammunition 3 anaesthetic 4 burp 5 fuel 6 good thing 7 nonsense 8 poison *v* 9 execute 10 talk nonsense *adj* 11 good

GASBAG *n* bag of wind, bull artist, bush-lawyer, expatiator, gusher, maunderer, windbag

GASEOUS *adj* effluvial, fluid, fluidal, fluidic, gasiform, pneumatic; **evaporative,** volatile; **vaporescent,** vaporific; **gassy,** fumelike, steamy, vaporous, vapoury

gash *n* → 1 cut 2 gap 3 groin 4 more 5 sex object 6 surplus *v* 7 cut

gasket *n* → plug

gasp *n* → 1 absorption 2 breathing *v* 3 absorb 4 breathe 5 speak

gastronome *n* → glutton

gate *n* → 1 access 2 camera part 3 cost 4 dam 5 door 6 entrance 7 gap 8 obstacle *v* 9 imprison

gatecrash *v* → 1 be present 2 enter

GATEWAY *n* archway, débouché *(Fort.)*, doorway, French door, torii

GATHER *v* amass, centralise, collect, congest *(Obs.)*, glean, ingather, rake, scramble up, throw together, whip in; **accumulate,** agglomerate, aggregate, conglomerate, cumulate, run; **hoard,** bank up, scavenge, sock away, stack away, stockpile; **cluster,** bale, bunch, bundle, clump, constellate; **heap,** lumber, pile, stack; **congregate,** assemble, band, forgather, group, mass, meet, regroup, sit, turn out; **crowd,** flock, herd, horde, huddle, pack, press, serry, throng; **convene,** call, convoke, muster, muster up, raise, rally, summon

gather *n* → 1 contraction *v* 2 attract 3 become greater 4 bulge 5 fold 6 gain 7 get 8 harvest 9 increase 10 order 11 prepare 12 reason 13 take

GATHERER *n* bundler, gleaner, heaper, herder, ingatherer, mobber, musterer, stacker; **assembler,** congregator, convoker; **collector,** amasser, raiser; **hoarder,** bowerbird, magpie, stockpiler; **scavenger,** beachcomber, emu *(Colloq.)*; **discophil,** epidopterist, ex-librist, philatelist, phillumenist, stamp-collector

GATHERING *n* association, bee, get-together, meet, muster, roll-up, turnout; **assembly,** assemblage, body, confluence, conflux, congregation, constellation, convocation; **meeting,** hui *(N.Z.)*, indaba *(S. African)*, witan, witenagemot; **group,** band, cohort, company, outfit, party, phalanx; **gang,** crew, emu parade, mob, pack, rabble, ruck, shower; **crowd,** crush, huddle, multitude, press, sea of faces, throng; **jam,** bunfight, squeeze; **corroboree;** **grouping,** class, college, school; **stable,** string; **pack,** pride; **bevy,** covey, flight, flock, gaggle; **herd,** drove, horde, troop; **shoal,** school; **association,** biome, climax community, colony, community, society; **congregativeness,** gregariousness, herd instinct, sociality; **centralisation,** centralism

gauche *adj* → 1 ill-bred 2 incompetent

gaudy *n* → 1 amusement *adj* 2 colourful 3 showy 4 ugly 5 vulgar

gauge *n* → 1 length 2 measurement 3 rule 4 tester 5 thickness *v* 6 assess 7 fold 8 homogenise 9 measure 10 regularise

gaunt *adj* → 1 thin 2 ugly

gauntlet *n* → 1 armour 2 glove 3 interlacement 4 railway *v* 5 cross

gauze *n* → 1 cloud 2 fluff 3 lace 4 textiles 5 transparent substance *v* 6 cloud

gavel *n* → 1 club 2 emblem of office *v* 3 hit

gawk *n* → 1 fool 2 incompetent *v* 3 look

gay *n* → 1 affected person 2 man 3 sexual type *adj* 4 colourful 5 happy 6 male 7 overindulgent 8 sexual

gaze *n* → 1 look *v* 2 look 3 wonder

gazebo *n* → room

gazette *n* → 1 list 2 newspaper 3 record *v* 4 list 5 publicise

gear *n* → 1 clothes 2 drug 3 equipment 4 groin 5 personal property 6 supplies 7 weapon *v* 8 borrow 9 equip 10 prepare *adj* 11 fashionable

GEIGER COUNTER *n* cloud chamber, counter, counter tube, dosimeter, scintillation counter, scintillometer

gel *n* → paste

geld *n* → 1 tax *v* 2 cut off 3 make infertile

gelding *n* → truncation

gelignite *n* → 1 ammunition 2 explosive

gem *n* → 1 good thing 2 jewel 3 jewellery

gender *n* → 1 class 2 sex

gene *n* → living thing

genealogy *n* → ancestry

GENERAL *adj* all, all-round, any, broad, catholic, ecumenical, every, universal, universalistic; **comprehensive,** across-the-board, all-embracing, blanket, broad-spectrum, collective, inclusive, omnibus, panoptic, panoramic, plenary, sweeping; **cosmopolitan,** azonic, global, worldwide; **exoteric,** broadcast, encyclical; **prevalent,** common, current, pandemic, prevailing, regnant, rife, ruling, ubiquitous, widespread

general *n* → 1 anaesthetic 2 ruler 3 servant 4 the public *adj* 5 customary 6 inclusive

GENERALISATION *n* abstraction, generality, universalisation; **conspectus,** bird's-eye view, broad spectrum, overview, panorama

GENERALISE *v* abstract, catholicise, universalise; **broadcast,** spread; **depersonalise,** impersonalise; **prevail,** be everywhere, obtain, rule

GENERALIST *n* all-rounder, jack-of-all-trades, one-man band, universalist

GENERALITY *n* catholicity, commonness, generalness, omnifariousness, prevailingness, prevalence, regnancy, ubiquitousness, ubiquity, universalism, universality, universalness; **cosmopolitanism,** cosmopolitism

generality *n* → 1 generalisation 2 inclusion 3 rule

GENERALLY *adv* across the board, everywhere, globally, high and low, sweepingly, ubiquitously, universally; **in general,** broadly, by and large, catholically, ecumenically, in the abstract, largely, on the whole, prevailingly, prevalently

general practitioner *n* → healer

generate *v* → 1 copy 2 create 3 make 4 reproduce

generation *n* → 1 age 2 ancestry 3 creation 4 duration 5 offspring 6 period 7 reproduction

generator *n* → 1 creator 2 procreator 3 vaporiser

generic *adj* → classificatory

GENEROSITY *n* bounteousness, bountifulness, charitableness, free-handedness, freeness, generousness, goodness, handsomeness, kindness, large-heartedness, largess, lavishness, liberality, liberalness, munificence, open-handedness, open-heartedness, princeliness, prodigality, soft-heartedness, unsparingness; **benefaction,** almsgiving, beneficence, bounty, charity, hospitality, philanthropy; **contribution,** act of charity, Christmas box, donation, favour, gift, good deed, good turn, largess, salvo, widow's mite; **open house,** liberty hall; **shout,** treat

GENEROUS *adj* beneficent, big, big-hearted, bounteous, bountiful, charitable, eleemosynary, free, free-handed, generous-spirited, grudgeless, handsome, hospitable, kindly, large, large-hearted, lavish, liberal, magnificent, munificent, open, open-handed, open-hearted, princely, prodigal, ungrudging, unsparing, unstinting; **touchable,** soft-hearted, susceptible

generous *adj* → 1 abundant 2 fertile 3 helpful 4 tasty 5 thick 6 tolerant 7 unselfish

GENEROUSLY *adv* a fair treat, a treat, beneficently, bounteously, bountifully, charitably, freely, handsomely, lavishly, liberally, magnanimously, magnificently, munificently, open-handedly, open-heartedly, prodigally, profusely, unsparingly, unstintingly, with open hand, without stint

genesis *n* → 1 creation 2 start

GENETIC *adj* genic, genotypic, idioplasmic, Mendelian; **hereditary,** descendible, hereditable, heritable, inheritable, inherited; **phyletic,** monophyletic, polyphyletic; **lineal,** direct, unilateral; **collateral,** indirect; **pedigreed,** blooded, well-bred; **purebred,** full-blooded, inbred, true, true-born, true-bred; **half-blooded,** half-breed, half-caste, miscegenetic; **hybrid,** crossbred, interbred, mongrel; **atavistic,** reversionary

genetic *adj* → creative

genetics *n* → evolution

genial *adj* → 1 friendly 2 happy 3 hot 4 kind 5 pleasant

genie *n* → mythical being

genitals *n* → groin

genius *n* → 1 character 2 characteristic 3 competence 4 influencer 5 intelligence 6 mind 7 mythical being 8 phantom 9 wise person

genocide *n* → 1 massacre 2 non-being 3 victimisation

genre *n* → class

genteel *adj* → 1 affected 2 courteous

gentile *n* → 1 foreigner 2 irreverent person *adj* 3 foreign 4 irreverent

gentility *n* → 1 aristocracy 2 courteousness 3 formality 4 good taste

gentle *v* → 1 make peace *adj* 2 courteous 3 kind 4 lenient 5 moderate 6 quiet

gentleman *n* → 1 aesthete 2 butler 3 courteous person 4 man

gentry *n* → aristocracy

genuflect *v* → 1 bow 2 pay homage 3 repose 4 worship

genuine *adj* → 1 correct 2 faithful 3 forthright 4 honest 5 true 6 truthful

genus *n* → class

geography *n* → textbook

geometry *n* → 1 mathematics 2 order 3 shape

geriatric *n* → 1 old people *adj* 2 aged

geriatrics *n* → age

germ *n* → 1 organism 2 poison 3 start

german *adj* → 1 apt 2 kindred

germane *adj* → 1 apt 2 topical

germinate *v* → 1 create 2 flower 3 give birth

gerrymander *n* → 1 dishonesty 2 electioneering *v* 3 act unfairly 4 politicise

gerund *n* → word

gestate *v* → 1 conceive 2 prepare

gestation *n* → pregnancy

gesticulate *v* → gesture

GESTURE *n* beau geste, business *(Theat.)*, gesticulation, motion, shrug, wave; **nod,** beck, beckon, eyewink, nictation, nictitation, wink; **mime,** charade, dumb show, pantomime; **thumbs up,** thumbs down, V-sign; **grimace,** mouth, mow *(Archaic)*, mug *(Brit.)*, smack

GESTURE *v* beckon, gesticulate, motion, point, recognise, shrug, wave; **mime,** pantomime, talk with one's hands; **cue,** peter *(Whist)*, telegraph one's punches, tick-tack *(Horseracing)*; **nod,** bob, give the nod, nictitate, shake one's head, wink; **grimace,** mouth, mow *(Archaic)*, mug *(Brit.)*, raise one's eyebrows

gesture *n* → move

GET *v* accept, accrue, acquire, adopt, be in receipt of, collect, come by, cop, gain, gather, have, obtain, pocket, receive, take off one's hands, win; **come to hand,** fall into one's hands, fall to one's lot; **inherit,** become heir to, come into, come into one's own, heir, step into a fortune, succeed; **receipt,** sign for; **be on the dole,** go on the dole, live on handouts

get *v* → 1 attack 2 be ill 3 buy 4 capture 5 cause 6 communicate 7 cook 8 gain 9 hear 10 kill 11 reproduce 12 understand

getaway *n* → 1 escape 2 starting line

get away *v* → 1 depart 2 escape 3 start

GET DIRTY *v* collect dust, foul up; **mildew,** moulder; **stagnate,** putrefy, rot; **draggle,** drabble; **pig it,** live in a pig sty; **wallow,** roll in the mud

GETTING *n* acceptance, acquirement, acquisition, attainment, collection, earning, gathering, landing, obtainment, procuration, procurement, purchase, receipt, receival, reception, recipience; **inheritance,** appanage, bequest, coinheritance, devise, entail, gift, heritage, heritance *(Archaic)*, jointure, legacy

geyser *n* → 1 heater 2 spring

ghastly *adj* → 1 colourless 2 deathlike 3 dreadful 4 ugly

ghetto *n* → 1 city 2 region

ghost *n* → 1 living 2 phantom 3 soul 4 writer *v* 5 haunt 6 write

GHOSTLY *adj* ghoulish, phantasmal, spectral, spirit, spiritual, supernatural; **angelic,** archangelic, celestial, cherubic, godly *(Archaic)*, heavenly, seraphic, spiritual; **nymphal,** chthonian *(Gk. Myth.)*, nymphean, satyric, sylphic; **impish,** elfin, faerie *(Archaic)*, fairy

ghoul *n* → 1 devil 2 thief 3 unpleasant person

GIANT *n* behemoth, biggie, boomer, bouncer, bumper, colossus, giantess, Goliath, hulk, husky *(U.S.)*, jumbo, Juno, leviathan, monster, monstrosity, snorter, the daddy of them all, the father and mother of a, titan, whopper

giant *n* → 1 expert 2 important person 3 mythical being 4 strong person 5 tall person *adj* 6 big 7 enormous 8 superior 9 tall

gibberish *n* → 1 code 2 nonsense 3 speaking

gibe *n* → 1 insult 2 joke 3 mockery *v* 4 mock

giddy *v* → 1 spin *adj* 2 capricious 3 feverish 4 foolish

GIFT *n* alms, bounty, Christmas hamper, Christmas stocking, compliment, contribution, donation, donative, favour, grant, handout, handsel, keepsake, largess, manna from heaven, mortuary *(Archaic)*, present, presentation, pressie, prezzie, remembrance, subscription; **offering,** oblation, offertory *(Rom. Cath. Ch.)*, peace-offering, sacrifice; **tip,** baksheesh, beer money, Christmas box, consideration, cumshaw, douceur, gratification *(Archaic)*, gratuity, pourboire; **prize,** award, reward; **bequest,** devise *(Law)*, dowry, endowment, foundation, grant, legacy, subsidy, subvention; **bonus issue,** bonus, capital distribution, capital issue, premium; **giveaway,** free sample, handout

gift *n* → 1 competence 2 easy thing 3 generosity 4 getting *v* 5 give

gifted *adj* → competent

gig *n* → 1 carriage 2 concert 3 contract 4 fool 5 job 6 look 7 looker 8 rowing boat 9 spear *v* 10 annoy 11 drive 12 fish 13 look 14 mock

gigantic *adj* → 1 big 2 enormous 3 tall

giggle *n* → 1 mirth *v* 2 laugh

gigolo *n* → 1 dancer 2 lover 3 prostitute

gild *v* → 1 coat 2 hide 3 redden 4 yellow

gilt *n* → 1 childless female 2 pig *adj* 3 coated 4 decorative 5 metallic 6 yellow

gilt-edged *adj* → 1 decorative 2 good

gimlet *n* → 1 piercer *v* 2 open

gimmick *n* → 1 expedient 2 illusion 3 method 4 stratagem

gin *n* → 1 brush 2 filter 3 woman *v* 4 start

ginger *n* → 1 liveliness 2 orange 3 red 4 vitality *v* 5 rob *adj* 6 brown 7 orange

gingerly *adj* → 1 cautious *adv* 2 affectedly

gipsy *n* → 1 traveller 2 wheel *adj* 3 travelling

giraffe *n* → tall person

gird *n* → 1 mockery *v* 2 enclose 3 restrain

girder *n* → 1 beam 2 shaft

girdle *n* → 1 edge 2 ring 3 tape 4 underwear *v* 5 cut 6 enclose 7 surround

girl *n* → 1 children 2 lover 3 servant 4 woman

girth *n* → belt

gist *n* → 1 authentication 2 essence 3 important thing 4 meaning

GIVE *v* accord, administer, assign, award, bestow, confer, cough up *(Colloq.)*, dedicate, donate, extend, gift, hand out, heap, make a present of, oblige with, portion, present, provide, sacrifice, shower, spare, tender; **contribute,** chip in, dob in, fork out, kick in, subscribe; **tip,** baksheesh, remember; **consign,** commit, delegate, deliver, dispense, dispose of, entrust, give into someone's keeping, hand in, hand over, make over, part with, pass into someone's charge, put into someone's hands, sign away, surrender, turn over to; **grant,** allow, concede, seise *(Law)*, vouchsafe, yield; **bequeath,** devise *(Law)*, dower, endow, leave, settle *(Law)*, vest, will; **sacrifice,** give up, offer, spend

give *n* → 1 pliability *v* 2 communicate 3 conjecture 4 occur 5 offer

GIVE BIRTH *v* bear, bring forth, bring into the world, deliver, drop a bundle *(Colloq.)*, have, produce, pullulate, teem *(Obs.)*; **lie in,** be confined; **labour,** travail; **abort,** cast, miscarry; **fruit,** berry, germinate, set; **drop,** calve, farrow, fawn, foal, kid, kitten, lamb, litter, pig, pup, spawn, throw, twin, whelp, yean; **slink,** slip; **brood,** clutch, cover *(Obs.)*, hatch, nest

given *adj* → 1 conjectural 2 known

GIVER *n* almoner *(Hist.)*, angel *(Colloq.)*, benefactor, benefactress, bestower, conferrer, contributor, dedicator, deviser, dispenser, donator, donor, endower, fairy godmother, fat cat *(Politics)*, grantor, imparter *(Archaic)*, legator, philanthropist, presenter, Santa Claus, testator, testatrix, tipper

gizzard *n* → abdomen

glacé *adj* → 1 coated 2 cold 3 smooth 4 sweet

glacial *adj* → cold

glacier *n* → ice

glad *v* → 1 make happy 2 please *adj* 3 agreeable 4 happy 5 pleased

gladden *v* → 1 make happy 2 please

gladiator *n* → fighter

glamour *n* → **1** allure **2** magic **3** pleasantness
glance *n* → **1** look **2** mineral **3** stroke *v* **4** see **5** shine
glare *n* → **1** angry act **2** brightness **3** look **4** polish *v* **5** be angry **6** look **7** shine *adj* **8** bright **9** smooth
glass *n* → **1** mirror **2** raw materials **3** smooth object **4** transparent substance *adj* **5** bright **6** brittle **7** hard
GLASSES *n* bifocals, eyeglasses, goggles, half-frames, lorgnette, pince-nez, specs, spectacles; **contact lenses,** hydrophilic contact lenses; **sunglasses,** dark glasses, polaroids, shades, sunnies; **goggles,** safety glasses; **monocle,** lorgnon. *See also* LENS
GLAZE *n* bloom, crust, finish, glost, laitance, lamella, patina, rust, salt glaze, scale, verdigris; **film,** filminess
glaze *n* → **1** ice **2** paint **3** polish *v* **4** coat **5** depict **6** smooth
gleam *n* → **1** fire **2** light **3** small amount *v* **4** appear **5** shine
glean *v* → **1** find out **2** gather **3** harvest
glee *n* → **1** happiness **2** joy **3** song
glen *n* → **1** gap **2** hollow
glib *adj* → easy
GLIDE *v* coast, free-fall, freewheel, glissade, run, skate, slide, slip, slur
glide *n* → **1** move **2** smoothness *v* **3** change **4** fly **5** move
glider *n* → **1** aircraft **2** dancer **3** pilot
glimmer *n* → **1** idea **2** light *v* **3** shine
glimpse *n* → **1** idea **2** light **3** look *v* **4** devise **5** see
glint *n* → **1** fire **2** light *v* **3** shine **4** speed
glisten *n* → **1** light *v* **2** shine
glitch *n* → hindrance
glitter *n* → **1** light **2** show **3** trimming *v* **4** shine **5** show off
gloat *v* → rejoice
globe *n* → **1** ball **2** emblem of office **3** heavenly body **4** representation *v* **5** round
globule *n* → bead
gloom *n* → **1** darkness **2** unhappiness *v* **3** make unhappy
gloomy *adj* → **1** distressing **2** dull **3** shadowy **4** unhappy
GLORIFY *v* aggrandise, chair, dignify, distinguish, emblaze *(Archaic)*, emblazon, exalt, extol, fame, honour, illuminate, illumine, lionise, put on the map, translate, uplift, upraise, venerate; **immortalise,** classicise
glorious *adj* → **1** beautiful **2** pleasant **3** reputable
glory *n* → **1** approval **2** contentedness **3** god **4** heaven **5** holy person **6** prayer **7** reputation **8** wealth *v* **9** brag **10** rejoice
gloss *n* → **1** appearances **2** brightness **3** clarification **4** commentary **5** shallow **6** written composition *v* **7** explain **8** illuminate
glossary *n* → **1** commentary **2** list **3** vocabulary
GLOVE *n* boxing glove, doeskins, gauntlet, kid gloves, mitt, mitten, muff, wristlet; **cuff,** finger, palm, thumb
glove *n* → armour
glow *n* → **1** emotion **2** fire **3** light *v* **4** be hot **5** feel emotion **6** shine
glower *n* → **1** angry act *v* **2** be angry **3** become irritated **4** misbehave
GLOWING *adj* ardent, candescent, flagrant *(Rare)*, incandescent
glucose *n* → sweetness
glue *n* → **1** adhesive *v* **2** stick together
glum *adj* → unhappy
glut *n* → **1** satisfaction **2** surplus *v* **3** bore **4** fill **5** oversupply **6** satisfy
gluten *n* → adhesive
glutinous *adj* → **1** sludgy **2** sticky
GLUTTON *n* beast, cormorant, garbage-guts, gorger, gormandiser, greedy-guts, gulper, guts, gutser, guzzle-guts, guzzler, hog, pig, trencherman; **epicure,** epicurean, gastronome, gourmand
glutton *n* → desirer
gnarled *adj* → **1** knobby **2** rough **3** stubborn
gnome *n* → **1** financier **2** proverb
gnomic *adj* → intelligent
go *n* → **1** attempt **2** bargain **3** health **4** period **5** sprightliness **6** success **7** vitality *v* **8** depart **9** die **10** extend **11** gamble **12** move **13** operate **14** sell **15** tend to **16** travel *adj* **17** operating
goad *n* → **1** incentive **2** piercer **3** propellant *v* **4** arouse **5** irritate
goal *n* → **1** aim **2** destination **3** finish
goanna *n* → piano
goat *n* → **1** fool **2** promiscuous person **3** sexual partner **4** sheep **5** voluptuary
go at *v* → attack
goatee *n* → beard
gob *n* → **1** excavation **2** mouth *v* **3** excrete
GO BACK *v* back, back-pedal, backwater, countermarch, ebb, recede, reflux, regorge, regress, regurgitate, retrocede, retrogress, reverse, track out *(Film)*; **return,** boomerang, do a Melba, get back, home, make a comeback, return to the fold, turn back; **backtrack,** retrace one's footsteps; **retreat,** back down, back off, back out, back-pedal, draw one's horns in, flinch, pull one's horns in, pull out, retire, retract, shrink, withdraw; **relapse,** backslide, degenerate; **revert,** hark back
gobble *n* → **1** birdcall *v* **2** absorb **3** capture **4** chirp **5** eat **6** gorge
gobbledegook *n* → language
go between *v* → mediate
go-between *n* → **1** delegate **2** mediator **3** procurer **4** wedding
GOD *n* atua *(N.Z.)*, daemon *(Greek Myth.)*, deity, demigod, demigoddess, demiurge, earthmother, goddess, lares, manes, mimen, penates, presence, snake-god, sun-god; **incarnation,** avatar, embodiment; **false god,** Baal, idol; **pantheon,** powers, thearchy; **godship,** blessedness, divineness, divinity, glory, godhead, godhood, godliness, grace, sacredness, sacrosanctity, sanctimony *(Obs.)*, sanctity, theomorphism
GOD *interj* à bas, begorrah *(Irish)*, by jingo, by Jove, Christ, Christ almighty, egad,

gadzooks *(Archaic)*, gosh, Jeez, Jesus, Jesus Christ, Od *(Archaic)*, perdie *(Archaic)*, zounds *(Archaic)*; **curses,** arse holes, blast, bloody hell, bugger, confound it, damn, damnation, darn, dash, drat, hell, hell's bells, hell's teeth, phut, pigs, the blazes, the hell with it, what the fuck, what the shit; **shit,** bugger me, bugger me dead, fuck me, fuck me dead, I'll be buggered, I'll be damned, I'll be hanged, I'll be jiggered, shit a brick; **bloody oath,** my colonial oath, my oath; **bull,** balls, bullshit, bullswool, crap; **curse you,** bash it, bore it up you, bugger you, fuck you, get fucked, get knotted, get shagged, go jump in the lake, go to blazes, go to buggery, go to hell, go to the devil, piss off, plague upon you *(Archaic)*, shove it, sod it, stick it, stick that for a lark, take a running jump, up cook's arse *(N.Z.)*, up you, upya, you can stick that for a joke; **may your chooks turn to emus,** and kick your dunny down

godchild *n* → child

goddess *n* → **1** beautiful person **2** god **3** good person **4** lover **5** woman

godly *adj* → **1** ghostly **2** reverent

godsend *n* → **1** good fortune **2** surpriser

goggle *n* → **1** look *v* **2** look

going *n* → **1** departure **2** stairs *adj* **3** growing **4** occurrent **5** operating **6** real

goitre *n* → bulge

gold *n* → **1** cash **2** mineral **3** recording **4** wealth **5** yellow *adj* **6** metallic **7** yellow

goldfield *n* → yard

gondola *n* → **1** aircraft **2** basket **3** rowing boat **4** watercraft

gone *adj* → **1** dead **2** excited **3** feverish **4** hopeless **5** lost **6** pregnant **7** weak

gong *n* → **1** award **2** emblem **3** warning *v* **4** warn

GOOD *n* advantage, benefit, boon, silver lining, virtue; **blessing,** benediction, benefaction, favour, mercy; **the common good,** commonweal, commonwealth *(Obs.)*, summum bonum, the public good, welfare

GOOD *adj* amazing, bang-up, bonny *(Scot.)*, bonzer, bosker, brave *(Archaic)*, braw *(Scot.)*, budgeree, capital, castor, copasetic *(U.S.)*, corking, crackerjack, cracking, crash-hot, daisy, dandy, decent, desirable, excellent, extra, extra grouse, extraordinaire, fabulous, famous, fantastic, fine, gas, gorgeous, grand, great, grouse, immense, kapai *(N.Z.)*, keen, magnificent, marvellous, nice, nobby, not bad, peachy, pie *(N.Z.)*, pretty *(Obs.)*, proper *(Archaic)*, ribuck *(Obs.)*, ripping, royal *(Obs.)*, ruby-dazzler, sensational, shining, slap-up, slashing, smashing, snifter, snodger *(Obs.)*, sollicking, spiffing *(Brit.)*, splendid, splendiferous, super, super-duper, superb, superfine, swell, swinging, terrif, terrific, tickety-boo *(Brit.)*, top, topping *(Brit.)*, trim *(Obs.)*, wizard *(Brit.)*, wonderful, you-beaut; **rare,** recherché, select, uncommon; **first-class,** A-1, ace, at one's best, best, champion, first-rate, five-star *(Brit.)*, front rank, front ranking, high-class, high-grade, in the first flight, in the front rank, of the first water, optimum, purler, supreme, tiptop, top-flight, top-hole *(Brit.)*, topnotch, unbeatable, up to par, up to scratch, up to standard, up to the knocker, up to the mark, world-class; **better,** superior; **ideal,** perfect; **premium,** bijou, blue-chip, choice, deluxe, elect, elegant, exquisite, finished, gilt-edged, goodly, hand-picked, polished, prime, select; **matchless,** especial, exceptional, irreplaceable, outstanding, peerless, prize; **sound,** A-OK *(U.S.)*, healthful, healthy, trim; **beneficial,** aidful, salutary; **hunky-dory,** all cush *(Obs.)*, all right, all serene, all Sir Garnet, fine and dandy, hunky, jake, jakerloo, okay, right, satisfactory; **sublime,** divine, dreamy, heavenly, insane, out of this world, unreal; **class,** golden, plummy, silk department, sterling, vintage; **helluva,** beaut, bully, hell of a, rum *(Archaic)*; **neat,** cool, nifty; **benevolent; virtuous**

good *n* → **1** usefulness *adj* **2** beautiful **3** competent **4** faithful **5** great **6** highly regarded **7** operating **8** perfect **9** satisfactory **10** superior **11** useable *interj* **12** well done

GOODBYE *interj* adieu, adios, aloha, arrivederci, au revoir, auf Wiedersehen, bon voyage, bonsoir, bye-bye, ciao, farewell, godspeed, good afternoon, good day, good evening, good morning, good night, hooroo, night-night, see you later, so long, ta-ta, vale, yickadee *(N.T.)*; **all aboard,** all ashore that's going ashore

goodbye *n* → **1** farewell *interj* **2** hello

GOOD FORTUNE *n* devil's own luck *(Brit.)*, happiness, luck, propitiousness, prosperity, rosiness, speed *(Archaic)*; **bonanza,** blessing, godsend, piece of good luck, snap, stroke of fortune, treasure-trove; **prosperousness,** blessedness, boom times, estate, flowering, fortunateness, luckiness, run of luck, serendipity, thriving, winning streak; **well-being,** weal *(Archaic)*, wealth *(Archaic)*, welfare; **break,** lucky streak

GOODNESS *n* choiceness, desirability, fineness, niceness; **excellence,** exceptionalness, exquisiteness, fabulousness, ideality, idealness, marvellousness, peerlessness, perfection, rareness, rarity, splendidness, supremeness, uncommonness, wonderfulness; **refinement,** class, elegance, finesse, finish, polish, selectness; **quality,** merit, preciousness, value, worth; **wholesomeness,** healthiness

GOOD PERSON *n* a bit of all right, a good sort, angel, beaut bloke, beaut sheila, bobby-dazzler, brick, card, cherub, Christian, cynosure of all eyes, demigod, dove, Galahad, goddess, good egg, good Joe *(U.S.)*, goodie, goody-goody, honey, impeccable, jewel, lion, model, one in a thousand, one of the best, perfection, rattler, ripsnorter, ruby-dazzler, saint, squarehead *(Prison)*, the pick of the bunch, the tops; **salt of the earth,** a good sport, ocker, one of nature's gentlemen, rough diamond, sportsman; **benefactor,** good and faithful servant, good master, just man, just woman, kind master, philanthropist, pillar of society, Robin Hood, worthy citizen; **hero,** amazon, champion, daredevil, great, hearty, heroine, one of the elite

GOODS *n* artefact, article, cargo, commodity, freight, merchandise, staple, stock, stock-in-trade, wares

GOOD TASTE *n* breeding, civilisation, civility *(Archaic)*, class, cultivation, culture, finesse, finish, genteelness, gentility, gentleness, politeness, refinement, seemliness, sensitivity; **taste,** appreciation, fancy, gusto, likes, liking, palate, penchant; **elegance,** bon ton, chic, choiceness, dapperness, dressiness, finery *(Rare)*, manners, poshness, savoir-faire, smartness, sophistication, style, tastefulness, tone, urbaneness, urbanity; **daintiness,** delicateness, fineness, rarefaction; **artistry,** virtuosity; **aesthetics,** delicacy, delicateness, discrimination, judgment, sensibility

GOOD THING *n* a bit of all right, beaut, beauty, bobby-dazzler, bottler, corker, cracker, crackerjack, daisy, dandy, dilly, dinkum, dinky, dinnyhayser, front-ranker, gas, gasser, honey, hot stuff, humdinger, just what the doctor ordered, knockout, miracle, peach, plum, purler, rube *(N.Z.)*, ruby-dazzler, sensation, sollicker, swan, topper, treasure, trimmer; **showpiece,** aristocrat, beauty, choice, flower, gem, jewel, masterpiece, masterwork, pearl, pink, pride, Rolls Royce; **beau ideal,** idea, ideal; **bijou,** titbit; **better,** superior; **the best,** acme, cap, climax, culmination, high point, high spot, ne plus ultra, the full two bob, the most, the mostest, tiptop, ultimate; **one in a million,** one in a thousand, the ant's pants, the bee's knees, the cat's pyjamas, the cat's whiskers, the glassy, the greatest, the icing on the cake, the oil *(N.Z.)*

goodwill *n* → **1** capital **2** friendship **3** happiness **4** kindness

goose *n* → **1** dissonance **2** fool **3** pat **4** stupid person

gore *n* → **1** bodily discharge **2** clothes **3** paste *v* **4** perforate

GORGE *v* be like vultures, bog in, cram, eat fit to bust, eat like a horse, gluttonise, gormandise, guts, have hollow legs, like one's food, make a pig of oneself, overeat, raven *(Obs.)*, stodge, stuff; **devour,** bolt, gobble, gulp, guzzle, ingurgitate, weigh into, wolf. *See also* EAT

gorge *n* → **1** binge **2** entrance **3** gap **4** meal **5** neck **6** rear *v* **7** eat **8** obstruct

gorgeous *adj* → **1** beautiful **2** good **3** pleasant

gorilla *n* → **1** popularity **2** recording **3** ugly person **4** violent person

gormandise *v* → gorge

gormless *adj* → stupid

gosling *n* → animal offspring

GO SLOWLY *v* amble, coast, crawl, drag, inch, plod, run like a hairy goat, stalk, trundle; **lag,** compound *(Horseracing)*, fall behind, run dead *(Horseracing)*, straggle, trail; **tarry,** be slow off the mark, dally, dawdle, delay, demur *(Obs.)*, hang fire, hesitate, linger, loiter, lounge about, potter, saunter, stall for time, stay, stroll, take one's time; **work to rule,** drag the chain

gospel *n* → **1** belief **2** certain thing **3** truth *adj* **4** religious

Gospel *n* → scripture

gossamer *n* → **1** thread **2** transparent substance *adj* **3** ethereal **4** light **5** thin

GOSSIP *n* gossipmonger, newsmonger, quidnunc, scandalmonger, whisperer; **talebearer,** dobber, informer, sneak, taleteller, tattler, tattletale, telltale, tittle-tattle, tittle-tattler

gossip *n* → **1** friend **2** news **3** parent **4** speaker **5** talk **6** talker *v* **7** noise abroad **8** talk

gouge *n* → **1** chisel **2** furrow *v* **3** cut **4** dig **5** hollow

gourd *n* → plant

gourmet *n* → aesthete

gout *n* → **1** cramp **2** small amount

govern *v* → **1** control **2** legislate **3** manage

governess *n* → teacher

government *n* → **1** authority **2** legislation **3** management

governor *n* → **1** boss **2** controlling device **3** manager **4** parent **5** ruler

governor-general *n* → agent

gown *n* → **1** dress **2** uniform

grab *n* → **1** hold **2** takings *v* **3** capture **4** influence **5** rob

grace *n* → **1** artistry **2** forgiving **3** god **4** gratefulness **5** interval **6** kindness **7** pity **8** pleasantness

Grace *n* → **1** mister **2** mythical being

graceful *adj* → **1** beautiful **2** forgiving **3** pleasant

gracious *adj* → **1** affected **2** courteous **3** fortunate **4** kind **5** pitying *interj* **6** oh

GRADATION *n* shading; **step,** degree, notch, peg, pitch, point, remove, stage, strain *(Rare)*; **graduation,** calibration, scale; **measurement system,** Celsius scale, centimetre-gram-second system, Fahrenheit scale, foot-pound-second system, imperial system, International System of Units, metric system; **unit,** denomination, fundamental unit, indication, measure, size

gradation *n* → **1** colour **2** series

GRADE *n* class, Dan, Kyu, level, order, rank, year; **level,** plane; **ranking,** footing, rate, standing, station, status; **shade,** nuance, shadow

grade *n* → **1** class **2** slope *v* **3** change **4** class **5** graduate **6** level **7** measure **8** reproduce **9** slope **10** smooth

gradient *n* → **1** ascent **2** curve **3** slope *adj* **4** sloping **5** walking

gradual *n* → **1** answer **2** breviary **3** musical score

GRADUALLY *adv* a little at a time, bit by bit, by degrees, inch by inch, little by little, step by step; **to some degree,** a bit, in some measure, somewhat, to some extent

GRADUATE *v* calibrate, divide, measure, scale; **grade,** class, rank, rate; **shade,** fade, melt into

graduate *n* → **1** bottle **2** intellectual **3** prisoner **4** pupil *v* **5** change

graffiti *n* → **1** drawing **2** writing form

graft *n* → **1** dishonesty **2** insertion **3** profit **4** toil *v* **5** insert **6** join **7** make an effort **8** reproduce **9** substitute **10** swindle

grail *n* → shrine

grain *n* → **1** bead **2** break **3** character **4** colour **5** fuel **6** hide **7** line **8** matter **9** powder **10** roughness **11** small amount *v* **12** bare **13** powder **14** roughen

grammar *n* → **1** essence **2** textbook

GRAMMATICAL ERROR *n* abusage, barbarism, error, illiteracy *(Rare)*, impropriety, lapsus linguae, malapropism, misusage, mixed metaphor, slip, solecism, unfelicity; **faulty language,** anacoluthia, anacoluthon, bad grammar, lack of concord, mispunctuation, misspelling, slipslop

gramophone *n* → sound system

grampus *n* → parent

granary *n* → **1** field **2** stable **3** storehouse

grand *adj* → **1** affected **2** beautiful **3** enormous **4** good **5** important **6** musical **7** reputable **8** tall **9** thorough

grandiloquent *adj* → eloquent

grandiose *adj* → **1** affected **2** beautiful **3** bombastic **4** eloquent **5** enormous

grandparent *n* → parent

grandstand *v* → **1** brag **2** show off

grant *n* → **1** charity **2** gift *v* **3** assent to **4** give

granular *adj* → **1** powdery **2** round **3** small

granulate *v* → **1** powder **2** round

granule *n* → **1** bead **2** matter **3** small amount

grape *n* → **1** ammunition **2** purple **3** red

graphic *adj* → **1** artistic **2** depictive

grapnel *n* → **1** anchor **2** holder **3** piercer

grapple *n* → **1** anchor **2** fight **3** hold *v* **4** fight **5** hold

grasp *n* → **1** competence **2** hold **3** knowledge **4** ownership *v* **5** attempt **6** fasten **7** hold **8** know

grasping *n* → **1** holding *adj* **2** avaricious **3** holding **4** predatory **5** striving

grass *n* → **1** farmland **2** informant **3** marijuana **4** plant **5** revealer *v* **6** cover **7** lower **8** report on

GRASSLAND *n* down, heath, meadow, moor, pampas, prairie, savanna, steppe, tundra

grate *n* → **1** covering **2** dissonance **3** fireplace **4** rack **5** screen *v* **6** be dissonant **7** displease **8** powder **9** rub

GRATEFUL *adj* appreciative, appreciatory, thankful; **thankyou,** recognitive, recognitory; **obliged,** beholden, indebted, much obliged; **thankworthy**

GRATEFULNESS *n* appreciation, appreciativeness, gratitude, hearty thanks, thankfulness, thanks; **thanksgiving,** celebration, eucharist, grace, grace before meals, praises; **acknowledgement,** bow, bread-and-butter letter, credit, credit line, recognition, sense of obligation, thankyou, tribute, vote of thanks; **requital,** recognition of one's services, return, return favour, reward, thankyou present, tip, token of one's gratitude

gratify *v* → **1** pay **2** please **3** satisfy

grating *n* → **1** interlacement **2** screen *adj* **3** abrasive **4** dissonant

gratis *adj* → **1** cheap **2** unpaid *adv* **3** cheaply

gratitude *n* → gratefulness

gratuitous *adj* → **1** agreeable **2** cheap **3** illogical **4** unfair

gratuity *n* → **1** gift **2** income

GRAVE *n* Davy Jones's locker, resting place; **tomb,** burial chamber, catacomb, confession *(Eccles.)*, crypt, cubiculum, dolmen, hypogeum, mastaba *(Egyptian Architecture)*, mausoleum, monument *(Obs.)*, sepulchre, sepulture *(Archaic)*, vault; **burial mound,** barrow, kurgan, tumulus; **headstone,** cairn, gravestone, ledger, stele, stone, tombstone; **cenotaph,** memorial, war memorial. *See also* CEMETERY

grave *v* → **1** clean **2** cut **3** engrave *adj* **4** important **5** sombre

GRAVECLOTHES *n* cerements, winding sheet; **mourning clothes,** half-mourning, mourning, sables, weeds

gravel *n* → rock

gravitate *v* → attract

gravitation *n* → **1** attraction **2** descent **3** point of view

gravity *n* → **1** attraction **2** importance **3** sombreness

gravy *n* → profit

graze *n* → **1** contact **2** cut **3** rubbing **4** touch *v* **5** contact **6** cut **7** farm **8** rub **9** touch

grazier *n* → farmer

grease *n* → **1** dirt **2** fat *v* **3** facilitate **4** oil

GREAT *adj* appreciable, big, biggish, considerable, extended, full-scale, good, good-sized, goodly, hearty, high, horse, king, king-size, large, large-scale, largish, mickle *(Scot.)*, mighty, much, muckle *(Scot.)*, old-man, respectable, sensible, sizeable, spacious, substantial, tidy; **abundant,** ample, considerable, copious, goodly, handsome, luxuriant, plenteous, plentiful, pretty, princely, rich, round, square, substantial, tall, tidy

great *n* → **1** good person **2** important person *adj* **3** big **4** enormous **5** good **6** important **7** reputable **8** superior *adv* **9** well *interj* **10** well done

GREATLY *adv* appreciably, considerably, in a big way, mightily, on a large scale, widely; **mostly,** for the most part, generally, in the main, largely, mainly, maximally, most, principally, substantially, to a degree; **much,** a lot, far, far and away, lots; **galore,** as all get-out, like anything, like buggery, like hell, like the devil, till it hurts, to the skies; **abundantly,** amply, by a long chalk, by far, by half, considerably, copiously, hand over fist, handsomely, in bulk, largely, luxuriantly, no end, opulently, richly, substantially, substantively, thickly, widely; **and how,** and a half, and then some; **absolutely,** downright, exceedingly, extremely, far and away, fully, hollow, ineffably, insuperably, invincibly, monumentally, out and away, out and out, overwhelmingly, perfectly, plain, plumb, quite, spaciously, stark, supremely, surpassing *(Obs. Poetic)*, surpassingly, toweringly, unutterably, utterly; **awesomely,** devastatingly, extra-specially, fabulously, fantastically, frighteningly, frightfully, horribly, impossibly, phenomenally, portentously, prodigiously, shockingly, stupendously; **grandiosely,** big, grandly, regally; **massively,** bulkily, solidly

GREED *n* avarice, avidity, concupiscence, cupidity, lust, rapacity; **greediness,** esurience, esuriency, gluttonousness, gluttony, hoggishness, over-eating, piggery, piggishness, swinishness; **voracity,** insatiability, ravening *(Obs.)*, ravenousness, voraciousness, wolfishness; **epicureanism,** gourmandise. *See also* OVERINDULGENCE

greed *n* → desire

GREEDY *adj* devouring, insatiable, rapacious, ravening *(Obs.)*, ravenous, voracious; **gluttonous,** gutsy, hoggish, hoglike, open-mouthed, piggish, swinish; **esurient,** epicurean, gastronomic, lickerish *(Archaic)*. *See also* OVERINDULGENT

GREEN *n* emerald, grass-green, jade green, leek green, vert *(Heraldry)*; **sea green,** aqua, aquamarine, beryl, Nile green, turquoise; **yellow-green,** chartreuse, lime-green, pea green, pistachio; **apple green,** almond green, celadon; **khaki,** bottle green, jungle green, olive, olive green; **grey-green,** mignonette, reseda, sage-green

GREEN *adj* glaucous, greenish, prasine, virescent, viridescent; **verdant,** grassy, green, leafy, verdurous

green *n* → **1** garden **2** sportsground *adj* **3** artless **4** colourless **5** floral **6** green **7** ignorant **8** incompetent **9** innocent **10** living **11** memorable **12** new **13** raw **14** separate **15** sour **16** youthful

greenery *n* → **1** garden **2** greenness

greengrocer *n* → **1** drug dealer **2** insect

greenhouse *n* → **1** breeding ground **2** garden

GREENNESS *n* verdancy, verdure, verdurousness, virescence, viridescence, viridity; **greenery,** verdure; **verdigris; green pigment,** bice, chlorophyll, chrome green, green verditer, Paris green, terre-verte, verditer, viridian

greet *v* → be sociable

GREETING *n* beck *(Scot.)*, bow, cheerio call, hongi *(N.Z.)*, salaam, salutation, the glad hand; **regards,** compliment, remembrances; **introduction,** debut, knockdown, presentation, presentment

greeting *adj* → sociable

gregarious *adj* → **1** accumulative **2** sociable

gremlin *n* → **1** fairy **2** mischief-maker

grenade *n* → ammunition

GREY *n* ash-grey, iron-grey; **charcoal-grey,** gunmetal, slate; **dove colour; drab,** beige, dun, fuscous, isabel, mouse-dun, putty, stone, taupe; **merle; pearl,** off-white, oyster white, pearl blue, pearl grey; **French grey,** sage-green; **grey-blue,** Copenhagen blue, steel blue, steel grey; **grizzle; grisaille; greyness,** hoariness, leadenness, lividness; **silver,** argent, frostiness, silveriness

GREY *adj* ash-grey, ashen, ashy, cinereous, greyish, grizzly; **blue-grey,** livid, slaty; **dove-coloured,** columbine; **dapple-grey,** merle; **leaden,** dusty, frosty, leady; **smoky,** fuliginous; **drab,** beige, dun, fulvous, isabel, putty; **pearl-grey,** griseous, off-white, pearl, pearly; **sage-green; silver,** argent, iron, penumbral, silvern *(Archaic)*, silvery, steel

grey *n* → **1** coinage *adj* **2** aged **3** dark **4** grey-haired **5** hairy **6** sombre

GREY-HAIRED *adj* canescent, grey, grey-headed, greying, grizzled, grizzly, hoar *(Archaic)*, hoary, pepper-and-salt, silver-haired, white-haired

greyhound *n* → **1** tobacco **2** watercraft

grid *n* → **1** bicycle **2** interlacement **3** starting line

griddle *v* → cook

grief *n* → **1** grieving **2** penitence

grievance *n* → complaint

GRIEVE *v* anguish, bleed for, deplore, grieve over, lament, pine *(Archaic)*, regret; **bemoan,** bewail, elegise, threnodise, weep over; **cry,** bawl, blub, blubber, boohoo, cry one's heart out, pipe one's eye, shed tears, snivel, snuffle, sob, tune one's pipes, weep; **moan,** croon *(Scot. Irish)*, groan, keen, sigh, ululate, wail; **whine,** howl, whimper; **mourn,** give someone a good send-off, hold a wake for, tangi *(N.Z.)*; **wear black,** don widows's weeds, go into mourning, wear sackcloth and ashes; **wring one's hands,** beat one's breast, rend one's garments; **half-mast the flag**

grieve *v* → **1** be unhappy **2** make unhappy **3** repress **4** wrong

GRIEVER *n* lamenter, mourner, sorrower; **weeper,** bawler, blubberer, cry-baby, sniveller, snuffler, wailer; **keener,** crooner *(Scot. Irish)*, monodist, threnodist; **groaner,** sigher; **pietà**

GRIEVING *n* broken heart, dole *(Archaic)*, dolour, grief, lamentation, misery, moan *(Archaic)*, mournfulness, sadness, sorrow, woe; **lament,** cri de coeur, plaint *(Archaic)*; **elegy,** coronach, dead march, dirge, epicedium, jeremiad, monody, taps *(U.S. Mil.)*, threnody; **wake,** exequies, tangi *(N.Z.)*, vigil; **mourning,** armband, black, half-mourning, hatband, sables, weeds. *See also* CRY

GRIEVING *adj* cut up, desolate, grief-stricken, heartbroken, lamenting, mourning, sorrowful, sorrowing; **mournful,** dolorous, lugubrious, plaintive, woebegone, woeful; **crying,** blubbering, snivelly, sobbing, tearful, watery, weeping; **groaning,** ululant, wailful, wailsome; **elegiac,** epicedial, epicedian, exequial, threnodial, threnodic

grievous *adj* → **1** bad **2** difficult **3** distressing **4** intense **5** repressive **6** unhappy

grill *n* → 1 kitchen 2 stove *v* 3 cook 4 heat 5 punish 6 question

grille *n* → 1 interlacement 2 opening

griller *n* → stove

grim *adj* → 1 dreadful 2 ferocious 3 frightening 4 sombre 5 strict 6 ugly

grimace *n* → 1 distortion 2 gesture *v* 3 gesture

grime *n* → 1 dirt *v* 2 dirty

grin *n* → 1 distortion 2 mirth *v* 3 laugh

grind *n* → 1 battler 2 dissonance 3 learning 4 pupil 5 sexual intercourse 6 toil 7 walk *v* 8 be dissonant 9 make an effort 10 persist 11 powder 12 rub 13 smooth

grindstone *n* → 1 bore 2 powderer 3 smoother

grip *n* → 1 bag 2 competence 3 hold 4 job 5 transporter *v* 6 capture 7 engross 8 fasten 9 hold

gripe *n* → 1 complaint 2 hold *v* 3 capture 4 complain 5 fasten 6 hold 7 pain 8 swerve

grisly *adj* → 1 dreadful 2 frightening 3 ugly

grist *n* → powder

grit *n* → 1 courage 2 persistence 3 powder *v* 4 be dissonant

grizzle *n* → 1 grey 2 hair *v* 3 complain

groan *n* → 1 boo 2 cry 3 dissonance 4 quiet sound *v* 5 be dissonant 6 grieve

grog *n* → alcohol

groggy *adj* → 1 drunk 2 unconscious 3 weak

GROIN *n* brush, crotch, mons pubis, mons veneris, mount of Venus, muff, pubes, pubic hair; **genitals,** genitalia, meat, nasties *(Brit.)*, perineum, private parts, privates, privy parts, pudenda; **female genitalia,** cervix, cherry, clitoris, Fallopian tubes, hymen, labia, maidenhead, nympha, ovary, tubes, uterus, womb, yoni; **vulva,** box, crack, cunt, date, dot, fanny, fork, furburger, gash, gear, growl, hole, honey pot, michael, mick, pudendum, pussy, quim, slit, snatch, tail, twat, vagina; **male genitalia,** cod, epididymis, foreskin, glans, linga, manhood, prepuce, prostate gland, scrotum, sporting equipment, vas deferens; **testicles,** aggots, balls, bollocks, cobblers, fun bags, gonads, goolies, knackers, Niagara falls, nuts, spermaries, stones *(Obs.)*, testes; **penis,** cock, dick, dickie, ding, dong, donger, dragon, fang, ferret, John, John Thomas, knob, mutton, old boy, old fellow, old man, one-eyed trouser snake, Percy, pizzle, prick, roger, short arm, tassel, the virile member, tonk, tool, wick, willie; **erection,** beef bayonet, beef bugle, fat, hard on, horn, phallus, pork sword, rod, shaft, stiff, stiffy, the bishop

groom *n* → 1 butler 2 spouse *v* 3 care for 4 prepare 5 tidy

groomsman *n* → 1 helper 2 wedding

groove *n* → 1 custom 2 furrow 3 niche 4 passageway 5 recording *v* 6 furrow

groovy *adj* → pleasurable

grope *v* → 1 bungle 2 eroticise 3 touch

groper *n* → Australian

gross *v* → 1 gain *adj* 2 big 3 fat 4 immoral 5 sickening 6 solid 7 thick 8 thorough 9 ugly 10 vulgar

grotesque *n* → 1 strange person 2 ugly person *adj* 3 distorted 4 strange 5 ugly

grotto *n* → cave

grotty *adj* → 1 bad 2 dirty 3 useless

grouch *n* → 1 complainer 2 irritable person *v* 3 complain 4 irritate

ground *n* → 1 cause 2 freight 3 land *v* 4 bowl over 5 electrify 6 initiate 7 prohibit 8 restrict 9 teach *adj* 10 bottom 11 land 12 powdered 13 rough

grounding *n* → knowledge

groundless *adj* → illogical

group *n* → 1 armed forces 2 class 3 gathering 4 mixture 5 musical band 6 society *v* 7 gather 8 inquire into

grouse *n* → 1 complaint *v* 2 complain *adj* 3 good

grout *n* → 1 adhesive 2 filler *v* 3 fill

grove *n* → forest

GROVEL *v* be at another's beck and call, bend before, bow and scrape, bow to, chum up to, eat crow *(U.S.)*, eat humble pie, eat one's words, eat out of someone's hand, fawn, get gravel rash, kneel to, kowtow to, lick the dust, piss in someone's pocket, pocket one's pride, prostrate oneself, slaver, smarm, stoop *(Rare)*, toady, truckle

grovel *v* → 1 be meek 2 obey

GROW *v* bloom, develop, rise, unfold; **accumulate,** accrete, accrue; **branch,** branch out, bush, extend, spread; **distend,** aggrandise, amplify, balloon, enlarge, expand, hypertrophy; **outgrow,** outreach; **overgrow,** dispread *(Archaic)*, grow like Topsy *(Colloq.)*, mushroom, outspread, outstretch, overreach, overrun, overspread, run wild; **advance,** progress, snowball. *See also* FLOWER

grow *v* → 1 become greater 2 farm 3 reproduce

GROWING *adj* anabolic, crescent, developing, going, proliferous, regenerative, rising; **accumulative,** accretive, cumulative; **developmental,** evolutional, evolutionary; **excrescent,** fungoid, gallic, intumescent, scirrhoid, scirrhous; **distensible,** distensile, enlargeable; **flourishing,** fulminant, hypertrophic, luxuriant, overgrown, rank, sturdy, wanton *(Poetic)*; **germinant,** germinative

growl *n* → 1 animal call 2 boom 3 groin *v* 4 be angry 5 call (of animals) 6 complain 7 menace

growth *n* → 1 cancer 2 enlargement 3 finished product

grub *n* → 1 food 2 insect *v* 3 dig 4 eat 5 farm 6 feed 7 make an effort 8 study

grubby *adj* → 1 dirty 2 unkempt

grudge *v* → 1 be angry 2 be jealous of 3 be unfriendly 4 be unwilling

gruel *v* → 1 be strict 2 punish 3 tire

gruelling *adj* → 1 strict 2 tiring

gruesome *adj* → 1 dreadful 2 ugly

gruff *adj* → 1 discourteous 2 quiet

grumble *n* → 1 boom 2 complaint 3 quiet sound *v* 4 be ungrateful 5 complain 6 speak

grumpy *adj* → 1 discontented 2 irritable

grunt *n* → 1 animal call 2 quiet sound *v* 3 call (of animals)

guarantee *n* → 1 contract 2 deed 3 insurance 4 surety

guaranty *n* → 1 contract 2 surety

guard *n* → 1 conservationist 2 gaoler 3 protector 4 safety *v* 5 imprison 6 protect 7 secure

guarded *adj* → 1 cautious 2 protected

guardian *n* → 1 conservationist 2 minder 3 protector *adj* 4 protective

guerilla *n* → 1 combat troops 2 dissident

guess *n* → 1 computation 2 conjecture *v* 3 conjecture 4 predict

guest *n* → 1 occupant 2 visitor

guffaw *n* → 1 mirth *v* 2 laugh

GUIDANCE *n* direction, guideline, recommendation, suasion; **consultation,** reference, referral; **advice,** briefing, counsel, counsel of perfection, words of wisdom; **hint,** piece of advice, pointer, points, suggestion, tip, word of advice; **exhortation,** charge, injunction, instruction, moralising; **criticism,** constructive criticism, correction, corrective; **admonition,** admonishment, earful, expostulation, protestation, warning

guidance *n* → teaching

GUIDE *n* assessor, consulter, director, exhorter, mentor; **adviser,** advocate, advocator, amicus curiae, consigliore, consultant, councillor, counsellor; **authority,** advisory body, brains trust, oracle, sage; **careers adviser,** extension worker *(N.Z.)*, family doctor, farm consultant *(Agric.)*, marriage guidance counsellor; **confidant,** confessor, father confessor; **admonisher,** corrector, expostulator, monitor, warner; **back-seat driver,** kibitzer *(U.S.)*

GUIDE *v* advise, advocate, commend, counsel, give advice, kibitz *(U.S.)*, prescribe, recommend; **suggest,** move, propose, submit; **exhort,** charge, urge; **admonish,** advise against, expostulate, put someone straight, remonstrate, set someone straight, warn

GUIDE *adj* advisory, assessorial, consultative, consulting, deliberative; **exhortative,** hortative, recommendatory, suasive, suasory; **admonitory,** correctional, corrective, directive, expostulatory, moralising, warning

guide *n* → 1 controlling device 2 indicator 3 informant 4 leader 5 model 6 reference book 7 teacher *v* 8 accompany 9 direct 10 introduce 11 manage

guild *n* → 1 institute 2 trade union

guile *n* → cunning

guillotine *n* → 1 cutter 2 means of killing 3 restraining order *v* 4 cut 5 execute 6 kill 7 restrain

GUILT *n* blood guilt, blood-guiltiness, complicity, fault, guilt by association, guiltiness; **blameworthiness,** censurableness, criminality, damnableness, delinquency; **shame,** ashamedness, contriteness, contrition, embarrassment, peccavi, qualms

guilt *n* → 1 accountability 2 penitence

GUILTILY *adv* damningly, in flagrante delicto, red-handed; **ashamedly,** contritely, repentantly

GUILTY *adj* at fault, blood-guilty, blood-stained, double-dyed, faulty *(Obs.)*, in fault, in the wrong, nocent, to blame; **damned,** impure, unaneled; **damnable,** condemnable, criminal, delinquent, punishable, reprehensible

guilty *adj* → penitent

guineapig *n* → tester

guise *n* → 1 appearances 2 fashion 3 method *v* 4 hide

gulf *n* → 1 bay 2 depth 3 gap *v* 4 absorb

gull *n* → 1 artiess person 2 victim *v* 3 trick

gullet *n* → 1 channel 2 excavation 3 neck

gullible *adj* → artless

gully *n* → 1 channel 2 gap 3 hollow

gulp *n* → 1 bit 2 eating *v* 3 absorb 4 eat 5 gorge

gum *n* → 1 adhesive 2 mouth 3 powder 4 timber

gumboot *n* → boot

gumption *n* → 1 vitality 2 wisdom

GUN *n* automatic, equaliser *(Colloq.)*, firearm, firelock, firer, flintlock, gat, ironmongery, joint, matchlock, muzzle-loader, over-under, piece, pump action, rapid-firer, repeater, roscoe, semiautomatic, shooter, shooting iron, side-arms, small arms, smoothbore; **pistol,** automatic pistol, bulldog, Colt, derringer, hand gun, heater *(U.S. Colloq.)*, horse pistol, iron *(Brit. Colloq.)*, revolver, rod, six-shooter; **rifle,** armalite, automatic rifle, breech-loader, carabin, carbine, chassepot, elephant gun, Enfield, Mauser, Winchester rifle; **shotgun,** chokebore, double *(Colloq.)*, fowling-piece, petronel, pump gun, sawn-off shotgun, side by side *(Colloq.)*; **machine-gun,** Bofors gun, Bren gun, Gatling gun, Lewis gun, Owen gun, pompom, pounder, sten gun, Thomson machine gun, Tommy gun *(Colloq.)*; **cannon,** basilisk, Big Bertha, bombard, chase-gun, chaser, culverin, falconet, field-gun, field-piece, heavy metal, howitzer, mortar, stern-chaser, trench mortar; **musket,** arquebus, blunderbuss, fusil, hackbut, harquebus; **blowgun,** blowpipe; **airgun,** air-rifle, BB gun, daisy gun, pea-shooter; **ray gun; spear gun; swivel gun; toy gun,** pop gun, water-pistol

gun *n* → 1 expert 2 fighter 3 hunter 4 rowing boat *v* 5 accelerate 6 hunt *adj* 7 competent

GUNFIRE *n* firepower, flak; **gunshot,** penetration, snapshot; **bombardment,** barrage, blitz, broadside, burst, dispersion, fusillade, round, salvo, whip

gunny *n* → 1 bag 2 excavation

gunpowder *n* → 1 ammunition 2 drink 3 explosive

gunwale *n* → 1 edge 2 side

gunyah *n* → shelter

gurgle *n* → 1 boom 2 quiet sound *v* 3 bubble

guru *n* → 1 enlightener 2 wise person

gush *n* → 1 bleeding 2 flow 3 stream 4 waffle *v* 5 feel emotion 6 flow 7 waffle

gusset *n* → 1 insert *v* 2 support

gust *n* → 1 flow 2 outburst 3 wind

gusto *n* → 1 enthusiasm 2 good taste 3 pleasure

gut *n* → 1 abdomen 2 gap *v* 3 cut off 4 destroy 5 fire 6 rob *adj* 7 emotional

gutless *adj* → 1 cowardly 2 powerless

gutsy *adj* → 1 courageous 2 greedy 3 intoxicating 4 tasty

gutter *n* → 1 channel 2 drain 3 frame 4 furrow 5 pigsty 6 working class *v* 7 flow

guttural *n* → dissonance

guy *n* → 1 butt 2 lover 3 man 4 portrait 5 steadier 6 ugly person *v* 7 hold 8 mock 9 steady

guzzle *v* → gorge

gym *n* → sportsground

gymkhana *n* → contest

gymnasium *n* → sportsground

gymnastic *adj* → athletic

gymnastics *n* → exercise

gynaecology *n* → healing

gyp *n* → 1 dishonesty 2 trick 3 trickster *v* 4 cheat 5 swindle

gypsy *n* → traveller

gyrate *v* → spin

gyre *n* → 1 circle 2 rotation

gyroscope *n* → 1 spin 2 steadier 3 wheel

Hh

habit *n* → **1** character **2** custom **3** drug addiction **4** point of view **5** shape **6** uniform *v* **7** clothe **8** inhabit
habitat *n* → **1** dwelling **2** surroundings
habitation *n* → dwelling
HABITUATE *v* acclimatise, accustom, condition, familiarise, harden, inure, naturalise, season
habituate *v* → be present
HABITUATION *n* acclimatisation, conditioning, hardening, inurement, naturalisation, seasoning, training
habitué *n* → visitor
hack *n* → **1** axe **2** car **3** cut **4** kick **5** platform **6** rack **7** shelf **8** writer *v* **9** cut **10** damage **11** dislike **12** kick **13** ride **14** roughen *adj* **15** mediocre
hackle *n* → **1** animal's coat **2** feather *v* **3** cut
hackneyed *adj* → **1** boring **2** customary **3** mediocre
hackwork *n* → work
haemoglobin *n* → colour
haemorrhage *n* → **1** bleeding *v* **2** bleed
hag *n* → **1** bad person **2** fairy **3** old people **4** ugly person **5** worshipper
haggard *adj* → ugly
haggle *v* → **1** annoy **2** contest **3** trade
HAIL *interj* all hail, good on you, here's to, long life to, long live, viva
HAIR *n* flue, fluff, fuzz, lanugo, pile, shag; **filament,** penicil, whisker, wire; **bristle,** arista, chaeta, gare, seta, setula, vibrissa, villus; **hair of the head,** bush, combings, dreadlocks, frizz, head, locks, mane, mat, mop, thatch, tousle *(Rare)*; **grizzle,** snow; **curl,** kiss-curl, lock, pin-curl, quiff, ringlet, strand, tag, tress *(Archaic)*; **elflock,** cowlick, feather, forelock, foretop *(Obs.)*, lovelock, topknot, tourbillion, widow's peak; **bang,** bob, braid, bun, bunches, chignon, cue, ducktail, fringe, horse tail, lovelock, pigtail, plait, plat, pompadour, ponytail, puff, queue, tail, topknot, tress *(Archaic)*; **eyebrow,** cilia, eyelash, falsies; **pubes,** short and curlies, short hairs; **blonde,** ash-blond, coppernob, coppertop, fair head, goldilocks, lemonhead, peroxide blonde, platinum blonde, redhead, strawberry blonde, towhead; **brunette;** **whitebeard,** greybeard; **hairy-legs; fungus face; croppy,** curlyhead, long-hair
hair *n* → small amount
hairdo *n* → hairdressing
HAIRDRESSER *n* barber, coiffeur, comber hairstylist, Sydney Harbour, wigmaker; **hairdresser's salon,** barber shop, beauty shop, wiggery
HAIRDRESSING *n* setting; **haircut,** afro, bob, clip *(Wool)*, crew cut, crop, cut, Eton crop, frizz, nana, pageboy, razor cut, shingle, trim; **hairstyle,** coiffure, hairdo, headdress *(Obs.)*, pouf, tire *(Archaic)*, tonsure; **wave,** blow-wave, cold wave, finger-wave, perm, permanent wave, root perm, water-wave
HAIRLIKE *adj* capillaceous, capillary, pileous, piliform, pilous; **bristlelike,** barbellate, penicillate, setaceous, setiform
HAIRPIECE *n* crepe hair, fall, postiche, switch, toupee; **wig,** bobwig, buzzwig, periwig, peruke, spencer, transformation *(Obs.)*
HAIRY *adj* bristly, brushy, chaetophorous, comate, comose, crinite, furred, furry, hirsute, hispid, maned, pileous, piliferous, pilose, rough, setaceous, setigerous, setose, setulose, shaggy, stubby, ulotrichous, whiskery, wire-haired; **fleecy,** downy, fluey, fluffy, fuzzy, lanuginose, tomentose; **flocculent,** bunchy, floccose, flocky, tufted, tufty; **arachnoid,** fimbrial, fimbriate, fimbrillate, pubescent, silky, villiform, villous; **long-haired,** bewigged, ringleted, shockheaded, tressed, wigged; **ash-blond,** blonde, brunette, carroty, fair-haired, peroxide blonde, red-headed, strawberry blonde, towheaded; **bearded,** barbate, barbed, black-browed, side-whiskered, whiskered; **grey,** grizzled, grizzly, hoary, white-haired, white-headed
halcyon *adj* → **1** birdlike **2** peaceful **3** pleasurable
hale *v* → **1** pull *adj* **2** healthy
HALF *n* equal part, fifty per cent, moiety; **halving,** bipartition, bisection, dichotomisation, dimidiation, division
half *n* → **1** alcohol container *adj* **2** halved
half-breed *n* → **1** descendant **2** hybrid *adj* **3** genetic
half-caste *n* → **1** descendant **2** hybrid *adj* **3** genetic **4** hybrid
half-hearted *adj* → apathetic
half-life *n* → atomic radiation
halfway *adj* → **1** central **2** partial
halitosis *n* → stench
HALL *n* antechamber, anteroom, corridor, foyer, galilee, hallway, lobby, loggia, narthex, parvis, porch *(U.S.)*, propylaeum, vestibule; **auditorium,** ballroom, chamber, concert-hall, council chamber, dance hall, divan, durbar, hall, lecture theatre, reception room, rotunda, saloon, stateroom, theatre, theatrette
hall *n* → **1** barracks **2** entrance **3** hall **4** house **5** kitchen **6** living room **7** path

hallelujah *interj* → well done
hallmark *n* → **1** emblem **2** label *v* **3** emblematise **4** label
hallow *v* → **1** consecrate **2** pursue **3** respect **4** shout **5** worship *interj* **6** cooee **7** hey
hallucinate *v* → delude oneself
hallucination *n* → **1** delusion **2** dream **3** madness **4** psychic disturbance
HALLUCINOGEN *n* angel dust, DET, dimethyltryptamine, DMT, PCP, phencyclidine, STP; **magic mushroom,** gold cap, gold top, psylocibin; **mescaline,** mesc, mescaline buttons, peyote; **LSD,** acid, lysergic acid, lysergic acid diethylamide, microdot, mike, ticket, trip. *See also* DRUG
halt *n* → **1** injury **2** stoppage *v* **3** stop **4** vacillate *adj* **5** injured *interj* **6** stop
halter *n* → **1** capital punishment **2** harness **3** killing **4** neckwear *v* **5** execute **6** restrain
HALVE *v* divide by two; **bisect,** cut in two, dichotomise, dimidiate, divide into halves, split in two; **go halves,** go fifty-fifty, share equally
HALVED *adj* bisected, cleft, cloven, divided, half; **in two parts,** bifid, bipartite, bisectional, dichotomous, dimerous, dimidiate
halyard *n* → **1** cord **2** puller
ham *n* → **1** actor **2** buttocks
hamlet *n* → **1** community **2** town
hammer *n* → **1** club **2** ear **3** gun part *v* **4** accuse **5** beat **6** decrease **7** hit **8** question **9** repeat
hammock *n* → pendant
hamper *n* → **1** basket **2** hindrance *v* **3** hinder
hamster *n* → animal's coat
hamstring *v* → injure
hand *n* → **1** applause **2** feeler **3** gamesman **4** height **5** help **6** indicator **7** labourer **8** person **9** side **10** wedding **11** writing
handbag *n* → case
handbill *n* → public notice
handbook *n* → reference book
handcuff *v* → **1** imprison **2** restrain
handicap *n* → **1** antecedence **2** hindrance **3** injury *v* **4** hinder
handicraft *n* → creativity
handiwork *n* → **1** finished product **2** work
handkerchief *n* → washer
handle *n* → **1** alcohol container **2** beer **3** name **4** touch *v* **5** hold **6** manage **7** touch **8** trade **9** trick
handout *n* → **1** charity **2** gift **3** news **4** public notice
hand out *v* → **1** give **2** share out
handsome *adj* → **1** accomplished **2** beautiful **3** generous **4** great
handwriting *n* → writing
handy *adj* → **1** competent **2** easy **3** expedient **4** useful
handyman *n* → **1** labourer **2** repairer
HANG *v* dangle, depend, pend, poise, swing; **overhang,** hang over, impend; **flow,** float, fly, stream; **hang down,** bag, blouse, droop, fall, flag, loll, lop, nod, sag, slouch; **drag,** draggle, sweep, trail; **suspend,** append, hang out, hang up, sling, string, string up
hang *n* → **1** exercise **2** hanging **3** meaning *v* **4** cook **5** execute **6** fasten **7** kill **8** tower **9** vacillate
hangar *n* → **1** airport **2** shelter
hang-glider *n* → **1** aircraft **2** pilot
HANGING *n* impendence, impendency, pendency, pendulousness, pensileness, pensility, suspense, suspension, suspensiveness; **bagginess,** flabbiness, flaccidity, flaccidness, slouchiness; **hang,** dangle, drape, droop, fall, sag, set, slouch, sweep
HANGING *adj* dangling, dependent, overhung, pendent, pending, pendulous, pensile, poised, suspended, suspensive; **overhanging,** imminent, impendent, impending, projecting; **drooping,** cernuous, deflexed, epinastic, flagging, nodding, sagging; **baggy,** droopy, flabby, flaccid, flaggy, slouchy; **flowing,** floating, flying, streaming
hangover *n* → **1** drunkenness **2** remnant
hang over *v* → hang
hang up *v* → **1** hang **2** stop
hang-up *n* → psychic disturbance
hank *n* → **1** curve **2** length **3** thread **4** twist
hanky-panky *n* → **1** cunning **2** endearments **3** sexual intercourse
haphazard *n* → **1** luck *adj* **2** lucky *adv* **3** by chance
hapless *adj* → unfortunate
happen *v* → **1** be **2** chance on **3** occur *adv* **4** possibly
HAPPINESS *n* blithesomeness, cheer, cheerfulness, cheeriness, enlivenment, exhilaration, festiveness, festivity, gladness, gladsomeness, glee, gleefulness, gleesomeness, good cheer, good humour, good nature, good-humouredness, good-naturedness, jolliness, joy, lightsomeness, merriness, sunniness, sunny side, sunshine; **liveliness,** airiness, animal spirits, animation, boyishness, breeziness, brightness, debonairness, exuberance, frolicsomeness, gaiety, high spirits, hilariousness, hilarity, insouciance, jauntiness, jocundity, joie de vivre, jollity, merriment, mirth, playfulness, sparkle, sportfulness, sportiveness, sprightliness, vivacity; **joviality,** cordiality, geniality, genialness, goodwill, mellowness, pleasantness; **buoyancy,** alacrity, bounce, elasticity, resilience, uplift; **levity,** flippancy, flippantness, frivolousness, kittenishness, lightheartedness, light-mindedness, lightness, tricksiness
HAPPY *adj* beaming, blithe, blithesome, buoyant, carefree, careless *(Archaic)*, cheerful, cheery, comfortable *(Obs.)*, elate, elated, full of beans, gay, glad, gladsome, happy as a sandboy, happy as Larry, hilarious, insouciant, jocund, joyful, joyous, light, lightsome, mirthful, pleasant, riant, rident; **genial,** backslapping, boon, bully, convivial, cordial, forward, good-humoured, good-natured, jolly, jovial, mellow, merry, rollicking; **lively,** airy, boyish, breezy, bright,

bright-eyed and bushytailed, carefree, chipper, chirpy, chirrupy, debonair, effervescent, exuberant, galliard *(Archaic)*, giocoso *(Music)*, jaunty, peart, perky, pert, radiant, spiritoso *(Music)*, spiritous *(Obs.)*, sprightly, vivacious; **hilarious,** bouncy, frolic, frolicsome, gamesome, tricksy, wanton *(Poetic)*; **sanguine,** irrepressible, rose-coloured, sunny, sunshine, up-beat; **frivolous,** flip, flippant, giggly, kittenish, light, light-hearted, light-minded, lightsome, playful, sportive; **exhilarating,** exhilarant, exhilarative

happy *adj* → **1** congruous **2** content **3** fortunate **4** joyful **5** pleased

HARANGUE *n* diatribe, exhortation, lecture, philippic, screed, sermon, tirade

harangue *v* → **1** speak **2** speak well **3** teach

HARANGUER *n* demagogue, phrase-monger, rabble-rouser, ranter, raver, rhetorician, soapbox orator, tub-thumper, word-monger

harass *v* → **1** annoy **2** attack **3** victimise

harbinger *n* → **1** forerunner **2** omen *v* **3** predict

HARBOUR *n* anchorage, harbour of refuge, harbourage, haven, mole, moorage, moorings, roads, roadstead; **port,** free port, outport, seaport; **basin,** marina, tidal basin, wet dock; **quay,** dock, jetty, pier, slip *(U.S.)*, staithe, wharf; **quayage,** wharfage. *See also* REFUGE; SHELTER

harbour *n* → **1** dwelling *v* **2** hide **3** shelter

HARD *adj* adamant, adamantine, bricklike, concrete, concretionary, flinty, glass, glasslike, glassy, granitic, gritty, iron, ironbound, marble, marbly, pebbly, petrous, rocklike, rocky, semivitreous, steel, steely, stone, stonelike, stony, vitreous, vitriform, wooden, woody; **bony,** bonelike, chitinous, corneous, horny, osseous, ossiferous, osteoid, scaley, scleritic, sclerodermatous, scleroid, sclerosal, sclerotic, sclerous, testaceous; **rigid,** erect, erectile, indurate, inflexible, springless, starched, starchy, stark, stiff, stiff as a poker, taut, unbending, uncrushable, wiry; **tough,** chewie, chewy, leathery; **solid,** compacted, consistent *(Obs.)*, dense, firm, imperviable, impervious, infusible, inpermeable, stout, stubborn, sturdy; **hardened,** high-speed *(Metall.)*, ironbound, prestressed, sealed, strain-hardened, tempered, weather-beaten, weathered, weatherworn; **hardening,** calcifying, indurative, ossifying, petrifactive, sclerosed

HARD *adv* inflexibly, rigidly, starkly, stiff, tautly, tight, tightly, unbendingly, woodenly; **solidly,** sturdily; **stonily,** flintily; **glassily,** vitreously

hard *adj* → **1** bad **2** callous **3** cash **4** difficult **5** effortful **6** intoxicating **7** strict **8** unfair **9** unpleasant *adv* **10** attentively **11** solidly **12** strictly **13** wholly **14** with effort

HARDEN *v* fix, set, solidify, stiffen, tauten, toughen; **consolidate,** bind, compact, concrete, condense, firm; **petrify,** bake, calcify, callus, carburise, case-harden, chill *(Metall.)*, cornify, crust, crystallise, encrust, fossilise, freeze, indurate, lignify, ossify, season, steel, temper, vitrify; **starch,** clear-starch

harden *v* → **1** be callous **2** become greater **3** be strict **4** habituate **5** steady **6** strengthen

hardly *adv* → **1** negligibly **2** unlikely

hardship *n* → **1** difficulty **2** misfortune

hardware *n* → **1** supplies **2** tool

hardy *n* → **1** chisel *adj* **2** courageous **3** persevering **4** rash **5** strong

hare *v* → speed

harem *n* → barracks

hark *v* → hear

harlot *n* → **1** promiscuous person **2** prostitute *adj* **3** promiscuous

HARM *n* bale *(Archaic)*, damage, hurt, ill, injury, mayhem, offence *(Obs.)*, trespass; **detriment,** a kick in the teeth, disadvantage, disservice, evil, mischief, prejudice; **ruin,** havoc, ravage, scathe *(Archaic)*, waste; **bomb damage,** blast effect, cratering, ground-shock effect. *See also* DAMAGE; INJURY

harm *v* → **1** act unkindly **2** injure **3** wrong

HARMFUL *adj* cariogenic, corrosive, damaging, deleterious, detrimental, evil, hurtful, injurious, mischievous, mutilative, nocent, nocuous, noxious, pernicious, ruinous, scorching, wearing; **bruising,** contusive; **pestilent,** pestiferous, pestilential, putrefactive, saprogenic

HARMFULLY *adv* damagingly, hurtfully, injuriously, nocuously, noxiously, pestiferously, pestilently, ruinously; **detrimentally,** corrosively, deleteriously, for the worse

harmonica *n* → wind instrument

harmony *n* → **1** agreement **2** congruity **3** music **4** peace **5** sound **6** tidiness

HARNESS *n* bellyband, bridle, britchen, halter, martingale, rein, surcingle, trace, tug. *See also* CORD

harness *n* → **1** armour **2** equipment

harp *n* → **1** guitar *v* **2** make music **3** speak

harpoon *n* → **1** piercer **2** spear *v* **3** kill

harridan *n* → **1** ugly person **2** violent person

harrow *n* → **1** digging implement *v* **2** farm **3** make unhappy **4** pain

harry *v* → **1** act unkindly **2** annoy **3** cause difficulties

harsh *adj* → **1** callous **2** difficult **3** dissonant **4** ill-bred **5** rough **6** sour **7** strict **8** unkind

HARVEST *v* crop, cut, gather, glean, head, ingather, mow, pick, reap, scythe, strip; **thresh,** fan, flail, willow, winnow; **bale,** bind, ensile, rick, stook, windrow. *See also* FARM

harvest *n* → **1** finished product **2** season **3** storage

hash *n* → **1** failure **2** jumble **3** marijuana **4** radio *v* **5** bungle **6** cut

hashish *n* → marijuana

hasp *n* → bolt

hassle *n* → **1** argument *v* **2** annoy

hassock *n* → support

haste *n* → **1** rashness **2** speed *v* **3** hurry

hasten *v* → hurry

hasty *adj* → **1** angry **2** capricious **3** irritable **4** rash **5** speedy

HAT *n* barrel, bell-topper, billycock, boater, bowler, boxer, broadbrim, bun hat *(N.Z.)*, busby, cabbage-tree hat, cady, chapeau, chimneypot, cocked hat, deerstalker, derby *(U.S.)*, digger hat, Dolly Varden, fedora, hard-hitter *(N.Z.)*, hard-knocker, high hat, homburg, lemon squeezer *(N.Z. Colloq.)*, lid, mitre, mortarboard, opera hat, Panama, petasus, picture hat, pillbox, plug *(U.S. Colloq.)*, pork-pie hat, red hat *(Rom. Cath. Ch.)*, shovel hat, slouch hat, snap-brim, sombrero, stetson, stovepipe, taj *(Islam)*, tall hat, tarpaulin, ten-gallon hat, titfer, top hat, topper, toque, trencher, trilby, turban, wide-awake; **sunhat,** sun-helmet, sunbonnet. *See also* HEADGEAR; CAP; HELMET

hat *n* → **1** ecclesiastic **2** employment

hatch *n* → **1** animal offspring **2** covering **3** entrance **4** line **5** opening *v* **6** darken **7** depict **8** fantasise **9** give birth **10** initiate **11** line **12** mark **13** plan **14** prepare

hatchet *n* → axe

HATE *n* abhorrence, allergy, despite *(Archaic)*, disgust, dislike, hatred, loathing, malice, nausea, odium, rancour, revolt, revulsion; **detestation,** abomination, animosity, embitterment, execration, nauseation, repugnance; **enmity,** alienation, bad blood, bad feeling, bitterness, combativeness, estrangement, hostility, ill feeling, implacability; **misanthropy,** misandry, misogyny, race-hatred, racism, xenophobia; **the creeps,** the heebie-jeebies, the willies

HATE *v* abhor, abominate, be unable to abide, bear a grudge against, detest, execrate, hate someone's guts, have a hate on, loathe, recoil from, shrink from, view with horror, view with loathing; **be disgusted,** keck, revolt against, revolt from; **burn in effigy,** hang in effigy, stick pins into

hate *v* → dislike

HATEFUL *adj* abhorrent, abominable, accursed, contemptible, damnable, damned, despiteful *(Archaic)*, despiteous *(Archaic)*, detestable, disgustful *(Archaic)*, disgusting, dislikeable, execrable, hateable, hated, heinous, invidious, loathsome, nauseous, odious, rancorous, repugnant, revolting; **love-hate,** ambivalent

HATER *n* abhorrer, detester, execrator, misanthrope, misogynist, racist, witch-hunter, xenophobe; **embitterer,** activist, stirrer; **enemy,** combatant

HATING *adj* antipathetic, bitter, combative, easily disgusted, embittered, execrative, hostile, inimical, misanthropic, misogynous, xenophobic; **spiteful,** execratory, malicious, viperish, viperous

haughty *adj* → **1** arrogant **2** discourteous **3** reputable

haul *n* → **1** amount **2** pull **3** takings *v* **4** pull **5** swerve

haunch *n* → **1** arch **2** buttocks **3** side

HAUNT *v* bedevil, ghost, possess, spook; **communicate from the dead,** rap out

haunt *n* → **1** position *v* **2** be present **3** partner **4** remember **5** visit

have *n* → **1** illusion **2** trick *v* **3** buy **4** cause **5** get **6** give birth **7** have sex **8** hold **9** include **10** own **11** permit **12** trick **13** undertake

HAVE A JOB *v* carry a cut-lunch, fill, hold a chair, hold a portfolio, hold an office, hold down a job, join the workforce, occupy a position, take up a position; **earn a living,** bring home the bacon, keep body and soul together, keep the wolf from the door, make a living, produce, support oneself, turn an honest penny, turn out; **practise,** be in, carry on, concern oneself with, do, follow, have to do with, occupy oneself with, ply, profess, pursue, serve time as, spend one's time on, work as

HAVE DIFFICULTY *v* buy into trouble, catch a Tartar, fall foul, have one's work cut out; **make it difficult,** do it the hard way, flounder on, go through the mill, make heavy weather of, rub along, scratch along, wade through

HAVE GOOD TASTE *v* have a nose for, have an ear for, have an eye for

haven *n* → **1** harbour *v* **2** shelter

HAVE NO HOPE *v* be doomed to failure, have a fat chance, have Buckley's, have Buckley's chance, have no chance, have one's fate sealed

haversack *n* → bag

HAVE SEX *v* consummate a marriage, copulate, couple, fornicate, frig, fuck, go all the way, have it away, have it off, have relations, make love, play tootsy, roll in the hay, root, swive *(Archaic)*, tread; **sleep with,** feature with, fuck, get off with, get with, have, hop into bed with, lay, lie with, make, pull, race, root, screw; **bed,** ball, bang, bull, do, do over, enjoy *(Archaic)*, get up someone, hump, knock off, mount, poke, possess, punch one through, roger, scrape, shag, slip it to, stuff, take; **bury the bishop,** crack it, dip one's wick, get into someone's pants, get one's end in, get one's wick wet, perform, pull a chick, score, sink the sausage, slip someone a length; **suck off,** dine at the Y, eat, give head, go down on, suck; **bugger,** buggerise, rim, seat; **commit buggery,** go Greek; **get any,** get a bit; **come across; commit adultery,** cuckold; **cohabit,** live together, live with, shack up with; **proposition,** crack onto, make a pass at, put the hard word on; **swing,** intrigue, sleep around; **captain; camp,** come out. *See also* EROTICISE

HAVE THE RIGHT *v* demand one's rights, stand on one's rights; **confer a right,** allow, entitle, ordain, sanction

havoc *n* → **1** destruction **2** harm **3** signal

hawk *n* → **1** attacker **2** extortionist **3** fighter **4** political ideologist **5** warmonger *v* **6** be loud **7** excrete **8** hunt **9** sell **10** shout

hawker *n* → **1** seller **2** traveller

hay *n* → cash

hay fever *n* → allergy

haywire *n* → **1** wire *adj* **2** disorderly
hazard *n* → **1** danger **2** gambling **3** obstacle **4** opening *v* **5** attempt **6** gamble **7** risk
haze *n* → **1** cloud **2** imprecision *v* **3** annoy
hazel *n* → **1** timber *adj* **2** brown
he *n* → **1** man *adj* **2** male
HEAD *n* bean, belfry, block, chump, cobbra *(Obs.)*, crown, cruet, crumpet, dome, loaf, lolly, melon, nob, noddle, noggin, noodle, nut, onion, pate, sconce, scone, top; **skull,** brainpan, calvaria, cranium, inion, pan; **scalp,** poll, vertex; **brow,** forehead, temple; **brain,** encephalon, grey matter, little grey cells, white matter; **forebrain,** cerebral hemisphere, cerebrum, corpus callosum, cortex, end brain, hippocampus, infundibulum, prosencephalon, sensorium, telencephalon; **midbrain,** corpora quadrigemina, diencephalon, hypothalamus, interbrain, mesencephalon, optic thalamus, peduncle, thalamencephalon, thalamus; **afterbrain,** cerebellum, epencephalon, hindbrain, medulla oblongata, metencephalon, myelencephalon, pons; **convolution,** fissure, gyrus, lobe, sulcus, ventricle; **fontanelle,** foramen magnum; **craniology,** bumpology, cephalometry, craniometry, phrenology. *See also* FACE; EYE; NOSE; EAR; MOUTH
head *n* → **1** advance **2** apex **3** boss **4** bubbling **5** bulge **6** clip **7** covering **8** drug user **9** flower **10** frame **11** front **12** hair **13** headland **14** holder **15** knob **16** length **17** manager **18** mind **19** musical score **20** news item **21** person **22** portrait **23** score **24** sore **25** spring **26** start **27** toilet **28** top *v* **29** cut **30** cut off **31** harvest **32** introduce **33** manage **34** surpass **35** swerve **36** top *adj* **37** front **38** top
headache *n* → **1** ache **2** difficulty **3** puzzle
HEADBAND *n* bandeau, chaplet, fillet, snood, sweat-rag, sweatband; **veil,** fly-net, flyveil, loup, mask, veiling; **earflap,** earlap, earmuff, lug; **hairnet,** net. *See also* HEADGEAR; HAT
HEAD FOR *v* bear down on, carry on, course, fetch, fetch about, make for, strike out towards; **ply a course,** pursue a course, run a course, stand a course, track a course, wend one's way; **follow,** fly the beam, go by, ride the beam
HEADGEAR *n* millinery; **headdress,** commode, cornet, crown, pinner, pouf, puggaree, tiara, tire *(Archaic)*, turban; **hood,** amice, balaclava, calash, capuche, capuchin, cowl, wimple. *See also* HAT; CAP; HELMET; HEADBAND
heading *n* → **1** direction **2** front **3** passageway **4** title
HEADLAND *n* cape, foreland, head, naze, point, promontory; **isthmus,** landbridge, neck, strait *(Rare)*, tombolo; **peninsula,** tied island, tongue
headland *n* → **1** edge **2** mound
headlight *n* → lighting
headline *n* → news item
head line *n* → fortune-telling
headlong *adj* → **1** rash **2** sloping **3** speedy *adv* **4** frontally **5** rashly **6** speedily
headmaster *n* → **1** leader **2** teacher
headmistress *n* → **1** leader **2** teacher
headquarters *n* → **1** battleground **2** centre **3** office **4** operator
head start *n* → **1** advance **2** antecedence **3** easy thing
headstone *n* → **1** grave **2** label **3** rock
headstrong *adj* → **1** capricious **2** rash **3** uncompromising
headwaters *n* → spring
headway *n* → **1** advance **2** interval **3** length
headwind *n* → wind
heady *adj* → **1** exciting **2** fragrant **3** intoxicating **4** rash
heal *v* → **1** atone for **2** clean **3** mediate **4** medicate **5** practise medicine
HEALER *n* cupper, curer, leech *(Archaic)*, therapeutist, therapist, treater; **doctor,** apothecary *(Archaic)*, barefoot doctor, biotechnologist, clinician, doc, doctoress *(Rare)*, doctress *(Rare)*, family doctor, flying doctor, G.P., general practitioner, hakim, medic *(U.S.)*, medico, physician, quack, radio doctor; **specialist,** Collins Street doctor, consultant, ENT specialist, firm, Harley Street doctor, honorary, Macquarie Street doctor, neurologist, orthotist, paediatrician, podiatrist, prosthetist, urologist, visiting medical officer; **resident,** intern, registrar; **surgeon,** chirurgeon *(Archaic)*, orthopaedic surgeon, orthopod, plastic surgeon, sawbones; **diagnostician,** aetiologist, pathologist; **gynaecologist,** accoucheur, accoucheuse, midwife, obstetrician; **anaesthetist; pharmacologist,** chemist, druggist *(U.S.)*, pharmacist; **physiotherapist,** massager, massageuse, massagist, masseur, masseuse, physio; **paramedic,** ambo, ambulanceman, hospital orderly, medical orderly, nursing aide, orderly, stretcher-bearer, zambuck; **nurse,** amah, bush nurse, charge nurse, district nurse, dresser, health visitor *(Brit.)*, hospitaller, Karitane nurse, matron, Plunket nurse, registered nurse, sister, Tresillian nurse, wardsman; **naturopath,** acupuncturist, bonesetter, chiropractor, herbalist, homoeopathist, hygienist, iridologist, naprapath, osteopath; **faith-healer; mountebank; dentist,** dental technician, endodontist, exodontist, gum-digger, orthodontist, prosthodontist; **veterinary surgeon,** farrier, vet, veterinarian
HEALING *n* folk medicine, internal medicine, medical science, medicine, physic *(Archaic)*, preventive medicine, therapeutics; **diagnostics,** aetiology, pathology, symptomatology; **acupuncture,** acupressure, chiropractic, herbalism, homeopathy, iridology, naprapathy, naturopathy, osteopathy, radionics, shiatsu; **allopathy,** dosology, homeopathy, iatrochemistry, pharmaceutics, pharmacology, pharmacy, posology; **psychosomatic medicine,** faith healing, mental heal-

ing; **surgery,** anaplasty, microsurgery, plastic surgery; **gynaecology,** gyniatrics, midwifery, obstetrics, tocology; **physiotherapy,** orthotics, physical therapy *(U.S.)*, physio, prosthetics; **dentistry,** bridgework, exodontia, odontology, orthodontics, periodontics, prosthodontics; **forensic medicine,** medical jurisprudence; **veterinary science**

HEALTH *n* bloom, clean bill of health, fitness, flourish *(Rare)*, good health, haleness, healthiness, normality, soundness, welfare, well-being; **robustness,** bonniness, buckishness, buxomness, freshness, go, heartiness, lustiness, red-bloodedness, strength, vigour; **condition,** constitution, form, tone, tonicity; **wholesomeness,** healthfulness, hygiene, salubriousness, salubrity, salutariness, sanitariness; **resilience,** recuperativeness

health *n* → congratulation

HEALTH CENTRE *n* health camp, health farm, hydro, quarantine, sanatorium, spa, watering-place

HEALTHY *adj* fine, fit as a fiddle, hale, hale and hearty, normal, resilient, right, right as rain, sane *(Obs.)*, sound, sound as a bell, well, whole; **flourishing,** blooming, bonny, bouncing, bright-eyed and bushytailed, buxom, fresh, full of beans, glowing, thriving; **fit,** buckish, fighting fit, hearty, in fine feather, in full feather, in high feather, in training, lusty, red-blooded, robust, strong, valid *(Archaic)*, vigorous; **tolerable,** all right, middling; **convalescent,** better, on the improve, on the mend, up and about

healthy *adj* → good

HEALTHY PERSON *n* ball of muscle, flourisher, thriver

heap *n* → **1** accumulation **2** discard **3** much *v* **4** add **5** gather **6** give

HEAR *v* catch, get, hark, hearken; **listen,** be all ears, get a load of, hear out, list, prick up one's ears; **sound,** auscultate; **lip-read,** interpret; **give ear,** give audience, interview, lend an ear *(Archaic)*; **overhear,** bug, eavesdrop, listen in, tap

hear *v* → **1** assent to **2** assess

HEARER *n* audience, audient, audile, auditor, hearkener, listener; **eavesdropper,** earwig, overhearer; **audiologist,** acoustician

HEARING *n* audience, audition, listening; **audibility,** earshot; **perception,** diplacusis, hyperacusis, monophony, quadrophony, stereophony; **audiology,** acoustics, audiometry; **auscultation,** stethoscopy

HEARING *adj* attentive, audient, listening; **auditory,** acoustic, audile, audiovisual, aural, auricular; **audible,** heard; **audiological,** audiometric; **monophonic,** quadraphonic, stereophonic

hearing *n* → **1** litigation **2** trial

HEARING AID *n* acoustic, audiphone, deaf-aid, dentiphone, ear trumpet, trumpet; **sign language,** dactylology, deaf-and-dumb language

HEARING DEVICE *n* headphone, headpiece, headset; **stethoscope,** audiometer, otoscope

hearsay *n* → news

hearse *n* → coffin

HEART *n* pump, ticker; **aortic valve,** atrium, auricle, endocardium, epicardium, mitral valve, myocardium, pacemaker, pulmonary valve, semilunar valve, tricuspid valve, ventricle

heart *n* → **1** centre **2** characteristics **3** courage **4** emotion **5** enthusiasm **6** important thing **7** inside **8** living **9** pity *v* **10** encourage **11** help

heartache *n* → unhappiness

heartburn *n* → **1** jealousy **2** nausea

hearten *v* → **1** embolden **2** make happy

heartfelt *adj* → emotional

hearth *n* → **1** dwelling **2** fireplace **3** heater **4** metalworks **5** rack

heartless *adj* → **1** callous **2** unkind

hearty *n* → **1** friend **2** good person **3** mariner *adj* **4** abundant **5** busy **6** enthusiastic **7** fertile **8** friendly **9** great **10** healthy **11** satisfactory

HEAT *n* caloric, caloricity, enthalpy, phlogiston, solar energy, temp, temperament *(Obs.)*, temperature, total heat; **warmth,** lukewarmness, tepidity, tepidness, warmness; **intense heat,** ardour, burning heat, causticity, ferventness, fervidness, fervour, fever heat, perfervidity, perfervidness, perfervour, torridity, torridness; **red heat,** afterheat, overheat, steam heat, superheat, white heat; **incandescence,** calefaction, decalescence, recalescence

HEAT *v* heat through, heat up, hot up, incubate, irradiate, preheat, tepefy, warm, warm through, warm up; **thaw,** de-ice, defrost, melt, sweal; **overheat,** seethe *(Obs.)*, stew, superheat, sweat; **bake,** broil, chafe *(Obs.)*, cook, decrepitate, grill, roast; **parch,** burn, calcine, carbonise, torrefy; **heat-treat,** anneal, cupel, cure, recalesce, reverberate, vulcanise; **stove,** fire, kiln, kiln-dry, underburn *(Pottery)*; **cast,** found, smelt; **steam,** autoclave, sterilise; **boil,** decoct, kier, simmer

heat *n* → **1** emotion **2** reproduction **3** season **4** sex **5** violent outburst

HEATED *adj* pyrogenous, roast, roasted; **gas-fired,** external-combustion, oil-fired, open-hearth

HEATER *n* incubator, superheater, warmer; **fireplace,** hearth, ingle; **room-heater,** convector, gas fire, heat reservoir, hypocaust, kerosene heater, open fire, radiator, space heater, storage heater, strip heater; **direct heating,** central heating, ducted heating, panel heating; **boiler,** califont *(N.Z.)*, chip heater, donkey, fire-tube boiler, geyser, hot-water service, immersion heater, water-back, water-tube boiler; **heat exchanger,** heat pipe, heat pump, heat sink, intercooler, recuperator; **demister,** de-icer; **water bath,** bain-marie, bath; **furnace,** afterburner, bosh, combustion chamber, combustion tube, converter, cupola, electric furnace, glass tank, muffle furnace, open-hearth furnace, regenerative furnace, regenerator, reverberatory furnace, solar furnace, tank furnace; **kiln,** brick-kiln, lehr, oast, oast-house, roaster; **brazier,** chauffer, cockle, devil; **blowtorch,** acetylene lamp, blowlamp, Bunsen burner, fantail, loggerhead, oxyacetylene burner, oxyhydrogen burner, pilot, pilot burner, pilot lamp, soldering iron; **sunglass,** argon laserphotocoagulator, burning-glass

heater *n* → gun

heath *n* → grassland

heathen *n* → **1** irreverent person *adj* **2** irreverent

HEATING *n* calefaction, incubation, insulation, tepefaction, thaw, warming; **calescence,** decalescence, incalescence; **boiling,** cooking, decoction, sterilisation; **incubation,** aluminothermy, eddy current heating, greenhouse effect, induction heating, open-hearth process, radiofrequency heating, reverberation; **heat therapy,** fomentation, insolation; **pyrolysis,** cupellation, destructive distillation, dry distillation, thermal cracking, torrefaction; **case-hardening,** cyanide hardening, vulcanisation; **steam treating,** crabbing; **sunbaking,** insolation, sunbathing

HEATING *adj* calefacient, calefactory, inflammatory, pyretic, pyrogenic, sudatory, warming; **incubatory,** incubational, slow; **burning,** calcinatory, caustic, pyrolytic; **calescent,** incalescent, recalescent

HEAT TRANSFER *n* advection, conduction, convection, radiation; **thermogenesis,** thermaesthesia, thermanaesthesia, thermolysis; **thermotropism,** thermotaxis, xerophily

heave *n* → **1** exercise **2** lifting **3** misplacement **4** pull **5** throw *v* **6** bulge **7** lift **8** misplace **9** move **10** pull **11** throw **12** toss

HEAVEN *n* Canaan, paradise; **Elysium,** Asgard, Avalon, Elysian fields, Elysian plains, empyrean, Happy Hunting Grounds, Hesperides, Islands of the Blessed, Olympus, Valhalla; **Zion,** kingdom come, New Jerusalem, Pearly Gates, the sky *(Obs.)*; **heavenliness,** bliss, divineness, glory. *See also* AFTERWORLD

heaven *n* → **1** a good time **2** pleasantness

HEAVENLY *adj* blissful, celestial, divine, Elysian, empyreal, empyrean, paradisiacal, supernal, superterrestrial; **ultramundane,** otherworldly

HEAVENLY BODY *n* ball, celestial body, globe, luminary, moon, orb *(Poetic)*, planet, satellite, sphere; **the earth,** lower world, terrene, the globe, world; **minor planet,** asteroid, planetoid; **planets,** Earth, Jupiter, Mars, Mercury, Neptune, Pluto, Saturn, Uranus, Venus; **asteroids,** Adonis, Apollo, Eros, Hermes, Icarus. *See also* STAR; SUN; MOON; METEOR

HEAVY *adj* heavier-than-air, leaden, leady, massive, ponderable, ponderous, preponderant, preponderating, stodgy, weighty; **hefty,** beefy, elephantine, hulking, lumbering, lumpy, overweight, solid; **burdensome,** cumbersome, cumbrous, oppressive, overburdensome; **heavy-laden,** burdened, loaded; **counterweighted,** equiponderant

heavy *n* → **1** actor **2** famous person **3** policeman **4** unpleasant person *v* **5** menace **6** oppose *adj* **7** big **8** cloudy **9** difficult **10** dramatic **11** effortful **12** forceful **13** important **14** incompetent **15** intellectual **16** intense **17** pregnant **18** sombre **19** thick **20** unhappy **21** vulgar *adv* **22** heavily **23** with effort

HEAVY DRINKER *n* alcoholic, alkie, bacchanal, bacchant, bacchante, bar fly, beer swiper, bibber, booze artist, booze hound, boozer, boozician, boozington, cheap drunk, compotator, dipso, dipsomaniac, drinking school, drunk, drunkard, grog artist, guzzleguts, guzzler, hard case, hard drinker, hophead, imbiber, indulger, inebriate, Jimmy Woodser, juice-freak, lolly legs, lush, lushington, metho, pisshead, pisspot, plonko, pot walloper, shicker, soak, sot, souse, stiff, swigger, taverner *(Brit. Obs.)*, tippler, toper, tosspot, two-pot screamer, winebibber, winedot, wineskin, wino

heckle *n* → **1** brush *v* **2** cut **3** mock

hectare *n* → area

hectic *n* → **1** fever *adj* **2** busy **3** excited **4** hot **5** muddled **6** short-winded

hector *n* → **1** arrogant person **2** forcer **3** vulgarian *v* **4** act unkindly **5** menace

hedge *n* → **1** fence **2** loophole **3** preparation *v* **4** avoid **5** enclose **6** gamble **7** invest **8** separate

hedonism *n* → **1** pleasure **2** voluptuousness

heed *n* → **1** attentiveness *v* **2** attend to **3** obey

heel *n* → **1** bad person **2** bottom **3** curve **4** footgear **5** leg *v* **6** slope

hefty *adj* → **1** fat **2** heavy **3** strong

hegemony *n* → **1** authority **2** precedence

heifer *n* → **1** animal offspring **2** cattle **3** woman

HEIGHT *n* dizzy height; **loftiness,** domination, eminence, grandness, hilliness, sublimity *(Poetic)*; **steepness,** precipitousness; **altitude,** almucantar, elevation; **stature,** hand *(Horses)*, tallness; **rise,** loft, pitch. *See also* APEX; MOUNTAIN; TOWER

height *n* → top

heinous *adj* → **1** hateful **2** immoral **3** wrong

heir *n* → **1** descendant **2** gainer **3** successor *v* **4** get

heirloom *n* → property

helicopter *n* → aircraft

helix *n* → **1** solid **2** twist

HELL *n* Gehenna, hellfire, inferno, Pandemonium, purgatory, sheol, Tartarus; **damnation,** perdition, tarnation; **abyss,** pit, the bottomless pit. *See also* AFTERWORLD

HELLO *interj* aloha, ave, bonjour, g'day, good afternoon, good day, good evening, good morning, greetings, haeremai *(N.Z.)*, heil, hi, how ya goin' (mate), how're the bots biting *(N.Z.)*, how're you going, how's things, how's tricks, how-de-do, how-do-you-do, howdy, tenakoe *(N.Z.)*, yickadee *(N.T.)*; **bon appétit,** all the best, cheers, chin-chin, good health, skol, to your health; **goodbye,** bon voyage, cheerio, ciao

hello *v* → **1** be sociable **2** call attention to *interj* **3** hey **4** oh

helm *n* → **1** helmet **2** steering wheel *v* **3** direct

HELMET *n* bash hat, basinet, bearskin, bump cap, burgonet, busby, casque, crash hat, crash-helmet, hard hat, headpiece, helm *(Archaic)*, morion, pith helmet, safety helmet, sallet, skidlid, tin hat, topee

helmet *n* → armour

HELP *n* aid, assistance; **backing,** advocacy, boost, championship, encouragement, promotion; **patronage,** auspices, favour, recourse, sponsorship; **support,** aliment, alimentation, fosterage, nurture, protection, sustainment, sustenance, sustention; **comfort,** charity, cheer, favourableness, moral support; **relief,** deliverance, succour, visitation; **service,** good turn, yeoman service; **altruism,** almsgiving, benefaction, beneficence, mercy, philanthropy, subvention, voluntaryism; **solicitude,** attendance, attention, ministration, ministry; **facilitation,** accommodation; **helpfulness,** cooperativeness, obligingness, preferential treatment, responsiveness; **favouritism,** abetment, complicity, partisanship; **resource,** facility; **helping hand,** a leg up, boost, crutch, hand, lift, springboard, stepping stone

HELP *v* aid, bestead *(Archaic)*, oblige; **sustain,** carry through, comfort *(Obs.)*, succour, support, tide over; **administer to,** attend, care for, fix someone up, minister, nurse, spoonfeed, visit; **strengthen,** buoy, carry, prop up, stay; **nurture,** aliment, provide for; **further,** accelerate, boost, cultivate, facilitate, feed, foment, foster, pilot, promote, prompt; **favour,** patronise, shine on, shine upon, smile on, smile upon; **champion,** befriend, defend, go all the way for, push someone's barrow, root for *(U.S.)*, side with, stick up for, take sides, take someone's part, throw in one's lot with; **serve,** be at someone's service, be of service, be useful, hold someone's hand, make oneself useful, stand by, stand with; **abet,** collaborate; **assist,** bear a hand, come forward, give a hand, help out, lend a hand, rally, second; **cheer,** encourage, heart *(Archaic)*; **sponsor,** back, back up, bankroll, finance, put someone on his feet, set someone on his feet, subsidise; **chip in,** come to the party, pass round the hat, put money in the tin, whip round

help *n* → **1** farmhand **2** helper **3** servant *v* **4** cooperate **5** improve **6** partner

HELPER *n* abetter, adjuvant, aider, ally, facilitator, help, obliger; **assistant,** adjutant, aide, aide-de-camp, assessor, assister, assistor *(Law)*, associate, best boy *(Films)*, bottle-holder *(Wrestling)*, coadjutor, coadjutress, croupier, deputy, handler, right hand, right-hand man, second, sidekick, yeoman *(Archaic)*; **auxiliary,** reinforcement, stand-by; **attendant,** acolyte, pursuivant; **servant,** domestic help, girl Friday, gopher, server, shitkicker, tweeny *(Obs.)*, yardman; **secretary,** private secretary, receptionist; **groomsman,** best man, bridesmaid, flower girl, matron of honour, pageboy, trainbearer; **benefactor,** angel, deliverer, easy touch, fairy godmother, favourer, intercessor, Lady Bountiful, paraclete, patron, patroness, provider, ready giver, Robin Hood, Santa Claus, soft touch, softie, subsidiser, sugar daddy; **supporter,** activist, advocate, backer, champion, fan, promoter, rooter; **nurturer,** administrant, carer, fosterer, fuzzy wuzzy angel, ministrant, nurse, succourer; **helpmate,** booster, companion, friend, friend in need, helpmeet *(Archaic)*, pal, vade mecum; **tower of strength,** Atlas, bastion, cheerer, comforter, moral support, pillar, prop, soldier, strengthener, support; **counsellor,** adviser, almoner, almsgiver, altruist, case worker, do-gooder, philanthropist, probation officer, settlement worker, social worker, voluntaryist

HELPFUL *adj* accommodating, cooperative, helping, obliging, responsive, well-disposed; **altruistic,** generous, patronal; **charitable,** eleemosynary, subventionary; **ministrative,** ministrant, visitational; **sustaining,** alimental, comfortable, nutrient, supporting; **auxiliary,** adjuvant, ancillary, assistant, subsidiary, supernumerary; **useful,** necessary *(Archaic)*, of service; **favourable,** advantageous, auspicial, beneficial, conducive to, propitious; **subsidised,** aided, backed; **contributary,** facilitatory, tributary

HELPFULLY *adv* altruistically, comfortingly, constructively, cooperatively, helpingly, obligingly, responsively; **on behalf of,** for the sake of, on someone's account; **by the aid of,** on the strength of, thanks to; **favourably,** favouringly

helpless *adj* → **1** ineffectual **2** weak

helpmate *n* → **1** companion **2** helper **3** partner **4** spouse

helter-skelter *n* → **1** amusement park **2** jumble **3** speed **4** tower *adj* **5** speedy *adv* **6** hurriedly **7** untidily

hemisphere *n* → arch

hemlock *n* → means of killing

hemp *n* → marijuana

hen *n* → **1** fool **2** woman

hence *adv* → **1** in the future **2** remotely *interj* **3** piss off *conj* **4** because

henchman *n* → **1** accomplice **2** dependant **3** servant

henna *n* → **1** brown **2** orange **3** yellow pigment *v* **4** redden

herald *n* → **1** forerunner **2** messenger **3** omen **4** publicist *v* **5** introduce **6** noise abroad **7** predict **8** publicise

herb *n* → **1** medication **2** plant *v* **3** speed **4** transport

herd *n* → **1** gathering **2** working class *v* **3** farm **4** gather

HERE *adv* herein, inside, out here; **there,** ad loc, o'er *(Poetic)*, over there, thereabouts, thereat, thereby, yon *(Archaic)*, yond *(Archaic)*, yonder; **at hand,** herein, in, on board, on hand, on the scene, on the spot, round, to hand; **locally,** in loc. cit., in loco, in one's tracks, in situ, on the spot; **op. cit.,** opere citato; **suo loco**

here *n* → **1** actuality *adv* **2** closely **3** particularly

hereby *adv* → **1** closely **2** how

hereditary *adj* → genetic

heredity *n* → ancestry

herein *adv* → **1** here **2** inside

HERESY *n* anathema, false doctrine, misbelief, miscreance *(Archaic)*; **unorthodoxy,** dissent, heterodoxy, schism, superstition *(Derog.)*, unconformity

HERETIC *n* anathema, heresiarch, miscreant *(Archaic)*, pervert, perverter; **dissenter,** nonconformist

HERETICAL *adj* excommunicate, heretic, miscreant *(Archaic)*, perverted, profane; **unorthodox,** heterodox, schismatic

heritage *n* → **1** getting **2** property

hermaphrodite *n* → **1** opposite meaning **2** sexual type *adj* **3** opposing **4** sexual

hermetic *adj* → **1** closed **2** independent **3** supernatural

hermit *n* → **1** believer **2** solitary

hernia *n* → bulge

HERO *n* champion, daredevil, dreadnought, heroine, lion, Spartan, stalwart, the brave, the good guys, tiger; **darer,** blood, gallant *(Archaic)*, sportsman, venturer

hero *n* → **1** famous person **2** fighter **3** good person **4** mythical being **5** ruler

HEROIC STORY *n* epic, epos, gest, saga

heroin *n* → narcotic

herpes *n* → sore

herringbone *v* → ascend

hesitate *v* → **1** be uncertain **2** be unwilling **3** go slowly **4** mispronounce **5** stop **6** vacillate

heterodox *adj* → **1** heretical **2** nonconformist

heterogeneous *adj* → **1** different **2** mixed

heterosexual *n* → **1** sexual type *adj* **2** sexual

heuristic *adj* → questioning

hew *v* → **1** cut **2** level

hex *n* → **1** bad thing **2** luck **3** magic spell **4** misfortune *v* **5** bewitch **6** swear

hexagon *n* → six

HEY *interj* ahem, ahoy, cooee, cop this, halloo, hallow, hello, hey there, hi, hist, I say, look here, N.B., nota bene, there, yack-ai, yoo-hoo; **look out,** fore, timber, watch that last step

heyday *n* → **1** luxury *interj* **2** hooray **3** how about that **4** oh

hiatus *n* → **1** gap **2** interruption **3** interval

hibernate *v* → **1** be inactive **2** seclude **3** sleep

hiccup *v* → breathe

hickory *n* → **1** stick **2** timber

HIDDEN *adj* blind, concealed, dark, dead *(Mil.)*, delitescent, perdu; **camouflaged,** apatetic, sugar-coated; **covered over,** blacked out, gilded, veiled; **private,** backstage, confidential, offstage, privy *(Archaic)*; **unadmitted,** ulterior; **unnoticed,** unmarked, unremarked, unwitnessed; **undercover,** deep-laid, gone to ground, hidden away, secluded, submerged, subterranean, underground; **covert,** anonymous, incognita, incognito, pseudonymous, secret; **obscure,** abstruse *(Obs.)*, arcane, occult, recondite, unilluminating; **cryptic,** cryptogrammic, cryptographic, enigmatic, shrouded in mystery, veiled in mystery

hidden *adj* → secluded

HIDE *n* cowhide, crop, fell, fur, greenhide, kid, pelt, peltry, woolfell *(Obs.)*; **animal skin,** bearskin, broadtail, buckskin, buff, calf, calfskin, cowskin, deerskin, doeskin, goatskin, horsehide, lambskin, pigskin, sealskin, snakeskin, swanskin; **leather,** grain, levant, mocha, morocco, morocco leather, ooze leather, shagreen, suede; **bootlace,** moult, pie piece, scarf, slough. *See also* SKIN

HIDE *v* blot, conceal, cover one's tracks, dissemble, dissimulate, hoodwink *(Obs.)*, hugger-mugger, hush up, mew up, obscure, occult, snooker *(Colloq.)*; **keep secret,** give nothing away, hold back, keep back, keep dark, keep one's own counsel, keep to oneself, let go no further, not breathe a syllable, not breathe a word; **envelop,** adumbrate, becloud, befog, blanket, cloak, clothe, draw the veil, enshroud, mantle, shade, shroud, smother, swallow up, veil; **cache,** bury, harbour, lock up, plant *(Colloq.)*, put out of sight, salt away, salt down, seclude, secrete, shut away, sink, stash, stow away, treasure; **cover,** curtain, cushion, ensconce, mask, screen, screen off; **erase,** efface, obliterate; **disguise,** camouflage, guise *(Scot.)*, mask, masquerade; **cover up,** black out, gild, paper over, whitewash; **watergate,** rort; **bamboozle,** snow; **censor,** suppress. *See also* LIE LOW

hide *n* → **1** area **2** arrogance **3** discourtesy **4** hiding place **5** skin *v* **6** keep secret **7** obscure

hidebound *adj* → **1** intolerant **2** restricted

hideous *adj* → ugly

HIDING *n* adumbration, concealment, covering, coverture, delitescence, effacement, retirement, screening, the dark; **anonymity,** pseudonymity; **secrecy,** covertness, darkness, hugger-mugger *(Archaic)*, retreat, secret, secretness, shade; **cover-up,** double blind, mystification, smokescreen, white lie, whitewash; **smokescreen,** blackout, brownout, dim-out *(U.S.)*, white-out

hiding *n* → **1** corporal punishment **2** hitting **3** losing

HIDING PLACE *n* covert, den, hide-out, hideaway, hidy-hole, lurk, mai mai *(N.Z.)*, mew, retreat; **cache,** plant *(Colloq.)*, stash; **concealed drawer,** false bottom; **hide,** priest-hole, snooker *(Colloq.)*; **ambush,** ambuscade, blind, suprise attack

hierarchy *n* → **1** angel **2** classification

hieroglyphic *n* → **1** letter **2** sign *adj* **3** unclear

HIGH *adj* aerial, aery *(Poetic)*, airy, aloft, apogeal, apogean, high-flying, high-level, midair, sky-high, skyey *(Poetic)*; **altitudinal,** hypsometric; **elevated,** highblocked, highset; **top,** topmost, upper, uppermost; **overhead,** hanging; **uphill,** upstairs. *See also* TALL

HIGH *adv* aerially, midair, overhead, uppishly, upwards; **on high,** aloft, o'er *(Poetic)*, on tiptoe; **loftily,** eminently, grandly, majestically; **mountainously,** precipitously, toweringly

high *n* → **1** atmospheric pressure **2** drug use **3** pleasure **4** school *adj* **5** deteriorated **6** distant **7** drugged **8** drunk **9** expensive **10** great **11** important **12** intense **13** joyful **14** pleased **15** pungent **16** rural **17** shrill **18** smelly **19** tall

highbrow *n* → **1** aesthete **2** intellectual *adj* **3** intellectual **4** knowledgeable **5** tasteful

high-class *adj* → good

HIGH COMMAND *n* generalissimo, supreme commander *(U.S.)*; **officer,** brass, brass hat, commandant, commissioned officer, constable *(Hist.)*, duty officer, ranker, red hat, staff officer, underofficer; **non-commissioned officer,** N.C.O., non-com. *See also* SOLDIER; SERVICEMAN; ARMED FORCES

high-fidelity *adj* → audio

high-handed *adj* → presumptuous

highland *n* → **1** mountain *adj* **2** mountainous

highlight *v* → **1** colour **2** display **3** emphasise

HIGHLY REGARDED *adj* dear, esteemed, good, in high esteem, in high regard, respected, revered, reverend; **respectable,** ancient *(Archaic)*, decent, decorous, estimable, time-honoured, venerable, worthy; **commendable,** commendatory, laudable; **awesome,** awe-inspiring, awful, compelling, dread, dreadful, fearful, impressive, redoubtable, redoubted

highly strung *adj* → worried

HIGH REGARD *n* devotion, esteem, estimation, honour, regard, respect, veneration; **respectfulness,** civility, comity, consideration, courtesy, good manners, regardfulness; **adoration,** hero-worship, homage, idolatry, idolisation, idolism, obsequiousness, piety, piousness, worshipfulness; **awe,** dread, fear, reverence

highway *n* → **1** road **2** route

highwayman *n* → thief

hijack *n* → **1** robbery *v* **2** rob

hike *n* → **1** inflation **2** walk *v* **3** travel

hilarious *adj* → **1** happy **2** humorous

hill *n* → **1** accumulation **2** mound

hillbilly *n* → **1** country dweller *adj* **2** provincial

himself *n* → boss

hind *adj* → rear

HINDER *v* disturb, drag the chain, filibuster, forestall, hold up, impede, incommode, inconvenience, let *(Archaic)*, put a spoke in someone's wheel, queer someone's pitch, retard, set back, spike someone's guns, stonewall; **hamper,** cumber, encumber, lumber, weigh; **handicap,** cramp, penalise, pinch; **thwart,** baffle, bilk, counterwork, cross, dash, dish, dish up, foil, frustrate, interfere, put paid to, snooker, spite, stymie, traverse; **prevent,** forbid, foreclose, interdict, oppose, preclude, prohibit, stop; **trip,** booby trap, cripple, disenable, hogtie *(U.S.)*, lame, mask, snag, tie down, tie someone's hands, trip up; **discourage,** damp, take the wind out of one's sails; **cramp one's style,** discomfit, embarrass. *See also* OBSTRUCT

hinder *v* → **1** incommode **2** restrain **3** stop *adj* **4** rear

HINDERER *n* backstop, baffler, impeder, interceptor, interferer, interposer; **obstructer,** blocker, defeater, dog in the manger, filibusterer, obstructionist, stonewaller; **handicapper,** cumberer, lumberer; **preventer,** counterworker, forbidder, forestaller, opposer, thwarter; **discourager,** damper, heckler, killjoy, spoilsport, wet blanket

HINDERING *adj* cumbersome, cumbrous, impedient, impedimental, impedimentary, impeditive, obstruent, retardative, retardatory; **obstructive,** bloody-minded, difficult, filibusterous; **interceptive,** counteractive, interferential, preclusive, preventive, prohibitive; **in the way,** discouraging, inconvenient, obvious *(Obs.)*

HINDRANCE *n* difficulty, impedient, impediment, let *(Archaic)*, obstruction, rub *(Archaic)*; **encumbrance,** clog, cumber, cumbrance, dead weight, deadwood, fardel, hamper, impedimenta, incubus, lumber, remora *(Archaic)*, weight; **burden,** dead hand, drag; **preventive,** counter measure, countercheck, defeat, penalty; **bar,** conclusion *(Law)*, estoppel; **handicap,** discommodity, embarrassment, inconvenience; **hitch,** embuggerance, fly in the ointment, glitch, nigger in the woodpile, snag, spanner in the works, stick *(Obs.)*; **setback,** check, damp, dash, drawback, facer, throwback; **delaying tactic,** filibuster, stall; **impasse,** brick wall, catch 22, deadlock, stalemate, sticking point, stumbling block, stymie, vicious circle; **bottleneck,** blockage, congestion, jam, shackle, trammels; **blind alley,** cul-de-sac, dead end; **bodycheck,** hand-off, intercept, stiff-arm tackle. *See also* OBSTACLE

hindsight *n* → remembering

hinge *n* → **1** bone **2** centre-line **3** necessities **4** qualification **5** rule **6** support *v* **7** join

hint *n* → **1** allusion **2** guidance **3** information **4** sign **5** signal **6** small amount *v* **7** inform **8** remind

hinterland *n* → **1** land **2** region **3** the bush *adj* **4** rural

hire *n* → **1** income **2** loan *v* **3** borrow **4** buy **5** depute **6** employ

hire-purchase *n* → **1** buying **2** debt **3** loan *v* **4** buy

hirsute *adj* → hairy

HISS *n* sigh, sough, whisper; **rush of air,** swish, whish, whistle, whiz, whoosh, zip; **sibilant,** affricative, aspirate, fricative; **puff,** chuff, chug; **fizz,** bubble, bubbling, fizzing, fizzle, hubble-bubble; **rustle,** crinkle, froufrou; **snuffle,** sneeze, sniffle, snore, snort, sob, souffle; **sizzle,** spatter, sputter; **suck,** slurp

HISS *v* affricate, aspirate, assibilate, blow, sibilate, whistle; **rustle,** crinkle, sigh, sough, swish, whisper; **whoosh,** whish, whiz, zip; **sniffle,** sneeze, sniff, snivel, snore, snuffle; **fizz,** effervesce, fizzle, frizzle, sizzle; **spit,** spatter, splutter, sputter; **hiss a performer,** give someone the bird

hiss *n* → **1** boo **2** breathing **3** insult **4** quiet sound *v* **5** disapprove of

HISSING *n* affrication, assibilation, audible friction, frication, sibilance, sibilancy; **effervescence,** effervescency

HISSING *adj* affricated, aspirated, crinkly, fricative, rushing, rustling, sibilant, wheezy; **fizzy,** effervescent, effervescible, fizzling

HISTORIAN *n* annalist, chronicler; **archaeologist,** Egyptologist, Etruscologist; **antiquarian,** antiquary

historic *adj* → famous

HISTORICAL *adj* annalistic, archival, biographical, hierogrammatic, philologic

historical *adj* → **1** correct **2** past **3** true

history *n* → **1** drama **2** memory **3** narrative **4** past **5** record

histrionic *adj* → **1** affected **2** dramatic **3** emotional **4** exaggerated

histrionics *n* → **1** acting **2** affectation **3** emotion **4** exaggeration

HIT *n* bash, bat, belt, blow, bong, clap, crack, dint *(Obs.)*, drub, knock, swipe; **punch,** biff, box, buff, buffet, clip, clock, clonk, clout, clump, conk, cuff, dong, facer, fisticuff, flea in someone's ear, floorer, job, knuckle sandwich, plug; **pound,** packet, pile-driver, slog, slosh, slug, smash, smasher, sock, wallop, wham, whop; **body blow,** backhander, bolo punch, combination, cross, flick, haymaker, hook, left, pivot punch, rabbit punch, rabbit-killer, rally *(Boxing)*, right, sideswipe, sidewinder *(U.S.)*, sucker punch, uppercut; **king hit,** chop, coup de grâce, death-blow, flattener, knockout, stunner, woodener; **smack,** flap, paddywhack, slap, spank, spat, swat, thwack, whack; **whip,** cut, lash, pandy *(Scot.)*, slash, stripe, swish, switch, thrash, welt; **loft,** flier. *See also* STROKE; TAP

HIT *v* bat, bong, chop, connect with, crease, crown, ding, dob, sideswipe, smite, strike, swat, sweep, swing at, swipe, zot; **tap,** bob, dab, dub, fillip, flap, flick, pat, peck, rap, spat, tip, touch; **drum,** percuss, thrum; **bang,** knock, rap, slam, slay *(Obs.)*, thud, thump, wham, whang; **smack,** clap, paddle *(U.S.)*, slap, slipper, snap, spank, thwack, whack; **bash,** belt, dash, pound, ram, slog, sock, thump, wallop, whop; **punch,** biff, bop, box, buffet, clip, clock, clonk, clout, clump, conk, cuff, dong, dot, fist, fisticuff, hang one on someone, job, mug, plug, roof, scone, slug, take a poke at, uppercut; **hammer,** beetle, gavel, knap, tamp. *See also* BEAT; CUDGEL

hit *n* → **1** drug use **2** mockery **3** success *v* **4** arrive **5** attack **6** contact **7** take drugs *adj* **8** famous

hitch *n* → **1** bond **2** disenchantment **3** hindrance **4** journey **5** military service **6** period **7** pull *v* **8** drive **9** marry **10** pull

hitchhike *v* → drive

hither *adj* → **1** close *adv* **2** closely

hitherto *adv* → in the past

HITTING *n* bashing, buffeting, pounding; **beating,** bastinado, belting, drubbing, hammering, hiding, lacing *(Brit.)*, larruping, milling *(Brit.)*, pasting, plastering, spanking, tanning, thrashing, towelling, trimming, walloping; **assault,** battery, corporal punishment, once-over, the works; **whipping,** bob, bull, canary, flagellation, flogging, fustigation *(Archaic)*, lashing, tester; **stoning,** lapidation, pelting. *See also* IMPACT

hive *n* → **1** animal dwelling **2** centre of activity **3** insect **4** many *v* **5** shelter

hives *n* → sore

hoard *n* → **1** accumulation **2** storage *v* **3** gather **4** store

hoarding *n* → public notice

hoarse *adj* → **1** dissonant **2** quiet

hoary *adj* → **1** aged **2** grey-haired **3** hairy **4** white

hoax *n* → **1** trick *v* **2** trick

hobble *n* → **1** dilemma **2** restraints **3** walking *v* **4** confuse **5** fasten **6** restrain **7** walk

hobby *n* → a good time

hobgoblin *n* → **1** fairy **2** frightener

hobnob *v* → **1** associate **2** be friends

hobo *n* → **1** poor person **2** traveller **3** worker

hock *n* → **1** buttocks **2** sexual type *v* **3** lend **4** sell

hocus pocus *n* → nonsense

hocus-pocus *n* → **1** illusion **2** magic spell **3** trickery *v* **4** trick

hod *n* → box

hoe *n* → **1** digging implement *v* **2** farm

hog *n* → **1** dirty person **2** glutton **3** self-seeker **4** watercraft *v* **5** curve **6** cut

hogget *n* → sheep

hogwash *n* → nonsense

hoi polloi *n* → working class

hoist *n* → **1** flag **2** lift **3** robbery *v* **4** lift **5** rob

HOLD *n* clench, clinch, close, grab, grapple, wrestle; **wrestling hold,** arm lock, body scissors, collar-and-elbow, grapevine, hammer lock, headlock, lock, maginnis, octopus clamp, scissors, toehold, wristlock; **grip,** bite, clutch, grasp, gripe, purchase; **eastern grip,** handshake grip; **hug,** bear hug, clasp, cuddle, embrace

HOLD *v* bite, clench, grip, gripe, handle, hold the road, nip; **hold down,** guy, immobolise; **grasp,** catch, catch at, clasp, clutch, clutch at, lay hold of, seize, strain; **clinch,** grapple, hang on, pin; **cling,** cleave, hold fast; **clamp,** cramp, vice; **reserve,** book, put aside; **detain,** buttonhole, collar; **withold,** deforce; **keep,** have, retain; **hug,** bosom, cuddle, embosom, embrace, fold, press; **nurse,** cradle, inarm

hold *n* → **1** fortress **2** influence **3** stand *v* **4** believe **5** disuse **6** imprison **7** include **8** operate **9** own **10** stick together **11** support

HOLDER *n* billy tongs, clams, forceps, lazy tongs, nippers, pincers, pliers, sugar tongs, tongs, tweezers; **clamp,** bitstock, bootjack, brace, bracing, clam, cramp, face-plate, head, jig, oarlock, tailstock, vice; **clasp,** catch, clip, split ring, tiepin, woggle; **clipboard,** copyholder, folder; **hook,** anchor, grapnel, grappling hook, grappling iron, jaw; **climbing irons,** chock-stone, clinker, piton

HOLDING *n* deforcement *(Law)*, retention, retentiveness, retentivity, tenaciousness, tenacity, tenure; **reservation,** booking, withholding; **prehension,** grasping, prehensility, retainment

HOLDING *adj* cheliform, grasping, griping, prehensile, raptorial; **tenacious,** clingy, retentive

holding *n* → ownership

HOLD IN LOW REGARD *v* belittle, depreciate, misesteem, misprise, underrate, underestimate, undervalue; **despise,** contemn *(Archaic)*, curl one's lip, disdain, disesteem, disprize *(Archaic)*, disvalue *(Rare)*, give someone the glassy eye, give someone the greasy eyeball, look down on, look down one's nose at, revile, scorn, snap one's fingers at, sneer at, sneeze at, sniff at, snuff at *(Obs.)*, thumb one's nose, turn one's nose up; **disrespect,** disregard, flout, make free with, profane, violate

hold up *v* → **1** defer **2** display **3** erect **4** hinder **5** rob **6** stop

hold-up *n* → **1** lateness **2** robbery

hole *n* → **1** animal dwelling **2** bay **3** buttocks **4** cabin **5** dilemma **6** groin **7** hollow **8** mouth **9** opening **10** prison **11** seclusion *v* **12** break **13** dig **14** open

HOLIDAY *n* bank holiday, day of rest, dies non, festa, fete, fete day, flex-day, flexiday, half-day, half-holiday, half-term *(Brit.)*, lay day *(Sport)*, long weekend, Lord's day, Picnic Day, public holiday, Sabbath, weekend; **leave,** bush week, Christmas holidays, Easter holidays, furlough, holidays, hollies, hols, leave of absence, long service leave, long vacation, maternity leave, R and R *(U.S. Mil.)*, rec leave, shore leave, time off, vac, vacation; **study leave,** sabbatical, stu vac, swot vac

holiday *n* → **1** festival **2** holy day *v* **3** rest *adj* **4** festive **5** resting

HOLLOW *n* calyx, cavity, cup, funnel; **hole,** kettle hole, pitfall, pot *(Scot.)*, pothole, tomo *(N.Z.)*; **pocket,** amygdale, druse, geode, vugh; **dish,** depression, scoop; **basin,** amphitheatre, bolson, bunker, caldera, cirque, coomb, corrie, crater, devil's punchbowl, doline, lap, pan, polje, retarding basin, river basin, saddle, salt flat, saltpan, shott, volcanic neck, walled plain; **valley,** dale, dell, dip, glen, gully, vale; **waterhole,** artesian basin, claypan, melon hole, namma hole, soak, soak hole, wallow, watering hole; **sink,** sinkhole, soakage pit, sump; **hollowness,** concaveness, concavity, curvature, sag. *See also* ORGANIC CAVITY; NICHE; CAVE; EXCAVATION; INDENTATION

HOLLOW *v* concave, dig out, dish, gouge, hollow out, scoop; **excavate,** burrow, drive, mine, open-cut, sink, tunnel, undermine; **pit,** crater, dimple; **drill,** dibble, rout; **dent,** depress, indent; **stamp,** impress, press in

HOLLOW *adj* cavernous, concave *(Obs.)*, cryptal, spelaean, tomblike; **sunken,** basined, dished, shallow; **concave,** amphicoelous, biconcave, concavo-concave, concavo-convex, plano-concave; **pitted,** craterous, dented, dimpled, dimply, foveal, foveate, foveolate, pockmarked, rimose, variolous; **crannied,** nooky; **cup-shaped,** arytenoid, cotyloid, cuplike, cupped, cyathiform, glenoid, infundibular; **bottle-shaped,** ampullaceal; **bladder-like,** bladdery, pouchy, vesicular, vesiculate; **navel-like,** umbilicate, umbiliform

hollow *adj* → **1** deceitful **2** hungry **3** quiet **4** resonant *adv* **5** greatly

holocaust *n* → **1** massacre **2** religious ceremony **3** ruin **4** victimisation

holster *n* → **1** arsenal **2** case

HOLY *adj* blessed, Christly, hallowed, sainted, saintly, supernal; **sacred,** sacrosanct, taboo, tapu *(N.Z.)*

holy *n* → place of worship

HOLY DAY *n* feast-day, festival, fete, fete day, harvest festival, holiday, jubilee, movable feast, vigil; **fast day,** Day of Atonement, fast, Lent, Ramadan, rogations; **Holy Week,** Christmas, Easter, Eastertide, epiphany, Lent, Passion Week, Passover, Pentecost, Pesach, Ramadan, Shrovetide, tide

HOLY PERSON *n* arhat, bodhisattva, hafiz, maharishi, mahatma, man of God, saint; **martyr,** Job, patron saint, stigmatic; **icon,** Madonna, Mater dolorosa, noli-me-tangere, pietà; **halo,** aureole, gloriole, glory, nimbus, stigma

homage *n* → **1** contract **2** high regard **3** obedience **4** obsequiousness *v* **5** be faithful to

home *n* → **1** animal dwelling **2** dwelling **3** house **4** nation **5** refuge *v* **6** direct **7** go back *adj* **8** domestic **9** national **10** resident

Home *n* → hospital

homeland *n* → nation

homely *adj* → **1** domestic **2** ugly

homesick *adj* → unhappy

homespun *n* → **1** textiles *adj* **2** simple

homestead *n* → **1** farm **2** house

homicide *n* → killing

homily *n* → oration

HOMOGENEOUS *adj* diffused, even, uniform; **solid,** monolithic, monomorphic, of a piece, unstratified; **constant,** monotonous, regular, steady; **monotone,** fleckless, immaculate *(Zool. Bot.)*, orthotropous *(Bot.)*, self-coloured; **identical,** identic *(Obs.)*, indistinguishable, same, selfsame

HOMOGENEOUSLY *adv* indistinguishably, solidly, uniformly; **constantly,** steadily, steady; **alike,** ibid, ibidem, identically

HOMOGENISE *v* gauge, identify, uniformalise *(Rare)*

homogenise *v* → mix

homogenous *adj* → simple

homologous *adj* → congruous

homonym *n* → **1** equivalent **2** name
Homo sapiens *n* → person
homosexual *n* → **1** man **2** sexual type *adj* **3** male **4** sexual
homosexuality *n* → sexuality
hone *n* → sharpener
HONEST *adj* aboveboard, all wool and a yard wide, authentic, bona fide, clean, downright, flat, legit, on the up and up *(U.S.)*, plain, scrupulous, square, straight, straight-out, straight-up, unfeigned, upright; **genuine,** dinkum, dinky, dinky-di, fair dinkum, true-hearted, truthful, veracious, veridical; **straightforward,** blunt, candid, earnest, frank, free-spoken, guileless, jonick, manly, open, outspoken, plain-spoken, round, simple-hearted, sincere, single, single-minded, unreserved, up-front; **reliable,** as good as one's word, sound, steadfast, true *(Archaic)*, trustworthy, trusty, upstanding; **fair,** disinterested, even-handed, honourable, virtuous
honest *adj* → **1** abstinent **2** fair **3** forthright **4** truthful
HONESTLY *adv* aboveboard, by fair means, fair and square, fairly, on the level, plainly, square, straight from the shoulder, unfeignedly; **straightforwardly,** candidly, frankly, from the bottom of one's heart, heart-to-heart, openly, outspokenly, sincerely, single-mindedly, straightly; **genuinely,** in all conscience, truthfully, veraciously, veridically, verily *(Archaic)*; **reliably,** trustily, trustworthily; **honourably,** virtuously, without fear or favour
HONESTLY *interj* blood oath, dicken, dinkum, fair dinkum, honest to God, honour bright, in truth, on my word
HONEST PERSON *n* flat *(Obs.)*, man of his word, man of honour, plain-dealer, square-shooter, straight talker, straightshooter, white man *(Brit.)*, woman of her word, woman of honour
HONESTY *n* incorruptness, integrity, plain dealing, plainness, probity, scrupulosity, sincerity, straightness; **straightforwardness,** candidness, candour, frankness, free-spokenness, openness, outspokenness, sincereness, single-mindedness, unreserve, unreservedness; **genuineness,** fact, reality, sooth *(Archaic)*, truth, truthfulness, unfeignedness, veraciousness, veracity, veridicality; **reliability,** bona fides, reliableness, soundness, trueness, trustiness, trustworthiness; **good faith,** uberrima fidei; **the genuine article,** the dinkum article, the drum, the full two bob, the good guts, the good oil, the griff, the real thing, the straight wire; **fairness,** honour, impartiality, manliness, virtue, virtuousness; **point of honour,** matter of principle
honey *n* → **1** good person **2** good thing **3** lover **4** sweetness **5** yellow *v* **6** kiss *adj* **7** beloved
honeymoon *n* → **1** contentedness **2** wedding
honk *n* → **1** birdcall **2** boom *v* **3** chirp **4** ring
honorarium *n* → cost
honorary *n* → **1** healer *adj* **2** cheap **3** unpaid
honorific *n* → name
honour *n* → **1** commemoration **2** faithfulness **3** high regard **4** honesty **5** mister **6** reputation **7** reverence *v* **8** congratulate **9** glorify **10** respect **11** worship
hood *n* → **1** criminal **2** emblem of office **3** headgear *v* **4** blind **5** cover
hoodlum *n* → **1** adolescent **2** criminal **3** destroyer **4** mischief-maker
hoodwink *v* → **1** blind **2** hide **3** trick
hoof *n* → leg
hook *n* → **1** allure **2** anchor **3** curve **4** fishing tackle **5** hit **6** holder **7** musical score **8** region **9** stroke *v* **10** beguile **11** capture **12** curve **13** deflect **14** marry **15** rob **16** sew
hookah *n* → **1** drug equipment **2** tobacco
hooked *adj* → **1** curved **2** married
hooligan *n* → **1** mischief-maker *adj* **2** badly-behaved
hoop *n* → **1** dress **2** ring **3** underwear *v* **4** surround
HOORAY *interj* alleluia, eureka, Glory be, heaven be praised, heyday *(Archaic)*, hosanna, hurrah, huzza, rah, saints be praised, whoopee
hooray *interj* → **1** congratulations **2** well done
hoot *n* → **1** animal call **2** compensation **3** mirth **4** mockery **5** shout *v* **6** be loud **7** call (of animals) **8** laugh **9** mock **10** shout
hop *n* → **1** dance **2** flight **3** jump **4** party *v* **5** dance **6** depart **7** jump **8** move **9** walk
HOPE *n* aspiration, belief, confidence, esperance *(Obs.)*, faith, hopefulness, trust; **optimism,** buoyancy, enterprise, insouciance, overconfidence, positivism; **anticipation,** contemplation, expectation, foresight, foretaste; **wishful thinking,** false optimism, micawberism; **dream,** pie in the sky, pious hope, pipedream, velleity, vision; **favourite,** comer, fancy *(Horseracing)*, hope, white hope; **silver lining,** relief, uplift
HOPE *v* aspire after, aspire to, believe, have faith, trust; **be hopeful,** catch at straws, gamble, hope against hope, keep one's fingers crossed, look on the bright side, look through rose-coloured glasses, optimise, rally; **expect,** anticipate, believe in, contemplate, count on, count one's chickens before they are hatched, count upon, hope for, hope in, lean on, lick one's chops, lick one's lips, pin one's hopes on, place one's trust in, put confidence in, trust in; **dream,** build castles in the air, fantasise, live in a fool's paradise
hope *n* → **1** expectation **2** hope *v* **3** depend on
HOPEFUL *adj* bullish, buoyant, optimistic, overconfident, positive, positivist, positivistic, rose-coloured, up-beat; **confident,** happy-go-lucky, insouciant, radiant, sanguine, starry-eyed; **aspiring,** aspirant *(Rare)*, would-be
hopeful *n* → **1** children **2** expected thing *adj* **3** expectant **4** favourable
HOPELESS *adj* beyond remedy, fatal *(Obs.)*, immedicable, incurable, inoperable, irrecoverable, irredeemable, irremeable, irre-

mediable, irreparable, irretrievable, irreversible; **desperate,** dead-end, futureless; **inevitable,** defeated, gone, unavoidable; **bleak,** black, comfortless, depressive, desolate, feral *(Archaic)*, funereal, unbearable

horde *n* → **1** gathering **2** many **3** relative *v* **4** gather

horizon *n* → **1** layer **2** level **3** limit

horizontal *n* → **1** level *adj* **2** level

horn *n* → **1** brass instrument **2** groin **3** knob **4** piercer **5** siren **6** sound system **7** warning

horoscope *n* → fortune-telling

horrendous *adj* → **1** dreadful **2** frightening

horrible *adj* → **1** dreadful **2** frightening

horrid *adj* → **1** dreadful **2** frightening **3** ugly

horrific *adj* → **1** dreadful **2** frightening

horrify *v* → **1** displease **2** frighten

horror *n* → **1** bad thing **2** fright **3** frightener **4** ugly person **5** unpleasant thing

horse *n* → **1** armed forces **2** stand *v* **3** ascend **4** cudgel *adj* **5** great

horseplay *n* → amusement

horsepower *n* → energy

horseshoe *n* → **1** curve **2** lucky charm *adj* **3** curved

hortatory *adj* → encouraging

horticulture *n* → gardening

hose *n* → **1** piping **2** tights *v* **3** wet

hosiery *n* → clothier

hospice *n* → **1** hospital **2** hotel **3** refuge

hospitable *adj* → **1** friendly **2** generous **3** sociable

HOSPITAL *n* base hospital, community hospital, cottage hospital, district hospital, general hospital, infirmary, institution, maternity hospital, pavilion, polyclinic *(Brit.)*, private hospital, public hospital, spital *(Obs.)*, teaching hospital; **field hospital,** clearing hospital, clearing station, dressing station; **clinic,** baby health centre, fertility clinic, health centre, prenatal clinic, STD clinic, the house that Jack built, V.D. clinic; **nursing home,** convalescent home, Home, hospice; **sanatorium,** isolation hospital, lazaretto, leprosarium; **sick room,** san, sanatorium, sick bay, solarium; **ward,** casualty, intensive care unit, labour ward, nursery, outpatients' department, private ward, public ward

hospitality *n* → **1** friendliness **2** generosity **3** sociability

host *n* → **1** armed forces **2** crowd **3** many

hostage *n* → surety

hostel *n* → hotel

hostess *n* → waiter

hostile *n* → **1** dissident *adj* **2** hating **3** unfriendly

HOT *adj* baking, blazing, blistering, furnace-like, hot as Hades, hot as Hay Hell and Booligal, roasting, scalding, scorching, sweltering; **fervent,** afire, aflame, ardent, fervid, fiery, perfervid; **incandescent,** candent, ignescent; **burning,** glowing, live, living; **heated,** caustic, overheated, piping hot, red-hot, superheated, white-hot; **fiery,** angry, inflammatory; **fevered,** febrile, feverish, hectic, pyrexial, pyrexic, subfebrile; **warm,** lukewarm, tepid, warmish; **summery,** summer, summer-like, sun-drenched; **fine,** balmy, fair, genial, mild, sunny, sunshiny, temperate; **humid,** close, muggy, oppressive, stifling, suffocating, sultry, sweltering; **tropical,** equatorial, semitropical, torrid, tropic, ultratropical

hot *adj* → **1** chain-reacting **2** close **3** colourful **4** emotional **5** fashionable **6** ferocious **7** new **8** obscene **9** pungent **10** stolen **11** voluptuous

hotbed *n* → **1** breeding ground **2** garden

hot-blooded *adj* → **1** excited **2** rash

hotchpotch *n* → **1** jumble **2** mixture

hotch-potch *adj* → mixed

hot dog *n* → **1** specialist **2** surfboard *interj* **3** oh **4** well done

HOTEL *n* convention centre, halfway house, hostel *(Archaic)*, hostelry *(Archaic)*, house, inn, lodge, motel, pub, public house, roadhouse, tavern; **hostel,** youth hostel; **boarding house,** guesthouse, hydro, lodging house, pension, resort, rooming house *(U.S.)*, spa; **bunkhouse,** charnel-house, dosshouse, flophouse; **poorhouse,** almshouse, beadhouse *(Brit.)*, hospice; **creche,** baby-farm; **accommodation,** bed, bed and board, bed and breakfast, billet, board, full board, housing, lodging, lodgment *(Rare)*, pension

hotel *n* → pub

HOTHEAD *n* bull at a gate, harum-scarum, hotspur, madcap, rusher; **daredevil,** adventurer, adventuress, fire-eater, gambler, Icarus, Promethean, scapegrace; **desperado,** bravo, destructo

hot-headed *adj* → rash

hothouse *n* → **1** breeding ground **2** garden *adj* **3** weak

hotplate *n* → stove

hound *n* → **1** bad person **2** dog **3** drug user *v* **4** act unkindly **5** arouse **6** be unfriendly **7** pursue

hour *n* → **1** crucial moment **2** time

HOUSE *n* home; **terrace house,** semi, town house, villa *(Chiefly Brit.)*, villa home, villa unit; **cottage,** bungalow, dower house, project house, tied cottage *(Brit.)*; **housing commission house,** council house *(Brit.)*, glebe house, state house *(N.Z.)*; **block,** duplex, mews, row, terrace; **housing estate,** cluster housing, council estate *(Brit.)*, estate, housing development; **homestead,** Government house *(Colloq.)*, grange, hacienda, hall, head station, ranch house, rancho, station house, the house; **country house,** chateau, court, dacha, manor, manor house, seat, villa; **bure,** donga *(Papua New Guinea)*, igloo, rondavel; **beehive house; adobe,** wattle and daub; **rectory,** manse, parsonage, presbytery, vicarage; **farmhouse,** farm; **bower,** bush house; **maisonette,** doll's house; **premises,** messuage; **lodge,** gatehouse, schoolhouse, tollhouse; **split-level house,** blockhouse, garrison, lake-dwelling, pile-dwelling; **palace,** castle, palazzo, seigneury, seigniory, seraglio. *See also* CABIN

HOUSE *v* accommodate, domicile, domiciliate; **lodge,** billet, board, put up, quarter, take in; **bed down,** sleep, stay at; **keep house,** run an establishment

house *n* → 1 ancestry 2 auditorium 3 community 4 council 5 fortune-telling 6 hotel 7 legislative body *v* 8 fasten 9 shelter *adj* 10 domestic

household *n* → 1 occupant *adj* 2 conventional 3 domestic

housekeeper *n* → 1 labourer 2 manager 3 servant 4 supplier

housewife *n* → 1 case 2 labourer 3 manager

housing *n* → 1 bedclothes 2 covering 3 hotel

hovel *n* → cabin

hover *n* → 1 lightness *v* 2 float 3 fly 4 tower 5 vacillate

HOW *adv* what *(Obs.)*, whereby; **however,** howsoever, howsomever; **any way,** by hook or by crook; **so,** thus; **hereby,** herewith; **in a manner,** after a fashion, in a fashion, in a manner of speaking

how *n* → 1 method *adv* 2 very 3 why

HOW ABOUT THAT *interj* can you beat that, fancy, garn, hush my mouth, I declare *(U.S.)*, I'll be a son of a gun *(U.S.)*, indeed, my hat, my sainted aunt, my word, well I never, will wonders never cease, you wouldn't read about it; **goodness,** ah, bless me, blimey, blow me down, bugger me, bugger me dead, by gum *(Brit.)*, fuck me, fuck me dead, goodness gracious, gorblimey, heavens, heigh-ho, hey-day *(Archaic)*, la *(Archaic)*, O, oh, shiver my timbers, starve the bardies, starve the crows, stiffen the crows, stone the crows, strike me dead, strike me lucky, strike me pink, strike-a-light, struth; **hell's bells,** for crying out loud, good grief, hell's teeth, holy cow, holy mackerel, holy Moses, I ask you, Jesus, Jesus Christ, lawks *(Archaic)*, the devil, what, what on earth; **far out,** fuck, gee, gee whiz, Glory be, golly, lo and behold, oh boy, phew, shit, whew, wow

however *adv* → 1 conditionally 2 how 3 nevertheless *conj* 4 still

howl *n* → 1 animal call 2 cry 3 loud sound 4 mirth 5 shout *v* 6 be loud 7 blow 8 call (of animals) 9 grieve 10 mock 11 shout

hub *n* → 1 centre 2 point of convergence

hubbub *n* → 1 commotion 2 loud sound 3 turbulence

huddle *n* → 1 gathering 2 jumble 3 secret society *v* 4 gather

hue *n* → 1 character 2 colour 3 shouting

huff *n* → 1 angry act 2 gas *v* 3 anger 4 breathe 5 pride oneself

hug *n* → 1 endearments 2 friendship 3 hold *v* 4 hold 5 kiss 6 love

huge *adj* → 1 big 2 enormous

hulk *n* → 1 discard 2 giant 3 incompetent 4 watercraft

hull *v* → bare

hullabaloo *n* → 1 commotion 2 loud sound

hum *n* → 1 animal call 2 asker 3 click 4 quiet sound 5 request *v* 6 be busy 7 beg 8 be smelly 9 call (of animals) 10 click 11 sing

HUMAN *adj* carnal, earthborn, mortal; **incarnate,** impersonate; **humanoid,** anthropoid anthropomorphous, australopithecine hominoid, pithecanthropoid; **racial,** ethnic interracial, intertribal, phyletic, phylogenic

human *n* → person

humane *adj* → 1 kind 2 lenient 3 pitying

humanitarian *n* → 1 pitier 2 unselfish person *adj* 3 kind 4 pitying

HUMANITY *n* generations of man, human family, human race, human society, human species, humankind, man, mankind, microcosm, the living; **the world,** the earth, the universe; **people,** brothers, fellow creatures, fellow man, folk, neighbours; **race,** ethnic group; **earthling,** earthman, postdiluvian tellurian; **humanness,** carnality, flesh, flesh and blood, human nature, manhood, subsistence *(Philos.)*

humanity *n* → 1 kindness 2 pity

HUMBLE *v* abase, abash, bastardise, bring down, chagrin, confound *(Archaic)*, confuse, crush, cut down to size, dash, flatten, give someone the arse, give someone the big A, give someone the bum's rush, humiliate, lower, mortify, put someone in his place, put out of countenance, put someone down, send away with a flea in one's ear, snub, take down, take down a peg, wipe the floor with

humble *adj* → 1 meek 2 regardful

humbug *n* → 1 fake 2 faker 3 trick *v* 4 trick

humdrum *n* → 1 bore 2 boringness 3 speaking *adj* 4 boring

humid *adj* → 1 hot 2 wet

humiliate *v* → 1 disgrace 2 humble 3 insult

humility *n* → 1 meekness 2 modesty

hummock *n* → mound

HUMORIST *n* amuser, cap and bells, clown, comedian, comedienne, comic, farceur, jester, mimic, stand-up comic; **joker,** card, dag, doer, hard case, hard doer, monkey, scream, wag; **practical joker,** buffoon, gagger, imp, japer, pantagruelist, prankster, Rabelaisian; **banterer,** josher, kidder, sporter; **wit,** punster, quipster, wisecracker, witling; **satirist,** lampooner, lampoonist

HUMOROUS *adj* amusing, Chaplinesque, comic, comical, droll, fun, funny, humoristic, laughable, risible; **hilarious,** killing, priceless, screaming, side-splitting, uproarious; **Rabelaisian,** pantagruelian; **seriocomic,** tragicomical; **farcical,** absurd, Gilbertian, ludicrous, zany; **slapstick,** custard-pie, prankish; **witty,** Attic, bright, clever, salty, scintillating; **ironic,** caustic, dry, facete *(Archaic)*, mordant, sarcastic, wry; **quizzical,** daggish, whimsical; **bantering,** facetious, playful, sly, sportful, tongue-in-cheek; **jesting,** jocose, jocular, merry, mirthful, pleasant, waggish

humorous *adj* → wet

HUMOUR *n* Attic salt, Attic wit, comedy, drollery, fun, salt, whimsy, wit; **humorousness,** amusingness, drollness, funniness, hilariousness, jocoseness, jocosity, jocularity, risibility, uproariousness; **merriness,** clownishness, funny bone, impishness, mirthfulness, playfulness, scintillation, sense of humour, sportfulness, waggery, waggishness; **absurdity,** absurdness, comicality, comicalness, ludicrousness, whimsicality, whimsicalness, zanyism; **wittiness,** dryness, epigramatism, facetiousness, saltiness, wryness. *See also* COMEDY; MIRTH; JOKE

humour *n* → **1** caprice **2** character *v* **3** be lenient

hump *n* → **1** bulge **2** mound **3** railway **4** surf *v* **5** bulge **6** have sex **7** transport

humpy *n* → **1** cabin **2** shelter *adj* **3** swollen

humus *n* → **1** fertile land **2** soil

hunch *n* → **1** anticipation **2** bulge **3** caprice **4** conjecture **5** idea *v* **6** bulge

HUNCHBACKED *adj* gibbous, humpbacked, roach-backed, round-shouldered

HUNDRED *n* century, hundredth, ton

HUNDRED *adj* centesimal, centuple, hundredfold, hundredth

hundred *n* → domain

HUNGER *n* edaciousness, edacity, hungriness, pecker, stomach, turophilia, voraciousness, voracity

HUNGER *v* have hollow legs, have the munchies; **thirst**

hunger *n* → desire

HUNGRY *adj* edacious, empty, famished, hollow, hungry as a hunter, peckish, ravening, ravenous, sharp-set, starveling, starving, voracious; **gluttonous,** bulimic, greedy

hungry *adj* → **1** avaricious **2** infertile **3** mean

hunk *n* → **1** man **2** part **3** sex object

HUNT *v* course, drive, follow the hounds, gun, prey, raven *(Obs.)*, ride to hounds, stalk, still-hunt *(U.S.)*; **ferret,** beagle, flight, hark back, hawk, run, scent; **trap,** ensnare, entrap, run to earth, run to ground, snare, springe, tree, wire; **rabbit,** beat, bird, fowl, frog, mouse, pigstick, rat, snipe, wolf

hunt *n* → **1** hunter **2** inspection **3** pursuit **4** ringing *v* **5** dismiss **6** flutter **7** pursue **8** repel

HUNTER *n* batfowler, beater, birder *(Colloq.)*, birdman, bounty hunter *(U.S.)*, chaser, chasseur, deerculler *(N.Z.)*, deerstalker, dog catcher, falconer, ferreter, field, fowler, fox-hunter, gun, harrier, hunt, huntress, huntsman, huntswoman, jaeger, mutton-birder, Nimrod, pigsticker, pink, pothunter, rabbiter, ranger, ratcatcher, shikari *(India)*, snarer, sportsman, sportswoman, stalker, trapper, trepanner, venerer *(Archaic)*, wildfowler, wirer, wolver, woodcraftsman *(U.S.)*, woodman *(Obs.)*, woodsman; **courser,** beagle, bloodhound, cry, gun dog, kangaroo dog, mouser, otterhound, pig-dog, preyer, ratter, retriever, sleuth, sleuthhound

HUNTING *n* bloodsport, course, coursing, deerstalking, dogging, falconry, flight shooting, fowling, fox-hunting, gunning, muttonbirding, pigsticking, sport, spotlighting, stalk, venery *(Archaic)*, wildfowling, woodcraft *(U.S.)*

hurdle *n* → **1** obstacle **2** sledge *v* **3** accomplish **4** jump

hurl *n* → **1** expulsion **2** throw *v* **3** speak **4** throw **5** vomit

hurricane *n* → **1** lighting **2** violent outburst **3** wind

HURRIEDLY *adv* cursorily, hastily, hectically, helter-skelter, hurriedly, hurry-scurry, hurryingly, in haste, on the fly *(U.S.)*, precipitantly, precipitately, summarily; **all at once,** pop, sharp, short, slam-bang, slap, slap-bang, smack; **promptly,** anon *(Archaic)*, directly, forthright *(Archaic)*, forthwith, in short order, presently *(Archaic)*, pronto, quick smart, smartly, soon, yarely; **express,** expeditiously, post, posthaste

HURRY *v* be quick off the mark, bicker, bust a gut, chase, come along, come on, dash, dispatch *(Archaic)*, get a move on, get a wriggle on, get the hell out of, haste *(Archaic)*, hasten, hie, hop to it, hurry-scurry, jump to it, lash, make haste, make it snappy, put one's best foot forward, rush, shake a leg, shoot, swash; **expedite,** express *(U.S.)*; **spur,** boot home *(Horseracing)*, brisk up, buck up, gee up, hustle, press, prick *(Archaic)*. *See also* SPEED

hurry *n* → speed

hurt *n* → **1** harm **2** insult **3** pain *v* **4** act unkindly **5** displease **6** injure **7** make unhappy **8** pain *adj* **9** acrimonious

hurtle *n* → **1** impact *v* **2** collide **3** speed **4** throw

husband *n* → **1** man **2** spouse *v* **3** farm **4** manage **5** save

husbandry *n* → **1** farming **2** management **3** thrift

hush *n* → **1** silence *v* **2** alleviate **3** clean **4** silence *adj* **5** silent *interj* **6** silence

husk *n* → **1** covering **2** skin *v* **3** separate

husky *n* → **1** giant **2** strong person *adj* **3** quiet **4** strong

hussy *n* → sexual partner

hustings *n* → **1** election **2** platform

hustle *n* → **1** busyness **2** vitality *v* **3** advance **4** arouse **5** be energetic **6** hurry **7** prostitute oneself **8** sell **9** swindle

hut *n* → **1** barracks **2** cabin **3** shelter *v* **4** inhabit

hutch *n* → **1** animal dwelling **2** cabin **3** container **4** cupboard **5** shelter *v* **6** store

HYBRID *n* creamie, cross, Eurasian, half-blood, half-breed, half-caste, heterozygote, mestizo, mongrel, mosaic *(Genetics)*, mulatto, mule, octoroon, quadroon; **bitser,** Heinz, melting pot, ten best breeds in town

HYBRID *adj* cross, half-blooded, half-caste, heterozygous, interbred, miscegenetic, mongrel, multi-racial

hybrid *n* → **1** descendant **2** offspring **3** something different *adj* **4** genetic

HYBRIDISE *v* cross, interbreed, mongrelise

hydraulic *adj* → liquid

hydrofoil *n* → **1** beam **2** motor vessel

hydroplane *n* → **1** aircraft **2** motor vessel

hydroponics *n* → farming

hygiene *n* → health
hygienic *adj* → 1 clean 2 wholesome
hymen *n* → groin
hymn *n* → 1 applause 2 poetry 3 song *v* 4 approve 5 rejoice 6 sing
hymnal *n* → breviary
hype *n* → 1 affectedness 2 drug equipment 3 drug user 4 incentive 5 inserter 6 piercer 7 publicity 8 trick *v* 9 trick
hyperbola *n* → curve
hyperbole *n* → 1 exaggeration 2 figure of speech
hypnosis *n* → 1 psychotherapy 2 sleeping 3 unconsciousness
hypocrisy *n* → 1 affectedness 2 fake
hypocrite *n* → 1 affected person 2 faker
hypodermic *n* → 1 drug equipment 2 inserter 3 medication *adj* 4 medicinal 5 skin
hypothesis *n* → 1 conjecture 2 qualification
hypothetical *adj* → 1 conditional 2 conjectural 3 empirical 4 uncertain
hysteria *n* → 1 excitement 2 psychic disturbance

Ii

ibidem *adv* → homogeneously

ICE *n* brash *(Naut.)*, cornice, dry ice, floe, frazil, glacier, icecap, icefall, icefield, icefloe, icepack, icesheet, iceshelf, water-ice; **anchor-ice,** dead ice, drift ice, glaze, glaze ice, glazed frost, ground ice, icefoot, icefront, pack-ice, pancake ice; **ice needles,** frost flower, graupel, hail, hailstone, sleet, soft hail; **icicle,** bollard, serac; **iceberg,** berg; **ice-cube,** iceblock, party ice; **icerink,** rink; **glaciology**

ice *n* → **1** formality **2** jewel **3** smooth object *v* **4** be cold **5** coat **6** cool

iceberg *n* → ice

icicle *n* → ice

icing *n* → covering

icon *n* → **1** holy person **2** painting

iconoclast *n* → **1** destroyer **2** irreverent person **3** nonconformist

icy *adj* → **1** callous **2** cold **3** formal **4** smooth **5** unsociable

IDEA *n* abstract, abstraction, apprehension, conceit, concept, conception, construct, form, generalisation, image, intellection, notion, recept, theory, thought; **fixed idea,** conceit, idée fixe, kink, obsession, vagary; **brainwave,** brainstorm, suggestion, tip, wrinkle *(Colloq.)*; **intuition,** feeling, gut feeling, gut reaction, hunch, inspiration, instinct, presentiment, sixth sense; **inkling,** glimmer, glimmering, glimpse, impression

idea *n* → **1** example **2** good thing **3** image **4** music **5** opinion **6** perfect thing **7** plan **8** portrait **9** the intangible

ideal *n* → **1** aim **2** example **3** good thing **4** perfect thing **5** the intangible *adj* **6** good **7** model **8** notional **9** perfect

idealise *v* → **1** etherealise **2** perfect

idealism *n* → fantasy

identical *adj* → **1** homogeneous **2** precise

identify *v* → **1** class **2** homogenise **3** label **4** particularise

identity *n* → **1** character **2** famous person **3** oneness **4** similarity

ideology *n* → **1** belief **2** conjecture **3** plan

idiom *n* → **1** characteristic **2** figure of speech **3** fine arts **4** language

idiosyncrasy *n* → **1** allergy **2** character **3** characteristic

idiot *n* → **1** fool **2** stupid person

IDLE *v* bludge, bum, coast along, donga, drowse, laze, lie, lie in, lie up, loaf, loll, lounge, moon about, not pull one's weight, rest, shirk, skulk, slack, sponge, swing the lead; **dawdle,** dally, delay, drag the chain, loiter, mooch, tarry, trail, wait; **bugger around,** arse about, arse around, boondoggle, bugger about, buggerise about, buggerise around, fart-arse, goof off, play silly buggers, trifle, twiddle. *See also* BE INACTIVE

IDLE *adj* bone-idle, faineant, indolent, lazy, oscitant, shiftless, slack, slothful, vacuous; **sluggardly,** dronish, effortless, inert, otiose, remiss, sluggard, sluggish, snail-like, work-shy. *See also* INACTIVE

idle *adj* → **1** inactive **2** purposeless **3** unimportant **4** useless

IDLENESS *n* accidie, acedia, effortlessness, faineance, indolence, inexertion, laziness, Mondayitis, oscitance, oscitancy, otiosity, shiftlessness, slackness, sloth, slothfulness, vacuousness; **lethargy,** anergy, languishment, languor, listlessness, sleepiness, sluggishness, spiritlessness, torpidity, torpidness, torpor. *See also* INACTION; PERIOD OF INACTION

IDLER *n* beat, bludger, bum, crawler, deadbeat, dole bludger, drone, faineant, layabout, loafer, lotus-eater, passenger, poler, shirk, shirker, skulk, skulker, slacker, sponger, trifler, waster, wastrel; **sluggard,** good-for-nothing, lazybones, log, log of wood, loller, recumbent, sleepyhead, snail, sooner; **dawdler,** dallier, delayer, lizard, loiterer, lounge lizard, lounger, tarrier; **paralytic,** catatonic, cot case

IDLY *adv* at a loose end, dallyingly, loiteringly, recumbently; **lazily,** indolently, languorously, otiosely, shiftlessly, slack, slackly, slothfully; **lethargically,** listlessly, mustily, passively, phlegmatically, spiritlessly, vacuously. *See also* INACTIVELY

IDOL *n* graven image, tin god; **zombie,** entellus, hanuman, uraeus; **fetish,** fertility symbol, juju, sun-disc; **betyl,** circle *(Archaeol.)*, henge; **churinga,** bullroarer, tchuringa, thunder stick

idol *n* → **1** god **2** image **3** lover **4** portrait **5** the intangible

idyll *n* → **1** a good time **2** musical piece **3** poetry **4** story

if *n* → **1** qualification *conj* **2** on condition that

igloo *n* → house

igneous rock *n* → rock

ignite *v* → **1** fire **2** illuminate **3** operate

ignition *n* → **1** burning **2** firing

ignoble *adj* → **1** disreputable **2** inferior **3** working-class

ignominy *n* → disrepute

IGNORAMUS *n* dogberry, doob, illiterate, lowbrow, nescient, simple; **boor,** alf, backwoodsman *(U.S.)*, barbarian, bog-Irish, clod, clodhopper, country bumpkin, country cousin, hayseed *(U.S.)*, hick, lout, ocker, ockerina, philistine, redneck, rube *(U.S.)*, troglodyte, yokel; **greenhorn,** amateur, babe, Johnny Raw, new chum, novice, parcel-post man, raw material, raw recruit, red-arse *(N.Z. Mil.)*, rookie, shlemiel, tabula rasa, tenderfoot, tyro, youngling; **outsider,** mushroom

IGNORANCE *n* blind spot, blindness, darkness, dogberryism, illiteracy, illiterateness, innumeracy, nescience, paralexia, simpleness; **unknowingness,** incognizance, unconsciousness, unwittingness; **inexperience,** artlessness, callowness, greenness, innocence, unadvisedness, unfamiliarity, unworldliness, verdancy, viridity; **boorishness,** barbarianism, barbarism, barbarity, illiberality, illiberalness, loutishness, ockerdom

IGNORANT *adj* backward, benighted, dark, dooby, natural, nescient, profane, simple, uneducated, unenlightened, unformed, uninformed, unlearned, unread, unscholarly, unschooled, unstudied, untaught, untutored; **unknowing,** in the dark, incognizant, insensible, unaware, unconscious, unwitting; **illiterate,** analphabetic, dyslectic, innumerate, paralexic, unlettered; **boorish,** backwoods, barbarian, barbarous, hick, illiberal, lowbrow, ocker, ockerish, philistine, redneck, troglodytic; **inexperienced,** amateur, armchair, artless, callow, clueless, fresh, freshwater, green, guiltless, home-town, inexpert, new-laid, raw, unexperienced, unseasoned, untravelled, unworldly, verdant, wet behind the ears, young

ignorant *adj* → discourteous

ignore *v* → **1** be unfriendly **2** defeat

ilk *n* → relative

ILL *adj* ailing, bad, crook, dicky, down, in the miseries, indisposed, lousy, not so hot, off, off-colour, out of sorts, poorly, R.S., ratshit, sick, sick as a dog, unwell, wonky; **invalid,** bedridden, feeble, infirm, laid up, senile; **sickly,** adynamic, asthemic, debilitated, malnourished, peaky, pimping, sickish, wan, weakly, weedy, white-livered

ILL-BRED *adj* base, baseborn, ill-conditioned, illiberal, low, low-minded, lowbred, philistine, pleb, plebeian, underbred; **indecorous,** unbecoming, uncivil, uncivilised; **parvenu,** non-U, nouveau-riche; **uncouth,** Maori *(N.Z.)*, raw, rough, rough-and-ready, rough-spoken, rude, tramontane, troglodytic, unkempt; **loutish,** lairy, oafish, rowdy, rowdyish; **rustic,** awkward, backwoods, barnyard, buffoonish, bush, clodhopping, country, gauche, gorblimey; **brutish,** barbarian, barbaric, barbarous, beastlike, boarish, brutal, harsh, heathenish, sensual, swinish. *See also* VULGAR

illegal *adj* → **1** anarchic **2** disobedient **3** prohibited **4** unlawful **5** wrong

illegible *adj* → unclear

illegitimate *n* → **1** offspring **2** population *adj* **3** casuistic **4** unlawful

ILL HEALTH *n* delicacy, infirmity, infirmness, invalidism, peakiness, poor health, senility, sickliness, unhealthiness, unsoundness; **weakness,** adynamia, atrophy, cachexia, carphology, consumption, decay *(Obs.)*, marasmus, myasthenia, phthisis, tabes, tabescence. *See also* ILLNESS

illicit *adj* → **1** prohibited **2** unlawful

illiterate *n* → **1** ignoramus *adj* **2** ignorant

ILLNESS *n* affection, affliction, ailment, complaint, discomfort, disease, disorder, distemper, idiopathy, indisposition, malady, malaise, morbidity, pip, sickness, trouble, upset; **breakdown,** atony, decay, dysfunction, shock; **symptom,** syndrome; **attack,** dose, paroxysm, touch, turn; **relapse; complication,** epiphenomenon, sequela; **infection,** auto-infection, Black Death, contagion, epidemic, exogenesis, murrain *(Archaic)*, pandemic, pest, pestilence, plague, zoonosis; **infectiousness,** contagiousness, deleteriousness, unwholesomeness; **infectious disease,** evil, felon, infection, sepsis, virus, zymosis; **wog,** bug, lurgi, lurgy, the dreaded lurgi. *See also* COLD; FEVER; NAUSEA; CRAMP; HEART DISEASE; MALNUTRITION VENEREAL DISEASE; TOOTHACHE; CANCER;

illness *n* → immorality

ILLOGICAL *adj* alogical, arbitrary, blind, capricious, discretionary, random; **irrational,** erroneous, fallacious, false, flimsy, gratuitous, groundless, ill-founded, incorrect, loose, post hoc, subreptitious, unaccountable, unreasonable, unreasoned, unscientific, unsound, weak, wrong; **groundless,** causeless, fond, implausible, reasonless, untenable; **contradictory,** antilogous, Irish, paradoxical, self-contradictory; **incompatible,** inconsistent, mutually exclusive; **absurd,** frivolous, harebrained, inept, insane, intuitive, nonsensical, scatterbrained; **fanciful,** emotional, fantastic, unreasoning; **incoherent,** disconnected, disjointed, lacking cohesion, rambling, unconnected, uncoordinated, wandering

ILLOGICALITY *n* ad hoc argument, false dilemma, false reasoning, illogicalness, inconsistency, irrationalism, irrationality, irrationalness, misjudgement, misology, reasonlessness, unreason, unreasonableness; **fallaciousness,** error, groundlessness, illegitimacy, inconsequence, sophisticalness, ungroundedness, unsoundness; **arbitrariness,** blindness, capriciousness, randomness, speciousness, unaccountability, unaccountableness; **absurdity,** absurdness, bull, claptrap, garbage, ineptitude, ineptness, mere words, nonsense, rubbish, solecism; **inconsistency,** antilogy, contradiction, contradiction in terms, contradictoriness, incompatability, incompatibles, self-contradiction; **fallacy,** elenchus, equivocation, false premise, flaw, ignoratio elenchi, non sequitur, paralogism, quibble, quillet *(Archaic)*, quirk, sophism, sophistication, sophistry, weak argument, weak case; **vicious circle,** begging the question, hysteron proteron, petitio principii; **casuistry,** chicanery, equivocation, hairsplitting, Jesuitism, mystification, quibbling, quiddity, sophistry, special pleading, subterfuge

ILL-TREAT *v* ill-use, kick about, kick around, knock about, knock around, maltreat, maul, mishandle, mistreat, put the boot into, rough up; **pervert,** corrupt, profane, prostitute; **misuse,** abuse, fool around with, misapply, misappropriate, misemploy, overuse, overwear, squandor, tamper with, violate, waste; **mismanage,** misgovern, misrule

ILLUMINATE *v* emblaze *(Archaic)*, floodlight, illume, illumine, light, relume, spotlight; **irradiate,** insolate, roentgenise, solarise, sun; **kindle,** ignite, inflame; **gloss,** burnish, lustre, polish, schillerise, shine, varnish, wax

illuminate *n* → **1** specialist *v* **2** clarify **3** depict **4** display **5** glorify *adj* **6** knowledgeable

ILLUSION *n* false perspective, FX, hocus-pocus, hokey-pokey, legerdemain, sleight of hand, special effects, trickery, trompe l'oeil; **trick,** gimmick *(U.S.)*, have *(Colloq.)*, spoof; **trick of the light,** aberration, distortion, reflection, refraction, virtual image. *See also* DELUSION

illusion *n* → **1** delusion **2** psychic disturbance

illustrate *v* → **1** clarify **2** depict **3** explain **4** represent **5** teach

illustrious *adj* → **1** bright **2** reputable

ILL WILL *n* animosity, enmity, malevolence; **malice,** despite *(Archaic)*, ill-naturedness, maliciousness, malignity, poisonousness, Schadenfreude, spite, venom, venomousness, virulence

ill will *n* → unfriendliness

IMAGE *n* conceit, crotchet, fiction, flight of fancy, idea *(Obs.)*, ideation, imagery, imago, notion, projection, representation, romance, vagary, vision, whimsy; **phantom,** eidolon, idol, little green men

image *n* → **1** appearance **2** character **3** emblem **4** figure of speech **5** idea **6** portrait **7** reflection **8** similar thing **9** soul *v* **10** devise **11** fantasise **12** represent

imagery *n* → **1** fantasy **2** figure of speech **3** image **4** representation

imaginary *adj* → **1** delusive **2** fantastic **3** numerical

imagination *n* → **1** fantasy **2** plan

imaginative *adj* → fantastic

imagine *v* → **1** believe **2** conjecture **3** delude oneself **4** devise **5** exaggerate **6** fantasise **7** plan

imbecile *n* → **1** fool **2** incompetent **3** stupid person *adj* **4** foolish **5** incompetent **6** stupid

imbibe *v* → **1** absorb **2** drink **3** drink alcohol **4** learn **5** wet

imbroglio *n* → **1** argument **2** tangle

imbue *v* → **1** disfigure **2** wet

IMITATE *v* ape, copy, do a *(Colloq.)*, duplicate, echo, emulate, follow, follow in someone's footsteps, follow suit, make like, mirror, take a leaf out of someone's book; **plagiarise,** counterfeit, forge; **mimic,** impersonate; **caricature,** burlesque, mock, monkey, parody, send up, spoof, take off, travesty; **feign,** affect, come the (something or someone) with, counterfeit, play at; **simulate,** represent, reproduce

imitate *v* → **1** copy **2** pose **3** represent

IMITATION *n* apery, apishness, duplication, echo, emulation, emulousness, foreignism *(U.S.)*, imitativeness, impersonation, impression, mimesis, mimicry, representation, rivalry, simulation; **plagiarism,** plagiary, stealing; **copying,** duplicating, photocopying, reproducing, xeroxing; **onomatopoeia,** echoism; **copy,** a chip off the old block, duplicate, effigy, facsimile, likeness, photocopy, record, recording, replication, representation, reproduction, semblance, transcript, xerox; **forgery,** counterfeit, sham; **caricature,** burlesque, cartoon, mockery, parody, pastiche, postiche, send-up, skit, spoof, take-off, travesty

imitation *n* → **1** repetition **2** similarity *adj* **3** fake **4** imitative

IMITATIVE *adj* apish, echoic, echolike, emulative, emulous, imitational, plagiaristic, pseudo, sequacious *(Archaic)*, simulative; **artificial,** counterfeit, dummy, ersatz, imitation, mock, simulant; **mimic,** mimetic, pantomimic

IMITATIVELY *adv* apishly, emulously, literally, reproductively, word for word; **à la,** after, in the manner of

IMITATOR *n* ape, copier, copycat, echoer, emulator, epigone, follower, following, kook *(Surfing)*, reproducer; **plagiariser,** magpie, plagiarist; **mimer,** caricaturist, impersonator, mimic, monkey, parodist, parrot; **feigner,** affecter, counterfeiter, simulant, simular, simulator; **forger,** short-story writer *(Prison Colloq.)*

immaculate *adj* → **1** clean **2** homogeneous **3** innocent **4** perfect

immanent *adj* → **1** inborn **2** present

immaterial *adj* → **1** intangible **2** unimportant **3** unrelated

immature *adj* → **1** early **2** imperfect **3** new **4** youthful

immediate *adj* → **1** close **2** current **3** following **4** momentary

immemorial *adj* → **1** old **2** past

immense *adj* → **1** big **2** enormous **3** good **4** infinite

immerse *v* → **1** dive **2** wet

immigrate *v* → **1** enter **2** travel

imminent *adj* → **1** dangerous **2** expected **3** future **4** hanging **5** protuberant

immoderate *adj* → **1** excessive **2** infinite **3** overindulgent

immodest *adj* → **1** discourteous **2** obscene **3** proud

immolate *v* → kill

IMMORAL *adj* corrupt, debauched, decadent, degenerate, degraded, depraved, ruined, unprincipled, vitiated; **disreputable,** knavish, louche, scoundrel *(Rare)*, scoundrelly, scrofulous, villainous, worthless; **indecent,** base, loose, profligate, wanton; **frail,** only human, weak; **reprobate,** abandoned, incorrigible, irredeemable, lost, naught *(Obs.)*, recidivous; **sinful,** Babylonian, black, black-hearted, dark, erring, evil, evil-minded, naughty *(Obs.)*, nefarious, peccant, pernicious, sinister, vicious, wicked; **godless,** impious, irreligious, profane, unblessed, ungodly, unhallowed, unholy, unrighteous; **devilish,** accursed, cloven-footed, cloven-hoofed, demoniac, demonian, demonic, diabolic, diabolical, fiendish, hellish, infernal, satanic; **foul,** abominable, filthy, nasty, polluted, putrid, rank, rotten, ulcerous, unclean, unhealthy, vile; **atrocious,** enormous, gross, heinous, inexpiable, iniquitous, unforgivable, unpardonable; **corruptive,** seductive

immoral *adj* → **1** promiscuous **2** wrong

IMMORALITY *n* corruption, debauch *(Obs.)*, debauchery, degeneracy, degeneration, degradedness, depravity, loose morals, moral turpitude, perversion, transgression, turpitude, vice; **foulness,** filthiness, nastiness, odiousness, rottenness, scrofulousness, uncleanliness, unhealthiness, vileness; **human frailty,** feet of clay, infirmity, looseness, the old Adam, wantonness, weakness, weakness of the flesh; **wickedness,** belial, blackness, corruptness, darkness, enormity, enormousness *(Archaic)*, evilness, heinousness, ill *(Archaic)*, illness *(Obs.)*, iniquitousness, iniquity, maleficence, nefariousness, perniciousness, sinfulness, sinisterness, ungodliness, unholiness, unrighteousness, viciousness; **damnation,** depths, perdition. *See also* EVILDOING

IMMORAL PERSON *n* blood, decadent, miscreant, profligate, reprobate, wretch; **backslider,** recidivist; **wrongdoer,** evildoer, malefactor, malefactress, sinner; **devil,** cloven foot, cloven hoof, demon, Mammon, Satan; **corrupter,** depraver, pander, polluter, seducer

immortal *n* → **1** eternity *adj* **2** changeless **3** eternal **4** famous

immovable *adj* → **1** changeless **2** uncompromising

immune *adj* → protected

immure *v* → **1** bury **2** enclose **3** imprison

immutable *adj* → changeless

IMPACT *n* concussion, impingement, impulse, jar, percussion, shock; **collision,** bang, bump, clash, conflict, confliction, crack-up, crash, elastic collision, hurtle *(Poetic)*, knock, slam, smash, stack, thud, thump, whang; **smash-up,** concertina crash, head-on, pile-up, stack-up; **prang,** ding, foul; **tackle,** bonecrusher, flying tackle, smother tackle; **rebound,** croquet, ricochet, roquet *(Croquet)*; **bounce,** dribble. *See also* HITTING

impact *n* → **1** influence *v* **2** collide **3** press

impair *n* → **1** deterioration *v* **2** damage

impale *v* → **1** enclose **2** execute **3** kill **4** perforate

impalpable *adj* → **1** intangible **2** powdered **3** unclear

impart *v* → **1** communicate **2** inform **3** reveal

impartial *adj* → **1** fair **2** neutral

impassable *adj* → **1** impossible **2** obstructed

impasse *n* → **1** dilemma **2** hindrance

impassioned *adj* → emotional

impassive *adj* → **1** apathetic **2** callous **3** composed

impatient *adj* → **1** desirous **2** irritable **3** rash

impeach *v* → **1** lay charges **2** litigate

impeccable *n* → **1** good person *adj* **2** perfect

impecunious *adj* → poor

impede *v* → hinder

impediment *n* → **1** hindrance **2** injury **3** prohibition

impel *v* → **1** encourage **2** thrust

IMPEND *v* approach, be imminent, be near at hand, draw near

impend *v* → hang

impenetrable *adj* → **1** closed **2** intolerant **3** solid **4** unclear

IMPENITENCE *n* brassiness, brazenness, impenitency, impenitentness, obduracy, obdurateness, obstinacy, recusancy, shamelessness, unblushingness

IMPENITENT *adj* remorseless, shameless, unashamed, unblushing, unreformed, unregenerate, unrepentant, unshriven; **obstinate,** brassy, brazen, brazen-faced, hardened, indurate, obdurate, recusant; **incorrigible,** irreclaimable, irredeemable.

IMPENITENT PERSON *n* constant offender, habitual criminal, hardened criminal, recidivist, recusant, self-confessed sinner

imperative *n* → **1** command **2** insistence **3** necessities *adj* **4** commanding **5** insistent **6** necessary **7** obligatory

imperceptible *adj* → **1** intangible **2** invisible

IMPERFECT *adj* incomplete, unideal; **defective,** bad, deficient, faulty, sketchy, unsound, vicious; **underdone,** immature, underdeveloped, unripe; **impure,** adulterated

imperfect *adj* → **1** deficient **2** ineffectual **3** partial

IMPERFECTION *n* defectiveness, faultiness, imperfectness, sketchiness, weakness; **underdevelopment,** immatureness, immaturity, unripeness; **contamination,** adulteration, impureness, impurity; **defect,** bug, failing, fault, fly in the ointment, shortcoming, vice; **weak point,** Achilles heel, chink in one's armour, faultiness, feet of clay, weak link in the chain, weakness; **impurity,** blemish, flaw

imperial *n* → **1** beard **2** box **3** ruler **4** soldier *adj* **5** aristocratic **6** authoritative **7** beautiful **8** national

imperialism *n* → nationalism

imperil *v* → endanger

imperious *adj* → **1** autocratic **2** commanding **3** powerful **4** presumptuous

IMPERMANENT *adj* casual, deciduous, lapsable, movable, semipermanent; **temporary,** acting, commendatory, de bene esse, fill-in, interim, make-do, makeshift, pro tem, pro tempore, provisional, provisory, temporal, working; **transitory,** cursory, ephemeral, evanescent, fleeting, fugacious, fugitive, here to-day and gone tomorrow, in transit, like a dream, passing, shifting, summary, transient volatile; **instant,** ad hoc, instantaneous, momentary; **short-lived,** mortal, perishable, primitive, short-life, spasmodic; **brief,** acute, brisk, meteoric, quick

impermeable *adj* → **1** closed **2** solid

IMPERSONAL *adj* anonymous, faceless, indefinite, indeterminate, of sorts, omnifarious, open, overhead, unmarked, unnamed, unspecified

impersonate *v* → **1** imitate **2** perform **3** pretend **4** represent *adj* **5** human

imperturbable *adj* → composed

impervious *adj* → **1** callous **2** closed **3** hard **4** solid

impetigo *n* → sore

impetuous *adj* → **1** capricious **2** energetic **3** rash

impetus *n* → **1** energy **2** motive **3** thrust

impinge *v* → **1** collide **2** contact

impious *adj* → **1** disdainful **2** immoral **3** irreverent

implacable *adj* → **1** callous **2** dissident

implant *v* → **1** farm **2** insert **3** reproduce **4** teach

implement *n* → **1** method **2** tool *v* **3** equip **4** operate **5** satisfy

implicate *v* → **1** imply **2** involve

implication *n* → **1** accusation **2** allusion **3** meaning **4** participation

implicit *adj* → **1** allusive **2** tangled **3** unconditional

implore *v* → entreat

IMPLY *v* allude to, get at *(Colloq.),* hint at, infer *(Colloq.),* insinuate, suggest; **implicate,** connote, involve, predicate

imply *v* → **1** accuse **2** be likely **3** fold **4** mean

impolite *adj* → **1** discourteous **2** insulting

impolitic *adj* → **1** foolish **2** inappropriate

import *n* → **1** enterer **2** importance **3** meaning *v* **4** absorb **5** be important **6** mean **7** obligate **8** trade

IMPORTANCE *n* account, concern, concernment, consequence, consequentiality, consideration, greatness, import, interest, magnitude, matter, moment, notability, notableness, noteworthiness, pith, significance, significancy, size, substance; **seriousness,** earnestness, eventfulness, fatefulness, graveness, gravity, momentousness, portentousness, solemnity, weight, weightiness; **essentiality,** essentialness, vitalness; **urgency,** acuteness, criticalness, pressure, primacy, priority; **profoundness,** deepness, profundity; **emphasis,** accent, accentuation, force, stress; **value,** goodness, worth; **eminence,** altitude *(Obs.),* distinction, egregiousness *(Obs.),* grandeur, grandiosity, grandness, mark, note, pre-eminence, prominence, stature, supremeness

IMPORTANT *adj* all-important, consequential, considerable, significant; **signal,** impressive, memorable, notable, noted, noteworthy, unforgettable; **emphasised,** pointed; **serious,** earnest, grave, heavy, weighty; **momentous,** climacteric, critical, eventful, fatal, fateful, portentous; **earth-shattering,** breathtaking, colossal, earth-shaking, epochmaking, shattering, stirring, world-shaking; **newsworthy,** big-time, front-page; **essential,** material, pivotal, to the point; **basic,** fundamental, indispensable, irreplaceable, key, necessary, primary; **vital,** acute, high-priority, insistent, pressing, top-priority, urgent; **major,** arch, capital, cardinal, chief, first, foremost, leading, main, paramount, pet, primal, prime, principal, staple; **prominent,** big, conspicuous, distingué, distinguished, egregious *(Obs.),* eminent, grand, great, noble, pre-eminent; **exalted,** august, high, high-level, high-up, lofty, senior, top-level; **dominant,** number one, supreme, top, top-line, uppermost

important *adj* → **1** annoying **2** persevering **3** reputable

IMPORTANT PERSON *n* arch *(Obs.),* bashaw *(Obs.),* big gun, big noise, big shot, big wheel, bigwig, brass, buzzwig, chief, dignitary, everybody who is anybody, giant, great, high-up, his nibs, magnate, magnifico, mogul, Mr Big, number one, numero uno, personage, pot, prince, principal, sire *(Obs.),* tall poppy, top brass, top dog, top-liner, V.I.P., visiting fireman, wheel, who's who; **star,** first fiddle, lead, leading light, prima donna; **key person,** anchorman, mainstay; **panjandrum,** boiled shirt, stuffed shirt

IMPORTANT THING *n* cardinal point, heart of the matter, issue, point, sixty-four dollar question, the thing; **climax,** climacteric, crisis, great divide, juncture, moment of truth, red-letter day, turning point; **key word,** punch line; **a matter of life and death,** a big deal, be-all and end-all, everything, importance *(Obs.),* no joke, no laughing matter, vital concern; **gist,** heart, substance, vitals, yolk; **basics,** bedrock, essentials, fundamentals, nitty-gritty, sine qua non; **cornerstone,** keynote, kingpin *(Colloq.),* linchpin; **pride of place,** face, front, head and front, spearhead; **notabilia,** notable *(Obs.),* rubric, something; **masterpiece,** centrepiece, chef-d'oeuvre, magnum opus, pièce de résistance

importunate *adj* → **1** annoying **2** begging **3** persevering **4** pestering

importune *v* → **1** annoy **2** encourage **3** entreat **4** persuade *adj* **5** annoying **6** persevering

IMPOSE *v* administer, agist, distrain, encroach, exact, inflict, lay a burden on, prescribe, put a responsibility on, require, wreak; **foist on,** land with, lumber, palm off on, saddle with, wish on; **requisition,** commandeer, levy, tax; **domineer,** command, demand, force, tyrannise

impose *v* → print

imposing *adj* → influential

IMPOSITION *n* administration, distrainment, distraint, enactment, enforcement, exaction, infliction; **demand,** burden, edict, impost, order, order of the day, ordination, requirement, requisition, tax, ukase

IMPOSSIBLE *adj* beyond the bounds of reason, contrary to reason, hopeless, no-go, not to be thought of, out of court, out of the question, uncome-at-able; **infeasible,** absurd, impracticable, inexecutable, out of reach, quixotic, unaccomplishable, unachievable, unattainable, unfeasible, unobtainable, unworkable; **inconceivable,** incredible, unimaginable, unthinkable; **insuperable,** impassable, inextricable, insurmountable

impossible *adj* → **1** bad **2** inappropriate **3** pestering **4** unmanageable

impostor *n* → faker

impotent *adj* → **1** incompetent **2** infertile **3** powerless

impound *v* → **1** enclose **2** take

IMPOVERISH *v* bankrupt, beggar, bleed white, clean out, pauperise, ruin, skin, take to the cleaners

impoverish *v* → **1** make infertile **2** take

impracticable *adj* → **1** impossible **2** inappropriate **3** stubborn **4** unmanageable

IMPRECISE *adj* approximate, inaccurate, inexact, proximate, wide of the mark; **vague,** amorphous, aoristic, blurred, blurry, dim, dreamy, faint, faraway, hazy, indefinable, indefinite, indeterminate, indistinct, intangible, loose, misty, muddy, mysterious, mystic, nebulous, nubilous, obscure, tenuous, uncertain, undefined, vaporous, vapoury, veiled; **shadowy,** airy, bleary, blurry, ghostlike, ill-defined, phantom, wraithlike; **inexplicit,** ambiguous, confused, cryptic, enigmatic, equivocal, woolly

IMPRECISELY *adv* dreamily, inaccurately, indefinitely, indeterminately, inexactly, loosely, tenuously, vaguely; **ambiguously,** inexplicitly, woollily; **indistinctly,** faintly, hazily, mistily, nebulously, obscurely, vaporously; **approximately,** about, in some sort, like, more or less, or so, proximately, roughly, sort of; **upwards of,** off the ballpark

IMPRECISION *n* approximation, bush reckoning, impreciseness, inaccuracy, inaccurateness, inexactitude, inexactness, inexplicitness, looseness, rule of thumb; **vagueness,** grey area, indefinableness, indefiniteness, indeterminancy, indeterminateness, indetermination, intangibility, intangibleness, tenuousness; **shapelessness,** amorphism, amorphousness; **indistinctness,** bleariness, blur, blurriness, dimness, faintness, fog, haze, haziness, mistiness, nebulousness, shadow, vaporousness; **uncertainty,** ambiguity, ambiguousness, incomprehensibility, obscureness, obscurity, open question, pig in a poke, waffle, woolliness

impregnable *adj* → durable

impregnate *v* → **1** conceive **2** insert **3** mix **4** wet *adj* **5** pregnant **6** wet

impress *n* → **1** emblem **2** forcefulness **3** label *v* **4** be approved **5** command respect **6** encourage **7** engrave **8** force **9** hollow **10** influence **11** label **12** press **13** rob **14** take

impression *n* → **1** idea **2** imitation **3** imprint **4** indentation **5** influence **6** memory **7** opinion **8** perception

impressionable *adj* → influenced

impressive *adj* → **1** alluring **2** highly regarded **3** important **4** reputable

IMPRINT *n* impression, print, stamp, touch *(Metall.)*

imprint *n* → **1** emblem **2** indentation **3** influence **4** label *v* **5** label **6** press

IMPRISON *v* gaol, immure, incarcerate, jug, lag, pound, put away, send down, send up, shut in, shut up, tuck away; **detain,** guard, hold, keep, keep in, remand, remit *(Obs.)*; **confine,** cabin, cloister, coop, cordon off, cramp, immure, lock in, lock up, pocket, restrain, secure, shut away, shut in, shut up; **intern,** gate; **slot,** slough up; **limit,** circumscribe; **cage,** corner, encage, hedge in, hem in, pound; **pen,** kraal *(S. African)*, paddock, stall; **fetter,** handcuff, manacle. *See also* ARREST

imprison *v* → **1** enclose **2** punish

IMPRISONED *adj* captive, incarcerate; **secured,** confined, fast, pent, pent-up; **cramped,** claustrophobic, close, limitative, limited, poky, strait *(Archaic)*; **penal,** custodial, institutional, non-parole, penitentiary; **maximum-security,** minimum-security

IMPRISONMENT *n* false imprisonment, immurement, incarceration, internment, lockup, prison; **arrest,** apprehension, arrestment, attachment, capture, cop, pinch; **order,** capias, capias ad satisfaciendum, commitment, mittimus, writ; **captivity,** confinement, constraint, durance, durance vile, duress, solitary; **custody,** detainment, detention, house arrest, keeping, protective custody, remand, restraint, safety *(Obs.)*, surveillance, ward; **commitment,** committal; **time,** bed and breakfast, bird, brick, clock, drag, lag, lagging, lost weekend, porridge, rest, sleep, snooze, spin, stretch, swy, zack; **life imprisonment,** the lot, the twist

improbable *adj* → unlikely

impromptu *n* → **1** caprice **2** musical piece *adj* **3** capricious **4** momentary *adv* **5** momentarily

improper *adj* → **1** badly-behaved **2** discourteous **3** incongruous **4** inconvenient **5** incorrect **6** strange **7** unfair

IMPROVE *v* ameliorate, amend, better, elaborate, enrich, fair *(Shipbuilding)*, fine, meliorate, perfect, refine on, transfigure, update, upgrade, uplift; **smarten,** brush up, chamfer up, detail, enhance, polish up, refurbish, touch up; **mend,** remodel, repair, retouch; **civilise,** cultivate, edify; **benefit,** facilitate, help; **advance,** be none the worse for, better oneself, climb, evolve, gain ground, make headway, progress, pull ahead, pull up; **reform,** go straight, mend one's ways, turn over a new leaf; **come good,** brighten, look up, pick up, rally, recover, recuperate, regenerate, take a turn for the better; **mellow,** develop, ripen

improve *v* → **1** farm **2** fertilise **3** use

IMPROVED *adj* better, enhanced, enriched, on the improve, on the mend, on the up and up, on the upgrade, reformed, regenerate, up-and-coming, upwardly mobile

IMPROVEMENT *n* amelioration, amendment, betterment, enhancement, melioration, pick-up, recovery, uplift; **reform,** counter-reformation, reformation, regeneracy, regeneration, self-improvement; **progress,** advancement, development, enrichment, preferment, progression, promotion; **change for the better,** transfiguration, transformation; **advance,** a leap forward, stride; **repair,** mend, renovation, retouch

IMPROVING *adj* ameliorative, amendatory *(U.S.)*, beneficial, civilising, corrective, edificatory, edifying, meliorative, reformational, reformative, reforming, remedial; **progressive,** Fabian, reformist; **improvable,** ameliorable, amendable, developable, mendable, perfectible, reformable

improvise *v* → **1** be impulsive **2** create **3** fantasise **4** make do **5** perform

imprudent *adj* → **1** foolish **2** rash

impudent *adj* → **1** arrogant **2** discourteous **3** insulting

impulse *n* → **1** caprice **2** electricity **3** energy **4** impact **5** incentive **6** point of view **7** thrust

impulsive *adj* → **1** capricious **2** encouraging **3** momentary **4** rash

IMPULSIVE PERSON *n* creature of impulse, goodtimer, tear-arse, tearaway

impure *adj* → **1** dirty **2** guilty **3** imperfect **4** mixed

IMPUTATION *n* accreditation, arrogation, ascription, assignation, assignment, attribution, buck-passing, projection, witch-hunting; **blame,** censure motion, head-hunting, rap, reproach

IMPUTE *v* affix, arrogate, ascribe, assign, attach, attribute, chalk up to, lay, lay at the door of, object *(Obs.)*, put down, put on, put to, sheet home, source; **charge,** accredit with, accuse, attack, blame, bring to account, call to account, challenge, pick on; **pass the buck,** sling the hook

impute *v* → lay charges

INACTION *n* cataplexy, inactivation, inactivity, inertness, inoperativeness, motionlessness, quiescence, repose, rest, spectator sport *(joc.)*, stagnancy, stagnation, stoniness, supineness; **abstention,** arrest, default, delay, forbearance; **sedentariness,** vegetation; **quietness,** calmness, depression *(Econ.)*, drowsiness, languidness, languor, quietude, stillness; **dawdling,** dalliance, tarriance *(Archaic)*; **recumbency,** disengagement, Edwardianism, inoccupation, vacancy *(Rare)*; **passiveness,** Fabianism, inactiveness, laissez faire, passion *(Rare)*, passivity. *See also* IDLENESS; PERIOD OF INACTION

INACTIVATE *v* becalm, calm, easy *(Rowing)*, put on the back burner, quiet, quieten, sedate; **paralyse,** palsy, petrify

INACTIVE *adj* abeyant, actionless, at a loose end, dummy, idle, in abeyance, inert, inoperative, noble *(Chem.)*, passive, quiescent, recumbent, silent, supine; **sedentary,** chairborne; **lethargic,** catatonic, coasty, indolent *(Pathol.)*, listless, musty, palsied, paralytic, phlegmatic, phlegmy, poppied, remiss, sleepy, slow, stonkered, thick, torpid; **dormant,** asleep, comatose, hibernating; **off-peak,** dead, dead-and-alive, drowsy, dull, dullish, easy, flat, inertial, languid, languishing, languorous, off-season, quiet, slack, sleepy, slow, sluggish, slumberous, stagnant; **out of action,** hors de combat, laid low, on the back burner, on the sidelines, run-down, u/s, unserviceable; **calm,** breathless, down, motionless, still, stock-still, stony, unmoving; **fogbound,** closed, icebound. *See also* IDLE

INACTIVELY *adv* down, inertly, on the back burner, quiescently, sedentarily, supinely; **sluggishly,** drowsily, languidly, languishingly, on ice, quietly, sleepily, torpidly; **at rest,** motionlessly, stagnantly, still, stonily. *See also* IDLY

inadequate *adj* → insufficient

inadvertent *adj* → inattentive

IN AGREEMENT *adj* accordant, according, ad idem *(Law)*, agreeable, agreed nem. con., agreeing, close-knit, compatible, concordant, congenial, consensual, consentaneous, consentient, empathetic, empathic, en rapport, harmonious, in accord, in tune, like-minded, of one accord, of one mind, simpatico, sympathetic, unanimous; **allied,** in cahoots, in league. *See also* ASSENTING

inalienable *adj* → own

IN A LOUD VOICE *adv* at the top of one's lungs, at the top of one's voice, screamingly, vociferously; **clamorously,** clangourously, noisily

inane *n* → **1** emptiness *adj* **2** empty **3** foolish

inanimate *adj* → dead

INAPPROPRIATE *adj* inadmissible, inapposite, inapt, ineligible, inopportune, out of place, unfit, unqualified, unsuitable, unsuited; **unwise,** crazy, ill-advised, impolitic, inadvisable; **inapplicable,** futile, impossible, impracticable, ineffective, infeasible, unpractical, vain

inappropriate *adj* → incongruous

INAPPROPRIATENESS *n* impropriety, inadvisability, inappositeness, inaptitude, inaptness, unfitness, unqualifiedness, unsatisfactoriness; **inapplicability,** futility, impracticability, impracticableness, inapplicableness, infeasibility, unpracticality, unpracticalness, vainness; **uselessness,** needlessness, unsuitability, unsuitableness; **unwiseness,** craziness, impoliticness

INARTICULATE *adj* aphasic, disconnected, disjointed, dysphonic, fumbling, hesitant, ineloquent, quavery; **mute,** aphonic, dumb, silent, speechless, tongue-tied

INARTICULATELY *adv* disconnectedly, disjointedly, ineloquently, lispingly, mutteringly; **stammeringly,** falteringly, fumblingly, hesitantly, hesitatingly, mumblingly, stutteringly; **dumbly,** mutely, speechlessly

IN ASTONISHMENT *adv* agape, amazedly, with open mouth, wonderingly

INATTENTIVE *adj* half asleep, inobservant, oscitant; **abstracted,** absent-minded, bemused, distracted, distrait, dreamy, lost in thought, moony, preoccupied; **unheeding,** disregardful, inadvertent, regardless; **thoughtless,** mindless, not switched on, on auto, scatty, unmindful, unthinking; **careless,** casual, cursory, neglectful, remiss, rough, scatterbrained, slaphappy, slipshod, superficial

INATTENTIVELY *adv* absently, abstractedly, abstractly, cursorily, distractedly, in a dream, in the clouds; **unheedingly,** inadvertently, mindlessly, thoughtlessly, unmindfully, unthinkingly

INATTENTIVENESS *n* absence of mind, absent-mindedness, disregard, inadvertence, inattention, inobservance, mindlessness, thoughtlessness, unmindfulness, unthinkingness; **abstractedness,** abstraction, brown study, daydreaming, doodling, dreaminess, oscitance, oscitancy, reverie, woolgathering; **carelessness,** neglect, neglectfulness, oversight, remissness

inaugurate *v* → **1** create **2** employ **3** initiate

inauspicious *adj* → calamitous

INBORN *adj* born, congenital, connate, connatural, inbred, indigenous, ingenerate *(Archaic)*, innate; **inherent,** built-in, constitutional, immanent, in-built, indigenous, inward, natural, radical; **personal,** complexional, specific, subjective, subjectivistic

inborn *adj* → characteristic

incalculable *adj* → **1** infinite **2** uncertain **3** unclear

in camera *adj* → **1** secret *adv* **2** in secret **3** secretly

incandescence *n* → **1** heat **2** light

incandescent *adj* → **1** glowing **2** hot

incantation *n* → magic spell

incapable *n* → **1** incompetent *adj* **2** incompetent **3** powerless **4** prohibited

incapacitate *v* → **1** injure **2** prohibit

incarcerate *v* → **1** enclose **2** imprison *adj* **3** imprisoned

incarnate *v* → **1** materialise **2** represent *adj* **3** human **4** real **5** red

incendiary *n* → **1** ammunition **2** destroyer **3** encourager **4** firer **5** fuel *adj* **6** encouraging **7** fiery

incense *n* → **1** fragrance *v* **2** anger

INCENTIVE *n* appetiser, carrot, prompt, spiff; **stimulus,** fillip, hurry-up, impellent, impulse, inducer, pep talk, prodder, prompter, provocative, recommender, stimulant *(Rare)*, stimulative, stimulator, urge; **spur,** ankus *(India)*, battery stick, cattle prod, goad, gully-raker, paroo dog *(Agric.)*, prick *(Archaic)*, prod, riding crop, sting, stockwhip, whip; **shout of encouragement,** cheer, hype, war dance; **promotion,** advertisement, advertising campaign, commercial, film clip *(T.V.)*, hard sell, loss leader, plug, promo, recommendation, sell, soft sell, teaser, trailer *(Film)*; **inducement,** bribery, consideration, reward; **cajolery,** blandishment, flattery

incentive *n* → **1** bribe **2** causer **3** motive *adj* **4** encouraging

inception *n* → start

incessant *adj* → **1** continual **2** eternal **3** frequent **4** repetitive

incest *n* → rape

inch *n* → **1** island **2** length **3** small amount *v* **4** go slowly

inchoate *adj* → **1** original **2** shapeless

incidence *n* → **1** being **2** influence **3** occurrence **4** presence

incident *n* → **1** act of war **2** occurrence *adj* **3** additional **4** related

incidental *n* → **1** luck *adj* **2** additional **3** occurrent

incinerate *v* → **1** destroy **2** fire

incipient *adj* → original

incise *v* → **1** cut **2** engrave

incision *n* → **1** cut **2** indentation

incisor *n* → mouth

incite *v* → arouse

inclement *adj* → climatic

incline *n* → **1** mound **2** slope *v* **3** slope **4** tend to

INCLUDE *v* comprehend, count in, cover, embrace, entail, incorporate, number, subsume, take in; **comprise,** consist of, contain, have, hold; **be included,** be in it, have a finger in the pie

INCLUSION *n* comprehension, comprisal, coverage, embracement, entailment, incorporation; **inclusiveness,** comprehensiveness, generality

INCLUSIVE *adj* across the board, all-embracing, comprehensive, general, incorporative, overall, sweeping, total, umbrella, wholesale; **all told,** all found, all-in, all-included, all-inclusive, all-up, in all

incognito *n* → **1** disguise *adj* **2** hidden

incoherent *adj* → **1** disorderly **2** illogical **3** incongruous **4** nonsensical **5** separate

INCOME *n* annuity, bread and butter, crust, disposable income, earnings, emolument, establishment *(Archaic)*, independent means, livelihood, meal ticket, money wages, nominal wages, pay, pay-packet, real wages, remuneration, revenue, salary, screw, secondary wage, sturt *(Mining)*, susso *(Obs.)*, take-home pay, total wage, truck, wage; **living,** benefice, fellowship, scholarship; **stipend,** bounty system *(Hist.)*, gratification *(Archaic)*, gratuity, pourboire, prebend *(Eccles.)*, recompense, reward; **basic wage,** award wage, industry award, living wage, minimum wage, ordinary pay; **penalty rate,** back pay, double time, half-pay, margin, overtime, piece rate, severance pay, sick pay, strike pay, time-and-a-half, triple time, weekend penalty rate; **blood money,** danger money; **allowance,** attraction money, climatic allowance, dirt money, district allowance, field allowance, heat money, height money, living allowance, loading, locality allowance, lost time allowance, meal allowance, mess allowance, mileage, per diem, percentage, separation allowance *(Mil.)*, shift allowance, subsistence allowance, tea money, tool allowance, war loading, weighting, zone allowance; **bonus,** bounty, cost-of-living bonus, perk, perquisite, premium; **advance,** sub *(Brit.)*; **royalty,** douceur, enfeoffment, farm, fee, levy, public lending right, retainer, retaining fee, retainment; **rent,** fair rent, farm *(English Hist.)*, hire, peppercorn rent, quitrent, rental; **pension,** child allowance, child endowment, disability allowance, super, superannuation, welfare; **unemployment benefit,** dole, sickness benefit, sit-down money, suss

income *n* → funds

INCOMMODE *v* be inexpedient, disadvantage, discommode, disoblige, embarrass, gum up the works, hinder, indispose, never do, not do, put out

incommode *v* → hinder

incommunicado *adj* → solitary

IN COMPANY WITH *adv* arm in arm, hand in hand, in convoy, side by side; **together,** jointly, unitedly; **in waiting,** in attendance

incomparable *adj* → **1** different **2** superior

INCOMPATIBLE *adj* inconsistent, insolvable, irresolvable, mutually exclusive, paradoxical, preclusive, self-contradictory

incompatible *adj* → **1** dissident **2** illogical **3** incongruous **4** unsociable

INCOMPETENCE *n* fumbling, ignorance, inaptness, ineffectuality, inefficiency, ineptitude, inexperience, inexpertness, maladministration, mismanagement; **Peter principle; incapacity,** apraxia *(Pathol.)*, disability, disablement, impotence, inaptitude, incapability, incapableness, incapacitation, unfitness; **artlessness,** amateurishness, amateurism, cubbishness, gaucheness, gaucherie, lubberliness, naivete, otherworldliness; **awkwardness,** angularness, bearishness, clumsiness, flat-footedness, gawkiness, heavy-handedness, left-handedness, lumpiness, lumpishness, maladdress, maladroitness, stiffness, ungainliness, ungracefulness, unhandiness, unskilfulness; **unprofessionalism,** lack of expertise, quackery; **hopelessness,** badness, poorness; **imbecility,** clownishness, folly, foolishness, goofiness; **uncouthness,** slovenliness, ungraciousness

INCOMPETENT *n* boggler, botcher, bungler, fumbler, incapable, misdoer, mismanager, mucker-up, muddler; **duffer,** bad shot, billygoat, clown, deadhead, dill, dunce, fart, fool, galoot, great ape, imbecile, lame dog, lame duck, palooka, rabbit *(Cricket)*, spastic, unco; **clumsy person,** blunderbuss, blunderer, bull in a china shop, bumpkin, butter-fingers, clodhopper, gawk, gazob, hobbledehoy, hulk, lubber, lummox, lump, mullocker, slab, the awkward squad; **bad workman,** backyarder, blackjack merchant *(Plumbing)*, bush carpenter, cobbler, cub, quack, snagger *(Shearing)*, wood butcher; **sloven,** slob, slouch; **dead loss,** hopeless case, no-hoper, the end, the living end, write-off; **dogberry,** bureaucrat, flunkey, lackey, seatwarmer

INCOMPETENT *adj* ineffectual, inefficient, inept; **incapable,** impotent, inapt, unfit; **unpractised,** backyard, fumbling, inexpert, ungifted, unskilful, unskilled, untalented; **amateurish,** artless, cubbish, cut-lunch, half-baked, home-made, landlubberly, lubberly, unprofessional; **untrained,** callow, green, inexperienced, raw, semi-skilled; **slovenly,** bearish, gauche, offhand, uncouth, ungracious *(Obs.)*, unhandy, unmechanical; **imbecile,** clownish, foolish, goofy, imbecilic, spastic, unco, uncool; **clumsy,** accident-prone, all thumbs, awkward, bumble footed, cack-handed, cacky-handed, clodhopping, elephantine, flat-footed, footless *(U.S. Colloq.)*, gawky, ham-fisted, heavy, heavy-handed, hipshot, hulking, left-handed, lumpish, lumpy, maladroit, ungainly, ungraceful, unwieldy. *See also* BADLY-DONE

incompetent *adj* → **1** prohibited **2** unworthy

incomplete *adj* → **1** deficient **2** imperfect **3** partial **4** raw

INCOMPREHENSION *n* inapprehension, incoherence, incomprehensiveness; **puzzlement,** bafflement, bamboozlement, bewilderment, confusion, mystification, perplexity

INCONGRUITY *n* anomalousness, incongruence, oddness, unnaturalness; **unaptness,** improperness, impropriety, infelicity, unbecomingness, unfitness, unseemliness, unsuitability, unsuitableness; **disagreement,** antinomy, disaccord, nonconformity, repugnance; **discord,** contention, discordance, disharmony, inconsonance; **irreconcilability,** incompatibleness; **antibiosis,** disoperation

INCONGRUOUS *adj* absonant, anomalistic, anomalous, incongruent, odd, unnatural; **discrepant,** contradictory, inconsistent, repugnant; **incompatible,** ill-assorted, incoherent, irreconcilable, off, unbecoming, unconformable, unfortunate, unhappy, unseemly; **inappropriate,** misplaced, out of character, out of keeping, out of place; **at variance,** at issue, at odds, contentious, controversial, in question; **unapt,** impertinent, improper, inept, infelicitous, irrelevant, unfit, unsuitable, unsuited, wrong; **dissonant,** discordant, disharmonious, inconsonant, out of phase, parataxic

incongruous *adj* → different

inconsequential *adj* → **1** nonsensical **2** unimportant

inconsistent *adj* → **1** different **2** illogical **3** incompatible **4** incongruous **5** indecisive **6** nonsensical **7** opposing

inconspicuous *adj* → invisible

incontinent *adj* → **1** liberated **2** nauseous **3** overindulgent

IN CONTRAST *adv* by way of contrast, contrarily, on the contrary, on the other hand, vice versa

INCONVENIENCE *n* disadvantageousness, discommodity, incommodiousness, incommodity, inexpedience, inexpediency, unprofitability, unprofitableness, untowardness; **disadvantage,** disutility, drawback, ill effect, ill fortune, infelicity, liability, misfortune, penalty, slug; **awkwardness,** clumsiness, ineptitude, ineptness, infelicity; **unhelpfulness,** disobligingness, impertinence, inimicality, uncooperativeness

INCONVENIENT *adj* incommodious, inexpedient; **disadvantageous,** bad, cross, improper, infelicitous, needless, nugatory, objectionable, undesirable, unfortunate, unprofitable, unsatisfactory, unseemly, untoward, useless, worthless; **awkward,** clumsy, de trop, inept, infelicitous, unmanageable; **unhelpful,** disobliging, impertinent, inimical, uncooperative

inconvenient *adj* → hindering

incorporate *v* → **1** associate **2** combine **3** include **4** join *adj* **5** intangible **6** societal

INCORRECT *adj* amiss, fallacious, faulty, wrong; **unworthy,** irregular, unchristian, unprofessional; **improper,** close to the wind, naughty, offensive, out-of-the-way, spicy, unacceptable, unbecoming, uncalled-for; **questionable,** censurable, reproachable; **unjustified,** undue. *See also* WRONG

incorrect *adj* → **1** false **2** illogical **3** ungrammatical

incorrigible *n* → **1** criminal **2** mischief-maker **3** stubborn person *adj* **4** badly-behaved **5** disobedient **6** immoral **7** impenitent **8** stubborn **9** wrong

INCREASE *n* accession, accretion, accumulation, addition, aggrandisement, amplification, appreciation, augmentation, bank-up, build-up, cumulation, enhancement, exacerbation, expansion, extension, gain, heterosis, increment, inflation, overfall, reinforcement; **intensification,** aggravation, concentration, crescendo, enrichment, escalation, exaggeration, intension, magnification, maximisation, regeneration, rise, swell; **proliferation,** elaboration, escalation, multiplication, propagation, pullulation, rash; **acceleration,** speed-up; **boom,** rally, revaluation, rise, upswing, upturn

INCREASE *v* accumulate, amplify, augment, boost, cumulate, double, enhance, enlarge, enrich, expand, redouble, reinforce, soup up, work up; **exaggerate,** add fuel to the fire, exacerbate, lay it on; **aggrandise,** beef up, blow up, broach, build up, bump up, clap on, deepen, develop, double, eke *(Archaic)*, escalate, extend, flash, flesh out, gross up, heighten, hot up, increment, lengthen, let out, magnify, maximise, multiply, pad out, piece out, propagate, space out, spin out, step up, thicken, turn up, up; **accelerate,** gather, pick up, speed, speed up; **revalue,** approve *(Law)*, bull, enhance, hike up, jump, load, mark up, pyramid, raise, raise the ante, rise, up the ante

increase *n* → **1** addition **2** offspring **3** profit **4** reproduction *v* **5** become greater **6** surpass

INCREASED *adj* blown, blubber, blubbery, enlarged, erect, expanded, inflated, swollen, tumescent, tumid, tympanitic; **intensified,** concentrate, concentrated, crash, intensive; **more,** other, plus; **exaggerated,** extended, souped-up

INCREASING *adj* crescendo, crescent, dilatant, dilative, expansive, growing, increscent, monotonic, multiplying, waxing; **enhancive,** concentrative, exaggerative, intensifying; **accelerative,** acceleratory, progressive; **augmentative,** accretive, accumulative, cumulative, exponential, multiplicative

incredible *adj* → **1** astonishing **2** impossible

incredulous *adj* → doubting

increment *n* → **1** addition **2** increase *v* **3** increase

incriminate *v* → lay charges

incubate *v* → **1** create **2** heat **3** prepare **4** shape

incubator *n* → **1** breeding ground **2** heater

inculcate *v* → teach

incumbent *n* → **1** ecclesiastic *adj* **2** obligatory

incur *v* → **1** cause **2** involve **3** undergo

incurable *adj* → **1** hopeless **2** unwholesome

incursion *n* → **1** attack **2** flow

IN DEBT *adj* encumbered, head over heels in debt, in arrears, in beyond one's depth, in difficulties, in financial difficulties, in the red, indebted, liable; **overdrawn,** behindhand, embarrassed, O/D, out of pocket; **bankrupt,** bust, insolvent, ruined

indebted *adj* → **1** grateful **2** in debt

INDEBTEDNESS *n* embarrassment, judgment, obligation, tribute; **arrears,** arrearage, default, non-payment; **account,** reckoning, score; **bankruptcy,** bust, bust-up, commercial failure, financial collapse, financial crash, insolvency, receivership

indecent *adj* → **1** immoral **2** obscene

INDECISION *n* aboulia, ambivalence, double-mindedness, doubtfulness, indecisiveness, tentativeness, uncertainness, undecidedness; **irresoluteness,** haltingness, inconsistency, infirmness, limpness, shakiness, unstableness, unsteadiness; **aimlessness,** unsettledness, unsettlement; **second thoughts,** pause, pendency, pendulousness, quandary, vacillation; **procrastination,** hesitation, temporisation; **evasion,** equivocation, prevarication, run-around; **capriciousness,** caprice, flightiness, skittishness, whimsicality

indecision *n* → uncertainty

INDECISIVE *adj* aboulic, ambivalent, double-minded, doubtful, halting, inconsistent, inconstant, pendulous, shaky, tentative, vacillating, vacillatory; **unsure,** open, piss-weak, uncertain, uncommitted, undecided, unsettled, weak, weak-willed; **perplexed,** at a loss, at one's wit's end, in a sweat, on the horns of a dilemma; **irresolute,** aimless, capricious, errant, fickle, flighty, objectless, skittish, unstable, unsteady, whimsical; **evasive,** non-committal

indeed *adv* → **1** actually **2** in fact *interj* **3** how about that

indefatigable *adj* → **1** busy **2** persevering

indefensible *adj* → **1** vulnerable **2** wrong

indefinable *adj* → imprecise

indefinite *adj* → **1** changeable **2** impersonal **3** imprecise **4** infinite **5** shapeless **6** uncertain

indelible *adj* → changeless

indelicate *adj* → vulgar

indemnify *v* → compensate

indemnity *n* → **1** compensation **2** forgiving **3** insurance **4** payment

indent *n* → **1** cut **2** deed **3** indentation *v* **4** cut **5** hollow **6** promise

INDENTATION *n* bingle, dent, depression, ding, dint, furrow, indent, puncture; **dimple,** pock; **pore,** crypt, domatium, fossa, fovea, foveola; **impression,** footprint, imprint, incision, print, toehold; **intaglio,** champlevé, cloisonné. *See also* HOLLOW

indenture *n* → **1** deed *v* **2** promise

INDEPENDENCE *n* autarchy, autocephaly, autonomy, home-rule, republicanism, self-determination, self-government, self-rule, separatism; **freedom,** discretion, free will, freedom of action, freedom of choice, liberty; **anarchy,** anarchism, libertarianism; **individualism,** individuality, self-expression; **self-sufficiency,** autarky, independent means, inner-direction, private means, self-reliance, toughness; **self-support,** private practice, self-employment, self-help

INDEPENDENT *adj* acephalous, autocephalous, autonomic, autonomous, free, hermetic, incoercible, indomitable, substantive; **self-determining,** self-governed, self-governing, self-regulating, self-ruling; **separatist,** isolationist, separate; **uncommitted,** detached, non-partisan, unattached, uninvolved; **anarchic,** anarchistic, libertarian; **single-handed,** sole, unconnected, undirected, unsupported. *See also* SELF-SUFFICIENT

independent *n* → **1** independent person **2** member of parliament *adj* **3** unconditional **4** unrelated

INDEPENDENTLY *adv* autonomically, autonomously, separately; **by oneself,** off one's own bat, on one's own, on one's own initiative, on one's own responsibility, on one's own undertaking, single-handedly, singly; **anarchically**

INDEPENDENT PERSON *n* autarkist, crossbencher, feme sole, free agent, free spirit, independent, individualist, lone hand, loner, mugwump *(U.S.)*, one's own person, rugged individualist, self-made man, separatist; **breakaway,** splinter group; **anarchist,** libertarian; **independent contractor,** freelance, freelancer, private practitioner, self-starter

indeterminate *adj* → **1** changeable **2** impersonal **3** imprecise **4** lucky **5** uncertain

index *n* → **1** book part **2** classification **3** indicator **4** list *v* **5** list **6** signify *adj* **7** brachial

Index *n* → **1** list **2** prohibition

indicate *v* → **1** confess **2** display **3** mean **4** predict **5** signify

INDICATIVE *adj* connotative, denotative, evincive, gesticulatory, indexical, indicant, significant, significative, suggestive; **symbolic,** emblematic, figurative, pantomimic, representative, symbolical, symbolist, typical; **symptomatic,** prodromal, semiotic, stigmatic

indicative *adj* → **1** allusive **2** meaningful **3** revealing

INDICATOR *n* barometer, guide, index, indicant; **marker,** benchmark, cairn, checkpoint, cue dot *(Films)*, guide-mark, landmark, mile post, milestone, post *(Horseracing)*, surface indication, target *(Survey)*, terminus, tidemark, vigia, witness mark *(Survey)*; **pointer,** arrow, cock, fingerpost, guidepost, hand, signpost; **buoy,** anchor buoy, bell buoy, cork; **buoyage,** balisage; **weathercock,** weathervane; **traffic sign,** fried egg, give-way sign, silent cop, stop sign, witch's hat; **traffic light,** amber light, green light, red light; **indicator light,** blinker, brakelight, hand signal, hazard lights, light, trafficator, turning-indicator, winker. *See also* SIGNAL; SIGN

indicator *n* → **1** pressure gauge **2** warner

indict *v* → **1** lay charges **2** litigate

indifferent *adj* → **1** apathetic **2** bored **3** mediocre **4** neutral **5** ordinary

IN DIFFICULTIES *adv* behind the eight ball, hard put, hard put to it, in a jam, in deep water, in dire straits, in hot water, in the cactus, in the cart, in the shit, in the soup, in trouble, on one's beam ends, on the hook, on the spot, over a barrel, up against it, up shit creek, up shit creek in a barbwire canoe, up shit creek without a paddle, up the booay, up the creek, up the pole, with one's back to the wall; **between wind and water,** between Scylla and Charybdis, between the devil and the deep blue sea, in a cleft stick, on the horns of a dilemma

indigenous *adj* → **1** inborn **2** resident

indigent *adj* → poor

indigestion *n* → nausea

indignant *adj* → **1** acrimonious **2** angry **3** displeased

indignation *n* → **1** anger **2** displeasure

indignity *n* → **1** disrepute **2** insult **3** unworthiness

indigo *n* → **1** blue **2** purple *adj* **3** purple

indirect *adj* → **1** deflective **2** genetic

INDIRECTNESS *n* aberrance, anfractuosity, circuitousness, circuity, circularity, deviousness, obliqueness, obliquity, refractiveness, tortuosity, tortuousness, wryness

indiscreet *adj* → **1** rash **2** revealing

indiscriminate *adj* → muddled

indispensable *adj* → **1** important **2** necessary

indisposed *adj* → **1** ill **2** unwilling

individual *n* → **1** one **2** organism **3** person *adj* **4** one

indolent *adj* → **1** idle **2** inactive

indomitable *adj* → **1** courageous **2** dissident **3** durable **4** independent

indoor *adj* → inside

indubitable *adj* → certain

induce *v* → **1** cause **2** encourage **3** persuade **4** reason

induct *v* → **1** employ **2** teach

induction *n* → **1** act **2** book part **3** cause **4** electricity **5** encouragement **6** radioactivation **7** start **8** written composition

indulge *v* → **1** be lenient **2** be pleased **3** drink alcohol **4** overindulge

industrial *n* → **1** worker *adj* **2** creative

INDUSTRIAL ACTION *n* ban, bans and limitations, black ban, boycott, demarcation dispute, general strike, go-slow, green ban, lockout, picket, picket line, rolling ban, rolling strike, shutout, sit-down, sit-down strike, stop-work meeting, strike, sympathy strike, walkout, wildcat strike, work-to-rule; **collective bargaining,** collective agreement

industrious *adj* → **1** busy **2** effortful

INDUSTRY *n* cottage industry, primary industry, secondary industry; **technology,** high tech, high technology, industrialisation, industrialism, sunrise industry

industry *n* → **1** effort **2** persistence **3** work

inedible *adj* → unsavoury

ineffable *adj* → **1** enormous **2** prohibited

INEFFECTUAL *adj* adiaphorous, brummy, cardboard cutout, helpless, imperfect *(Law)*, in chancery, ineffective, inefficacious, inept, non-effective, nugatory, null, null and void, unarmed, unmanned, void

INEFFECTUAL PERSON *n* alf, dead duck, deadhead, milksop, nine day wonder, old woman, paper tiger, sissy, spado, wimp; **has-been,** disso, non-effective, retread; **dud,** brummie, fizzer

inefficient *adj* → **1** incompetent **2** infertile

inept *adj* → **1** illogical **2** incompetent **3** incongruous **4** inconvenient **5** ineffectual

INEQUALITY *n* asymmetry, disequilibrium, disparity, disproportion, disproportionateness, dissymmetry, imbalance, imparity, irregularity, overbalance, unbalance, unequalness, unevenness; **lopsidedness,** bias, list; **unequals,** mismatch, odds

inert *adj* → **1** apathetic **2** idle **3** inactive **4** insensible

inertia *n* → **1** apathy **2** sleepiness

inescapable *adj* → inevitable

inestimable *adj* → **1** infinite **2** uncertain

INEVITABILITY *n* fatality, ineluctability, inevitableness, predetermination, sureness, unavoidability, unavoidableness; **fatalism,** karma, predestinarianism; **fatefulness,** feyness. *See also* FATE

INEVITABLE *adj* fatal, fated, ineluctable, ineludible, inescapable, predestinate, predeterminate, predetermined, sure, unavoidable; **doomed,** fatal *(Obs.)*, fey, starred. *See also* FATEFUL

inevitable *n* → **1** certain thing *adj* **2** certain **3** hopeless

IN EXCHANGE FOR *adv* in lieu of, in loco parentis, instead of

inexorable *adj* → **1** callous **2** changeless **3** persevering **4** stubborn

IN FACT *adv* actually, certainly, certes *(Archaic)*, definitely, for a fact, forsooth *(Archaic)*, in faith *(Archaic)*, in reality, in truth, indeed, just, quite, really, soothly, too *(Colloq.)*, truly, verily *(Archaic)*; **factually,** accurately, aright, correctly, justly, literally; **genuinely,** authentically, legitimately, veritably; **in effect,** de facto, effectively, essentially, in substance, realistically, to all intents and purposes; **validly,** logically, rigorously, soundly, tenably; **self-evidently,** axiomatically, undeniably

infallible *adj* → **1** correct **2** perfect

infamous *adj* → **1** disreputable **2** punished

infant *n* → **1** offspring **2** starter *adj* **3** youthful

infanticide *n* → killing

infantile *adj* → youthful

infantry *n* → armed forces

infatuated *adj* → **1** foolish **2** loving

infect *v* → **1** dirty **2** disease **3** poison *adj* **4** unwholesome

infection *n* → **1** illness **2** poison

infectious *adj* → **1** influential **2** unwholesome

infer *v* → imply

INFERIOR *n* adjunct, assistant, cog, junior, minor, number one, number two, second, second class, second tenor, secondary, sub, subaltern, subordinate, subsidiary, underling, yeoman *(Archaic)*; **supporting artist,** backing group, ensemble, session musician, studio musician; **stand-in,** replacement, substitute, understudy

INFERIOR *adj* junior, minor, of lesser importance, puisne, puny *(Obs.)*, secondary, thrown in the shade, under, yeoman, young, younger; **subordinate,** assistant, associate, attendant, auxiliary, subaltern, subordinative, subservient, subsidiary; **lowly,** base, below the salt, common, degrading, ignoble, infra dig, low, mean, non-U, of low caste, ordinary, peasant, poor, simple, vassal, vile, worse off; **less,** last, least *(Archaic)*, lesser, littler, minimal, smaller, worse, worst; **second-class,** not the full quid, second-best, second-rate, secondary, sub, subnormal, substandard, third-rate; **adulterated,** adulterate, broken-down, watery; **of less height,** inferior, lower, subjacent

inferior *adj* → **1** bad **2** bodily **3** bottom **4** inferior

INFERIORITY *n* baseness, coarseness, ignobility, ignobleness, imperfection, lowness, meanness, mediocrity, vileness; **debasement,** adulteration, minimisation, subordination; **lowliness,** lack of position, lack of rank, lack of standing, poorness; **ordinariness,** scrubbiness, shoddiness; **subnormality,** bottom, low tide; **minimum,** least, less, lesser, worse, worst; **inferiority complex,** cultural cringe, feeling of inadequacy, sense of inadequacy

INFERIORLY *adv* lowly, secondarily, subordinately; **on the wrong side of the tracks,** in a humble station, in a low station, in lowly circumstances, in poor circumstances

INFERNAL *adj* chthonian, nether, stygian; **hellish,** purgatorial; **Dantean,** Dantesque, pandemoniac, pandemonic, sulphurous

infernal *adj* → **1** bad **2** immoral

inferno *n* → hell

INFERTILE *adj* barren, fruitless, sterile, unfruitful, unproductive; **arid,** desert, desolate, dried up, dry, exhausted, hungry, poor, sheep-sick *(Agric.)*, sick, stony, submarginal, waste; **uncultivated,** fallow, unseeded, untilled, unused; **unprofitable,** abortive, academic, dead, dead-end, effete, ineffective, non-productive, Sisyphean, useless, vain; **counterproductive,** inefficient, uneconomic; **childless,** non-parous, nulliparous, without issue; **impotent,** castrated, neuter, sexless, spayed; **not reproducing,** acarpous *(Bot.)*, anovulatory, celibate, farrow, seedless, shy, unjoined, virgin, virginal; **contraceptive,** abortifacient

infest *v* → flood

infidel *n* → **1** doubter **2** irreverent person *adj* **3** irreverent

infidelity *n* → **1** irreverence **2** unfaithfulness

infiltrate *n* → **1** insert *v* **2** enter

INFINITE *adj* immense, immoderate *(Obs.)*; **boundless,** endless, illimitable, indefinite, limitless, never-ending, perpetual, shoreless, spaceless, termless, unbounded, uncounted, unlimited, unmeasured, untold; **immeasurable,** countless, incalculable, incomputable, inestimable, inexhaustible, innumerable, interminable, myriad, numberless, transfinite, umpteen, uncountable, unfathomable, unmeasurable, without end, without measure, without number

infinite *n* → **1** infinity **2** sky *adj* **3** perfect

infinitesimal *adj* → smallest

INFINITY *n* endlessness, eternity, immenseness, immensity, infiniteness, infinitude, perpetuity; **boundlessness,** illimitability, illimitableness, immeasurability, immeasurableness, unboundedness, unlimitedness; **infinite,** eternal, omnipotent; **abyss,** bottomless deep, bottomless pit. *See also* ETERNITY

infirm *v* → **1** cancel *adj* **2** ill **3** weak

infirmary *n* → hospital

inflame *v* → **1** anger **2** arouse **3** disease **4** emotionalise **5** illuminate **6** redden

inflammable *n* → **1** lighter *adj* **2** excited **3** fiery

inflammation *n* → **1** encouragement **2** fire **3** redness

inflate *v* → **1** air **2** become greater **3** pride oneself

INFLATION *n* cost-push inflation, credit squeeze, demand economy, demand-pull inflation, inflationary spiral, price spiral, stagflation; **appreciation,** capital appreciation, revaluation, upvaluation; **rise,** advance, hike, jump, mark-up; **surcharge,** extra, overcharge, rip-off, slug

inflation *n* → increase

inflection *n* → **1** accent **2** bend **3** change **4** curve

inflexible *adj* → **1** callous **2** changeless **3** hard **4** straight **5** strict **6** stubborn

inflict *v* → impose

INFLUENCE *n* affection, atmosphere, charisma, force, hold, imposingness, impression, imprint, leverage, mana, operation, penetration, potency, potentness, power, powerfulness, pressure, push, spell, sway, weight, whammy; **impact,** effect, impingement, incidence; **predominance,** ascendancy, predomination, prevailingness, regnancy; **patronage,** auspices, dominion, good offices, interest *(Obs.)*; **nepotism,** pull, string-pulling, wire-pulling. *See also* PERSUASION

INFLUENCE *v* act on, act upon, affect, bear on, decide, determine, impinge on, militate, move, move to, operate on, work on; **predominate,** hold the balance of power, hold the reins, preponderate, prevail, surmount; **pull rank,** pull strings *(Colloq.)*, pull the braid, pull wires *(U.S.)*, throw one's weight about, throw one's weight around; **be influential,** carry weight, grab, have a drag *(U.S. Colloq.)*, have pull, impress, make an impact on, strike, tell with, tip the scales, touch. *See also* PERSUADE

influence *n* → **1** encouragement *v* **2** encourage

INFLUENCED *adj* affected, coloured, interested; **responsive,** exorable, impressible, impressionable, other-directed, pervious, plastic, sensitive, soft, susceptible, susceptive; **amenable,** adaptable, compliant, convincible, easy, facile, flexile, open, persuadable, persuasible, pliable, pliant, suggestible, tractable

INFLUENCER *n* affecter, assurer, catalyst, convincer, inspirer, reasoner; **persuader,** arguer, blandisher, cajoler, coaxer, pleader, swayer, sweet-talker, urger, wheedler; **brainwasher,** conditioner, hypnotiser, manipulator, mesmeriser, mesmerist; **lobbyist,** operator, string-puller, wire-puller; **lobby,** connections, pressure group; **influential person,** backer, backroom boy, big wheel, éminence grise, genius, high priest, patron, power, power behind the throne; **determinative,** determinant, organiser *(Embryol.)*

INFLUENTIAL *adj* active, decisive, far-reaching, impingent, imposing, intervenient, seminal, strong, weighty; **predominant,** ascendant, preponderant, preponderating, prepotent, prevailing, regnant; **charismatic,** infectious, manipulative, manipulatory, mesmeric; **convincing,** coaxing, luculent, persuasive, silver-tongued

influx *n* → **1** arrival **2** entrance **3** flow

INFORM *v* acquaint, apprise, circumstance *(Obs.)*, convey, drum up, fill in, give to understand, oil up, put in the picture, put wise; **brief,** communicate, direct, elaborate on, enlighten, impart, instruct, make known, show; **advertise,** propagandise, publicise; **notify,** advise, circularise, keep posted, notice *(U.S.)*, warn; **hint,** insinuate, intimate

inform *v* → encourage

INFORMAL *adj* unceremonious, unofficial; **casual,** easy, easygoing, free and easy, nonconformist, offhand, offhanded, relaxed, unbuttoned, unconcerned, unconventional; **uninhibited,** bohemian, permissive, unembarrassed; **colloquial,** conversational; **casually dressed,** déhabillé, in dishabille

informal *adj* → **1** nonconformist **2** useless

INFORMALITY *n* approachability, approachableness, intimacy, intimateness, lack of ceremony; **casualness,** bohemianism, ease, easiness, lack of inhibition, offhandedness, permissiveness, unconventionality; **anomie,** social vacuum; **casual dress,** dishabille, fatigues, mufti, undress

INFORMANT *n* conveyor, informer, intelligencer *(Archaic)*, notifier, promoter *(Obs.)*, teller; **source,** adviser, authority, consultant, referral; **guide,** cicerone, courier; **grapevine,** channel; **tipster,** a little bird, urger; **pimp,** blabber, chocolate frog, copper's nark, dobber, dog, golliwog, grass, grasser, nark, shelf, silvertail, snitch, squealer, stool pigeon *(U.S.)*, supergrass, telltale, welsher; **spy,** eavesdropper, plant, scout, security police, sleeper, spook, wire-tapper *(U.S.)*

INFORMATION *n* change, dope, drum, gen, good guts, griff *(N.Z.)*, griffin *(N.Z.)*, hot tip, info, inside information, intelligence, lowdown, news, run-down, the dinkum oil, the facts, the good oil, the goods; **advice,** lead, tip, tip-off, warning, word, word in the ear; **hint,** clue, inkling, intimation, sidelight, suggestion, suspicion; **propaganda,** agitprop, PR, public relations; **report,** brief, case history, document, follow-up, praecipe, statement, story, summary, white paper; **bulletin,** circular, communiqué, memorandum, newsletter, notice; **message,** dispatch, dispatch note *(Brit.)*, line, note; **databank,** card file, card index, catalogue, clipping service, database, dossier, file, reference library, teletext; **data,** block *(Computers)*, datum, details *(Archaic)*, material, source material; **bit,** byte, field, word *(Computers)*; **baud**

information *n* → **1** knowledge **2** news

INFORMATIVE *adj* directive, directory, documentary, encyclopaedic, informational, instructional, instructive, intelligential; **communicative,** chatty, communicatory, newsy

INFORMED *adj* abreast of, au courant, cluedup, cluey, enlightened, in on, in the know, in the picture, up on, up-to-date, wellinformed; **advised,** briefed, instructed, posted, primed, told

informer *n* → **1** gossip **2** informant **3** spy

infrastructure *n* → building

infrequent *adj* → **1** few **2** irregular **3** rare

infringe *v* → **1** contravene **2** disobey

infuriate *v* → **1** anger **2** annoy *adj* **3** angry

infuse *v* → **1** cook **2** liquefy

ingenious *adj* → **1** fantastic **2** intelligent

ingenuous *adj* → artless

ingest *v* → **1** absorb **2** eat **3** learn

ingot *v* → shape

ingrate *n* → **1** ungratefulness *adj* **2** ungrateful

ingratiate *v* → welcome

ingratitude *n* → ungratefulness

ingredient *n* → part

ingress *n* → **1** attack **2** entrance **3** right of way

INGROWING *adj* accrete, ingrown; **geophilous,** epigenous, epigeous

INHABIT *v* affect, domicile at, habit *(Obs.)*, indwell, live in, occupy, reside in, squat, tenant; **move in,** settle in; **stay,** lie *(Archaic)*, sojourn, visit; **lodge,** board, quarter, room; **flat,** bach, bachelorise, pad down; **live out,** sleep out; **live together,** cohabit, live with, muck in, shack up with; **camp,** bivouac, bivvy, encamp, tent; **kennel,** nest, stable, stall, sty; **cabin,** barrack, hut; **caravan,** campervan; **dwell,** abide, bide *(Archaic)*, hang out, live, reside, stay, use *(Archaic)*, won *(Archaic)*; **come from,** belong to, hail from; **colonise,** people, plant, populate; **settle,** anchor, pitch *(Rare)*, swallow the anchor

INHABITANT *n* abider, denizen, dweller, habitant, indweller, outlier, parishioner, resident, residentiary; **neighbour,** local; **frontiersman,** borderer, marcher; **inlander,** bogtrotter, highlander, islander, isthmian, lowlander, mainlander, mountaineer, sylvan, ultramontane, woodlander; **cave-dweller,** caveman, troglodyte; **terrestrial,** earthling, earthman, tellurian. *See also* OCCUPANT; POPULATION

inhale *v* → **1** absorb **2** breathe

inherent *adj* → **1** characteristic **2** inborn

inherit *v* → get

inhibit *v* → **1** prohibit **2** restrict **3** stop

inhuman *adj* → **1** callous **2** unkind

inimical *adj* → **1** hating **2** inconvenient **3** unfriendly

inimitable *adj* → **1** perfect **2** superior

iniquity *n* → **1** immorality **2** unfairness

initial *n* → **1** bookbinding **2** letter *v* **3** assent to **4** label *adj* **5** new **6** original

INITIATE *v* auspicate *(Obs. Rare)*, bring in, bring into use, create, float, give birth to, give rise to, handsel, hatch, inaugurate, initialise *(Computers)*, innovate, instigate, introduce, launch, phase in, pioneer, premiere, set on foot, trigger, turn on; **establish,** found, ground, institute, set up; **baptise,** blood, christen; **prime,** clutch-start, crank, fetch, kick-start, set going, turn over. *See also* START

initiate *n* → **1** believer **2** member **3** starter *v* **4** activate **5** innovate **6** offer **7** teach

initiative *n* → **1** doing **2** foundation *adj* **3** original

inject *v* → insert

injunction *n* → **1** command **2** guidance **3** insistence **4** prohibition **5** restraining order

INJURE *v* harm, hurt, traumatise; **wound,** beat up, concuss, disfeature, draw first blood, give someone a facial, run over, shatter, sprain, strain, wing; **maim,** bemaul, deface, deform, disfigure, make mincemeat of, mangle, mutilate; **bruise,** contuse, jam; **stab,** bayonet, bite, carve up, feather, pike, prick, run-through, spur, tusk; **cripple,** disable, hamstring, incapacitate, lame, nobble, scotch. *See also* DAMAGE

INJURED *adj* battle-scarred, bruised, corked, maimed, winged, wounded; **frozen,** frostbitten; **handicapped,** crippled, developmentally disabled, disabled, flat-footed, game, gammy, halt *(Archaic),* hipshot, incapacitated, lame

INJURY *n* Blighty *(Brit.),* breach *(Obs.),* flesh wound, lesion, maim *(Rare),* microtrauma, trauma, traumatism, wound; **specific injury,** bite, bruise, burn, contusion, fracture, march fracture, scratch, shiner, sprain, stab, strain, welt; **grievous bodily harm,** G.B.H.; **disability,** handicap, impediment; **limp,** cork knee, cork leg, flatfoot, halt *(Archaic).* *See also* DAMAGE; HARM

injury *n* → **1** crime **2** harm **3** pain **4** unfairness

injustice *n* → **1** crime **2** unfairness

in justice *adv* → fairly

ink *n* → **1** alcohol **2** disguise **3** dye *v* **4** colour **5** depict

inkling *n* → **1** conjecture **2** idea **3** information

inland *n* → **1** inside **2** land **3** region *adj* **4** inside **5** land **6** national *adv* **7** inside

in-law *n* → relative

inlay *n* → **1** insert **2** medication *v* **3** insert

inlet *n* → **1** bay **2** entrance *v* **3** insert

inmate *n* → **1** occupant **2** prisoner

inn *n* → **1** barracks **2** hotel **3** pub **4** restaurant

innards *n* → **1** abdomen **2** inside

innate *adj* → **1** characteristic **2** inborn **3** natural

inner *n* → **1** aim *adj* **2** characteristic **3** inside **4** secret

innings *n* → **1** land **2** period **3** repair **4** swamp

INNOCENCE *n* blamelessness, guiltlessness; **purity,** candour, immaculacy, immaculateness, maidenhead, maidenhood, maidenliness, pureness, sinlessness, state of grace, virginity, virtue, whiteness; **artlessness,** dupability, guilelessness, inexperience, simpleness, simplicity

INNOCENT *n* child, child of nature, cleanskin, dove, ingenue, lamb, newborn babe

INNOCENT *adj* blameless, clean, clean-handed, clear, guiltless, inculpable, irreproachable, not guilty, offenceless, reproachless, white-handed; **pure,** dovelike, immaculate, incorruptible, lamblike, lilywhite, maidenly, sinless, unsullied, untouched, virginal, virtuous, white; **artless,** dupable, green, inexperienced, simple, uncalculating, unworldly

innocent *n* → **1** artless person **2** butt **3** children **4** stupid person *adj* **5** artless **6** clean

innocuous *adj* → **1** moderate **2** safe

INNOVATE *v* break new ground, initiate, inspirit, originate, turn over a new leaf; **swing,** be with it; **modernise,** bring up to date, freshen, furbish up, refurbish, revamp, revive, update

innovate *v* → **1** create **2** initiate

INNOVATION *n* bright idea, innovativeness, modernity, neologism, neology, newie, note *(Colloq.),* novation *(Rare),* novelty, originality, wrinkle; **renovation,** re-creation, rebirth, recast, renaissance, renewal, revival, reviviscence, update; **modernisation,** aggiornamento, revivification, updating; **latest fashion,** the last word, the latest

INNOVATIVE *adj* innovational, innovatory, newfangled, novel, original, state-of-the-art, unconventional, unprecedented; **futuristic,** avant-garde, high-tech, sunrise, ultramodern; **modern,** contemporary, current, fashionable, fresh as a daisy, just out, late-model, latest, live, mod, modernist, modernistic, neological, neoteric, new-fashioned, recent, redbrick, swinging, trendy, ultrafashionable, up-to-date, up-to-the-minute, with-it

INNOVATOR *n* innovationist, neologist, original, original thinker, originator, trailblazer; **moderniser,** freshener, refurbisher, restorer, reviver, revolutionary, Young Turk; **modern,** bright young thing, junior, modernist, swinger, trendy; **nouveau riche,** parvenu, upstart; **new wave,** a breath of fresh air, avant-garde, ginger group, nouvelle vague, young blood; **youth,** infancy, spring, springtime

innuendo *n* → **1** accusation **2** allusion **3** slander

innumerable *adj* → **1** infinite **2** many **3** uncertain

inoculate *v* → **1** fertilise **2** insert **3** medicate **4** protect

inoffensive *adj* → pleasant

IN ONE'S POSSESSION *adv* at call, in hand, in one's clutches, in one's own hands, on hand, to hand, to one's credit, to one's name, to the good

inopportune *adj* → inappropriate

inordinate *adj* → **1** excessive **2** liberated

in-patient *n* → patient

input *n* → insert

inquest *n* → **1** court of law **2** jury **3** trial

inquire *v* → question

INQUIRE INTO *v* examine, investigate, probe, review, scrutinise, study; **analyse,** anatomise, appraise, assay, assess, break down, catalogue, classify, codify, derive, digest, file, group, interpret, list, order, pull apart, pull to pieces, rank, reduce to order, sift, sort, unravel, winnow; **dissect,** prosect, randomise, segment

inquisition *n* → **1** questioning **2** trial

inquisitive *n* → **1** morbid curiosity *adj* **2** curious

IN RETURN *adv* back, in compensation

inroad *n* → **1** attack **2** entrance

insane *adj* → **1** astonishing **2** good **3** illogical **4** mad **5** psychologically disturbed

insatiable *adj* → **1** avaricious **2** greedy

inscribe *v* → **1** list **2** record

inscrutable *adj* → **1** composed **2** unclear

IN SECRET *adv* backstage, behind someone's back, behind the scenes, by the back door, cagily, clandestinely, close, closely, furtively, invisibly, on the q.t., on the quiet, on the side, secretly, sneakily, sneakingly, stealthily, surreptitiously, through the back door, under one's hat, under the table, underhand, up one's sleeve; **covertly,** clandestinely, collusively, under cover, underground; **confidentially,** between ourselves, between you and me, entre nous; **privately,** in camera, in confidence, in private, intimately, sub rosa, under the rose

INSECT *n* bitie, bloodsucker, borer, bug, creepy-crawly, daddy-long-legs, grub, hexapod, imago; **larva,** instar; **insect colony,** hive, termitarium, vespiary; **invertebrate,** arthropod, articulate *(Rare),* segmented invertebrate; **cicada,** black prince, double drummer, floury baker, green Monday, greengrocer, red-eye, Union Jack, yellow Monday; **worm,** annelid, earthworm, helminth, leech, tube worm, vermicule

insect *n* → bad person

insecticide *n* → poison

insecure *adj* → **1** changeable **2** uncertain **3** vulnerable

inseminate *v* → **1** conceive **2** insert

insensate *adj* → **1** insensible **2** prejudiced **3** stupid

INSENSIBILITY *n* blockishness, dullness, impassiveness, impassivity, imperception, imperceptiveness, imperceptivity, impercipience, insensateness, insensitiveness, insensitivity, insentience, insusceptibility, obtuseness, unawareness; **senselessness,** anosmia, hypaesthesia, numbness, paralysis, sensory deprivation. *See also* UNCONSCIOUSNESS; ANAESTHESIA

INSENSIBLE *adj* hypaesthesic, imperceptive, impercipient, insensate, insensitive, insentient, insusceptible, lost to, obtuse, unaware; **numb,** dead, inert, lifeless, paralysed; **blockish,** blocked, dull, dullish, thick-skinned, unalive; **senseless,** anosmatic, tasteless *(Rare)*

insensible *adj* → **1** apathetic **2** callous **3** ignorant

INSERT *n* Dutchman *(Carp.),* embolism, enclosure, fold-out, gusset, infiltrate, infusion, inlay, inlay graft, input, inset, interlining, noddy *(T.V. Colloq.),* peg, stuffing, suppository, tibby; **injection,** enema, fuel-injection, infiltration, infusion, instillation, instilment, intrusion, jab, shot, skinpop

INSERT *v* catheterise, ease in, infix, inlet, inset, intercalate, interleaf, interleave, interlineate, introduce, intromit, jug, margin, overstuff, package, peg, pile, plug, pocket, pot, pouch, put in, rowel *(Vet. Science),* sandwich, sheathe, slip in, slot in, stuff, tabernacle, thrum, tip in *(Print.),* trench *(Obs.),* tuck, whack in, work in; **interpolate,** insinuate, interject; **enclose,** bag, barrel, bottle, box, encapsulate; **embed,** bury; **enter,** enrol, file, fill in; **implant,** bed, embed, engraft, enroot, graft, heel in *(Bot.),* impregnate, infix, inlay, inoculate, inseminate, plant, root, tub, vaccinate, variolate; **inject,** instil, intrude *(Geol.),* mainline, shoot, skinpop, syringe

insert *n* → inside

INSERTER *n* bottler, canner, enroller, grafter, implanter, infuser, inoculator, introducer, packer, stinger, vaccinator; **injector,** fuel-injector, hype, hypo, hypodermic, hypodermic needle, infiltrator, needle, spike, vaccine gun; **drill,** diamond drill, perforator

INSERTION *n* embolism, epenthesis, grafting, infixion, insinuation, intercalation, interpolation, introduction, intromission, putting in; **implantation,** embedding, embedment, emboly, engraftation, engraftment, graft, grafting, impregnation, inoculation, insemination, vaccination, vaccinisation, variolation

inset *n* → **1** act **2** flow **3** insert **4** inside *v* **5** insert

INSIDE *n* belly, bottom, bowels, contents, entrails, guts, innards, insides, interior, internal organs, interns *(Archaic),* intestines, pith, viscera, vitals, within; **innermost,** core, endocrine, heart, kernel, marrow, penetralia; **inland,** dead heart, heartland, outback, red centre, up-country; **inwardness,** innerness, inscape, interiority, internality; **inset,** chine, concavity, fissure, insert, interstice, recess

INSIDE *adj* deep-seated, enclosed, inmost, inner, innermost, interior, intern *(Archaic),* internal, interstitial, intestinal, intestine, subcutaneous, visceral; **inland,** up-country; **inward,** endoreic, incurrent, ingrowing, re-entrant; **indoor,** domestic, in-house, inboard *(Naut.),* ingrown, intimate, intramural; **inlying,** endogenous, intratelluric

INSIDE *adv* aboard, herein, in, inboard, indoors, therein, within, withindoors *(Obs.)*; **inward,** centripetally, hereinto, inly *(Archaic),* inwards; **internally,** endogenously, interiorly, inwardly; **inland,** up-country; **at home,** in the bosom of one's family, in the family

inside *n* → **1** characteristics **2** clique **3** essence **4** secret society **5** side *adv* **6** here

insidious *adj* → **1** cunning **2** deceitful **3** invisible

insight *n* → **1** discrimination **2** learning **3** understanding

insignia *n* → emblem

insignificant *n* → **1** unimportant person **2** unimportant thing *adj* **3** nonsensical **4** smallest **5** unimportant

insinuate *v* → **1** accuse **2** beguile **3** imply **4** inform **5** insert

INSIPID *adj* flavourless, floury, milk-and-water, savourless, tasteless, undistinguished, unseasoned, vapid; **watery,** diluted, washy, wishy-washy; **flat,** dead, plastic; **mild,** bland, plain, unflavoured, unspiced

insipid *adj* → **1** boring **2** moderate

INSIPIDITY *n* blandness, insipidness, mildness, plainness, tastelessness, vapidity, washiness, weak flavour; **milk and water,** pap

insist *v* → assert

INSISTENCE *n* clamorousness, clamour, hue and cry, importunacy, insistency, public outcry; **demand,** call, claim, counterclaim, exaction, request, requisition, ultimatum; **order,** behest, command, decree, fiat, imperative, injunction, stipulation, ukase; **writ,** quo warranto, warrant; **levy,** burden, imposition, requirement, strain, tax; **bill,** dun, final demand, invoice, notice

INSISTENT *adj* demanding, exacting, exigent, imperative, stipulatory, urgent

insistent *adj* → **1** assertive **2** important **3** uncompromising

INSIST ON *v* ask, call for, deliver an ultimatum, demand, order, require, stipulate; **claim,** counterclaim, postulate; **exact,** impose on, levy, make heavy demands on, requisition, tax; **bill,** dun, exact payment, foreclose, invoice

insolent *n* → **1** disdainer *adj* **2** arrogant **3** discourteous **4** dissident **5** insulting

insolvent *n* → **1** defaulter *adj* **2** in debt **3** non-paying

insomnia *n* → waking

inspect *v* → **1** examine **2** look

INSPECTION *n* field day, field trip, recce, reconnaissance, review *(Mil.)*, snoop, visit, visitation; **search,** dig, digging, exploration, hunt, potholing, quest, treasure hunt; **body-search,** frisk, house-search, ramp *(Prison)*; **legal search,** requisitions on title. *See also* INVESTIGATION; TEST

inspire *v* → **1** breathe **2** cause **3** embolden **4** encourage **5** enliven

install *v* → **1** employ **2** position

instalment *n* → magazine

instance *n* → **1** example **2** importunacy **3** litigation

instant *n* → **1** moment **2** the present *adj* **3** current **4** impermanent **5** momentary

instantaneous *adj* → **1** impermanent **2** momentary

instep *n* → leg

in step *adv* → **1** aptly **2** conventionally **3** simultaneously

instigate *v* → **1** arouse **2** initiate

instil *v* → insert

instinct *n* → idea

INSTITUTE *n* academy, college, faculty, institution; **guild,** chapel, confraternity, craft, livery company, lodge, mystery *(Archaic)*, trades union; **fellowship,** brotherhood, fraternity *(U.S.)*, sisterhood, sodality, sorority; **friendly society,** benevolent association, benevolent society, cooperative society, housing association, service club

institute *n* → **1** college **2** custom **3** rule *v* **4** create **5** employ **6** initiate **7** operate

institution *n* → **1** college **2** creation **3** custom **4** hospital **5** institute **6** rule **7** start

instruct *v* → **1** command **2** inform **3** teach

instrument *n* → **1** agency **2** deed **3** measurement **4** method **5** tool

instrumental *adj* → musical

insubordinate *n* → **1** disobeyer *adj* **2** disobedient

insufferable *adj* → unbearable

INSUFFICIENCY *n* dearth, defect, deficiency, half-measure, lack, meagreness, pitifulness, scantiness, scarceness, scarcity, scrimpiness, shortage, want; **inadequacy,** inadequateness, incommensurateness, jejuneness, scragginess; **deficit,** deficiency, shortage, shortfall, ullage; **scarcity,** privation; **need,** penury, poorness, poverty

INSUFFICIENT *adj* deficient, inadequate, jejune, lean, light on *(Colloq.)*, measly, scant, scanty, scarce, scrimp, scrimpy, short, slim, wanting; **poor,** incommensurate, meagre, piss-weak, scraggy, unequal to, weak

insular *adj* → **1** intolerant **2** land **3** one **4** solitary

insulate *v* → cover

insulation *n* → **1** building materials **2** conservation **3** heating **4** quietener

INSULT *n* affront, disparagement, flout, humiliation, hurt, indignity, outrage, put-down, revilement, slight, smack in the eye, snub, spurn, violation; **gibe,** taunt; **hiss,** boo, catcall; **V-sign,** thumbs up; **leer,** smirk

INSULT *v* blister, call names, humiliate, jeer at, slight, taunt, trample on, twit; **ridicule,** cheek, laugh at, put down, sauce, slang, tell someone a thing or two; **snub,** cut dead, disoblige, give someone the cold shoulder, set down, turn one's back on; **affront,** mortify; **be rude,** be lacking in courtesy, show disrespect; **snigger,** laugh, leer, sneer, snort; **gesture rudely,** cock a snoot at, look cross-eyed at, make a face at, poke out one's tongue at, thumb one's nose at

insult *n* → **1** arrogance **2** disrepute

INSULTING *adj* abusive, injurious, scurrile, scurrilous; **cheeky,** airy, breezy, cavalier, flip, flippant, impertinent, off-hand, saucy; **impolite,** discourteous, familiar, rude, unceremonious, uncivil; **insolent,** audacious, impudent, presumptuous

insuperable *adj* → impossible

IN SUPPLY *adv* in hand, in reserve, in stock, in the pipeline, on tap, on the menu

INSURANCE *n* assurance, coinsurance, consequential loss insurance, coverage, endowment insurance, fire insurance, protection, protective trust, public liability insurance, reinsurance, tontine, valued policy; **indemnity,** counterindemnity, guarantee, indemnification, security; **policy,** cover note, floating policy; **superannuation,** annuity, provident fund

insurance *n* → **1** contract **2** expedient **3** surety

insure *v* → be cautious

insurgent *n* → **1** disobeyer **2** dissident *adj* **3** anarchic **4** disobedient **5** dissident **6** revolutionary **7** sea

insurrection *n* → **1** dissidence **2** mutiny **3** revolution

intact *adj* → **1** abstinent **2** perfect **3** whole

intake *n* → **1** absorption **2** contraction **3** entrance **4** thinness

INTANGIBILITY *n* abstractness, disembodiment, immateriality, immaterialness, impalpability, imponderability, imponderableness, incorporeity, inessentiality, intangibleness, invisibility, unreality; **ethereality,** airiness, etherealness, vaporosity, vaporousness; **evanescence,** fugitiveness, transience; **insubstantiality,** flimsiness, tenuousness, thinness

INTANGIBLE *adj* bodiless, disembodied, ectoplasmic, immaterial, impalpable, imperceptible, inappreciable, incorporate, incorporeal, insubstantial, invisible, unreal, untouchable; **supersensory,** imponderable, inconceivable, inessential, supersensible, supersensual, unessential, unknowable; **internal,** mental, subjective; **abstract,** conceptual, metaphysical, metempiric, metempirical, theoretical. *See also* ETHEREAL

intangible *adj* → **1** imprecise **2** nonexistent

integer *n* → number

integral *n* → **1** number **2** part *adj* **3** constituent **4** numerical

integrate *v* → **1** combine **2** compute **3** join **4** make whole

integrity *n* → **1** faithfulness **2** honesty

intellect *n* → mind

INTELLECTUAL *n* academic, academician, blue, bluestocking, bookman, bookworm, Brahman, classicalist, classicist, diplomate, doctor, don *(Brit.)*, fellow, graduate, humanist, licentiate, pandit *(India)*, postgraduate, professor, rabbi, rabbin, researcher, sage, scholar, scholastic, schoolman, sophist; **highbrow,** connoisseur, Dryasdust, egghead, pedant; **bohemian,** long-hair

INTELLECTUAL *adj* academic, cerebral, learned, scholarly, scholastic; **highbrow,** bluestocking, bohemian, bookish, heavy, ivory tower, long-haired, pedantic

intellectual *n* → **1** wise person *adj* **2** intelligent **3** mental

INTELLECTUAL PROPERTY *n* copyright, patent, petty patent, public lending right, trademark

INTELLIGENCE *n* ambidexterity, braininess, brains, brightness, brilliance, brilliantness, capacity, cleverness, genius, luminousness, smartness, strong-mindedness, understanding, wit; **sharp-wittedness,** acumen, aptitude, esprit, keenness, knowingness, penetration, penetrativeness, perspicacity, sharp-sightedness, sharpness; **nimbleness,** precociousness, precocity. *See also* WISDOM

intelligence *n* → **1** communication **2** information **3** investigation **4** mind **5** news

Intelligence *n* → phantom

INTELLIGENT *adj* able, brainy, bright, brilliant, capable, clever, cleverish, conceited *(Obs.)*, ingenious, intellective, intellectual, intelligential, knowledgeable, luminous, neat, smart, understanding; **quick on the uptake,** apprehensive, apt, nimble, precocious, quick, ready, ready-witted, receptive; **sharp-witted,** acuminous, acute, Attic, fly *(Colloq.)*, gnomic, keen, knowing, parlous *(Obs.)*, penetrating, perspicacious, quick-witted, sharp, sharp-sighted, wide-awake. *See also* WISE

intelligent *adj* → **1** knowing **2** mental

intelligentsia *n* → wise person

intelligible *adj* → **1** clear **2** easy

intemperate *adj* → **1** climatic **2** liberated **3** overindulgent

INTEND *v* calculate, choose, destine, mean to, plan, vow; **have a good mind to,** have a great mind to, have half a mind to, think fit; **consider,** contemplate, meditate, think about; **desire,** list *(Archaic)*, long for, will, wish, yearn for

intend *v* → **1** aim at **2** desire

INTENSE *adj* bad, dense, exquisite, frightful, grievous, heavy, high, keen, particular, perfervid, poignant, profound, severe, sharp, special, terrible, terrific, violent, vivid

intense *adj* → **1** emotional **2** energetic **3** opaque **4** perceptive

INTENSELY *adv* amain *(Archaic)*, dearly, deeply, grievously, highly, intensively, keenly, perfervidly, poignantly, resoundingly, severely, sharply, so, violently, vividly, with a vengeance

intensify *v* → **1** become greater **2** photograph

intensity *n* → **1** colour **2** pitch

intensive *adj* → **1** increased **2** thorough

intent *n* → **1** meaning **2** plan **3** will *adj* **4** attentive **5** careful **6** uncompromising

intention *n* → **1** aim **2** plan **3** will

INTERACT *v* alternate, be a function of, be proportional to, come together, correlate, correspond, cut across one another, give and take, intercross, interflow, interlock, intermarry, intermingle, interplay, interrelate, intersect, intertwine, interweave, marry, mutualise, reciprocate; **exchange,** come and go between, commute, interchange, intercommunicate, interconnect; **cause to interact,** interface

INTERACTION *n* alternation, bilateralism, bilateralness, exchange, interchange, interconnection, intercourse, interdependence, interplay, interrelation, mutuality, reciprocality, reciprocation, reciprocity, relationship; **mutualism,** biocenology, communion, symbiosis; **direct ratio,** correlation, correspondence, direct relation, functional relationship, inverse ratio, inverse relation; **barter,** trade; **toing and froing,** coming and going, commutation *(U.S.)*, commuting; **exchange of ideas,** cross fertilisation, cultural exchange

INTERACTIVE *adj* bilateral, commutative, interfacial, internecine, mutual, reciprocal, reciprocative; **interdependent,** alternate, interchangeable, interconnected; **international,** inter-dominion, inter-island, intercollegiate, interdepartmental, intermundane, interpersonal, interracial, interstate, intertribal

intercede *v* → **1** entreat **2** mediate

intercept *n* → **1** hindrance **2** stoppage *v* **3** come between **4** converge **5** obstruct **6** stop

interchange *n* → **1** communication **2** exchange **3** interaction *v* **4** alternate **5** exchange **6** interact

intercom *n* → telecommunications

intercourse *n* → **1** communication **2** interaction **3** sexual intercourse **4** talk

interdict *n* → **1** prohibition **2** punishment *v* **3** hinder **4** prohibit **5** punish

interest *n* → **1** attentiveness **2** capital **3** debt **4** importance **5** influence **6** motive **7** ownership **8** participation **9** profit **10** share **11** stocks and shares *v* **12** be important **13** engross **14** involve

INTERESTING *adj* absorbing, arresting, conspicuous, engrossing, eye-catching, fascinating, gripping, juicy, newsworthy, noteworthy, noticeable, readable, remarkable, showy, striking

interesting *adj* → alluring

interface *n* → **1** contact **2** wall *v* **3** interact **4** sew

interfere *v* → **1** hinder **2** interrupt **3** meddle

interference *n* → **1** electricity **2** obstructiveness **3** radio **4** rape **5** reflection

INTERIM *adj* intercurrent, intermediate, intermissive, interregnal, interspatial, intervenient, intervening

interim *n* → **1** interval *adj* **2** impermanent

interior *n* → **1** inside **2** land **3** region *adj* **4** inside **5** national **6** secret **7** spiritual

INTERIORISE *v* embed, internalise, put inside; **introvert,** withdraw into oneself

interject *v* → **1** add **2** insert **3** interrupt **4** shout

INTERLACE *v* braid, enlace, entangle, intercross, intertwine, intervolve, interweave, plait, plash, pleach, reticulate, weave; **mat,** mesh; **trellis,** wattle

interlace *v* → mix

INTERLACEMENT *n* enlacement, entanglement, intertwinement, interweavement, matting, mesh, meshes, meshwork, netting, network, reseau, reticulation, wattling, webbing; **net,** bird netting, chain mesh, chain wire, drag-net, fishnet, mosquito net, purse seine, screen, seine, wire gauze, wire netting, wirecloth; **grid,** gauntlet *(Railways)*, grating, gridiron, grillage, grille, reticle; **latticing,** latticework, treillage, wickerwork; **trellis,** trelliswork, wattle; **plait,** braid, wreath; **skein,** cat's cradle; **crisscross,** crackle, craze, frostwork; **shutter,** jalousie, wicket; **crosshair,** crosswire

interlock *v* → **1** fit **2** interact **3** join

interlope *v* → come between

interlude *n* → **1** act **2** drama **3** interruption **4** interval **5** musical piece **6** rest

intermediary *n* → **1** mediator *adj* **2** central

intermediate *adj* → **1** central **2** interim **3** intervenient **4** rocky

interminable *adj* → **1** changeless **2** continual **3** eternal **4** infinite

intermission *n* → **1** interruption **2** interval **3** irregularity

intermittent *adj* → **1** interrupted **2** irregular **3** rare

intern *n* → **1** healer **2** prisoner *v* **3** imprison *adj* **4** inside

internal *adj* → **1** inside **2** intangible **3** national

international *n* → **1** sportsman *adj* **2** interactive **3** sports

International Phonetic Alphabet *n* → letter

internecine *adj* → **1** interactive **2** murderous

interplay *n* → **1** interaction *v* **2** interact

interpolate *v* → **1** add **2** insert

interpose *v* → **1** add **2** come between **3** interrupt **4** mediate **5** obstruct

interpret *v* → **1** clarify **2** explain **3** hear **4** inquire into

INTERPRETER *n* constructionist, construer, deconstructionist, exegete, explainer, exponent, expounder, glossator *(Old Eng. Law)*; **semiotician,** hermeneutist, hierophant, oneirocritic, solarist, symbolist; **paraphrast,** paraphraser, renderer; **commentator,** critic, editorialist, reviewer; **annotator,** glosser, scholiast

INTERPRETIVE *adj* explanatory, explicative, exponential, expository, illustrative, interpretational, interpretative; **paraphrastic,** transcriptive; **exegetic,** anagogic, anagogical, hermeneutic, hierophantic; **commentarial,** annotative, editorial, glossarial

interregnum *n* → **1** interruption **2** interval **3** temporary appointment

interrogate *v* → question

interrogative *adj* → questioning

INTERRUPT *v* break into, bust up, cut, disconnect, disturb, punctuate, stop; **pause,** hold it; **interfere,** barge in, break in, burst in, butt in, chime in, chip in, cut in, horn in, intrude, irrupt; **interject,** cut someone short, get a word in edgeways, interpose, intervene

interrupt *v* → **1** meddle **2** stop

INTERRUPTED *adj* broken, desultory, disconnected, discontinuous, discrete, disjunctive, episodic, few and far between, fitful, intermittent, spasmodic, striated; **unconformable,** faulty

INTERRUPTEDLY *adv* at intervals, by snatches, desultorily, discontinuously, falteringly, fitfully, in fits and starts, spasmodically

INTERRUPTION *n* anacoluthon, discontinuation, discontinuity, disjunction, disturbance, embuggerance, embuggery, interposition, intrusion; **unconformity,** chasm, fault *(Geol.)*; **pause,** abeyance, break, caesura, gap, hiatus, interlude, intermission, interregnum, interval, lacuna, rest, spell; **interjection,** digression, episode, exclamation, interposal, irrelevance, parenthesis; **commercial break,** station break

intersect *v* → **1** cross **2** interact

intersection *n* → **1** crossing **2** join **3** road

intersperse *v* → **1** disperse **2** mix

interstate *adj* → **1** interactive **2** regional *adv* **3** away

interstice *n* → **1** gap **2** inside **3** opening

INTERVAL *n* gap, hiatus, interim, interruption, interspace, meantime, parenthesis, space, time; **interlude,** antimasque, entr'acte, episode, intermission, wait; **moratorium,** abeyance, cease-fire, grace *(Law),* interregnum, prorogation, suspension, truce; **lull,** break, breather, breathing space, dwell *(Mach.),* let-up, pause, recess, remission *(Med.),* respite, rest, shoot *(Rowing),* smoko, spell, tea-break; **lag,** dead time *(Elect.),* headway *(Railways),* hysteresis *(Physics),* lead *(Engineering),* response time, saros *(Astron.),* time-lag

interval *n* → **1** difference **2** gap **3** interruption **4** stoppage

intervene *v* → **1** come between **2** entreat **3** interrupt **4** mediate

INTERVENIENT *adj* interjacent, intermediate, interposed, intervening, interventional, irruptive, mesne, middle, sandwiched; **meddlesome,** busy, curious, interfering, nosy, obstructive, officious, stickybeaking

interview *n* → **1** assignation **2** questioning **3** talk *v* **4** hear **5** question

intestine *adj* → **1** inside **2** national

IN THE FRESH AIR *adv* alfresco, in the open air, out of doors, under the stars

IN THE FUTURE *adv* at length, eventually, finally, in the fullness of time, one of these days, sooner or later, ultimately; **imminently,** at any moment, before long, by and by, momentarily *(U.S.),* pendently, presently, shortly, soon; **onwards,** afterwards, forth, forwards, from this time on, hence *(Archaic),* henceforth, off, onwards in time, thence, thenceforth, thenceforward, thereafter; **some day,** mañana, one day, sometime, tomorrow, tonight; **next,** near, nigh; **in waiting,** a day off, a week off, in store, in the offing, in the wind, some time off; **yet,** still; **then,** thereon, thereupon, therewith, with that

IN THE PAST *adv* ago, already *(U.S.),* back, before now, beforetime *(Archaic),* by, erenow *(Archaic),* formerly, hitherto, since, sometime, sometimes *(Obs.),* then, whilom *(Archaic)*; **before that time,** theretofore, thitherto *(Rare)*; **yesterday,** last century, last week, last year, lately, latterly, recently, the other day, the other night, yesteryear *(Poetic)*; **long ago,** at one time, early, erst *(Archaic),* erstwhile *(Archaic),* historically, immemorially, in the year dot, langsyne *(Scot.),* late, once, once upon a time, sometime, wayback

intimate *n* → **1** friend *v* **2** confess **3** inform **4** publicise *adj* **5** essential **6** friendly **7** inside **8** secret **9** sexy

intimidate *v* → **1** force **2** menace

intolerable *adj* → unbearable

INTOLERANCE *n* blindness, bumbledom, impenetrability, impenetrableness, narrow-mindedness, opinionativeness; **bigotry,** anti-Semitism, apartheid, colour-bar, colour prejudice, commie bashing, Jew-baiting, Jim Crowism, McCarthyism, poofter-bashing, racialism, racism, segregation, union bashing; **chauvinism,** ageism, jingoism, misoneism, sexism; **pettiness,** illiberality, illiberalness, littleness, small-mindedness, smallness; **parochialism,** clannishness, insularism, insularity, micrology, provincialism, sectionalism; **puritanism,** bowdlerism, Grundyism; **prejudice,** bias, preconception, prenotion, slant, warp; **deep north,** cracker-barrel, deep south, parish pump

INTOLERANT *adj* blind, blinkered, impenetrable, narrow, narrow-minded, unenlightened; **small-minded,** black-and-white, dogmatic, illiberal, Lilliputian, little, one-eyed, one-track, opinionated, opinionative, petty, picky, small; **parochial,** blue-rinse, conservative, fogram, hidebound, mealy-mouthed, old-line, puritan, puritanical, straitlaced; **insular,** clannish, home-town, jingoistic, parochial, provincial; **suburban,** parish-pump, poky; **bigoted,** anti-Semitic, chauvinist, chauvinistic, fascist, misoneist, sexist; **biased,** affectionate *(Obs.),* ex parte, one-sided, partial, prejudiced, unfair, unilateral, warped

intolerant *adj* → **1** prejudiced **2** unsociable

INTOLERANT PERSON *n* anti-Semite, bigot, closed mind, fascist, Jew-baiter, racialist, racist, segregationist; **chauvinist,** alf, male chauvinist, male chauvinist pig, ocker, poofter-basher; **wowser,** bible-basher, bowdleriser, jingoist, puritan; **fogy,** blimp *(Brit.),* doctrinaire, fogram, fuddy-duddy, mossback, ramrod, stick-in-the-mud; **provincial,** Lilliputian, suburbanite

intonation *n* → speaking

intone *v* → **1** sing **2** speak

INTOXICATE *v* befuddle, besot, fox *(Obs.),* fuddle, go to one's head, inebriate, liquor up, souse, wine

intoxicate *v* → excite

INTOXICATING *adj* alcoholic, hard, inebriant, intoxicant, intoxicative, spiritous *(Obs.),* spirituous; **strong,** gutsy, heady, high-proof, nappy *(Brit.),* neat, overproof, short, stiff; **winy,** beery, vinaceous, vinic, vinous; **proof,** single *(Archaic),* underproof

intractable *adj* → **1** stubborn **2** unmanageable

intransigent *n* → **1** strict person **2** stubborn person *adj* **3** strict **4** stubborn

intrastate *adj* → regional

intravenous *adj* → medicinal

intrepid *adj* → courageous

intricate *adj* → **1** complex **2** difficult

intrigue *n* → **1** conspiracy **2** cunning **3** love affair **4** narrative **5** secrecy **6** sexual relationship **7** trickery *v* **8** allure **9** beguile **10** conspire **11** engross **12** have sex **13** involve **14** keep secret **15** make do

intrinsic *adj* → essential

INTRODUCE *v* herald, preface, prelude, premise, usher in; **pioneer,** blaze a trail, go ahead, guide, head, lead the way

introduce *v* → **1** be sociable **2** initiate **3** insert **4** teach

INTRODUCTION *n* exordium, foreword, frontispiece, intro, lead-up, preamble, preface, preliminary, prelims, proem, prolegomena, prologue, prolusion, proposition *(Archaic),* protasis, recitals *(Law)*; **prelude,**

overture, voluntary; **curtain-raiser,** pre-release, teaser

introduction *n* → 1 assignation 2 book part 3 greeting 4 insertion 5 start

introspection *n* → thinking

introvert *n* → 1 solitary *v* 2 interiorise *adj* 3 solitary

intrude *v* → 1 insert 2 interrupt

intuition *n* → 1 conjecture 2 idea

IN TWOS *adv* à deux, in pairs, tete-a-tete; **dually,** bilaterally, binately, bipartitely, doubly, geminately; **double,** as much again, bis, in duplicate, twice, twofold

inundate *v* → 1 flood 2 flow 3 wet

inure *v* → habituate

IN USE *adj* live, living; **occupied,** busy *(U.S.),* engaged

invade *v* → 1 advance 2 attack 3 enter 4 wage war

invalid *n* → 1 patient *v* 2 be ill *adj* 3 ill 4 useless 5 weak

invaluable *adj* → expensive

invariable *n* → 1 number *adj* 2 changeless 3 level

invasion *n* → 1 act of war 2 advance 3 attack 4 entrance 5 flood

invective *n* → 1 disapproval 2 slander 3 swearing *adj* 4 accusatory 5 slanderous

inveigle *v* → allure

invent *v* → 1 create 2 fantasise

invention *n* → 1 creation 2 finished product 3 lie 4 musical piece

inventory *n* → 1 account 2 classification 3 list *v* 4 account 5 list

inverse *n* → 1 opposite meaning 2 opposite position *v* 3 overturn *adj* 4 opposing 5 overturned

INVERT *v* contrapose, oppose, polarise; **confront,** face, subtend

invert *n* → 1 bottom *v* 2 contrast 3 overturn *adj* 4 sexual

invertebrate *n* → insect

INVEST *v* average down, average up, bear, bull, buy in, close out, embark, hedge, hive off, job, operate, overbuy, play the market, play the stock market, scalp, speculate

invest *v* → 1 attack 2 clothe 3 cover 4 employ 5 pay 6 wear

INVESTIGATE *v* anatomise, delve into, dig, dissect, experiment, explore, fossick out, hunt up, look into, look up, plumb, pull apart, pull to pieces, reconnoitre, research, see how the land lies, see into; **check,** countercheck, go over, go through, road-test, sample, screen, snuff, swab *(Horseracing),* vet; **survey,** case, have a good look around, hunt about, hunt around, look over, nose around, observe, overlook, oversee *(Obs.),* peruse *(Archaic),* review, see over, shop around, sweep *(Naut.),* traverse, view. *See also* EXAMINE

investigate *v* → inquire into

INVESTIGATION *n* check, inquiry; **examination,** probe, review, reviewal, scrutiny, survey; **research,** experiment, R and D, research and development; **analysis,** anatomisation, appraisal, assay, criticism, diagnosis, dissection, evaluation, form criticism *(Theol.),* overhaul, qualitative analysis, quantitative analysis, scan, spectrum analysis; **screening,** airing, gallup poll, market research, mass observation, opinion poll, poll, questionnaire, random sampling, straw vote; **field study,** case study, field work, sampling; **cost-benefit analysis,** environmental impact study, feasibility study, systems analysis, time and motion study; **spot check,** countercheck, fatigue test, going-over, look, look-over, looksee, quality control, rummage, shakedown *(U.S.),* trip-check, view; **self-examination,** soul-searching; **identification parade,** police line-up; **spying,** cloak-and-dagger stuff, counterespionage, counterintelligence, espionage, intelligence, wire-tapping. *See also* QUESTIONING; INSPECTION; TEST

investiture *n* → employment

investment *n* → employment

invidious *adj* → 1 disreputable 2 hateful 3 unfair 4 vexing

invigorate *v* → energise

invincible *adj* → durable

inviolable *adj* → durable

inviolate *adj* → 1 perfect 2 safe 3 whole

INVISIBILITY *n* imperceptibleness, inconspicuousness, latency, latescence, obscureness, obscurity, smoke; **indistinctness,** blurriness, dimness, fogginess, shadowiness, umbrage *(Rare)*; **obscuration,** eclipse, immergence, immersion *(Astron.)*; **invisible ink,** sympathetic ink

INVISIBLE *adj* imperceptible, inconspicuous, insidious, latent, latescent, obscure, out of sight, sightless, viewless; **unseen,** unsighted; **obscured,** dead *(Mil.),* fogbound, occult *(Obs.)*; **indistinct,** blurry, darkling *(Poetic),* dim, faint, foggy, shadowy; **asymptomatic**

invisible *n* → 1 phantom *adj* 2 intangible 3 nonexistent 4 secret

INVISIBLY *adv* behind the scenes, imperceptibly, inconspicuously, latently, viewlessly; **indistinctly,** blurrily, darkly *(Archaic),* dimly, foggily, obscurely; **asymptomatically**

invite *n* → 1 entreaty *v* 2 allure 3 arrange 4 be sociable 5 entreat

inviting *adj* → 1 alluring 2 desirable 3 encouraging

invoice *n* → 1 account 2 bill 3 insistence 4 list *v* 5 insist on

invoke *v* → entreat

involuntary *adj* → unwilling

INVOLVE *v* catch up, commit, compromise, concern, condemn, entangle, entrap, implicate, incur, intervolve, overcommit, put up to, rope in; **interest,** intrigue

involve *v* → 1 cause difficulties 2 complicate 3 cover 4 engross 5 imply 6 signify 7 surround

inward *adj* → 1 entering 2 inborn 3 inside 4 quiet 5 spiritual *adv* 6 inside

inwards *adv* → inside

ion *n* → atom

iota *n* → small amount
IOU *n* → 1 bill 2 cheque
irascible *adj* → 1 angry 2 irritable
irate *adj* → angry
ire *n* → anger
iridescent *adj* → 1 bright 2 colourful
iris *n* → eye
irk *v* → 1 annoy 2 bore 3 tire
iron *n* → 1 club 2 gun 3 harshness 4 labeller 5 metal 6 press *v* 7 press 8 smooth *adj* 9 durable 10 fastened 11 grey 12 hard 13 metallic 14 strict
ironic *adj* → 1 figurative 2 humorous
iron lung *n* → breathing
irony *n* → 1 comedy 2 figure of speech 3 mockery 4 opposite meaning 5 surpriser 6 trickery
irradiate *v* → 1 heat 2 illuminate *adj* 3 bright
irrational *adj* → 1 illogical 2 numerical 3 rash 4 stupid
irrefutable *adj* → certain
IRREGULAR *adj* acyclic, agogic, aperiodic, arrhythmic, broken, catchy, desultory, discontinuous, fitful, fluttery, on-off, stop-go, uncertain, unequal, uneven, unrhythmical, unsteady, variable; **sporadic,** casual, erratic, flickering, fulgurating, infrequent, intermissive, intermittent, odd, periodic, remittent, snatchy, spasmodic, sporadical, unsystematic; **jerky,** abrupt, jolty, rickety, rough, unequal; **ragged,** patchy, scraggly, scraggy
irregular *n* → 1 combat troops 2 foreigner 3 freak 4 nonconformist *adj* 5 foreign 6 incorrect 7 nonconformist 8 rough 9 strange 10 unequal 11 unlawful
IRREGULARITY *n* abruptness, aperiodicity, arrhythmia, casualness, desultoriness, fitfulness, fluctuation, inconstancy, jerkiness, patchiness, raggedness, randomness, uncertainness, unequalness, unevenness, unsteadiness, variability; **intermittence,** intermission, jump, remittence, remittency, surge
IRREGULARLY *adv* brokenly, by fits and starts, desultorily, fitfully, flutteringly, in fits and starts, infrequently, now and then, on and off, patchily, raggedly, uncertainly, unequally, unevenly, unsteadily; **intermittently,** at intervals, intermittingly, now and again, now and then, periodically, remittently, spasmodically, sporadically, whiles *(Archaic)*; **jerkily,** abruptly, roughly, unequally
irrelevant *adj* → 1 incongruous 2 unimportant 3 unrelated
irreparable *adj* → hopeless
irreplaceable *adj* → 1 good 2 important
irrepressible *adj* → 1 happy 2 liberated
irreproachable *adj* → 1 clean 2 correct 3 innocent
irresistible *adj* → 1 alluring 2 encouraging
irresolute *adj* → indecisive
irrespective *adj* → unconditional
irresponsible *n* → 1 anarchist 2 mischief-maker *adj* 3 anarchic 4 badly-behaved 5 neglectful
irretrievable *adj* → hopeless
IRREVERENCE *n* impiety, impiousness, irreligion; **profanity,** blasphemousness, blasphemy, desecration, iconoclasm, pollution, profanation, profaneness, sacrilege, simony, violation; **godlessness,** fall from grace, unblessedness, ungodliness, unholiness; **faithlessness,** agnosticism, atheism, free thought, indifferentism, irreligion, lack of faith, nescience, nihilism, scepticism, secularisation; **paganism,** heathendom, heathenism, heathenry, infidelity, pagandom; **secularism,** secularity, worldliness
IRREVERENT *adj* blasphemous, iconoclastic, impious, profanatory, sacrilegious, unregenerate, violative *(U.S.)*; **profane,** ungodly, unhallowed, unholy, unsanctified; **apostate,** accursed, churchless, creedless, faithless, godforsaken, godless, unredeemed; **unreligious,** agnostic, anti-church, anti-religious, antichristian, anticlerical, atheist, freethinking, irreligious, nescient, sceptic, sceptical, unbelieving, unchristian, uncircumcised, undevout; **heathen,** gentile *(Obs.)*, heathenish, infidel, pagan, paganish; **secular,** carnal, mundane, secularistic, unspiritual, worldly
IRREVERENT PERSON *n* blasphemer, desecrater, freethinker, iconoclast, polluter, profaner, simoniac, simonist, the ungodly, the unrighteous, violator; **unbeliever,** agnostic, atheist, irreligionist, materialist, nescient, nullifidian, sceptic, secular humanist *(Derog.)*, seculariser, secularist; **pagan,** gentile, heathen, infidel; **antichristian,** antichrist
irreversible *adj* → 1 changeless 2 hopeless
irrigate *v* → 1 channel 2 wet
IRRITABLE *adj* aggravated, apoplectic, atrabilious, bad-tempered, bilious, brittle, cantankerous, captious, crabbed, crabby, cranky, cross, cross-grained, crotchety, crusty, fiery, fractious, fretful, grumpy, hot-tempered, huffish, huffy, ill-humoured, ill-natured, ill-tempered, impatient, lemony, like a bear with a sore head, on edge, out of humour, peevish, peppery, pettish, petulant, quarrelsome, querulous, ratty, scotty, shirty, shitty, shitty-livered, short-tempered, snappish, snappy, snarly, snitchy, snuffy, sore, sour, spiky, spleenful, spleenish, splenetic, temperamental, terse, uptight, verjuice, vexed, vinegary, viraginous, virago-like, vixenish, waspish, waspy; **moody,** broody, glowering, ill-conditioned, lowering, morose, saturnine, sullen, surly; **irascible,** hasty, prickly, scratchy, testy, tetchy, touchy
irritable *adj* → perceptive
IRRITABLENESS *n* atrabiliousness, bile, biliousness, cantankerousness, captiousness, crabbiness, crankiness, crossness, crotchetiness, crustiness, distemper, edginess, exasperation, fieriness, fractiousness, fretfulness, grouchiness, grumpiness, huffiness, ill humour, ill nature, ill temper, ill-naturedness, ill-temperedness, impatience, irritability, moodiness, moroseness, peevishness, per-

verseness, perversity, pettishness, petulance, prickliness, querulousness, shit on liver, snappishness, sourness, spleen, sulkiness, sullenness, surliness, terseness, vexedness, vinegar, vixenishness, waspishness; **irascibility,** hastiness, irascibleness, pepperiness, testiness, tetchiness, touchiness

IRRITABLE PERSON *n* bat, cow, crabstick, crosspatch, curmudgeon, grouch, iron maiden, scowler, sourpuss, virago, vixen, wasp, xanthippe

IRRITATE *v* aggravate, bug, chafe, chagrin, crap someone off, drive someone up the wall, fret, gall, get on someone's nerves, get on someone's quince, get under someone's skin, get up someone's nose *(Brit.)*, give someone the irrits, give someone the shits, goad, jangle, nark, peeve, pique, provoke, rankle, rasp, rile, roil, tease, vex; **nag,** air-raid, grouch, scold, snap someone's head off

irritate *v* → **1** anger **2** annoy **3** discontent

IRRITATING *adj* aggravating, infuriating, irritative, narky, provoking, vexatious *(Law)*

IRRITATION *n* aggravation, annoyance, chafe, fret, gall *(Archaic)*, provocation, rub, vexation; **fit of pique,** act, blow-up, cob *(N.Z.)*, pet, sulk, tantrum, temper, the hump, tiff

ISLAND *n* atoll, cay, coral island, holm *(Brit.)*, inch *(Scot.)*, isle, islet, key; **archipelago; reef,** barrier reef, bombora, coral reef; **sandbank,** bar, barrier, sandbar, shoal, spit, swash

island *n* → **1** mound *v* **2** separate

isle *n* → island

ism *n* → **1** belief **2** conjecture

isobar *n* → pressure unit

ISOLATE *v* alienate, cold-shoulder, freeze out, give the cold shoulder, ostracise, reject, send to Coventry, shut out, spurn; **banish,** excommunicate, exile, expatriate, send away, send packing, unchurch; **disinherit,** cut off without a penny, cut off without a shilling, foreclose. *See also* EXCLUDE; BOYCOTT

isolate *n* → **1** solitary *v* **2** distil **3** seclude **4** separate

isometric *adj* → **1** athletic **2** equal

isosceles *adj* → equal

issue *n* → **1** departure **2** exit **3** flow **4** important thing **5** magazine **6** offspring **7** profit **8** publicity **9** result **10** sharing out **11** subject matter *v* **12** circulate **13** discharge **14** flow **15** publicise **16** publish **17** share out

isthmus *n* → headland

it *n* → **1** allure **2** sexuality

italic *n* → letter

itch *n* → **1** desire **2** touch

item *n* → **1** account **2** concert **3** news item **4** particulars *v* **5** memorise **6** record *adv* **7** additionally **8** similarly

itemise *v* → **1** list **2** particularise

itinerant *n* → **1** traveller *adj* **2** travelling **3** wandering

itinerary *n* → **1** reference book **2** route *adj* **3** travelling

IT'S TRUE *interj* by jingo, fair dinkum, honestly, my oath, perdie *(Archaic)*, so help me, straight up, struth, too right

ivory *n* → **1** white *adj* **2** white

Jj

jab *n* → **1** insert **2** medication **3** pat

jabber *n* → **1** nonsense **2** speaking *v* **3** speak **4** talk **5** talk nonsense

jack *n* → **1** armour **2** bar **3** beam **4** coinage **5** electric circuit **6** flag **7** lift **8** man **9** mariner **10** policeman **11** venereal disease *v* **12** plan *adj* **13** tired

Jack *n* → bird

jackass *n* → **1** fool **2** plug **3** stupid person

jackeroo *n* → **1** farmhand *v* **2** farm

JACKET *n* banian, bedjacket, blazer, blouse, bumfreezer *(Brit. Colloq.)*, camisole, cassock, coat, doublet, Eton jacket, jerkin, jupon, kirtle *(Archaic)*, loafer *(Brit.)*, monkey-jacket, Norfolk jacket, sack, sack coat, sacque, slop, smoking-jacket, soutane, spencer, sports jacket, tunic, waistcoat, weskit; **heavy jacket,** anorak, battle jacket, donkey jacket *(Brit.)*, duffle coat, lumber-jacket, parka, pea jacket, reefer, tabard; **dress coat,** claw-hammer coat, coat-tails, dinner jacket, hacking jacket, mess jacket, morning coat, swallow-tailed coat, tail coat, tails; **cardigan,** cardie, twin-set; **bodice,** basque, bolero, vest, waistcoat; **straitjacket; life jacket,** Mae West. *See also* OVERCOAT

jacket *n* → **1** animal's coat **2** book part **3** covering **4** skin **5** wrapper *v* **6** cover

jackhammer *n* → **1** club **2** digging implement **3** piercer

jackknife *n* → **1** knife *v* **2** fold **3** jump

jackpot *n* → funds

jade *v* → **1** bore **2** satisfy **3** tire

jaded *adj* → **1** bored **2** composed **3** satisfied **4** tired

jag *n* → **1** binge **2** drinking session **3** extravagance **4** knob *v* **5** cut

jagged *adj* → **1** bent **2** cutting **3** drunk **4** knobby **5** rough

jail *n* → prison

jalopy *n* → car

jam *n* → **1** concert **2** gathering **3** hindrance **4** pressing *v* **5** fill **6** injure **7** obstruct **8** press

jamb *n* → side

jamboree *n* → **1** celebration **2** crowd

jangle *n* → **1** dissonance **2** fight *v* **3** be angry **4** be dissonant **5** contest **6** irritate **7** ring

janitor *n* → protector

jar *n* → **1** alcohol container **2** dissonance **3** fight **4** impact **5** vessel **6** vibration *v* **7** be dissonant **8** displease **9** vibrate

jargon *n* → **1** language **2** nonsense *v* **3** talk nonsense

jaundice *n* → **1** jealousy **2** prejudice *v* **3** yellow

jaunt *n* → **1** journey *v* **2** travel

jaunty *n* → **1** seaman *adj* **2** beautiful **3** fashionable **4** happy

javelin *n* → **1** spear *v* **2** perforate

jaw *n* → **1** face **2** holder **3** reprimand **4** speaking *v* **5** scold **6** speak **7** talk

jay *n* → **1** fool **2** marijuana **3** stupid person

jaywalk *v* → walk

jazz *v* → **1** dance **2** enliven *adj* **3** musical

JEALOUS *adj* covetous, envious, green with envy, green-eyed

jealous *adj* → careful

JEALOUSY *n* covetousness, enviousness, envy, green-eyed monster, grudgingness, heartburn, heartburning, jaundice, jealousness, penis envy *(Psychol.)*, rivalry, sour grapes, yellows *(Obs.)*; **apple of discord,** bone of contention

jeans *n* → trousers

jeep *n* → truck

jeer *n* → **1** machine **2** mockery **3** puller **4** slander *v* **5** mock

jelly *n* → **1** explosive **2** paste **3** rubber

jellyfish *n* → weakling

jemmy *n* → **1** bar **2** machine *v* **3** open

jeopardise *v* → endanger

jeopardy *n* → danger

jerk *n* → **1** bad person **2** fool **3** lifting **4** move **5** pat **6** pull **7** stupid person **8** thrust *v* **9** conserve **10** fluctuate **11** move **12** pull **13** react **14** throw

jersey *n* → jumper

jest *n* → **1** action **2** joke **3** mockery *v* **4** joke **5** mock

jester *n* → humorist

jet *n* → **1** aeroplane **2** black **3** flow **4** stream *v* **5** flow *adj* **6** black

jettison *n* → **1** discard *v* **2** abandon **3** disuse **4** eject

jetty *n* → **1** harbour *adj* **2** black

jew *n* → **1** miser *v* **2** trade

JEWEL *n* bijou, cameo, doublet, gem, gemstone, girandole, precious stone, stone, toadstone; **cut jewel,** baguette, brilliant, briolette, cabochon, chip, rose, star, table, triplet; **diamond,** adamant, brilliant, ice, rough diamond, solitaire, sparkler; **opal,** black opal, cleanskin, colour, fire opal, flash, girasol, harlequin, hydrophane, nobby, solid, streak; **mother-of-opal,** Andamooka matrix, matrix

jewel *n* → **1** good person **2** good thing **3** jewellery

JEWELLERY *n* bijouterie, costume jewellery, paste, tomfoolery; **jewel,** brilliant, gem, pearl, precious stone, rock *(Colloq.)*, scarab, scarabaeus, solitaire, sparkler; **brooch,** anaglyph, breastpin, breastplate *(Judaism)*, cameo, fibula, ouch *(Archaic)*, pin, scatter pin, stickpin *(U.S.)*, tiepin; **bracelet,** anklet, armlet, bangle, wristlet; **ring,** circle, circus *(Obs.)*, engagement ring, eternity ring, nosering; **necklace,** beads, chain, chaplet, choker, collar, collaret, dog-collar, locket, peag, rivière, rope, strand, string, torque, wampum; **bead,** bugle bead, charm, drop, girandole, pear drop, pendant; **earring,** eardrop, labret, sleeper; **crown,** circlet, coronal, coronet, diadem, tiara; **parure,** equipage; **filigree,** engrailment, gadroon; **enamelwork,** champlevé, cloisonné, enamel, enamelling, Fabergé, japan, japanning, lacquer, tole, varnish

b *v* → **1** avoid **2** be unwilling **3** swerve

ffy *n* → moment

g *n* → **1** holder **2** joke *v* **3** be absent **4** dance **5** vibrate

gger *n* → **1** alcohol container **2** pole **3** support **4** tool *v* **5** ruin

ggle *n* → **1** turbulence *v* **2** agitate

llaroo *n* → farmhand

lt *n* → **1** abandoner *v* **2** abandon

ngle *n* → **1** carriage **2** poetry **3** ringing **4** song *v* **5** ring **6** versify

ngoism *n* → **1** intolerance **2** nationalism **3** warmongering

nx *n* → **1** bad thing **2** luck *v* **3** risk

ve *n* → **1** language *v* **2** dance

OB *n* avocation, business, calling, career, craft, follow-the-job occupation, game, gig, grip, lurk, metier, mystery *(Archaic)*, occupation, practice, private practice, profession, pursuit, racket *(Colloq.)*, trade, vocation, walk of life, work; **position,** a sweet cop, appointment, billet, engagement, incumbency, office, place, post, posting, province, rank, role, sinecure, situation, station, vacancy; **field,** area of expertise, bailiwick, beat, department, domain, line of work, orbit, specialty, sphere, sphere of activity; **duty,** care, charge, chore, commission, concern, errand, obligation, responsibility, task; **the press of business,** the demands of one's job

ob *n* → **1** affair **2** difficulty **3** finished product **4** hit **5** obligation **6** robbery **7** undertaking **8** work *v* **9** hit **10** invest **11** swindle **12** work

ob *n* → **1** holy person **2** patient person **3** unfortunate

ockey *n* → **1** rider *v* **2** cheat **3** make do

ockstrap *n* → underwear

ocular *adj* → humorous

ocund *adj* → happy

odhpurs *n* → trousers

oey *n* → **1** animal offspring **2** children **3** kangaroo

og *n* → **1** pat **2** walking *v* **3** advance **4** remind **5** walk

OIN *n* bond, close, connection, coupling, junction, juncture, nexus; **link,** connective, copula, interlink; **confluence,** abutment, concurrence, meeting point; **intersection,** cloverleaf, cusp, spinode; **attachment,** affix, appendage, appendant, appendicle; **chemical bond,** closed chain, conjugated bond, coordinate bond, coordinate covalent bond, covalent bond, dative bond, semipolar bond, triple bond, triplet, valency bond

JOIN *v* catenate, compact, concatenate, conjoin, connect, contact, couple, interconnect, interlink, link, match, mate, partner, unite; **bridge,** span; **bracket,** hyphenate; **interlock,** engage, fit, mesh; **fuse,** ankylose, intercommunicate, knit, marry; **merge,** ally, federalise, incorporate, integrate, lump together, roll into one; **couple,** conjugate *(Obs.)*, copulate, kiss, osculate, pair; **attach,** affix, annex, append, apply, fasten; **tie,** lace, seam, sew, string; **splice,** graft, hook up with, inarch, inosculate; **hinge,** articulate; **joint,** butt, dovetail, fay, mortise, tenon

join *v* → **1** arrive **2** combine **3** contact **4** converge **5** fight **6** join up **7** marry **8** participate

JOINING *n* conjunction, conjuncture *(Obs.)*, joinder; **union,** conjugation, copulation; **linkage,** catenation, concatenation, hyphenation, linkwork; **annexation,** affixture, appendance; **contact,** communication, hookup, intercommunication, interconnection, networking, tie-up; **fusion,** combination, polymerisation; **splicing,** contingence, grafting, inarching, inosculation; **connectedness,** connectivity, inseparability, inseparableness, unitedness

joint *n* → **1** bone **2** break **3** dwelling **4** gun **5** marijuana **6** pub **7** restaurant *v* **8** join **9** separate *adj* **10** combined **11** joined **12** related **13** shared **14** societal

JOIN UP *v* enlist, join, join the colours, take the king's shilling, volunteer

joist *n* → **1** beam **2** shaft

JOKE *n* funny, gag, jape, jest, jocularism, laugh, one-liner, punch line, shaggy dog story, wheeze; **prank,** antic, apery, apple-pie bed, berley, caper, capriccio, hotfoot *(U.S.)*, jig *(Obs.)*, leg-pulling, monkey tricks, monkeyshine *(U.S.)*, play, practical joke, short sheet, sport; **pun,** equivoque, paranomasia, play on words, quibble, word play; **witticism,** bon mot, boutade, crack, epigram, facetiae, in-joke, jeu d'esprit, nifty *(U.S.)*, quip, sally, wisecrack; **malapropism,** blooper, spoonerism; **banter,** badinage, chaff, gibe, josh *(U.S.)*, kid, persiflage, pleasantry, raillery, repartee, riposte; **dirty joke,** blue story, double entendre; **stale joke,** chestnut; **comics,** comic strip, funnies, strip cartoon. *See also* HUMOUR; COMEDY

JOKE *v* farce *(Obs.)*, fun, gag, jape *(Archaic)*, jest, pun, quip, repartee *(Obs.)*, wisecrack; **play the wag,** antic *(Obs.)*, fool, play; **amuse,** make someone laugh, slay; **banter,** chaff, josh *(U.S.)*, kid, pull someone's leg, rag; **satirise,** epigrammatise, lampoon

joke *n* → **1** mockery **2** unimportant thing

joker *n* → **1** bull artist **2** humorist **3** man **4** trickster

jolly *n* → **1** flattery *adj* **2** happy **3** joyful **4** pleasant **5** sociable *adv* **6** very

jolt *n* → **1** move **2** pat **3** period *v* **4** fluctuate
jostle *n* → **1** pat **2** thrust *v* **3** collide **4** thrust
jot *n* → **1** bit **2** small amount *v* **3** memorise
joule *n* → energy
journal *n* → **1** account **2** diary **3** magazine **4** newspaper
journalism *n* → the media
JOURNALIST *n* correspondent, cub reporter, newshawk, newshound, newsman, paparazzo, photojournalist, pressman, reporter, roundsman, special correspondent, stringer, war correspondent; **newsreader,** newscaster; **columnist,** editor, feature writer, gossip columnist, sob-sister; **newsagent,** newsdealer, newsstand, newsvendor; **news desk,** city desk *(Brit.)*, newsroom; **press agent,** flack *(U.S.)*, P.R.O., press officer, press secretary, public relations officer, publicity agent
JOURNEY *n* expedition, odyssey, travels; **trip,** drive, daytrip, excursion, fang, jaunt, joy-ride, junket, outing, round trip, sally, spin; **tour,** grand tour, lecture tour, mystery tour, package tour; **pilgrimage,** hajj *(Islam.)*; **lift,** hitch, pick-up; **patrol,** round; **swim,** bathe, skinny-dip, wade; **ski,** skate
journey *v* → travel
joust *n* → **1** stroke *v* **2** fight
jovial *adj* → happy
jowl *n* → **1** face **2** side
JOY *n* exaltation *(Obs.)*, felicity, festiveness, gaiety, glee, gleefulness, gleesomeness, gratulation *(Archaic)*, joyfulness, joyousness, mirth, paradise, ravishment, rejoicing; **joie de vivre,** charivari, excess of spirits, exuberance; **elation,** elatedness, rapture, rapturousness; **triumph,** exultation, jubilance, jubilation; **revelry,** carousal, good cheer, jollification, merrymaking. *See also* CELEBRATION; FESTIVAL
joy *n* → **1** happiness **2** pleasure *v* **3** please **4** rejoice
JOYFUL *adj* blithe, cock-a-hoop, elate, elated, elevated, enrapt, exuberant, gleeful, gleesome, glowing, happy, high, high as a kite, in raptures, jolly, joyous, mirthful, on top of the world, overjoyed, rapturous, rejoicing
jube *n* → **1** room **2** wall
jubilant *adj* → celebratory
jubilee *n* → **1** anniversary **2** festival **3** forgiving **4** holy day
JUDGE *n* adjudicator, arbiter, awarder, beak, justice, magistrate, referee, sentencer; **judiciary,** bench, court, Full Bench, judicature, syndicate; **wise judge,** a Daniel, a Daniel come to judgment, Solomon; **alcalde,** archon *(Greek Hist.)*, bailie *(Scot.)*, burgomaster, cadi *(Islam)*, chancellor, Chief Justice, circuit judge, coroner, Family Court judge, Federal Court judge, High Court judge, J.P., judge advocate, judge advocate general, Justice of the Peace, master, prefect *(Rom. Cath. Ch.)*, puisne judge, registrar, seneschal *(Archaic)*, squire *(U.S.)*, stipendiary magistrate, Supreme Court judge, syndic. *See also* JURY
judge *n* → **1** adjudicator **2** aesthete **3** assessc **4** ruler **5** specialist *v* **6** assess **7** determin **8** legislate **9** predict
JUDGMENT *n* account, adjudgment, adjud cation, arbitrament, arbitration *(Law)*, cor clusion, condemnation, deliverance, dia nosis, discrimination, reckoning, resolutio umpirage; **ruling,** decision, determinatio doom, mark, order, pronouncement; **verdic** award, class resolution, declaration, decre decretal, finding, non prosequitur, nonsui ratio decidendi, sentence; **justice,** judicatur jurisprudence
judgment *n* → **1** assessment **2** good taste **3** ir debtedness **4** mind **5** obligation **6** predictio **7** punishment
Judgment *n* → fortune-telling
judicial *adj* → **1** assessorial **2** discriminatin **3** lawful
judiciary *n* → **1** judge *adj* **2** assessorial
judicious *adj* → **1** discriminating **2** expedier **3** moderate **4** wise
jug *n* → **1** prison **2** vessel *v* **3** cook **4** impriso **5** insert
juggernaut *n* → **1** destroyer *v* **2** advanc **3** force
juggle *n* → **1** trick *v* **2** fake
juice *n* → **1** alcohol **2** electricity **3** essenc **4** fuel **5** liquid **6** strength *v* **7** extract
juicy *adj* → **1** interesting **2** liquid **3** living **4** ob scene **5** wet
jukebox *n* → sound system
JUMBLE *n* clutter, dog's breakfast, dog's dir ner, hash, huddle, hugger-mugger, litte mess, mix, muddle, muss *(U.S.)*, tumble, up set; **mess-up,** a fine kettle of fish, a prett kettle of fish, balls-up, boggle, cock-up, foul up, frig-up, fuck-up, mix-up; **hotchpotcl** gallimaufry, mishmash; **bustle,** bun rush helter-skelter, hurry-scurry, scramble
jumble *n* → **1** mixture *v* **2** mix **3** muddl **4** tangle **5** untidy
jumbo *n* → **1** aeroplane **2** giant *adj* **3** big
jumbuck *n* → sheep
JUMP *n* bounce, bound, flier, flying jump hop, hop skip and jump, leap, pounce spring, take-off; **caper,** frisk, gambol, prance skip; **buck,** capriole, croupade, curve gambado, tittup; **jumping,** buckjumping hurdling, leapfrogging, leaping, saltation transilience, vaulting; **long jump,** broa jump, Fosbury flop, high jump, hop step an jump, polevault, straddle, triple jump, vaul western roll; **ski-jump,** axel; **volte,** demivol *(Horseriding)*
JUMP *v* bound, galumph, leap, lollop, ram about, start, tumble, vault; **caper,** bol around, bob up and down, cavort, dance exult *(Obs.)*, frisk, gambol, hop, prance, skip **pounce,** spring; **buck,** buckjump, capriole curvet, fence, jackknife, kangaroo, rear tittup; **trampoline,** bounce; **jump over,** clear hurdle, leapfrog, over *(Rare)*, overleap, top vault
jump *n* → **1** advantage **2** fall **3** inflation **4** ir regularity **5** obstacle **6** sexual intercourse

7 ascend **8** attack **9** become greater **10** capture **11** change **12** descend **13** dive **14** escape **15** gamble **16** increase **17** move **18** pain **19** take **20** worry

JUMPER *n* jersey, pullover, skinny rib, skivvy, sloppy joe, sweater, windcheater, windjammer, woolly

jumper *n* → **1** dress **2** sledge **3** thief

jumpy *adj* → **1** excited **2** frightened **3** turbulent **4** worried

junction *n* → **1** contact **2** convergence **3** crossing **4** join **5** mixture **6** road

juncture *n* → **1** important thing **2** join **3** moment

jungle *n* → **1** commotion **2** forest **3** muddle

junior *n* → **1** children **2** inferior **3** innovator **4** lawyer **5** pugilist **6** pupil **7** sportsman *adj* **8** following **9** inferior **10** new **11** youthful

junk *n* → **1** discard **2** drug **3** sailing ship **4** waste *v* **5** refuse

junket *n* → **1** celebration **2** journey **3** meal *v* **4** eat **5** rejoice **6** travel

junkie *n* → drug user

junta *n* → **1** council **2** legislation

jurisdiction *n* → **1** authority **2** domain **3** power

jurisprudence *n* → **1** judgment **2** law

jurist *n* → lawyer

juror *n* → **1** adjudicator **2** jury

JURY *n* grand jury *(U.S.)*, hung jury, inquest, panel, petty jury, quest, tales; **juror,** ambidexter *(Archaic)*, foreman, jurat, juryman, petty juror, talesman. *See also* JUDGE

jury *n* → **1** adjudicator *adj* **2** expedient

just *adj* → **1** correct **2** fair **3** rightful **4** smallest **5** true *adv* **6** in fact **7** negligibly **8** precisely

justice *n* → **1** judge **2** judgment

JUSTIFIABILITY *n* defensibility, defensibleness; **veniality,** excusableness, venialness

JUSTIFIABLE *adj* defensible, pleadable, warrantable; **excusable,** pardonable, venial

JUSTIFICATION *n* allegation *(Law)*, apologia, apology, authority, burden of proof, defence, plea, pleading, reply, self-defence *(Law)*, self-justification, theodicy *(Theol.)*, title, vindication, warrant; **excuse,** alibi *(Colloq.)*, colour *(Law)*, denial, extenuating circumstance, pretext, salvo *(Rare)*, sob-story; **extenuation,** alleviation, cover-up, mitigation, palliation, snow job, whitewashing

JUSTIFY *v* authorise, be a reason for, be an excuse for, explain, give the devil his due, plead ignorance, rationalise, set right, set the score right, vindicate, warrant; **excuse,** acquit, clear, exculpate, exonerate; **extenuate,** gloss over, make allowances, palliate, put a good face on, put in a good word for, speak up for, varnish over, whitewash

justify *v* → **1** acquit **2** forgive **3** print **4** tidy

JUT *v* basset, beetle, exsert, flange, jut out, outcrop, outgrow, point out, poke out, thrust out; **protrude,** pout, project, shoot out; **stand out,** start, stick out, stick up; **protract,** extend; **bunch,** calk, clump, spike. *See also* BULGE

jut *n* → knob

juvenile *n* → **1** actor **2** adolescent **3** animal offspring *adj* **4** youthful

juxtapose *v* → **1** be close **2** contact **3** flank

Kk

kanaka *n* → subject

KANGAROO *n* big red, blue flier, boomer, joey, kanga, old man, roo

kangaroo *n* → **1** gaoler *v* **2** defecate **3** jump **4** repose

kaput *adj* → **1** damaged **2** ruined

kayak *n* → rowing boat

keel *n* → **1** amount **2** red dye **3** sailing ship

keen *n* → **1** cry *v* **2** grieve *adj* **3** desirous **4** enthusiastic **5** good **6** intelligent **7** intense **8** perceptive **9** sharp

keep *n* → **1** charity **2** fortress *v* **3** care for **4** conserve **5** hold **6** imprison **7** obey **8** protect **9** protract **10** store

keeping *n* → **1** care **2** imprisonment **3** restraints

KEEP SECRET *v* black out, classify, hide, hush up, sit on, smother, withhold; **keep a secret**, clam up, hold one's tongue, keep one's mouth shut, keep one's own counsel, let it go no further, not breathe a word; **be secretive**, cabal, collude, hugger-mugger, intrigue, manoeuvre, plot, tick-tack

keg *n* → alcohol container

kennel *n* → **1** animal dwelling **2** cell **3** shelter *v* **4** inhabit **5** shelter

kerb *n* → **1** kerbing *v* **2** limit

KERBING *n* capstone, coaming, coping, kerb, kerbstone; **roadside**, nature strip, shoulder, wayside; **building alignment**, alignment, building line

kernel *n* → **1** centre **2** inside *v* **3** enclose

kero *n* → fuel

kerosene *n* → fuel

ketch *n* → sailing ship

ketchup *n* → beer

key *n* → **1** clarification **2** classification **3** explanation **4** island **5** nail **6** opener **7** reference book **8** restraints **9** roughness **10** solution *v* **11** roughen *adj* **12** fundamental **13** important

khaki *n* → **1** green *adj* **2** brown

kibble *n* → **1** vessel *v* **2** powder *adj* **3** powdered

kibbutz *n* → **1** community **2** farm

KICK *n* balloon, banana kick, boot, crosskick, drop kick, garryowen, hack, header, place kick, punt, rainmaker, scissors kick, spiral punt, spurn *(Obs.)*, stab, stab kick, tap-kick, torp, torpedo punt, up-and-under

KICK *v* crosskick, foot *(Obs.)*, hack, knee, put in the boot, put the boot into someone, spurn *(Obs.)*, toe; **stamp**, stomp

kick *n* → **1** complaint **2** excitement **3** pleasure **4** reaction **5** vitality *v* **6** oppose **7** react **8** refuse

kidnap *v* → **1** capture **2** rob

kidney *n* → **1** character **2** class

KILL *v* account for, bag, be in for the kill, do away with, do for, fordo *(Archaic)*, halal, kill off, make away with, shed blood, slay, smite, spiflicate *(Joc.)*, transport *(Obs.)*, zot; **murder**, assassinate, blow away, bump off, burke, croak, do in, get, knock off, liquidate, remove, rub out, take for a ride, waste *(U.S.)*; **execute**, condemn to death, dispatch, do to death, put to death, sign the death warrant of; **asphyxiate**, axe, bayonet, behead, blow the brains out, bone, brain, burn, choke, club, cut the throat of, dangle, decapitate, decollate, drown, electrocute, garrotte, gibbet, guillotine, hang, harpoon, impale, jugulate, knife, lapidate, lynch, neck, overlie, pick off, pike, pith, point the bone at, poison, poleaxe, pot *(Hunting)*, sabre, scalp, scrag, shoot, shoot down, sing, slaughter, smother, spear, spike, stick, stifle, stiletto, stone, strangle, strangulate, string up, suffocate, supercollate, tomahawk, turn off *(Obs.)*, wring the neck of; **suicide**, blow one's brains out, commit harakiri, do oneself in, fall on one's sword, go off the bars, go off the tub, jump overboard, jump the Gap, kill oneself, o.d., put one's head in the oven, self-immolate, slit one's wrists, take poison; **sacrifice**, immolate; **put down**, destroy, put away, put out of misery, put to sleep. *See also* MASSACRE

kill *n* → **1** victim *v* **2** prohibit

KILLER *n* assassin, assassinator, bravo, butcher, Cain, cutthroat, decapitator, decimator, decollator, depopulator, dispatcher, gangster, gunman, hatchet man, headhunter, hired killer, hit man, hit squad, manslaughterer, manslayer, massacrer, murderer, murderess, poisoner, purger, scalper, slaughterer, slayer, strangler, thug; **executioner**, deathsman *(Archaic)*, firing party, firing squad, garrotter, guillotiner, hangman, headsman; **sacrificer**, immolator; **butcher**, chainman *(N.Z.)*, gun-chain *(N.Z.)*, harpooner, knacker, slaughterman; **toreador**, bullfighter, matador, torero

KILLING *n* blood-letting, bloodshed, the kill; **murder**, assassination, chance-medley *(Law)*, dispatch, first-degree murder, foul play, manslaughter, manslaying, second-degree murder, violent death; **strangulation**, asphyxiation, jugulation, suffocation, thuggee; **homicide**, aborticide, exposure of infants, filicide, foeticide, fratricide, infanticide, matricide, parricide, patricide, regicide, sororicide, tyrannicide, uxoricide; **suicide,** bushido, felo-de-se, harakiri, Russian roulette, self-destruction, self-murder; **sacrifice,** hecatomb, immolation, ritual killing, suttee; **execution,** beheading, capital punishment, crucifixion, decapitation, decollation, electrocution, garrotte, halter, hanging, lapidation, lynching, stoning; **deicide; euthanasia,** mercy killing. *See also* MASSACRE; MEANS OF KILLING; PLACE OF KILLING

KILLING *adj* asphyxiant, deadly, death-dealing, fatal, lethal, manslaying, mortiferous, poisonous, suffocative, toxic; **germicidal,** bactericidal, insecticidal. *See also* MURDEROUS

kiln *n* → 1 heater *v* 2 heat

kilojoule *n* → energy

kilometre *n* → length

kilt *n* → 1 dress *v* 2 fold 3 lift

kilter *n* → condition

kimono *n* → dress

kin *n* → 1 relative *adj* 2 kindred

KIND *adj* considerate, kindly, nice, open-hearted, regardful, solicitous, sweet, sweet-tempered, tactful, tender-hearted, thoughtful, warm-hearted, well-meaning; **benevolent,** beneficent, benignant, big-hearted, gracious, kind-hearted, mild *(Obs.)*, well-disposed, well-wishing; **sympathetic,** caring, consolatory, involved; **gentle,** benign, compassionate, forgiving, humane, lenient, mild, propitious, soft; **amiable,** decent, friendly, genial, good-hearted, grandfatherly, warm; **altruistic,** charitable, Christianly, humanitarian, philanthropic; **overkind,** paternalistic, smothery, well-meaning

kind *n* → 1 class *adj* 2 loving

kindergarten *n* → 1 nursery 2 school

kindle *v* → 1 emotionalise 2 fire 3 illuminate

KINDNESS *n* considerateness, consideration, goodness, kind-heartedness, loving-kindness, niceness, regardfulness, solicitousness, solicitude, sweetness, tender-heartedness, thoughtfulness, warm-heartedness; **goodwill,** benevolence, grace, kindliness; **altruism,** charitableness, generosity, humanitarianism, philanthropy, unselfishness; **friendliness,** amiability, amiableness, geniality, good-heartedness, warmness, warmth; **gentleness,** benignancy, benignity, candour *(Obs.)*, graciosity, graciousness, humaneness, humanity, leniency, mildness, propitiousness, softness; **paternalism,** patronage

KINDRED *adj* kin, near, of kin, once removed, related, twice removed; **consanguine,** adoptive, agnate, agnatic, cognate, collateral, consanguineous, enate, german, half-blooded; **familial,** familiar *(Rare)*, family; **nepotic,** clannish, incestuous; **tribal,** tribalist, tribalistic

kindred *n* → relative

kinetic *adj* → moving

king *n* → 1 aristocrat 2 expert 3 wealthy person *adj* 4 big 5 great

kingdom *n* → 1 class 2 domain 3 nation

kingpin *n* → 1 important thing 2 nail

kink *n* → 1 distortion 2 idea 3 strangeness

KINSHIP *n* agnation, clanship, cognation, consanguinity, filiation, nick *(Horse breeding)*, relation; **familial relationship,** brotherhood, fatherhood, fraternalism, fraternity, maternity, motherhood, parenthood, paternity, sisterhood; **cousinhood,** cosinage *(Law)*, cousinship; **kinship system,** matriarchy, patriarchy; **tribalism,** clannishness, nepotism

kiosk *n* → 1 shop 2 telecommunications

kip *n* → sleep

kipper *v* → 1 conserve 2 cook

kirk *n* → church

kismet *n* → fate

KISS *v* bill, blow a kiss, buss, lip *(Obs.)*, osculate, pash off, peck, smack; **embrace,** bosom, clasp, clip *(Archaic)*, cuddle, enfold, fold in one's arms, hug, lap, nestle, nuzzle, snuggle, squeeze; **caress,** chuck, chuck under the chin, coax *(Obs.)*, dandle, fondle, pat, stroke; **coo,** honey *(U.S. or Archaic)*, murmur sweet nothings; **make love,** bill and coo, bundle, canoodle, neck, pash, pet, smooch, smoodge, spoon

kiss *n* → 1 contact 2 endearments 3 friendship *v* 4 contact 5 join

kit *n* → 1 basket 2 case 3 equipment *v* 4 equip 5 prepare

KITCHEN *n* bakehouse, bakery, butlery, caboose *(Naut.)*, cook-shop *(N.Z.)*, cookhouse, cuisine, dairy, gallery, galley, grill, grillroom, kitchenette, scullery, servery; **dining room,** breakfast room, cenacle, dinette, frater, hall, morning room; **dining hall,** bar, butlery, cocktail bar, cocktail lounge, dive, grillroom, lounge, mess, public bar, refectory, saloon bar, soup kitchen, swill, tearoom, wardroom

kite *n* → 1 aircraft 2 crook 3 extortionist 4 newspaper 5 the intangible *v* 6 move

kitsch *n* → 1 vulgarism *adj* 2 vulgar

kitten *n* → 1 animal offspring 2 cat 3 woman *v* 4 give birth

kitty *n* → 1 animal offspring 2 charity 3 funds

klaxon *n* → 1 siren 2 warning

kleptomania *n* → robbery

knack *n* → 1 competence 2 expedient

knacker *n* → killer

knapsack *n* → bag

knave *n* → 1 butler 2 crook

knead *v* → 1 press 2 pulp 3 touch

knee *n* → 1 leg *v* 2 kick 3 repose

kneecap *n* → 1 armour 2 leg

kneel *v* → 1 pay homage 2 repose 3 worship

knell *n* → 1 funeral rites 2 ringing *v* 3 publicise 4 ring

knickerbockers *n* → trousers

knick-knack *n* → 1 trinket 2 unimportant thing

KNIFE *n* breadknife, carver, carving knife, case-knife, clicking knife, drawknife, drawshave, French knife, hunting knife, paperknife, pigsticker, sheath-knife, shiv *(Brit.)*, steel; **dagger,** kris, kukri, poniard, skean; **clasp-knife,** dover, flick-knife, jack-knife, penknife, pocket-knife, switchblade; **heavy knife,** cradle, cradle-scythe, froe, machete, panga, pruning hook, pruning knife, scythe, sickle, swingle; **scalpel,** bistoury, lance, lancet; **razor,** cutthroat, safety razor, shaver; **blade,** edge, edge tool, knife edge, runner, slice bar, tool

knife *n* → **1** sword *v* **2** cut **3** kill

knight *n* → fighter

knit *n* → **1** textiles *v* **2** fold **3** join **4** sew

KNOB *n* bunch, head, knobble, knop, nub, nubbin, nubble, pinhead, prominence, stub, umbo; **burl,** bump, burr, emergence, gallnut, gnarl, knot, knur, node, nodule, nut-gall, trabecula, whelp; **process,** ala, apophysis, berry, bosset, calcar, calk, caruncle, condyle, cornu, coronoid process, hyperostosis, nose, osteophyte, wing; **jut,** cog, dent, dentation, denticle, denticulation, fang, finger, flange, joggle, languet, pallet, ratchet, serration, serrulation, tappet, tongue, tooth; **projection,** gargoyle, jag, limb, lip, peak, point, snag, spade, spout, thorn, toe; **saddle bow,** horn, pommel, pummel. *See also* BULGE

knob *n* → **1** groin **2** mound

KNOBBY *adj* bony, bossy, burled, condylar, condyloid, gangliate, gangliated, ganglionic, gnarled, jointed, knobbed, knobbly, knurled, knurly, moniliform, nodal, nodose, nodular, nodulous, nubbly, osteophytic, ridged, torose, umbonate, umbonic, warty; **cusped,** bicorn, bicuspid, calcariferous, corniculate, cornuted, cuspidal, cuspidate, tricorn, tricuspid; **goosepimply,** goosy; **bumpy,** hummocky, lumpy, pebbly, snaggy; **jagged,** dentate, denticulate, dentirostral, jaggy, peaked, pointed, saw-toothed, serrated, toothed; **clumpy,** clumpish, lobate, lobular, multilobular, stubbed, stubby, tussocky. *See also* PROTUBERANT; SWOLLEN

knock *n* → **1** boom **2** hit **3** impact **4** mockery *v* **5** collide **6** disapprove of **7** hit

knockout *n* → **1** beautiful person **2** good thing **3** hit **4** winner *adj* **5** anaesthetic **6** competitive **7** exclusive

knock out *v* → **1** anaesthetise **2** bowl over

knoll *n* → **1** mound *v* **2** publicise **3** ring

knot *n* → **1** accumulation **2** bulge **3** difficulty **4** knob **5** tangle **6** velocity *v* **7** bulge **8** fasten **9** tangle

KNOW *v* can *(Obs.)*, cognise, intuit, ken *(Archaic)*, remember, savvy, wis *(Archaic)*, wit *(Archaic)*; **be familiar with,** have at one's finger tips; **grasp,** accept, apperceive, appreciate, apprehend, comprehend, digest, know by sight, perceive, read, recognise, see, sense, take; **know the score,** awake, be in the picture, have an ear to the ground, know how many beans make five, know the ropes not have come down in the last shower; **be informed,** get wind of, get word of, hear of. *See also* UNDERSTAND

know *v* → discriminate

KNOWING *adj* apperceptive, cognitive, enlightened, insightful, perceptive, percipient switched-on, understanding; **in the know,** au courant, cluey, hep, hip, not born yesterday on the ball, on the beam, up on, with-it **aware,** apprised, cognisant, informed, intelligent *(Rare)*, sensible, witting *(Archaic)*; **self-aware,** self-conscious

KNOWLEDGE *n* cognition *(Obs.)*, enlightenment, illumination, information, ken knowingness, light, science, technology, wisdom; **omniscience,** encyclopaedism, pansophy; **mastery,** apprehension, comprehension, experience, expertise, expertness grasp, mastership, realisation, uptake; **rudimentary knowledge,** equipment, grounding propaedeutics, rudiments; **smattering,** sciolism, smatter; **esotery,** privity, specialty, technicality; **common knowledge,** a household word, ancient history, open secret; **folklore** folk memory, lore; **sophistication,** savoir-faire, savoir-vivre, urbaneness, urbanity worldliness; **familiarity,** acquaintance, conversance, conversancy, intimateness; **study of knowledge,** architectonics, epistemology exact science, pantology, science. *See also* UNDERSTANDING

knowledge *n* → **1** competence **2** sexual intercourse

KNOWLEDGEABLE *adj* Alexandrian *(Class Antiq.)*, cultivated, educated, enlightened highbrow, illuminate *(Obs.)*, informed learned, lettered, read, skilled, versed, well-informed, well-read; **erudite,** classical clerkly *(Archaic)*, humanistic, virtuoso, wise **omniscient,** all-knowing, pansophic; **experienced,** able, expert, knowing, proficient salted, savvy, sciential, versed in; **worldly-wise,** not born yesterday, sophisticated, urbane; **awake up to,** on to, privy to; **familiar** acquainted, at home, au fait, big on, conversant, intimate with, no stranger to

KNOWN *adj* given *(Maths)*, unspoken; **well-known,** familiar, famous, noted, notorious old, proverbial; **perceptual,** identifiable, objective, perceptional, supraliminal; **esoteric** gnostic

known *adj* → revealed

knuckle *v* → attack

kosher *n* → food

kowtow *n* → **1** obsequiousness **2** pose **3** tribute *v* **4** pay homage **5** repose **6** worship

kow-tow *n* → **1** courtesy *v* **2** bow

kudos *n* → reputation

Ll

LABEL *n* car sticker, sticker, tab, tag; **hallmark,** countermark, frank, impress, imprint *(Bibliog.),* plate-mark, postmark, remarque *(Engraving),* seal, stamp, surcharge *(Philately),* touch *(Metall.),* touchmark, watermark; **brand,** blaze, chop *(India),* crop, earmark, fryingpan brand, logo, logotype, moko *(N.Z.),* raddle, rubber stamp, tattoo, trademark; **inscription,** legend, rubric; **identification,** badge, calling card, credentials, dead meat ticket, dog tag, ID, ID card, identity disc *(Mil.),* marking tape, meat tag, meat (ticket), name tag, OK card, papers, placecard, ration-card, register *(Comm.),* union card, visiting card; **nameplate,** bookplate, doorplate, escutcheon *(Naut.),* numberplate, shingle; **serial number,** call number, Dewey number, flight number *(Aeron.),* IBN, postcode, pressmark *(Bibliog.),* shelf mark; **station identification,** call sign *(Naut.),* signature tune; **ticket,** check *(U.S.),* docket *(U.S.),* excursion ticket, firemark, jetton *(Brit.),* meal ticket, platform ticket, price-tag, season ticket, transfer, transfer-ticket, voucher; **stamp,** health stamp *(N.Z.),* postage stamp, precancel, provisional; **notice,** clapperboard, clappers *(Films),* facia, noticeboard, signboard; **tombstone,** headstone

LABEL *v* identify, mark, personalise, tab, tag, ticket; **brand,** blaze, designate, earmark, fingerprint, notch, raddle, sear, stigmatise, tattoo; **stamp,** frank, hallmark, impress, imprint, postmark, print, roulette, rubricate, seal, surcharge *(Philately),* watermark; **sign,** autograph, consign *(Obs.),* initial, put one's mark on, re-sign, signature; **countersign,** countermark, ratify, undersign, underwrite

label *n* → **1** addition **2** name *v* **3** class

laboratory *n* → **1** tester **2** workplace

laborious *adj* → **1** difficult **2** effortful

labour *n* → **1** birth **2** effort **3** trade unionist **4** work **5** workers *v* **6** emphasise **7** farm **8** give birth **9** make an effort **10** roll **11** work

laboured *adj* → **1** affected **2** careful **3** effortful

LABOURER *n* blue-collar worker, bohunk *(U.S.),* coolie, day labourer, fellah, hand, hunky *(U.S.),* manual labourer, offsider, unskilled worker; **handyman,** blue-tongue, bogtrotter, factotum, fix-it man, jack-of-all-trades, odd-job man, rouseabout; **artisan,** artificer, artist *(Obs.),* craftsman, fabricant, master-craftsman; **fettler,** hairy-legs, jobber, permanent-way man, platelayer, sleeper cutter, snake-charmer, trackman *(U.S.),* trackwalker *(U.S.),* woollynose; **wharfie,** disso, dock labourer, docker, longshoreman *(U.S.),* lumper, seagull *(N.Z.),* stevedore, waterside worker, wharf labourer; **housekeeper,** hausfrau, home-maker, housemaid, housewife; **plumber,** blackjack merchant, drainer, turd strangler. *See also* WORKER

labyrinth *n* → **1** disorder **2** muddle **3** tangle

LACE *n* Alençon lace, binche lace, bobbin lace, bobbinet, brussels lace, cascade, Chantilly, cluny lace, drawn-thread work, duchesse lace, filet lace, gauze, guipure, lacework, macramé, Mechlin lace, mesh, needlepoint lace, net, orris, pillow lace, point, reseau, tatting, tiffany, torchon lace, valenciennes; **embossment,** enlacement, moiré, morrie; **trimmings,** appliqué, bias binding, elastic, flouncing, goffer, lastings, piping, rickrack, ruche, ruching, ruffle, soutache, stripe, tape, tinsel *(Obs.)*

lace *n* → **1** a drink **2** belt **3** string **4** trimming *v* **5** beat **6** brew **7** cord **8** fasten **9** join

lacerate *v* → **1** cut **2** pain *adj* **3** cutting

lack *n* → **1** absence **2** deficiency **3** insufficiency *v* **4** fall short

lackadaisical *adj* → **1** apathetic **2** composed

LACK COURAGE *v* be unable to say boo to a goose; **chicken out,** dingo, funk, go to water, have cold feet, pike out, show the white feather, skulk; **quail,** boggle, cower, flinch, shrink, waver

lackey *n* → **1** butler **2** crawler **3** incompetent **4** obeyer **5** servant **6** subject *v* **7** work

LACK OF CLARITY *n* abstruseness, ambiguity, ambiguousness, deepness, double meaning, reconditeness; **mysteriousness,** anagrammatism, elusiveness, inscrutability, vagueness; **incomprehensibility,** impalpability, impenetrability, impenetrableness, incomprehensibleness, inexplicability, inexplicableness, unaccountability, unaccountableness, unfathomableness, unintelligibility, unintelligibleness; **obscurity,** encryption, obscureness, opacity; **insolubility,** indecipherability, insolubleness, insolvability; **illegibility,** crabbedness, illegibleness, unreadability, unreadableness

LACK OF SAVOUR *n* unpalatability, unpalatableness, unsavouriness; **nastiness,** noisomeness, offensiveness, rankness, unwholesomeness; **rancidity,** brackishness, gaminess, tinniness; **pig-swill,** guk, gunk, pig-tucker *(N.Z.),* slops; **bread and water,** prison fare, stodge

laconic *adj* → **1** concise **2** reticent

lacquer *n* → **1** jewellery **2** paint *v* **3** coat

lactate *v* → excrete

lad *n* → **1** adolescent **2** man **3** promiscuous person
ladder *n* → **1** classification **2** means of escape **3** stairs
lady *n* → **1** aesthete **2** courteous person **3** Ms **4** owner **5** ruler **6** spouse **7** woman *adj* **8** courteous **9** female
Lady *n* → aristocrat
lady-in-waiting *n* → **1** aristocrat **2** servant
lag *n* → **1** criminal **2** imprisonment **3** interval **4** period **5** prisoner **6** slowness *v* **7** go slowly **8** imprison **9** lay charges **10** punish **11** wane
lager *n* → beer
laggard *n* → **1** slowcoach *adj* **2** slow
lagoon *n* → lake
LAIC *adj* churchmanly, impropriate, laical, lay, secular, temporal, tertiary
lair *n* → **1** affected person **2** animal dwelling **3** man **4** vulgarian *v* **5** rest
laissez faire *n* → **1** inaction **2** liberalism
laissez-faire *adj* → liberated
laity *n* → religious follower
LAKE *n* inland sea, lagoon, landlocked water, loch *(Scot.)*, lough, mere, overflow lake; **salt lake,** broad *(Brit.)*, drowned valley, playa, shott; **basin,** anabranch, confluence, conflux; **dam,** arched dam, gravity dam, lock, milldam, reservoir, sluice, tank, turkey's-nest tank; **billabong,** backwater, bayou *(U.S.)*, lunette, plunge *(U.S.)*; **waterhole,** bogeyhole, bogie, wallow, watering hole; **pool,** dike *(Brit.)*, linn *(Scot.)*, millpond, oxbow, pond, tarn, tidal pool; **swimming pool,** baths, pool; **fish pond,** fish ladder; **puddle,** plash, sump; **standing water,** dead water, mickery country, stagnant water, still water
lake *n* → dye
lama *n* → **1** monastic **2** ruler
lamb *n* → **1** animal offspring **2** artless person **3** innocent *v* **4** give birth **5** swindle
LAME *adj* hipshot; **arthritic,** gouty, rheumatic, rheumatoid, stiff; **paralysed,** paraplegic, quadriplegic; **dislocated,** out of joint
lame *v* → **1** hinder **2** injure *adj* **3** injured
lament *n* → **1** grieving **2** poetry **3** song *v* **4** grieve
laminate *v* → **1** separate *adj* **2** layered
lamp *n* → **1** lighting **2** moon *v* **3** look
lampoon *n* → **1** comedy **2** mockery *v* **3** joke **4** mock
lance *n* → **1** knife **2** piercer **3** soldier **4** spear *v* **5** cut
LAND *n* earth, real estate, terra, terra firma; **continent,** country, landmass, main, mainland; **terrain,** country; **ground,** floor *(Colloq.)*; **inland,** heartland, hinterland, interior, midland; **lithosphere,** asthenosphere, barysphere, centrosphere, crust, sial; **delta,** bird's-foot delta, fan delta; **flood plain,** doab, holm *(Brit.)*, warpland; **lowland,** innings, polder. *See also* SOIL
LAND *adj* earthy, geophilous, telluric, terraqueous, terrene, terrestrial; **ground,** ashore, shore, surface; **continental,** inland, landlocked; **coastal,** littoral, longshore, onshore, seaside; **insular,** archipelagic; **peninsular,** isthmian; **riverside,** deltaic, riparian, riverine
land *n* → **1** nation **2** real estate **3** region **4** wealth *v* **5** arrive **6** descend **7** dismount **8** fish **9** gain **10** transport
landing *n* → **1** arrival **2** descent **3** floor **4** flying **5** getting
landlady *n* → **1** lender **2** owner
landlocked *adj* → **1** enclosed **2** land
landlord *n* → **1** aristocrat **2** lender **3** owner
landlubber *n* → novice
landmark *n* → **1** indicator **2** signpost
landscape *n* → **1** painting **2** view
LANDSLIDE *n* ash fall, ash flow, avalanche, cave-in, earthflow, landslip, mudslide, rockfall, slide, snowslip, soil creep, subsidence; **sinkage,** settlement, settling
landslide *n* → success
lane *n* → **1** channel **2** path **3** road **4** route
LANGUAGE *n* acrolect, basilect, code, competence, creole, dialect, idiolect, idiom, langue, lect, lingua franca, matrilect, mother tongue, parlance, parole, patois, performance, pidgin, regional dialect, register, social dialect, sociolect, speech, speech variety, tongue; **standard English,** formal English, good English, good grammar, literary language, prestige dialect, prestige form, the King's English, the Queen's English; **jargon,** argot, baby talk, back slang, cant, colloquialism, expletive, flash *(Obs.)*, hobson-jobson, informal language, jive, lingo, patter, rhyming slang, slang, swear word, taboo term, vernacular, vulgar; **gobbledegook,** cablese, commercialese, euphuism, jabberwocky, journalese, legalese, officialese, technical language, telegraphese, trade name; **terminology,** nomenclature, technology, trade description; **code,** clear, cypher, microdot, scrambled message; **language family,** family, group of languages, stock, subfamily; **language type,** agglutinating language, analytic language, artificial language, interlanguage, isolating language, metalanguage, object language, protolanguage, synthetic language, target language, tone language, universal language
language *n* → **1** animal call **2** speaking **3** swearing **4** vocabulary **5** writing
languid *adj* → **1** apathetic **2** inactive **3** slow **4** weak
languish *n* → **1** bad mood **2** weakness *v* **3** be inactive **4** be tired **5** be unhappy **6** desire **7** weaken
lank *adj* → **1** long **2** thin
lanolin *n* → fat
lantern *n* → **1** lighting **2** room
lap *n* → **1** circle **2** fold **3** hollow **4** leg **5** length **6** quiet sound **7** smoother *v* **8** absorb **9** care for **10** flank **11** flow **12** fold **13** kiss **14** overtake
lapel *n* → **1** addition **2** fold **3** neckwear
lapidary *n* → **1** craftsman **2** reference book *adj* **3** written
lapse *n* → **1** descent **2** error **3** evildoing **4** failure **5** neglectfulness **6** stoppage *v* **7** be

immoral **8** be neglected **9** descend **10** err **11** fail **12** fall into disuse **13** misbehave

larceny *n* → robbery

lard *n* → **1** fat *v* **2** cook **3** oil

larder *n* → cupboard

large *adj* → **1** big **2** generous **3** great **4** windy *adv* **5** windward

largess *n* → **1** generosity **2** gift

lark *n* → amusement

larrikin *n* → **1** adolescent **2** mischief-maker

larva *n* → **1** animal offspring **2** insect

larynx *n* → neck

lascivious *adj* → **1** obscene **2** voluptuous

laser *adj* → audio

lash *n* → **1** club **2** cord **3** eye **4** fight **5** hit **6** sexual intercourse *v* **7** cudgel **8** fasten **9** hurry **10** scold **11** slander

lass *n* → **1** adolescent **2** lover **3** woman

lassitude *n* → **1** tiredness **2** weakness

lasso *n* → **1** cord *v* **2** cord

last *n* → **1** finish **2** model *v* **3** be **4** be adequate **5** continue **6** eternalise *adj* **7** final **8** inferior **9** late **10** remnant *adv* **11** finally **12** late

latch *n* → bolt

LATE *adj* belated, latish, serotine *(Rare)*; **dilatory,** backward, behindhand, slow, tardif, tardy; **overdue,** belated, in retard *(Obs.)*; **last-minute,** eleventh-hour; **last,** latest, lattermost; **later,** latter, Upper *(Geol.)*

LATE *adv* belatedly, tardily; **latterly; last**

late *adj* → **1** dead **2** past **3** untimely *adv* **4** in the past

lately *adv* → in the past

LATENESS *n* backwardness, belatedness, tardiness; **last minute,** eleventh hour; **delay,** demurrage, detainment, hold-up, procrastination, retard, retardation, tarriance *(Archaic)*, wait

latent *adj* → **1** allusive **2** invisible

lateral *n* → **1** passageway *adj* **2** side

lath *n* → **1** coating **2** shaft **3** stand **4** thinness

lathe *n* → cutter

lather *n* → **1** bodily discharge **2** bubbling **3** builder *v* **4** beat **5** bubble **6** coat **7** excrete

latitude *n* → **1** astronomic point **2** length **3** liberty **4** thickness **5** tolerance

latrine *n* → toilet

latter *adj* → **1** final **2** following **3** late **4** two

lattice *n* → building

laud *n* → **1** applause *v* **2** approve

LAUGH *v* chortle, chuckle, guffaw, haw-haw; **giggle,** laugh in one's sleeve, laugh up one's sleeve, snicker, snigger, teehee, titter; **shriek,** cackle, hoot, roar, scream, shout, snort; **fall about,** break up, cachinnate, convulse, kill oneself, laugh fit to kill, laugh like a drain, laugh one's socks off, piss oneself, split one's sides; **smile,** grin

laugh *n* → **1** joke **2** mirth *v* **3** be pleased **4** call (of animals) **5** insult

laughable *adj* → humorous

LAUGHINGLY *adv* merrily, mirthfully; **banteringly,** playfully, sportfully; **jocularly,** facetiously, jestingly, jocosely, jokingly, pleasantly

launch *n* → **1** watercraft *v* **2** initiate **3** move **4** offer **5** throw **6** thrust **7** undertake

launder *n* → **1** bath *v* **2** change **3** clean

laundry *n* → **1** bath **2** room

lavatory *n* → **1** basin **2** bath **3** room **4** toilet

lavender *n* → **1** purple *adj* **2** purple

lavish *v* → **1** be generous *adj* **2** abundant **3** extravagant **4** generous

LAW *n* Aboriginal law, case law, civil law, commercial law, common law, consumer protection, criminal law, crown law, equity, family law, international law, Islamic law, law merchant, law of nations, law of the jungle, legislation, lex, maritime law, martial law, military law, natural law, organic law, penal code, Roman law, statute law, sumptuary law, unwritten law; **code,** canon, capitularies *(Frankish)*, Code Napoléon, corpus juris, Decalogue, judicature system, pandect, Ten Commandments, the Digest; **act,** act of Parliament, assize *(Archaic)*, bill, by-law, caption, charter, consolidation, dead letter, decree, edict, enactment, ex post facto law, measure, ordinance, ordonnance, private act, private bill, private member's bill, public bill, regulation, rescript, rider *(Parl. Proc.)*, standing order, statute, statutory instrument, ways and means *(Govt)*; **amendment,** novel *(Civil Law)*; **precedent,** authority, nice point, precept, ruling; **jurisprudence,** codification, jurimetrics, medical jurisprudence, nomography, nomology, rule of law

law *n* → **1** antecedence **2** authority **3** command **4** legal profession **5** litigation **6** rule

LAWFUL *adj* according to the law, allowable, authorised, chartered, constitutional, legal, legit, legitimate, licit, permitted, statutory, unalienable, valid, very *(Archaic)*; **paralegal,** quasi-judicial; **judicial,** forensic, jural, juridical, juristic, justiciary; **jurisprudential,** jurisprudent, nomographic, nomographical, nomological

lawsuit *n* → litigation

LAWYER *n* articled clerk, jurisconsult, jurisprudent, jurist, legal adviser, legal eagle, legist, limb of the law, nomographer, nomologist, proctor *(Archaic)*, procurator, publicist, trial lawyer; **crooked lawyer,** ambidexter *(Archaic)*, pettifogger, shyster; **barrister,** advocate *(Scot. Law)*, barrister-at-law, bencher *(Brit.)*, counsel, counsellor *(U.S.)*, junior, K.C., King's Counsel, leader, mouthpiece, pleader, Q.C., Queen's Counsel, senior, silk, utter barrister; **prosecutor,** crown prosecutor, district attorney *(U.S.)*, fiscal, police prosecutor, public prosecutor; **solicitor,** attorney *(U.S.)*, attorney at law *(U.S.)*, chamber magistrate, clerk of the peace, commissioner for oaths, conveyancer, duty solicitor, notary, notary public, scrivener *(Archaic)*, shopfront lawyer; **attorney-general,** prothonotary, solicitor-general. *See also* LEGAL PROFESSION

lawyer *n* → ecclesiastic

lax *adj* → **1** lenient **2** neglectful **3** soft

lay *n* → **1** poetry **2** sex object **3** share **4** song *v* **5** direct **6** gamble **7** have sex **8** impute **9** level **10** lower **11** moderate **12** place **13** position **14** reproduce **15** smooth *adj* **16** laic

lay-by *n* → **1** buying **2** debt *v* **3** buy

LAY CHARGES *v* appeal *(Obs.)*, arraign, article, attaint *(Archaic)*, book, bring to book, carpet, charge, do for, hang something on, have up, impeach, implead, impute, incriminate, inculpate, indict, lag, lay a complaint, place on the mat, precondemn, prefer charges, press charges, swear out, throw the book at; **countercharge,** recriminate. *See also* ACCUSE

LAYER *n* flake, folium, interleaf, lamina, slice, thickness, tier; **band,** course, cross reef, flookan, flucan, frieze, friezing, line, lode, panel, reef, rib, schlieren, seam, stage, streak, string, string-course; **stratum,** bar, bone bed, cap rock, colluvium, counter, disconformity, floor, hardpan, horizon, killas, lamella, lithosphere, litter, mantle, mantle rock, pan, roadbed, sial, sill, sima, subsoil, substrate, substratum, superstratum, unconformity, underlay, varve, watertable; **strata,** coal measures, cross-course, measures, series

layer *v* → reproduce

LAYERED *adj* cross-bedded, laminated, multilaminate, stratiform, tegular, three-ply; **split-level,** decked, double-deck, double-decker, storeyed; **stratal,** crustal, crusty, desmoid, substrative, superincumbent, superjacent, supernatant; **laminate,** clinker, flaggy, laminose; **striped,** sliced, vittate; **filmy,** membranous

layette *n* → **1** outfit **2** supplies

layman *n* → religious follower

layout *n* → **1** diagram **2** order

lay out *v* → **1** bowl over **2** bury **3** display **4** line **5** pay **6** plan **7** tidy

laze *n* → **1** period of inaction *v* **2** idle

lazy *adj* → **1** idle **2** purposeless **3** slow

leach *v* → liquefy

leaden *adj* → **1** boring **2** dull **3** grey **4** heavy **5** metallic **6** slow **7** unhappy

LEADER *n* captain, cheerleader *(U.S.)*, driver, guide, helmsman, pilot, standard-bearer, trailblazer, wheelman; **mastermind,** brains, éminence grise, father, power behind the throne, wheeler-dealer; **leading light,** cock, prime mover, protagonist, ringleader, ruling spirit, top dog; **chairperson,** chair, chairman, chairwoman, master of ceremonies, moderator, prolocutor, symposiarch, toastmaster, toastmistress, whip; **principal,** chancellor, dean, headmaster, headmistress, provost, rector, rectorate, regent, scholarch, vice-chancellor, warden; **orchestra leader,** bandmaster, concertmaster, conductor, coryphaeus, first violin, kapellmeister; **pioneer,** pathfinder, scout; **bellwether,** Judas goat, Judas sheep; **scout leader,** akela, brown owl, group leader, guider, scouter, scoutmaster, tawny owl, troop leader. *See also* MANAGER

leader *n* → **1** antecedent **2** conductor **3** forerunner **4** lawyer **5** news item **6** ruler **7** steerer

leaf *n* → **1** book part **2** coating

leaflet *n* → public notice

league *n* → **1** alliance **2** class **3** contract **4** length **5** society *v* **6** associate **7** promise *adj* **8** societal **9** sports

leak *n* → **1** exit **2** opening **3** revelation **4** urination *v* **5** discharge **6** open up **7** urinate

lean *n* → **1** point of view **2** slope *v* **3** slope *adj* **4** insufficient **5** thin

leap *n* → **1** dancing **2** jump *v* **3** jump **4** speed

LEARN *v* absorb, audit, compass, digest, experience, get down pat, get the hang of, get the knack of, imbibe, infix, ingest, know by heart, learn by rote, learn the ropes, master, memorise, pick up, take in; **get wise,** cut one's eyeteeth, cut one's teeth, get one's feet wet, live and learn, pick someone's brains, serve one's apprenticeship. *See also* STUDY

learn *v* → **1** excel **2** memorise

learned *adj* → **1** educated **2** intellectual **3** knowledgeable

LEARNER *n* greenhorn, improver, kid, novice, probationer, raw recruit, rookie, tenderfoot, tyro; **beginner,** abecedarian, abecedary, cadet, fresher, freshette, freshman, underclassman *(U.S.)*; **trainee,** apprentice, articled clerk, prentice *(Archaic)*; **neophyte,** catechumen, disciple, follower, proselyte; **catechist,** chela *(India)*, ritualist, scholastic, seminarian, seminarist, theolog *(Colloq.)*. *See also* PUPIL

LEARNING *n* book-learning, bookishness, culture, erudition, latent learning *(Psychol.)*, lore, scholarship, studiousness; **comprehension,** absorption, assimilation, digestion, infixion, ingestion, insight, mastery, taking-in, understanding; **study,** boning up, brainwork, conning, cram, grind, homework, lucubration, memorisation, overstudy, prep, preparation, swotting, training. *See also* LESSON; COURSE

lease *n* → **1** loan *v* **2** borrow

leash *n* → **1** cord **2** three *v* **3** fasten

least *n* → **1** inferiority **2** small amount *adj* **3** inferior **4** smallest

leather *n* → **1** hide *v* **2** cudgel *adj* **3** skin

leave *n* → **1** absence **2** farewell **3** holiday **4** liberty **5** permission *v* **6** avoid **7** depart **8** give **9** resign

leaven *v* → change

lecher *n* → **1** promiscuous person **2** sexual partner **3** voluptuary

lectern *n* → church

lecture *n* → **1** harangue **2** lesson **3** oration **4** reprimand **5** warning *v* **6** scold **7** speak well **8** teach

ledge *n* → **1** edge **2** mineral **3** rock outcrop

ledger *n* → **1** account **2** grave **3** list

lee *n* → **1** remnant **2** side

leech *n* → **1** extortionist **2** extractor **3** healer **4** insect

leer *n* → **1** insult **2** look *v* **3** insult

EFT *n* left wing, verso; **left-hander,** cackyhander, left-footer, leftie, mollydooker, southpaw; **port,** larboard *(Naut. Obs.)*, nearside, on *(Cricket)*, on side, prompt-side *(Theat.)*; **rule of the road**

EFT *adj* left-hand, left-wing, leftward, sinister, sinistral, sinistrous; **left-handed,** cack-handed, cacky-handed, southpaw; **port,** larboard *(Naut. Obs.)*, near, nearside, nigh *(Archaic)*, on *(Cricket)*, onside

EFT *adv* aport, leftward, leftwards, on the left, sinisterwise, sinistrally

eft *n* → **1** hit *adj* **2** remnant

eftist *n* → political ideologist

EG *n* calf, crus, gam, lap, pins, props, shank, shin, stumps, thigh; **knee,** genu, kneecap, kneepan, marrowbones, pan, patella; **foot,** ankle, dogs *(Colloq.)*, footsy, heel, hoof, instep, mundowie, pettitoes, podium, sole, tarsus; **toe,** big toe, hallux, little toe, minimus, pinkie, tootsy

egacy *n* → **1** getting **2** gift **3** property **4** result

egal *adj* → lawful

EGALISE *v* authorise, decriminalise, enact, legitimate, legitimatise, legitimise, ordain, validate; **formulate,** codify

egate *n* → **1** ambassador **2** messenger **3** religious dignitary **4** ruler

egatee *n* → gainer

egation *n* → agency

egend *n* → **1** clarification **2** commentary **3** label **4** story

egible *adj* → **1** clear **2** readable

egion *n* → **1** armed forces **2** many *adj* **3** many

EGISLATE *v* administer, govern, hold office, hold power, judge *(Jewish Hist.)*

egislate *v* → command

EGISLATION *n* government, law-making, lawgiving, policy *(Rare)*, polity; **administration,** bureaucracy, civil service, commissariat, officialism, public service, quango, semi-government authority, statutory authority; **regime,** ancien régime, Canberra, junta, kiap *(Papua New Guinea)*, Kremlin, ministry, politburo, Quirinal, raj, regimen, the government, White House, Whitehall

egislation *n* → law

EGISLATIVE *adj* cabinet, comitial, congressional, curial, law-making, legislatorial, parliamentary, Quirinal; **unicameral,** bicameral; **governmental,** county, federal, municipal, state; **bureaucratic,** administrative

EGISLATIVE BODY *n* assembly, congress, cowards' castle, legislature, moot *(Old Eng. Law)*, parliament, soviet, talking shop *(Colloq.)*; **administrative committee,** agora *(Greek Hist.)*, board, caucus, comitia *(Roman Hist.)*, commission, conclave, convocation, curia *(Roman Hist.)*, duma *(Russian Hist.)*, executive, executive council, meeting, presidium *(Russia)*, senate, standing committee, subcommittee, synod; **municipal council,** borough council *(U.K.)*, corporation *(U.K.)*, county council, local authority, local government, municipality, shire, shire council, town council; **place of assembly,** chamber, house, parliament house

legislature *n* → legislative body

legitimate *n* → **1** prisoner *v* **2** legalise **3** permit *adj* **4** fair **5** lawful **6** logical **7** true

legume *n* → plant

leisure *n* → rest

leisurely *adj* → **1** resting **2** slow *adv* **3** restfully

lemon *n* → **1** complainer **2** failure **3** fool **4** sourness **5** ugly person **6** unhappy person **7** unpleasant thing **8** yellow *adj* **9** sour **10** yellow

lemonade *n* → drink

LEND *v* advance, loan; **rent,** demise, hire out, lease out, let, re-lease, rent out, sublease, sublet, underlet; **mortgage,** bond; **fund,** accommodate, finance, re-finance, refund; **pawn,** hock, pledge, pop

lend *v* → add

LENDER *n* advancer, creditor, discounter, Ikey Mo, kulak, loan shark, loaner, money-lender, mortgagee, pawnbroker, uncle, usurer; **lessor,** landlady, landlord, rack-renter, sublessor; **credit union,** building society, permanent building society; **pawnshop,** hockshop, mont-de-piété, pop-shop

LENGTH *n* distance, expanse, extent, fetch, piece *(U.S.)*, range, reach, scope, space, spacing, span, straddle; **extension,** coextension, elongation, expansion, lankiness, lankness, lengthiness, linearity; **linear measure,** altitude, angular distance, chainage, easting, footage, latitude, long measure, longitude, mileage, northing, southing, surveyor's measure, westing; **trajectory,** arrowshot, bowshot, cannon shot, carry, cast, flight, gunshot, outreach, shot, throw; **hand's-breadth,** canvas, digit, finger, footstep, hank, head, march, neck, nose, pace, palm, step, stride; **yarn length,** bundle, hank, lea, spindle; **calibre,** bore, gauge; **miscellaneous length,** clearance, draw *(Mining)*, drift, drop, epoch *(Astron.)*, focal length, focus, freeboard, frontage, gap *(Aeron.)*, headway *(Railways)*, lap, overhang, overlap, pitch, recoil, setback, slippage, travel, traverse, wheelbase; **unit of length,** air mile, angstrom, astronomical unit, barleycorn, centimetre, chain, cubit, degree, ell, em, fathom, foot, furlong, inch, international nautical mile, kilometre, league, light-year, meridional part, metre, microinch, micrometre, micron, mil, mile, millimetre, minute, module, nail, nautical mile, parsec, perch, pole, rod, sea mile, thou, verst, yard

length *n* → **1** duration **2** part **3** textiles

LENGTHWAYS *adv* along, at length, axially, fore-and-aft, from end to end, from stem to stem, in extenso, lengthwise, longitudinally, meridionally, out, tandem

LENIENCE *n* gentleness, leniency, lenity, mildness, moderation, temperance, toleration; **charitableness,** clemency, compassion, fellow feeling, forbearance, mercifulness, mercy, quarter; **relaxation,** unbending; **lax-**

ness, elasticity, indiscipline, indulgence, laxity, liberalness, looseness, permissive society, Rafferty's rules; **dispensation,** days of grace, moratorium, reprieve

LENIENT *adj* agreeable, charitable, clement, complaisant, easy, easygoing, forgiving, gentle, humane, indulgent, kindly, liberal, merciful, mild, obliging, soft, soft-hearted, tolerant, uncritical, unexacting; **lax,** elastic, free and easy, loose, permissive, slack, un-buttoned, wide-open *(U.S. Law)*

lenient *adj* → 1 alleviant 2 composed 3 kind 4 moderate 5 pitying

LENIENT PERSON *n* a good sport, indulger, liberaliser, loosener, mollycoddler, wittol *(Obs.)*

LENS *n* burning-glass, eyepiece, hand glass, magnifier, magnifying glass, meniscus, sunglass; **prism,** Wollaston prism; **microscope,** compound microscope, dark microscope, dark-field microscope, electron microscope, phase contrast microscope, polar-ising microscope, simple microscope, ultra-microscope, ultraviolet microscope; **telescope,** comet-finder, Gregorian telescope, Newtonian telescope, reflecting telescope, refracting telescope, spyglass, zenith tube; **binoculars,** field-glasses, opera glasses, tele-stereoscope; **periscope,** camera lucida, cam-era obscura; **projector,** magic lantern, planet-arium, stereopticon, wheel of life, zoetrope; **hydroscope,** waterglass; **gastroscope,** phar-yngoscope, proctoscope, urethroscope. *See also* GLASSES

lens *n* → 1 mineral 2 rock outcrop

Lent *n* → 1 fast 2 holy day

leonine *adj* → animal-like

leotard *n* → tights

leper *n* → patient

leprechaun *n* → fairy

lesbian *n* → 1 sexual type *adj* 2 sexual

Lesbian *n* → woman

lesion *n* → injury

LESS *prep* bar, except, excluding, failing, minus, save, wanting, without

less *n* → 1 inferiority *adj* 2 decreased 3 in-ferior 4 unimportant *adv* 5 decreasingly

lessee *n* → borrower

lessen *v* → 1 decrease 2 slander 3 subtract

lesser *n* → 1 inferiority *adj* 2 decreased 3 in-ferior

LESSON *n* class, lecture, module, object lesson, practical, section *(N.Z.),* seminar, ser-mon, session, teach-in, tute, tutorial; **drill,** boat drill, dismounted drill, exercise, exercitation, fire drill, haute école *(Eques-trian),* pack drill, practice, rehearsal, rifle drill, rote learning, skeleton exercise, square bashing *(Mil.).* *See also* LEARNING; COURSE

lesson *n* → 1 punishment 2 warning *v* 3 scold

lessor *n* → lender

lest *conj* → on condition that

let *n* → 1 hindrance 2 loan *v* 3 cause 4 hinder 5 lend 6 permit

lethal *adj* → 1 deadly 2 killing

lethargy *n* → 1 apathy 2 boredom 3 idlenes 4 sleepiness

LET ONESELF GO *v* do as one pleases, d what one likes, find one's feet, freewheel have one's fling, have one's own way, let all hang out, let off steam, let one's hai down, play, run about, run riot, run wild wanton; **deliver oneself from,** break free break loose, cast off the trammels, get rid of shake off the yoke, slip, slip the collar, throw off

LETTER *n* character, grapheme, hiero glyphic, homophone, ideogram, ideograph numeral, pictogram, rune, sign, sphenogram stenograph; **alphabet,** ABC, abecedary futhorc, International Phonetic Alphabet phonetic alphabet, Roman alphabet; **charac tery,** alphabetisation, kana, notation, sylla bary, transliteration; **cipher,** cuneiform, let tering, monogram, ogham, script, stencil stenotype; **cardinal vowel,** consonant, con tinuant, digraph, diphthong, polyphone, tri graph, vowel; **capital letter,** block capital block letter, capital, caps, print, upper case **character face,** blockletter, bold, Gothic italic, roman, small capitals, uncial; **smal letter,** lower case, majuscule, minuscule **superscript,** subindex, superior; **letter par** ascender, cock-up, descender, initial

letter *n* → message

lettuce *n* → cash

leukaemia *n* → cancer

levee *n* → 1 celebration 2 crowd 3 dam 4 em bankment

LEVEL *n* flat, plane, stratum, table; **horizon tal,** artificial horizon, false horizon, geoid horizon, mean sea-level, sea-level, true level

LEVEL *v* barrel, bed, cut, cut down, fell, flat ten, floor, hew, hew down, knock end wise knock endways, landplane, lay, lay down mow down, raze, shake down; **even,** float flush, garden, grade, pat, plane, planish plaster, roll, smooth, square

LEVEL *adj* equal, even, flat, flattish, flush *(Print.),* horizontal, invariable, plane, reg ular, smooth, square, straight, table-top tabular, uniplanar; **levelled,** compressed flattened, pitch-faced *(Bldg Trades);* **recum bent,** accumbent, fallen, horizontal, lolling lolling about, lying down, procumbent prone, prostrate, reclining, sprawling, supine

level *n* → 1 grade *v* 2 bowl over 3 direc 4 equal 5 lower *adj* 6 composed 7 equa 8 precise 9 straight *adv* 10 equally

LEVELLER *n* evener, flattener, flatter, float garden roller, grader, heavy roller, plane planer, planisher, road roller, roll, roller steamroller; **surveyor's level,** alidade bubble chalk-line, gimbals, plumb-rule, stringline wye level

LEVELNESS *n* evenness, flatness, planeness straightness; **recumbency,** accumbency proneness, prostration, reclination, recum bent, supineness; **loll,** lounge

lever *n* → 1 lift 2 machine *v* 3 lift

leverage *n* → 1 influence 2 lifting 3 power

leviathan *n* → giant
levitate *v* → 1 ascend 2 float
levity *n* → 1 happiness 2 lightness
levy *n* → 1 income 2 insistence 3 obligation 4 tax *v* 5 beg 6 charge 7 impose 8 insist on 9 take
lewd *adj* → obscene
lexicon *n* → 1 list 2 reference book 3 vocabulary
liability *n* → 1 debt 2 feasibility 3 inconvenience 4 obligation 5 point of view
liable *adj* → 1 feasible 2 in debt 3 obligated 4 predisposed
liaison *n* → 1 communication 2 love affair 3 relationship 4 sexual relationship
LIAR *n* belier, fabricator, falsifier, fibber, fibster, forswearer, misinformant, misreporter, mythomaniac, pathological liar, perjurer, storyteller
libel *n* → 1 misrepresentation 2 slander *v* 3 litigate 4 misinterpret 5 slander
liberal *n* → 1 libertarian 2 political ideologist *adj* 3 generous 4 lenient 5 liberated 6 tolerant
LIBERALISM *n* broad-mindedness, existentialism, informality, laissez faire, liberality, liberalness, non-intervention, non-restraint, toleration, tolerationism, unbiasedness
LIBERATE *v* deliver, emancipate, extricate, free, manumit, rescue, spring; **acquit,** absolve, affranchise, clear, discharge, disengage, disentail, dispense with, exempt, exonerate, frank, free, parole, ransom, release, unburden, vindicate *(Obs.)*; **let be,** leave alone, let alone, let go, remit *(Obs.)*; **unleash,** decontrol, give someone his head, loose, release, unbind, unbridle, uncage, unchain, unhand, unloose, unmuzzle, unscrew, unshackle, untie
liberate *v* → 1 rob 2 separate
LIBERATED *adj* emancipated, exonerated, free, free of the country *(Convict)*, free on the ground *(Convict)*, freeborn, released, scot-free; **freehold,** allodial; **liberal,** liberalist, liberalistic, non-restrictive, open-handed; **unbridled,** abandoned, all-in, anarchic, anarchistic, boisterous, facile, incoercible, incontinent, inordinate, intemperate, irrepressible, loose, outspoken, unbent, unbidden, unbitted, unbowed, unbroken, uncrossed, wanton, wild, wild and woolly; **uninhibited,** expansive, free, spontaneous, unashamed, unconventional, unembarrassed, unfettered, unreserved; **unlimited,** arbitrary, broad, common, laissez-faire, open, rampant, unbounded, unchartered, unclassified, unconditional, undetermined, unstructured, untrammelled
LIBERATION *n* affranchisement, deliverance, delivery, emancipation, enfranchisement, manumission, ransom, release; **acquittal,** absolution, exoneration, redemption; **discharge,** bail, bailment, dismissal, parole, remission; **disengagement,** decontrol, extrication; **freedom from conditions,** acquittance, disentailment, exemption, quittance; **unboundedness,** unaccountability, unbrokenness, unconditionality, unconditionalness, unlimitedness
LIBERATOR *n* emancipationist, emancipator, emancipist, libber, liberationist; **deliverer,** absolvent, acquitter, discharger, exonerator, manumitter, Messiah, ransomer, redeemer
LIBERTARIAN *n* civil libertarian, existentialist, liberal, liberaliser, liberalist, noninterventionist, tolerationist
libertine *n* → 1 dissipater 2 promiscuous person *adj* 3 anarchic 4 promiscuous
LIBERTY *n* autonomy, freedom, freeness, independence, self-determination; **licence,** familiarity, outspokenness, spontaneity, spontaneousness, unrestraint; **abandon,** anarchism, anarchy, incontinence, incontinency, indiscipline, inordinacy, intemperateness, irrepressibility, irrepressibleness, libertarianism, looseness, openhandedness, wantonness, wildness; **latitude,** breadth, elbow room, leg room, margin, option, play, poetic licence, tolerance; **leave,** exequatur, permission; **free hand,** blank cheque, fling, free rein, free swing, licence, open go, open slather, public domain; **immunity,** academic freedom, free speech, freedom of the seas; **sanctuary,** diplomatic immunity, franchise; **open door,** egress, entrance, entree, entry; **parole,** bail, cartel, force majeure, out, ransom, release, remission, ticket-of-leave; **the outside,** open *(Prison)*, rules *(Brit.)*, the outer *(Prison)*
liberty *n* → 1 independence 2 permission
libido *n* → 1 desire 2 living 3 psyche 4 sex 5 vitality 6 voluptuousness
library *n* → 1 book 2 storage
libretto *n* → musical score
licence *n* → 1 certificate 2 liberty 3 permission 4 power to act 5 promiscuity
license *v* → permit
licentious *adj* → 1 anarchic 2 obscene 3 overindulgent 4 promiscuous
lichen *n* → plant
licit *adj* → lawful
lick *n* → 1 small amount *v* 2 defeat 3 surpass 4 taste
lid *n* → 1 covering 2 eye 3 hat
LIE *n* alias, canard, disinformation, distortion, equivocation, evasion, exaggeration, fable, fabrication, factoid, fairytale, falsehood, fib, fiction, half-truth, invention, legal fiction, misinformation, misreport, misrepresentation, misstatement, perjury, pretext, prevarication, story, tale, tarradiddle, untruth, white lie, whopper
LIE *v* cant, dud up, fable, fabricate, fib, forswear oneself, lie like a trooper, perjure oneself; **equivocate,** not give a straight answer, palter, prevaricate, quibble; **exaggerate,** overstate, strain the truth, understate; **distort,** bend the truth, garble, misreport, pervert, tell a white lie
lie *n* → 1 direction *v* 2 be 3 direct 4 idle 5 inhabit 6 position 7 recline

LIE LOW *v* burrow, go to ground, hole up, lie doggo, make oneself scarce, retire, retreat, take to the hills; **ambush,** couch, lie in wait, lurk. *See also* HIDE

life *n* → **1** being **2** bubbliness **3** duration **4** liveliness **5** living **6** period **7** record **8** savour **9** sprightliness

lifeline *n* → **1** arm **2** cord **3** fortune-telling **4** route

LIFESAVER *n* beach inspector, beltman, life-guard, reelman, surf-lifesaver

lifesaver *n* → repairer

LIFT *n* elevator, fork hoist, fork lift, goods lift, grain elevator, hoist, noria, service lift; **pulley,** block and tackle, capstan, cat, winch, windlass; **crane,** derrick, goliath crane, luffing crane, tower crane; **lever,** jack, screwjack, wallaby jack, well sweep

LIFT *v* elevate, lever, prise, raise, up-end, upheave, uplift, upraise; **hoist,** advance *(Archaic),* exalt *(Archaic),* fly *(Theat.),* masthead, run up, sway up, up; **erect,** build, set up; **boost,** heighten, prop, stilt, underlay; **heave,** heft, hoick, pick up; **toss,** fork, lob, loft, sky, throw; **hitch up,** kilt, perk up, take up, tuck up; **wind up,** dredge up, fish up, haul up, jack up, pull up, winch, windlass; **trip anchor,** weigh anchor

lift *n* → **1** amount **2** coating **3** conveyor **4** elevator **5** gravimetry **6** help **7** journey **8** lifting *v* **9** emphasise **10** repair **11** rob **12** transport

LIFTING *n* Assumption, cranage, elevation, erection, exaltation *(Archaic),* leverage, levitation, take-up, upheaval, uplift, upliftment, uptake; **boost,** a leg up, raise; **lift,** dead lift, deep knees bend, heave, jerk, press, snatch

ligament *n* → bond

ligature *n* → **1** bond **2** musical phrase **3** musical score **4** tape

LIGHT *n* illuminance, illumination, luminance; **lamplight,** candlelight, firelight, gaslight, torchlight; **limelight,** Bengal light, calcium light, magnesium light, red fire; **beam,** irradiation, moonbeam, pencil, phlegethon, ray, shaft, sunbeam, sunray; **glow,** candescence, gleam, incandescence, lustre, radiance, refulgence; **flash,** arc, blaze, flare, flare-up, fulguration; **sparkle,** blink, coruscation, flicker, gleam, glimmer, glimmering, glimpse *(Archaic),* glint, glisten, glister *(Archaic),* glitter, scintillation, shimmer, spark, twinkle, twinkling, wink; **daylight,** broad day, day, daytime, sun, sunburst, sunlight, sunniness, sunshine; **dawn,** daybreak, false dawn, first light, sunrise; **aurora,** aurora australis, aurora borealis, northern lights, polar lights; **airglow,** afterglow, alpenglow, blink *(Meteorol.),* gegenschein, green flash, ice-blink, rainbow, snowblink, sunbow, sundog, white-out; **moonlight,** earthlight, earthshine, moonshine, starlight, zodiacal light; **will-o'-the-wisp,** friar's lantern, ignis fatuus, jack-o'-lantern, marsh light, wildfire; **parhelion,** mock moon, mock sun, paraselene, photosphere; **halo,** aureole, circle, corona. *See also* BRIGHTNESS

LIGHT *adj* airy-fairy, delicate, feathery, filmy, fine, flimsy, floaty, flossy, fluffy, fuzzy, gauzy, gossamer, papery, papyraceous; **airy,** aerial, aery, ethereal, rare, rarefied, spiritual, spirituel, spirituelle, tenuous, thin; **unsubstantial,** imponderable, lightweight, weightless

light *n* → **1** appearance **2** indicator **3** knowledge **4** lighter **5** morning **6** seeing **7** signal **8** window **9** wise person *v* **10** dismount **11** fire **12** illuminate *adj* **13** amusing **14** bright **15** changeable **16** colourless **17** easy **18** few **19** foolish **20** happy **21** powdered **22** promiscuous **23** small **24** thin **25** unimportant **26** white *adv* **27** lightly

LIGHTER *n* anarchist, friction match, fusee, light, lucifer, match, safety match, slow match, vesta; **flint,** steel; **taper,** fuse, proximity fuse, spill, touchpaper, touchwood, train, wick; **torch,** firebrand, firestick; **firebox,** tinderbox; **detonator,** primer; **tinder,** amadou, combustible, ignescent, inflammable, punk *(U.S.)*

LIGHT-FOOTED *adj* agile, alacritous, alert, lambent, lightsome, nimble, tripping, volant, volante

lighthouse *n* → **1** lighting **2** signal **3** signpost

LIGHTING *n* illumination, irradiation; **electric light,** arc lamp, arc light, bulb, city lights, fluorescent tube, gas lamp, gaslight, glow lamp, harbour lights, incandescent lamp, mercury-vapour lamp, neon lamp, port light, port lights, quartz-iodine lamp, starboard light, tungsten lamp; **chandelier,** corona, cresset, lustre, pendant; **concealed lighting,** indirect lighting, panel lighting, strip lighting, strobe lighting; **lamp,** Aldis lamp, dark lantern, droplight, flashlight, hurricane, hurricane lamp, lampion, lantern, night-light, slush lamp, standard lamp, storm-lantern *(Brit.),* Tilley lamp, torch, wall-washer; **safety lamp,** Davy lamp; **Chinese lantern,** fairy lights, jack-o'-lantern; **streetlight,** lamp standard, lamppost, pavement light; **footlights,** floats, floodlight, foots, klieg light, limelight, spot, spotlight, sunlamp; **headlight,** courtesy light, flasher, flickers, fog lamp, headlamp, indicator light, sidelight, stoplight, tail-light; **searchlight,** star shell, Very light; **lighthouse,** leads *(Naut.),* pharos; **flashbulb,** electronic flash, flash, flashcube, flashgun, flashlight, photoflash lamp, photoflood lamp, strobe; **safelight; floodlight projector,** up-lighter

LIGHTLY *adv* filmily, flimsily, fluffily, fuzzily, light; **airily,** ethereally, tenuously, thinly; **agilely,** lambently, light-footedly, lightly, lightsomely, volante

LIGHTNESS *n* filminess, fineness, flimsiness, fluffiness, fuzziness, gauziness; **airiness,** ethereality, etherealness, rarefaction, rareness, rarity, tenuousness, thinness; **weightlessness,** imponderability, imponderableness, levity, zero gravity; **buoyancy,** floatability, flotage, flotation, hover, poise, wafture; **agility,** lambency, light-footedness, lightsomeness, nimbleness

light-year *n* → length

lignite *n* → fuel

like *v* → **1** desire **2** enjoy *adj* **3** equal **4** likely **5** similar *adv* **6** imprecisely

LIKELIHOOD *n* every chance, good chance, good prospect, likeliness, probability, promise, reason to hope, reasonable chance, well-founded view; **credibility,** plausibility, verisimilitude; **expectation,** conditional probability, normal curve, presumption, probability curve, reasonable hope; **favourite,** best bet, goer, great white hope, the one most likely to succeed

LIKELY *adj* apparent, like *(Archaic)*, odds-on, on the cards, presumable, probable, promising, to be expected; **liable to,** apt to, in line, incident to, incidental to, like to *(Archaic)*, likely to, ready to; **credible,** easy to believe, ostensible, plausible, verisimilar

LIKELY *adv* apparently, belike *(Archaic)*, doubtless, doubtlessly, easily, in all likelihood, in all probability, like as not, London to a brick, no doubt, ostensibly, presumably, probably, seemingly, ten to one, to all appearances

likely *adj* → favourable

liken *v* → compare

likeness *n* → **1** imitation **2** portrait **3** similarity

likewise *adv* → **1** additionally **2** similarly

lilac *n* → **1** purple *adj* **2** purple

lilt *n* → **1** music **2** rhythm *v* **3** sing

lily *n* → **1** man **2** plant **3** white *adj* **4** clean

LIMB *n* appendage, extremity, manus, member. *See also* ARM; LEG

limb *n* → **1** flower **2** knob

limber *n* → **1** arsenal *adj* **2** pliable

limbo *n* → **1** afterworld **2** prison

lime *v* → fertilise

limelight *n* → **1** light **2** lighting

limerick *n* → **1** abridgment **2** poetry **3** pornography

LIMIT *n* measure, mete, pale, precincts, riverside; **demarcation,** delimitation, partition, Rubicon; **boundary,** by-line, dead-ball line, ditch, goal line, line, score, sideline, tramlines; **deadline,** cut-off, term *(Archaic)*, time limit; **terminus,** farthest reaches, termination, the ends of the earth, ultima Thule; **horizon,** equator, skyline; **upper limit,** ceiling, high-water mark, limitations, strings; **lower limit,** dead finish, low water mark, the end of one's tether, threshold. *See also* EDGE

LIMIT *v* circumscribe, conscribe, contain, define, delimit, draw the line, terminate; **demarcate,** beat the bounds, mark out, peg, zone; **bound,** bank, kerb

limit *n* → **1** region *v* **2** imprison **3** qualify **4** restrict

limited *adj* → **1** imprisoned **2** limiting **3** restricted

LIMITING *adj* borderline, cut-off, delimitative, extreme, limitary, limitative, restrictive, terminational, terminative; **limited,** definite, finite, restricted

limousine *n* → car

limp *n* → **1** injury *v* **2** walk *adj* **3** weak

limpid *adj* → **1** clear **2** transparent

LIMPLY *adv* droopingly, flabbily, flaccidly, flaggingly, flimsily, loosely, slack, slackly, tenuously; **shakily,** groggily, totteringly, tremulously

LINE *n* axis, band, bar, canal *(Astron.)*, crossbar, dash, guideline, hatch, outline, ray, ribbon, rule, straight, streak, stria, strip, stroke, swath, tail, thread, track, trail, vein, veinlet; **row,** file, hedgerow, Indian file, orthostichy, procession, queue, rank, single file, train, windrow; **geometric line,** asymptote, chord, circumference, curve, diameter, directrix, median, perimeter, radius, secant, tangent; **equator,** great circle, meridian, parallel; **lineation,** crosshatching, grain, hatching, ruling, striation, veining; **specific line,** baseline, buttock line, condensation trail, contour, contour line, em rule, fall line *(Geog.)*, International Date Line, load line, magistral *(Fort.)*, magistral line *(Fort.)*, pinstripe, pitch line, Plimsoll line, ridge, service line, sideline, taw *(Marbles)*, thalweg, touchline, vapour trail, waterline

LINE *v* band, crosshatch, hatch, ray, rule, rule off, streak, striate, strip, stripe, vein; **align,** collimate, lay out, range, rank, rectify, windrow; **line up,** defile, queue, string, string out, trail

line *n* → **1** ancestry **2** aristocracy **3** armed forces **4** battleground **5** cord **6** direction **7** fold **8** information **9** layer **10** limit **11** method **12** musical score **13** plan **14** position **15** railway **16** road **17** route **18** series **19** sign **20** song **21** thread **22** trick **23** wire *v* **24** cover **25** fill **26** fold **27** portray **28** position

lineage *n* → **1** ancestry **2** aristocracy

lineal *adj* → genetic

liner *n* → **1** coating **2** cosmetics **3** watercraft

linger *v* → **1** go slowly **2** rest

lingerie *n* → **1** manchester **2** underwear

lingo *n* → language

liniment *n* → medication

link *n* → **1** bond **2** candle **3** join *v* **4** join

lint *n* → **1** medication **2** remnant **3** textiles

lintel *n* → beam

lion *n* → **1** famous person **2** good person **3** hero **4** strong person

Lion *n* → member

lipstick *n* → **1** cosmetics **2** dye

LIQUEFACTION *n* deliquescence, dispersion, dissolution, emulsification, fluidisation, fusion; **leaching,** lixiviation, percolation, washing away

LIQUEFIABLE *adj* eutectic, eutectoid, fusible, thixotropic; **soluble,** dissoluble, dissolvable, dissolvent, solvable, water-soluble; **deliquescent,** liquescent; **hydrophilic,** hydrophobic, hydrotropic; **solvent,** anticoagulant

LIQUEFIER *n* fluidiser, liquefacient; **solvent,** alkahest, anticoagulant, antifreeze, dispersion medium, dissolvent, dissolver, emulsifier, menstruum, thinner

LIQUEFY *v* deliquesce, melt, run, sweal, thaw; **dissolve,** disintegrate, disperse; **liquidise,** fluidise, flux, fuse, render, smelt, try; **soak,** infuse, leach, lixiviate, percolate, steep

LIQUID *n* aqua, condensate, dew, effusion *(Pathol.)*, emulsion, fluid, grume, juice, liquor, moisture, sap, wet; **solution,** colloidal solution, decoction, distillate, emulsion, emulsoid, hydrosol, infusion, lixivium, lye; **bath,** dip, soak, souse, steep, wash; **drop,** bead, blob, dewdrop, drip, droplet; **melt,** metal *(Glassmaking)*, thaw; **spillage,** spill, splash; **percolate,** leachate, seepage, soakage; **water-divining,** dowsing, rhabdomancy. *See also* WATER

LIQUID *adj* emulsive, fluctuant *(Med.)*, fluent *(Rare)*, fluid, fluidal, fluidic, molten, run, running, runny; **watery,** aqueous, hydrogenous, hydrous, hygric, juicy, sappy, serous, succulent, water, waterish, waterlike, wishy-washy; **dissolved,** in solution, liquefied, solute, uncongealed; **hydraulic,** hydrodynamic, hydrokinetic, hydrologic, hydromechanical, hydrostatic

liquid *adj* → **1** cash **2** transparent

liquidate *v* → **1** account **2** cash **3** destroy **4** kill **5** massacre **6** pay

LIQUIDITY *n* fluidity, fluidness, flux, liquidness, serosity, wateriness; **solubility,** dissolubility, dissolubleness, dissolvableness, solubleness, solvability, solvableness; **fusibility,** fusibleness, thixotropy; **hydrology,** fluid mechanics, hydraulics, hydrodynamics, hydrokinetics, hydromechanics, hydrostatics

liquor *n* → **1** alcohol **2** liquid

lisp *v* → mispronounce

lissom *adj* → **1** beautiful **2** busy **3** pliable

LIST *n* beadroll, catalogue, inventory, listing, record, register, scroll, tally; **table,** chart, scale; **calendar,** almanac, atlas, gazette, gazetteer, yearbook; **word list,** concordance, dictionary, glossary, lexicon, syllabary, synonymy, thesaurus, vocabulary; **contents,** bibliography, bibliotheca, corrigenda, errata, index, sigla, syllabus, synposis; **account,** invoice, ledger, receipt; **waybill,** basket *(Econ.)*, bill of lading, bill of quantities, check list, manifest, price-list, stocktaking; **roll,** accession list, active list, army list, book *(Racing)*, cartulary, census, class list, class roll, electoral roll, empanelment, enrolment, file, law list, mailing list, muster roll, necrology, panel, payroll, peerage, poll, racecard, roster, rota, short list, sick list, slate, studbook, ticket *(Politics)*, transfer list, waiting list, waitlist; **credits,** directory, list of contributors; **roll of honour,** honour board, honour scroll; **list of saints,** canon, hagiology, martyrology; **telephone directory,** pink pages *(Obs.)*, teledex, yellow pages; **black list,** black book, Index *(R.C. Church)*; **conduct sheet,** charge sheet *(Law)*, crime sheet *(Mil.)*

LIST *v* accession, book, catalogue, index, inventory, table, tabularise, tabulate, take stock; **enrol,** empanel, inscribe, matriculate, poll, register; **black-list,** short-list, waitlist; **enumerate,** docket *(Law)*, itemise, recount, run through; **schedule,** bill, calendar, gazette

list *n* → **1** frame **2** inequality **3** slope *v* **4** desire **5** edge **6** hear **7** inquire into **8** intend **9** please **10** slope

listen *v* → **1** attend to **2** hear

LISTING *n* analysis, assay, breakdown, citation, enumeration, itemisation, recountal, tabularisation, tabulation

listless *adj* → **1** apathetic **2** bored **3** inactive

litany *n* → bore

literal *n* → **1** error *adj* **2** forthright **3** precise **4** true

literate *adj* → educated

literature *n* → **1** public notice **2** writing

lithe *adj* → **1** beautiful **2** pliable

lithography *n* → **1** engraving **2** printing

LITIGANT *n* alleger, appellant, complainant, libellant, party, plaintiff, privy, suer, suitor; **accused,** codefendant, defendant, libellee, respondent; **witness,** crown witness, defence witness, interested party

litigant *adj* → litigious

LITIGATE *v* bring an action against, bring to justice, bring to trial, file a suit against, fit, go to law, implead, proceed against, process, prosecute, put on trial, replevy, settle out of court, sue, take to court; **arraign,** accuse, bring in, charge, cite, convene, give in charge, impeach, indict, libel, plead *(Obs.)*, serve with a writ, subpoena, summon

LITIGATION *n* action, audit *(Archaic)*, case, cause, dispute, hearing, instance, law, lawsuit, legal proceeding, petition, plea, proceeding, process, question *(Obs.)*, reference, suit; **legal action,** assumpsit, cattle trespass, class action, commercial cause, cross-action, fender case *(Colloq.)*, interpleader, praemunire *(Brit.)*, remand, remanet, repetition, replevin, test case, trover, wager of law *(Old Eng.)*; **summons,** arraignment, citation, compurgation *(Obs.)*, detainer, habeas corpus, impeachment, subpoena, writ

LITIGIOUS *adj* quarrelsome; **litigant,** trial; **summonsed to appear,** due in court, for the high jump, subpoenaed; **actionable,** appealable, committable, issuable, judicable, justiciable, reviewable, suable, triable

litter *n* → **1** animal offspring **2** fertile land **3** jumble **4** layer **5** waste *v* **6** cover **7** give birth **8** untidy

litterbug *n* → dirty person

little *adj* → **1** few **2** intolerant **3** short **4** small **5** weak *adv* **6** rarely

LIVE *v* be, breathe, endure, exist, keep body and soul together, persist, subsist, survive; **come to life,** be born, light up, lighten; **revive,** awaken, come to, quicken, resurge, resurrect, rise

live *v* → **1** be **2** behave **3** be pleased **4** inhabit *adj* **5** busy **6** colourful **7** current **8** energetic **9** explosive **10** hot **11** innovative **12** in use **13** living **14** moving **15** operating

livelihood *n* → income

IVELINESS *n* animation, ebullience, ebulliency, effervescence, effervescency, friskiness, ginger *(Colloq.)*, life, vibrancy

ively *adj* → **1** bright **2** bubbly **3** busy **4** colourful **5** energetic **6** exciting **7** happy **8** powerful *adv* **9** busily **10** energetically

iven *v* → enliven

very *n* → **1** emblem of office **2** uniform

ivid *adj* → **1** angry **2** black **3** blue **4** grey

IVING *n* existence, modus vivendi, struggle for existence, subsistence, survival, sustentation; **life,** being, creation, nature; **course of life,** days, expectation of life, life cycle, life-expectancy, race *(Archaic)*; **longevity,** long life, survivorship, viability; **animation,** a new lease of life, quickening, reanimation, resurgence, resurrection, revival, reviviscence, vitalisation, vivification; **vital force,** anima, animus, atman, ghost *(Obs.)*, libido, life force, pneuma, prana, psyche, soul, spirit, vital fluid, vital spark, zombie; **lifeblood,** blood, breath, heart, heart's blood, heartblood, marrow, pith, pulse

IVING *adj* above ground, animate, breathing, existent, in the flesh, in the land of the living, live, on deck, quick *(Archaic)*, surviving, to the fore; **alive,** alive and kicking, red-blooded, vital; **long-lived,** longeval, vivacious *(Archaic)*; **viable,** capable of life; **resurgent,** renascent, resurrectional, resurrectionary, reviviscent; **vital,** animated, full of life, jazzy, peppy, pert, proud, snappy, spirited, vivacious, vivid, zingy, zippy; **green,** blooming, fresh, juicy, sappy, verdant; **life-giving,** animating, animative, quickening, vivifying

iving *n* → **1** behaviour **2** income *adj* **3** current **4** hot **5** in use **6** real **7** realistic **8** whole

IVING ROOM *n* calefactory, club, clubroom, common room, drawing room, green room, hall, lounge, lounge room, megaron, mess, misericord, parlour, rest room, salon, sitting room, solar, staffroom; **sunroom,** snuggery, solarium, sunlounge; **smoking room,** divan, smokeroom; **nursery,** playroom, rumpus room; **conservatory,** gallery, saloon

LIVING THING *n* biota, nature, organic matter; **chromatin,** chromosome, DNA, double helix, gene, genetic material, plasmagene, spireme; **biotype,** genotype, phenotype

izard *n* → **1** farmhand **2** idler **3** reptile **4** scissors **5** shears

LO *interj* behold, look, watch

oad *n* → **1** ammunition **2** amount **3** contents **4** electricity **5** toil **6** venereal disease *v* **7** fill **8** increase **9** oversupply **10** place **11** transport **12** weigh

oading *n* → **1** income **2** placement

oaf *n* → **1** easy thing **2** head **3** mind **4** period of inaction **5** rest *v* **6** idle

oam *n* → **1** soil *v* **2** cover **3** fill

LOAN *n* accommodation, advance, boomerang *(Colloq.)*, bridging finance, imprest, permanent loan, soft loan, terminating loan, touch *(Colloq.)*; **lease,** lease-back, leveraged lease, let, location *(Civil Law)*, sublease, under-lease; **rent,** bond money, Duke of Kent *(Colloq.)*, farm *(English Hist.)*, ground rent, hire, rack-rent; **mortgage,** encumbrance, equitable mortgage, first mortgage, home loan, monkey *(N.Z. Colloq.)*, poultice *(Colloq.)*; **tenancy,** lessee-ship, undertenancy; **charter,** hire; **hire-purchase,** credit foncier, H.P., never-never *(Orig. Brit.)*; **usury,** pawnbroking, usance *(Obs.)*

loan *v* → lend

loath *adj* → unwilling

loathe *v* → **1** dislike **2** hate

lob *n* → **1** stroke **2** throw *v* **3** lift **4** throw

lobby *n* → **1** hall **2** influencer **3** society *v* **4** entreat **5** persuade **6** politicise

lobe *n* → **1** bulge **2** head

lobster *n* → soldier

local *n* → **1** anaesthetic **2** inhabitant **3** newspaper **4** pub **5** society **6** trade union *adj* **7** regional **8** resident

locale *n* → **1** position **2** region

localise *v* → position

locality *n* → **1** position **2** region

locate *v* → **1** find **2** place **3** position

location *n* → **1** computer record **2** loan **3** placement **4** position **5** region **6** surroundings

loch *n* → lake

lock *n* → **1** bolt **2** chute **3** dam **4** hair **5** hold **6** lake **7** textiles *v* **8** fasten **9** straighten **10** transport

locker *n* → **1** box **2** container **3** cupboard **4** fastener

locket *n* → jewellery

lockup *n* → **1** imprisonment **2** prison

lock up *v* → **1** hide **2** imprison

locomotion *n* → move

locomotive *n* → **1** puller **2** train *adj* **3** moving

locum *n* → substitute

locus *n* → **1** curve **2** position

locution *n* → speaking

lode *n* → **1** diggings **2** layer **3** mineral **4** rock outcrop

lodge *n* → **1** animal dwelling **2** cabin **3** hotel **4** house **5** institute **6** shelter *v* **7** house **8** inhabit **9** place **10** pursue **11** shelter

lodging *n* → hotel

loft *n* → **1** height **2** hit **3** room **4** tower *v* **5** lift

lofty *n* → **1** tall person *adj* **2** arrogant **3** eloquent **4** important **5** proud **6** reputable **7** tall

log *n* → **1** diary **2** fool **3** fuel **4** idler **5** length-measurer **6** marijuana **7** speedometer **8** timber **9** watercraft *v* **10** account **11** cut **12** record **13** remove

LOGIC *n* cogency, coherence, equipollence, equipollency, legitimacy, legitimateness, logicality, modality, rationalisation, rationality, reasonableness, syllogisation, unanswerableness, undeniability, validation, validity, validness; **the Enlightenment; sense,** common sense, pragmatism, reason. *See also* REASONING

logic *n* → reasoning

LOGICAL *adj* cogent, coherent, consequent, consequential, deductive, dianoetic, discursive, illative, inferential, legitimate, ratiocinative, rational, reasonable, reasoned, skilful *(Obs.)*, sound, tenable, valid; **deducible,** extractable, inferable

logistics *n* → transport

LOINCLOTH *n* breechcloth, breechclout, dhoti *(India)*, futah, G-string, lap-lap, loin-clout, lungi *(India)*

loiter *v* → **1** go slowly **2** idle

loll *n* → **1** levelness **2** period of inaction **3** rest *v* **4** hang **5** idle **6** recline **7** rest

lollipop *n* → act

lollop *v* → jump

lolly *n* → **1** cash **2** fool **3** head

lone *adj* → **1** one **2** single **3** solitary

lonely *adj* → **1** remote **2** solitary **3** unhappy

lonesome *adj* → **1** solitary **2** unhappy

LONG *adj* elongate, elongated, expanded, expansive, extended, farthest, lengthy; **lengthwise,** axial, endlong *(Arch.)*, fore-and-aft, full-length, longitudinal, overall, whole-length; **extendable,** expansible, expansile, extensible, extensile; **metric,** kilometric, kilometrical, milliary, sesquipedalian, uncial; **lank,** gangling, gangly, lanky, rangy

long *adj* → **1** distant **2** propertied *adv* **3** then

longevity *n* → **1** age **2** living

longhand *n* → writing

longitude *n* → length

longwinded *adj* → verbose

LOOK *n* bo-peep, butchers, Captain, Captain Cook, cook, dek, dekko, eye, eyeful, gander, gaze, geek, geez, gig, gink, optic, regard, screw, shooftee, squiz, view; **glimpse,** sight; **peek,** peep, pry, squint; **glance,** aspect *(Archaic)*, blink, eyebeam, eyeshot, eyewink; **stare,** gape, glare, goggle; **leer,** ogle; **look of disdain,** greasy eyeball, hairy eyeball, the glassy eye; **inspection,** look-over, once-over, recce, reconnaissance, reconnoitre, review, scan, survey; **sheep's eyes.** *See also* SEEING

LOOK *v* embrace, eye, get a load of, gig, have an optic at, lamp, look, look after, look at, look on, observe, preview, regard, rubberneck, sit in on, spy on, tout, twig, watch; **ogle,** leer at, perv on; **inspect,** case, eyeball, look over, rake, reconnoitre, study, survey, sweep; **keep watch,** invigilate, keep a weather eye open, keep one's eyes open, keep one's eyes peeled, keep one's eyes skinned, oversee, overwatch, sentinel, wake *(Archaic)*, watch, watch over; **glance at,** glimpse at, run one's eye over, scan, skew, skim, squiz; **peek,** have a sticky, have a sticky beak, peep, peer, pry, squint; **stare,** gape, gawk, gawp, glare, goggle, have eyes only for, quiz *(Obs.)*; **have a view of,** command, overlook; **gaze,** contemplate, pore; **see through,** pierce, see into; **look for,** keep an eye out for, look out for, watch out for. *See also* SEE

look *n* → **1** appearance **2** investigation *v* **3** appear **4** look *interj* **5** lo

LOOKER *n* argus, audience, beholder, bystander, contemplator, eyewitness, gazer, gig, invigilator *(Obs.)*, looker-on, observer, onlooker, sightseer, spectator, spier, viewer, watcher, witness, witnesser; **starer,** gaper, rubberneck, sticky beak; **descrier,** espier, seer *(Rare)*; **peeping Tom,** gubba, leerer, ogler, peeper, spy, voyeur; **spotter,** birdwatcher, racegoer, televiewer, supertwitcher, theatregoer, twitcher; **lookout,** watch

LOOKOUT *n* captive balloon, conning tower, crow's-nest, observation post, observatory, outlook, viewpoint

lookout *n* → **1** looker **2** seeing **3** tower **4** warner

look out *interj* → **1** beware **2** hey

loom *n* → **1** appearance **2** stick *v* **3** appear **4** sew

loop *n* → **1** circle **2** contraception **3** curve **4** fool **5** opening **6** railway **7** ring **8** trimming *v* **9** curve **10** fly **11** overturn **12** surround

LOOPHOLE *n* bypass, conscience clause, doubletalk, escape clause, escape mechanism, sidestep; **tax lurk,** tax haven, tax shelter; **quibble,** chicanery, equivocation, fencing, hedge, prevarication, procrastination, quibbling, quillet *(Archaic)*, quip, quirk, salvo *(Rare)*, temporisation

loophole *n* → **1** expedient **2** means of escape **3** opening *v* **4** open

loose *v* → **1** liberate **2** separate **3** weaken *adj* **4** illogical **5** immoral **6** imprecise **7** lenient **8** liberated **9** promiscuous **10** separate **11** sexy **12** soft **13** unused **14** weak *adv* **15** at liberty **16** separately

LOOT *n* boodle *(U.S.)*, booty, earn *(Prison)*, pickings, plunder, spoils, stolen goods, swag

loot *n* → **1** cash *v* **2** rob

lop *v* → **1** hang **2** subtract

lope *n* → **1** rate **2** walking *v* **3** speed **4** walk

lopsided *adj* → **1** sloping **2** unequal

loquacious *adj* → **1** talkative **2** verbose

lord *n* → **1** aristocrat **2** manager **3** owner **4** spouse *interj* **5** oh

Lord *n* → **1** aristocrat **2** mister

lore *n* → **1** knowledge **2** learning

lorgnette *n* → glasses

lorry *n* → **1** supply vehicle **2** truck

LOSE *v* be all up, bite the dust, come off second best, come off worst, get the worst of it, go down, go under, lose out, meet one's match, meet one's Waterloo, overreach, take a tumble; **give in,** break down, drop one's bundle, say uncle, sky the towel, throw in one's hand, throw in the sponge, throw in the towel, throw it in, yield; **fail,** be among the also-rans, bomb, bomb out, collapse, get the thumbs down, get the wooden spoon, give up the ghost, give way, go down, go to the wall, have had it, win the wooden spoon

lose *v* → **1** advance **2** fail

LOSE COLOUR *v* blanch, blench, change colour, discolour, etiolate, fade, go green at the gills, go white, go white at the gills, sallow, tarnish, turn pale, wan *(Poetic)*; **dull,** dilute, pale, subdue; **decolour,** achromatise, bleach, decolourise

LOSER *n* also-ran, defeatist, has-been, non-starter, underdog, victim, wooden spooner

OSING *n* annihilation, confusion *(Obs.)*, conquest, defeat, discomfiture, downfall, downthrow, overthrow, overturn, pulverisation, rout, subdual, subjection, subjugation; **drubbing,** beating, checkmate, confutation, hiding, licking, punishment, shellacking, sui, suimate, thrashing, towelling, trimming *(U.S.)*, walloping; **reversal,** check, foil *(Archaic)*, repulse, reverse, upset; **whitewash**

OSING *adj* beat, beaten, bested, creamed, defeated, dished, dished up, done like a dinner, down, down-and-out, downfallen, euchred, gone a million, lost, outclassed, outmanoeuvred, pipped at the post, subdued

oss *n* → **1** absence **2** failure

OST *adj* bereft, bushed, cast, forfeit, gone, in limbo, irreclaimable, irrecoverable, irredeemable, lost to, slewed

ost *adj* → **1** confused **2** failed **3** immoral **4** losing **5** past **6** ruined

ot *n* → **1** accumulation **2** amount **3** condition **4** fate **5** gambling **6** luck **7** many **8** much **9** part **10** person **11** share **12** yard *v* **13** separate **14** share out

otion *n* → **1** fat **2** medication

ottery *n* → gambling

otus *n* → forgetter

OUD *adj* big, deafening, deep, forte, fortissimo, full, sonorous, strong, voiceful; **audible,** distinct; **crescendo,** rising; **resounding,** echoing, reboant, resonant; **shrill,** piercing, strident, ululant; **powerful,** deep-throated, stentorian; **vociferous,** loudmouthed, vociferant; **howling,** roaring; **thunderous,** clamorous, clangourous, fulminant, fulminatory, fulminous, strepitous, sulphurous, thundering

oud *adj* → **1** colourful **2** resonant **3** showy **4** vulgar *adv* **5** loudly **6** showily **7** vulgarly

OUDLY *adv* aloud, forte, fortissimo, loud

OUDMOUTH *n* blusterer, boyo, clamourer, noise maker, raver, roarer, roisterer, stentor, vociferant, vociferator, yammerer, yawper

OUDNESS *n* audibility, distinctness, forte, volume; **crescendo,** rise, swell; **noisiness,** boisterousness, clamorousness, obstreperousness, riotousness, tumultuousness, unquietness, uproariousness, vociferousness

OUD SOUND *n* babel, ballyhoo, bedlam, bluster, brawl, broil, brouhaha, bruit *(Archaic)*, bust-up, clamour, clangour, din, hubbub, hullabaloo, hurly, hurly-burly, melee, noise, outcry, pandemonium, pother, racket, rough-house, rout, row, ruckus, rumpus, shemozzle, tumult, turmoil, uproar; **bang,** blast, clap, clash, crash, explosion, report; **clang,** beep, blare, clarion call, peal; **thunder,** roar, roaring, roll, sonic boom, thunderclap, thunderpeal; **slurp,** snore, snort, stridor; **howl,** shriek, ululation; **vociferance,** vociferation, yammer, yap, yawp; **cachinnation,** belly laugh; **noisy place,** bear garden, pandemonium

oudspeaker *n* → microphone

lounge *n* → **1** auditorium **2** couch **3** kitchen **4** levelness **5** living room **6** period of inaction **7** pub *v* **8** idle **9** recline

louse *n* → bad person

lousy *n* → **1** bad mood *adj* **2** bad **3** ill **4** unkempt **5** unpleasant

lout *n* → **1** ignoramus **2** man **3** stupid person **4** violent person **5** vulgarian

louvre *n* → **1** airway **2** door

LOVE *n* adoration, affection, attachment, calf love, devotion, fondness, love at first sight, passion, puppy love; **infatuation,** crush, dotage, pash; **spiritual love,** agape, caritas, charity, courtly love, platonic love, platonism; **Venus,** eros; **cupid,** amoretto, amorino

LOVE *v* be enamoured of, be smitten with, be soft on someone, care for, carry a torch for; **fall in love,** adore, be nuts on, be nuts over, do one's balls on, do one's nuts over, dote on, fall for, have got it bad for, idolise, lose one's heart to, take a shine to; **lust after,** have the hots for; **embrace,** caress, cuddle, embosom, fondle, hug; **infatuate,** besot, smite

love *n* → **1** desire **2** friend **3** nothing **4** pleasure **5** religious ceremony **6** reverence **7** worship *v* **8** enjoy **9** flirt **10** respect

LOVE AFFAIR *n* affair, affaire de coeur, amour, eternal triangle, flirtation, intrigue, liaison, romance; **date,** assignation, tryst

lovelorn *adj* → **1** abandoned **2** flirtatious **3** loving **4** unhappy

lovely *adj* → **1** beautiful **2** pleasant

LOVER *n* admirer, adorer, beloved, captive, darling, doter, fair *(Archaic)*, favourite, flame, idoliser, light-o'-love, mash *(Obs. Colloq.)*, paramour, spoony, steady, sweetheart, sweeting *(Archaic)*, truelove, valentine; **lovebirds,** couple, pair; **boyfriend,** beau, boy, bully *(Obs.)*, follower *(Obs.)*, gallant *(Archaic)*, guy, inamorato, spark, swain *(Poetic)*; **amorist,** casanova, Don Juan, fancy man, gay Lothario, gigolo, ladies' man, lady-killer, philanderer, rake, Romeo, sugar daddy, womaniser; **de facto,** tallyman; **catamite,** cat, minion; **girlfriend,** babe *(U.S)*, baby *(U.S)*, donah, dulcinea, girl, inamorata, ladylove, lass, leman *(Archaic)*, potato peeler, sheila; **mistress,** fancy woman, gun-moll, kept woman, moll, tallywoman, woman; **ex,** lost love; **love-object,** apple of the eye, dreamboat, goddess, heart-throb, idol; **honey,** chérie, chuck *(Archaic)*, darl, dear, duck, ducky, luv, mavourneen, pet, precious, snooks, snookums, sugar, sweet, sweetie, tootsy

lover *n* → **1** desirer **2** enjoyer **3** flirt **4** friend **5** sexual partner

LOVING *adj* adoring, affectionate, amoroso, devoted, fond, kind *(Archaic)*, loving, tender; **amatory,** amorous, erotic, passionate, romantic, sportive *(Obs.)*; **infatuated,** at someone's feet, besotted, captive, doting, gaga, gone on, in love, lovelorn, lovesick, lovey-dovey, shook on, smitten, struck on, stuck on, sweet on, uxorious; **love-hate,** ambivalent

LOVINGLY *adv* affectionately, amoroso, con amore, dearly, fondly, tenderly; **adoringly,** amorously, passionately

LOVINGNESS *n* affectionateness, amorousness, lovesickness, passionateness, tenderness; **dearness,** adorableness

low *n* → 1 animal call 2 atmospheric pressure 3 bottom *v* 4 call (of animals) *adj* 5 bad 6 bare 7 bottom 8 ill-bred 9 inferior 10 past 11 quiet 12 shallow 13 unhappy 14 weak 15 working-class 16 wrong *adv* 17 below 18 quietly

lowboy *n* → cupboard

LOWER *v* abase *(Archaic)*, bring down, douse *(Naut.)*, let down, pull down, strike *(Naut.)*, take down; **set down,** drop off; **knock down,** bring down, deck, down, drop, fell, grass *(Football)*, lay, level, overthrow, run down, sling *(Football)*, throw, topple, tumble, wooden; **dump,** deposit, ditch, plonk, precipitate, throw down; **bow,** bob, crouch, curtsy, dip, duck, nod, stoop

lower *v* → 1 decrease 2 humble 3 quieten 4 vulgarise *adj* 5 bottom 6 inferior

lower case *n* → letter

low-key *adj* → 1 restricted 2 reticent

lowly *adj* → 1 bottom 2 inferior 3 meek *adv* 4 inferiorly

LOW REGARD *n* disesteem, dishonour, disregard, disrespect; **disdain,** contempt *(Law)*, contumely, cynicism, despite, misprision, ridicule, scorn; **disrespectfulness,** contemptuousness, contumeliousness, derisiveness, flippancy, flippantness, impiety, impiousness, irreverence, scurrility, scurrilousness, superciliousness; **insolence,** audacity, cheek, cheekiness, effrontery, gall, impudence, presumption; **impoliteness,** discourtesy, unceremoniousness, incivility

loyal *adj* → 1 conservative 2 faithful 3 obedient

lozenge *n* → 1 heraldry 2 medication

lubber *n* → 1 incompetent 2 novice 3 stupid person

lubricate *v* → oil

lucid *adj* → 1 bright 2 clear 3 sane 4 transparent

LUCK *n* cess *(Irish)*, Chinaman's luck, fortune, the luck of the Irish; **chance,** fortune, half a chance, hap *(Archaic)*, lot, plight, potluck; **fluke,** accident, act of God, coincidence, fortuity, haphazard, happenstance, incidental, stroke of fortune, the luck of the draw; **pot shot,** break, chance, look-in, risk, show *(U.S.)*, spin, throw; **a run of good luck,** a good trot; **bonanza,** pianola *(Cards)*, windfall; **bad luck,** ambs-ace, misadventure, mischance, misfortune, the deuce, the devil; **jinx,** hex, hoodoo, jonah, mozzle, schlemiel

luck *n* → 1 fate 2 good fortune

LUCKINESS *n* fortuitism, fortuitousness, fortuity, fortunateness, serendipity; **haphazardness,** accidentalness, adventitiousness, arbitrariness, casualness, flukiness, hazardousness, indeterminacy, promiscuousness, ticklishness

LUCKY *adj* arsy, tinny; **happy-go-lucky,** ad venturous, careless; **fortunate,** providentia **chance,** accidental, adventitious, aleatory, a bitrary, casual, chanceful, chancy, circum stantial, fortuitous, indeterminate, promiscu ous, scratch, unmeant; **haphazard,** arbitrar coincidental, desultory, fluky, hit-and-mis hit-or-miss, random, sporting

lucky *adj* → fortunate

LUCKY CHARM *n* birthstone, four-leaf cl ver, good luck charm, good omen, hors shoe, mascot, merrythought, rabbit's foo talisman, wishbone

LUCKY PERSON *n* child of fortune, luck dog, rising man, tin-arse

lucrative *adj* → profitable

lucre *n* → 1 cash 2 profit 3 wealth

ludicrous *adj* → 1 foolish 2 humorous

lug *n* → 1 headband 2 pull *v* 3 make musi 4 pull

luggage *n* → equipment

lugger *n* → 1 bore 2 sailing ship

lugubrious *adj* → 1 distressing 2 grieving

lukewarm *adj* → 1 apathetic 2 hot

lull *n* → 1 interval 2 rest 3 silence 4 stoppage 5 rest 6 silence

lullaby *n* → 1 sleeping 2 song

lumbago *n* → cramp

lumber *n* → 1 hindrance 2 timber 3 waste 4 arrest 5 cut 6 gather 7 hinder 8 impos 9 walk 10 weigh

luminary *n* → 1 famous person 2 heavenl body

luminescence *n* → brightness

luminous *adj* → 1 bright 2 clear 3 intelligent

lump *n* → 1 bulge 2 incompetent 3 pa 4 shapelessness 5 solid body *v* 6 bulg 7 transport

lunacy *n* → 1 foolishness 2 madness

LUNAR *adj* circumlunar, lunarian, moon sublunary, superlunary, translunary

lunar *adj* → 1 curved 2 metallic

lunatic *n* → 1 mad person *adj* 2 mad 3 psy chologically disturbed

lunch *n* → 1 meal *v* 2 burp 3 eat

luncheon *n* → meal

lung *n* → neck

lunge *n* → 1 cord 2 exercise 3 stroke

lurch *v* → swerve

lure *n* → 1 allure 2 attractor *v* 3 allure 4 a tract

lurid *adj* → 1 bright 2 colourful 3 colourles 4 exciting

lurk *n* → 1 dishonesty 2 hiding place 3 job 4 lie low

luscious *adj* → 1 delicious 2 pleasant 3 swee

lush *n* → 1 alcohol 2 drinking session 3 heav drinker *v* 4 drink alcohol *adj* 5 allurin 6 fertile 7 floral 8 soft 9 wet

lust *n* → 1 desire 2 greed 3 pleasure 4 se 5 voluptuousness

lustre *n* → 1 brightness 2 light 3 lightin 4 paint 5 reputability *v* 6 illuminate 7 polis

lusty *adj* → 1 desirous 2 energetic 3 health 4 strong

lute *v* → make music

luxuriant *adj* → **1** decorative **2** fertile **3** great **4** growing

luxuriate *v* → **1** be pleased **2** overindulge

LUXURY *n* a bed of roses, a place in the sun, easy street, good living, life of Riley, plenty, the fat of the land, the good life; **heyday**, golden age, good old days, good times, halcyon days, happy days, summer, sunshine

luxury *n* → **1** pleasure **2** surplus **3** voluptuousness *adj* **4** surplus

lynch *v* → **1** execute **2** kill

lyric *n* → **1** poetry *adj* **2** musical **3** poetic

lysis *n* → destruction

Mm

macabre *adj* → **1** deathlike **2** dreadful
macadam *n* → **1** paving **2** road
macaroni *n* → **1** affected person **2** nonsense
mace *n* → **1** emblem of office **2** stick
macerate *v* → **1** cook **2** separate **3** soften **4** thin **5** wet
machete *n* → **1** knife **2** sword
machinate *v* → **1** beguile **2** conspire
MACHINE *n* apparatus, appliance, attachment, bitser, contraption, contrivance, device, engine, mechanical device, unit; **mechanism,** action, appurtenances, assembly, clockwork, movement, parts, rig, subassembly, works; **motor,** motor drive, prime mover, servo, servomechanism, servomotor; **plant,** assembly line, enginery, equipment, machinery, tooling; **simple machine,** inclined plane, screw, wedge, wheel and axle; **lever,** crow, crowbar, jemmy, pinch-bar; **winch,** block and tackle, burton, capstan, cat *(Naut.)*, coffee grinder *(Naut.)*, deadeye *(Naut.)*, garnet, headgear *(Mining)*, jeer, luff tackle, parbuckle, pulley, sheave, sheave-block *(Naut.)*, snatch block, wharve, whim, whip, winder, windlass; **waterwheel,** water-motor, watermill, windmill; **automaton,** auto, automatic, humanoid, robot
machine *n* → agency
machine-gun *n* → gun
machinery *n* → **1** machine **2** operation **3** stage
machismo *n* → **1** manliness **2** show **3** strength
macho *n* → **1** show-off **2** strong person *adj* **3** male **4** showy **5** strong
mackintosh *n* → **1** raincoat **2** textiles
macramé *n* → lace
macrobiotic *adj* → wholesome
macrocosm *n* → **1** matter **2** sky **3** surroundings
MAD *adj* barmy, barmy as a bandicoot, bats, batty, bonkers, certifiable, certified, crack-brained, cracked, crackers, crackpot, crazed, crazy, cuckoo, daffy, daft, demented, deranged, dilly, dingbats, dotty, far gone, frantic *(Archaic)*, gaga, gonzo, insane, kinky, loco *(U.S.)*, loony, loopy, lunatic, luny, mad as a cut snake, mad as a gumtree full of galahs, mad as a hatter, mad as a March hare, mad as a meataxe, madding, maniac, maniacal, manic, mental, moonstruck, non compos, nuts, nutty, nutty as a fruitcake, odd, off one's block, off one's face, off one's head, off one's nut, off one's onion, off one's pannikin, off one's rocker, off one's saucer, off one's scone, off one's tile, off one's trolley, off the air, off the beam, off the rails, off the wall, off-centre, original, out of one's head, out of one's mind, out of one's tree, over the edge, peculiar, porangi *(N.Z.)*, potty, psycho, queer, round the bend, round the twist, schizo, screwed up, soft in the head, starkers, strange, troppo, unbalanced, unhinged, up the pole, wrong in the head, yarra; **frenzied,** beresk, berko, berserk, beside oneself, distraught, frantic, frenetic, maddened, maddening, possessed, rabid, uncontrollable, violent
mad *adj* → **1** angry **2** celebratory **3** enthusiastic **4** excited **5** ferocious **6** foolish **7** rash
madam *n* → **1** Ms **2** prostitute
MADDEN *v* craze, dement, derange, frenzy, loco *(U.S.)*, overthrow *(Obs.)*, turn someone's mind, unbalance
made *adj* → **1** fortunate **2** sexy **3** successful
MADNESS *n* craziness, daftness, derangement, franticness *(Archaic)*, insaneness, insanity, looniness, lunacy, queerness, rage *(Obs.)*, strangeness, unbalance, unreason, unsoundness of mind, wildness; **nervous breakdown,** mental illness, mental instability; **delirium,** deliration, deliriousness, hallucination, morbidity, morbidness, raving; **mental flaw,** aberration, crack; **brainstorm,** fit, frenzy, pink fit; **craze,** mania, obsession
MAD PERSON *n* basket case, bedlamite *(Archaic)*, crackbrain, crackpot, demoniac, dingbat, energumen, fruit cake, loco *(U.S.)*, loony, lunatic, luny, madman, madwoman, maenad, maniac, nut, nutter, odd bod, phrenetic, psycho, schizo, schizoid, schizophrenic
madrigal *n* → **1** poetry **2** song
maelstrom *n* → **1** current **2** muddle **3** spin **4** violent outburst
maestro *n* → **1** conductor **2** expert **3** mister
MAGAZINE *n* annals, annual, bimonthly, bulletin, dreadful, fanzine, fashion journal, fashion magazine, fortnightly, girlie magazine, glossy, house journal, house magazine, illustrated, journal, monthly, periodical, pictorial, publication, quarterly, review, semimonthly, semiyearly, slick *(U.S.)*, trade journal, trade magazine, weekly; **issue,** back number, back-run, number; **serial,** continuation, instalment, part, sequel
magazine *n* → **1** ammunition **2** arsenal **3** case **4** film **5** storehouse
maggot *n* → **1** animal offspring **2** caprice
MAGIC *n* alchemy, bewitchery, bewitchment, black art, black magic, conjuration, diablerie, diabolism, enchantment, fetishism, glamour, hoodoo, kadaicha magic *(Aborig.)*, sorcery, sortilege, sympathetic magic

thaumaturgy, theurgy, voodoo, white magic, witchcraft, witchery, witching, wizardry; **prestidigitation,** legerdemain, pass, sleight of hand

MAGIC *adj* magical, mystic, sorcerous, thaumaturgic, theurgic, theurgical, witching, wizard, wizardly; **alchemical,** alchemic, alchemistic, alchemistical; **voodooistic,** fetishistic, talismanic

magic *n* → **1** allure **2** the supernatural *adj* **3** alluring

magician *n* → bewitcher

MAGIC SPELL *n* hex, mozz, spell; **incantation,** abracadabra, hocus-pocus, hokey-pokey, mumbo jumbo; **charm,** amulet, fetish, grigri, juju, obeah, obi, phylactery *(Archaic),* talisman; **wand,** Aladdin's lamp, black cat, broomstick, kadaicha shoes *(Aborig.),* kurdaitcha shoes *(Aborig.),* magic carpet, philosopher's stone, witch's cauldron; **magic potion,** philtre, potion; **crystal ball,** mirror *(Archaic)*; **pentagram,** magic circle, magic square

magisterial *adj* → **1** powerful **2** presumptuous

magistrate *n* → judge

magma *n* → **1** medication **2** pulp **3** sludge

magnanimous *adj* → **1** forgiving **2** unselfish

magnate *n* → **1** famous person **2** important person **3** member of parliament **4** wealthy person

magnet *n* → **1** allurer **2** attractor **3** desideratum

magnetic tape *n* → sound system

magnification *n* → **1** copy **2** increase **3** reflection

magnificent *adj* → **1** beautiful **2** generous **3** good **4** superior

magnify *v* → **1** approve **2** emphasise **3** exaggerate **4** increase **5** worship

magnitude *n* → **1** astronomic point **2** importance **3** number **4** size

magnum *n* → bottle

magpie *n* → **1** Australian **2** bull artist **3** gatherer **4** imitator **5** talker

maharaja *n* → mister

mahogany *n* → **1** timber *adj* **2** brown **3** red

maid *n* → **1** adolescent **2** servant **3** woman

maiden *n* → **1** adolescent **2** woman *adj* **3** new

maiden name *n* → name

mail *n* → **1** armour **2** train *v* **3** secure **4** send a message

maim *n* → **1** injury *v* **2** injure

main *n* → **1** contest **2** land **3** piping **4** sea **5** strength **6** violent outburst **7** wire *adj* **8** important **9** most **10** strong

mainland *n* → land

mainstay *n* → important person

maintain *v* → **1** assert **2** equip **3** protract

maintenance *n* → **1** allowance **2** charity **3** continuation **4** divorce **5** payment **6** supply

maize *n* → yellow

majesty *n* → **1** aristocracy **2** aristocrat **3** reputability

major *n* → **1** course **2** subject matter *adj* **3** aged **4** important

majority *n* → **1** age **2** entitlement **3** much **4** part **5** score *adj* **6** most

MAKE *v* compound, do, effect, effectuate, fashion, form, generate, mould, prepare, produce, set, shape, synthesise, work; **construct,** build, erect, fabricate, forge, frame, knock together, knock up, make up, manufacture, mock up, prefabricate, raise, turn out, whip up; **constitute,** compose, form, make up. *See also* CREATE

make *n* → **1** amount **2** character **3** finished product **4** structure *v* **5** accomplish **6** allure **7** arrive **8** be timely **9** build **10** cause **11** combine **12** compute **13** employ **14** flow **15** force **16** have sex **17** order **18** write

MAKE AN EFFORT *v* bend the bow, exert oneself, keep at it, pull one's weight, put one's shoulder to the wheel, roll up one's sleeves, take the labouring oar, tax oneself; **spare no effort,** bend over backwards, burst one's boiler, bust a gut, bust one's boiler, do all in one's power, do all one can, do one's darnedest, do one's utmost, do or die, do the best one can, fall over backwards, go all out, go eyes out, go out of one's way, go to great lengths, lean over backwards, leave no stone unturned, move heaven and earth, pull out all the stops, sink or swim; **work at,** beaver away at, belabour *(Obs.),* buckle down to, buckle into, bullock at, cope with, elaborate, get stuck into, grapple with, have the bit between one's teeth, hoe into, hop into, knuckle down to, lay out to, pitch into, plough into, put one's back into, stick to, take to, turn to, wade into; **toil,** burn the midnight oil, do double duty, drudge, graft, grind, grub, keep one's nose to the grindstone, labour, lucubrate, moil, outwork, plod, plug, slave, slog, sweat blood, tiger, tug, work, work day and night, work like a dog, work like a galley slave, work like a horse, work like a Trojan, work like Jacky, work one's guts out, work one's slot out; **take pains,** agonise over; **battle,** scrabble, scramble, scrimmage, scuffle, strive, struggle; **get moving,** bestir oneself, get cracking, pull one's finger out, pull one's socks up, set to, strike a blow

MAKE DO *v* adapt, extemporise, improvise, shift, think on one's feet; **take advantage of,** be in the right place at the right time, benefit, clean up, fall back on, find a loophole, fish in troubled waters, get mileage out of, jockey, make a good thing out of, make the best of, make the most of, profit, resort to, seize an opportunity, strike while the iron is hot, turn to one's advantage; **make every post a winning post,** climb on the bandwagon, get with the strength; **play a waiting game,** bide one's time, trim; **connive,** arrange, contrive, intrigue, plot, wangle, wriggle

MAKEFAST *n* anchorage, dolphin, moorage, moorings; **bollard,** bitt, post, timberhead

MAKE HAPPY *v* elate, elevate, enliven, exhilarate, glad *(Archaic),* gladden, hearten, jollify, revive

MAKE HISTORY *v* go down in history, hit the headlines, make a noise in the world, make one's mark, raise one's head, set the world on fire; **star,** blaze, resound, shine

MAKE INFERTILE *v* exhaust, impoverish, overcrop; **sterilise,** castrate, fix, geld, neuter, spay

MAKE PEACE *v* bury the hatchet, come to terms with, compromise, hold out the olive branch, make it up, make up, negotiate terms, patch up a quarrel, shake hands, turn swords into ploughshares; **pacify,** bring peace, bring to terms, bring to the table, demilitarise, denuclearise, disarm, offer the hand of peace, pacificate, quiet, quieten, reconcile, restore harmony, temper *(Obs.)*; **appease,** assuage, becalm, defuse, gentle *(Rare)*, mollify, pour oil on troubled waters, subdue, tranquillise; **retreat,** turn the other cheek, withdraw; **be at peace,** keep the peace, live in harmony

MAKE PLEASANT *v* dulcify, please, sauce, sweeten, zest

MAKE POSSIBLE *v* afford, allow, capacitate, enable, permit

makeshift *n* → **1** expedient *adj* **2** expedient **3** impermanent

MAKE UNHAPPY *v* break the heart of, distress, grieve, harrow, hurt, rend the heart of, upset; **depress,** dash, deject, get someone down, sadden; **darken,** cloud, dampen, gloom, oppress

make up *v* → **1** account **2** be penitent **3** create **4** make **5** make peace **6** mediate **7** prepare

make-up *n* → **1** character **2** cosmetics **3** dye **4** making **5** order **6** structure

MAKE WHOLE *v* complement, fill, fill a gap, fill in, fill out, make good, round off, supplement; **integrate,** piece together, synthesise, synthetise, totalise; **complete,** accomplish, consummate, finish, perfect, perform *(Obs.)*, put the finishing touches; **follow through,** carry through, explore every avenue, follow up, go the whole hog, go through with, tie up the loose ends; **finalise,** clench, clinch, close, come full circle, settle; **mature,** flower, fulfil

MAKING *n* building, construction, contrivance, crystallisation, development, elaboration, erection, fabrication, facture, fashion *(Obs.)*, formation, manufacture, manufacturing, output, prefabrication, preparation, production, synthesis, synthesisation, turning, turnout, twinning *(Crystall.)*, working; **structure,** composition, constitution, construction, make-up, reconstruction. *See also* CREATION

malady *n* → illness

malapropism *n* → **1** bungle **2** error **3** figure of speech **4** grammatical error **5** joke **6** word

malcontent *n* → **1** complainer **2** revolutionary *adj* **3** discontented **4** revolutionary

MALE *adj* gentlemanly, he, positive, yang; **masculine,** macho, manlike, manly, potent, virile; **bull,** buck, hunky, stag, well-endowed, well-hung; **mannish,** amazonian, butch, unfeminine, unwomanly; **boyish,** coltish; **homosexual,** camp, effeminate, gay, high-camp

male *n* → **1** man **2** sex *adj* **3** sexual

malefactor *n* → immoral person

malevolent *adj* → **1** bad **2** unfriendly **3** unkind

malformation *n* → distortion

malice *n* → **1** hate **2** ill will

malign *v* → **1** slander *adj* **2** bad

malignant *adj* → **1** dangerous **2** deadly **3** unkind

malinger *v* → pretend

mall *n* → **1** road **2** shop

malleable *adj* → **1** soft **2** variable

mallee *n* → **1** plant **2** remote place

mallet *n* → **1** club **2** timber

MALNUTRITION *n* avitaminosis, beri-beri, chlorosis, deficiency disease, kwashiorkor, marasmus, milk fever, pellagra, rickets, scurvy

malpractice *n* → **1** crime **2** misbehaviour **3** misuse **4** wrong

malt *n* → **1** beer *v* **2** brew

maltreat *v* → **1** act unkindly **2** ill-treat

mama *n* → parent

Mammon *n* → **1** immoral person **2** wealth

mammoth *adj* → **1** big **2** enormous

MAN *n* brave, he, husband, male; **mankind,** menfolk; **bloke,** bastard, bugger, chap, chappie, codger, coot, cove, cully *(Archaic)*, dandy, dog, dude *(U.S.)*, feller, fellow, geezer, guy, hombre, jack, johnny, joker, scout, skate *(U.S.)*, snoozer *(Obs.)*, tomcat, wallah, whoreson *(Obs.)*; **he-man,** alf, apeman, bronzed Aussie, bull, butch, caveman, jock, macho man, male chauvinist, male chauvinist pig, MCP, ocker, rugger-bugger; **buck,** blade, blood, bodgie, homo, lair, lout, son of a gun, stag, Teddy Bear; **a good sort,** hunk, spunk, stud; **gentleman,** gent, rye, squire; **lad,** boy, bucko, colt, cub, gossoon *(Irish)*, jackanapes, nipper, urchin, youth; **sissy,** aunty, dude *(U.S.)*, eunuch, gussie, lily, little Lord Fauntleroy, milksop, nancy boy, old woman, pansy, ponce, wimp; **homosexual,** camp, faggot, gay, poonce, pork 'n bean, queen

man *n* → **1** butler **2** friend **3** humanity **4** mister **5** servant **6** subject *v* **7** defend **8** strengthen

manacle *n* → **1** restraints *v* **2** imprison **3** restrain

MANAGE *v* administer, administrate, be in charge of, carry on, conduct, direct, handle, keep in order, overlook, oversee, run, see to, steward, superintend, supervise; **control,** be in the chair, govern, guide, head, head a team, lead, preside over, steer, take over, take the reins; **domineer,** boss *(Colloq.)*; **sweat,** drive; **organise,** get up, mastermind, package *(Finance)*; **manage one's resources,** economise, husband

manage *v* → **1** control **2** operate **3** persuade

MANAGEMENT *n* admin, administration, dispensation *(Theol.)*, economy, government, organisation; **supervision,** conduct, direction, handling, intendance, intendancy, oversight, running, superintendence, superintendency, surveillance; **managership,** chairmanship, chairpersonship, commission, superintendentship, supervisorship; **housekeeping,** economy *(Archaic)*, housewifery, husbandry, ménage; **bureaucracy,** apparatus, board, body corporate, bureau, directorate, umbrella organisation *(Comm.)*

anagement *n* → **1** operation **2** operator

ANAGER *n* administrator, adminstratrix, bureaucrat, burgrave, commissar, commissary, commissioner, comptroller, controller, curator, director, director-general, directress, directrix, dispensator, engineer, entrepreneur, executive, executor, functionary, governor, Grand Master, head, inspector, inspector-general, intendant, manageress, master, monitor, office-bearer, officer, president, principal, procurator, secretary-general, super, superintendent, supervisor, surveillant, taskmaster, taskmistress; **boss,** boss cocky, chief, employer, gaffer, pannikin boss, slavedriver, sweater *(Colloq.)*, two-bob boss; **overseer,** charge hand, forelady, foreman, foreperson, forewoman, headman, supervisor; **official,** agent, dignitary, silvertail, vizier; **master,** lord, matriarch, mistress, padrone *(U.S.)*, patriarch, patron; **housekeeper,** bailiff, castellan, chamberlain, chatelaine, factor, housewife, land agent *(Brit.)*, major-domo, manciple *(Brit.)*, matron, park ranger, ranger, reeve *(Hist.)*, seneschal, steward; **hotelier,** innkeeper, motelier, publican, restauranteur, restaurateur. *See also* LEADER

anager *n* → boss

ANAGERIAL *adj* administrative, bureaucratic, directorial, dispensational, entrepreneurial, executive, governmental, hegemonic, organisational, superintendent, supervisory, surveillant

ANCHESTER *n* dry goods, lingerie *(Archaic)*, mercery, napery, piece goods, soft goods; **drape,** arras, curtain, drapery, runner, tapestry; **soft furnishings,** curtains, drapes, hangings, upholstery; **upholstery fabric,** chintz, frisé, madras muslin, tabaret; **carpet,** Aubusson carpet, Axminster carpet, hooked rug, Wilton carpet

andarin *n* → **1** bureaucrat **2** ruler

andate *n* → **1** authority **2** command **3** contract **4** nation *v* **5** authorise

andatory *adj* → **1** commanding **2** necessary

ane *n* → **1** animal's coat **2** hair

angle *n* → **1** drier **2** press *v* **3** cut **4** injure **5** press

anhandle *v* → **1** be violent **2** transport

anhole *n* → opening

ania *n* → **1** desire **2** madness **3** psychic disorder **4** psychic disturbance

aniac *n* → **1** mad person *adj* **2** mad **3** psychologically disturbed

anifest *n* → **1** list **2** public notice **3** record *v* **4** authenticate **5** display **6** record *adj* **7** apparent **8** blatant **9** obvious

anifesto *n* → public notice

manifold *n* → **1** copy *v* **2** copy *adj* **3** different **4** many

manipulate *v* → **1** arrange **2** beguile **3** change **4** medicate **5** persuade **6** touch

mankind *n* → **1** humanity **2** man

MANLINESS *n* animus, gentlemanliness, machismo, maleness, manhood, mannishness, masculineness, masculinity, unfeminineness, virtue *(Obs.)*; **virility,** manly vigour, potency, virileness; **male chauvinism,** male supremacy, masculism, paternalism; **boyishness,** coltishness

mannequin *n* → portrait

manner *n* → **1** affectation **2** behaviour **3** character **4** custom **5** method **6** pose

mannered *adj* → **1** affected **2** courteous

mannerism *n* → **1** affectation **2** behaviour **3** characteristic

manoeuvre *n* → **1** action **2** stratagem *v* **3** keep secret **4** wage war

manor *n* → **1** house **2** real estate

manse *n* → **1** church **2** house

mansion *n* → **1** dwelling **2** moon

manslaughter *n* → killing

mantelpiece *n* → shelf

mantle *n* → **1** cloak **2** covering **3** fuel **4** layer **5** shelf *v* **6** bubble **7** cover **8** hide **9** redden

manual *n* → **1** car **2** reference book *adj* **3** brachial

manufacture *n* → **1** finished product **2** making *v* **3** make

manure *n* → **1** dung *v* **2** fertilise

manuscript *n* → **1** book **2** model **3** writing **4** written composition *adj* **5** authorial

MANY *n* a big mob, a good few, a good many, a great many, a hatful, a heap, loads, lot, lots *(Colloq.)*, mass, more than one can poke a stick at, more than one can shake a stick at, myriad, pile, quite a few, some few, stacks, tons; **crowd,** army, array, battalion, bevy, cloud, fleet, flock, forest, hive, horde, host, legion, mob, multitude, power *(Colloq.)*, ruck, swarm, throng, tribe, troop; **numbers,** billions, dozens, hundreds, millions, quintillions, scores, thousands, zillions

MANY *adj* any number of, biggest mobs of *(Colloq.)*, bulk, considerable, countless, innumerable, multiple, multiplex, multiplicate, numerous, plural, pluralist, umpteen, uncounted, untold, various; **multifarious,** all-round, manifold, many-sided; **abounding,** abundant, affluent, ample, aplenty, copious, easy *(Comm.)*, plenteous, plentiful, profuse, prolific, rife, superabundant; **teeming,** alive with, aswarm, crawling with, crowded, legion, multitudinous *(Poetic)*, populous, stiff with, thick with

MAP *v* blueprint, chart, contour, diagram, diagrammatise, draft, outline, plat *(U.S.)*, plot, protract, represent, schematise, trace. *See also* DIAGRAM

map *n* → diagram

maple *n* → **1** timber *adj* **2** brown

marathon *n* → **1** race *adj* **2** distant

maraud *n* → **1** robbery *v* **2** rob

MARBLE *n* acker *(S.A.)*, agate, aggie, alley, bottler, bottley, connie, doog, fat, glassy, peewee, taw

marble *n* → **1** sculpture **2** smooth object *adj* **3** callous **4** cold **5** hard

mare *n* → **1** devil **2** moon

margarine *n* → fat

margin *n* → **1** edge **2** equal **3** income **4** liberty **5** more **6** remnant **7** surplus *v* **8** edge **9** explain **10** insert

MARIJUANA *n* bhang, cannabis, dope, ganja, grass, hemp, Indian hemp, kef, kif, Mary Jane, pot, shit, tea, the herb, the weed; **hash,** hashish; **hash oil,** THC; **joint,** jay, log, number, reefer, roach, scoob, stick. *See also* DRUG

marina *n* → harbour

marinade *n* → **1** wetting *v* **2** wet

marinate *v* → **1** cook **2** wet

marine *n* → **1** armed forces **2** painting **3** seaman **4** watercraft *adj* **5** nautical **6** resident **7** sea

MARINER *n* boatie, hearty, jack, lascar, matelot, raftsman, sailor, salt, sea-dog, seafarer, shellback, shipman *(Archaic)*, shipmate, submariner, tar, tarpaulin *(Rare)*; **ship's crew,** company, complement, crew, ship; **navy,** mercantile marine, merchant marine, merchant navy, senior service; **yachtsman,** rock-hopper, sailor, windsurfer, yachtswoman, yachty, yottie; **windjammer,** reefer, sheethand; **ferryman,** bargee, boatman, bumboatman, gondolier, lighterman, wherryman; **oarsman,** bow, bow oar, bowhand, bowman, canoeist, galley slave, oar, paddler, punter, rower, sculler, stroke, waterman; **rowing crew,** bank, eight, four. *See also* SEAMAN

marionette *n* → **1** portrait **2** puppet

MARITAL *adj* concubinary, conjugal, connubial, matrimonial; **nuptial,** bridal, epithalamic, hymeneal, postnuptial, spousal; **wifely,** matronly, uxorial; **bigamous,** digamous, endogamous, exogamic, exogamous, leviratic, leviratical, monandrous, monogamistic, monogamous, polyandrous, polygamous, polygynous

maritime *adj* → sea

MARK *v* chalk, chalk up, direct, dot, hatch, mark up, overscore, pencil, red-pencil, rule, score, touch, underline, underscore, write; **check,** check off, cross, cross off, record, tally, tick, tick off; **punctuate,** accent, accentuate, dagger, hyphenate, hyphenise, lemmatise, obelise, point, star, subscribe, superscribe

mark *n* → **1** abdomen **2** aim **3** characteristic **4** depth **5** importance **6** judgment **7** reputation **8** sign **9** title *v* **10** attend to **11** class **12** cut off **13** label **14** particularise **15** reveal

marked *adj* → visible

market *n* → **1** cost **2** shop **3** trade *v* **4** buy **5** sell **6** trade

marksman *n* → **1** fighter **2** signer

maroon *n* → **1** ethnic **2** red **3** signal **4** solitary *v* **5** abandon **6** separate *adj* **7** red

marquee *n* → shelter

MARRIAGE *n* conjugal bliss, conjugalit connubiality, matrimony, unitedness, we ded bliss, wedlock; **wifehood,** matronag wifedom, wifeliness; **match,** alliance, unio **mismatch,** mésalliance, misalliance, mi marriage; **type of marriage,** endogamy, e ogamy, group marriage, levirate, sororat **arranged marriage,** mariage de convenanc marriage of convenience, morganatic ma riage; **de facto marriage,** cohabitatio common-law marriage, companionate ma riage, concubinage, living in sin, trial ma riage; **mixed marriage,** intermarriage, mi cegenation; **remarriage,** deuterogamy; **lo match; bigamy,** digamy, monandry, mono amy, monogyny, polyandry, polygamy, pc ygyny. *See also* WEDDING

marriage *n* → **1** mixture **2** relation

MARRIAGEABILITY *n* eligibilit marriageableness, nubility

MARRIED *adj* hitched, hooked, one, splice united, wedded

marrow *n* → **1** centre **2** durability **3** essen **4** inside **5** living

MARRY *v* espouse, make an honest woma of, take to wife, wed, wive *(Rare)*; **get ma ried,** become one, go off, settle down; **elop** run away; **pair off,** ally with, cohabit, matc mate, set up housekeeping; **intermarry,** mi cegenate; **remarry,** commit bigamy; **propos** offer, pop the question; **betroth,** affianc contract matrimony, engage, hook, lead the altar, precontract, promise, win; **join marriage,** conjugate *(Obs.)*, declare man an wife, hitch, join, splice, tie, tie the kno unite; **give in marriage,** give away, marry o

marry *v* → **1** interact **2** join *interj* **3** oh

marsh *n* → **1** sludge **2** stream **3** swamp

marshal *n* → **1** policeman *v* **2** emblemati **3** tidy **4** wage war

mart *n* → shop

MARTIAL *adj* amazonian, combatan combative, filibusterous, pugilistic, pugn cious, warlike; **soldierly,** soldierlike

martial *adj* → warlike

martinet *n* → strict person

martyr *n* → **1** holy person **2** unhappy perso **3** unselfish person **4** victim

marvel *v* → wonder

marvellous *adj* → **1** astonishing **2** good

mascara *n* → **1** cosmetics **2** dye **3** powder

mascot *n* → lucky charm

masculine *adj* → **1** male **2** strong

mash *n* → **1** lover **2** pulp *v* **3** flirt **4** mix **5** pu

mask *n* → **1** armour **2** disguise **3** dram **4** headband **5** party **6** portrait *v* **7** cove **8** hide **9** hinder

masochism *n* → **1** pain **2** psychic disord **3** sexuality

mason *n* → **1** builder *v* **2** build

Mason *n* → member

masquerade *n* → **1** costume **2** disguis **3** party *v* **4** hide **5** pretend

mass *n* → **1** accumulation **2** many **3** matte **4** much **5** part **6** prayer **7** shapelessness **8** so id body *v* **9** abound **10** gather

MASSACRE *n* battue, bloodbath, butchery, carnage, holocaust, shambles, slaughter; **genocide,** ethnocide, race murder; **purge,** decimation, depopulation, pogrom. *See also* KILLING

MASSACRE *v* butcher, cut down, cut to pieces, mow down, put to the sword, slaughter; **purge,** annihilate, commit genocide, decimate, depopulate, exterminate, liquidate, wipe out. *See also* KILL

massacre *n* → **1** act of war **2** victimisation *v* **3** victimise

massage *n* → **1** medical treatment **2** rubbing **3** touch *v* **4** medicate **5** touch

masseur *n* → healer

massive *adj* → **1** astonishing **2** big **3** enormous **4** heavy

master *n* → **1** boss **2** children **3** expert **4** judge **5** manager **6** model **7** owner **8** seaman **9** teacher **10** winner **11** wise person *v* **12** defeat **13** excel **14** learn *adj* **15** accomplished **16** authoritative **17** predominant

mastermind *n* → **1** creator **2** leader **3** wise person *v* **4** beguile **5** manage **6** plan

masterpiece *n* → **1** good thing **2** important thing **3** the best **4** work of art

masticate *v* → **1** eat **2** pulp

masturbate *v* → eroticise

masturbation *n* → sexuality

mat *n* → **1** cloak **2** frame **3** hair **4** tangle *v* **5** edge **6** interlace **7** scold **8** tangle

matador *n* → **1** fighter **2** killer

match *n* → **1** contest **2** copy **3** cord **4** equal **5** equivalent **6** lighter **7** marriage **8** similar thing **9** two *v* **10** adjust **11** be similar **12** copy **13** counteract **14** double **15** equal **16** equalise **17** fit **18** join **19** marry

mate *n* → **1** friend **2** mister **3** partner **4** servant **5** similar thing **6** spouse *v* **7** defeat **8** fit **9** join **10** marry **11** partner

material *n* → **1** information **2** matter **3** textiles *adj* **4** fundamental **5** important **6** tangible

MATERIALISE *v* body forth, embody, incarnate, objectify, objectivise, reify, substantialise; **crystallise,** degrade, fix, fractionate, neutralise

materialise *v* → appear

maternity *n* → **1** kinship *adj* **2** pregnant

MATHEMATICAL *adj* algebraic, arithmetic, geometric, geometrical, trigonometric, trigonometrical; **statistical,** demographic; **computable,** calculable, countable, enumerable, integrable, numerable

MATHEMATICIAN *n* algebraist, arithmetician, geometrician; **statistician,** actuary, demographer, demographist; **counter,** computer, estimator, figurer, integrator, numerator, scorer, tallier, teller

MATHEMATICS *n* algebra, analytical geometry, analytics, arithmetic, binary arithmetic, calculus, combinatorial analysis, coordinate geometry, differentiation, Euclidean geometry, floating point arithmetic, geometry, higher mathematics, infinitesimal calculus, integral calculus, maths, number theory, quadratics, quaternions, relaxation, set theory, theoretical arithmetic, trigonometry; **applied mathematics,** biometrics, biometry, Boolean algebra, computational linguistics, critical-path analysis, dead reckoning, factor analysis, Fourier analysis, mathematical logic, mensuration, Monte Carlo method, numerical analysis, statistics

maths *n* → mathematics

matinee *n* → performance

matriarch *n* → **1** manager **2** old people **3** ruler

matriculate *n* → **1** pupil *v* **2** list

matriculation *n* → examination

matrimony *n* → marriage

matrix *n* → **1** essence **2** jewel **3** model **4** order **5** printing press **6** shape

matron *n* → **1** healer **2** manager **3** woman

matted *adj* → **1** dull **2** rough **3** tangled

MATTER *n* antimatter, material, stuff, substance; **mass,** block, body, concrete; **grain,** crystal, granule, micron, particle, sand, seed crystal; **thing,** anything, article, doodackie *(N.Z.)*, doodah, doofer, doohickie, doover, dooverlackie, object, phenomenon, something, thingummybob, thingummyjig, wigwam for a goose's bridle; **the tangible,** being, concreteness, corporality, corporeality, corporealness, corporeity, earthliness, embodiment, existence, fleshliness, materialisation, materiality, materialness, naturalness, palpability, substantiality, substantiation, tangibility; **cosmos,** creation, macrocosm, nature, plenum, universe, world

matter *n* → **1** accusation **2** affair **3** amount **4** bodily discharge **5** cause **6** difficulty **7** evidence **8** importance **9** meaning *v* **10** be important **11** excrete

matter-of-fact *adj* → **1** forthright **2** realistic **3** simple

mattock *n* → **1** digging implement **2** piercer

mattress *n* → bed

mature *v* → **1** age **2** make whole **3** perfect **4** prepare **5** taste *adj* **6** aged **7** unwholesome **8** whole

maudlin *adj* → **1** drunk **2** emotional **3** unhappy

maul *n* → **1** club *v* **2** ill-treat **3** separate

mausoleum *n* → grave

mauve *n* → **1** purple *adj* **2** purple

maw *n* → **1** abdomen **2** mouth **3** neck

mawkish *adj* → **1** emotional **2** nauseous

maxim *n* → **1** proverb **2** rule

maximise *v* → increase

maximum *n* → **1** fullness **2** much *adj* **3** most

may *v* → be permitted to

maybe *adv* → possibly

mayhem *n* → **1** act of war **2** fight **3** harm

mayor *n* → member of parliament

maze *n* → **1** muddle **2** tangle *v* **3** confuse

mead *n* → **1** drink **2** farmland **3** field

meadow *n* → **1** farmland **2** field **3** grassland

meagre *adj* → **1** deficient **2** insufficient **3** small **4** thin

MEAL *n* agape, banquet, barbecue, barby, blow-out, buffet, chew-'n'-spew, clambake, collation, cookout *(U.S.)*, feast, feed, gorge, hangi *(N.Z.)*, junket, kai, love feast, luau, mess, midnight feast, nosh-up, picnic, refection, regale, repast, short order *(U.S.)*, smorgasbord, spread, table d'hôte, tuck-in, TV dinner; **snack,** afternoon tea, bite, coffee break, continental breakfast, crib, Devonshire tea, elevenses *(Brit. Colloq.)*, little lunch, morning piece *(W.A.)*, morning tea, munchies, nibble, nosh, playlunch, refreshment, scroggin; **breakfast,** brekkie, brunch, bush breakfast, déjeuner, wedding breakfast; **lunch,** big lunch, counter lunch, cut-lunch, fork luncheon, luncheon, oslo lunch, packed lunch, ploughman's lunch *(Brit.)*, pub lunch, tiffin *(India)*; **dinner,** din-din, din-dins, dinnies, fork dinner, high tea *(Brit.)*, progressive dinner, supper, tea; **course,** afters, antipasto, dessert, dish, entree, entremets, fork dish, hors d'oeuvre, pièce de résistance, plat du jour, pudding, savoury, side-dish, soupe du jour, starters, sweets. *See also* FOOD

meal *n* → powder

mealy-mouthed *adj* → **1** affected **2** cowardly **3** flattering **4** intolerant

MEAN *v* betoken, connote, denote, designate, express, imply, import, indicate, purport, represent, signify, stand for

MEAN *adj* careful, cheeseparing, churlish, close, close-fisted, mangy, mingy, miserly, near, niggard, niggardly, nigh *(Archaic)*, parsimonious, penny-ante, penny-pinching, penurious, pinchpenny, skimpy, small, stingy, tight, tight-arsed, tight-fisted; **avaricious,** greedy, hard-fisted, hungry, Ikey Mo, iron-fisted, money-grubbing, sordid; **ungenerous,** grudging, illiberal *(Rare)*, shabby, uncharitable, unhandsome. *See also* MISER; BE MISERLY

mean *n* → **1** average **2** centre *v* **3** signify *adj* **4** angry **5** bad **6** capable **7** inferior **8** mediocre **9** meek **10** ordinary **11** pestering **12** smallest **13** ugly **14** unkind **15** unmanageable **16** wrong

meander *n* → **1** circuitousness **2** decoration *v* **3** flow **4** travel **5** vacillate

MEANING *n* content, drift, effect, force, gist, hang, import, importance *(Obs.)*, intendment *(Law)*, intent, matter, message, point, purport, sense, significance, signification, substance, tenor, the strong of, value; **connotation,** implication, nuance, polysemy; **denotation,** acceptation, application, definition, designation, extension *(Logic)*, indication, signification, usage; **synonymousness,** equivalence, synonymity, synonymy; **ambiguity,** double meaning

meaning *n* → **1** essence *adj* **2** meaningful

MEANINGFUL *adj* pithy, pointed, portentous, pregnant, profound, significant; **connotative,** allusive, evocative, suggestive; **denotative,** designative, explicit, expressive, indicative, meaning, notional, presentive, significative; **synonymous,** equivalent, synonymic, synonymical; **ambiguous,** polysemous; **semantic,** semasiological

MEANINGFULLY *adv* pointedly, portentously, pregnantly, profoundly, significantly

MEANLY *adv* churlishly, mangily, parsimoniously, penuriously, stingily, tightly; **avariciously,** hungrily; **ungenerously,** shabbily, uncharitably, unhandsomely, with a sparing hand

MEANNESS *n* cheeseparing, churlishness, closeness, manginess, miserliness, niggardliness, parsimony, penuriousness, stinginess, tightness; **avarice,** avariciousness, greediness, hungriness, sordidness; **ungenerosity,** illiberality, shabbiness, smallness, uncharitableness, ungenerousness, unhandsomeness

MEANS OF ESCAPE *n* back door, bolthole, Davis apparatus, escape hatch, escape lock, fire-escape, ladder; **loophole,** cop-out, let-out; **vent,** safety-valve. *See also* ESCAPE

MEANS OF KILLING *n* coup de grâce, deathblow, dispatch, quietus; **death warrant,** auto-da-fé, death penalty; **gallows,** bough *(Archaic)*, drop, gibbet, high jump, long drop, rope, rope's end; **guillotine; gas chamber,** Auschwitz, Belsen, Dachau, gas oven; **electric chair,** chair, hot seat; **poison,** arsenic, asphyxiant, cyanide, hemlock, poison cart

means test *n* → examination

MEANWHILE *adv* betweenwhiles, intermediately, meantime, whiles *(Obs.)*

MEASURABLE *adj* assessable, gaugeable, mensurable, quantifiable, rateable, surveyable

MEASURE *v* dial, gauge, mete *(Archaic)*, meter, quantify; **rate,** assess, evaluate, grade, revalue, score; **calibrate; pace,** calliper, cube, fathom, sound, span, step, tape, titrate, walk; **survey,** shoot, triangulate; **scale,** plot, prick off

measure *n* → **1** amount **2** example **3** gradation **4** law **5** limit **6** measurement **7** musical score **8** rhythm *v* **9** graduate **10** quantify

MEASUREMENT *n* admeasurement, measure, mensuration, quantification; **exact science,** metrology; **evaluation,** analysis, rating; **calibration; dimensions,** size, vital statistics; **gauge,** dial, digital readout, instrument, LCD, measure, meter, recording instrument, VU meter

measurement *n* → assessment

MEASURING *adj* dimensional, mensural, mensurative, metrical, quantitative

meat *n* → **1** essence **2** food **3** groin

MECHANICAL *adj* mechanistic, motor, motored, powered; **robotic,** bionic, robotistic; **automatic,** self-acting, self-adjusting, semiautomatic, servo-assisted, servomechanical

mechanical *adj* → **1** tangible **2** unwilling

mechanics *n* → **1** method **2** movement

MECHANISATION *n* automation, automatism, engineering, industrialisation, motorisation, robotism

MECHANISE *v* automate, motorise; **tool up,** gear up

mechanism *n* → **1** machine **2** method
medal *n* → **1** commemoration **2** emblem
medallion *n* → **1** emblem **2** moulding
MEDDLE *v* have a finger in the pie, interfere, intermeddle, mess in, nose about, nose into, poach *(Tennis)*, poke one's nose into, put in, put one's bib in, stick one's bib in, stick one's nose in, sticky-nose, stickybeak, weigh in with; **interrupt,** barge in, bib in, butt in, get a word in edgeways, put one's oar in
media *n* → **1** centre **2** telecommunications
medial *adj* → **1** central **2** ordinary
median *n* → **1** average **2** centre **3** line *adj* **4** central
MEDIATE *v* arbitrate, conciliate, decide, go between, intercede, interpose, intervene, negotiate, umpire; **appease,** compromise *(Obs.)*, propitiate, temporise; **settle,** arrange, bring together, bury the hatchet, compose, heal, make up, pacify, patch things up, pour oil on troubled waters, smooth things over
mediate *adj* → mediatory
MEDIATION *n* arbitrament, arbitration, compromise, conciliation, diplomacy, good offices, healing, intercession, intermediacy, intermediation, interposal, interposition, intervention, negotiation, pacification, propitiation, reconcilement, temporisation, treaty *(Rare)*, troubleshooting; **peace-making ceremony,** armistice, makarrata, parley, treaty, truce; **peace-pipe,** calumet, flag of truce, olive branch, white flag
MEDIATOR *n* arbiter, arbitrator, arbitress, conciliation committee, conciliator, diplomat, diplomatist, firefighter, interceder, intercessor, intermediator, intervener, interventionist, negotiator, propitiator, referee, troubleshooter, ump, umpie, umpire; **reconciler,** healer, paraclete; **compromiser,** temporiser; **intermediary,** go-between, mouthpiece, next friend, proxy
MEDIATORY *adj* arbitral, arbitrational, arbitrative, conciliatory, diplomatic, intercessional, intercessory, intervenient, interventional, mediate, mediative, propitiative, propitiatory, reconciliatory
MEDICAL *adj* biomedical, clinical, doctoral, iatric, paramedic, paramedical, premedical, prosthetic; **Aesculapian,** Galenic, Hippocratic; **allopathic,** homeopathic; **diagnostic,** diacritic; **surgical,** chirurgic, chirurgical, operating, operative, post-operative; **dental,** orthodontic; **medicable,** curable, operable
MEDICAL TREATMENT *n* first aid, intervention, spontaneous cure, therapy, treatment; **nursing,** after-care, care, intensive care, rest cure; **physiotherapy,** manipulation, massage, massotherapy, mechanotherapy, orthoptic exercises, physio; **occupational therapy,** diversionary therapy, O.T.; **speech therapy,** speech pathology; **heat therapy,** diathermy, heliotherapy, insolation, phototherapy, radiothermy, thermotherapy; **hydrotherapy,** hydropathy, pneumatotherapy, water cure; **lavage,** irrigation, toilet, wash-out; **artificial respiration,** kiss of life, mouth-to-mouth resuscitation, resuscitation; **surgery,** ablation, excision; **radiotherapy,** irradiation, X-ray therapy; **immunisation,** auto-immunisation, auto-inoculation, immunotherapy, inoculation, mithridatism, pasteurism, prophylaxis, take, tuberculisation, vaccination, vaccinisation, variolation; **transfusion,** blood transfusion, exchange; **blood-letting,** cupping, phlebotomy, venesection, venipuncture; **transplantation,** grafting, implantation, plastic surgery, skin graft; **dialysis,** haemodialysis; **chemotherapy,** chelation therapy, organotherapy; **electrotherapy,** cardioversion, cataphoresis, defibrillation, faradism, fulguration, galvanism; **hypnotherapy; cauterisation,** cautery, cryocautery, cryosurgery, cryotherapy, electrodessication, electrolysis, hypothermia
MEDICATE *v* dispense, dose, physic, prescribe, treat; **cure,** doctor, heal, nurse, rehabilitate, remedy, restore; **resuscitate,** revive, revivify; **operate,** ablate, amputate, curette, cut, debride, decerebrate, excise, operate on, resect, set, spay; **inoculate,** mithridatise, pasteurise, tuberculise, vaccinate, variolate; **drench,** fog, footrot, spray; **massage,** manipulate, percuss
MEDICATION *n* alterant, alterative *(Obs.)*, curative, drug, medicament, medicine, physic, prescription, specific; **dose,** dosage, draught, drench; **botanical,** herb, simple *(Archaic)*; **adjuvant,** synergist; **materia medica,** pharmacopoeia; **pharmacy,** pharmaceutics, pharmacognosy, pharmacology; **dispensary,** chemist, drug store; **cure,** arcanum, boot *(Obs.)*, bush cure, catholicon, cup, cure-all, faith cure, folk remedy, mithridate *(Obs.)*, nostrum, panacea, placebo, proprietary; **prophylactic,** antiserum, antivenene, preventive, remedy, serum, vaccine; **antidote,** alexipharmic, bezoar *(Obs.)*, counterpoison, theriac, treacle *(Obs.)*; **application,** bath, cold pack, compress, corn plaster, eyewash, fomentation, hot pack, icepack, icebag, mud bath, mustard plaster, poultice, stupe, wash, wet pack; **dressing,** bandage, bandaid, blister plaster, court plaster, diachylon, dossil, elastoplast, frog plaster, lint, plaster, pledget, shin plaster *(U.S. Obs.)*, sticking plaster, swab; **suture,** stitch; **ointment,** abirritant, balm, balsam, cerate, counterirritant, demulcent, emollient, hand cream, inunction, liniment, lotion, magma, salve, unction, unguent; **powder,** fuller's earth, pomander, triturate; **pessary,** bougie, implantation, suppository; **pill,** bolus, cap, capsule, durule, football, pilule, tab, tablet, tabloid, time-release capsule, troche, wafer; **lozenge,** cachou, confection, excipient, masticatory, pastille; **elixir,** decoction, drops, electuary, philtre, potion, ptisan, tincture, tisane; **inhalation,** errhine, vaporisation; **injection,** booster, hypodermic, jab, needle, shot; **sling,** plaster, plaster cast, spica, suspensor, tourniquet; **surgical appliance,** caliper, crutch, or-

thosis, peg leg, prosthesis, truss, wooden leg; **filling,** bridge, cap, crown, inlay

MEDICINAL *adj* curative, healing, panacean, remedial, sanatory, sanitive, therapeutic; **active,** alterant, alterative *(Obs.)*; **antidotal,** alexipharmic, antitoxic, prophylactic, theriacal; **adjuvant,** synergetic, synergic, synergistic; **nervine,** tetanic; **tonic,** roborant; **calmative,** sedative, tranquilising; **endermic,** hypodermic, intravenous, parenteral, topical; **ethical,** magistral, officinal

medicine *n* → **1** healing **2** medication *v* **3** practise medicine

MEDIOCRE *adj* half-pie, indifferent, mean, middling, nothing to boast of, nothing to write home about, undistinguished; **so-so,** average, fifty-fifty, much of a muchness; **tolerable,** fair, fair to middling, goodish, moderate, not bad, not so dusty, passable, unobjectionable; **no great shakes,** minor, not so hot, not too hot, nothing out of the box, of sorts, second-best, second-class, second-rate; **commonplace,** colourless, conventional, mill-run, mundane, nondescript, ordinary, pedestrian, run-of-the-mill; **hackneyed,** common, deja vu, hack, tired, trite; **bourgeois,** middle-of-the-road, middlebrow

mediocre *adj* → ordinary

meditate *v* → **1** aim at **2** assess **3** intend **4** think **5** worship

medium *n* → **1** dwelling **2** method **3** occultist **4** ordinariness **5** surroundings *adj* **6** central **7** ordinary

medley *n* → **1** mixture *adj* **2** mixed

MEEK *adj* abashed, ashamed, browbeaten, cheap, crestfallen, guidable, humbled, lowly, mean, out of countenance, shamefaced, sheepish, small, struck all of a heap; **humble,** abject, flunkeyish, intropunitive, self-critical, self-effacing, servile, submissive, supple, wormlike; **obsequious,** sycophantic, toadyish

meek *adj* → patient

MEEKLY *adv* abjectly, cap in hand, crawlingly, humbly, on bended knee, servilely; **crestfallenly,** ashamedly, ignominiously, shamefacedly, sheepishly, with one's tail between one's legs

MEEKNESS *n* abasement, humbleness, lowliness, resignation, self-abasement, self-effacement, sense of shame, worm's eye view; **humility,** abashment, abjectness, chagrin, cheapness, confusion, crestfallenness, modesty; **servility,** flattery, flunkeyism, obsequiousness, servileness, suppleness, sycophancy, toadyism

meet *n* → **1** contest **2** gathering *v* **3** agree **4** argue **5** associate **6** be sociable **7** contact **8** converge **9** fight **10** gather **11** undergo *adj* **12** apt **13** expedient

MEET AN OBSTACLE *v* back up, baulk at, come up against, refuse, seize, seize up, stick at, stop at

meeting *n* → **1** assignation **2** contact **3** contest **4** convergence **5** crowd **6** gathering **7** legislative body **8** prayer *adj* **9** contacting

MEETING PLACE *n* casino, chapterhouse community centre, community hall

megalith *n* → rock outcrop

megaphone *n* → microphone

megaton *n* → explosion

melancholy *n* → **1** despair **2** sombreness **3** unhappiness *adj* **4** bored **5** despairing **6** sombre **7** unhappy

melanin *n* → **1** brown **2** colour

melee *n* → **1** act of war **2** fight **3** loud sound **4** muddle **5** tangle

meliorate *v* → improve

mellifluous *adj* → **1** musical **2** pleasant

mellow *v* → **1** age **2** improve **3** soften **4** taste *adj* **5** happy **6** musical **7** soft **8** tasty

melodic *adj* → musical

melodious *adj* → musical

melodrama *n* → **1** drama **2** emotion **3** exaggeration

melody *n* → music

melon *n* → **1** fool **2** head **3** stupid person

melt *n* → **1** liquid *v* **2** change **3** disappear **4** fail **5** heat **6** liquefy

MEMBER *n* charter member, clubman clubwoman, committeeman, committeewoman, communitarian; **new member,** entrant initiate; **federator,** federalist, internationalist, leaguer, uniter; **Mason,** Apexian, billy goat rider, communicant, conventicler Freemason, guildsman, Jaycee, Lion, liveryman *(Brit.)*, Oddfellow, Rechabite Rosicrucian, Rotarian, Soroptimist

member *n* → **1** limb **2** part

MEMBER OF PARLIAMENT *n* backbencher congressman, congresswoman, deputy, honourable member, law-maker, legislator legislatress, magnate, Member of the House of Representatives, MHR, MP, oncer, parliamentarian, representative, senator; **alderman,** bailie *(Scot.)*, burgess *(Hist.)*, burgomaster, city father, councillor, lord mayor, mayor, mayoress, provost *(Scot.)*, town councillor; **independent,** crossbencher, freelance, mugwump *(U.S.)*; **minister,** administrator, attorney-general, cabinet minister, foreign secretary *(Brit.)*, frontbencher, member of cabinet, minister without portfolio, postmaster general, secretary, secretary of state *(U.S.)*, shadow minister, speaker, state secretary, statesman, stateswoman, statist *(Obs.)*, treasurer; **prime minister,** P.M., premier; **power behind the throne,** éminence grise, grey eminence; **party whip,** numbers man. *See also* POLITICIAN

membrane *n* → **1** coating **2** skin

MEMENTO *n* keepsake, relic, remembrance, remembrancer, souvenir, token, trophy, **commemoration,** auld lang syne, commemorative, testimonial; **memorial,** cenotaph, chantry, cornerstone, epitaph, foundation stone, pantheon, Tomb of the Unknown Soldier, tombstone, tope, war memorial

memo *n* → reminder

MEMORABLE *adj* catchy, eidetic, haunting, recallable, recognisable, retainable; **unforgotten,** fresh, graven, green, unforgettable

memorable *adj* → important

MEMORABLY *adv* unforgettably; **reminiscently,** nostalgically; **in memoriam,** commemoratively, memorially, pro memoria

memorandum *n* → 1 deed 2 information 3 record 4 reminder

memorial *n* → 1 commemoration 2 grave 3 memento *adj* 4 commemorative 5 past

MEMORISE *v* commit to memory, embalm, etch in one's memory, fix in one's mind, learn; **revise,** refresh one's memory, rub up on; **note,** item, jot, minute; **know by ear,** know by heart, know by rote

memorise *v* → learn

MEMORY *n* collective memory, long-term memory, memory span, recall, retainment, retention, retentiveness, retentivity, short-term memory; **remembrance,** engram, impression, memory, trace *(Psychol.)*; **flashback,** association of ideas, recapture, recurrence; **memoirs,** anecdotes, autobiography, biography, history, memorabilia, reminiscences. *See also* REMEMBERING

memory *n* → 1 computer record 2 memory 3 psyche 4 reputation

MENACE *n* commination, sword of Damocles, threat; **menaces,** intimidation, standover tactics, strongarm methods; **bluster,** defiance, fulmination; **blackmail,** embracery; **gunboat diplomacy,** mailed fist; **war cloud,** dark clouds, gathering clouds, thunder; **fearsomeness,** minaciousness, minacity, ominousness, sinisterness, ugliness

MENACE *v* intimidate, look daggers, look daggers at, overhang, shake the fist at, threaten; **bully,** badger, blackjack, blackmail, bludgeon, bullyrag, do a heavy, heavy, hector, put pressure on, stand over; **bark,** growl, snarl; **bluster,** fulminate, talk big, tell someone what for, thunder; **overawe,** concuss, cow, have under threat; **have hanging over one**

menace *n* → 1 annoyance 2 danger *v* 3 endanger

MENACER *n* bludgeoner, blusterer, bucko, bully, standover man, standover merchant, threatener; **blackmailer,** embraceor

MENACING *adj* baleful, black, comminatory, intimidating, minacious, minatory, Tammany-Hall, threatening, ugly; **foreboding,** boding ill, ominous; **sinister,** slinky, stealthy

MENACINGLY *adv* darkly, minaciously, minatorily, threateningly; **sinisterly,** balefully, uglily; **forebodingly,** bodingly, ominously

mend *n* → 1 improvement 2 repair *v* 3 improve 4 repair

menial *n* → 1 servant *adj* 2 obsequious

menopause *n* → age

menses *n* → 1 bleeding 2 bodily discharge 3 regularity

menstruate *v* → 1 bleed 2 excrete

mensuration *n* → 1 mathematics 2 measurement

MENTAL *adj* cerebral, intellectual, intelligential, noetic, phrenic, psychic, psychobiological, psychological, psychophysiological; **conscious,** apprehensive, cognitive, perceptional, perceptive, percipient, sensible; **intelligent,** clever, intellective, rational, reasonable, sane; **psychogenetic**

mental *adj* → 1 foolish 2 intangible 3 mad

mentality *n* → mind

mention *v* → 1 name 2 speak

mentor *n* → 1 guide 2 teacher

menu *n* → 1 agenda 2 choice

mercenary *n* → 1 fighter 2 self-seeker 3 servant *adj* 4 selfish

merchandise *n* → 1 goods 2 supplies *v* 3 trade

merchant *n* → 1 seller 2 trader

merchant navy *n* → 1 mariner 2 watercraft

merciful *adj* → 1 lenient 2 pitying

merciless *adj* → 1 callous 2 strict 3 unkind

mercurial *adj* → changeable

mercury *n* → messenger

Mercury *n* → heavenly body

mercy *n* → 1 good 2 help 3 lenience 4 pity

mere *n* → 1 club 2 lake *adj* 3 one 4 simple 5 smallest

merge *v* → 1 associate 2 combine 3 join 4 mix

merger *n* → 1 amalgamation 2 combine 3 mixture

meridian *n* → 1 circle 2 line *adj* 3 daily 4 top

merit *n* → 1 goodness *v* 2 deserve

mermaid *n* → 1 mythical being 2 sea nymph

merry *adj* → 1 drunk 2 happy 3 humorous 4 pleasant

merry-go-round *n* → 1 amusement park 2 busyness

mesh *n* → 1 allure 2 interlacement 3 lace 4 stratagem *v* 5 allure 6 contact 7 interlace 8 join *adj* 9 crossed

mesmerise *v* → 1 allure 2 bewitch 3 persuade

mess *n* → 1 barracks 2 dilemma 3 dirt 4 dung 5 food 6 jumble 7 kitchen 8 living room 9 meal 10 muddle 11 paste 12 tangle *v* 13 eat

MESSAGE *n* communication, notification, piece of information, word; **correspondence,** exchange of letters; **letter,** aerogram, air letter, billet-doux, brief *(Obs.)*, communication, covering letter, dead letter, dispatch, encyclical, epistle, express letter, favour *(Obs.)*, love letter, missive, note, writing; **bread-and-butter letter,** follow-up, reply; **card,** lettercard, notelet, postal *(U.S.)*, postal card *(U.S.)*, postcard, Valentine; **circular,** advertisement, bulletin, dodger, form letter, junk mail, open letter, pamphlet, petition, round robin; **telegram,** cable, cablegram, express, gorillagram, heliogram, phonogram, radiotelegram, strippergram, telex, wire; **postal order,** bank draft, money order, postal note; **postal chess,** correspondence chess, postal shoot, postal vote. *See also* MAIL

message *n* → 1 information 2 meaning 3 signal

MESSENGER *n* herald, mercury, officer at arms, orderly, peon, pursuivant; **envoy,** ambassador, legate; **bellboy,** bellhop, callboy, devil, errand boy, gopher, leg man, messenger boy, pageboy *(Brit.)*; **doorman,** commissionaire; **courier,** dispatch bearer, dispatch rider, express, runner; **carrier pigeon,** homing pigeon; **postman,** mail sorter, mailman, postboy, postie *(Colloq.)*, postmaster, postmaster general, postmistress, postrider, telegraph boy; **telegraphist,** telegrapher, wirer

messenger *n* → **1** cord **2** puller

metabolism *n* → change

metal *n* → **1** liquid **2** raw materials *v* **3** work metal

METALLIC *adj* bimetallic, metalline, mineral; **golden,** aureate, auric, aurous, gilded, gilt, gold; **brass,** brassy, brazen; **bronzy; copper,** coppery, cupreous, cupric, cuprous; **iron,** ferric, ferritic, ferrous; **lead,** leaden, plumbeous, plumbic, plumbous; **silver,** argent, argental, argentic, argentine, argentous, lunar, lunarian, silvery; **platinum,** platinic, platinoid; **steel,** steely; **tinny,** stannic, stannous; **zinc,** zincic, zincky, zincous

METALLURGIC *adj* metallurgical, mineralogical, vulcanian; **ductile,** eutectic, eutectoid, forgeable, mitis, self-annealing, self-hardened, self-hardening, weldable

METALWORKER *n* coiner, gilder, metal fabricator, pewterer; **smith,** blacksmith, founder, galvaniser, gold-beater, goldsmith, ironmaster, ironsmith, ironworker, plumber, silversmith, smelter, steelworker, tinman, tinner, tinsmith, welder, whitesmith; **metallurgist,** alchemist, mineralogist

METALWORKS *n* foundry, ironworks, rolling mill, smelter, smithery, smithy, stannary, steelworks, strip mill, tinworks, wireworks; **furnace,** blast furnace, finery, hearth

metamorphosis *n* → **1** change **2** shape

metaphor *n* → **1** figure of speech **2** similarity

metaphysical *adj* → **1** fantastic **2** intangible

mete *n* → **1** limit *v* **2** measure

METEOR *n* bolide, falling star, fireball, shooting star; **meteorite,** meteoroid, siderite, siderolite; **comet,** Halley's comet; **nucleus,** coma, tail, train. *See also* STAR; HEAVENLY BODY

meteor *n* → **1** rainfall **2** weather

meteorite *n* → **1** meteor **2** rock

METEOROLOGIST *n* climatologist, skywonkie, weather forecaster, weatherman

meter *n* → **1** measurement *v* **2** measure

methane *n* → gas

metho *n* → **1** alcohol **2** heavy drinker

METHOD *n* guise, manner, mode, procedure, sort, technics, technique, way, wise *(Archaic)*; **line,** approach, tack; **avenue,** channel, course, highroad, path, road, stepping stone, track; **means,** agent, how, implement, instrument, medium, tool, vehicle, way, ways and means, wherewithal; **process,** mechanics, mechanism, modus operandi, operation; **expedient,** device, gimmick, nostrum; **customary method,** custom, practice, routine, usual way

method *n* → **1** behaviour **2** classification **3** expedient **4** order

methodical *adj* → ordered

methylated spirits *n* → alcohol

meticulous *adj* → precise

metre *n* → **1** figure of speech **2** length

metric *adj* → **1** long **2** poetic

metronome *n* → rhythm

metropolis *n* → city

mettle *n* → **1** characteristics **2** courage **3** pride

mew *n* → **1** animal call **2** hiding place **3** seclusion *v* **4** bare **5** call (of animals) **6** enclose

mews *n* → **1** animal dwelling **2** house **3** pen

mezzanine *n* → storey

microbe *n* → organism

microcosm *n* → **1** humanity **2** small thing

microfiche *n* → **1** photograph **2** record

MICROPHONE *n* bug, hydrophone, mike, radiophone, thermophone; **resonator,** reverberator, sound post, sounding-board; **public-address system,** bullhorn, loudhailer, loudspeaker, megaphone, PA, speaking trumpet, tannoy *(Brit.)*

microphone *n* → radio

microscope *n* → lens

microscopic *adj* → small

midair *adj* → **1** high *adv* **2** high

midday *n* → **1** noon *adj* **2** daily

middle *n* → **1** abdomen **2** centre **3** ordinariness *v* **4** centralise *adj* **5** central **6** intervenient

MIDDLE CLASS *n* bourgeoisie, equites, lower middle class, petite bourgeoisie, professional class, upper middle class; **member of the middle class,** bourgeois, businessman, capitalist, employer, petit bourgeois, professional, rentier, yeoman; **upstart,** nouveau riche, parvenu, social climber

MIDDLE-CLASS *adj* comfortably well-off, non-U, petit-bourgeois, risen from the ranks, untitled, upwardly mobile

middleman *n* → **1** seller **2** trader

middle man *n* → delegate

middling *adj* → **1** healthy **2** mediocre **3** ordinary *adv* **4** ordinarily

middy *n* → **1** alcohol container **2** seaman

midge *n* → small person

midget *n* → small person

midnight *n* → **1** night *adj* **2** dark **3** nightly

midriff *n* → **1** abdomen **2** centre

midshipman *n* → seaman

midst *n* → **1** centre *prep* **2** amid

MIDWIFE *n* accoucheur, accoucheuse, deliverer, gynaecologist, obstetrician

midwife *n* → healer

mien *n* → **1** appearance **2** behaviour **3** character

might *n* → **1** power **2** strength

mighty *adj* → **1** big **2** great **3** powerful **4** strong *adv* **5** very

migraine *n* → ache

migrant *n* → **1** arriver **2** population **3** traveller *adj* **4** resident **5** travelling

migrate *v* → **1** depart **2** travel

mild *n* → **1** beer *adj* **2** bright **3** composed **4** courteous **5** hot **6** insipid **7** kind **8** lenient **9** moderate **10** soft **11** tasty
mildew *n* → **1** dirt *v* **2** get dirty
mile *n* → length
mileage *n* → **1** income **2** length
milestone *n* → indicator
milieu *n* → surroundings
militant *n* → **1** fighter **2** warmonger *adj* **3** aggressive **4** dissident **5** warlike
MILITARISE *v* activate *(U.S.)*, arm, crusade, embattle, mobilise, put on a war footing; **recruit,** call up, conscript; **enlist,** join up; **soldier,** bear arms, campaign, go on active service; **prepare for action,** clear the decks
military *n* → armed forces
MILITARY SERVICE *n* active service, hitch *(U.S. Colloq.)*, soldiering; **recruitment,** call-up, conscription, draft, national service, selective service. *See also* WAR
militia *n* → serviceman
milk *n* → **1** drink **2** white *v* **3** extract **4** farm **5** use
milk tooth *n* → mouth
mill *n* → **1** extractor **2** powderer **3** press **4** pub *v* **5** agitate **6** edge **7** furrow **8** powder **9** press
millennium *n* → **1** anniversary **2** last day **3** pleasantness
milliner *n* → clothier
millionaire *n* → wealthy person
millstone *n* → powderer
mime *n* → **1** comedy **2** gesture *v* **3** gesture **4** perform
mimic *n* → **1** humorist **2** imitator *v* **3** imitate **4** represent *adj* **5** imitative
minaret *n* → **1** church **2** sharp point **3** tower
mince *v* → **1** attitudinise **2** cook **3** cut **4** walk
mincing *adj* → affected
MIND *n* belfry, breast, consciousness, head, headpiece, loaf, psyche, sconce, sentient, skull, upper storey; **intellect,** brains, capacity, faculties, genius, grey matter, intelligence, judgment, lights, mentality, percipience, powers, psychology, rationality, reason, saneness, sanity, sense, thought, understanding, wit, wits
mind *n* → **1** character **2** desire **3** emotion **4** opinion **5** perception **6** soul *v* **7** attend to **8** be cautious **9** care for **10** dislike **11** feel emotion **12** obey **13** remember **14** undertake
MINDER *n* attendant, ayah, baby-sitter, carer, childminder, fosterer, guardian, housefather, housemother, houseparent, keeper, nanny, nurse, parent; **ministrant,** cherisher, mollycoddler; **fusser,** fusspot, old woman
mindful *adj* → **1** attentive **2** careful
mine *n* → **1** diggings **2** excavation **3** explosive **4** factory *v* **5** dig **6** extract **7** hollow
MINER *n* burrower, quarrier, sapper, tunneller; **potholer,** caver, speleologist
miner *n* → **1** digger **2** soldier
MINERAL *n* ore; **reef,** bloom, bushoo, deep ground, deposit, jeweller's shop, ledge, lens, lode, mother lode, ore body, ore shoot, outcrop, pipe, pocket, quartz reef, surface reef, underset, vein, winning; **gold-bearing soil,** alluvial, alluvial cone, alluvial fan, alluvial ground, bar, pay-dirt, placer, wash, washing; **colour,** glance, opacite; **metal dust,** dust, gold dust, platinum black, sponge; **nugget,** floater, slug; **gold,** fool's gold, iron pyrites, yellow metal
mineral *n* → **1** raw materials *adj* **2** metallic
mineral water *n* → drink
mingle *v* → **1** associate **2** mix
miniature *n* → **1** sculpture **2** small thing *adj* **3** decreased **4** small
minim *n* → **1** bit **2** small amount **3** unimportant thing *adj* **4** smallest
minimise *v* → **1** belittle **2** decrease
minimum *n* → **1** adequacy **2** inferiority **3** small amount *adj* **4** smallest
minion *n* → **1** friend **2** lover **3** sexual type *adj* **4** beautiful
minister *n* → **1** ambassador **2** ecclesiastic **3** member of parliament **4** ruler *v* **5** help
mink *n* → animal's coat
minnow *n* → unimportant person
minor *n* → **1** course **2** inferior *adj* **3** inferior **4** mediocre **5** smallest **6** unimportant **7** youthful
minority *n* → **1** a few **2** foreigner **3** youth
minstrel *n* → **1** poet **2** singer
mint *n* → **1** much **2** treasury **3** wealth *v* **4** circulate **5** create *adj* **6** new
minus *adj* → **1** absent *prep* **2** less **3** without
minuscule *n* → **1** letter *adj* **2** small
minute *n* → **1** account **2** crucial moment **3** length **4** moment **5** reminder *v* **6** memorise **7** record **8** time **9** write *adj* **10** momentary **11** precise **12** small
minx *n* → **1** children **2** discourteous person **3** disdainer **4** flirt **5** woman
miracle *n* → good thing
mirage *n* → **1** delusion **2** dream **3** the intangible
mire *n* → **1** sludge **2** swamp *v* **3** cause difficulties **4** dirty
MIRROR *n* cheval glass, distorting mirror, glass, hand glass, looking glass, magic mirror, pier glass, rear-vision mirror, reflector, speculum, wing mirror
mirror *n* → **1** example **2** magic spell *v* **3** imitate
MIRTH *n* laughing, laughter, merriment; **smile,** grin; **giggle,** snicker, snigger, teehee, the giggles, titter; **laugh,** belly laugh, cachinnation, convulsion, guffaw, haw-haw, horse laugh, roar; **shriek,** cackle, chortle, hoot, howl, shout. *See also* HUMOUR
mirth *n* → **1** happiness **2** joy
misadventure *n* → **1** luck **2** misfortune
misappropriate *v* → **1** ill-treat **2** take
MISBEHAVE *v* act up, be up to no good, blackguard, commit transgressions, corrupt others, cut up nasty, cut up rough, deviate from the straight and narrow, forget oneself, go astray, lapse, misconduct oneself, muck up, play up, rogue, sell oneself short, sow wild oats, trespass; **cheat,** duckshove, indulge in sharp practice, swindle; **make mis-**

chief, be up to monkey business, be up to monkey tricks, make trouble, mess about, mess around, play hob; **riot,** brutalise, destroy property, rough-house, run riot, smash property, vandalise; **overstep the mark,** ask for it, ask for trouble, go too far; **lose one's temper,** carry on, glower, sulk

MISBEHAVIOUR *n* bad behaviour, bad manners, delinquency, dereliction, improperness, impropriety, malfeasance, malpractice, malversation, misconduct, misdoing, naughtiness, pertness; **rascality,** bastardry, caddishness, cruelty, devilment, doggery, knavishness, malefaction, obstreperousness, waywardness; **disrespect,** discourtesy, impudence, incivility, insolence, lese-majesty *(Joc.)*, tactlessness; **mischievousness,** devilment, elfishness, impishness, mischief, mischief-making, roguery, roguishness; **slyness,** archness, kittenishness, tricksiness; **bad temper,** acerbity, acrimony, asperity, bad language, bad looks, harsh words, tartness, unparliamentary language, virulence; **sullenness,** moroseness, rudeness, stubbornness; **hooliganism,** criminality, irresponsibility, irresponsibleness, juvenile delinquency, larrikinism, restiveness, rowdyism, rudeness, ruffianism, vulgarity; **infamous conduct,** bestiality, blackguardism, brutality, brutishness, conduct unbecoming, infamy

miscarriage *n* → **1** birth **2** failure

miscarry *v* → **1** be early **2** be infertile **3** fail **4** give birth

miscellaneous *adj* → mixed

miscellany *n* → **1** book **2** mixture

mischief *n* → **1** devil **2** harm **3** misbehaviour

MISCHIEF-MAKER *n* elf, gremlin, imp, jackanapes, monkey, muck-up, pickle, prankster, rogue, scallywag, scamp; **enfant terrible,** perisher, tyke, Young Turk; **gamin,** gamine, guttersnipe, mudlark *(Brit. Colloq.)*; **bastard,** bear, blackguard, bugger, whoreson; **hooligan,** bovver boy *(Brit. Colloq.)*, disorderly person, goon, hellion, hoodlum, hoon, irresponsible, juvenile delinquent, larrikin, rugger-bugger, scourer *(Brit. Hist.)*; **wrongdoer,** delinquent, duckshover, hard case, incorrigible, recidivist, wrong 'un

misconduct *n* → **1** misbehaviour *v* **2** bungle

misdeed *n* → **1** crime **2** wrong

MISDEMEANOUR *n* evil deeds, peccadillo, slip, transgression, trip, wrongdoing; **escapade,** caper, capriccio, caprice, monkey tricks, monkeyshine, prank, trick; **disorder,** disorderliness, disorderly conduct, riot, rough-house, rumble

misdemeanour *n* → **1** crime **2** wrong

MISER *n* cheapskate, churl, codger, curmudgeon, death adder, dog in the manger, Ikey Mo, jew *(Derog.)*, meanie, money-grubber, niggard, penny pincher, pinchpenny, screw, scrooge, Shylock, skinflint, tightwad; **piker,** last of the big spenders

miser *n* → **1** piercer **2** unfortunate **3** unhappy person

miserable *adj* → **1** bad **2** pitiable **3** poor **4** unfortunate **5** unhappy

misery *n* → **1** grieving **2** poverty **3** sobersides **4** unfortunateness **5** unhappiness **6** unhappy person

misfit *n* → **1** anomaly **2** fish out of water **3** nonconformist **4** strange person

MISFORTUNE *n* accident, ambs-ace, bale *(Archaic)*, clap *(Obs.)*, contretemps, evil, evil chance *(Archaic)*, hard lines, hard luck story, ill, infortune *(Obs.)*, misadventure, mischance, raw deal, setback; **mishap,** mess-up, slip; **calamity,** blight, catastrophe, debacle, disaster, plague, tragedy, visitation; **blow,** body blow, kick in the arse, king hit, peripeteia, reversal, reverse, slump, smack in the eye, turnabout; **hard lines,** hard cheddar, hard cheese, hard luck, just one's luck, stiff cheddar, stiff cheese, stiff luck, the deuce, the devil, tough luck; **mixed blessing; run of bad luck,** bad trot, chapter of accidents, hard times, night, rainy day; **evil star,** bad fairy, cross, curse, fire, hex, mozz, scourge; **black-letter day,** Black Friday; **disaster area,** Pandora's box; **adversity,** asperity, hard life, hardship, rough end of the pineapple, sorrow, trouble, worriment; **ruination,** kiss of death, the worst; **fate worse than death**

misfortune *n* → **1** inconvenience **2** luck

misgiving *n* → **1** doubt **2** fright **3** uncertainty

MISGUIDANCE *n* bum steer, furphy, misdirection, wrong advice; **debauchment,** debauchery *(Obs.)*, depravation, perversion

MISGUIDE *v* give a false impression, give someone a bum steer, lead astray, lead into error, misadvise, miscounsel, misdirect, misinform, mislead, misrepresent, misteach; **deprave,** debauch, deceive, demoralise, empoison, lead astray, pervert, subvert; **confuse,** bewilder, mystify, throw someone off the scent; **fool,** give someone the wrong idea, lead a merry dance, lead by the nose, lead someone up the garden path

mishap *n* → misfortune

mishmash *n* → jumble

MISINTERPRET *v* belie, caricature, distort, falsify, flatter, garble, libel, miscolour, misdescribe, misquote, misreport, misrepresent, parody, portray falsely, put a false construction on, skew, slant, travesty, twist

MISJUDGE *v* be unable to see the wood for the trees, fly in the face of facts, go off half-cocked, have a bias, jump to the wrong conclusion, misapprehend, miscalculate, misconceive, misconstrue, misestimate, misreckon, mistake, misvalue, not see beyond one's nose, overestimate, overplay one's hand, overrate, overvalue, prejudge, presume, presumise, reckon without, underestimate, underrate

MISJUDGED *adj* based on false premises, exaggerated, ill-judged, injudicious, misunderstood, overestimated, overrated, overvalued, superficial, underestimated, underrated, undervalued, unsound, wrong, wrong-headed

MISJUDGMENT *n* error, hasty conclusion, jaundiced view, misapprehension, miscalculation, misconception, miscue, misestimate, misestimation, mistake, misunderstanding, overestimate, overestimation, underestimate, underestimation, warped judgment

mislead *v* → **1** beguile **2** misguide **3** trick

MISLEADER *n* false prophet, will-o'-the-wisp; **debaucher,** depraver; **debauchee,** pervert

misnomer *n* → name

misogyny *n* → hate

MISPLACE *v* misarrange, misdeliver, misfile; **displace,** antevert, buck, dislodge, disseat, heave *(Geol.)*, spill, unbalance, unhorse, unsaddle, unseat; **dislocate,** disjoint, luxate; **decentre,** unbalance

MISPLACED *adj* ectopic *(Pathol.)*, erratic *(Geol.)*, heterotopic, parallactic; **displaced,** adventitious *(Bot. Zool.)*, astray, dislocated, unbalanced; **homeless,** houseless, stateless, unaccommodated; **eccentric,** off-centre, skew-whiff, wonky

MISPLACEMENT *n* disturbance, ectopia, epeirogenesis, epeirogeny, heave *(Geol.)*, heterotopia, malposition, prolapse, spill, spillage, version; **displacement,** adventitiousness *(Bot. Zool.)*, dislocation, dislodgment, driftage, eluviation, luxation; **homelessness,** no-man's-land, statelessness, vagrancy

misprint *n* → error

MISPRONOUNCE *v* clip, lisp, nasalise, slur; **stammer,** falter, fumble, haw, hem, hesitate, hum and haw, mumble, mutter, quaver, stutter; **splutter,** clutter, gabble, sputter, swallow one's words

MISREPRESENTATION *n* distortedness, distortion, exaggeration, false portrayal, falsehood, falsification, garble, libel, misdescription, misinterpretation, misquotation, misquote, misreport, perversion, violence; **bad likeness,** anamorphosis, burlesque, caricature, parody, travesty

miss *n* → **1** children **2** failure **3** neglectfulness *v* **4** avoid **5** be inattentive **6** fail **7** mistime

Miss *n* → Ms

misshapen *adj* → **1** disfigured **2** distorted **3** ugly

missing *adj* → **1** absent **2** nonexistent

mission *n* → **1** act of war **2** agency **3** aim **4** delegate **5** domain **6** obligation **7** undertaking **8** work

missionary *n* → **1** enlightener **2** preacher *adj* **3** ecclesiastic

missive *n* → message

mist *n* → **1** cloud **2** shade *v* **3** cloud

mistake *n* → **1** bungle **2** error **3** misjudgment **4** pregnancy *v* **5** err **6** misjudge

MISTER *n* bung, Esq., esquire, goodman *(Archaic)*, herr, m'sieur, monsieur, Mr, Mynheer, sahib, san, señor, signor, signore, sir; **sir,** aga, Alhaji, Dan *(Archaic)*, dignity, Doctor, dom, Don, effendi, emir, Grace, honour, imperator, landgrave, Lord, maestro, maharaja, milord, mirza, monseigneur, nawab, pasha, seignior *(Archaic)*, Serenity, swami, Tunku, tycoon, worship, your lordship; **Grace,** dom, Holiness, Lord, Monsignor, Reverence; **mate,** blue, bluey, boss, cobber, comrade, dig, digger, Mack *(U.S.)*, man, matey, old fruit *(Brit.)*, sirrah, skeeter, snow, snowy, son, sonny, uncle; **so-and-so,** what's-his-face, what's-his-name

MISTIME *v* go off at half-cock, go off half-cocked, miscue, miss, overtime *(Photog.)*, shoot one's bolt; **lose an opportunity,** blow it, let a chance slip through one's fingers, miss the boat, miss the bus; **misdate,** antedate, postdate, predate

mistress *n* → **1** boss **2** lover **3** manager **4** Ms **5** owner **6** sexual partner **7** spouse **8** teacher

mistrust *n* → **1** doubt *v* **2** doubt

misty *adj* → **1** cloudy **2** imprecise **3** shadowy

MISUNDERSTAND *v* be all at sea, be at cross purposes, have one's wires crossed, make little of, make neither head nor tail of, make nothing of, misinterpret, miss the point, see through a glass darkly

MISUSE *n* abusage, abuse, improper use, maladministration, misapplication, misappropriation, misdirection, misemployment, mismanagement, misusage, overuse, waste; **malpractice,** barbarism, corruption, malversation, perversion, prostitution, simony, violation; **maltreatment,** ill usage, ill use, ill-treatment, mishandling, mistreatment, misuse *(Obs.)*

misuse *n* → **1** misuse *v* **2** ill-treat

mite *n* → **1** coinage **2** offspring **3** small person

mitigate *v* → **1** alleviate **2** decrease **3** ease **4** moderate

mitre *n* → **1** hat *v* **2** employ **3** take the cloth

mitten *n* → glove

MIX *v* blunge, dash, mash, paddle, puddle *(Mining)*, roil, shake, shake up, stir; **blend,** admix, emulsify, fold, homogenise, impregnate, interblend, interlard; **compound,** brew, prepare; **amalgamate,** alloy, conglomerate, fuse, merge; **diversify,** assort; **shuffle,** jumble, scramble; **mingle,** commix, immingle, immix, interfuse, interlace, interlard, intermingle, intermix, intersperse; **adulterate,** contaminate, debase, sophisticate, vitiate; **temper,** attemper, doctor, season, tincture, water, water down

mix *n* → **1** combine **2** jumble **3** mixture *v* **4** be sociable **5** combine

MIXED *adj* assorted, kaleidoscopic, mingled, miscellaneous, motley, multifarious; **jumbled,** diversiform, farraginous, hotchpotch, macaronic *(Obs.)*, medley, muddled, scrappy, unclassified, unsorted; **diverse,** daedal *(Poetic)*, diversified, many-sided, multi-racial, multicultural, pluralist, pluralistic; **heterogeneous,** eclectic, heteromerous, multilingual, polyglot, promiscuous; **fifty-fifty,** half-and-half, Jekyll-and-Hyde, pepper-and-salt; **conglomerate,** complex, composite, conglomeritic; **adulterated,** commercial, cut, sophisticated; **impure,** foul, tainted, vitiated

MIXER *n* amalgamator, blender, food processor, jumbler, mingler, shuffler, vitamiser; **paddle,** blunger *(Pottery)*, egg whisk, egg-beater, larry *(Bldg Trades)*, palette knife, puddling machine, rabble; **adulterator,** adulterant, vitiator

mixer *n* → sound system

MIXTURE *n* assortment, medley, melange, miscellany, mix; **jumble,** bag of tricks, catch-all, fantasia, farrago, flotsam and jetsam, gallimaufry, grab bag, hodgepodge, hotchpotch, medley, mixed bag, motley, odds and ends, olio, omnium gatherum, paraphernalia, patchwork, pell-mell, polyglot, potpourri, rummage, salmagundi, shandygaff, smorgasbord; **assemblage,** album, assembly, box, bundle, collection, congeries, group; **pastiche,** cento *(Archaic)*, collage, infusion, pasticcio, patchwork, tincture; **musical medley,** macaronic verse; **mingling,** admixture, amalgamation, blending, commixture, conglomeration, diffusion, fusion, immixture, integration, interfusion, interlarding, interpolation, junction, marriage, merger, mixing, stirring, transfusion; **intermixture,** entanglement, interlacement, interminglement, interspersion, lacing; **synaeresis,** crasis, synaesthesia, synaloepha *(Phonet.)*; **miscibility; adulteration,** admixture, contamination, corruption, debasement, sophistication, vitiation; **hybridisation,** hybridism, interbreeding, miscegenation, mixed marriage, mongrelisation, mongrelism, mosaicism *(Genetics)*

mixture *n* → **1** addition **2** combination

mix up *v* → **1** disorder **2** muddle

mix-up *n* → **1** fight **2** jumble

mnemonic *n* → **1** reminder *adj* **2** reminiscent

moan *n* → **1** complaint **2** grieving **3** quiet sound *v* **4** be unhappy **5** complain **6** grieve

moat *n* → **1** channel **2** fortification **3** furrow

mob *n* → **1** gathering **2** many **3** untidy person **4** working class *v* **5** attack *adj* **6** public

mobile *n* → **1** sculpture *adj* **2** changeable **3** flowing **4** moving

mobilise *v* → **1** militarise **2** move **3** use

moccasin *n* → footgear

MOCK *v* chuck off at, debunk, deride, fleer at, flout, gibe, gig, have a shot at, heckle, jeer, jest, monkey, scoff, take the micky out of; **ridicule,** laugh at, make a fool of, make a monkey of, make fun of, poke borak at, poke fun at, poke mullock at, rib, sport; **taunt,** barrack, burl, gird at, guy, howl down, joe, laugh out of court, rubbish; **banter,** chaff, chiack, get a rise out of, josh, pull someone's leg, quiz *(Obs.)*, rag, rally, take a rise out of, tease, twit; **hoot,** howl; **satirise,** befool, burlesque, lampoon, send up, squib, travesty; **pillory,** blister, gibbet, pasquinade, razz, roast

mock *n* → **1** mockery *v* **2** imitate **3** trick *adj* **4** imitative

MOCKER *n* cynic, derider, flouter, jeerer, ridiculer, scoffer, sneerer; **taunter,** barracker, giber, heckler, twitter; **banterer,** chaffer, leg-puller, teaser; **satirist,** caricaturist, lampooner, parodist, pasquinader, satiriser

MOCKERY *n* borak *(Aborig.)*, derision, derisiveness, name-calling, razz, ridicule; **sarcasm,** irony, satiricalness; **taunting,** heckling, heehaw, ribaldry; **chaff,** chiack, chiacking, teasing; **banter,** badinage, persiflage, raillery; **satire,** burlesque, caricature, cartoon, iambic *(Gk Lit.)*, lampoon, parody, pasquil, pasquinade, send-up, skit, squib, travesty; **rogue's march; mock,** crack, dig, flout, gibe, gird *(Archaic)*, hit, knock, rub, scoff, witticism; **taunt,** fleer, jeer, twit; **jest,** joke, leg-pull; **howl of derision,** hoot

mockery *n* → **1** anomaly **2** imitation

MOCKING *adj* deriding, derisive, fleering, Hudibrastic, jeering, nipping, quizzical, sarcastic, sardonic, sarky, scoffing; **bantering,** sportful, teasing; **satiric,** burlesque, satirical

mock up *v* → make

mock-up *n* → model

mode *n* → **1** appearance **2** condition **3** custom **4** method **5** structure

MODEL *n* copy *(Archaic)*, dummy, exemplar, mock-up, mount, pattern, pilot, working model; **template,** form, guide, mitre box, shape; **mould,** cast, casting, core, dariole, deckle, die, matrix, roughcast; **stamp,** engraving, pig, pig-bed, plate, seal, stamper, woodblock, woodcut; **design,** cartoon, sinopia; **block,** last; **original,** archetype, manuscript, master, parent, protocol, prototype, stock, the copy

MODEL *adj* classic, classical, ideal; **standard,** formulaic, normal, normative, sample, typical; **original,** archetypal, archetypical, prototypal; **exemplary,** citatory, copybook, exemplificative, paradigmatic, paradigmatical, precedential

model *n* → **1** antecedent **2** copy **3** good person **4** perfect thing **5** portrait **6** prostitute **7** representation **8** rule *v* **9** depict **10** shape

MODERATE *v* attemper, milden, mitigate, modify, modulate, palliate, qualify, season, soften, temper, tone down, turn down; **restrain,** allay, appease, assuage, lay, mollify, slake, soothe, staunch *(Archaic)*; **calm,** cool down, cool off, defuse, pacify, quell, quiet, quieten, stay, still, tranquillise; **abate,** attenuate, bate, relax, relent, remit, slack, slacken, wane; **dull,** blunt, buff, cushion, deaden, tame

MODERATE *adj* judicious, middle-of-the-road, modest, non-extreme, reasonable, restrained, temperate; **mild,** balmy, gentle, kindly, lenient, smooth, soft, tempered; **calm,** cool, even, peaceful, quiet, stormless, tranquil; **soothing,** assuasive, attenuant, lenitive, mitigative, mitigatory, modulative, palliative; **dull,** dullish, innocuous, insipid, tame

moderate *n* → **1** moderator **2** neutral **3** political ideologist *v* **4** decrease *adj* **5** mediocre **6** ordinary

MODERATELY *adv* in moderation, modestly, restrainedly, temperately, to a degree; **calm-**

ly, coolly, evenly, quietly; **mildly,** balmily, gently, leniently; **dully,** innocuously, tamely

MODERATION *n* golden mean, judiciousness, moderateness, modesty, reasonableness, restraint, self-control, temperance, temperateness; **mildness,** balminess, gentleness; **calmness,** coolness, quietness, subduedness; **dullness,** innocuousness, insipidity, tameness

MODERATOR *n* damper, deadener, restrainer, seasoner, temperer; **assuager,** allayer, lenitive *(Rare)*, mitigator, modulator, mollifier, palliative, palliator, queller, quieter, relaxer, soother, tranquilliser; **middle-of-the-roader,** Menshevik, moderate, non-extremist; **neutraliser,** buffer, cushion, dashpot *(Mach.)*

modern *n* → **1** innovator *adj* **2** current **3** innovative

MODEST *adj* backward, backward in coming forward, bashful, blushful, blushing, coy, demure, diffident, nice *(Obs.)*, reserved, restrained, retiring, sheepish, shy, skittish, verecund *(Rare)*, withdrawn; **self-effacing,** self-deprecating, unassuming, unobtrusive, unostentatious, unpretending, unpretentious; **decent,** chaste, missish, prim and proper, prudish, pure, virtuous

modest *adj* → moderate

MODESTLY *adv* backwardly, bashfully, blushingly, coyly, demurely, sheepishly, shyly; **self-effacingly,** self-deprecatingly, unassumingly, unostentatiously, unpretendingly, unpretentiously, with no fuss or bother, without ceremony

MODEST PERSON *n* blusher, effacer, shrinking violet, wallflower

MODESTY *n* backwardness, bashfulness, constraint, coyness, demureness, diffidence, humility, pudency, reserve, shamefacedness, sheepishness, shyness, timidity; **self-effacement,** effacement, self-deprecation, unassumingness, unobtrusiveness, unpretentiousness; **decency,** chastity, decorum, purity

modicum *n* → small amount

modify *v* → **1** change **2** differ **3** moderate

modulate *v* → **1** change **2** moderate

module *n* → **1** length **2** lesson **3** part **4** thickness

mogul *n* → **1** important person **2** mound **3** train

mohair *n* → animal's coat

moiety *n* → **1** ancestry **2** half **3** part

moist *adj* → wet

moisture *n* → **1** liquid **2** wetness

molar *n* → mouth

mole *n* → **1** disfigurement **2** harbour **3** mound **4** spy

molecule *n* → **1** atom **2** small amount

molest *v* → victimise

mollify *v* → **1** alleviate **2** make peace **3** moderate

mollycoddle *v* → **1** be lenient **2** care for

molten *adj* → liquid

MOMENT *n* a brace of shakes, breath, crack, flash, instant, jiffy, minute, mo, sec, second, shake, split second, tick, trice, twinkle, twinkling, whipstitch *(U.S.)*, wink; **point,** article *(Archaic)*, epoch *(Astron.)*, juncture, point of time, time

moment *n* → **1** average **2** crucial moment **3** importance

MOMENTARILY *adv* for a moment, momently; **soon,** after a bit, anon *(Archaic)*, awhile, before long, erelong *(Archaic)*, in a bit; **in a moment,** all at once, in a brace of shakes, in half a mo, in less than no time, in no time, in no time at all, in two shakes of a dog's tail, in two ticks, quickly, readily; **instantly,** at once, at sight, forthright *(Archaic)*, forthwith, here and now, immediately, instantaneously, on sight, on the spot, shortly, with this; **suddenly,** abruptly, all at once, at the drop of a hat, extempore, impromptu, impulsively, on the spot, on the spur of the moment, out of hand, without notice

MOMENTARINESS *n* abruptness, suddenness, transience; **instantaneity,** immediacy, immediateness, instancy *(Rare)*, instantaneousness, quickness

MOMENTARY *adj* passing, transient; **instantaneous,** immediate, instant, overnight, present *(Obs.)*, quick, split-second; **minute,** ready-made; **sudden,** abrupt, ad hoc, impromptu, impulsive, snap

momentary *adj* → impermanent

momentous *adj* → important

momentum *n* → energy

monarchy *n* → nation

monastery *n* → **1** abbey **2** seclusion

MONASTIC *n* ascetic, bodhisattva, bonze, brother, caloyer, canon regular, canoness, coenobite, enthusiast, fakir, Flagellant, flagellator, Fra, frère, friar, holy Joe, incluse, lama, lay brother, maharishi, mendicant, monk, nun, out sister, recluse, regular, religious, shaveling *(Archaic)*, sister, stylite, vestal, vower; **novice,** canon, canonry, neophyte, ordinand, postulant, scholastic, seminarian, seminarist; **tertiary,** regular tertiary, secular tertiary; **provost,** abbé, abbess, abbot, hegumen *(Greek Orthodox)*, monk, mother, mother superior, prior, prioress, rector, Reverend Mother, right reverend, superior, votaress, votary, votress; **dervish,** Calender, dancing dervish, fakir, howling dervish, sheikh, spinning dervish, whirling dervish; **dalai lama.** *See also* ECCLESIASTIC

MONASTIC *adj* ascetic, ascetical, claustral, cloistral, institutionary, monachal, monasterial, professed, regular, religious, tonsured; **conventual,** abbatial, coenobitic, coenobitical, monkish, rectorial, succursal

MONASTICISM *n* coenobitism, monachism; **religious order,** congregation, discipline, lamasery *(Buddhism)*, major order, minor order, monkery, monkhood, observance, rule, veil

monetary *adj* → cash

money *n* → **1** cash **2** profit **3** wealth
money order *n* → **1** cash **2** message
mongrel *n* → **1** bad person **2** descendant **3** hybrid **4** offspring *adj* **5** bad **6** genetic **7** hybrid
monitor *n* → **1** controlling device **2** guide **3** manager **4** reminder **5** television **6** tester **7** warner **8** watercraft *v* **9** control **10** examine **11** test
monk *n* → **1** abstainer **2** monastic **3** solitary
monkey *n* → **1** animal's coat **2** humorist **3** imitator **4** loan **5** mischief-maker **6** press *v* **7** imitate **8** mock
monochrome *n* → **1** dyeing **2** painting **3** photograph
monocle *n* → glasses
monogamy *n* → marriage
monogram *n* → **1** letter **2** sign
monolith *n* → **1** post **2** rock outcrop **3** support
monologue *n* → **1** act **2** oration
monoplane *n* → aeroplane
monopolise *v* → **1** buy **2** control **3** own
monopoly *n* → **1** corporation **2** economy **3** ownership
monosyllable *n* → word
monotone *n* → **1** accent *adj* **2** boring **3** homogeneous
monotonous *adj* → **1** boring **2** frequent **3** homogeneous **4** repetitive
monsoon *n* → **1** rainfall **2** season **3** wind
monster *n* → **1** bad person **2** giant **3** mythical beast **4** strange person **5** ugly person **6** unkind person *v* **7** disapprove of *adj* **8** big
monstrous *adj* → **1** bad **2** big **3** dreadful **4** strange **5** ugly
montage *n* → work of art
monument *n* → **1** grave **2** sculpture
monumental *adj* → **1** big **2** enormous
mooch *v* → **1** be present **2** idle **3** rob **4** trick
mood *n* → **1** character **2** emotion
moody *adj* → **1** discontented **2** emotional **3** irritable **4** unhappy
MOON *n* earth satellite, lamp *(Poetic)*, Paddy's lantern *(N.Z.)*, Phoebe; **paraselene,** mock moon; **phase,** first quarter, interlunation, last quarter, mansion, quadrature, quarter; **crater,** mare, mascon, ray, rill, sea, walled plain; **crescent,** full moon, gibbous moon, half-moon, harvest moon, moonrise, new moon, old moon, waning moon, waxing moon; **moons,** Amalthea *(Jup.)*, Callisto *(Jup.)*, Charon *(Pluto)*, Deimos *(Mars)*, Europa *(Jup.)*, Galilean satellites *(Jup.)*, Ganymede *(Jup.)*, Io *(Jup.)*, Phoebus *(Mars)*, Titan *(Sat.)*, Triton *(Nep.)*
moon *n* → **1** ball **2** heavenly body *v* **3** be inattentive **4** be indifferent
moonlight *n* → **1** light *v* **2** work *adj* **3** bright **4** nightly
moonshine *n* → **1** alcohol **2** light **3** nonsense
moor *n* → **1** grassland *v* **2** fasten
moot *n* → **1** committee **2** court of law **3** legislative body *v* **4** reason **5** theorise
mop *n* → **1** absorber **2** brush **3** hair *v* **4** clean **5** dry
mope *n* → **1** apathetic person **2** unhappy person *v* **3** be indifferent **4** be unhappy
mopoke *n* → **1** complainer **2** stupid person
moraine *n* → **1** mound **2** rock outcrop **3** soil
MORAL *adj* axiological, casuistic, ethic; **moralistic,** carping, conscience-stricken, puritan, sermonising, wowserish; **ethical,** clean, decent, honourable, snowy
moral *n* → **1** certain thing **2** morality *adj* **3** abstinent **4** correct
morale *n* → emotion
MORALISER *n* moralist, nag, puritan, wowser
MORALITY *n* cardinal virtues, ethics, moral philosophy, morals, natural law, professional ethics, right, rightness; **ethic,** moral, moral code, moralism, standard
morality *n* → **1** correctness **2** dutifulness
MORAL SENSE *n* categorical imperative, conscience, mens rea *(Law)*, superego
morass *n* → swamp
moratorium *n* → **1** bad debt **2** interval **3** lenience **4** peace **5** stoppage
morbid *adj* → **1** psychologically disturbed **2** unwholesome
MORBID CURIOSITY *n* prurience, voyeurism; **curio,** conversation piece, peepshow; **curious person,** buttinski, earwig, eavesdropper, inquisitive, nosy parker, peeping Tom, prier, pry, quidnunc, rubberneck, stickybeak, voyeur; **thirst for knowledge,** inquiring mind
mordant *n* → **1** dye **2** steadier *v* **3** colour *adj* **4** coloured **5** humorous
MORE *n* a bit on the side, allowance, another, anotherie, gash, margin, over, seconds; **extra,** etceteras, plus, supernumerary, supplement, supplementary. *See also* ADDITION; POSTSCRIPT
more *adj* → **1** additional **2** increased *adv* **3** additionally
moreover *adv* → additionally
mores *n* → custom
morgue *n* → **1** cemetery **2** room
moribund *adj* → **1** dead **2** finished
MORNING *n* a.m., dayspring *(Poetic)*, forenoon, midmorning, morn *(Poetic)*, morrow *(Archaic)*; **dawn,** break of day, cockcrow, dawning, daybreak, light, sparrow fart, spring *(Archaic)*, sun-up, sunrise; **small hours,** matins, prime; **breakfast-time,** brunch, elevenses *(Brit.)*, playtime
morning *n* → **1** start *adj* **2** daily
moron *n* → stupid person
morose *adj* → **1** irritable **2** solitary **3** unhappy **4** unsociable
morphology *n* → structure
morrow *n* → **1** future **2** morning
morse code *n* → code
morsel *n* → **1** part **2** small amount *v* **3** share out
mortal *n* → **1** person *adj* **2** dead **3** deadly **4** human **5** impermanent **6** most
mortality *n* → the dead
mortar *n* → **1** adhesive **2** building materials **3** gun **4** powderer
mortarboard *n* → hat

mortgage *n* → **1** debt **2** loan **3** surety *v* **4** lend **5** promise

mortice *n* → **1** niche *v* **2** fasten

mortify *v* → **1** humble **2** insult

mortuary *n* → **1** cemetery **2** gift *adj* **3** funereal

mosaic *n* → **1** fine arts **2** hybrid **3** multicolour

Mosaic *adj* → scriptural

mosque *n* → church

moss *n* → plant

MOST *adj* best, consummate, extreme, maximal, maximum, maximus, supreme, top, utmost, uttermost, veriest; **majority**, dominant, main, ruling; **all-time**, absolute, almighty, arrant, awful, bally, blank, bleeding, bloody, blooming, bumper, downright, effing, fantastic, father and mother of a, flagrant, flaming, flipping, flopping, frigging, fucking, hang of a, howling, humming, mortal, out-and-out, passing, plain, plumb, positive, rank, rattling, resounding, smacking, sollicking, some, spanking, stark, stinking, surpassing, swingeing, tearing, thoroughgoing, thumping, thundering, uncommon, unmitigated, unqualified, utter, walloping, whacking

most *n* → **1** much *adv* **2** almost **3** greatly

mostly *adv* → greatly

mote *n* → **1** powder **2** small amount

motel *n* → hotel

mothball *v* → disuse

mother *n* → **1** bad person **2** bad thing **3** creator **4** monastic **5** old people **6** parent **7** procreator *v* **8** care for **9** reproduce

mother-in-law *n* → parent

mother-of-pearl *n* → **1** coating **2** white *adj* **3** multicoloured

motif *n* → **1** decoration **2** subject matter

motion *n* → **1** defecation **2** entreaty **3** gesture **4** move **5** movement **6** offer **7** plan **8** point of view *v* **9** direct **10** gesture

motivate *v* → encourage

MOTIVE *n* arrière-pensée, drive, impetus, incentive, interest, raison d'être, reason, the why and the wherefore, ulterior motive, what makes one tick

motive *v* → **1** encourage *adj* **2** encouraging **3** moving

motley *n* → **1** costume **2** mixture *adj* **3** mixed **4** multicoloured

motor *n* → **1** machine *v* **2** drive *adj* **3** mechanical **4** moving

motor car *n* → car

motorcycle *n* → bicycle

motorist *n* → driver

MOTOR VESSEL *n* flyboat, hot-water boat, motor boat, oil-burner, powerboat, rubber duckie, runabout, speedboat; **steamship**, paddle-steamer, paddleboat, side-wheeler, steamboat, steamer,. stern-wheeler; **cabin cruiser**, cruiser, houseboat; **hydrofoil**, hydroplane, seaplane *(U.S.)*; **ferry**, car ferry, ferryboat, punt, wherry *(Brit.)*; **wetbike**; **submarine**, bathyscaphe, bathysphere, minisub, sub, submersible, U-boat

motto *n* → **1** proverb **2** rule

mould *n* → **1** character **2** copy **3** destroyer **4** dirt **5** model **6** shape **7** soil *v* **8** copy **9** decorate **10** depict **11** make **12** shape

moulder *v* → **1** get dirty **2** powder

moulding *n* → **1** copy **2** frame

moult *n* → **1** hide *v* **2** bare

MOUND *n* ant heap, ant hill, barrow, burial mound, dene, effigy-mound, embankment, hummock, hump, kurgan, midden, mogul, molehill, monticule, moraine, niggerhead, salt dome, seif-dune, stage, tell, tope *(Buddhism)*, tumulus, upthrow *(Geol.)*; **rampart**, bulwark, dike, mole; **hill**, barchan, bill, butte *(U.S. Canada)*, down, drumlin, dune, foothill, gentle Annie *(N.Z.)*, headland, hencackle *(N.Z.)*, hill site, hillock, hilltop, holt *(Poetic)*, hurst, incline, island, knob, knoll, kop *(S. African)*, kopje *(S. African)*, mesa, monadnock, outcrop, promontory, rise, sand dune, sand hill, skillion, swell, tor, wold. *See also* MOUNTAIN; APEX; HEIGHT

mound *n* → **1** accumulation **2** embankment **3** fortification

mount *n* → **1** ascent **2** fortune-telling **3** model **4** mountain *v* **5** ascend **6** become greater **7** have sex **8** stage **9** support **10** top **11** tower

MOUNTAIN *n* alp, ben *(Scot.)*, bluff, cliff, cone, crag, crag-and-tail, escarpment, fjeld, massif, mount, nunatak, peak, pinnacle, plateau, precipice, prominence, table, tableland, volcano, wall *(Mountaineering)*; **mountain range**, alps, chain, continental divide, cordillera, ghats *(India)*, interfluve, palisades *(U.S.)*, sierra, slopes, the tops, tiers *(Tas.)*; **ridge**, esker, horseback, offset, os, rand *(S. African)*, sideling *(N.Z.)*, siding *(N.Z.)*, spur, watershed; **high country**, highland, paramo, the heights, uplands. *See also* MOUND; APEX; HEIGHT

mountain *n* → **1** much *adj* **2** enormous **3** mountainous

mountaineer *n* → **1** climber **2** inhabitant *v* **3** ascend

MOUNTAINOUS *adj* alpine, cordilleran, high-country, highland, montane, mountain, rangy, subalpine *(Phys. Geog.)*, upland, volcanic, vulcanian; **precipitous**, cliffy, cragged, ridgy, steep; **hilly**, hillocky, hummocky. *See also* HIGH; TALL

mourn *v* → grieve

mournful *adj* → **1** distressing **2** grieving **3** unhappy

mourning *n* → **1** funeral rites **2** graveclothes **3** grieving *adj* **4** grieving

mouse *n* → **1** computer controls **2** worrier *v* **3** hunt **4** pursue

moustache *n* → **1** animal's coat **2** beard **3** feather

mousy *adj* → **1** colourless **2** silent

MOUTH *n* cakehole, chook's bum, gob, hole, kisser, maw, moosh, mug, north and south, puss, rattletrap, trap; **lip**, labium, labrum; **tooth**, choppers, clackers, denticle, dentition, fang, pearly gates, snag, snaggle-tooth, tusk; **eyetooth**, baby tooth, bicuspid, canine, carnassial, cheektooth, grinder, incisor, laniary, microdont, milk tooth, molar, premolar, wisdom tooth; **false teeth,** denture, falsies, plate, tatters, tatts; **tongue,** clapper, glossa, lingua; **gum,** faucal pillars, fauces, gingiva, hard palate, palate, alveolus, soft palate, tooth ridge, velum, uvula

mouth *n* → **1** exit **2** gesture **3** opening **4** speaking **5** stream *v* **6** gesture **7** speak well

mouthful *n* → **1** bit **2** small amount

mouthpiece *n* → **1** armour **2** lawyer **3** mediator **4** newspaper **5** orator

MOVE *n* action, business *(Theat.)*, gesture, motion, movement; **gait,** footfall, footwork, locomotion, pace, step, stride, walk; **bounce,** bob, dip, gurgitation, nod, nutation, prance, shrug; **jerk,** cant, jolt, snatch, stamp, start, stroke, whip; **slide,** fishtail, flap, glide, skid, slip, slither, stroke, swim; **wriggle,** squirm, writhe; **course,** drift, march, run, sweep, tack, way *(Naut.)*; **circuit,** circle, circulation, orbit, traverse

MOVE *v* go, heave *(Naut.)*, make one's way, run, stir, surge, walk *(Obs.)*; **ply,** plough, truck; **bounce,** bob, dap, hop, jump, nod, noddle, prance, surge; **jerk,** flitter, flutter, play, skitter, squib, waver, winnow *(Archaic)*; **slide,** aquaplane, plane, skid, skim, slip, slither; **glide,** bowl, coast, cruise, kite, ride, roll, roll along, sail, skim, spank, sweep; **wriggle,** squirm, writhe; **mobilise,** agitate, animate; **budge,** give way, shift, work; **start,** clutch-start *(Motor Vehicles)*, flip, launch, let rip, rev up, turn over

move *n* → **1** action **2** transport *v* **3** advance **4** agitate **5** assert **6** depart **7** emotionalise **8** encourage **9** guide **10** influence **11** operate **12** sell **13** theorise **14** transport

MOVEMENT *n* action, Brownian motion, evolution, motion, perpetual motion, perpetuo moto; **mobility,** agility, degree of freedom *(Mech Engineering)*, manoeuvrability, motility, movability; **tropism,** galvanotropism, geotropism, heliotaxis, heliotropism, negative geotropism, nyctitropism, photokinesis, phototaxis, phototropism, positive geotropism, sleep-movement, thermotaxis, thigmotaxis; **mobilisation,** dislocation *(Geol.)*; **dynamics,** hydrokinetics, kinematics, kinesiology, kinetics, mechanics; **Newton's laws,** Einstein's general theory of relativity, Einstein's special theory of relativity

movement *n* → **1** advance **2** defecation **3** machine **4** move **5** musical piece **6** point of view **7** society

movie *n* → film

MOVING *adj* automobile, automotive, locomotive, locomotor, motile, self-moving; **in motion,** astir, away, live, off, running, shifting, volitant; **motor,** psychomotor, sensorimotor; **circulatory,** ambient, circulative; **tropic,** geotropic, heliotactic, heliotropic, nutational, photokinetic, phototropic, thermotaxic, thigmotactic; **mobile,** dynamic, kinematic, kinematical, kinetic, manoeuvrable, motive

mow *n* → **1** gesture *v* **2** cut **3** gesture **4** harvest

MS *n* dame, Donna, frau, fraulein, goodwife, goody, lady, ma'am, madam, Madame, mademoiselle, Madonna, Miss, missus, mistress, Mrs, señora, señorita, signora, Tengku, your ladyship

MUCH *n* abundance, copiousness, flood, heap, lot, mass, mountain, muchness, ocean, peck, pile, plenty, power, profusion, quantity, quiverful, raft, rain, sea, sight, store, torrent, volume, wealth, world; **a great deal,** acres, any amount, bags, big mobs, biggest mobs, lashings, mint, neckful, no end, oodles, reams, scads, stacks, tons, whips; **most,** best part, bulk, majority, the lion's share; **maximum,** peak, the full bore; **extreme,** extremeness, extremity, the nth degree, the nth power, utmost, uttermost

much *adj* → **1** great *adv* **2** greatly

muck *n* → **1** dirt **2** dung **3** soil **4** unpleasantness **5** waste *v* **6** dirty **7** spoil

muck up *v* → **1** bungle **2** fail **3** misbehave **4** spoil

muck-up *n* → **1** failure **2** mischief-maker

mucous *adj* → sludgy

mud *n* → **1** adhesive **2** sludge **3** swamp

MUDDLE *n* balls-up, kettle of fish, mess, mess-up, no-man's-land, shambles, shemozzle; **disturbance,** babel, bouleversement, furore, hullaballoo, jungle, madhouse, maelstrom, melee, picnic, pother, riot, shindig, shindy, song and dance, tumult, turmoil, uproar, upset; **disorder,** clutter, confusedness, messiness, pandemonium, tumultuousness, turbidity, turbulence; **entanglement,** embranglement, embroilment, enravelment, ravelment, tangle; **maze,** labyrinth

MUDDLE *v* ball up *(U.S. Brit.)*, balls-up, embrangle, embroil, entangle, fuck up, jumble, make a mess of, mix up, overset, ravel, screw up

muddle *n* → **1** bungle **2** failure **3** jumble *v* **4** agitate **5** bungle **6** confuse

MUDDLED *adj* at sixes and sevens, in a mess, in a muddle, in disorder, indiscriminate, messy; **riotous,** hectic, pandemonic, tumultuary, tumultuous, turbid, turbulent, wild; **snafu,** situation normal all fucked up

muddy *v* → **1** dirty **2** dull *adj* **3** colourless **4** dirty **5** dull **6** imprecise **7** opaque **8** sludgy **9** wet

muff *n* → **1** failure **2** feather **3** glove **4** groin *v* **5** bungle **6** fail

muffle *n* → **1** cloak **2** quietener *v* **3** cover **4** silence

muffler *n* → neckwear

mufti *n* → informality

mug *n* → **1** face **2** fool **3** gesture **4** mouth **5** victim *v* **6** attack **7** gesture **8** hit **9** photograph **10** rob *adj* **11** foolish **12** stupid

muggy *adj* → **1** dull **2** hot

mulatto *n* → **1** descendant **2** hybrid

mulch *v* → fertilise

mule *n* → **1** horse **2** hybrid **3** sandal **4** stubborn person **5** transporter

mulga *n* → 1 armour 2 timber
mull *n* → 1 wrapper *v* 2 fail
mullock *n* → 1 diggings 2 remnant 3 waste *v* 4 bungle
MULTICOLOURED *adj* bicolour, dichroic, dichromatic, dichromic, particoloured, pavonine, polychromatic, polychrome, prismatic, psychedelic, rainbow, trichroic, trichromatic, tricolour, tricoloured, two-tone, varicoloured, varied, variegated; **versicolour,** changeable *(Archaic),* chatoyant, cloudy, moiré, mother-of-pearl, nacreous, opalescent, opaline, shot, watered; **motley,** harlequin, heather-mixture, heterochromatic, heterochromous, mealy, pepper-and-salt; **brindled,** black-and-blue, calico *(U.S.),* dapple-bay, dapple-grey, dappled, flea-bitten, merle, mickey mouse, mottled, piebald, pied, pinto *(U.S.),* roan, skewbald, tabby, tortoiseshell; **spotted,** blotchy, dotted, speckled, splashy, spotty, stippled, variolitic; **barred,** banded, candy-striped, fasciate, paly *(Heraldry),* ring-streaked, ringed, striped; **veined,** marbled, streaky; **check,** checked, chequered, compony *(Heraldry),* tessellate; **ocellated,** bird's-eye, eyed; **plaid,** argyle, plaided, tattersall
multicultural *adj* → mixed
multifarious *adj* → 1 many 2 mixed
multipartite *adj* → partial
multiple *adj* → many
multiplicity *n* → numerousness
multiply *v* → 1 become greater 2 compute 3 flower 4 increase 5 reproduce
multitude *n* → 1 gathering 2 many 3 working class
mum *n* → 1 parent *v* 2 perform 3 silence *adj* 4 silent *interj* 5 silence
mumble *v* → 1 eat 2 mispronounce
mummy *n* → 1 parent 2 the dead
MUM'S THE WORD *phr* it must go no further, keep it under your hat, no-one will be the wiser
munch *v* → eat
mundane *adj* → 1 irreverent 2 mediocre 3 ordinary
municipal *adj* → 1 legislative 2 regional
municipality *n* → 1 administrative area 2 city 3 domain 4 legislative body
munition *v* → supply
mural *n* → painting
murder *n* → 1 difficulty 2 killing *v* 3 kill
MURDEROUS *adj* bloodthirsty, butcherly, cutthroat, homicidal, slaughterous, thuggish; **sanguinary,** blood-guilty, bloodstained, bloody, crimson, internecine, red-handed; **fratricidal,** deicidal, filicidal, foeticidal, genocidal, matricidal, parricidal, patricidal, regicidal, sororicidal, tyrannicidal, uxoricidal; **suicidal,** banzai, kamikaze, self-destructive; **sacrificial,** capital, immolatory. *See also* KILLING
murmur *n* → 1 complaint 2 quiet sound *v* 3 complain 4 speak
muscle *n* → 1 effort 2 force 3 strength
muse *v* → 1 be inattentive 2 think
museum *n* → display case
mush *n* → 1 emotionality 2 walk *v* 3 walk
mushroom *n* → 1 bulge 2 ignoramus *v* 3 bulge 4 grow *adj* 5 swollen
MUSIC *n* accord, consonance, ensemble, harmony, unison; **melody,** air, chime, klangfarbenmelodie, lilt, sonance *(Obs.),* strain, theme, tune; **subject,** countersubject, idea, principal, subsidiary; **musicality,** canorousness, harmoniousness, lyricalness, lyricism, mellifluousness, melodiousness, sweetness, tunefulness; **accompaniment,** alberti bass, backing, bass, basso continuo, basso ostinato, boogie bass, bourdon, burden, continuo, drone, figured bass, ground bass, obbligato, stride piano, thoroughbass, tutti, vamp, walking bass. *See also* SINGING
music *n* → musical score
MUSICAL *adj* consonant, harmonic, perfect; **melodious,** canorous, harmonious, Lydian, lyrical, mellifluous, mellow, Orphean, songful, sweet, tunable *(Archaic),* tuneful; **melodic,** diapasonic, homophonic, monodic, monophonic; **instrumental,** grand, orchestral, symphonic; **unaccompanied,** secco, solo; **vocal,** choral, choric, lyric, melic, operatic; **treble,** falsetto, piping, reedy; **bass,** continuo; **classical,** baroque, romantic; **jazz,** bottleneck, cool, hep *(U.S.),* hip *(U.S.),* honky-tonk; **pop,** calypso; **threnodic,** epicedial, epicedian, threnodial; **rhapsodical,** quodlibetical; **figurate,** florid; **through-composed,** strophic
MUSICALLY *adv* canorously, harmoniously, lyrically, mellifluously, melodiously, rhapsodically, rhythmically, sweetly, tunefully; **polyphonically,** contrapuntally, fugally; **vocally,** chorally, operatically; **tonally,** achromatically, diatonically, harmonically; **atonally,** chromatically, enharmonically
MUSICAL PHRASE *n* figure, phrase, repetend, riff; **passage,** break, episode, fill, middle eight, period; **cadence,** buzz bar, close, feminine cadence, half-cadence, imperfect cadence, interrupted cadence, perfect cadence, plagal cadence; **tone row,** retrograde inversion, row, series; **coda,** codetta, stretta, tag; **slur,** ligature, melisma
MUSICAL PIECE *n* composition, cycle, morceau, movement, opus, opuscule, potboiler, standard, work; **study,** étude, five-finger exercise, gradus; **arrangement,** realisation, rifacimento, setting, transcription, transposition; **fanfare,** bravura, fanfaron, flourish, tucket; **overture,** concert-overture, praeludium, prelude; **interlude,** entr'acte, intermezzo, ritornello, verset *(Archaic)*; **finale,** postlude; **refrain,** chorus, derry, falderal, ritornello, tag; **character piece,** arabesque, bagatelle, ballade, capriccio, caprice, fantasia, humoresque, idyll, impromptu, invention, legende, nocturne, novelette, pastorale, perpetual motion, perpetuo moto, pibroch, potpourri, quodlibet, reverie, rhap-

sody, romance, scherzo, sketch, toccata. *See also* SONG; OPERA

MUSICAL SCORE *n* charts, chord chart, full score, gradual, head, music, part, prick-song *(Hist.)*, sheet music, short score, top lines, vocal score; **libretto,** book, wordbook; **stave,** bar, double bar, leger line, line, measure *(U.S.)*, space, staff; **note,** bind, dot, hook, stem, tail, tie; **direction,** expression mark, fermata, ligature, presa, rest, segno, signature, slur, time signature; **notation,** neumes, solfa, solfège, solfeggio, solmisation, staff notation, tablature, tonic sol-fa

MUSICIAN *n* artiste, concert artist, duettist, executant, muso, performer, sessionman, soloist, studio musician, virtuoso; **jazz player,** bebopper, cat, hepcat, swinger; **rhythmist,** syncopator; **accompanist,** répétiteur, vamper; **tuner,** temperer; **composer,** arranger, contrapuntist, dodecaphonist, harmonist, madrigalist, melodiser, melodist, monodist, scorer, singer-songwriter, songwriter, symphonist, transposer, writer; **hymnologist,** hymnist, hymnodist, psalmist, psalmodist, threnodist; **musicologist; tin-pan alley.** *See also* INSTRUMENTALIST; SINGER; CONDUCTOR

MUSICIANSHIP *n* articulation, ensemble, execution, feeling, music appreciation, musicality, touch, virtuosity; **musicology,** doctrine of affection, ethnomusicology, harmonics, hymnology, melodics, rhythmics

musket *n* → gun

must *n* → **1** destroyer **2** dirt **3** necessities *v* **4** necessitate

mustard *n* → yellow

muster *n* → **1** crowd **2** farming **3** gathering **4** shout *v* **5** farm **6** gather

musty *adj* → **1** inactive **2** old **3** smelly

mutant *adj* → evolutionary

mutate *v* → change

mutation *n* → change

mute *n* → **1** entertainer **2** quietener **3** string instrument **4** undertaker *v* **5** silence *adj* **6** inarticulate **7** silent

mutilate *v* → **1** cut **2** cut off **3** disfigure **4** injure

MUTINY *n* act of defiance, insurrection, outbreak, rebellion, resistance, revolt, revolution, sedition, unauthorised march, unauthorised stoppage, uprising, violation of the law, wildcat strike

mutiny *n* → **1** revolution *v* **2** anarchise **3** disobey **4** revolt

mutt *n* → stupid person

mutter *v* → **1** complain **2** mispronounce

mutton *n* → groin

mutton-bird *n* → Australian

mutton-chops *n* → beard

mutual *adj* → **1** interactive **2** related **3** societal

muzzle *n* → **1** saddlery *v* **2** restrain **3** silence

myopia *n* → faulty sight

myriad *n* → **1** many *adj* **2** infinite

mysterious *adj* → **1** imprecise **2** uncertain **3** unclear

mystery *n* → **1** arcanum **2** institute **3** job **4** puzzle **5** religious ceremony **6** trade union **7** uncertain thing

mystic *n* → **1** believer **2** worshipper *adj* **3** arcane **4** imprecise **5** magic **6** religious **7** supernatural **8** unclear

mysticism *n* → reverence

mystify *v* → **1** confuse **2** misguide **3** puzzle

mystique *n* → arcanum

myth *n* → **1** belief **2** delusion **3** story

MYTHICAL BEAST *n* androsphinx, basilisk, bunyip, centaur, Cerberus, Charybdis, chimaera, cockatrice, criosphinx, Cyclops, dragon, dragoness, easter bunny, Echidna, Gorgon, Grendel, griffin, gryphon, harpy, hippocampus, hippogriff, Hydra, Kraken, Loch Ness monster, Medusa, Minotaur, monster, monstrosity, Nessie, Pegasus, phoenix, Python, roc, salamander, Scylla, sea-monster, sea-serpent, seahorse, snark, sphinx, unicorn, wampus, wyvern; **abominable snowman,** alma, big-foot *(North America)*, sasquatch *(North America)*, yeti

MYTHICAL BEING *n* baresark, berserker, hero, superman; **mermaid,** merman, naiad, nereid, nix, nixie, seamaid, undine, water nymph; **Grace,** Aglaia, Euphrosyne, Thalia; **nymph,** dryad, hamadryad, numen, nymphette, oread, satyr, silvan, sylvan, wood nymph, wood spirit; **genie,** djinn, genii, genius, jinn, jinnee; **giant,** Aegir, Argus, Atlas, Brobdingnagian, Cyclops, Fafnir, Fasolt, Gog, Goliath, Heracles, Hercules, Magog, Pantagruel, Polyphemus, Titan. *See also* FAIRY; PHANTOM

mythology *n* → the supernatural

Nn

nab *v* → capture

nadir *n* → **1** astronomic point **2** bottom

nag *n* → **1** moraliser *v* **2** annoy **3** discontent **4** irritate

NAIL *n* brad, ceiling dog, clasp-nail, clout nail, dog nail, dog spike, doornail, drawing-pin, panel pin, skewnail, sparable, spike, sprig, stub nail, tack, tintack; **screw,** dowel screw, grubscrew, Phillips screw, screw-eye, self-tapping screw, setscrew, thumbscrew, woodscrew; **pin,** belaying pin, bodkin, cotter, dowel, forelock, hatpin, headpin, key, kingpin, nog, pintle, safety pin, split pin, stickpin *(U.S.)*, stud, swivel pin, tap-bolt, tiepin, treenail, trunnel, wedge, wristpin; **rivet,** explosive rivet

nail *n* → **1** animal part **2** length **3** piercer *v* **4** capture **5** fasten **6** reveal

naive *adj* → artless

naked *adj* → **1** bare **2** blatant **3** simple **4** vulnerable

NAKEDLY *adv* au naturel, en déshabillé, in one's birthday suit, in the altogether, in the bollock, in the bollocky, in the bols, in the buff, in the nick, in the nuddy, in the nude, in the raw, nudely, starkers, starkly

NAME *n* appellation, compellation, courtesy title, handle, honorific, hypocorism, moniker, style, title; **common name,** binomial, homonym *(Biol.)*, polynomial *(Zool. Bot.)*, synonym, tautonym, vernacular, vox barbara; **denomination,** designation, homonym, proper name, tag; **given name,** Christian name, family name, first name, forename, middle name, namesake, pet name, praenomen; **surname,** byname, cognomen, family name, maiden name, metronymic, patronymic; **eponym,** patrial, titular; **nickname,** addition *(Obs.)*, agnomen *(Class. Antiq.)*, byname, cognomen, epithet, sobriquet; **alias,** anonym, bodgie *(Colloq.)*; **pseudonym,** allonym, codename, cryptonym, nom de guerre, nom de plume, pen-name, stage-name; **trade name,** business name, style; **placename,** toponym; **byword,** synonym; **misnomer; brand,** label, trade name, trademark

NAME *v* baptise, call, christen, clepe *(Archaic)*, entitle, nickname, surname, title; **designate,** codename, denominate, denote, dub, hail, mention, nominate, style, tag, term; **sign,** autograph, endorse, subscribe

name *n* → **1** relative **2** reputation *v* **3** depute **4** employ **5** scold **6** speak

NAMED *adj* hight *(Archaic)*, nee, nominate, y-clept *(Archaic)*

namely *adv* → particularly

namesake *n* → name

nanny *n* → **1** minder **2** parent **3** servant

nanny-goat *n* → sheep

nap *n* → **1** bedclothes **2** prediction **3** sleep *v* **4** be inattentive **5** predict **6** sew **7** sleep

napalm *n* → **1** ammunition **2** fuel

nape *n* → neck

napery *n* → manchester

napkin *n* → washer

NAPPY *n* diaper *(U.S.)*, pilchers, swaddle, swaddling clothes

nappy *n* → **1** washer *adj* **2** intoxicating **3** worried

narcissism *n* → **1** braggartism **2** pride **3** selfishness

narcosis *n* → **1** drug use **2** sleepiness

narcotic *n* → **1** anaesthetic **2** drug **3** sleeping-pill *adj* **4** soporific

nark *n* → **1** complainer **2** informant *v* **3** annoy **4** discontent **5** irritate **6** report on

NARRATE *v* chronicle, fable, recite, recount, relate, report, set forth, story *(Rare)*, tell, write; **describe,** delineate, depict, depicture, outline, paint, picture, represent, sketch; **fictionalise,** mythologise, novelise, romance, spin a yarn, yarn

NARRATIVE *n* account, annals, chronicle, history, record, report, statement; **plot,** action, argument, continuity *(Broadcasting)*, counterplot, fable *(Archaic)*, intrigue, scenario, story-line, subplot, synopsis, underplot; **narration,** delineation, depiction, description, picture, portrayal, profile, recital, relation, representation, sketch, voice-over *(Films)*, word-painting. *See also* STORY

NARRATIVE *adj* delineative, depictive, descriptive; **fictional,** anecdotal, anecdotic, legendary, mythical, mythopoeic, romantic

narrative *adj* → reminiscent

narrow *n* → **1** thinness *v* **2** thin *adj* **3** intolerant **4** thin

nasal *n* → armour

nascent *adj* → **1** new **2** original

nasty *adj* → **1** dirty **2** immoral **3** smelly **4** unkind **5** unpleasant **6** unsavoury

natal *adj* → pregnant

NATION *n* buffer state, city, city-state, commonweal *(Archaic)*, commonwealth, democracy, nation-state, polity, republic, respublica, sovereignty, state; **kingdom,** monarchy, princedom, principality, realm, royalty; **dictatorship,** autocracy, despotism, police state, tyranny; **plutocracy,** pentarchy, tetrarchy, theocracy; **superpower,** atomic power, land power, nuclear power, power, sea-power, superstate, suzerain, world power; **third world country,** banana republic, developing country; **confederation,** bloc, Commonwealth, federation; **empire,** colony, dominion, empery *(Poetic)*, lebensraum; **territory,** condominium, independency, mandate, protectorate, trust territory; **country,** fatherland, land, shore, soil; **homeland,** home, home country, motherland, native land, old country

nation *n* → ancestry

NATIONAL *n* citizen, compatriot, countryman, patrial; **patriot,** nationalist, stalwart; **jingoist,** chauvinist, mafficker *(Brit.)*, minute man *(U.S.)*, supernationalist

NATIONAL *adj* country, patrial, state, territorial; **supranational,** imperial, metropolitan, supernational; **domestic,** civil, home, inland, interior, internal, intestine; **nationwide,** transnational

NATIONALISM *n* love of country, nationality, patriotism, public spirit, supernationalism; **regionalism,** parochialism, provincialism; **symbol of nationhood,** Anzac, Australia Day, national flag, national song, slouch hat; **jingoism,** chauvinism, flag-wagging, flag-waving; **imperialism,** colonialism, expansionism

NATIONALIST *adj* patriotic, public-spirited; **jingoistic,** chauvinist, chauvinistic, flag-wagging, flag-waving

NATIONALITY *n* aboriginality, citizenship, compatriotism; **nationhood,** statehood, territoriality

nationality *n* → nationalism

native *n* → **1** population *adj* **2** characteristic **3** natural **4** resident **5** simple

nativity *n* → start

natter *n* → **1** talk *v* **2** talk

natty *adj* → fashionable

NATURAL *adj* innate, instinctive, normal, unformed, unschooled; **primitive,** in a state of nature, native, savage, uncivilised, unlearned; **wild,** feral, ladino, tameless, warrigal, wilding *(Archaic)*, wildish; **undeveloped,** rough, trackless, unimproved, untouched, waste

natural *n* → **1** winner *adj* **2** artless **3** congruous **4** ignorant **5** inborn **6** raw **7** simple **8** tangible

naturalise *v* → **1** evolve **2** habituate

NATURALIST *n* bionomist, ecologist, physiographer; **nature lover,** comservationist, greenie

NATURALLY *adv* wild; **primitively,** savagely, wildly; **instinctively,** by birth, innately

NATURE *n* the great outdoors, the wild, tiger country, waste, wilderness, wilderness area; **balance of nature,** ecosystem; **ecology,** autecology, bionomics, natural history, natural science, nature study, physic *(Obs.)*, physiography, synecology

nature *n* → **1** character **2** essence **3** living **4** living thing **5** matter **6** sky

NATURE RESERVE *n* chase, flora and fauna reserve, game reserve, national park, sanctuary

naught *n* → **1** failure **2** nothing *adj* **3** immoral **4** ruined **5** useless

naughty *n* → **1** sexual intercourse *adj* **2** badly-behaved **3** disobedient **4** immoral **5** incorrect **6** obscene

NAUSEA *n* airsickness, altitude sickness, Barcoo spews, biliousness, carsickness, jet lag, mal de mer, mawkishness, morning sickness, mountain sickness, nauseousness, regurgitation, seasickness, trainsickness; **indigestion,** dyspepsia, dysphagia, heartburn, hyperacidity, hypoacidity, waterbrash; **stomach-ache,** colic, collywobbles, gripes, painter's colic; **diarrhoea,** amoebic dysentery, bloody flux, dysentery, food poisoning, gastro, gastroenteritis, Jimmy Brits, the runs, the shits, tomtits, trots

nausea *n* → hate

NAUSEOUS *adj* airsick, bilious, green at the gills, mawkish, seasick, squeamish, trainsick, upset, warby, white at the gills; **constipated,** costive; **incontinent; jacked-up**

NAUTICAL *adj* marine, naval, shipboard; **floating,** afloat, sailing, waterborne; **seaworthy,** A1 at Lloyd's, fit for sea, shipshape and Bristol fashion, watertight; **ocean-going**

naval *adj* → nautical

nave *n* → **1** centre **2** church

navel *n* → **1** abdomen **2** centre

navigate *v* → **1** beat a path **2** fly

navvy *n* → digger

navy *n* → **1** armed forces **2** blue **3** mariner **4** watercraft

nay *n* → **1** denial **2** disagreement *adv* **3** additionally *interj* **4** no

neap *n* → **1** current *adj* **2** sea

NEAR *prep* about, around, beside, by, nigh, on, round, towards

near *v* → **1** come close *adj* **2** close **3** future **4** kindred **5** left **6** mean **7** similar *adv* **8** closely **9** in the future **10** windward

nearby *adj* → **1** close *adv* **2** closely

nearly *adv* → **1** almost **2** similarly

neat *n* → **1** cattle *adj* **2** competent **3** good **4** intelligent **5** intoxicating **6** simple **7** tidy

nebula *n* → faulty sight

nebulous *adj* → **1** cloudy **2** ethereal **3** imprecise

NECESSARILY *adv* crucially, indispensably, obligatorily, perforce, requisitely

NECESSARY *adj* indispensable, necessitative, needful, requisite; **essential,** all-important, apodictic, crucial, exigent, imperative, mandatory, obbligato *(Music)*, obligate *(U.S.)*, pressing, urgent, vital; **obligatory,** de rigueur, prerequisite

necessary *n* → **1** necessities *adj* **2** forced **3** helpful **4** important **5** obligatory

NECESSITATE *v* ask, call for, claim, demand, need, oblige, require, take, want; **must,** have to, need to, needs must, should; **need,** can do with, could do with, crave

NECESSITIES *n* bare necessities, estovers, necessaries, occasions *(Obs.)*; **need,** call, use, want; **requirement,** essential, exigency, hinge, imperative, must, necessary, postulate, prerequisite, requisite, requisition, sine qua non

NECESSITY *n* compulsion, indispensability, indispensableness, matter of life and death, needfulness, requisiteness, urgency

necessity *n* → poverty

NECK *n* nape, nucha, scrag, scruff; **throat,** gorge, gullet, little red lane, maw, pharynx; **air passage,** bronchial tubes, bronchiole, bronchus, lung, pipes, trachea, tube, windpipe; **larynx,** Adam's apple, epiglottis, glottis, vocal cords, voice box

neck *n* → **1** channel **2** headland **3** length **4** thinness *v* **5** kill **6** kiss

neckerchief *n* → neckwear

necklace *n* → jewellery

NECKWEAR *n* boa, comforter, fichu, fraise, muffler, neckband, neckcloth, neckerchief, neckpiece, ruff; **collar,** bertha, chitterling *(Obs.)*, choker, collaret, collet, dicky, Eton collar, facings, front, guimpe, jabot, lapel, mandarin collar, peter pan collar, revers, roll-collar, stock, Vandyke collar, wing collar; **tie,** black tie, bow tie, choker, cravat, necktie, old school tie, white tie, Windsor tie; **clerical collar,** bands, dog-collar, Geneva bands; **scarf,** babushka, bandanna, barb, fascinator, four-in-hand, kerchief, madras, mantilla, nubia, tippet, victorine; **neckline,** décolletage, halter, halter-neck, polo-neck, scoop neck, turtleneck, V-neck

necromancy *n* → the supernatural

nectar *n* → drink

nee *adj* → named

need *n* → **1** deficiency **2** desire **3** insufficiency **4** necessities **5** poverty *v* **6** desire **7** fall short **8** necessitate

needle *n* → **1** direction finder **2** inserter **3** medication **4** piercer **5** rock outcrop **6** sewing machine **7** sharp point **8** worry *v* **9** annoy **10** arouse

needless *adj* → inconvenient

needlework *n* → sewing

needy *adj* → poor

nefarious *adj* → immoral

negate *v* → deny

negative *n* → **1** denial **2** disagreement **3** photograph *v* **4** deny **5** refuse *adj* **6** denying **7** female **8** numerical **9** unwilling

NEGLECT *v* default, disregard, evade, forget, forgo *(Archaic)*, leave out, let slide, let slip, not do, omit, overlook, pigeonhole, pretermit, scamp, shut one's eyes to, turn one's back on; **treat neglectfully,** mismother *(Agric.)*; **skim,** cut corners, huddle up, skimp

neglect *n* → **1** inattentiveness **2** neglectfulness **3** unreadiness

NEGLECTED *adj* derelict, in limbo, ragged, run-down, undone *(Archaic)*

NEGLECTED PERSON *n* cinderella, gamin, grass widow, gutter-snipe, latchkey child, mudlark *(Brit.)*, street Arab, street urchin, urchin

NEGLECTFUL *adj* careless, casual, disregardful, dizzy, forgetful, heedless, lax, mindless, negligent, omissive, regardless, slack, slipshod, thoughtless; **irresponsible,** delinquent, derelict, reckless, remiss

NEGLECTFULNESS *n* carelessness, casualness, forgetfulness, hastiness, heedlessness, irresponsibility, irresponsibleness, laxness, mindlessness, recklessness, remissness, slackness, thoughtlessness; **negligence,** delinquency, disregard, evasion, mismothering *(Agric.)*, preterition, pretermission, waste *(Law)*; **neglect,** conduct conducing, default, dereliction, lapse, laxity, miss *(Colloq.)*, nonfeasance, omission; **laches,** res ipsa loquitur

negligee *n* → nightwear

negligible *adj* → smallest

NEGLIGIBLY *adv* inconsiderably, infinitesimally, microscopically, vestigially; **scantily,** exiguously, skimpily, slightly, sparingly, sparsely; **merely,** alone, only, simply; **at least,** in the least; **just,** by degrees, by inches, by the skin of one's teeth, hardly; **in a nutshell,** in miniature

negotiate *v* → **1** mediate **2** talk **3** trade

neigh *n* → **1** animal call *v* **2** call (of animals)

neighbour *n* → **1** friend **2** inhabitant *v* **3** be close *adj* **4** close

neighbourhood *n* → **1** closeness **2** friendship **3** region

nemesis *n* → **1** avenger **2** punishment

neologism *n* → **1** innovation **2** word

neophyte *n* → **1** defector **2** learner **3** monastic **4** religious follower **5** starter

nephew *n* → relative

nepotism *n* → **1** dishonesty **2** influence **3** kinship **4** unfairness

nerve *n* → **1** arrogance **2** courage **3** durability **4** strength **5** vitality *v* **6** embolden **7** strengthen

nervous *adj* → **1** excitable **2** frightened **3** worried

nervy *adj* → **1** courageous **2** excited **3** strong **4** worried

nest *n* → **1** accumulation **2** animal dwelling **3** birth **4** shelter *v* **5** give birth **6** inhabit

nestle *v* → kiss

net *n* → **1** headband **2** interlacement **3** lace **4** sportsground **5** stratagem *v* **6** fish **7** gain *adj* **8** crossed **9** final **10** remnant

nether *adj* → **1** bottom **2** infernal

nettle *v* → annoy

network *n* → **1** interlacement **2** number system **3** tangle **4** telecommunications station

neuralgia *n* → ache

neurology *n* → body

neurosis *n* → psychic disorder

neuter *n* → **1** neutral *v* **2** make infertile *adj* **3** infertile **4** neutral

NEUTRAL *n* abstainer, civilian, fence-sitter, isolationist, moderate, mugwump, neuter *(Archaic)*, neutralist, non-belligerent, noncombatant

NEUTRAL *adj* apathetic, apolitical, detached, disinterested, even-handed, impartial, indifferent, neuter *(Archaic)*, non-aligned, noncommittal, non-involved, non-partisan, uncommitted

neutral *adj* → 1 colourless 2 peaceful

NEUTRALITY *n* abstention, apathy, detachment, disinterestedness, even-handedness, impartiality, indifference, isolation, isolationism, lack of involvement, neutralism, nonaggression, non-alignment, non-involvement; **neutral country,** neutral territory, no-man's-land, open city

NEUTRALLY *adv* disinterestedly, impartially

neutron bomb *n* → atomic bomb

never *adv* → 1 rarely *interj* 2 no

NEVERTHELESS *adv* all the same, anyhow, anyway, howbeit, however, just the same, non obstante, nonetheless, notwithstanding, regardless, still, though, withal *(Archaic)*, yet

NEW *adj* brand-new, fresh, green, hot, mint, new-laid, piping hot, red-hot, spick-and-span, unworn, virgin, virginal; **emergent,** nascent, newly-formed, promising, raw, renascent, reviviscent, up-and-coming; **first,** initial, maiden, pioneer; **young,** fledgling, immature, junior, newish, redbrick *(Brit.)*, untried, youngish; **inventive,** creative, enactory *(Law)*, initiatory

new *adj* → 1 additional *adv* 2 newly

NEWLY *adv* emergently, fresh, freshly, new, virginally; **modernly,** neoterically, not long ago, recently, swingingly; **innovatively,** for the first time, inspiritingly, novelly, originally, unprecedentedly

NEWNESS *n* change, curiousness, freshness, new look, novelty; **modernity,** modernism, modernness, recency, recentness, up-to-dateness

NEWS *n* information, intelligence, sound *(Obs.)*, tidings; **rumour,** ana, blue duck, bruit *(Archaic)*, buzz, dirt, gossip, hearsay, noise *(Archaic)*, renown *(Obs.)*, tale, talk, tattle, whisper; **bulletin,** announcement, communiqué, dispatch, handout, press conference, press release; **the latest,** stop press, the score; **gossiping,** tale-bearing, taletelling

news *n* → information

NEWS ITEM *n* a good spread, beat-up, cover story, exclusive, feature story, flash, item, leading article, personal *(U.S.)*, report, scoop, sensation, story, write-up; **newscast,** newsreel; **column,** editorial, gossip column, leader; **advertisement; headline,** banner, caption, head, side heading, streamer

NEWSPAPER *n* biweekly, blatt, broadsheet, buster *(N.Z. Obs.)*, daily, extra, final, gazette, journal, kite *(Colloq.)*, local, mouthpiece, news-sheet, newsletter, organ, paper, print, publication, rag, semiweekly, sheet, softcover, supplement, tabloid, triweekly, weekly; **comic,** feuilleton, funnies, horror comic, strip; **fourth estate,** press, print media, print press, the daily blatts, yellow press

newsreel *n* → 1 film 2 news item

newton *n* → energy

next *adj* → 1 close 2 following *adv* 3 after 4 in the future

nexus *n* → join

nib *n* → sharp point

nibble *n* → 1 meal 2 part *v* 3 eat

nice *adj* → 1 accomplished 2 delicious 3 discriminating 4 good 5 kind 6 modest 7 pleasant 8 precise 9 promiscuous

nicety *n* → 1 distinction 2 precision

NICHE *n* alcove, ambry, angle, apse, apsis, bay window, cockpit, columbarium, conch, inglenook, nook, pigeonhole, recess, set-off, setback, tabernacle; **socket,** caisson, groove, mortice, rebate. *See also* HOLLOW

niche *n* → compartment

nick *n* → 1 departure 2 furrow 3 kinship 4 prison 5 rest *v* 6 arrest 7 be precise 8 cheat 9 cut 10 furrow 11 record 12 reproduce 13 rob

nickel *v* → coat

nickname *n* → 1 name *v* 2 name

nicotine *n* → tobacco

niece *n* → relative

nifty *n* → 1 joke *adj* 2 good 3 tasteful

niggard *n* → 1 miser *adj* 2 mean

niggle *v* → annoy

nigh *adj* → 1 close 2 future 3 left 4 mean *adv* 5 closely 6 in the future *prep* 7 near

NIGHT *n* weeknight; **night-time,** dead of night, graveyard shift *(Mining Colloq.)*, midnight, moonrise, overnight, the witching hour; **the small hours,** piccaninny daylight. *See also* EVENING

night *n* → 1 dark 2 evening 3 misfortune

nightcap *n* → 1 a drink 2 cap

nightclub *n* → pub

NIGHTLY *adj* acronychal, all-night, nightlong, noctivagant, nocturnal, overnight, owl-like, owlish; **midnight,** midnightly; **evening,** goodnight, vesper, vespertine; **twilight,** crepuscular, duskish, moonlight

NIGHTLY *adv* all night, midnightly, nightlong, nights, nocturnally, overnight, under the stars

nightmare *n* → 1 devil 2 dream 3 unpleasant thing

NIGHT OWL *n* all-nighter, night-bird, nighthawk, nightwalker, owl

NIGHTWEAR *n* nightclothes; **dressing-gown,** bathrobe, beach robe, brunch coat, negligee, nightrobe, peignoir, robe, shave coat, shaving coat, shaving jacket; **pyjamas,** jamas, jamies, nightdress, nightgown, nightrobe, nightshirt, P.J.s

nihilism *n* → 1 anarchy 2 doubt 3 irreverence

nil *n* → nothing

nimble *adj* → 1 athletic 2 competent 3 cunning 4 intelligent 5 light-footed 6 speedy

nimbus *n* → 1 cloud 2 holy person 3 ring

NINE *n* ennead, ninth, nonet; **nonagon,** enneagon

NINE *adj* enneadic, ninefold, ninth, nonagonal

nine *n* → 1 alcohol container 2 sportsman

ninny *n* → 1 fool 2 stupid person

nip *n* → 1 a drink 2 coldness 3 pressing 4 pressure 5 slander 6 small amount 7 taste *v* 8 depart 9 hold 10 pain 11 press 12 remove 13 rob

nipple *n* → **1** bulge **2** chest
nippy *adj* → **1** cold **2** speedy
nirvana *n* → **1** afterworld **2** peace
nit *n* → **1** fool **2** stupid person
nitrogen *n* → air
nitroglycerine *n* → explosive
nitty-gritty *n* → **1** essence **2** important thing **3** particulars
nitwit *n* → **1** fool **2** stupid person
nix *n* → **1** mythical being **2** nothing *interj* **3** no
NO *interj* like hell, nae *(Scot.)*, nary *(U.S. Brit.)*, nay, never, nix, no such luck, no way, nope, not a bit of it, not by a long sight, not for quids, not on your life, noway, nowise, scarcely; **pigs,** baal *(Aborig.)*, balls, like fun, not on your nelly, nuts, phooey, speak for yourself, up you, upya
nob *n* → **1** aristocrat **2** coinage **3** head
nobble *v* → injure
nobility *n* → aristocracy
noble *n* → **1** aristocrat *adj* **2** aristocratic **3** enormous **4** important **5** inactive **6** reputable **7** steady **8** unselfish
nobody *n* → unimportant person
nocturnal *adj* → nightly
nod *n* → **1** gesture **2** move **3** sleep *v* **4** be inattentive **5** gesture **6** hang **7** lower **8** move
node *n* → **1** astronomic point **2** bulge **3** centre **4** difficulty **5** knob **6** point of convergence **7** steadiness
nodule *n* → **1** bulge **2** knob
noggin *n* → **1** alcohol container **2** head
noise *n* → **1** loud sound **2** news **3** radio **4** sound *v* **5** noise abroad
NOISE ABROAD *v* bruit, herald, noise, retail; **gossip,** chew the fat, fly a kite, rumour; **tattle,** inform on, pimp, tell tales
noisome *adj* → **1** bad **2** poisonous **3** sickening **4** unsavoury
NOISY *adj* blustery, boisterous, bouncing, hurly-burly, obstreperous, pandemoniac, pandemonic, pell-mell, rackety, rambunctious *(U.S. Colloq.)*, riotous, rip-roaring, roisterous, rumbustious, tumultuary, tumultuous, unquiet, uproarious
noisy *adj* → shouting
nom de plume *n* → **1** disguise **2** name
nomenclature *n* → **1** classification **2** language
nominal *adj* → **1** cheap **2** satisfactory
nominate *v* → **1** depute **2** employ **3** name *adj* **4** named
nominee *n* → appointee
NONACHIEVER *n* cipher, disaster area, failure, gutless wonder, no-hoper, nonentity, underachiever; **dud,** crookie, dead duck, debacle, disaster, lost cause; **loser,** also-ran, autumn leaf *(Horseracing Colloq.)*, bad shot, booby, easybeats, ferret *(Cricket)*, flop, hairy goat, lapser, non-starter, stiff *(Horseracing)*
nonagon *n* → nine
NON-BEING *n* inexistence, inexistency, nonexistence, nonentity, nullity; **nothingness,** absence, blank, blankness, negation, nihility, nowhere, vacuum, void, voidness; **insubstantiality,** abstractness, intangibility, intangibleness, invisibility, nebulousness, the intangible; **annihilation,** abolition, abrogation, annulment, defeasance, dematerialisation, destruction, disannulment, elimination, erasure, expunction, extermination, extinction, genocide, obliteration, removal. *See also* NOTHING
nonchalant *adj* → apathetic
non-committal *adj* → **1** elusive **2** indecisive **3** neutral **4** reticent
NONCONFORMIST *n* beat, beatnik, bodgie, bohemian, drop-out, flowerchild, hippie, hipster, long-hair, Promethean, sharpie; **eccentric,** a one, bird, card, case, caution, character, crank, dag, ding-a-ling, dingbat, enfant terrible, erratic, freak, fruit cake, geezer, half-axe, hangman *(N.Z.)*, kook, nut, nut case, odd bod, oddball, original, poon, queer fish, ratbag, screwball, wack, weirdo; **deviant,** bent, deviate *(U.S.)*, pervert; **radical,** angry young man, Bolshevik *(Derog.)*, dissenter, extremist, iconoclast, rebel, Red, reformist; **misfit,** fish out of water, no-hoper, square peg in a round hole; **exception,** curiosity, freak, heteroclite, irregular, odd one out, oddity, rarity; **bohemia,** beat generation, beautiful people, cafe society, demimonde, hip-hop culture, the Push
NONCONFORMIST *adj* anomalous, heteroclite, heterodox, informal, irregular, nonstandard, nonconforming, unconformable, uncustomary, unorthodox, unusual; **exceptional,** extraordinary, tremendous, unexampled, unheard-of, unique; **aberrant,** aberational, abnormal, bent, deviant, freakish, kinky, perverted, quirky, unnatural; **eccentric,** bizarre, crank, cranky, crazy, daggish, daggy, erratic, kooky, mad as a meataxe, maggoty, odd, odd-bod, oddball, off-beat, pixilated, queer, ratbaggy, ratty, screwy, singular, wacky, way-out; **unconventional,** alternative, beat, bohemian, unfashionable; **radical,** bold, iconoclastic, reformist
nondescript *adj* → **1** mediocre **2** shapeless
none *adj* → nonexistent
nonentity *n* → **1** nonachiever **2** non-being **3** unimportant person
nonetheless *adv* → nevertheless
NONEXISTENT *adj* absent, blank, extinct, inexistent, missing, napoo, unhistorical; **intangible,** abstract, insubstantial, invisible, metempiric, theoretical, unessential, virtual; **no,** none *(Archaic)*, null
NONFLAMMABLE *adj* athermanous, fireproof, fire-resistant, flame-proof, incombustible, thermoduric
nong *n* → **1** fool **2** stupid person
NON-PAYING *adj* bankrupt, behind, behindhand, broken, gazetted, in arrears, insolvent, ruined, unable to make both ends meet, unable to pay
NON-PAYMENT *n* avoidance, default, dishonour, evasion, moonlight flit, repudiation; **tax avoidance,** bottom-of-the-harbour scheme, dry Slutzkin, tax dodge, tax evasion, tax evasion scheme, tax haven, tax lurk, tax

shelter, underground economy, wet Slutzkin; **bankruptcy,** bust, failure, insolvency, insufficiency of funds, overdrawn account, receivership

NONSENSE *n* abracadabra, babble, bizzo, blah, blather, chatter, double-dutch, fable, falderal, fandangle, fiddle-faddle, fiddlesticks, flapdoodle, flim-flam, flummery, footle, froth and bubble, fustian, gaff *(Rare)*, gas, Greek, guff, gunk, guyver, hocus pocus, hokum *(U.S.)*, hooey, jabber, jabberwocky, jargon, kid-stakes, macaroni, malarky, mere words, moonshine, mumbo jumbo, pack of nonsense, palaver, pap, patter, persiflage, rant, rave, rhubarb, rigmarole, slipslop, sound and fury, stuff and nonsense, tarradiddle, tongue, tosh, trash, tripe, trumpery, twaddle, verbiage, waffle, yak, yawp; **absurdity,** amphigory, bagatelle, contradiction, exaggeration, imbecility, inanity, inconsistency, paradox, platitude, quibble, sophism, triviality, vagueness, verbalism; **nonsense verse,** derry; **tomfoolery,** jiggery-pokery, monkey tricks, mummery, practical joke, shenanigans; **bullshit,** a load of old cobblers, balderdash, balls, baloney, bilge, bollocks, bosh, bull, bulldust, bullo, bullswool, bumf, bunk, bunkum, claptrap, cock-and-bull, codswallop, crap, drivel, eyewash, farmyard confetti, Flemington confetti, fudge, gammon, gammon and spinach, garbage, gibberish, heifer dust, hogwash, horseshit *(U.S.)*, hot cock, kybosh, piffle, poppycock, rot, rubbish, shit, tommyrot

nonsense *n* → **1** foolishness **2** illogicality **3** waffle

NONSENSICAL *adj* absurd, cockeyed, crappy, extravagant, fantastic, foolish, inconsistent, jumbled, macaronic *(Obs.)*, paradoxical, piffling, preposterous, rich, ridiculous, sophistical, too-too; **meaningless,** amphigoric, insignificant, moonshiny, pointless, senseless, unmeaning, without rhyme or reason; **inconsequential,** babbly, farcical, flim-flam, futile, gassy, incoherent, inconsequent, quibbling, raving, rubbishy, windy

non sequitur *n* → illogicality

NON-USER *n* boycotter, discarder, rejecter, shepherd, sparer

noodle *n* → **1** fool **2** head **3** stupid person *v* **4** pursue

nook *n* → **1** compartment **2** niche **3** seclusion

NOON *n* lunchtime, mean noon, midday, midnoon, noonday, noontide, noontime

no-one *n* → nothing

noose *n* → ring

norm *n* → **1** example **2** ordinariness

Norm *n* → apathetic person

normal *n* → **1** average **2** ordinariness *adj* **3** bent **4** conventional **5** customary **6** erect **7** healthy **8** model **9** natural **10** ordinary **11** sane

north *n* → wind

NOSE *n* beak, boko, bracket, bugle, button, conk, hooter, nozzle, proboscis, schnozzle, smeller, snoot, snout, snoz; **nostrils,** nares, olfactories

nose *n* → **1** finding **2** knob **3** length **4** person **5** smell *v* **6** contact

nosedive *n* → **1** fall *v* **2** dive **3** fail

nose-dive *n* → failure

nosegay *n* → **1** fragrance **2** plant

NOSTALGIA *n* ; **retrospectivity** retroactivity, retrospect, retrospection, review; **flashback,** repeat, replay; **time machine**

nostalgia *n* → **1** desire **2** remembering

nostrum *n* → **1** expedient **2** medication **3** method **4** plan

nosy *adj* → **1** curious **2** intervenient

notable *n* → **1** famous person **2** important thing *adj* **3** accomplished **4** effortful **5** famous **6** important **7** obvious **8** thrifty

notary *n* → lawyer

notation *n* → **1** letter **2** musical score **3** record

notch *n* → **1** access **2** cut **3** furrow **4** gradation **5** record *v* **6** cut **7** label

NOTCHED *adj* biserrate, crenate, crenulated, deckle-edged, dentate, denticulate, double serrate, fringed, knurled, ridged, scalloped, serrate, serrated, serriform, serrulate, toothed, warded; **indented,** broken, erose, etched, gnawed away, gorgy, grooved, gullied, incised, valleyed

note *n* → **1** account **2** attentiveness **3** birdcall **4** cash **5** clarification **6** importance **7** information **8** innovation **9** message **10** musical score **11** particulars **12** postscript **13** record **14** reminder **15** reputation **16** shout **17** sign **18** sound **19** surpriser **20** written composition *v* **21** account **22** add **23** attend to **24** memorise **25** record

noted *adj* → **1** famous **2** important **3** known

NOTHING *n* aught *(Obs.)*, bugger all, damn-all, F.A., fuck-all, naught *(Archaic)*, nihil, nil, nix, no-one, not a sausage, not hide nor hair, nought, nowt, s.f.a., sweet F.A., zilch; **zero,** duck *(Cricket)*, duck's egg *(Cricket)*, love *(Tennis)*. *See also* NON-BEING

nothing *n* → **1** unimportant person **2** unimportant thing

notice *n* → **1** assessment **2** attentiveness **3** dismissal **4** information **5** insistence **6** label **7** publicity **8** public notice **9** seeing **10** warning *v* **11** attend to **12** inform **13** see

notify *v* → **1** inform **2** publicise **3** send a message

notion *n* → **1** caprice **2** idea **3** image **4** opinion

NOTIONAL *adj* conceptual, ideal, ideate, ideational, inspirational, intellective

notorious *adj* → **1** disreputable **2** famous **3** known **4** obvious

NOTWITHSTANDING *prep* after all, despite, for all, in despite of, in spite of, in the face of

notwithstanding *adv* → **1** nevertheless *conj* **2** still

nought *n* → nothing

noun *n* → word

nourish *v* → **1** encourage **2** feed

nous *n* → wisdom

novel *n* → **1** book **2** law **3** story *adj* **4** innovative

novelty *n* → **1** innovation **2** newness

NOVICE *n* beginner, greenhorn, raw recruit; **amateur,** calf, dabbler, dilettante, dilutee, landlubber *(Naut.)*, landsman, lilywhite *(Sport)*, lubber, potterer, tinkerer

novice *n* → **1** defector **2** ignoramus **3** learner **4** monastic **5** starter

novitiate *n* → **1** course **2** starter

NOW *adv* at present, at the present moment, at this point in time, before one's very eyes, currently, here and now, just now, nowadays, presently, still, under one's very eyes; **as of now,** for the nonce, for the time being, in the short run; **directly,** outright, right, straight; **today,** nowadays, tonight; **to date,** as yet; **already,** yet; **immediately,** anon *(Archaic)*, at once, on the spur of the moment, right away, straightaway, straightway

now *n* → the present

nowadays *n* → **1** the present *adv* **2** now

nowhere *n* → non-being

NO WORRIES *interj* no problem, no probs, no sweat

noxious *adj* → **1** harmful **2** poisonous **3** sickening

nozzle *n* → **1** exit **2** nose

nuance *n* → **1** colour **2** distinction **3** grade **4** meaning

nub *n* → **1** essence **2** knob

nubile *adj* → aged

nuclear *adj* → **1** atomic **2** central **3** chain-reacting

nucleus *n* → **1** atom **2** centre **3** meteor

nude *n* → **1** nudist **2** painting *adj* **3** bare

nudge *n* → **1** pat *v* **2** thrust

NUDIST *n* artiste, disrober, jaybird, naturist, skinny-dipper, streaker, stripper; **nude,** beefcake, centrefold, cheesecake, full-frontal, pin-up

nugget *n* → **1** bit **2** mineral **3** short person **4** strong person

nuisance *n* → **1** annoyance **2** bore **3** unpleasant thing

null *adj* → **1** ineffectual **2** nonexistent

nulla-nulla *n* → club

nullify *v* → **1** annihilate **2** cancel **3** deny

numb *v* → **1** anaesthetise *adj* **2** apathetic **3** insensible

NUMBER *n* digit, figure, value; **numeral,** chapter *(Horol.)*, cipher, lining figure *(Print.)*, modern figure *(Print.)*; **integer,** binary digit, binary number, natural number, perfect number, whole number; **cardinal number,** ordinal number; **decimal number,** compound number, decimal fraction, floating point number, half-integer, mixed number, real number, recurring decimal, repeating decimal, transcendental; **imaginary number,** complex number, composite number; **prime number,** square number; **surd,** irrational number; **variable,** dependent variable, independent variable, unknown, X; **constant,** invariable, invariant; **absolute value,** magnitude, modulus; **factor,** common factor, divisor, submultiple; **coefficient,** regression coefficient; **square,** cube, exponential, factorial, root mean square; **square root,** cube root, root; **mathematical function,** binomial, expression, form, formula, integral, polynomial, potential, quadratic, quadrinomial, quantic, quintic, step function, trinomial; **mathematical series,** arithmetic progression, geometric progression, harmonic progression, time series; **continuum,** domain, field; **number element,** characteristic, decimal place, decimal point, exponent, mantissa, repetend, significant figures; **fraction,** common fraction, complex fraction, compound fraction, continued fraction, improper fraction, proper fraction, recurring fraction, simple fraction, vulgar fraction; **denominator,** common denominator, lowest common denominator; **numerator**

NUMBER *v* numerate; **paginate,** foliate, folio, page

number *n* → **1** act **2** amount **3** concert **4** magazine **5** marijuana **6** rhythm *v* **7** age **8** compute **9** include **10** quantify

NUMBERING *n* foliation, numeration, pagination

numberless *adj* → infinite

numeral *n* → **1** letter **2** number *adj* **3** numerical

numerate *v* → **1** compute **2** number

numerator *n* → **1** mathematician **2** number

NUMERICAL *adj* alphanumeric, numeral, numerary, numeric; **integral,** digital, prime, round, whole; **real; fractional,** half-integral, rational; **imaginary,** even, odd; **negative,** positive, subtractive; **exponential,** differential, irrational, logarithmic, logometric; **cardinal,** ordinal; **decimal,** binary, duodecimal, duodenary, hexadecimal, octal, quinary, sexagesimal, uncial, undecimal; **submultiple,** aliquant *(Obs.)*, aliquot *(Obs.)*; **reciprocal,** complementary

numerous *adj* → many

NUMEROUSNESS *n* innumerability, innumerableness, multiplicity, pluralism, plurality; **abundance,** affluence, ampleness, amplitude, copiousness, plenteousness, plentifulness, profusion, thickness; **multitudinousness,** manifoldness, many-sidedness, multifariousness

numismatics *n* → coinage

nun *n* → **1** abstainer **2** monastic

nunnery *n* → **1** abbey **2** seclusion

nuptial *adj* → marital

nurse *n* → **1** healer **2** helper **3** minder *v* **4** care for **5** feed **6** help **7** hold **8** medicate **9** practise medicine

NURSERY *n* creche, day nursery, kindergarten

nursery *n* → **1** amusement park **2** breeding ground **3** garden **4** hospital **5** living room **6** school

nurture *n* → **1** help **2** teaching *v* **3** encourage **4** feed **5** help **6** rear

nut *n* → **1** bead **2** bolt **3** fool **4** head **5** mad person **6** nonconformist

nutrient *n* → **1** food *adj* **2** helpful **3** nutritive

nutriment *n* → food

nutrition *n* → food
NUTRITIVE *adj* alible, alimental, alimentative, nutrient, nutritional, sustentative, trophic
nuzzle *v* → **1** contact **2** kiss
nymph *n* → **1** animal offspring **2** beautiful person **3** mythical being **4** woman
nymphomania *n* → sexuality

Oo

oaf *n* → **1** stupid person **2** substitute **3** vulgarian

oak *n* → **1** timber *adj* **2** brown

oar *n* → **1** mariner **2** propellant

oasis *n* → fertile land

oath *n* → **1** contract **2** swearing

obdurate *adj* → **1** callous **2** impenitent **3** strict **4** stubborn

OBEDIENCE *n* compliance, deference, nonresistance, observance, observation *(Obs.)*, passiveness, passivity, subjection, submission; **dutifulness,** ductility, duteousness, duty, fealty, homage, loyalty, obsequiousness, orderliness, servility, submissiveness, towardliness *(Archaic)*, tractability, yieldingness; **compulsion,** domination, enforcement

OBEDIENT *adj* compliant, devoted, obsequious *(Rare)*, puppet, servile, yielding; **dutiful,** duteous, faithful, law-abiding, leal *(Archaic)*, loyal, observant, orderly; **tractable,** controllable, docile, guidable, henpecked, nonresistant, passive, pliant, subservient, towardly *(Archaic)*, under control

obeisance *n* → **1** obsequiousness **2** tribute

obelisk *n* → post

obese *adj* → **1** fat **2** thick

OBEY *v* do someone's bidding, do what one is told, follow, follow someone's lead, grovel, jump through hoops, play second fiddle, serve, submit, toe the line; **comply,** answer the helm, carry out, carry out orders, clear *(Naut.)*, comply with, defer to, fulfil, heed, keep, mind, observe, shape up or ship out

obey *v* → conform

OBEYER *n* clean potato, complier, follower, fulfiller, non-resistant, observant, observer; **yes-man,** arse-licker, brown-nose, lackey, puppet, slave, stooge, teacher's pet

obituary *n* → **1** funeral rites **2** public notice *adj* **3** funereal

object *n* → **1** actuality **2** aim **3** matter **4** subject matter *v* **5** impute

objection *n* → disagreement

objectionable *adj* → **1** inconvenient **2** unfair **3** unpleasant

objective *adj* → **1** artistic **2** fair **3** known **4** real **5** tangible **6** visible

oblation *n* → **1** gift **2** offering **3** religious ceremony

OBLIGATE *v* astrict, bind, oblige, tie; **be one's duty to,** be incumbent on, be up to, befit, behove, devolve, fall to one's lot, import, rest in, rest on, rest upon, rest with; **be obligated,** had better, have got to, ought, should

OBLIGATED *adj* beholden, bound, duty-bound, fain *(Archaic)*, in duty bound, obligate *(U.S.)*, obliged, under a compliment to someone, under an obligation to someone; **liable,** accountable, amenable, answerable, charged, responsible, saddled with

OBLIGATION *n* bounden duty, charge, devoir *(Archaic)*, duty, incumbency, onus, ought, responsibility; **bond,** agreement, astriction, band, call of duty, categorical imperative, contract, faith, personal responsibility, tie, trust, white man's burden; **liability,** burden *(Comm.)*, judgment *(Law)*, levy, service due, tax, tithe, tribute, vassalage; **job,** assignment, calling, commission, function, mission, office, part, role, task, undertaking, vocation; **quota,** darg, production target

obligation *n* → **1** contract **2** indebtedness **3** job

OBLIGATORY *adj* binding, bounden, de rigueur, imperative, incumbent, irremissible, necessary, obliging, peremptory *(Law)*, required

oblige *v* → **1** help **2** necessitate **3** obligate **4** promise

obliging *adj* → **1** helpful **2** lenient **3** obligatory

oblique *n* → **1** slope *v* **2** deflect **3** slope *adj* **4** allusive **5** bent **6** deflective **7** elusive **8** sloping **9** unequal

obliterate *v* → **1** hide **2** remove

oblivion *n* → **1** forgetfulness **2** sleeping **3** unconsciousness

oblivious *adj* → **1** forgetful **2** unconscious **3** ungrateful

oblong *n* → plane figure

obloquy *n* → **1** disapproval **2** disrepute **3** slander **4** swearing

obnoxious *adj* → **1** unpleasant **2** vulnerable **3** wrong

OBSCENE *adj* blue, filthy, foul, ithyphallic, lascivious, lewd, licentious, pornographic, rank, ripe, salacious, scabrous, scatalogical, thersitical, vile; **vulgar,** bawdy, broad, Corinthian, Cyprian, dirty, earthy, Fescennine, fruity, Rabelaisian, racy, raffish, rakish, randy, ribald, salty, smutty; **suggestive,** borderline, close to the bone, close to the knuckle, daring, juicy, naughty, near the bone, near the knuckle, risque, spicy, titillating; **erotic,** hot, phallic, priapic, sexy; **indecent,** coarse, curious, indecorous, off-colour; **unprintable,** unrepeatable, unspeakable; **foul-minded,** foul-mouthed, prurient, voyeuristic; **immodest,** flaunting, revealing, scarlet, shameless

OBSCENITY *n* bawdiness, filthiness, foulness, lasciviousness, lewdness, obsceneness, profanity, rankness, salaciousness, scabrousness, vileness; **indecency,** bawdry, coarseness, dirtiness, ribaldry, vulgarness, wantonness; **foul-mindedness,** prurience, scopophilia, skeptophilia, voyeurism; **suggestiveness,** earthiness, raciness, raffishness, smuttiness; **immodesty,** impudicity, indecorousness, shamelessness; **impureness,** impurity, unchasteness; **dirty word,** four-letter word, vulgarism. *See also* PORNOGRAPHY

OBSCURE *v* black out, blot, darken, darkle, fog, hide

obscure *v* → **1** darken **2** hide *adj* **3** allusive **4** dark **5** disreputable **6** dull **7** hidden **8** imprecise **9** invisible **10** secluded **11** uncertain **12** unclear **13** unimportant **14** working-class

OBSEQUIOUS *adj* menial, parasitic, servile, slavish, slimy, smarmy, sycophantic, toadyish, wormlike, wormy; **submissive,** acquiescent, amenable, compliant, concessionary, concessive, corrigible, deferent, deferential, ductile, easily managed, flexible, manageable, obedient, pliant, tractable, yielding; **bowed,** broken, browbeaten, cowed, crushed, downtrodden, henpecked, humbled, prostrate, subjective *(Obs.)*

obsequious *adj* → **1** flattering **2** meek **3** obedient **4** regardful

OBSEQUIOUSLY *adv* cap in hand, deferentially, in obedience to, meekly, menially, slavishly, slimily, subserviently, tamely, trucklingly; **submissively,** acquiescingly, amenably, compliably, compliantly, corrigibly, flexibly, in compliance with, on bended knee, resignedly, yieldingly

OBSEQUIOUSNESS *n* humbleness, self-abasement, servility, slavishness, sliminess, submissiveness, subservience, subserviency, suppleness; **deference,** genuflection, homage, kowtow, obeisance, prostration, salaam, slime, smarm; **sycophancy,** toadyism

observance *n* → **1** behaviour **2** conformity **3** custom **4** dutifulness **5** formal occasion **6** monasticism **7** obedience **8** rule **9** seeing **10** tribute

observant *n* → **1** obeyer *adj* **2** attentive **3** dutiful **4** obedient **5** perceptive **6** sharp-eyed

observatory *n* → lookout

observe *v* → **1** attend to **2** command respect **3** investigate **4** look **5** obey **6** perceive **7** see **8** speak

obsess *v* → remember

obsession *n* → **1** certainty **2** desire **3** idea **4** madness **5** psychic disturbance

obsolescent *adj* → **1** disused **2** old **3** untimely **4** useless

obsolete *adj* → **1** antique **2** disused **3** old **4** powerless **5** untimely **6** useless

OBSTACLE *n* barrier, baulk, block, hurdle, stop, traverse; **barricade,** abatis, balloon barrage, barbed wire, barrage, blockade, booby trap, caltrop, cheval-de-frise, concertina wire, fence, gabionade, trou-de-loup, wire entanglement; **gate,** cattle ramp, cattlegrid, cattlestop *(N.Z.)*, portcullis, turnpike, turnstile; **roadblock,** boom gate, humps, judder bar *(N.Z.)*, speed bumps, speed-trap, tollbar; **crash barrier,** bollard, guardrail; **dam,** boom, breakwater, dyke, embankment, sandbank, sandbar, sudd, weir; **chock,** doorstop, floor stop, trig, wedge; **deflector,** baffle, baffle plates, breakweather, breakwind, stopping *(Mining)*, windbreak; **airlock,** air-trap, P trap, vapour lock; **bunker,** hazard, sandtrap; **jump,** crossbar, fence *(Showjumping)*, oxer, water-jump; **obstacle race,** debil-debil country, obstacle course. *See also* HINDRANCE

obstacle *n* → **1** discourager **2** unwillingness

obstetrics *n* → healing

obstinate *adj* → **1** impenitent **2** stubborn

obstreperous *adj* → **1** badly-behaved **2** noisy

OBSTRUCT *v* intercept, interpose, obtrude; **block,** arrest, bar, barricade, blockade, close, dam, embank, hedge in, snow in, stop; **choke,** clog, congest, foul, gorge, gum up, jam, occlude, oppilate, stop up; **chock,** trig, wedge; **bunker,** trap; **bodycheck,** backstop, box in, hem in. *See also* HINDER

obstruct *v* → **1** come between **2** oppose

OBSTRUCTED *adj* air-bound, choked, clogged, congested, fitchered, icebound, impassable, insurmountable, snowbound; **blocked off,** barricaded, dead-end; **frustrated,** confounded, dished, stopped

obstruction *n* → **1** closure **2** dissidence **3** hindrance

OBSTRUCTIVENESS *n* bloody-mindedness, obstructionism; **interference,** forestalment, interception, interposal, interposition, interruption, mental block; **prevention,** forbiddance *(Rare)*, limitation, preclusion, restriction; **discouragement,** crossing, frustration, oppilation, thwarting; **cumbrousness,** awkwardness, unwieldiness

obtain *v* → **1** buy **2** gain **3** generalise **4** get

obtrude *v* → obstruct

obtuse *adj* → **1** blunt **2** curvilinear **3** insensible

obverse *n* → **1** front *adj* **2** front

OBVIOUS *adj* apparent, appreciable, black-and-white, broad, clean-cut, clear, clear as day, clear-cut, distinct, evident, in the foreground, manifest, notable, noticeable, palpable, pellucid, plain, plain as a pikestaff, plain as the nose on your face, unmistakable, vivid; **conspicuous,** outstanding, prominent, pronounced, salient, splendent, striking, under one's nose; **glaring,** flagrant, notorious, shroudless, unshaded; **self-evident,** axiomatic, incontestable, self-explanatory, truistic

obvious *adj* → **1** blatant **2** clear **3** hindering **4** simple **5** visible

OBVIOUSLY *adv* appreciably, clear, clearly, evidently, in evidence, manifestly, noticeably, palpably, plainly; **conspicuously,**

prominently, pronouncedly; **self-evidently,** axiomatically

occasion *n* → **1** cause **2** occurrence **3** opportunity *v* **4** cause

occasional *adj* → **1** causal **2** occurrent **3** rare

occlude *v* → **1** absorb **2** close **3** contact **4** obstruct

occult *n* → **1** arcanum *v* **2** come between **3** hide *adj* **4** arcane **5** hidden **6** invisible **7** supernatural

OCCULTIST *n* cabbalist, demonologist, occulter, pythoness, Rosicrucian, shaman, sibyl, sorcerer, sorceress, spiritist, spiritualist, supernaturalist, warlock, witch, wizard; **mind-reader,** telepath, telepathist, thought-reader; **medium,** clairaudient, clairsentient, clairvoyant, evocator, necromancer, oracle, psychic, seer, spirit-rapper, spiritist; **demoniac,** energumen, zombie

OCCUPANT *n* cotenant, homesteader, householder, leaseholder, occupier, tenant; **homemaker,** homebody; **household,** family, ménage; **cohabitant,** cohabitator, flatmate, inmate *(Archaic)*; **lodger,** boarder, hosteller, paying guest, roomer *(U.S.)*; **guest,** commensal, sojourner, visitor. *See also* INHABITANT; POPULATION

occupant *n* → **1** filler **2** owner

occupation *n* → **1** capture **2** fullness **3** job **4** presence

occupy *v* → **1** be present **2** engross **3** fill **4** inhabit **5** own

OCCUR *v* arise, arrive *(Obs.)*, be, break out, brew, come about, come one's way, come to pass, come up, fall, give, hap *(Archaic)*, happen, offer, pop up, rise, see the light of day, take place, transpire, turn up; **bechance,** befall, betide, come over, worth *(Archaic)*; **turn out,** come off, fall out, fare, go off, go on, pass off, prove

occur *v* → be

OCCURRENCE *n* circumstance, contingency, contingent, episode, event, experience, hap *(Archaic)*, happening, incident, occasion, passage *(Archaic)*, phenomenon; **incidence,** advent, incurrence, occasion. *See also* AFFAIR; SITUATION

OCCURRENT *adj* actual, afoot, emergent, going, happening, in progress, incidental, occasional, occurring, on, passing, up; **phenomenal,** empirical, experiential, experimental, practical

ocean *n* → **1** much **2** sea

ochre *n* → **1** powder **2** soil **3** yellow *v* **4** colour *adj* **5** yellow

ocker *n* → **1** Australian **2** discourteous person **3** good person **4** ignoramus **5** intolerant person **6** man **7** vulgarian *adj* **8** ignorant

octagon *n* → plane figure

octet *n* → **1** musical band **2** theatrical company

ocular *adj* → optical

odd *n* → **1** freak **2** one **3** remnant *adj* **4** incongruous **5** irregular **6** mad **7** nonconformist **8** numerical **9** remnant **10** strange

oddball *n* → **1** nonconformist **2** strange person *adj* **3** nonconformist

oddity *n* → **1** nonconformist **2** strangeness

oddment *n* → remnant

odds *n* → **1** advantage **2** gambling **3** inequality

odds-on *adj* → likely

ode *n* → poetry

odious *adj* → **1** bad **2** disreputable **3** hateful **4** ugly **5** unpleasant **6** vexing

odium *n* → **1** disapproval **2** dislike **3** disrepute **4** hate

odour *n* → **1** reputation **2** smell **3** stench

ODOURLESS *adj* inodorous, scentless; **deodorant; anosmatic**

ODOURLESSNESS *n* freshness, inodorousness, lack of smell, ring of confidence, scentlessness; **deodorisation; deodoriser,** activated charcoal, deodorant; **anosmia,** inability to smell

odyssey *n* → journey

oesophagus *n* → abdomen

off *n* → **1** right *adj* **2** absent **3** deteriorated **4** ill **5** incongruous **6** moving **7** resting **8** right **9** sea **10** unsavoury *adv* **11** absently **12** away **13** decreasingly **14** deflectively **15** in the future **16** remotely **17** restfully **18** wanderingly *prep* **19** without

off-beat *adj* → nonconformist

off-colour *adj* → **1** ill **2** obscene

off-cut *n* → remnant

offence *n* → **1** attack **2** crime **3** harm **4** wrong

offend *v* → **1** act unkindly **2** annoy **3** be immoral **4** contravene **5** displease **6** wrong

offensive *n* → **1** attack *adj* **2** aggressive **3** annoying **4** dirty **5** incorrect **6** sickening **7** smelly

OFFER *n* bid, overbid, proffer, proposal, proposition, psychic bid *(Bridge)*, tender, underbid; **recommendation,** suggestion; **approach,** feeler, opener, overture; **formal proposal,** motion; **last offer,** ultimatum

OFFER *v* bargain, bid, extend, give, hold out, overbid, tender, underbid; **propose,** advance, hawk an idea, initiate, lay a plan before, make a suggestion, move a motion, present, project, proposition, propound, put forward, put up, raise a matter, sponsor, submit, suggest; **make an overture,** approach, launch, make oneself available, offer oneself, overture, put oneself at another's disposal, sound out, stand for, volunteer; **proposition,** crack onto, put the hard word on *(Colloq.)*; **advocate,** recommend, stand for; **toast**

offer *n* → **1** assertion **2** attempt **3** cost **4** wedding *v* **5** appraise **6** give **7** marry **8** occur **9** sell **10** theorise

OFFERER *n* bidder, presenter, tenderer; **proposer,** proponent, propounder, sponsor; **bargainer,** underbidder

OFFERING *n* candidature, presentation, presentment; **launching,** sponsorship; **bidding,** calling; **oblation,** propitiation, sacrifice

offering *n* → **1** allowance **2** gift **3** religious ceremony

offhand *adj* → **1** incompetent **2** informal

off-hand *adj* → **1** apathetic **2** arrogant **3** discourteous **4** insulting

OFFICE *n* boardroom, chamber, chancellery, composing room, confined space, consulting room, counting room, headquarters, operations room, orderly room, registry, registry office, salesroom, studio, surgery, tally-room

office *n* → **1** company **2** employment **3** funeral rites **4** information agency **5** job **6** obligation **7** recorder **8** shop **9** workers **10** workplace

officer *n* → **1** high command **2** manager

official *n* → **1** bureaucrat **2** manager *adj* **3** agential **4** authoritative **5** commanding **6** formal

OFFICIALLY *adv* authoritatively, ex cathedra, from the horse's mouth; **in the name of,** by the authority of, in virtue of

officious *adj* → **1** intervenient **2** presumptuous

offing *n* → **1** remote place **2** sea

off-limits *adj* → **1** exclusive **2** prohibited

OFF ONE'S GUARD *adv* on the hop, unawares, with one's pants down

off-peak *adj* → inactive

off-putting *adj* → discouraging

off-season *n* → **1** period of inaction *adj* **2** inactive

offset *n* → **1** compensation **2** copy **3** counterbalance **4** curve **5** error **6** mountain **7** start *v* **8** be adequate **9** compensate **10** counteract **11** print *adj* **12** compensatory

offshoot *n* → **1** ancestry **2** descendant **3** offspring

offshore *adj* → **1** distant **2** sea *adv* **3** at sea **4** remotely **5** windward

offsider *n* → **1** labourer **2** partner **3** workers

OFFSPRING *n* family, fruit of the womb, generation, increase, issue, posterity, progeny, seed, team *(Obs.)*, young; **scion,** cadet, clone, daughter, descendant, firstborn, firstling, hybrid, mongrel, offshoot, pigeon pair, son, sprig, sprout; **twin,** quad, quadruplet, quintuplet, sextuplet, triplet; **illegitimate,** basket *(Euph.)*, bastard, by-blow, git, love child, whoreson *(Obs.)*; **orphan,** orphanage *(Archaic)*; **baby,** a little stranger, babe, bairn, blue baby, bottle baby, bub, infant, neonate, nursling, papoose, premmie, test-tube baby, the little stranger, war baby; **toddler,** mite, tot. *See also* CHILD; ANIMAL OFFSPRING

often *adj* → **1** frequent *adv* **2** frequently

ogle *n* → **1** endearments **2** look *v* **3** flirt **4** look

ogre *n* → **1** bad person **2** fairy

OH *interj* bejesus, blimey, boy, by George, by gum *(Brit.)*, coo *(Brit.)*, cor, crikey, cripes, dear, egad, God almighty, gorblimey, gosh, gracious, gramercy *(Archaic)*, Great Scott, ha-ha, hello, heyday *(Archaic)*, ho, hot dog *(U.S.)*, I say, jeepers creepers *(U.S.)*, Jesus, jiminy, jingaloes, lord, marry *(Archaic)*, my, my word, oops, struth, the dickens, well, what, whoops, why, woops, yikes, yow. *See also* HOW ABOUT THAT

oh *interj* → how about that

OIL *n* aromatic oil, fixed oil, oleoresin, volatile oil

OIL *v* grease, lubricate; **butter,** lard; **anoint,** baste

oil *n* → **1** bribe **2** flattery **3** fuel *v* **4** bribe **5** flatter

oilskin *n* → textiles

OILWELL *n* gusher, step-out, step-out well; **grasspay sandstone**

OILY *adj* greasy, lubricous, slick, slippery, soapy; **unctuous,** balsamic, chrismal, oleaginous, unguinous; **lubricant,** antifriction, lubricative; **fatty,** buttery, butyraceous, fat, lardaceous, lardlike, lardy, pinguescent, pinguid, stearic; **mono-unsaturated,** polyunsaturated; **adipose,** blubbery; **sebaceous,** waxy

oily *adj* → **1** flattering *adv* **2** flatteringly

ointment *n* → **1** fat **2** medication

okay *n* → **1** affirmation *v* **2** assent to *adj* **3** approved **4** good **5** satisfactory *adv* **6** satisfactorily **7** well

OLD *adj* aboriginal, age-old, ancient, antediluvian, antemundane, antique, as old as Adam, as old as Methuselah, as old as the hills, fossil, fossil-like, original, out of the ark, preadamite, preglacial, prehistoric, primitive, primordial, pristine; **immemorial,** long-gone, of yore, olden *(Archaic)*; **outmoded,** antiquated, archaic, archaistic, behind the times, dated, demoded, discontinued, extinct, moss-grown, obsolescent, obsolete, out of date, out of fashion, outdated, passé, slow, square, steam *(Colloq.)*; **vintage,** antique, classic, classical, dateless, former, rancio, ripe, veteran; **timeworn,** crumbling, decayed, decrepit, moth-eaten, threadbare; **burnt out,** beat-up, clapped-out; **stale,** fusty, mouldy, mucid, musty, rancid; **second-hand,** hand-me-down, preloved, pre-owned, third-hand

old *n* → **1** beer *adj* **2** accomplished **3** aged **4** colourless **5** dilapidated **6** dull **7** frequent **8** known **9** past **10** wise

olden *adj* → **1** early **2** old **3** past

OLDNESS *n* agedness, anecdotage, antiqueness, elderliness, hoariness, old age; **great age,** ancientness, antiquarianism, antiquity, archaism, classicality, classicism, medievalism; **ageing,** fossilisation; **decrepitude,** obsolescence, primitiveness, ruin; **staleness,** fustiness, mouldiness, mucidness, mustiness, rancidity, rancidness

OLD PEOPLE *n* Dad's army, old guard, older generation, the aged, the ageing, the old; **old person,** ancient, antediluvian, dotard, fogram, fossil, geri, geriatric, has-been, methuselah, museum piece, old bird, old crock, old fogy, old identity, old stager, old thing, oldie, oldster, relic, senior, senior citizen, wrinklie; **old man,** colonel blimp, father, gaffer *(Brit.)*, grandsire, grey beard, old boy, old codger, old fellow, old-timer, whitebeard; **old woman,** beldam, biddy, carline *(Scot.)*, crone, dame, gammer *(Brit. Archaic)*, grandam, granny, grimalkin, hag, harpy, mother, old boiler, old chook, old girl, old maid; **elder,** doyen, elder statesman, grand old man, matriarch, Nestor, patriarch; **centenarian,** nonagenarian, octogenarian, quinquagenarian, septuagenarian, sexagenarian

oleaginous *adj* → oily

olive *n* → **1** green **2** pacification *adj* **3** arboreal

Olympian *adj* → **1** reputable **2** superior

OMEN *n* augury, auspice, boding, foreboding, forerunner, forewarning, harbinger, herald, portent, presage, prodigy *(Rare)*, sign, signifier, type, writing on the wall; **harbinger of evil,** death knell, premonition of death, time bomb; **destiny,** fate, fortune

omen *n* → **1** warning *v* **2** predict

ominous *adj* → **1** calamitous **2** dangerous **3** menacing **4** predictive **5** warning

omit *v* → **1** exclude **2** neglect

omnibus *n* → **1** book **2** truck *adj* **3** general

omnipotent *n* → **1** infinity *adj* **2** powerful

omnipresent *adj* → present

omniscient *adj* → knowledgeable

on *n* → **1** left *adj* **2** left **3** occurrent **4** operating *adv* **5** continually **6** forward *prep* **7** concerning **8** near

ON BEHALF OF *prep* for, in the name of; **by,** of *(Archaic)*

once *adv* → **1** in the past **2** only **3** rarely *conj* **4** while

ON CONDITION THAT *conj* and *(Archaic)*, as, as long as, if, on the understanding that, provided, provided that, providing, so as, so long as, so that *(Obs.)*, sobeit *(Archaic)*, though; **unless,** except *(Archaic)*, excepting *(Archaic)*, lest, nisi, save *(Archaic)*, without *(Brit. Colloq.)*; **if and only if,** iff *(Logic)*

ON CREDIT *adv* on account, on H.P., on hire-purchase, on lay-by, on the never-never, on the nod, on tick

ON DISPLAY *adv* demonstratively, for all to see, from the housetops, in the open, on show, on view, open to the public, openly, publicly; **manifestly,** blatantly, obviously, patently

ONE *n* ace, ane *(Scot.)*; **single item,** monad, none other than, odd, odd one, one-off, singleton, solo, the one and only, unicum *(Rare)*, unit; **individual,** one, one-man band, one-man show, soloist; **loner,** crusoe, hatter, Jimmy Woodser, lone wolf, odd man out

ONE *adj* a, an, ane *(Scot.)*, any, unit, unitarian, unitary; **single,** exclusive, individual, mere *(Law)*, one-off, only, only-begotten, singular, sole, unique; **unilateral,** azygous, haploid, unipolar; **unifying,** unific; **lone,** insular, one-out, single-handed, solitary, solo, unaccompanied, unattended

ONE *pron* ane *(Scot.)*, any, each

one *n* → **1** one **2** person *adj* **3** congruous **4** married **5** particular

one-eyed *adj* → **1** intolerant **2** prejudiced **3** unfair

ONENESS *n* conjugation, conjunction, ecumenicalism, identicalness, identity, indivisibility, indivisibleness, solidarity, unification, unity; **singleness,** aloneness, exclusiveness, individuality, oddness, solitariness, unicity, uniqueness; **loneliness,** isolation, seclusion, solitude

onerous *adj* → **1** difficult **2** pestering

one-upmanship *n* → superiority

ON FOOT *adv* afoot, on footback, on shanks's pony

onion *n* → **1** head **2** sexual partner

ONLY *adv* solely; **once,** for the nonce

only *adj* → **1** one **2** smallest *adv* **3** negligibly **4** simply

onomatopoeia *n* → **1** figure of speech **2** imitation **3** rhyme **4** sound

onset *n* → **1** attack **2** start

onslaught *n* → **1** attack **2** reprimand

ON THE MOVE *adv* on the go, on the wing, under way, under weigh *(Naut.)*, up and about; **to and fro,** back and forth, hither and thither

on to *adj* → knowledgeable

onus *n* → obligation

onward *adj* → **1** advanced *adv* **2** forward

onwards *adv* → **1** forward **2** in the future

oomph *n* → **1** allure **2** sexuality **3** vitality

ooze *n* → **1** sea **2** sludge **3** swamp *v* **4** discharge **5** flow

OPACITY *n* denseness, density, opaqueness, solidity, thickness; **turbidity,** cloudiness, muddiness

opal *n* → jewel

OPAQUE *adj* dense, intense, thick; **turbid,** cloudy, muddy, roily

opaque *n* → **1** darkener **2** dye *v* **3** darken **4** dull *adj* **5** dark **6** stupid **7** unclear

OPEN *v* reopen, throw open, unbar, unbolt, unclench, unclose, uncork, undo, unglue, unhook, unlatch, unlock, unplug, unseal, unstop, unwrap, unzip; **pierce,** bore, breach, broach, buttonhole, drawbore, drill, eat into, eye, eyelet, gimlet, hole, loophole, peck, perforate, pin-prick, pink, prick, prickle, prong, rebore, roulette, scuttle *(Naut.)*, stab, stave, tunnel, wimble, window; **tear,** gap, slash, slit; **force,** jemmy, pick

OPEN *adj* agape, ajar, dehiscent, expanded, overt *(Her.)*, undone, unsealed, wide-open; **gaping,** expanded, oscitant, patulous, rictal, ringent, wide; **perforated,** cancellate, holey, porous

OPEN *adv* ajar; **wide,** gapingly, patulously, yawningly

open *n* → **1** air **2** contest **3** liberty **4** opportunity **5** sea **6** space *v* **7** bare **8** gape **9** reveal **10** separate **11** start **12** weaken *adj* **13** bare **14** displayed **15** feasible **16** forthright **17** gaping **18** generous **19** honest **20** impersonal **21** indecisive **22** influenced **23** liberated **24** predisposed **25** revealed **26** spacious **27** tolerant **28** uncertain **29** undetermined **30** visible

OPEN-AIR *adj* alfresco, exposed, plein air

OPENER *n* key, latchkey, latchstring, ripcord *(Aeron.)*, skeleton key, tin-opener, undoer; **drill,** borer, broach, cardpunch *(Computers)*, driller, hole puncher, perforator, piercer, trepan, wimble

OPENING *n* aperture, chink, cranny, gap, gape, hole, interstice, ostiole, perforation, pinhole, pinprick, pit, prick, slit, slot, yawn; **orifice,** blastopore, blowhole, fistula, foramen, foramen magnum, jaws, meatus, micropyle, mouth, os, osculum, pore, stoma; **breach,** break, crack, fissure, leak, puncture, rent, rift, wash-out; **bore,** blowhole, borehole, mofette, Mohole, quarry, winning; **manhole,** drop, hatch, hatchway *(Naut.)*, stokehole, trap, trapdoor, vampire *(Theat.)*; **scupper,** hawse, hawsehole, lubber's hole, scuttle; **escape lock,** David apparatus; **peephole,** hagioscope, judas hole, peep, spy-hole, squint; **miscellaneous opening,** airbrick, airhole, core, core hole, embrasure, grille *(Royal Tennis)*, gunport, hazard *(Royal Tennis)*, loop *(Archaic)*, loophole, machicolation, port *(Mil.)*, service hatch, sleeve, weephole

opening *n* → **1** entrance **2** exit **3** gap **4** opportunity **5** start

open-minded *adj* → tolerant

OPENNESS *n* gape, oscitance, oscitancy, patulousness, rictus

OPEN UP *v* become open, bilge *(Naut.)*, break, crevasse, dehisce, fissure, leak, pop, reopen, rift; **gape,** expand, loosen, open out, run, spread, undouble, unfold, unfurl, yawn

operable *adj* → medical

OPERATE *v* be operative, function, go, play, run, serve; **work,** act, be in operation, be in working order, be under way, take effect, tell; **actuate,** act on, erect, float, functionalise, gear up, ignite, make work, move, ply, run in, summon up, switch on, wind up; **administer,** administrate, apply, command, drive, hold, manage; **drive,** force *(Obs.)*, operate, power; **apply,** exercise; **implement,** bring to bear, institute

operate *v* → **1** invest **2** medicate **3** operate **4** wage war

OPERATING *adj* effectual, in effect, operant, operational; **going,** acting, afloat, alive, at work, effective, efficient, go, in force, in motion, in play, in the pipeline, in the system, live, on, on deck, on stream, operational, operative, up, working; **running,** A-OK, going strong, good; **functional,** applied, economic, expedient, practical, useful

OPERATION *n* action, activity, application; **function,** affair, cycle, exercise, procedure, process; **actuation,** effectuation, implementation, making; **governance,** administration, control, management, treatment; **machinery,** order

operation *n* → **1** act of war **2** agency **3** capability **4** influence **5** method **6** trade **7** undertaking

operational *adj* → **1** operating **2** prepared

operative *n* → **1** hider **2** policeman **3** worker *adj* **4** capable **5** medical **6** operating

OPERATOR *n* actuator, administrant, agent, applier, commission, effecter, force, operant; **headquarters,** command, management, operations branch

operator *n* → **1** computer programmer **2** financier **3** influencer **4** powerful person

ophthalmic *adj* → optical

opiate *n* → **1** anaesthetic **2** sleeping-pill *v* **3** anaesthetise

opine *v* → **1** believe **2** think

OPINION *n* conception, conclusion, conviction, editorial, estimate, idea, impression, mind, notion, preconception, prejudice, prenotion, prepossession, rooted opinion, sentence *(Obs.)*, sentiment, surmise, theory, thinking, thought; **public opinion,** ground swell, vox pop, vox populi; **viewpoint,** position, school of thought, stance, standpoint, view, Weltanschauung, world view. *See also* BELIEF

opinion *n* → **1** approval **2** assessment **3** point of view

opinionated *adj* → **1** certain **2** intolerant **3** stubborn

opponent *n* → **1** dissident **2** enemy *adj* **3** dissident **4** opposite

opportune *adj* → **1** expedient **2** timely

OPPORTUNISM *n* craftiness, cunning, gamesmanship, political skill, shiftiness, timeserving; **back scratching,** flattery, sycophancy

opportunism *n* → selfishness

OPPORTUNIST *n* carpetbagger, self-seeker, timeserver, trimmer *(Politics)*; **flatterer,** back scratcher, gamesman, sycophant; **wangler,** conniver, Machiavellian, wriggler; **improviser,** adaptor, extemporiser, improvisator

OPPORTUNIST *adj* artful, crafty, cunning, devious, resourceful, shifty; **self-seeking,** fawning, flattering, servile, sycophant, timeserving; **scheming,** astute, calculating, deceitful, deliberate, Machiavellian, manipulative, ruthless

OPPORTUNITY *n* chance, occasion, open, open go, opening, potency *(Obs.)*, potential, potentiality, resource, room, scope; **psychological moment,** high time, right moment, right time

opportunity *n* → crucial moment

opportunity shop *n* → shop

OPPOSE *v* answer back, be set against, contend against, counter, fall foul of, make a stand against, object to, obstruct, rebut, recalcitrate, repugn *(Obs.)*, resist, set one's face against, side against, stand against, stand out against, strive against, take on, talk back to, tangle with, withstand; **defy,** beard, brave, brave it out, brazen out, breast, champion *(Obs.)*, check, face, hold out against, kick against the pricks, persist, reluct *(Archaic)*, stand one's ground, stand up to, stick up to; **outface,** call someone's bluff, dare, fly in the face of, heavy, hurl defiance at, laugh to scorn, outstare, put it on someone, set at naught, thumb one's nose; **challenge,** bare one's teeth, bluster, call in question, show fight, threaten, throw down the gauntlet; **rebel,** buck, find fault, kick

oppose *v* → **1** contrast **2** hinder **3** invert

OPPOSING *adj* antagonistic, antithetic, antithetical, conflicting, contradictory, contrary, contrasted, ditheistic, inconsistent, like chalk and cheese, mutually exclusive, opposed, opposite, oppositional, paradoxical, the other, tother *(Archaic)*; **antonymic,** opposite in meaning; **inverse,** arsy-versy, back-to-front, converse, inversive, reverse; **on opposite sides,** antipodean, at cross purposes, at opposite poles, like oil and water; **ambivalent,** ac-dc, bisexual, hermaphrodite, hermaphroditic, hermaphroditical, two-edged

OPPOSITE *adj* diametrically opposite, face to face, vis-a-vis; **opposed,** contrary, counter, cross, foul, opposable, polarised; **adverse,** contrapositive, opponent; **polar,** bipolar; **antipodal,** antipodean

OPPOSITE *adv* dos-à-dos, oppositely, overleaf, vis-a-vis; **contrarily,** adversely, contrariwise, counter, per contra; **bilaterally,** distichously

OPPOSITE *prep* against *(Obs.)*, anent *(Archaic)*, face to face with, facing, vis-a-vis; **against,** over against

opposite *n* → **1** contrast **2** dissident *adj* **3** bad **4** opposing

OPPOSITE MEANING *n* antipode *(U.S.)*, antipodes, antithesis, contraposition, contrary, converse, the other extreme; **inverse,** contrary, counter, reverse; **antonym; enantiosis,** a contradiction in terms, adversative, irony, paradox, sarcasm; **hermaphrodite**

OPPOSITE POSITION *n* antithesis, inverse, reverse; **contraposition,** adverseness, confrontment, contrariness, opposition; **polarity,** bilateralism, bilateralness, bipolarity, dissymetry, polarisation; **pole,** antipode *(U.S.)*; **opposite number,** flip side, verso, vis-a-vis

opposition *n* → **1** astronomic point **2** dislike **3** dissidence **4** opposite position **5** unfriendliness

oppress *v* → **1** be unfriendly **2** make unhappy **3** repress **4** victimise

optic *n* → **1** look *adj* **2** optical

OPTICAL *adj* ocular, ophthalmic, optic, photopic, visual; **binocular,** emmetropic, orthoptic, orthoscopic, stereoscopic, stereoscopical; **audiovisual**

OPTICS *n* dioptrics, geometrical optics; **fibre optics,** catoptrics

optimism *n* → **1** expectation **2** hope

OPTIMIST *n* bull, positivist, truster; **aspirant,** aspirer, young hopeful

optimum *adj* → good

option *n* → **1** choice **2** liberty

OPTIONAL *adj* alternative, discretional, elective, facultative, permissive, selective, volitional, volitionary, voluntary, votive *(Rom. Cath. Ch.)*; **multiple-choice,** either-or, two-way; **eclectic**

OPTIONALLY *adv* ad libitum, alternatively, at one's discretion, discretionally, electively, volitionally; **eclectically,** preferentially, selectively; **rather,** by choice, first, preferably, sooner, voluntarily

opulent *adj* → wealthy

opus *n* → **1** musical piece **2** work of art **3** written composition

or *prep* → before

oracle *n* → **1** guide **2** occultist **3** predictor **4** revealer **5** shrine **6** wise person

oral *adj* → spoken

ORANGE *n* amber, cadmium orange, tangerine; **orange-red,** ginger, henna, poppy, rust, scarlet; **orange-brown,** terracotta; **peach,** apricot, coral, yellow-pink; **brass,** copper, old gold

ORANGE *adj* amber, carroty, scarlet, tangerine, terracotta; **ginger,** rusty; **peach,** apricot, coralline, luteous. *See also* YELLOW

orange *adj* → red

ORATION *n* address, address-in-reply *(Parl. Proc.)*, allocution, declamation, defence, discourse, effusion, homily, inaugural, King's speech, lecture, maiden speech, monologue, narration, panegyric, Queen's speech, sermon, soliloquy, speech, spiel; **recitation,** reading, recital, set speech; **prologue,** exordium, peroration; **funeral oration,** valediction, valedictory; **eulogy,** encomium; **speechifying,** homiletics, sermonising

ORATOR *n* declaimer, demagogue, elecutionist, haranguer, homilist, lecturer, mouthpiece, narrator, oratress, oratrix, polemicist, rabblerouser, ranter, reader, rhapsodist, rhetor, rhetorician, soap-box orator, speaker, spokesperson, stump orator, stylist, tub-thumper, valedictorian *(U.S.)*, word-spinner, Yarra banker; **spieler,** amster, deipnosophist, poet, smart talker, spruiker; **public speaker,** after-dinner speaker, toastmaster, toastmistress; **preacher,** Amen snorter, bible-basher, gospeller, holy Joe, hot-gospeller, pulpiteer, sermoniser

oratory *n* → **1** bombast **2** eloquence **3** shrine

orb *n* → **1** ball **2** emblem of office **3** eye **4** heavenly body **5** rotation **6** space *v* **7** enclose **8** rotate **9** round

orbit *n* → **1** astronomic point **2** circle **3** direction **4** eye **5** job **6** move **7** rotation **8** route *v* **9** rotate

orchard *n* → garden

orchestrate *v* → order

orchid *n* → **1** plant **2** purple

ORDAIN *v* foreordain, order, predestinate, predestine, predetermine, preordain; **doom,** destine, foredoom

ordain *v* → **1** command **2** elect **3** employ **4** have the right **5** legalise

ordeal *n* → **1** pain **2** test

ORDER *n* combination, configuration, conformation, form, geometry, Gestalt *(Psychol.)*, matrix, method, shape, structure, syntax *(Obs.)*, system, taxis; **arrangement,** arrayal, calibre, cast, collation, collocation, composition, dispensation, disposal, disposition, disposure *(Rare)*, distribution, layout, line-up, make-up, ordination, permutation, placement; **battle formation,** battleline, close-order, echelon, flight formation; **brick arrangement,** bond, colonialbond, English bond, Flemish bond, four-and-a-half bond, garden-wall bond, half bond, hit-and-miss brickwork, stack bond, stretcher bond, toothing; **floral formation,** aestivation, anthotaxy, phyllotaxis, vernation

ORDER *v* compose, fix, form, gather *(Bookbinding)*, make *(Print.)*, permute, range, rank, set, settle; **arrange,** coordinate, orchestrate, permutate, program *(Computers)*, rotate, seed *(Sport)*, set to rights, structure, tabularise, tabulate, timetable; **rearrange,** re-format, re-sort, readjust, recast, recompose, redeploy, reorder; **systematise,** alphabetise, codify, coordinate, methodise, organise, rationalise, regularise, systemise

order *n* → **1** angel **2** cash **3** class **4** command **5** community **6** conformity **7** grade **8** imposition **9** imprisonment **10** insistence **11** judgment **12** operation **13** rule **14** uniform *v* **15** class **16** command **17** inquire into **18** insist on **19** ordain

ORDERED *adj* architectonic, structured; **orderly,** businesslike, methodical, scientific, streamlined, systematic, tight-knit, well-regulated; **harmonious,** cosmic, organic; **sequential,** chronological, seriate, synchronistic, tabular

ORDERING *n* alphabetisation, orchestration, organisation, rationalisation, recomposition, redeployment, schematisation, systematisation, systemisation; **coordination,** imposition *(Print.)*, regimentation, regularisation, subjunction; **systematics,** architectonics, methodology, systematology

ORDERLY *adv* harmoniously, harmonistically, regularly, systematically, systemically; **sequentially,** in order, just so, seriately, step by step, stepwise

orderly *n* → **1** healer **2** messenger **3** servant *adj* **4** obedient **5** ordered

ordinance *n* → **1** command **2** law **3** rule

ORDINARILY *adv* averagely, indifferently, middling, middlingly, moderately, on the average; **commonly,** exoterically, medially, mundanely, prosaically, tritely, usually

ORDINARINESS *n* commonness, commonplaceness, exotericism, mediocrity, pedestrianism, prosaicness, triteness, triviality, trivialness; **average,** medium, middle, norm, normal, normality, par, standard; **commonplace,** banality, cliché, platitude, prosaism, trivialism, triviality; **standardisation**

ORDINARY *adj* average, fair to middling, indifferent, mediocre, medium, middling, moderate, normal, par, par for the course, standard; **mean,** medial; **common,** banal, common-or-garden, commonplace, day-to-day, everyday, exoteric, middle-of-the-road, middlebrow, mill-run, moderate, mundane, pedestrian, prosaic, run-of-the-mill, tired, tolerable, trite, trivial, vulgar

ordinary *n* → **1** ecclesiastic **2** heraldry **3** religious ceremony *adj* **4** conventional **5** customary **6** inferior **7** mediocre **8** simple **9** ugly

ORDINARY PERSON *n* middle-of-the roader, middlebrow; **everyman,** Aussie battler, Joe *(U.S.)*, Joe Bloggs, Joe Blow, John Citizen, the man in the street

ordination *n* → **1** employment **2** imposition **3** order **4** power to act

ordure *n* → defecation

ore *n* → **1** mineral **2** raw materials

organ *n* → **1** newspaper **2** wind instrument

organic *adj* → **1** bodily **2** farming **3** ordered

organisation *n* → **1** corporation **2** management **3** ordering

organise *v* → **1** associate **2** combine **3** manage **4** order **5** plan

ORGANISM *n* animalcule, individual, zooid; **micro-organism,** aerobe, anaerobe, anaerobiont, coenocyte, infusorian, intestinal flora, microbe, microfauna, microparasite, monad, nanoplankton, protist, protistan, protozoan; **pathogen,** bacillus, bacteria, bacteriophage, bacterium, bug, germ, parvovirus, PPLO, rickettsia, virus, wog; **cell,** corpuscle, protoplast; **culture,** plate, pure culture, subculture; **colony,** clump, coenobium, plasmodium, zoogloea

orgasm *n* → **1** excitement **2** sexual intercourse *v* **3** eroticise

orgy *n* → **1** binge **2** sexual intercourse **3** voluptuousness

orient *n* → **1** brightness *adj* **2** ascending **3** bright

oriental *adj* → bright

orientation *n* → **1** direction **2** positioning

orifice *n* → **1** exit **2** opening

origami *n* → **1** fine arts **2** folding

origin *n* → **1** ancestry **2** being **3** creation **4** start

ORIGINAL *adj* conceptive, exordial, first, fontal, front-end, inaugural, inceptive, incipient, initial, initiative, initiatory, instigative, institutive, primary, radical, unprecedented; **germinal,** elementary, embryo, embryonic, nascent, seminal; **rudimentary,** abecedarian, basic, foundation, fundamental, introductory; **primeval,** early, inchoate, inchoative *(Rare)*, primigenial, primitive, primordial, pristine, protomorphic; **cosmogonic,** cosmogonical, cosmological

original *n* → **1** antecedent **2** creator **3** innovator **4** model **5** nonconformist **6** strange person *adj* **7** creative **8** fundamental **9** innovative **10** mad **11** model **12** old **13** real

originate *v* → **1** create **2** innovate

ornament *n* → **1** decoration **2** equipment **3** trinket *v* **4** decorate

ornate *adj* → **1** decorative **2** spectacular

orphan *n* → **1** break **2** offspring

orphanage *n* → **1** dwelling **2** offspring

orthodontics *n* → healing

orthodox *adj* → **1** conservative **2** correct **3** religious **4** strict

oscillate *v* → **1** flutter **2** vacillate

osmosis *n* → flow
ossify *v* → 1 be prejudiced against 2 harden
ostensible *adj* → 1 apparent 2 fake 3 likely 4 revealed
ostentation *n* → 1 display 2 showiness
osteoarthritis *n* → cramp
osteopathy *n* → healing
ostracise *v* → 1 be unfriendly 2 isolate 3 prohibit
other *adj* → 1 different 2 increased 3 past 4 remnant
otherwise *adj* → different
ottoman *n* → 1 couch 2 support
ouch *n* → 1 button 2 jewellery
ought *n* → 1 obligation *v* 2 obligate
ounce *n* → 1 bit 2 small amount
oust *v* → 1 dismiss 2 eject
outback *n* → 1 inside 2 remote place *adj* 3 remote 4 rural *adv* 5 remotely
outbreak *n* → 1 commotion 2 exit 3 flood 4 mutiny 5 outburst
outbuilding *n* → 1 break 2 building
OUTBURST *n* blaze, burst, ebullition, flaw *(Obs.)*, gust, outbreak, outrage *(Obs.)*, riot, start *(Archaic)*, tornado, torrent, whiff, willy; **flush,** swell, wave
outburst *n* → 1 exit 2 explosion
outcast *n* → 1 outsider 2 traveller 3 waste *adj* 4 excluded
outcome *n* → result
outcrop *n* → 1 mineral 2 mound *v* 3 jut
outcry *n* → 1 challenge 2 loud sound 3 shout 4 shouting *v* 5 shout
outdo *v* → surpass
outdoor *adj* → outside
outdoors *adv* → outside
outer *n* → 1 gambling hall *adj* 2 outside
OUTFIT *n* change, ensemble, layette, separates, trousseau, turnout; **suit,** bag of fruit, dinner suit, dress suit, evening suit, lounge suit, monkey suit, morning dress, pants-suit, safari suit, slacks suit, three-piece, tuxedo, two-piece; **overalls,** boilersuit, coogans, dungarees, ovaries *(Colloq.)*. *See also* UNIFORM; FINERY; DRESS
outfit *n* → 1 clique 2 corporation 3 drug equipment 4 equipment 5 gathering *v* 6 equip
outflank *v* → 1 flank 2 succeed 3 wage war
outgoing *n* → 1 exit *adj* 2 emergent 3 friendly 4 sociable
outgrow *v* → 1 disuse 2 grow 3 jut
outgrowth *n* → 1 bulge 2 result
outhouse *n* → 1 building 2 toilet
outing *n* → 1 journey 2 remote place 3 sea
outlandish *adj* → 1 foreign 2 remote 3 strange 4 vulgar
outlaw *n* → 1 anarchist 2 criminal 3 disobeyer 4 prohibition *v* 5 boycott 6 prohibit
outlay *n* → 1 cost 2 payment *v* 3 pay
outlet *n* → 1 exit 2 shop
outline *n* → 1 abridgment 2 diagram 3 drawing 4 edge 5 line 6 outside 7 plan *v* 8 abbreviate 9 depict 10 edge 11 map 12 narrate
outlook *n* → 1 lookout 2 point of view 3 view
outlying *adj* → 1 outside 2 remote
outmoded *adj* → 1 old 2 untimely
OUT OF PLACE *adv* adventitiously *(Bot. Zool.)*, astray, in no-man's-land, on the streets, out, out of joint
outpatient *n* → patient
outpost *n* → 1 combat troops 2 dwelling 3 fortress 4 remote place
output *n* → 1 amount 2 fertilisation 3 finished product 4 making
outrage *n* → 1 crime 2 insult 3 outburst 4 wrong *v* 5 be violent 6 rape
outright *adj* → 1 thorough 2 unconditional *adv* 3 freely 4 now 5 wholly
outset *n* → start
OUTSIDE *n* exterior, external, outward, superficies, surface, top; **face,** facade, facia, front; **covering,** crust, epidermis, rind, shell, skin, superstratum; **outline,** boundary, circumference, periphery, profile, silhouette
OUTSIDE *adj* exoteric, exterior, external, extrinsic, out, outer, outward; **surface,** covering, crustal, crusty, epidermal, epidermic, epigene, epigenic, superficial, top; **out-of-doors,** alfresco, extramural, field, open-air, outdoor; **peripheral,** boundary, circumjacent, surrounding; **extraneous,** outlying
OUTSIDE *adv* out, outward, outwards, thereout *(Archaic)*, without; **on the outside,** externally, extrinsically, on the face of it, on the surface, outwardly, superficially; **out of doors,** abroad, alfresco, en plein air, in the open air, out the back, outdoors, withoutdoors *(Obs.)*
OUTSIDE *prep* beyond, out, round, without *(Archaic)*
outside *n* → 1 sea *adj* 2 foreign *prep* 3 except
OUTSIDER *n* fringe dweller, harijan *(India)*, Ishmael, lost soul, marginal man, outcast, outlander, pariah, reprobate, social leper; **exile,** alien, expatriate, refugee
outsider *n* → 1 competitor 2 foreigner 3 ignoramus
outsize *n* → 1 size *adj* 2 fat 3 strange
outskirts *n* → 1 edge 2 town
outspoken *adj* → 1 assertive 2 callous 3 honest 4 liberated
outstanding *adj* → 1 good 2 obvious 3 owing 4 separate 5 unpaid
outstrip *v* → 1 advance 2 overtake
outward *n* → 1 appearance 2 outside 3 pose *adj* 4 apparent 5 outside 6 surrounding *adv* 7 at sea 8 outside 9 remotely
OUTWARDNESS *n* exteriority, externality, extrinsicality, superficiality, superficialness
outweigh *v* → 1 predominate 2 succeed 3 weigh
outwit *v* → 1 beguile 2 surpass
OVAL *n* ellipse, ellipsoid, geoid; **ovoid,** almond, amygdala *(Anat.)*, cartouche *(Archit.)*, egg, ovum *(Archit.)*
OVAL *adj* ecliptic, egg-shaped, ellipsoid, ellipsoidal, elliptical, obovate, obovoid, olivary, ovate, oviform, ovoid, pear-shaped, pineal, piriform, spatulate *(Bot.)*, testiculate, vesical
ovary *n* → 1 flower 2 groin

ovate *adj* → oval
ovation *n* → applause
oven *n* → stove
overall *n* → **1** overcoat *adj* **2** inclusive **3** long **4** thorough *adv* **5** wholly
overarm *n* → swimming
overawe *v* → **1** command respect **2** menace
overbalance *n* → **1** inequality *v* **2** fall **3** overturn **4** weigh
overcast *v* → **1** cloud **2** darken *adj* **3** cloudy **4** shadowy
overcharge *n* → **1** inflation *v* **2** exaggerate **3** weigh
OVERCOAT *n* balmacaan, box coat, buff, cutaway, dreadnought, frockcoat, gaberdine, greatcoat, jubbah, matinee coat, pelisse, peplos, petersham, Prince Albert, raglan, redingote, surcoat, topcoat, ulster; **overgarment,** frock, outer garments, overclothes, overdress, paletot, tabard, toga, vestment, wrapper; **coverall,** cover-up, dustcoat, duster *(U.S.)*, housecoat, overall; **apron,** bib, feeder, pinafore, pinny, smock. *See also* CLOAK; RAINCOAT; JACKET
overcome *v* → **1** defeat **2** repress *adj* **3** captivated
overdo *v* → **1** bore **2** exaggerate
overdose *n* → **1** amount **2** drug use **3** surplus *v* **4** oversupply **5** take drugs
overdraft *n* → debt
overdraw *v* → **1** be in debt **2** cash **3** distort **4** exaggerate
overdrive *v* → be excessive
overdue *adj* → late
overflow *n* → **1** flood **2** spring **3** surplus *v* **4** be surplus **5** flood **6** flow
overhang *n* → **1** length *v* **2** hang **3** menace **4** tower
overhaul *n* → **1** investigation **2** repair *v* **3** advance **4** examine **5** overtake **6** prepare **7** repair **8** separate **9** set sail
overhead *adj* → **1** high **2** impersonal *adv* **3** above **4** high
overhear *v* → hear
OVERINDULGE *v* burn the candle at both ends, carouse, debauch, dissipate, go on the tiles, go round the traps, go to town, indulge, live fast, live hard, live high on the hog, luxuriate, paint the town red, racket, riot, run riot, sow one's wild oats, surfeit, wallow, wanton; **give oneself up to,** give free rein to
OVERINDULGENCE *n* bacchanalianism, crapulousness, debauchery, dissipatedness, dissipation, dissoluteness, excess, immoderacy, intemperance, intemperateness, profligacy, profligateness, rakishness, riotousness, self-indulgence, unrestraint, wantonness, wildness. *See also* GREED
OVERINDULGENT *adj* abandoned, crapulous, dionysian, immoderate, incontinent, orgiastic, profligate, rakehelly *(Archaic)*, saturnalian, unbridled, uncontrolled, unmeasured, unrestrained; **dissipated,** Corinthian, debauched, dissolute, gay, goliardic, licentious, rakish, riotous, wanton; **self-indulgent,** compulsive, indulgent, intemperate. *See also* GREEDY
overjoyed *adj* → **1** joyful **2** pleased
overkill *n* → **1** exaggeration **2** surplus *v* **3** exaggerate
overlap *n* → **1** length **2** surplus *v* **3** cross
overleaf *adv* → opposite
overlook *v* → **1** be inattentive **2** bewitch **3** forgive **4** investigate **5** look **6** manage **7** neglect **8** top **9** tower
overly *adv* → excessively
overnight *n* → **1** night *adj* **2** momentary **3** nightly *adv* **4** nightly
overpass *n* → **1** bridge **2** road
overpower *v* → repress
overreach *v* → **1** cheat **2** grow **3** lose **4** succeed
overrun *n* → **1** flood **2** surplus *v* **3** fill **4** flood **5** grow **6** overtake **7** own **8** print *adj* **9** flooded
overseas *adj* → **1** remote **2** sea *adv* **3** at sea **4** away
oversee *v* → **1** investigate **2** look **3** manage
overshadow *v* → **1** belittle **2** darken **3** surpass **4** top **5** tower
overshoot *v* → overtake
oversight *n* → **1** error **2** forgetfulness **3** inattentiveness **4** management
overstate *v* → **1** exaggerate **2** lie
OVERSUPPLY *v* cloy, congest, cram, drug, engorge, fill to overflowing, glut, OD, overdose, overfill, sate, satiate, stuff, surfeit; **deluge,** flood, glut the market, load, overwhelm, plaster, riddle, smother, swamp; **overproduce,** overstock, pile up
overt *adj* → **1** open **2** visible
OVERTAKE *v* catch up with, forereach, gain upon, lap, overhaul, ride down; **leave behind,** beat, forerun *(Obs.)*, leave at the post, leave standing, outdistance, outpace, outrun, outstrip, shoot ahead; **pass,** go beyond, go past, move past, shoot by, shoot past, whistle by, whistle past, whizz by, whizz past; **skirt,** slide past, slip past; **overshoot,** go further, move ahead, override, overrun, overshoot the mark, overstand *(Naut.)*, overstep, overstride
overtake *v* → **1** advance **2** come close **3** surprise
overthrow *n* → **1** dismissal **2** losing **3** overturn *v* **4** defeat **5** destroy **6** dismiss **7** lower **8** madden **9** overturn
overtime *n* → **1** income **2** time *v* **3** mistime
overtone *n* → allusion
overture *n* → **1** introduction **2** musical piece **3** offer *v* **4** offer
OVERTURN *n* bouleversement, careen *(Naut.)*, overset, overspill, overthrow, tip, turnover, upset; **headstand,** cartwheel, somersault, topsy-turvy; **topsy-turviness,** topsy-turvydom
OVERTURN *v* overset *(Rare)*, overthrow, skittle, tip, tip over, tip up, turn over, upset, upturn; **invert,** inverse *(Rare)*, put the cart before the horse; **overbalance,** capsize, careen *(Naut.)*, keel over, loop *(Canoeing)*, overspill,

pitch pole, somersault, stand on one's head, tumble, turn cartwheels, turn turtle

overturn *n* → **1** losing *v* **2** bowl over **3** counteract **4** defeat

OVERTURNED *adj* arse-up, arsy-versy, back-to-front, topsy-turvy, upset, upside down, upturned, wrong side up; **inverted,** awkward *(Obs.)*, backward, inversive, reversionary; **converse,** inverse

overview *n* → generalisation

overweening *adj* → **1** arrogant **2** excessive

overwhelm *v* → **1** abound **2** astonish **3** defeat **4** flood **5** oversupply **6** weigh

overwrought *adj* → **1** complex **2** decorative **3** excited **4** tired **5** worried

ovine *adj* → animal-like

ovoid *n* → **1** oval *adj* **2** oval

ovulate *v* → reproduce

ovum *n* → **1** moulding **2** oval

owe *v* → be in debt

OWING *adj* chargeable, due, floating, outstanding, payable, undischarged, unpaid

owl *n* → **1** night owl **2** sobersides **3** wise person

OWN *v* be worth, bear, command, enjoy, enjoy the use of, have, have all to oneself, have in hand, hold, hold in fee, possess; **gain possession of,** enfeoff, get one's hands on, occupy, overrun, squat in; **corner,** engross, monopolise, privatise

OWN *adj* ain *(Scot.)*, appropriative, belonging, inalienable; **of one's own,** exclusive, personal, private, privy, proper; **claimed,** bespoke, previously claimed, spoken for; **of the house,** maison; **pre-owned,** pre-loved, secondhand, used

own *adj* → particular

OWNER *n* capitalist, franklin, joint owner, monopolist, occupant, possessor, proprietary, proprietor, proprietress, riparian, tenant, tenant in common; **holder,** claimholder, coparcener, copyholder, freeholder, impropriator, squatter; **landlord,** absentee landlord, body corporate, land-holder, landlady, landowner; **lord,** lady, laird, master, mistress, seignior; **alienee,** cestui que vie

OWNERSHIP *n* demesne, domain, easement, estate, grasp, holding, interest, occupancy, possession, proprietary, proprietorship, stake, tenure, vested interest; **lordship,** lairdship, landownership, landowning, seigniority; **monopoly,** corner *(Finance)*, monopolisation, monopolism; **use,** coparcenary, copyhold, exclusive right, freehold, gavelkind, impropriation *(Eccles. Law)*, leasehold, mortmain, seigniorage, seisin, socage *(Archaic)*, tenancy, vacant possession, villeinage *(Archaic)*; **title,** company title, copyright, fee, fee simple, fee tail, feoff, feud, patent, reversion, title deed, Torrens title, trust instrument

ox *n* → cattle

oxidise *v* → **1** coat **2** deteriorate

oxygen *n* → air

ozone *n* → air

Pp

pace *n* → **1** length **2** move **3** platform **4** rate **5** walking *v* **6** measure **7** ride **8** speed **9** walk

pacemaker *n* → **1** example **2** heart **3** speedster

pacific *adj* → peaceful

PACIFICATION *n* appeasement, assuagement, conciliation, détente, frank and free discussion, meaningful exchange, mediation, mollification, negotiation, peacekeeping, reconciliation, tranquillisation; **peace-offering,** calumet, compromise, dove, olive, olive branch, overtures, peace-pipe, pipe of peace; **white flag,** flag of truce; **demilitarisation,** non-proliferation

PACIFISM *n* ahimsa, disarmament, peace march, peace movement; **peaceableness,** amicability, amicableness, anti-militarism, friendship

pacify *v* → **1** make peace **2** mediate **3** moderate **4** satisfy

pack *n* → **1** amount **2** bag **3** gathering *v* **4** cover **5** fill **6** gather **7** press **8** transport **9** weigh *adj* **10** transport

package *n* → **1** accumulation **2** bag *v* **3** cover **4** insert **5** manage

packet *n* → **1** accumulation **2** bag **3** drug **4** hit

packing *n* → **1** filler **2** placement

pact *n* → **1** arrangement **2** contract

pad *n* → **1** armour **2** bed **3** bedroom **4** click **5** dwelling **6** path **7** propellant **8** room **9** thief **10** writing materials **11** yard *v* **12** fill **13** secure **14** soften **15** walk

paddle *n* → **1** corporal punishment **2** door **3** mixer **4** propellant *v* **5** hit **6** mix **7** touch

paddock *n* → **1** farmland **2** field **3** pen **4** sportsground *v* **5** enclose **6** imprison

paddy *n* → **1** angry act **2** farmland

paddywhack *n* → **1** angry act **2** back **3** corporal punishment **4** hit

padlock *n* → bolt

padre *n* → ecclesiastic

pagan *n* → **1** foreigner **2** irreverent person **3** worshipper *adj* **4** foreign **5** irreverent **6** worshipful

page *n* → **1** book part **2** butler **3** period **4** shout *v* **5** number

pageant *n* → **1** entertainment **2** festival **3** platform **4** representation **5** show **6** stage

pagoda *n* → **1** church **2** tower

pail *n* → vessel

PAIN *n* affliction, discomfort, hurt, injury, malaise; **irritation,** thorn in one's flesh, trouble; **suffering,** passion *(Archaic),* pathos *(Obs.),* travail; **agony,** anguish, distress, excruciation, hell, slow death, torment, torture, tortures; **ordeal,** baptism of fire, gethsemane, Golgotha, trial; **martyrdom,** crucifixion; **algolagnia,** masochism, sadism, sadomasochism; **algometry,** algometer. *See also* ACHE

PAIN *v* ache, anger *(Obs.),* give one gip, gripe, hurt, jump, play hell, play merry hell, smart, throb, tingle, trouble, twinge; **sting,** urticate; **chafe,** fret, gall, pinch, rub; **fester,** rankle; **cause pain,** afflict, anguish, cut up, distress, excruciate, harrow, hurt, rack, torment, vex *(Archaic),* wring; **wound,** bite, lacerate, nip, prick, stab, sting, tear; **torture,** crucify, excruciate; **prolong the agony,** kill by inches

pain *n* → **1** ache **2** annoyance **3** bore **4** perception **5** unpleasantness **6** unpleasant thing

PAINFUL *adj* afflictive, distressful, distressing, harrowing, heart-rending, piquant *(Archaic),* poignant; **excruciating,** torturous; **biting,** bitter, burning, cruel, nipping, piercing, shooting, stabbing, throbbing; **griping,** colicky, fulgurating; **sore,** exposed, raw, tender; **achy,** footsore, footworn, headachy, saddle-sore; **suffering,** aching, racked with pain

painstaking *adj* → **1** attentive **2** busy **3** effortful

PAINT *n* acrylic paint, antifouling, clobber, colourwash, couch, daub, distemper, dope, duco, emulsion paint, estapol, gesso, glair, glaze, glazing, graining, ground colour, impastation, japan, kalsomine, lacquer, luminous paint, lustre *(Pottery),* metalflake duco, oil-paint, overglaze, paintwork, plastic paint, poster colour, poster paint, primer, sealant, size, slip *(Pottery),* spirit varnish, splash coat, thixotropic paint, tiger's-eye, varnish, wash, water-paint, whitewash; **undercoat,** undercoating, underseal

paint *n* → **1** dye *v* **2** coat **3** colour **4** depict **5** narrate **6** place **7** portray

painter *n* → **1** artist **2** colourist **3** cord

PAINTING *n* bark painting, batik, cave painting, daubery, drip painting, portraiture; **picture,** diptych, icon, lunette, panel, pastiche, polyptych, predella, triptych; **portrait,** figure, half-face, half-length, nude, profile, self-portrait, silhouette, torso; **study,** landscape, marine, moonscape, nocturne, pastoral, scene, seascape, still life, tableau, townscape, view, waterscape; **kakemono,** tanka; **fresco,** frieze, mural; **painting technique,** alla prima, chiaroscuro, direct painting, encaustic, gouache, grisaille, sfumato, sgraffito, stipple; **painting medium,** acrylics, aquarelle, monochrome, oils, poster colour,

stereochrome, tempera, wash, watercolour; **canvas,** easel, picture plane, support; **palette,** oils, paintbox, paints
painting *n* → 1 fine arts 2 portrait
pair *n* → 1 arrangement 2 lover 3 rowing boat 4 similar thing 5 spouse 6 two *v* 7 double 8 join
pal *n* → 1 friend 2 helper *v* 3 be friends
palace *n* → 1 auditorium 2 house
palatable *adj* → 1 delicious 2 pleasant
palate *n* → 1 good taste 2 mouth 3 pleasure 4 taste
palatial *adj* → 1 big 2 wealthy
palaver *n* → 1 discussion 2 flattery 3 nonsense 4 talk 5 waffle *v* 6 flatter 7 talk
pale *n* → 1 limit 2 region 3 shaft *v* 4 enclose 5 lose colour *adj* 6 colourless 7 dull 8 weak 9 white
palette *n* → 1 armour 2 colour 3 painting
palindrome *n* → figure of speech
paling *n* → shaft
palisade *n* → 1 fortification 2 shaft *v* 3 defend
pall *n* → 1 cloak 2 coffin 3 covering 4 shade *v* 5 be unpalatable 6 bore 7 cover 8 satisfy
pallbearer *n* → 1 transporter 2 undertaker
pallet *n* → 1 bed 2 knob 3 platform
palliate *v* → 1 alleviate 2 justify 3 moderate
pallid *adj* → colourless
palmistry *n* → fortune-telling
palpable *adj* → 1 obvious 2 tactile 3 tangible
palpate *v* → 1 examine 2 touch
palpitate *v* → 1 toss 2 vibrate
palsy *n* → 1 period of inaction *v* 2 disease 3 inactivate
paltry *adj* → 1 bad 2 smallest 3 unimportant
pamper *v* → satisfy
pamphlet *n* → 1 book 2 message 3 public notice
panacea *n* → medication
panache *n* → 1 artistry 2 feather 3 show 4 trimming
pancake *n* → cosmetics
pandemonium *n* → 1 anarchy 2 commotion 3 loud sound 4 muddle
Pandemonium *n* → hell
pander *n* → 1 immoral person 2 procurer 3 prostitute *v* 4 prostitute oneself
panegyric *n* → 1 applause 2 flattery 3 oration
panel *n* → 1 bookbinding 2 coating 3 committee 4 council 5 jury 6 layer 7 list 8 painting 9 part 10 photograph *v* 11 employ
pang *n* → ache
panic *n* → 1 fright *v* 2 be frightened *adj* 3 frightened
pannier *n* → 1 bag 2 underwear
panoply *n* → 1 armour 2 covering 3 display
panorama *n* → 1 generalisation 2 representation 3 view
pansy *n* → 1 man 2 sexual type *v* 3 feminise 4 walk
pant *n* → 1 breathing *v* 2 breathe 3 desire 4 vibrate
pantechnicon *n* → 1 storehouse 2 truck
pantheon *n* → 1 church 2 god 3 memento
pantihose *n* → tights
pantomime *n* → 1 drama 2 gesture *v* 3 gesture
pantry *n* → cupboard
pants *n* → 1 trousers 2 underwear
papa *n* → parent
papacy *n* → period
papal *adj* → ecclesiastic
paper *n* → 1 cash 2 examination 3 newspaper 4 plaster 5 raw materials *v* 6 coat 7 rub *adj* 8 ethereal 9 thin
paperback *n* → book
papilla *n* → bulge
papoose *n* → offspring
papyrus *n* → writing materials
par *n* → 1 equality 2 ordinariness 3 written composition *adj* 4 equal 5 ordinary
parable *n* → 1 figure of speech 2 proverb 3 representation 4 story
parabola *n* → curve
parachute *n* → 1 aircraft *v* 2 descend 3 fly 4 transport
parade *n* → 1 crowd 2 road 3 show *v* 4 display 5 show off 6 walk
paradigm *n* → example
paradise *n* → 1 a good time 2 heaven 3 joy 4 pleasantness
paradox *n* → 1 nonsense 2 opposite meaning 3 puzzle
paraffin *n* → fuel
paragon *n* → example
paragraph *n* → written composition
parallel *n* → 1 comparison 2 equal 3 equivalent 4 fortification 5 line 6 similar thing *v* 7 be similar 8 equal 9 fit *adj* 10 comparable 11 congruous 12 similar
parallelogram *n* → plane figure
paralyse *v* → 1 disease 2 inactivate
paralysis *n* → 1 insensibility 2 period of inaction 3 powerlessness
paramedical *adj* → medical
parameter *n* → particulars
paramount *n* → 1 ruler *adj* 2 important 3 predominant
paramour *n* → 1 lover 2 sexual partner
paranoia *n* → psychic disorder
parapet *n* → 1 embankment 2 fortification
paraphernalia *n* → 1 accumulation 2 equipment 3 mixture 4 personal property
paraphrase *n* → 1 translation *v* 2 translate
paraplegia *n* → period of inaction
parasite *n* → 1 accomplice 2 dependant 3 extortionist 4 plant
parboil *v* → cook
parcel *n* → 1 accumulation 2 bag 3 part *v* 4 cover *adv* 5 partially
parch *v* → 1 cook 2 dry 3 heat
parchment *n* → 1 writing materials 2 written composition
pardon *n* → 1 acquittal 2 forgiving *v* 3 acquit 4 forgive
pare *v* → 1 bare 2 decrease
PARENT *n* oldie, olds, parents, the olds; **foster-parent,** godparent, gossip *(Archaic),* step-parent; **mother,** mama, mamma, mammy, mater, mater dolorosa, materfamilias, mom, mum, mummy, old girl,

old lady, old woman; **foster-mother,** godmother, mother-in-law, stepdame *(Archaic),* stepmother; **father,** begetter, dad, daddy, gaffer *(Brit. Colloq.),* genitor, governor, old boy, old man, pa, papa, pappy, pater, paterfamilias, patriarch, père, pop, poppa; **foster-father,** father-in-law, godfather, stepfather; **grandparent,** great-grandfather, great-grandmother, great-grandparent; **grandmother,** beldam *(Archaic),* gran, grandam, grande dame, grandma, grandmamma, granny, nanna, nanny; **grandfather,** grampers, gramps, grampus, grandad, grandpa, grandpapa, grandsire *(Archaic),* pop, poppa

parent *n* → **1** creator **2** minder **3** model

parenthesis *n* → **1** figure of speech **2** interruption **3** interval

pariah *n* → outsider

parietal *adj* → side

parish *n* → **1** city **2** domain

parity *n* → **1** congruity **2** equality **3** pregnancy **4** similarity

park *n* → **1** amusement park **2** field **3** garden *v* **4** position

parka *n* → jacket

parlance *n* → **1** discussion **2** language

parley *n* → **1** discussion **2** mediation *v* **3** talk

parliament *n* → **1** committee **2** council **3** legislative body

PARLIAMENTARY *adj* congressional, senatorial; **consistorial,** convocational, synodal

parlour *n* → living room

parochial *adj* → **1** intolerant **2** public **3** regional

parody *n* → **1** comedy **2** exaggeration **3** imitation **4** misrepresentation **5** mockery *v* **6** imitate **7** misinterpret

parole *n* → **1** contract **2** language **3** liberation **4** liberty **5** signal *v* **6** liberate

paroxysm *n* → **1** emotion **2** illness **3** turbulence **4** violent outburst

parrot *n* → **1** imitator **2** stupid person *v* **3** repeat

parry *v* → **1** avoid **2** repel

parsimony *n* → meanness

parson *n* → ecclesiastic

PART *n* canton, fraction, moiety, percentage, portion, proportion; **constituent,** component, detail, element, ingredient, integral, integrant, member, module, particular; **section,** compartment, department, desk, division, panel, partition, segment, subdivision, subsection; **cross-section,** example; **allotment,** allocation, allowance, contingent, cut, dividend, helping, length, lot, parcel, quantum, quota, rake-off, share, whack; **chunk,** dollop, hunk, lump; **slice,** cantle, finger, shive *(Archaic),* wedge; **greater part,** body, bulk, majority, mass; **particle,** bite, crumb, driblet, morceau, morsel, nibble, nubbin *(U.S.),* nubble; **fragment,** bit, catch, chip, flake, flinders, fritter, piece, scrap, shiver, shrapnel, shred, sliver, snatch, spill, splinter, split, whittling; **bits and pieces,** fragmentation, odds and ends, smithereens

partake *v* → share out

PARTIAL *adj* halfway, imperfect, incomplete, part; **fragmentary,** bitty, disjointed, fragmental, piecemeal, scrap, scrappy, splintery; **partite,** bipartite, compartmentalised, departmentalised, divided, dividual *(Archaic),* divisional, divisionary, multipartite, sectional, segmental, segmentary, segmented, volumed; **articulated,** modular

partial *adj* → **1** deficient **2** desirous **3** intolerant **4** predisposed **5** prejudiced **6** unfair

PARTICIPATE *v* be up to one's neck in, become committed, buy in, buy into, enter, enter into, get into, get involved, get up to, go the whole hog, have a hand in, have an interest in, join, join in, make a stand, mix up in, partake in, share, stand up, step in, take a stand, take part, take sides

participate *v* → **1** cooperate **2** partner **3** share out

PARTICIPATING *adj* concerned with, hands-on, implicated, in the same boat, in the thick of, involved; **interested,** concerned, engaged, for, full of, rapt in, wrapped up in

PARTICIPATION *n* accessoriness, affiliation, commitment, complicity, concernment, engagement, entanglement, immixture, implication, interest, interestedness, involution, involvement, stake, sympathy

participle *n* → word

particle *n* → **1** matter **2** part **3** powder **4** small amount **5** word

PARTICULAR *adj* certain, circumstantial, definite, deictic, especial, one, peculiar, precise, special, specific, such, such and such, that, this, what, which; **for a particular occasion,** ad hoc, magistral *(Pharm.)*; **bespoke,** custom-built, custom-made, customised, made-to-measure, made-to-order, specially made, tailor-made; **respective,** appropriate, different, distributive, dividual *(Archaic),* each, ilka *(Scot.),* proper, separate, several; **of one's own,** one's, own, personal, private, unipersonal; **specifiable,** assignable, circumscriptive, definable, differentiable, identifiable, isolable

particular *n* → **1** part *adj* **2** intense **3** precise

PARTICULARISE *v* characterise, customise, define, determine, distinguish, have someone tabbed, identify, individualise, mark, specialise, type; **circumstantiate,** circumstance *(Obs.),* detail, differentiate, elaborate, itemise; **specify,** assign, designate

PARTICULARLY *adv* ad hoc, ad hominem, circumstantially, e.g., especially, in detail, in particular, namely, peculiarly, specially, specifically, to wit, videlicet, viz.; **for my part,** as far as I am concerned, in my opinion, on all counts, speaking for myself; **there,** here, locally, where; **respectively,** apart, apiece, bit by bit, each, individually, separately, severally; **differentially,** diacritically, dividually *(Archaic)*

PARTICULARS *n* article, circumstance, detail, element, fine print, item, minutiae, nitty-gritty, note, parameter, part, piece, point, portion, property, small print

partisan *n* → **1** accomplice **2** combat troops **3** spear *adj* **4** predisposed **5** unfair

partition *n* → **1** limit **2** part **3** sharing out **4** wall *v* **5** come between **6** separate **7** share out

partly *adv* → partially

PARTNER *n* associate, bedfellow, colleague, compeer, confrère, copartner, duumvir, fellow, mate *(Archaic)*, offsider, peer; **silent partner,** sleeping partner; **assistant,** acolyte, adjunct, adjutant, aide, attaché, attendant, chaperone, right hand, second, secondary; **helpmate,** helping hand, helpmeet *(Archaic)*; **comrade,** brethren, brother, frère, sister; **workfellow,** messmate, shipmate, team-mate, workmate, yokefellow; **compatriot,** countryman, countrywoman, townsman, townswoman. *See also* ACCOMPLICE

PARTNER *v* accompany, associate, assort *(Archaic)*, chaperone, company *(Archaic)*, consociate, consort, mate, squire; **ally with,** go into business with, hang around with, hang with, keep company with, latch on to, mess with, pal up with, string along with, take up with, tie up with; **haunt,** follow, shadow; **assist,** attend, have a hand in, help, participate, take a hand in

partner *n* → **1** companion **2** cooperator **3** dancer **4** friend **5** sexual partner **6** spouse **7** workers *v* **8** accompany **9** associate **10** join

parturition *n* → birth

PARTY *n* après-ski, at-home, bottle party, celebration, conversazione, cracker night, festivity, get-together, house-warming, potlatch, reunion, revel, revelry, rout, send-off, shivoo, singsong, social, social occasion, soiree, tea-party, third half, turn, turnout, twenty-first, wayzgoose; **dance,** ball, barn-dance, dinner-dance, fancy-dress ball, fandango *(U.S.)*, hoedown *(U.S.)*, hop, mask, masked ball, masquerade, ridotto; **house party,** blanket party, pyjama party, slumber party; **barbecue,** barby, clambake *(U.S.)*, cookout *(U.S.)*, fry *(U.S.)*, luau, picnic, picnic races; **rort,** bust-up, destroy party, destructo, ding, hooley, hui *(N.Z.)*; **booze-up,** beer-up, boozeroo *(N.Z.)*, bowl, carousal, carouse, cocktail party, drinks, grog-on, wassail; **wedding breakfast,** bridal *(Archaic)*, reception; **bucks' party,** bucks' night, girls' night out, hen's party, hens' night, kitchen tea, shower tea, stag party

party *n* → **1** armed forces **2** celebration **3** gathering **4** litigant **5** participant **6** person **7** subject matter

passable *adj* → mediocre

passage *n* → **1** access **2** advance **3** bay **4** bridge **5** defecation **6** entrance **7** exchange **8** fight **9** musical phrase **10** occurrence **11** path **12** transport **13** travelling **14** written composition

PASSAGEWAY *n* adit, draft tube, drift, heading, lateral, tunnel; **airway,** air-drive, airduct, airshaft, breezeway, port, porting, shaft, slot, snorkel, upcast, uptake, ventiduct, windsail; **furrow,** crevice, flue, flute, fulgurite, groove; **chimney,** chimneypot, flue, funnel, smokestack, stack, tallboy

passbook *n* → account

passé *adj* → **1** antique **2** old

PASSENGER *n* back-seat driver, cabbie's jockey, fare, hitcher, pillion, swinger; **hitchhiker,** stowaway

passenger *n* → idler

passion *n* → **1** anger **2** desire **3** emotion **4** enthusiasm **5** inaction **6** love **7** pain **8** sex

passionate *adj* → **1** acrimonious **2** desirous **3** emotional **4** excited **5** loving **6** rash

passive *adj* → **1** apathetic **2** composed **3** inactive **4** obedient

passport *n* → **1** certificate **2** permission

PASS THROUGH *v* pass, pick one's way, plough through, ply, thread one's way, transit; **percolate,** perfuse, perk *(Colloq.)*, permeate, soak in, soak through

password *n* → **1** answer **2** signal

PAST *n* antiquity, auld lang syne, bygone, days of old, days of yore, Dreamtime *(Aborig.)*, foretime, history, horse-and-buggy age, langsyne, the good old days, time immemorial, time out of mind, yesterday, yore *(Archaic)*; **earliness,** antiqueness, historicity

PAST *adj* back, bygone, dead-and-buried, departed, erstwhile, foregone, former, historical, late, lost, of yore, old-time, olden, one-time, other, over, quondam, sometime, whilom *(Archaic)*, yesterday; **nostalgic; retrospective,** memorial, retroactive; **perfect,** perfective, pluperfect, preterite; **primeval,** atavistic, primal, pristine; **early,** mythical, old, olden *(Archaic)*; **ancient,** classical, immemorial, preadamite, premillennial, venerable; **prehistoric,** antediluvian, Archaean, archaeological, Archaeozoic, azoic, eolithic, Neanderthal, palaeogeographical, palaeogeological, Palaeolithic, preglacial, prehuman, primeval, primitive, primordial, protolithic; **fossil,** fossil-like, fossiliferous; **postdiluvian,** postclassical, postwar; **recent,** latter-day, low, of late

past *n* → disrepute

PASTE *n* clobber, dope, goo; **clag,** mess; **gore,** clot; **syrup,** tear-arse, treacle; **semifluid,** colloid, semisolid; **gel,** gelatinoid, glair, jelly. *See also* SLUDGE

paste *n* → **1** adhesive **2** jewellery **3** pulp *v* **4** beat **5** coat **6** scold **7** stick together

pastel *adj* → colourless

pasteurise *v* → medicate

pastiche *n* → **1** imitation **2** mixture **3** painting

pastime *n* → **1** a good time **2** amusement

pastor *n* → ecclesiastic

pastoral *n* → **1** emblem of office **2** painting **3** poetry *adj* **4** ecclesiastic **5** farming **6** poetic **7** rural

pasture *n* → **1** farmland *v* **2** farm

pasty *n* → **1** underwear *adj* **2** colourless **3** pulpy

PAT *n* bob, dab, fillip, flick, flip, peck, rap, tap, tip, touch; **stamp,** appel *(Fencing)*, tamp; **prod,** attaint *(Obs.)*, bunt, butt, dig, goose, jab, jerk, poke, stab; **push,** jog, jolt, jostle, nudge, stir; **accolade,** dubbing. *See also* HIT; STROKE

patch *n* → **1** emblem **2** garden **3** period **4** repair **5** small amount *v* **6** electrify **7** repair

patchwork *n* → **1** mixture **2** sewing

pate *n* → head

patella *n* → leg

patent *n* → **1** intellectual property **2** ownership **3** record **4** restraining order *adj* **5** blatant

paternity *n* → kinship

PATH *n* bikeway, bridle-track, bridlepath, cycleway, pack-track, pathway, ride, towpath; **footpath,** banquette *(U.S.)*, causeway, flagging, flags, flagstones, footway, pavement, paving, roadside, side path, sidewalk *(U.S.)*, walk, walkway, wayside; **lane,** alley, alleyway, pall-mall, passage, passageway; **aisle,** ambulatory, bay, corridor, hall; **arcade,** cloister, colonnade, gallery, loggia, ropewalk, slype; **arch,** archway; **subway,** tunnel, underpass; **manway,** catwalk, duckboard, gangboard, gangway, logway, ridgeway; **bridge,** aerobridge, drawbridge, floating bridge, footbridge, pontoon, span, viaduct, walkway; **track,** bush track, fire trail, nature trail, snigging track, trail, walking track; **course,** cinder track, dirt track, drag strip, dromos, gallop, home straight, home stretch, racecourse, racetrack, sandtrack, straight, straightaway *(U.S.)*, the turf, track; **ramp,** cattle ramp, cattlepit, cattlestop *(N.Z.)*; **chute,** crush, drafting race, race; **walk,** pad, sheepwalk. *See also* ROUTE; ROAD; ACCESS

pathetic *adj* → **1** bad **2** distressing **3** emotive **4** pitiable **5** powerless **6** useless

pathology *n* → healing

pathos *n* → **1** pain **2** pitifulness **3** unhappiness

PATIENCE *n* endurance, enduringness, forbearance, fortitude, long-suffering, longanimity, meekness, resignation, stoicalness, sufferance, sustainment, tolerance, toleration

patience *n* → composure

PATIENT *n* case, day-patient, in-patient, invalid, lame duck, outpatient, private patient, public patient, subject, T.P.I., valetudinarian, victim, wreck; **sufferer from specific complaint,** arthritic, asthmatic, bleeder, diabetic, haemophiliac, lazar *(Archaic)*, leper, paraplegic, quadriplegic, spastic; **convalescent,** recuperator

PATIENT *adj* enduring, forbearing, long-suffering, meek, stoical, tolerant; **persevering,** diligent, persistent

PATIENT PERSON *n* Griselda, Job, long-sufferer, Stoic

patina *n* → **1** colour **2** glaze **3** plating

patio *n* → field

patriarch *n* → **1** ecclesiastic **2** manager **3** old people **4** parent **5** starter

patriarchy *n* → **1** ancestry **2** community **3** kinship

patrician *n* → **1** aristocrat *adj* **2** aristocratic

patricide *n* → killing

patrimony *n* → property

patriot *n* → national

patrol *n* → **1** journey **2** protector **3** warner *v* **4** protect **5** travel **6** warn

patron *n* → **1** buyer **2** encourager **3** helper **4** influencer **5** manager **6** protector

patronise *v* → **1** be arrogant **2** buy **3** help **4** pride oneself

patter *n* → **1** language **2** nonsense **3** quiet sound **4** selling **5** speaking *v* **6** disperse **7** speak **8** talk nonsense

pattern *n* → **1** decoration **2** diagram **3** drawing **4** example **5** model **6** shape *v* **7** decorate **8** shape

paucity *n* → deficiency

paunch *n* → abdomen

pauper *n* → poor person

pause *n* → **1** indecision **2** interruption **3** interval **4** rest **5** silence **6** stoppage *v* **7** interrupt **8** rest **9** stop **10** vacillate

pave *v* → **1** coat **2** explain **3** smooth

pavement *n* → **1** path **2** paving

pavilion *n* → hospital

PAVING *n* clinker, cobble, cobblestone, pavement, paviour, quarry tile, tile, tiling; **bitumen,** asphalt, blacktop, macadam, seal, surface dressing, tarmac, tarmacadam, tarseal; **concrete,** cement, Leichhardt grass, Leichhardt lawn

paw *n* → **1** animal part **2** feeler *v* **3** touch

pawn *n* → **1** surety **2** victim *v* **3** lend

pawnbroker *n* → lender

PAY *v* advance, defray, disburse, dispend *(Archaic)*, expend, invest, lay out, outlay, overpay, prepay, refund, remit, render payment, spend; **pay up,** alley up, ante up, cash up *(Obs.)*, dip into one's pocket, fork out, loosen the purse strings, part up, pay one's way, pony up *(U.S.)*, shell, shell out, stump up, subscribe, untie the purse strings; **settle,** acquit, adjust, amortise, clear, compound, discharge, extinguish *(Law)*, liquidate, pay off, redeem, satisfy, square, square up; **pay the bill,** bear the costs, foot the bill, pay the costs, pay the piper, pick up the tab, stand the costs, stand treat; **contribute,** club in, tithe *(Obs.)*; **make payable,** declare; **remunerate,** cross someone's palm with silver, gratify *(Obs.)*, grease someone's palm, recompense, recoup, reimburse, reward, tickle someone's palm; **yield,** return; **deposit,** plank down, put down

pay *n* → **1** income *v* **2** coat

PAYABLE *adj* collect, defrayable, disbursable, dischargeable, due, expendable, penal, prepayable, redeemable, remittable, renderable; **taxable,** customable, declarable, dutiable, excisable, leviable

PAY HOMAGE *v* abase oneself, bend the knee, bow, bow and scrape, congratulate

(Obs.), dip one's lid, fall down before, fire a twenty-one gun salute, genuflect, humble oneself, kiss the hem of another's garment *(Archaic)*, kneel, kowtow, present arms, prostrate oneself, pull one's forelock, remove one's hat, salaam, salute, touch one's forelock, tug one's forelock, uncap, uncover; **defer to,** keep one's distance, make up to, make way for, stand aside for, stand back for

PAYMENT *n* aid *(Europ. Hist.)*, amortisation, amortisement, claim, commission, composition, cop, defrayal, disbursement, discharge, down payment, drawback, foregift, handsel, hansel, imprest, key money, maintenance, overpayment, perpetuity, prepayment, quarterage, redundancy, remittance, satisfaction, soft dollars, spot cash, time payment, token payment, valuable consideration; **expenditure,** capital expenditure, cost, current expenses, expense, expenses, incidentals, outgo, outgoings, outlay, pump priming; **contribution,** benevolence *(Eng. Hist.)*, indemnity, Peter's pence, subscription, subsidy, tribute; **settlement,** extinguishment, recoup, recoupment, redemption, requital, return, settling; **pay-off,** baksheesh, blackmail, kickback, touch; **refund,** drawback, recompense

payola *n* → **1** bribe **2** dishonesty

payroll *n* → list

pea *n* → small amount

PEACE *n* agreement, amnesty, bloodlessness, compromise, concord, harmony, neutrality, non-belligerency, non-resistance, non-violence, nonaggression, peaceful coexistence; **peacefulness,** quiet, quietness, sereneness, serenity, tranquillity, tranquilness; **peacetime,** halcyon days, nirvana; **armistice,** cease-fire, moratorium, rest, retirement, retreat, suspension of hostilities, truce, withdrawal; **demilitarised zone,** no-man's-land

peace *n* → **1** period of inaction **2** rest **3** silence

PEACEFUL *adj* amicable, bloodless, eirenic, harmonious, irenic, non-violent, nonaggression, pacific, subdued; **peaceable,** calm, halcyon, pacific, peacetime, quiet, retired, serene, tranquil; **anti-war,** anti-militarist, dovish, neutral, non-combatant, nonproliferation, pacifist; **peacekeeping,** pacificatory; **appeaseable,** mollifiable, subduable

PEACEMAKER *n* appeaser, arbitrator, assuager, compromiser, conciliator, dove, make-peace *(Rare)*, mediator, mollifier, nonresistant, pacificator, pacifier, quieter; **pacifist,** conch, conchie, conscientious objector, flowerchild, non-belligerent, noncombatant, peacenik

peach *n* → **1** good thing **2** orange *v* **3** report on *adj* **4** orange **5** red

peacock *n* → **1** affected person **2** arrogant person **3** show-off *v* **4** attitudinise **5** buy

peak *n* → **1** knob **2** mountain **3** much **4** rough **5** top *v* **6** be ill **7** bulge **8** thin **9** top **10** wane

peal *n* → **1** explosion **2** loud sound **3** ringing *v* **4** be loud **5** explode **6** make music

peanut *n* → unimportant person

pearl *n* → **1** bead **2** brightness **3** good thing **4** grey **5** jewellery **6** white *v* **7** pursue *adj* **8** bright **9** grey

peasant *n* → **1** country dweller **2** farmer **3** population **4** vulgarian *adj* **5** farming **6** inferior **7** provincial **8** working-class

peat *n* → **1** fuel **2** soil

pebble *n* → **1** dissident **2** rock *v* **3** cudgel

peccadillo *n* → **1** evildoing **2** misdemeanour **3** unimportant thing **4** wrong

peck *n* → **1** bit **2** endearments **3** much **4** pat *v* **5** hit **6** kiss **7** open

peculiar *adj* → **1** mad **2** particular **3** strange

pecuniary *adj* → cash

pedagogue *n* → **1** precisionist **2** teacher

pedal *n* → **1** accelerator **2** steering wheel *v* **3** thrust *adj* **4** brachial

pedant *n* → **1** affected person **2** bore **3** intellectual **4** precisionist **5** teacher

peddle *v* → sell

pederasty *n* → sexuality

pedestal *n* → **1** bottom **2** toilet

pedestrian *n* → **1** walker *adj* **2** boring **3** mediocre **4** ordinary **5** walking

pedigree *n* → **1** ancestry **2** aristocracy

pediment *n* → top

pedlar *n* → **1** seller **2** traveller

pee *n* → **1** urination *v* **2** urinate

peek *n* → **1** look *v* **2** look

peel *n* → **1** fortress **2** skin **3** tower *v* **4** bare **5** undress

peep *n* → **1** look **2** opening *v* **3** appear **4** chirp **5** look **6** speak

peevish *adj* → **1** dissident **2** irritable **3** stubborn

peewee *n* → marble

peg *n* → **1** clip **2** gradation **3** insert **4** rod *v* **5** defeat **6** insert **7** limit **8** restrict **9** throw

pejorative *n* → **1** slander *adj* **2** disapproving **3** disdainful **4** slanderous

pellet *n* → **1** ammunition **2** bead **3** small amount **4** vomit *v* **5** cudgel **6** round

pellucid *adj* → **1** clear **2** obvious **3** transparent

pelt *n* → **1** hide **2** stroke *v* **3** attack **4** beat **5** cudgel **6** fire on **7** rain **8** scold **9** shower **10** speed

PEN *n* bullpen, byre, cattlepen, compound, corral, fold, holding paddock, kraal, mews, paddock, piggery, pigsty, pinfold, pound, sheepcote, sheepfold, stable, stall, stockade, stockyard, sty, walk; **holding pen,** catching pen, counting-out pen, creep feeder, crush, crush-pen, dip, drafting yard, draining pen, farrowing house, forcing pen, sheep dip; **barrier stall,** starting box, starting grid, swabbing stall

penal *adj* → **1** imprisoned **2** payable **3** punishing

penalise *v* → **1** hinder **2** punish

penalty *n* → **1** force **2** hindrance **3** inconvenience **4** punishment

penance *n* → **1** abstinence **2** atonement

penchant *n* → **1** desire **2** good taste **3** point of view

pencil *n* → **1** cosmetics **2** dye **3** light **4** writing materials *v* **5** colour **6** depict **7** mark **8** write

PENDANT *n* drop, hanging ornament; **swing,** cuddle seat, hammock, trapeze; **pendulum,** bob, bobber, lead; **tassel,** bobble, dangle, fandangle; **hanging,** curtains, drapery, drapes, tapestry, wall-hanging; **skirt,** tail, tippet *(Hist.)*, train; **flap,** flapper, lappet

pendant *n* → **1** cord **2** jewellery **3** lighting

pending *adj* → **1** expected **2** future **3** hanging **4** undetermined

pendulous *adj* → **1** hanging **2** indecisive **3** vibrating

pendulum *n* → pendant

penetrate *v* → **1** perforate **2** understand

penguin *n* → aeroplane

peninsula *n* → headland

penis *n* → groin

PENITENCE *n* attrition, contriteness, contrition, guilt, mortification, repentance, self-reproach, soul-searching; **remorse,** abashment, grief, remorsefulness, shame, sorrow, sorrowfulness; **regret,** compunction, regretfulness, rue *(Archaic)*, sorriness; **apology,** beg-pardon, by-your-leave; **regrets,** apologies, excuse

PENITENT *n* a sadder and a wiser man, magdalen, penitential, prodigal son

PENITENT *adj* abashed, ashamed, contrite, repentant, self-accusing, shamefaced; **regretful,** afraid, bad, compunctious, guilty, remorseful, rueful, ruthful *(Archaic)*, sorry; **apologetic,** deprecatory

penitent *n* → **1** abstainer **2** believer **3** requiter *adj* **4** ashamed **5** compensatory

penitentiary *n* → **1** prison *adj* **2** imprisoned **3** punishing

penknife *n* → knife

pennant *n* → flag

penniless *adj* → poor

pension *n* → **1** charity **2** hotel **3** income **4** school

pensive *adj* → thinking

pentagon *n* → plane figure

penthouse *n* → roof

pent-up *adj* → **1** imprisoned **2** restricted

penumbra *n* → **1** shade **2** sun

penury *n* → **1** insufficiency **2** poverty

people *n* → **1** community **2** humanity **3** relative **4** the public *v* **5** inhabit

pep *n* → **1** vitality *v* **2** enliven

pepper *v* → **1** cook **2** fire on **3** shower

peppermint *n* → fat

pep talk *n* → incentive

perambulate *v* → walk

per capita *adv* → each

PERCEIVE *v* apperceive, appreciate, become aware of, become conscious of, cognise, drink in, experience, feel, observe, savour, sense, suffer, taste *(Archaic)*; **regain consciousness,** come back to one's senses, come to

perceive *v* → **1** find **2** know

percentage *n* → **1** cost **2** income **3** part **4** profit **5** relationship

perceptible *adj* → **1** clear **2** visible

PERCEPTION *n* affect *(Obs.)*, apperception, appreciation, aura *(Pathol.)*, experience, impression, mental impulse, observation, percept, sensation, sense, sense datum, undersense; **perceptiveness,** aesthesia, anabiosis, awareness, conscience *(Obs.)*, consciousness, feeling, mind, passibility, sense, sensuousness, sentience, wits; **feeling,** feel, feelings, ferment, flutter, frisson, hot flush, inner glow, irritation, pain, prick, quiver, reaction, stir, thrill, tingle, tingling, tremor; **five senses,** five wits, sensorium

perception *n* → **1** hearing **2** understanding

PERCEPTIVE *adj* affected, alive to, anabiotic, apperceptive, aware, cognisant, conscious, feeling, passible, protopathic, sensate, sensible, sentient, touched, ware *(Archaic)*; **percipient,** observant, paraesthetic, sensitive; **supersensitive,** acute, exquisite, hyperaesthetic, hypersensitive, intense, irritable, keen, miffy, prickly, thin-skinned, ticklish, touchy

perch *n* → **1** animal dwelling **2** length **3** stick **4** tower *v* **5** dismount **6** place **7** rest **8** tower

perchance *adv* → **1** by chance **2** possibly

percolate *n* → **1** liquid *v* **2** become known **3** cook **4** flow **5** liquefy **6** pass through

percussion *n* → **1** impact **2** musical band

perdition *n* → **1** hell **2** immorality **3** ruin

peremptory *adj* → **1** assertive **2** autocratic **3** commanding **4** obligatory

perennial *n* → **1** plant *adj* **2** changeless **3** continual **4** eternal **5** repetitive

PERFECT *v* bring to perfection, complete, consummate, idealise, leave nothing to be desired, redintegrate, round off; **purify,** polish; **ripen,** mature

PERFECT *adj* absolute, consummate, hundred-per-cent, infinite, quintessential; **whole,** complete, entire, finished, intact; **sublime,** beautiful, heavenly, ideal, superb; **unparalleled,** inimitable; **flawless,** blotless, clean, clear, copperplate, fair, faultless, fine, good, immaculate, impeccable, incorrupt, inviolate, pure, spotless, stainless, unblemished, unimpaired, unscratched, unspoilt, unsullied, unworn, white; **infallible,** indefectible, inerrable, sound, watertight

perfect *v* → **1** excel **2** finish **3** improve **4** make whole *adj* **5** apt **6** certain **7** good **8** musical **9** past **10** precise **11** simple **12** unconditional **13** whole

PERFECTION *n* absoluteness, completeness, entireness, ideality, idealness, infiniteness, infinitude; **prime,** bloom, matureness, maturity; **consummation,** completion, redintegration; **purity,** cleanness, faultlessness, flawlessness, immaculacy, immaculateness, impeccability, incorruptness, pureness; **infallibility,** indefectibility, inerrability, inerrableness, infallibleness, watertightness

PERFECTLY *adv* consummately, ideally, superbly; **flawlessly,** faultlessly, immaculately, impeccably; **infallibly,** indefectibly, inerrably; **to a turn,** to perfection

ERFECT THING *n* acme, apotheosis, beau ideal, culmination, idea *(Philos.)*, ideal, ideal type, quintessence, summit, the Absolute, the abstract, top; **classic,** model, standard; **utopia**

erfidy *n* → betrayal

ERFORATE *v* bite, crack, dub, gore, impale, javelin, penetrate, pierce, pike, prick, prickle, prong, reach, rowel, run through, stab, stick, sting, thrust, transfix, work into

erforate *v* → open

ERFORATION *n* impalement, inburst *(Rare)*, penetration, prick, stab, sting, transfixion

ERFORM *v* act, appear in, clown, improvise, mime, mum, outact, play, play-act, show, tread the boards, ventriloquise, walk a slackwire, walk a tightrope, wing; **portray,** come *(Colloq.)*, emote *(Colloq.)*, impersonate, personate, represent; **recite,** busk, do a number, put across, regale with; **support,** co-star, compere, second; **go on the stage,** go on the road, have one's name in lights, make one's bow, star, tour; **overact,** ham it up, rant

erform *v* → **1** accomplish **2** be angry **3** behave **4** do **5** have sex **6** make whole

ERFORMANCE *n* command performance, flop, sell-out; **premiere,** debut, first night, matinee, one-night stand; **crowd-pleaser,** potboiler, smash, smash-hit, tear-jerker, weepie; **preview,** off-Broadway run, tryout; **rehearsal,** clambake *(U.S)*, run-through

erformance *n* → **1** accomplishment **2** action **3** language

erfume *n* → fragrance

erfunctory *adj* → **1** apathetic **2** deficient **3** formal **4** purposeless

ergola *n* → **1** building **2** roof **3** shelter

erhaps *adv* → **1** by chance **2** possibly

eril *n* → **1** danger *v* **2** endanger

erimeter *n* → **1** frame **2** line

ERIOD *n* season, space, span, term, time, tract; **period of duty,** hours, session, stint, stretch; **reign,** diaconate, dictatorship, papacy, regency, sitting, tenancy, tenure; **bout,** go, innings, round, shift, turn; **run,** patch, spell, streak; **era,** age, culture, cycle, day, epoch, generation, siècle, times, Yuga *(Hinduism)*; **episode,** page, stage; **academic year,** Lent term, Michaelmas term, semester, term, trimester, Trinity term; **prison sentence,** bird, clock, dream, hitch, jolt, Kath, lag, life, stretch, time; **prison term,** a brick, a clock, a drag, a sleep, a spin, a swy, a zack, the lot

period *n* → **1** bleeding **2** bodily discharge **3** finish **4** musical phrase **5** regularity *adj* **6** antique

periodic *adj* → **1** irregular **2** regular

periodical *n* → **1** magazine *adj* **2** regular

PERIOD OF INACTION *n* abeyance, cold storage, latent period, laying-off season, low season, off-season, sit-down strike, strike, vacation, waiting; **calm,** Irishman's hurricane, peace, slack, slumber, slump; **dormancy,** aestivation, diapause, hibernation, sleep, suspended animation, torpor; **loaf,** laze, loll *(Archaic)*, lounge, slack, wait; **paralysis,** atropism, catatonia, diplegia, hemiplegia, palsy, panplegia, paralysation, paraplegia

peripheral *adj* → **1** boundary **2** outside **3** unimportant

periphery *n* → **1** frame **2** outside

periscope *n* → lens

perish *v* → **1** collapse **2** deteriorate **3** die

perishable *adj* → **1** dead **2** impermanent

perjury *n* → lie

perk *n* → **1** income *v* **2** be arrogant **3** flow **4** pass through

permanent *adj* → **1** changeless **2** eternal

permeate *v* → **1** flood **2** pass through

PERMISSION *n* dispensation, go-ahead, green light, imprimatur, leave, passport, planning permission, release, sanction, thumbs up, vouchsafement; **licence,** authorisation, clearance *(Football)*, empowerment, faculty *(Eccles.)*, indult, nihil obstat, permit, pratique, the call, warrant; **free hand,** blank cheque, carte blanche, liberty; **consent,** acquiescence, appro, approbation, approval, courtesy

permission *n* → liberty

permissive *adj* → **1** informal **2** lenient **3** optional **4** sexy **5** tolerant

PERMIT *v* admit, allow, consent to, countenance, give one's permission, give the nod to, have, let, sanction, suffer, tolerate, vouchsafe; **license,** authorise, clear, empower, legitimate, privilege, warrant

permit *n* → **1** permission **2** power to act *v* **3** make possible

PERMITTED *adj* allowed, authorised, granted, sanctioned; **permissible,** admissible, allowable, lawful

permutation *n* → **1** change **2** order

pernicious *adj* → **1** bad **2** destructive **3** harmful **4** immoral

perpendicular *n* → **1** erectness *adj* **2** bent **3** erect

perpetrate *v* → do

perpetual *adj* → **1** continual **2** eternal **3** infinite

perpetuate *v* → eternalise

perplex *v* → **1** cause difficulties **2** complicate **3** confuse **4** puzzle

perquisite *n* → income

perse *n* → **1** blue *adj* **2** purple

per se *adv* → essentially

persecute *v* → **1** act unkindly **2** annoy **3** be unfriendly **4** punish **5** repress **6** victimise

PERSEVERANCE *n* diligence, persistence, stamina, staying power

PERSEVERE *v* bear with, crack hardy, crack hearty, endure, forbear, hang in, have patience with, hold the line, last the distance, persist, ride out, see through, sit tight, stay with, stick at, stick it out, stick to one's guns, sustain, weather the storm; **bear up,** bite one's lip, cool one's heels, grin and bear it, grit one's teeth, hold one's tongue, keep one's cool, keep one's temper, kick one's heels, put on a brave front, roll with the punches, take it on the chin, take the rough with the smooth; **bear,** abide, accept, bide *(Archaic)*, brook, cop, digest, hack it, lump it, put up with, stomach it, suffer, support, swallow, take, take it, tolerate

persevere *v* → **1** continue **2** persist

PERSEVERING *adj* assiduous, consistent, diligent, dogged, perseverant, sedulous, single-minded, strong-willed, tenacious, uncompromising; **steadfast,** enduring, firm, hardy, heart of oak, indefatigable, inexorable, staunch, stout, stout-hearted, sturdy, tough; **persistent,** determined, high-pressure, important *(Obs.)*, importunate, importune, pertinacious, unflagging, unremitting

PERSEVERINGLY *adv* firm, firmly, like grim death, manfully, pertinaciously, sedulously, staunchly, stout-heartedly, stoutly, tenaciously, through thick and thin, uncompromisingly; **assiduously,** diligently; **persistently,** doggedly, inexorably

PERSIST *v* box on, hang in, hang in there, keep at it, keep on, keep up, lay in, lay in there, persevere, plod on, plug on, push, rub along, rub on, rub through, see through, soldier on, stay, stick it out, stick out for; **apply oneself,** dig in, grind, peg away at, plough through, toil, work at; **endure,** bear up, hang on, hold on, not take no for an answer, sit pat, stand one's ground, stick to one's guns, worry along, worry through

persist *v* → **1** continue **2** live **3** oppose **4** persevere

PERSISTENCE *n* doggedness, firmness, grit, inexorability, inexorableness, perseverance, pertinaciousness, pertinacity, resoluteness, resolution, resolve, tenaciousness, tenacity; **assiduity,** application, assiduousness, diligence, industry, push, sedulity, sedulousness, single-mindedness; **indefatigability,** endurance, indefatigableness, persistence, stamina, stay *(U.S.)*, staying power, steadfastness, stoutness, tirelessness

persistent *adj* → **1** changeless **2** continual **3** dissident **4** patient **5** persevering

PERSON *n* individual, lot, one, party, persona, personage, personality, presence, wight *(Archaic)*; **human being,** being, hominoid, Homo, Homo sapiens, human, mortal; **head,** hand, nose; **character,** bird, bleeder *(Brit.)*, blighter, bod, body, card, cookie, creature, cuss *(U.S.)*, customer, element, fellow, gink, kiddo, stick, type; **worthy,** Christian, soul. *See also* ETHNIC

person *n* → portrait

persona *n* → **1** character **2** disguise **3** person **4** portrait

personable *adj* → beautiful

personage *n* → **1** famous person **2** important person **3** person

personal *n* → **1** news item **2** public notice *adj* **3** inborn **4** own **5** particular **6** secret **7** slanderous

personality *n* → **1** character **2** characteristic **3** essence **4** famous person **5** person **6** slander

PERSONAL PROPERTY *n* belongings, collectibles, effects, equipment, gear, goods, goods and chattels, household goods, lares and penates, moveables, paraphernalia, personal effects, personalty, stock-in-trade, tangibles, things; **article of personal property,** chattel, chattel personal, chose *(Law)*, fixture *(Law)*, moveable *(Law)*. *See also* PROPERTY

personify *v* → represent

personnel *n* → **1** recorder **2** workers

perspective *n* → **1** drawing **2** relationship

perspicacious *adj* → **1** discriminating **2** intelligent **3** sharp-eyed

perspicuous *adj* → clear

perspire *v* → excrete

PERSUADE *v* bounce, convince, handrush, induce, lead, lead someone on, lobby, overpersuade, put up to, talk around, talk into, wrangle; **urge,** blandish, blarney, cajole, carry away, coax, importune, solicit, sweet-talk, wheedle; **manipulate,** bias, brainwash, condition, impose on, manage, mesmerise, pervert, prejudice, prepossess, psych, seed, sway, swing, tamper with, twist round one's little finger; **argue,** assure, plead, reason, talk. *See also* INFLUENCE

persuade *v* → encourage

PERSUASION *n* agitation, agitprop, brainwashing, cajolery, conditioning, convincement, emotional blackmail, hypnotisation, lobbyism, manipulation, mesmerisation, mesmerism, psychological warfare, salesmanship, suggestion; **argument,** hard sell, persuasive, pitch, propaganda, sales talk, soft sell, spiel. *See also* INFLUENCE

pert *adj* → **1** badly-behaved **2** busy **3** discourteous **4** happy **5** living

pertain *v* → fit

pertinacious *adj* → **1** persevering **2** stubborn

pertinent *adj* → **1** apt **2** related **3** topical

perturb *v* → **1** confuse **2** deflect

peruse *v* → **1** investigate **2** read

pervade *v* → **1** disperse **2** flood

perverse *adj* → **1** badly-behaved **2** casuistic **3** disobedient **4** displeased **5** dissident **6** false **7** stubborn **8** wrong

perversion *n* → **1** change **2** immorality **3** misguidance **4** misrepresentation **5** misuse **6** sexuality **7** strangeness

pervert *n* → **1** heretic **2** misleader **3** misuser **4** nonconformist **5** sexual type **6** strange person *v* **7** change **8** ill-treat **9** lie **10** misguide **11** persuade

pessary *n* → **1** contraception **2** medication

pessimism *n* → **1** despair **2** unhappiness

pest *n* → **1** annoyance **2** deterioration **3** illness

pester *v* → annoy

PESTERING *adj* bothersome, importunate, onerous, oppressive, teasing, tormenting; **bloody-minded,** bad-tempered, bitchy, cantankerous, doggish, icky, ill-natured, impossible, liverish, mean, ornery. *See also* UNPLEASANT

pesticide *n* → poison

pestilence *n* → illness
pestilent *adj* → 1 annoying 2 badly-behaved 3 harmful 4 poisonous
pestle *n* → 1 powderer 2 press *v* 3 powder 4 press
pet *n* → 1 friend 2 irritation 3 lover *v* 4 eroticise 5 kiss *adj* 6 chosen 7 important
petal *n* → flower
peter *n* → 1 box 2 cell 3 treasury *v* 4 gesture
petite *adj* → small
petition *n* → 1 entreaty 2 litigation 3 message *v* 4 entreat
petrify *v* → 1 astonish 2 frighten 3 harden 4 inactivate
petrol *n* → fuel
petroleum *n* → 1 fat 2 fuel
petrology *n* → metallurgy
petticoat *n* → 1 underwear 2 woman *adj* 3 female
pettifog *v* → 1 disagree 2 swindle
petty *adj* → 1 intolerant 2 smallest 3 unimportant
petty cash *n* → funds
petulant *adj* → irritable
petunia *n* → purple
pew *n* → church
phalanx *n* → 1 crowd 2 flower 3 gathering
phallus *n* → groin
PHANTOM *n* apparition, appearance, astral, astral body, embodiment, Intelligence, invisible, materialisation, phantasm, presence, spectre, supernatural, wight *(Archaic)*, wraith; **ghost,** poltergeist, revenant, spook, wandoo, zombie; **soul,** manes, psyche, shade, shades, spirit; **attendant spirit,** familiar, familiar spirit, genius
phantom *n* → 1 image 2 soul *adj* 3 delusive 4 fantastic 5 imprecise
Pharaoh *n* → ruler
pharmacology *n* → 1 healing 2 medication
pharmacy *n* → 1 healing 2 medication
pharynx *n* → neck
phase *n* → 1 appearance 2 condition 3 moon 4 reproduction
phenomenal *adj* → 1 astonishing 2 enormous 3 occurrent 4 tangible
phenomenon *n* → 1 appearance 2 matter 3 occurrence
phial *n* → bottle
philander *v* → 1 be promiscuous 2 flirt
philanthropy *n* → 1 generosity 2 help 3 kindness
philistine *n* → 1 ignoramus 2 vulgarian *adj* 3 ignorant 4 ill-bred
philology *n* → writing
philosophical *adj* → 1 composed 2 epistemological
philosophy *n* → 1 belief 2 conjecture
phlegm *n* → 1 apathy 2 slowness
phlegmatic *adj* → 1 apathetic 2 composed 3 inactive
phobia *n* → 1 fright 2 psychic disturbance
phoenix *n* → 1 beautiful person 2 mythical beast
phone *n* → telecommunications
phonetics *n* → speaking
phoney *n* → 1 faker *adj* 2 fake
phosphoresce *v* → shine
phosphorescence *n* → brightness
photocopy *n* → 1 copy 2 imitation
photogenic *adj* → bright
PHOTOGRAPH *n* bromide, contact print, drop-out, facsimile, frame, glossy, photo, pickie, picture, positive, print, proof, shooter, shot, snap, snapshot, still, visual, wirephoto; **slide,** lantern slide, microfiche, trannie *(Colloq.)*, transparency; **black-and-white,** colour photo, monochrome, sepia, vignette; **negative; composite photograph,** double exposure; **portrait,** candid, mug shot; **close-up,** blow-up, enlargement, long shot, reduction; **photomural,** panel, photomontage; **ambrotype,** anaglyph, autoradiograph, autotype, blueprint, calotype, cyanotype, daguerreotype, ferrotype, gravure, heliotype, hologram, macrograph, microdot, microform, micrograph, microphotograph, photochronograph, photogram, photomicrograph, platinotype, radiograph, roentgenogram, schlieren photograph, shadowgraph, stereophotograph, telephotograph, tintype, tomogram, X-ray photograph
PHOTOGRAPH *v* film, mug *(U.S.)*, shoot, snap; **develop,** enlarge, fix, print, reduce; **tone,** fog, intensify, sensitise, solarise, tint; **expose,** overexpose, underdevelop, underexpose
photograph *n* → 1 portrait *v* 2 portray
PHOTOGRAPHER *n* cameraman, cinematographer, daguerreotyper, daguerreotypist, photojournalist, shutterbug, snapshotter; **photoresearcher**
photography *n* → representation
photon *n* → energy
photostat *n* → 1 copy *v* 2 copy
phrase *n* → 1 dance 2 figure of speech 3 musical phrase 4 speaking
phrenetic *n* → 1 mad person *adj* 2 excited
phrenology *n* → head
phylum *n* → class
physical *adj* → 1 bodily 2 tangible
physician *n* → healer
physics *n* → energy
physiognomy *n* → 1 appearance 2 characteristics 3 face
physiology *n* → body
physiotherapy *n* → 1 healing 2 medical treatment
physique *n* → 1 body 2 structure
pianoforte *n* → piano
pianola *n* → luck
picador *n* → fighter
pick *n* → 1 anchor 2 choice 3 digging implement 4 dirt 5 drug equipment 6 guitar 7 piercer 8 sewing machine 9 thread *v* 10 choose 11 cook 12 eat 13 harvest 14 make music 15 open 16 remove 17 rob 18 sew
picket *n* → 1 industrial action 2 shaft 3 warner *v* 4 fasten 5 protect
pickle *n* → 1 children 2 condition 3 dilemma 4 mischief-maker *v* 5 clean 6 conserve 7 cook 8 sour

pickpocket *n* → thief
picnic *n* → 1 a good time 2 easy thing 3 meal 4 muddle 5 party
pictorial *n* → 1 magazine *adj* 2 artistic 3 depictive
picture *n* → 1 beautiful person 2 example 3 film 4 narrative 5 painting 6 photograph 7 portrait *v* 8 fantasise 9 narrate 10 portray
picturesque *adj* → 1 artistic 2 beautiful 3 eloquent
piddle *n* → 1 urination *v* 2 bungle 3 urinate
pidgin *n* → language
pie *n* → 1 alliance *adj* 2 good *interj* 3 well done
piebald *adj* → multicoloured
piece *n* → 1 affair 2 bit 3 drama 4 essay 5 example 6 gun 7 length 8 part 9 particulars 10 poetry 11 textiles 12 woman
pièce de résistance *n* → 1 important thing 2 meal
piecemeal *adj* → 1 partial *adv* 2 slowly
pied *adj* → multicoloured
pier *n* → harbour
pierce *v* → 1 be loud 2 look 3 open 4 perforate
PIERCER *n* aiguille, antler, awl, brochette, caltrop, claw, cock, eyeleteer, fork, glover's needle, hayfork, horn, knitting needle, marlinespike, nail, pigsticker, point, prick *(Obs.)*, rapier, skewer, stiletto, stylet, tooth; **spur,** goad, prick *(Archaic)*, prod, rowel, sting; **hypodermic needle,** hype, hypo, spike, vaccine point; **spear,** arrow, arrowhead, assegai, grains, harpoon, lance, pile, shaft, spearhead; **needle,** acicula, aciculum, pin, point, ram, rostellum, rostrum, spicula, spicule, spiculum, spine, spinule; **spike,** crampon, creeper, grapnel, grappling iron, pike, piton, pricket, prong, spit, sticker, tenaculum, tine; **sting,** aculeus, emergence, stinger; **pick,** ice-axe, icepick, pickaxe, yam stick; **bit,** borer, brace and bit, bradawl, burin, centre-bit, diamond point, drill, gimlet, jackhammer, mattock, miser, pneumatic drill, post-hole digger, power drill, sticker, stopper, twist drill, wimble; **punch,** centre-punch, pirri point, puncheon; **barb,** barbule, beard, flue, fluke, pinnula, pinnule; **thorn,** aculeus, prickle, snag, spica
piety *n* → 1 high regard 2 reverence 3 worship
piffle *n* → 1 nonsense *v* 2 talk nonsense
pig *n* → 1 alcohol container 2 bottle 3 dirty person 4 glutton 5 model 6 policeman 7 stubborn person *v* 8 give birth
pigeon *n* → victim
pigeonhole *n* → 1 animal dwelling 2 compartment 3 niche *v* 4 class 5 neglect 6 place
piggyback *n* → 1 transport *v* 2 add
pig-headed *adj* → stubborn
piglet *n* → animal offspring
pigment *n* → dye
PIGSTY *n* Augean stables, pigpen, sty; **fleapit,** plague-spot; **rubbish heap,** dunghill, garbage bin; **cesspool,** cloaca, gutter, sewer, slough
pigtail *n* → 1 hair 2 tobacco 3 wire
pike *n* → 1 piercer 2 sharp point 3 spear *v* 4 injure 5 kill 6 perforate 7 speed
pile *n* → 1 accumulation 2 arsenal 3 building 4 fuel 5 funeral rites 6 hair 7 many 8 much 9 piercer 10 post 11 thread 12 tower 13 wealth 14 weave *v* 15 gather 16 insert 17 strengthen 18 support
pilfer *v* → rob
pilgrim *n* → 1 believer 2 traveller 3 worshipper
pill *n* → 1 ball 2 bead 3 bore 4 medication 5 unpleasant person *v* 6 rob 7 round 8 undress
pillage *n* → 1 act of war 2 attack 3 capture 4 robbery *v* 5 attack 6 rob 7 wage war
pillar *n* → 1 helper 2 post 3 tower *v* 4 support
pillion *n* → passenger
pillory *n* → 1 cell 2 restraints *v* 3 disgrace 4 mock 5 punish 6 restrain
pillow *v* → 1 soften 2 support
PILOT *n* ace, aircrew, airman, airwoman, aviator, aviatress, aviatrix, birdman, bush-pilot, captain, copilot, crew, flier, flight engineer, high-flier, navigator, observer, paraflier, sky pilot *(U.S.)*, skyman, test pilot; **cabin crew,** air hostess, flight attendant, steward, stewardess; **aeronaut,** balloonist, parachutist; **glider,** hang-glider, soarer; **astronaut,** cosmonaut, spaceman, spacewoman; **aeroplane passenger,** pax
pilot *n* → 1 heater 2 leader 3 model 4 seaman 5 steerer 6 test *v* 7 direct 8 fly 9 help *adj* 10 test
pimp *n* → 1 bad person 2 informant 3 procurer 4 prostitute *v* 5 noise abroad 6 prostitute oneself
pimple *n* → 1 bulge 2 disfigurement
pin *n* → 1 aim 2 jewellery 3 nail 4 piercer 5 rod 6 surfboard *v* 7 hold 8 support
pinafore *n* → overcoat
pince-nez *n* → glasses
pincers *n* → 1 extractor 2 holder
pinch *n* → 1 bar 2 bit 3 imprisonment 4 pressing 5 railway 6 robbery 7 small amount *v* 8 arrest 9 be miserly 10 cut 11 damage 12 enclose 13 hinder 14 pain 15 press 16 rob 17 set sail
pineapple *n* → 1 ammunition 2 bomb
pinion *n* → 1 feather 2 rod 3 wheel *v* 4 cut off 5 restrain
pink *n* → 1 good thing 2 hunter 3 political ideologist 4 red 5 watercraft *v* 6 bare 7 click 8 cut 9 decorate 10 open 11 shear *adj* 12 red
pinnacle *n* → 1 mountain 2 top *v* 3 top
pinpoint *n* → 1 sharp point 2 unimportant thing *v* 3 be precise 4 position
pint *n* → alcohol container
pin-up *n* → 1 allurer 2 nudist 3 sex object *adj* 4 alluring
pioneer *n* → 1 forerunner 2 leader 3 soldier 4 starter *v* 5 initiate 6 introduce *adj* 7 new
pious *adj* → 1 regardful 2 reverent
pip *n* → 1 emblem 2 illness 3 signal *v* 4 annoy 5 chirp 6 cudgel 7 shrill

ipe *n* → **1** alcohol container **2** birdcall **3** mineral **4** piping **5** tobacco **6** wind instrument *v* **7** channel **8** sew **9** shrill

ipedream *n* → **1** dream **2** hope

ipeline *n* → piping

IPING *n* blowpipe, gas main, gas pipe, main, pipe, pipeline, service pipe, steampipe, umbilical cord *(Aerospace)*, water main, waterworks; **agricultural pipe,** boom spray, sprinkler system; **stinkpipe,** exhaust pipe, tailpipe; **navel pipe,** spurling pipe; **hose,** hosepipe; **siphon; tube,** straw, sucker, tubulure

iping *n* → **1** birdcall **2** frame **3** lace **4** trimming *adj* **5** musical **6** shrill

ipsqueak *n* → **1** small person **2** unimportant person

iquant *adj* → **1** alluring **2** encouraging **3** painful **4** pleasant **5** pungent

ique *n* → **1** anger *v* **2** anger **3** enthuse **4** irritate

IRATE *n* buccaneer, corsair, freebooter, picaroon, rover *(Archaic)*, sea-robber, sea-rover, Viking

irate *n* → **1** thief **2** violent person *v* **3** rob

irouette *n* → **1** turn *v* **2** dance **3** rotate

iscatorial *adj* → pursuing

iscine *adj* → fishy

iss *n* → **1** beer **2** urination *v* **3** urinate *adv* **4** very

ISS OFF *interj* aroint thee *(Archaic)*, arsehole off, avaunt *(Obs.)*, away, away with you, be off, beat it, begone, bugger off, buzz off, fuck off, get fucked, get knotted, get lost, get nicked, get rooted, get stuffed, go jump in the lake, go to blazes, go to buggery, hence *(Archaic)*, hop it, nick off, rack off, rack off hairy legs, scat, scram, shove it, skedaddle, vamoose; **exeunt,** exeunt omnes, exit

istachio *n* → green

istil *n* → flower

istol *n* → gun

iston *n* → tap

it *n* → **1** bank **2** danger **3** diggings **4** disfigurement **5** excavation **6** hell **7** opening **8** stage *v* **9** bury **10** dig **11** disfigure **12** hollow **13** subtract

itch *n* → **1** amount **2** gradation **3** height **4** length **5** persuasion **6** plan **7** position **8** positioning **9** slope **10** sportsground **11** throw *v* **12** erect **13** fall **14** inhabit **15** position **16** slope **17** sound **18** throw

itcher *n* → **1** thrower **2** vessel

itchfork *v* → throw

iteous *adj* → **1** pitiable **2** pitying

itfall *n* → **1** danger **2** hollow **3** stratagem

ith *n* → **1** centre **2** characteristics **3** essence **4** importance **5** inside **6** living **7** strength *v* **8** kill

ithy *adj* → **1** concise **2** meaningful **3** soft

ITIABLE *adj* miserable, pathetic, piteous, pitiful, poor, rueful, ruthful *(Archaic)*, sorry, wretched

ITIER *n* bleeding heart, condoler, softie, sympathiser; **humanitarian,** philanthropist

itiful *adj* → **1** bad **2** pitiable

PITIFULNESS *n* miserableness, piteousness, pitiableness, wretchedness; **pathos,** touchingness

pittance *n* → small amount

PITY *n* feeling, fellow feeling, graciosity, heart, humaneness, humanity, ruefulness, ruthfulness, soft-heartedness, sorriness, tender-heartedness, tenderness; **compassion,** bowels of compassion *(Archaic)*, charity, clemency, compassionateness, grace, mercifulness, mercy, misericordia, quarter, remorse *(Obs.)*, rue *(Archaic)*, ruth *(Archaic)*; **sympathy,** commiseration, condolence, consolation, empathy; **compassionate leave**

PITY *v* be cruel to be kind, be moved, compassion, compassionate, enter into, feel for, feel with, have a heart, soften, sympathise with, take pity on; **bleed for,** bemoan, feel sorry for; **condole,** commiserate, send one's condolences; **humanise**

PITYING *adj* bleeding, feeling, humane, humanitarian, rueful, ruthful *(Archaic)*, sorry; **compassionate,** clement, gracious, merciful, piteous *(Archaic)*, sparing; **sympathising,** commiserative, condolatory; **soft-hearted,** lenient, sympathetic, tender-hearted

pivot *n* → **1** causer **2** centre-line **3** rod **4** support *v* **5** support

pixy *n* → fairy

placard *n* → public notice

PLACE *v* lay, locate, lodge, perch, position, post, put, set, station, stick; **deposit,** bank, put down, set down; **table,** prefer, present, put forward; **put on,** apply, paint, slap on, slather, slosh, superpose, trowel; **store,** bestow, load, pigeonhole, stack, stow, truck

place *n* → **1** class **2** condition **3** dwelling **4** employment **5** field **6** job **7** position **8** road *v* **9** employ **10** position **11** remember **12** tidy

placebo *n* → medication

PLACEMENT *n* emplacement, location, lodgment, placing, positioning, posting, postposition, reposition, setting, settlement, settling, stationing; **putting down,** deposit, deposition; **tabling,** preferment, presentation; **putting on,** application, superposition; **storage,** bestowal, bestowment, loading, packing, stowage

placenta *n* → flower

PLACE OF KILLING *n* abattoirs, butchery, knackery, shamble, slaughterhouse; **arena,** bullring, mort *(Hunting)*; **death cell,** death row; **battlefield,** battleground

PLACE OF WORSHIP *n* bora *(Aborig.)*, high place, holy, sacred place, sacred site, sanctuary, stupa; **Holy City,** Fatima, Holy Land, Jerusalem, Lourdes, Mecca, Medina, Varanasi, Vatican City. *See also* CHURCH; ABBEY; SHRINE

placid *adj* → composed

plagiarise *v* → imitate

plague *n* → **1** annoyance **2** flood **3** illness **4** misfortune *v* **5** annoy **6** flood

plaid *n* → **1** cloak *adj* **2** multicoloured

plain *v* → **1** complain *adj* **2** acoustic **3** clear **4** forthright **5** honest **6** insipid **7** most **8** obvious **9** simple **10** tasty **11** ugly **12** visible *adv* **13** clearly **14** greatly

plaintiff *n* → **1** accuser **2** litigant

plaintive *adj* → **1** distressing **2** grieving

plait *n* → **1** fold **2** hair **3** interlacement *v* **4** interlace

PLAN *n* counsel, design, device, idea, intent, intention, project, proposal, proposition, scheme; **suggestion,** cogitation, conception, contemplation, imagination *(Archaic),* motion, thought; **program,** agenda, arrangements, book, budget, démarche, format, nostrum, outline, regime, regimen, schedule, schema, schematism, syllabus, system, timetable; **policy,** ideology, line, platform; **tactics,** card, commander's concept, concept of operations, dart, healy *(Prison Colloq.),* pitch, ploy, stratagem, strategic plan, strategy, tactic. *See also* CONSPIRACY

PLAN *v* arrange, engineer, forecast, frame, jack *(N.Z.),* mastermind, organise, tee up; **schedule,** bill, budget, slate, timetable; **map out,** chalk out, chart, lay out, set out; **devise,** cast, cast about for, cogitate, compass, concert, concoct, contrive, design, hatch, imagine *(Archaic),* project, propose; **systemise,** systematise. *See also* CONSPIRE

plan *n* → **1** act of war **2** diagram **3** expedient **4** preparation **5** undertaking *v* **6** intend

plane *n* → **1** aeroplane **2** condition **3** grade **4** level **5** leveller **6** smoother *v* **7** fly **8** level **9** move **10** smooth *adj* **11** level

planet *n* → **1** fortune-telling **2** heavenly body

plank *n* → **1** belief **2** coating **3** shaft **4** support **5** timber *v* **6** cook

plankton *n* → fish

PLANNED *adj* concerted, devised, prearranged, projected, put-up; **systematic,** schedular, schematic; **strategic,** tactical; **teleological,** destined, telic

PLANNER *n* architect, delineator, designer, draughtsman, plotter; **cartographer,** mapmaker, mapper, surveyor

PLANT *n* amphibian, annual, ant-house plant, biennial, bine, broom, bulb, bush, carnivore, climber, corm, creeper, cushion plant, endophyte, ephemeral, epiphyll, epiphyte, ericoid, evergreen, fan palm, forb, geophyte, halophyte, herb, liana, liane, mallee, microphyte, monocarp, palm, parasite, perennial, rambler, rosette, runner, sand-binder, saprophyte, sedge, shrub, succulent, trailer, tree, tumbleweed, tussock, twiner, vine, whipstick, winder; **ornamental plant,** bouquet, boutonniere, cacoon, calabash, corsage, gourd, gum tips, jequirity, job's-tears, nosegay, posy, wreath; **plant classification,** acotyledon, acrogen, alga, angiosperm, bacteria, blue-green algae, brown algae, bryophyte, club moss, conifer, cormophyte, cryptogam, cyanobacterium, cyanophyte, cycad, dicotyledon, endogen, eukaryote, exogen, fern, fungus, green algae, gymnosperm, hepatic, lichen, liverwort, monocotyledon, moss, phanerogam, prokaryote, protist, pteridophyte, red algae, schizophyte, seed plant, spermatophyte, thallophyte, vascular plant; **flowering-plant family,** amaryllid, araliad, aroid, asclepiad, bromeliad, cactus, chenopod, composite, crucifer, cucurbit, daisy, dipterocarp, epacrid, goosefoot, grass, labiate, legume, lily, orchid, palm, sedge, umbellifer

plant *n* → **1** conspiracy **2** embezzlement **3** factory **4** hiding place **5** informant **6** machine **7** trick *v* **8** create **9** farm **10** hide **11** inhabit **12** insert **13** position

plantation *n* → **1** dwelling **2** farm

plaque *n* → **1** covering **2** emblem **3** heart disease **4** toothache

plasma *n* → gas

PLASTER *n* cement render, drummy, facing, gyprock, parget, plastering, pricking coat, render, revetment, roughcast, setting coat, skimming coat, wattle; **veneer,** brick veneer, burlwood veneer, panelling, wainscot; **wallpaper,** dado, flock paper, lining paper, paper

plaster *n* → **1** adhesive **2** building materials **3** medication **4** powder *v* **5** beat **6** coat **7** fill **8** fire on **9** level **10** oversupply

plastic *n* → **1** capital **2** explosive *adj* **3** fake **4** influenced **5** insipid **6** pliable **7** restorative **8** soft

plastic surgery *n* → **1** healing **2** medical treatment

plate *n* → **1** beam **2** brace **3** circle **4** coating **5** copy **6** electric circuit **7** engraving **8** metal **9** model **10** mouth **11** organism **12** plating **13** racing **14** smooth object *v* **15** coat **16** conserve **17** smooth **18** work metal

plateau *n* → mountain

PLATFORM *n* apron *(Theat.),* bandstand, barbette, bema *(Greek Antiq.),* bridge, pageant *(Hist.),* stage; **podium,** dais, footpace, hustings *(Politics),* pace, pulpit, rostrum, soapbox, tribune; **docking,** boatswain's chair, bosun's chair, cradle, jiggerboard, springboard *(Timber Industry),* **pallet,** hack, skidway *(Timber Industry),* staddle

platform *n* → **1** belief **2** entrance **3** footgear **4** plan **5** public notice

PLATING *n* case *(Metall.),* casing, electroplating, enamel, enamelling, enamelwork, foliation, galvanisation, gilding, gold plate, leading, nickel plate, overlay, oxidation, oxidisation, patina, plate, rolled gold, silvering, silverplate, tarnish, vitreous enamel

plating *n* → coating

platinum *adj* → metallic

platitude *n* → **1** bore **2** nonsense **3** ordinariness **4** proverb

platonic *adj* → friendly

platoon *n* → armed forces

plaudit *n* → applause

plausible *adj* → **1** believable **2** deceitful **3** likely

play *n* → **1** amusement **2** behaviour **3** doing **4** drama **5** joke **6** liberty **7** space *v* **8** amuse oneself **9** contest **10** do **11** fish **12** gamble **13** joke **14** let oneself go **15** move **16** operate **17** perform **18** speed **19** use

playboy *n* → **1** squanderer **2** wealthy person

PLAYFULLY *adv* friskily, frolicsomely, gamesomely, sportively; **for fun,** for kicks, in fun; **amusingly,** enjoyably

plaza *n* → field

plea *n* → **1** entreaty **2** justification **3** litigation

plead *v* → **1** entreat **2** litigate **3** persuade

PLEASANT *adj* acceptable, agreeable, bland, compatible, enjoyable, inoffensive, nice, offenceless, palatable, piacevole, pleasing, sapid, simpatico, to one's taste, welcome; **amiable,** adorable, benign, courteous, genial, good-natured, good-tempered, kindly, likeable, lovable, sweet-tempered; **charming,** attractive, beautiful, becoming, comely, cute, easy on the eyes, engaging, glam, glamorous, graceful, piquant, pretty, taking, winning, winsome; **cheerful,** cosy, jolly, merry *(Archaic)*; **delightful,** delectable, delicious, delightsome *(Archaic)*, fragrant, gladsome, glorious, goluptious, gorgeous *(Colloq.)*, heavenly, lovely *(Colloq.)*, luscious; **sweet,** bittersweet, dulcet, mellifluous

pleasant *adj* → **1** beautiful **2** happy **3** humorous **4** pleasurable

PLEASANTLY *adv* acceptably, agreeably, amiably, inoffensively, nicely, piacevole, pleasingly; **charmingly,** attractively, becomingly, delectably, deliciously, delightfully, delightsomely *(Archaic)*, engagingly, piquantly, sweetly

PLEASANTNESS *n* acceptability, acceptableness, agreeableness, amenity, blandness, inoffensiveness, likeability, likeableness, niceness, palatability, palatableness, pleasingness; **amiability,** amiableness, lovability, lovableness; **charm,** attractiveness, comeliness, cuteness, douceur, glam *(Colloq.)*, glamour, grace, gracefulness, loveliness; **cheerfulness,** cosiness; **delightfulness,** delectability, delectableness, deliciousness, delightsomeness *(Archaic)*, gloriousness, gorgeousness, heavenliness, lusciousness, luxuriousness, mellifluousness, sweetness; **pleasant place,** Eden, Elysium, heaven, millennium, paradise

pleasantry *n* → joke

PLEASE *v* divert, elicit a positive response, gratify, grow on, list *(Archaic)*, pleasure, rub up the right way, tickle; **enchant,** beguile, charm, delectate, enrapture, entrance; **gladden,** beatify, delight, glad *(Archaic)*, imparadise, joy *(Obs.)*, thrill to bits, transport

PLEASE *interj* for God's sake, for goodness sake, for heaven's sake, I beg of you, pray, prithee *(Archaic)*

please *v* → **1** be pleasant **2** make pleasant **3** satisfy

PLEASED *adj* glad, happy, happy as a bastard on Father's Day, happy as Larry, joyful, joyous; **enchanted,** charmed; **delighted,** chuffed, enrapt, overjoyed, pleased as Punch, rapt, stoked, thrilled, tickled pink, tickled to bits, tickled to death; **euphoric,** beatific, blissful, ecstatic, enraptured, high, high as a kite, in raptures, on a high, rapturous, raving; **enjoying oneself,** in the groove, turned on

PLEASURABLE *adj* appealing, enjoyable, funky, groovy, likeable, mild-mannered, pleasant; **pleasing,** entertaining, gratifying, satisfying; **idyllic,** Edenic, Elysian, halcyon, paradisiacal

PLEASURE *n* delight, delightedness, gladness, gladsomeness, happiness, joy, joyfulness, joyousness, lust *(Obs.)*, pleasance *(Archaic)*; **enjoyment,** delectation, recreation, refreshment; **gratification,** fulfilment, satisfaction, sensuality, voluptuosity, voluptuousness; **indulgence,** epicureanism, feasting, festivity, hedonics, hedonism, luxuriation, luxuriousness, luxury, pleasure principle; **pleasurableness,** enjoyableness, pleasantness, thrillingness; **creature comforts,** cakes and ale, comfort, cosiness, ease, snugness, well-being; **liking,** fancy, palate, partiality, predilection, propensity *(Obs.)*, relish, taste; **appreciation,** admiration, love; **joie de vivre,** gusto, zest, zestfulness; **rapture,** abandonment, bliss, ecstasy, exaltation, rapturousness, transport; **seventh heaven,** beatification, beatitude, blessedness, blissfulness; **enchantment,** beguilement, bewitchment, ravishment, titillation; **euphoria,** ecstatics, raptures, transports; **thrill,** buzz, charge, kick; **high,** trip, upper

pleasure *n* → **1** amusement **2** voluptuousness **3** will *v* **4** please

PLEASURE-LOVING *adj* high-stepping, indulgent, luxurious, pleasure-seeking, sybaritic, voluptuary, voluptuous; **hedonistic,** epicurean, hedonic

pleat *n* → **1** fold *v* **2** contract **3** fold

plebeian *n* → **1** vulgarian *adj* **2** ill-bred **3** working-class

plebiscite *n* → election

pledge *n* → **1** contract **2** surety *v* **3** lend **4** promise **5** rejoice

plenary *adj* → **1** general **2** whole

plenipotentiary *n* → **1** delegate **2** powerful person *adj* **3** powerful **4** whole

plenitude *n* → **1** abundance **2** fullness

plentiful *adj* → **1** abundant **2** great **3** many

plenty *n* → **1** abundance **2** fertility **3** fullness **4** luxury **5** much *adv* **6** fully **7** very

plethora *n* → surplus

PLIABILITY *n* flexibility, flexibleness, limberness, lissomness, litheness, pliableness, pliancy, pliantness, suppleness, tone, twistability; **resilience,** bounce, bounciness, buoyancy, rebound, renitency, spring, springiness, temper, tension, tonicity, torsibility; **elasticity,** aero-elasticity, give, plasticity, sponginess; **stretchability,** ductility, stretchiness, tensility, tractility, Young's modulus; **elasticisation,** jellification, plasticisation

PLIABLE *adj* bendable, bendy, double-jointed, flexible, flexile, flippant *(Obs.)*, limber, lissom, lithe, pliant, springy, supple, twistable, twisty, whippy, willowy, wristy; **resilient,** bouncy, buoyant, inflated, renitent, spring, spring-loaded, spring-loading, tonic;

elastic, aero-elastic, al dente, boneless, elastomeric, gelatinous, indiarubber, jellied, rubbery; **mouldable,** fictile, plastic, thermoplastic; **stretchable,** ductile, stretch, stretchy, tensible, tensile, tractile

pliable *adj* → **1** conventional **2** influenced **3** soft

pliant *adj* → **1** influenced **2** obedient **3** obsequious **4** pliable **5** soft

pliers *n* → **1** extractor **2** holder

plight *n* → **1** condition **2** luck **3** surety *v* **4** promise

plinth *n* → bottom

plod *n* → **1** click **2** record **3** time sheet **4** walking *v* **5** go slowly **6** make an effort **7** walk

plonk *n* → **1** alcohol **2** click **3** wine *v* **4** lower *adv* **5** precisely

plop *n* → **1** fall **2** splash *v* **3** shower **4** splash

plot *n* → **1** conspiracy **2** diagram **3** expedient **4** garden **5** narrative **6** position **7** secrecy **8** stratagem **9** yard *v* **10** beat a path **11** beguile **12** conspire **13** cooperate **14** keep secret **15** make do **16** map **17** measure

plough *n* → **1** digging implement **2** electric circuit **3** failure **4** farmland **5** farm machinery *v* **6** dig **7** farm **8** furrow **9** move

ploy *n* → **1** plan **2** stratagem

pluck *n* → **1** courage **2** pull *v* **3** extract **4** pull

PLUG *n* bathplug, bung, cork, fipple, gasket, jackass *(Naut.)*, shive, spigot, spile, spill, stop, stopper, stopple *(Archaic)*, stuffing box, tap; **cap,** bottle top, crown cap, crown seal, screw-top; **sealing wax,** cachet, cane, seal; **sealing strip,** weather strip *(Bldg. Trades)*, weather-stripping; **wad,** tampion *(Gunnery)*, tampon

plug *n* → **1** electric circuit **2** electric generator **3** hat **4** hit **5** horse **6** incentive **7** public notice **8** tap **9** tobacco *v* **10** approve **11** close **12** fill **13** hit **14** insert **15** make an effort

plum *n* → **1** good thing **2** purple

plumage *n* → feather

plumb *n* → **1** erectness *v* **2** close **3** erect **4** investigate *adj* **5** erect **6** most *adv* **7** erectly **8** greatly **9** precisely

plumber *n* → **1** labourer **2** metalworker

plumbing *n* → depth

plumbline *n* → erectness

plume *n* → **1** feather **2** trimming *v* **3** feather

plummet *n* → **1** erectness *v* **2** dive

plump *n* → **1** fall *v* **2** fall *adj* **3** fat **4** thick

plunder *n* → **1** loot **2** robbery *v* **3** attack **4** rob

plunge *n* → **1** dive **2** lake *v* **3** dive **4** gamble

plural *adj* → many

plus *n* → **1** more **2** profit *adj* **3** additional **4** increased *conj* **5** and

plush *adj* → expensive

plutocracy *n* → **1** nation **2** wealthy person

pluvial *n* → **1** cloak **2** uniform

ply *n* → **1** point of view **2** thread *v* **3** entreat **4** have a job **5** move **6** operate **7** pass through **8** supply **9** travel **10** use

pneumatic *adj* → **1** airy **2** beautiful **3** fat **4** gaseous

poach *v* → **1** cook **2** meddle **3** rob

pock *n* → **1** bulge **2** disfigurement **3** indentation

POCKET *n* bin *(Colloq.)*, fob, hip-pocket, poke *(Archaic)*, pouch *(Scot.)*, sporran

pocket *n* → **1** airflow **2** amount **3** funds **4** hollow **5** mineral **6** region *v* **7** be inactive **8** capture **9** enclose **10** get **11** imprison **12** insert

pod *n* → **1** bag **2** covering *v* **3** bare **4** bulge

poddy *n* → **1** animal offspring **2** cattle *adj* **3** swollen **4** thick

podium *n* → **1** bottom **2** flower **3** leg **4** platform

poem *n* → poetry

POET *n* ballad-monger, bard, dithyrambist, elegist, hymnist, hymnodist, idyllist, imagist, jongleur, laureate, lyricist, lyrist, maker *(Archaic)*, metrician, metrifier, metrist, minnesinger, minstrel, monodist, poet laureate, poetaster, poetess, prosodist, rhymer, rhymester, scop, singer, skald, songster, songwriter, sonneteer, troubadour, trouvère, vers librist, versifier

poet *n* → **1** fantasiser **2** orator

POETIC *adj* bardic, Parnassian; **lyric,** elegiac, idyllic, lyrical, melic, odic; **heroic,** Dantesque, epic, Homeric; **bucolic,** pastoral; **satiric,** mock-heroic; **metric,** measured, metrical, prosodic, prosodical, quantitative, rhythmical, scannable; **versicular,** stanzaic, stichic, strophic, systolic

POETRY *n* poesy, verse; **balladry,** concrete poetry, goliardery, hymnody, hymnology, minstrelsy, namby-pamby, nonsense verse, satire; **poetic art,** ars poetica, poetics, prosody, the Muse; **poem,** lines, monostrophe, piece, prose poem, rhyme, rime, song, strain; **book of poetry,** anthology, chapbook, divan *(Obs.)*, Parnassus; **lyric,** ballade, canzone, cento, Cowleian ode, dithyramb, ditty, eclogue, epode, erotic, Horatian ode, idyll, irregular ode, ithyphallic, madrigal, monody, ode, pantun, Pindaric ode, Pseudo-Pindaric ode, regular ode, rondeau, rondel, roundel, rune, Sapphic ode, sestina, sextain, sonnet, tanka, villanelle, virelay; **ballad,** broadsheet, bush ballad, doggerel, fit, jingle, macaronic, nursery rhyme, singsong; **epic,** chanson de geste, épopée, epopoeia, epos, heroic verse, heroics, rhapsody; **romance,** ballad, fabliau, gest *(Archaic)*, lay, roman, romaunt; **georgic,** bucolic, pastoral; **elegy,** dirge, lament; **epithalamium,** prothalamion; **hymn,** psalm; **epigram,** acrostic, charm, clerihew, gnomic verse, haiku, limerick

poetry *n* → figure of speech

pogrom *n* → massacre

poignant *adj* → **1** distressing **2** emotive **3** intense **4** painful **5** pungent

point *n* → **1** animal part **2** electric circuit **3** essence **4** face **5** finish **6** gradation **7** headland **8** important thing **9** knob **10** lace **11** meaning **12** moment **13** particulars **14** piercer **15** position **16** sharp point **17** sign **18** small amount **19** string *v* **20** bulge **21** cheat **22** direct **23** fill **24** gesture **25** mark **26** set sail **27** sharpen

point-blank *adj* → **1** direct *adv* **2** directly

POINTED *adj* acuate, aculeate, acuminate, acute, bicorn, cornuted, cultrate, cusped, cuspidal, cuspidate, ericoid, fastigiate, obeliscal, oxy, subacute, superacute; **barbed,** pinnular, pinnulate, pinnulated; **beaked,** beaky, lipped; **spearlike,** lanceolate, oblanceolate; **arrowy,** harpoonlike, sagittal, sagittate; **cone-shaped,** coniform. *See also* SHARP; SPINY

pointer *n* → **1** dog **2** guidance **3** indicator

POINT OF CONVERGENCE *n* crunode, cusp, focus, hub, node, vanishing point; **line of convergence,** asymptote, confluent, spoke

POINT OF VIEW *n* attitude, opinion, outlook, pose, position, stance, stand, thing, view, viewpoint; **inclination,** bent, bias, cast, impulse, lean, leaning, penchant, ply, prejudice, set, slant, tenor, turn; **predisposition,** amenability, diathesis, disposition, exposure, habit, liability, liableness, susceptibility, susceptibleness, susceptiveness, susceptivity, tendency, weakness; **affinity,** affect *(Obs.),* affection *(Obs.),* appetence, aptitude, liking, partiality, predilection, proclivity, proneness, propensity, readiness, talent *(Obs.)*; **trend,** climate, course, current, direction, drift, gravitation, motion, movement, stream, tide, undercurrent, wave, wind

poise *n* → **1** composure **2** equality **3** lightness **4** rest *v* **5** equal **6** hang **7** support **8** weigh

POISON *n* autotoxin, bait, bane, endotoxin, exotoxin, intoxicant, potion, toxicant, toxin, toxoid; **venom,** snakebite, sting, venin, zootoxin; **germ,** infection, virus; **biocide,** agent orange, agent purple, agent white, anticrop agent, defoliant, fungicide, herbicide, picloran, weedicide, weedkiller; **chemical agent,** biological weapon, nerve agent, phosgene, sternutator, yellow rain; **radiation,** fallout, strontium-90; **poison gas,** adamsite, arsine, asphyxiant, damp, diphosgene, effluvium, gas, mephitis, miasma, mofette, mustard gas, vapours; **pesticide,** acaricide, arsenicals, chlordane, DDT, dichlorodiphenyltrichloroethane, dieldrin, insecticide, malathion, metaldehyde, miticide, Paris green, pyrethrum, rotenone; **dichlorophenoxyacetic acid,** 2, 4-D; **trichlorophenoxyacetic acid,** 2, 4, 5-T, dioxin, toxaphene; **poisonousness,** nocuousness, noisomeness, noxiousness, toxicity, venomousness, virulence

POISON *v* drug, empoison, envenom, hocus, venom *(Archaic)*; **bait,** cyanide *(N.Z.),* loco *(U.S.)*; **sting,** urticate; **contaminate,** denature, denaturise, infect; **biomagnify**

poison *n* → **1** destroyer **2** means of killing *v* **3** destroy **4** kill *adj* **5** poisonous

POISONOUS *adj* baited, baneful, contaminative, germ-laden, mephitic, miasmal, miasmatic, miasmatical, miasmic, nocuous, noisome, noxious, pestilent, pestilential, poison, venenose *(Rare),* venomous, vicious *(Obs.),* virulent; **toxic,** autotoxic, carcinogenic, cyanic, epipastic, escharotic, fungicidal, strychnic, toxicant, toxicogenic, zootoxic

poke *n* → **1** bag **2** pat **3** pocket **4** sexual intercourse *v* **5** have sex **6** thrust

poky *adj* → **1** imprisoned **2** intolerant **3** small

polar *adj* → **1** attractive **2** opposite

polarise *v* → invert

POLE *n* barber's pole, beanpole, caber, flagpole, jackstaff, maypole, totem pole; **telegraph pole,** breakaway, frangible, Stobie pole, utility pole; **barge pole,** catching pole, roping pole; **mast,** jigger, jiggermast, jury mast, mizzenmast, royal mast, samson post, topmast; **boom,** bowsprit, bumpkin, dolphin striker, gaff, jackyard, jib boom, jockey pole, martingale, spar, sprit, steeve, traveller, yard

pole *n* → **1** area **2** astronomic point **3** extremity **4** length **5** opposite position **6** road

poleaxe *n* → **1** sword *v* **2** kill

polemic *n* → **1** discussion **2** reasoning *adj* **3** eloquent

polemics *n* → reasoning

POLICE *n* armed constabulary, CIB, CID, coastguard, commissary, consorting squad, constabulary, customs, dog squad, drug squad, ducks and geese, FBI *(U.S.),* filth *(Brit.),* flying squad, force, fuzz, gendarmerie, military police, Scotland Yard, secret police, the boys in blue, the law, the long arm of the law, vice squad, water police

police *n* → **1** cleansing *v* **2** clean

POLICEMAN *n* bobby, bull, constable, convict constable, cop, copper, customs officer, demon, detective, farm constable *(Convict),* flat, flatfoot, gendarme, heavy, inspector, jack, Joe, john, jonnop, lawman *(U.S.),* Mickey, mountie *(Canada),* narc, operative *(U.S.),* patrolman, peeler *(Obs.),* pig *(Colloq.),* pointsman *(N.Z.),* police constable, police officer, policewoman, provost marshal, ranger, roundsman *(U.S.),* rozzer, screw, sergeant, speed-cop, super, superintendent, trap, trooper, walloper; **proctor,** attendance officer, bulldog, prison officer, provost, screw, truant officer, warden *(U.S. Prison),* warder; **parking policeman,** brown bomber, grey ghost, meter maid *(Brit. Colloq.),* traffic warden *(Brit.)*; **posse,** posse comitatus, vigilance committee *(U.S.),* vigilance man *(U.S.),* vigilante *(U.S.)*; **peace officer,** marshal *(U.S.),* sheriff, special, special constable

policy *n* → **1** expedient **2** gambling **3** insurance **4** legislation **5** plan **6** wisdom

POLISH *n* bull *(Mil.),* glare, glaze, shine, shoeshine

POLISH *v* beeswax, buff, burnish, dub, furbish, lustre, planish, rub up, shine, wax

polish *n* → **1** brightness **2** goodness **3** smoother *v* **4** approve **5** clean **6** illuminate **7** perfect

polite *adj* → **1** courteous **2** cultivated

politic *adj* → **1** cunning **2** expedient **3** wise

POLITICAL IDEOLOGIST *n* centrist, coalitionist, democrat, federalist, fusionist, liberal, liberalist, moderate, ochlocrat, reformist, small-l liberal, technocrat, unicameralist; **left-winger,** bolshevik bolshevist, bolshie, collectivist, com, commie, commo, communalist, communist, comrade, leftie, leftist, Leninist, Maoist, Marxist, nationaliser, parlour pink *(Colloq.)*, pink, pinkie, pinko *(U.S.)*, progressive, radical, red, republican, socialist, sovietist, syndicalist, Trotskyite, weekend revolutionary *(Derog.)*; **revolutionary,** Jacobin, terrorist, urban guerilla; **nationalist,** free-stater *(Brit.)*, home-ruler, Little Englander, separatist; **feminist,** radical feminist, suffragette, suffragist, women's libber; **conservationist,** environmentalist, greenie; **right-winger,** capitalist, capitalist roader *(Derog.)*, conservative, counter-revolutionary, fundamentalist, grouper, legitimist, mossback *(U.S.)*, reactionary, revisionist, right-to-lifer, tory, true blue; **fascist,** absolutist, Caesarist, czarist, elitist, feudalist, imperialist, monarchist, monocrat, neo-fascist, royalist, stratocrat, territorialist, theocrat, totalitarian, tsarist; **hawk,** cold warrior

POLITICIAN *n* agitprop, agro-politician, barnstormer, candidate, canvasser, crusader, crypto, favourite son *(U.S.)*, fellow traveller, king maker *(U.S.)*, lobbyist, political activist, political enthusiast, politico, pollie, strategist, stump orator, tub-thumper. *See also* MEMBER OF PARLIAMENT

POLITICISE *v* agitate, propagandise, raise consciousness; **lobby,** pressure; **redistribute,** gerrymander

POLITICS *n* class warfare, lobbyism, mugwumpery, party politics, political football, power structure, statecraft, statesmanship, statism *(Obs.)*, war conducted by other means; **diplomacy,** balance of power, brinkmanship, cold war, domino theory, escalation, gunboat diplomacy, irredentism, power politics, Realpolitik, shuttle diplomacy, summitry, ultimatum; **political science,** geopolitics

politics *n* → cunning

polka *v* → dance

poll *n* → 1 election 2 head 3 investigation 4 list *v* 5 cut 6 cut off 7 list

pollen *n* → 1 flower *v* 2 reproduce

pollinate *v* → reproduce

pollute *v* → 1 dirty 2 profane

poltergeist *n* → phantom

poltroon *n* → coward

polyandry *n* → marriage

polygamy *n* → marriage

polyglot *n* → 1 breviary 2 mixture *adj* 3 mixed

polygyny *n* → marriage

polyhedron *n* → solid

polyp *n* → bulge

polyunsaturated *adj* → oily

pomegranate *n* → arriver

pommel *n* → 1 knob *v* 2 beat

pomp *n* → show

pompom *n* → 1 bead 2 gun 3 trimming

pompous *adj* → 1 bombastic 2 showy

ponce *n* → 1 affected person 2 man 3 prostitute *v* 4 feminise 5 prostitute oneself 6 tomfool

poncho *n* → cloak

pond *n* → lake

ponder *v* → 1 assess 2 think

ponderous *adj* → 1 boring 2 heavy

pontiff *n* → ecclesiastic

pontificate *v* → pride oneself

pontoon *n* → 1 bridge 2 float 3 gambling 4 path 5 raft 6 support

pony *n* → 1 alcohol container 2 robbery 3 shearer

ponytail *n* → hair

poofter *n* → 1 coward 2 sexual type 3 weakling

pool *n* → 1 company 2 contest 3 corporation 4 funds 5 lake 6 sportsground 7 storage *v* 8 associate

poop *n* → 1 defecation *v* 2 flood 3 tire

POOR *adj* badly off, depressed, disadvantaged, distressed, dowerless, down at heel, down on one's arse, down on one's luck, down to the bottom dollar, down to the last crust, fortuneless, gone to Gowings, hard up, indigent, landless, miserable, miserable as a bandicoot, needful, needy, on one's beam-ends, on one's uppers, out at elbows, poor as a bandicoot, poor as a church mouse, underprivileged, without; **destitute,** beggarly, done for, down and out, impoverished, living on queer street, mendicant, on skid row, on the streets, penurious, poverty-stricken, slummy, starveling, vagrant, wretched; **broke,** bled white, broke to the wide, dead motherless broke, flat broke, impecunious, on the beach, on the outer, on the strap, out of pocket, penniless, skint, skun, stiff, stiff as a crutch, stony, stony-broke, strapped, stumped up; **bankrupt,** broken, stumered

poor *adj* → 1 bad 2 cowardly 3 inferior 4 infertile 5 insufficient 6 pitiable 7 thin 8 unfortunate

POORHOUSE *n* almshouse; **slums,** dump, shantytown; **depressed area,** distressed area

POORLY *adv* comfortlessly, impecuniously, indigently, miserably, on the wrong side of the tracks, penuriously, wretchedly; **from hand to mouth,** at subsistence level, on a shoestring, on the breadline, on the downgrade

poorly *adj* → 1 ill *adv* 2 incompetently

POOR PERSON *n* beadsman, beadswoman, cracker *(U.S.)*, derelict, dero, down-and-out, garreteer, have-not, needer, pauper, poor white *(U.S.)*; **beggar,** almsman, almswoman, beggarman, hobo, mendicant, starveling, tatterdemalion, vag, vagabond; **ragamuffin,** Arab, cinderella, guttersnipe, street Arab; **the poor,** poor white trash *(Derog.)*, the have-nots, the other half

pope *n* → 1 ecclesiastic 2 ruler

poplar *n* → timber

poppy *n* → 1 orange 2 red

populace *n* → working class

POPULAR *adj* best-selling, chartbound, commercial *(Music)*, hit-bound, pop

popular *adj* → 1 approved 2 desirable 3 famous 4 public

POPULARITY *n* mass appeal; **popular success,** gorilla *(U.S.)*, rage, smash, smash-hit, top of the pops

populate *v* → inhabit

POPULATION *n* citizenry; **towndweller,** burgess, burgher, citizen, city dweller, fringe dweller, metropolitan, slummer, townie, townsman, townswoman; **suburbanite,** commuter, exurbanite; **townspeople,** suburbia, townsfolk, township *(Brit. Hist.)*, village; **countrydweller,** back-countryman, backblocker, backwoodsman, bushie, bushman, bushwhacker *(U.S.)*, cottager, cottar *(Scot.)*, cottier, countryman, countryside, countrywoman, hatter, peasant, provincial, ryot, villager; **settler,** colonist, currency lad, currency lass, illegitimate, overstraiter *(Hist.)*, soldier settler, squatter; **migrant,** alien, black hat, ethnic, ethno, immigrant, New Australian, new chum, reffo; **native,** aborigine, autochthon, indigene. *See also* INHABITANT; OCCUPANT

populous *adj* → many

porch *n* → 1 entrance 2 hall 3 room

pore *n* → 1 indentation 2 opening *v* 3 look

pork *n* → bribery

PORNOGRAPHY *n* blue movie, child pornography, dirty postcard, filth, hard porn, hot stuff, obscenity, skin-flick, smut, soft porn; **pornographic writing,** banned book, curiosa *(U.S.)*, erotica, ithyphallic, yellowback; **bawdy yarn,** double entendre, limerick; **indecent exposure,** hambone, poppy show, strip, striptease. *See also* OBSCENITY

pornography *n* → sex aid

porridge *n* → imprisonment

port *n* → 1 case 2 door 3 entrance 4 harbour 5 left 6 opening 7 passageway 8 pose 9 side 10 town 11 window *v* 12 transport *adj* 13 left 14 red

portable *adj* → transportable

portal *n* → 1 door 2 entrance

portcullis *n* → 1 door 2 obstacle

portend *v* → predict

porter *n* → 1 beer 2 butler 3 religious dignitary 4 transporter

portfolio *n* → case

porthole *n* → window

portico *n* → entrance

portion *n* → 1 bit 2 part 3 particulars 4 property 5 share 6 small amount 7 supplies *v* 8 give 9 share out

portly *adj* → 1 enormous 2 fat 3 thick

portmanteau *n* → box

PORTRAIT *n* copy, counterfeit *(Obs.)*, delineation, depiction, drawing, engraving, etching, facsimile, half-face, half-length, idea *(Obs.)*, identikit, image, likeness, painting, photograph, picture, presentment, projection, representation, semblance, silhouette, sketch, speaking likeness, study; **caricature,** cartoon, comic, comic strip; **statue,** antic *(Archaic)*, bronze, bust, effigy, gargoyle, glyph, head, herm, sculptured figure; **effigy,** automaton, doll, dummy, figurine, guy, jackstraw, manikin, mannequin, marionette, model, puppet, robot, waxwork; **totem,** churinga, idol, tiki, totem pole; **mask,** character, disguise, person, persona

portrait *n* → 1 painting 2 photograph

PORTRAY *v* catch a likeness, delineate, depict, depicture, draw, engrave, etch, hold the mirror up to nature, just hit off, line, paint, picture, write; **caricature,** cartoon; **photograph,** X-ray; **carve,** cast, sculpt

portray *v* → 1 depict 2 perform 3 write

POSE *n* antic, attitude, position, posture; **bearing,** carriage, deportment, manner, outward, port, set; **stance,** stand; **accumbency,** couching, decumbence, decumbency, prostration, recumbency; **sitting,** seat, seating, sedentariness, straddle; **bending,** bow, curtsy, kneeling, kowtow, squat, stoop; **slouch,** droop, sprawl

POSE *v* imitate, position oneself, posture, posturise, square off *(Boxing)*, square one's shoulders, stand up properly, stand up straight, strike a pose; **bear oneself,** carry oneself; **stand erect,** be upstanding, draw oneself up, stand up

pose *n* → 1 affectation 2 point of view *v* 3 assert 4 attitudinise 5 position 6 question 7 represent

poseur *n* → 1 affected person 2 show-off

posh *adj* → tasteful

POSITION *n* line *(Mil.)*, locus, pitch, place, plot, point, possie, set, set-up, site, situation, situs, spot, station; **location,** address, whereabouts; **locale,** haunt, locality, post, setting, stamping ground; **rendezvous,** tryst, trysting place, venue

POSITION *v* allocate, bung, determine, draw, emplace, establish, install, instate, localise, locate, park, pinpoint, pitch, place, plank down, plant, pose *(Archaic)*, posit, reposition, site, situate, stage, station; **deploy,** collocate, dispose, line, range; **lie,** rest, sit, stand, take one's place; **lay,** plank down, plonk down, whack down

position *n* → 1 condition 2 educational office 3 job 4 opinion 5 point of view 6 pose 7 reputation *v* 8 place

POSITIONED *adj* bestead *(Archaic)*, disposed, located, placed, sited, situate *(Archaic)*, situated

POSITIONING *n* collocation, configuration, deployment, deposition, distribution, emplacement, establishment, installation, instatement, localisation, orientation, pitch, placement; **echolocation,** echo ranging, fix *(Colloq.)*, radiolocation; **radar,** asdic, Doppler radar, loran, magnetron, minitrack *(Aerospace)*, radar scanner, radio beacon, radio-compass, sonobuoy

positive *n* → 1 photograph *adj* 2 assertive 3 certain 4 hopeful 5 male 6 most 7 numerical 8 real 9 unconditional 10 unrelated

possess *v* → **1** capture **2** haunt **3** have sex **4** own **5** remember
possessed *adj* → **1** mad **2** resting **3** supernatural
possession *n* → **1** habitation **2** ownership
possessive *adj* → **1** repressive **2** selfish
possible *adj* → feasible
POSSIBLY *adv* by chance, haply *(Archaic)*, happen *(Brit. Colloq.)*, maybe, mayhap *(Archaic)*, peradventure *(Archaic)*, perchance *(Archaic)*, perhaps, potentially, practicably
possum *n* → fool
POST *n* bedpost; **pile,** block *(Qld.)*, piling, stilt; **gatepost,** gradient post, heelpost, hitching post, quintain, strainer, strainer post, winning post; **bollard,** barrel, bitt, loggerhead; **column,** anta, atlantes, gnomon, monolith, obelisk, pilaster, pillar, pylon, shaft, verge; **dado,** die, scape, trunk
postage *n* → freight
postcode *n* → label
postdate *v* → **1** be late **2** mistime
poster *n* → public notice
posterior *n* → **1** buttocks **2** rear *adj* **3** bodily **4** following **5** rear
posterity *n* → offspring
postgraduate *n* → **1** intellectual **2** pupil
posthaste *n* → **1** speed *adv* **2** hurriedly
posthumous *adj* → deathlike
post-mortem *n* → **1** questioning *adj* **2** deathlike
postpone *v* → defer
POSTSCRIPT *n* allonge, annex, annexure, appendix, codicil, embolism, endorsement, rider, schedule, subjunction, subscription; **epilogue,** addendum, corollary, envoy, excursus, follow-up; **footnote,** end note, note, protocol, scholium. *See also* ADDITION
postscript *n* → addition
postulate *n* → **1** conjecture **2** entreaty **3** necessities **4** proverb *v* **5** conjecture **6** employ **7** insist on
posture *n* → **1** condition **2** pose *v* **3** attitudinise **4** pose
posy *n* → plant
pot *n* → **1** abdomen **2** alcohol **3** alcohol container **4** cookware **5** fishing tackle **6** gambling **7** gambling equipment **8** hollow **9** important person **10** marijuana **11** shot **12** toilet **13** vessel *v* **14** conceive **15** conserve **16** cook **17** farm **18** insert **19** kill **20** shoot **21** urinate
potbelly *n* → **1** abdomen **2** bulge
potent *adj* → **1** male **2** powerful **3** strong
potentate *n* → ruler
potential *n* → **1** electricity **2** number **3** opportunity *adj* **4** allusive **5** feasible **6** powerful **7** strong
pothole *n* → **1** borehole **2** hollow
potion *n* → **1** magic spell **2** medication **3** poison
potluck *n* → **1** food **2** luck
potpourri *n* → **1** book **2** fragrance **3** mixture **4** musical piece
potter *n* → **1** bungle **2** craftsman *v* **3** bungle **4** go slowly
potty *n* → **1** toilet *adj* **2** foolish **3** mad **4** smallest **5** unimportant
pouch *n* → **1** case **2** pocket *v* **3** insert
poultice *n* → **1** loan **2** medication
pounce *n* → **1** absorber **2** dive **3** drier **4** fall **5** jump **6** powder *v* **7** bulge **8** dive **9** jump **10** speed
pound *n* → **1** cash **2** cell **3** explosion **4** hit **5** pen *v* **6** be loud **7** enclose **8** explode **9** hit **10** imprison **11** powder **12** vibrate **13** walk
pour *n* → **1** amount **2** flow **3** rainfall *v* **4** flow **5** rain
pout *n* → **1** bulge **2** scowl *v* **3** become irritated **4** dislike **5** jut
POVERTY *n* destitution, distress, impecuniosity, impecuniousness, indigence, miserableness, misery, necessity, need, neediness, pauperism, penuriousness, penury, poorness, privation, starvation, want, wretchedness; **impoverishment,** deprivation, pauperisation; **beggardom,** beggarhood, beggarliness, beggary, hoboism, mendicancy, mendicity; **poverty line**
poverty *n* → insufficiency
POW *n* → prisoner
POWDER *n* bulldust *(Colloq.)*, coaldust, cosmic dust, crocus, diamond dust, dust, flowers of sulphur *(Chem.)*, glacial meal, grit, ground glass, gum *(Coal Mining)*, icing sugar, platinum black *(Chem.)*, pounce, powdered chalk, powdered charcoal, pumice, rockflour, sawdust, slack *(Coal Mining)*, streak *(Mineral.)*, triturate; **ash,** ash fall, cinder, flyash, volcanic ash; **sand,** black sand, greensand, shingle; **flour,** bran, grist, grits, meal; **plaster,** cement, flock, petuntse *(Geol.)*, terra alba *(Geol.)*; **ochre,** kamala *(Bot.)*, kohl, mascara, rouge; **talcum powder,** face powder, sachet; **bloom,** efflorescence; **speck,** corn, detritus, filing, fine *(Mining)*, fines, grain, mote, particle, seed, spore, sporule
POWDER *v* abrade, bray, bruise, comminute, crumble, crunch, crush, levigate, pound, pulverise, rasp, triturate; **dolly,** pestle, puddle; **grind,** file, grate, kibble, mill; **granulate,** corn, grain; **effloresce,** come to dust, disintegrate, fall to dust, moulder, reduce to powder
powder *n* → **1** medication *v* **2** coat **3** decorate **4** disperse
POWDERED *adj* attrite *(Obs.)*, desiccated, ground, kibble, milled, pulverised, sifted, stoneground; **fine,** crumby, impalpable, light, pulverisable
POWDERER *n* file, grater, grinder, pouncer, pulveriser, rasp; **pestle,** dolly, posser; **millstone,** ball mill, grindstone, mortar, muller, puddling box, puddling tub, spider; **mill,** flour mill, gristmill, hand mill, quern; **konometer**
POWDERINESS *n* friability, friableness, mealiness; **grittiness,** sabulosity, sandiness
POWDERY *adj* branlike, efflorescent, flocculent, furfuraceous, granular, pruinose, pulverulent; **floury,** farinaceous, flourlike, mealy; **ashy,** ashen; **sandy,** arenaceous, dusty, gritty, sabulous

POWER *n* authority, force, forcefulness, might, mightiness, potence, potency, potentness, powerfulness, puissance *(Archaic)*, strength; **dominion,** danger *(Obs.)*, domain, empire, jurisdiction, rule, sovereignty, sway; **force,** action, activity, clout, effect, energy, leverage, teeth, thrust, vigorousness, vigour, virtue, wallop *(Colloq.)*

power *n* → **1** artistry **2** authority **3** capability **4** electricity **5** energy **6** entitlement **7** force **8** influence **9** influencer **10** many **11** much **12** nation **13** reflection **14** strength *v* **15** electrify **16** operate

POWERFUL *adj* all-powerful, almighty, armipotent, elemental, mighty, omnipotent, plenipotent, plenipotentiary, potent, potential *(Rare)*, puissant *(Archaic)*, strong; **authoritative,** commanding, magisterial, masterful; **domineering,** autocratic, dictatorial, imperious, overruling, tyrannical; **energetic,** emphatic, exertive, high-performance, high-powered, knockdown, knockdown drag-out, lively, punchy, raunchy, sledge-hammer, spunky, telling, vigorous

POWERFUL PERSON *n* autocrat, baron, big brother, boss cocky, cock of the walk, crowner of kings, dictator, dynamo, éminence grise, force majeure, grey eminence, head sherang, high priest, high-flier, Mr Big, operator, oppressor, plenipotentiary, predominator, prime mover, robber baron, strong man, top dog, tycoon, tyrant; **the Establishment,** vested interests

POWERLESS *adj* emptied, feeble, impotent, impuissant, incapable, unable, void, weak; **incapacitated,** buggered, castrated, crippled, debilitated, enervate, enervated, fucked, neutralised, paralysed, screwed up, shot, washed-out, washed-up; **ataxic,** asthenic, atactic, avirulent; **decrepit,** obsolete, over the hill, past it, senile, superannuated; **good-for-nothing,** gutless, milky, milquetoast, pathetic, prostrate, sissy, useless

POWERLESSNESS *n* asthenia *(Path.)*, brewer's droop, debility, decrepitude, exhaustion, helplessness, impotence, impuissance, inability, inanition, incapability, incapableness, incapacity, incompetence, ineptitude, milkiness, senility, weakness; **enervation,** ataxia, caducity, debilitation, decay, enfeeblement, impalement, impoverishment, incapacitation, paralysis, slough, wane

POWER TO ACT *n* charter, empowerment, licence, permit, power of attorney; **appointment,** installation, nomination, ordination

practicable *adj* → **1** feasible **2** useable

practical *n* → **1** lesson *adj* **2** busy **3** competent **4** expedient **5** occurrent **6** operating **7** useable

practical joke *n* → **1** joke **2** nonsense **3** trick

practically *adv* → almost

practice *n* → **1** action **2** custom **3** exercise **4** job **5** lesson **6** method **7** preparation **8** repetition

practise *v* → **1** be accustomed to **2** conspire **3** do **4** have a job **5** repeat **6** study

PRACTISE LAW *v* advise, assist, brief, defend, do conveyancing, plead cases, prepare briefs, prosecute, represent; **take silk,** be called to the bar

PRACTISE MEDICINE *v* cure, doctor, heal, medicine, treat; **nurse,** special; **have a good bedside manner; diagnose,** auscultate, sound, succuss

practitioner *n* → **1** agent **2** doer

pragmatic *adj* → **1** accomplished **2** busy **3** proud **4** realistic

prairie *n* → **1** grassland **2** swamp

praise *n* → **1** approval *v* **2** approve **3** be grateful **4** worship

prance *n* → **1** jump **2** move *v* **3** attitudinise **4** dance **5** jump **6** move **7** ride

prang *n* → **1** attack **2** impact **3** ruin *v* **4** break **5** collide **6** fire on

prank *n* → **1** caprice **2** joke **3** misdemeanour **4** trick *v* **5** decorate **6** show off

prate *n* → **1** talk *v* **2** talk

prattle *n* → **1** quiet sound **2** talk *v* **3** talk

prawn *v* → fish

pray *v* → **1** atone for **2** entreat **3** worship *interj* **4** please

prayer *n* → **1** entreaty **2** worship

preach *v* → teach

PREACHER *n* evangel, evangelist, hot-gospeller, missionary, missioner, predicant *(Obs.)*, pulpiteer *(Derog.)*, revivalist, Sal, Sallie, Salvation Army, Salvationist, Salvo; **acolyte,** deacon, deaconess, diaconate, exorcist; **catechist,** catechiser. *See also* ECCLESIASTIC

preamble *n* → introduction

precarious *adj* → **1** dangerous **2** uncertain

precaution *n* → **1** anticipation **2** preparation **3** safety

PRECEDE *v* antecede, antedate, beat, come before, foredate, forego, forerun, predate; **anticipate,** predict, prevent *(Obs.)*, prophecy

precede *v* → advance

PRECEDENCE *n* ascendancy, predominance, predomination, prerogative *(Obs.)*, pride of place, priority, seniority; **primacy,** headship, hegemony, leadership, lordship, overlordship, paramountcy, sovereignty, supereminence, supremacy; **preponderance,** preponderation, prevailingness, prevalence

precedence *n* → **1** antecedence **2** rights

precedent *n* → **1** example **2** law *adj* **3** preceding

PRECEDING *adj* antecedent, anterior, early, former, precedent, precessional, precursive, prevenient, previous, prior, yester *(Archaic)*; **aforesaid,** above, aforementioned, foregoing, said, which; **prefixal,** preposed, prepositive

precept *n* → **1** command **2** law **3** rule

precinct *n* → **1** administrative area **2** church **3** city **4** domain **5** region

precious *n* → **1** lover *adj* **2** affected **3** beloved **4** expensive **5** rocky *adv* **6** very

precipice *n* → mountain

precipitate *n* → **1** rainfall *v* **2** cause **3** lower **4** rain **5** separate **6** throw **7** thrust *adj* **8** rash **9** speedy **10** surprising

precipitation *n* → **1** cause **2** expulsion **3** fall **4** rainfall **5** rashness **6** separation **7** speed

precipitous *adj* → **1** mountainous **2** rash **3** sloping **4** surprising

precis *n* → abridgment

précis *n* → translation

precis *v* → **1** abbreviate **2** decrease

PRECISE *adj* accurate, bang-on, exact, in focus, on the beam, pat, perfect, point-device *(Archaic)*, right on, sharp, sharp-cut, spot-on; **unambiguous,** definite, univocal, unmistakable; **minute,** fine, particular; **measured,** calculated, determinate, mathematical, nicely calculated, strict, unerring, well-defined; **explicit,** elaborate, elaborative, express, identical, very; **true,** even, flush, level; **made-to-measure,** made-to-order, precut, ready-made; **punctilious,** fastidious, meticulous, punctual, rigorous, scrupulous, severe; **pedantic,** donnish, pedantical; **refined,** correct, nice, proper, pukka, right; **literal,** letter-perfect, technical, verbal *(Rare)*, verbatim, word perfect

precise *adj* → **1** affected **2** clear **3** concise **4** formal **5** particular

PRECISELY *adv* accurately, minutely, squarely, strictly, to a nicety, to a T, unerringly, with clockwork precision; **exactly,** dead, dead-centre, even, flat, full, giusto *(Music)*, just, plonk, plumb, slap-bang, square; **measuredly,** mathematically, scientifically; **flush,** even, true; **punctiliously,** punctually, scrupulously; **pedantically,** donnishly; **verbatim,** ad litteram, ad verbum, explicitly, literally, literatim, off pat, pat, sic, to the letter, word for word

PRECISION *n* accuracy, accurateness, correctness, niceness, nicety, preciseness, squareness, unerringness; **exactness,** definitude, exactitude, fidelity, punctiliousness, truth, veracity; **alignment,** face edge, face side, register *(Print.)*, tram *(Mach.)*, true, trueness, working edge, working face; **sharpness,** definition *(Optics)*; **regulation,** adjustment, calibration, ensendation; **formulation,** formularisation, formulisation; **literality,** explicitness, literalism, literalness, the letter of the law; **strictness,** pedantry, scrupulosity, severeness, severity; **punctilio,** technicality

PRECISIONIST *n* elaborator, formulator, formuliser, literaliser, literalist, pedagogue, pedant, perfectionist, refiner

preclude *v* → **1** exclude **2** hinder

precocious *adj* → **1** early **2** intelligent

preconceive *v* → anticipate

precursor *n* → forerunner

PREDATORY *adj* bloodsucking, confiscatory, dispossessory, predacious, prehensile, privative, raptorial, ravening; **extortionary,** extortive, grasping, greedy, leechlike, on the make, on the take, parasitic, rapacious, vampirish, vulture-like

predatory *adj* → **1** aggressive **2** pursuing **3** thieving

predecessor *n* → forerunner

predestine *v* → ordain

predicament *n* → **1** condition **2** danger **3** dilemma

predicate *n* → **1** assertion *v* **2** assert **3** imply *adj* **4** avowed

PREDICT *v* cast, divine, forecast, foresee, foretell, harbinger, herald, presignify, prognosticate, prophesy, read, see, shadow forth, soothsay, vaticinate; **promise,** augur, auspicate *(Archaic)*, bid fair to, point to, raise expectations, raise hopes; **signify,** indicate, suggest; **tell someone's fortune,** cast a horoscope; **cross someone's palm with silver,** have one's fortune told; **warn,** bode, forebode, omen, portend, presage; **prefigure,** pretypify; **tip,** nap *(Horseracing)*; **estimate,** cost, guess, judge, take a stab at

predict *v* → **1** anticipate **2** precede

PREDICTION *n* bodement, prophecy, self-fulfilling prophecy; **forecast,** cast, prognosis, prognostic; **estimate,** approximation, cost estimate, cost-benefit analysis, guesstimate, judgment, predicted cost, quantity survey; **tip,** nap *(Horseracing)*; **promise,** reason to hope, something to look forward to. *See also* FORTUNE-TELLING

PREDICTIVE *adj* prefigurative, prognosticative, prophetic, significative; **prophetic,** all-seeing, augural, auspicial, divinatory, fatal *(Obs.)*, mantic, oracular, prognostic, vatic, vaticinal, weatherwise; **auspicious,** promising; **ominous,** boding, disastrous *(Archaic)*, fateful, foreboding, ill-boding, sinister

PREDICTOR *n* augur, Chaldean, diviner, foreboder, foreteller, geomancer, haruspex, oneiromancer, oracle, presager, prognosticator, prophesier, prophet, seer, soothsayer, vaticinator; **prophet of doom,** Cassandra, jeremiah. *See also* FORTUNE-TELLER

predilection *n* → **1** choice **2** pleasure **3** point of view **4** prejudice

PREDISPOSED *adj* apt to, capable of, disposed, given to, in a fair way to, inclined, partial, prone, ready, tending; **biased,** affectionate *(Obs.)*, appetent, partisan, prejudiced, tendentious; **tempered,** minded, spirited; **susceptible,** accessible, amenable, diathetic, exposed, liable, open, subject, susceptive, vulnerable; **inclinational,** inclinatory

PREDOMINANCE *n* almightiness, ascendancy, omnipotence, predomination, preponderance, preponderation, superhumanity, supremacy, supremeness; **autocracy,** dictatorship, lordship, tyranny

PREDOMINANT *adj* absolute, ascendant, eminent, high-flying, master, paramount, pre-eminent, preponderant, preponderating, prepotent, sovereign, supreme

PREDOMINATE *v* command, have carte blanche, hold in fee, hold sway over, hold the balance of power, put the maginnis on, ride, rule; **preponderate,** outman, outvote, outweigh; **surmount,** be in the ascendant, have one's day, triumph

predominate *v* → influence

pre-eminent *adj* → 1 important 2 predominant 3 reputable
pre-empt *v* → 1 anticipate 2 buy
preen *v* → 1 decorate 2 feather 3 pride oneself
preface *n* → 1 book part 2 introduction 3 religious ceremony 4 written composition *v* 5 introduce
prefect *n* → 1 judge 2 pupil 3 ruler
prefer *v* → 1 choose 2 place 3 promote
preference *n* → 1 choice 2 rights 3 the best
prefix *n* → 1 antecedent *v* 2 arrange
PREGNANCY *n* foetation, gestation, gravidity, interesting condition, sitting; **parity,** multiparity, oviparity, ovoviviparity, polycyesis, primiparity, viviparity; **unwanted pregnancy,** mistake, unplanned pregnancy. *See also* CONCEPTION; BIRTH; REPRODUCTION
PREGNANT *adj* banged-up, big, enceinte, expectant, gone, gravid, heavy, impregnate, in pod, in the family way, in the pudding club, in trouble, knocked-up, preggers, up the duff, with child, with young; **brood,** stud; **natal,** congenital, parturient, peri-natal, postpartum, postnatal, prenatal, puerperal; **lying-in,** maternity, obstetric; **broody,** clucky, in season, oestrous, on heat, philoprogenitive; **biparous,** fissiparous, live-bearing, multiparous, oviparous, ovoviviparous, primiparous, pupiparous, uniparous, viviparous; **ecbolic,** oxytocic
pregnant *adj* → 1 abundant 2 concise 3 fertile 4 meaningful
prehensile *adj* → 1 holding 2 predatory
prehistoric *adj* → 1 old 2 past
PREJUDICE *n* bias, fixed idea, idée fixe, partisanship, predilection, predisposition, prepossession; **preconception,** prejudgment, prenotion, presumption, presupposal, presupposition, presurmise; **wrong-headedness,** blind spot, doublethink, injudiciousness, jaundice, self-deception
prejudice *n* → 1 harm 2 intolerance 3 opinion 4 point of view *v* 5 damage 6 persuade
PREJUDICED *adj* doctrinaire, intolerant, one-eyed, one-sided, partial, predisposed, self-opiniated, stupid, unbalanced, unreasonable; **insensate,** blind, boss-eyed, purblind, self-deceptive, short-sighted
prelate *n* → ecclesiastic
preliminary *n* → 1 introduction *adj* 2 prototypal 3 teaching
prelude *n* → 1 introduction 2 musical piece *v* 3 introduce
premarital *adj* → single
premature *adj* → 1 early 2 rash 3 raw 4 untimely
premeditate *v* → aim at
premier *n* → 1 member of parliament 2 ruler *adj* 3 early 4 successful
premiere *n* → 1 actor 2 performance 3 start *v* 4 initiate 5 stage
premise *n* → 1 assertion 2 conjecture 3 qualification *v* 4 introduce
premium *n* → 1 gift 2 income *adj* 3 good 4 reputable
premonition *n* → 1 anticipation 2 warning
PREPARATION *n* alertness, anticipation, concert pitch, preparedness, readiness; **preparations,** address *(Obs.)*, arrangements, hedge, make-ready *(Print.)*, plan, precaution, preparative, provision, scramble *(Mil.)*; **groundwork,** foundation, training; **rehearsal,** dress rehearsal, drill, knock-up, practice, run-through, trial run, warm-up; **stand-by,** red alert; **countdown,** lead time
preparation *n* → 1 anticipation 2 foundation 3 learning 4 making
PREPARE *v* address *(Obs.)*, arm, dight *(Archaic)*, equip, fit, fit out, furbish, furnish, gear, gear up, get into working order, get ready, kit, make ready, make up, overhaul, prep *(Med.)*, prime, refit, win *(Mining)*; **prime,** cock, unlimber; **dress,** curry, forward *(Bookbinding)*, gather *(Bookbinding)*, lick into shape, taw; **bring to readiness,** brew, concoct, gestate, hatch, incubate, mature, ripen; **rehearse,** bring up to form, bring up to scratch, drill, groom, run through, teach, train, warm up; **make preparations,** address oneself to, arrange, close ranks, cook up a plan, do one's homework, draw up, gather together, get up, lead up to, make provision, take steps, tee up; **prepare oneself,** buckle down, clear the decks, get into harness, gird up one's loins, go into training, roll up one's sleeves, serve an apprenticeship, set one's house in order; **anticipate,** foresee, keep one's powder dry, lay in stores, look ahead, provide against a rainy day, provide for the future
prepare *v* → 1 anticipate 2 cook 3 make 4 mix 5 teach
PREPARED *adj* bound *(Archaic)*, expedite *(Obs.)*, fit, in readiness, in working order, on one's toes, on tap, operational *(Mil.)*, raring to go, ready, set, yare *(Archaic)*; **forearmed,** armed to the teeth, booted and spurred, in battle array, in battle-readiness, prep, prompt, sword in hand; **in best bib and tucker,** dressed to the nines, dresses to kill, with one's warpaint on; **previously prepared,** already prepared, canned *(U.S.)*, forthcoming, prerecorded, ready-made
PREPAREDLY *adv* at hand, at the ready, in hand, in the wings, on call, on ice, on stand-by, on the qui vive; **ready and waiting,** in the pipeline, in the press, under consideration, up one's sleeve; **in preparation,** afoot, in embryo, in train, on the drawing board, on the stocks
preponderant *adj* → 1 heavy 2 influential 3 predominant
preposition *n* → word
prepossessing *adj* → 1 alluring 2 approved
preposterous *adj* → 1 foolish 2 nonsensical
prepuce *n* → groin
prerequisite *n* → 1 necessities 2 qualification *adj* 3 necessary
prerogative *n* → 1 authority 2 precedence 3 rights *adj* 4 rightful

presage *n* → 1 anticipation 2 omen *v* 3 anticipate 4 predict
prescribe *v* → 1 codify 2 command 3 guide 4 impose 5 medicate
prescription *n* → 1 command 2 diagram 3 medication 4 rights
PRESENCE *n* appearance, immanence, immanency, occupancy, occupation; **attendance,** audience, durbar *(India Hist.)*, turn-up; **omnipresence,** incidence, ubiquitousness, ubiquity
presence *n* → 1 appearance 2 being 3 closeness 4 companionship 5 god 6 person 7 phantom
PRESENT *adj* as large as life, attendant; **immanent; omnipresent,** ubiquitous
presentiment *n* → 1 anticipation 2 idea 3 warning
presently *adv* → 1 hurriedly 2 in the future 3 now
PRESERVE *v* salvage, salve, save; **save one's bacon,** bear a charmed life
preserve *n* → 1 field *v* 2 commemorate 3 conserve 4 cook 5 protract
PRESERVED *adj* alcoholic, canned, corned, cured, frozen, pickled, potted, salt, salted, sun-cured, tinned, vacuum-packed; **coated,** rainproof, showerproof, waterproof; **fireproof,** fire-resistant, flame-resistant, flameproof; **stuffed,** taxidermal, taxidermic
president *n* → 1 manager 2 ruler
PRESS *n* ball mill, box iron, calender, clothes press, cylinder, cylinder press, garbage compactor, mangle, mill, monkey, oilpress, pestle, ram, road-roller, roll, rolling mill, rolling pin, stamp mill, stamp-head, steamroller, supercalender, wine press, wool press; **iron,** cramp, cramp iron, flatiron, fluting iron, hot-press, steam iron; **stamp,** clicking press, imprinter, puncheon, stamper; **presser,** ironer, trampler, treader; **compressor,** pump, supercharger; **extruder,** crush, crusher, squasher, squeezer, squelcher, wringer; **tourniquet; clamp,** clench, clip, nipper, pincher
PRESS *v* beat out, calender, iron, iron out, mangle, mill, pestle, steamroller, supercalender; **pressurise,** squelch, supercharge *(Mach.)*, trample, tread; **compress,** affix, astringe, clamp, clench, clip, constrict, depress, detrude, impact, jam, knead, nip, pack, pinch, pug *(Agric.)*, scrunch, squash, squeeze, strangulate, vice; **squeeze out,** crush, express, extrude, wring off, wring out; **impress,** imprint, incuse, print, stamp, touch *(Metall.)*, trace
PRESSED *adj* adpressed, compressed, dense, extrusive *(Geol.)*, impacted, incuse, milled, superdense
PRESSING *n* constriction, detrusion, expression, extrusion, impaction, ironing, jam, milling, nip, pinch, press, scrunch, squash, squeeze, strangulation *(Pathol. Surg.)*, trample, vellication
pressing *n* → 1 recording *adj* 2 important 3 necessary
pressure *n* → 1 force 2 importance 3 influence 4 repression *v* 5 politicise
pressurise *v* → press
prestige *n* → 1 reputation *adj* 2 affected 3 reputable
presume *v* → 1 be arrogant 2 believe 3 be likely 4 conjecture 5 misjudge
PRESUMPTUOUS *adj* assuming, assumptive, audacious, blushless, brazen, bumptious, familiar, forward, hubristic, shameless; **highhanded,** bossy, dictatorial, dogmatic, domineering, imperious, magisterial, magistral *(Rare)*, officious, overbearing, pushy, self-assertive, swashbuckling; **dismissive,** dismissory
pretence *n* → 1 affectation 2 appearances 3 fake
PRETEND *v* boggle, cry wolf, dissemble, dissimulate, feign, fudge, keep up appearances, lead a double life, masquerade, pay lip-service to, play a part, put on an act, sham; **impersonate,** pass oneself off as, personate; **malinger,** swing the lead
pretend *v* → 1 delude oneself 2 fantasise 3 trick
pretension *n* → 1 affectation 2 arrogance 3 assertion
pretentious *adj* → 1 affected 2 bombastic 3 proud 4 showy 5 verbose
pretext *n* → 1 disguise 2 justification 3 lie 4 trickery
pretty *v* → 1 beautify *adj* 2 beautiful 3 courageous 4 cultivated 5 good 6 great 7 pleasant *adv* 8 very
prevail *v* → 1 be 2 generalise 3 influence
prevalent *adj* → general
prevaricate *v* → 1 avoid 2 lie 3 vacillate
prevent *v* → 1 expect 2 hinder 3 precede 4 prohibit 5 stop
preventive *n* → 1 contraception 2 hindrance 3 medication 4 stoppage *adj* 5 hindering
preview *n* → 1 display 2 performance *v* 3 look 4 stage
previous *adj* → 1 early 2 preceding
prey *n* → 1 victim *v* 2 hunt
price *n* → 1 cost 2 tax *v* 3 appraise
priceless *adj* → 1 expensive 2 humorous
prick *n* → 1 bad person 2 groin 3 incentive 4 opening 5 perception 6 perforation 7 piercer 8 sword 9 unpleasant person *v* 10 arouse 11 copy 12 cut 13 hurry 14 injure 15 open 16 pain 17 perforate
prickle *n* → 1 bubbliness 2 piercer 3 sharp point *v* 4 bubble 5 erect 6 open 7 perforate 8 touch
PRIDE *n* amour-propre, crest, high spirit, mettle, self-respect, stomach *(Obs.)*; **self-esteem,** conceit, immodesty, narcissism, self-conceit, self-congratulation, self-importance, self-love, self-opinion, self-regard, self-satisfaction, vanity, wind; **conceitedness,** boastfulness, vainness; **condescension,** inflatedness, loftiness, lordliness, malapertness, overconfidence
pride *n* → 1 arrogance 2 decoration 3 gathering 4 good thing 5 sex

PRIDE ONESELF *v* claim, credit to oneself; **have a good opinion of oneself,** be above oneself, be too big for one's boots, be up oneself, boast, fancy oneself, fish for compliments, have a swelled head, have tickets on oneself, think oneself Christmas; **talk down to,** condescend, lord it over, patronise; **lord it,** pontificate, put on dog, put on side, stand on one's dignity; **preen,** bloat, huff *(Archaic)*, inflate, plume oneself, primp, put on airs, put on airs and graces, swell with pride

priest *n* → ecclesiastic

prig *n* → affected person

primacy *n* → **1** importance **2** precedence

prima facie *adv* → apparently

primal *adj* → **1** important **2** past

primary *n* → **1** election **2** feather **3** the best *adj* **4** fundamental **5** important **6** original **7** prototypal

primate *n* → **1** ecclesiastic **2** ruler

prime *n* → **1** age **2** morning **3** perfection **4** race **5** season **6** start *v* **7** coat **8** fuel **9** initiate **10** prepare **11** supply *adj* **12** fundamental **13** good **14** important **15** numerical **16** prototypal

prime minister *n* → **1** member of parliament **2** ruler

primer *n* → **1** dye **2** explosive **3** lighter **4** paint **5** textbook

primeval *adj* → **1** original **2** past

primitive *n* → **1** artless person *adj* **2** impermanent **3** natural **4** old **5** original **6** past

primordial *adj* → **1** creative **2** old **3** original **4** past

primrose *n* → yellow

prince *n* → **1** aristocrat **2** ecclesiastic **3** important person

princess *n* → aristocrat

principal *n* → **1** actor **2** beam **3** capital **4** competitor **5** conductor **6** criminal **7** important person **8** leader **9** manager **10** music **11** property **12** ruler **13** teacher *adj* **14** important

principality *n* → nation

principle *n* → **1** causer **2** characteristics **3** conjecture **4** correctness **5** essence **6** foundation **7** proverb **8** rule

PRINT *v* print out, pull, run off, type; **go to press,** put to bed; **lithograph,** engrave, italicise, linotype, offset, overlay, photoengrave, photolithograph; **set,** compose, filmset, handset, impose, typeset; **justify,** lead, overrun, overset, white

print *n* → **1** copy **2** engraving **3** imprint **4** indentation **5** letter **6** newspaper **7** photograph **8** printing **9** sign *v* **10** engrave **11** label **12** photograph **13** press **14** publish **15** write

PRINTING *n* engraving, letterpress, lithography, print, screen-printing, silk-screening, typography; **typesetting,** composition, computer typesetting, filmsetting, photocomposition, phototypesetting

prior *n* → **1** monastic *adj* **2** preceding

priority *n* → **1** antecedence **2** importance **3** precedence

prise *v* → **1** lift **2** remove

prism *n* → **1** colour **2** lens **3** solid

PRISON *n* bagnio, bin, bird, birdcage, boob, booby hatch *(U.S.)*, caboose, cage, calaboose *(U.S.)*, choky, clink, college, cooler, coop, factory *(Hist.)*, female factory *(Convict)*, gaol, hole, hoosegow *(U.S.)*, jail, jailhouse *(U.S.)*, jug, limbo, nick, pen, penitentiary, pokey, quad, quod, rock college, roundhouse *(Obs.)*, salt mines, slammer, state prison *(U.S.)*, stir, the can, the logs *(Convict)*, tower; **compound,** concentration camp, internment camp, labour camp, penal settlement, prison farm, prison-camp, rules *(Brit.)*, stalag, stockade *(U.S.)*; **Botany Bay,** Bastille, Devil's Island, Fort Denison, Moreton Bay, Norfolk Island, Pinchgut, Port Arthur, the establishment, the Ocean Hell, the Tench, the Tower *(Brit.)*; **lockup,** brig, bullpen *(U.S.)*, detention centre *(Brit.)*, dock, watch-house; **reform school,** Borstal *(Brit.)*, reformatory, training school; **prison ship,** hulks. *See also* CELL

prison *n* → imprisonment

PRISONER *n* boobhead, crim, criminal, gaolbird, gaolie, graduate *(Colloq.)*, jailbird, keyman, lag, lifer, prisoner of the crown, probation pass-holder, state prisoner *(U.S.)*, trusty; **convict,** canary, canary bird, cockatoo, Cockatoo Islander, con, croppy, demon, Derwent duck, emancipist, expiree, government man, Hawkesbury duck, inmate, legitimate, old hand, prisoner servant, ticket-of-leaver, transportee, vandemonian; **inmate,** intern *(U.S.)*, internee; **prisoner of war,** POW; **periodic detainee,** shitkicker, short-timer, toe-ragger, weekender; **chain-gang,** gaol gang, iron gang; **captive,** detainee

prissy *adj* → affected

pristine *adj* → **1** clean **2** old **3** original **4** past

private *adj* → **1** hidden **2** own **3** particular **4** secluded **5** secret

privation *n* → **1** insufficiency **2** poverty **3** taking

privilege *n* → **1** advantage **2** rights *v* **3** permit

privy *n* → **1** litigant **2** toilet *adj* **3** hidden **4** own **5** secluded **6** secret

prize *n* → **1** contest **2** gift **3** takings *v* **4** appraise **5** approve **6** respect *adj* **7** good **8** superior

probability *n* → likelihood

probable *adj* → likely

probate *n* → **1** authentication **2** record *adj* **3** testimonial

probation *n* → authentication

probe *n* → **1** investigation **2** test *v* **3** inquire into **4** question

probity *n* → **1** faithfulness **2** honesty

problem *n* → **1** annoyer **2** difficulty **3** puzzle **4** uncertain thing *adj* **5** badly-behaved

proboscis *n* → nose

procedure *n* → **1** behaviour **2** custom **3** method **4** operation

proceed *v* → **1** advance **2** continue **3** do **4** start

proceeding *n* → **1** action **2** litigation *adj* **3** advanced

process *n* → **1** action **2** advance **3** knob **4** litigation **5** method **6** operation *v* **7** litigate

procession *n* → 1 commemoration 2 line 3 religious ceremony 4 sequence 5 series
proclaim *v* → 1 prohibit 2 publicise 3 signify
proclivity *n* → point of view
procrastinate *v* → 1 avoid 2 be late 3 vacillate
procreate *v* → 1 create 2 reproduce
PROCREATOR *n* breeder, broodbitch, brooder, engenderer, fertiliser, generator, impregnator, propagator, sitter, springer, stud, venter; **mother,** mother-to-be, multipara, primigravida, primipara
procure *v* → 1 accomplish 2 buy 3 gain 4 prostitute oneself
PROCURER *n* arranger, bawd, fixer, go-between, maquereau, pander, panderer, pimp, procuress
prod *n* → 1 incentive 2 pat 3 piercer *v* 4 arouse
prodigal *n* → 1 squanderer *adj* 2 abundant 3 extravagant 4 fertile 5 generous
prodigious *adj* → 1 astonishing 2 big 3 enormous 4 strange
prodigy *n* → 1 children 2 expert 3 omen 4 strange person 5 winner 6 wise person
produce *n* → 1 finished product *v* 2 accomplish 3 be fertile 4 cause 5 display 6 give birth 7 have a job 8 make 9 stage
producer *n* → 1 causer 2 creator
product *n* → finished product
PROFANE *v* defile, deflower, desecrate, dishallow, pollute, violate; **blaspheme,** swear; **deconsecrate,** excommunicate, secularise
profane *v* → 1 hold in low regard 2 ill-treat *adj* 3 heretical 4 ignorant 5 immoral 6 irreverent 7 vulgar
profess *v* → 1 assert 2 believe 3 have a job
profession *n* → 1 assertion 2 job
professional *n* → 1 expert 2 middle class 3 worker *adj* 4 accomplished 5 sports 6 working
professor *n* → 1 intellectual 2 teacher
proffer *n* → offer
proficient *n* → 1 expert *adj* 2 competent 3 knowledgeable
profile *n* → 1 appearance 2 diagram 3 edge 4 narrative 5 outside 6 painting 7 side *v* 8 depict
PROFIT *n* advantage, fruit of one's labours, gain, remuneration; **financial profit,** bunce, capital gains, clean-up, clearings, commission, dibs, dividend, divvies, earnings, earnings per share *(Stock Exchange)*, earnings yield *(Stock Exchange)*, gains, graft, gravy, grist for the mill, gross profit *(Comm.)*, increase, interest, issue *(Law)*, money, net profit *(Comm.)*, percentage, plus, proceeds, rake-off, return, revenue *(Econ.)*, share, take, takings, the main chance, use *(Obs.)*, velvet, yield; **spoils,** a fast buck, booty, filthy lucre, lucre, something that fell off the back of a truck, theft, unjust enrichment; **money-spinner,** a sprat to catch a mackerel
PROFIT *v* advantage, cash in on, clean up, make capital of, make money, profiteer, reap great reward
profit *n* → 1 advantage *v* 2 make do 3 take advantage
PROFITABLE *adj* advantageous, engrossing, gainful, lucrative, productive, remunerative, worthwhile; **making a profit,** ahead, better off, in pocket, running at a profit, showing a profit, to the good
profiteer *n* → 1 extortionist *v* 2 profit
profligate *n* → 1 dissipater 2 immoral person 3 promiscuous person 4 squanderer *adj* 5 extravagant 6 immoral 7 overindulgent 8 promiscuous
profound *n* → 1 depth 2 sea *adj* 3 deep 4 emotional 5 intense 6 meaningful 7 wise
profuse *adj* → 1 abundant 2 extravagant 3 fertile 4 many
progeny *n* → offspring
prognosis *n* → prediction
prognosticate *v* → predict
PROGRAM *n* chat show, docu-drama, game show, live broadcast, mini-series, quiz show, radio play, radio program, serial, series, soap, soap opera, soapie, talent quest, talk show, talk-back program, telefilm, telethon
program *n* → 1 agenda 2 course 3 plan 4 undertaking *v* 5 order
progress *n* → 1 action 2 advance 3 continuation 4 evolution 5 improvement *v* 6 advance 7 grow 8 improve
progression *n* → 1 advance 2 continuation 3 improvement 4 sequence 5 series
progressive *n* → 1 political ideologist *adj* 2 advanced 3 following 4 improving 5 increasing 6 unwholesome
PROHIBIT *v* ban, blue-pencil, bowdlerise, censor, clip the wings of, enjoin, forbid, forfend, inhibit, interdict, prevent, proclaim, proscribe; **debar,** banish, bar, disbar, disqualify, exclude, expel, ground, interdict, rule out, send down, shield *(Obs.)*, shut, shut out, unchurch, unfrock, warn off; **disallow,** black-list, forbid the banns, kill, make taboo, outlaw, repress, veto; **disqualify,** disable, incapacitate; **blackban,** blackball, boycott, declare black, embargo, ostracise, send to Coventry
prohibit *v* → hinder
PROHIBITED *adj* black, forbidden, impermissible, inadmissible, ineffable, not to be countenanced, not to be thought of, off-limits, out of bounds, verboten; **contraband,** banned, illegal, illicit, unauthorised, unlicensed; **taboo,** unclean; **ineligible,** incapable, incompetent *(Law)*; **closed,** close *(Sport)*
PROHIBITER *n* blackball, dry *(U.S. Colloq.)*, forbidder, inhibiter, jeremiah, prohibitionist, proscriber, teetotaller, vetoer, wowser; **censor,** bowdleriser, Lord Chamberlain
PROHIBITION *n* ban, charging order *(Law)*, enjoiner *(Law)*, enjoinment, injunction, interdict, writ of prohibition; **debarment,** bar, inhibition, interdict, veto; **black ban,** black list, boycott, embargo, Expurgatory Index, Index, Index of Prohibited Books; **prohibited item,** contraband, forbidden fruit, ineligible, no-no, outlaw, restricted exhibition;

taboo, juju; **disqualification,** disability, impediment, impedimenta, incapability, incapableness, incapacity; **censorship,** bowdlerisation, bowdlerism; **repression,** extinction, hindrance, interdiction, proscription, restriction, suppression; **disablement,** exclusiveness, inadmissibility, incapacitation, ineligibility; **impermissibility,** forbiddance *(Rare)*

prohibitive *adj* → 1 discouraging 2 expensive 3 hindering

project *n* → 1 plan 2 undertaking *v* 3 communicate 4 fantasise 5 jut 6 offer 7 plan 8 thrust

projectile *n* → 1 ammunition *adj* 2 protuberant

projector *n* → 1 camera 2 lens

prolapse *n* → 1 descent 2 misplacement *v* 3 fall

proletariat *n* → working class

proliferate *v* → 1 become greater 2 be fertile 3 flower

prolific *adj* → 1 abundant 2 fertile 3 many

prolix *adj* → verbose

prologue *n* → 1 act 2 entertainer 3 introduction 4 oration

prolong *v* → protract

promenade *n* → 1 road 2 walk *v* 3 dance 4 display 5 walk

prominent *adj* → 1 important 2 obvious 3 protuberant 4 reputable

PROMISCUITY *n* licence, looseness, promiscuousness, unchasteness, unchastity; **profligacy,** profligateness, raffishness, rakishness; **lechery,** goatishness, lecherousness, libertinage, libertinism

PROMISCUOUS *adj* easy, fast, free, free-living, immoral, libertine, licentious, lickerish, light, loose, nice *(Obs.)*, slack, unchaste, unvirtuous, vicious; **harlot,** fallen, sluttish, whorish; **lecherous,** goatish, profligate, raffish, rakehelly *(Archaic)*, rakish, satyric

promiscuous *adj* → 1 capricious 2 lucky 3 mixed 4 sexy

PROMISCUOUS PERSON *n* bike, Cyprian, easy lay, floozy, goodtime girl, harlot, jezebel, man-eater, prostitute, scarlet woman, scrubber *(Brit.)*, slack, slut, town bike, tramp, wanton, wench *(Archaic)*, working girl; **lecher,** Don Juan, goat, lad, libertine, Lothario, philanderer, profligate, rake, rakehell *(Archaic)*, satyr, wencher, wolf, womaniser

PROMISE *v* agree, give one's word, mortgage, pledge, plight, swear, vow, wager *(Hist.)*; **contract,** arrange, bind, commit, engage, lend-lease, oblige, pre-engage, precontract, subcontract, tie, undertake; **article,** bind out, indent, indenture; **bargain,** come to terms, covenant, dicker *(Politics)*, do a deal, go in with, settle, strike a bargain, tut; **stipulate,** give terms, make conditions; **league,** accede, ally

promise *n* → 1 contract 2 favourableness 3 likelihood 4 prediction 5 surety 6 wedding *v* 7 be likely 8 marry 9 predict

promising *adj* → 1 favourable 2 fortunate 3 likely 4 new 5 predictive

promissory note *n* → bill

promontory *n* → 1 headland 2 mound

PROMOTE *v* advance, brevet, kick upstairs, prefer, upgrade; **exalt,** elevate, raise

promote *v* → 1 encourage 2 help 3 publicise

PROMOTION *n* advance, advancement, brevet, preferment; **Peter principle**

prompt *n* → 1 incentive 2 reminder *v* 3 arouse 4 help 5 remind *adj* 6 agreeable 7 busy 8 prepared 9 speedy 10 timely

promulgate *v* → 1 publicise 2 teach

prone *adj* → 1 level 2 predisposed 3 sloping

prong *n* → 1 piercer *v* 2 open 3 perforate

pronoun *n* → word

pronounce *v* → 1 assert 2 publicise 3 speak

pronounced *adj* → 1 blatant 2 obvious 3 spoken

pronunciation *n* → speaking

proof *n* → 1 copy 2 engraving 3 evidence 4 photograph 5 reasoning 6 solution 7 winemaking *v* 8 conserve 9 strengthen *adj* 10 closed 11 intoxicating

proofread *v* → correct

propaganda *n* → 1 information 2 persuasion 3 teaching 4 war

propagate *v* → 1 increase 2 publicise 3 reproduce

propane *n* → fuel

propel *v* → thrust

PROPELLANT *n* boost, impellent, reaction propulsion; **catapult,** dinger, ging, shanghai, sling, slingshot, trap; **launch complex,** cosmodrome, launching pad, pad *(Aerospace)*, silo *(Mil.)*, slips *(Shipbuilding)*, ways; **paddle,** float, oar, scull, sweep; **spur,** ankus *(India)*, crop, gad, goad, stick, whip; **propeller,** bow thruster *(Naut.)*, paddlewheel, prop, rotor, screw, screw-propeller, tail rotor

propellant *n* → 1 ammunition 2 explosive 3 fuel

propeller *n* → 1 propellant 2 spin

propensity *n* → 1 desire 2 pleasure 3 point of view

proper *adj* → 1 affected 2 apt 3 beautiful 4 correct 5 courteous 6 expedient 7 good 8 own 9 particular 10 precise 11 thorough

PROPERTY *n* appanage, assets, capital, endowment, holdings, one's all, peculium, possessions, principal, proprietary, resources, salvage, settlement *(Law)*, substance, temporalities, temporals, thirds *(Law)*; **dowry,** dot, dower, dower house, jointure, marriage portion, marriage settlement, portion; **estate,** deceased estate, heirloom, hereditament, heritage, legacy, patrimony, reversion; **after-acquired property,** escheat; **fixed assets,** capital assets, capital goods; **liquid assets,** current assets, floating assets, liquidity; **stocks and shares,** blue chip, capital stock, gilt-edged investment. *See also* PERSONAL PROPERTY; REAL ESTATE

property *n* → **1** essence **2** farm **3** particulars **4** supplies
prophecy *n* → **1** prediction *v* **2** precede
prophesy *v* → predict
prophet *n* → **1** enlightener **2** forerunner **3** predictor
prophylactic *n* → **1** contraception **2** medication *adj* **3** medicinal
propinquity *n* → **1** closeness **2** relation **3** similarity
propitiate *v* → **1** atone for **2** mediate
propitious *adj* → **1** favourable **2** fortunate **3** helpful **4** kind
proponent *n* → offerer
proportion *n* → **1** amount **2** comparison **3** part **4** relationship **5** share
propose *v* → **1** assert **2** guide **3** marry **4** offer **5** plan **6** theorise
proposition *n* → **1** assertion **2** conjecture **3** introduction **4** offer **5** plan *v* **6** flirt **7** have sex **8** offer
propound *v* → **1** offer **2** theorise
proprietary *n* → **1** medication **2** owner **3** ownership **4** property
proprietor *n* → owner
propriety *n* → **1** aptness **2** conformity **3** correctness **4** dutifulness **5** expedience
propulsion *n* → thrust
pro rata *adj* → **1** related *adv* **2** relatively
prorogue *v* → **1** defer **2** stop
prosaic *adj* → **1** boring **2** conventional **3** ordinary **4** simple
proscenium *n* → stage
proscribe *v* → **1** boycott **2** prohibit
prose *n* → writing
prosecute *v* → **1** litigate **2** practise law
proselyte *n* → **1** defector **2** learner
prosody *n* → poetry
prospect *n* → **1** diggings **2** expected thing **3** view *v* **4** pursue
prospective *adj* → **1** expected **2** future
prospectus *n* → public notice
PROSPER *v* be on to a good thing, cotton *(Obs.)*, do a roaring trade, go from rags to riches, have never had it so good, have the Midas touch, live high, live on milk and honey, make one's pile, soar, speed *(Archaic)*, strike it lucky, strike it rich, strike oil, succeed, thrive; **boom**, be on the crest of the wave, be on the make, be on the up and up, bloom, blossom, flourish, rise in the world, thrive; **be in luck**, be born under a lucky star, be born with a silver spoon in one's mouth, be in clover, be in the silk, be in velvet, be on a good wicket, be sitting pretty, bear a charmed life, cop it sweet, fall on one's feet, have it made, have the ball at one's feet, live off the fat of the land
prosper *v* → be wealthy
prosperous *adj* → **1** fortunate **2** wealthy
prostate gland *n* → groin
prosthesis *n* → medication
PROSTITUTE *n* aspro, bagswinger, battler, callgirl, chromo, cocotte, courtesan, Cyprian *(Obs.)*, doxy *(Archaic)*, drab, fallen woman, fancy woman, gun-moll, harlot, hooker, hustler *(U.S.)*, kelly, kewpie, light o' love *(Brit. U.S.)*, lowheel, model, moll, painted lady, painted woman, pro, prossie, quean, scarlet woman, second-hand Sue, streetwalker, strumpet, tart, town bike, trollop, wench, white slave, whore, worker, working girl; **gigolo; procuress**, bawd, madam; **pimp**, bludger, bully, fancy man, hoon, pander, ponce, poofter-rorter, procurer, white-slaver; **whoremonger**, crack, whoremaster
prostitute *n* → **1** promiscuous person *v* **2** ill-treat **3** spoil
PROSTITUTE ONESELF *v* crack it, walk the streets, whore; **solicit**, accost, hustle; **procure**, bludge, live on immoral earnings, pander, pimp, ponce; **whore**, wench *(Archaic)*
PROSTITUTION *n* business, harlotry, solicitation, streetwalking, the game, whoredom; **procuration**, procurement
prostrate *v* → **1** defeat **2** repose **3** repress **4** tire **5** weaken *adj* **6** bottom **7** level **8** obsequious **9** powerless **10** repressed **11** tired **12** unhappy **13** weak
protagonist *n* → leader
protean *adj* → changeable
PROTECT *v* bulwark, defend, forfend *(U.S.)*, guard, keep, ward *(Archaic)*, watch over; **patrol**, picket *(Mil.)*; **immunise**, inoculate, vaccinate; **bless**, charm, sain *(Archaic)*
protect *v* → secure
PROTECTED *adj* guarded, immune, secure, under one's wing
PROTECTION *n* backstop, bulwark, defence, screen, umbrella; **safe-conduct**, air cover, convoy, escort, protective custody; **custody**, aegis, auspices, care, cover, coverture, fatherly eye, safekeeping, tutelage, ward, wardship; **guardianship**, custodianship, wardenry, wardenship
protection *n* → **1** bribe **2** bribery **3** defence **4** help **5** insurance **6** safety **7** surety
PROTECTIVE *adj* alimentary *(Law)*, custodial, guardian, tutelary
protective *adj* → safe
PROTECTOR *n* committee *(Law Obs.)*, father, genius loci, guardian, patron *(Roman Hist.)*, patroness, protectress, tutelary, tutor *(Archaic)*; **guard**, air-raid warden, coast-watcher, coastguard, concierge, conservator, curator, custodian, fire warden, firewatcher, janitor, night watch, patrolman, security guard, security officer, sentinel, sentry; **bodyguard**, convoy, escort, patrol, safeguard; **defender**, harbourer, keeper, shelterer, shielder
protectorate *n* → nation
protégé *n* → dependant
protest *n* → **1** bad debt **2** challenge **3** disagreement **4** discouragement **5** public notice *v* **6** assert **7** be unable to pay **8** discourage
protestant *n* → disputant
protocol *n* → **1** contract **2** custom **3** formality **4** model **5** postscript **6** rule *v* **7** record
protoplasm *n* → start
PROTOTYPAL *adj* archetypal, archetypical, embryo, first, primary, prime, protoplastic; **introductory**, inaugural, isagogic, precursory,

prefatory, preliminary, prelusive, prelusory, preparatory, proemial, prolegomenous, prolusory, propaedeutic; **advance,** ahead of one's time, fore, forehand, headmost, leading, up-front; **anticipatory,** anticipative

prototype *n* → 1 antecedent 2 model

PROTRACT *v* prolong, prolongate *(Rare)*, string out; **maintain,** keep, preserve, retain, sustain; **resume,** renew, take up; **outlast,** outlive, survive

protract *v* → 1 bore 2 jut 3 map 4 waffle

protrude *v* → jut

PROTUBERANT *adj* beetle, beetling, exserted, extant *(Archaic)*, extrusive, imminent, obtrusive, overhanging, pendent, prognathous, projectile, projecting, prominent, protractile, protrudent, protrusile, protrusive, rostral, salient, tumular; **raised up,** eminent, erect, proud; **spined,** calcarate, horned, horny, muricate, spurred, thorny; **popeyed,** bug-eyed, exophthalmic; **tentacled,** tentacular, vibracular, villiform. *See also* SWOLLEN; KNOBBY

PROUD *adj* bloated, conceited, condescending, consequential, inflated, jumped-up, lofty, lordly, malapert, narcissistic, overblown, overproud, patronising, pragmatic, puffed-up, self-conceited, self-important, self-loving, self-opinionated, self-satisfied, smug, snubby, stuck-up, tight-arsed, vain; **boastful,** immodest, prideful, self-congratulatory; **purse-proud,** house-proud; **ostentatious,** pretentious; **high-spirited,** mettlesome

proud *adj* → 1 arrogant 2 courageous 3 energetic 4 enormous 5 living 6 protuberant 7 reputable

prove *v* → 1 authenticate 2 conserve 3 cook 4 examine 5 occur 6 test

provenance *n* → 1 record 2 start

provender *n* → 1 food 2 supplies

PROVERB *n* adage, byword, dictum, saying, truth, word *(Obs.)*; **maxim,** aphorism, apophthegm, epigram, gnome, logion, notabilia, saw, sentence *(Obs.)*; **axiom,** postulate, principle, theorem; **apologue,** moralism, parable; **device,** catchword, motto, poesy *(Obs.)*, slogan, tag; **platitude,** banality, bromide, cliche, commonplace, prosaism, truism

PROVERB *v* aphorise, apophthegmatise, epigrammatise

proverb *n* → figure of speech

provide *v* → 1 give 2 qualify 3 supply

provided *conj* → on condition that

providence *n* → 1 anticipation 2 care 3 fate 4 thrift

provident *adj* → 1 anticipatory 2 thrifty

province *n* → 1 administrative area 2 domain 3 dwelling 4 job 5 region

PROVINCIAL *adj* boorish, churlish, cloddish, clodhopping, hayseed, hick, hillbilly, peasant, rube, yeoman, yokel, yokelish; **country-born,** country-bred, Dad'n'Dave, folksy, swainish. *See also* RURAL

provincial *n* → 1 country dweller 2 ecclesiastic 3 intolerant person 4 population *adj* 5 artless 6 boring 7 intolerant 8 regional

provision *n* → 1 deed 2 employment 3 preparation 4 qualification 5 supply *v* 6 supply

provisional *n* → 1 label *adj* 2 conditional 3 empirical 4 impermanent 5 uncertain

proviso *n* → qualification

provocative *n* → 1 causer 2 doer 3 incentive *adj* 4 alluring 5 causal 6 encouraging 7 vexing

provoke *v* → 1 activate 2 anger 3 annoy 4 arouse 5 cause 6 irritate

PROVOKE HATRED *v* alienate, cause bad blood, disaffect, embitter, estrange, incur enmity, incur wrath, make another see red, raise someone's ire, set by the ears, sow dissension, stir up bad blood; **be anathema to,** disgust, go against the grain, make someone's flesh creep, nauseate, revolt, stink in one's nostrils, turn someone's stomach

provost *n* → 1 gaoler 2 leader 3 member of parliament 4 monastic 5 policeman 6 ruler 7 teacher

prow *n* → 1 front 2 watercraft

prowess *n* → 1 competence 2 courage

prowl *n* → 1 pursuit *v* 2 pursue

proximity *n* → closeness

proxy *n* → 1 delegate 2 mediator

prudence *n* → 1 anticipation 2 thrift 3 wisdom

prune *v* → 1 cut 2 decrease 3 subtract

prurient *adj* → obscene

pry *n* → 1 look 2 morbid curiosity *v* 3 be curious 4 look 5 search

psalm *n* → 1 poetry 2 prayer *v* 3 sing 4 worship

pseudonym *n* → 1 disguise 2 name

PSYCHE *n* libido, motive force, pneuma, self, soul, vital impulse; **ego,** id, superego; **the unconscious,** collective unconscious, inner space, preconscious, subconscious; **preconsciousness,** coconsciousness, subconsciousness; **engram,** memory, trace; **motivation,** drive

psyche *n* → 1 living 2 mind 3 phantom

psychedelic *n* → 1 drug *adj* 2 colourful 3 delusive 4 multicoloured

psychic *n* → 1 occultist *adj* 2 anticipatory 3 mental 4 supernatural

PSYCHIC DISORDER *n* alienation, anomie, craze, deliration, dementia, derangement, insanity, maladjustment, mania, neuropsychosis, neurosis, psychopathy, psychosis, schizothymia; **dementia praecox,** hebephrenia; **nervous breakdown,** breakdown, collapse; **paranoia,** hallucinosis; **dissimulation,** simulation; **amnesia,** fugue; **masochism,** sadism, sadomasochism; **psychosomatic disorder,** hysterical fever, hysterical pregnancy, phantom pregnancy; **specific learning difficulty,** agraphia, alexia, alogia, amentia, aphasia, dysarthria, dysgraphia, dyslexia, dysphasia, dysphemia, glossolalia, paralexia, strephosymbolia, stuttering, word blindness; **mental deficiency,** autism, cretinism, Down's syndrome, idiocy, imbecility, mental retardation, Mongolism, moronity

PSYCHIC DISTURBANCE *n* complex, fetish, fixation, fixed idea, hang-up *(Colloq.)*, obsession, phobia; **mania,** cacoethes, compulsion, craze; **hallucination,** delusion, illusion; **inhibition,** censor, censorship, repression, suppression; **Freudian slip,** parapraxis; **regression,** reversion; **schizophrenia,** battle fatigue, culture shock, identity crisis, multiple personality, shell shock, split personality; **shock,** trauma; **hysteria,** frenzy, hysterics

psychoanalysis *n* → psychotherapy

PSYCHOLOGICALLY DISTURBED *adj* fixated, maladjusted; **insane,** deranged, disordered, lunatic, maniac, maniacal, unbalanced; **compulsive,** manic, obsessional; **manic-depressive,** cycloid, cycloidal, cyclothymic; **depressive,** atrabilious, hypochondriac, melancholiac, melancholic, morbid, phobic; **neurotic,** hung-up *(Colloq.)*, hysteric, hysterical, neuropathic, psychasthenic; **psychotic,** paranoid, psycho *(Colloq.)*, psychopathic, schizo *(Colloq.)*, schizoid, schizophrenic; **delusional,** expansive; **shell-shocked; boob happy,** stir-crazy; **mentally deficient,** autistic, cretinous, mentally handicapped, mongoloid, retarded, subnormal

PSYCHOLOGIST *n* analyst, behaviourist, Freudian, Jungian, nomologist, psychoanalyser, psychoanalyst, psychobiologist, psychopathologist, sensationist; **third force; hypnotist,** hypnotiser; **psychiatrist,** alienist *(Obs.)*, headshrinker, orthopsychiatrist, psychotherapist, shrink, trick cyclist

psychology *n* → **1** character **2** mind

psychosis *n* → psychic disorder

psychosomatic *adj* → unwholesome

PSYCHOTHERAPY *n* aversion therapy, behaviour therapy, catharsis, E.C.T., electroconvulsive therapy, narcosynthesis, psychotherapeutics, shock treatment, therapy, treatment; **counselling,** child guidance; **group therapy,** encounter group, T-group; **psychodrama,** acting out; **psychoanalysis,** analysis, hypnoanalysis, psychognosis; **psychograph,** psychometer; **personality test,** Binet test, free association test, ink-blot test, Rorschach test; **hypnosis,** hypnotisation, hypnotism; **certification,** stultification; **mental hospital,** bedlam, booby hatch, funny farm, giggle factory, loony bin, lunatic asylum, madhouse, nut factory, nuthouse, psychiatric hospital, rat factory *(N.Z. Colloq.)*, retreat

PUB *n* beer-hall *(S. African)*, boozer, boozeroo *(N.Z.)*, bunny club, drinking-house, free house, grog shop, hotel, inn, local, off-licence *(Brit.)*, opera house, pisser, porterhouse *(Archaic)*, public house, rubbidy, rubbidy-dub, shypoo joint *(W.A.)*, tap *(Brit.)*, taphouse, tavern, tied house, watering hole, watering-place; **shanty,** bloodhouse, gin palace, joint; **wineshop,** bottle department, bottle shop, cellars; **sly-grog shop,** honky-tonk, shebeen *(Irish Scot.)*, speak-easy; **bar,** beer garden, bistro, bodega, clipjoint, cocktail bar, groggery, hot spot, ladies' lounge, ladies' parlour, lounge, lounge bar, nightclub, nineteenth hole, private bar, public bar, saloon, saloon bar, taproom *(Brit.)*, wine bar; **brewery,** distillery, mill, still, winery

pub *n* → hotel

puberty *n* → youth

pubes *n* → **1** abdomen **2** groin **3** hair

PUBLIC *adj* common, communal, demotic, mob, popular, vernacular, vulgar; **folk,** grassroots, parish-pump, parochial

public *adj* → **1** displayed **2** formal **3** revealed

PUBLICAN *n* innkeeper, lamber-down, licensee, shanty-keeper, taverner *(Brit.)*, vintner; **barman,** barkeeper, barmaid, bartender, cellarmaster, wine waiter

publican *n* → **1** manager **2** tax collector

publication *n* → **1** book **2** magazine **3** newspaper **4** publicity **5** the media

PUBLICISE *v* advertise, ballyhoo, bark, bawl, bill, build up, cry up, pamphleteer, promote, puff, tout; **announce,** annunciate, celebrate, declare, enounce, enunciate, intimate, preconise, proclaim, report; **decree,** adjudge, expedite, gazette, pronounce; **publish,** ask *(Archaic)*, blaze, blazon, broadcast, circulate, divulgate, give out, go the rounds, hawk about, herald, issue, promulgate, propagate, voice; **trumpet,** blare, call, count, knell, knoll *(Archaic)*, resound, ring, ring in, ring out, sound, tick, toll, trump; **tell,** out with, rap out, speak, utter; **notify,** apprise of, post, stir *(Rare)*

PUBLICIST *n* adman, advertiser, billposter, bullsticker, copywriter, pamphleteer, placarder, plugger; **announcer,** declarer, divulgater, enunciator, notifier, proclaimer, promulgator, warner; **herald,** barker, bawler, bellman, crier, officer at arms, sandwichman, spieler, town crier, trumpeter, vaunt-courier *(Archaic)*; **toastmaster,** toastmistress

PUBLICITY *n* build-up, daylight, notice, promotion; **advertising,** ballyhoo, billing, hype; **publication,** broadcast, divulgation, gazettal, issuance, issue, notification, promulgation, propagation

publicity *n* → revealing

PUBLIC NOTICE *n* announcement, annunciation *(Rare)*, banns, celebration, cry *(Obs.)*, declaration, enouncement, enunciation, hue and cry, intimation, proclamation, protest, report; **notice,** bill, bulletin, green paper, notice paper; **advertisement,** ad, advert, blurb, classified ad, classifieds, commercial, plug, promo, teaser ad, trailer, want ad; **personal column,** obit, obituary, personal *(U.S.)*; **poster,** banner, placard, wanted poster; **handbill,** broadsheet, broadside, brochure, circular, flier, flyer, handout, leaflet, literature, pamphlet, playbill, prospectus, showbill, throwaway, ticket *(Rare)*; **sticker,** bumper sticker, car sticker; **billboard,** bulletin board *(U.S.)*, corkboard, hoarding, noticeboard, Ritchie board, sandwich board; **edict,** ban, decree, deliverance, dictum, diktat, manifest, manifesto, platform, pronouncement, rescript

PUBLISH *v* feature, issue, lay before the public, print, run; **report,** cover, reveal, write up; **broadcast,** radio, relay, telecast, televise; **scoop; edit,** prepare copy, put to bed, sub, subedit

publish *v* → **1** publicise **2** reveal

puce *adj* → brown

puck *n* → **1** circle **2** fairy

pucker *n* → **1** fold *v* **2** fold

pudding *n* → **1** fool **2** meal **3** short person **4** stupid person

puddle *n* → **1** lake **2** spin *v* **3** coat **4** confuse **5** dirty **6** mix **7** powder **8** wet

puerile *adj* → **1** foolish **2** unimportant **3** youthful

puff *n* → **1** absorption **2** bragging **3** breathing **4** bulge **5** cloud **6** exaggeration **7** gas **8** hair **9** hiss **10** tobacco **11** wind *v* **12** brag **13** breathe **14** flatter **15** publicise

pug *n* → **1** pugilist **2** sign *v* **3** fill **4** press **5** pursue **6** quieten

PUGILIST *n* boxer, bruiser, ex-pug, fisticuffer, infighter, palooka, prize-fighter, pug, slugger, sparring partner; **bantamweight,** featherweight, flyweight, heavyweight, middleweight, welterweight; **bludgeoner,** buffeter, cudgeller; **wrestler,** grappler, junior; **judoist,** ju-jitsuist, judoka. *See also* FIGHTER

pugnacious *adj* → **1** martial **2** unfriendly **3** warlike

PULL *n* drag, draw, haul, heave *(Naut.)*, lug, tow, tug; **wrench,** tear, twist, wrest; **hitch,** jerk, pluck, tweak, twitch, yank

PULL *v* bowse *(Naut.)*, brail *(Naut.)*, clew *(Naut.)*, drag, draw, hale, haul, heave, lug, rouse away *(Naut.)*, snig, trice; **tow,** kedge, tug, warp; **trail,** daggle *(Obs.)*, draggle; **wrench,** tear, wrest; **strain at,** tear at; **jerk,** pluck, twitch, yank; **hitch,** hike up; **winch,** purchase, wind up, windlass

pull *n* → **1** absorption **2** advantage **3** attraction **4** extraction **5** influence **6** pulling **7** tobacco **8** vitality *v* **9** attract **10** bare **11** bungle **12** have sex **13** print

PULLER *n* haler, hauler, tugger; **towrope,** hawser, messenger, towline; **winch,** capstan, coffee-grinder winch, davit, parbuckle, whim *(Mining)*, windlass; **pulley,** block and tackle, crab, garnet, halyard, jeer, shearlegs; **prime mover,** bank engine *(Railways)*, banker *(Railways)*, caterpillar, locomotive, tow truck, towboat, towie, traction engine, tractor, tug, tugboat

pulley *n* → **1** lift **2** machine **3** puller

PULLING *n* draught, drawing, haulage, pull, stress, towage, traction, tractive power *(Railways)*

pullover *n* → jumper

pull over *v* → deflect

PULP *n* chyme, mash, pap, pomace, slops, sop, squash, squelch; **dough,** magma *(Chem.)*, paste, sponge

PULP *v* knead, mash, masticate, sodden, sop, squash, squish

pulp *n* → **1** bad thing *v* **2** soften

pulpit *n* → **1** church **2** platform

PULPY *adj* doughy, pappy, pasty, sodden, soggy, sopping, spongy, squashy, squishy

pulsate *v* → vibrate

pulse *n* → **1** emotion **2** enlargement **3** ephemeral **4** living **5** vibration *v* **6** vibrate

pulverise *v* → **1** defeat **2** destroy **3** powder

puma *n* → animal's coat

pumice *n* → **1** powder *v* **2** smooth

pummel *n* → **1** knob *v* **2** beat

pump *n* → **1** airway **2** extractor **3** footgear **4** heart **5** press *v* **6** extract **7** question **8** vibrate

pun *n* → **1** figure of speech **2** joke **3** similarity *v* **4** joke

punch *n* → **1** drink **2** hit **3** piercer *v* **4** hit

punctilious *adj* → precise

punctual *adj* → **1** precise **2** timely

punctuate *v* → **1** come between **2** interrupt **3** mark

puncture *n* → **1** indentation **2** opening

PUNGENCY *n* acridity, acridness, gaminess, piquancy, poignancy, raciness, saltiness, spicery, spiciness; **bite,** edge, race, sting, strength, tang; **pepperiness,** fieriness, sharpness; **roughness,** harshness

PUNGENT *adj* acrid, ammoniacal, penetrating, sharp, strong; **piquant,** fiery, hot, poignant, racy, savoury; **spicy,** alliaceous, garlicky, gingery, peppery, salty, tangy; **gamy,** earthy, high, rank

pungent *adj* → **1** distressing **2** emotive **3** sharp

PUNISH *v* afflict, condemn, gruel, penalise, visit *(Obs.)*; **discipline,** bring to book, castigate, chasten, chastise, come down on, correct, give someone a lesson, have a rod in pickle, lay it on, scold, strafe, throw the book at, vindicate *(Obs.)*; **sentence,** blanket, imprison, lag, pillory, stock *(Obs.)*; **fine,** amerce, estreat, mulct; **keelhaul,** duck, masthead; **persecute,** have heads over, have someone's head, make an example of, tar and feather, victimise; **excommunicate,** attaint, damn, interdict, rusticate; **torture,** break on the wheel, excruciate, give the third degree, grill, rack, thumbscrew

punish *v* → defeat

PUNISHABLE *adj* statutable, statutory; **visitational,** amerceable, excommunicable, excommunicative, excommunicatory

PUNISHED *adj* disenfranchised, excommunicate, infamous *(Law)*, penalised; **convicted,** damned, for it, for the high jump, in for it, off tap

PUNISHER *n* amercer, condemner, sentencer; **discipliner,** castigator, chastener, chastiser, corrector, excommunicator, persecutor; **caner,** flogger, fustigator *(Archaic)*, lasher, scourger, swinger, thrasher, walloper, whipper; **executioner,** bow-stringer, crucifier, deathsman *(Archaic)*, firing squad, garrotter, hangman, headsman, lynch mob, lyncher, lynching party; **torturer,** inquisitor; **avenger,** vindicator

PUNISHING *adj* castigatory, corrective, disciplinary, penal, penitentiary, penological, punitive; **correctional,** baculine, fire-and-brimstone, flagellant; **amercing,** confiscatory, expropriatory, mulctuary *(Obs.)*; **retributive,** persecutional, persecutive, persecutory, vindicatory *(Obs.)*, vindictive; **comminatory,** damning, interdictory

PUNISHMENT *n* condemnation, disciplinary action, penalisation, penalty; **forfeiture,** amercement, attainder, attaint, praemunire; **chastisement,** castigation, chastening, correction, discipline, dressing-down, the treatment, what-for; **retribution,** nemesis, poetic justice; **retaliation,** comeuppance, reprisal, requital, vengeance, wrath; **judgment,** day of judgment, day of reckoning, doom, visitation; **banishment,** anathema, commination, excommunication, exile, interdict, monition, outlawing, proscription, transportation; **hellfire,** Gehenna, purgatory; **persecution,** victimisation; **fine,** forfeit, lesson, mulct, parking ticket, penalty, sanction; **imposition,** impost, infliction, lines, task

punitive *adj* → **1** punishing **2** strict

punnet *n* → basket

punt *n* → **1** gamble **2** kick **3** motor vessel **4** rowing boat *v* **5** gamble **6** transport

puny *adj* → **1** inferior **2** small **3** unimportant **4** weak

pup *n* → **1** adolescent **2** animal offspring **3** braggart **4** stupid person *v* **5** give birth

pupa *n* → animal offspring

PUPIL *n* boarder, child, day pupil, dayboy, daygirl, high-schooler, junior, kindergartener, schoolboy, schoolgirl, schoolkid; **student,** autodidact, bursar, co-ed, collegian, day student, evening student, exhibitioner *(Archaic)*, external student, imbiber, learner, mature age student, part-time student, postgraduate student, practiser, scholar, scholarship holder, sophomore *(U.S.)*, undergrad *(U.S.)*, undergraduate; **bookworm,** grind, swot; **slow-learner; prefect,** head boy, head girl, school captain, senior; **graduate,** diplomate, fellow, graduand, licentiate, matriculant, matriculate, postgraduate; **classmate,** alumna, alumnus, fellow student, former student, old boy, old girl. *See also* LEARNER

pupil *n* → eye

PUPPET *n* finger puppet, glove puppet, hand puppet, marionette, Punch and Judy, shadow puppet

puppet *n* → **1** obeyer **2** portrait **3** subject **4** victim *adj* **5** obedient

puppy *n* → **1** adolescent **2** animal offspring **3** braggart **4** stupid person

purchase *n* → **1** buying **2** getting **3** hold *v* **4** bribe **5** buy **6** pull

pure *adj* → **1** abstinent **2** clean **3** innocent **4** modest **5** perfect **6** simple **7** unconditional

puree *v* → cook

purgative *n* → **1** cleanser *adj* **2** cleansing

purgatory *n* → **1** hell **2** punishment **3** unpleasant place *adj* **4** cleansing **5** compensatory

purge *n* → **1** alcohol **2** atonement **3** cleanser **4** massacre **5** removal *v* **6** acquit **7** atone for **8** clean **9** excrete **10** massacre

purify *v* → **1** clean **2** perfect

puritan *n* → **1** abstainer **2** believer **3** intolerant person **4** moraliser **5** strict person *adj* **6** intolerant **7** moral **8** strict

purl *n* → **1** quiet sound **2** spin **3** string **4** trimming *v* **5** sew

purloin *v* → rob

PURPLE *n* burgundy, magenta, orchid, petunia, plum, purpure *(Heraldry)*, raspberry; **lilac,** lavender, mauve, violet; **amethyst,** heliotrope; **cerise,** carmine, grape, solferino; **indigo,** indigo blue, raisin, royal purple

PURPLE *adj* aubergine, magenta, purpure *(Heraldry)*; **purplish,** amaranthine, amethystine, vinaceous, violescent; **lilac,** lavender, lilaceous, mauve, violet; **cerise,** carmine, vinous; **indigo,** perse

purple *n* → **1** aristocracy *adj* **2** aristocratic **3** colourful **4** eloquent

purport *n* → **1** aim **2** meaning *v* **3** mean

purpose *n* → **1** aim **2** usefulness **3** will *v* **4** aim at **5** undertake

PURPOSELESS *adj* aimless, collar-proud, idle, lazy, perfunctory, tardy, unambitious, unenterprising, work-shy; **unwitting,** unconscious, unintentional, unpremeditated, unwilled

purr *n* → **1** animal call **2** click *v* **3** be content **4** be pleased **5** call (of animals) **6** click

purse *n* → **1** case **2** funds *v* **3** fold

purser *n* → **1** accountant **2** seaman

pursuant *adj* → **1** pursuing *adv* **2** aptly

PURSUE *v* chase, chivvy *(Brit.)*, course, dog, follow up, halloo, hallow, hound, hunt, hunt down, lie in wait, shadow, take after *(U.S.)*, tree; **track,** dog, lodge, nose after, nose out, pug, sleuth, spoor, trail, wind; **search,** explore *(Obs.)*, forage, foray, fossick, mouse, noodle *(Mining)*, pearl, prospect, prowl, quest, rake, scout, scrimmage, seek

pursue *v* → **1** flirt **2** have a job

PURSUER *n* blacktracker, bounty hunter *(U.S.)*, chaser, hunter, prowler, spoorer, tracer, tracker; **searcher,** fossicker, noodler, pearler, prospector, rummager, seeker

PURSUING *adj* hunting, piscatorial, piscatory, predatory, preying, pursuant, raptorial, venatic

PURSUIT *n* chasings, derry, hide-and-seek, hidings, hue and cry, man-hunt, prowl, stern chase, tiggy touchwood, wild-goose chase; **hunt,** battue, beat, chase, chivvy, drag hunt, kangaroo drive, safari, still hunt *(U.S.)*. *See also* HUNTING

purulent *adj* → unwholesome

purvey *v* → supply

pus *n* → bodily discharge

push *n* → **1** advance **2** attack **3** clique **4** dismissal **5** effort **6** influence **7** pat **8** persistence

9 thrust 10 vitality *v* 11 arouse 12 collide 13 persist 14 sell 15 thrust

pushover *n* → easy thing

pushy *adj* → presumptuous

pusillanimous *adj* → cowardly

puss *n* → 1 cat 2 face 3 mouth 4 woman

pustule *n* → 1 bulge 2 sore

put *n* → 1 throw *v* 2 gamble 3 place

putative *adj* → conjectural

putrefy *v* → 1 deteriorate 2 get dirty

putrid *adj* → 1 bad 2 deteriorated 3 immoral 4 sickening 5 smelly 6 wrong

putty *n* → 1 adhesive 2 grey *v* 3 coat *adj* 4 brown 5 grey

PUZZLE *n* conundrum, headache, mystery, paradox, pons asinorum, poser, problem, puzzler, sealed book, sticker, stickler, stumper, teaser, tickler; **crossword,** acrostic, anagram, cryptic crossword, cryptonym, logogriph, rebus, Rubik's cube, tangram

PUZZLE *v* amuse *(Obs.)*, anagrammatise, baffle, bamboozle, confuse, elude, mystify, perplex, riddle, stick, throw off the scent

puzzle *n* → 1 amusement *v* 2 confuse

pygmy *n* → 1 fairy 2 small person 3 unimportant person

pyjamas *n* → 1 nightwear 2 trousers

pylon *n* → 1 post 2 signpost 3 tower

pyramid *n* → 1 solid 2 tower *v* 3 increase

pyre *n* → 1 accumulation 2 fire 3 fuel

pyromania *n* → firing

pyrotechnics *n* → 1 display 2 entertainment

Python *n* → mythical beast

Qq

quack *n* → 1 birdcall 2 faker 3 healer 4 incompetent *v* 5 cheat 6 chirp
quad *n* → 1 arch 2 field 3 four 4 offspring 5 prison 6 square 7 train
quadrangle *n* → 1 field 2 plane figure
quadrant *n* → curve
quadratic *n* → 1 mathematical operation 2 number *adj* 3 binomial
quadrilateral *n* → 1 fortress 2 square *adj* 3 square
quadruple *n* → four
quadruplet *n* → 1 four 2 offspring
quaff *v* → drink
quagmire *n* → 1 dilemma 2 swamp
quail *v* → 1 be frightened 2 lack courage
quaint *adj* → 1 competent 2 strange 3 wise
quake *n* → 1 turbulence 2 vibration *v* 3 toss 4 vibrate
QUALIFICATION *n* but, condition, if, limitation, modification, provision, proviso, qualifier, rider, strings; **precondition,** hinge, hypothesis, premise, prerequisite; **reservation,** afterthought, arrière-pensée, reserve; **conditional clause,** article, codicil, condition precedent, condition subsequent, fine print, in terrorem clause, small print, stipulation, tail
QUALIFY *v* condition, limit, provide, stipulate
qualify *v* → 1 be adequate 2 change 3 moderate 4 teach
qualitative *adj* → essential
quality *n* → 1 character 2 condition 3 essence 4 goodness 5 superiority *adj* 6 superior
qualm *n* → 1 ache 2 fright
quandary *n* → 1 dilemma 2 indecision 3 uncertain thing
QUANTIFY *v* amass, measure, number, preponderate, reach, take stock
quantify *v* → measure
quantitative *adj* → 1 measuring 2 poetic
QUANTITATIVELY *adv* volumetrically; **so much,** a bit of, as far as, better than, that, upwards of
quantity *n* → 1 amount 2 much
quantum *n* → 1 amount 2 energy 3 part 4 share
quarantine *n* → health centre
quarrel *n* → 1 argument 2 chisel 3 fight *v* 4 argue 5 be unfriendly
quarry *n* → 1 diggings 2 excavation 3 opening *v* 4 dig
quarter *n* → 1 direction finder 2 four 3 lenience 4 moon 5 pity 6 region 7 season 8 side *v* 9 emblematise 10 execute 11 house 12 inhabit 13 separate 14 turn
quarterly *n* → magazine
quartermaster *n* → 1 storeman 2 supplier
quartet *n* → 1 four 2 theatrical company
quarto *n* → book part
quash *v* → 1 cancel 2 repress
quaternary *n* → four
quaver *n* → 1 vibration *v* 2 mispronounce 3 sing 4 vibrate
quay *n* → harbour
queen *n* → 1 aristocrat 2 man 3 sexual type
queer *n* → 1 sexual type *v* 2 spoil *adj* 3 bad 4 mad 5 nonconformist 6 sexual 7 strange
quell *v* → 1 moderate 2 repress
quench *v* → 1 extinguish 2 satisfy
querulous *adj* → 1 discontented 2 irritable
query *n* → 1 question 2 uncertain thing *v* 3 doubt 4 question
quest *n* → 1 inspection 2 jury 3 undertaking *v* 4 pursue
QUESTION *n* a good question, awkward question, challenge, demand, dorothy dixer, feeler, inquiry, interrogatory, leading question, moot point, poser, query, question on notice, question without notice
QUESTION *v* ask, challenge, demand, enquire, inquire, query, seek an answer, survey; **interview,** audition, examine; **interrogate,** catechise, cross-examine, cross-question, debrief, give the third degree, grill, hammer, pick someone's brains, pose, probe, pump, put to the question, quiz, re-examine *(Law)*, sift the evidence, sweat
question *n* → 1 litigation 2 uncertain thing *v* 3 doubt
questionable *adj* → 1 disreputable 2 incorrect 3 uncertain 4 undetermined
QUESTIONER *n* asker, catechiser, demander, enquirer, inquirer, inquisitor, interrogator, interviewer, querist, question-master, quizzer, re-examiner, seeker; **investigator,** field worker, researcher, scout; **pollster,** canvasser, sampler; **examiner,** analyst, appraiser, assayer, checker, critic, dissector, examinant, observer, prober, scanner, scrutiniser, surveyor; **auditor,** datary *(Rom. Cath. Ch.)*, head-hunter, health inspector, inspector, reviewer, scrutator, scrutineer, systems analyst, talent scout; **committee,** court of inquiry, Royal Commission, standing committee, working party; **examinee,** catechumen, interviewee
QUESTIONING *n* catechisation, catechism, debriefing, interrogation, interview; **cross-examination,** cross-questioning, quiz, re-examination, trial; **inquisition,** dialectic, dialogue, discussion, post-mortem, socratic

method. *See also* INVESTIGATION; INSPECTION; TEST

QUESTIONING *adj* inquisitional, inquisitorial, interrogational, interrogative, interrogatory, searching; **inquiring,** curious, snoopy; **investigative,** analytic, appraising, diagnostic, exploratory, fact-finding, heuristic, laboratorial, observational, research, scientific, scrutinising; **inspectional,** check, inspective

questionnaire *n* → **1** agenda **2** investigation

queue *n* → **1** hair **2** line **3** series *v* **4** line

quibble *n* → **1** figure of speech **2** illogicality **3** joke **4** loophole **5** nonsense *v* **6** avoid **7** lie **8** talk nonsense

quick *n* → **1** essence *adj* **2** busy **3** energetic **4** impermanent **5** intelligent **6** living **7** momentary **8** speedy

quicksand *n* → **1** sludge **2** swamp

quiescent *adj* → **1** inactive **2** silent

QUIET *adj* dreamy, gentle, sedate, softspoken; **whispering,** murmuring, murmurous, susurrant; **husky,** croaky, groaning, gruff, hoarse, hollow, roupy, thick, throaty; **tinkling,** humming, ripply, twittery; **soft,** dim, low, low-pitched, small, still, stilly; **faint,** distant, inaudible, indistinct, inward, muffled, muted; **unstressed,** unaccented, unemphasised, weak; **whispered,** stealthy; **dull,** dead, tinny, tubby; **deadening,** dulling, tempering

quiet *n* → **1** peace **2** rest **3** silence *v* **4** inactivate **5** make peace **6** moderate **7** quieten **8** rest **9** silence *adj* **10** inactive **11** moderate **12** peaceful **13** reticent **14** silent

QUIETEN *v* lower, quiet, shush, soften; **temper,** damp, deaden, drown, dull, overdamp, pug, soft-pedal; **devocalise,** devoice; **become quieter,** die away, drop, fade

QUIETENER *n* damper, deadener, muffle, mute, overdamper, silencer, soft pedal, softener, sordino, sourdine, temperer; **deadening,** acoustic tile, insulation

QUIETLY *adv* dimly, inwardly, low, small, soft, softly, stilly; **sotto voce,** under one's breath, with bated breath; **piano,** calando, decrescendo, diminuendo, pianissimo; **gently,** dreamily, sedately; **murmuringly,** cooingly, groaningly, moaningly, murmurously; **huskily,** gruffly, hollowly, thickly, throatily, tinnily

QUIETNESS *n* faintness, inaudibility, indistinctness, softness; **gentleness,** dimness, dreaminess, sedateness; **dullness,** deadness, tinniness; **huskiness,** frog, gruffness, hoarseness, hollowness, lowness, roup, throatiness; **devocalisation,** ecthlipsis

QUIET SOUND *n* burble, burr, croon, hum, murmur, murmuration, murmuring; **whisper,** aside, susurration, susurrus, undertone; **sigh,** breath, hiss, sniff, swish, waft; **moan,** groan, grumble, grunt, whine; **babble,** prattle, twitter; **lap,** gurgle, plash, purl, ripple; **rustle,** ruffle, scroop, stir; **scratch,** scuff, squeak; **click,** tick; **tinkle,** clink, tinkling; **pitter-patter,** pat, patter, pitapat

quill *n* → **1** feather **2** rod **3** writing materials

quilt *n* → **1** bedclothes **2** beds **3** sewing *v* **4** sew

quince *n* → sexual type

quintessence *n* → **1** essence **2** perfect thing

quintet *n* → **1** musical band **2** theatrical company

quintuplet *n* → offspring

quip *n* → **1** freak **2** joke **3** loophole **4** speaking *v* **5** joke

quire *n* → **1** book part **2** singer

quirk *n* → **1** curve **2** decoration **3** illogicality **4** loophole

quisling *n* → **1** accomplice **2** betrayer

quit *v* → **1** back out **2** depart **3** resign **4** stop

quite *adv* → **1** fully **2** greatly **3** in fact **4** wholly *interj* **5** yes

quits *adj* → equal

quiver *n* → **1** arsenal **2** case **3** perception **4** vibration *v* **5** flutter

quixotic *adj* → **1** delusive **2** impossible

quiz *n* → **1** contest **2** questioning *v* **3** look **4** mock **5** question

quizzical *adj* → **1** humorous **2** mocking **3** strange

quoit *n* → **1** buttocks **2** fool **3** ring

quorum *n* → **1** adequacy **2** chooser **3** committee **4** score

quota *n* → **1** obligation **2** part **3** score **4** share

quotation *n* → **1** gambling **2** repetition **3** value **4** written composition

quote *n* → **1** repetition **2** value *v* **3** appraise **4** repeat **5** speak

Rr

rabbi *n* → **1** ecclesiastic **2** intellectual

rabbit *n* → **1** beer **2** failure **3** fool **4** incompetent *v* **5** hunt

rabble *n* → **1** gathering **2** mixer **3** untidy person **4** working class *v* **5** attack **6** disorder

rabid *adj* → **1** enthusiastic **2** ferocious **3** mad

RACE *n* course *(Archaic)*, trial; **footrace,** Bay to Breakers, city to surf, cross-country, dash, egg-and-spoon race, fun run, hare and hounds, marathon, obstacle race, relay, running race, sack-race, scurry, sprint, three-legged race, walking race, wheelbarrow race; **slalom,** dauerlauf, downhill, rallycross, stock-car race; **swimming race,** iron-man race, medley relay, relay, surf race; **boat race,** bumping race *(Brit.)*, head of the river, regatta, repechage, sculls; **car race,** drag, drag race, Grand Prix, hill climb, motocross, motorkhana, MX, rally; **cycle race,** devil take the hindmost, madison, prime, pursuit, roller race, scramble, stage race, tour, Tour de France; **soapbox derby,** billycart race

race *n* → **1** advance **2** ancestry **3** chute **4** class **5** community **6** current **7** humanity **8** living **9** path **10** pungency **11** taste **12** time *v* **13** accelerate **14** contest **15** have sex **16** speed

RACECOURSE *n* birdcage, collecting ring, flat, ring, stretch, track

racial *adj* → human

racism *n* → **1** hate **2** intolerance

RACK *n* hack; **stand,** inkstand, penholder, tantalus, umbrella stand, whatnot; **grate,** brazier, chauffer, firebox, hay oven, haybox, hearth

racket *n* → **1** crime **2** dishonesty **3** job **4** loud sound *v* **5** be happy **6** be loud **7** be sociable **8** overindulge

raconteur *n* → storyteller

racquet *n* → **1** club **2** footgear

racy *adj* → **1** alluring **2** busy **3** energetic **4** obscene **5** pungent

radar *n* → **1** defence **2** positioning **3** warner

radial *n* → **1** wheel *adj* **2** divergent

radiant *n* → **1** astronomic point *adj* **2** beautiful **3** bright **4** happy **5** hopeful **6** thermal

radiate *v* → **1** disperse **2** diverge **3** expel **4** shine *adj* **5** divergent

radiation *n* → **1** divergence **2** expulsion **3** heat transfer **4** poison

radiator *n* → **1** cooler **2** heater

radical *n* → **1** atom **2** enthusiast **3** nonconformist **4** political ideologist *adj* **5** bottom **6** excessive **7** fundamental **8** inborn **9** nonconformist **10** original

RADIO *n* crystal set, earphone, gibson girl, pedal wireless, radio receiver, radio set, receiver, receiving set, steam radio, trannie, transceiver, transistor, walkie-talkie, wireless, wireless set; **transmitter,** racon, radio beacon, radio transmitter, transmitting set; **modulator,** tuner; **microphone,** cans *(Colloq.)*, carbon microphone, dial, pick-up; **valve,** beam tube, dynatron, pentode, tickler coil, triode; **airplay,** air, airshift; **interference,** hash, jitter, noise, whistler; **modulation,** demodulation, diplexer, duplexer, heterodyne method, phase modulation, pulse-time modulation, superheterodyne method, synchrodyne method; **amplitude modulation,** AM, FM, frequency modulation

RADIOACTIVATION *n* activation, breeding, capture, conversion, excitation, induction, initiation, ionisation, multiplication, spallation, transformation, transition; **fission,** binary fission, photofission; **fusion,** fusion reaction, nuclear fusion, thermonuclear reaction; **reaction,** chain-reaction, nuclear reaction, pair production; **meltdown,** China syndrome, critical mass. *See also* ATOMIC RADIATION; NUCLEAR ENERGY; ATOMIC BOMB

radioactive *adj* → chain-reacting

radioactivity *n* → atomic radiation

radius *n* → **1** branch **2** circle **3** line **4** thickness

raffish *adj* → **1** obscene **2** promiscuous **3** vulgar

raffle *n* → gambling

RAFT *n* balsa, cat, catamaran, float, kon-tiki *(N.Z. Angling)*, life raft, scow; **floating bridge,** bateau, pontoon, stakeboat; **buoy,** lifebuoy

raft *n* → **1** float **2** much **3** support *v* **4** transport

rafter *n* → **1** beam **2** shaft *v* **3** cover

rag *n* → **1** bad person **2** bad thing **3** denigrator **4** newspaper **5** small amount **6** textiles *v* **7** annoy **8** joke **9** mock **10** scold **11** trick

ragamuffin *n* → **1** children **2** poor person **3** untidy person

rage *n* → **1** anger **2** angry act **3** celebration **4** desire **5** emotion **6** entertainment **7** enthusiasm **8** fashion **9** madness **10** popularity **11** violent outburst *v* **12** be angry **13** be pleased **14** be sociable **15** be violent **16** blow **17** desire **18** feel emotion

ragged *adj* → **1** dilapidated **2** dissonant **3** irregular **4** neglected **5** rough

raglan *n* → overcoat

ragout *v* → cook

raid *n* → **1** act of war **2** attack *v* **3** attack **4** fire on

rail *n* → **1** bar **2** edge **3** railway **4** restraints *v* **5** support **6** transport

railing *n* → frame

raillery *n* → **1** joke **2** mockery

RAILWAY *n* branch line, feeder, hump, line, loop, main line, permanent way, plate rail, rack-railway, rail, railway line, road *(U.S.)*, scenic railway, section, sidetrack *(U.S.)*, siding, switchback, third rail, track, trackage, trunk, trunk line; **tramline,** pinch, tramway; **underground,** metro, tube *(Brit.)*, underground railway; **cableway,** teleferic; **cable railway,** cable tramway, funicular, funicular railway; **points,** gauntlet, switch *(U.S.)*

raiment *n* → clothes

RAIN *v* precipitate; **drizzle,** shower, spit, sprinkle; **pour,** bucket, deluge, pelt, piss down, rain cats and dogs, storm *(U.S.)*, teem

rain *n* → **1** much **2** rainfall *v* **3** shower

rainbow *n* → **1** colour **2** light *adj* **3** multicoloured

RAINCOAT *n* burberry, camlet, Drizabone, mac, mackintosh, oiler *(U.S.)*, oilskins, rubbers *(U.S.)*, slicker, trench coat, waterproof. *See also* CLOAK; OVERCOAT

RAINFALL *n* hydrometeor, meteor *(Obs.)*, precipitation, water cycle; **rain,** blood rain, convectional rain, drizzle, precipitate, serein, virga, water, wet; **raindrop; shower,** flurry, spit, sprinkle; **downpour,** cloudburst, cockeye bob, deluge, equinoctial, pour, rainstorm, spate, storm, the Deluge *(Bible)*, thundershower, thunderstorm, torrent, waterspout; **rainy season,** bogaduck weather, monsoon, the wet

rainforest *n* → forest

raise *n* → **1** lifting *v* **2** build **3** bulge **4** care for **5** communicate **6** compute **7** cook **8** erect **9** gamble **10** gather **11** increase **12** lift **13** make **14** promote **15** stop **16** wake up

RAISE UP *v* elevate, erect, heighten, uplift, upraise, uprear

raisin *n* → purple

rake *n* → **1** allurer **2** dissipater **3** flirt **4** lover **5** promiscuous person **6** slope **7** smoother *v* **8** cut **9** farm **10** gather **11** look **12** pursue **13** slope **14** smooth

rally *n* → **1** crowd **2** hit **3** increase **4** race **5** recovery *v* **6** accelerate **7** associate **8** be healthy **9** gather **10** help **11** hope **12** improve **13** mock **14** strengthen **15** tidy

ramble *v* → **1** flood **2** flower **3** travel **4** waffle

ramification *n* → divergence

ramp *n* → **1** angry act **2** ascent **3** descent **4** dishonesty **5** inspection **6** path **7** slope *v* **8** ascend **9** be angry **10** be violent

rampage *n* → **1** angry act *v* **2** be angry **3** be violent **4** speed

rampant *adj* → **1** abundant **2** angry **3** erect **4** ferocious **5** fertile **6** liberated **7** risen **8** voluptuous

rampart *n* → **1** embankment **2** fortification **3** mound *v* **4** defend

ramrod *n* → **1** intolerant person **2** stick **3** washer

ramshackle *adj* → dilapidated

R.A.N. *n* → **1** armed forces **2** watercraft

ranch *n* → **1** farm *v* **2** farm

rancid *adj* → **1** old **2** sickening **3** unsavoury

rancour *n* → **1** acrimony **2** hate **3** unfriendliness

random *adj* → **1** disorderly **2** illogical **3** lucky **4** uncertain

randy *adj* → **1** captivated **2** desirous **3** obscene **4** sexy

range *n* → **1** class **2** difference **3** dwelling **4** length **5** mathematical operation **6** pitch **7** region **8** remoteness **9** space **10** stove **11** whole *v* **12** change **13** class **14** direct **15** farm **16** line **17** order **18** position **19** straighten **20** travel

ranger *n* → **1** classer **2** hunter **3** manager **4** policeman **5** traveller

rank *n* → **1** class **2** condition **3** grade **4** job **5** line **6** reputation **7** series *v* **8** assess **9** class **10** graduate **11** inquire into **12** line **13** order **14** surpass *adj* **15** bad **16** growing **17** immoral **18** most **19** obscene **20** pungent **21** sickening **22** smelly **23** unsavoury

rank and file *n* → working class

rankle *v* → **1** annoy **2** displease **3** irritate **4** pain

ransack *v* → **1** rob **2** search

ransom *n* → **1** liberation **2** liberty **3** repair *v* **4** buy **5** compensate **6** liberate **7** repair

rant *n* → **1** angry act **2** nonsense *v* **3** be angry **4** be violent **5** perform **6** talk nonsense **7** waffle

rap *n* → **1** accusation **2** bit **3** boom **4** coinage **5** imputation **6** pat **7** small amount **8** talk *v* **9** accelerate **10** dance **11** hit **12** talk

rapacious *adj* → **1** avaricious **2** greedy **3** predatory **4** thieving

RAPE *n* defilement, fate worse than death, pack-rape, ravishment, statutory rape *(U.S.)*, violation; **indecent assault,** assault, interference; **incest; seduction,** ruin *(Archaic)*

RAPE *v* defile, outrage, ravish, violate; **pack-rape,** stir the porridge; **seduce,** deflower, ruin, wrong; **assault,** interfere with

rape *n* → **1** attack **2** forcefulness **3** remnant *v* **4** be promiscuous **5** destroy **6** rob

rapid *adj* → speedy

rapier *n* → **1** piercer **2** sword

rapine *n* → robbery

rapport *n* → **1** agreement **2** relation

rapt *adj* → **1** approving **2** attentive **3** emotional **4** pleased

rapture *n* → **1** joy **2** pleasure

RARE *adj* few, few and far between, rare as hen's teeth, scarce, uncommon, unheard-of; **rarefactive; infrequent,** seldom *(Obs.)*; **sporadic,** intermittent, occasional; **unusual,** almost unheard-of, unprecedented

rare *adj* → **1** few **2** good **3** light **4** strange

RARELY *adv* hardly ever, infrequently, little, once, once in a blue moon, scarcely, scarcely ever, seldom; **at times,** every now and again, every now and then, every once in a while, every so often, from time to time, now and again, now and then, occasionally, on occasion, once in a blue moon, once in a month of Sundays, once in a while, sometime *(Rare)*, sometimes; **never,** nevermore

RARENESS *n* fewness, rarity, scarceness, scarcity, uncommonness; **rarefaction; infrequency,** seldomness; **rarity,** bibelot, collector's item, rara avis, rare bird, rare book; **intermittence,** discontinuity

rarity *n* → **1** air **2** freak **3** goodness **4** lightness **5** nonconformist **6** rareness

rascal *n* → crook

RASH *adj* brash, foolhardy, hardy, harum-scarum, headlong, ill-advised, ill-judged, imprudent, irrational, unadvised, unconsidered, unwise; **headstrong,** ardent, harebrained, heady, heedless, hot-blooded, hot-headed, impatient, impetuous, incautious, indiscreet, mad, madcap, passionate, warm-blooded; **overconfident,** confident, overbold, presumptuous; **hasty,** improvident, impulsive, precipitant, precipitate, precipitative, precipitous, premature; **audacious,** bold, cavalier, daredevil, devil-may-care, free-and-easy, reckless, temerarious, wildcat; **unreasonable,** crazy, trigger-happy, wanton, wild; **blind,** blindfold, desperate; **suicidal,** banzai, kamikaze

rash *n* → **1** increase **2** sore

RASHLY *adv* audaciously, foolhardily, harum-scarum, heedlessly, ill-advisedly, improvidently, imprudently, incautiously, indiscreetly, recklessly, temerariously, unadvisedly; **adventurously,** for the hell of it; **headstrongly,** head over heels, headfirst, headily, headlong, hot-headedly; **overconfidently,** boldly, confidently; **hastily,** impetuously, impulsively, precipitantly, precipitately, precipitously, prematurely; **unreasonably,** crazily, wantonly, wildly; **pell-mell,** at full fling, neck or nothing, to the hilt; **blindly,** blind, desperately

RASHNESS *n* foolhardiness, headiness, heedlessness, hot-headedness, improvidence, imprudence, incaution, incautiousness, indiscreetness, indiscretion, lack of caution, thoughtlessness, unadvisedness; **haste,** hastiness, impetuosity, impetuousness, precipitancy, precipitateness, precipitation, precipitousness, prematurity, rush; **audacity,** audaciousness, boldness, overconfidence, presumption, recklessness, temerariousness, temerity, wildcatting; **adventurousness,** adventurism, daredevilry; **unreasonableness,** craziness, madness, unreason, wantonness; **blindness,** desperateness, desperation; **rash act,** leap in the dark

rasp *n* → **1** abrasive **2** dissonance **3** powderer **4** smoother *v* **5** be dissonant **6** irritate **7** powder **8** roughen **9** rub **10** speak

raspberry *n* → **1** boo **2** purple

rat *n* → **1** abandoner **2** bad person **3** soldier *v* **4** hunt **5** rob

ratbag *n* → **1** crook **2** nonconformist **3** strange person

ratchet *n* → knob

RATE *n* cadence *(Mil.)*, pace, tempo, time; **quick time,** double time, quick march; **rush,** career, tantivy, whirl; **scamper,** dart, scoot, scud, scurry, scutter, whisk; **gallop,** canter, clip, lope, romp, sprint; **run,** burn, fang, hit out, schuss, spin; **walking pace,** footpace. *See also* SPEED; VELOCITY

rate *n* → **1** cost **2** grade *v* **3** appraise **4** assess **5** class **6** deserve **7** graduate **8** measure **9** scold

rather *adv* → **1** optionally *interj* **2** yes

ratify *v* → **1** assent to **2** label

rating *n* → **1** assessment **2** classification **3** measurement **4** reprimand **5** seaman

ratio *n* → **1** relationship **2** value

ration *n* → **1** share *v* **2** restrict **3** share out **4** supply

rational *adj* → **1** logical **2** mental **3** numerical **4** sane

rationale *n* → reasoning

rationalise *v* → **1** clarify **2** compute **3** justify **4** order

rattan *n* → stick

rattle *n* → **1** breathing **2** click **3** crackle **4** vibrator *v* **5** be loud **6** click **7** confuse **8** speed **9** talk **10** vibrate **11** worry

ratty *adj* → **1** dilapidated **2** irritable **3** nonconformist

raucous *adj* → dissonant

raunchy *adj* → **1** powerful **2** sexy **3** vulgar

ravage *n* → **1** destruction **2** harm *v* **3** damage **4** destroy **5** wage war

rave *n* → **1** approval **2** celebration **3** nonsense *v* **4** be excited **5** be loud **6** enjoy **7** enthuse **8** talk nonsense *adj* **9** approving

ravel *n* → **1** tangle *v* **2** deteriorate **3** muddle **4** separate **5** simplify **6** tangle

raven *n* → **1** black **2** robbery *v* **3** absorb **4** be hungry **5** gorge **6** hunt *adj* **7** black

ravenous *adj* → **1** greedy **2** hungry

ravine *n* → gap

ravish *v* → **1** be promiscuous **2** emotionalise **3** enchant **4** rape

ravishing *adj* → **1** alluring **2** beautiful

RAW *adj* crude, green, in the rough, incomplete, premature, rough, rude; **untreated,** en déshabille, in a state of nature, natural, undressed, unlaid, untilled. *See also* UNREADY

raw *adj* → **1** cold **2** fundamental **3** ignorant **4** ill-bred **5** incompetent **6** new **7** painful **8** realistic **9** unfair

RAW MATERIALS *n* producer goods, raw stock, resources, staple, stuff, substance; **raw material,** bone, clay, fibre, glass, metal, mineral, ore, paper, plastics, timber, wax. *See also* TIMBER; BUILDING MATERIALS; PAPER

ray *n* → **1** atomic radiation **2** flower **3** light **4** line **5** moon **6** thinness *v* **7** line **8** shine

raze *v* → **1** cut **2** destroy **3** level

razor *n* → **1** knife *v* **2** cut

reach *n* → **1** channel **2** length **3** rod **4** stream *v* **5** arrive **6** come close **7** compute **8** extend **9** gain **10** perforate **11** quantify

REACT *v* answer, reply, respond, take it; **shy,** curl *(Colloq.)*, jerk, prop, start, wince; **overreact,** freak out; **recoil,** cannon, kick, ricochet; **rebound,** boomerang, come home to roost, redound, spring back

REACTION *n* answer, echo, feedback, reply, response, return; **reflex,** knee jerk, shy, start, wince; **recoil,** backlash, boomerang, kick, kickback, rebound, repercussion, reverberation; **backstroke,** cannon, carom, ricochet

reaction *n* → **1** action **2** answer **3** change **4** conformist behaviour **5** counteraction **6** perception **7** radioactivation

reactionary *n* → **1** conformer **2** political ideologist *adj* **3** conservative

REACTIVE *adj* corresponsive, responsive, sensitive, tropistic; **reflex,** boomerang, feedback, repercussive; **hyperreactive,** supersensitive

READ *v* bury oneself in, go over, peruse, pore over, study, wade through; **scan,** browse, dip into, leaf through, look at, run through, skim, speed read, taste, thumb through

read *n* → **1** reading *v* **2** explain **3** know **4** predict **5** speak **6** speak well **7** study *adj* **8** knowledgeable

READABLE *adj* decipherable, legible, perusable, written

READER *n* bibliophile, bookworm, browser, peruser; **readership,** readers, subscribers; **proofreader,** copyreader, proofer, taster

readily *adv* → **1** easily **2** momentarily **3** willingly

READING *n* perusal, read; **literacy,** reading ability; **readableness,** decipherability, legibility, legibleness, readability; **machine reading,** bar coding, MICR encoding, OCR, optical character reading

ready *n* → **1** cash **2** conspiracy *adj* **3** agreeable **4** easy **5** equipped **6** intelligent **7** predisposed **8** prepared **9** useable

reagent *n* → tester

REAL *adj* actual, concrete, de facto, factual, incarnate, objective, positive, solid, substantival, substantive; **existent,** contemporary, current, extant, going, ingenerate, living, original, pre-existent, self-existent, surviving, uncaused

real *adj* → **1** correct **2** numerical **3** realistic **4** true *adv* **5** very

REAL ESTATE *n* country seat, demesne, domain, dominant estate, dominant tenement, entail, fee simple, fee tail, fief, freehold, immoveables *(Law)*, land *(Law)*, lordship *(Hist.)*, manor, mesnalty, real property, realty, seigneury, seigniory, servient tenement, tenement, thanage

real estate *n* → land

realise *v* → **1** accomplish **2** be realistic **3** cash **4** gain **5** make music **6** sell

REALISM *n* commonsense, earthiness, factualism, factualness, sense, soberness; **reality,** hardpan, the facts of life, the harsh reality, the truth of the matter, tintacks; **worldliness,** hard-headedness, pragmatism, worldly-mindedness; **naturalism,** cinéma-vérité, mimesis, social realism, verism

REALIST *n* factualist, hardhead, nuts-and-bolts man, pragmatist, utilitarian, verist

REALISTIC *adj* banausic, bread-and-butter, commonsensical, down-to-earth, fanciless, matter-of-fact, no-nonsense, pragmatic, sober, utilitarian, worldly, worldly-minded; **naturalistic,** factual, lifelike, living, mimetic, photographic, real, three-dimensional, true to life, truthful; **earthy,** kitchen-sink, raw, verist, veristic, warts-and-all

reality *n* → **1** actuality **2** honesty **3** realism **4** truth

really *adv* → in fact

realm *n* → **1** domain **2** nation **3** subject matter

realty *n* → real estate

reap *v* → **1** cut **2** harvest **3** take

REAR *n* arrear *(Archaic)*, background, backside, gorge, stern; **back,** B-side, reverse, smooth *(Tennis)*, tail, verso; **backside,** behind, breech, butt, buttocks, dorsum, hindquarter, posterior, rump, tail, tail end; **posteriority,** postposition; **rearguard; retroflexion,** resupination, retroversion

REAR *v* breed, bring up, discipline, house-train, nurture, teach manners to, toilet-train

REAR *adj* aft, after *(Naut.)*, epaxial, hind, hinder, posterior, tail; **hindmost,** aftermost, backmost, rearmost, sternmost; **background; backstage,** upstage; **back,** reverse, tail; **backward,** hindward, rearward; **retroflex,** resupinate, retrorse, retroussé, revolute

rear *n* → **1** buttocks **2** combat troops *v* **3** ascend **4** care for **5** erect **6** jump

REASON *v* argue, chop logic, contend, debate, moot *(Obs.)*, ratiocinate, refine on, refine upon, subtilise; **deduce,** collect *(Rare)*, conclude, derive, figure, gather, induce

reason *n* → **1** cause **2** logic **3** mind **4** motive **5** reasoning **6** sanity **7** wisdom *v* **8** persuade

reasonable *adj* → **1** adequate **2** fair **3** logical **4** mental **5** moderate **6** sane **7** wise

REASONING *n* argument, argumentation, assumption, consecution, debate, dialectic, discursion, discursiveness, discussion, disputation, exercise, illation, philosophism, polemic, proof, ratiocination, rationale, reason, refinement, subtilisation, syllogism, synthesis; **logic,** apologetics, Aristotelian logic, Aristotelianism, dialectics, formal logic, mathematical logic, methodology, polemics, propositional calculus, symbolic logic, syntax. *See also* LOGIC

rebate *n* → **1** furrow **2** niche *v* **3** furrow **4** subtract

rebel *n* → **1** disobeyer **2** dissident **3** nonconformist **4** revolutionary *v* **5** anarchise **6** disobey **7** oppose **8** revolt *adj* **9** disobedient **10** revolutionary

rebellion *n* → **1** mutiny **2** revolution

rebound *n* → **1** impact **2** pliability **3** reaction *v* **4** bounce **5** react

rebuff *n* → **1** disapproval **2** refusal **3** repulsion *v* **4** refuse **5** repel

rebuke *n* → **1** reprimand *v* **2** scold

rebut *v* → **1** answer **2** deny **3** disprove **4** oppose

recalcitrant *n* → **1** disobeyer *adj* **2** disobedient **3** dissident

recall *n* → 1 cancellation 2 command 3 memory *v* 4 cancel 5 dismiss 6 remember 7 remind 8 repair
recant *v* → deny
recapitulate *v* → repeat
recede *v* → 1 cancel 2 go back
receipt *n* → 1 account 2 cookery 3 diagram 4 getting 5 list *v* 6 get
receive *v* → 1 absorb 2 be sociable 3 gain 4 get 5 welcome
receiver *n* → 1 agent 2 appointee 3 container 4 gainer 5 radio 6 telecommunications
recent *adj* → 1 innovative 2 past
receptacle *n* → 1 container 2 electric circuit 3 flower
reception *n* → 1 celebration 2 crowd 3 getting 4 party 5 wedding
receptionist *n* → helper
receptive *adj* → 1 absorbent 2 intelligent 3 tolerant
recess *n* → 1 furrow 2 inside 3 interval 4 niche 5 rest *v* 6 rest 7 stop
recession *n* → 1 cheapness 2 compensation 3 decrease 4 religious ceremony
recherché *adj* → good
recidivism *n* → unlawfulness
recipe *n* → 1 cookery 2 diagram
recipient *n* → 1 absorber 2 gainer *adj* 3 absorbent
reciprocal *adj* → 1 interactive 2 numerical 3 regular 4 related 5 retaliatory
reciprocate *v* → 1 alternate 2 exchange 3 flutter 4 interact 5 relate 6 retaliate
recital *n* → 1 concert 2 narrative 3 oration 4 speaking
recite *v* → 1 narrate 2 perform 3 speak
reckless *adj* → 1 capricious 2 neglectful 3 rash
reckon *v* → 1 assess 2 compute 3 depend on 4 devise 5 think
reclaim *n* → 1 repair *v* 2 convert 3 repair
RECLINE *v* lie, lie down, loll, loll about, lounge, measure one's length, prostrate oneself, repose, shake, spinebash, sprawl, stretch out
recline *v* → rest
recluse *n* → 1 monastic 2 solitary *adj* 3 solitary
recognise *v* → 1 approve 2 assent to 3 be sociable 4 find 5 gesture 6 know 7 remember 8 see
recoil *n* → 1 counteraction 2 length 3 reaction *v* 4 react
recollect *v* → remember
recommend *v* → 1 approve 2 encourage 3 guide 4 offer
recompense *n* → 1 compensation 2 income 3 payment *v* 4 compensate 5 pay
reconcile *v* → 1 adjust 2 make peace
recondite *adj* → 1 arcane 2 hidden 3 unclear
reconnaissance *n* → 1 inspection 2 look
reconnoitre *n* → 1 look *v* 2 investigate 3 look
RECORD *n* account, annal, autobiography, bio, biography, chronicle, commentary, curriculum vitae, document, history, life, track record, travels; **annals,** archives, commentaries, oral history, reminiscences, transactions; **notes,** adversaria, brief, cahier, case history, case record, detail *(Archaic)*, dictation, minutes; **note,** billet, chit, chitty, entry, memorandum, notation, observation, registration, sidenote; **file,** card catalogue, card file, card index, fiche, field book, filing card, form, microfiche, notebook, pocket-book, scribble block, scribble pad, slip, stub, table book, tablet, work sheet; **parish register,** family Bible, vestry book; **register,** cartulary, logbook, manifest, plod, service rdcord, visitors' book; **scorebook,** scoreboard, scorecard, scoresheet; **score,** notch, return, **quipu,** pictograph; **legal record,** act, breve, cadastre, charter, corpus, court roll, discharge, docket, gazette, grant of probate, Hansard, law report, memorandum, muniments, patent, power of attorney, praecipe, presents, probate, provenance, statute, statute book, terrar, terrier, title deed, transcript, transumpt, will, writ; **electoral register,** census *(Class. Antiq.)*, electoral roll. *See also* DIARY; CERTIFICATE
RECORD *v* book, calendar, card, catalogue, chronicle, diarise, enrol, enter, inscribe, item, journalise, keep tabs on, keep track of, log, manifest, minute, notate, note, protocol, put down, register; **file,** archive; **tally,** mark up, nick, notch up, put on the slate, rack, score
record *n* → 1 account 2 analysis 3 computer record 4 imitation 5 list 6 narrative 7 recording 8 reminder *v* 9 account 10 mark *adj* 11 superior
RECORDER *n* amanuensis, annalist, biographer, chaser, chronicler, clerk, diarist, filer, hagiographer, historian, jerquer, rapporteur, registrar, scorer, secretary, tallyclerk, tallyman; **personnel,** office, secretariat; **recording instrument,** black box, flight recorder
recorder *n* → sound system
RECORDING *n* album, disc, pressing, record, soundtrack, take; **LP,** A-side, black disc, B-side, CD, compact disc, digital disc, EP, extended play, flip side, forty-five, laser disc, mono, quadradisc, seventy-eight, single, thirty-three; **track,** cut, groove, microgroove, run-in groove; **smash-hit,** bullet, chart-buster, gold, gold record, gorilla *(U.S.)*, number one, platinum record, top forty, top ten; **sound library,** discography
record-player *n* → sound system
recount *v* → 1 compute 2 list 3 narrate
re-count *n* → 1 computation *v* 2 compute
recoup *n* → 1 compensation 2 payment *v* 3 compensate 4 pay
recourse *n* → 1 expedient 2 help
recover *v* → 1 be healthy 2 compensate 3 gain 4 improve 5 revive 6 use
RECOVERY *n* amends *(Obs.)*, convalescence, cure, rally, recruitment, recuperation, rehabilitation, sanation
recreation *n* → 1 amusement 2 pleasure 3 return to normal
re-creation *n* → 1 creation 2 innovation
recriminate *v* → lay charges

recruit *n* → **1** serviceman **2** starter *v* **3** be healthy **4** militarise **5** repair
rectangle *n* → plane figure
rectify *v* → **1** change **2** correct **3** line
rectitude *n* → **1** correctness **2** straightness
rector *n* → **1** ecclesiastic **2** leader **3** monastic **4** teacher
rectum *n* → abdomen
recumbent *n* → **1** idler **2** levelness *adj* **3** inactive **4** level
recuperate *v* → **1** be healthy **2** improve
recur *v* → **1** alternate **2** remind **3** repeat
recycle *v* → use
RED *n* blood red, carnation, Chinese red, chrome red, cinnabar, Congo red, crimson, flame colour, ginger, Indian red, pompadour, Pompeian red, poppy, ruby, rust, titian, Turkey red, Venetian red; **maroon,** grape, murex, murrey; **pink,** flesh, flesh colour, hot pink, peachblow, rose, shocking pink
RED *adj* cardinal, cherry, laky, ruddy, stammel *(Obs.)*; **crimson,** carmine, cerise, claret, cramoisy *(Obs.)*, garnet, incarnadine, incarnate, ruby; **scarlet,** vermeil, vermilion; **blood-red,** bloodied, bloodlike, bloodstained, bloody, ensanguined, gory, sanguine, sanguineous, sanguinolent; **magenta,** murex, port, vinous, wine; **pink,** blush, carnation, damask; **rose,** rosaceous, rose-coloured, roseate, roselike, rosy; **salmon,** apricot, coral, coralline, peach, salmon pink, sandy; **pinkish,** flamingo, flesh-coloured; **carroty,** flame-coloured, gingery, orange; **russet,** brick red, lateritious, mahogany, maroon, rubiginous, rusty, testaceous
red *n* → political ideologist
Red *n* → nonconformist
red-blooded *adj* → **1** busy **2** healthy **3** living
REDDEN *v* bloody, crimson, ensanguine, gild *(Obs.)*, raddle, rubricate; **rouge,** henna; **flush,** blush, change colour, colour, colour up, have the blood rush to one's cheeks, inflame, mantle, rose
REDDISH *adj* erubescent, rubicund, rubrical *(Obs.)*, ruddy, rufescent, rufous, rutilant *(Rare)*, strawberry, warm; **inflamed,** angry *(Med.)*, bloodshot, erythematous, erythrismal, inflammatory, injected, rubefacient; **red-faced,** blowzy, blushing, florid, flushed, high-coloured, raddled, rosy-cheeked, rouged, rubescent, rubicund; **red-headed,** carroty, sandy
redeem *v* → **1** buy **2** compensate **3** pay **4** repair
red-handed *adj* → **1** murderous *adv* **2** guiltily
red herring *n* → unimportant thing
REDNESS *n* colour, floridity, floridness, gules, reddishness, rubicundity, ruddiness; **rosiness,** pinkness; **bloodiness,** angriness, erythema *(Pathol.)*, erythrism, erythroderma, erythrophobia, flush, hectic flush, inflammation, sanguineness
redolent *adj* → fragrant
redoubtable *adj* → **1** frightening **2** highly regarded
redound *n* → **1** result *v* **2** react
redress *n* → compensation
re-dress *v* → wear
red tape *n* → tape
reduce *v* → **1** abstain **2** cheapen **3** compute **4** decrease **5** photograph **6** repair **7** repress **8** subtract **9** thin
redundant *adj* → **1** repetitive **2** surplus **3** useless **4** verbose
redwood *n* → timber
reed *n* → **1** moulding **2** wind instrument
reefer *n* → **1** cooler **2** digger **3** jacket **4** marijuana **5** mariner **6** tobacco
reek *n* → **1** gas **2** stench *v* **3** be smelly **4** cloud **5** expel **6** wet
reel *n* → **1** amount **2** sound system *v* **3** roll up
refectory *n* → **1** kitchen **2** restaurant
referee *n* → **1** adjudicator **2** judge **3** mediator
reference *n* → **1** authentication **2** guidance **3** litigation
REFERENCE BOOK *n* atlas, calendar, dictionary, digest, directory, encyclopaedia, fauna, gazetteer, gradus, key, lapidary, lexicon, source book, thesaurus, wordbook, yearbook; **guidebook,** guide, itinerary, roadbook; **handbook,** companion, enchiridion, manual, phrasebook, stylebook, vade mecum, writer *(Obs.)*; **bibliography,** catalogue, reading list
referendum *n* → election
refine *v* → **1** beautify **2** be precise **3** clean **4** discriminate
refined *adj* → **1** beautiful **2** clean **3** courteous **4** cultivated **5** discriminating **6** precise
reflect *v* → **1** deflect **2** shine
REFLECTION *n* total internal reflection; **refraction,** birefringence, diffraction, interference, refringence; **polarisation,** coma, fringe; **aberration,** achromatism, aplanatism, chromatic aberration, spherical aberration, stigmatism; **angle of incidence,** angle of reflection, angle of refraction, cardinal points, centre of curvature, focal plane, focal point, focus, image, mirror image, nodal point, principal axis, principal focus, principal points; **focal length,** critical angle, depth of field, depth of focus, dioptre, magnification, numerical aperture, power, resolution, resolving power
reflex *n* → **1** action **2** reaction *v* **3** fold *adj* **4** reactive **5** unwilling
reform *n* → **1** correction **2** improvement *v* **3** atone for **4** be penitent **5** convert **6** improve
re-form *v* → create
reformatory *n* → **1** prison *adj* **2** corrective
refraction *n* → **1** deflection **2** illusion **3** reflection
refractory *adj* → **1** disobedient **2** stubborn **3** unmanageable
refrain *n* → **1** musical piece **2** repetition *v* **3** abstain **4** be inactive **5** restrain oneself
refreshment *n* → **1** meal **2** pleasure **3** return to normal
refrigerate *v* → **1** conserve **2** cool
refrigerator *n* → **1** box **2** cooler

REFUGE *n* asylum, bolthole, cot, cover, covert, coverture, funk-hole, hide-out, hideaway, place of safety, sanctuary; **hospice,** home, hospitium, imaret, retreat, spital *(Obs.)*; **traffic island.** *See also* SHELTER; HARBOUR

refuge *n* → 1 almshouse 2 seclusion

refugee *n* → 1 arriver 2 escapee 3 foreigner 4 outsider 5 traveller

refund *n* → 1 compensation 2 payment *v* 3 lend 4 pay

refurbish *v* → 1 improve 2 innovate 3 repair

REFUSAL *n* declension, declination *(Obs.)*, declinature, denial, first refusal, negation, no, non-compliance, point-blank refusal, rebuff; **negativity,** disapproval, discountenance, negativeness, negativism; **veto,** disallowance, pocket veto *(U.S.)*, thumbs down

refusal *n* → choice

REFUSE *v* abnegate, begrudge, deny, not come at, not hear of, reject, repel, repulse, slam the door in someone's face; **baulk at,** beg off, chicken out, jack up, kick, kick against; **veto,** decline, disallow, negative, send back, withhold consent from; **give up,** kick the habit, pass up, renounce; **deprive,** dispossess, divest, strip; **rebuff,** disapprove, discountenance, knock back, not have a bar of it, not have any of it, repudiate, stick in one's throat, throw out, turn away, turn down; **draw the line at,** have nothing to do with, have second thoughts, not be in it, send away with a flea in the ear, set one's face against, turn a deaf ear to, turn one's back on, wash one's hands of; **reject,** cast away, cast off, discard, disown, forswear, junk

refuse *n* → 1 dirt 2 waste *v* 3 be inactive 4 meet an obstacle *adj* 5 useless

refute *v* → disprove

regain *n* → 1 wetness *v* 2 arrive

regal *adj* → 1 aristocratic 2 beautiful 3 enormous

regale *n* → 1 meal *v* 2 be sociable 3 feed

regalia *n* → 1 emblem of office 2 formal dress 3 rights

regard *n* → 1 attentiveness 2 courtesy 3 friendship 4 high regard 5 look 6 reputation *v* 7 attend to 8 look 9 respect

REGARDFUL *adj* bareheaded, cap in hand, deferent, deferential, humble, obeisant, obsequious, pious, respectful, reverential, suppliant, tributary; **awe-struck,** adoring, worshipful

regardless *adj* → 1 inattentive 2 neglectful 3 unconditional *adv* 4 nevertheless

regatta *n* → race

regenerate *v* → 1 become greater 2 convert 3 create 4 defect 5 improve 6 repair *adj* 7 improved

regent *n* → leader

regime *n* → 1 legislation 2 plan 3 weather

regimen *n* → 1 legislation 2 plan

regiment *n* → 1 armed forces 2 crowd *v* 3 regularise 4 tidy

REGION *n* area, corner, country, district, extent, land, limit *(Obs.)*, locale, locality, location, natural region, neck of the woods, pale parts, precinct, province, purlieu, quarter, redevelopment area, restricted area, scope, stretch, swath, time zone, tract, tract of land, zone, zonule; **subdistrict,** subregion *(Geog.)*; **neighbourhood,** precincts, purlieus, vicinage, vicinity; **territory,** beat, range, terrain; **quarter,** colony, ghetto, pocket; **borderland,** border, bounds, corridor, enclave, exclave, frontier *(U.S.)*, hook, march, no-man's-land; **lowland,** mickery country, surge area, surge line, tideland, warpland; **top end,** upstate *(U.S.)*; **Eastern States,** northland, southland, west; **inland,** heartland, hinterland, interior, midland, up-country

REGIONAL *adj* areal, subregional, territorial, topographic, topographical, zonal; **local,** municipal, parochial, topical; **provincial,** cantonal, county, departmental, diocesan, divisional, eparchial, prefectural; **interstate,** intrastate, upstate *(U.S.)*; **neighbouring,** vicinal

register *n* → 1 account 2 analysis 3 computer record 4 label 5 language 6 list 7 precision 8 printwork 9 record *v* 10 adjust 11 arrive 12 be precise 13 list 14 make music 15 record

registrar *n* → 1 healer 2 judge 3 recorder

registry *n* → office

regress *v* → go back

REGRESSIVE *adj* backward, recessional *(Eccles.)*, recurrent *(Anat.)*, refluent, retroactive, retrograde, retrogressive, reverse; **reversionary,** atavistic, retrospective

regret *n* → 1 complaint 2 penitence *v* 3 be penitent 4 grieve

REGULAR *adj* equinoctial, even, isochronal, isochronous, measured, menstrual, oscillating, periodic, periodical, pulsating, recurrent, rhythmic, rhythmical, seasonal, sequential, serial, synchronous, systolic, throbbing, tidal, tidelike; **alternate,** alternant, bicyclic, cyclic, every other, peristaltic, reciprocal, revolving, rotary, rotatable, rotational, rotative, rotatory, successive

regular *n* → 1 monastic 2 soldier *adj* 3 changeless 4 customary 5 frequent 6 homogeneous 7 level 8 monastic 9 thorough 10 tidy

REGULARISE *v* gauge, normalise, right, socialise, standardise, uniformalise *(Rare)*; **stylise,** classicise, reduce to order, stereotype, style; **adjust,** align, bowdlerise, bring into line, expurgate, fit, regiment, regulate, set, set to rights

REGULARITY *n* frequency, isochronism, natural frequency, periodicity, rhythm, rhythmics, rotation, sequacity, synchronisation, synchronousness, timing, uniformity; **biorhythms,** alternation of generations, circadian rhythms, course, courses, life cycle, menses, menstrual cycle, monthly, oestrus cycle, period

REGULARLY *adv* in phase, isochronally, isochronously, like clockwork, measuredly, periodically, rhythmically, sequaciously, serially, steadily, steady, synchronously; **alter-**

nately, about, at intervals, by rote, by turns, every other day, in rotation, in turn, seasonally, to-and-fro, turn and turn about; **round,** through

regulate *v* → 1 be precise 2 control 3 regularise

regulation *n* → 1 command 2 law 3 precision 4 rule

regurgitate *v* → 1 go back 2 vomit

rehabilitate *v* → 1 be healthy 2 medicate 3 repair 4 teach

rehearse *v* → 1 prepare 2 repeat 3 study

reign *n* → 1 authority 2 period

reimburse *v* → 1 compensate 2 pay

rein *n* → 1 controlling device 2 harness

reinforce *v* → 1 increase 2 strengthen 3 supply 4 support

reinstate *v* → 1 employ 2 repair

reiterate *v* → repeat

reject *n* → 1 discard 2 rejection *v* 3 abandon 4 disuse 5 eject 6 isolate 7 refuse 8 repel 9 vomit

REJECTION *n* dismissal, heave-ho, knock-back, repudiation, repulse, the big A, unrequitedness; **cast-off,** abnegation, discard, reject, throw-out, throwaway

REJOICE *v* clap hands, exult, fling one's cap in the air, have one's heart leap for joy, hug oneself, jollify, joy, jubilate, jump for joy, make merry, thank one's lucky stars, tread on air, walk on air; **celebrate,** commemorate, jubilate, maffick *(Brit.)*; **fete,** shivaree *(U.S.)*; **triumph,** crow, exalt *(Obs.)*, gloat, glory; **carol,** gratulate *(Archaic)*, hail, hymn, sing for joy; **congratulate,** pledge, toast; **go wild,** be on the tiles, carouse, dance the night away, go to town, jollify, paint the town red, revel, roister, whoop it up; **banquet,** feast, junket, kill the fatted calf

rejoice *v* → be pleased

REJOICER *n* caroller, celebrant, celebrator, exalter *(Obs.)*, mafficker, merrymaker, reveller, roisterer, wassailer; **feaster,** bacchant, banqueter, junketer

rejoin *v* → answer

rejoinder *n* → answer

rejuvenate *v* → revive

relapse *n* → 1 illness 2 reversion *v* 3 be ill 4 go back

RELATE *v* ally, associate, connect, mutualise, tie in; **concern,** appertain to, apply to, be in respect of, have regard to, have to do with, pertain to, refer to, touch; **interrelate,** cohere, correlate; **reciprocate,** mutualise *(U.S.)*

relate *v* → narrate

RELATED *adj* affined, affinitive, akin, analogous, appendant, associated, connected, connectional, correspondent, incident, interrelated, relational, relative; **proportional,** commensurate, correlative, pro rata, proportionate; **common,** joint, shared; **correlative,** correlate *(Rare)*, interrelated, mutual, mutually related, reciprocal, reciprocative; **relevant,** applicable, apposite, appurtenant, apropos, in point, pertinent, suitable, to the point

RELATION *n* affinity, alliance, apposition, association, cognation, coherence, communality, connation, connection, correlation, correspondence, marriage, nearness, propinquity, proportionality, rapport, relativity, respondence; **compatibility,** analogousness, appositeness, compatibleness, correlativeness, relativeness; **interrelation,** intercommunion, interrelationship, reciprocality, reciprocation

relation *n* → 1 kinship 2 narrative 3 relationship 4 relative

RELATIONSHIP *n* affiliation, alliance, ascription, association, connection, filiation, habitude *(Obs.)*, liaison, relation, tie, tie-up; **transitive relation,** class inclusion; **something in common,** common denominator; **ratio,** correlation, perspective, proportion, scale; **commensuration,** percentage

RELATIVE *n* clansman, clanswoman, enate, in-law, kinsman, kinswoman, next of kin, relation, tribesman; **kin,** clan, flesh, flesh and blood, gens *(Anthrop.)*, horde, kindred, kinsfolk, kith and kin, name, parentage, people, sept, tribe *(Joc.)*; **family,** blended family, extended family, family circle, folks, gens *(Roman Hist.)*, ilk, nuclear family; **tribalist,** nepotist; **blood relation,** agnate, cognate, collateral, connection, connexion; **aunt,** aunty, great-aunt; **uncle,** grand-uncle, great-uncle; **niece,** grand-niece, great-niece; **nephew,** grand-nephew, great-nephew; **cousin,** country cousin, cousin-german, first cousin, first cousin once removed, full cousin, second cousin. *See also* PARENT; SIBLING; KINSHIP

relative *adj* → 1 comparable 2 related 3 topical

RELATIVELY *adv* according as, commensurately, in proportion, pro rata, proportionally; **reciprocally,** answerably, appositely, correlatively, in common, mutually, together

relax *v* → 1 be informal 2 be lenient 3 compose oneself 4 decrease 5 moderate 6 rest 7 soften 8 weaken

relay *n* → 1 race 2 substitute *v* 3 communicate 4 publish 5 transport

release *n* → 1 acquittal 2 death 3 liberation 4 liberty 5 permission *v* 6 display 7 forgive 8 liberate 9 reveal

re-lease *v* → lend

relegate *v* → 1 demote 2 seclude

relent *v* → 1 be lenient 2 moderate

relentless *adj* → 1 callous 2 strict 3 strong

relevant *adj* → 1 apt 2 related 3 topical

reliable *adj* → 1 faithful 2 honest

reliant *adj* → dependent

relic *n* → 1 memento 2 old people 3 remnant

relief *n* → 1 abatement 2 charity 3 help 4 hope 5 sculpture 6 substitute

relieve *v* → 1 alleviate 2 dismiss 3 ease 4 substitute

RELIGION *n* belief, church, connection, covenant, denomination, discipleship, faith, inspiration, persuasion, rule; **state religion,** established church, establishment; **theology,**

divinity, ecclesiology, eschatology, hagiography, hagiology, ontology, soteriology, theodicy

religion *n* → reverence

RELIGIOUS *adj* deistic, deistical, ditheistic, monolatrous, monotheistic, pantheistic, polytheistic, spiritual, supernaturalistic, theandric, theanthropic, theist, theistic, theocentric, tritheistic; **evangelical,** born-again, charismatic, evangelistic, gospel, kerugmatik, mystic, Pentecostal, perseverant, redemptive, redemptory; **fundamentalist,** fire-and-brimstone; **theological,** ecclesiastical, eschatological, hagiographic, ontological; **canonical,** credal, creedal, divine, ecclesiologic, ecclesiological, orthodox, patristic, subscriptive; **denominational,** schismatic, sectarian; **interdenominational,** catholic, reunionistic, subjectivistic

religious *n* → **1** monastic *adj* **2** dutiful **3** monastic **4** reverent

RELIGIOUS CEREMONY *n* celebration, ceremonial, common, procession, recession, rite, ritual, solemnities, thanksgiving; **consecration,** Alleluia, canon, celebration, collect, Communion, confiteor, epiclesis, Epistle, Eucharist, eulogia, fraction, introit, Kyrie eleison, lavabo, mystery, oblation, offertory, ordinary, preface, sacrifice, sanctification, Secret, the Lord's Supper; **initiation,** anabaptism, aspersion, baptism, christening, circumcision, confirmation, dedication, immersion, initiation ceremony, insufflation, lustrum, paedobaptism, palingenesis, simple vow, vow; **offering,** donary, flagellation, holocaust, immolation, libation, offertory, sacrifice, thank-offering, victim; **benediction,** benison *(Archaic)*, blessing, love; **last sacraments,** anointment, extreme unction, viaticum; **love feast,** agape, Chaburah, Seder; **corroboree,** bora, ceremony, tabi song *(Aborig.)*

RELIGIOUS DIGNITARY *n* beadle, church commissioner, churchwarden, elder, moderator, presbyter, proctor, sexton, sidesman, verger, vestryman, warden; **elders,** classis, colloquy, parish council, presbytery; **deputy,** acolyte, curate, impropriator, oblate, ostiary, porter, surrogate; **papal envoy,** ablegate, apostolic delegate, friary, legate, nuncio; **vicar choral,** cantor, chanter, chazzan, precentor, succentor; **pardoner,** simoniac, simonist. *See also* ECCLESIASTIC

RELIGIOUS FOLLOWER *n* believer, biblicist, churchgoer, disciple, elect, evangelical, evangelist, follower, fundamentalist, saint, sectary, subjectivist; **neophyte,** catechumen; **congregation,** flock, fold, the faithful; **layperson,** charge, churchman, churchwoman, civilian, diocesan, laic, layman, laywoman, papal knight, parishioner, secular; **lay preacher,** acolyte, lay reader; **server,** altar boy, parish clerk, sacristan; **laity,** brother, brotherhood, confraternity, regular tertiaries, secular tertiaries, sidesman, sodality, tertiary

RELIGIOUS PERSON *n* believer, churchgoer, the faithful; **dogmatist,** apologist, dogmatiser; **crusader,** bible-banger, bible-basher, biblicist, bibliolater, evangelical, evangeliser, evangelist, fundamentalist, hot-gospeller, Sal, Sallie, Salvo

relinquish *v* → abandon

relish *n* → **1** desire **2** pleasure **3** savour **4** taste *v* **5** enjoy **6** taste

reluctant *adj* → **1** dissident **2** unwilling

remain *v* → **1** be **2** continue

remainder *n* → **1** remnant *v* **2** sell **3** throw out *adj* **4** remnant

remand *n* → **1** imprisonment **2** litigation *v* **3** command **4** imprison

remark *n* → **1** attentiveness *v* **2** attend to **3** speak

remarkable *adj* → **1** astonishing **2** interesting **3** strange

remedy *n* → **1** expedient **2** medication *v* **3** counteract **4** medicate

REMEMBER *v* be mindful of, bethink oneself of *(Archaic)*, conjure up, live in the past, relive, retrace, revive, think of; **retain,** hold in mind, keep in mind, mind *(Archaic)*; **recollect,** place, recall, recognise; **reminisce,** flashback, hark back to, rake up the past; **haunt,** obsess, possess; **have a good memory,** have a memory like an elephant

remember *v* → **1** command respect **2** give **3** know **4** remind

REMEMBERING *n* anamnesis, hindsight, nostalgia, recognition, recollection, reminiscence, retrospection, review; **memorisation,** learning, mnemonics, mnemotechnics, rote learning. *See also* MEMORY

REMIND *v* admonish, jog someone's memory, refresh someone's memory, remember *(Archaic)*; **prompt,** cue, hint, jog; **be on the tip of one's tongue,** come back, recur; **evoke,** be reminiscent of, breathe of, bring back, call to mind, call up, put in mind of, recall, remind of, ring a bell, strike a chord

REMINDER *n* admonishment, admonition; **prompt,** autocue, cue card, prompter, teleprompter; **cue,** dorothy dixer, leading question; **aide-mémoire,** hurry-up, jotting, memento mori, memo, memorandum, memory-jogger, minute, mnemonic, monitor, note, phylactery *(Archaic)*, record, round robin

reminisce *v* → remember

reminiscence *n* → remembering

REMINISCENT *adj* anecdotal, narrative, nostalgic; **evocative,** redolent of, remindful; **recollective,** mnemonic, recognitive, recognitory

remiss *adj* → **1** idle **2** inactive **3** inattentive **4** neglectful

remission *n* → **1** abatement **2** acquittal **3** forgiving **4** interval **5** liberation **6** liberty **7** stoppage

remit *v* → **1** acquit **2** be lenient **3** capitulate **4** compensate **5** defer **6** forgive **7** imprison **8** liberate **9** moderate **10** pay **11** transport

remittance *n* → payment

REMNANT *n* bob, butt, counterfoil, end, fag, fag-end, frazzle, rump, shred, stub, stump, tail; **remains,** flotsam and jetsam, oddment, odds and ends, relics, relicts, residue; **remainder,** balance, carryover, hangover, hold-over *(U.S.)*, leaving, margin, odd, remanet, residual, residuum, rest, surplus; **leftovers,** orts, scrag end, scraps; **vestige,** relic, scrap, skeleton, trace; **leavings,** dross, foot, foots, grounds, heeltap, sediment, sludge, snuff, waste; **debris,** flotsam, jetsam, shipwreck, wreck, wreckage; **dregs,** alluvium, crust, deposit, dottle, draff, fur, geest, lee, lees, marc, scum, spent grains; **clippings,** borings, filings, grass clippings, paring, peelings, sawdust, scrapings, scraps, swarf; **tailings,** dump, mullock, spoil; **tartar,** wine stone; **off-cut,** cutting, docking, off-cuts; **pomace,** chum, rape, trash; **ash,** bone ash, bone earth, boneblack, calx, cinders, dust; **scruff,** salamander, scale, scoria, sow, sprue, tap-cinder; **weapon debris; cotton waste,** lint, strass; **tree stump,** stool, stub, stump; **sewage,** sewage farm, sewerage, sullage, sullage pit, waste product; **bombsite,** rubble, ruins; **earthly remains,** ashes, clay, dust, earth, mortal remains

REMNANT *adj* last, left, left behind, left over, net, odd, other, remainder, remaining, remanent, surviving; **vestigial,** residual, residuary, rudimentary

remnant *n* → **1** a few **2** discard

remonstrate *v* → **1** disagree **2** discourage **3** guide

remorse *n* → **1** penitence **2** pity

REMOTE *adj* devious, godforsaken, lonely, out, out-of-the-way, outlandish, outlying, wayback; **outback,** back-country, backblock, backwoods; **inaccessible,** unapproachable, unreachable, untouchable; **overseas,** o.s., transalpine, transoceanic, transpacific, ultramontane; **ultramundane,** beyond the universe, out of this world. *See also* DISTANT

remote *adj* → **1** secluded **2** separate **3** unsociable

REMOTELY *adv* deviously, outlandishly; **far,** a long way away, a long way off, afar, afield, deeply, distantly, far and near, far and wide, far away, in the distance, not within cooee, off to billyo, off to buggery, offshore, on the horizon; **away,** awa *(Scot.)*, distally, forth, hence *(Archaic)*, off, out, outward, recessively; **outback,** back of beyond, beyond the black stump, up the booay; **aloof,** aloofly, at arm's length, wide; **too far,** out of range, out of reach; **yonder,** over there, thither, yon *(Archaic)*, yond *(Archaic)*

REMOTE PLACE *n* back of beyond, back of Bourke, back of the black stump, Bandywallop, Bullamakanka, jumping-off place *(U.S.)*, never-never, Outer Mongolia, Timbuktu, wayback, Woop Woop, wopwops *(N.Z.)*; **end,** antipodes, ends of the earth, infinity, outer limits, Thule, ultima Thule, utmost, uttermost; **back country,** backblocks, backwoods, booay, boondocks *(U.S.)*, goat country, mallee, outback, the waybacks *(N.Z.)*, tiger country; **outpost,** back-station, out-station; **back run,** back paddock, outrun, run-off *(N.Z.)*; **offing,** outing

REMOVAL *n* abstraction, avulsion, deracination, dislodgment, eradication, exsection, extirpation, extraction, purge, remotion, remove, ripping out, shift, stripping, uprooting, withdrawal; **disinterment,** disentombment, exhumation; **obliteration,** erasure, rubbing out, wiping out; **clearance,** clean sweep, clearing, sweep; **brushing away,** Australian salute, Barcoo salute; **emptying,** drainage, unfouling, venting; **unloading,** deconsolidation, offloading, unpacking; **clear-felling,** back-burning, burning-off, bush bashing, bush-burning *(N.Z.)*, bush-falling *(N.Z.)*, cabling, chaining-off, clear-cutting, double-logging, frilling, logging, mullenising, ringbarking, scrub-cutting, scrub-rolling, scrub bashing, sucker-bashing

removalist *n* → transporter

REMOVE *v* grub out, root out, scrub, strike, strip, take away, take down, take off, thin out, uproot; **take out,** abstract, aspirate, bale out, prescind, withdraw; **disinter,** disentomb, exhume; **obliterate,** blank, blank out, erase, rub off, rub out, wipe off, wipe out; **cut out,** excide, excise, extirpate; **pull off,** nip, pick, pick out, prise, pull up, put off; **unload,** debark, deconsolidate, off-load, unpack; **get rid of,** brush aside, clear, clear away, get shot of, make a clean sweep, make away with, see the back of, ship, shuffle off, shunt, sweep away, swish off, swoop up, whisk away; **clear of,** free from, purge of, rid of; **clear-fell,** backburn, cable, chain off, clear-cut, frill, log, mullenise, ringbark

remove *n* → **1** gradation **2** removal **3** transport *v* **4** dismiss **5** extract **6** kill **7** subtract **8** transport

removed *adj* → **1** different **2** distant **3** separate

remunerate *v* → **1** compensate **2** pay

renaissance *n* → **1** innovation **2** return to normal

renal *adj* → bodily

rend *v* → separate

render *n* → **1** plaster *v* **2** be faithful to **3** coat **4** compensate **5** extract **6** liquefy **7** translate

rendezvous *n* → **1** assignation **2** position *v* **3** arrange **4** associate

renegade *n* → **1** betrayer **2** defector *v* **3** defect *adj* **4** unfaithful

renege *v* → **1** defect **2** deny

renew *v* → **1** protract **2** repeat **3** revive

renounce *n* → **1** change *v* **2** abandon **3** abstain **4** cancel **5** deny **6** refuse

renovate *v* → repair

renown *n* → **1** news **2** reputation

rent *n* → **1** break **2** gap **3** income **4** loan **5** opening *v* **6** borrow **7** buy **8** lend *adj* **9** gaping

rental *n* → income

renunciation *n* → 1 abandonment 2 cancellation 3 defection 4 denial

REPAIR *n* darn, mend, patch; **overhaul,** careenage, checkup, drop test *(Joc.)*, refit, service; **restoration,** cannibalisation, renovation, reparation, vamp; **reclamation,** innings, land reclamation, reafforestation, reclaim, rescue, retrieval, revegetation, salvage; **replenishment,** recruitment, reinforcement; **redemption,** postliminy, ransom, restitution

REPAIR *v* cannibalise, careen, cicatrise, clobber *(Obs.)*, doctor, fix, make whole, overhaul, reassemble, redintegrate, refit, restore, service, tinker; **cobble,** fox, half-sole, resole, vamp; **renovate,** bodgie up, do over, do up, fix up, freshen up, jack up *(N.Z.)*, lift, make over, reface, refurbish, revamp, touch up, vamp up; **mend,** darn, patch, piece up, reduce *(Surg.)*, sew; **reclaim,** reafforest, reforest, retrieve; **replenish,** recruit; **redeem,** ransom; **rehabilitate,** put someone on his feet, recondition, regenerate, reinstate; **revive,** bring to life, reanimate, recall *(Poetic)*, recreate, resurrect, resuscitate, revitalize, revivify

repair *n* → 1 improvement *v* 2 atone for 3 improve 4 repeat 5 travel

REPAIRER *n* fix-it man, fixer, handyman, renovator, repairman, restorer, service man; **mender,** careener, cobbler, darner, patcher, piecer, spiderman, steeplejack, tailor, tinker, vamper; **rejuvenator,** reclaimant, reclaimer, recoverer, resurrectionist, salvager; **restorative,** febrifuge, freshener, lifesaver, pick-me-up, pick-up, refresher, shot in the arm, tonic

reparation *n* → 1 compensation 2 repair

repartee *n* → 1 answer 2 eloquence 3 joke 4 talk *v* 5 answer 6 joke

repast *n* → meal

repatriate *n* → traveller

repay *v* → compensate

repeal *n* → 1 cancellation 2 denial *v* 3 cancel 4 deny

REPEAT *v* encore, parrot, replay, retake, run through again; **echo,** re-echo, resound, reverberate; **ding,** drum; **do to death,** beat into the ground, cuckoo, hammer, harp upon, thrash out; **come again,** ditto, go over, go over the same ground, quote, reword; **practise,** re-act, re-enact, reconstruct, redraft, reduplicate, rehearse, remake, reproduce; **recommence,** reappear, repair, restore; **renew,** reopen, resume; **iterate,** circulate *(Maths Obs.)*, come back to, ingeminate, recapitulate, recapture, recur, redouble, reiterate, return to, revert to, run, tautologise

repeat *n* → 1 copy 2 nostalgia 3 repetition *v* 4 activate 5 burp 6 resonate

REPEATEDLY *adv* again and again, cyclically, day by day, day in day out, in-and-in, morning noon and night, over and over, perennially, till doomsday, time and time again, without end, year after year; **afresh,** again, anew, bis, da capo, dal segno, ditto, once more, over *(Brit.)*, over again; **repetitiously,** constantly, pleonastically, tautologically

REPEL *v* avert, beat off, chase away, dispel, drive away, drive back, drive off, fight off, force away, force back, force off, frighten away, frighten off, hand off, parry, put the frighteners on *(Brit.)*, repulse, scare away, scare off, send away, stave off, stink out, ward off; **rebuff,** arsehole, cut, give the arse, give the big A, give the bum's rush, keep at a distance, keep at arm's length, see someone about his business, snub, spurn, turn away, turn down, turn one's back on; **dismiss,** bundle off, bundle out, cast away, cast off, cast out, exile, fling aside, pack off, put off, reject; **shed,** burke, ditch, doff, get rid of, give the flick, hunt, piss off, wipe

repel *v* → 1 defend 2 displease 3 refuse 4 seclude

repent *v* → 1 be penitent 2 defect *adj* 3 bottom

repercussion *n* → 1 reaction 2 resonance 3 result

repertoire *n* → agenda

repertory *n* → 1 agenda 2 storage 3 theatrical company

REPETITION *n* ingemination, iterance, iteration, recurrence, recursion, reiteration, renewal, resumption, return, series, succession; **repeat,** action replay, duplication, encore, re-enactment, re-run, reappearance, recapitulation, reconstruction, redraft, reduplication, remake, repeat performance, retake, return season; **reprise,** burden, canon, chorus, fugue, imitation, ostinato, passacaglia, recapitulation, refrain, repeat, repetend, ritornells, rondo, round; **practice,** rehearsal, rote learning, training; **twin,** clone, copy, duplicate, Xerox; **anaphora,** anadiplosis, dittography, emphasis, gemination, pleonasm, redundancy, tautology, twinning; **repetitiousness,** periodicity; **repetend,** circulating decimal *(Obs.)*, recurring decimal, repeating decimal; **ditto,** ditto marks, quotation, quote

repetition *n* → 1 copying 2 figure of speech 3 litigation

re-petition *v* → entreat

REPETITIVE *adj* ding-dong, dittographic, iterant, iterative, monotonous, pleonastic, redundant, reiterant, reiterative, repetitious, resumptive, tautological, tick tock; **repeated,** continual, habitual, incessant, invariant, perennial, reconstructive, recurrent, recurring, recursive, reduplicate, reduplicative, reiterated, return, twice-told, unvarying, usual; **echolike,** recapitulative, recapitulatory, repercussive, reverberative, reverberatory; **anaphoric,** abovementioned, aforementioned, aforesaid, cataphoric, exophoric

repine *v* → complain

replace *v* → 1 compensate 2 substitute

replenish *v* → 1 fill 2 repair 3 supply

replete *adj* → 1 full 2 satisfied

replica *n* → copy

reply *n* → 1 answer 2 justification 3 message 4 reaction 5 retaliation *v* 6 answer 7 react 8 resonate

report *n* → **1** answer **2** assessment **3** explosion **4** information **5** loud sound **6** narrative **7** news item **8** public notice **9** reputation *v* **10** appear **11** narrate **12** publicise **13** publish

reporter *n* → **1** journalist **2** storyteller

REPORT ON *v* blow the whistle on, delate, dob in, dob on, drop, drop in, give up, grass, nark, peach *(Brit.)*, put in, put someone's weights up, put the finger on, rat on, shelf, shelve, shop, sing, squeak, squeal, tell on, tip off, tip someone the wink, top off, welsh; **expose,** blow, drop a bundle

REPOSE *v* couch, lie down, prostrate, spread-eagle, stretch out; **sit,** sit up; **straddle,** sit astride, spraddle, sprawl; **kneel,** bow, curtsy, genuflect, have one's knees fold beneath one, knee *(Obs. Poetic)*, kowtow, sink; **squat,** crouch, kangaroo *(Colloq.)*; **slouch,** stoop

repose *n* → **1** composure **2** inaction **3** rest **4** sleeping *v* **5** depend on **6** die **7** recline **8** rest **9** sleep

repository *n* → storage

repossess *v* → take

reprehensible *adj* → **1** guilty **2** wrong

REPRESENT *v* allegorise, emblematise, emblemise, express, figure, illustrate, image, prefigure, stand for, symbol, symbolise, type, typify; **personify,** assume a character, characterise, imitate, impersonate, incarnate, mimic, personate, play charades, pose

represent *v* → **1** act for **2** depict **3** imitate **4** map **5** mean **6** narrate **7** perform **8** practise law **9** signify

REPRESENTATION *n* expression, symbolisation, symbolism, symbology, typology; **impersonation,** characterisation, enactment, mimesis, personation, personification; **allegory,** fable, imagery, parable; **typification,** prefiguration, prefigurement; **portrayal,** art, iconography, iconology, imagery, photography, portraiture, sculpture; **graphics,** design work, ichnography, photocopying, tracing; **cartography,** cosmography, hypsography, hypsometry; **model,** diorama, pageant, panorama, tableau, tableau vivant; **planetarium,** georama, globe

representative *n* → **1** agent **2** ambassador **3** member of parliament **4** seller **5** traveller *adj* **6** agential **7** indicative **8** sports

REPRESS *v* crush, put down, quash, quell, smother, squash, squelch, stifle, tame; **persecute,** burden, grieve *(Obs.)*, grind under, lade, oppress, trample on, tyrannise; **enslave,** enfeoff, enthral, feudalise, imperialise, mediatise, slave, thrall *(Archaic)*, yoke *(Obs.)*; **subdue,** beat down, bring down, bring someone to his knees, bring to heel, bring to terms, bring under, compel, down, kneel on, overcome, overpower, prostrate, reduce, stoop *(Archaic)*, strangle, strangulate, vanquish; **keep down,** have at one's beck and call, have by the balls, have by the short and curlies, have by the short hairs, keep on a string, keep under, put the maginnis on; **domineer,** browbeat, henpeck, overbear, overlord, override, tread on, treat like dirt, walk all over

repress *v* → **1** forget **2** prohibit **3** restrain

REPRESSED *adj* at one's beck and call, at one's feet, downtrodden, henpecked, under the thumb; **enslaved,** aggrieved, subject to, thrall *(Archaic)*; **servile,** controllable, hierodulic, prostrate, slavish, subduable, submissive, wormlike

REPRESSER *n* authoritarian, despot, oppressor, overrider, persecutor, queller, subjugator, trampler, tyranniser, tyrant; **conqueror,** coloniser, enthraller, vanquisher; **slaveholder,** enslaver, slave-trader, slaver

REPRESSION *n* subjection, subjugation; **oppression,** persecution, pressure; **subdual,** colonisation, conquest, quelling; **feudal system,** assignment system, colonialism, feudalisation, helotism, helotry, heteronomy, peonage, serfdom, serfhood, vassalage, villeinage; **slavery,** bondage, chains, enslavement, enthralment, servitude, thraldom, thrall; **slave trade,** blackbirding, corvée, forced labour, slave-trading

REPRESSIVE *adj* domineering, on top, overbearing, overpowering, possessive; **oppressive,** burdensome, despotic, grievous *(Archaic)*, persecutional, persecutive, persecutory, tyrannic, tyrannical, tyrannous; **authoritarian,** hard-handed, heavy-handed

reprieve *n* → **1** acquittal **2** forgiving **3** lenience *v* **4** acquit **5** alleviate **6** be lenient **7** forgive

REPRIMAND *n* admonishment, lecture, rebuke, reproach, reproof, reproval, schooling *(Archaic)*, scolding, upbraiding; **tongue-lashing,** a flea in one's ear, a kick in the pants, a piece of one's mind, bagging, blast, chip, counterblast, dressing-down, earful, jaw, lashing, pasting, rating, razz, roast, roasting, rocket, rub, scorcher, serve, slam, slap, talking-to, the rounds of the kitchen, the treatment, trimmings, wigging *(Brit.)*; **tirade,** diatribe, jeremiad, philippic; **attack,** broadside, onslaught. *See also* DISAPPROVAL; BOO

reprimand *v* → scold

reprisal *n* → **1** punishment **2** retaliation

reproach *n* → **1** accusation **2** denigration **3** imputation **4** reprimand *v* **5** disgrace **6** scold

reprobate *n* → **1** immoral person **2** outsider *v* **3** scold *adj* **4** immoral

REPRODUCE *v* breed, procreate, propagate; **beget,** bring forth, engender, father, generate, get, mother, sire; **lay,** oviposit, ovulate, spawn, spore; **fertilise,** cross-fertilise, cross-pollinate, fecundate, pollen, pollinate, superfetate; **breed,** backcross, clone, crossbreed, duplicate, grade, grow, hybridise, inbreed, interbreed, intercross, milt, mongrelise, multiply, nick, outbreed, propagate; **graft,** engraft, inarch, layer; **implant,** nidate. *See also* CONCEIVE; GIVE BIRTH

reproduce *v* → 1 copy 2 flower 3 imitate 4 repeat

REPRODUCTION *n* bearing, engenderment, generation, increase, procreation, propagation, pullulation; **sexual reproduction,** allogamy, amphimixis, autogamy, cleistogamy, entomophily, exogamy, gamogenesis, hydrophily, isogamy, karyogamy, oogamy, syngamy, syngenesis, xenogamy, zoogamy; **biogenesis,** cainogenesis, palingenesis *(Obs.)*; **neoteny,** paedogenesis; **asexual reproduction,** agamogenesis, apogamy, apomixis, blastogenesis, duplication, fission, gemmation, parthenogenesis, schizogenesis, vegetativeness, virgin birth; **maturation,** abstriction *(Bot.)*, gametogenesis, heterospory, oogenesis, ovulation, spermatogenesis, sporogenesis, sporogony; **digenesis,** metagenesis; **epigenesis,** germ theory, pangenesis, preformation; **cell-division,** crossing over, crossover, cytogenesis, cytogenetics, cytokinesis, haplosis, meiosis, metaphase, mitosis, phase, prophase, synapsis; **oestrous cycle,** heat, rut. *See also* CONCEPTION; PREGNANCY; BIRTH

reproof *n* → reprimand

reprove *v* → 1 disprove 2 scold

re-prove *v* → authenticate

REPTILE *n* reptilian; **snake,** Joe Blake; **lizard,** saurian

reptile *n* → 1 bad person 2 flatterer 3 unpleasant person *adj* 4 reptilian

republic *n* → nation

republican *n* → political ideologist

repudiate *v* → 1 abandon 2 be unable to pay 3 cancel 4 deny 5 refuse

repugnant *adj* → 1 hateful 2 incongruous 3 unpleasant

repulse *n* → 1 losing 2 rejection 3 repulsion *v* 4 refuse 5 repel

REPULSION *n* antipathy, aversion *(Obs.)*, dislike, distaste, repellence; **dismissal,** brush-off, cold shoulder, cut, rebuff, repulse, snub, spurning

repulsive *adj* → 1 ugly 2 unpleasant

REPUTABILITY *n* creditableness, respectability, respectableness, worthiness; **exaltedness,** augustness, illustration *(Rare)*, illustriousness, venerability, venerableness; **majesty,** dignity, gloriousness, grandeur, impressiveness, splendidness, splendour, stateliness; **brilliance,** dazzle, halo, lustre, radiance

REPUTABLE *adj* admirable, considerable, estimable, honourable, of good reputation, respectable, respected, valued, well-thought-of; **eminent,** celebrated, distingué, distinguished, exalted, great, illustrious, important, pre-eminent, prestigious, prominent, splendid, splendorous, star, venerable, worthy; **special,** premium, prestige; **noble,** august, dignified, glorious, grand, great, haughty *(Archaic)*, impressive, lofty, lordly, majestic, Olympian, princely, proud, stately, sublime, uplifted

REPUTATION *n* account, attribute *(Obs.)*, character, conceit *(Archaic)*, esteem, estimation, memory, name, odour, regard, report, repute, store, value, worth; **rank,** footing, form, position, standing, station, status, stock; **good reputation,** credit, distinction, good name, good report, good repute, high repute, honour, worship *(Archaic)*; **renown,** fame, famousness, mark, note, notedness, noteworthiness, notoriety; **importance,** altitude, consequence, consideration, distinction, eminence, pre-eminence, superiority; **prestige,** cachet, eclat, face, kudos; **glory,** exaltation, stardom

repute *n* → reputation

REQUEST *n* claim, demand, requisition, ultimatum; **cadge,** bite, hum, sting, touch; **begging letter,** agony column, classified ad, personal column, want ad

request *n* → 1 command 2 insistence *v* 3 entreat

requiem *n* → funeral rites

require *v* → 1 command 2 desire 3 entreat 4 impose 5 insist on 6 necessitate

requisite *n* → 1 necessities *adj* 2 necessary

requisition *n* → 1 command 2 imposition 3 insistence 4 necessities 5 request *v* 6 impose 7 insist on

requite *v* → compensate

REQUITER *n* indemnifier, redresser, restorer, satisfier; **penitent,** atoner, expiator, mourner *(U.S.)*, purger

rescind *v* → 1 cancel 2 deny

rescue *n* → 1 repair *v* 2 alleviate 3 liberate

research *n* → 1 investigation *v* 2 investigate *adj* 3 questioning

resemble *v* → 1 be similar 2 compare

reservation *n* → 1 dwelling 2 exclusion 3 holding 4 qualification 5 unwillingness

reserve *n* → 1 dwelling 2 field 3 formality 4 modesty 5 qualification 6 reticence 7 serviceman 8 solitude 9 storage 10 unsociability *v* 11 be reticent 12 disuse 13 hold

reserved *adj* → 1 formal 2 modest 3 restricted 4 unsociable 5 unwilling

reserve price *n* → cost

reservoir *n* → 1 basin 2 lake 3 storage

reside *v* → inhabit

residence *n* → dwelling

RESIDENT *adj* indwelling, quartered, residentiary; **native,** aboriginal, autochthonous, indigenous; **first-generation,** currency, native-born; **home,** domestic, local; **migrant,** alien, ethnic, naturalised; **parasitic,** entophytic, entozoan, entozoic, epizoic, inquiline, inquilinous; **commensal,** symbiotic; **aerial,** arboreal, arenicolous, epigeal, fenny, geophilous, marine, riparian, terrestrial, terricolous

resident *n* → 1 ambassador 2 healer 3 inhabitant *adj* 4 essential

residue *n* → remnant

RESIGN *v* bow out, chuck it in, give the tube away *(Shearing)*, go into retirement, leave, quit, retire, roll over *(Politics)*, sign off, snatch one's time, step down, take off, tender one's resignation, vacate a position; **abdicate,** give up the throne, lay down the burden of office

resign *v* → back out
re-sign *v* → label
resigned *adj* → assenting
resilient *adj* → **1** healthy **2** pliable
resist *n* → **1** conservation *v* **2** abstain **3** be inactive **4** oppose
resistance *n* → **1** defence **2** dislike **3** dissidence **4** electricity **5** mutiny
Resistance *n* → secret society
resolute *adj* → **1** faithful **2** serious **3** uncompromising
resolution *n* → **1** faithfulness **2** judgment **3** persistence **4** reflection **5** separation **6** simplification **7** wilfulness
resolve *n* → **1** persistence *v* **2** choose **3** clarify **4** determine **5** discriminate **6** see **7** simplify **8** solve
RESONANCE *n* fullness, fullness of tone, hollowness, resonation, reverberation, rotundity, rotundness; **echo,** re-echo, repercussion, replication; **plangency,** sonority, sonorousness, vibrancy
RESONANT *adj* echoic, echolike, repercussive, resounding, reverberant, reverberative, reverberatory; **sonorous,** fruity, gonglike, plummy, rotund, round, sounding, vibrant, voiceful; **plangent,** loud, reboant, wiry; **hollow,** cavernous, sepulchral; **rumbly,** rolling, stertorous, thundering, thunderous
resonant *adj* → **1** fluttery **2** loud
RESONATE *v* resound, reverberate, ring out; **echo,** re-echo, re-sound, redouble, repeat *(Horol.)*, reply, revoice
RESONATOR *n* cavity resonator, echo chamber, echo unit, reverberation unit, reverberator, rhumbatron; **clacker,** chimer, clicker, honker, hummer, rattler, thrummer; **bell,** carillon, chime, cowbell, sacring bell, shark bell, sleighbell, tenor, tom, treble; **clapper,** tongue; **alarum,** buzzer
resort *n* → **1** expedient **2** hotel
re-sort *v* → order
resound *v* → **1** be loud **2** make history **3** publicise **4** repeat **5** resonate
re-sound *v* → resonate
resource *n* → **1** competence **2** expedient **3** help **4** opportunity
resourceful *adj* → **1** competent **2** opportunist
RESPECT *v* consider highly, esteem, have a high opinion of, hold in high esteem, hold in high regard, honour, regard, revere, reverence, think highly of, think much of, think well of, weigh *(Obs.)*; **idolise,** adore, hallow, hero-worship, look up to, venerate, worship; **prize,** cherish, love, take to one's bosom, treasure; **fear,** dread *(Obs.)*, hold in awe
respect *n* → **1** courtesy **2** high regard **3** reverence
RESPECTABILITY *n* admirableness, respectableness, venerability, venerableness; **awesomeness,** dreadfulness, fearfulness, redoubtableness; **estimableness,** value, worth, worthiness
respectable *adj* → **1** great **2** highly regarded **3** reputable
RESPECTER *n* commemorator, honourer, observer, tributary, tributer, valuer, venerator; **honourer,** adorer, fan club, genuflector, hero-worshipper, idoliser, kowtower, saluter
RESPECTFULLY *adv* deferentially, regardfully; **in deference to,** with all respect, with respect; **adoringly,** piously, worshipfully
respective *adj* → **1** particular **2** shared
respiration *n* → breathing
respire *v* → **1** absorb **2** be relieved **3** breathe
respite *n* → **1** deferment **2** interval **3** rest **4** stoppage *v* **5** alleviate **6** stop
resplendent *adj* → **1** beautiful **2** bright
respond *v* → **1** answer **2** behave **3** feel emotion **4** react
respondent *n* → **1** accused **2** answerer **3** litigant
response *n* → **1** answer **2** behaviour **3** reaction **4** retaliation
responsibility *n* → **1** accountability **2** job **3** obligation
responsible *adj* → **1** obligated **2** sane
responsive *adj* → **1** emotional **2** helpful **3** influenced **4** reactive
REST *n* bange, camp, ease, leisure, loaf, Maori P.T. *(N.Z. Colloq.)*, relaxation, spinebash, spinebashing, vacancy *(Obs.)*; **lull,** abeyance, cessation, fallow, interlude, pause, recess, respite, spell; **break,** blow, boil-up, breath, breather, breathing space, half-time, loll *(Archaic)*, nick, pit stop, pull-in, sit-down, time-out; **calm,** equilibrium, peace, quiet, quietude, reposal, repose; **calmness,** composedness, composure, downiness, easefulness, heart's ease, leisureliness, poise, quietness, reposefulness, restfulness; **sick leave,** m.d.o. *(N.Z. Colloq.)*, sickie; **meal break,** brew-up, coffee break, dinnertime, lemons *(Sport)*, lunch hour, lunchtime, orange time, playlunch, playtime, smoko, tea-break
REST *v* compose oneself, fallow, lull, quiet, quieten, settle, sit; **have a rest,** bange, breathe, camp, curl up, die down, have a break, have a spell, lie down, lie fallow, pause, put one's feet up, recess, settle down, sit down, spell, take a seat; **relax,** ease, unbend, unbrace, wind down; **take it easy,** coast along, hang loose, lie at ease, linger, live on one's fat, rest on one's laurels, rest on one's oars; **lie at rest,** couch, lair, loll, perch, recline, repose, roost, spinebash; **pause,** boil the billy, take five; **holiday,** camp, flex, flex off, get away from it all, shut up shop, vacation
rest *n* → **1** imprisonment **2** inaction **3** interruption **4** interval **5** musical score **6** peace **7** remnant **8** silence **9** sleeping **10** stand **11** support *v* **12** be inactive **13** be silent **14** continue **15** die **16** do easily **17** farm **18** idle **19** position **20** sleep **21** stop
RESTAURANT *n* B.Y.O., bevery, bistro, brasserie, buffet, buffet car *(Railways)*, caf, cafe, cafeteria, canteen, chophouse *(Brit. U.S.)*, coffee bar, coffee house, coffee shop, diner, dining car *(Railways)*, dining hall,

dining room, eatery, eating house, el cheapo, greasy spoon, grillroom, hash house, inn *(Brit.)*, joint, luncheonette, meals on wheels, pizzeria, pull-in *(Brit.)*, refectory, restaurant car, road house, self-service, snack bar, soda fountain *(U.S.)*, soup kitchen, steakhouse, takeaway, tavern, tearoom, teashop *(Brit.)*, trattatoria

RESTER *n* camper, holiday-maker, lady of leisure, lingerer, loller, lotus eater, relaxer, spinebasher

restful *adj* → resting

RESTFULLY *adv* at ease *(Mil.)*, at rest, easefully, reposefully; **calmly,** composedly, leisurely, quietly, soothingly; **at leisure,** at one's leisure, off, off duty

RESTING *adj* still; **fallow,** off, off-duty; **restful,** leisured, leisurely; **calm,** composed, poised, possessed; **sabbatical,** ferial, holiday

restitution *n* → **1** compensation **2** repair

restive *adj* → **1** badly-behaved **2** stubborn **3** unmanageable

restless *adj* → **1** awake **2** badly-behaved **3** discontented **4** excitable **5** turbulent

RESTORATIVE *adj* recreational, redintegrative, refreshing, regenerative, rejuvenescent, reparative; **plastic,** anaplastic *(Surg.)*

restore *v* → **1** compensate **2** medicate **3** repair **4** repeat **5** take

RESTRAIN *v* bate, button down, chastise *(Archaic)*, check, circumscribe, clip someone's wings, constrain, control, curb, detain, enjoin *(Law)*, hinder, hobble, hopple, stop, tether; **repress,** bite back, bottle up, keep back, put down, sit on, stifle, strangle, suppress; **hold back,** choke, contain, hold in, keep down, rein back, rein in; **silence,** burke, gag, guillotine *(Parl. Proc.)*, muzzle; **chain,** collar, enchain, enfetter, fetter, gyve, handcuff, jess *(Falconry)*, leg-rope, manacle, put in irons, shackle, trammel; **bail,** bail up, crib, pillory, stock *(Obs.)*; **bit,** bridle, curb, halter; **tie up,** astrict, bind, cord, gird, hogtie, pinion, rope, swaddle, truss, wire; **anchor,** cast anchor, skid, stay

restrain *v* → **1** be reticent **2** control **3** discourage **4** imprison **5** moderate

RESTRAINER *n* binder, inhibiter, retainer; **controller,** constrainer, limiter, obstructionist, stinter, withholder

RESTRAINING *adj* binding, inhibitory, limitative, restrictive; **repressive,** inhibiting, suppressive

RESTRAINING ORDER *n* covenant, D-notice, embargo, injunction *(Law)*, patent, prohibition, tail, writ; **gag,** guillotine *(Parl. Proc.)*

RESTRAIN ONESELF *v* bite one's lip, get a hold on oneself, hold one's horses, let sleeping dogs lie, pull one's punches, refrain; **play gooseberry**

RESTRAINT *n* astriction, censorship, comstockery *(U.S.)*, containment, control, inhibition, repression, restriction, suppression; **limitation,** clampdown, rationing, squeeze, stint, stranglehold; **self-control,** moderation; **bondage,** binding, enchainment; **curfew,** custody, detainment, detention, tuition *(Archaic)*

restraint *n* → **1** composure **2** discourager **3** imprisonment **4** moderation **5** restraints

RESTRAINTS *n* ball and chain, bands, bilbo, bracelet, chains, darbies *(Prison Colloq.)*, fetters, gyves, handcuffs, hobble, hobblechain, manacle, nippers, shackle, tether, trammel; **pillory,** bail, crib, stocks, trave; **restraint,** bind, bond, brake, chain, check, constraint, cramp, curb, dead hand, stop; **keeper,** keeping, key, sprag, sprig, tie; **doorstop,** chock, skid; **roofguard,** snowguard; **rail,** fiddle *(Naut.)*, throatlatch, tug

RESTRICT *v* confine, constrict, contain, cramp, embargo, ground, inhibit, stop, withhold; **limit,** peg, ration, stint, straiten

RESTRICTED *adj* constrained, limited; **repressed,** hidebound, pent-up; **bound,** affined *(Obs.)*, confined, corded, detained, earthbound, fast, fenced-in, housebound, icebound, imprisoned, jessed, stormbound; **restrained,** discreet, low-key, low-profile, measured, reserved

RESULT *n* effect, ensemble, resultant, turnout; **consequence,** apodosis, attendant, consequent, bottom line, fallout, flowthrough, issue, legacy, outcome, outgrowth, pay-off, repercussion, side-effect; **conclusion,** crystallisation, end, event, foregone conclusion, realisation, redound, termination; **sequel,** after-effect, aftermath, aftertaste, sequence, sequent, train; **development,** elaboration, evolution

RESULT *v* end, pan out, terminate in, turn out; **follow,** attend, ensue, proceed from; **emanate,** issue from

result *n* → **1** coming after *v* **2** follow

RESULTANT *adj* appendant, attendant, consecutive, consequent, consequential, flowthrough, sequent, sequential, terminational, terminative; **derivative,** derivate, secondary; **emanative,** emanatory

résumé *n* → abridgment

resumé *n* → translation

resume *v* → **1** protract **2** repeat **3** start **4** take

resurgent *adj* → living

resurrect *v* → **1** live **2** repair **3** use

resuscitate *v* → **1** medicate **2** repair

retail *v* → **1** disperse **2** noise abroad **3** sell *adv* **4** commercially

retain *v* → **1** hold **2** protract **3** remember

retainer *n* → **1** income **2** restrainer **3** servant

RETALIATE *v* fight back, give as good as one gets, make payment, pay off, pay out, reciprocate, retort, return enemy fire, return the compliment, riposte, take the law into one's own hands, turn on; **get even with,** call it quits, fix someone, get back at, get one's own back, have someone's guts for garters, pay back, pay back in the same coin, pay off a score, pay off old scores, settle a debt, settle a score, square off with, turn the tables on; **re-**

venge, avenge, have revenge, pay a debt, venge *(Archaic)*, vindicate *(Archaic)*

retaliate *v* → attack

RETALIATION *n* avengement, paying back, quid pro quo, reciprocation, reciprocity, reprisal, retorsion, retortion, retribution, return, revenge, utu *(N.Z.)*, vendetta; **vengefulness,** revanchism, revengefulness, vengeance, vindictiveness, wrath; **counter-terrorism,** counterblast; **reply,** response, retort, riposte; **tit for tat,** a dose of one's own medicine, a game that two can play, a kick in the arse, a Roland for an Oliver, a taste of one's own medicine, an eye for an eye, blow for blow, give-and-take, talion, the biter bit; **unwritten law,** lex talionis

RETALIATORY *adj* reciprocal, recriminatory, retributive, revengeful, vengeful; **returnable,** requitable

retard *n* → 1 lateness *v* 2 defer 3 hinder

retarded *adj* → 1 psychologically disturbed 2 slow 3 stupid

retch *n* → 1 burp *v* 2 vomit

retentive *adj* → holding

RETICENCE *n* aloofness, low profile, undemonstrativeness, understatement; **speechlessness,** dumbness, silence, taciturnity, unexpressiveness; **reserve,** backwardness, bashfulness, shyness; **secrecy,** closeness, incommunicativeness, secretiveness

RETICENT *adj* aloof, low-key, low-profile, quiet, self-contained, undemonstrative, underplayed, unexpressive; **shy,** backward, bashful, in the wings; **tight-lipped,** close, close-lipped, dark, incommunicative, noncommittal, secret, secretive; **taciturn,** incommunicative, laconic, monosyllabic, of few words; **silent,** dumb, inarticulate, speechless, tongue-tied

reticent *adj* → 1 silent 2 unsociable

retina *n* → eye

retinue *n* → 1 sequence 2 servant

retire *v* → 1 depart 2 disuse 3 go back 4 lie low 5 resign 6 sleep

retired *adj* → 1 aged 2 disused 3 peaceful

retiring *adj* → 1 modest 2 unsociable

retort *n* → 1 accusation 2 answer 3 bottle 4 retaliation *v* 5 answer 6 retaliate

retrace *v* → remember

retract *v* → 1 cancel 2 contract 3 deny 4 go back

retreat *n* → 1 hiding 2 hiding place 3 peace 4 psychotherapy 5 refuge 6 seclusion 7 timepiece 8 unsociability *v* 9 depart 10 go back 11 lie low 12 make peace 13 seclude

retrench *v* → 1 decrease 2 defend 3 dismiss 4 subtract

retribution *n* → 1 punishment 2 retaliation

retrieve *v* → 1 compensate 2 repair

retriever *n* → hunter

retroactive *adj* → 1 past 2 regressive

retrograde *v* → 1 deteriorate *adj* 2 deteriorated 3 regressive

retrospect *n* → nostalgia

retrospective *n* → 1 commemoration *adj* 2 past 3 regressive

return *n* → 1 account 2 answer 3 compensation 4 gratefulness 5 payment 6 profit 7 reaction 8 record 9 repetition 10 retaliation *v* 11 answer 12 compensate 13 elect 14 go back 15 pay *adj* 16 repetitive

RETURN TO NORMAL *n* recovery, reestablishment, regression, rehabilitation, reinstatement, remitter, return to normal; **revival,** reanimation, rebirth, recreation, renaissance, resurgence, resurrection, resuscitation; **renewal,** Indian summer, instauration, redintegration, refreshment, regeneracy, regeneration, rejuvenation, rejuvenescence, second youth, urban renewal

reunion *n* → 1 clique 2 party

revalue *v* → 1 appraise 2 circulate 3 increase 4 measure

REVEAL *v* come out with, disclose, discover *(Archaic)*, display, enucleate, impart, shew *(Archaic)*, show, unfold, unroll; **expose,** bare, bring out, bring to light, disinter, flush out, give air to, make public, mark, open, publish, rake up, root up, show up, smoke out, take the lid off, turn up, unbrick, uncase, uncloak, unclothe, uncover, unlock; **release,** compromise *(Mil.)*, declassify; **enlighten,** undeceive; **unmask,** give the lie to, nail, reveal in true colours, strip off a disguise, unveil; **blurt out,** blow the gaff, blunder, drop a bundle, let on, let out, let slip, let the cat out of the bag, noise off, shoot off one's mouth, spill the beans, tell; **blab,** babble, blabber, give away, sneak, spill, split on, tattle, tell on, tell tales, tell tales out of school, tittle-tattle. *See also* CONFESS

reveal *v* → 1 display 2 publish

REVEALED *adj* bare, exposed, full-frontal, unconcealed; **current,** known, reported; **professed,** confessed, ostensible, ostensive, self-confessed; **public,** open, semipublic

REVEALER *n* betrayer, discloser, displayer, divulger, enlightener, expresser, imparter, oracle, revelationist, revelator, undeceiver, unmasker; **confessor,** admitter, unbosomer; **telltale,** blabber, blabbermouth, blower, blunderer, grass, ratter, sieve, stool pigeon, supergrass, tattler, tittle-tattler

REVEALING *n* communication, disclosure, divulgement, divulgence, enucleation, impartation, impartment, intimation; **exposure,** disinterment, overexposure, unfoldment, unveiling; **revelation,** apocalypse, discovery, enlightenment, epiphany; **confession,** admission, shrift *(Archaic)*; **revealment,** daylight, publicity; **exposedness,** bareness, openness

REVEALING *adj* indicative, telltale; **revelatory,** apocalyptic, explanatory, oracular; **confessional,** confessionary *(Eccles.)*; **indiscreet,** gossipy, leaky, tattletale

reveille *n* → 1 signal 2 timepiece 3 waking

revel *n* → 1 party *v* 2 rejoice

REVELATION *n* a foot in the mouth, betrayal, Freudian slip, give-away, indiscretion, telltale sign; **eye-opener,** bibful, exposé, startling disclosure; **leak,** blab, leakage, tattle, verbal; **whole truth,** clean breast

revelation *n* → 1 finding 2 revealing

revenge *n* → 1 retaliation *v* 2 retaliate

revenue *n* → 1 funds 2 income 3 profit

reverberate *v* → 1 heat 2 repeat 3 resonate

REVERE *v* adore, reverence, venerate, worship; **fear God,** keep the faith

revere *v* → 1 respect 2 worship

REVERENCE *n* adoration, dedication, devotedness, devotement, devotion, devoutness, faith, honour, love, respect, trust, veneration; **piety,** cardinal virtues, godliness, good life, goodness, pietism, piousness, religiousness, righteousness, services, virtue; **prayerfulness,** communion, contemplation, meditation, mysticism, religion *(Obs.)*, religiosity; **religious frenzy,** beatitude, ecstasy, enthusiasm, gift of tongues, jerks *(U.S.)*, theopathy, zealotry; **pilgrimage,** hajj; **ecclesiasticism,** bibliolatry, churchmanship, fundamentalism, orthodoxy; **crusading spirit,** missionary zeal; **spirituality,** earnestness, inwardness, otherworldliness, spiritualism

reverend *n* → 1 ecclesiastic *adj* 2 ecclesiastic 3 highly regarded 4 worshipful

REVERENT *adj* believing, devoted, devotional, devout, faithful, god-fearing, godly, pious, prayerful, religious; **spiritual,** contemplative, meditative, spiritualist, spiritualistic, supermundane, vatic

reverie *n* → 1 delusion 2 inattentiveness 3 musical piece

reverse *n* → 1 contrast 2 losing 3 misfortune 4 opposite meaning 5 opposite position 6 rear *v* 7 cancel 8 contrast 9 go back 10 swerve *adj* 11 opposing 12 rear 13 regressive

REVERSION *n* atavism, backsliding, degeneration, devolution *(Biol.)*, relapse

revert *v* → go back

review *n* → 1 analysis 2 assessment 3 commentary 4 inspection 5 investigation 6 look 7 magazine 8 nostalgia 9 remembering *v* 10 assess 11 discourse 12 examine 13 inquire into 14 investigate 15 study 16 think

revile *v* → 1 hold in low regard 2 slander

revise *n* → 1 change *v* 2 change 3 correct 4 memorise 5 study

revival *n* → 1 innovation 2 living 3 return to normal 4 staging 5 use

REVIVE *v* be restored, come to life, get one's second wind, make a comeback, pick up, recover, rejuvenate, renew, return to life, return to normal

revive *v* → 1 activate 2 innovate 3 live 4 make happy 5 medicate 6 remember 7 repair 8 use

revoke *v* → cancel

REVOLT *v* agitate, mutiny, rebel, rise up, rise up in arms, storm the barricades

revolt *n* → 1 hate 2 mutiny 3 revolution *v* 4 displease 5 provoke hatred

revolting *adj* → 1 hateful 2 revolutionary 3 sickening 4 unpleasant

REVOLUTION *n* blood in the streets, counter-revolution, coup d'état, insurgence, insurgency, insurrection, mutiny, palace revolution, rebellion, revolt, riot, rising, subversion, upheaval, uprising

revolution *n* → 1 astronomic point 2 change 3 mutiny 4 rotation

REVOLUTIONARY *n* activist, agent provocateur, agitator, counter-revolutionary, dynamiter, insurrectionary, insurrectionist, malcontent, rebel, rioter, subversive, subverter

REVOLUTIONARY *adj* counter-revolutionary, subversive; **rebellious,** insurgent, insurrectional, insurrectionary, malcontent, rebel, revolting

revolutionary *n* → 1 anarchist 2 innovator 3 political ideologist

revolutionise *v* → change

revolve *v* → 1 alternate 2 rotate

revolver *n* → gun

revue *n* → entertainment

revulsion *n* → hate

reward *n* → 1 compensation 2 gift 3 gratefulness 4 incentive 5 income *v* 6 compensate 7 pay

rewarding *adj* → satisfactory

rhapsody *n* → 1 accumulation 2 musical piece 3 poetry

rhetoric *n* → 1 bombast 2 eloquence *adj* 3 figurative

rheumatism *n* → cramp

rhombus *n* → 1 solid 2 square

rhubarb *n* → 1 commotion 2 nonsense

RHYME *n* alliteration, alliterativeness, assonance, clink, crambo *(Derog.)*, eye rhyme, female rhyme, feminine rhyme, half rhyme, internal rhyme, masculine rhyme, onomatopoeia, perfect rhyme, rhyme scheme

rhyme *n* → 1 figure of speech 2 poetry 3 similarity 4 sound *v* 5 versify

RHYTHM *n* beat, lilt, number *(Obs.)*, swing, tempo, time; **rhythm type,** cross rhythm, hemiola, isorhythm, polyrhythm, singsong, syncopation; **common time,** common measure, duple rhythm, measure, quadruple time, simple time, triple measure, triple rhythm, triple time, triplex; **up-beat,** anacrusis, arsis; **down-beat,** thesis; **syncopator,** timekeeper; **metronome**

rhythm *n* → 1 figure of speech 2 regularity

RHYTHMICAL *adj* driving, eurythmic, measured, rhythmic, singsong, up-tempo; **metronomic; iambic,** anapaestic, dactylic, ithyphallic, spondaic, tribrachic, trochaic

rib *n* → 1 bookbinding 2 book part 3 chest 4 gun part 5 layer 6 spouse *v* 7 annoy 8 mock 9 sew 10 strengthen 11 support

ribald *n* → 1 vulgarian *adj* 2 obscene 3 vulgar

ribbon *n* → 1 belt 2 emblem 3 line 4 tape *v* 5 cut 6 separate

rich *adj* → 1 abundant 2 colourful 3 decorative 4 expensive 5 fertile 6 fragrant 7 great 8 nonsensical 9 showy 10 tasteful 11 tasty 12 wealthy

riches *n* → wealth
rick *v* → harvest
rickets *n* → malnutrition
rickety *adj* → **1** irregular **2** ugly
ricochet *n* → **1** impact **2** reaction *v* **3** react
riddle *n* → **1** code **2** disguise **3** figure of speech *v* **4** oversupply **5** puzzle **6** slander
RIDE *v* canter, gallop, hack, jogtrot, pace, prance, rack, single-foot, trot
ride *n* → **1** path *v* **2** drive **3** move **4** predominate **5** top
RIDER *n* buckjumper, cavalier, cavalry, equestrian, horseman, horsewoman, jockey, post, postboy, postilion, postrider
rider *n* → **1** law **2** postscript **3** qualification
RIDGE *n* anticline, arris, bank, carina, costa, embankment, isocline, knurl, razorback, ripple, ripple-mark, stop-ridge, striation, strix; **corrugation,** carination; **corrugated iron,** corrugated board, corrugated paper; **corduroy road**
ridge *n* → **1** atmospheric pressure **2** line **3** mountain **4** top *v* **5** fold *adj* **6** correct **7** true
ridicule *n* → **1** low regard **2** mockery *v* **3** insult **4** mock
ridiculous *adj* → **1** foolish **2** nonsensical **3** stupid
rife *adj* → **1** current **2** flooding **3** frequent **4** general **5** many
rifle *n* → **1** furrow **2** gun *v* **3** cut **4** furrow **5** rob
rift *n* → **1** break **2** gap **3** opening *v* **4** open up **5** separate
rig *n* → **1** carriage **2** clothes **3** equipment **4** machine **5** truck *v* **6** act unfairly **7** be promiscuous **8** fake **9** swindle
rigging *n* → **1** cord **2** equipment
RIGHT *n* ; **starboard** bowside, off side; **recto; forehand; off; dexterity,** dextrality, righthandedness; **righthander**
RIGHT *adj* dexter, dextral, right-hand; **right-handed,** dexterous, dextral; **forehand,** forehanded; **off; starboard,** offside, rightward
RIGHT *adv* dextrally, on the right, on the starboard bow, rightwards, starboard
right *n* → **1** correctness **2** entitlement **3** hit **4** morality **5** political spectrum **6** stocks and shares *v* **7** deal fairly **8** erect **9** regularise **10** tidy *adj* **11** apt **12** conservative **13** correct **14** easy **15** equipped **16** fair **17** front **18** good **19** healthy **20** precise **21** satisfactory **22** straight **23** true *adv* **24** aptly **25** now **26** straight **27** well
righteous *adj* → correct
RIGHTFUL *adj* entitled, just, prerogative, titled, true, welcome; **jural,** prescriptible, prescriptive, usufructuary
RIGHT OF WAY *n* access, appurtenance *(Law)*, easement, ingress, ingression
RIGHTS *n* claim, droit, entitlement, jus, lien, prescription *(Law)*, say, title, toll *(Obs.)*; **authority,** parliamentary privilege, power of appointment, precedence, prerogative, privilege; **charter,** bill of rights, muniments; **civil rights,** civil liberty, freedom, human rights, individualism; **franchise,** ballot, secret ballot, suffragetism, universal suffrage; **birthright,** heirship, inheritance *(Obs.)*, primogeniture, ultimogeniture; **royal prerogative,** droit de seigneur, escheatage, preference, regalia, regality; **state rights,** land rights; **specific claim,** ancient light, angary, beach claim *(Mining)*, cabotage, crop lien, fishery, profit a prendre, reef claim, right of search, servitude, trackage *(U.S. Railways)*, turbary, uti possidetis, water right; **title deed,** strata title, Torrens title, user *(Law)*, usufruct
rigid *adj* → **1** callous **2** hard **3** straight **4** strict
rigmarole *n* → **1** nonsense **2** tangle
rigor mortis *n* → death
rigour *n* → **1** coldness **2** difficulty **3** fever **4** hardness **5** sombreness
rile *v* → **1** annoy **2** irritate
rim *n* → **1** circle **2** edge *v* **3** edge **4** have sex **5** roll
rind *n* → **1** coating **2** covering **3** outside **4** skin
RING *n* annulet, annulus, areola, areole, circle; **band,** belt, collar, girdle, headband, ruff, torques *(Zool.)*; **garland,** daisy-chain, wreath; **bracelet,** bangle, chaplet, circlet, circus *(Obs.)*, cirque *(Poetic)*, coronet, crown, earring, garland *(Naut.)*, keeper, ringlet, wristlet; **hoop,** quoit *(Games)*, rubber ring; **loop,** noose, piston ring, terry *(Textiles)*, washer; **grummet,** gudgeon, terret, traveller *(Naut.)*; **corona,** halo, nimbus *(Art)*, photosphere. *See also* CIRCLE; WHEEL
RING *v* carillon, chime, dong, knell, knoll *(Archaic)*, ring the changes, toll; **jingle,** chink, clank, clink, jangle, tinkle; **clang,** clangour, ding; **twang,** ping, plunk, sing, thrum; **trumpet,** blare, honk, trump; **trill,** vibrate
ring *n* → **1** buttocks **2** button **3** corporation **4** gambling hall **5** jewellery **6** racecourse **7** ringing **8** sportsground **9** telecommunications *v* **10** be loud **11** clean **12** enclose **13** publicise **14** rotate **15** shear **16** signal **17** telephone
ringbark *v* → **1** cut **2** remove
ringer *n* → **1** expert **2** faker **3** farmhand **4** shearer **5** the best
ring in *v* → **1** publicise **2** substitute
ring-in *n* → **1** anomaly **2** substitute
RINGING *n* clang, clangour, ding, ding-dong, knell, peal, ring, stroke, ting, tintinnabulation, toll, whang; **jingle,** ting-a-ling, tinkle, tinkling, trill; **bellringing,** campanology, change-ringing; **peal,** bob, change, dodge, hunt, ring, rounds, touch
RINGING *adj* amphoric, bell-like, jingly, silvery, tinkling, tintinnabular; **twangy,** clangourous, zingy; **rattly,** abuzz; **clumpy,** clumpish, wooden
ringleader *n* → leader
ring leader *n* → encourager
ringlet *n* → **1** curl **2** hair **3** ring
rink *n* → **1** corporation **2** ice **3** sportsground
rinse *n* → **1** cleanser **2** cleansing **3** dye **4** wetting *v* **5** clean
riot *n* → **1** celebration **2** commotion **3** display **4** misdemeanour **5** muddle **6** outburst **7** rev-

olution *v* **8** be violent **9** misbehave **10** overindulge
ripcord *n* → **1** cord **2** opener
ripe *adj* → **1** drunk **2** expedient **3** obscene **4** old **5** smelly **6** timely
ripen *v* → **1** age **2** flower **3** improve **4** perfect **5** prepare **6** taste
rip off *v* → separate
rip-off *n* → **1** embezzlement **2** inflation
riposte *n* → **1** answer **2** joke **3** retaliation *v* **4** answer **5** retaliate
ripper *n* → **1** separator **2** the best
ripple *n* → **1** quiet sound **2** ridge **3** roughness **4** sewing machine **5** spin **6** surf *v* **7** furrow **8** sew **9** toss
rise *n* → **1** ascent **2** astronomic point **3** height **4** increase **5** inflation **6** loudness **7** mound **8** start *v* **9** appear **10** ascend **11** become greater **12** be happy **13** come close **14** cost **15** erect **16** flower **17** grow **18** increase **19** live **20** occur **21** start **22** stop **23** succeed **24** tower **25** wake up
RISEN *adj* emersed, uplifted; **erect,** issuant, jessant, rampant; **erectile,** erective; **scansorial**
rising *n* → **1** ascent **2** revolution *adj* **3** ascending **4** growing **5** loud *adv* **6** almost
RISK *v* be in the running, chance, chance one's arm, do on the off-chance, gamble, give it a go, have a go, run a risk, sail close to the wind, take a pot shot, venture; **hit the jackpot,** be one's lucky day, fall on one's feet, land on one's feet, live a charmed life; **jinx,** hoodoo, jonah, kill a Chinaman, put the mocker(s) on
RISK *v* chance, hazard; **dare,** court disaster, enter the lion's den, gamble, live dangerously, run the gauntlet, tempt fate, tempt providence, venture, walk into the dragon's mouth; **play with fire,** be between Scylla and Charybdis, be in dire straits, be on the brink, be on the precipice, be out on a limb, bell the cat, dice with death, hang by a thread, play chicken, ride for a fall, run the gauntlet, run the risk of, sail too near the wind, skate on thin ice, take one's life in one's hands, walk a slackwire, walk a tightrope
risk *n* → **1** danger **2** luck *v* **3** act rashly
risqué *adj* → obscene
rite *n* → **1** custom **2** formal occasion **3** religious ceremony
ritual *n* → **1** custom **2** formal occasion **3** religious ceremony **4** rule *adj* **5** formal **6** ritualistic
RITUALLY *adv* ceremonially, ceremoniously, ritualistically, traditionally
rival *n* → **1** competitor **2** enemy *v* **3** contest **4** equal *adj* **5** dissident
rive *v* → separate
river *n* → **1** channel **2** separator **3** stream
rivet *n* → **1** nail *v* **2** fasten
rivulet *n* → stream
ROAD *n* carriageway, drag, frog and toad, roadway, street, thoroughfare; **the bitumen,** blacktop, macadam, metal road, sumpbuster, tarmac; **highway,** arterial road, distributor, divided road, dual carriageway, highroad, postroad, priority road, ring-road, trunk road, turnpike *(U.S.)*; **expressway,** autobahn, fast road, freeway, motorway; **beefroad; avenue,** boulevard, mall, parkway, place, row, terrace; **promenade,** alameda *(U.S.)*, esplanade, front, parade, seafront; **back road,** backtrack, bypass, byroad, cart track, detour, line, side road; **backstreet,** alley, bypath, bystreet, byway, side street, sideway; **dead end,** blind alley, cul-de-sac; **dirt road,** gravel road, unmade road, unsealed road, unsurfaced road; **access road,** feeder, service road, turn-off; **cross-street,** crossroad, crossway, slip-road *(Brit.)*; **junction,** bottleneck, intersection, roundabout; **crossover,** overbridge, overpass; **causeway,** dyke, stepping stones; **zigzag,** switchback; **tollway,** turnpike; **stock-route,** drove, lane, long paddock; **lane,** fast lane, laneway, overtaking lane, pole *(Racing)*, traffic lane, transit lane, turnout. *See also* PATH; ROUTE
road *n* → **1** method **2** railway
roam *n* → **1** walk *v* **2** travel
roan *adj* → **1** brown **2** multicoloured
roar *n* → **1** animal call **2** loud sound **3** mirth *v* **4** be loud **5** be violent **6** call (of animals) **7** laugh
roast *n* → **1** reprimand *v* **2** be hot **3** cook **4** disapprove of **5** fire **6** heat **7** mock *adj* **8** heated
ROB *v* bail up, clean out, hold up, mug, reave *(Archaic)*, roll, stick up, strongarm *(U.S.)*, waylay; **burgle,** barber *(Prison)*, blindstab *(Prison)*, burglarise *(U.S.)*, bust; **steal,** abstract, acquire, annex, appropriate, bag, bone, clout on, convey *(Obs.)*, cop, filch, finger, flog, frisk, get down on, ginger, grab, half-inch, heist, hoist, hook, knock off, liberate, lift, make away with, make off with, milk the till, mooch, nick, nim *(Archaic)*, nip, nonch *(Prison)*, oozle, palm, pick, pick pockets, pilfer, pinch, purloin, race off with, rat *(Mining)*, reef off, rifle, run off with, shake, shanghai, shoplift, snaffle, sneak, snitch, snowdrop, souvenir, spirit away, swipe, take, tea-leaf, thieve, thump, walk off with, whip off; **plunder,** carry off, depredate, despoil, gut, loot, maraud, pill *(Archaic)*, pillage, prey upon, ransack, rape, rifle, sack, spoil *(Archaic)*, spoliate, strip, strip bare; **freeboot,** buccaneer, picaroon, pirate, run, smuggle, take to the road *(Obs.)*; **kidnap,** abduct, hijack, shanghai, skyjack; **impress,** crimp, press; **duff,** gully-rake, lift cattle, poach, rustle
ROBBERY *n* appropriation, rapacity, sacrilege, stealing, subreption, theft, thievery, thievishness; **larceny,** crib, fingering, five-finger discount, kleptomania, nonch *(Prison)*, petty larceny, pilferage, pilfering, pinch, pony *(U.S.)*, shoplifting; **burglary,** bust, crack, heist, hoist, housebreaking, job; **cattle stealing,** cattleduffing, horse-duffing, poddy-dodging, rustling; **body-snatching,** resurrectionism *(Hist.)*; **banditry,** bushrang-

ing, highway robbery, hold-up, robbery under arms, smash-and-grab, snatch, stick-up, thuggee, thuggery; **piracy,** buccaneering, hijack, kidnapping, privateering, skyjack; **pillage,** brigandage, brigandry, depredation, despoilment, despoliation, maraud, mosstrooping, plunder, plunderage, rapine, raven *(Obs.)*, sack, spoliation

robe *n* → **1** cupboard **2** dress **3** nightwear *v* **4** clothe

robot *n* → **1** machine **2** portrait

robust *adj* → **1** healthy **2** strong

roc *n* → mythical beast

ROCK *n* igneous rock, metamorphic rock, mylonite, sedimentary rock, siliceous rock, ultrabasic rock, ultramafic rock, volcanic rock; **boulder,** bomb, erratic, eruptive, floater, gibber; **stone,** billy boulder, boondy *(W.A.)*, brinnie, chinaman, cobble, cobblestone, drake stone, goolie, niggerhead, pebble, yonnie; **standing stone,** betyl, cairn, cromlech, dolmen, headstone, menhir, orthostat, tombstone; **fossil,** belemnite, thunder egg, thunderbolt, thunderstone; **meteorite,** aerolite; **gravel,** brash, debris, lapilli, rubble, scree, shingle

rock *n* → **1** bottom **2** jewellery *v* **3** dance **4** emotionalise **5** vibrate

rocker *n* → **1** adolescent **2** support **3** vessel

rockery *n* → garden

rocket *n* → **1** fireworks **2** reprimand **3** signal *v* **4** become greater **5** speed

Rocket *n* → train

ROCK OUTCROP *n* basset, blow, boss, inlier, roche moutonnée; **concretion,** dogger, septarium, spherulite; **rock stack,** aiguille, dyke, needle, yardang, zeuge; **stalactite,** column, stalagmite, stylolite; **megalith,** monolith; **batholith,** laccolith, xenolith; **stratum,** aquifer, basement, basement complex, bed, bedding, bedrock, bone bed, cap rock, confined aquifer, footwall, ledge, lens, lode, shelf, sill, vein; **moraine,** glacial meal, rock flour, till; **rock formation,** series, shield

ROCKY *adj* lithic, lithoid, marmoreal, petrous, stone, stony; **fragmental,** clastic, conglomerate, crystalloid, crystalloidal, pyroclastic, secondary; **crystalline,** asteriated, crystalliferous, idiomorphic, microcrystalline; **volcanic,** tuffaceous; **stratiform,** stratigraphic; **sedimentary,** aqueous, arenaceous; **intrusive,** hypabyssal, irruptive; **acid,** acidic, basic, felsic, intermediate, mafic; **precious,** diamantine, sapphirine, semiprecious

rococo *adj* → **1** decorative **2** vulgar

ROD *n* connecting rod, piston rod, pitman *(U.S.)*, reach, tie rod; **shaft,** countershaft, crankshaft, jackshaft, prop shaft, propellor shaft, quill, quill shaft, rockshaft, shafting, tail shaft; **axle,** arbor, axis, axletree, mandrel, pinion, pintle, spindle; **pin,** break pin, broach, fid, hob, linchpin, peg, pivot, shear pin, stem, toggle, tongue; **skewer,** brochette

rod *n* → **1** authority **2** car **3** club **4** community **5** emblem of office **6** fuel **7** groin **8** gun **9** length **10** stick **11** straight edge

rodeo *n* → contest

roger *n* → **1** groin *v* **2** have sex

rogue *n* → **1** crook **2** freak **3** mischief-maker **4** traveller *v* **5** cheat **6** misbehave

role *n* → **1** behaviour **2** job **3** obligation

ROLL *n* backflip, cartwheel, eskimo roll *(Canoeing)*, esquimautage *(Canoeing)*, flick-roll *(Aeoronautics)*, flip, neckroll, snap-roll, somersault, tumble

ROLL *v* somersault, troll, tumble; **wallow,** labour; **bowl,** burl, devolve *(Archaic)*, rim *(Sport)*, roll along (down); **wheel,** trundle

roll *n* → **1** birdcall **2** boom **3** cash **4** curve **5** leveller **6** list **7** loud sound **8** press **9** sexual intercourse **10** textiles **11** thrust **12** twist **13** vibration **14** walking *v* **15** advance **16** boom **17** bowl over **18** defeat **19** flutter **20** fly **21** gamble **22** level **23** move **24** rob **25** smooth **26** thrust **27** twist

roller *n* → **1** leveller **2** shearer

roller skate *n* → **1** bicycle **2** footgear

ROLL UP *v* belay, clew, marl, reel, rewind, scroll, spool; **entwine,** entwist, enwind, twine, twirl, wisp *(Rare)*; **convolve,** circumflex, fold, gnarl

roly-poly *adj* → fat

romance *n* → **1** flirtation **2** image **3** love affair **4** musical piece **5** poetry **6** story *v* **7** exaggerate **8** fantasise **9** narrate

romantic *n* → **1** emotionalist *adj* **2** emotional **3** flirtatious **4** loving **5** musical **6** narrative **7** unrealistic

romp *n* → **1** amusement **2** easy thing **3** rate **4** woman *v* **5** amuse oneself **6** do easily **7** speed

roo *n* → kangaroo

ROOF *n* cupola, curb roof, dome, drop ceiling, gambrel roof, hip roof, hipped roof, mansard roof, northlight roof, pop-top, roofing, rooftree, saddle roof, sawtooth roof, shell, skillion roof, southlight roof, span roof; **pergola,** marquise, penthouse; **canopy,** baldachin *(Relig.)*, ciborium, tester; **tarpaulin,** dustcover, dustsheet, fly, oilcloth, pool blanket, tarp, throwover, tilt, tonneau

roof *n* → **1** dwelling **2** top *v* **3** cover **4** hit

rook *n* → **1** crook *v* **2** cheat

rookery *n* → **1** animal dwelling **2** birth **3** dishonesty

rookie *n* → **1** ignoramus **2** learner **3** serviceman **4** starter

ROOM *n* apartment, atrium, attic, basement, chamber, cockloft, compartment, garret, pad, shovel *(Colloq.)*, solar, suite; **veranda,** piazza *(U.S.)*, porch *(U.S.)*, sleep-out; **gallery,** box, choir loft, clerestory, dedans, floor, gazebo, jube, lantern, loft, loge, loggia, parvis, traverse, tribune; **bathroom,** bath, caldarium, comfort station, en suite, laundry, lav, lavatory, lavvy, powder room, public convenience, rest room, sauna, steam room, washroom; **clinic,** cas *(Colloq.)*, sick room, solarium, surgery, theatre, ward; **dressing-**

room, change room, fitting room, tiring room *(Archaic)*; **darkroom,** bio-box, booth, projection room; **cell,** black hole, black peter, dummy *(N.Z.)*, fleapit, guardroom, oubliette, slot, slough; **booth,** bower, cabin, carport, crib, den, skillion, stall; **capsule,** airlock, caisson, cockpit, cofferdam, command module, cuddy *(Naut.)*, engine-room, recompression chamber, stank; **compartment,** carrel, cubicle, phone box, polling booth, signal box, telephone booth, waiting room, well; **cellar,** basement, coal cellar, coal hole, crypt, sub-basement, subcellar, undercroft, vault; **strongroom,** vault; **gunroom,** casemate; **schoolroom,** classroom, study; **crypt,** mastaba, morgue, vault; **chapel,** ante choir, antechapel, athenaeum, bema, cella, chancel, choir, naos, sacristy, vestry. *See also* LIVING ROOM; KITCHEN; BEDROOM; HALL

room *n* → **1** opportunity **2** space *v* **3** inhabit

roost *v* → **1** rest **2** sleep

root *n* → **1** ancestry **2** descendant **3** essence **4** foundation **5** number **6** sexual intercourse *v* **7** flower **8** have sex **9** insert **10** ruin **11** steady **12** tire

rope *n* → **1** cord **2** jewellery **3** means of killing *v* **4** cord **5** fasten **6** restrain

ropeable *adj* → angry

rort *n* → **1** celebration **2** drinking session **3** party **4** stratagem *v* **5** control **6** hide

rosary *n* → garden

rosette *n* → plant

roster *n* → list

rostrum *n* → **1** church **2** piercer **3** platform **4** stage

rosy *adj* → **1** beautiful **2** coloured **3** favourable **4** fortunate **5** red

rot *n* → **1** deterioration **2** dirt **3** nonsense *v* **4** deteriorate **5** get dirty **6** wet

rotary *adj* → **1** regular **2** spinning

ROTATE *v* brace *(Naut.)*, circumrotate, circumvolve, revolve, turn, windmill *(Aeron. Colloq.)*; **circle,** circuit, circulate, circumnavigate, encircle, orb, orbit, ring, transit; **spiral,** corkscrew; **turn,** about-face, about-turn, caracole, pirouette, turn around, wheel; **jibe,** slew around, swing, yaw; **turn over,** flip, pronate, supinate. *See also* SPIN

rotate *v* → **1** alternate **2** order

ROTATION *n* autorotation, circulation, circumrotation, circumvolution, free rotation, precession, revolution, rolling, turning; **pronation,** supination; **turning power,** torque; **circuit,** circle, compass, cycle, equatorial, gyre, orb *(Rare)*, orbit. *See also* SPIN; ROLL

rotisserie *n* → stove

rotten *adj* → **1** bad **2** deteriorated **3** drunk **4** immoral **5** sickening

rotund *adj* → **1** fat **2** resonant

rotunda *n* → hall

rouge *n* → **1** cosmetics **2** dye **3** powder *v* **4** redden

ROUGH *n* sumpbuster, tiger country; **white water,** chop, haystack *(Canoeing)*, overfall, turbulence; **crag,** peak

ROUGH *adj* bitty, bullate, bumpy, gnarled, knaggy, knotty, lumpy, nodular, pebbly, roughish, rubbly, rugose, spotty, stubbed, uneven, wrinkled; **jagged,** chopping, choppy, hackly, irregular, jaggy, muricate, rafferty *(N.Z.)*, ragged, scraggy, squarrose, tattered, turbulent; **craggy,** cragged, ironbound, rocky, rugged, savage; **jolty,** bumpy, rough, uneven; **coarse,** coarse-grained, cross-grained, grainy, ground, harsh, matted, rough-hewn, rude, shaggy, shagreen, shagreened, unfinished, unpolished; **scaly,** furfuraceous, scabrous, scurfy; **bristly,** bushy, ciliate, fimbriate, hispid, prickly, spiniferous, spinous, spiny, thorny, tufted

rough *n* → **1** drawing **2** vulgarian *v* **3** roughen *adj* **4** badly-behaved **5** calamitous **6** climatic **7** discourteous **8** dissonant **9** hairy **10** ill-bred **11** inattentive **12** irregular **13** natural **14** raw **15** rough **16** sour **17** turbulent **18** ugly **19** unpleasant **20** unsavoury **21** violent *adv* **22** roughly

roughage *n* → food

ROUGHEN *v* coarsen, grain, hack, rasp, rough, rough up, shag; **key,** knurl, scabble, stab; **rumple,** rub the wrong way, ruffle; **chap,** rub

ROUGHLY *adv* irregularly, rough, rudely, unevenly; **bumpily,** spottily; **craggily,** ruggedly; **jaggedly,** raggedly, scraggily; **dentately,** crenately, denticulately; **coarsely,** harshly, scabrously, shaggily

roughly *adv* → **1** imprecisely **2** irregularly **3** violently

ROUGHNESS *n* asperity, brokenness, rudeness, rugosity; **bumpiness,** inequality, irregularity, key *(Bldg Trades)*, lumpiness, nodosity, spottiness, stubbedness, unevenness; **cragginess,** jaggedness, ruggedness, savageness, scragginess; **crenulation,** corrugation, dentation, denticulation, ripple, serration, serrulation; **coarseness,** bite, grain, graininess, granulation, harshness, scratchiness, texture; **shagginess,** hispidity, raggedness, scabrousness, scaliness

roulette *n* → **1** gambling **2** wheel *v* **3** label **4** open

ROUND *v* ball, conglobate, globe, orb, sphere; **roll up,** clew, coil up; **granulate,** pellet, pelletise, pill *(Textiles)*

ROUND *adj* conglobate, conglomerate, conglomeratic, coniform, cylindric, cylindrical, globate, globoid, globose, globular, moony, orbicular, orbiculate, orby *(Rare)*, spheral, spheric, spherical, spheroid, spheroidal, spherular, sphery; **capitate,** clavate, claviform, club-shaped, mooned; **beady,** gibbous, granular, pea-like, pilular, pisiform; **buttony,** discal, disclike, discoid, discoidal, platelike, scutate

round *n* → **1** circle **2** gunfire **3** journey **4** period **5** repetition **6** sculpture **7** sequence **8** share **9** shot **10** song *v* **11** shape **12** surround **13** travel *adj* **14** domed **15** great **16** honest **17** numerical **18** resonant **19** swollen **20** unconditional **21** whole **22** written *adv* **23** deflectively **24** here **25** regularly *prep* **26** across **27** during **28** near **29** outside

undabout *n* → **1** amusement park **2** crossway **3** road *adj* **4** deflective **5** twisting **6** verbose

undly *adv* → strictly

undsman *n* → **1** journalist **2** policeman **3** traveller **4** visitor

und-up *n* → farming

use *n* → **1** signal **2** waking *v* **3** activate **4** anger **5** arouse **6** wake up

useabout *n* → **1** farmhand **2** labourer

ut *n* → **1** commotion **2** crowd **3** losing **4** loud sound **5** party **6** working class *v* **7** defeat **8** disperse **9** eject **10** furrow **11** hollow

OUTE *n* beat, channel, course, highway, lane, line, march, path, tack, track, wake; **itinerary**; **short cut**, crosscut, cut-off, direttissimo; **trade route**, lifeline; **air-route**, air structure, air-corridor, airlane, airline, airway, flight path, glide path, great circle route, kangaroo route; **trajectory**, orbit; **sea lane**, shipping lane. *See also* PATH; ROAD; RAILWAY; ACCESS

ute *v* → arrange

utine *n* → **1** act **2** custom **3** dance **4** method **5** rule

ve *n* → **1** thread *v* **2** cord **3** travel

w *n* → **1** argument **2** house **3** line **4** loud sound **5** musical phrase **6** road *v* **7** argue **8** be loud **9** contest **10** scold **11** transport

wdy *n* → **1** untidy person **2** violent person **3** vulgarian *adj* **4** disorderly **5** ill-bred

OWING BOAT *n* bateau, caique, coble, dinghy, dinky, double scull, eight, felucca, flattie, gig, gun, longboat, outrigger, pair, rowboat, scull, shell, skiff, surfboat, toothpick, wherry *(U.S.)*, whiff; **canoe**, dugout, faltboat, foldboat, kayak, piragua, pirogue, surf ski; **coracle**, bidarka, umiak; **punt**, gondola, sampan; **galley**, bireme, galleass, galliot, longship, quinquereme, trireme

wlock *n* → support

oyal *adj* → **1** aristocratic **2** good

oyalist *n* → political ideologist

oyalty *n* → **1** aristocracy **2** funds **3** income **4** nation

UB *v* embrocate, flannel, rub down, stroke, towel; **rub away**, abrade, degrade, denude, erode, fret, sculpture *(Phys. Geog.)*; **sandpaper**, fray, glasspaper, grate, graze, grind, paper, rasp, sand, sandblast, scuff, shave, stone, strop, whet; **chafe**, rub together; **scrabble**, claw, scrape, scratch

ub *n* → **1** difficulty **2** hindrance **3** irritation **4** mockery **5** reprimand **6** rubbing **7** slander **8** touch *v* **9** clean **10** dry **11** pain **12** roughen **13** touch

ubber *n* → **1** contraception **2** sandal **3** smoother

UBBING *n* effleurage, embrocation, frottage, massage, rub, rub-down; **rubbing away**, abrasion, attrition, denudation, erosion, fret, scraping, wearing away; **graze**, abrasion, scrape, scratch, scuff

rubbish *n* → **1** bad thing **2** illogicality **3** nonsense **4** waste *v* **5** mock

RUBBISH BIN *n* ash can *(U.S.)*, ashtray, car tidy, dustbin *(Brit.)*, dustpan, garbage bin, hell, hell box, kitchen tidy, litter-bin, pedal bin, pig-bucket, rubbish tin, tidy, w.p.b., wastebasket, wastepaper basket; **catchpit**, catch-basin, silt pit; **spittoon**, cesspit, cuspidor, grease trap, slop-basin, slop-bucket, sullage pit

rubble *n* → **1** building materials **2** remnant **3** rock

rubicund *adj* → **1** coloured **2** reddish

rubric *n* → **1** command **2** important thing **3** label **4** title **5** written composition

ruby *n* → **1** red *adj* **2** red

ruck *n* → **1** gathering **2** many **3** working class *v* **4** fold

rucksack *n* → bag

ruction *n* → argument

rudder *n* → steering wheel

ruddy *adj* → **1** beautiful **2** red **3** reddish *adv* **4** very

rude *adj* → **1** badly-behaved **2** brutal **3** discourteous **4** dissonant **5** ill-bred **6** insulting **7** raw **8** rough **9** strong **10** ugly

rudiments *n* → **1** course **2** foundation **3** knowledge

rue *n* → **1** penitence **2** pity **3** unhappiness *v* **4** be penitent

ruff *n* → **1** fold **2** neckwear **3** ring

ruffian *n* → **1** anarchist **2** violent person *adj* **3** anarchic

ruffle *n* → **1** boom **2** confusion **3** edge **4** fold **5** lace **6** quiet sound *v* **7** annoy **8** feather **9** roughen **10** toss **11** untidy

rufous *adj* → reddish

rug *n* → bedclothes

rugged *adj* → **1** calamitous **2** difficult **3** dissonant **4** folded **5** rough **6** strict **7** strong **8** violent

RUIN *n* belial *(Eccles.)*, comedown, defeat, doom, downfall, fall, fate, labefaction, perdition, ruination, ruinousness, undoing, watergate, Waterloo; **collapse**, crash, crunch; **smash**, destruct *(Mil.)*, prang, shipwreck; **conflagration**, holocaust, incineration; **blast effect**, ground-shock effect, scorched earth *(Mil.)*; **ruins**, ashes, rack, wrack, wreck, wreckage; **disaster**, avalanche, calamity, catastrophe, debacle, fatality; **the end**, the beginning of the end, the crunch, the finish, the last straw, the living end, the moment of truth, the road to ruin. *See also* DESTRUCTION

RUIN *v* bugger up, bust up, cook someone's goose, do in, frig up, fuck up, jigger, play havoc with, put paid to, root; **break**, break down, graunch *(N.Z.)*, shatter, wreck; **scuttle**, scupper, shipwreck, sink, torpedo. *See also* DESTROY

ruin *n* → **1** damage **2** destruction **3** harm **4** oldness **5** rape **6** unfortunate *v* **7** be promiscuous **8** impoverish **9** rape **10** spoil

RUINED *adj* buggered, bust, busted, done for, done up, downfallen, fallen, fucked, gone to Gundy, had it, jiggered up, kaput, lost, naught *(Archaic)*, no good to Gundy, rooted, stonkered, stuffed, undone, up the spout

RULE *n* axiom, canon, convention, custom, dictate, formula, generality, golden rule, ground rule, hard and fast rule, hinge, institute, institution, law, maxim, model, motto, natural order, observance *(Rom. Cath. Ch.)*, order, ordinance, precept, prescript, principle, procrustean bed, regulation, routine, rule of thumb, standing order, sutra *(Sanskrit)*, theorem; **discipline,** bushido *(Jap. Hist.)*, dos and don'ts, ethics, protocol, ritual; **tenets,** articles, articles of association, code, constitution, elements, organon *(Philos.)*, ruling, teaching; **standard,** criterion, determinant, double standard, gauge, yardstick

rule *n* → **1** authority **2** command **3** line **4** mathematical operation **5** monasticism **6** power **7** religion **8** straight edge *v* **9** determine **10** generalise **11** line **12** mark **13** predominate

RULER *n* administrator, arch *(Obs.)*, archon, ataman, begum, cacique, caliph, caudillo, chief, chieftain, dame *(Archaic)*, dato, elder, elector, eponym, ethnarch, gerent, hero *(Gk. Antiq.)*, hetman, jarl *(Scand. Hist.)*, judge *(Jewish Hist.)*, lady, laird, liege, lord (of the manor), lord temporal, matriarch, overlord, pendragon, plutocrat, potentate, primate *(Rare)*, principal, seignior *(Archaic)*, sire *(Obs.)*, suzerain, tribal elder; **bureaucrat,** apparatchiki, aristocrat, hierocrat, panjandrum *(Colloq.)*, Pooh-Bah *(Colloq.)*, technocrat; **civilian official,** alcalde, director, politician, provost, syndic; **governor,** area commander, bashaw, bey, captain, commissar, constable *(Brit.)*, department head, eparch, exarch, gauleiter, grand vizier *(Islam)*, legate *(Rom. Hist.)*, mandarin, minister, pasha, prefect, proconsul, satrap, stadtholder, tetrarch; **military commander,** admiral, general, leader; **church ruler,** archbishop, imam, lama, pope; **the authorities,** officialdom, the government, the powers that be; **head of government,** chancellor, consul *(Rom. Hist.)*, doge, duumvir, P.M., premier, president, president-elect, prime minister, protector, triumvir; **emperor,** Caesar, czar, czarina, empress, imperator, imperial, Kaiser, Mikado, Negus, Padishah, Pharaoh, tsar, tsarina; **autocrat,** absolute monarch, ayatollah *(Colloq.)*, Big Brother, despot, dictator, dictatress, dictatrix, Duce, feudal lord, Führer, oligarch, paramount, robber baron, shogun, supremo, tyrant, war lord

ruler *n* → straight edge

rum *n* → **1** alcohol *adj* **2** good **3** strange

rumble *n* → **1** boom **2** fight **3** misdemeanour **4** vessel *v* **5** boom **6** fight **7** find out

ruminant *n* → **1** cattle *adj* **2** thinking

ruminate *v* → think

rummage *n* → **1** investigation **2** mixture **3** search

rummy *n* → **1** gambling *adj* **2** strange

rumour *n* → **1** allusion **2** news **3** uncertai[n] thing *v* **4** communicate **5** noise abroad

rump *n* → **1** buttocks **2** rear **3** remnant

rumple *n* → **1** fold *v* **2** contract **3** fo[ld] **4** roughen **5** untidy

rumpus *n* → **1** commotion **2** loud sound

run *n* → **1** move **2** period **3** rate **4** series *v* **5** a[l]ternate **6** cash **7** contest **8** discharge **9** d[...] **10** elude **11** excrete **12** extend **13** farm **14** f[...] **15** flow **16** flower **17** gather **18** glide **19** hu[...] **20** liquefy **21** manage **22** move **23** open u[...] **24** operate **25** publish **26** repeat **27** ro[...] **28** speed **29** stage **30** surpass **31** transpo[rt] **32** walk *adj* **33** liquid

run down *v* → lower

run-down *n* → **1** abridgment **2** informatio[n] *adj* **3** inactive **4** neglected **5** tired **6** unhappy

rune *n* → **1** letter **2** poetry

rung *n* → **1** stairs **2** support

run in *v* → operate

run-in *n* → **1** argument **2** fight **3** finish

runner *n* → **1** covering **2** flooring **3** footgea[r] **4** knife **5** manchester **6** messenger **7** pla[nt] **8** support **9** walker

runner-up *n* → competitor

running *n* → **1** management **2** trade *adj* **3** as[]cending **4** current **5** liquid **6** moving **7** operating **8** sequential **9** written

runny *adj* → liquid

runoff *n* → exit

run off *v* → **1** depart **2** print

run-off *n* → **1** contest **2** farmland **3** flow **4** re[]mote place

run-of-the-mill *adj* → **1** mediocre **2** ordinary

runt *n* → **1** bad person **2** small person

runway *n* → **1** access **2** airport

rupture *n* → **1** break *v* **2** be unfriendly **3** separate

RURAL *adj* agrarian, agricultural, country, exurban, rustic, village, villatic; **outback,** back-country, backwoods, high, hinterland, up-country; **country-style,** countrified, country-fashion; **pastoral,** Arcadian, bucolic, sylvan, woodland. *See also* PROVINCIAL

rural *adj* → farming

RURALLY *adv* bucolically, pastorally, provincially, rustically; **beyond the black stump,** back of beyond, from the sticks, in the mulga, up the booay, up the mulga

ruse *n* → stratagem

rush *n* → **1** advance **2** attack **3** busynes[s] **4** rashness **5** rate **6** speed **7** stroke *v* **8** advance **9** attack **10** be busy **11** force **12** hurr[y] **13** transport *adj* **14** speedy

russet *adj* → **1** brown **2** red

rust *n* → **1** brown **2** deterioration **3** glaz[e] **4** orange **5** red *v* **6** brown **7** deteriorate **8** fal[l] into disuse

rustic *n* → **1** artless person **2** country dweller *adj* **3** artless **4** farming **5** ill-bred **6** rural

rustle *n* → **1** hiss **2** quiet sound *v* **3** hiss **4** rob

rusty *adj* → 1 brown 2 deteriorated 3 dilapidated 4 disused 5 orange 6 red

rut *n* → 1 custom 2 furrow 3 reproduction *v* 4 conceive 5 furrow

ruthless *adj* → 1 callous 2 opportunist 3 unkind

rye *n* → man

Ss

Sabbath *n* → holiday
sabbatical *n* → 1 absence 2 holiday *adj* 3 resting
sable *n* → 1 animal's coat 2 black *adj* 3 black 4 dark
sabotage *n* → 1 damage 2 dissidence *v* 3 damage
sabre *n* → 1 soldier 2 sword *v* 3 attack 4 kill
sac *n* → bag
saccharin *n* → sweetness
sachet *n* → 1 bag 2 fragrance 3 powder
sack *n* → 1 bag 2 dress 3 jacket 4 robbery *v* 5 dismiss 6 enclose 7 rob
sacrament *n* → 1 contract 2 sign
sacred *adj* → holy
sacrifice *n* → 1 gift 2 killing 3 offering 4 religious ceremony 5 victim *v* 6 give 7 kill
sacrilege *n* → 1 irreverence 2 robbery
sacrosanct *adj* → holy
sad *adj* → 1 bad 2 colourless 3 dull 4 shadowy 5 unhappy
sadden *v* → 1 displease 2 make unhappy
saddle *n* → 1 hollow 2 stand
sadism *n* → 1 pain 2 psychic disorder 3 sexuality 4 unkindness
safari *n* → 1 pursuit 2 walk
SAFE *adj* all right, cocksure *(Obs.)*, fail-safe, inviolate, right as rain, safe and sound, safe as houses, secure, shockproof, sure *(Archaic)*; **harmless,** innocuous, innoxious; **low-toxicity,** hypo-allergenic; **protective,** childproof, flameproof, shark-proof, waterproof; **armoured,** armour-plated, bulletproof, ironclad, loricate, mailed, panoplied, shellproof
safe *n* → 1 box 2 cupboard *adj* 3 cautious
safeguard *n* → 1 defence 2 protector 3 safety *v* 4 secure
SAFETY *n* safeness, secureness, security; **harmlessness,** innocence, innocuousness, innoxiousness; **safety margin,** factor of safety; **safeguard,** guard, precaution, protection; **immunity,** active immunity
safety *n* → imprisonment
saffron *n* → yellow
sag *n* → 1 decrease 2 descent 3 hanging 4 hollow *v* 5 capitulate 6 curve 7 fall 8 hang 9 wane
saga *n* → 1 heroic story 2 story
sagacious *adj* → 1 discriminating 2 wise
sage *n* → 1 enlightener 2 guide 3 intellectual 4 wise person *adj* 5 wise
said *adj* → preceding
sail *n* → 1 sailing ship *v* 2 depart 3 move 4 set sail
SAILING SHIP *n* barque, barquentine, brig, brigantine, caravel, carvel, catboat, clipper, cutter, dandy, dogger, fore-and-after, galleon, hermaphrodite brig, hoy, ketch, lugger, polacca, schooner, sloop, smack, tartan, three-decker, three-master, topsail schooner, two-master, yawl, xebec; **sailing boat,** auxiliary, carrack, dhow, dory, drogher, dromond, felucca, junk, keel, keelboat, knockabout, pinnace, proa, sabot, sail, sailboard, sailboat, sailer, sharpie, windjammer, windsurfer, yacht; **catamaran,** cat, trimaran
sailor *n* → mariner
saint *n* → 1 good person 2 holy person 3 religious follower 4 unselfish person *v* 5 consecrate 6 worship
sake *n* → aim
salacious *adj* → obscene
salamander *n* → 1 mythical beast 2 remnant 3 stove
salary *n* → income
sale *n* → 1 bargain 2 selling
salient *n* → 1 fortification *adj* 2 obvious 3 protuberant
sallow *v* → 1 lose colour 2 yellow *adj* 3 colourless 4 yellow
sally *n* → 1 attack 2 busyness 3 combat troops 4 exit 5 joke 6 journey *v* 7 attack 8 exit
salmon *adj* → red
salon *n* → 1 clique 2 living room
saloon *n* → 1 car 2 hall 3 living room 4 pub
salt *n* → 1 humour 2 mariner *v* 3 conserve 4 cook 5 sour *adj* 6 cooked 7 preserved 8 sour
salt-petre *n* → ammunition
salubrious *adj* → wholesome
salutary *adj* → 1 good 2 wholesome
salutation *n* → 1 courtesy 2 greeting 3 tribute
salute *n* → 1 congratulation 2 courtesy 3 tribute *v* 4 pay homage 5 signal
salvage *n* → 1 compensation 2 property 3 repair *v* 4 preserve
salve *n* → 1 alleviator 2 fat 3 medication *v* 4 alleviate 5 preserve
salvo *n* → 1 applause 2 attack 3 congratulation 4 explosion 5 generosity 6 gunfire 7 justification 8 loophole
Salvo *n* → 1 preacher 2 religious person
same *adj* → 1 congruous 2 equal 3 homogeneous
sampan *n* → rowing boat
sample *n* → 1 example *v* 2 investigate 3 taste 4 test *adj* 5 model
sanatorium *n* → 1 health centre 2 hospital
sanctify *v* → 1 clean 2 command respect 3 consecrate

sanctimonious *adj* → 1 deceitful 2 godlike
sanction *n* → 1 affirmation 2 approval 3 command 4 force 5 permission 6 punishment *v* 7 approve 8 assent to 9 authorise 10 have the right 11 permit
sanctity *n* → god
sanctuary *n* → 1 liberty 2 nature reserve 3 place of worship 4 refuge 5 seclusion 6 shrine
sand *n* → 1 extinguisher 2 matter 3 powder 4 soil 5 yellow *v* 6 disperse 7 rub 8 smooth
SANDAL *n* espadrille, flip-flop, jandal *(N.Z.)*, rubber *(Colloq.)*, slaps, thong, zori; **slipper,** carpet slipper, mule, pantofle, scuff. *See also* FOOTGEAR
sandal *n* → tape
sandalwood *n* → timber
sandpaper *n* → 1 abrasive 2 smoother *v* 3 rub 4 smooth
sandshoe *n* → footgear
sandsoap *n* → cleanser
sandwich *v* → insert
SANE *adj* all there, clear-headed, compos mentis, lucid, normal, present, rational, reasonable, sound of mind; **sober,** responsible, self-possessed, well-balanced
sane *adj* → 1 healthy 2 mental
SANELY *adv* lucidly, rationally; **in one's right mind,** in possession of one's faculties, responsibly, soberly
sanguine *adj* → 1 ferocious 2 happy 3 hopeful 4 red
sanitary *adj* → 1 clean 2 wholesome
SANITY *n* lucidity, lucidness, normalcy, normality, rationality, reason, saneness, soundness of mind; **soberness,** responsibleness, sobriety
sap *n* → 1 diggings 2 fool 3 furrow 4 liquid 5 stupid person *v* 6 come close 7 defend 8 dig 9 furrow 10 weaken
sapling *n* → adolescent
sapphire *n* → blue
sarcasm *n* → 1 comedy 2 mockery 3 opposite meaning
sarcophagus *n* → coffin
sardonic *adj* → 1 figurative 2 mocking
sari *n* → dress
sarong *n* → 1 dress 2 textiles
sarsaparilla *n* → drink
Satan *n* → 1 devil 2 immoral person
satanic *adj* → 1 devilish 2 immoral
satchel *n* → bag
sate *v* → 1 oversupply 2 satisfy
satellite *n* → 1 accomplice 2 companion 3 dependant 4 flatterer 5 heavenly body 6 subject
satiate *v* → 1 oversupply 2 satisfy
satin *n* → 1 smooth object *adj* 2 bright 3 smooth
satire *n* → 1 comedy 2 figure of speech 3 mockery 4 poetry
satirise *v* → 1 joke 2 mock
SATISFACTION *n* fulfilment, gratification, implementation *(Archaic)*; **satisfactoriness,** suitability, suitableness; **contentment,** comfort, content, contentedness; **appeasement,** assuagement; **fullness,** impletion *(Obs.)*, repleteness, repletion; **satiation,** jadedness, satiety; **sufficiency,** bellyful, fill, glut
satisfaction *n* → 1 adequacy 2 compensation 3 contentedness 4 payment 5 pleasure
SATISFACTORILY *adv* all cush, all right, okay, very well, well; **satisfyingly,** gratifyingly; **comfortably,** contentedly
SATISFACTORY *adj* all right, fair enough, good enough, jake, jakerloo, nominal *(U.S.)*, okay; **up to scratch,** good, right, well-done; **satisfying,** gratifying, rewarding; **square,** hearty
SATISFIED *adj* comfortable, content, contented, thirstless; **satiated,** full as a butcher's pup, full as a goog, full up, replete, sated; **jaded,** blasé
SATISFY *v* deliver the goods, fill the bill, fulfil, hit the nail on the head, hit the spot, implement *(Archaic)*, rise to the occasion, serve, suffice, suit; **appease,** assuage, content, gratify, pacify; **pander to,** pamper, please; **satiate,** feed, fill, glut, quench, sate, slake, stay; **pall,** cloy, jade
satisfy *v* → 1 compensate 2 do one's duty 3 fit 4 pay 5 solve
saturate *v* → 1 fill 2 fire on *adj* 3 full
saturnine *adj* → 1 irritable 2 unhappy
satyr *n* → 1 mythical being 2 promiscuous person 3 sexual partner
sauce *n* → 1 arrogance 2 discourtesy *v* 3 cook 4 energise 5 insult 6 make pleasant
saucy *adj* → 1 arrogant 2 discourteous 3 fashionable 4 insulting
sauna *n* → 1 bathroom 2 cleansing 3 room
saunter *n* → 1 walk 2 walking *v* 3 go slowly 4 walk
sausage *n* → aircraft
sauté *v* → cook
savage *n* → 1 bad person 2 unkind person 3 vulgarian *v* 4 attack *adj* 5 angry 6 ferocious 7 natural 8 rough 9 unkind
SAVE *v* go easy on, husband, make every penny work, put it all down south, scrape by on, squirrel; **skimp on,** stint on; **be sparing,** cut one's coat according to one's cloth, economise, keep costs down, keep within one's budget, make both ends meet
save *v* → 1 care for 2 disuse 3 preserve 4 store *prep* 5 except 6 less *conj* 7 on condition that
saving *n* → 1 thrift *adj* 2 thrifty
saviour *n* → defender
SAVOUR *n* deliciousness, lusciousness, mellowness, niceness, palatability, palatableness, sapidity, savouriness, tastiness, toothsomeness; **relish,** life, tang, zest
SAVOUR *v* lap up, lick one's fingers, smack the lips; **taste good,** tickle the palate
savour *n* → 1 fragrance 2 taste *v* 3 enjoy 4 perceive 5 smell out 6 taste
savoury *n* → 1 meal *adj* 2 correct 3 delicious 4 fragrant 5 pungent
savvy *n* → 1 wisdom *v* 2 know 3 understand *adj* 4 knowledgeable
saw *n* → 1 proverb *v* 2 be dissonant 3 cut

say *n* → **1** rights **2** speaking *v* **3** speak **4** theorise
saying *n* → proverb
SAY WHAT ONE THINKS *v* be without guile, call a spade a spade, have nothing to hide, let it all hang out, wear one's heart on one's sleeve
scab *n* → **1** betrayer **2** sore *v* **3** deteriorate **4** work
scabbard *n* → **1** arsenal **2** case **3** covering
scaffold *n* → **1** building *v* **2** support
scald *v* → **1** cook **2** fire
SCALES *n* balance, jockey scales, microbalance, spring balance, steelyard, weighbridge
scallop *n* → **1** curve *v* **2** cook **3** curve
scallywag *n* → mischief-maker
scalp *n* → **1** head *v* **2** cut **3** invest **4** kill
scalpel *n* → knife
scamp *n* → **1** mischief-maker *v* **2** disorder **3** neglect
scamper *n* → **1** rate *v* **2** speed
scan *n* → **1** analysis **2** investigation **3** look *v* **4** examine **5** look **6** read **7** versify
scandal *n* → **1** bad thing **2** disrepute **3** slander **4** talk *v* **5** slander **6** talk
scandalise *v* → wrong
scant *v* → **1** decrease *adj* **2** adequate **3** deficient **4** few **5** insufficient **6** small
scape *n* → **1** escape **2** post
scapegoat *n* → **1** unfortunate **2** victim
scar *n* → **1** disfigurement *v* **2** disfigure
scarab *n* → **1** amulet **2** jewellery
scarce *adj* → **1** few **2** insufficient **3** rare
scarcely *adv* → **1** rarely **2** unlikely *interj* **3** no
scare *n* → **1** fright *v* **2** frighten
scarecrow *n* → **1** frightener **2** thin person **3** ugly person **4** untidy person
scarf *n* → **1** furrow **2** hide **3** neckwear
scarify *v* → **1** cut **2** disapprove of **3** farm **4** flower **5** furrow
scarlet *n* → **1** orange *adj* **2** obscene **3** orange **4** red
scat *n* → **1** defecation *v* **2** depart *interj* **3** piss off
scathing *adj* → disapproving
scatter *n* → **1** drinking session *v* **2** disperse **3** diverge
scavenge *v* → **1** clean **2** gather
scenario *n* → **1** narrative **2** situation
scene *n* → **1** act **2** excitement **3** painting **4** situation **5** stage **6** surroundings **7** view
scenery *n* → **1** stage **2** surroundings
scenic *adj* → dramatic
scent *n* → **1** fragrance **2** smell *v* **3** find **4** hunt **5** smell out
sceptic *n* → **1** doubter **2** irreverent person *adj* **3** irreverent
sceptre *n* → **1** authority **2** emblem of office
schedule *n* → **1** agenda **2** clarification **3** classification **4** plan **5** postscript **6** time sheet **7** written composition *v* **8** list **9** plan
schematic *n* → **1** diagram *adj* **2** planned
scheme *n* → **1** expedient **2** plan **3** shape *v* **4** beguile **5** conspire
SCHEMER *n* complotter, conspirator, conspiratress, contriver, designer, framer, hatcher, intriguer, machinator, plotter; **planner,** arranger, deviser, strategist systematiser, systematist, systemiser, tactician, teleologist
scheming *adj* → opportunist
schism *n* → **1** break **2** heresy
schizophrenia *n* → **1** fantasy **2** psychic disturbance
schmalz *n* → affectation
scholar *n* → **1** intellectual **2** pupil **3** specialist
scholarship *n* → **1** allowance **2** charity **3** income **4** intellectualism **5** learning
scholastic *n* → **1** intellectual **2** learner **3** monastic *adj* **4** educated **5** intellectual
SCHOOL *n* area school, blackboard jungle bush school, central school, comprehensive school, consolidated school, dame school demonstration school, district school, educational institution, feeder school, hospital school, one-teacher school, rural school, secondary modern school *(Brit.)*, state school **independent school,** charity school *(Brit.)* G.P.S., non-government school, non-state school, parish school, pension, private school, public school, ragged school *(Brit.)* **opportunity school,** special school; **boarding school,** day school; **open school,** alternative school, open classroom, open planning, progressive school; **correspondence school** school of the air; **summer school,** finishing school; **girls' school,** heifer paddock; **alma mater,** old school; **convent,** seminary; **Sunday school,** Sabbath school; **kindergarten,** creche day care, infants' school, nursery, nursery school, preschool; **primary school,** grade school *(U.S.)*, junior school, prep, prepatory school; **secondary school,** grammar school high, high school, junior college *(U.S.)* junior high school, lycée, selective high school, technical school. *See also* COLLEGE
schooner *n* → **1** alcohol container **2** sailing ship
science *n* → **1** competence **2** knowledge
science fiction *n* → story
scientific *adj* → **1** epistemological **2** ordered **3** questioning
scientist *n* → **1** specialist **2** tester
scintillate *v* → shine
scion *n* → **1** child **2** descendant **3** offspring
SCISSORS *n* clippers, nail scissors; **shears,** b-bows, bog-eye, bogghi, bows, clips, daggers, grass-clippers, hand shears, handpiece, jingling Johnnies, lizard, pinking shears, pruning shears, secateurs, snips, swords, tinsnips, wire-cutter, wool-shears
scissors *n* → **1** exercise **2** hold
scoff *n* → **1** food **2** mockery *v* **3** eat **4** mock
SCOLD *v* admonish, chasten, chastise, chide, give someone a bad mark, go on at, name *(Parl. Proc.)*, rebuke, remonstrate with, reprehend, reprimand, reproach, reprobate, reprove, rouse at, rouse on, tick off, tongue, twit, wig *(Brit.)*; **lecture,** chat, jaw *(Colloq.)*, lesson, rag *(Colloq.)*, read someone a lecture, school *(Archaic)*, tutor; **scold severely,** attack,

baste, bawl out, be on at, berate, blast, blast hell out of, blow up, bore up, carpet, castigate, denounce, denunciate, dress down, flay, fulminate against, give a pay, give beans, give gip, give heaps, give someone hell, give someone Larry Dooley, give someone what for, give the rough side of one's tongue, give the rounds of the kitchen, go crook at, go crook on, go to town on, haul over the coals, hoe into, keelhaul, lash, make mincemeat of, mat, objurgate, paste, pelt, play hell with, put on the mat, put the boot into, rail at, rap over the knuckles, rate, row *(Obs.)*, sally up *(N.Z.)*, take a piece out of, take to task, tongue-lash, upbraid, whip; **jump on,** jump down someone's throat, pull up. *See also* DISAPPROVE OF

scold *n* → **1** bad person **2** disapprover **3** violent person *v* **4** irritate **5** punish

scone *n* → **1** head *v* **2** hit

scoop *n* → **1** cash **2** digging implement **3** hollow **4** news item *v* **5** dig **6** hollow **7** publish

scoot *n* → **1** rate *v* **2** speed

scooter *n* → **1** bicycle *v* **2** drive

scope *n* → **1** length **2** opportunity **3** region **4** size **5** space

scorch *v* → **1** disapprove of **2** fire **3** speed **4** wage war

SCORE *n* aggregate, circulation, count, head, raw score, strength, tally, total; **attendance,** enrolment; **majority,** quorum, quota

score *n* → **1** account **2** cost **3** cut **4** furrow **5** indebtedness **6** limit **7** record **8** winner *v* **9** cut **10** disapprove of **11** furrow **12** have sex **13** mark **14** measure **15** record **16** succeed

scorn *n* → **1** arrogance **2** disapproval **3** low regard *v* **4** be arrogant **5** hold in low regard

scotch *n* → **1** cut *v* **2** cut **3** injure **4** stop

scot-free *adj* → **1** cheap **2** liberated

scoundrel *adj* → immoral

scour *n* → **1** cleansing *v* **2** clean **3** excrete **4** speed **5** walk

scourge *n* → **1** club **2** destroyer **3** misfortune *v* **4** cudgel

scout *n* → **1** informant **2** leader **3** man **4** questioner *v* **5** consult **6** pursue

SCOWL *n* flounce, frown, lour, pout, snarl

scowl *n* → **1** boo *v* **2** become irritated **3** dislike

scrabble *v* → **1** make an effort **2** rub

scraggly *adj* → irregular

scraggy *adj* → **1** insufficient **2** irregular **3** rough **4** thin

scram *v* → **1** depart *interj* **2** piss off

scramble *n* → **1** jumble **2** preparation **3** race *v* **4** cook **5** drive **6** make an effort **7** mix **8** speed **9** walk

scrape *n* → **1** dilemma **2** fight **3** rubbing *v* **4** be dissonant **5** have sex **6** rub **7** smooth

scratch *n* → **1** disfigurement **2** dissonance **3** furrow **4** injury **5** quiet sound **6** rubbing **7** shallow **8** starting line **9** writing *v* **10** back out **11** be dissonant **12** cudgel **13** cut **14** disfigure **15** furrow **16** rub **17** touch **18** write *adj* **19** lucky

scrawl *n* → **1** writing *v* **2** write

scrawny *adj* → thin

scream *n* → **1** humorist **2** shout *v* **3** laugh **4** shout

screech *n* → **1** animal call **2** birdcall **3** shout *v* **4** call (of animals) **5** shout **6** shrill

screed *n* → **1** harangue **2** written composition

SCREEN *n* sconce *(Obs.)*, windbreak; **awning,** brise-soleil, dodger *(Naut.)*, heat shield, shade, sunblind, sunbreak; **fireguard,** cowl *(Railways)*, fire-curtain, firebreak, firescreen, firewall, safety curtain; **bar,** bollard, buffer, bull-bar, bumper, bumper bar, cowcatcher, crash barrier, fender, grate, grating, guardrail, handrail, kangaroo bar, sponson, stone shield

screen *n* → **1** combat troops **2** defence **3** interlacement **4** protection **5** wall **6** watercraft *v* **7** hide **8** investigate **9** secure **10** separate **11** stage

screw *n* → **1** distortion **2** gaoler **3** income **4** look **5** machine **6** miser **7** nail **8** policeman **9** propellant **10** sexual intercourse **11** spiral **12** twist *v* **13** extort **14** fasten **15** force **16** have sex **17** spoil **18** twist *adj* **19** spinning

scribble *n* → **1** writing *v* **2** sew **3** write

scribe *n* → **1** sharp point **2** teacher **3** writer *v* **4** cut **5** write

scrimp *v* → **1** be miserly *adj* **2** insufficient

scrip *n* → **1** bag **2** diagram **3** dispensary

script *n* → **1** letter **2** writing **3** written composition

scroll *n* → **1** decoration **2** list **3** spiral **4** twist **5** writing materials **6** written composition *v* **7** roll up **8** write

scrooge *n* → miser

scrotum *n* → groin

scrounge *v* → borrow

scrub *n* → **1** cleansing **2** forest *v* **3** arouse **4** cancel **5** clean **6** remove

scruff *n* → **1** dirty person **2** neck **3** remnant **4** untidy person

scruffy *adj* → **1** unkempt **2** untidy

scrumptious *adj* → delicious

scruple *n* → **1** small amount **2** unwillingness *v* **3** be unwilling

scrupulous *adj* → **1** correct **2** honest **3** precise **4** unwilling

scrutineer *n* → **1** questioner *v* **2** examine

scrutinise *v* → **1** examine **2** inquire into

scrutiny *n* → **1** analysis **2** investigation **3** seeing

SCUBA *n* → breathing

scud *n* → **1** cloud **2** rate *v* **3** set sail **4** speed

scuff *n* → **1** quiet sound **2** rubbing **3** sandal *v* **4** deteriorate **5** rub

scuffle *n* → **1** fight *v* **2** fight **3** make an effort

scull *n* → **1** propellant **2** rowing boat

scullery *n* → kitchen

SCULPTURE *n* ceroplastics, modelling, statuary; **carving,** woodcarving, woodwork; **statue,** bronze, bust, figurine, marble, monument *(Obs.)*, plaster cast, stabile, statuette; **relief,** alto-rilievo, bas-relief, basso-rilievo, demirelief, glyph, high relief, low relief, mezzo-rilievo, relievo, round; **petroglyph,**

rock carving, rock engraving; **mobile,** kinetic art; **cameo,** miniature

sculpture *n* → **1** fine arts **2** representation *v* **3** depict **4** rub

scum *n* → **1** bad person **2** covering **3** dirt **4** remnant **5** working class

scurrilous *adj* → **1** insulting **2** vulgar

scurry *n* → **1** race **2** rate *v* **3** speed

scurvy *n* → **1** malnutrition *adj* **2** wrong

scuttle *n* → **1** basket **2** opening *v* **3** fall **4** open **5** ruin **6** speed

scythe *n* → **1** knife *v* **2** cut **3** harvest

SEA *n* brine, briny, Davy Jones's locker, ditch, Neptune, ocean, profound, the blue, the deep, the drink, wave *(Archaic)*; **open sea,** blue water, main, open, seaway, seven seas, the high seas; **waters,** territorial waters; **offing,** outing, outside; **shallow,** low water, tidewater *(U.S.)*; **sea-floor,** benthos, ooze; **marine habitat,** euphotic zone, water-column. *See also* BAY; SURF; LAKE

SEA *adj* aquatic, halophilous *(Zool. Bot.)*, marine, Neptunian, oceanic, pelagic, sea-born, seawater, thalassic; **maritime,** deep-water, ocean-going, seaborne, seafaring, sea-going; **deep-sea,** abyssal, benthic, deepwater, demersal *(Zool.)*; **underwater,** subaquatic, subaqueous, submarine, suboceanic, undersea; **surfy,** insurgent, surgy; **tidal,** luni-tidal, neap; **neritic; littoral,** circumlittoral, inlying, inshore, seagirt *(Poetic)*; **offshore,** off, outward-bound, seaward; **overseas,** surface, transmarine, transoceanic, transpacific, ultramarine

sea *n* → **1** blue **2** moon **3** much

seagull *n* → **1** colourist **2** labourer **3** transporter

seahorse *n* → mythical beast

seal *n* → **1** animal's coat **2** emblem **3** label **4** model **5** paving **6** plug *v* **7** assent to **8** authorise **9** close **10** coat **11** emblematise **12** fish **13** label **14** smooth

seam *n* → **1** furrow **2** layer *v* **3** deflect **4** furrow **5** join

SEAMAN *n* a.b., able seaman, able-bodied seaman, artisan, bluejacket, bunting tosser, deckhand, Jack Tar *(Brit.)*, leatherneck *(U.S.)*, lime-juicer, limey, lower deck, marine, ordinary seaman, rating, topman; **ship's officer,** admiral, captain, captain, commander, commodore, deck officer, engine-room artificer, engineer officer, ensign *(U.S.)*, first mate, first officer, flag captain, flag officer, lieutenant commander, master, master mariner, number one, officer of the watch, privateer, rear admiral, sea-captain, second mate, shipmaster, skipper, vice-admiral, wardroom; **petty officer,** bo's'n, boatswain, bosun, jaunty, master-at-arms, steward *(U.S.)*, yeoman; **helmsman,** cox, coxswain, leadsman, navigator, pilot, steersman, wheelman *(U.S.)*; **midshipman,** middy; **purser,** supercargo; **cabin boy,** powder monkey. *See also* MARINER

seamstress *n* → sewer

seamy *adj* → bad

SEA NYMPH *n* bathing beauty, Lorelei, mermaid, nereid, sea witch, siren, undine, watersprite; **Neptune,** merman, the old man of the sea, Triton

sear *v* → **1** be callous **2** cook **3** dry **4** fir[e] **5** label

SEARCH *v* comb, leave no stone unturned, ransack, rat through, rummage; **cast about,** seek a clue; **look for,** cherchez la femme, keep an eye out for, nose after, nose for, seek, suss out; **frisk,** shake; **spy,** drag out, draw out, fish out, fly a kite, nose about, nose into, poke about, poke around, poke one's nose into, pry, smell out, sniff out, snoop, sound out; **explore,** fossick, geologise, wildcat

search *n* → **1** inspection **2** undertaking **3** pursue

SEARCHER *n* ransacker, rummager; **detective,** bloodhound, dick, frisker, gumshoe *(U.S.)*, private eye, private investigator, shamus, sleuth, tec; **ticket inspector,** snapper, ticket snapper; **explorer,** fossicker, hunter, potholer, prospector, search party, sourdough *(U.S.)*, spelunker, wildcatter *(U.S.)*

seasickness *n* → nausea

SEASIDE *n* coast, seaboard, seacoast, seafront, waterfront, waterfrontage; **shore,** bank, beach, dene, dunes, foreshore, sands, seashore, shingle, shoreline, strand, strandline, wash, wharf *(Obs.)*; **seabed,** bed, bottom, wavecut platform

SEASON *n* equinox, quarter, seedtime, solstice, tide, time of the year; **spring,** blossomtime, Maytide, Maytime, prime, springtime, vernal equinox, vernal point; **summer,** dog days, heat, heat wave, height of summer, Indian summer, midsummer, silly season, summer solstice, summeriness, summertime; **autumn,** autumnal equinox, autumnal point, fall *(U.S.)*, harvest, harvest home; **winter,** depth of winter, freeze, freeze-up, midwinter, winter solstice, wintertime, wintriness; **the wet,** monsoon; **the dry**

season *n* → **1** period *v* **2** cook **3** dry **4** habituate **5** harden **6** mix **7** moderate

SEASONAL *adj* equinoctial, solsticial; **seasonable,** in, in season; **spring,** vernal; **summer,** aestival, estival *(U.S.)*, midsummer, summer-like, summery; **autumn,** autumnal; **winter,** brumal, hibernal, midwinter, wintry

seasoning *n* → habituation

seat *n* → **1** bottom **2** buttocks **3** electorate **4** house **5** pose *v* **6** employ **7** fasten **8** have sex **9** support

seaweed *n* → surfer

secant *n* → **1** line *adj* **2** crossing

secateurs *n* → scissors

SECLUDE *v* cloister, closet, insulate from, isolate, relegate, rusticate, sequester, sequestrate *(Archaic)*, shut away; **retreat,** go to ground, hibernate, hole up, pull one's head in, shut out the world, skulk; **repel,** hold off, insulate oneself from, keep a low profile, keep at arm's length, keep away, withdraw from; **be isolated,** be in a world of one's own, be off the beaten track; **be antisocial,** go it alone, keep one's distance, keep one's own counsel, keep oneself to oneself

seclude *v* → hide

SECLUDED *adj* claustral, cloister-like, cloistered, cloistral, monachal, monasterial, monastic, monkish, seclusive, sequestered; **secret,** closet, private, privy *(Archaic)*; **remote,** desolate, distant, isolated, obscure, unmanned; **unfrequented,** buried, godforsaken, hidden, off the beaten track, out-of-the-way, tucked-away. *See also* SOLITARY

SECLUSION *n* isolation, privacy, privity *(Obs.)*, purdah, secrecy; **asylum,** a world of one's own, backwater, cloister, corner, hermitage, hideaway, ivory tower, refuge, retreat, sanctuary, sanctum; **private place,** cloister, closet, convent, holy of holies, inner sanctum, mew, monastery, monkery, nook, nunnery, sanctum sanctorum; **the back of beyond,** desert island, dump, hole, shell, the end of the earth. *See also* SOLITUDE

secondary *n* → **1** coming after **2** feather **3** inferior **4** partner *adj* **5** inferior **6** resultant **7** rocky **8** two **9** unimportant

second class *n* → inferior

second-class *adj* → **1** inferior **2** mediocre

second cousin *n* → relative

second-hand *adj* → **1** dilapidated **2** old **3** own **4** used up

SECRECY *n* caginess, closeness, covertness, dark, hugger-mugger *(Archaic)*, privacy, privateness, privity *(Obs.)*, secretness; **confidentiality,** confidence, confidentialness; **clandestineness,** collusiveness, furtiveness, slyness, sneakiness, stealth, stealthiness, surreptitiousness; **conspiracy,** cabal, collusion, conjuration *(Obs.)*, intrigue, plot; **code,** argot, cant, cipher, tick-tack

SECRET *n* classified information, confidence, dark secret, official secrets; **skeleton in the cupboard,** family skeleton, skeleton in the closet; **silent number**

SECRET *adj* classified, close, confidential, intimate, irrevealable, personal, private, privy *(Archaic)*, snug *(Obs.)*, top-secret; **hush-hush,** backroom, cabinet, cameral, closet, in camera, inner, interior; **unlisted,** concealed, ex-directory, invisible, unadmitted, unnamed

secret *n* → **1** cause **2** code **3** hiding *adj* **4** hidden **5** reticent **6** secluded **7** supernatural

Secret *n* → religious ceremony

secretariat *n* → recorder

secretary *n* → **1** desk **2** helper **3** member of parliament **4** recorder **5** writer

secrete *v* → **1** excrete **2** hide

SECRETIVE *adj* cagey, cloak-and-dagger, collusive, furtive, hole-and-corner, hugger-mugger, obreptitious, sly, sneaking, sneaky, stealthy, surreptitious, tiptoe, underhand; **clandestine,** backdoor, backstairs, bootleg *(U.S.)*, undercover, under-the-counter, underground

SECRETLY *adv* cryptically, on the side, under the counter; **privately,** behind closed doors, behind the scenes, between ourselves, between you and me, confidentially, entre nous, in camera, in confidence, in secret, in the background, on the q.t., sub rosa, under the rose; **stealthily,** behind one's back, like a thief in the night

SECRET PLACE *n* conclave, conventicle, corner, hideaway, recesses; **closed court,** camera *(Law)*

secret service *n* → spy

SECRET SOCIETY *n* backroom boys, cabal, huddle, inner circle, inside; **Resistance,** maquis *(French Hist.)*, underground *(Europ. Hist.)*

sect *n* → clique

section *n* → **1** armed forces **2** book part **3** coating **4** cut **5** diagram **6** lesson **7** musical band **8** part **9** railway *v* **10** cut

sector *v* → separate

secular *n* → **1** religious follower *adj* **2** ecclesiastic **3** irreverent **4** laic

SECURE *v* cocoon, cover, guard, pad, protect, safeguard, screen, shade, shadow, shield, wrap; **armour,** bard, cuirass, mail, visor; **defilade,** sconce

secure *v* → **1** fasten **2** gain **3** imprison **4** steady *adj* **5** certain **6** composed **7** fastened **8** protected **9** safe **10** steady

security *n* → **1** capital **2** composure **3** defence **4** insurance **5** safety **6** surety

sedan *n* → car

sedate *v* → **1** inactivate *adj* **2** composed **3** quiet **4** sombre

sedative *n* → **1** alleviator **2** anaesthetic **3** sleeping-pill *adj* **4** alleviant **5** anaesthetic **6** composed **7** medicinal

sedentary *adj* → inactive

sediment *n* → **1** remnant **2** soil

sedition *n* → **1** commotion **2** dissidence **3** encouragement **4** mutiny

seduce *v* → **1** allure **2** be promiscuous **3** encourage **4** flirt **5** rape

seductive *adj* → **1** alluring **2** attractive **3** encouraging **4** immoral **5** sexy

sedulous *adj* → **1** attentive **2** busy **3** effortful **4** persevering

SEE *v* behold, observe, view, witness; **catch sight of,** clap eyes on, glance *(Obs.)*, glimpse, lay eyes on, set eyes on, sight, twig, view *(Hunting)*; **discern,** descry, detect, distinguish, espy, ken *(Archaic)*, notice, recognise, resolve, scry *(Archaic)*, spot, spy; **visualise,** envisage, vision; **vide,** vide ante, vide infra, vide post, vide supra. *See also* LOOK

see *n* → **1** domain *v* **2** accompany **3** be friends **4** clarify **5** equal **6** find **7** flirt **8** know **9** predict **10** understand **11** visit

seed *n* → **1** bubble **2** offspring **3** powder **4** secretion **5** start **6** the chosen *v* **7** disperse **8** farm **9** order **10** persuade

seedy *adj* → dilapidated

seek *v* → **1** attempt **2** desire **3** pursue **4** search

seem *v* → appear

seemly *adj* → 1 beautiful 2 correct 3 cultivated 4 well-behaved *adv* 5 correctly
seep *n* → 1 exit 2 flow 3 wetness *v* 4 discharge 5 flow
seer *n* → 1 looker 2 occultist 3 predictor 4 wise person
seesaw *n* → 1 amusement park 2 flutter *v* 3 flutter 4 vibrate
seethe *n* → 1 turbulence *v* 2 complain 3 cook 4 extract 5 feel emotion 6 heat 7 toss
segment *n* → 1 curve 2 part *v* 3 inquire into 4 separate
segregate *v* → 1 separate *adj* 2 separate
seismic *adj* → vibrating
seize *v* → 1 arrest 2 capture 3 fasten 4 hold 5 meet an obstacle 6 use
seizure *n* → capture
seldom *adj* → 1 rare *adv* 2 rarely
select *v* → 1 choose *adj* 2 chosen 3 good
selection *n* → 1 choice 2 competitor 3 conception 4 farm 5 written composition
self-confidence *n* → certainty
self-conscious *adj* → 1 knowing 2 worried
self-defence *n* → 1 defence 2 justification
self-evident *adj* → 1 certain 2 obvious 3 true
self-government *n* → independence
self-interest *n* → selfishness
SELFISH *adj* asocial, egocentric, egoistic, egoistical, egotistic, egotistical, narcissistic, self-absorbed, self-aware, self-centred, self-loving, self-regarding; **self-indulgent,** incogitant, inconsiderate, possessive, self-pitying, spoilt; **mercenary,** base, calculating, hoggish, hoglike, self-interested, self-seeking, small, sordid, venal
selfish *adj* → avaricious
SELFISHNESS *n* egocentricity, egoism, egomania, egotism, narcissism, self-absorption, self-awareness, self-interest, self-love, self-regard, self-seeking; **self-indulgence,** hoggishness, inconsiderateness, inconsideration, possessiveness, self-pity, wank; **mercenariness,** baseness, careerism, cupboard love, opportunism, sordidness, venality
self-made *adj* → self-sufficient
self-opinionated *adj* → 1 proud 2 stubborn
self-possessed *adj* → 1 composed 2 sane
self-respect *n* → pride
SELF-SEEKER *n* brute, egocentric, egoist, egomaniac, egotist, hog, road-hog; **wanker,** spoilt brat; **mercenary,** careerist, opportunist; **sponge,** bludger, fortune-hunter, gimme girl, gold-digger, sponger
self-service *n* → restaurant
SELF-SUFFICIENT *adj* autarkical, individualistic, inner-directed, self-contained, self-made, self-reliant, self-supported, self-supporting, self-sustaining; **freelance,** self-employed. *See also* INDEPENDENT
SELL *v* auction, dispose of, flog, hock, market, offer, outsell, oversell, realise, regrate, resell, retail, sell out, sell short, sell up, short, turn over, wholesale; **peddle,** hawk, offer for sale, put on the market, send to market, tout, vend; **push,** hard-sell, hustle *(U.S.)*; **sell off,** discount, dump, knock down, remainder, undersell, unload; **be sold,** go, go like hc cakes, go under the hammer, move
sell *n* → 1 disenchantment 2 incentive 3 selling 4 trick *v* 5 encourage 6 trick
SELLER *n* broker, commission agent, commission merchant, dealer, discounter, flogger, merchant, middleman, regrater, reseller, retailer, stockist, tallyman, trader, trafficker, vendor, warehouseman, wholesaler; **travelling salesman,** agent, bagman, chapman *(Brit.)*, cheapjack, colporteur, commercial traveller, drummer, faker *(U.S.)*, Ghan, hawker, huckster, packman, pedlar, pitchman *(U.S.)*, rep, representative, sutler, traveller; **shopkeeper,** bourgeois, cashier, chandler, checkout chick, checkout operator, clerk *(U.S.)*, counterjumper, salesclerk *(U.S.)*, salesgirl, saleslady, salesman, salesperson, saleswoman, shop assistant, shopgirl, shopman *(Rare)*, storekeeper; **spieler,** barker, tout, touter; **auctioneer; dishonest trader,** black marketeer, blackbirder, bootlegger, dud-dropper, fence, short, slaver
SELLING *n* inertia selling, marketing, merchandising, pyramid selling, runout campaign, sales promotion, vendition; **auction,** crown auction, Dutch auction, public auction, vendue; **sale,** bazaar, clearance sale, clearing sale, closing-down sale, disposal, fete, fire sale, garage sale, jumble sale, reduction sale, resale, rummage sale, tie-in sale *(U.S.)*, walk-in walk-out sale; **sales talk,** colportage, hard sell, patter, sales pitch, salesmanship, sell, soft sell, spiel
selvedge *n* → edge
semantic *adj* → meaningful
semaphore *n* → 1 communication *v* 2 signal
semblance *n* → 1 appearances 2 copy 3 imitation 4 portrait 5 similarity
semen *n* → secretion
semester *n* → period
seminal *adj* → 1 creative 2 influential 3 original
seminar *n* → 1 discussion 2 lesson
seminary *n* → 1 college 2 school 3 start
semitrailer *n* → 1 supply vehicle 2 truck
senate *n* → 1 council 2 legislative body
send *n* → 1 thrust *v* 2 excite 3 thrust 4 transport
SEND A MESSAGE *v* leave word, pass information, send word; **correspond,** communicate with, correspond with, drop a line to, respond to, write; **circularise,** advise, file a report, notify; **mail,** consign, letterbox, post; **telegraph,** cable, telephone, telex, wire; **address,** direct, redirect
senile *adj* → 1 aged 2 ill 3 powerless 4 stupid
senior *n* → 1 boss 2 lawyer 3 old people 4 pupil 5 sportsman *adj* 6 aged 7 important
sensation *n* → 1 emotion 2 excitement 3 good thing 4 news item 5 perception
sensational *adj* → 1 exciting 2 good 3 violent
sense *n* → 1 competence 2 direction 3 logic 4 meaning 5 mind 6 perception 7 realism 8 translation 9 understanding 10 wisdom *v* 11 know 12 perceive

ensibility *n* → 1 emotionality 2 good taste 3 susceptibleness 4 understanding

ensible *adj* → 1 emotional 2 great 3 knowing 4 mental 5 perceptive 6 wise

ensitive *adj* → 1 cultivated 2 emotional 3 influenced 4 perceptive 5 reactive

ensual *adj* → 1 alluring 2 ill-bred 3 sexy 4 voluptuous

ensuous *adj* → beautiful

entence *n* → 1 judgment 2 opinion 3 proverb *v* 4 determine 5 punish

ententious *adj* → 1 assessorial 2 bombastic 3 boring 4 concise

entient *n* → 1 mind *adj* 2 emotional 3 perceptive

entiment *n* → 1 emotion 2 opinion

entimental *adj* → 1 desirous 2 emotional

entinel *n* → 1 defender 2 protector 3 soldier 4 warner *v* 5 look

entry *n* → 1 defender 2 protector 3 soldier 4 warner

EPARATE *v* crumble, decompose, disintegrate, dissociate, explode, fall apart, fall to pieces, shatter, spall, splinter, spring, start; **disconnect,** break away, disarticulate, disassemble, disengage, disjoin, dismount, disunite, loose, loosen, overhaul, splay, unbind, unbuckle, unbutton, unclasp, uncouple, unfasten, unfix, ungird *(Archaic)*, unglue, unhasp, unhinge, unhitch, unhook, unlay, unlimber, unlink, unpick, unplug, unravel, unsolder, unstick, untuck, unwind, unyoke; **sever,** abscind, cut, detach, disbranch, disbud, dissever; **part company,** break up, bust up, disband, divorce, opt out, part, sell dearly, split up; **break off,** calve, chip, cut off, destalk, hew off, sever, shear, slice, slice off, snip, strip, sunder; **rupture,** breach, break, cleave, crack, crash, crevasse, dash, disrupt, divide, divorce, fault, fissure, fracture, maul *(U.S.)*, open, part, rift, rip, rive, slit, split, sunder, wedge; **dismember,** break up, carve up, cut up, decartelise, decollate, departmentalise, disaffiliate, disband, disperse, dissect, dissolve, disunite, factionalise, quarter, segment, segregate, trisect; **disjoint,** dismantle, dismember, dissect, dissever, divide, enucleate, joint, knock down, macerate, ravel, ribbon, riffle, separate; **cast loose,** cast off *(Naut.)*, slip, unbend, unloose, untie; **bisect,** bifurcate, dichotomise, divide, fork, furcate; **allot,** chapter, compartment, compartmentalise, cut, demarcate, divide, fence off, fraction, fractionise, hedge, lot, mark off, part, partition, screen, sector, separate, serialise, shut off, size, space, spread, subdivide, wall; **detach,** break away, cull, distinguish from, draft, extract, hive off, maroon, pair off, sequester, sequestrate *(Archaic)*, shut off; **disassociate,** atomise, blanch, centrifugalise, centrifuge, cream, decompound, demulsify, desorb, dialyse, dissociate, distil, electrolyse, flake, hydrolyse, liberate, precipitate, screen, segregate, sleave; **partition,** Balkanise, dismember, divide and rule; **shred,** fractionate, gad, knap, spall, tease, ultracentrifuge; **pull apart,** dilacerate, dynamite, fritter, lancinate, rend, rip, rip off, scrap, siit, sliver, stave, tear, tear to pieces, tear up; **flake,** cast, exfoliate, foliate, husk, laminate, shed, slough; **isolate,** exile, island; **double-declutch,** double-shuffle; **be divisible into,** fall into

SEPARATE *adj* apart, detached, disconnected, discrete, disjunct, distinct, dividual *(Archaic)*, segregate; **loose,** free, loose leaf, unattached, unbolted, unbuttoned, unconnected, yokeless; **adrift,** castaway, cut loose; **divided,** cleft, compartmental, creviced, cut, diffractive, dipartite, disjointed, disrupt, dissected, episodic, multifid, parted, partite, ripped, riven, ruptured, split; **cleft in two,** bifid, bifurcate, bilobed, bilocular, bipartite, cloven, dichotomous, dimerous, forficate, forked, furcate, swallow-tailed; **trifurcate,** trifid, trifurcated, triparted, tripartite; **alienated,** disembodied, remote, removed, segregated; **cracked,** broken, crazed, fractural, fragmentary, fragmented, splintery; **clastic,** fragmental, green *(Metall.)*; **unmixible,** immiscible, incoherent; **freestanding,** outstanding, singular; **crumbly,** crumby, exfoliative, flaky, splitting; **parting,** ripping

separate *v* → 1 gape 2 separate *adj* 3 different 4 independent 5 particular

SEPARATOR *n* breaker-down, detacher, disarticulator, dismemberer, disperser, divider, harrower, ripper, subdivider, sunderer, zootomist; **screener,** cutter-out, dry-blower, rippler, scutcher, thresher, winnower; **dag picker,** dagger; **splitter,** mauler *(U.S.)*, river

sepia *n* → 1 photograph *adj* 2 brown 3 colourless

sepsis *n* → illness

septic *n* → 1 toilet *adj* 2 bad 3 dirty 4 unwholesome

septic tank *n* → toilet

septum *n* → wall

sepulchre *n* → 1 church 2 grave *v* 3 bury

sequel *n* → 1 coming after 2 drama 3 magazine 4 result

SEQUENCE *n* catena, chain, concatenation, consecution, continuation, continuity, course, cycle, prolongation, round, series, succession; **following,** cavalcade, column, cortege, procession, progression, retinue, string, suite, trail, train; **single file,** Indian file, tandem

sequence *n* → 1 act 2 classification 3 result 4 series

SEQUENTIAL *adj* consecutive, on end, processional, progressional, running, sequent, serial, seriate, successive; **unbroken,** direct, entire, flowing, indiscrete, run-on, solid, steady, straight

sequester *v* → 1 seclude 2 separate 3 take

sequin *n* → trimming

serenade *n* → 1 concert *v* 2 sing

serendipity *n* → 1 finding 2 good fortune 3 luckiness

serene *n* → 1 space *adj* 2 peaceful

serf *n* → 1 servant 2 subject

sergeant *n* → policeman

serial *n* → 1 magazine 2 program *adj* 3 regular 4 sequential

serial number *n* → label

SERIES *n* continuum, gradation, one thing after another, progression, sequence, succession; **line,** chain, column, file, Indian file, procession, queue, rank, run, stream, string, train; **arithmetical progression,** arithmetic series, geometric progression, geometric series

series *n* → 1 book 2 layer 3 musical phrase 4 program 5 repetition 6 rock outcrop 7 sequence 8 whole

SERIOUS *adj* earnest; **decisive,** certain *(Obs.)*, constant, single-minded, stable, staunch, steadfast, steady, steady of purpose, stout, stout-hearted, sturdy; **resolute,** decided, determinate, determined, firm, resolved

serious *adj* → 1 attentive 2 dangerous 3 important 4 sombre

sermon *n* → 1 bore 2 figure of speech 3 harangue 4 lesson 5 oration

serpent *n* → 1 bad person 2 brass instrument 3 cunning person 4 devil

serum *n* → 1 medication 2 secretion

SERVANT *n* menial, server, servitor, underservant, wallah; **domestic,** abigail, au pair, ayah, bedmaker, chambermaid, char, charlady, charwoman, cleaning lady, daily, domestic help, general *(Obs.)*, girl, handmaid, help, home aid, home help, houseboy, housekeeper, housemaid, lady's maid, maid, maidservant, old Dutch, parlourmaid, sadie, slavey, soubrette, tweeny *(Obs.)*, woman; **nursemaid,** amah, mammy *(U.S.)*, mother's help, nanny; **washerwoman,** dhobi, laundress, washerman; **lady-in-waiting,** gentlewoman *(Hist.)*; **bondservant,** assignee, blackbird, bondman, bondsman, bondwoman, carl *(Obs.)*, helot, Nubian, prisoner servant, serf, slave, thrall, vassal *(Archaic)*, villain, villein *(Hist.)*; **concubine,** odalisque; **attendant,** bumboy, camp follower, follower, hatchet man, henchman *(Obs.)*, lackey, mercenary, roadie; **aide-de-camp,** ADC, aide, batman *(Mil.)*, orderly *(Mil.)*, squire; **armour-bearer,** armiger, caddie, caddy, linkboy, mate; **beadle,** verger; **retainer,** liege, liegeman, man, samurai; **entourage,** attendance, cortege, retinue, varletry *(Archaic)*, villeinage. *See also* BUTLER

servant *n* → 1 helper 2 subject 3 supplier

serve *n* → 1 reprimand 2 supplies *v* 3 be adequate 4 be expedient 5 be of service 6 be sociable 7 cover 8 do one's duty 9 feed 10 help 11 obey 12 operate 13 satisfy 14 twist 15 work

servery *n* → kitchen

service *n* → 1 help 2 repair 3 supply 4 twist 5 usefulness *v* 6 conceive 7 repair

serviceable *adj* → 1 careful 2 durable 3 useable 4 useful

SERVICEMAN *n* effective, enlisted ma *(U.S.)*, servicewoman; **conscript,** chocc chocolate soldier, draftee *(U.S.)*, nasho, se ectee *(U.S.)*; **national service,** conscriptio draft; **recruit,** rookie, sprog, substitute, vo unteer; **militiaman,** armed constabular *(N.Z. Obs.)*, Dad's army, Home Guard, mi itia, minute man *(U.S.)*, reserve, reservis state trooper, territorial; **ex-serviceman,** cam paigner, old soldier, returned soldier, RSI vet *(U.S.)*, veteran, warhorse; **non-combatan** base wallah, base walloper *(N.Z.)*, shiny arse, tin soldier; **military policema** gendarme. *See also* SOLDIER; COMBA TROOPS; ARMED FORCES

serviette *n* → washer

servile *adj* → 1 flattering 2 meek 3 obedien 4 obsequious 5 opportunist 6 repressed

servitude *n* → 1 repression 2 rights

session *n* → 1 centre of activity 2 cour session 3 lesson 4 period

set *n* → 1 accumulation 2 book 3 clas 4 dance 5 direction 6 distortion 7 hangin 8 point of view 9 pose 10 position 11 simila thing 12 stage 13 surf 14 television *v* 15 command 16 cost 17 dance 18 decorate 19 descend 20 direct 21 flow 22 give birth 23 harden 24 make 25 make music 26 medicat 27 order 28 place 29 print 30 regularis 31 sharpen 32 steady 33 support *adj* 34 conventional 35 faithful 36 prepared 37 steady

SET AN EXAMPLE *v* lead the way, provide model, set the pace, show the way

SET SAIL *v* get under way, put to sea, sai weigh anchor; **go to sea,** cruise, follow th sea, ship, voyage; **picaroon,** buccaneer; **mak way,** beat, luff, make heavy weather, pinch point, sail close to the wind, scud, thrash **tack,** bear away, broach, ease off, go about harden sheets, haul up, overlay, overstand **shorten sail,** back and fill, blanket, fill away jibe, reef; **make sail,** overhaul, sheet home **dismast,** unrig

settee *n* → couch

setting *n* → 1 hairdressing 2 musical piec 3 placement 4 position 5 stage 6 surroundings

settle *n* → 1 couch *v* 2 account 3 agree 4 arrange 5 dismount 6 fall 7 finish 8 give 9 inhabit 10 make whole 11 mediate 12 orde 13 pay 14 promise 15 rest 16 steady

settlement *n* → 1 adjustment 2 agreemen 3 almshouse 4 arrangement 5 contrac 6 dwelling 7 finish 8 landslide 9 paymen 10 placement 11 property 12 town

settler *n* → population

SEVEN *n* hebdomad, heptad, heptameter heptarchy, septenary, septet, septuplet, seventh; **heptagon,** heptahedron

SEVEN *adj* heptagonal, heptahedral, heptamerous, septenary, septuple, sevenfold, seventh

sever *v* → 1 cut 2 separate

several *adj* → 1 few 2 particular

severe *adj* → 1 callous 2 difficult 3 intense 4 precise 5 strict 6 violent

EW *v* darn, fine-draw, hem; **stitch,** buttonhole; **embroider,** appliqué, broider *(Archaic)*, crochet, enlace, hook, tat, work; **interface,** buckram, interline; **brocade,** damask, emboss, quilt; **pipe,** goffer; **weave,** beetle, bolt, card, comb, garnet, loom *(Rare)*, pick, ripple, scribble, scutch, spin, spindle, tease, teasel, throw, twill, willow; **felt,** nap, tack; **knit,** purl, rib

ew *v* → **1** join **2** repair

ewage *n* → **1** bodily discharge **2** dirt **3** remnant

EWER *n* darner, dressmaker, hemmer, machinist, needlewoman, seamstress, tailor; **weaver,** knitter, spinster *(Obs.)*, tatter; **textile worker,** comber, flaxie *(N.Z. Colloq.)*, napper, rippler, teaseller

ewer *n* → **1** butler **2** clothier **3** den of vice **4** drain **5** pigsty **6** toilet

ewerage *n* → **1** remnant **2** toilet

EWING *n* appliqué, broderie anglaise, broidery *(Archaic)*, contexture, couching, crewelwork, crochet, cutwork, darning, dressmaking, embroidery, Florentine trapunto, invisible mending, knitting, needlepoint, needlework, overcasting, patchwork, petit point, quilt, quilting, sampler, smocking, tapestry, trapunto; **spinning,** beating-up, carding, combing, crabbing, felting, filature, intertwining, interweaving, picking, shedding; **lacing,** tatting; **weaving**

SEX *n* female, gender, male, opposite sex; **bisexualism,** androgyny, hermaphroditism, virilism; **sexlessness,** asexuality; **lust,** arousal, concupiscence, excitement, heat, horniness, hotpants, libido, oestrus, passion, pride *(Obs.)*

SEX AID *n* dildo, vibrator; **aphrodisiac,** cantharides, love philtre, love potion, love-juice, powdered blister beetles, Spanish fly; **sex shop,** porn shop; **sexploitation,** sex-sell; **pornography,** hard-core, hard-core pornography, porno, soft-core pornography

sexist *adj* → intolerant

SEX OBJECT *n* arse, black velvet, crumpet, cunt, fuck, gash, lay, snatch, tail, talent, twat, yellow satin; **stud,** cunthook, hunk; **sex symbol,** cover girl, pin-up

SEXUAL *adj* female, gamic, male, sexed; **hermaphroditic,** androgynous, epicene, hermaphrodite, hermaphroditical, intersexual; **sexless,** asexual; **heterosexual,** unisexual; **bisexual,** ac-dc, bi; **homosexual,** camp, fruity, gay, high-camp, invert, lesbian, queer; **transsexual; paraphiliac,** algolagnic, anilingual, bestial, masochistic, onanistic, pederastic, sadist, sadistic, transvestite, voyeuristic; **incestuous**

SEXUAL INTERCOURSE *n* carnal knowledge, coition, coitus, commerce, congress, connection, consummation, copulation, favours, funny business, intercourse, intimacy, jigjig, knowledge *(Law Archaic)*, lovemaking, sex, twat; **act of sexual intercourse,** a tumble in the hay, bang, fuck, grind, jump, kneetrembler, lash, morning glory, naughty, nooky, poke, quickie, roll, root, screw, shag; **sexual behaviour,** facts of life, love-life; **illicit sex,** a bit on the side, adultery, forbidden fruit, fornication; **loveplay,** feel, foreplay, fumble, hanky-panky, slap-and-tickle; **oral sex,** anilingus, blow job, cunnilingus, fellatio, furburger, hair pie, sixty-nine, soixante-neuf; **missionary position; coitus interruptus; orgy,** gang bang, gang slash, gang splash, gangie, group grope, group stoop, team cream; **orgasm,** climax, ejaculation, nocturnal emission, the big O, wet dream

SEXUALITY *n* alloerotism, carnality, earthiness, eroticisation, eroticism, lewdness, sensuality, venery; **sexiness,** alluringness, bedworthiness, bedroom eyes, cheesecake, erogeneity, it, oomph, seductiveness, sex appeal; **promiscuity,** amorism, bawdry, whorishness; **erotomania,** nymphomania, satyriasis; **frigidity,** coldness, frigidness; **heterosexuality,** unisexuality; **bisexuality; homosexuality,** inversion, pederasty, queerness; **lesbianism,** sapphism, tribadism; **transvestism,** eonism; **sodomy,** bestiality, buggery; **paraphilia,** necrophilia, perversion, scopophilia, voyeurism; **indecent exposure,** exhibitionism; **sadomasochism,** algolagnia, b. and d., bondage, discipline, masochism, sadism; **fetishism; masturbation,** autoerotism, jerk-off, onanism, self-abuse, wank

SEXUAL PARTNER *n* bedfellow, cohabitant, cohabiter, paramour, partner, pick-up, sleeping partner; **fornicator,** adulterer, adultress, amorist, cicisbeo, co-respondent, erotic, eroticist, fucker, hotpants, shagger; **erotomaniac,** nympho, nymphomaniac, satyr; **swinger,** gang banger, onion; **lover,** fancy man, sugar daddy; **womaniser,** Bluebeard, easy rider *(U.S.)*, goat, lecher, pants man, ruiner, seducer, sheikh; **premature ejaculator,** minute man; **cradle-snatcher,** baby snatcher; **gin burglar,** gin jockey; **mistress,** concubine, demimondaine, hetaera, leman *(Archaic)*, woman; **seductress,** mantrap, vamp; **cockteaser,** prick-teaser, teaser; **hussy,** bike, floozy, gunnie, scrubber *(Brit.)*, wanton; **groupie,** band moll; **fridge**

SEXUAL RELATIONSHIP *n* affair, amour, intrigue, involvement, liaison, love affair, ménage à trois, one-night stand; **dirty weekend,** lost weekend, naughty forty-eight

SEXUAL TYPE *n* hetero, heterosexual; straight; **bisexual,** epicene, hermaphrodite, switch hitter; **homosexual,** arse bandit, aunty, bimbo, bronzer, cat, catamite, dung puncher, effeminate, fag, faggot, fairy, flit, fruit, Ganymede, gay, hock, homo, horse's hoof, minion, nancy boy, nut man, pansy, pederast, poof, poofter, poonce, poove, punk, quean *(Obs.)*, queen, queer, quince, second-hand Sue, shirt-lifter, swish, tonk; **lesbian,** butch, dyke, femme, les, lezz, lezzy, tribade; **transsexual; sodomite,** bugger, bummer, sod; **muff-diver; paraphiliac,** fetishist, necrophiliac, peeping tom, pervert, porno, secco, transvestite, voyeur; **exhibitionist,** flasher; **sadomasochist,** algolagnist, masochist, sadist; **masturbator,** jerk-off, rod-walloper, wanker

SEXY *adj* alluring, bed-worthy, beddable, erogenous, oomphy, seductive; **erotic,** alloerotic, anatomical, aphrodisiac, autoerotic, carnal, earthy, erotogenic, fruity, sensual; **aroused,** excited, horny, on heat, randy, raunchy, ruttish, toey; **lecherous,** evil-minded *(Joc.)*, libidinous, on the make, oversexed, randy; **in like Flynn,** made; **permissive,** loose, promiscuous, swinging; **pornographic,** porno; **copulative,** intimate, orgastic, venereal

sexy *adj* → **1** alluring **2** beautiful **3** obscene

shabby *adj* → **1** dilapidated **2** mean **3** ugly

shack *n* → cabin

shackle *n* → **1** hindrance **2** restraints *v* **3** fasten **4** restrain

SHADE *n* penumbra, shadow, umbra, umbrage *(Obs.)*; **cloud,** fog, lour, mist, murk, smog, smoke; **pall,** covering, shroud. *See also* DARKNESS

shade *n* → **1** darkener **2** grade **3** hiding **4** phantom **5** screen *v* **6** change **7** cover **8** darken **9** depict **10** graduate **11** hide **12** secure

shadow *n* → **1** black **2** companion **3** danger **4** drawing **5** friend **6** grade **7** imprecision **8** shade **9** small amount *v* **10** cloud **11** darken **12** depict **13** partner **14** pursue **15** secure

SHADOWY *adj* adumbral, bosky, bowery, darkened, penumbral, shaded, shady, tenebrific, tenebrous, umbrageous, umbriferous; **twilight,** crepuscular, dusk, duskish; **dim,** caliginous *(Rare)*, darkish, wan *(Archaic)*; **dull,** bleary, cloudy, dingy, dirty, dismal, foggy, gloomy, hazy, lack-lustre, lowering, misty, murk *(Archaic)*, murky, overcast, sad, smoky, sombre, subfusc, sunless. *See also* DARK

shady *adj* → **1** dishonest **2** disreputable **3** ethereal **4** shadowy

SHAFT *n* lath, pale, paling, palisade, picket, slat, slip, spline, stake, stave; **board,** chump, floorboard, skirt, skirting, skirting board; **plank,** deal, gangplank, gangway, skid, wale; **beam,** baulk, binder, couple, dead shore, flitch beam, girder, joist, rafter, rolled steel joist, RSJ, sleeper, stanchion, straining beam, timber, tree; **crossbeam,** collar tie, summer, tie beam, transom, traverse

shaft *n* → **1** bridge **2** excavation **3** feather **4** groin **5** light **6** passageway **7** piercer **8** post **9** rod **10** slope **11** spear **12** stick *v* **13** demote

shag *n* → **1** hair **2** sexual intercourse **3** tobacco *v* **4** have sex **5** roughen **6** sharpen **7** tire

shaggy *adj* → **1** hairy **2** rough **3** untidy

shake *n* → **1** drink **2** flutter **3** gap **4** moment **5** timber **6** turbulence **7** vibration *v* **8** agitate **9** agree **10** be frightened **11** elude **12** escape **13** extort **14** mix **15** recline **16** rob **17** search **18** vibrate **19** weaken

shale *n* → coating

SHALLOW *n* bank, bar, bombora, coral reef flat, ford, low-water mark, reef, sandbank sandbar, shallows, shelf, shoal; **shallowness** superficiality, superficialness; **scratch** pinprick; **thin coat,** gloss, skin, veneer

SHALLOW *v* flatten, shoal, silt up

SHALLOW *adj* flat, low, shoal, shoaly; **superficial,** ankle-deep, knee-deep, skin-deep slight

shallow *n* → **1** sea *adj* **2** foolish **3** hollow **4** stupid **5** unimportant

sham *n* → **1** fake **2** imitation *v* **3** pretend *adj* **4** fake

shamble *n* → **1** place of killing **2** walking **3** walk

shambles *n* → **1** massacre **2** muddle **3** untidiness

shame *n* → **1** disrepute **2** guilt **3** penitence *v* **4** disgrace

shampoo *n* → **1** cleanser **2** cleansing *v* **3** clean

shandy *n* → beer

shanghai *n* → **1** propellant **2** transport *v* **3** rob **4** transport

shank *n* → **1** leg *v* **2** walk

shanty *n* → **1** cabin **2** pub **3** song

SHAPE *n* fashion, figuration, figure, form, lines, mould, turn; **design,** pattern, schematism, scheme; **geometry,** spherics, topology; **multiformity,** dimorphism, heteromorphism, heteromorphy, metamorphosis, polymorphism, pseudomorphism, stereo-isomerism, trimorphism; **polymorph,** dimorph, habit, trimorph; **cast,** die, formwork, matrix, swage block. *See also* STRUCTURE

SHAPE *v* fashion, figure, form, model, pattern; **structure,** define, develop, formalise, formulate, frame, incubate; **design,** geometrise, round, square, style, tailor; **mould,** block, cast, found, ingot, tree; **sculpt,** carve, chisel, cut, rough-hew, trim, whittle; **forge,** beat out, dolly, hammer out, smith; **turn,** blow, spin, throw; **stamp,** die, swage, tool

shape *n* → **1** condition **2** model **3** order *v* **4** adjust **5** make

SHAPELESS *adj* amorphous, baggy, blobby, featureless, formless, inchoate, indefinite, indigested, nondescript; **unshaped,** rudimentary, uncut, unformed, unhewn

SHAPELESSNESS *n* amorphia, amorphism, amorphousness, formlessness; **lump,** agglomeration, aggregation, cloud, mass, smudge

shapely *adj* → beautiful

SHARE *n* a slice of the action, a slice of the cake, allotment, allowance, bit, bunce, chop, cut, darg, deal *(Obs.)*, dividend, dole, fraction, helping, interest, lay *(Fishing)*, lot, portion, preallotment, proportion, quantum, quota, rake-off, ration, round, split, stint, whack

share *n* → **1** part **2** profit **3** small amount *v* **4** participate **5** share out

SHARED *adj* common, divided, dividual *(Archaic)*, joint, participable, split; **distribut-**

able, apportionable, commonable, dividable, divisible; **distributive,** distributional, respective

HARE OUT *v* admeasure, administer, allocate, allot, apportion, assign, assort, average out, carve up, deal, demark, detail, dish out, dispense, distribute, divide, divvy up, dole out, give out, hand out, issue, lot, mete out, morsel, parcel out, partition, portion, ration, redistribute, repartition, serve out, subdivide, unlock the land *(Hist.)*; **share,** divvy, go Dutch, go halves, go into, split, whack up; **participate,** get in for one's chop, get one's corner, get one's share, partake

HARING OUT *n* cavil *(Mining)*, communalism, communism, Dutch shout, Dutch treat, job sharing, profit sharing, sharing, socialism, tontine; **distribution,** admeasurement, administration, allocation, allotment, apportionment, appropriation, assignation, assignment, assortment, carve-up, chop-up, deal, dispensation, divide, division, issue, participation, partition, partitionment, rationing, redistribution, repartition, shareout

shark *n* → crook

SHARP *adj* acuate, acute, cultrate, fine, keen, sharp-edged, trenchant *(Poetic)*; **biting,** acid, acidulous, acrid, acrimonious, bitter, cutting, mordacious, penetrating, piercing, pointed, pungent, shrewd *(Archaic)*, shrill *(Poetic)*; **double-edged,** two-edged; **self-sharpening.** *See also* POINTED; SPINY

sharp *n* → **1** crook *adj* **2** attentive **3** cold **4** cunning **5** deflective **6** dissonant **7** enthusiastic **8** intelligent **9** intense **10** precise **11** pungent **12** shrill **13** sloping **14** sour **15** speedy **16** strict **17** unpleasant *adv* **18** attentively **19** hurriedly **20** speedily **21** timely

SHARPEN *v* acuminate, edge, point, put kinchella on *(Shearing)*, set, spike, strap *(Obs.)*, whet; **point,** barb, shag, Vandyke

SHARPENER *n* hone, pencil-sharpener, slip, strap, strickle, strop, whetstone

SHARP-EYED *adj* clear-eyed, clear-sighted, eagle-eyed, far-seeing, far-sighted, hawk-eyed, lyncean, lynx-eyed, perspicacious *(Archaic)*, sharp-sighted; **watchful,** argus-eyed, observant, open-eyed, surveillant, wakeful; **voyeuristic**

SHARPNESS *n* acumination, acuteness, keenness; **pointedness,** prickliness, spininess, spinosity, thorniness; **acuity,** acuteness, shrewdness, subtleness, subtlety

SHARP POINT *n* cusp, mucro, neb, nib, pike, pinpoint, point, prickle, tip; **spire,** flèche, minaret, steeple; **stylus,** needle, scribe, scriber, style, stylo pen

shatter *v* → **1** injure **2** ruin **3** separate

shave *n* → **1** cut *v* **2** come close **3** cut **4** cut off **5** rub

shaving *n* → **1** coating **2** small amount

shawl *n* → cloak

she *n* → woman

sheaf *n* → accumulation

SHEAR *v* barber, barrow, chop, cut, pink, poke off, ring, tomahawk, undress; **dag,** belly, channel, crutch, ring, wig; **ring the board,** do a Jimmy Gibbs, ring the shed, swing the gate

shear *n* → **1** amount **2** cut *v* **3** cut **4** separate

SHEARER *n* bladeshearer, bladesman, brute, gouger, greasy, jingling Johnny, sheepshearer, stooper, stud, tiger, woolhawk; **ringer,** deuce artist, deucer, dreadnought, good iron, gun shearer, ryebuck shearer, shed-boss; **learner,** barrowman, Cunnamulla gun, drummer, snagger; **shedhand,** baler, board boy, broomie, brownie gorger, hummer, penner *(N.Z.)*, picker, picker-up, pony, sheepo, tarboy; **dagpicker,** dag boy, dagger; **fleece-picker,** fleece-oh, fleecie, fleecy, piece-picker, table hand; **roller,** fleeceroller, skirter, woolroller; **expert,** squirt; **wool classer,** con man, guesser, wool sorter, wool stapler

SHEARING *n* barrowing, sheepshearing; **Barcoo challenge,** throwing the belly wool; **wool classing,** bulk classing, core testing

sheath *n* → **1** arsenal **2** case **3** contraception **4** covering **5** dress **6** skin

sheathe *v* → **1** enclose **2** insert

sheen *n* → **1** brightness *adj* **2** beautiful **3** bright

SHEEP *n* barebelly, bellwether, carry-over lamb, cobbler, cosset, crock, ewe, fat lamb, flock ewe, flock ram, full-mouth, hogget, joe, jumbuck, prime lamb, ram, sandy cobbler, shearer, shornie, sound-mouth, spring lamb, teg, treble fleece, tup, wet sheep, woolly, yeo; **goat,** billy, billygoat, kid, nanny-goat, nubian goat

sheep *n* → coward

sheepish *adj* → **1** meek **2** modest

sheer *n* → **1** curve *v* **2** deflect *adj* **3** bright **4** simple **5** sloping **6** transparent **7** unconditional *adv* **8** slopingly

sheikh *n* → **1** allurer **2** monastic **3** sexual partner

sheila *n* → **1** friend **2** lover **3** woman

SHELF *n* bookrack, cupboard, étagère *(Furnit.)*, gradin *(Eccles.)*, hob, mantelpiece, mantelshelf, mantle, shelving, whatnot; **rack,** hack, hayfeeder *(Agric.)*

shelf *n* → **1** informant **2** rock outcrop **3** shallow *v* **4** report on

SHELTER *n* air-raid shelter, Anderson shelter, bunker, fallout shelter, hardened site, storm cellar *(U.S.)*; **hut,** beach hut, gunyah, humpy *(Aborig.)*, mia-mia *(Aborig.)*, Nissen hut, wurley *(Aborig.)*; **shed,** booth, box, bus-shelter, picnic shelter, press-box, sentry-box, shelter-shed; **tent,** awning, bell tent, hutchie, marquee, pup tent, stock-camp, tarpaulin; **arbour,** bower, mai mai *(N.Z.)*, pergola, summerhouse; **garage,** boathouse, boatshed, carport, coach-house, depot, hangar, hoverport, running shed *(Railways)*; **den,** burrow, cote, earth, hutch, kennel, lodge, nest, sett. *See also* REFUGE; HARBOUR

SHELTER *v* ensconce, harbour, haven, house, lodge, shroud *(Obs.)*; **garage,** embower, hive, kennel, shed

shelter *n* → **1** almshouse **2** dwelling

shelve *v* → **1** avoid **2** dismiss **3** report on **4** slope

shemozzle *n* → **1** loud sound **2** muddle

shenanigan *n* → **1** stratagem **2** trickery

shepherd *n* → **1** ecclesiastic **2** farmhand **3** non-user *v* **4** care for **5** disuse

sherbet *n* → **1** beer **2** bubbling

sheriff *n* → policeman

shield *n* → **1** armour **2** coating **3** defence **4** rock outcrop **5** wall *v* **6** prohibit **7** secure

shift *n* → **1** centre of activity **2** change **3** dress **4** exchange **5** expedient **6** period **7** removal **8** stratagem **9** transport **10** trick **11** workers *v* **12** make do **13** move **14** speed **15** transport **16** wear

shiftless *adj* → **1** idle **2** unready

shifty *adj* → **1** cunning **2** dishonest **3** opportunist

shimmer *n* → **1** light *v* **2** shine

shin *n* → **1** leg *v* **2** ascend

SHINE *v* beam, beat, effulge, glare, outshine *(Rare)*, overshine; **glow,** halo *(Rare)*, incandesce; **sparkle,** bicker, blink, coruscate, flicker, glance, gleam, glimmer, glint, glisten, glister *(Archaic)*, glitter, scintillate, shimmer, spangle, spark, twinkle, wink; **flash,** fulgurate, lighten; **radiate,** diffract, ray, reflect, refract; **luminesce,** fluoresce, phosphoresce; **burn,** blaze, flame, flare

shine *n* → **1** amusement **2** brightness **3** polish **4** weather *v* **5** be obvious **6** illuminate **7** make history **8** polish **9** succeed

shiner *n* → injury

shingle *n* → **1** building materials **2** coating **3** hairdressing **4** label **5** powder **6** rock **7** seaside *v* **8** cover **9** cut

shining *adj* → **1** bright **2** good

ship *n* → **1** aircraft **2** mariner **3** watercraft *v* **4** absorb **5** remove **6** set sail **7** transport

shipment *n* → **1** amount **2** trade

shipshape *adj* → **1** tidy *adv* **2** tidily

shiralee *n* → accumulation

shire *n* → **1** administrative area **2** domain **3** legislative body

shirk *n* → **1** avoider **2** idler *v* **3** avoid **4** be unwilling **5** idle

shirr *n* → **1** fold *v* **2** cook **3** fold

SHIRT *n* banian, body shirt, boiled shirt *(Colloq.)*, byrnie, cilice, Crimean shirt, jac shirt, sark *(Scot. Archaic)*, sports shirt, sweatshirt, T-shirt, tank top, tee-shirt, top; **blouse,** boob tube, chemisette, guimpe, overblouse, stomacher; **shirt-tail,** Australian flag *(Colloq.)*, flag

shirty *adj* → irritable

shit *n* → **1** bad person **2** defecation **3** marijuana **4** nonsense *v* **5** anger **6** defecate *interj* **7** God **8** how about that

shiver *n* → **1** coldness **2** part **3** vibration *v* **4** be cold **5** vibrate

shoal *n* → **1** fish **2** gathering **3** island **4** shallow *v* **5** shallow *adj* **6** shallow

shock *n* → **1** illness **2** impact **3** psychic dis turbance **4** surprise **5** violent outburst **6** electrify **7** surprise *adj* **8** surprising

shocking *adj* → **1** bad **2** dreadful **3** surprisin **4** ugly

shoddy *n* → **1** affectation *adj* **2** bad

shoe *n* → **1** boot **2** footgear

shoot *n* → **1** contest **2** interval **3** shot **4** stem **5** appear **6** cinematise **7** explode **8** fire o **9** flower **10** hurry **11** insert **12** kill **13** measur **14** photograph **15** take drugs **16** throw

SHOP *n* establishment, outlet, point of sal p.o.s., store, tallyshop *(Brit.)*; **market,** bazaa exchange, flea market, marketplace, mart **supermarket,** cash and carry, hypermarke *(Brit. U.S.)*, superette; **shopping centre,** ar cade, mall, shopping complex, shopping pre cinct *(Brit.)*, shoppingtown; **stall,** barrow booth, counter, stand; **salesroom,** floo space, shopwindow; **department store,** chain store, emporium, retail store; **general store** army surplus store, chaff-and-grain store, co op, corner shop, disposal store, duty-fre shop, prodgie, produce store, trading post **food shop,** bakery, butchery, macellaria charcuterie, dairy, deli, delicatessen, dellie fair, grocery, ham-and-beef shop, pie-car rialto, sweetshop, tuckshop; **bookshop** bookstall, bookstand, newsagency, news stand, stationer; **clothes shop,** boutique jeanery, slopshop; **haberdashery,** mercery **hardware store,** ironmongery; **second-hand shop,** junk shop, op-shop, opportunity shop thrift shop; **tobacconist; toyshop; pawnshop** hockshop *(U.S.)*, Moscow, pop-shop; **bar** bodega, bottle department, bottle shop, cellars, grog shop, speak-easy, wine bar wineshop; **café,** bistro, coffee bar, coffee house, coffee shop, espresso bar, estaminet gelataria, kiosk, milk bar, tea-garden, teahouse, tearoom, teashop *(Brit.)*; **saleyard** birdcage *(N.Z.)*, caryard, timber yard; **booking office,** box office *(Theat.)*, office; **vending machine,** automat, slot machine

shop *n* → **1** factory *v* **2** betray **3** buy **4** report on

shoplift *v* → rob

shop steward *n* → trade unionist

shore *n* → **1** beam **2** coastline **3** nation **4** seaside *v* **5** support *adj* **6** land

SHORT *adj* brief, cut-off, short and sweet, truncate, truncated; **little,** dwarfed, knee-high to a grasshopper, pint-size, snub, snubby, stunted, undersized; **stocky,** nuggetty, squat; **tubby,** fubsy, podgy, stodgy; **low-rise**

short *n* → **1** absence **2** electric circuit **3** film **4** seller *v* **5** sell *adj* **6** brittle **7** concise **8** deficient **9** discourteous **10** insufficient **11** intoxicating **12** small *adv* **13** hurriedly

shortage *n* → **1** deficiency **2** insufficiency

short-change *v* → cheat

shortcoming *n* → **1** deficiency **2** imperfection

SHORTEN *v* abbreviate, curtail, cut, epitomise, telescope; **cut down,** crop, cut, detruncate, truncate; **cut across,** cut corners, cut off a corner

ıorten *v* → **1** cook **2** decrease

ıorthand *n* → writing

ıortly *adv* → **1** concisely **2** in the future **3** momentarily

IORT PERSON *n* dwarf, little person, nugget *(Colloq.)*, pigmy, pudding, short arse, shortie, stodge

ıorts *n* → trousers

ıort-sighted *adj* → **1** prejudiced **2** stupid

IORT-WINDED *adj* asthmatic, chesty, wheezy; **catarrhal,** allergic, stuffed up, stuffy; **consumptive,** hectic, tubercular, wasting; **pneumonic,** pleuritic

IOT *n* cannon shot, cannonry, discharge, gunshot, pot, pot shot, round, shoot, shooting, snipe; **volley,** blaze, bombardment, cannonade, fire, firing, fusillade, rapid fire

ıot *n* → **1** a drink **2** ammunition **3** attack **4** attempt **5** ball **6** conjecture **7** explosive **8** insert **9** length **10** medication **11** photograph **12** stroke *adj* **13** multicoloured **14** powerless

ıotgun *n* → gun

ıould *v* → **1** necessitate **2** obligate

ıoulder *n* → **1** bulge **2** kerbing **3** surf *v* **4** support **5** thrust

HOUT *n* bawl, bellow, holler, whoop, yell; **howl,** cry, outcry, squall, squawk, wail, whimper, whine, yawp, yelp, yowl; **shriek,** scream, screech, squeal; **cheer,** encore, huzza; **call,** azan, clarion, hoot, muster, mustering, note, page, rollcall, summons; **hail,** cooee, oyez; **distress call,** alarm, alarum; **war cry,** battle cry, watchword

HOUT *v* bell *(Obs.)*, bellow, clamour, clangour, hawk, holler, outcry, scream blue murder, sing out, sound off, vociferate, yell; **whoop,** crow, hoot, tally-ho, whistle; **scream,** screech, shriek, shrill, sing *(Convict)*, skirl *(Scot.)*, squall, squeal; **howl,** bark, bawl, bray, hoot, yawp, yelp, yowl; **pule,** mewl, waul, whimper; **call out,** cry out, exclaim, interject; **hail,** call, cooee, give a hoy, halloo, hallow, summon, yo-ho, yoo-hoo; **cheer,** encore, huzza

hout *n* → **1** generosity **2** mirth *v* **3** be loud **4** buy **5** drink alcohol **6** laugh **7** speak

HOUTING *n* calling, clamour, clangour, cry, hue, hue and cry, outcry, vociferance, vociferation; **exclamation,** ejaculation, interjection

HOUTING *adj* clamant, clamorous, clangourous, noisy, uproarious, vociferant, vociferous; **exclamatory,** interjectional, interjectory

hove *n* → **1** thrust *v* **2** thrust

hovel *n* → **1** digging implement **2** dwelling **3** room *v* **4** dig

HOW *n* demonstration, fanfare, fanfaron, gala performance, pageant, parade, razzle-dazzle, spectacle, spread; **pomp,** display, eclat, gimmickry, glitter, pageantry, pomp and circumstance, pomposity, razzamatazz, wallow; **flourish,** bravura, flash, flaunt; **style,** panache, pizzazz; **flamboyance,** flamboyancy, machismo; **finery,** best, frippery, full dress, gaudery, war paint

show *n* → **1** appearances **2** display **3** entertainment **4** festival **5** luck **6** sign **7** situation **8** small amount *v* **9** appear **10** authenticate **11** be third **12** display **13** evidence **14** inform **15** perform **16** reveal **17** teach

showdown *n* → **1** argument **2** gambling

SHOWER *v* beat, cascade, hail, pelt, pepper, plop, rain, snow

shower *n* → **1** amount **2** bath **3** cleansing **4** covering **5** gathering **6** rainfall *v* **7** be generous **8** clean **9** give **10** rain **11** wet

shower tea *n* → party

SHOWILY *adv* flamboyantly, flashily, flauntingly, floridly, garishly, gaudily, loud, loudly, obtrusively, vulgarly; **ostentatiously,** overelaborately, pompously, pretentiously

SHOWINESS *n* beadledom, fineness, flashiness, obtrusiveness, ostentation, ostentatiousness, pomposity, pompousness, pretentiousness, sharpness; **garishness,** floridity, floridness, gaudiness, loudness, overelaborateness, sportiness, vulgarity, vulgarness

SHOW OFF *v* call attention to oneself, camp it up, cut a dash, flounce, glitter, grandstand, hog the limelight, keep a high profile, lair it up, maintain a high profile, make a figure, make a spectacle of oneself, strut; **flaunt,** display, flash, flourish, parade, play to the gallery, show off to the best advantage, sport; **dress up,** bedeck, doll up in, lair up, overdress, overelaborate, prank, primp, tart up, trick out in, trick up in; **sensationalise,** lairise

show off *v* → **1** act pretentiously **2** display

SHOW-OFF *n* actor, actress, duchess, exhibitionist, flaunter, macho, peacock, Pooh-Bah, poser, poseur, turkey cock, wallower, Woolloomooloo Yank; **silvertail,** glitterati, social climber

SHOWY *adj* done for effect, exhibitionistic, flash, flashy, flaunty, florid, frilly, garish, gaudy, gimmicky, glittering, lairy, loud, obtrusive, rich, sporty, tarted up, tinsel, tizzy, vulgar; **ostentatious,** chichi, extravagant, flamboyant, high-camp, high-flown, overelaborate, pompous, pretentious, upmarket; **macho; dressed to the nines,** dressed fit to kill, dressed up like a sore toe, in one's glad rags

showy *adj* → **1** interesting **2** spectacular **3** ugly

shrapnel *n* → **1** ammunition **2** coinage **3** part

shred *n* → **1** part **2** remnant *v* **3** separate

shrew *n* → **1** angry person **2** violent person

shrewd *adj* → **1** cunning **2** sharp **3** unkind **4** wise

shriek *n* → **1** loud sound **2** mirth **3** shout *v* **4** be loud **5** laugh **6** shout **7** shrill

shrift *n* → **1** atonement **2** forgiving **3** revealing

SHRILL *v* pipe, skirl *(Scot.)*; **screech,** caterwaul, shriek, squawk, squeal; **whine,** pule, sing, wail; **toot,** flute, stridulate, tootle;

whistle, blow, wheeze, wolf-whistle; **squeak,** beep, bleep, creak, pip

SHRILL *adj* clarion, ear-piercing, ear-splitting, high, piercing, sharp, strident, stridulatory, stridulous; **screeching,** screaming, screechy, wailsome; **piping,** pipy, reedy; **squeaky,** creaky, scrannel *(Archaic)*, thin, tinny; **whining,** puling; **high-pitched,** acute, alto, falsetto, high, high-frequency, high-toned, shrill, soprano, treble

shrill *v* → 1 shout *adj* 2 loud 3 sharp 4 shrill

SHRILLNESS *n* creakiness, flutiness, high frequency, reediness, sharpness, squeakiness, stridor, stridulation, stridulousness, thinness, tinniness, wheeziness

shrimp *n* → 1 small person *v* 2 fish

SHRINE *n* aedicule, chantry, chapel, feretory, Lady Chapel, martyry, oratory; **sanctuary,** adytum, ark of the covenant, cella, holy of holies, naos, oracle, presbytery, sacrarium, sanctum, sanctum sanctorum, tabernacle; **altar,** bema, chancel, high altar, prothesis, the Lord's table; **altarpiece,** antependium, baldachin, ciborium, reredos; **ambry,** almery, credence, fenestella; **reliquary,** phylactery; **font,** baptistery, laver, stoup; **grail,** chalice, lune, lunette, monstrance, pyx; **thurible,** censer; **sacring bell; purificator; menorah,** paschal candle

shrine *n* → 1 container *v* 2 enclose

shrink *n* → 1 contraction 2 psychologist *v* 3 be modest 4 contract 5 decrease 6 go back 7 lack courage

shrivel *v* → 1 be infertile 2 contract 3 deteriorate 4 dry 5 fold

shroud *n* → 1 cord 2 covering 3 funeral rites 4 shade *v* 5 bury 6 cover 7 hide 8 shelter

shrub *n* → plant

shrug *n* → 1 gesture 2 move *v* 3 gesture

shudder *n* → 1 coldness 2 fright 3 turbulence *v* 4 be cold 5 be frightened 6 vibrate

shuffle *n* → 1 avoidance 2 walking *v* 3 dance 4 mix 5 tangle 6 untidy 7 walk

shun *v* → avoid

shunt *n* → 1 byroad 2 transport *v* 3 deflect 4 remove 5 transport

shush *v* → 1 quieten 2 silence *interj* 3 silence

shut *n* → 1 closure *v* 2 close 3 prohibit *adj* 4 closed

shutter *n* → 1 covering 2 door 3 interlacement *v* 4 close

shuttle *v* → flutter

shuttlecock *v* → flutter

shy *n* → 1 reaction 2 throw *v* 3 be frightened 4 react 5 swerve 6 throw 7 worry *adj* 8 frightened 9 infertile 10 modest 11 reticent 12 solitary 13 unwilling

shyster *n* → 1 crook 2 lawyer

sibilant *n* → 1 hiss *adj* 2 hissing

SIBLING *n* cater-cousin *(Archaic)*, fraternal twin, half-blood, identical twin, Siamese twins, sib, twin; **littermate; brother,** binghi *(Aborig.)*, blood brother, brer *(U.S.)*, brother-german, brother-in-law, bud *(U.S.)*, foster-brother, frater, frère, full brother, half-brother, stepbrother, whole brother; **sister,** blister, foster-sister, full sister, half-siste sister-german, sister-in-law, skin and bliste stepsister, whole sister

sic *adv* → precisely

sick *n* → 1 vomit *adj* 2 angry 3 colourle 4 damaged 5 ill 6 infertile

SICKENING *adj* abominable, chunderou daggy, deformed, foul, frowzy, gooey, ick messy, nauseating, offensive, revoltin scungy, sticky, untouchable, yucky, yu **tasteless,** fulsome, gross, in bad taste, insi cere; **poisonous,** insalubrious, noxious, pes lential, slimy, toxic; **rank,** dirty, evil smel ing, filthy, frowsty, mephitic, noisome, c the nose, pissy, poohey, putrid, ranci reeky, rotten, stinking, stinko. *See al.* UNPLEASANT; UNBEARABLI DREADFUL; PESTERING

sickie *n* → 1 absence 2 rest

sickle *n* → 1 curve 2 knife

sickly *v* → 1 colour *adj* 2 colourless 3 i 4 sweet 5 weak

SIDE *n* border, cheek, edge, flank, han jowl, temple, wing; **jamb,** haunch; **profil** half-face, silhouette; **sidepiece,** edge *(Skiing* **winger,** flanker, outrider, postilio **weatherside,** lee, leeside, leeward, sunny sid **starboard,** beam, bulwark, gunwale, larbo *(Obs.)*, port, quarter, saxboard, weathe board; **closed side,** inside, open sid *(Skating)*

SIDE *adj* by, collateral, flanking, latera sidelong, sidling, skirting, stoss; **sideway** half-face, in silhouette, side-on; **costal,** pa ietal

side *n* → 1 affectation 2 ancestry 3 arrogan 4 corporation 5 slope 6 spin 7 sportsman

sideboard *n* → 1 beard 2 cupboard

sidecar *n* → bicycle

sidelevers *n* → beard

sidelong *adj* → 1 side *adv* 2 deflectively

sideshow *n* → 1 amusement park 2 entertair ment 3 unimportant thing

sidestep *n* → 1 avoidance 2 loophole *v* 3 as cend 4 avoid

sidetrack *n* → 1 byroad 2 railway *v* 3 deflec

SIDEWAYS *adv* askance, askew, besid broadside on, collaterally, edgeways, hal face, laterally, to lee-ward, to wind-warc **alongside,** abeam, aboard, abreast, aside, b ex parte, on all sides, on beam-ends, on th left, on the right; **side by side,** cheek by jow

sideways *adj* → 1 deflective 2 side *ad* 3 deflectively

siding *n* → 1 byroad 2 mountain 3 railway

sidle *v* → 1 ascend 2 deflect 3 flank 4 trick

siege *n* → 1 act of war *v* 2 attack 3 wage wa

siesta *n* → sleep

sieve *n* → revealer

sift *v* → 1 disperse 2 inquire into

sigh *n* → 1 breathing 2 cry 3 hiss 4 quie sound *v* 5 grieve 6 hiss 7 speak

sight *n* → 1 freak 2 gun part 3 look 4 muc 5 ugly person 6 understanding *v* 7 direc 8 see

SIGN *n* allegory *(Obs.)*, emblem, ensign, figure, manifestation, sacrament, symbol, taw, tessera, token, totem; **character,** colophon, hieroglyphic, hierogram, ideogram, ideograph, logogram, logograph, monogram, note *(Music)*; **mark,** black mark, block *(Cricket)*, chalk, check *(U.S.)*, cross, diacritic, dot, engram *(Biol.)*, erasure, fingermark, line, lineation, marking, note, point, print, tick, tittle, trace, underline, underscore; **signature,** autograph, countersignature, henry; **spoor,** fingerprint, footmark, footprint, footstep, ichnite *(Palaeontol.)*, pug, tracks, trail, vapour trail *(Aerospace)*; **trace,** hint, smell, soupçon, suggestion, suspicion, vestige, vestigium, waft *(Naut.)*, waif *(Naut.)*; **evidence,** appearances, face; **symptom,** attribute *(Fine Arts)*, characteristic, denotation, determinative, diagnostic, indication, prodrome *(Pathol.)*, show *(Pathol.)*, significant *(Archaic)*, signifier; **sign of the times,** straw in the wind; **stigma,** broad arrow, mark of Cain. *See also* SIGNAL; INDICATOR; GESTURE

sign *n* → **1** fortune-telling **2** letter **3** omen **4** small amount *v* **5** assent to **6** direct **7** label **8** name **9** signal

SIGNAL *n* catchword, clew, clue, cue, hint, lead, message, selah *(Bible)*, sennet, the office; **password,** countersign, parole *(U.S. Mil.)*, secret sign, watchword, word; **warning signal,** cone, red flag; **alarm,** air alert, alarum *(Archaic)*, all clear, burglar alarm, fire alarm, fog signal, tocsin; **distress signal,** distress call, distress rocket, Mayday, pan, SOS; **railway signal,** distant signal, home signal; **light signal,** Aldis lamp, amber, anchor light, balefire *(Archaic)*, beacon, Belisha beacon, bonfire, flare, flash, heliograph, light, lighthouse, localiser beacon, magnesium light, maroon, pharos, pilot lamp, pilot light, red fire, riding light, rocket, storm signals *(Naut. Meteorol.)*, tracer, Very light, watch-fire; **radio beam,** beam, blip, localiser *(Aeron.)*; **telephone ring,** dial tone, engaged signal; **beep,** bleep, gating signal *(Elect.)*, pinger, pip, time signal; **military signal,** advance, assembly, boots and saddles *(U.S.)*, call, charge, havoc *(Archaic)*, last post, last trump, lights out, reveille, rollcall, rouse *(Obs.)*, taps *(U.S.)*, tattoo; **death knell,** muffled drum, passing bell. *See also* INDICATOR; SIGN

SIGNAL *v* beacon, beam *(Radio)*, flag, flag down, flare, semaphore, sign *(Obs.)*, wigwag *(Navy)*; **sound the alarm,** beat the drum, beat the gong, ring, whistle; **lower the flag,** dip the flag, half-mast, salute, strike *(Naut.)*; **show the way,** blaze a trail, buoy *(Naut.)*, demarcate, mark the way, point the way

signal *n* → **1** telecommunications station *v* **2** communicate *adj* **3** important

signatory *n* → **1** assenter *adj* **2** assenting

signature *n* → **1** book part **2** musical score **3** sign **4** song **5** title *v* **6** label

signet *n* → **1** emblem *v* **2** emblematise

significance *n* → **1** importance **2** meaning

SIGNIFY *v* bespeak, connote, denote, design *(Obs.)*, feature, index, indicate, involve, mean, point to, proclaim, signalise; **symbolise,** betoken, emblematise, emblemise, represent, symbol, typify

signify *v* → **1** be important **2** mean **3** predict

SIGNPOST *n* arrow, beacon, beam, beckon, landmark, lighthouse, lodestar, pharos, pylon, traffic sign, vane, weathercock

SILENCE *n* hush, lull, peace, quiescence, quiet, quietness, stillness; **period of silence,** pause, rest, tacet; **dead space,** anechoic chamber, cone of silence, soundproof box; **soundlessness,** inaudibility, noiselessness; **muteness,** dumbness, voicelessness; **speechlessness,** reticence, sullenness, tacitness, taciturnity

SILENCE *v* hush, lull, mum, quiet, quieten, shush, still; **suppress,** burke, play down, soft-pedal, squash, squelch, stifle, subdue; **mute,** drown the noise, gag, muffle, muzzle, tongue-tie; **soundproof,** deaden

SILENCE *interj* hist, hush, mum, mum's the word, sh, shush, shut up, shut your face, shut your mouth, shut your mouth there's a bus coming, soft *(Archaic)*, whist

silence *n* → **1** forgetfulness **2** reticence **3** unsociability *v* **4** answer **5** restrain **6** stop

SILENT *adj* hush *(Archaic)*, hushed, quiescent, quiet, quiet as the grave, still, stilly; **unsounded,** tacit, unsaid, unspoken, unuttered, unvoiced; **inaudible,** noiseless, soundless, subsonic, supersonic; **silenced,** muffled, subdued; **soundproof,** anechoic, echoless; **inarticulate,** coy *(Obs.)*, mousy, quiet as a mouse, tongue-tied; **speechless,** dumb, mum, mute, songless, tuneless, voiceless, wordless; **tight-lipped,** dark, po-faced, pokerfaced, reticent, sullen, taciturn

silent *adj* → **1** inactive **2** inarticulate **3** reticent

SILENTLY *adv* inaudibly, noiselessly, quiescently, quietly, soundlessly, still, stilly, subduedly; **speechlessly,** dumbly, mutely; **reticently,** sullenly, tacitly, taciturnly, voicelessly

silhouette *n* → **1** outside **2** painting **3** portrait **4** side *v* **5** darken

silk *n* → **1** lawyer **2** smooth object *adj* **3** bright **4** corded

sill *n* → **1** beam **2** layer **3** rock outcrop

silly *n* → **1** fool *adj* **2** close **3** foolish **4** stupid **5** unconscious **6** weak

silo *n* → **1** propellant **2** stable **3** storehouse **4** tower *v* **5** conserve

silt *v* → **1** fill **2** solidify

silver *n* → **1** coinage **2** grey **3** white *adj* **4** eloquent **5** grey **6** metallic **7** white

SIMILAR *adj* akin, alike, all of a piece, analogical, cut from the same cloth, like, not unlike, reminiscent of, semblable, suggestive of, tarred with the same brush; **comparable,** conformable, correspondent, homothetic, parallel, suchlike; **assimilable; approximate,** approaching, bastard, close, much the same, near, pseudo, quasi; **congeneric,** cognate, congenerous, connatural, consanguineous; **isomorphic,** isologous

SIMILARITY *n* analogousness, analogy, closeness, comparableness, conformableness, conformance, correspondence, isomorphism, likeness, resemblance, semblance, similitude; **approximation,** affinity, approach, imitation *(Biol.)*, nearness, parallelism, propinquity; **rhyme,** alliteration, assonance, metaphor, pun, simile; **conformity,** equality, equivalence, identity, parity

SIMILARLY *adv* analogically, analogously, comparably, conformably, connaturally, correspondently, correspondingly, nearly, semblably; **likewise,** by the same token, in kind, item *(Obs.)*; **approximately,** in the neighbourhood of, nearly

SIMILAR THING *n* approximation, close match, match, parallel; **perfect match,** alter ego, another, chip off the old block, clone, dead spit, doppleganger, double, image, look-alike, mate, mirror image, second self, spit, spitting image, twin; **analogue,** counterpart, isomorph, opposite number; **class,** community, family, subset; **set,** birds of a feather, matching pair, matching set, pair, peas in a pod, pigeon pair, Siamese twins, twins, two of a kind; **peer,** equal, fellow, peer group

simile *n* → **1** comparison **2** figure of speech **3** similarity

simmer *v* → **1** cook **2** heat

simper *n* → **1** affectation *v* **2** attitudinise

SIMPLE *adj* Attic, common-or-garden, commonplace, everyday, homespun, mere, obvious, ordinary, plain, sheer, simplex, single, very, workaday; **elementary,** back-to-basics, basic, elemental, fundamental, rudimentary; **no-frills,** bare, matter-of-fact, naked, prosaic, unadorned, undecorated, unfancy; **pure,** absolute, au naturel, entire *(Obs.)*, homogenous, native, natural, neat, perfect, stark, straight, unadulterated, unalloyed, uniform, unmixed, unsophisticated, virgin; **straightforward,** direct, resolvable, straight, uncomplicated; **simplistic,** oversimplified

simple *n* → **1** fool **2** ignoramus **3** medication *adj* **4** artless **5** easy **6** fundamental **7** ignorant **8** inferior **9** innocent **10** stupid **11** teaching **12** unimportant **13** working-class

simpleton *n* → **1** fool **2** stupid person

SIMPLICITY *n* elementariness, ordinariness, resolvability, resolvableness, rudimentariness, simpleness; **purity,** homogeneity, homogeneousness, pureness, unsophisticatedness, unsophistication; **straightforwardness,** directness, plainness, straightness

SIMPLIFICATION *n* degradation *(Chem.)*, denouement, disembarrassment, disentanglement, resolution, solution, streamlining, unravelment; **simplism,** oversimplification, reductionism

SIMPLIFY *v* clarify, clear, make plain, streamline; **disentangle,** disembarrass, disembroil, disentwine, ravel, sort out, uncoil uncross, unknit, unlash, unloose, unmix, untangle, untie, unwind; **comb,** brush, card; **resolve,** break down, degrade *(Chem.)*, disintegrate, dissociate; **oversimplify,** popularise

simplify *v* → translate

simplistic *adj* → simple

SIMPLY *adv* downright, merely, only, ordinarily, plainly, purely; **straightforwardly** commonly, elementarily, naturally rudimentarily, unmixedly, unsophisticatedly; **simplistically**

simply *adv* → **1** negligibly **2** stupidly **3** wholly

simulate *v* → **1** copy **2** imitate *adj* **3** fake

simulator *n* → imitator

SIMULTANEOUS *adj* accompanying coetanious, coeternal, coeval, coexisting, coextensive, coincident, coincidental, coinstantaneous, concomitant, concurrent, contemporaneous, contemporary, coseismal inseparable, intercurrent, isochronal, isochronous, synchronic, synchronistic, synchronous; **twin,** twinborn

SIMULTANEOUSLY *adv* at once, at the same moment, at the same time, coevally, coincidentally, coincidently, concurrently, contemporaneously, ensemble *(Obs.)*, hand in hand, in concert, in step, in sync, in unison, isochronally, isochronously, neck and neck, synchronistically, synchronously, together

sin *n* → **1** evildoing **2** wrong *v* **3** be immoral **4** wrong

SIN-BIN *n* carnal car, frigmobile, fuck truck, shaggin' wagon

since *adv* → **1** after **2** in the past *prep* **3** during *conj* **4** because

sincere *adj* → **1** emotional **2** forthright **3** honest **4** truthful

sine *prep* → without

sinecure *n* → job

sinew *n* → **1** strength *v* **2** strengthen

SING *v* anthem, carol, croon, descant, discourse, hum, hymn, lilt, outsing, precent, psalm, quaver, solfa, troll, vocalise, warble, yodel; **chorus,** chime in, choir, consort *(Obs.)*; **intone,** chant; **serenade,** shivaree *(U.S.)*

singe *v* → fire

SINGER *n* cantatrice, chanter, chanteuse, choirboy, chorister, crooner, descanter, hummer, serenader, singer-songwriter, solfaist, songbird, songster, torch-singer, troller, vicar choral, vocaliser, vocalist, voice, warbler; **folk singer,** balladeer, bard, carol-singer, caroller, folkie, gleeman *(Archaic)*, jongleur, minnesinger, minstrel, troubadour, yodeller; **soprano,** coloratura, diva, dramatic soprano, prima donna; **contralto,** alto, mezzo, mezzosoprano, second; **tenor,** heldentenor, heroic tenor; **countertenor,** castrato, falsetto; **bass,** baritone, base *(Obs.)*, basso, basso profundo; **cantor,** chanter, chazzan, coryphaeus, precentor; **choir,** cantoris, chorale *(U.S.)*, chorus, consort, liedertafel, quire *(Archaic)*, waits

NGLE *adj* celibate, chaste, lone, partnerless, unattached, unmarried, unwedded, virgin; **spinsterish,** old-maidish, on the shelf; **widowed,** vidual; **premarital**

ngle *n* → 1 recording *adj* 2 honest 3 intoxicating 4 one 5 simple

ngle file *n* → 1 line 2 sequence

ngle-handed *adj* → 1 independent 2 one

ngle-minded *adj* → 1 artless 2 honest 3 persevering 4 serious

INGLE PERSON *n* bachelor, bachelor girl, back, feme sole, lonely heart, misogamist, old maid, spinster, tabby, virgin; **divorcee,** divorcer; **single parent; widow,** dowager, grass widow *(U.S.),* grass widower *(U.S.),* relict, widower; **widow's weeds,** black, mourning band; **singles bar,** dating service *(U.S),* lonely hearts' club, marriage bureau, parents without partners club

INGLE STATE *n* bachelorhood, bachelorship, celibacy, maidenhood, misogamy, single blessedness, singleness, spinsterhood, virginity

inglet *n* → underwear

ingsong *n* → 1 concert 2 party 3 poetry 4 rhythm *adj* 5 frequent 6 rhythmical

ingular *adj* → 1 astonishing 2 nonconformist 3 one 4 separate 5 solitary 6 strange

inister *adj* → 1 calamitous 2 immoral 3 left 4 menacing 5 predictive

ink *n* → 1 bath 2 borehole 3 den of vice 4 hollow 5 toilet *v* 6 be tired 7 decrease 8 deteriorate 9 dig 10 eat 11 exclude 12 fall 13 hide 14 hollow 15 repose 16 ruin 17 slope 18 sound 19 weaken

inker *n* → fishing tackle

inuous *adj* → 1 deflective 2 twisting

inus *n* → 1 bladder 2 curve 3 sore

ip *v* → 1 absorb 2 drink

iphon *n* → 1 piping *v* 2 channel

ir *n* → 1 aristocrat 2 mister

ire *n* → 1 aristocrat 2 important person 3 ruler *v* 4 reproduce

IREN *n* beeper, bell, foghorn, hooter, horn, klaxon, whistle

iren *n* → 1 allurer 2 encourager 3 fairy 4 sea nymph 5 warning 6 woman *adj* 7 alluring

issy *n* → 1 coward 2 ineffectual person 3 man *adj* 4 powerless

ister *n* → 1 healer 2 monastic 3 partner 4 sibling

ister-in-law *n* → sibling

it *v* → 1 be inactive 2 care for 3 gather 4 position 5 repose 6 rest

ite *n* → 1 position *v* 2 position

ituate *v* → 1 position *adj* 2 positioned

ITUATION *n* circumstances, conjuncture, kettle of fish, scenario, scene, set-up, shebang, show, state of affairs. *See also* AFFAIR; OCCURRENCE

ituation *n* → 1 condition 2 job 3 position

IX *n* half-a-dozen, half-dozen, hexad, hexameter, hexarchy, sextet, sextuplet, sixth; **hexagon,** hexagram, hexahedron

SIX *adj* half-a-dozen, half-dozen, hexadic, hexagonal, hexahedral, hexamerous, senary, sexpartite, sextuple, sixfold, sixth

SIZE *n* capacity, dimensions, extent, magnitude, proportions, scale, scope, volume; **hugeness,** enormousness, giantism, giganticness, immenseness, immensity, mightiness, monstrousness, outsize, oversize, prodigiousness, sizeableness, vastitude, vastness, voluminousness; **amplitude,** ampleness, breadth, extensiveness, spaciousness, spread, sweepingness; **bulk,** beefiness, bulkiness, burliness, buxomness, corpulence, dumpiness, embonpoint, fatness, flesh, fleshiness, grossness, heftiness, massiness, massiveness, obeseness, obesity, plumpness, rotundity, rotundness, squatness, steatopygia, tubbiness

size *n* → 1 adhesive 2 gradation 3 importance 4 measurement 5 paint *v* 6 class 7 control 8 separate 9 stick together

sizeable *adj* → 1 big 2 great

sizzle *n* → 1 hiss *v* 2 fire 3 hiss

skate *n* → 1 journey 2 man 3 sledge *v* 4 do easily 5 glide

skateboard *n* → bicycle

skein *n* → 1 interlacement 2 thread 3 twist

skeleton *n* → 1 bone 2 building 3 diagram 4 essence 5 remnant 6 thin person *adj* 7 fundamental

skeleton key *n* → opener

skerrick *n* → small amount

sketch *n* → 1 act 2 comedy 3 diagram 4 drawing 5 musical piece 6 narrative 7 portrait 8 written composition *v* 9 depict 10 narrate

skew *n* → 1 slope *v* 2 fasten 3 look 4 misinterpret 5 swerve *adj* 6 bent 7 deflective 8 sloping

skewer *n* → 1 piercer 2 rod

ski *n* → 1 journey 2 sledge

skid *n* → 1 move 2 restraints 3 shaft 4 support *v* 5 move 6 restrain 7 swerve

skilful *adj* → 1 competent 2 logical

skill *n* → 1 cause 2 competence 3 understanding

skim *n* → 1 dirt *v* 2 be inattentive 3 look 4 move 5 neglect 6 read 7 throw

skimp *v* → 1 be miserly 2 neglect

skimpy *adj* → 1 few 2 mean 3 small

SKIN *n* bark, buff *(Colloq.),* epicarp, fur, hide, integument, peel, pericarp, rind, sheath, shell; **membrane,** caul, cortex, film, fraenulum, indusium, lamella, pellicle, scale, squama, tela, tunic, web, webbing; **corium,** cuticle, cuticula, cutis, derma, dermatome, epidermis, scarfskin; **hangnail,** agnail; **marsupium,** epicanthus; **peel,** husk, jacket, peeling, zest. *See also* HIDE

SKIN *adj* cutaneous, cuticular, dermal, dermatomic, dermic, epicanthic, epidermal, epidermic, membranaceous, membranous, subcutaneous; **dermatoid,** dermoid; **hypodermic,** endermic, percutaneous; **cortical,** corticate, lamellar, lamellate, pellicular, scutellate; **crustaceous,** crusty, scurfy;

leather, cordovan, coriaceous, leathern *(Archaic)*, shagreen, shagreened
skin *n* → **1** bag **2** coating **3** contraception **4** covering **5** outside **6** shallow *v* **7** bare **8** impoverish
skindiving *n* → swimming
skinflint *n* → miser
skinny *adj* → thin
skip *n* → **1** boss **2** dancing **3** jump **4** train *v* **5** depart **6** escape **7** exclude **8** jump
skipper *n* → **1** boss **2** seaman
skirmish *n* → **1** act of war **2** fight *v* **3** fight **4** wage war
skirt *n* → **1** bottom **2** dress **3** edge **4** pendant **5** shaft **6** woman *v* **7** border **8** flank **9** overtake
skirting board *n* → **1** frame **2** shaft
skit *n* → **1** act **2** comedy **3** imitation **4** mockery
skite *n* → **1** braggart *v* **2** brag
skittish *adj* → **1** excitable **2** indecisive **3** modest **4** worried
skittle *v* → **1** bowl over **2** overturn
skivvy *n* → jumper
skulduggery *n* → dishonesty
skulk *n* → **1** bad person **2** coward **3** idler *v* **4** idle **5** lack courage **6** seclude
skull *n* → **1** head **2** mind
skunk *n* → **1** animal's coat **2** bad person *v* **3** defeat
SKY *n* azure, canopy, celestial sphere, cope, ether, firmament, heavens, solar system, sphere, welkin *(Archaic)*; **stratosphere,** Appleton layer, atmosphere, chemosphere, E-layer, exosphere, Heaviside layer, inversion layer, ionosphere, Kenelly-Heaviside layer, lower atmosphere, magnetosphere, troposphere, upper atmosphere, Van Allen belt; **space,** aerospace, deep space, infinite, inner space, outer space, plenum; **cosmos,** creation, macrocosm, nature, universe, world
sky *n* → **1** air **2** cloud *v* **3** lift
skydiving *n* → **1** dive **2** fall
skylark *v* → amuse oneself
skylight *n* → window
skyscraper *n* → tower
slab *n* → **1** bit **2** coating **3** incompetent **4** tall person *v* **5** support
slack *n* → **1** period of inaction **2** powder **3** promiscuous person **4** waste *v* **5** be unwilling **6** decrease **7** idle **8** moderate **9** weaken *adj* **10** idle **11** inactive **12** lenient **13** neglectful **14** promiscuous **15** slow **16** weak *adv* **17** idly **18** limply
slacks *n* → trousers
slag *n* → **1** secretion **2** waste *v* **3** excrete **4** slander
slake *v* → **1** be inactive **2** moderate **3** satisfy **4** weaken
slalom *n* → race
slam *n* → **1** closure **2** explosion **3** impact **4** reprimand *v* **5** close **6** disapprove of **7** explode **8** hit **9** slander
SLANDER *n* calumny, dirt, innuendo, insinuation, libel, malediction, personality, scandal; **invective,** attack, obloquy; **jeer,** backhander, barb, fling, flout, nip, put-down, ru **smear-word,** byword, epithet, pejorative, slu smear; **denigration,** aspersion, assassinatio backbiting, calumniation, character assassi ation, decrial, defamation, objurgation, r vilement, sledging *(Cricket)*, vilification; **di paragement,** abuse, assailment, criticism, d traction, excoriation, vituperation; **muckra ing,** dirty tricks, smear campaign; **re baiting,** poofter-bashing
SLANDER *v* asperse, backbite, badmout belie, calumniate, defame, denigrate, libe malign, put the knife into, shitcan, squib, tr duce, vilify, vilipend; **blacken,** besmirch, b spatter, empty the bucket on, muckrake, p shit on, scandal *(Archaic)*, sling mud a smear, throw mud at, tip the bucket on; **re vile,** abuse, assail, attack, be personal, b labour, blackguard, bullyrag, excoriate, flir out, fulminate against, get stuck into, las make mincemeat of, objurgate, slag *(U.S.* slag off at, slam, slate, sling off at, slur, snip at, throw off at, vituperate; **disparage,** b little, cry down, damn, decry, demean, d preciate, diminish, dispraise, disvalue *(Rare* downgrade, lessen, make little of, poo pooh, riddle, slight, sneer at
SLANDERER *n* backbiter, backstabber, b lier, calumniator, defamer, libeller, maligne traducer; **scandalmonger,** blackener, muck raker, mud-slinger, tabby; **disparager,** d crier, denigrator, depreciator, detractor, di praiser, knocker, vilipender; **vilifier,** abuse asperser, assailant, assailer, assassinator, a tacker, railer, reviler, vituperator
SLANDEROUS *adj* calumnious, defamator libellous, scandalous; **abusive,** denunciator invective, maledictory, objurgatory, oppro brious, vituperative; **disparaging,** belittling contemptuous, derogative, derogatory, de tractive, pejorative, personal, slighting, snid
slang *n* → **1** language **2** vulgarism *v* **3** insult
slant *n* → **1** intolerance **2** point of vie **3** slope **4** translation *v* **5** misinterpret **6** slop
slap *n* → **1** corporal punishment **2** explosio **3** hit **4** reprimand *v* **5** hit *adv* **6** hurriedl **7** straight
slapstick *n* → **1** comedy **2** drama **3** stick *ad* **4** dramatic **5** humorous
slash *n* → **1** cut **2** hit **3** stroke **4** urinatio **5** waste *v* **6** cudgel **7** cut **8** decrease **9** ope **10** subtract
slat *n* → **1** chest **2** coating **3** shaft
slate *n* → **1** blue **2** building materials **3** coat ing **4** grey **5** list **6** writing materials *v* **7** disap prove of **8** employ **9** plan **10** slander
slather *v* → place
slaughter *n* → **1** massacre *v* **2** defeat **3** ki **4** massacre **5** wage war
slave *n* → **1** obeyer **2** servant **3** subje **4** worker *v* **5** make an effort **6** repress
slaver *n* → **1** represser **2** seller **3** watercraft **4** excrete **5** grovel
slay *v* → **1** destroy **2** hit **3** joke **4** kill
sleazy *adj* → **1** bad **2** unkempt **3** untidy
sled *n* → **1** sledge *v* **2** drive

SLEDGE *n* bob, bobsled, bobsleigh, catamaran *(N.Z.)*, coaster *(U.S.)*, fart machine, hurdle, ice-yacht, iceboat, jumper, koneke *(N.Z.)*, skibob, skidboard, skidoo, sled, sleigh, toboggan, troika; **ski,** ice skate, skate; **land yacht,** land sailer, sandyacht

sledge *v* → 1 cudgel 2 drive

sledge-hammer *n* → 1 club *v* 2 cudgel *adj* 3 forceful 4 powerful

sleek *v* → 1 smooth *adj* 2 bright 3 courteous 4 smooth

SLEEP *n* beauty sleep, camp, kip *(Brit.)*; **nap,** catnap, doze, forty winks, nod, siesta, snooze, zizz; **sleep-in,** lie-in

SLEEP *v* be dead to the world, dream, push up zeds, repose, sleep like a log, sleep like a top, slumber, stack zeds; **nap,** catnap, doze, drowse, rest, snooze, take a nap, take forty winks; **hibernate,** lie dormant; **go to sleep,** crash, die on someone, doss down, drop off, fall asleep, fall off, flake, flake out, go to the land of nod, nod off; **go to bed,** bed down, bunk, camp, get between the sheets, go to beddy-byes, hit the hay, hit the sack, jump into bed, kip down, retire, roll in, roost, settle down for the night, turn in; **sleep in,** lie in, oversleep

sleep *n* → 1 imprisonment 2 period of inaction 3 unconsciousness *v* 4 become unconscious 5 be inactive 6 be inattentive 7 die 8 house

SLEEPER *n* dosser, dreamer, slumberer, snorer; **sleepyhead,** dozer, napper; **sleepwalker,** somnambulant, somnambulator, somnambulist

sleeper *n* → 1 beam 2 bed 3 bedroom 4 informant 5 jewellery 6 shaft 7 success 8 train

SLEEPINESS *n* doziness, drowse, drowsiness, oscitance, yawn, yawning; **lethargy,** inertia; **snoring,** tossing and turning, zzz; **sleepwalking,** somnambulation, somnambulism, somniloquy; **sleeping sickness,** encephalitis lethargica, narcolepsy, narcosis

SLEEPING *n* bye-byes, shut-eye, somnolence; **rest,** lie-down, reposal, repose; **dormancy,** aestivation, coma, hibernation, sopor, torpor; **oblivion,** dream, hypnosis, trance; **land of nod,** dreamland, sandman; **lullaby,** berceuse, cradle song

SLEEPING-PILL *n* depressant, hypnotic, narcotic, opiate, sedative, sleeping-draught, soporific, stopper, torpedo

sleet *n* → 1 ice *v* 2 be cold

sleeve *n* → opening

sleigh *n* → 1 sledge *v* 2 drive

sleight *n* → trick

slender *adj* → 1 small 2 thin

sleuth *n* → 1 hunter 2 searcher *v* 3 pursue

slew *v* → swerve

slice *n* → 1 layer 2 part 3 stroke *v* 4 bungle 5 cut 6 deflect 7 separate

slick *n* → 1 magazine 2 wheel *v* 3 smooth *adj* 4 bright 5 busy 6 competent 7 courteous 8 cunning 9 eloquent 10 oily 11 smooth

slide *n* → 1 amusement park 2 descent 3 guitar 4 landslide 5 move 6 photograph 7 pitch *v* 8 change 9 deteriorate 10 glide 11 move

slide rule *n* → computer

slight *n* → 1 insult *v* 2 belittle 3 insult 4 slander *adj* 5 ethereal 6 shallow 7 small 8 smallest 9 thin 10 unimportant 11 weak

slim *v* → 1 thin *adj* 2 cunning 3 insufficient 4 small 5 thin

slime *n* → 1 dirt 2 obsequiousness 3 sludge 4 unpleasantness *v* 5 dirty 6 flatter

slimy *adj* → 1 dirty 2 obsequious 3 sickening 4 sludgy

sling *n* → 1 bribe 2 medication 3 propellant 4 tape 5 wire *v* 6 bribe 7 hang 8 lower 9 throw

slink *n* → 1 animal offspring *v* 2 give birth 3 trick *adj* 4 early

slip *n* → 1 bedclothes 2 break 3 ceramics 4 children 5 error 6 escape 7 failure 8 fall 9 grammatical error 10 harbour 11 misdemeanour 12 misfortune 13 move 14 paint 15 record 16 shaft 17 sharpener 18 underwear 19 wrong *v* 20 be immoral 21 be inattentive 22 deteriorate 23 err 24 fall 25 farm 26 give birth 27 glide 28 let oneself go 29 move 30 separate 31 speed 32 wane

slipper *n* → 1 sandal *v* 2 hit

slippery *adj* → 1 changeable 2 dishonest 3 elusive 4 escaped 5 oily 6 smooth 7 uncertain 8 unfaithful

slippery dip *n* → 1 amusement park 2 descent 3 slope

slipshod *adj* → 1 inattentive 2 neglectful 3 ungrammatical 4 untidy

slipstream *n* → airflow

slit *n* → 1 cut 2 gap 3 groin 4 opening *v* 5 cut 6 open 7 separate *adj* 8 gaping

slither *n* → 1 move *v* 2 move 3 walk

sliver *n* → 1 part 2 small amount 3 thread *v* 4 cut 5 separate

slob *n* → 1 incompetent 2 sludge 3 swamp 4 vulgarian

slobber *n* → 1 secretion *v* 2 excrete 3 feel emotion 4 wet

slog *n* → 1 hit 2 toil *v* 3 hit 4 make an effort 5 walk

slogan *n* → 1 proverb 2 word

sloop *n* → sailing ship

slop *n* → 1 jacket 2 surf 3 trousers *v* 4 swim 5 wet

SLOPE *n* bank, banking, brae *(Scot.)*, cant, couloir, crag-and-tail, escarp, grade, gradient, hillside, icefront, oblique, obliquity, side, slant, steep, superelevation, tilt, ubac, versant; **ramp,** chamfer, chute, counter, counterscarp, escarp, gangway, glacis, nursery slope, raked floor, shaft, ski run, ski-jump, skidboard, skidway, slippery dip, slipway, stepped floor, talus, tambour; **pitch,** anhedral, attitude, bank, batter, camber, cant, chandelle, dihedral, dip, knockdown, lean, list, rake, skew, wane; **incline,** acclivity, ascent, inclination, jump-up, upgrade *(U.S.)*, uphill, upsweep; **declivity,** anticline, declension, declination, descent, dip, downgrade, drop, drop-off, fall, geanticline, icefall, isocline, monoclinal, monocline, nappe, preponderation, syncline

SLOPE *v* bank, be at an angle, cant, lean, list, oblique, shelve, slant, splay, steeve, sway, tilt, tip, verge; **grade,** bank, batter, chamfer, decline, escarp, hade, heel, pitch, rake, weather; **climb,** incline, steepen, uprise *(Archaic),* uptilt; **fall,** delve, descend, dip, preponderate, sink

slope *n* → **1** ascent *v* **2** travel

SLOPING *adj* cant, declivous, inclinatory, inclining, leaning, lopsided, on her beam ends, preponderating, skew, slanting, slantwise, weathered; **banking,** anhedral, dihedral; **anticlinal,** centroclinal, isoclinal, monoclinal, synclinal; **aslant,** aslope, atilt, declivitous, gradient, inclined, oblique, prone; **steep,** abrupt, critical, gorgy, headlong *(Archaic),* precipitous, sharp, sheer, uphill

SLOPINGLY *adv* preponderatingly, slantingly, slantwise; **aslope,** aslant, atilt; **steeply,** abruptly, obliquely, precipitously, pronely, sharply, sheer, sheerly

sloppy *adj* → **1** dirty **2** emotional **3** foolish **4** sludgy **5** untidy **6** wet

slosh *n* → **1** alcohol **2** hit *v* **3** disperse **4** place

slot *n* → **1** cell **2** furrow **3** opening **4** passageway **5** room *v* **6** imprison

sloth *n* → idleness

slouch *n* → **1** hanging **2** incompetent **3** pose *v* **4** hang **5** repose **6** walk

slouch hat *n* → **1** hat **2** nationalism

slough *n* → **1** cell **2** discard **3** hide **4** pigsty **5** powerlessness **6** room **7** sludge **8** swamp *v* **9** separate

sloven *n* → **1** dirty person **2** incompetent **3** untidy person

SLOW *adj* deliberate, languid, languorous, lazy, leisured, leisurely, low-geared; **sluggish,** leaden, lymphatic, phlegmy *(Obs.),* retarded, slack, sullen *(Obs.),* torpid; **snail-like,** bumper-to-bumper, lumbering, slow-motion, snail-paced, tardigrade; **dilatory,** laggard, lagging, tardy, unready; **retardative,** retardatory

slow *adj* → **1** boring **2** heating **3** inactive **4** late **5** old **6** stupid **7** untimely

SLOWCOACH *n* ambler, crawler, dallier, dawdler, delayer, laggard, lingerer, plodder, potterer, slowpoke, slug, snail, straggler, Sunday driver, tarrier, tortoise

slowcoach *n* → stupid person

SLOWLY *adv* at one's leisure, bumper-to-bumper, deliberately, languidly, languorously, lazily; **gradually,** bit by bit, by degrees, by easy stages, by inches, inch by inch, inchmeal, little by little, piecemeal, poco a poco, step by step; **dilatorily,** dallyingly, laggardly, loiteringly, potteringly, tardily; **sluggishly,** leadenly, lumberingly, ploddingly, slackly, sullenly

SLOWNESS *n* deliberateness, deliberation, flat-footedness, lack of speed, laggardness, leadenness, phlegm *(Obs.),* sluggishness; **delay,** dilatoriness, lag, latency *(Computers),* retardation, tardiness, tarriance *(Archaic)*; **hesitation,** demur *(Obs.),* hesitancy; **slackness,** languidness, languor, leisureliness; **go-slow,** work-to-rule; **deceleration,** brakeage, calando, moderation *(Physics),* slowdown, slowup

SLUDGE *n* activated sludge, guck, heavy mud *(Geol.),* mud, ooze, slime, slob *(Irish),* slush; **bog,** marsh, mire, quicksand, slough, swamp; **magma,** eruption; **viscosity,** creaminess, gelatinousness, glairiness, glutinosity, glutinousness, gooiness, mucosity, ropiness, sloppiness, stringiness, thickness, threadiness, toughness, treacliness, viscidity, viscidness, viscousness; **gelatinisation,** gelation, impastation, thickening. *See also* PASTE

sludge *n* → **1** remnant **2** snow

SLUDGY *adj* miry, muddy, slimy, sloppy, slushy; **viscous,** claggy, close *(Rare),* clotted, colloidal, curdled, gelatinoid, gelatinous, glairy, glutinous, gooey, lyophilic *(Chem.),* magmatic, melting, mucous, oozy, semifluid, semisolid, soupy, syruplike, thick, treacly, unset, viscid, viscoid; **stringy,** ropy, thready, tough; **boggy,** boggish

slug *n* → **1** a drink **2** ammunition **3** circle **4** coinage **5** hit **6** inconvenience **7** inflation **8** mineral **9** slowcoach *v* **10** hit

sluggard *n* → **1** idler *adj* **2** idle

sluggish *adj* → **1** apathetic **2** idle **3** inactive **4** slow

sluice *n* → **1** bath **2** chute **3** cleansing **4** dam **5** lake *v* **6** clean **7** extract **8** flow

slum *n* → **1** cabin *v* **2** bungle

slumber *n* → **1** period of inaction *v* **2** be inactive **3** sleep

slump *n* → **1** cheapness **2** failure **3** fall **4** misfortune **5** period of inaction *v* **6** be cheap **7** be out of luck **8** be unhappy **9** fail **10** fall

slur *n* → **1** denigration **2** musical phrase **3** musical score **4** slander *v* **5** dirty **6** glide **7** make music **8** mispronounce **9** slander **10** speak

slurp *n* → **1** hiss **2** loud sound *v* **3** drink **4** eat

slush *n* → **1** dirt **2** sludge **3** snow **4** swamp

slut *n* → **1** dirty person **2** promiscuous person **3** untidy person

sly *adj* → **1** badly-behaved **2** cunning **3** humorous **4** secretive

smack *n* → **1** corporal punishment **2** endearments **3** gesture **4** hit **5** narcotic **6** sailing ship **7** small amount **8** taste **9** watercraft *v* **10** click **11** hit **12** kiss *adv* **13** hurriedly **14** straight

SMALL *adj* baby, diminutive, dinky, ickle, itsy-bitsy, little, microscopic, mini, miniature, minuscule, minute, pint-size, teeny, teeny-weeny, tiny, two-by-four *(U.S.),* wee, weeny; **petite,** dainty, dapper, delicate, elfin, gamin, light, mignon, slender, slight, slim; **undersized,** puny, runty, short, stunted; **scant,** abbreviated, brief, exiguous, meagre, scanty, skimpy, spare, sparing, sparse, wisplike, wispy; **compact,** desktop, microcosmic, pocket size, small-scale; **Lilliputian,** dwarfish, gnomish, pygmaean; **squat,** squab, stumpy; **incommodious,** poky; **beady,** grainy, granular

small *adj* → **1** few **2** intolerant **3** mean **4** meek **5** quiet **6** selfish **7** thin **8** unimportant **9** weak **10** youthful *adv* **11** quietly

SMALL AMOUNT *n* ambs-ace, least, minimum, minimus; **next to nothing,** a fat lot, bugger-all, cat's whisker, damn-all, fuck-all, s.f.a., sweet F.A.; **tinge,** lick, smack, strain, taste, tincture, touch; **trace,** cast, dab, dash, hint, shadow, show, sign, suspicion, thought, vestige; **skerrick,** inch, iota, jot, patch, pea, peppercorn, rag, rap, scrap, straw, tap, tittle, whit; **spark,** gleam, scintilla; **hair's-breadth,** ace, hair, hairbreadth, whisker; **sprinkling,** handful, sprinkle; **pittance,** mess of pottage, peanuts, starvation wages; **modicum,** bit, pennyworth, pinch, scantling, smidgin, snip, snippet, soupçon, stiver, tot, trifle; **drop,** dribble, driblet, gout *(Archaic)*, nip; **point,** dot, pinhead; **crumb,** break, chip, droob, morceau, morsel; **sliver,** paring, shaving, snippet; **grain,** granule, nubbin *(U.S.)*, nubble, pellet; **atom,** atomy *(Archaic)*, molecule, mote, particle; **speck,** fleck, flyspeck, spot; **ounce,** minim, pennyweight, scruple; **portion,** share, tithe; **mouthful,** spoonful, thimbleful

SMALLEST *adj* least, minim, minimum, slightest; **inconsiderable,** fractional, inappreciable, infinitesimal, insignificant, insubstantial, light-weight, marginal, minimal, minor, negligible, vestigial; **measly,** halfpenny, mere, paltry, pelting *(Archaic)*, petit, petty, potty, trifling; **mean,** niggardly, stingy; **slight,** certain; **cursory,** superficial, tenuous; **just,** bare, mere, no more than, only

SMALL PERSON *n* dwarf, fingerling, half-pint, hop-o'-my-thumb, manikin, midge, midget, mite, pipsqueak, pygmy, shrimp, squab, Tom Thumb; **elf,** elfin, gamine, minikin, wisp; **lightweight,** bantam, feather, featherweight, skeeter, titch; **runt,** squirt, stunt

SMALL THING *n* diminutive, miniature; **minutiae,** details; **splinters,** flinders, matchwood; **microcosm,** Lilliput

smarmy *adj* → **1** flattering **2** obsequious

smart *v* → **1** pain *adj* **2** beautiful **3** busy **4** clothed **5** competent **6** cunning **7** eloquent **8** fashionable **9** intelligent **10** speedy **11** tasteful

smarten *v* → improve

smash *n* → **1** explosion **2** failure **3** hit **4** impact **5** performance **6** popularity **7** ruin **8** stroke *v* **9** break **10** collide **11** destroy

smashing *adj* → good

smattering *n* → knowledge

smear *n* → **1** denigration **2** slander *v* **3** coat **4** dirty **5** disgrace **6** slander

SMELL *n* aroma, bouquet, fume, odour; **waft,** breath *(Obs.)*, vapour, whiff; **scent,** drag *(Hunting)*, sniff, snuff, trace, trail; **sense of smell,** flair, hyperosmia, nose, olfaction. *See also* FRAGRANCE; STENCH

smell *n* → **1** sign **2** stench *v* **3** be smelly

SMELL OUT *v* breathe, get wind of, savour, scent, sniff, snuff, whiff

SMELLY *adj* a bit on the nose, bilgy, cacodylic, cheesy, fetid, funky *(U.S.)*, high, malodorous, mephitic, nasty, offensive, on the bugle, on the nose, pongo, pongy, putrid, rammish, rank, reeky, ripe, stinking, stinko, whiffy; **stuffy,** airless, frowsty, frowzy, fusty, musty; **effluvial,** miasmal, miasmatic, miasmatical, miasmic

smelly *n* → burp

smelt *v* → **1** distil **2** heat **3** liquefy

smidgin *n* → small amount

smile *n* → **1** mirth *v* **2** be pleased **3** laugh

smirk *n* → **1** insult *v* **2** attitudinise

smite *v* → **1** allure **2** damage **3** destroy **4** emotionalise **5** hit **6** kill **7** love

smith *n* → **1** creator **2** metalworker *v* **3** shape

smitten *adj* → **1** beaten **2** captivated **3** flirtatious **4** loving **5** unfortunate

smock *n* → overcoat

smog *n* → **1** cloud **2** shade

smoke *n* → **1** cloud **2** fire **3** gas **4** invisibility **5** shade **6** the intangible **7** tobacco *v* **8** blacken **9** catch fire **10** cloud **11** conserve **12** cook **13** disinfect **14** take drugs

smoodge *v* → **1** flatter **2** kiss

SMOOTH *v* even, face, fettle, planish, pumice, rub down, sleek, slick, smoothen, strike, worm *(Naut.)*; **sandpaper,** crop *(Textiles)*, drove, file, glasspaper, grind, plane, sand, scrape, trim *(Carp.)*; **comb,** rake; **coat,** glaze, lay, plate, surface; **pave,** macadamise, seal; **flatten,** bulldoze, float, grade, trowel; **press,** calender, iron, iron out, roll; **unwrinkle,** sironise

SMOOTH *adj* alabaster, soft, velvet, velvet-like, velvety; **sleek,** ganoid, glacé, polished, satin, satiny, sericeous, shiny, silken, silky, sleeky, slick, smug; **glassy,** glare, glazy, icy; **slippery,** greasy, slithery; **streamlined,** fastback, flowing, fluent, profluent; **glissando,** gliding, legato; **creamy,** lubricous; **even,** fair, flat, platelike, tabular, tabulate, unruffled; **bald,** baldish, bare, glabrate, glabrous, waterworn; **ratite; cold-rolled,** coated; **crease-resistant,** siroset

smooth *n* → **1** rear **2** smooth object *v* **3** level *adj* **4** bald **5** composed **6** courteous **7** deceitful **8** easy **9** eloquent **10** level **11** moderate **12** soft **13** tasty *adv* **14** easily **15** smoothly

SMOOTHER *n* comber, filer, glazer, grinder, planer, planisher, surfacer, trimmer *(Carp.)*, troweller; **polisher,** furbisher, lapper, waxer; **putty powder,** polish, rottenstone; **file,** bastard file, block plane, compass plane, cropper, crosscut file, drove, emery board, emery cloth, emery paper, facer, facing tool, grinder, grinding wheel, grindstone, jack plane, land plane, nailfile, plane, rasp, riffler, rubber, sander, sanding machine, sandpaper, smoothing plane, stone, trimmer; **abrasive,** abradant, carborundum; **smoothing device,** battledore, bulldozer, calender, comb, float, grader, jointer *(Carp.)*, lap, rake, rolling pin, slicker *(Foundry)*, smoothing-iron

SMOOTHLY *adv* smooth; **silkily,** glassily, sleekly, slickly; **flowingly,** fluently, glidingly, legato; **evenly,** even

SMOOTH OBJECT *n* alabaster, glass, ice, marble, plate, satin, silk, slickensides, smooth, velvet

smorgasbord *n* → **1** choice **2** meal **3** mixture

smother *n* → **1** cloud **2** fire **3** flood *v* **4** cover **5** enclose **6** extinguish **7** flood **8** hide **9** keep secret **10** kill **11** oversupply **12** repress **13** suffocate **14** welcome

smoulder *n* → **1** cloud **2** fire *v* **3** catch fire **4** feel emotion

smudge *n* → **1** cloud **2** dirt **3** shapelessness *v* **4** blacken **5** dirty

smug *adj* → **1** arrogant **2** proud **3** smooth **4** tidy

smuggle *v* → **1** cheat **2** rob **3** trade

smut *n* → **1** dirt **2** pornography *v* **3** dirty

snack *n* → **1** easy thing **2** meal

snag *n* → **1** hindrance **2** knob **3** mouth **4** piercer *v* **5** hinder

snail *n* → **1** farmhand **2** idler **3** slowcoach

snake *n* → **1** bad person **2** betrayer **3** enemy **4** reptile *v* **5** twist

snap *n* → **1** button **2** click **3** easy thing **4** good fortune **5** photograph **6** vitality *v* **7** break **8** call (of animals) **9** click **10** hit **11** photograph **12** speak *adj* **13** momentary *adv* **14** speedily

snapper *n* → **1** searcher **2** thin person

snapshot *n* → **1** gunfire **2** photograph

snare *n* → **1** allure *v* **2** hunt

snarl *n* → **1** animal call **2** distortion **3** scowl **4** tangle *v* **5** call (of animals) **6** engrave **7** menace **8** speak **9** tangle

snatch *n* → **1** groin **2** lifting **3** move **4** part **5** robbery **6** sex object **7** takings *v* **8** capture **9** fluctuate

sneak *n* → **1** bad person **2** gossip *v* **3** reveal **4** rob **5** trick

sneaker *n* → **1** bad person **2** footgear

sneer *n* → **1** boo *v* **2** insult

sneeze *n* → **1** breathing **2** hiss *v* **3** breathe **4** drink alcohol **5** hiss

snib *n* → bolt

snick *n* → **1** click **2** cut **3** stroke *v* **4** click **5** cut

snide *adj* → **1** disapproving **2** disdainful **3** slanderous

sniff *n* → **1** breathing **2** quiet sound **3** smell *v* **4** breathe **5** hiss **6** smell out

sniffle *n* → **1** breathing **2** hiss *v* **3** hiss

snigger *n* → **1** mirth *v* **2** insult **3** laugh

snip *n* → **1** bit **2** click **3** cut **4** small amount **5** success *v* **6** borrow **7** cut **8** separate

snipe *n* → **1** shot *v* **2** hunt

snippet *n* → **1** bit **2** small amount **3** unimportant person

snitch *n* → **1** betrayer **2** informant *v* **3** rob

snivel *n* → **1** affectation **2** cry *v* **3** attitudinise **4** be unhappy **5** excrete **6** grieve **7** hiss **8** speak

snob *n* → **1** affected person **2** arrogant person

snooker *n* → **1** hiding place *v* **2** hide **3** hinder

snoop *n* → **1** inspection **2** spy *v* **3** search

snooze *n* → **1** imprisonment **2** sleep *v* **3** sleep

snore *n* → **1** breathing **2** dissonance **3** hiss **4** loud sound *v* **5** be dissonant **6** hiss

snorkel *n* → **1** passageway *v* **2** swim

snort *n* → **1** a drink **2** breathing **3** crackle **4** hiss **5** loud sound *v* **6** be loud **7** insult **8** laugh **9** take drugs

snout *n* → **1** bulge **2** exit **3** nose **4** tobacco

SNOW *n* firn, névé, snow cap, snow country, snowdrift, snowfield, snowflake, snowline, virga; **sludge,** slush; **snowstorm,** avalanche, blizzard, flurry, hailstorm, snowfall; **snowball,** snowman; **frost,** black frost, freeze, hoar, hoarfrost, Jack Frost, permafrost, rime, silver frost, white frost; **absolute zero,** degrees of frost, freezing point, frost point

snow *n* → **1** hair **2** mister **3** narcotic **4** white *v* **5** be cold **6** hide **7** shower

snub *n* → **1** insult **2** repulsion **3** stoppage *v* **4** be unfriendly **5** humble **6** insult **7** repel **8** stop *adj* **9** short

snuff *n* → **1** breathing **2** remnant **3** smell **4** tobacco **5** waste *v* **6** breathe **7** investigate **8** smell out **9** subtract

snuffle *n* → **1** accent **2** breathing **3** hiss *v* **4** attitudinise **5** breathe **6** grieve **7** hiss **8** speak

snug *adj* → **1** content **2** secret **3** tidy *adv* **4** easily **5** tidily

snuggle *n* → **1** endearments *v* **2** kiss

so *adv* → **1** how **2** intensely *interj* **3** stop *conj* **4** because

soak *n* → **1** absorber **2** drinking session **3** heavy drinker **4** hollow **5** liquid **6** wetting *v* **7** cook **8** extract **9** liquefy **10** wet

soap *n* → **1** cleanser **2** program *v* **3** clean

soapbox *n* → **1** platform **2** wagon

soap opera *n* → program

soar *v* → **1** ascend **2** fly **3** prosper **4** succeed **5** tower

sob *n* → **1** cry **2** hiss *v* **3** grieve

sober *adj* → **1** abstinent **2** colourless **3** realistic **4** sane **5** sombre

SOBERSIDES *n* boy scout, owl, straight man; **wowser,** damper, Job's comforter, killjoy, misery, party pooper, snufflebuster, sourpuss, streak of misery, wet blanket

SOCIABILITY *n* companionableness, conviviality, good fellowship, gregariousness, hospitableness, hospitality, party spirit, sociableness, sociality; **cordiality,** advances, approachability, approachableness, backslapping, bonhomie, cordialness, expansiveness, gladhanding, joviality, mellowness; **social relations,** commerce, companionship, company, comradeship, fellowship, routs and revels, social intercourse, socialness, society; **open house,** welcome

SOCIABLE *adj* approachable, chummy, clubbable, companionable, cordial, folksy *(U.S.)*, gregarious, hospitable, neighbourly, outgoing, social; **convivial,** Anacreontic, backslapping, boon, expansive, hail-fellow-well-met, jolly; **welcoming,** greeting, salutatory

social *n* → **1** party *adj* **2** sociable **3** societal

socialise *v* → **1** associate **2** be sociable **3** democratise **4** regularise

socialism *n* → **1** economy **2** sharing out

socialite *n* → fashionable person

social work *n* → charity

SOCIETAL *adj* associational, associative, comitial, curial, institutional, institutionary, organisational; **communal,** collective, common, cooperative, mutual, social; **allied,** associated, coalition, joint; **federal,** confederative, federalist, fusionist, league, unitarian, united; **corporate,** corporative, incorporate, incorporated; **fraternal,** comradely, freemasonic, masonic; **intercommunity,** interclub, interdepartmental; **congregational,** tribal, tribalist, tribalistic; **cliquey,** clannish, cliquish, incestuous

SOCIETY *n* association, auxiliary, club, foundation, group, movement, sewing circle; **alliance,** affiliation, affinity group, alignment, axis, bloc, camp, coalition, combination, front, union, united front; **interest group,** lobby; **federation,** commonwealth, confederacy, confederation, consociation, league, umbrella organisation; **branch,** chapter, local *(U.S.)*. *See also* COMMUNITY; INSTITUTE; COMMITTEE; CLIQUE; CORPORATION

society *n* → **1** friendship **2** gathering **3** sociability **4** the public **5** wealthy person

SOCK *n* alberts *(Colloq.)*, almonds *(Colloq.)*, ankle-sock, bobbysock *(U.S.)*, bootee, gaiter, leggings, toe sock

sock *n* → **1** hit *v* **2** hit

socket *n* → niche

sod *n* → **1** bad person **2** bit **3** sexual type *v* **4** cover

soda *n* → **1** drink **2** easy thing **3** success

soda-water *n* → drink

sodden *v* → **1** pulp **2** wet *adj* **3** boring **4** pulpy **5** stupid **6** thick **7** wet

sodomy *n* → sexuality

sofa *n* → couch

SOFT *adj* cottony, downy, floccose, flocculent, flocky, flossy, piled, pillow-like, pillowy, silky, spongy, velutinous, velvet, velvet-like, velvety; **delicate,** lacerable, tender; **crumbly,** crumby, floury, friable, loose, mealy; **plastic,** ductile, flexible, flexile, floppy, lax, malleable, mouldable, pliable, pliant, pulvinar, semiplastic, supple, thermoplastic, tractable, tractile, waxen, whippy, willowy; **creamy,** smooth; **mushy,** dozy, fleshy, fluctuant, lush, marshy, pithy, pulpy, splashy, spongy, springy, unset; **doughy,** stodgy; **emollient,** mollescent, softening; **mellow,** mild

soft *adj* → **1** dull **2** emotional **3** flattering **4** influenced **5** kind **6** lenient **7** moderate **8** quiet **9** smooth **10** weak *adv* **11** carefully **12** quietly *interj* **13** silence **14** stop

softball *n* → ball

soft drink *n* → drink

SOFTEN *v* emolliate, macerate, pulp, tenderise, thaw; **cushion,** ease, pad, pillow, upholster; **mellow,** milden; **relax,** supple, unbend, unbrace

SOFTLY *adv* delicately, silkily, tenderly; **flexibly,** floppily, laxly; **pliably,** plastically, pliantly, supplely, supply, tractably; **mildly,** mellowly; **mushily,** lushly

SOFTNESS *n* downiness, flocculence, silkiness, velvetiness; **suppleness,** ductility, flexibility, flexibleness, floppiness, malleability, malleableness, plasticity, pliability, pliableness, pliancy, pliantness, tractability, tractableness, tractility; **delicateness,** tenderness; **laxness,** laxation, laxity, mellowness, mildness; **tenderness,** soft-heartedness; **friableness,** mealiness; **creaminess,** smooth texture; **mushiness,** doziness, fleshiness, pulpiness, rottenness, sectility, sponginess; **stodginess,** doughiness; **softening,** emollition, laxation, maceration, mollescence

soggy *adj* → **1** boring **2** pulpy **3** stupid **4** wet

SOIL *n* dirt, earth, loam, mould *(Poetic)*, rhizosphere, topsoil, zonal soil; **ochre,** chestnut soil, red earth, terra rossa, umber; **subsoil,** bind, hardpan, underclay, undersoil; **clay,** adobe, argil, bole, china clay, fuller's earth, kaolin, potter's clay; **marl,** black cotton soil, black earth, chernozem, malm, regur, rendzina, tropical black earth; **sand,** diatomaceous earth, kieselguhr, mineral sand; **deposit,** alluvium, eluvium, geest, loess, sediment, warp, wash; **humus,** black soil, brown forest soil, duff, mould, muck, muck soil, peat; **podsol,** gleisoil, gumbo *(U.S.)*; **drift,** apron, boulder clay, diluvium, moraine, till; **calcrete,** caliche, capstone; **acid soil,** alkali soil, azonal soil, intrazonal soil. *See also* LAND

soil *n* → **1** bodily discharge **2** dirt **3** nation *v* **4** dirty **5** uglify

soirée *n* → concert

soiree *n* → party

sojourn *n* → **1** visit *v* **2** inhabit **3** visit

solace *v* → alleviate

solar *n* → **1** living room **2** room

solar plexus *n* → abdomen

solder *n* → **1** adhesive *v* **2** stick together

SOLDIER *n* Anzac, blue-bonnet, crunchie, desert rat, digger, doughboy *(U.S.)*, Federal *(U.S.)*, G.I., galloglass, Hun, imperial, Jerry, Joe *(U.S.)*, lobster, man-at-arms, pongo *(N.Z.)*, rat, redcoat, regular, sepoy *(India)*, tommy, Tommy Atkins, trooper, Unknown Soldier, Yankee; **infantryman,** foot soldier, footman *(Obs.)*, footslogger, janissary, peon, pioneer; **artilleryman,** bazookaman, bombardier, bomber, cannoneer, gunner, powder monkey, spotter, strafer; **rifleman,** carabineer, fusilier, grenadier, harquebusier, musketeer, pistoleer; **swordsman,** halberdier, lance, paviser, pikeman, sabre, spear, spearman; **archer,** arbalester, bowman, crossbowman; **cavalryman,** bashibazouk, cameleer, carabin, carabineer, cavalier, cuirassier, demon, dragoon, guardsman *(Brit.)*, horse marine *(U.S.)*, horseman, hussar, lancer, light-horseman, trooper, uhlan; **centurion,** flanker, legionary, manipular, palatine; **standard-bearer,** colour company, colour party, colour sergeant, cornet, ensign, guidon, vexillary; **sentinel,** sentry; **bodyguard,** fugleman; **drill sergeant,** drillmaster, drum-major; **engineer,** miner *(Obs.)*, sapper, signalman, specialist *(U.S.)*. *See also* SERVICEMAN; COMBAT TROOPS; ARMED FORCES; HIGH COMMAND

soldier *n* → **1** helper *v* **2** militarise

sole *n* → **1** bottom **2** coating **3** footgear **4** leg *adj* **5** independent **6** one

solecism *n* → **1** discourtesy **2** error **3** figure of speech **4** grammatical error **5** illogicality

solemn *adj* → **1** formal **2** sombre

solicit *v* → **1** desire **2** entreat **3** persuade **4** prostitute oneself

solicitor *n* → lawyer

solicitous *adj* → **1** careful **2** desirous **3** kind

SOLID *n* decahedron, dodecahedron, heptahedron, icosahedron, octahedron, pentahedron, polyhedron, prism, pyramid, trisoctahedron; **hexahedron,** cube, cuboid, dice, parallelpiped, rhombohedron, rhombus; **tesseract,** hypercube; **sphere,** cone, conoid, cylinder, oblate spheroid, prolate spheroid, solid of revolution, toroid, torus, tube, ungula; **helix,** spiral; **crystal,** baguette, brilliant, rose

SOLID *adj* bushy, caked, close, close-grained, concentrated, condensed, consolidate *(Archaic)*, dense, gross, massy, so thick you can cut it with a knife, stodgy, thick, thickish, thickset; **concretionary,** constringent; **impenetrable,** concrete, impermeable, impervious; **clotted,** clotty, coagulated, curdy, grumous; **condensable,** congealable

solid *n* → **1** jewel *adj* **2** enormous **3** full **4** hard **5** heavy **6** homogeneous **7** real **8** sequential **9** sticky **10** thick **11** wealthy

solidarity *n* → **1** agreement **2** cooperation **3** friendship **4** oneness

SOLID BODY *n* body *(Geom.)*, cake, cluster, concrete, concretion, condensate, conglomerate, conglomeration, grume, hard core, lump, mass; **clot,** blood clot, thrombosis; **curd,** coagulum, congelation

SOLIDIFIER *n* coagulant, coagulator, condenser, congealer, thickener, thickening; **densimeter,** hydrometer, pycnometer

SOLIDIFY *v* cluster, cohere, conglomerate, full; **clot,** coagulate; **curdle,** clabber, curd; **thicken,** cake, concentrate, concrete, condense, congeal, inspissate, silt, silt up

SOLIDITY *n* closeness, cohesion, compaction, concentration, condensation, congealment, congelation, constringency, denseness, density, grossness, relative density, solidness, specific gravity, stodginess, thick, thickness, tightness; **solidification,** concentration, eburnation, gelation, inspissation, thickening; **impenetrability,** impenetrableness, impermeability, impermeableness, imperviousness

soliloquy *n* → oration

solitaire *n* → **1** jewel **2** jewellery

SOLITARILY *adv* alone, aloof, aloofly, distantly, lonelily, lonesomely, on one's pat, out on a limb, remotely; **antisocially,** insularly

SOLITARY *n* hatter *(Colloq.)*, introvert, isolate, lone wolf, loner, maverick, skulker, troglodyte; **hermit,** anchoress, anchorite, ascetic, eremite, monk, recluse, seclusionist, solitary; **castaway,** maroon; **lonely heart,** a rose on the rubbish tip, wallflower; **isolationist,** little Englander

SOLITARY *adj* anchoritic, ascetic, ascetical, eremitic, eremitical, eremitish, hermitic, hermitical, monkish; **antisocial,** asocial, morose, troglodytic, unfriendly, withdrawn; **aloof,** friendless, incommunicado, lone, out of circulation, recluse, reclusive, singular *(Obs.)*, stand-offish, strange, unapproachable; **lonely,** insular, introversive, introvert, isolative, like a shag on a rock, lone *(Poetic)*, lonesome, lorn, misanthropic, shy, unfriended. *See also* SECLUDED

solitary *n* → **1** imprisonment **2** solitary *adj* **3** one

SOLITUDE *n* desolateness, desolation, friendlessness, isolation, loneliness, lonesomeness, obscureness, obscurity, reclusion, remoteness, secludedness, solitariness; **aloofness,** distance, insularity, introversion, reserve, secrecy; **withdrawal,** hibernation, relegation, retirement, rustication, segregation, sequestration *(Archaic)*. *See also* SECLUSION

solitude *n* → oneness

solo *n* → **1** actor **2** bicycle **3** flight **4** one *adj* **5** dramatic **6** musical **7** one *adv* **8** alone

solstice *n* → **1** astronomic point **2** season

soluble *adj* → liquefiable

SOLUTION *n* conclusion, deduction, determination, explanation, generalisation, illation, key, proof, solvent. *See also* ANSWER

solution *n* → **1** explanation **2** liquid **3** simplification

SOLVE *v* crack *(Colloq.)*, deduce, explain, figure out, find the key to, get out, hammer out, puzzle out, thrash out, turn the scales, work out, zero in; **resolve,** clear up, conclude, extract, find; **answer a need,** meet a requirement, satisfy

solve *v* → **1** clarify **2** translate

solvent *n* → **1** liquefier **2** solution *adj* **3** liquefiable

SOMBRE *adj* black, bleak, cheerless, dismal, dispiriting, grey, melancholy, sour, wintry; **solemn,** awful, deep, grave, grim, heavy; **sedate,** demure, owl-like, owlish, serious, sober, soberminded, staid; **stern,** dour, frowning, humourless, mirthless

sombre *adj* → **1** black **2** colourless **3** shadowy

SOMBRENESS *n* bleakness, dismalness, greyness, grimness, melancholy, sourness, wintriness; **austereness,** austerity, harshness, rigorousness, rigour, severeness, severity; **sternness,** dourness, mirthlessness; **soberness,** demureness, sedateness, sobermindedness, sobriety; **solemnity,** deepness, depth, graveness, gravity, seriousness, solemness; **solemnification,** solemnisation

sombrero *n* → hat

some *adj* → most

somebody *n* → famous person

somersault *n* → **1** exercise **2** overturn **3** roll *v* **4** overturn **5** roll

something *n* → **1** important thing **2** matter

SOMETHING DIFFERENT *n* a whole new ball game, horse of another colour, something else, something else again, this that or the other, variations on a theme; **another,** anotherie, change, choice, hybrid, modification, otherie, tertium quid, variety

somewhat *adv* → gradually

somewhere *adv* → then

somnambulism *n* → **1** sleepiness **2** walking

somnolent *adj* → asleep

son *n* → **1** child **2** mister **3** offspring

SONG *n* anthem, ballad, barcarolle, calypso, cantata, cantilena, canto, cantus, canzone, canzonet, chanson, chant, comeallyers, descant, ditty, folk song, frottola, hit song, hymn, lay, lied, national anthem, nursery rhyme, patter song, penillion, shanty, song cycle, tabi song *(Aborig.)*, torch song, vocal, vocalise, Volkslied, waiata *(N.Z.)*, warble; **part-song,** canon, glee, madrigal, villanella; **round,** catch, roundelay, troll; **aria,** arietta, cabaletta, cavatina, concert aria; **yodel,** styrienne; **lullaby,** berceuse, cradlesong; **drinking song,** brindisi, wassail *(Obs.)*; **marriage song,** epithalamium, hymeneal, prothalamion; **dirge,** coronach, elegy, epicedium, lament, lamentation, monody, threnody; **theme song,** jingle, leitmotiv, signature, signature tune, theme tune; **part,** canto, canto fermo, cantus firmus, chart, descant, fundamental bass, line, organum, second, secondo, vocals, voice part

song *n* → **1** birdcall **2** poetry

sonic *adj* → acoustic

son-in-law *n* → child

sonnet *n* → poetry

sonorous *adj* → **1** eloquent **2** loud **3** resonant

sook *n* → **1** cattle **2** coward

soon *adv* → **1** hurriedly **2** in the future **3** momentarily

soot *n* → **1** dirt **2** fire

soothe *v* → **1** alleviate **2** ease **3** moderate

sop *n* → **1** bribe **2** coward **3** pulp **4** weakling *v* **5** pulp **6** wet

sophisticated *adj* → **1** complex **2** composed **3** courteous **4** knowledgeable **5** mixed **6** tasteful

SOPORIFIC *adj* hypnotic, narcotic, somniferous, somnific, soporiferous, torporific

soporific *n* → sleeping-pill

sopping *adj* → **1** pulpy **2** wet

soppy *adj* → **1** affected **2** emotional **3** wet

soprano *n* → **1** singer *adj* **2** shrill

sorcery *n* → **1** magic **2** the supernatural

sordid *adj* → **1** mean **2** selfish **3** unkempt

SORE *n* abscess, blain, boil, canker, carbuncle, cold sore, fester, furuncle, gathering, gumboil, scab, sinus, stigma, ulcer, weal, whitlow; **pustule,** blackhead, bulla, eruption, head, wen, whelk; **contusion,** haematoma; **rash,** barber's itch, barber's rash, gravel rash, prickly heat, shaving rash; **acne,** herpes, impetigo, pimples, school sores, zits; **dermatitis,** brigalow itch, cradle cap, eczema, hives, uredo, urticaria

sore *n* → **1** disfigurement *adj* **2** discontented **3** displeased **4** irritable **5** painful

sorrow *n* → **1** grieving **2** misfortune **3** penitence **4** unhappiness *v* **5** be unhappy

sorry *adj* → **1** ashamed **2** bad **3** penitent **4** pitiable **5** pitying **6** unhappy

sort *n* → **1** character **2** class **3** example **4** method **5** woman *v* **6** class **7** differ **8** inquire into

SOS *n* → signal

sot *n* → heavy drinker

sotto voce *adv* → quietly

souffle *n* → hiss

SOUL *n* atman, inner being, mind, monad, self, spirit, spiritual self; **life force,** breath of life, ectoplasm *(Spiritualism)*, etheric body, etheric force, vital force; **phantom,** apparition, astral body, astral spirit, eidolon, ghost, image, spirit, vapour *(Archaic)*, wraith

soul *n* → **1** characteristics **2** emotion **3** encouragement **4** essence **5** living **6** person **7** phantom **8** psyche

SOUND *n* audition *(Rare)*, noise, note, sonance *(Obs.)*, tone, tune *(Obs.)*, vox; **complex sound,** chord, combination tone; **sonority,** consonance, euphonicalness, euphoniousness, euphony, harmonisation, harmony, sonorousness, symphony *(Archaic)*, syntony; **assonance,** alliteration, onomatopoeia, rhyme, stave *(Pros.)*

SOUND *v* cipher, phonate, strike, strike up; **tune,** euphonise, pitch, syntonise, tone; **lower the pitch,** depress, sink; **raise the pitch**

sound *n* → **1** bay **2** channel **3** news *v* **4** appear **5** dive **6** examine **7** hear **8** make music **9** measure **10** practise medicine **11** publicise **12** speak *adj* **13** good **14** healthy **15** honest **16** logical **17** perfect **18** true

SOUND SYSTEM *n* audio system, hi-fi system, music system, playback, stack, stereo; **gramophone,** jukebox, nickelodeon, phonautograph, phonograph *(U.S.)*, record-changer, record-player, stereogram, turntable; **stylus,** cartridge, crystal, pick-up; **radio,** radio-cassette, radiogram, tuner, wireless, wireless set; **amplifier,** amp, box, brick, preamp, preamplifier, preselector; **speaker,** horn, tweeter, woofer; **tone control,** Dolby system, fuzz box, graphic equaliser, mixer; **tape-recorder,** cassette deck, dictaphone, magnetic recorder, recorder, recording head, reel-to-reel, tape deck, wire recorder; **reel,** cartridge, cassette, spool, take-up spool; **electromagnetic tape,** magnetic tape, tape, tape loop

soundtrack *n* → recording

SOUR *v* acetify, acidify, acidulate, brine, pickle, salt

SOUR *adj* acetous, acid, acidic, acidulous, acidy, astringent, lemon, sharp, sourish, subacid, tart, tartish, vinegar-like, vinegarish, vinegary; **bitter,** acerbic, bitterish, bittersweet; **salty,** brackish, brinish, briny, salt, saltlike; **dry,** brut, demi-sec, flinty, sec, unsweetened; **rough,** austere, harsh; **unripe,** green

sour *adj* → **1** irritable **2** sombre

source *n* → **1** creator **2** informant **3** spring **4** start *v* **5** impute

SOURNESS *n* acidity, astringency, austereness, sharpness, subacidity, subacidness, tartness; **bitterness,** acerbity; **saltiness,** brackishness, brininess, salinity; **acidulation,** acidification; **acid,** bitters, brine, gall, lemon, vinegar

souse *n* → **1** dive **2** flying **3** heavy drinker **4** liquid **5** wetting *v* **6** cook **7** dive **8** drink alcohol **9** fly **10** intoxicate **11** wet

south *n* → wind

souvenir *n* → **1** memento *v* **2** rob

sovereign *n* → **1** aristocrat *adj* **2** authoritative **3** predominant

sow *n* → **1** pig **2** remnant *v* **3** disperse **4** farm

SO WHAT *interj* big deal, che sarà sarà, do tell, for aught one cares, hard cheddar, hard cheese, it's all one to me, stiff cheddar, stiff cheese, that's the way the cookie crumbles, what of it, what the hell, who cares

spa *n* → **1** bath **2** health centre **3** hotel **4** sportsground **5** spring

SPACE *n* accommodation, air space, elbowroom, floor space, head room, houseroom, lebensraum, leg room, play, room, room to breathe, room to move, sea room, serene *(Archaic)*, standing room; **scope,** ambit, compass, orb *(Astrol.)*, range, verge; **expanse,** area, continuum, open; **storage,** roomage, stowage; **roominess,** commodiousness, spaciousness, wideness; **spatiality,** 3-D, three-dimensionality; **vacuum,** free space, vacuity, void; **space-time,** four-dimensional continuum, Minkowski world. *See also* AREA

space *n* → **1** gap **2** interval **3** length **4** musical score **5** period **6** sky *v* **7** gape **8** separate *adj* **9** spacious

SPACIOUS *adj* commodious, expansive, open, roomy, wide; **spatial,** space, three-dimensional

spacious *adj* → **1** big **2** great **3** thick

spade *n* → **1** digging implement **2** knob *v* **3** dig

spadework *n* → foundation

span *n* → **1** bridge **2** length **3** path **4** period *v* **5** extend **6** join **7** measure **8** surround **9** traverse

spangle *n* → **1** trimming *v* **2** shine

spaniel *n* → crawler

spank *n* → **1** corporal punishment **2** hit *v* **3** hit **4** move **5** speed

spanking *n* → **1** corporal punishment **2** hitting *adj* **3** energetic **4** most **5** speedy

spar *n* → **1** contest **2** pole *v* **3** fight

spare *n* → **1** equipment *v* **2** acquit **3** disuse **4** ease **5** forgive **6** give *adj* **7** abstinent **8** small **9** thin **10** thrifty

sparing *adj* → **1** abstinent **2** pitying **3** small **4** thrifty

spark *n* → **1** affected person **2** electricity **3** fire **4** light **5** lover **6** small amount *v* **7** catch fire **8** electrify **9** flirt **10** shine

sparkle *n* → **1** artistry **2** fire **3** happiness **4** light *v* **5** be happy **6** bubble **7** excel **8** shine

sparse *adj* → **1** dispersed **2** few **3** small

spasm *n* → **1** contraction **2** distortion **3** emotion **4** turbulence

spasmodic *adj* → **1** contracted **2** impermanent **3** interrupted **4** irregular

spastic *n* → **1** incompetent **2** patient *adj* **3** contracted **4** incompetent **5** stupid

spat *n* → **1** animal offspring **2** fight **3** hit *v* **4** fight **5** hit **6** wet

spate *n* → **1** flow **2** rainfall

spatial *adj* → spacious

spatter *n* → **1** hiss **2** splash *v* **3** crackle **4** disperse **5** hiss

spawn *n* → **1** animal offspring *v* **2** be fertile **3** give birth **4** reproduce

spay *v* → **1** cut off **2** make infertile **3** medicate

SPEAK *v* articulate, chin, emit, enounce, enunciate, give tongue to, give voice to, phonate, pronounce, pyalla, say, sound, syllable, tongue, utter, vent, vocalise, voice; **think aloud,** soliloquise; **recite,** intonate, intone; **dictate,** deliver, give out, read, trot out; **speak of,** mention, name, tell, tell of; **comment,** allow *(U.S.)*, express, observe, outspeak, pass comment, pass comment on, pass comment upon, quote, remark, state, talk off the top of one's head, ventilate, weigh one's words; **quoth; talk,** bend someone's ear, blow down someone's lug, chew someone's ear, earbash, get on one's soapbox, get up on the stump, harangue, harp, jaw, jawbone, preach at, talk nineteen to the dozen; **exclaim,** ejaculate, gasp; **chatter,** babble, blab, blabber, blather, burble, clack, drivel, gab, gabble, jabber, jaw, patter, smatter *(Obs.)*, twaddle, yap; **blurt,** come out with, drop, jerk out; **snap,** hurl, rasp, snarl, spit, spit it out, throw out; **whine,** bleat, blubber, cant, grumble, snivel, snuffle; **whisper,** breathe, lip, murmur, peep, sigh; **shout,** raise one's voice, yell; **slur,** burr, drawl, twang; **buzz,** croak, drone, thrum

speak *v* → **1** call (of animals) **2** publicise **3** speak well **4** talk

SPEAKER *n* native speaker, sayer, talker, vocaliser, voicer; **exclaimer,** ejaculator, quipster; **reciter,** articulator, deliverer, elocutionist, enunciator; **drawler,** snuffler; **babbler,** blabber, blabbermouth, clacker, earbasher, gabber, gossip, patterer, twaddler, whisperer; **ranter,** blusterer, haranguer

speaker *n* → **1** member of parliament **2** orator **3** sound system

SPEAKING *n* breath, language, locution, mouth, speech, tongue, utterance, vocalisation, voice; **expression,** cadence, delivery, intonation, reading, recital, tone; **talk,** pyalla, say, words; **comment,** ejaculation, exclamation, interjection, observation, phrase, quip; **babble,** blab, blather, burble, clack, doubletalk, drivel, gab, gabble, gibberish, humdrum, jabber, jaw, patter, spiel, twaddle, yap; **whisper,** aside, stage whisper; **somniloquy; emphasis,** accent, stress; **fluency,** articulateness, competence, loquacity, vocalism, vocality, vocalness; **pronunciation,** articulation, diction, enouncement, enunciation, phonation; **phonetics,** acoustic phonetics, articulatory phonetics, orthoepy, perceptual phonetics, phonemics, phonics, phonography, phonology, spelling pronunciation, syllabism

SPEAK WELL *v* have the gift of the gab; **declaim,** hold forth, mouth, orate, pour forth, pull out all the stops, reel off, smart talk, spiel, spout, spruik; **address,** apostrophise, call, have one's say, have the floor, hold forth, read, speak; **harangue,** give someone an earful, lecture, perorate, preach at, say a mouthful, sermonise, trawl

SPEAR *n* assegai, dart, eelspear, gaff, gidgee, gig, harpoon, javelin, leister, trident, woomera; **lance,** bill, gisarme, halberd, partisan, pike, shaft, spontoon, twibill, vouge; **boomerang,** kylie, throwing stick; **flail,** thunderbolt

spear *n* → **1** dismissal **2** piercer **3** soldier **4** surfboard *v* **5** kill **6** speed

special *n* → **1** bargain **2** policeman **3** textbook **4** train *v* **5** practise medicine *adj* **6** intense **7** particular **8** reputable

specialise *v* → **1** change **2** particularise

SPECIALIST *n* authority, boffin, buff, consultant, crack, expert, hot dog *(U.S.)*, judge, old hand, sophisticate, stager, technician, veteran, virtuoso; **connoisseur,** appreciator, apprehender, cognoscente, maven, perceiver, percipient, recognisor; **generalist,** illuminate *(Archaic)*, illuminist, pansophist, pantologist, scientist, wake-up; **scholar,** clerk *(Archaic)*; **illuminati,** clerisy, faculty, literati

speciality *n* → **1** characteristic **2** course **3** the best

specialty *n* → **1** deed **2** job **3** knowledge **4** subject matter

species *n* → class

specific *n* → **1** characteristic **2** medication *adj* **3** inborn **4** particular

specify *v* → particularise

specimen *n* → example

specious *adj* → **1** apparent **2** beautiful **3** ugly

speck *n* → **1** powder **2** small amount **3** smallgoods

speckle *n* → **1** disfigurement *v* **2** disfigure

spectacle *n* → **1** display **2** entertainment **3** show

SPECTACULAR *adj* gala, panoplied, splendid; **showy,** blazing, dashing, dashy, eyecatching, for show, ornate, ostentatious, phantasmagorical, pyrotechnic, splashy, triumphal

spectacular *n* → entertainment

spectator *n* → looker

spectre *n* → phantom

spectrum *n* → **1** colour **2** diagram **3** difference

speculate *v* → **1** attempt **2** gamble **3** invest **4** think

speech *n* → **1** language **2** oration **3** speaking

SPEED *n* celerity, fastness, fleetness, quickness, rapidity, speediness, swiftness; **promptness,** dispatch, expedition, expeditiousness, immediateness, promptitude, smartness, summariness; **haste,** cursoriness, hastiness, helter-skelter, hurriedness, hurry, hurry-scurry, posthaste *(Archaic)*, precipitancy, precipitateness, precipitation, rush, stampede; **briskness,** activeness, agility, alacrity, lightness, mercurialness, nimbleness, sharpness, slippiness, snappiness. *See also* RATE; VELOCITY

SPEED *v* bat, bowl, clip, flash, fleet, fly, hightail it, hurtle, lope, pike, post, romp, scud, shift, skirr, skitter, slip, spank, spear, spear on, spin, tear, travel, whip, whirl, whiz, zap, zip, zoom; **drive fast,** barrel along, beetle along, belt, break the sound barrier, burl, burn, crack on sail, do a ton *(Obs.)*, fang, flat-chat, give it a rap, go like a bomb, go like a cut cat, go like a rocket, go through on the padre's bike, herb, hunt along, pelt, rip, rocket, scorch, streak; **dart,** dive, flit, glint, leap, play, pop, pounce, scoot; **scamper,** clatter, rattle, scramble, scurry, scutter, scuttle; **run,** chevy, chivvy, double *(Mil.)*, double-time, gallop, hare, hotfoot it, make the running, pace, race, run like a hairy goat, schuss, scour, sprint, step out; **stampede,** bolt, career, rampage. *See also* HURRY

speed *n* → **1** good fortune *v* **2** facilitate **3** increase **4** prosper

SPEEDILY *adv* apace, at a fair bat, at a rate of knots, by leaps and bounds, fast, fleetly, hotfoot, like a bat out of hell, like a bird, like a house on fire, like a shot, like billyo, like mad, like one thing, meteorically, pell-mell, quickly, rathe *(Archaic)*, swiftly; **briskly,** actively, agilely, nimbly, sharp, snap, snappily; **flittingly,** dartingly, trippingly; **flat out,** amain *(Archaic)*, at full speed, flat chat, flat out like a lizard drinking, for the lick of one's life, full chat, full fling, full pelt, full sail, full tilt, headlong, hell for leather, in nothing flat, tantivy; **in double time,** at the double, doppio movimento, double-quick; **accelerando,** allegretto, allegro, mosso, prestissimo, presto, veloce, vivace

SPEEDSTER *n* darter, dasher, fleer, flier, flitter, galloper, goer, Jehu, racer, rattler, rusher, scorcher *(Obs.)*, speed-merchant, speeder, speeler, sprinter; **pacesetter,** pacemaker, pacer; **express,** blue streak, clipper, flier, hot rod; **expediter,** hastener, rusher

SPEEDY *adj* arrowy, blistering, express, fast, flighty *(Rare)*, high-speed, jet-propelled, meteoric, nippy, quick, rapid, swift, tantivy, toey, ton-up *(Brit.)*, wingy; **spanking,** clipping, cracking, double-quick, furious, headlong, raking, tripping; **brisk,** alacritous, briskish, expeditious, prompt, sharp, smart, snappy, yare *(Archaic)*; **hurried,** hasty, helter-skelter, hurry-scurry, precipitant, precipitate, rush, sudden *(Archaic)*; **nimble,** active, agile, alert, fleet, fleet-footed, flitting, flying, light on one's feet, slippy, swift-footed, whippy, wing-footed *(Archaic)*, zippy; **rakish,** clipper-built, racing, streamlined; **transonic,** hypersonic, relativistic, subsonic, supersonic

spell *n* → **1** allure **2** centre of activity **3** influence **4** interruption **5** interval **6** magic spell **7** period **8** rest *v* **9** rest **10** substitute

spellbound *adj* → **1** attentive **2** captivated

spencer *n* → **1** hairpiece **2** jacket **3** underwear

spend *v* → **1** give **2** pay **3** use up

spendthrift *n* → squanderer

spent *adj* → **1** extinguished **2** tired **3** used up

spew *v* → vomit

sphere *n* → **1** ball **2** dwelling **3** heavenly body **4** job **5** sky **6** solid **7** surroundings *v* **8** round

spice *n* → **1** eloquence **2** fragrance *v* **3** cook

spick-and-span *adj* → **1** clean **2** new **3** tidy

spider *n* → **1** allurer **2** belt **3** carriage **4** contest **5** drink **6** powderer **7** stand **8** support

spiel *n* → **1** oration **2** persuasion **3** selling **4** speaking *v* **5** encourage **6** speak well

spigot *n* → **1** plug **2** tap

spike *n* → **1** flower **2** fortification **3** inserter **4** nail **5** piercer *v* **6** be infertile **7** brew **8** jut **9** kill **10** sharpen

spill *n* → **1** dismissal **2** lighter **3** liquid **4** misplacement **5** part **6** plug *v* **7** discharge **8** disperse **9** flood **10** flow **11** misplace **12** reveal

SPIN *n* backspin, English *(U.S. Billiards)*, overspin, side *(Billiards)*, tail spin, top, top spin, twist *(Cricket Baseball)*, underspin; **twist,** twiddle, twirl, whirl, whirlabout; **spinning,** burling, centrifugation, gyration, hunting, twisting, whirling, winding; **swirl,** puddle *(Rowing)*, purl, ripple; **eddy,** maelstrom, vortex, whirlpool; **catherine-wheel,** girandole, pinwheel; **propeller,** impeller; **waterwheel,** flywheel, windmill; **spinner,** gyroscope, peg top, teetotum, top, twirler; **cyclone,** tornado, tourbillion, twister, typhoon, whirlwind, willy-willy. *See also* ROTATION; ROLL

SPIN *v* gyrate, twirl, whirl, whirr; **eddy,** centrifugalise, centrifuge, swirl; **whip,** stir; **dizzy,** giddy. *See also* ROTATE

spin *n* → **1** affair **2** atom **3** confusion **4** excitement **5** imprisonment **6** journey **7** luck **8** rate *v* **9** cord **10** fish **11** sew **12** shape **13** speed

spindle *n* → **1** length **2** rod **3** support *v* **4** flower **5** sew *adj* **6** female **7** patriarchal

spine *n* → **1** back **2** bulge **3** piercer **4** wrapper

SPINNING *adj* circulative, circulatory, gyroscopic, gyrostatic, orbital, precessional, rotational, rotatory, trochal; **revolving,** gyratory, planetary *(Mach.)*, rolling, rotary, rotative, swirly, swivel-like, vortical, vorticose, vortiginous, whirlabout; **clockwise,** anticlockwise, counterclockwise, dextrorotatory, laevorotatory; **stem-winding,** paddle-wheel, screw, stern-wheel *(Naut.)*, twin-screw

spinning wheel *n* → wheel

spin-off *n* → finished product

spinster *n* → **1** sewer **2** single person

SPINY *adj* acanthoid, acanthous, echinate, echinated, echinoid, spiculate, spined, spinescent, spiniferous, spinose, spinous; **prickly,** acanthaceous, brambly, burry, snaggy, spurred, thistlelike, thistly, thorny; **spiky,** apiculate, mucronate, spicate, spikelike, spinelike, spinulose, spiny, spurlike, thornlike; **needle-shaped,** acerose, acicular, aciculate, aciform, fanglike, needlelike, spiculate. *See also* SHARP; POINTED

spiny *adj* → **1** difficult **2** rough **3** spiny

SPIRAL *n* screw, thread, turbinate; **curl,** scroll, verticil, whorl; **convolution,** circination, involution *(Bot.)*, obvolution

SPIRAL *adj* circinate, curled, involute, involutional, obvolute, obvolutive, rolled, turbinate

spiral *n* → **1** circle **2** solid **3** twist *v* **4** rotate **5** twist *adj* **6** circular **7** twisted

spire *n* → **1** church **2** sharp point **3** tower *v* **4** ascend

spirit *n* → **1** character **2** courage **3** emotion **4** essence **5** living **6** phantom **7** soul **8** sprightliness **9** vitality *v* **10** encourage *adj* **11** ghostly

spirited *adj* → **1** busy **2** capricious **3** courageous **4** energetic **5** living **6** predisposed

SPIRITUAL *adj* extramundane, ghostly *(Archaic)*, hyperphysical, interior, inward, otherworldly, spiritous *(Obs.)*, supernatural, superphysical, transcendent, transcendental, translunary, transmundane, unworldly

spiritual *adj* → **1** ghostly **2** light **3** religious **4** reverent **5** supernatural

spit *n* → **1** island **2** piercer **3** rainfall **4** similar thing **5** stove *v* **6** disperse **7** excrete **8** expel **9** hiss **10** rain **11** speak

spite *n* → **1** ill will **2** unfriendliness *v* **3** be unfriendly **4** hinder **5** victimise

spitfire *n* → **1** angry person **2** violent person

spittoon *n* → rubbish bin

SPLASH *n* dash, drip, plop, spatter, splat, splatter, squash, squelch, squish, swash, wash

SPLASH *v* plash, plop, sputter, squash, squelch, squish

splash *n* → **1** cleansing **2** display **3** liquid **4** wetting *v* **5** dirty **6** disperse **7** flow **8** squander **9** wet

splatter *n* → **1** splash *v* **2** wet

splay *v* → **1** diverge **2** separate **3** slope *adj* **4** divergent

spleen *n* → **1** irritableness **2** unhappiness **3** unsociability

splendid *adj* → **1** astonishing **2** beautiful **3** good **4** reputable **5** spectacular

splendour *n* → **1** brightness **2** reputability

splice *n* → **1** knot *v* **2** join **3** marry

splint *n* → **1** timber *v* **2** support

splinter *n* → **1** part *v* **2** separate

split *n* → **1** break **2** exercise **3** gap **4** part **5** share *v* **6** depart **7** gape **8** separate **9** share out *adj* **10** gaping **11** separate **12** shared

splurge *n* → **1** binge **2** display **3** extravagance *v* **4** squander

splutter *n* → **1** code **2** fight *v* **3** crackle **4** disperse **5** hiss **6** mispronounce

SPOIL *v* addle, befoul, blast, blight, canker, contaminate, deflower, empoison, sully, taint, tarnish, vitiate; **corrupt,** adulterate, bastardise, commercialise, prostitute; **wreck,** arse up, bitch, botch, break, bugger up, bungle, cook, crab, cruel, cruel one's pitch, foul up, frig, fuck up, graunch *(N.Z.)*, gum up, gum up the works, louse up, make a hash of, make a muck of, muck, muck up, pakaru *(N.Z.)*, puckeroo, queer, ruin, screw. *See also* DAMAGE

spoil *n* → **1** diggings **2** remnant *v* **3** rob **4** uglify

spoilsport *n* → **1** discourager **2** hinderer

spoke *n* → **1** branch **2** point of convergence

SPOKEN *adj* articulate, nuncupative, oral, parol, phonatory, speaking, verbal, viva-voce, vocal; **voiced,** accented, pronounced, sonant, sonantal, tonic; **speakable,** enunciable, pronounceable, utterable, vocable; **pronunciational,** orthoepic; **interjectory,** ejaculative, ejaculatory, exclamatory, interjectional; **phonal,** phonemic, phonetic, phonic, phonogrammatic, phonologic, vocalic; **homophonous,** dissimilative; **voiceless,** breathed, unvoiced

spokesperson *n* → **1** agent **2** orator

sponge *n* → **1** absorber **2** cleansing **3** extortionist **4** mineral **5** pulp **6** self-seeker **7** washer *v* **8** clean **9** dry **10** idle

sponsor *n* → **1** offerer *v* **2** help **3** offer

spontaneous *adj* → **1** agreeable **2** capricious **3** liberated

spoof *n* → **1** illusion **2** imitation *v* **3** imitate

spook *n* → **1** informant **2** phantom *v* **3** haunt

spool *n* → **1** sound system *v* **2** roll up

spoon *v* → **1** fish **2** kiss

spoonerism *n* → **1** figure of speech **2** joke

spoor *n* → **1** sign *v* **2** pursue

sporadic *adj* → **1** dispersed **2** irregular **3** rare

spore *n* → **1** powder *v* **2** reproduce

sporran *n* → pocket

sport *n* → **1** a good time **2** amusement **3** endearments **4** exercise **5** freak **6** gambler **7** hunting **8** joke *v* **9** amuse oneself **10** display **11** mock **12** show off **13** wear

sporting *adj* → **1** fair **2** gambling **3** lucky

SPORTINGLY *adv* athletically, sportfully

SPORTS *adj* sportful; **sports grade,** amateur, friendly, international, league, national, Olympic, pro-am, professional, representative, state

sports car *n* → car

SPORTSGROUND *n* arena, cockpit, pitch, playing field, sports complex, stadium; **playing area,** ballpark *(U.S.)*, bowling green, clay court *(Tennis)*, covered court, grass court *(Tennis)*, green *(Bowls)*, hard court *(Tennis)*, icerink, links *(Golf)*, net *(Cricket)*, paddock *(N.Z.)*, piste *(Fencing)*, practice range *(Golf)*, prize ring, ring *(Boxing)*, rink *(Bowling Curling)*, shooting gallery, squared ring (circle), tennis court, velodrome *(Cycling)*; **gymnasium,** gym; **pool,** lido *(Brit.)*, natatorium *(U.S.)*, spa; **test cricket ground,** Adelaide Oval, Brisbane Cricket Ground *(The Gabba)*, Edgbaston *(Birmingham)*, Headingley *(Leeds)*, Lord's *(London)*, Melbourne Cricket Ground *(M.C.G.)*, Old Trafford *(Manchester)*, Sydney Cricket Ground *(S.C.G.)*, The Oval *(London)*, Trent Bridge *(Nottingham)*, Western Australian Cricket Ground *(The WACA)*

SPORTSMAN *n* amateur, athlete, Corinthian, first string, gamesman, jock *(U.S.)*, junior, player, pothunter, reserve grade, senior, sporter, sportswoman, tourneyer; **international player,** cap, international, tourist; **team,** eighteen *(Aus. Rules)*, eleven, fifteen *(Rugby Union)*, nine *(Baseball)*, side, squad

sportsman *n* → **1** good person **2** hero **3** hunter

SPORTSWEAR *n* all-in-one, casuals, creams, jogging suit, jumpsuit, playsuit, romper suit, rompers, slipsuit, sports uniform, strip, sunsuit, sweatsuit, tracksuit, trog suit, tunic, whites

spot *n* → **1** a drink **2** dilemma **3** disfigurement **4** lighting **5** position **6** small amount *v* **7** clean **8** dirty **9** disfigure **10** disperse **11** find **12** see

spotlight *n* → **1** lighting *v* **2** display **3** illuminate

SPOUSE *n* affinity, better half, consort, helpmate, helpmeet *(Archaic)*, mate, partner, yokefellow; **wife,** feme covert, goodwife *(Archaic)*, lady, missus, old Dutch, old lady, old woman, rib, the little woman, the old ball and chain, trouble and strife, woman; **husband,** goodman *(Archaic)*, his lordship, hubby, lord *(Archaic)*, lord and master, old man; **newlywed,** benedick, blushing bride, eloper, honeymooner, war bride; **de facto,** concubine, de facto husband, de facto wife, mistress; **marrier,** bigamist, deuterogamist, monogamist, polygamist; **couple,** Darby and Joan, husband and wife, man and wife, pair; **bridal pair,** bride, bridegroom, groom

spout *n* → **1** drain **2** exit **3** knob **4** spring *v* **5** discharge **6** expel **7** flow **8** speak well

sprain *n* → **1** cramp **2** injury *v* **3** injure

sprawl *n* → **1** disorder **2** pose *v* **3** flood **4** recline **5** repose **6** untidy

spray *n* → **1** bubbling **2** flow **3** fragrance *v* **4** disperse **5** medicate

spread *n* → **1** area **2** bedclothes **3** covering **4** farm **5** flood **6** growth **7** meal **8** show **9** size **10** thickness *v* **11** coat **12** disperse **13** diverge **14** extend **15** flood **16** generalise **17** grow **18** open up **19** separate *adj* **20** thick

spread-eagle *v* → **1** bowl over **2** repose *adj* **3** braggart

spree *n* → **1** amusement **2** binge **3** celebration **4** drinking session **5** extravagance

sprig *n* → **1** adolescent **2** child **3** nail **4** offspring **5** restraints

SPRIGHTLINESS *n* alacrity, animation, briskness, dapperness, dash, enlivenment, fastness, go, hurriedness, liveliness, quickness, raciness, spryness, verve; **restlessness,** exhaustlessness, inquietude, nervous energy, pottering, skittishness, tinkering, unquietness; **vigour,** eagerness, energy, heartiness, life, red-bloodedness, spirit, spiritedness, vigorousness, vivacity; **hyperactivity,** overactivity

sprightly *adj* → **1** busy **2** happy *adv* **3** busily

SPRING *n* fount, fountainhead, headspring, source, springhead, springlet, well, wellspring; **headwaters,** head, headstream, riverhead; **fountain,** conduit *(Archaic)*, font *(Archaic)*, fount; **bubbler,** drinking fountain; **geyser,** hot spring, thermae, thermal springs; **mineral spring,** salina, spa, waters; **waterfall,** cascade, cataract, chute, falls, Niagara, overflow, rapids, spout. *See also* FLOW; CURRENT; STREAM

spring *n* → **1** cord **2** elastic **3** innovator **4** jump **5** morning **6** pliability **7** season **8** start *v* **9** appear **10** attack **11** bounce **12** explode **13** find out **14** flower **15** jump **16** liberate **17** separate *adj* **18** pliable **19** seasonal

springboard *n* → **1** elastic **2** help **3** platform **4** starting line

sprinkle *n* → **1** flow **2** rainfall **3** small amount *v* **4** disperse **5** rain **6** wet

sprint *n* → **1** busyness **2** race **3** rate *v* **4** speed

sprite *n* → fairy

sprout *n* → **1** child **2** offspring *v* **3** flower

spruce *n* → **1** timber *adj* **2** fashionable

spry *adj* → busy

spud *n* → **1** chisel **2** digging implement *v* **3** dig

spume *n* → **1** bubbling *v* **2** bubble

spunk *n* → **1** beautiful person **2** courage **3** man **4** reproductive agent **5** vitality

spur *n* → **1** bulge **2** emblem **3** flower **4** incentive **5** mountain **6** piercer **7** propellant *v* **8** arouse **9** hurry **10** injure

spurious *adj* → **1** delusive **2** fake

spurn *n* → **1** insult **2** kick *v* **3** isolate **4** kick **5** repel

spurt *n* → **1** busyness **2** ephemeral **3** flow **4** stream *v* **5** flow

sputter *n* → **1** crackle **2** hiss *v* **3** coat **4** crackle **5** disperse **6** expel **7** hiss **8** mispronounce **9** splash

SPY *n* beagle, counterspy, double agent, informer, mole, secret agent, snoop, snooper, spier, undercover agent, wire-tapper; **secret service,** A.S.I.O., A.S.I.S., C.I.A., intelligence organisation, J.I.O., K.G.B., M.I.5, S.A.S.

spy *n* → **1** informant **2** looker *v* **3** search **4** see

squabble *n* → **1** fight *v* **2** contest

squad *n* → **1** armed forces **2** crowd **3** sportsman **4** workers

squadron *n* → **1** armed forces **2** flight **3** watercraft *v* **4** associate

squalid *adj* → **1** bad **2** ugly **3** unkempt

squall *n* → **1** commotion **2** shout **3** violent outburst **4** wind *v* **5** blow **6** shout

squalor *n* → dirtiness

SQUANDER *v* be prodigal, blow, blue, burn up one's capital, kill the goose that laid the golden eggs, knock down, lamb down, lash out, pay through the nose, run through, spend freely, spend money like water, splash, splurge; **waste,** confound *(Obs.)*, consume, dilapidate, fritter, fritter away, make ducks and drakes of, misspend, riot away, throw away; **gamble away,** game away, sport away; **dissipate,** burn the candle at both ends

squander *n* → extravagance

SQUANDERER *n* big spender, dissipater, fritterer, jetsetter, misspender, playboy, prodigal, profligate, scattergood, spendthrift, two-bob millionaire, waster, wastrel

square *n* → **1** area **2** armed forces **3** field **4** number **5** plane figure **6** protractor *v* **7** account **8** compute **9** fit **10** level **11** pay **12** shape **13** swerve *adj* **14** bent **15** equal **16** erect **17** fair **18** great **19** honest **20** level **21** old **22** satisfactory *adv* **23** angularly **24** fairly **25** honestly **26** precisely

square dance *n* → dance

square-dance *v* → dance

square root *n* → number

squash *n* → **1** drink **2** pressing **3** pulp **4** splash *v* **5** press **6** pulp **7** repress **8** silence **9** splash

squat *n* → **1** dwelling **2** pose *v* **3** inhabit **4** repose *adj* **5** fat **6** short **7** small

squatter *n* → **1** aristocrat **2** owner **3** population

squaw *n* → woman

squawk *n* → **1** birdcall **2** complaint **3** shout *v* **4** chirp **5** complain **6** shrill

squeak *n* → **1** escape **2** quiet sound *v* **3** chirp **4** report on **5** shrill

squeal *n* → **1** complaint **2** shout *v* **3** complain **4** report on **5** shout **6** shrill

squeamish *adj* → nauseous

squeeze *n* → **1** copy **2** dilemma **3** endearments **4** friendship **5** gathering **6** pressing **7** restraint *v* **8** copy **9** extract **10** force **11** kiss **12** press

squelch *n* → **1** pulp **2** splash *v* **3** press **4** repress **5** silence **6** splash

squint *n* → **1** faulty sight **2** look **3** opening *v* **4** look

squire *n* → **1** aristocrat **2** judge **3** man **4** servant *v* **5** accompany **6** partner

squirm *n* → **1** move *v* **2** feel pain **3** move

squirrel *n* → **1** animal's coat *v* **2** save

squirt *n* → **1** arrogant person **2** shearer **3** small person *v* **4** flow **5** wet

SS *n* → combat troops

stab *n* → **1** attempt **2** cut **3** injury **4** kick **5** pat **6** perforation *v* **7** injure **8** open **9** pain **10** perforate **11** roughen

STABLE *n* bails, cowshed, offices *(Brit.)*; **shed,** board, depot shed, shearing shed, stand, woolshed; **barn,** granary, hayshed, hopper, pit silo *(U.S.)*, silage pit, silo

stable *n* → **1** animal dwelling **2** factory **3** gathering **4** pen *v* **5** inhabit **6** store *adj* **7** changeless **8** composed **9** serious **10** steady

stack *n* → **1** accumulation **2** arsenal **3** flight **4** impact **5** passageway **6** sound system

7 storage *v* **8** act unfairly **9** collide **10** gather **11** place **12** store

stadium *n* → sportsground

staff *n* → **1** club **2** emblem of office **3** musical score **4** stick **5** workers

stag *n* → **1** defaulter **2** financier **3** man **4** trader *adj* **5** male

STAGE *n* boards, false stage, footlights, pageant, rostrum, scene *(Class. Antiq.)*; **apron,** coulisses, curtain, downstage, flies, fly gallery, fly-floor, fly-loft, forestage, gridiron, parterre *(U.S.)*, pit, proscenium, slips, stage left, stage right, tormentor, wing; **backdrop,** cyclorama, decor, flat, flown scenery, mise en scène, scenery, set, set piece, setting, special effects, stage effect; **machinery,** animation, effect, projection room, sound effects; **green room,** dressing room

STAGE *v* direct, mount, premiere, present, produce, put on, run, screen, serialise, stage-manage; **cast,** audition, typecast; **preview,** try out; **dramatise,** farcify, melodramatise, ring down the curtain, ring up the curtain, theatricalise

stage *n* → **1** carriage **2** gradation **3** layer **4** mound **5** period **6** platform **7** spacecraft **8** surroundings *v* **9** create **10** drive **11** position **12** undertake

stagecoach *n* → carriage

stagger *v* → **1** astonish **2** be tired **3** walk

STAGING *n* adaptation, dramatisation, dramaturgy, improvisation, mounting, presentation, production, recitation, revival, screening, serialisation, stage-management, stichomythia

stagnant *adj* → **1** dirty **2** inactive

stagnate *v* → **1** be inactive **2** be infertile **3** get dirty **4** stop

staid *adj* → **1** changeless **2** sombre

stain *n* → **1** denigration **2** dirt **3** dye *v* **4** colour **5** disfigure **6** disgrace

stair *n* → stairs

staircase *n* → stairs

STAIRS *n* apples, companionway, escalator, flight, spiral staircase, staircase, stairway, steps; **stair,** curtail step, doorstep, footstep, gradin, horseblock, step; **tread,** going *(Building Trades)*, nosing, riser; **ladder,** rope-ladder, scale *(Obs.)*, stepladder, turret *(Fort.)*, wall bars; **rung,** ratline, rundle

stake *n* → **1** fortification **2** ownership **3** participation **4** shaft *v* **5** fasten **6** gamble **7** support

stalactite *n* → rock outcrop

stalagmite *n* → rock outcrop

stale *n* → **1** urination *v* **2** be old **3** bore *adj* **4** boring **5** frequent **6** old

stalemate *n* → **1** hindrance **2** stoppage *v* **3** stop

stalk *n* → **1** hunting *v* **2** advance **3** go slowly **4** hunt

stall *n* → **1** animal dwelling **2** factory **3** hindrance **4** pen **5** room **6** shop **7** stoppage *v* **8** avoid **9** imprison **10** inhabit **11** stop

stalwart *n* → **1** hero **2** national **3** strong person *adj* **4** courageous **5** strong

stamina *n* → **1** durability **2** perseverance **3** persistence

stammer *v* → mispronounce

stamp *n* → **1** character **2** imprint **3** label **4** model **5** move **6** pat **7** press *v* **8** engrave **9** hollow **10** kick **11** label **12** press **13** shape

stampede *n* → **1** escape **2** speed *v* **3** be violent **4** disperse **5** escape **6** speed

stance *n* → **1** opinion **2** point of view **3** pose

STAND *n* bipod, coaster, crutch, easel, hallstand, hatstand, high hat *(Films Television)*, music stand, spider, stretcher *(Painting)*, tank-stand *(Engineering)*, top hat, tripod, trivet *(Cookery)*, valet; **holder,** candelabra, candelabrum, candlestick, chandelier, flambeau, frog, gasolier, girandole, hold; **andiron,** barbecue, dog, firedog, pothook, toast-rack, trammel; **shipway,** chock *(Naut.)*, dogshore *(Naut.)*, rest, saddle *(Naut.)*; **frame,** chassis, clothes drier, clothes hanger, clothes horse, clothes prop, coathanger, fadge frame, hanger, headframe *(Mining)*, headgear *(Mining)*, horse *(Gymnastics)*, lath *(Bldg. Trades)*, lathing *(Bldg. Trades)*, sawhorse *(Carp.)*, skids, stocks, thorough brace *(U.S. Vehicles)*, trestle; **anvil,** armature, horse, stithy

stand *n* → **1** dissidence **2** point of view **3** pose **4** rack **5** shop **6** stable **7** stoppage *v* **8** be inactive **9** conceive **10** electioneer **11** erect **12** position **13** stop **14** tend to **15** undertake **16** wage war

standard *n* → **1** class **2** currency **3** example **4** flag **5** flower **6** fuel **7** morality **8** musical piece **9** ordinariness **10** perfect thing **11** rule **12** tester *adj* **13** model **14** ordinary

standardise *v* → **1** average **2** regularise

stand by *v* → **1** attend to **2** be faithful to **3** be patient **4** help

stand-by *n* → **1** helper **2** preparation

stand in *v* → substitute

stand-in *n* → **1** actor **2** inferior **3** substitute

standing *n* → **1** condition **2** duration **3** grade **4** reputation *adj* **5** changeless **6** continual **7** erect **8** unused

standstill *n* → stoppage

staple *n* → **1** clip **2** goods **3** raw materials **4** supplies *v* **5** class **6** fasten *adj* **7** important

stapler *n* → classer

star *n* → **1** actor **2** emblem **3** famous person **4** fate **5** fortune-telling **6** important person **7** jewel *v* **8** make history **9** mark **10** perform *adj* **11** reputable

starboard *n* → **1** right **2** side *adj* **3** right *adv* **4** right

starch *n* → **1** formality *v* **2** harden

stare *n* → **1** look *v* **2** look

stark *adj* → **1** bare **2** hard **3** most **4** simple **5** strict **6** thorough *adv* **7** greatly **8** wholly

starling *n* → wall

START *n* alpha, beginning, commencement, early days, epoch, exordium, inception, inchoation, incipience, lead-off, offset, onset, opening, origin, origination, outset, square one; **dawn,** dawning, morning, prime, spring, springtide, springtime, youth, zero hour;

Dreamtime, alcheringa; **opening time; genesis,** birth, birthplace, derivation, nascence, nativity, provenance, provenience, womb; **source,** fount, fountain, fountainhead, head, headspring, headstream, rise, riverhead, seminary, spring, springhead, well, wellhead, wellspring; **germ,** bud, conception, embryo, primordium, protoplasm, seed; **primitiveness,** fundamentality; **first cause,** big bang theory, cosmogony, cosmology; **inauguration,** establishment, induction, initiation, instigation, institution, introduction; **debut,** coming out, inaugural, maiden speech, premiere, unveiling

START *v* bundy on, clock on, fall to, fire away, get away, get cracking, get going, get off on the right foot, get off on the wrong foot, get weaving, hit off, hoe in, kick off, lead off, pitch in, ring up the curtain, rip in, set to, set to work, set up shop, shove off, sign on, start the ball rolling, wade in; **begin,** belt into, commence, ease into, embark on, enter into, get stuck into, gin *(Archaic)*, open, rip into, set about, set on foot, wade into; **arise,** burst forth, come, come into the world, crop up, dawn, proceed, rise, set in, spring up, well up; **come out,** make one's debut; **start again,** make a fresh start, recommence, resume, take up. *See also* INITIATE

start *n* → **1** advance **2** advantage **3** antecedence **4** busyness **5** departure **6** fright **7** move **8** outburst **9** reaction *v* **10** be frightened **11** be surprised **12** extract **13** feel pain **14** jump **15** jut **16** move **17** react **18** separate **19** worry

STARTER *n* commencer, instigator, launcher, opener, promoter; **beginner,** abecedarian, infant, initiate, neophyte, new chum, novice, novitiate, recruit, red-arse, rookie, tyro; **debutante,** deb; **spearhead,** apostle, pioneer, trendsetter, vanguard; **founder,** Adam, First Fleet, founding father, inaugurator, initiator, institutor, introducer, originator, patriarch, progenitor; **first,** aborigines *(Rare)*, firstling

STARTING LINE *n* grid, mobile barrier, scratch, starting gate, starting mark, tape; **flying start,** getaway, kick-off, Le Mans start, send-off, standing start; **jumping-off place,** springboard, threshold

startle *n* → **1** surprise **2** turbulence *v* **3** agitate **4** surprise **5** worry

starve *v* → **1** be hungry **2** die

stash *n* → **1** hiding place *v* **2** hide

state *n* → **1** administrative area **2** condition **3** domain **4** excitement **5** formality **6** nation **7** the public *v* **8** assert **9** speak *adj* **10** formal **11** legislative **12** national **13** sports

stately *adj* → **1** beautiful **2** formal **3** reputable

statement *n* → **1** account **2** assertion **3** evidence **4** information **5** narrative

statesman *n* → member of parliament

static *n* → electricity

station *n* → **1** barracks **2** condition **3** factory **4** farm **5** grade **6** job **7** position **8** reputation **9** telecommunications station *v* **10** place **11** position

stationery *n* → writing materials

station wagon *n* → car

statistics *n* → mathematics

statue *n* → **1** portrait **2** sculpture

statuesque *adj* → beautiful

stature *n* → **1** height **2** importance

status *n* → **1** condition **2** grade **3** reputation

status quo *n* → condition

statute *n* → **1** deed **2** law **3** record

staunch *n* → **1** flow *v* **2** moderate **3** stop *adj* **4** dry **5** faithful **6** friendly **7** persevering **8** serious **9** strong

stave *n* → **1** club **2** musical score **3** shaft **4** sound **5** stick *v* **6** break **7** cut **8** open **9** separate

stay *n* → **1** cord **2** persistence **3** stoppage **4** support **5** timber **6** visit *v* **7** be present **8** continue **9** gamble **10** go slowly **11** help **12** inhabit **13** moderate **14** persist **15** restrain **16** satisfy **17** stop **18** strengthen **19** support **20** swerve **21** visit

stead *v* → be of service

steadfast *adj* → **1** changeless **2** faithful **3** honest **4** persevering **5** serious **6** steady

STEADIER *n* balancer, bracer, entrencher, fixative, mordant, securer, stabiliser, tightener; **stabilising device,** air foil, aerofoil, aileron, anti-roll bar, automatic gain control, brace, castor, cowcatcher, drag-anchor, drag-sheet, dragsail, drift anchor, drift sail, drogue, fiddle, guestrope, guy, gyroscope, gyrostabiliser, gyrostat, hygrostat, outrigger, pyrostat, sea-anchor, sponson, tailplane, thermostat; **ballast,** kentledge

STEADILY *adv* fixedly, indissolubly, irreducibly, steadfastly, unblinkingly; **stably,** firm, foursquarely, gyrostatically, securely, steady; **fast,** firm, firmly, hard and fast, tight, tightly; **even,** evenly, isostatically, on an even keel

STEADINESS *n* determinateness, entrenchment, firmness, foursquareness, secureness, sureness, tightness; **stability,** fastness, fixedness, fixity, indissolubility, indissolubleness, inexorability, inextensibility, irreducibility, irreducibleness, stableness, steadfastness, thermostability, unalterableness, viscosity; **fixture,** footing, rootage; **climax,** ground state, node; **statics,** aerostatics, thermostatics

STEADY *v* balance, ballast, brace, build on a rock, compact, firm, fix, guy, root, secure, settle, stabilise, tighten; **firm,** harden, set; **be steady,** have one's sea legs, hold the road, retain one's equilibrium

STEADY *adj* roadholding, secure, sure, surefooted; **stable,** critical *(Physics)*, earthbound, foursquare, indissoluble, inextensible, irreducible, monostable, noble *(Metall.)*, stabile, thermostable, windless; **even,** balanced, homeostatic, isostatic, magnetostatic; **steadfast,** fixed, unblinking; **set,** consistent *(Obs.)*, fast, firm, fixed, hard-set, impacted, stiff, tight

steady *n* → **1** lover *v* **2** support *adj* **3** abstinent **4** composed **5** erect **6** homogeneous **7** sequential **8** serious *adv* **9** homogeneously **10** regularly **11** steadily

steal *n* → **1** bargain *v* **2** rob **3** take **4** trick

stealth *n* → **1** secrecy **2** trickery

steam *n* → **1** breathing **2** cloud **3** gas **4** vitality **5** wine *v* **6** cloud **7** heat *adj* **8** old

steamroller *n* → **1** forcer **2** leveller **3** press *v* **4** advance **5** force **6** press *adj* **7** forceful

steel *n* → **1** knife **2** lighter **3** metal **4** sword *v* **5** harden **6** strengthen **7** work metal *adj* **8** durable **9** grey **10** hard **11** metallic

steep *n* → **1** liquid **2** slope **3** wetting *v* **4** cook **5** liquefy **6** wet *adj* **7** expensive **8** mountainous **9** sloping

steeple *n* → **1** church **2** sharp point **3** tower

steer *n* → **1** cattle *v* **2** direct **3** manage

STEERER *n* aimer, cox, coxswain, driver, helmsman, leader, manoeuvrer, pilot, wheelman *(U.S.)*; **automatic pilot,** automatic flight control system, beam-riding, celestial guidance, command guidance, inertial guidance, inertial navigation, radio control, talkdown

STEERING WHEEL *n* accelerator, brake, choke, clutch, pedal; **joystick,** aileron, elevator, flaps, tab, throttle; **ship's wheel,** engine-room-controls, helm, rudder, ship's telegraph

stem *n* → **1** ancestry **2** musical score **3** rod *v* **4** advance **5** close **6** stop **7** swerve

STENCH *n* fetor, funk *(U.S.)*, niff, odour, pong, reek, smell, stink; **malodorousness,** cheesiness, fetidity, fetidness, nastiness, noisomeness, offensiveness, rancidity, rankness, ripeness; **miasma,** cacodyl, effluvium, exhalation, malodour, mephitis; **mustiness,** frowziness, fustiness, stuffiness; **body odour,** BO, halitosis; **stink bomb; stinker,** reeker, smeller, stinkpot

stencil *n* → letter

stenographer *n* → writer

stentorian *adj* → loud

stepladder *n* → stairs

steppe *n* → grassland

stereophonic *adj* → **1** audio **2** hearing

stereotype *n* → **1** conformist behaviour *v* **2** regularise

sterile *adj* → **1** clean **2** infertile

sterling *n* → **1** currency *adj* **2** good

stern *n* → **1** rear *adj* **2** sombre **3** strict

stethoscope *n* → hearing device

stevedore *n* → **1** labourer **2** transporter *v* **3** transport

stew *n* → **1** contest **2** stratagem **3** trick **4** worry *v* **5** cook **6** heat **7** worry

steward *n* → **1** manager **2** pilot **3** seaman **4** supplier **5** waiter *v* **6** manage

STICK *n* broomstick, crab stick, hickory, rattan; **birch,** ferula, ferule, swish, switch; **rod,** cue, divining rod, perch, stave; **walking-stick,** alpenstock, cane, crutch, ski-pole, stilts, supplejack, sword cane, swordstick; **dolly,** copper stick, posser, washing dolly; **digging stick,** yam stick; **slapstick,** bauble; **bullroarer,** churinga, thunder stick; **yardstick,** tally; **staff,** baton, club, distaff, fescue *(Obs.)*, loom, mace, pikestaff, shaft, singlestick, swagger stick, tipstaff, truncheon *(Archaic)*, wand, warder; **ramrod,** pontil, probang, punty, toby

stick *n* → **1** adhesive **2** club **3** difficulty **4** gambling equipment **5** hindrance **6** marijuana **7** musical instrument **8** person **9** propellant **10** stoppage **11** timber *v* **12** confuse **13** fasten **14** kill **15** perforate **16** place **17** puzzle **18** support

sticker *n* → **1** battler **2** label **3** piercer **4** public notice **5** puzzle **6** sword

STICKINESS *n* adhesiveness, glutinosity, glutinousness, tackiness, viscidity, viscidness, viscosity, viscousness; **cohesiveness,** glueyness, tack, tenaciousness, tenacity; **cohesion,** adherence, adhesion, agglutination, binding, cementation, coherence, colligation, concretion, conglutination, fixation, fusion, sizing, solidification

stickler *n* → **1** conformer **2** puzzle **3** strict person

STICK TOGETHER *v* agglutinate, cement, conglutinate, glue, paste, size; **solder,** bind, bond, fix, frit, fuse, sweat, unite, wattle; **cohere,** adhere, cleave, clog, gum up, stick together, take; **cling,** hold, hold on

STICKY *adj* claggy, cloggy, gluey, gluggy, glutenous, glutinous, gummy, icky, mucilaginous, tacky, tenacious, viscid, viscoid, viscous; **cohesive,** adherent, adhesive, agglutinant, agglutinate, agglutinative, clingy, coherent, conglutinate, conglutinative, consistent *(Obs.)*; **fast,** bonded, fixed, solid, tight

sticky *adj* → **1** difficult **2** sickening **3** wet

stickybeak *n* → **1** morbid curiosity *v* **2** be curious **3** meddle

sticky beak *n* → looker

stiff *n* → **1** groin **2** heavy drinker **3** non-achiever **4** the dead *adj* **5** calamitous **6** difficult **7** drunk **8** excessive **9** formal **10** hard **11** intoxicating **12** lame **13** poor **14** steady **15** strict **16** stubborn **17** ugly **18** windy *adv* **19** hard

stifle *v* → **1** kill **2** repress **3** restrain **4** silence **5** suffocate

stigma *n* → **1** denigration **2** disfigurement **3** flower **4** holy person **5** sign **6** sore

stile *n* → entrance

stiletto *n* → **1** piercer **2** sword *v* **3** kill

STILL *conj* e'en *(Poetic)*, e'en so, even, for aught, no matter what, notwithstanding, yet; **although,** albeit, howbeit *(Obs.)*, however; **at all events,** in any case, in any event, in spite of everything, on all counts, under any circumstances

still *n* → **1** bottle **2** cleanser **3** photograph **4** pub *v* **5** brew **6** distil **7** moderate **8** silence *adj* **9** inactive **10** quiet **11** resting **12** silent *adv* **13** continually **14** inactively **15** in the future **16** nevertheless **17** now **18** silently

stillbirth *n* → **1** birth **2** death

still life *n* → painting

stilt *n* → **1** post *v* **2** lift

stilted *adj* → 1 bombastic 2 formal
stimulant *n* → 1 alcohol 2 incentive *adj* 3 encouraging
stimulate *v* → 1 enchant 2 encourage 3 energise
stimulus *n* → incentive
sting *n* → 1 a drink 2 incentive 3 perforation 4 piercer 5 poison 6 pungency 7 request 8 trick *v* 9 annoy 10 arouse 11 beg 12 cheat 13 pain 14 perforate 15 poison
stingy *adj* → 1 mean 2 smallest
stink *n* → 1 busyness 2 disrepute 3 stench *v* 4 be of no repute 5 be smelly
stint *n* → 1 period 2 restraint 3 share 4 stoppage *v* 5 be miserly 6 restrict 7 stop
stipend *n* → income
stipple *n* → 1 painting *v* 2 depict
stipulate *v* → 1 insist on 2 promise 3 qualify
stir *n* → 1 busyness 2 excitement 3 pat 4 perception 5 prison 6 quiet sound *v* 7 agitate 8 annoy 9 emotionalise 10 mix 11 move 12 publicise 13 spin
stirrup *n* → cord
stitch *n* → 1 cramp 2 medication *v* 3 fasten 4 sew
stock *n* → 1 agenda 2 ancestry 3 class 4 goods 5 gun part 6 handle 7 language 8 model 9 neckwear 10 reputation 11 storage 12 stupid person 13 support 14 timber *v* 15 farm 16 punish 17 restrain 18 store *adj* 19 customary
stockade *n* → 1 embankment 2 fortification 3 pen 4 prison *v* 5 defend
stockbroker *n* → financier
stocking *n* → tights
stockman *n* → 1 farmer 2 farmhand 3 storeman
stockpile *n* → 1 storage *v* 2 gather 3 store
stocky *adj* → 1 fat 2 short 3 strong 4 thick
stodgy *adj* → 1 boring 2 heavy 3 short 4 soft 5 solid 6 thick
stoic *adj* → 1 callous 2 composed
Stoic *n* → patient person
stoke *n* → 1 texture *v* 2 agitate 3 fuel
stole *n* → 1 cloak 2 dress
stolid *adj* → composed
stomach *n* → 1 abdomen 2 courage 3 desire 4 hunger 5 pride *v* 6 be angry with 7 eat
stone *n* → 1 abrasive 2 bead 3 building materials 4 grave 5 grey 6 jewel 7 rock 8 smoother *v* 9 kill 10 rub *adj* 11 hard 12 rocky
stoned *adj* → 1 drugged 2 drunk
stony *adj* → 1 callous 2 hard 3 inactive 4 infertile 5 poor 6 rocky
stooge *n* → 1 accomplice 2 butt 3 obeyer 4 subject
stool *n* → 1 defecation 2 remnant 3 toilet *v* 4 flower
stoop *n* → 1 curvature of the spine 2 descent 3 dive 4 flying 5 pose *v* 6 be meek 7 be of no repute 8 curve 9 dive 10 grovel 11 lower 12 repose 13 repress
STOP *v* arrest, bail up, bait, baulk, becalm, blow up *(N.Z.)*, bring up with a jolt, buttonhole, check, estop *(Law)*, foil *(Archaic)*, gag *(Parl. Proc.)*, hinder, hold up, inhibit, intercept, interrupt, prevent, pull the plug on, pull up, pull up short, rise, snub, stunt, suppress; **staunch,** stay, stem; **discontinue,** abandon, abate *(Law)*, abort, break, break off, break up, bug, choke, close, closure *(Parl. Proc.)*, cut, cut short, do away with, end, estop, interrupt, knock on the head, kybosh, nip in the bud, prorogue *(Parl. Proc.)*, put the kybosh on, scotch, sideline, silence, sit on, snub *(U.S.)*, stint *(Archaic)*, wind up; **cease,** bundy off, call it a day, call it off, call it quits, chuck it, chuck it in, chuck one's hand in, come to a full stop, come to a halt, come to a standstill, declare *(Cricket)*, give it away, give it up as a bad job, give over, give up, pack it in, pack the game in, shut down, shut up shop; **desist,** abort, break *(Boxing)*, cut it out, discontinue, draw up, drop, fetch up, freeze, halt, hang up, hesitate, hold it, hold on, intermit, lay off, leave it at that, leave off, let up, mark time, pause, prop, quit, raise, recess, respite, rest, rest on one's oars, sign off, snatch one's time, stagnate, stand, stay *(Archaic)*, stint *(Archaic)*, stop in one's tracks, stow it, surcease *(Archaic)*, walk out, wind down; **knock off,** break off, down tools, knock it off; **deadlock,** be at a standstill, stalemate; **brake,** anchor, back and fill, hit the anchors; **switch off,** shut off, turn off; **cast anchor,** bring to, heave to, lay to, snub *(Naut.)*; **stall,** feather *(Aeron.)*, whipstall
STOP *interj* avast *(Naut.)*, belay, halt, whoa, wo; **enough,** barley *(Brit. Obs.)*, break it down, come off it, cut it out, enough's enough, hold it, knock it off, lay off, so, soft *(Archaic)*, steady on, stop it, stow it, turn it up
stop *n* → 1 angle 2 bad debt 3 camera part 4 closure 5 cord 6 discourager 7 obstacle 8 plug 9 restraints 10 stopper 11 tap 12 visit *v* 13 be inactive 14 be present 15 close 16 defeat 17 discourage 18 fill 19 hinder 20 interrupt 21 make music 22 obstruct 23 restrain 24 restrict
stopgap *n* → 1 expedient *adj* 2 expedient
STOPPAGE *n* abatement, abruption, arrest, break-up, breakdown, cease *(Obs.)*, check, close, closure, desistence, freeze, shutdown, snarl-up, suspension, tie-up; **halt,** abscission, bait *(Archaic)*, break, catch, cessation, dead stop, deadlock, discontinuance, discontinuation, full stop, inter-house deadlock *(Parl. Proc.)*, prop, stalemate, stand, standstill, stint *(Obs.)*, stopping, stunt, suppression; **respite,** armistice, forbearance, intercept, interception, moratorium, pause, pretermission, prorogation; **interruption,** abeyance, interval, lapse, let-up, lull, remission, stay, stick *(Obs.)*, surcease, truce; **stall,** whipstall; **stagnation,** stagnancy; **prevention,** check, estoppage, inactivation, suppression, suspension; **preventive,** gag *(Parl. Proc.)*, kangaroo closure, snub, walkout; **notice to quit,** caveat *(Law)*, declaration *(Cricket)*
stop press *n* → news
stopwatch *n* → timepiece

STORAGE *n* deposition, reposition, stowage, tankage, wharfage; **refill,** refit; **store,** bank, cache, clamp *(Brit.)*, depot, dump, fond *(Obs.)*, fund, library, pool, repertory, repository, reservoir, stack, stock; **reserve,** backlog, backup, bulk, hoard, nest egg, savings, spare parts, stockpile; **cornucopia,** harvest

storage *n* → **1** freight **2** placement **3** space

STORE *v* bank, keep, put by, reposit, stow, tun; **stable,** barn, dump, garage, warehouse, wharf; **stock,** amass, get in, hoard, hutch, lay in, mount up, salt away, save, stack, stock up, stockpile

store *n* → **1** adequacy **2** computer record **3** much **4** reputation **5** shop **6** storage *v* **7** place

STOREHOUSE *n* bond store, godown, magazine, pantechnicon, thesaurus, treasure house, warehouse; **supply depot,** base *(Mil.)*, commissariat, commissary *(U.S.)*, logistics branch, public utility, quonset hut *(U.S. Mil.)*, railhead; **treasury,** bursary, exchequer; **granary,** elevator, silo; **coalbunker,** coal cellar, coalhole, coaling station

STOREMAN *n* caterer, chandler *(Obs.)*, provedore, provider, providore, purveyor, stockman *(U.S.)*, storekeeper, supplier, victualler; **quartermaster,** sutler

STOREY *n* basement, belvedere, cellar, clerestory, entresol, flat *(Obs.)*, floor, ground floor, hayloft, mezzanine, piano nobile, roof garden, rooftop garden, story *(U.S.)*, upstairs

storm *n* → **1** attack **2** explosion **3** rainfall **4** violent outburst **5** weather **6** wind *v* **7** be angry **8** be violent **9** blow **10** fire on **11** rain

STORY *n* anecdote, episode, fit, gest *(Archaic)*, idyll, nouvelle, novelette, novella, romance, short story, tale, yarn; **novel,** antinovel, fiction, roman, roman à clef, sci-fi, science fiction, shocker, stream-of-consciousness novel, thriller, western, whodunit; **allegory,** apologue, bestiary, exemplum, fable, parable; **legend,** fable, fairytale, folk story, folktale, myth, old wive's tale; **saga,** epic, romance, romaunt; **cycle,** legendary, legendry; **biography,** autobiography. *See also* NARRATIVE

story *n* → **1** history **2** information **3** lie **4** news item **5** storey *v* **6** narrate

STORYTELLER *n* anecdotist, annalist, chronicler, fabler, fabulist, jongleur, magsman, narrator, raconteur, relater, reporter, romancer, teller; **fictionist,** mythologist, novelist, short-story writer

stout *n* → **1** beer *adj* **2** courageous **3** fat **4** hard **5** persevering **6** serious **7** strong **8** thick

STOVE *n* cooker *(Brit.)*, cook-top, fuel stove, gas cooker, gas range, gas ring, gas stove, kitchener, oilstove, pot-belly stove, range, spirit stove, stovette, wetback *(N.Z.)*, wood stove; **oven,** charcoal-burner, colonial oven, Dutch oven, gas oven, hangi *(N.Z.)*, hay oven, haybox, Maori oven *(N.Z.)*, micro-oven, microwave oven, one-fire stove, two-fire stove, umu; **spit,** roasting spit, rotisserie; **griller,** broiler, grill, toaster; **camp fire,** barbecue, barby, hibachi, primus, salamander; **hotplate,** element; **burner,** combustor, gas burner, gas jet, gaslight, oil-burner

stove *v* → heat

stow *v* → **1** fill **2** place **3** store

stowaway *n* → **1** foreigner **2** passenger

stow away *v* → **1** drive **2** hide

straddle *n* → **1** jump **2** length **3** pose *v* **4** repose

strafe *n* → **1** attack *v* **2** fire on **3** punish **4** wage war

straggle *v* → **1** disperse **2** go slowly

STRAIGHT *adj* agonic, direct, even, level, rectilinear, right, true, waveless; **rigid,** erect, inflexible, soldierlike, unbent, unbowed

STRAIGHT *adv* directly, due, right, slap, smack; **in line**

straight *n* → **1** conformer **2** line **3** path **4** sexual type *adj* **5** concise **6** conservative **7** correct **8** direct **9** erect **10** faithful **11** honest **12** level **13** sequential **14** simple **15** true **16** unconditional *adv* **17** continually **18** correctly **19** directly **20** now **21** tidily **22** wholly

straightaway *n* → **1** path *adj* **2** direct *adv* **3** now

STRAIGHTEN *v* extend, lock, set straight, unbend, uncross, uncurl, untwine, untwist, unwind; **align,** line up, range

straightforward *adj* → **1** clear **2** direct **3** forthright **4** honest **5** simple

strain *n* → **1** ancestry **2** character **3** class **4** condition **5** cramp **6** distortion **7** effort **8** gradation **9** injury **10** insistence **11** music **12** poetry **13** small amount **14** tiredness *v* **15** cook **16** distort **17** flow **18** hold **19** injure **20** tire

strainer *n* → post

strait *n* → **1** access **2** bay **3** channel **4** headland **5** thinness *adj* **6** imprisoned **7** strict **8** thin

straitjacket *n* → jacket

straitlaced *adj* → **1** contracted **2** intolerant **3** strict

strand *n* → **1** coastline **2** hair **3** jewellery **4** seaside **5** thread *v* **6** abandon **7** cord

STRANGE *adj* abnormal, absonant, anomalous, atypical, borderline, different, iffy, improper, odd, oddish, out of character, peculiar, queer, unclassifiable, unconformable; **unusual,** amazing, esoteric, exotic, extraordinary, freak, out-of-the-way, outlandish, outré, outsize, rare, raving, remarkable, singular, sui generis, thumping, thundering, unaccustomed, uncommon, unexampled, unheard-of, unique, unparalleled, unprecedented, unwonted *(Archaic)*, way-out, without parallel; **eccentric,** antic *(Obs.)*, bizarre, crazy, fanciful, fantastic, far-out, funny, gonzo, off the rails, outlandish, Pickwickian, quaint, quizzical, rum, rummy, screwy; **freakish,** bastard, freaky, grotesque, malformed, monstrous, preterhuman, prodigious, teratoid, unnatural; **erratic,** aberrant, irregular, variable; **perverted,** deviant, kinky, psychopathic, wayward; **uncanny,**

eerie, eldritch *(Scot.)*, fey, preternatural, supernatural, supernormal, transnormal, unco *(Scot.)*, unearthly, weird; **teratological,** teratogenic

strange *adj* → **1** foreign **2** mad **3** solitary **4** unknown

STRANGENESS *n* anomalousness, bizarreness, eccentricity, esotericism, exceptionalness, exoticism, extraordinariness, fancifulness, freakiness, freakishness, funniness, grotesqueness, incongruousness, kinkiness, oddness, outlandishness, quaintness, queerness, ratbaggery, singularness, uncommonness, unconformity, uncouthness, unusualness, unwontedness; **abnormality,** aberrance, aberrancy, aberration, abnormity, anomaly, exception, incongruity, irregularity, isolated instance, oddity, peculiarity, peloria, singularity, special case, supernormality; **monstrousness,** enormity, enormousness, grotesqueness, prodigiousness; **eeriness,** feyness, preternaturalism, uncanniness, unearthliness, unnaturalness, weirdness; **perversion,** deviation, kink, pica, twist; **teratology,** teratologist. *See also* FREAK

STRANGE PERSON *n* deviant, eccentric, grotesque, kook, misfit, monster, nonconformist, odd bod, oddball, original, pervert, prodigy, queer fish, ratbag

stranger *n* → **1** arriver **2** foreigner **3** unknown **4** visitor

strangle *v* → **1** execute **2** kill **3** repress **4** restrain **5** suffocate

strap *n* → **1** belt **2** club **3** sharpener **4** tape *v* **5** cudgel **6** fasten **7** sharpen

S-trap *n* → drain

strapper *n* → **1** butler **2** strong person **3** tall person

strapping *n* → **1** corporal punishment **2** tape *adj* **3** big **4** strong **5** tall

strata *n* → layer

STRATAGEM *n* artifice, arts, catch, con, contrivance, craft, dodge, double, fake, fakement *(Obs.)*, game, gimmick, legerdemain, little game, manoeuvre, plot, roughie, ruse, shenanigan, shift, shrewdie, sleight of hand, trepan *(Archaic)*, trick, wangle, wheeze *(Brit. Colloq.)*, wrinkle; **bluff,** diversion, evasion, feint, ploy, rort, stew, subterfuge; **trap,** ambush, contrivance, mesh, net, pitfall, web

stratagem *n* → plan

strategy *n* → **1** act of war **2** cunning **3** plan

STRATIFICATION *n* bedding, delamination, interlamination, interstratification, lamination; **scaliness,** flakiness, foliation, imbrication, squamation, squamousness, superimposition, superincumbence, superincumbency, superposition

stratify *v* → **1** class **2** farm

stratosphere *n* → sky

stratum *n* → **1** class **2** community **3** layer **4** level **5** rock outcrop

straw *n* → **1** piping **2** small amount **3** unimportant thing

strawberry *adj* → reddish

stray *n* → **1** foreigner *v* **2** be immoral *adj* **3** foreign

streak *n* → **1** addition **2** character **3** characteristics **4** jewel **5** layer **6** line **7** period **8** powder **9** tall person **10** thin person *v* **11** line **12** speed **13** undress

STREAM *n* arroyo, creek, englacial stream, flow, fresh, freshet, tail; **streamlet,** beck *(Brit.)*, brook, brooklet, burn *(Scot.)*, millstream, rill, rivulet, runlet, runnel; **river,** thoroughfare, torrent, trunk, watercourse; **tributary,** affluent, anabranch, arm, branch, confluent, distributary, effluent, feeder, influent, reach, wadi; **underground river,** subartesian water, underdrainage, vein; **gush,** flush, jet, spurt, surge, upsurge; **confluence,** conflux, estuary, mouth; **slack water,** backwater, fan delta, marsh, stagnant pool, swamp. *See also* CURRENT; FLOW; SPRING

stream *n* → **1** advance **2** class **3** direction **4** point of view **5** series *v* **6** class **7** flow **8** hang

streamer *n* → **1** decoration **2** flag **3** news item **4** string

streamlined *adj* → **1** ordered **2** smooth **3** speedy

street *n* → **1** community **2** road

STRENGTH *n* arm, force, main, might, mightiness, muscle, potence, potency, potentness, power, powerfulness; **muscularity,** beef, brawn, brawniness, heftiness, huskiness, robustness, stalwartness, steeliness, sthenia; **wiriness,** athleticism, stringiness; **vigour,** juice, nerve, pith, sinew; **machismo,** lustiness, manliness, robustness, rudeness, ruggedness, vigorousness; **sturdiness,** stockiness, stoutness

strength *n* → **1** characteristics **2** faithfulness **3** force **4** health **5** power **6** pungency **7** score

STRENGTHEN *v* fortify, harden, reinforce, sinew, steel, stiffen, tone up; **consolidate,** build up, confirm; **brace up,** fortify, man, nerve, rally; **reinforce,** brace, pile, rib, riprap, stay *(Archaic)*, support, sustain; **fortify,** arm, reinforce, sconce *(Obs.)*; **harden,** anneal, steel, temper; **proof,** weatherproof

STRENGTHENER *n* brace, bracer, fortifier, reinforcement, stiffener

strenuous *adj* → effortful

stress *n* → **1** assertiveness **2** distortion **3** effort **4** energy **5** importance **6** pressure **7** pulling **8** speaking *v* **9** be loud **10** emphasise

stretch *n* → **1** direction **2** enlargement **3** imprisonment **4** period **5** racecourse **6** region *v* **7** become greater **8** execute **9** extend *adj* **10** pliable

stretcher *n* → **1** beam **2** bed **3** beds **4** brace **5** stand **6** support

strew *v* → disperse

stricken *adj* → **1** beaten **2** damaged **3** unfortunate **4** victimised

STRICT *adj* martinetish, no-nonsense, rigid, Spartan, tight, unswerving; **hard and fast,** binding, infrangible, ironclad, irrefrangible, strictly enforced, unbreakable; **puritanical,**

ascetic, ascetical, austere, Calvinistic, dour, hard on oneself, orthodox, prudish, puritan, straight-arrow, straitlaced; **harsh,** a bit much, a bit solid, demanding, draconian, draconic, exacting, exigent, fierce, gruelling, rigoristic, rigorous, searching, severe, strait *(Archaic)*, stringent; **unmerciful,** hard-baked, hard-headed, inflexible, intransigent, iron-handed, merciless, obdurate, relentless, unbending, uncompromising, unrelenting, unsparing, unyielding; **astringent,** cruel, cutting, sharp; **persecutory,** discriminatory, down on, persecutive, punitive, rough on; **firm,** grim, hard, hard as nails, iron, rugged, stark *(Archaic)*, stern, stiff

strict *adj* → **1** conservative **2** precise

STRICTLY *adv* according to the book, literally, rigidly, strictly speaking, technically, to the letter, verbatim, word for word; **harshly,** cruelly, grimly, hard, intransigently, mercilessly, relentlessly, roundly, ruggedly, unmercifully, unrelentingly, unsparingly, with a heavy hand; **stringently,** severely, sharply, starkly, sternly; **exactingly,** draconically, rigorously, straitly; **firmly,** infrangibly, irrefrangibly, stiffly, unbendingly; **puritanically,** ascetically, astringently, austerely, dourly

STRICT PERSON *n* disciplinarian, Dutch uncle, formalist, hanging judge, hard master, hard taskmaster, martinet, slavedriver, tyrant; **intransigent,** die-hard, rigorist, stickler; **puritan,** ascetic, Calvinist, Hole and Corner man *(Hist.)*, Spartan

stricture *n* → disapproval

stride *n* → **1** improvement **2** length **3** move *v* **4** walk

strident *adj* → **1** dissonant **2** loud **3** shrill

strife *n* → disagreement

STRIKE *n* ban, black ban, green ban, limitation, sit-down, sit-down strike, sit-in, walkout, wildcat strike

strike *n* → **1** failure **2** finding **3** industrial action **4** period of inaction **5** stroke *v* **6** arrive **7** be inactive **8** depart **9** find **10** fish **11** flower **12** hit **13** influence **14** lower **15** make music **16** remove **17** signal **18** smooth **19** sound

striking *adj* → **1** alluring **2** blatant **3** contacting **4** interesting **5** obvious

STRING *n* aglet, apron-strings, bootlace, bride, cordon, drawstring, fillet, lace, lacing, latchstring, petersham, point *(Archaic)*, shoelace, streamer, tie; **twine,** cordelier, purl, spun yarn, tatting, torsade, whipcord, whipping; **ornamental cord,** aiguillette, braid. *See also* CORD; TAPE; THREAD

string *n* → **1** belt **2** gathering **3** jewellery **4** layer **5** sequence **6** series *v* **7** cord **8** hang **9** join **10** line

stringent *adj* → strict

stringy *adj* → **1** corded **2** sludgy **3** strong

strip *n* → **1** coating **2** colour **3** line **4** newspaper **5** pornography **6** sportswear **7** thinness *v* **8** bare **9** capture **10** farm **11** harvest **12** line **13** refuse **14** remove **15** rob **16** separate **17** take **18** undress

stripe *n* → **1** character **2** coating **3** corporal punishment **4** emblem **5** hit **6** lace **7** thinness *v* **8** line

striptease *n* → **1** pornography **2** undressing

strive *v* → **1** argue **2** be energetic **3** contest **4** make an effort **5** wage war

STRIVER *n* conchie, doer, endeavourer, perfectionist; **battler,** grinder, lucubrator, plodder, plugger; **workhorse,** a beggar for punishment, a tiger for punishment, grafter, heaver, labourer, party hack, toiler

STRIVING *adj* conative, grasping, struggling; **last-ditch,** all-out, desperate; **effortful,** essayistic

STROKE *n* agricultural, backhand, backstroke, bunt, cover drive, drive, half-volley, lob, outstroke, pelt, rush, slash, smash, strike, swash, swipe, volley; **slice,** back cut, chop, chop stroke, cross-shot, cut, glance, late cut, leg glance, pitch shot, sweep; **hook,** edge, snick, top; **shot,** break *(Billiards)*, bricole, cannon, carom, follow, massé; **thrust,** bind, botte *(Fencing)*, home thrust, joust, lunge, tilt. *See also* HIT; TAP; KICK

stroke *n* → **1** accomplishment **2** action **3** attempt **4** corporal punishment **5** endearments **6** line **7** mariner **8** move **9** ringing **10** touch *v* **11** kiss **12** rub **13** touch

stroll *n* → **1** walk *v* **2** go slowly **3** walk

stroller *n* → **1** pram **2** walker

STRONG *adj* barrel-chested, brawny, built like a brick, built like a brick shithouse, bull, bullish, bullocky, hefty, husky, mesomorphic *(Physiol.)*, muscly, muscular, nuggetty, powerful, staunch, sthenic, stocky, stout, strong as a mallee bull, strong as an ox, sturdy, well-built; **mighty,** armipotent, main *(Obs.)*, potent, potential *(Rare)*; **herculean,** Atlantean, titanic; **athletic,** able-bodied, amazonian, hard-fisted, sinewy, strapping, stringy, thewy, wiry; **robust,** bouncing, doughty, full-blooded, hardy, lustful *(Archaic)*, lusty, nervy, robustious, rude, rugged, stalwart, two-fisted *(U.S.)*, vigorous; **virile,** macho, manly, masculine; **inexhaustible,** fatigueless, relentless, staminal, tireless, unstoppable, untiring, unwearied

strong *adj* → **1** assertive **2** colourful **3** courageous **4** execratory **5** faithful **6** forceful **7** fragrant **8** healthy **9** influential **10** intoxicating **11** loud **12** powerful **13** pungent **14** tasty **15** unsavoury **16** vulgar **17** windy *adv* **18** powerfully **19** strongly

stronghold *n* → fortress

STRONG PERSON *n* athlete, Atlas, ball of muscle, ball of strength, behemoth, bruiser, bull, butch, gangster *(N.Z. Colloq.)*, giant, Goliath, he-man, Hercules, husky *(U.S.)*, iron man, lion, macho, muscle man, Samson, stalwart, strapper, strongman, superman, Tarzan, titan; **nugget,** mesomorph; **giantess,** Amazon, Boadicea, virago

strontium-90 *n* → poison

strop *n* → **1** abrasive **2** sharpener *v* **3** rub

stroppy *adj* → dissident

STRUCTURAL *adj* architectonic, architectural, constructional, constructive, tectonic; **skeletal,** anatomical, osteological, physiological; **prefabricated,** demountable, modular

STRUCTURE *n* composition, constitution, contexture, make, make-up, microstructure, morphology, ordonnance, workings; **build,** anatomy, frame, physique; **architecture,** mode, style; **crystal lattice,** macrostructure, space lattice; **formation,** crystallisation, figuration. *See also* SHAPE

structure *n* → **1** building **2** making **3** order **4** tangle *v* **5** order **6** shape

struggle *n* → **1** attempt **2** contest **3** difficulty *v* **4** fight **5** make an effort

strumpet *n* → prostitute

strut *n* → **1** beam **2** walking *v* **3** show off **4** support **5** walk

stub *n* → **1** knob **2** record **3** remnant *v* **4** farm

STUBBORN *adj* adamant, diehard, dogged, impracticable, inexorable, inflexible, intractable, obdurate, obstinate, opinionated, opinionative, pertinacious, self-opinionated, self-willed, stiff, stiff-necked, tenacious, uncompromising, unshakeable, unswayed; **determined,** hard-bitten, hard-set, hardened, hell-bent, recusant, tough; **perverse,** bloody, bloody-minded, bolshie, contumacious, cross-grained, cussed, difficult, gnarled, gnarly, incorrigible, intransigent, peevish *(Obs.)*, refractory, restive, thwart *(Archaic)*, unmanageable, unreasonable, untoward *(Archaic)*, wilful, wrong-headed; **mulish,** asinine, boneheaded, bull-headed, bullet-headed, bullish, ornery *(U.S.)*, pig-headed, piggish

stubborn *adj* → hard

STUBBORNNESS *n* contumacy, doggedness, impracticability, inconvincibility, inexorability, inexorableness, inflexibility, inflexibleness, intractability, intractableness, intransigence, intransigency, obduracy, obdurateness, obstinacy, obstinateness, recusancy, refractoriness, tenaciousness, tenacity; **self-will,** piggery, piggishness, pigheadedness, wilfulness; **bloody-mindedness,** cussedness, incompliancy, perverseness, perversity, restiveness, wrong-headedness; **asininity,** mulishness

STUBBORN PERSON *n* bolshie, hard nut to crack, hardliner, hardnose, incorrigible, intransigent, trac *(Prison Colloq.)*; **bonehead,** bullet-head, bullhead, donkey, mule, pig

stud *n* → **1** allurer **2** bulge **3** button **4** man **5** moulding **6** nail **7** procreator **8** sex object **9** shearer **10** timber *v* **11** bulge **12** decorate *adj* **13** pregnant

student *n* → pupil

studio *n* → **1** office **2** telecommunications station **3** workplace

STUDY *v* burn the midnight oil, con, cram, gen up, grind away at, grub, ingrain, lucubrate, mug up, overstudy, swot, swot up; **revise,** bone up on, brush up on, read, restudy, review; **practise,** cultivate, drill, familiarise, knock up, rehearse, run through, train; **major in,** do honours in, minor in *(U.S.)*, read specialise in. *See also* LEARN

study *n* → **1** analysis **2** course **3** learning **4** musical piece **5** painting **6** portrait **7** room **8** workplace *v* **9** attempt **10** attend to **11** examine **12** inquire into **13** look **14** read

stuff *n* → **1** cash **2** characteristics **3** equipment **4** essence **5** finished product **6** matter **7** raw materials **8** textiles *v* **9** close **10** conserve **11** cook **12** fill **13** gorge **14** have sex **15** insert **16** oversupply

stuffing *n* → insert

stuffy *adj* → **1** arrogant **2** boring **3** short-winded **4** smelly

stumble *n* → **1** error **2** fall **3** wrong *v* **4** bungle **5** confuse **6** err **7** fall

stump *n* → **1** bottom **2** remnant **3** walking *v* **4** confuse **5** defeat **6** electioneer **7** farm

stun *v* → **1** anaesthetise **2** astonish **3** confuse

stung *adj* → drunk

stunning *adj* → beautiful

stunt *n* → **1** action **2** small person **3** stoppage *v* **4** stop

stuntman *n* → actor

stupefy *v* → **1** anaesthetise **2** astonish

stupendous *adj* → **1** astonishing **2** enormous

STUPID *adj* addlebrained, addlepated, anserine, asinine, barmy, blind, boneheaded, boobyish, bull-headed, bullet-headed, bullish, cloddish, clueless, crass, daggy, dead from the neck up, dense, dippy, dizzy, doltish, drippy, drooby, dumb, dunderheaded, empty, empty-headed, fat-witted, fatheaded fatuous, foolish, fuckwitted, goofy, gormless, headless, insensate, irrational, lubberly, mindless, muddleheaded, mug, nutty, oafish, opaque, pudding-headed, punch-drunk, punchy, ridiculous, silly, silly as a hatful of worms, silly as a snake, silly as a two-bob watch, silly as a wet hen, silly as a wheel, sodden, soft in the head, soft-headed, soggy, spastic, thick, thickheaded, thick-skulled, thick-witted, troglodytic, unthinking, unwise, vacuous, wooden-headed; **slow-witted,** a brick short, a brick short of a load, backward, barren, blockish, blunt, brainless, dead-and-alive, dim, dimwitted, doltish, dopey, dull, dullish, half-witted, inapt, not the full quid, purblind, short a sheet of bark, slow, slow on the uptake, thick as two short planks, three bangers short of a barbie, unapt, unwitting, weak-minded, without enough brains to give oneself a headache, witless; **unintelligent,** a shingle short, anile, cretinous, defective, doddering, doting, feeble-minded, gaga, imbecile, imbecilic, in one's second childhood, ineducable, mentally deficient, mentally handicapped, moronic, retarded, senile, simple, simple-minded, subnormal, unteachable, weak in the upper storey; **superficial,** facile, fatuitous, fluffy, frivolous, shallow, shallow-minded, short-sighted; **stultifying,** retardative, retardatory

stupid *n* → **1** stupid person *adj* **2** boring **3** prejudiced **4** unconscious

STUPIDITY *n* bêtise, blockishness, brainlessness, cloddishness, crassitude, crassness, denseness, density, doltishness, dullness, dumbness, gormlessness, half-wittedness, lubberliness, mindlessness, oafishness, opacity, silliness, simplicity, soft-headedness, sogginess, stupidness, thickheadedness, thickness, unintelligence, vacancy, vacuity, vacuousness, witlessness, woodenheadedness, woodenness; **low intelligence,** amentia, anility, defectiveness, dotage, feeble-mindedness, idiocy, idiotism, imbecility, insanity, madness, mental deficiency, moronism, retardation, senility, simplemindedness, simpleness, subnormality, unreason, weak-mindedness; **foolishness,** dogberryism, folly, impoliticness, imprudence, insipience, madness, unreason, unwisdom, unwiseness; **superficiality,** fatuity, shallowness, short-sightedness, superficialness

STUPIDLY *adv* asininely, blankly, blockishly, crassly, densely, doltishly, dully, dumbly, glassily, half-wittedly, mindlessly, oafishly, sillily, simple-mindedly, simply, thickly, unintelligently, unthinkingly, unwisely, vacantly, vacuously, witlessly, woodenly

STUPID PERSON *n* ass, automaton, blockhead, blunderbuss, boob, booby, boofhead, bullet-head, bullhead, cement head, changeling *(Archaic)*, clod, clodpate, clodpole, clot, cuckoo, cully *(Archaic)*, deadshit, dick, dickhead, dill, dillpot, dimwit, dodo, dolt, donkey, dope, doter, doughie, drongo, droob, duffer, dullard, dumb Dora, dumbbell, dumbcluck, dumbo, dumdum, dummy, dunce, dunderhead, egg roll, fathead, flathead, fool, Fred Nerk, fuckwit, galah, gazob, git, goof, goon, goose, gup *(Aborig.)*, imbo, innocent, jackass, jay, jerk, jerk-off, juggins, knucklehead, loggerhead, loghead, loon, lout, lowbrow, lubber, lunkhead *(U.S.)*, meat-head *(U.S.)*, melon, melonhead, moo *(Brit.)*, mooncalf, mopoke, moron, mutt, mutton-head, nerd, nig-nog, nincompoop, ning-nong, ninny, nit, nitwit, noddy, nong, noodle, numbskull, nutter, oaf, one-ten, parrot, peabrain, pinhead, poon, pudding, pudding head, pup, puppy, rock-ape, sap, saphead, schmuck, shithead, shmo, silly-billy, simpleton, slow-learner, slowcoach, slowpoke, spoony, stock, stupid, subman, thick, thickhead, tomfool, trog, troglodyte, twerp, twit, wally, woodenhead, zany; **imbecile,** ament, cretin, defective, halfwit, idiot, mental defective, moron, subnormal

stupor *n* → **1** apathy **2** drug use **3** unconsciousness

sturdy *adj* → **1** durable **2** growing **3** hard **4** persevering **5** serious **6** strong

stutter *v* → **1** fluctuate **2** mispronounce

sty *n* → **1** animal dwelling **2** disfigurement **3** pen **4** pigsty *v* **5** enclose **6** inhabit

style *n* → **1** artistry **2** character **3** fashion **4** fine arts **5** flower **6** good taste **7** name **8** sharp point **9** show **10** structure *v* **11** clothe **12** name **13** regularise **14** shape

stylise *v* → regularise

stylish *adj* → **1** accomplished **2** fashionable **3** tasteful

stylus *n* → **1** sharp point **2** sound system **3** writing materials

suave *adj* → **1** composed **2** courteous

subaltern *n* → **1** inferior *adj* **2** inferior

subconscious *n* → psyche

subcontract *n* → **1** contract *v* **2** act for **3** promise

subcutaneous *adj* → **1** inside **2** skin

subdivide *v* → **1** separate **2** share out

subdue *v* → **1** defeat **2** farm **3** lose colour **4** make peace **5** repress **6** silence **7** victimise

subeditor *n* → corrector

subheading *n* → title

SUBJECT *n* liegeman, man, serf, vassal; **servant,** assigned servant, dogsbody, flunkey, forced labourer, kanaka, lackey; **slave,** captive, chattel, galley slave, helot, hierodule, peon, serf, thrall, villein; **puppet,** creature, satellite, stooge

subject *n* → **1** actuality **2** music **3** patient **4** subject matter **5** tester *adj* **6** predisposed

subjective *adj* → **1** false **2** inborn **3** intangible **4** obsequious

SUBJECT MATTER *n* controversy, flute, issue, subject, substance, talk of the town, talking point, topic, topic of the day; **theme,** burden, motif; **text,** article, tirade; **field,** area, domain, field of interest, major *(Educ.)*, realm, specialty, territory; **quadrivium,** trivium; **person referred to,** party, subject; **thing referred to,** object, referent

subjugate *v* → defeat

sublimate *v* → **1** extract **2** psychoanalyse

sublime *v* → **1** extract *adj* **2** astonishing **3** good **4** perfect **5** reputable **6** superior **7** tall

submarine *n* → **1** motor vessel **2** watercraft *adj* **3** sea

submerge *v* → **1** dive **2** wet

submissive *adj* → **1** meek **2** obsequious **3** repressed

submit *v* → **1** assert **2** be meek **3** capitulate **4** compose oneself **5** guide **6** obey **7** offer **8** theorise

subordinate *n* → **1** inferior *v* **2** belittle *adj* **3** inferior **4** unimportant

subpoena *n* → **1** litigation *v* **2** command **3** litigate

subscribe *v* → **1** give **2** mark **3** name **4** pay

subscription *n* → **1** affirmation **2** gift **3** payment **4** postscript **5** title

subsequent *adj* → following

subservient *adj* → **1** flattering **2** inferior **3** obedient **4** useable

subside *v* → **1** fall **2** wane **3** weaken

subsidiary *n* → **1** inferior **2** music *adj* **3** additional **4** helpful **5** inferior **6** unimportant

subsidy *n* → **1** allowance **2** charity **3** gift **4** payment

subsist *v* → **1** be **2** live

substance *n* → **1** actuality **2** essence **3** importance **4** important thing **5** matter **6** meaning **7** property **8** raw materials **9** subject matter

substantial *n* → **1** actuality *adj* **2** essential **3** fundamental **4** great **5** tangible **6** wealthy

substantiate *v* → authenticate

substantive *n* → **1** word *adj* **2** essential **3** independent **4** real

SUBSTITUTE *n* a poor excuse for, alternate, ersatz, fudge, locum, ossia, pinch-hitter, relay, relief, replacement, ring-in, second string, stand-in, sub, surrogate; **changeling,** elfchild, oaf. *See also* EXCHANGE

SUBSTITUTE *v* dub, replace, ring in, subrogate, surrogate; **relieve,** pinch-hit, sit in for, spell, stand in, sub; **graft,** transplant. *See also* EXCHANGE

substitute *n* → **1** actor **2** agent **3** expedient **4** inferior **5** serviceman **6** word

subsume *v* → **1** codify **2** include

subterfuge *n* → **1** illogicality **2** stratagem **3** trickery

subterranean *adj* → hidden

subtitle *n* → **1** title **2** written composition

subtle *adj* → **1** accomplished **2** cunning **3** discriminating **4** thin **5** wise

SUBTRACT *v* abate, deduct, subduct *(Rare)*, take, take away; **decrease,** apocopate, bang, clip, curtail, cut, cut back, decimate *(Obs.)*, diminish, dock, lessen, lop, pare down, prune, reduce, retrench, snuff, trash, trim, truncate, whittle; **excise,** core, enucleate, exscind, exsect, extirpate, pit, remove; **discount,** allow, knock off, rebate, slash; **detract,** derogate. *See also* CUT OFF

subtract *v* → **1** compute **2** take

suburb *n* → city

subvert *v* → **1** argue **2** destroy **3** misguide

subway *n* → path

SUCCEED *v* arrive, be in the box seat, bring home the bacon, carry all before one, carry the day, click, come through, crack it, curl the mo, do the trick, get a guernsey, get it together, have it made, make good, make the grade, pass, pull oneself up by the bootstraps, put it across, ride it out, set the world on fire, shine, steal the show, take the cake, triumph, win one's spurs; **win,** carry off, carve out, crack, gain, score, sew up, take; **go like a bomb,** clean up *(Sport)*, get it in one, go great guns, guess it in one, have it in one, romp home, romp in, shit it in, sweep the board, walk away with, walk off with, win at a canter, win by a neck; **land on one's feet,** be on to a good thing, hit the jackpot, strike pay-dirt; **have it both ways,** kill two birds with one stone; **outmatch,** come off best, get the better of, have the better of, have the last laugh on, one-up, outflank, outgo, outperform, outweigh, overmaster, overreach; **get ahead,** be ahead, be going places, distance, draw first blood, gain ground, get to first base, go far, go places, go to town, leave someone for dead, rise, soar, take off

succeed *v* → **1** accomplish **2** follow **3** get **4** prosper

SUCCESS *n* do *(N.Z.)*, go, hit, killing, sleeper *(Colloq.)*, winner, wow; **win,** conquest, game set and match, triumph, vanquishment, victory; **walkover,** landslide, snip, soda, walk-up start, walkaway; **Pyrrhic victory**

success *n* → accomplishment

SUCCESSFUL *adj* first-past-the-post, fruitful, home and hosed, home on the pig's back, in like Flynn, made, on top, triumphal, triumphant, unbeaten, victorious; **winning,** premier, up

SUCCESSFULLY *adv* conqueringly, effectually, like a charm, swimmingly, with a bang; **triumphantly,** victoriously

SUCCESSFULNESS *n* favourable issue, flying colours, victoriousness, winning; **first place,** first, honours, line honours; **band wagon**

succession *n* → **1** aristocracy **2** exchange **3** repetition **4** sequence **5** series

successive *adj* → **1** following **2** regular **3** sequential

SUCCESSIVELY *adv* in array, in file, in line, in tandem, one by one, sequentially, seriation, successionally, tandem

SUCCESSOR *n* descendant, follower, heir, incomer, succeeder, superseder, supplanter

succinct *adj* → **1** concise **2** enclosed

succour *n* → **1** help *v* **2** help

succulent *n* → **1** plant *adj* **2** delicious **3** desirable **4** liquid **5** wet

succumb *v* → **1** capitulate **2** die

such *adj* → particular

SUCH IS LIFE *phr* that's the way it goes, that's the way the cookie crumbles, them's the breaks

suck *n* → **1** absorption **2** hiss *v* **3** drink **4** extract **5** have sex

sucker *n* → **1** absorber **2** animal offspring **3** artless person **4** extractor **5** piping **6** victim

suckle *v* → **1** care for **2** feed

suction *n* → **1** absorption **2** extraction

sudden *n* → **1** surpriser *adj* **2** momentary **3** speedy **4** surprising *adv* **5** surprisingly

suds *n* → **1** beer **2** bubbling

sue *v* → **1** flirt **2** litigate

suede *n* → hide

suet *n* → fat

suffer *v* → **1** dislike **2** feel pain **3** perceive **4** permit **5** persevere

sufferance *n* → patience

suffice *v* → **1** be adequate **2** satisfy

sufficient *adj* → adequate

suffix *v* → add

SUFFOCATE *v* asphyxiate, choke, drown, smother, stifle, strangle, strangulate

suffocate *v* → **1** die **2** kill

SUFFOCATION *n* apnoea, asphyxiation, breathlessness, choking, drowning, smothering

suffrage *n* → **1** election **2** electorate

suffuse *v* → flood

sugar *n* → **1** lover **2** sweetness *v* **3** cook

suggest *v* → **1** assert **2** encourage **3** guide **4** imply **5** offer **6** predict

suggestible *adj* → influenced

suggestive *adj* → **1** allusive **2** indicative **3** meaningful **4** obscene
suicide *n* → **1** death **2** killing *v* **3** kill
suit *n* → **1** class **2** dress **3** entreaty **4** flirtation **5** litigation **6** outfit *v* **7** fit **8** satisfy
suitable *adj* → **1** apt **2** expedient **3** related
suitcase *n* → case
suite *n* → **1** room **2** sequence
suitor *n* → **1** flirt **2** litigant
sulk *n* → **1** angry act **2** irritation *v* **3** be angry **4** be unfriendly **5** misbehave
sullage *n* → **1** dirt **2** remnant
sullen *adj* → **1** acrimonious **2** badly-behaved **3** cloudy **4** irritable **5** silent **6** slow **7** unhappy **8** unsociable
sully *n* → **1** dirt *v* **2** dirty **3** disgrace **4** spoil
sulphur *n* → yellow
sultan *n* → aristocrat
sultana *n* → aristocrat
sultry *adj* → hot
summary *n* → **1** abridgment **2** information *adj* **3** impermanent
summer *n* → **1** age **2** luxury **3** season **4** shaft **5** top *adj* **6** hot **7** seasonal
summit *n* → **1** apex **2** committee **3** perfect thing **4** top
summon *v* → **1** command **2** gather **3** litigate **4** shout
summons *n* → **1** act of war **2** litigation **3** shout
sump *n* → **1** basin **2** hollow **3** lake
sumptuous *adj* → **1** beautiful **2** expensive **3** wealthy
SUN *n* daystar *(Poetic)*, eye of the day *(Poetic)*, midnight sun, Phoebus *(Poetic)*, sundisc; **aureole,** corona, halo, photosphere, rainband, sunglow; **parhelion,** mock sun; **sunspot,** facula, flocculus, penumbra, solar flare, solar wind, umbra. *See also* STAR
SUNBAKE *v* bask *(Archaic)*, insolate, sun, sunbathe
sunder *v* → separate
sundial *n* → timepiece
sundowner *n* → **1** a drink **2** traveller
sundries *n* → **1** accumulation **2** any
sunglasses *n* → **1** darkener **2** glasses
sunken *adj* → **1** bottom **2** fallen **3** hollow
sunny *adj* → **1** bright **2** happy **3** hot
sunshine *n* → **1** happiness **2** light **3** luxury *adj* **4** bright **5** happy
sunspot *n* → sun
superannuation *n* → **1** income **2** insurance
superb *adj* → **1** astonishing **2** beautiful **3** good **4** perfect
supercilious *adj* → **1** arrogant **2** discourteous **3** disdainful
superficial *adj* → **1** apparent **2** deficient **3** inattentive **4** misjudged **5** outside **6** shallow **7** smallest **8** stupid **9** unimportant
superfluous *adj* → **1** extravagant **2** surplus **3** useless
superhuman *adj* → supernatural
SUPERIOR *adj* best, crack, crackerjack, cracking, excellent, first, first-rate, giant, good, great, greatest, maximal, of the first water, ripping, spiffing *(Brit.)*, super, superduper, superfine, superlative, top, top-flight, topping *(Obs.)*; **above average,** a cut above, head and shoulders above, in a different class, in a different league, more than a match for, streets ahead; **incomparable,** beyond compare, inapproachable, inimitable, matchless, nonpareil, Olympian, out of this world, supereminent, superordinate, unapproachable, unbeatable, unequalled, unmatched, unparalleled, unrivalled, unsurpassed, untouchable, world-beating; **supreme,** divine, magnificent, sublime, supernal, surpassing, transcendent, transcendental; **classy,** blue-chip, blue-ribbon, classic, deluxe, export, high-toned, quality, silk department, up-market; **elect,** chosen; **prize,** prize-winning, record, record-breaking, winning
superior *n* → **1** good thing **2** letter **3** monastic *adj* **4** arrogant **5** bodily **6** good
SUPERIORITY *n* distinction, eminence, excellence, excellency, first class, meliority, pre-eminence, prominence, superlativeness; **matchlessness,** divineness, divinity, inapproachability, incomparability, incomparableness, loftiness, sublimeness, sublimity, supremeness, surpassingness, transcendence, transcendentness, ultimateness, unapproachableness; **quality,** goodness, value, worth; **one-upmanship**
SUPERIORLY *adv* best, excellently, sublimely, supereminently, superlatively, supernally, supremely, surpassing *(Obs. Poetic)*, surpassingly, transcendentally, transcendently; **incomparably,** inapproachably, matchlessly, unapproachably; **above,** beyond, extra, far and away, head and shoulders above, out and away, over; **par excellence,** beyond compare; **in the ascendant,** one jump ahead
superlative *adj* → superior
supermarket *n* → shop
SUPERNATURAL *adj* hyperphysical, miraculous, mythical, paranormal, preternatural, psychic, superhuman, supernaturalist, supernaturalistic, supersensual, transcendental; **occult,** cabbalistic, cryptic, esoteric, hermetic, masonic, mystic, mystical, occultist, Rosicrucian, secret; **spiritistic,** spiritual, spiritualist, spiritualistic, unfleshly; **parapsychological; unearthly,** eerie, spooky, uncanny, weird; **clairvoyant,** canny *(Archaic)*, clairaudient, clairsentient, mediumistic, second-sighted, telepathic; **telekinetic,** psychokinetic; **shamanic,** sibylic, sibylline; **witching,** wizard, wizardly; **bedevilled,** bewitched, possessed, unlaid; **haunted,** ghost-ridden
supernatural *n* → **1** phantom *adj* **2** ghostly **3** spiritual **4** strange
superpower *n* → nation
supersede *v* → follow
supersonic *adj* → **1** acoustic **2** silent **3** speedy
superstition *n* → **1** belief **2** delusion **3** fright **4** heresy
superstructure *n* → building
supervise *v* → manage

supine *adj* → **1** apathetic **2** inactive **3** level

supper *n* → meal

supplant *v* → follow

supple *v* → **1** soften *adj* **2** beautiful **3** changeable **4** meek **5** pliable **6** soft

supplement *n* → **1** more **2** newspaper *v* **3** add **4** make whole

suppliant *n* → **1** asker *adj* **2** begging **3** regardful

supplicate *v* → entreat

SUPPLIER *n* accommodator, caterer, endower, equipper, fitter, furnisher, maintainer, organiser, outfitter, provider, provisioner, purveyor; **quartermaster,** camp follower, commissary, feeder, sutler, victualler, vivandière; **housekeeper,** butler, cellarman, manciple *(Brit.)*, servant, steward

SUPPLIES *n* allowance, ammunition *(Obs.)*, G.I. *(U.S. Army Colloq.)*, necessities, needs, resources, stores, viaticum, wherewithal; **commodity,** sideline, staple; **property,** matériel, merchandise, stock-in-trade, wares; **equipment,** baggage, gear, hardware, impedimenta; **provisions,** canteen, commons *(Brit.)*, groceries, grubstake, iron rations, provender, rations, victuals *(Archaic)*; **portion,** helping, serve; **trousseau,** layette, whites *(Brit.)*

SUPPLY *n* aid, endowment, fitment, furnishing, maintenance, provision, purveyance, service, subvention, suppliance, sustentation; **supply bill,** advance, civil list *(Brit.)*; **airdrop,** airlift, tanker service

SUPPLY *v* bring home the bacon, fill, make good, munition, plenish *(Scot.)*, prime, provision, ration, reinforce, replenish, restock, victual; **provide,** afford, come to light with, come up with, feed, find, furnish, lay on, line up, minister to *(Archaic)*, ply, present, purvey; **provide for,** allow for, cater for, do for, fend for, make provision for

supply *n* → **1** amount **2** electricity **3** funds *v* **4** fill *adj* **5** electric *adv* **6** pliantly **7** softly

SUPPLY VEHICLE *n* baggage train, cargo ship, container ship, container terminal, freight ship, freighter, lorry, road train, RORO, semitrailer, supply train

SUPPORT *n* brace, crutch, prop, rest, stay; **base,** basement, basis, bed, bedding, bedrock, box bed, drum, foundation, groundwork, hardcore, pigsty *(Railways)*, putlog, socle, step *(Naut.)*, stock, stylobate, substratum *(Biol.)*, substruction, substructure; **keystone,** cornerstone, foundation stone, monolith, raft, springer; **wall,** embankment, retaining wall; **float,** pontoon, raft; **fulcrum,** arbor *(Mach.)*, axis, axle, hinge, oarlock, pivot, racer *(Gunnery)*, rowlock, spindle, swivel *(Gunnery)*, thole *(Naut.)*, tholepin, trunnion *(Gunnery)*; **runner,** rocker, trundle, undercarriage *(Vehicles)*; **rest,** arm, armrest, back rest, cantle, chinrest *(Music)*, headrest, ladder back *(Furnit.)*; **bridge,** jigger, rest *(Billiards)*, spider; **footrest,** footboard, footing, footstool, hassock, horseblock, ottoman *(Furnit.)*, plank, pouf, rung, running board, scarcement, skid, step, stretcher *(Rowing)*, tread, tuffet

SUPPORT *v* base, bear, endure, prop, shoulder, stay, sustain, take the strain, upbear *(Rare)*, uphold; **bolster,** buttress, chock *(Naut.)*, corbel *(Archit.)*, jack up, pile, pillar, rail, reinforce, rib, shore, shore up, slab, spile, stanchion, steady, stick, strengthen, strut, timber, trig, truss, underlay, underpin, underprop, underset; **hold,** pin, stake; **brace,** bracket, clamp, cleat, gusset, traverse *(Naut.)*; **mount,** block, frame, set, step *(Naut.)*; **scaffold,** espalier, trellis; **crutch,** splint; **cushion,** pillow, seat; **pivot,** poise, stabilise

support *n* → **1** actor **2** affirmation **3** approval **4** charity **5** companionship **6** divorce **7** help **8** helper **9** painting **10** underwear *v* **11** be faithful to **12** encourage **13** equip **14** help **15** perform **16** persevere **17** strengthen

SUPPORTING *adj* sustentacular; **structural,** skeletal; **base,** foundation

suppose *v* → **1** be likely **2** conjecture **3** devise **4** expect **5** think

suppository *n* → **1** insert **2** medication

suppress *v* → **1** be reticent **2** hide **3** restrain **4** silence **5** stop **6** victimise

suppurate *v* → **1** excrete **2** expel

supreme *adj* → **1** authoritative **2** final **3** good **4** important **5** most **6** predominant **7** superior

surcharge *n* → **1** gravimetry **2** inflation **3** label *v* **4** label **5** weigh

sure *adj* → **1** certain **2** competent **3** faithful **4** inevitable **5** safe **6** steady *adv* **7** certainly *interj* **8** bullshit

surely *adv* → certainly

SURETY *n* assurance, bond, cover, coverage, insurance, protection, security; **guarantee,** avouchment, guaranty, promise, warrant, warranty; **pledge,** bail, collateral, deposit, earnest, gage, hostage, pawn, plight *(Rare)*, wage *(Obs.)*; **trust,** discretionary trust, fixed trust, flexible trust, trust corporation; **mortgage,** equitable mortgage, hypothec *(Roman Law)*, hypothecation, legal mortgage, stock mortgage; **suretyship,** bailment, sponsion, sponsorship; **offsetting,** covering, crossholding, safeguarding

surety *n* → certainty

SURF *n* choppy water, comb, head sea, shoulder, tube; **wave,** billow, bore, eagre, surge, swell, tidal wave, tsunami; **breaker,** beach comber, beacher, hump, shore break, slop; **greenback,** close-out, comber, greenie; **whitecap,** haystack, white horse; **ripple,** beach break, set; **wake,** backwash. *See also* SEA

surf *n* → **1** bubbling **2** current

surface *n* → **1** appearances **2** outside *v* **3** appear **4** arrive **5** clean **6** dig **7** smooth **8** wake up *adj* **9** apparent **10** land **11** outside **12** sea

SURFBOARD *n* board, body board, boogie board, downrailer, elephant gun, hot dog, kickboard, kneeboard, malibu board, pin, pintail, pop-out, spear, stubby, surf mat, surfoplane

surfeit *n* → **1** surplus *v* **2** overindulge **3** oversupply

SURFER *n* aquanaut, boardie, clubbie, goofy-foot, hot-dogger, natural foot, seaweed, skindiver, surfie, water-baby, water-rat, wax-head

surge *n* → **1** advance **2** current **3** flow **4** irregularity **5** stream **6** surf *v* **7** advance **8** move

surgeon *n* → healer

surgery *n* → **1** cutting **2** healing **3** medical treatment **4** office **5** room

surly *adj* → **1** discourteous **2** irritable **3** unsociable

surmise *n* → **1** conjecture **2** opinion *v* **3** conjecture

surmount *v* → **1** accomplish **2** ascend **3** influence **4** predominate **5** surpass **6** top **7** tower

surname *n* → **1** name *v* **2** name

SURPASS *v* exceed, excel, head, rise to the occasion, surmount *(Obs.)*, top, tower over; **eclipse,** extinguish, overshadow, overshine, steal the show, transcend; **lead the way,** break the record, gain ground, go ahead, never miss a trick, not miss a trick, outpace, outrange, outrun, pull ahead, run; **show up,** cast in the shade, put in the shade, take the shine out of; **outclass,** knock spots off, lick, outdo, outrank, rank *(U.S.)*, ring the board, ring the shed, run rings round someone, wipe the floor with; **outact,** outbrave, outsing; **best,** beat, defeat, encompass *(Obs.)*, get the better of, have someone on the hip, have the laugh on, jump the gun, outmanoeuvre, outplay, outwit, score off, steal a march on; **better,** cap, euchre *(U.S.)*, improve on, increase, overtop, trump, up

surplice *n* → **1** cloak **2** uniform

SURPLUS *n* deluge, drug *(Comm.)*, excess, flood, nimiety, outpouring, overflow, overplus *(U.S.)*, overrun, overstock, oversupply, pile-up, plethora, superfluity, superflux, surplusage; **more than enough,** bellyful, glut, gutful, surfeit, too much, too much of a good thing; **overdose,** OD, overkill; **luxury,** fruit for the sideboard, luxury article, luxury item, milk and honey, more than is needed; **overlap,** allowance, margin, over; **something extra,** bonus, fringe benefit, gash; **extra person,** odd man out, super, supernumerary

SURPLUS *adj* excess, luxury, overabundant, redundant, superabundant, supererogatory, superfluous, supernumerary, uncalled-for, unnecessary, waste; **overfull,** bursting, congested, crammed, engorged, flown *(Archaic)*, flush, inflated, overcrowded, plethoric, rolling in, smothery, stuffed, turgid; **extra,** over, ultra

surplus *n* → **1** remnant *adj* **2** additional

SURPRISE *n* amaze *(Archaic)*, amazement, astonishment, surprisal, wonder; **alarm,** shock, startle. *See also* ASTONISHMENT

SURPRISE *v* amaze, astonish, astound, bowl over, make someone open his eyes; **shock,** alarm, appal, startle, take aback; **take by surprise,** ambush, bushwhack, catch, catch off-guard, catch out, catch unawares, get the jump on, king-hit, overtake. *See also* ASTONISH

surprise *n* → **1** astonishment **2** attack *v* **3** astonish **4** attack **5** capture **6** find out *adj* **7** surprising

SURPRISED *adj* alarmed, like a stunned mullet, startled, taken aback; **astonished,** astounded, bushwhacked, thunderstruck. *See also* ASTONISHED

SURPRISER *n* dumbfounder, eye-opener, shocker, startler; **bombshell,** bolt out of the blue, sucker punch *(Boxing)*, thunderbolt; **bonus,** dark horse, godsend, manna from heaven; **irony,** bricole, note, sudden, surprise ending, turn-up, turn-up for the books

SURPRISING *adj* precipitant, precipitate, precipitative, precipitous, sudden, unpremeditated; **astonishing,** amazing, shock, shocking, spooky, startling; **surprise,** extemporary *(Obs.)*, uncalculated, unexpected, unforeseen, unguessed, unheralded; **bonus,** too good to be true, unhoped-for, unlooked-for. *See also* ASTONISHING

SURPRISINGLY *adv* amazingly, astonishingly, startlingly; **unexpectedly,** against all expectations, by surprise, contrary to all expectations, in an unguarded moment, like a thief in the night, out of the blue, unawares, without warning; **suddenly,** all at once, all of a sudden, amain *(Archaic)*, precipitantly, precipitately, precipitously, sudden *(Poetic)*; **strange to say,** marvellous to relate, mirabile dictu. *See also* ASTONISHINGLY

surrender *n* → **1** abandonment *v* **2** back out **3** capitulate **4** give

surreptitious *adj* → secretive

surrogate *n* → **1** agent **2** religious dignitary **3** substitute *v* **4** substitute

SURROUND *v* box in, compass, encircle, enclose, hem in, stake out; **circle,** embrace, encompass, involve, round, wreathe; **engird,** encincture, enlace, girdle, hoop, loop, span; **enfold,** swathe, wrap

surround *n* → **1** enclosure **2** frame *v* **3** enclose

SURROUNDING *adj* all-round *(U.S.)*, ambient, background, circumambient, circumfluent, circumfluous, circumjacent, outward

SURROUNDINGS *n* entourage, environs, geographic environment *(Sociol.)*, precincts, purlieu, surrounds; **environment,** habitat, medium, milieu; **element,** sphere, world; **ecosphere,** ecosystem, macrocosm; **encirclement,** encincture, encompassment, enlacement; **aureole,** border, halo; **setting,** background, location *(Films)*, mise en scène, scene, scenery, stage; **context,** frame of reference; **atmosphere,** aura, climate, vibes, vibrations; **ambience,** circumambience, circumfluence, circumfusion

surtax *n* → **1** tax *v* **2** tax

surveillance *n* → **1** imprisonment **2** management **3** seeing
survey *n* → **1** agenda **2** investigation **3** look *v* **4** assess **5** investigate **6** look **7** measure **8** question
survive *v* → **1** be **2** continue **3** escape **4** live **5** protract
susceptible *adj* → **1** emotional **2** generous **3** influenced **4** predisposed
SUSCEPTIBLENESS *n* exorability, impressibility, impressionability, impressionableness, persuasibility, pliability, pliancy, sensibility, sensitiveness, sensitivity, suggestibility, suggestiveness, susceptibility, susceptiveness, susceptivity, tractability, tractableness; **amenability,** amenableness, other-directedness, other-direction, perviousness
suspect *n* → **1** accused *v* **2** conjecture **3** doubt *adj* **4** disreputable
suspend *v* → **1** be unable to pay **2** be uncertain **3** boycott **4** defer **5** dismiss **6** fasten **7** hang
suspender *n* → belt
suspense *n* → **1** expectation **2** hanging **3** uncertainty
suspension *n* → **1** bad debt **2** cancellation **3** dissonance **4** disuse **5** hanging **6** interval **7** stoppage
suspicion *n* → **1** conjecture **2** doubt **3** information **4** sign **5** small amount
suspicious *adj* → disreputable
sustain *v* → **1** authenticate **2** equip **3** help **4** persevere **5** protract **6** strengthen **7** support
sustenance *n* → **1** food **2** help
suture *n* → **1** fruit **2** medication
svelte *adj* → thin
swab *n* → **1** bad person **2** bodily discharge **3** medication **4** washer *v* **5** absorb **6** clean **7** dry **8** investigate
swaddle *n* → **1** nappy *v* **2** clothe **3** cover **4** restrain
swag *n* → **1** bag **2** equipment **3** loot *v* **4** travel
swagger *n* → **1** arrogance **2** bragging **3** traveller *v* **4** be arrogant **5** brag **6** walk
swagman *n* → traveller
swallow *n* → **1** eating *v* **2** absorb **3** believe **4** drink **5** eat **6** persevere
swami *n* → **1** enlightener **2** mister
SWAMP *n* alluvion, bog, flat, flow *(Scot.)*, gluepot, innings, marish *(Archaic)*, marsh, mire, morass, mudflat, quagmire, quicksand, slob *(Irish)*, slough, wallow, wash; **fen,** bayou *(U.S.)*, everglade *(U.S.)*, salina, salt marsh, shott, wet ground; **swampland,** maremma, marshland, wetlands; **paddy field,** prairie *(U.S.)*; **mud,** mire, ooze, slush
swamp *n* → **1** sludge **2** stream *v* **3** fall **4** fill **5** flood **6** oversupply **7** walk **8** weaken **9** wet
swan *n* → **1** beautiful person **2** good thing
swank *n* → **1** arrogance **2** fashion *v* **3** act pretentiously **4** be arrogant *adj* **5** affected
swan song *n* → **1** birdcall **2** death
swap *n* → **1** exchange *v* **2** exchange
sward *v* → cover
swarm *n* → **1** many *v* **2** abound **3** be fertile **4** flood **5** fly
swarthy *adj* → **1** black **2** dark
swastika *n* → cross
swat *n* → **1** club **2** hit *v* **3** hit
swathe *v* → **1** cover **2** surround
sway *n* → **1** authority **2** flutter **3** influence **4** power *v* **5** encourage **6** flutter **7** persuade **8** slope **9** vacillate
SWEAR *v* abuse, anathematise, ban *(Archaic)*, bitch and bind, blacken, blackguard, blaspheme, bugger, confound, curse, cuss *(U.S.)*, damn, darn, drat, imprecate, let rip, mozz, swear, swear like a trooper, thunder against, use bad language, use foul language, vilify; **put a curse on someone,** beshrew *(Archaic)*, curse, execrate, hex, imprecate, put the mozz on; **call down curses on,** curse up hill and down dale
swear *n* → **1** contract *v* **2** assert **3** profane **4** promise **5** swear **6** testify
SWEARING *n* abuse, abusiveness, billingsgate, bullocky, cursing, damnation, dirt, filth, foul language, invective, language, obloquy, unparliamentary language, vilification, vituperation; **blasphemy,** blasphemousness, profanity; **execration,** anathema, anathematisation, ban, excommunication, malediction, proscription; **curse,** commination, cuss *(U.S.)*, dirty word, epithet, imprecation, oath, profanity, scurrility, swearword; **the great Australian adjective,** blankety blank, the big f.
sweat *n* → **1** bodily discharge **2** exercise **3** toil **4** worry *v* **5** excrete **6** extort **7** heat **8** manage **9** question **10** stick together **11** wet **12** work **13** worry
sweater *n* → **1** jumper **2** manager
sweep *n* → **1** advance **2** bar **3** cleansing **4** cord **5** direction **6** gambling **7** hanging **8** move **9** propellant **10** removal **11** stroke **12** thrust *v* **13** advance **14** clean **15** curve **16** hang **17** hit **18** investigate **19** look **20** move **21** walk
sweepstake *n* → **1** gambling **2** racing
SWEET *adj* ambrosial, dulcet *(Archaic)*, luscious, nectareous; **syrupy,** cloying, saccharine, sickly, sugary, sweetish, syruplike; **sweetened,** candied, cream, glacé, honied
sweet *n* → **1** fragrance **2** lover *adj* **3** beloved **4** easy **5** fragrant **6** kind **7** musical **8** pleasant
sweetheart *n* → **1** friend **2** lover
SWEETNESS *n* lusciousness, saccharinity, sickliness, sugariness, sweetishness; **sweetener,** honey, sweetening, syrup, topping; **sugar,** cyclamate, dextrose, fructose, fruit sugar, glucose, saccharin; **sweets,** candy, confectionary, guk, gunk, junk food, lollies, toffies; **sweet tooth; sugar concentration,** brix
swell *n* → **1** aristocrat **2** bulge **3** enlargement **4** fashionable person **5** increase **6** loudness **7** mound **8** outburst **9** pitch **10** surf *v* **11** be arrogant **12** become greater **13** bulge **14** flow *adj* **15** fashionable **16** good **17** tasteful
swelling *n* → **1** bulge **2** enlargement *adj* **3** eloquent
swelter *v* → **1** be hot **2** excrete

SWERVE *v* jink *(Rugby)*, lurch, prop, skew, skid *(Aeron.)*, slew, twist, wheel, whirl; **veer,** broach *(Naut.)*, gripe *(Naut.)*, hang in *(Horseracing)*, hang out *(Horseracing)*, haul, haul off *(Naut.)*, jib, jibe, run off the track, run via the Cape *(Horseracing)*, shy, stay *(Naut.)*, tack, wear *(Naut.)*, weathercock, yaw; **turn,** angle, bear away, bend, claw *(Naut.)*, corner, face *(Mil.)*, fade *(Surfing)*, fall away *(Naut.)*, fleet *(Naut.)*, head, put about *(Naut.)*, square, turn away, warp; **turn round,** about-face, back, back water, box, boxhaul, bring about, chuck a U-ie, go about *(Naut.)*, reverse, stem *(Skiing)*

swift *adj* → speedy

swill *n* → **1** dirt **2** kitchen *v* **3** clean **4** drink

SWIM *v* bathe, body-shoot, body-surf, breaststroke, drift, fleet *(Obs.)*, float, skinny-dip, snorkel, strike out, tread water; **wade,** slop

swim *n* → **1** journey **2** move *v* **3** float **4** wet

SWIMMER *n* aquanaut, bather, skindiver, skinny-dipper, surfer, wader

SWIMMING *n* body-surfing, natation, skindiving; **swimming stroke,** Australian crawl, backstroke, butterfly, butterfly stroke, crawl, dog paddle, dolphin kick, overarm, scissors kick

SWIMMING *adj* natant, natatorial, pinnigrade

SWIMWEAR *n* bathers, bathing suit, bathing trunks, bikini, cossie, costume, cozzie, diving suit, maillot, monokini, neck-to-knees, string bikini, swimmers, swimming costume, swimming trunks, swimsuit, togs, trunks, waders, vees

SWINDLE *v* chicane, fleece, graft, gyp, hustle *(U.S.)*, job, lamb, make a fast buck, pettifog, racketeer, wangle; **feather one's own nest,** look after number one, look out for number one, take care of oneself; **cheat,** fix, play with marked cards, rig, tamper; **deceive,** deliberately mislead, speak with double tongue, speak with forked tongue, trick out of

swindle *n* → **1** dishonesty **2** embezzlement **3** trick *v* **4** cheat **5** fail to pay **6** misbehave

swine *n* → **1** bad person **2** voluptuary **3** vulgarian

swing *n* → **1** amusement park **2** flutter **3** pendant **4** rhythm *v* **5** be promiscuous **6** be punished **7** deflect **8** die **9** flutter **10** hang **11** have sex **12** innovate **13** persuade **14** rotate **15** vacillate

swipe *n* → **1** bar **2** hit **3** stroke *v* **4** hit **5** rob

swirl *n* → **1** spin *v* **2** flow **3** spin

swish *n* → **1** hiss **2** hit **3** quiet sound **4** sexual type **5** stick *v* **6** cudgel **7** hiss *adj* **8** fashionable

switch *n* → **1** animal's coat **2** change **3** club **4** hairpiece **5** hit **6** railway **7** stick **8** telecommunications *v* **9** change **10** cudgel **11** divert **12** exchange **13** transport

switchboard *n* → telecommunications

swivel *n* → support

SWOLLEN *adj* blubber, blubbery, puffy, strumose, strumous, tumefacient, tumescent, tumid, tumorous; **bulgy,** bulbaceous, bulbous, bunchy, busty, chubby, mushroom, round, turgent *(Obs.)*, turgescent, ventricose; **billowy,** balloon, bloused, blown, bursiform; **potbellied,** poddy *(Brit. Colloq.)*; **humped,** gibbous, humpbacked, humpy, hunchbacked; **blistery,** blebby, bullate, condylomatous, eruptive, scabby, scabrous, torose, vesicular, vesiculate; **crested,** caruncular, carunculate, carunculous, cristate; **tubercular,** polypoid, tuberculate, tuberculoid, tuberculose, tuberculous, tuberose, tuberous, verrucose. *See also* PROTUBERANT; KNOBBY

swollen *adj* → **1** bombastic **2** increased

SWOLLENNESS *n* billowiness, rotundity, rotundness, tuberosity, tumefaction, tumescence, tumidity, turgor; **lumpiness,** bumpiness, gibbousness, nodality, nodosity, tuberculation, verrucosity, vesication, vesiculation; **convexity,** crenation, crenature, entasis, ventricosity; **protrusion,** evagination, exsertion, extrusion, herniation, protraction, salience, saliency

swoon *n* → **1** unconsciousness *v* **2** become unconscious **3** be ill **4** enjoy

swoop *n* → **1** dive **2** fall *v* **3** dive **4** fly

SWORD *n* backsword, bayonet, blade, brand, broadsword, claymore, cold steel, cutlass, épée, estoc, falchion, foil, glaive, hanger, pigsticker, prick *(Obs.)*, rapier, sabre, scimitar, simitar, smallsword, snickersnee, steel, sticker, sword bayonet, Toledo, tuck, yataghan; **sword part,** chape, cross-guard, foible, forte, quillon, roundel; **knife,** anlace, barong, bowie knife, crease, creese, dagger, dirk, flick-knife, kris, kukri, machete, misericord, panga, parang, poniard, sheath-knife, shiv *(Brit. Colloq.)*, skean, stiletto, stylet, ulu; **axe,** battleaxe, broadaxe, poleaxe, tomahawk, tommyaxe, tommyhawk, twibill *(Archaic)*

sword *n* → fighter

sworn *adj* → avowed

swot *n* → **1** pupil *v* **2** study

sybarite *n* → **1** enjoyer **2** voluptuary **3** wealthy person

sycophant *n* → **1** crawler **2** crook **3** flatterer **4** opportunist *adj* **5** opportunist

syllable *v* → speak

syllabus *n* → **1** course **2** list **3** plan

syllogism *n* → reasoning

symbiosis *n* → **1** combination **2** interaction

symbol *n* → **1** emblem **2** sign *v* **3** represent **4** signify

symbolise *v* → **1** represent **2** signify

symbolism *n* → **1** figure of speech **2** representation

symmetry *n* → equality

sympathetic *adj* → **1** approving **2** congruous **3** emotional **4** friendly **5** in agreement **6** kind **7** pitying

sympathise *v* → **1** agree **2** approve **3** feel emotion **4** fit

sympathy *n* → **1** agreement **2** approval **3** congruity **4** friendship **5** participation **6** pity

symphony *n* → sound

symposium *n* → 1 committee 2 discussion
symptom *n* → 1 illness 2 sign 3 warning
symptomatic *adj* → indicative
synagogue *n* → church
synchronise *v* → adjust
syncopate *v* → make music
syndicate *n* → 1 corporation 2 council 3 judge
syndrome *n* → illness
synod *n* → 1 council 2 legislative body
synonym *n* → 1 equivalent 2 name
synopsis *n* → 1 abridgment 2 narrative
syntax *n* → 1 classification 2 order 3 reasoning
synthesis *n* → 1 combine 2 making 3 reasoning 4 whole
synthesise *v* → 1 combine 2 make 3 make whole
synthetic *adj* → combined
syringe *n* → 1 washer *v* 2 clean 3 insert
syrup *n* → 1 flattery 2 paste 3 sweetness *v* 4 sweeten
system *n* → 1 body 2 classification 3 combine 4 order 5 plan 6 tangle 7 whole
systematic *adj* → 1 classificatory 2 ordered 3 planned
systemic *adj* → bodily
systole *n* → contraction

Tt

tabby *n* → **1** cat **2** single person **3** slanderer **4** woman *adj* **5** multicoloured

tabernacle *n* → **1** church **2** container **3** dwelling **4** niche **5** shrine *v* **6** insert

table *n* → **1** analysis **2** classification **3** food **4** jewel **5** level **6** list **7** mountain *v* **8** list **9** place

tableau *n* → **1** painting **2** representation

tableland *n* → mountain

tablet *n* → **1** medication **2** record **3** writing materials

TABLEWARE *n* china, chinaware, crockery, dinner service, dinner set, ironware, tea-set; **bowl,** coupe, dariole, eggcup, epergne, fingerbowl, mortar, porringer, ramekin, rice bowl, soup plate, sugar basin, tazza; **saucer,** bonbonnière, coquille, scallop, shell; **tureen,** crater, monteith, punchbowl; **plate,** bombe, butterdish, dish, sizzle plate; **platter,** ashet *(Scot.)*, charger, paten, patina *(Rom. Antiq.)*; **tray,** salver; **cone,** cornet, cornucopia; **coolamon,** pitchi

tabloid *n* → **1** medication **2** newspaper

taboo *n* → **1** exclusion **2** prohibition *v* **3** boycott *adj* **4** holy **5** prohibited

tabulate *v* → **1** list **2** order *adj* **3** smooth

tacit *adj* → **1** allusive **2** silent

taciturn *adj* → **1** reticent **2** silent

tack *n* → **1** cord **2** direction **3** food **4** method **5** move **6** nail **7** route **8** stickiness **9** turn *v* **10** fasten **11** set sail **12** sew **13** swerve **14** turn

tackle *n* → **1** cord **2** equipment **3** impact **4** thread *v* **5** attempt **6** bowl over **7** undertake

tacky *adj* → **1** bad **2** dilapidated **3** sticky

tact *n* → **1** discrimination **2** touch

tactic *n* → **1** act of war **2** plan

tactics *n* → **1** act of war **2** plan

TACTILE *adj* haptic, tactual, textural; **palpable,** tangible, touchable; **touching,** tangent; **handled,** felt, touched

tadpole *n* → animal offspring

tag *n* → **1** addition **2** animal's coat **3** contact **4** extremity **5** finish **6** hair **7** label **8** musical phrase **9** musical piece **10** name **11** proverb **12** working class **13** written composition *v* **14** add **15** appraise **16** label **17** name

tail *n* → **1** bottom **2** buttocks **3** extremity **4** groin **5** hair **6** line **7** meteor **8** musical score **9** pendant **10** qualification **11** rear **12** remnant **13** restraining order **14** sex object **15** stream *v* **16** be fastened **17** capture **18** cut off **19** direct **20** farm *adj* **21** rear

tailor *n* → **1** clothier **2** repairer **3** sewer *v* **4** clothe **5** shape

taint *n* → **1** colour **2** denigration **3** deterioration *v* **4** colour **5** dirty **6** disgrace **7** spoil

TAKE *v* adopt, annex, arrogate, assume, borrow, enter *(Law)*, jump *(Mining)*, misappropriate, nim *(Archaic)*; **retake,** repossess, restore, resume; **appropriate,** commandeer, confiscate, convert *(Law)*, expropriate, impound, impress, impropriate, possess oneself of, sequester *(Law)*, sequestrate *(Law)*, usurp; **tax,** attach, distrain, garnishee, levy; **dispossess,** disseise, divest, flit *(Archaic)*, forjudge; **disinherit,** cut off without a cent; **deprive,** bankrupt, beggar, beguile of, bereave, divest *(Archaic)*, do out of *(Colloq.)*, fleece, impoverish, reave *(Archaic)*, steal, strip *(Archaic)*, take from; **crop,** cull, gather, reap, subtract

take *n* → **1** amount **2** medical treatment **3** profit **4** recording **5** takings **6** trick *v* **7** absorb **8** advance **9** be ill **10** buy **11** capture **12** choose **13** eat **14** examine **15** explain **16** flower **17** have sex **18** know **19** necessitate **20** persevere **21** rob **22** stick together **23** subtract **24** succeed **25** transport

TAKE ADVANTAGE *v* benefit, profit, work a point; **get the jump on,** gain ascendancy over, get someone's measure, get to the windward of, pull rank, pull the braid

TAKE ADVANTAGE OF *v* bludge on, come it a bit much, let in for, pole on, put in the fangs, put in the hooks, put in the nips, put in the screws, put on, put the acid on, put upon; **leave someone holding the baby,** die on someone, leave in the lurch, not play the game

TAKE DRUGS *v* drop *(Colloq.)*; **turn on,** blow one's mind, bomb out, drop acid, fly high, goof, smoke, snort, trip; **hit up,** hit, mainline, shoot, shoot up, skinpop; **OD,** overdose

take over *v* → **1** control **2** gain **3** manage

TAKER *n* appropriator, enterer, grabber, harpy, Indian giver *(Colloq.)*, snatcher, wrester; **depriver,** confiscator, dispossessor, disseisor, distrainer, expropriator, impounder, sequestrator, usurper; **capturer,** abductor, captor, catcher, conqueror, rapist, ravisher, seizer, seizor *(Law)*

TAKE REFUGE *v* go to ground, lay to *(Naut.)*, put in *(Naut.)*, take cover, take shelter

TAKE SHAPE *v* crystallise, jell, shape up

TAKING *n* annexation, appropriation, arrogation, attachment, confiscation, conversion, dispossession, distrainment, distraint, distress, entry *(Law)*, escheatment, expropriation, forcible entry, impoundage, impoundment, misappropriation, reprise *(Law)*, resumption, sequestration, usurpation; **tax,** deduction, impost; **extortion,** blackmail *(Law)*, Rachmanism, rapacity, shakedown, usury, vampirism; **deprivation,** bereavement, divestiture, divestment, divesture, privation

TAKINGS *n* boot, booty, catch, grab, haul *(Colloq.)*, prize, snatch, spoils, take

tale *n* → **1** computation **2** lie **3** news **4** story **5** talk **6** whole

talent *n* → **1** competence **2** expert **3** point of view **4** sex object

talisman *n* → **1** amulet **2** lucky charm **3** magic spell

TALK *n* civilities, commerce *(Obs.)*, commune, communion, confab, confabulation, conversation, conversazione, converse, dialogue, discourse, give-and-take, intercourse, interlocution, repartee, shop talk, small talk, table talk, tale *(Obs.)*, yabber; **chat,** causerie, chinwag, coze *(Obs.)*, rap, wongi, yarn; **interview,** press conference; **heart-to-heart,** duologue, tete-a-tete; **telephone call,** call, galah session, person-to-person; **chatter,** cackle, chitchat, claver *(Scot.)*, gab, natter, palaver, persiflage, prate, prattle; **gossip,** dirt, furphy, gossiping, scandal, scuttlebutt, tattle. *See also* DISCUSSION

TALK *v* commune, confab, confabulate, confer, converse, dialogue, discourse, get together, have a word with, palaver, parley, pass the flute, pass the kip, powwow, speak, talk shop, wongi, yabber; **negotiate,** talk over; **chat,** bat the breeze, claver *(Scot.)*, coze *(Obs.)*, natter, palaver, pass the time of day, rap, visit *(U.S.)*, yarn; **gossip,** chew the fat, chew the rag, scandal *(Archaic)*, tattle; **gab,** gasbag, go on, jaw, jawbone; **chatter,** cackle, clatter, jabber, mag, prate, prattle, rattle; **discuss,** canvass, controvert, debate, have it out, kick about, kick around, korero *(N.Z.)*, thrash out; **argue,** argy-bargy, bicker

talk *n* → **1** animal call **2** news **3** speaking *v* **4** call (of animals) **5** persuade **6** speak

TALKATIVE *adj* chatty, communicative, garrulous, gassy, gossipy, loquacious, of many words, voluble; **conversational,** conferential, north-south interlocutory; **talkback,** open-line

TALKER *n* collocutor, colloquist, conversationalist, converser, debater, dialogist, dialoguer, discourser, interlocutor, interlocutrice, interlocutrix; **windbag,** bag of wind, big mouth, buttonholer, fluter, gasbag, rattletrap, yabberer; **interviewer,** interviewee; **negotiator,** negotiant; **chatterbox,** cackler, chatterer, flibbertigibbet, gabber, magger, magpie, prater, prattler; **gossip,** gossiper, gossipmonger, newsmonger, scandalmonger, tattler

TALK NONSENSE *v* babble, blather, chatter, crap, crap on, fudge, gabble, gammon, garble, gas, gibber, jabber, jargon, jargonise, mag, maunder, patter, piffle, quibble, rabbit on, rant, rave, signify little, talk rubbish, talk through one's arse, talk through one's hat, talk through the back of one's neck, twaddle, waffle, yak, yawp

TALL *adj* lanky, rangy, strapping, tallish; **towering,** all-highest, beetling, colossal, dominating, dominative, eminent, exalted, giant, gigantic, grand, high, high-rise, lofty, majestic, overhanging, soaring, sublime *(Poetic)*, supernal, topless, towery, uplifted; **spired,** spirelike, spiry, tower-like, towery, turrical, turriculate. *See also* HIGH; MOUNTAINOUS

tall *adj* → **1** exaggerated **2** great

tallow *n* → fat

TALL PERSON *n* beanpole, beanstalk, colossus, giant, giraffe, lofty, lolly legs, long streak of misery, long streak of pelican shit, longshanks, six-footer, slab, strapper, streak, yard of drink water

tally *n* → **1** account **2** computation **3** list **4** score **5** stick *v* **6** account **7** compute **8** fit **9** mark **10** record

talon *n* → **1** bird part **2** bolt

tame *v* → **1** defeat **2** moderate **3** repress *adj* **4** boring **5** cowardly **6** moderate

tamper *v* → swindle

tampon *n* → **1** absorber **2** plug *v* **3** close

tan *v* → **1** brown *adj* **2** brown

tandem *n* → **1** bicycle **2** carriage **3** sequence *adv* **4** lengthways **5** successively

tang *n* → **1** brace **2** fragrance **3** pungency **4** savour **5** taste

tangent *n* → **1** line *adj* **2** contacting **3** tactile

tangerine *n* → **1** orange *adj* **2** orange

TANGIBLE *adj* bodily, concrete, concretive, corporal, corporeal, cosmic, external *(Metaphys.)*, fleshly, material, mechanical, natural, objective, palpable, phenomenal, physical, spatiotemporal, substantial

tangible *adj* → tactile

TANGLE *n* bob, can of worms, disorder, dog's breakfast, dog's dinner, knot, mat, mess, nodus, ravel, shakings *(Naut.)*, snarl, twine; **maze,** Chinese puzzle, labyrinth, wheels within wheels. *See also* COMPLEXITY; **imbroglio,** fracas, melee; **rigmarole,** ins and outs, involution; **complex,** composite, compound, network, structure, system, tissue

TANGLE *v* convolute, disorder, embrangle, enmesh, entangle, entrammel, fall foul of, foul, jumble, knot, mat, ravel, shuffle, snarl, wind

tangle *n* → **1** argument **2** disorder **3** muddle

TANGLED *adj* afoul, cotted *(Wool)*, disordered, entangled, foul, implicit *(Obs.)*, inextricable, kaleidoscopic, knotted, knotty, matted, perplexed, tangly; **mazelike,** labyrinthine, mazy. *See also* COMPLEX

tango *v* → dance

tank *n* → **1** barrel **2** basin **3** lake **4** truck

tankard *n* → **1** alcohol container **2** drinking vessel

tanker *n* → **1** aeroplane **2** watercraft

tantalise *v* → **1** allure **2** disenchant

tantamount *adj* → equal

tantrum *n* → **1** angry act **2** irritation

TAP *n* bung, faucet *(U.S.)*, plug, spigot, stop; **valve,** ball valve, butterfly valve, check valve, inlet valve, mixing valve, needle valve, piston *(Music)*, slide valve, throttle valve; **cock,**

ballcock, bib cock, petcock, stopcock, turncock

tap *n* → **1** beer **2** boom **3** cutter **4** drink **5** exit **6** pat **7** plug **8** pub **9** small amount **10** touch *v* **11** cash **12** cut **13** extract **14** hear **15** hit **16** touch **17** use

TAPE *n* ferret, inkle, marking tape, masking tape, red tape, ribbon, strapping; **band,** sandal, sling, snood, strap, thong; **bandage,** brace, breeching, ligature, tourniquet; **belt,** belting, girdle, tie

tape *n* → **1** finish **2** lace **3** sound system **4** starting line *v* **5** measure

taper *n* → **1** candle **2** decrease **3** lighter **4** thinness *v* **5** decrease **6** thin

tape-recorder *n* → sound system

tapestry *n* → **1** fine arts **2** manchester **3** pendant **4** sewing

tar *n* → mariner

tardy *adj* → **1** late **2** purposeless **3** slow

tare *n* → **1** counterbalance **2** heaviness *v* **3** weigh

target *n* → **1** aim **2** armour **3** indicator

tariff *n* → **1** agenda **2** tax *v* **3** tax

tarmac *n* → **1** access **2** airport **3** paving **4** road *v* **5** coat

tarnish *n* → **1** colourlessness **2** deterioration **3** disfigurement **4** plating *v* **5** disgrace **6** dull **7** lose colour **8** spoil

tarpaulin *n* → **1** hat **2** mariner **3** roof **4** shelter

tarry *n* → **1** visit *v* **2** be late **3** be present **4** expect **5** go slowly **6** idle **7** visit

tart *n* → **1** prostitute **2** woman *adj* **3** sour

tartan *n* → sailing ship

tartar *n* → **1** remnant **2** violent person

task *n* → **1** difficulty **2** job **3** obligation **4** punishment **5** tax **6** toil **7** undertaking **8** work *v* **9** tax **10** tire

tassel *n* → **1** groin **2** pendant **3** trimming *v* **4** flower

TASTE *n* aftertaste, degustation *(Obs.)*, finish; **flavour,** body, flavouring, race, sapor, savour; **tang,** nip, smack, soupçon, tinge; **tastiness,** delicateness, flavoursomeness, freshness, mellowness, palatability, richness, sapidity, savouriness; **palate,** relish, tastebuds, tooth; **acquired taste,** foretaste, prelibation; **gustation,** tea-tasting, wine-tasting

TASTE *v* eat, lick, relish, sample, savour, smack one's lips, try; **taste of,** smack of; **mellow,** age, mature, ripen; **flavour,** tinge

taste *n* → **1** desire **2** discrimination **3** good taste **4** pleasure **5** small amount *v* **6** absorb **7** eat **8** enjoy **9** perceive **10** read **11** test **12** touch

TASTEFUL *adj* choice, exquisite, fancy, fine; **chic,** dapper, dressy, elegant, nifty, nobby; **stylish,** smart, sophisticated, urbane; **upmarket,** aristocratic, classy, deluxe, highbrow, posh, rich, silken, swell, toffy

TASTY *adj* agreeable, appetizing, delicate, delicious, flavorous, flavourful, flavoursome, fresh, sapid, yummy; **full-bodied,** big, foxy, fruity, generous, gutsy, rancio, rich, strong, vintage; **mellow,** creamy, smooth; **plain,** mild

tasty *adj* → delicious

tatting *n* → **1** lace **2** sewing **3** string

tattle *n* → **1** news **2** revelation **3** talk *v* **4** noise abroad **5** reveal **6** talk

tattoo *n* → **1** label **2** signal *v* **3** label

taunt *n* → **1** challenge **2** insult **3** mockery *v* **4** insult **5** mock

taut *adj* → **1** hard **2** tidy

tautology *n* → **1** figure of speech **2** repetition **3** waffle

tavern *n* → **1** hotel **2** pub **3** restaurant

taw *n* → **1** line **2** marble **3** sign *v* **4** cudgel **5** prepare

tawdry *adj* → **1** cheap **2** vulgar

tawny *n* → **1** yellow *adj* **2** brown **3** yellow

TAX *n* cess *(Brit.)*, clawback *(Colloq.)*, dues, farm *(Obs.)*, geld, price *(Archaic)*, scot *(Archaic)*, ship money *(Hist.)*, tallage *(Hist.)*, taxation, tithe, tithing; **income tax,** capital gains tax, gift tax, indirect tax, supertax, surtax, wealth tax, withholding tax; **duty,** countervailing duty, death duty, droit, estate duty, reprise, stamp duty, valuation; **excise,** consumption tax, customs, customs duties, fair trade *(Brit.)*, primage, purchase tax *(Brit.)*, sales tax, tariff, V.A.T., value added tax; **levy,** contribution, custom, impost, task *(Obs.)*, toll, tribute; **poll tax,** capitation, head money

TAX *v* assess, excise, overtax, surtax, tariff, task *(Obs.)*

tax *n* → **1** imposition **2** insistence **3** obligation **4** taking *v* **5** charge **6** disapprove of **7** impose **8** insist on **9** take **10** tire **11** weigh

taxation *n* → tax

TAX COLLECTOR *n* assessor, farmer, inspector, publican *(Rom. Antiq.)*, taxman; **customs officer,** exciseman, gauger

taxi *n* → **1** car *v* **2** drive

taxidermy *n* → conservation

taxonomy *n* → classification

tea *n* → **1** drink **2** marijuana **3** meal

TEACH *v* coach, cram, cultivate, drill, edify, educate, enlighten, ground, illumine, instruct, prepare, qualify, school, sophisticate, spoon-feed, team-teach, train, tutor; **induct,** apprentice, familiarise, implant, inculcate, indoctrinate in, initiate, introduce; **lecture,** harangue, preach, promulgate, proselytise, sermonise; **illustrate,** demonstrate, show, work at the chalkface; **examine,** assess, catechise; **re-educate,** rehabilitate

teach *v* → **1** convert **2** prepare

TEACHER *n* academic, educationalist, educationist, educator, guide, heurist, instructor, mentor, pedagogue, preceptor, scribe *(Jewish Hist.)*, seminarian, sophist *(Greek Antiq.)*; **schoolteacher,** beak, boss, chalkie, crammer *(Brit.)*, dame, dominie, form master, form mistress, governess, guzinter, headmaster, headmistress, housemaster, housemistress, master, mistress, P.T. instructor, pedant *(Obs.)*, principal, relief teacher, remedial teacher, schoolie, schoolman, schoolmarm, schoolmaster, schoolmistress, sportsmaster, sportsmistress, subprincipal; **tutor,** supervisor, teacher aide, usher *(Brit. Archaic)*; **professor,** aspro, associate professor, chancellor, dean, don, emeritus, proctor, prof, provost, reader, rector, senior lecturer, vice-chancellor, visiting professor; **lecturer,** docent *(U.S.)*, senior tutor, teaching fellow; **rhetor,** rhetorician; **teaching staff,** cadre, department, faculty, school; **coach,** catechiser, catechist, drillmaster, riding master, trainer; **animal trainer,** breaker, horsebreaker, lion tamer; **disciplinarian,** discipliner. *See also* ENLIGHTENER

TEACHING *n* catechesis, direction, drilling, edification, exegesis, explanation, implantation, inculcation, indoctrination, initiation, instruction, manual training, preaching, promulgation, propaganda, proselytism, schooling, spoon-feeding, training, tuition, tutelage, tutorage; **guidance,** consciousness raising, edification, enlightenment; **rearing,** breeding, bringing-up, civilisation, cultivation, house-training, nurture, parenting, potty-training, toilet-training, up-bringing; **didacticism,** didactics, doctrinism, pedagogics, pedagogy, scholasticism. *See also* EDUCATION

TEACHING *adj* catechetical, catechistic, consciousness-raising, didactic, edificatory, educational, exegetical, exponential, indoctrinatory, instructional, instructive, mind-expanding, pedagogic, pedagogical, preceptive, sermonic, tuitionary; **introductory,** preliminary, propaedeutic, simple; **advanced,** difficult

team *n* → **1** ancestry **2** animal offspring **3** corporation **4** offspring **5** sportsman *v* **6** transport

tease *n* → **1** annoyance **2** annoyer **3** flirt *v* **4** annoy **5** flirt **6** irritate **7** mock **8** separate **9** sew

teat *n* → chest

tech *n* → college

technical *adj* → **1** epistemological **2** precise

technicality *n* → **1** knowledge **2** precision

technician *n* → **1** craftsman **2** specialist

technicolour *n* → **1** film *adj* **2** colourful

technique *n* → **1** artistry **2** method

technology *n* → **1** industry **2** knowledge **3** language

tectonic *adj* → **1** creative **2** structural

tedious *adj* → **1** boring **2** verbose

tee *n* → **1** aim **2** cross

teem *v* → **1** abound **2** be fertile **3** conceive **4** discharge **5** flower **6** give birth **7** rain

teen *adj* → youthful

teenager *n* → adolescent

teeter *n* → **1** flutter *v* **2** flutter

teeth *n* → power

teetotal *adj* → abstinent

TELECAST *v* beam *(Radio)*, broadcast, colourcast, newscast, televise, transmit

telecast *n* → **1** telecommunications *v* **2** publish

TELECOMMUNICATIONS *n* communications, electronic media, media, telecine; **public broadcasting; community radio; broadcast,** colourcast, feature, newscast, outside broadcast, phone-in, satellite broadcast, simulcast, talkback, telecast, telefilm, teleplay, telethon, transcription, transmission; **telephone,** blower, extension, handpiece, handset, hot line, intercom, intercommunication system, interphone, party line, pay phone *(U.S.)*, phone, processor, public telephone, receiver, red phone, tie line, videophone; **telephone call,** bell, buzz, international call, ISD call, person-to-person call, reverse-charge call, ring, STD call, tingle, tinkle, trunk call; **international subscriber dialling,** ISD code, STD code, subscriber trunk dialling; **exchange,** central *(U.S.)*, PABX, PBX, Private Automatic Branch Exchange, private branch exchange, step-by-step, telephone exchange, trunks; **switchboard,** crossbar switch, switch; **telephone box,** callbox *(Brit.)*, kiosk *(Brit.)*, pay station *(U.S.)*; **telegraphy,** telegraphics; **teleprinter,** teletype, teletypewriter, telex. *See also* TELEVISION; RADIO

TELECOMMUNICATIONS STATION *n* citizen band radio, earth station, pirate radio, radio station, relay station, station, studio, television station; **network,** hook-up, radio link, radio relay; **landline,** transmission line; **communication satellite,** comsat; **signal,** airwaves, carrier, carrier wave, continuous waves, direct ray, direct wave, ground wave, medium wave, radio signal, radio wave, sky wave; **crystal,** cat's whisker, crystal detector, crystal rectifier; **control room**

telegram *n* → message

telegraph *v* → send a message

telepathy *n* → **1** communication **2** the supernatural

TELEPHONE *v* bell, buzz, call, dial, get through to, ring, ring up

telephone *n* → **1** telecommunications *v* **2** communicate **3** send a message

teleprinter *n* → telecommunications

telescope *n* → **1** lens *v* **2** abbreviate **3** shorten

TELEVISION *n* black-and-white, boob tube, cable television, closed-circuit television, colour television, idiot box, monitor, satellite television, set, small screen, tellie, the box, tube, TV, video *(U.S.)*; **video cassette recorder,** teleplayer, VCR, video recorder; **phototelegraphy,** telephotography, teletext; **teleprompter,** autocue

telex *n* → **1** message **2** telecommunications *v* **3** send a message

tell *n* → **1** mound *v* **2** be important **3** command **4** compute **5** discriminate **6** narrate **7** operate **8** publicise **9** reveal **10** speak

teller *n* → **1** informant **2** mathematician **3** storyteller

telltale *n* → **1** gossip **2** informant **3** revealer *adj* **4** revealing **5** warning

temerity *n* → **1** discourtesy **2** rashness

temper *n* → **1** anger **2** character **3** condition **4** emotion **5** irritation **6** pliability *v* **7** combine **8** ease **9** harden **10** make peace **11** mix **12** moderate **13** quieten **14** strengthen

tempera *n* → 1 dye 2 painting
temperament *n* → 1 abatement 2 character 3 heat
temperance *n* → 1 abstinence 2 composure 3 lenience 4 moderation
temperate *adj* → 1 abstinent 2 hot 3 moderate
temperature *n* → heat
tempest *n* → 1 commotion 2 turbulence 3 violent outburst 4 wind *v* 5 agitate
template *n* → model
temple *n* → 1 church 2 head 3 side
tempo *n* → 1 rate 2 rhythm
TEMPORAL *adj* chronological, fourth-dimensional, space-time, time
temporal *adj* → 1 impermanent 2 laic
TEMPORARILY *adv* ad hoc, for the moment, for the nonce, for the time being, in the interim, in the meantime, pro tempore, provisionally; **transitorily,** ephemerally, fleetingly, flickeringly, fugaciously, fugitively, transiently; **in passing,** by the way, casually, en passant; **briefly,** acutely, in the twinkling of an eye, meteorically
TEMPORARINESS *n* changeableness, currency, impermanence, impermanency, temporality; **transitoriness,** caducity, evanescence, fleetingness, fugacity, fugitiveness, transience, transientness, volatileness, volatility
temporary *n* → 1 temporary appointment 2 worker *adj* 3 impermanent
TEMPORARY APPOINTMENT *n* commendam, interim council, interregnum, regency, temporals; **temporary,** ad hoc committee, casual, temp, transient; **temporary thing**
temporise *v* → 1 avoid 2 capitulate 3 mediate 4 vacillate
tempt *v* → 1 enchant 2 test
tenable *adj* → 1 logical 2 true
tenacious *adj* → 1 holding 2 persevering 3 sticky 4 stubborn
tenant *n* → 1 borrower 2 occupant 3 owner *v* 4 inhabit
tend *v* → care for
tendentious *adj* → predisposed
tender *n* → 1 cash 2 offer 3 train 4 watercraft *v* 5 give 6 offer *adj* 7 brittle 8 loving 9 painful 10 soft 11 weak 12 youthful
tenderfoot *n* → 1 ignoramus 2 learner
tendril *n* → 1 stem 2 thread
TEND TO *v* go, gravitate towards, have in the blood, incline, lean towards, look towards, stand, trend, verge towards
tenement *n* → 1 dwelling 2 real estate
tenet *n* → belief
tenon *n* → 1 bulge *v* 2 join
tenor *n* → 1 meaning 2 point of view 3 resonator 4 singer
tense *adj* → 1 contracted 2 worried
tensile *adj* → pliable
tension *n* → 1 electricity 2 excitement 3 pliability 4 worry
tent *n* → 1 camp 2 shelter *v* 3 inhabit
tentacle *n* → 1 bulge 2 feeler 3 thread
tentative *adj* → 1 cautious 2 empirical 3 indecisive
tenuous *adj* → 1 ethereal 2 imprecise 3 light 4 smallest 5 thin 6 unimportant 7 weak
tenure *n* → 1 holding 2 ownership 3 period
tepee *n* → camp
tepid *adj* → hot
term *n* → 1 finish 2 limit 3 period 4 word *v* 5 name
terminal *n* → 1 electric circuit 2 finish 3 moulding *adj* 4 boundary 5 deadly 6 distant 7 final
terminate *v* → 1 finish 2 limit
terminology *n* → language
terminus *n* → 1 finish 2 indicator 3 limit
tern *n* → 1 gambling 2 three
ternary *n* → 1 three *adj* 2 third
terrace *n* → 1 field 2 house 3 road
terracotta *n* → 1 orange *adj* 2 brown 3 orange
terra firma *n* → land
terrain *n* → 1 land 2 region
terrarium *n* → 1 animal dwelling 2 box 3 breeding ground
terrestrial *n* → 1 inhabitant *adj* 2 land 3 resident
terrible *adj* → 1 bad 2 enormous 3 frightening 4 intense
terrier *n* → record
terrific *adj* → 1 frightening 2 good 3 intense
terrify *v* → frighten
terrine *n* → smallgoods
territory *n* → 1 domain 2 nation 3 region 4 subject matter
terror *n* → 1 annoyance 2 bad person 3 fright 4 frightener
terrorise *v* → 1 force 2 frighten
terse *adj* → 1 concise 2 discourteous 3 irritable
tertiary *n* → 1 feather 2 monastic 3 religious follower *adj* 4 laic 5 third
TEST *n* ascertainment, assay, bio-assay, check, crucible, drill stem test, flame test, herd testing, mantoux test, titration, touch; **experiment,** control experiment, inquiry, leap in the dark, probe; **trial,** field trial, pilot, pilot film, pilot study, run-through, test case, trial run, tryout, walk-through, war game, work-out; **trial by ordeal,** acid test, baptism of fire, ordeal
TEST *v* approve *(Obs.)*, essay, put to the test, tempt *(Obs.)*, trial, try out; **try,** discuss *(Rare)*, sample, taste; **hypothesise,** explore every avenue, fly a kite, try out an idea; **experiment,** ascertain, assay, prove, titrate; **monitor,** control, evaluate
TEST *adj* pilot, probative, trial; **probational,** on appro, on approval, on probation, on trial, verificatory
testament *n* → 1 breviary 2 command 3 contract
TESTER *n* analyst, assayer, empiricist, essayist, experimentalist, experimenter, gauger, herd tester, researcher, sampler, scientist; **testing agent,** determinative, gauge, litmus paper, monitor, reagent, test paper, touch-

stone; **test group,** guineapig, pilot plant, subject; **control group,** criterion, standard, touchstone, yardstick; **laboratory,** insectary, proving ground, test tube, wind-tunnel

testes *n* → groin

TESTIFIER *n* attestor, crown witness, deponent, deposer, earwitness, eyewitness, identifier, informant, swearer, voucher, witness, witnesser; **verifier,** affirmant, affirmer, authenticator, compurgator, corroborant, corroborator, establisher

TESTIFY *v* affirm, attest, bear witness, depone *(Archaic)*, depose, give evidence, jump the box, swear, witness; **argue,** adduce evidence, allege, exhibit, go on, lead evidence

TESTIMONIAL *adj* a posteriori, demonstrable, demonstrational, deposable, documentary, evidential, evidentiary, manifestable, probative, substantiative; **confirmatory,** corroborative, corroboratory, probate, verificative, verifying

testimonial *n* → **1** approval **2** evidence **3** memento

testimony *n* → evidence

test tube *n* → tester

testy *adj* → irritable

tetanus *n* → contraction

tete-a-tete *n* → **1** talk *adv* **2** in twos

tether *n* → **1** cord **2** restraints *v* **3** fasten **4** restrain

text *n* → **1** subject matter **2** textbook **3** vocabulary **4** written composition

TEXTBOOK *n* ABC, arithmetic, catechism, geography, grammar, hornbook, institutes, primer, reader, schoolbook, special, speller, spelling book, text; **workbook,** copybook

TEXTILES *n* cloth, contexture, fabric, homespun, material, stuff, texture, tissue; **knit,** knitting, stockinet; **cotton print,** batik, challis, chiné, futah, India print, persiennes, sarong; **rag,** bribe, fag-end, flock, lock, necks, tatter, thrum, waste; **lining,** buckram, fleece, interfacing, interlining, venetian; **padding,** bombast *(Obs.)*; **suiting,** blanketing, coating, sacking, shirting, skirting, towelling, vesting *(U.S.)*; **waterproof,** camlet, japara, mackintosh, nettlecloth, oilcloth, oiled silk, oilskin, tammy; **lint,** gauze, jaconet; **swatch,** bolt, length, piece, roll, web. *See also* WEAVE; LACE; SEWING; MANCHESTER

TEXTURE *n* fabric *(Textiles Geol.)*, finish, wale *(Textiles)*; **viscosity,** consistency; **unit of viscosity,** centipoise, centistokes, stoke, stokes

texture *n* → **1** roughness **2** textiles

thank *v* → be grateful

THANKYOU *interj* gramercy *(Archaic)*, merci, merci beaucoup, ta, thanks, thanks a bunch, thanks a million; **Deo gratias,** praise be to God, thanks be to God

that *adj* → **1** particular *adv* **2** quantitatively

thatch *n* → **1** building materials **2** hair *v* **3** cover

thaw *n* → **1** heating **2** liquid *v* **3** heat **4** liquefy **5** soften

theatre *n* → **1** audience **2** auditorium **3** hall **4** room

theatrical *adj* → **1** affected **2** dramatic **3** emotional

THEATRICAL COMPANY *n* circus, ensemble, rep, repertory, stock company *(U.S.)*, troop *(Rare)*, troupe; **cast,** characters, dramatis personae; **chorus,** duo, nonet, octet, quartet, quintet, septet, sextet, trio

THE AUTHORITIES *n* Big Brother, faceless men, officialdom, the administration, the elite, the establishment, the powers that be, the ruling classes, them

THE BEST *n* the acme, the cap, the crème de la crème, the cream, the fat, the first, the pick, the pink, the pride; **the ultimate,** the crest, the glassy, the height, the maximum, the noon, the noontide, the sublime of, the summit, the top, the tops; **first choice,** preference, primary; **nonpareil,** beauty, classic, clinker, clipper, collector's item, cracker, crackerjack, dilly, dinkum, dinky, doozey, dynamite, nonesuch, one out of the box, ringer, ripper, ripsnorter, something else, something else again, something extra *(U.S.)*, speciality, top-liner, topnotcher; **masterpiece,** chef d'oeuvre, magnum opus, masterwork

THE BUSH *n* city surroundings, countryside, meadows and pastures, the country, the land, the open, the provinces, the soil; **bushcountry,** brush, bushland, the brigalow, the donga, the mallee, the mulga, the saltbush, the scrub, tiger country, weald *(Archaic)*, woodlands, woods; **back country,** back of beyond, back of Bourke, back of the black stump, backblocks, backwoods, booay, boondocks *(U.S.)*, cactus, goat country, hinterland, never-never, the outback, the sticks; **dead centre,** dead heart, the centre, the red centre. *See also* RURALISM

THE DEAD *n* dearly departed, ghosts, loved ones, shades, the deceased, the defunct, the departed, those who have gone before; **corpse,** ashes, body, cadaver, carcass, corps *(Obs.)*, last remains, mummy, relics, stiff; **casualty,** fatality; **zombie,** walking dead; **death rate,** casualty list, death register, death toll, deathroll, mortality, mortality rate, necrology, road toll; **war dead,** the fallen, the slain

theft *n* → **1** capture **2** dishonesty **3** profit **4** robbery

THE INTANGIBLE *n* the abstract, the imponderable, the unknowable; **abstraction,** concept, conception, idea, ideal, supposition; **figment,** bubble, idol, imagining, mirage, smoke; **straw company,** kite *(Comm.)*

them *n* → the authorities

theme *n* → **1** music **2** subject matter

THE MEDIA *n* electronic media, Fleet Street, fourth estate, print media, the press; **press gallery,** press-box; **journalism,** coverage, photojournalism, reportage; **publication,** syndication; **news agency,** news syndicate, press agency, press office; **newsiness,** newsworthiness

THEN *adv* at that time, there, with that; **during that time,** the while; **sometime,** far, long, somewhere

then *adv* → **1** in the future **2** in the past *conj* **3** because

thence *adv* → in the future

theology *n* → religion

theorem *n* → **1** proverb **2** rule

theoretical *adj* → **1** conjectural **2** intangible **3** nonexistent

THEORISE *v* hypothesise, philosophise; **propound,** argue, moot, move, offer, propose, put up a case, say, submit

THEORIST *n* armchair philosophiser, armchair revolutionary, assumer, conjecturer, doctrinaire, doctrinarian, philosopher, philosophiser, presumer, supposer, surmiser, theoretician, theoriser

theory *n* → **1** conjecture **2** idea **3** opinion

THE PRESENT *n* here and now, instant, now, nowadays, the present juncture, the present moment, the present time, the times, the twentieth century, today, tonight; **immediacy,** immediateness, instancy

THE PUBLIC *n* body politic, common *(Obs.)*, commonalty, commonweal *(Archaic)*, commonwealth, community, community at large, country, democracy, general *(Archaic)*, general public, people, people in general, state; **society,** age, everyone, world

therapeutic *adj* → medicinal

therapy *n* → **1** medical treatment **2** psychotherapy

thereabouts *adv* → **1** almost **2** here

thereby *adv* → here

therefore *conj* → because

thereupon *adv* → **1** after **2** in the future

THERMAL *adj* caloric, calorific, phlogistic *(Obs.)*, thermic; **thermometric,** calorimetric, calorimetrical, pyrometric, pyrometrical, thermometrical, thermoscopic, thermoscopical; **thermodynamic,** geothermic, photothermic, thermodynamical, thermostatic; **adiabatic,** diathermanous, diathermic, isenthalpic, isocheimal, isotheral, isothermal; **radiant,** convectional, decalescent, endothermic, exothermic; **thermophilic,** thermotaxic, thermotropic

thermal *n* → airflow

thermos *n* → bottle

thermostat *n* → steadier

thesaurus *n* → **1** list **2** reference book **3** storehouse **4** treasury

thesis *n* → rhythm

THE SUPERNATURAL *n* cabbala, magic, the occult, the spiritism; **occultism,** animism, cabbalism, esotericism, esotery, spiritualism, supernaturalism; **witchcraft,** black magic, black mass, demonology, devilry, diablerie, sorcery, witchery, wizardry; **psychomancy,** demonomancy, mythology, necromancy, spirit-rapping; **ESP,** clairaudience, clairsentience, clairvoyance, extrasensory perception, psychometry, second sight, sixth sense; **telepathy,** mind-readng, thought transference, thought-reading; **psychic research,** parapsychology, psychokinetics, psychosophy; **unearthliness,** weirdness

THICK *adj* blocky, bold, bold-face, chunky, full-faced *(Print.)*, thickish; **wide,** broad, deep, expansive, extensive, outspread, spacious, spread, widish; **spatular,** spatulate; **bloated,** blubbery, puffy; **full,** ample, baggy, generous; **broad,** beamy, broad across the beam, broadish, steatopygic, wide-hipped; **fat,** adipose, corpulent, crass, fatly, fatted, fattish, gross, obese, overweight, paunchy, plump, poddy *(Brit.)*, podgy, porky, portly, pursy, stout, well-built, well-fed, well-rounded; **thickset,** bulky, bull-necked, fubsy, stocky, stubbed, stubby, stumpy; **solid,** dense, heavy, sodden, stodgy

thick *n* → **1** solidity **2** stupid person *adj* **3** cloudy **4** dark **5** friendly **6** inactive **7** opaque **8** quiet **9** sludgy **10** solid **11** stupid *adv* **12** solidly

THICKENING *n* callosity, callus, coagulation, dilatation, dilation, varicosity; **chunk,** chump, clog, clot

thicket *n* → forest

THICKNESS *n* amplitude, beam, breadth, depth, latitude, third dimension, tread, wideness, width; **diameter,** bore, calibre, gauge, module *(Archit.)*, radius; **extent,** expanse, extensiveness, spread; **bulk,** body, bulkiness; **fullness,** bagginess

thickset *adj* → **1** fat **2** solid **3** thick

THIEF *n* abstracter, acquirer, appropriator, boodler *(U.S.)*, bumper, cribber, cutpurse, dip *(Prison)*, filcher, fingerer, flogger, forty, frisker, head-puller, hoister, jumper *(Mining)*, kleptomaniac, kway, light fingers, lurcher, peter thief *(Prison)*, pickpocket, pilferer, purloiner, pussy-footer, ratter *(Mining)*, robber, shoplifter, sneakthief, snowdropper, stealer, tea-leaf, water-rat *(U.S.)*; **burglar,** cat-burglar, cracksman, housebreaker, picklock, yegg *(U.S.)*; **safebreaker,** safeblower, tankman *(Prison)*; **fence,** receiver of stolen goods; **bandit,** bravo, brigand, bushranger, dacoit, Dick Turpin, footpad, highwayman, knight of the road, mosstrooper, Ned Kelly, pad, poofter-rorter, Robin Hood, thug, waylayer; **pirate,** buccaneer, corsair, filibuster, freebooter, hijacker, marauder, picaroon, privateer, rover *(Archaic)*, sea-robber, sea-rover, skyjacker, viking, wrecker; **looter,** depredator, despoiler, forayer, harpy, marauder, pillager, plunderer, predator, ransacker, rifler, robber baron, sacker, spoiler, spoliator; **kidnapper,** baby snatcher; **body-snatcher,** ghoul, resurrectionist; **cattleduffer,** duffer, gully-raker, horse-duffer, poacher, poddy-dodger, rustler, tea-and-sugar bushranger

thief *n* → extortionist

thieve *v* → rob

THIEVING *adj* burglarious, kleptomaniac, larcenous, light-fingered, stealing; **crooked,**

bent; **piratical,** bushranging, predatory, rapacious, thuggish

thigh *n* → leg

THIN *v* attenuate, fall away, fine, fine-draw, taper; **slim,** count calories, diet, lose weight, reduce, slenderise, take off weight; **emaciate,** extenuate *(Archaic)*, macerate, peak; **narrow,** confine, constrict, straiten

THIN *adj* angular, bony, cadaverous, gaunt, hatchet-faced, lank, meagre, peaked, peaky, poor, raw-boned, scraggy, scrannel *(Archaic)*, scrawny, skinny, thin as a lath, thin as a rail, thin as a rake; **slender,** attenuate, ectomorphic, gracile, lean, light, slight, slim, small, spare, spindly, wiry, wisplike, wispy, wraithlike; **svelte,** hourglass, slinky, waisted, wasp-waisted, waspish, willowish, willowy; **stalky,** asthenic, gangling, gangly, lanky, rangy, spindle-legged, spindle-shanked, spindling; **skeletal,** atrophied, marasmic, tabescent, wasted, weedy; **narrow,** close, cramped, strait *(Archaic)*; **wafer-thin,** eggshell, fine-drawn, paper, papery, papyraceous, wafery; **threadlike,** capreolate, spidery, tendrilous; **bladelike,** lathlike, lathy; **fine,** fine-spun, gossamer, hair's-breadth, hairbreadth, hairline, spiry, subtle, tenuous, terete

thin *v* → **1** disperse **2** etherealise *adj* **3** colourless **4** ethereal **5** few **6** light **7** shrill *adv* **8** intangibly **9** thinly

thing *n* → **1** actuality **2** affair **3** any **4** emotion **5** matter **6** point of view **7** undertaking

THINK *v* allow *(U.S.)*, bash one's brains out, be in a brown study, bethink oneself of *(Archaic)*, brood, cast about, cerebrate, chew over, chew the cud, cogitate, concentrate, conceptualise, consider, contemplate, cudgel one's brains, deliberate, dream of, envisage, free-associate, ideate, introspect, meditate, mull over, muse, opine, perpend *(Archaic)*, ponder, pore over, put on one's thinking cap, reckon, reflect on, reflect upon, revolve in one's mind, ruminate, run upon, speculate, suppose, take into consideration, take it into one's head, take to heart, think out, think over, think through, turn over in one's mind, use one's loaf, use one's noodle, ween *(Archaic)*, weigh up, wonder; **philosophise,** theologise; **rethink,** reconsider, review

think *v* → **1** believe **2** devise **3** expect

THINKER *n* brooder, cogitator, concentrator, contemplator, deliberator, headworker, meditator, muser, philosophiser, puzzler, ruminator

THINKING *n* brown study, cerebration, cogitation, concentration, contemplation, deliberation, free association, headwork, ideation, intellectualisation, introspection, lateral thinking, meditation, musing, philosophism, preoccupation, reconsideration, reflection, rumination, stream of consciousness, thought, wool-gathering; **thoughtfulness,** contemplativeness, deliberativeness, introspectiveness, meditativeness, pensiveness, percept, profoundness, profundity, reflectiveness, transcendentalism

THINKING *adj* cerebral, cogitative, considerate *(Archaic)*, contemplative, deliberative, meditative, museful, musing, pensive, phrenic, preoccupied, reflective, ruminant, ruminative, speculative, thoughtful

THINNESS *n* angularness, cadaverousness, emaciation, gauntness, gracility, lankness, lean and hungry look, marasmus, meagreness, peakiness, poorness, scragginess, scrawniness, skinniness, tabescence; **leanness,** lankiness, slenderness, slightness, slimness, spareness, stalkiness, wiriness; **fineness,** attenuation, foliation, maceration; **tenuousness,** subtleness, subtlety, tenuity; **slimming,** calorie-counting, reducing, slenderising, weight-watching; **narrowing,** intake; **narrowness,** bottleneck, choke, narrow, neck, strait *(Archaic)*; **hairbreadth,** hairline, hairstroke; **blade,** lath, shim, spline, taper, thong; **strip,** belt, fascia, fillet, ray, stripe

THIN PERSON *n* a mere shadow of one's former self, bag of bones, beanpole, beanstalk, Belsen horror, cornstalk, ectomorph, hatchet face, lolly legs, long streak of pelican shit, scarecrow, scrag, skeleton, skin and bones, snapper, spindlelegs, spindleshanks, spindling *(Rare)*, streak, sylph, weed, wisp, wraith; **slimmer,** calorie counter, reducer, weight watcher

THIRD *adj* ternary, tertiary, triennial; **antepenultimate,** third last; **three,** threefold, treble

thirst *n* → **1** desire *v* **2** hunger

THIRSTY *adj* droughty, drouthy, dry, dry as a nun's nasty, dry as a pommy's towel, parched

this *adj* → particular

thither *adj* → **1** distant *adv* **2** remotely

thong *n* → **1** sandal **2** tape **3** thinness

thorax *n* → chest

thorn *n* → **1** annoyance **2** knob **3** piercer

thorny *adj* → **1** annoying **2** difficult **3** protuberant **4** rough **5** spiny

THOROUGH *adj* all-out, all-up, boots-and-all, deep-dyed, dyed-in-the-wool, in-depth, out-and-out, outright, overall, regular *(Colloq.)*, thoroughgoing, thoroughpaced, wholesale; **utter,** arrant, crashing, extreme, grand, gross, proper, stark, unmitigated; **extensive,** broad, clean, clear, cross-country, house-to-house, macroscopic, sweeping, wall-to-wall; **comprehensive,** detailed, encyclopaedic, exhaustive, intensive; **completive,** complemental, complementary, consummative, suppletory. *See also* WHOLE

thorough *adj* → **1** effortful **2** unconditional

thoroughbred *n* → **1** expert *adj* **2** accomplished **3** aristocratic **4** beautiful

thoroughfare *n* → **1** access **2** channel **3** road **4** stream

THOROUGHLY *adv* broadly, comprehensively, exhaustively, extensively, in depth, intensively, sweepingly; **throughout,** across the board, from A to Z, from arsehole to breakfast time, from beginning to end, from end to end, from head to foot, from top to bottom, from top to toe, over, through, through and through; **clear,** broad, clean, hands down, well, wide. *See also* WHOLLY

thou *n* → length

though *adv* → **1** conditionally **2** nevertheless *conj* **3** on condition that

thought *n* → **1** care **2** expected thing **3** idea **4** mind **5** opinion **6** plan **7** small amount **8** thinking

thoughtless *adj* → **1** inattentive **2** neglectful **3** unkind

thrall *n* → **1** repression **2** servant **3** subject *v* **4** repress *adj* **5** repressed

thrash *n* → **1** hit *v* **2** beat **3** defeat **4** set sail

THREAD *n* combed yarn, hank, noil, oakum, pack-thread, pick, pile, ply, rope yarn, rove, roving, sleave, sliver, slub, strand, thrum, tops, tram, yarn; **fibre,** fibril, filament, filum; **man-made fibre,** acetate fibre, carbon fibre, lurex, monofil, tinsel; **floss,** dental floss; **tendril,** byssus *(Zool.)*, chalaza, chord, cobweb, crosshair, gossamer, neurofibril, promycelium *(Bot.)*, tentacle, vegetable silk; **skein,** ball, clew, cop *(Textiles)*, hank; **fishing line,** dropline, gut line, line, tackle, trawl line; **fibrillation.** *See also* CORD; STRING

thread *n* → **1** line **2** spiral **3** twist **4** weave *v* **5** advance **6** cook **7** cord **8** cut

threadbare *adj* → old

threat *n* → **1** challenge **2** command **3** danger **4** force **5** menace **6** warning

THREE *n* hat-trick, leash *(Sport)*, tern, ternary, ternion, threesome, triad, trilogy, trine, trinity, trio, triple, triunity; **triarchy,** trimester, triumvirate, troika; **triplet,** triplicate; **triennium; three-piece,** triplex

three *adj* → third

three-dimensional *adj* → **1** realistic **2** spacious

thresh *v* → **1** cudgel **2** harvest

threshold *n* → **1** airport **2** limit **3** starting line

thrice *adv* → triply

THRIFT *n* abstemiousness, chariness, forehandedness *(U.S.)*, frugality, frugalness, saving, spareness, sparingness, thriftiness; **economy,** carefulness, husbandry, providence, prudence; **economisation,** cost cutting, economies of scale, good housekeeping

THRIFTY *adj* economic, economical, frugal, money-conscious, notable *(Archaic)*, penny-wise, provident, saving; **abstemious,** careful, chary, forehanded *(U.S.)*, spare, sparing

thrill *n* → **1** excitement **2** perception **3** pleasure **4** vibration *v* **5** excite **6** feel emotion **7** vibrate

thriller *n* → **1** book **2** story

thrive *v* → **1** become greater **2** be healthy **3** be wealthy **4** flower **5** prosper

throat *n* → neck

throb *n* → **1** ache **2** vibration *v* **3** feel emotion **4** pain **5** vibrate

throe *n* → **1** ache **2** emotion **3** turbulence

thrombosis *n* → solid body

throne *n* → **1** authority **2** chair

throng *n* → **1** gathering **2** many *v* **3** abound **4** fill **5** gather

throttle *n* → **1** accelerator **2** steering wheel

through *adv* → **1** regularly **2** thoroughly *prep* **3** at **4** during **5** inclusive of

throughout *adv* → **1** thoroughly *prep* **2** during

THROW *n* cast, chuck, fling, flirt, heave, hurl, incurve *(Baseball)*, put, shy, toss, upcast; **bowl,** bumper, chinaman, delivery, flier, flipper, floater, full pitch, full toss, gazunder, googly, half-volley, inswinger, leg break, leg spinner, leggie, lob, off break, off spinner, outswinger, pitch, topspinner, wrong 'un, yorker; **pass,** flick pass *(Aus. Rules)*, flickback *(Rugby Football)*, flip pass *(Ice Hockey)*

THROW *v* bung, cant, cast, chuck, dart, dash, detrude, fling, flip, heave, hoy, hurl, hurtle, jerk, launch, let fly, lob, pass, peg, pitch, pitchfork, shoot, shy, skim, sling, toss, whirl *(Obs.)*; **bowl,** deliver, flight, pitch; **flop,** dump, flump, plunk, precipitate, whop

throw *n* → **1** bedclothes **2** length **3** luck *v* **4** astonish **5** confuse **6** give birth **7** lift **8** lower **9** sew **10** shape

THROWER *n* caster, flinger, heaver, hurler, impeller, pitcher, precipitator, tosser; **bowler,** deliverer, pace bowler, paceman, spinner

THROW OUT *v* file in the w.p.b., put on the scrap-heap, remainder, scrap

thrum *n* → **1** click **2** edge **3** textiles **4** thread *v* **5** cord **6** hit **7** insert **8** ring **9** speak

THRUST *n* detrusion, jerk, jostle, push, ram, shove, upthrust; **impetus,** drift, drive, impulse, impulsion, jet propulsion, projection, propulsion, send *(Naut.)*, sweep; **trundle,** roll

THRUST *v* boot home, crowd, jostle, push, ram, shoulder, shove; **propel,** drive, impel, launch, precipitate, project, send; **roll,** pedal, trundle, wheel; **edge,** elbow, nudge, poke; **flick,** fillip, flirt

thrust *n* → **1** attack **2** energy **3** power **4** stroke *v* **5** perforate

thud *n* → **1** boom **2** impact *v* **3** boom **4** hit

thug *n* → **1** killer **2** thief **3** violent person **4** vulgarian

thumb *n* → **1** glove *v* **2** dirty **3** touch

thump *n* → **1** boom **2** explosion **3** impact *v* **4** be loud **5** boom **6** explode **7** fight **8** hit **9** rob **10** walk

thunder *n* → **1** boom **2** explosion **3** loud sound **4** menace **5** weather *v* **6** be angry **7** be loud **8** be violent **9** boom **10** explode **11** menace

thunderbolt *n* → **1** angry person **2** destroyer **3** frightener **4** rock **5** spear **6** surpriser

thus *adv* → **1** after **2** how

thwart *n* → **1** crosspiece *v* **2** argue **3** discourage **4** disenchant **5** hinder *adj* **6** calamitous **7** crossing **8** stubborn

thyroid *adj* → bodily

tiara *n* → **1** headgear **2** jewellery

tic *n* → cramp

tick *n* → **1** click **2** moment **3** quiet sound **4** sign *v* **5** click **6** mark **7** publicise

ticket *n* → **1** account **2** hallucinogen **3** label **4** list **5** public notice *v* **6** label

tickle *n* → **1** touch *v* **2** amuse **3** arouse **4** please **5** touch

ticklish *adj* → **1** difficult **2** perceptive **3** uncertain **4** undetermined

tidal wave *n* → **1** current **2** surf

tiddler *n* → **1** animal offspring **2** children **3** fish

tide *n* → **1** crucial moment **2** current **3** holy day **4** point of view **5** season

TIDILY *adv* neatly, shipshape, snug, snugly, straight, to rights, trim

TIDINESS *n* apple-pie order, eutaxy, harmony, methodicalness, neatness, orderliness, regularity, snugness, systematism, tautness, trim, trimness

tidings *n* → news

TIDY *v* do up, dress, fettle *(Archaic)*, groom, neaten, put one's house in order, set one's house in order, straighten, tidy up, trig; **array,** file, interfile, lay out, place, set out; **dispose,** align, collate, collocate, distribute, justify *(Print)*, right; **marshal,** draw up, dress, form up *(Mil.)*, rally, regiment, troop *(Mil.)*

TIDY *adj* feat *(Archaic)*, just so, neat, regular, smug, snug, tiddly *(Naut.)*, trig, trim, well-groomed; **well-ordered,** shipshape, spick-and-span, taut, trim; **disciplined,** obedient, well-behaved

tidy *n* → **1** covering **2** rubbish bin *adj* **3** great

tie *n* → **1** belt **2** bond **3** combine **4** equal **5** musical score **6** neckwear **7** obligation **8** relationship **9** restraints **10** string **11** tape *v* **12** cord **13** equal **14** fasten **15** join **16** marry **17** obligate **18** promise

tier *n* → **1** fastener **2** layer

tiff *n* → **1** irritation *v* **2** contest

tiger *n* → **1** hero **2** shearer *v* **3** make an effort *interj* **4** cooee

tight *adj* → **1** difficult **2** drunk **3** few **4** full **5** mean **6** steady **7** sticky **8** strict *adv* **9** hard **10** steadily

tightrope *n* → cord

TIGHTS *n* bodystocking, leg warmers, leotard, maillot; **stocking,** hose, nylons, pantihose. *See also* UNDERWEAR

tiki *n* → portrait

tile *n* → **1** building materials **2** coating **3** paving *v* **4** cover

till *n* → **1** box **2** rock outcrop **3** soil **4** treasury *v* **5** farm **6** furrow *conj* **7** while

tiller *n* → **1** bar **2** farmhand *v* **3** flower

tilt *n* → **1** roof **2** slope **3** stroke *v* **4** attack **5** fight **6** slope

TIMBER *n* bentwood, cabinet wood, driftwood, hardwood, matchwood, millwork, softwood, stumpage *(U.S.)*, veneer, wood, wrought timber; **woodchips,** wood flour, wood pulp, woodwool; **lumber,** clog, fascine, flitch, four-by-two, log, nog, plank, rollway *(U.S.)*, sawlog, scantling, shake, splint, stay, stick, stock, stud, two-by-four, yule log; **chipboard,** beaverboard *(U.S.)*, boxboard, cane-ite, corkboard, Gibraltar board *(N.Z.)*, particle board, pegboard, strawboard; **woods,** amboyna, bamboo, basswood, beech, birch, black locust, black pine, box, briarroot, briarwood, brushwood, calabash, calamander, calamus, camphorwood, candlewood, cedar, cypress, durmast, ebony, elm, fir, gopherwood, greenheart, guaiacum, gum, hazel, hickory, Huon pine, ironwood, kingwood, lancewood, larch, lignum vitae, loblolly, logwood, longleaf pine, mahogany, mallet, maple, Monterey pine, mulga, myall, oak, padauk, partridge-wood, pine, poon, poplar, red bean, red beech, red cedar, red fir, red oak, redwood, rosewood, saffronheart, sandalwood, santal, satinwood, shagbark, shittim wood, spruce, sumach, tamarack, teak, tupelo, wainscot, walnut, white birch, white cedar, white pine, white poplar, whitewood, wicopy *(U.S.)*, willow, yew, yiel-yiel, zebrawood

timber *n* → **1** character **2** raw materials **3** shaft *v* **4** support *interj* **5** hey

TIME *n* Father Time, fourth dimension, Kronos, race *(Archaic)*, sands of time, space-time, years; **fixed time,** chronogram, date, hour, obit, operative date *(Law)*, pull date, zero hour; **office hours,** flexitime, gliding time, overtime

TIME *v* clock, keep time, minute; **date; bundy on,** clock in, clock on, punch the bundy; **periodise**

time *n* → **1** accomplishment **2** birth **3** crucial moment **4** death **5** finish **6** imprisonment **7** interval **8** moment **9** period **10** rate **11** rhythm *adj* **12** temporal

timeless *adj* → eternal

TIMELINESS *n* good timing, opportuneness, propitiousness, seasonableness; **punctuality,** promptitude, promptness, punctualness

TIMELY *adj* opportune, pat, ripe, seasonable, synchronised, well-timed; **punctual,** prompt; **crucial,** critical; **last-minute,** eleventh-hour

TIMELY *adv* critically, in due course, in season, opportunely; **punctually,** in good time, on cue, on the beat, on the dot, on the knocker, on the nail, on the tick, on time, promptly, seasonably, sharp; **in the nick of time,** betimes, in time

timely *adj* → **1** early **2** expedient *adv* **3** early

TIMEPIECE *n* clepsydra, horologe, sundial, timekeeper, water-clock; **clock,** alarm clock, astronomical clock, atomic clock, caesium clock, chronograph, chronometer, cuckoo clock, digital clock, grandfather clock, grandmother clock, photochronograph; **watch,** block, digital watch, hunter, hunting watch, repeater, stem-winder, ticker, wristwatch; **biological clock,** biological timeclock; **timer,** autotimer, bundy, chronopher, chronoscope, chronotron, eggtimer, hourglass, parking meter, sandglass, stopwatch, time clock; **time signal,** curfew, last post, pips, retreat, reveille, taps *(U.S. Mil.)*, wait *(Obs.)*

TIME SHEET *n* cheat sheet, plod, schedule, timebook, timecard, timetable

timetable *n* → 1 agenda 2 classification 3 plan 4 time sheet *v* 5 order 6 plan

timid *adj* → 1 cowardly 2 frightened 3 unwilling

TIMIDLY *adv* basely, cravenly, faintheartedly, fearfully, fearsomely, in a blue funk, in a funk, nervelessly, pusillanimously, recreantly, spinelessly, tamely

timing *n* → 1 regularity 2 simultaneity

timorous *adj* → frightened

tin *n* → 1 drinking vessel *v* 2 coat 3 conserve *adj* 4 bad

tincture *n* → 1 dye 2 medication 3 mixture 4 small amount *v* 5 colour 6 mix

tinder *n* → 1 fuel 2 lighter

tine *n* → piercer

tinge *n* → 1 colour 2 small amount 3 taste *v* 4 colour 5 taste

tingle *n* → 1 perception 2 telecommunications 3 touch 4 turbulence *v* 5 pain

tinker *n* → 1 repairer *v* 2 bungle 3 repair

tinkle *n* → 1 quiet sound 2 ringing 3 telecommunications *v* 4 ring 5 urinate

tinny *n* → 1 drinking vessel *adj* 2 lucky 3 metallic 4 quiet 5 shrill 6 unsavoury

tinsel *n* → 1 lace 2 thread 3 trimming *v* 4 vulgarise *adj* 5 cheap 6 showy 7 vulgar

tint *n* → 1 colour *v* 2 colour 3 depict 4 photograph

tiny *adj* → small

tip *n* → 1 allowance 2 extremity 3 garbage dump 4 gift 5 gratefulness 6 guidance 7 idea 8 information 9 overturn 10 pat 11 prediction 12 sharp point 13 top *v* 14 give 15 hit 16 overturn 17 predict 18 slope

tipple *n* → 1 a drink *v* 2 drink alcohol

tipsy *adj* → drunk

tiptoe *v* → 1 be cautious 2 trick *adj* 3 expectant 4 secretive

tirade *n* → 1 harangue 2 reprimand 3 subject matter 4 written composition

TIRE *v* do in, exhaust, fag, fatigue, knock up, poop, prostrate, root, take it out of, tucker, use up, weary, whack; **jade,** frazzle, irk; **overwork,** drive, gruel, outwear, overwear, put through the mangle, shag, strain, task, tax, wear

tire *n* → 1 clothes 2 hairdressing 3 headgear *v* 4 be bored with 5 bore 6 clothe 7 decorate

TIRED *adj* bug-eyed, dull, fatigued, footsore, heavy-eyed, heavy-laden, jaded, jadish, on one's last legs, overweary, sleepy, toilworn, war-weary, wayworn, weariful, weary, worn, worn-out; **exhausted,** fordone *(Archaic)*, overwrought, prostrate, psychasthenic, rundown, spent, strained, stretched, wrung-out; **all in,** beat, beaten, blown, buggered, bushed, bushwhacked, clapped-out, dead, dog-tired, done for, done in, euchred, fagged, far gone, flat as a tack, flat out, fucked, jack, jiggered up, knackered, knocked-up, out for the count, pooped, R.S., ratshit, rooted, shagged, stonkered, washed-out, washed-up, wasted, whacked, wrecked, zapped, zonked; **like death,** green at the gills, half-dead, like death warmed up, white at the gills

tired *adj* → 1 mediocre 2 ordinary

TIREDNESS *n* fatigue, lassitude, wearifulness, weariness; **jadedness,** jadishness, staleness; **over-tiredness,** frazzle, psychasthenia, strain; **exhaustion,** battle fatigue, collapse, combat fatigue, inanition, limit of endurance, prostration, wornness

tiresome *adj* → 1 annoying 2 boring 3 tiring

TIRING *adj* exhaustive, gruelling, irksome, killing, tiresome, wearing, wearisome

tissue *n* → 1 coating 2 tangle 3 textiles 4 tobacco

tit *n* → 1 bulge 2 chest

titbit *n* → good thing

tithe *n* → 1 obligation 2 small amount 3 tax *v* 4 charge 5 pay

titian *n* → 1 red *adj* 2 brown

titillate *v* → 1 allure 2 arouse 3 eroticise

titivate *v* → decorate

TITLE *n* bastard title, caption, half-title, heading, masthead, rubric, subheading, subtitle, titlepage; **signature,** autograph, by-line, endorsement, henry, mark, subscription

title *n* → 1 book 2 church 3 entitlement 4 evidence 5 justification 6 name 7 ownership 8 rights *v* 9 name

titter *n* → 1 mirth *v* 2 laugh

tittle *n* → 1 bit 2 sign 3 small amount

tittle-tattle *n* → 1 gossip *v* 2 reveal

titular *n* → name

tizz *n* → 1 confusion 2 worry

T.N.T. *n* → 1 ammunition 2 explosive

toad *n* → 1 bad person 2 ugly person

toady *n* → 1 crawler 2 flatterer *v* 3 flatter 4 grovel

toast *n* → 1 a drink 2 applause 3 congratulation 4 tribute *v* 5 approve 6 brown 7 cook 8 drink alcohol 9 fire 10 offer 11 rejoice

TOBACCO *n* baccy, flat *(Prison)*, nicotine, snout, weed; **plug,** nailrod, niggerhead, pigtail, quid, twist; **broadleaf,** caporal, cavendish, perique, shag; **snuff,** maccaboy, rappee; **cigarette,** african, cancer stick, ciggie, coffin nail, dart, durry, fag, gasper *(Brit.)*, O.P., reefer, skag, smoke; **tailor-made,** filter, filter tip; **roll-your-own,** greyhound, racehorse, rollie; **the makings,** cigarette paper, filler, tissue, wrapper; **fag-end,** bumper, butt, dottle; **cigar,** cheroot, cigarillo, claro, panatella, perfecto, toby jug *(U.S.)*; **pipe,** briar, briar-root, briarwood, chibouk, churchwarden, clay pipe, corncob, doodie, dudeen *(Irish)*, matchbox, meerschaum; **water pipe,** bong, chillum, hookah, hubble-bubble, kalian, narghile; **peace-pipe,** calumet, pipe of peace; **pipestem,** bowl; **drag,** drawback, puff, pull, toke, whiff

tobacconist *n* → shop

toboggan *n* → sledge

today *n* → 1 the present *adv* 2 now

toddle *n* → 1 walking *v* 2 walk

to-do *n* → 1 busyness 2 commotion

toe *n* → 1 extremity 2 knob 3 leg *v* 4 kick

toey *adj* → **1** desirous **2** enthusiastic **3** excited **4** frightened **5** sexy **6** speedy **7** worried

toff *n* → wealthy person

tog *v* → clothe

toga *n* → overcoat

TOGETHER *adv* at one blow, jointly; **collectively,** associatively, conjointly, conjunctionally, coordinately

together *adj* → **1** competent *adv* **2** accumulatively **3** closely **4** collectively **5** cooperatively **6** in company with **7** relatively **8** simultaneously

toggle *n* → **1** button **2** rod

TOIL *n* donkey work, drudgery, fag, graft, grind, moil, slavery, slog, sweat, swink *(Archaic)*; **laboriousness,** arduousness, burdensomeness, operoseness, strenuosity, strenuousness, sweatiness, toilsomeness; **burden,** backbreaker, chore, fatigue, load, task

toil *n* → **1** act of war **2** contest *v* **3** make an effort **4** persist **5** walk **6** work

TOILET *n* bathroom, bog, brasco, can *(U.S.)*, carzey *(Brit.)*, crapper, did, diddy, dumpty, dunny, dyke, euphemism, garderobe *(Archaic)*, head *(Naut.)*, jakes *(Archaic)*, jerry, john, la, la-di-da, latrine, lav, lavatory, little girls' room, loo, low-down suite, Mary's room, pan, pedestal, pisser, roundhouse, smallest room, the throne, toot, urinal, water-closet, WC; **outhouse,** backhouse *(U.S.)*, boghouse, cloaca, dunny, earth closet, pissaphone, privy, shed, shithouse, shouse, stool, the little house; **public toilet,** amenities, convenience, gents, ladies, powder room, public convenience, rest room, toilet facilities; **sanitary can,** chemical toilet, dry pan, dunny can, honey pot, thunderbox; **bedpan,** bedroom mug, bottle, chamber, chamber-pot, commode, gozunder, jerry, pot, potty, thunder-mug, tub *(Prison)*; **cesspool,** cess, cesspit, sink *(Rare)*; **sewerage,** sep, septic, septic system, septic tank, sewage farm, sewer; **sanitary man,** Dan, sanny man; **night cart,** dunny cart, honey cart, seventeen door sedan; **kitty litter,** deep litter

toilet *n* → **1** cleansing **2** medical treatment

toiletry *n* → cleanser

token *n* → **1** memento **2** sign

told *adj* → informed

tolerable *adj* → **1** bearable **2** healthy **3** mediocre **4** ordinary

TOLERANCE *n* broad-mindedness, cosmopolitanism, cosmopolitism, open-mindedness, receptiveness, receptivity, unbiasedness; **latitude,** toleration; **liberality,** breadth, catholicity, generosity, generousness, large-mindedness, liberalness; **liberalism,** latitudinarianism, tolerationism

TOLERANT *adj* generous, open, open-minded, receptive, unbiased, unprejudiced; **broad-minded,** cosmopolitan, large-minded, latitudinous, permissive; **liberal,** catholic, freethinking, latitudinarian, liberal-minded, liberalist, liberalistic

tolerate *v* → **1** permit **2** persevere

toll *n* → **1** rights **2** ringing **3** tax *v* **4** allure **5** publicise **6** ring

tomahawk *n* → **1** axe **2** sword *v* **3** cut **4** kill **5** shear

tomb *n* → **1** cave **2** grave *v* **3** bury

tomboy *n* → **1** children **2** woman

tombstone *n* → **1** grave **2** label **3** memento **4** rock

tome *n* → book

TOMFOOL *v* act the angora, act the goat, antic *(Obs.)*, arse about, arse around, arsehole about, bugger around, fart about, fuck around, make a joe of oneself, mess around, muck around, play silly buggers, ponce

tomfoolery *n* → **1** foolery **2** jewellery **3** nonsense

tomorrow *n* → **1** future *adv* **2** in the future

tom-tom *n* → boom

ton *n* → hundred

tone *n* → **1** character **2** colour **3** fashion **4** fine arts **5** good taste **6** health **7** perceptivity **8** pliability **9** sound **10** speaking *v* **11** colour **12** photograph **13** sound

tongs *n* → holder

tongue *n* → **1** footgear **2** headland **3** knob **4** language **5** mouth **6** nonsense **7** resonator **8** rod **9** speaking *v* **10** contact **11** scold **12** speak

tonic *n* → **1** drink **2** repairer *adj* **3** encouraging **4** medicinal **5** pliable **6** spoken **7** wholesome

tonight *n* → **1** future **2** the present *adv* **3** in the future **4** now

tonnage *n* → **1** contents **2** freight

tonsillitis *n* → cold

tonsure *n* → **1** hairdressing *v* **2** bare **3** take the cloth

too *adv* → **1** additionally **2** excessively **3** in fact **4** very

TOOL *n* artefact, implement, instrument, utensil; **gadget,** gismo, jigger; **stock-in-trade,** haberdashery, hardware, ironmongery, ironware, notions

tool *n* → **1** groin **2** knife **3** method **4** victim *v* **5** cut **6** drive **7** shape

toot *n* → **1** birdcall **2** toilet *v* **3** shrill

tooth *n* → **1** animal part **2** knob **3** leaf **4** mouth **5** piercer **6** taste *v* **7** contact

TOP *n* acme, apex, apogee, cap, crown, foreside, head, height, ne plus ultra, peak, pinnacle, summit, tip, tiptop, upper limit, vertex, zenith; **top layer,** ceiling, housetop, roof, rooftop, treetop, watertable; **topside,** bridge, upperdeck, upside; **topping,** coating, surfacing; **crownpiece,** abacus *(Archit.)*, capital, capitulum, capstone, chapiter, copestone, coping, crest, crown, crowner, head, headpiece, pediment, summer; **crest,** arête, cap, cop *(Obs.)*, cope, lip, ridge, watershed; **climax,** crest of the wave, culmination, high point, peak

TOP *v* cap, crest, crown, head, overlook, overshadow, overtop; **surmount,** bestraddle, bestride, mount, pinnacle, ride, scale, transcend; **climax,** culminate, peak

TOP *adj* apical, apogeal, apogean, ceiling *(Colloq.)*, climactic, culminant, head, meridian, supermedial, tiptop, topmost, zenithal; **overtopping,** overlooking, superincumbent, transcendent, transcending

top hat *n* → **1** hat **2** stand

topiary *n* → gardening

topic *n* → subject matter

TOPICAL *adj* apposite, bearing on the matter, germane, pertinent, relative, relevant

topical *adj* → **1** bodily **2** medicinal **3** regional

topology *n* → shape

topple *v* → **1** fall **2** lower

topside *n* → top

topsoil *n* → **1** fertile land **2** soil *v* **3** cover

topsy-turvy *n* → **1** overturn *adj* **2** disorderly **3** overturned *adv* **4** oppositely **5** untidily

tor *n* → mound

torch *n* → **1** candle **2** criminal **3** lighter **4** lighting

toreador *n* → **1** fighter **2** killer

torment *n* → **1** annoyance **2** corporal punishment **3** pain **4** turbulence **5** victimisation *v* **6** act unkindly **7** agitate **8** annoy **9** pain

TORMENTOR *n* afflicter, crucifier, harmer, sadomasochist, torturer

tornado *n* → **1** busyness **2** explosion **3** outburst **4** spin **5** violent outburst **6** weather **7** wind

torpedo *n* → **1** ammunition **2** sleeping-pill *v* **3** explode **4** fall **5** ruin **6** wage war

torpor *n* → **1** apathy **2** idleness **3** period of inaction **4** sleeping

torque *n* → **1** energy **2** jewellery **3** rotation

torrent *n* → **1** flow **2** much **3** outburst **4** rainfall **5** stream

torrid *adj* → **1** dry **2** emotional **3** hot

torsion *n* → circuitousness

torso *n* → **1** chest **2** painting

tort *n* → **1** crime **2** wrong

tortoise *n* → **1** armour **2** fortification **3** slowcoach

tortoiseshell *n* → **1** cat *adj* **2** multicoloured

tortuous *adj* → **1** deceitful **2** deflective **3** twisting

torture *n* → **1** corporal punishment **2** pain *v* **3** act unkindly **4** distort **5** pain **6** punish

TOSS *v* roll about, toss and turn, twist, welter *(Obs.)*, writhe; **seethe,** boil, churn, fret, heave; **flutter,** flitter, quake, ripple, ruffle; **convulse,** palpitate

toss *n* → **1** gambling **2** throw **3** turbulence *v* **4** create **5** flutter **6** gamble **7** lift **8** throw

toss-up *n* → gambling

tot *n* → **1** a drink **2** alcohol container **3** computation **4** offspring **5** small amount

total *n* → **1** addition **2** computation **3** score **4** whole *v* **5** compute *adj* **6** inclusive **7** unconditional **8** whole

totalisator *n* → **1** computer **2** gambling hall

totalitarian *n* → **1** political ideologist *adj* **2** autocratic

totality *n* → whole

tote *v* → transport

totem *n* → **1** emblem **2** portrait **3** sign

totter *n* → **1** flutter *v* **2** flutter **3** walk **4** weaken

TOUCH *n* contact, feel, handle; **stroke,** brush, chuck, flick, graze, pat, tap, trait *(Rare)*; **feeling,** fingering, handling, manipulation, palpation; **massage,** rub, rub-down, squeezing; **sense of touch,** palpability, tact, tactility; **touch sensation,** itchiness, pins-and-needles, ticklishness; **tickle,** itch, tingle. *See also* TEXTURE

TOUCH *v* feel, palp *(Obs.)*, palpate; **handle,** fiddle with, finger, manipulate, thumb, twiddle; **tickle,** kittle *(Brit.)*, prickle, scratch; **pat,** chuck, tap; **stroke,** brush, graze, knead, massage, paddle, pat, rub; **grope,** feel up, grabble, palm, paw, taste *(Obs.)*

touch *n* → **1** characteristics **2** contact **3** fine arts **4** illness **5** imprint **6** label **7** loan **8** musicianship **9** pat **10** payment **11** request **12** ringing **13** small amount **14** test *v* **15** beg **16** borrow **17** change **18** contact **19** hit **20** influence **21** mark **22** press **23** relate

touching *adj* → **1** contacting **2** emotive **3** encouraging **4** tactile

touchstone *n* → tester

touchy *adj* → **1** dangerous **2** emotional **3** fiery **4** irritable **5** perceptive

tough *n* → **1** violent person *adj* **2** brutal **3** callous **4** difficult **5** durable **6** hard **7** persevering **8** sludgy **9** stubborn **10** unpleasant *adv* **11** angrily

toupee *n* → hairpiece

tour *n* → **1** journey **2** race **3** visit *v* **4** perform **5** travel **6** visit

tourist *n* → **1** sportsman **2** traveller **3** visitor

tournament *n* → contest

tourniquet *n* → **1** medication **2** press **3** tape

tousle *n* → **1** hair **2** untidiness *v* **3** be violent **4** untidy

tout *n* → **1** seller *v* **2** gamble **3** look **4** publicise **5** sell

tow *n* → **1** cord **2** pull *v* **3** pull *adj* **4** yellow

toward *adj* → **1** apt **2** favourable **3** future

towards *prep* → **1** concerning **2** near

towel *n* → **1** drier *v* **2** beat **3** defeat **4** dry **5** rub

towelling *n* → **1** hitting **2** losing **3** textiles

TOWER *n* acropolis, beacon, belfry, bell-tower, belvedere, broach spire, campanile, column, conning tower, cooling tower, cupola, dome, elevator, helter-skelter *(Brit.)*, Martello tower, minaret, pagoda, peel *(Brit.)*, pile, pillar, pylon, pyramid, shot tower, silo, skyscraper, spire, steeple, transmission tower, turret, watchtower; **perch,** coign of vantage, crow's nest, eyrie, lookout, vantage point; **loft,** attic, garret, hayloft, mansard roof, upstairs. *See also* APEX; HEIGHT

TOWER *v* bestride, command, crown, dominate, domineer, overhang, overlie, overlook, overshadow, overtop, rise above, stand over, surmount, tower above; **soar,** ascend, climb, mount, rise; **have a bird's-eye view,** be suspended, hang, hover, perch

tower *n* → **1** fortress **2** prison *v* **3** ascend

TOWN *n* boom town, closed town, company town, exurb, fishing town, ghost town, growth centre, home town, market town, mining town, outport, port, rail town, satellite town, seaport, township; **country town,** Bandywallop, Bullamakanka, clachan, county town *(Brit.)*, hamlet, kainga *(N.Z.)*, kampong *(S.E. Asia)*, kraal *(Africa)*, one-horse town, pa *(N.Z.)*, settlement, subtopia *(Brit.)*, village, whistlestop *(U.S.)*; **main street,** outskirts, pedestrian plaza, shopping centre, shopping mall, shopping precinct *(Brit.)*. *See also* CITY

town *n* → **1** administrative area **2** community

town house *n* → house

township *n* → **1** population **2** town

toxin *n* → poison

toy *n* → **1** amusement **2** flirt **3** unimportant thing *v* **4** amuse oneself

trachea *n* → neck

trachoma *n* → faulty sight

track *n* → **1** direction **2** line **3** method **4** path **5** racecourse **6** railway **7** recording **8** route **9** transporter *v* **10** adjust **11** beat a path **12** extend **13** pursue

tracksuit *n* → sportswear

tract *n* → **1** essay **2** period **3** prayer **4** region

tractable *adj* → **1** easy **2** influenced **3** obedient **4** obsequious **5** soft

traction *n* → **1** friction **2** pulling

tractor *n* → **1** aeroplane **2** puller **3** vehicle

TRADE *n* adventure, barter, big business, biz, business, buying and selling, concern, dealings, exchange, market, operation, trading, traffic, venture; **commerce,** brokerage, commercialism, marketing, mercantilism, merchandising; **export,** drop shipment, exportation, re-exportation, shipment, shipping; **importation; smuggling,** free trade *(Obs.)*, running

TRADE *v* barter, cheapen *(Archaic)*, deal, dicker *(U.S.)*, export, fair-trade, go offshore, handle, import, jew *(Derog.)*, market, merchandise, overtrade, re-export, recapitalise, smuggle, trade in, traffic, wheel and deal; **negotiate,** bargain, chaffer, haggle, higgle, huckster

trade *n* → **1** exchange **2** interaction **3** job **4** trader *v* **5** exchange

trade in *v* → trade

trade-in *n* → exchange

trademark *n* → **1** emblem **2** intellectual property **3** label **4** name

trade name *n* → **1** language **2** name

TRADER *n* bourgeois, chandler, chapman *(Archaic)*, dealer, free-trader, kulak *(Russian Hist.)*, marketeer, merchant, merchant prince, middleman, monger; **tradespeople,** private sector, trade; **businessman,** adventurer, businesswoman, commercialist, entrepreneur, little man, mercantilist, merchandiser, small businessman, tycoon, wheeler-dealer; **broker,** agent, forwarding agent, ship-broker, syndic; **barterer,** bargainer, exchanger, stag; **smuggler,** courier, drug-runner, free-trader *(Obs.)*

trader *n* → **1** seller **2** watercraft

TRADE UNION *n* artel, brotherhood, guild, industrial union, labour union, mystery *(Archaic)*; **chapel,** local *(U.S.)*; **shop committee,** works committee

TRADE UNIONIST *n* guildsman, labour, redfed *(Colloq.)*, syndicalist, unionist, Wobbly; **union delegate,** delegate, delo, organiser, rep, shop steward; **striker,** picketer

tradition *n* → custom

traffic *n* → **1** exchange **2** trade **3** transport *v* **4** contravene **5** trade **6** transport

tragedy *n* → **1** drama **2** misfortune

tragic *adj* → **1** calamitous **2** distressing **3** dramatic

trail *n* → **1** line **2** path **3** second **4** sequence **5** sign **6** smell *v* **7** beat a path **8** flood **9** go slowly **10** hang **11** idle **12** line **13** pull **14** pursue

trailer *n* → **1** antecedent **2** caravan **3** film **4** incentive **5** plant **6** public notice **7** wagon

TRAIN *n* boat-train, cane train, container train, division, freight train, goods train, mail, metro, mixed train, picker-up, rattler *(U.S. Colloq.)*, special, sweeper, tube train *(Brit.)*, unit *(N.Z.)*; **locomotive,** bank engine, banker, chuff-chuff, chuffer, diesel, engine, iron horse *(Archaic)*, loci *(N.Z.)*, loco, mogul, puffer; **rolling stock,** bogie cattle wagon, bogie sheep van, boxcar *(U.S.)*, brake van, buffet car, caboose *(U.S.)*, car, carriage, coach, corf, couchette, day coach *(U.S.)*, dining car, display van, dogbox carriage, flat-top, freight car *(U.S.)*, goods wagon, guard's van, hopper car, louvre van, luggage van, observation car, railcar, railcarriage, railcoach, railmotor, restaurant car, roomette *(U.S.)*, saloon car, skip, sleeper, sleeping car, smoker, tank wagon, tender, tin hare, truck, van, wagon, wagon-lit, water-carrier; **section car,** flivver, kalamazoo, quad, quadracycle, velocipede *(N.Z. Railways)*; **Chips,** Fish, Ghan, Indian Pacific, Newcastle Flier, Overlander, Prospector, Puffing Billy, Rocket, Silver Fern *(N.Z.)*, Southern Aurora, Spirit of Progress, Sunlander, The Alice, XPT

train *n* → **1** explosive **2** lighter **3** line **4** meteor **5** pendant **6** result **7** sequence **8** series *v* **9** direct **10** drive **11** prepare **12** study **13** teach

trainee *n* → learner

traipse *v* → walk

trait *n* → **1** character **2** characteristic **3** touch

traitor *n* → **1** betrayer **2** disobeyer **3** enemy

trajectory *n* → **1** curve **2** direction **3** length **4** route

TRAM *n* buckjumper, cable car, cable tram, dreadnought, dummy, inclinator, streetcar *(U.S.)*, toast-rack, trailing tram, tramcar, trolley, trolley car *(U.S.)*, trolleybus; **cable car,** telpher

tram *n* → **1** precision **2** thread *v* **3** be precise **4** drive

trammel *n* → **1** restraints **2** stand *v* **3** restrain

tramp *n* → **1** click **2** promiscuous person **3** traveller **4** walk **5** watercraft *v* **6** travel **7** walk

trample *n* → **1** pressing *v* **2** press **3** walk

trampoline *v* → jump
trance *n* → 1 sleeping 2 unconsciousness
tranquil *adj* → 1 composed 2 moderate 3 peaceful
tranquilliser *n* → 1 drug 2 moderator
transact *v* → 1 accomplish 2 do
transcend *v* → 1 etherealise 2 surpass 3 top
transcendental *n* → 1 number *adj* 2 delusive 3 fantastic 4 spiritual 5 superior 6 supernatural
transcribe *v* → 1 change 2 copy 3 translate
transfer *n* → 1 copy 2 defection 3 defector 4 label 5 transport *v* 6 transport
transfigure *v* → 1 change 2 improve 3 worship
transfix *v* → perforate
transform *n* → 1 mathematical operation *v* 2 change
transformer *n* → changer
transgress *v* → 1 be immoral 2 disobey
transient *n* → 1 temporary appointment *adj* 2 ethereal 3 impermanent 4 momentary
transistor *n* → 1 radio *adj* 2 electric
transit *n* → 1 change 2 protractor 3 transport *v* 4 pass through 5 rotate
transition *n* → 1 change 2 pitch 3 radioactivation
transitive *adj* → variable
transitory *adj* → 1 changeable 2 dead 3 ethereal 4 impermanent
TRANSLATE *v* render, transcribe, transliterate, turn, vernacularise; **decipher,** decode, demystify, solve, unravel; **rephrase,** metaphrase, paraphrase, reword, simplify, spell out; **lip-read**
translate *v* → 1 change 2 glorify 3 transport
TRANSLATION *n* transcript, transcription, transliteration, vernacularisation; **paraphrase,** abridgement, epitome, metaphrase, précis, resumé, rewording, simplification; **version,** lection, reading, rendering, rendition, varia lectio; **construction,** angle, construe, sense, slant, understanding
TRANSLATOR *n* dragoman, lip-reader, transcriber, vernacularist; **decoder,** decipherer
translucent *adj* → transparent
transmission *n* → 1 dissemination 2 telecommunications
transmit *v* → 1 communicate 2 telecast 3 transport
transmute *v* → change
transom *n* → 1 beam 2 shaft 3 window
TRANSPARENCY *n* diaphaneity, diaphanousness, pellucidity, pellucidness, penetrability, sheerness, transparence; **clearness,** clarity, limpidity, limpidness, liquidness, lucence *(Archaic)*, lucency *(Archaic)*, lucidity, lucidness; **glassiness,** vitreosity, vitreousness; **semi-transparency,** translucence, translucency, translucidity
transparency *n* → 1 clarity 2 photograph
TRANSPARENT *adj* diaphanous, pellucid, see-through, sheer; **semitransparent,** semitranslucent, translucent, translucid; **clear,** bright, limpid, liquid, lucent *(Archaic)*, lucid; **glasslike,** crystal, crystalline, glassy, hyaline, hyaloid, vitreous
transparent *adj* → 1 bright 2 clear
TRANSPARENT SUBSTANCE *n* crystal, glass, hyaline; **gossamer,** gauze, sheer silk
transpire *v* → 1 be revealed 2 excrete 3 occur
transplant *v* → 1 farm 2 substitute
TRANSPORT *n* airlift, cabotage, carriage, cartage, commissariat, conveyance, drayage, entrainment, express, expressage, ferriage, forwarding, handling, haulage, passage, piggyback, portage, traffic, transit, transportation, truckage, trucking, wagonage *(Archaic)*, waterage; **transfer,** move, removal, remove, shanghai *(Prison Colloq.)*, shift, shunt, transferal, transference, translation, translocation, transmittal, transmittance; **logistics; delivery,** collection, courier service, deliverance, dispatch, express delivery, paradrop, special delivery; **dink,** donkey *(S.A.)*, double, double-bank
TRANSPORT *v* carry, convey, frank, freight, lift, move, relocate, remove, run, shanghai *(Prison Colloq.)*, shift, take, traffic, transfer, translate, translocate, transmit, transpose *(Rare)*; **send,** check *(U.S.)*, consign, dispatch, forward, pass on, relay, remit, transmit; **express,** herb *(Colloq.)*, rush; **deliver,** bail, discharge, drop, dump, land, off-load; **collect,** bring, fetch; **cart,** dray, jitney, rail, railroad *(U.S.)*, team *(U.S.)*, trolley, truck, wagon, wheelbarrow; **ship,** barge, boat, canoe, ferry, flume *(U.S.)*, lighter, lock, punt, raft, row, wherry; **shunt,** reship, switch *(U.S.)*, tranship; **airfreight,** airlift, fly, parachute; **manhandle,** bear, frogmarch *(Brit. U.S.)*, hump, lump, pack, pikau *(N.Z.)*, port, tote; **stevedore,** load, unload; **dink,** donkey *(S.A.)*, double, double-bank, double-dink
TRANSPORT *adj* airborne, logistic *(Mil.)*, overland, pack, portative, roll-on roll-off, windborne
transport *n* → 1 aeroplane 2 emotion 3 pleasure 4 truck 5 watercraft *v* 6 eject 7 emotionalise 8 kill 9 please
TRANSPORTABLE *adj* consignable, conveyable, deliverable, dischargeable, movable, portable, portative, remissible, remittable, transferable, translatable, transmissible, transmittable
TRANSPORTER *n* consignor, dispatcher, remitter, sender, transmitter; **carrier,** carter, common carrier, conveyor, courier, deliverer, fetcher, forwarder, freighter, haulier, mover, packman *(N.Z.)*, removalist, remover, shifter, shipper, track *(Prison Colloq.)*, transferrer, transporter, trucker *(U.S.)*, water-carrier; **porter,** bearer, bheesti, grip *(Films Television)*, pallbearer, stretcher-bearer; **driver,** bullock-puncher, bullocker, bullocky, cameleer, Ghan; **stevedore,** loader, longshoreman *(U.S.)*, seagull *(Colloq.)*, wharf labourer, wharfie; **coalman,** coal-heaver, collier *(Obs.)*; **beast of burden,** ass, burro, camel, donkey, moke, mule, packhorse, packtrain

transpose *v* → 1 change 2 compute 3 exchange 4 transport

transsexual *n* → 1 sexual type *adj* 2 sexual

transverse *n* → 1 crosspiece *adj* 2 crossing 3 deflective

trap *n* → 1 allure 2 carriage 3 danger 4 door 5 fortification 6 mouth 7 opening 8 policeman 9 propellant 10 stratagem *v* 11 arrest 12 cover 13 hunt 14 obstruct

trapdoor *n* → 1 door 2 entrance 3 opening

trapeze *n* → pendant

trapezium *n* → square

trappings *n* → 1 addition 2 bedclothes 3 clothes 4 equipment

trash *n* → 1 bad person 2 bad thing 3 nonsense 4 remnant 5 waste *v* 6 subtract

trauma *n* → 1 injury 2 psychic disturbance

travail *n* → 1 birth 2 effort 3 pain *v* 4 feel pain 5 give birth

TRAVEL *v* buzz about, do, fare *(Archaic)*, gang *(Scot.)*, get about, get around, go, go around, journey, make one's way, peregrinate, repair, run up (over) (round), see the world, slope *(Colloq.)*, take oneself, tour, wade *(Obs.)*; **migrate,** come out, emigrate, immigrate; **gallivant,** excurse, gad about, jaunt, joy-ride, junket, trip *(Rare)*; **roam,** circumambulate, extravagate, go walkabout, have itchy feet, hump the bluey, knock about, knock around, meander, range, rove, swag, waltz Matilda, wander; **ply,** commute, itinerate, patrol, round, whistlestop; **hike,** bushwalk, ramble, tramp, trek

travel *n* → 1 length 2 travelling *v* 3 speed

TRAVELLER *n* journeyer, peregrinator, voyager, wayfarer; **tourist,** excursionist, globetrotter, jetsetter, joy-rider, junketer, tourer, tripper; **migrant,** boat people, emigré, immigrant, Jimmy Grant, migrator, refugee, repatriate; **wanderer,** bedouin, Egyptian, gippo, gipsy, gypsy, peripatetic, rambler, ranger, roamer, Romany, rover, travelling labour, Wandering Jew; **hiker,** bushwalker; **itinerant,** bird of passage, bogtrotter, rolling stone; **pilgrim,** hajji, palmer, visitant; **tramp,** bagman, battler, beachcomber, bender, bum, coaster, coiler, deadbeat, drummer, hobo, Murrumbidgee whaler, outcast, overlander, rogue, street Arab, sundowner, swagger *(N.Z.)*, swaggie, swagman, swamper, toeragger, tramper, vag, vagabond, vagrant, whaler; **explorer,** trekker; **travelling salesman,** hawker, pedlar, rep, representative, roundsman; **commuter,** kiss-and-ride commuter, season ticket holder, straphanger; **drover,** Afghan, bullock-puncher, bullocker, bullocky, cameleer, Ghan, mahout, muleskinner *(U.S.)*, muleteer, overlander, swamper *(U.S.)*; **skater,** ice-skater, langlaufer, skier, sleigher, snowshoer, tobogganer, tobogganist; **skateboarder,** rollerskater, skater; **rower,** sculler

TRAVELLING *n* itinerancy, itineration, passage, peregrination, staging, travel, wayfaring; **commuting,** commutation *(U.S.)*, straphanging; **tourism,** globetrotting; **migration,** immigration, nomadism, repatriation, transhumance; **vagabondism,** excursiveness, fugitiveness, vagabondage, vagrancy, vagrantness, walkabout; **wanderlust**

TRAVELLING *adj* globetrotting, seafaring, touring; **migratory,** anadromous, immigrant, migrant, migrational, nomadic, transhumant; **expeditionary,** odyssean; **peripatetic,** ambulant, arrant *(Obs.)*, deadbeat, Egyptian, errant, excursive, extravagant *(Obs.)*, gippo, gipsy, gipsy-like, itinerant, itinerary *(Rare)*, of no fixed address, rambling, romany, vagabond, vagarious, vagrant

travelogue *n* → film

TRAVERSE *v* cross, crosscut, cut across, cut through, ford, over *(Rare)*, pass over, voyage; **bridge,** span

traverse *n* → 1 crosspiece 2 denial 3 fence 4 fortification 5 length 6 move 7 obstacle 8 room 9 shaft *v* 10 cross 11 deny 12 direct 13 hinder 14 investigate 15 support *adj* 16 crossing *adv* 17 across 18 crosswise

travesty *n* → 1 imitation 2 misrepresentation 3 mockery *v* 4 imitate 5 misinterpret 6 mock

trawl *v* → 1 fish 2 speak well

tray *n* → tableware

treachery *n* → betrayal

treacle *n* → 1 affectation 2 medication 3 paste

tread *n* → 1 circle 2 click 3 stairs 4 support 5 thickness 6 walking *v* 7 dance 8 have sex 9 press 10 walk

treadle *n* → bicycle

treadmill *n* → bore

treason *n* → 1 betrayal 2 defection

treasure *n* → 1 good thing 2 wealth *v* 3 hide 4 respect

treasurer *n* → 1 member of parliament 2 treasury

TREASURY *n* bank, chamber *(Obs.)*, coffers, exchequer, fisc, mint, thesaurus; **cash desk,** cash register, checkout, peter, point-of-sale terminal, p.o.s. terminal, till; **strongroom,** strongbox, vault; **moneybox,** piggy bank; **money market,** foreign exchange market; **treasurer,** bursar, cashier, collector

treasury *n* → storehouse

treat *n* → 1 generosity *v* 2 behave 3 discourse 4 medicate 5 practise medicine

treatise *n* → written composition

treaty *n* → 1 contract 2 entreaty 3 mediation

treble *n* → 1 resonator *adj* 2 musical 3 shrill 4 third

tree *n* → 1 ancestry 2 cross 3 number system 4 plant 5 shaft *v* 6 cause difficulties 7 hunt 8 pursue 9 shape

trek *n* → 1 walk *v* 2 travel

trellis *n* → 1 building 2 interlacement *v* 3 interlace 4 support

tremble *n* → 1 coldness 2 fright *v* 3 be cold 4 be excited 5 be frightened 6 vibrate

tremendous *adj* → 1 astonishing 2 enormous 3 nonconformist

tremolo *n* → vibration

tremor *n* → 1 coldness 2 fright 3 perception 4 vibration 5 weakness 6 worry

tremulous *adj* → **1** excited **2** fluttery **3** frightened **4** turbulent **5** weak **6** worried

trench *n* → **1** channel **2** diggings **3** excavation **4** fortification **5** furrow *v* **6** cut **7** defend **8** furrow **9** insert

trenchant *adj* → **1** concise **2** sharp

trencher *n* → **1** food **2** hat

trend *n* → **1** direction **2** fashion **3** point of view *v* **4** tend to

trendy *n* → **1** fashionable person **2** innovator *adj* **3** fashionable **4** innovative

trepidation *n* → **1** fright **2** vibration **3** worry

trespass *n* → **1** advance **2** crime **3** entrance **4** evildoing **5** harm **6** wrong *v* **7** be immoral **8** contravene **9** enter **10** misbehave **11** wrong

tress *n* → hair

trestle *n* → stand

triad *n* → three

TRIAL *n* appeal, coronial inquiry, court martial, hearing, impeachment, inquest, inquiry, inquisition, mistrial, nisi prius, prosecution, retrial, show trial, state trial, trial by jury

trial *n* → **1** annoyance **2** attempt **3** contest **4** examination **5** pain **6** questioning **7** race **8** test *v* **9** test *adj* **10** litigious **11** test

triangle *n* → **1** plane figure **2** protractor

tribe *n* → **1** ancestry **2** class **3** crowd **4** many **5** relative

tribunal *n* → court of law

tributary *n* → **1** approver **2** payer **3** respecter **4** stream *adj* **5** approving **6** helpful **7** regardful

TRIBUTE *n* approbation, attention, commendations, compliments, congratulations, toast; **respects,** court, deference, devoirs, duty, fealty, loyalty, obedience; **bow,** congé, curtsy, genuflection, kneeling, kowtow, obeisance, observance *(Archaic)*, presenting arms, prostration, reverence, salaam, salutation, salute. *See also* COMMEMORATION

tribute *n* → **1** applause **2** gratefulness **3** indebtedness **4** obligation **5** payment **6** tax

trice *n* → **1** moment *v* **2** pull

TRICK *n* angle, bubble, caper, cheat, chizz *(Brit.)*, con, confidence trick, do, effect *(Theat.)*, fakement, fastie, feint, fetch, fiddle, finesse, flim-flam, frost, gyp, have, hype *(U.S.)*, juggle, line, plant, put-on, sell, set-up, shift, slanter, sleight *(Rare)*, smokescreen, snow job, stew, sting *(U.S.)*, swiftie, swindle, swiz, swizzle, take, take-down, trepan *(Archaic)*, wrinkle; **hoax,** berley, humbug, kid, kid-stakes, leg-pull, practical joke, prank, prankery; **legerdemain,** sleight of hand

TRICK *v* abuse *(Archaic)*, baffle *(Obs.)*, bamboozle, befool, bluff, bull, catch, cheat on, cog the dice, come the double on, come the raw prawn, come the uncooked crustacean, deceive, delude, dupe, equivocate, fast-talk, foist in, foist into, foist on, fool, fox, gull, handle, have, have a lend of, have someone on, hocus-pocus, hoodwink, humbug, hype *(U.S.)*, impose on, lead up the garden path, load the dice, misinform, mislead, pull a fast one, pull a fastie, pull a swiftie, pull the wool over someone's eyes, put it across, put one over, put over a fast one, put shit on, seel *(Archaic)*, sell, sophisticate, string along, swift-talk, take for a ride, take in, throw dust in someone's eyes, two-time; **hoax,** gag, gammon, hocus, kid, make a fool of, mock, play a joke on, pull someone's leg, rag, send on a fool's errand, sport with, trifle with; **counterfeit,** fake; **sneak,** gumshoe *(U.S.)*, mooch, sidle, slink, steal, tiptoe; **feint,** pretend

trick *n* → **1** behaviour **2** expedient **3** illusion **4** misdemeanour **5** stratagem *adj* **6** cunning

TRICKERY *n* abuse *(Archaic)*, archness, bamboozlement, beguilement, bluff, chenanigan, cozenage, craft, cunning, deceit, deception, defraudation, delusion, dupery, equivocation, eyewash, fast-talking, forgery *(Archaic)*, four-flush, hocus-pocus, hokey-pokey, indirection, intrigue, irony, jiggery-pokery, jugglery, monkey business, pretext, sharp practice, shenanigan, stealth, subterfuge, wiles; **false pretences,** impersonation, personation; **deceitfulness,** duplicity, sneakiness, speciousness, stealthiness, surreptitiousness

trickle *n* → **1** a few **2** flow *v* **3** flow

TRICKSTER *n* adventurer, adventuress, bamboozler, beguiler, bluffer, cheat, cheater, cozener, defrauder, deluder, diddler, duper, feigner, fiddler, finagler, flim-flammer, front man, gyp, gypper, hoodwinker, hotpointer, impersonator, juggler, personator, slyboots, stealer, swindler, swizzler, trepanner *(Archaic)*, tricker, twister, welsher; **deceiver,** gay deceiver, Mata Hari; **con man,** balancer, confidence man, dud-dropper, false-pretencer, gypster, illywhacker, lurk man, mouthman, paperhanger, rorter, share-pusher, slicker, thimblerigger; **leg-puller,** kidder, ragger; **dissembler,** actor; **hoaxer,** gagger, joker, leg-puller, practical joker, prankster, spoofer

tricky *adj* → cunning

tricycle *n* → bicycle

trident *n* → spear

triennial *n* → **1** anniversary *adj* **2** third

trifle *n* → **1** small amount **2** unimportant thing *v* **3** amuse oneself **4** belittle **5** idle

trigger *v* → initiate

trigonometry *n* → mathematics

trill *n* → **1** accent **2** birdcall **3** ringing *v* **4** chirp **5** ring

trilogy *n* → **1** drama **2** three

trim *n* → **1** clothes **2** condition **3** covering **4** display **5** equipment **6** hairdressing **7** tidiness **8** trimming *v* **9** change **10** clothe **11** cover **12** cut **13** decorate **14** defeat **15** exercise restraint **16** fly **17** make do **18** shape **19** smooth **20** subtract *adj* **21** equipped **22** good **23** tidy *adv* **24** tidily

trimaran *n* → sailing ship

TRIMMING *n* border, clock, edging, fixings, fringe, lace, orphrey, passementerie, piping, torsade, trim, whipping; **flounce,** caparison, falbala, frill, furbelow, valance; **braid,** binding, braiding, galloon, gimp; **loop,** picot, purl; **tassel,** bobble, fandangle, pompom, zizith; **spangle,** gilding, glitter, gold leaf, ormulu, paillette, pearly, sequin, tinsel; **gold braid,** aiguillette, bullion, cordon, epaulet, gimp, lace, sword knot; **plume,** aigrette, crest, panache

trimming *n* → 1 hitting 2 losing

trinity *n* → three

TRINKET *n* bauble, bibelot, bijou, bric-a-brac, doodad, fallal, garden gnome, gaud, gewgaw, gimcrack, gingerbread, knick-knack, ornament, pretties, scrimshaw, trumpery

trinket *n* → unimportant thing

trio *n* → 1 theatrical company 2 three

trip *n* → 1 drug use 2 error 3 fall 4 hallucinogen 5 journey 6 misdemeanour 7 pleasure 8 wrong *v* 9 dance 10 enjoy 11 fall 12 hinder 13 take drugs 14 travel 15 walk 16 wrong

tripartite *adj* → separate

tripe *n* → nonsense

triple *n* → three

triplet *n* → 1 jewel 2 join 3 offspring 4 three

triplicate *n* → 1 three *v* 2 triple

TRIPLY *adv* threefold, thrice, trebly; **tripartitely,** ternately; **triangularly,** trilaterally

tripod *n* → stand

triptych *n* → 1 painting 2 writing materials

trite *adj* → 1 boring 2 customary 3 mediocre 4 ordinary

triumph *n* → 1 joy 2 success *v* 3 predominate 4 rejoice 5 succeed

triumvirate *n* → three

trivia *n* → unimportant thing

troglodyte *n* → 1 ignoramus 2 inhabitant 3 solitary 4 stupid person 5 vulgarian

troll *n* → 1 fairy 2 song *v* 3 fish 4 roll 5 sing

trolley *n* → 1 tram 2 wagon *v* 3 transport

trollop *n* → prostitute

trombone *n* → brass instrument

troop *n* → 1 armed forces 2 crowd 3 gathering 4 many 5 theatrical company *v* 6 abound 7 display 8 tidy 9 walk

trooper *n* → 1 policeman 2 soldier 3 watercraft

trope *n* → figure of speech

trophy *n* → memento

tropic *n* → 1 astronomic point *adj* 2 hot 3 moving

trot *v* → ride

troth *n* → 1 contract 2 faithfulness 3 truth 4 wedding

troubadour *n* → 1 poet 2 singer

trouble *n* → 1 annoyance 2 annoyer 3 commotion 4 difficulty 5 effort 6 illness 7 misfortune 8 pain 9 turbulence 10 worry *v* 11 agitate 12 alarm 13 annoy 14 displease 15 pain

trough *n* → 1 atmospheric pressure 2 basin 3 bath 4 channel 5 furrow

trounce *v* → 1 beat 2 defeat

troupe *n* → 1 crowd 2 theatrical company

TROUSERS *n* applecatchers, baggies, bags, breeches, britches, buckskins *(U.S.)*, chaps, cords, corduroys, crawlers, creepers, daks, denims, drainpipes, duds, flannels, flares, galligaskins, gauchos, hipsters, jeans, jodhpurs, knee breeches, knickerbockers, knickers, knicks, Levis, long'uns, Oxford bags, pantaloons, pants, peg tops, plus-fours, pyjamas, riding breeches, slacks, slop, strides, trews *(Scot.)*, trunk hose, tweeds, velveteens; **shorts,** bermuda shorts, board shorts, Bombay bloomers, boxer shorts, hotpants, lederhosen, trunks *(Obs.)*

trousseau *n* → 1 outfit 2 supplies

trout *n* → ugly person

trowel *n* → 1 digging implement *v* 2 place 3 smooth

truant *n* → 1 absentee 2 avoider 3 escapee *v* 4 be absent *adj* 5 absent 6 escaped

truce *n* → 1 contract 2 interval 3 mediation 4 peace 5 stoppage

TRUCK *n* lorry, mini-van, pantechnicon, table-top, taxi truck, transit van, utility van, van; **semitrailer,** artic *(N.Z. Colloq.)*, articulated lorry, low-loader, prime mover, rig, road train, semi, transport; **tip-truck,** dump truck, dumper, tip-cart; **convoy,** beef train, caravan, motorcade, wagon train *(U.S.)*; **armoured car,** blitz buggy, jeep, panzer, tank, troop-carrier; **bus,** charabanc, coach, double-decker, green cart, minibus, motor coach, motorbus, omnibus, service car, single-decker

truck *n* → 1 contract 2 income 3 train 4 wagon 5 wheel *v* 6 move 7 place 8 transport 9 walk

truculent *adj* → 1 aggressive 2 ferocious

trudge *v* → walk

TRUE *adj* accurate, certain, correct, dead set, definite, dinkum, dinky-di, fair dinkum, for real, inerrant, ridge, ridgy-didge, right, sooth *(Archaic)*, veritable *(Rare)*; **genuine,** actual, authentic, factual, historical, legit, legitimate, literal, real, veritable, very; **verifiable,** affirmable, authenticable, certifiable, checkable; **realistic,** recognisable, true to life, true to nature; **valid,** just, logically true, rigorous, sound, straight, tenable; **verified,** authenticated, proved; **self-evident,** a priori, axiomatic, tautological, truistic, undeniable

true *n* → 1 precision *v* 2 be precise *adj* 3 congruous 4 conventional 5 correct 6 direct 7 essential 8 faithful 9 genetic 10 honest 11 precise 12 rightful 13 straight 14 truthful *adv* 15 conventionally 16 precisely 17 truthfully

true blue *n* → 1 blue pigment 2 political ideologist

true-blue *adj* → faithful

truism *n* → 1 proverb 2 truth

trump *n* → 1 brass instrument 2 fortune-telling 3 gaoler *v* 4 make music 5 publicise 6 ring 7 surpass

trumpery *n* → 1 nonsense 2 trinket *adj* 3 cheap 4 decorative 5 useless

trumpet *n* → 1 animal call 2 brass instrument 3 hearing aid *v* 4 brag 5 call (of animals) 6 make music 7 publicise 8 ring

truncate *v* → 1 shorten 2 subtract *adj* 3 short 4 truncated

TRUNCATED *adj* castrated, couped, crop-eared, cut short, docked, lopped, poley, premorse, truncate

TRUNCATION *n* attrition, curtailment, decrement, deduction, dockage, enucleation, evisceration, excision, expurgation, exsection, extirpation, removal, subduction *(Rare)*, subtraction; **castration,** elastration, emasculation, gelding, the unkindest cut of all; **circumcision,** clitoridectomy; **epilation,** depilation; **amputation,** mutilation

truncheon *n* → **1** club **2** emblem of office **3** stick *v* **4** cudgel

trundle *n* → **1** support **2** thrust **3** wheel *v* **4** go slowly **5** roll **6** thrust **7** walk

trunk *n* → **1** box **2** chest **3** post **4** railway **5** stem **6** stream

trunk line *n* → railway

truss *n* → **1** accumulation **2** brace **3** building **4** medication *v* **5** cook **6** restrain **7** support

trust *n* → **1** belief **2** care **3** hope **4** obligation **5** reverence **6** surety *v* **7** believe **8** hope

trustworthy *adj* → **1** believable **2** faithful **3** honest

TRUTH *n* actuality, fact, reality, sooth *(Archaic)*, the Absolute *(Metaphys.)*, troth *(Archaic)*, what's what; **self-evident truth,** axiom, first principle, truism; **the truth,** gospel, griff, griffin *(N.Z.)*, the drum, the full two bob, the genuine article, the lowdown, the real McCoy, the real thing, the strong of it, the true, the whole truth and nothing but the truth; **factualness,** actualness, historicity, realness, trueness, verity; **correctness,** accuracy, accurateness, infallibility, rightness, rigorousness, soundness, tenableness, validity; **genuineness,** authenticity, legitimacy, legitimateness

truth *n* → **1** actuality **2** faithfulness **3** honesty **4** precision **5** proverb

TRUTHFUL *adj* honest, true *(Archaic)*, veracious, veridical; **sincere,** candid, downright, frank, genuine, plain-spoken, unfeigned

TRUTHFULLY *adv* dead set, honestly, true, veraciously, veridically; **sincerely,** candidly, frankly, genuinely, unfeignedly

TRUTHFULNESS *n* honesty, straightness, veracity; **sincerity,** genuineness, unfeignedness; **candour,** downrightness, frankness, plain-speaking

try *n* → **1** attempt *v* **2** assess **3** attempt **4** authenticate **5** bore **6** examine **7** liquefy **8** taste **9** test

trying *adj* → **1** annoying **2** difficult

TRYST *n* assignation, lover's meeting; **love-letter,** billet-doux, love knot, valentine; **love potion,** aphrodisiac, philtre

tryst *n* → **1** assignation **2** love affair **3** position *v* **4** arrange

tsar *n* → **1** aristocrat **2** ruler

T-shirt *n* → shirt

tub *n* → **1** basin **2** bath **3** toilet **4** watercraft *v* **5** clean **6** insert

tuba *n* → brass instrument

tubby *adj* → **1** fat **2** quiet **3** short

tube *n* → **1** alcohol container **2** bladder **3** drinking vessel **4** flower **5** neck **6** piping **7** railway **8** solid **9** surf **10** television

tuber *n* → **1** bulge **2** root

tubercle *n* → bulge

tuck *n* → **1** clothes **2** dive **3** fold **4** food **5** sword *v* **6** contract **7** cover **8** fold **9** insert

tucker *n* → **1** food *v* **2** tire

tuckshop *n* → shop

tuft *n* → **1** animal's coat **2** button *v* **3** feather

tug *n* → **1** extraction **2** fight **3** harness **4** pull **5** puller **6** restraints **7** watercraft *v* **8** make an effort **9** pull

tuition *n* → **1** cost **2** restraint **3** teaching

tumble *n* → **1** fall **2** jumble **3** roll *v* **4** disorder **5** fall **6** jump **7** lower **8** overturn **9** roll **10** wane

tumbler *n* → **1** bolt **2** circus performer **3** dog **4** drier **5** drinking vessel **6** gun part

tumescent *adj* → **1** increased **2** swollen

tumid *adj* → **1** bombastic **2** increased **3** swollen

tumour *n* → **1** bulge **2** cancer

tumult *n* → **1** anarchy **2** commotion **3** loud sound **4** muddle **5** turbulence

tundra *n* → grassland

tune *n* → **1** emotion **2** music **3** sound *v* **4** sound

tuner *n* → **1** musician **2** radio **3** sound system

tunic *n* → **1** dress **2** jacket **3** leaf **4** skin **5** sportswear **6** stem **7** uniform

tunnel *n* → **1** animal dwelling **2** bridge **3** channel **4** diggings **5** passageway **6** path *v* **7** dig **8** hollow **9** open

turban *n* → **1** hat **2** headgear

turbid *adj* → **1** muddled **2** opaque

TURBULENCE *n* agitation, convulsion, ferment, inquietude, tempest, torment, trouble, turmoil, unquietness, unrest, vexedness; **commotion,** ado, bobberie, cataclysm, catastrophe, disturbance, fuss, hubbub, hurly-burly, much ado about nothing, song and dance, tumult, volcanicity; **convulsion,** palpitation, paroxysm, spasm, throe, welter; **flurry,** jactation, jiggle, joggle, jounce, popple, shake, shaking, startle, succussion, tingle, toss; **excitement,** ebullience, ebulliency, tempestuousness; **boil,** churning, ebullition, seethe, vortex; **quake,** shudder; **the shakes,** delirium tremens

TURBULENT *adj* agitated, jittery, restless, rough, tempestuous, troublous *(Archaic)*, unquiet; **excited,** ebullient, palpitant; **vexed,** disturbed, unquiet; **fluttery,** jumpy, quaky, saltatory, shaky, tremulous; **convulsant,** convulsionary, convulsive, paroxysmal

tureen *n* → tableware

turf *n* → **1** bit **2** fuel *v* **3** cover

turgid *adj* → **1** bombastic **2** surplus

turkey *n* → **1** failure **2** fool

turmoil *n* → **1** anarchy **2** disorder **3** loud sound **4** muddle **5** turbulence

TURN *n* about-face, about-turn, caracole, christiania *(Skiing)*, facing *(U.S. Mil.)*, kick turn *(Skiing)*, left turn, pirouette, right turn, tack, three-point turn, volte *(Manège)*, volte-face, yaw

TURN *v* corner, quarter, tack; **zigzag,** Major-Mitchell, wind

turn *n* → 1 celebration 2 change 3 circle 4 crucial moment 5 curve 6 exercise 7 fright 8 illness 9 party 10 period 11 point of view 12 shape 13 stocks and shares 14 twist 15 walk *v* 16 alternate 17 be unpalatable 18 blunt 19 change 20 create 21 curve 22 defect 23 deteriorate 24 rotate 25 shape 26 swerve 27 translate

turncoat *n* → defector

TURNING INSIDE-OUT *n* evagination, eversion, extroversion

turnover *n* → overturn

turn over *v* → 1 initiate 2 move 3 overturn 4 rotate 5 sell

turnstile *n* → 1 entrance 2 obstacle

turntable *n* → sound system

turpentine *n* → fat

turpitude *n* → 1 immorality 2 wrongfulness

turquoise *n* → 1 blue 2 green

turret *n* → 1 stairs 2 tower

turtle *v* → fish

turtleneck *n* → neckwear

tusk *n* → 1 mouth *v* 2 injure

tussle *n* → 1 fight *v* 2 fight

tussock *n* → plant

tutelage *n* → 1 dependence 2 protection 3 teaching

tutor *n* → 1 protector 2 teacher *v* 3 be strict 4 scold 5 teach

tutorial *n* → lesson

tutu *n* → dress

tuxedo *n* → outfit

TV *n* → television

twaddle *n* → 1 nonsense 2 speaking 3 waffle *v* 4 speak 5 talk nonsense

twain *n* → two

twang *n* → 1 accent 2 click 3 faulty speech 4 vibration *v* 5 make music 6 ring 7 shoot 8 speak 9 vibrate

tweak *n* → pull

twee *adj* → affected

'tween *prep* → between

tweezers *n* → 1 extractor 2 holder

twice *adv* → in twos

twiddle *n* → 1 spin *v* 2 idle 3 touch

twig *v* → 1 look 2 see 3 understand

twilight *n* → 1 dark 2 evening *adj* 3 nightly 4 shadowy

twill *v* → sew

twin *n* → 1 offspring 2 repetition 3 sibling 4 similar thing 5 two *v* 6 double 7 give birth *adj* 8 simultaneous 9 two

twine *n* → 1 circuitousness 2 disorder 3 string 4 tangle *v* 5 edge 6 flower 7 roll up

twinge *n* → 1 ache *v* 2 pain

twinkle *n* → 1 light 2 moment 3 urination *v* 4 shine

twinkling *n* → 1 light 2 moment

twin-set *n* → jacket

twirl *n* → 1 spin 2 twist *v* 3 roll up 4 spin

TWIST *n* crinkle, curl, curlicue, gyrus, slub, torsade, tortuosity, turn, twirl, verticil, volute *(Zool.)*, whorl, wind; **convolution,** circumflex roll, winding; **coil,** clew, flake, hank, service *(Naut.)*, skein; **helix,** double helix, right-handed helix, right-handed spiral, screw screw thread, scroll, spiral, square thread thread, volute, worm; **coil spring,** balance spring, hairspring

TWIST *v* circumnutate, coil, convolve, corkscrew, crinkle, intort, screw, serve *(Naut.)* spiral, whip, wind, wrap, wrench, wring, **snake,** squiggle, vermiculate, weave, wriggle, writhe; **curl,** braid, crimp, crimple, crisp, frizz, frizzle, roll, wave

twist *n* → 1 ammunition 2 change 3 curve 4 distortion 5 pull 6 spin 7 strangeness 8 tobacco *v* 9 change 10 contact 11 dance 12 distort 13 fake 14 misinterpret 15 swerve 16 toss

TWISTED *adj* cochleate, coiled, convolute, convoluted, snaily-horn, turreted, verticillate, whorled; **spiral,** corkscrew, dextral, helical, helicoid, helicoidal, screwed, sinistrorse, tortile, turbinate

TWISTING *adj* anfractuous, circuitous, circular, flexuose, flexuous, peristaltic, roundabout, serpentine, sinuate, sinuous, snaky, tortuous, voluminous *(Obs.)*, winding; **tendril-like,** capreolate, tendrillar, vinelike; **curly,** crimpy, crinkly, crisp, crispate, crispy, frizzy; **wriggly,** rolling, sigmate, squiggly, vermicular, vermiculate, volute, wiggly

twitch *n* → 1 ache 2 pull *v* 3 feel pain 4 pull

twitter *n* → 1 birdcall 2 excitement 3 mocker 4 quiet sound 5 vibration 6 worry *v* 7 be excited 8 chirp 9 vibrate

'twixt *prep* → between

TWO *n* binary, brace, couple, couplet, deuce *(Cards)*, doublet, duad, duumvirate, dyad, pair, pigeon pair, twa *(Scot.)*, twain *(Archaic)*, twosome, yoke; **twin,** fellow, match, pair; **twins,** Castor and Pollux, fraternal twins, Gemini, identical twins, Siamese twins, Tweedledum and Tweedledee

TWO *adj* binary, both, dual, dyad, dyadic; **twinned,** binate *(Bot.)*, conjugate, coupled, dizygotic *(Embryol.)*, geminate, paired, twin; **double,** biparous, diploid, duple, duplex, duplicate, duplicative, twofold; **two-sided,** amphibious, bicameral, biform, bilateral, binucleate, dimorphous, double-sided, two-handed, two-piece, twosome; **second,** alternate, every other, latter, secondary

two-faced *adj* → 1 deceitful 2 dishonest

two-time *v* → 1 betray 2 trick

two-up *n* → gambling

tycoon *n* → 1 boss 2 mister 3 powerful person 4 trader 5 wealthy person

type *n* → 1 ancestry 2 character 3 class 4 conformist behaviour 5 essence 6 example 7 omen 8 person *v* 9 particularise 10 print 11 represent 12 write

typecast *v* → 1 stage *adj* 2 changeless

typescript *n* → 1 copy 2 written composition

typeset *v* → print

typhoon *n* → 1 spin 2 wind

typical *adj* → **1** apt **2** characteristic **3** classificatory **4** conventional **5** essential **6** indicative **7** model

typify *v* → **1** represent **2** signify

typist *n* → writer

typography *n* → printing

tyranny *n* → **1** authority **2** forcefulness **3** nation **4** predominance **5** unfairness

tyrant *n* → **1** forcer **2** powerful person **3** represser **4** ruler **5** strict person

tyre *n* → wheel

tyro *n* → **1** ignoramus **2** learner **3** starter

Uu

ubiquity *n* → **1** being **2** generality **3** presence

UFO *n* → aircraft

UGLIFY *v* blemish, contort, deface, deform, disfigure, distort, marr, soil, spoil, vandalise

UGLINESS *n* dreadfulness, haggishness, hideousness, ill-favouredness, unsightliness; **unattractiveness,** plainness, unhandsomeness, unloveliness; **grotesqueness,** deformity, distortion, grotesquerie; **dowdiness,** frumpiness, frumpishness, homeliness, manginess; **uglification,** disfigurement; **inelegance,** gracelessness, horsiness, stiffness

UGLY *adj* dreadful, foul, frightful, grotesque, hideous, horrid, monstrous, not fit to be seen, odious, toadlike, ugly as sin, with a face like a bagful of arseholes, with a face like the back of a bus, with a face that would stop a clock; **unattractive,** beer-sodden, bloated, coarse, common, crooked, disfigured, distorted, favourless *(Archaic)*, gaunt, graceless, haggard, hard-favoured, hard-featured, ill-favoured, ill-looking, ill-proportioned, ill-shaped, inelegant, lumbering, misshapen, repellant, repulsive, shapeless, stiff, unbeauteous, unbeautiful, uncomely, uncouth, ungainly, ungraceful, unhandsome, unlovely, unprepossessing, unseemly *(Obs.)*, unshapely, unsightly; **mean,** clumsy, dingy, foul, mangy, rickety, rough, rude, scrubby, squalid; **ghastly,** cadaverous, Gothic *(Lit.)*, grim, grisly, gruesome, shocking; **plain,** blemished, homely, ordinary; **horsy,** horse-faced; **haggish,** haggy; **dowdy,** dowdyish, drack, dumpy, frumpish, frumpy, gawky, shabby, shapeless; **showy,** crude, garish, gaudy, gross, overdecorated, overdone, specious

ugly *adj* → **1** menacing **2** unpleasant

UGLY PERSON *n* baboon, bag, beldam *(Archaic)*, cow, eyesore, face-ache, fright, gorgon, gorilla, hag, harpy, harridan, hellcat, horror, lemon, old bag, old cow, old trout, scarecrow, sight, toad, trout, ugly duckling, witch; **grotesque,** guy, monster, monstrosity, Punchinello; **frump,** dowdy, fleabag, hausfrau

ulcer *n* → sore

ulterior *adj* → **1** following **2** hidden

ultimate *n* → **1** finish **2** good thing *adj* **3** distant **4** final **5** fundamental

ultimatum *n* → **1** command **2** finish **3** insistence **4** offer **5** politics **6** request

ultramarine *n* → **1** blue *adj* **2** sea

ululate *v* → **1** be loud **2** call (of animals) **3** grieve

umber *n* → **1** brown **2** soil *v* **3** colour *adj* **4** brown

umbilical cord *n* → piping

umbilicus *n* → **1** abdomen **2** centre **3** seed

umbrage *n* → **1** displeasure **2** invisibility **3** shade

umbrella *n* → **1** covering **2** defence **3** protection *adj* **4** inclusive

umpire *n* → **1** adjudicator **2** mediator *v* **3** mediate

unanimous *adj* → in agreement

unassuming *adj* → modest

unattached *adj* → **1** independent **2** separate **3** single

UNAVAILABLE *adj* elusive, inaccessible, irretraceable, not to be had, unobtainable, unrealisable; **vain,** futile, unavailing, unlikely

unaware *adj* → **1** ignorant **2** insensible

unawares *adv* → **1** off one's guard **2** surprisingly

unbalanced *adj* → **1** confused **2** mad **3** misplaced **4** prejudiced **5** psychologically disturbed **6** unequal

UNBEARABLE *adj* enough to drive one mad, enough to try the patience of Job, insufferable, intolerable, more than flesh and blood can bear, not to be borne, not to be put up with, past bearing, unendurable, unsupportable; **distressing,** afflicting, comfortless, depressing, disheartening, harrowing, heartbreaking, heart-rending. *See also* UNPLEASANT; SICKENING; DREADFUL; PESTERING

unbending *n* → **1** lenience *adj* **2** hard **3** strict **4** uncompromising

unbridled *adj* → **1** anarchic **2** liberated **3** overindulgent

uncalled-for *adj* → **1** incorrect **2** surplus **3** unfair

uncanny *adj* → **1** strange **2** supernatural

UNCERTAIN *adj* arguable, changeable, debatable, doubtable, doubtful, dubersome *(Brit. and U.S.)*, dubious, dubitable, facultative, fallible, in doubt, in the air, insecure, open, precarious, problematic, questionable, random, rocky, slippery, suspenseful, ticklish, unauthenticated, unconfirmed, unpredictable, unreliable, unsourced, unstable, untrustworthy; **ambiguous,** amphibolic, amphibological, amphibolous, aoristic, apocryphal, cloudy, cryptic, enigmatic, equivocal, indefinite, indistinct, mysterious, obscure, oracular, paradoxical, undefined, vague, veiled; **marginal,** borderline, cliff-hanging; **conditional,** casual *(Obs.)*, chancey, chancy, contingent, dependent on circumstances, provisional, subject to circumstances; **unknown,** hypothetical, uncounted, undetermined, unmeasured, unnumbered, unresolved, unsettled, unsure, untold, without number; **indeterminable,** incalculable, indemonstrable, indeterminate, indiscernible, inestimable, innumerable, unknowable, unmeasurable; **unsure,** aimless, ambivalent, at one's wit's end, dithering, dithery, halting, hesitant, hesitative, indecisive, nonplussed, perplexed, puzzled, suspensive, unassured, undecided, undetermined, unresolved, unsettled, vacillating; **doubtful,** agnostic, dubitative

uncertain *adj* → **1** changeable **2** imprecise **3** indecisive **4** irregular **5** undetermined

UNCERTAIN THING *n* borderland, borderline, chance, cliff-hanger, conjecture, contingency, contingent, leap in the dark, lineball, neither fish nor fowl, pig in a poke, possibility, problem, rumour, the joker in the pack, unknowable, unknown, unknown factor, variable, x *(Maths)*; **open question,** enigma, matter of opinion, moot point, mystery, obscureness, obscurity, query, question; **quandary,** dilemma

UNCERTAINTY *n* ambivalence, bewilderment, doubtfulness, haltingness, hesitancy, hesitation, indecision, indecisiveness, misgiving, pendency, perplexity, self-distrust, undecidedness, unresolvedness, unsettledness, unsureness, vacillation; **doubt,** agnosticism, dubiety, dubitation, incertitude; **indeterminancy,** incalculability, incalculableness, indemonstrability, indiscernibleness, unknowability, unknowableness, unpredictability, unpredictableness, unreliability, untrustworthiness; **indeterminateness,** dependence, dubiousness, fallibility, fortuitousness, peradventure *(Archaic)*, precariousness, suspense, uncertainness; **ambiguity,** ambiguousness, amphibology, amphiboly, cloudiness, double meaning, equivocalness, vagueness

uncle *n* → **1** lender **2** mister **3** relative

unclean *adj* → **1** dirty **2** immoral **3** prohibited **4** wrong

UNCLEAR *adj* abstract, abstruse, confused, dark, deep, dim, equivocatory, esoteric, hazy, mystical *(Rare)*, obscure, opaque, recondite; **puzzling,** baffling, bewildering, beyond comprehension, challenging, confusing, difficult, elusive, paradoxical, past comprehension, perplexing; **inapprehensive,** incomprehensive; **mysterious,** arcane, cryptic, enigmatic, inscrutable, mystic; **Delphic,** Delphian, oracular; **incomprehensible,** all Greek, beyond one's depth, clear as mud, fathomless, impalpable, impenetrable, inapprehensible, unintelligible; **insoluble,** impenetrable, incalculable, inexplicable, insolvable, unaccountable, unexplainable, unfathomable, unknowable, unscrutable, unsearchable; **illegible,** crabbed, cramped, hieroglyphic, ill-defined, indecipherable, unreadable

uncomfortable *adj* → **1** unpleasant **2** worried

UNCOMPROMISING *adj* confirmed, immovable, insistent, iron-fisted, resolute, strong-willed, unbending, vocal; **wilful,** headstrong, self-willed, wanton; **intent,** bent on, bound to, hell-bent on, intent on, set on

UNCONDITIONAL *adj* clear, cool *(Colloq.)*, round, straight, straight-out, termless, unqualified; **categorical,** definitive, unexceptional; **regardless,** independent, irrespective; **utter,** absolute, flat, implicit, out-and-out, outright, perfect, unmitigated; **total,** arrant, complete, downright, positive, pure, sheer, thorough

unconditional *adj* → **1** liberated **2** whole

UNCONDITIONALLY *adv* categorically, clear, clearly, come hell or high water, implicitly, unexceptionally, unmitigatedly, unqualifiedly, with no strings attached; **utterly,** absolutely, arrantly, completely, definitively, easily, flat, flatling *(Archaic)*, flatly, purely, soever, totally; **independently,** irrespectively; **unequivocably,** explicitly, in so many words, unquestionably

unconscionable *adj* → **1** excessive **2** wrong

UNCONSCIOUS *adj* asleep, comatose, oblivious, out cold, out like a light, syncopic; **dazed,** bleary, bleary-eyed, blurry, groggy, non compos, silly, stunned, stupid, stuporous; **punch-drunk,** concussed, like a stunned mullet, punchy; **drugged,** blind, dopey; **hypnotic,** autohypnotic, hypnagogic, hypnoid, hypnologic, hypnopompic, trancelike

unconscious *adj* → **1** drunk **2** feverish **3** ignorant **4** purposeless

UNCONSCIOUSNESS *n* Lethe, lifelessness, nothingness, oblivion, sleep; **grogginess,** amazement *(Obs.)*, bleariness, blindness, concussion, daze, stupefaction, stupidness, stupor, subconsciousness; **faint,** blackout, catalepsy, coma, epilepsy, fit, grand mal, petit mal, swoon, swound *(Archaic)*, syncope, trance; **hypnotism,** animal magnetism *(Obs.)*, autohypnosis, hypnogenesis, hypnosis. *See also* INSENSIBILITY; ANAESTHESIA

unconventional *adj* → **1** informal **2** innovative **3** liberated **4** nonconformist

uncouth *adj* → **1** discourteous **2** ill-bred **3** incompetent **4** ugly

uncover *v* → **1** bare **2** display **3** pay homage **4** reveal **5** undress

unction *n* → **1** fat **2** medication

unctuous *adj* → **1** affected **2** flattering **3** oily

undeniable *adj* → **1** certain **2** true

UNDER *prep* beneath, neath *(Scot. Poetic)*, underneath

UNDER ATTACK *adv* between two fires, on the receiving end, under fire, under siege

undercarriage *n* → **1** bottom **2** building **3** support

undercover *adj* → **1** hidden **2** secretive

under cover *adv* → in secret

undercurrent *n* → **1** allusion **2** point of view

undercut *n* → **1** cut *v* **2** beguile **3** cheapen **4** cut

underdog *n* → **1** loser **2** unfortunate

UNDERGO *v* bechance, befall, come upon, encounter, endure, experience, fare, incur, meet, meet with, run across, run into, run up against, stumble on, stumble upon, walk into

undergraduate *n* → pupil

underground *n* → **1** bottom **2** dissident **3** railway **4** secret society *adj* **5** bottom **6** hidden **7** secretive *adv* **8** below **9** in secret

undergrowth *n* → forest

underhand *adj* → **1** cunning **2** secretive *adv* **3** in secret

underline *n* → **1** sign *v* **2** emphasise **3** mark

underling *n* → inferior

undermine *v* → **1** damage **2** destroy **3** dig **4** hollow

underneath *n* → **1** bottom *adv* **2** below *prep* **3** under

underpin *v* → support

underprivileged *adj* → **1** poor **2** unfortunate **3** working-class

UNDERSTAND *v* bottom, catch on, click, comprehend, cotton on, fathom, follow, get, get inside, get the message, get the picture, have someone taped, healy, jerry to, make head or tail of, penetrate, savvy, see, see the light, take a tumble to, take a wake-up, take in, the penny drops, trick to, tumble to, twig. *See also* KNOW

understand *v* → **1** believe **2** explain

UNDERSTANDING *n* insight, sight *(Obs.)*, skill *(Obs.)*; **awareness,** apperception, cognisance, consciousness, initiation, recognisance, recognition, self-awareness, self-consciousness, self-knowledge, sense; **perception,** cognition, noesis, observation, percept, perceptiveness, perceptivity, percipience, sensibility. *See also* KNOWLEDGE

understanding *n* → **1** agreement **2** arrangement **3** contract **4** friendship **5** intelligence **6** learning **7** mind **8** translation *adj* **9** emotional **10** intelligent **11** knowing

understate *v* → lie

understudy *n* → **1** actor **2** inferior

UNDERTAKE *v* assume, attempt, come to holts with, do, engage in, fix, go ahead with, have, launch, mind, purpose, set up, stage, stand, tackle, take on, take upon oneself, work; **break new ground,** cross the Rubicon, embark, enter on, launch forth, venture upon; **have irons in the fire,** have a lot on one's plate; **get on with the job,** do someone's dirty work, get a grip on, get one's teeth into, get stuck into, go to it, hop into, make bold to, put one's hand to the plough, put one's shoulder to the wheel, square up to, take in hand, take the bit between one's teeth, take upon one's shoulders, throw oneself into, turn one's hand to; **attempt the impossible,** square the circle

undertake *v* → **1** attempt **2** fight **3** promise

UNDERTAKER *n* burier, cremationist, embalmer, funeral director, grave-digger, mortician, sexton; **pallbearer,** mourner, mute

undertaker *n* → contractor

UNDERTAKING *n* affair, enterprise, operation, program, thing, venture, voyage *(Obs.)*; **assignment,** commission, engagement, job, plan, project, task, work; **campaign,** adventure, crusade, emprise *(Archaic)*, mission, quest, search; **forlorn hope,** leap in the dark, tall order; **embarkation,** assumption, candidature, commitment, espousal

undertone *n* → **1** colour **2** quiet sound

undertow *n* → current

UNDERWEAR *n* chiton, combinations, dishabille, flannels *(Obs.)*, lingerie, long johns, smalls *(Brit. Colloq.)*, underclothes, undergarment, underthings, undies, unmentionables; **camisole,** bodice *(Obs.)*, chemise, diaper shirt, hoop, hoop skirt, sark *(Scot. Archaic)*, spencer, undershirt *(U.S.)*, undersleeve; **petticoat,** balmoral, bustle, crinoline, farthingale, half-slip, pannier *(Obs.)*, slip, underskirt; **foundation garment,** boob tube, bra, brassiere, busk, corset, corsetry, cup, easies *(N.Z.)*, falsies, girdle, pasty, roll-ons, stays, step-ins; **singlet,** Jacky Howe, Jimmy Howe, undervest, vest; **panties,** bloomers, briefs, drawers, gorgeous gussies, grundies, gussies, knickers, pantalets, pants, scanties; **underpants,** boxer shorts, grundies, jockey shorts, jockeys, jocks, reginalds, underdaks, Y-fronts; **supporter,** athletic support, codpiece, jock, jockstrap, support; **figleaf,** cache-sexe. *See also* TIGHTS

underworld *n* → **1** afterworld **2** criminal

underwrite *v* → **1** finance **2** label

undesirable *n* → **1** bad person *adj* **2** bad **3** inconvenient **4** unpleasant

UNDETERMINED *adj* in the air, inconclusive, open, pendent, pending, uncertain, undecided; **perplexing,** debatable, paradoxical, problematical, questionable, ticklish

undo *v* → **1** cancel **2** counteract **3** destroy **4** open

UNDRESS *v* bare, debag, dishelm *(Archaic)*, disrobe, divest, do a hambone, expose oneself, peel, pill *(Archaic)*, strip, uncover, unhood; **go naked,** chuck a brown-eye, flash, jaybird, skinny-dip, streak

undress *n* → **1** informality **2** uniform *v* **3** bare **4** cut **5** shear

UNDRESSING *n* dismantlement, disrobement, divestiture, divestment, divesture, exposure, indecent exposure, poppy show, striptease

undue *adj* → **1** excessive **2** incorrect

undulate *v* → curve

unearth *v* → **1** dig **2** find

unearthly *adj* → **1** foolish **2** strange **3** supernatural

uneasy *adj* → **1** discontented **2** formal **3** worried

uneducated *adj* → ignorant

unemployed *adj* → dismissed

UNEQUAL *adj* anisotropic, asymmetrical, disparate, irregular, unbalanced, uneven; **disproportional,** disproportionate, out of proportion; **lopsided,** anisometric, dissymetric, dissymmetrical, oblique, one-sided, secund, unilateral; **perissodactyl,** perissodactylous; **scalene**

unequal *adj* → **1** different **2** irregular
unequivocal *adj* → certain
unerring *adj* → **1** correct **2** direct **3** precise
unfailing *adj* → **1** certain **2** changeless **3** continual **4** faithful
UNFAIR *adj* a bit rough, bloody, hard, inofficious, invidious, loaded, on the cuff *(N.Z.)*, raw, unjust, unjustified, unrighteous, wanton; **undeserved,** gratuitous, improper, uncalled-for, unearned, unexpected, unfitting; **discriminatory,** biased, nepotic, one-eyed, one-sided, partial, partisan; **unauthorized,** unconstitutional, unsanctioned, unwarrantable, unwarranted; **foul,** dirty, unsportsmanlike; **unpardonable,** inexcusable, objectionable, unjustifiable; **oppressive,** extortionate, inequitable, iniquitous, injurious
unfair *adj* → intolerant
UNFAIRLY *adv* below the belt, dirtily, foul; **unjustly,** extortionately, gratuitously, iniquitously, injuriously, inofficiously, invidiously, oppressively, unrighteously, wantonly; **unworthily,** improperly, unfitly
UNFAIRNESS *n* gratuitousness, inequality, inequity, iniquitousness, iniquity, injury, invidiousness; **discrimination,** bias, cronyism, favouritism, leaning, nepotism, onesidedness, partiality, preferential treatment; **injustice,** dirtiness, inofficiousness, miscarriage of justice, misjudgment, rum go, unjustness, wrong; **oppression,** abuse, bloodiness, dirtiness, injuriousness, oppressiveness, tyranny, unrighteousness, wantonness; **head-hunting,** kangaroo court, McCarthyism, Star Chamber, witch-hunting
UNFAITHFUL *adj* disloyal, faithless, false, forsworn, recreant, slippery, unreliable, untrue; **treacherous,** apostate, double-dealing, false-hearted, feline, perfidious, renegade, snaky, traitorous, treasonable, treasonous; **adulterous,** adulterine
UNFAITHFULNESS *n* disloyalty, faithlessness, falseness, falsity, infidelity, untrueness; **treacherousness,** apostasy, doubleness, felineness, felinity, insidiousness, perfidiousness, recreance, recreancy, tergiversation, traitorousness, treasonableness. *See also* BETRAYAL
UNFASTEN *v* disyoke, unbrace, unfetter, unfix, unfreeze, unharness, unhasp, unhitch, unhook, unmoor, unpeg, unpen, unpin, unscrew, unsling, unsnap, unstick, unyoke
unfeeling *adj* → callous
unfit *adj* → **1** inappropriate **2** incompetent **3** incongruous **4** unworthy **5** useless
unfold *v* → **1** display **2** explain **3** grow **4** open up **5** reveal
unforeseen *adj* → surprising
UNFORTUNATE *n* bad news, Job, lame duck, miser *(Obs.)*, poor cow, poor fish, ruin, scapegoat, schlemiel *(U.S.)*, underdog, victim, wreck, wretch; **deadbeat,** derelict, dero, down-and-out, toe-ragger, vagrant
UNFORTUNATE *adj* badly off, hapless, miserable, poor, stricken, underprivileged, unhappy, wretched; **luckless,** out of luck, star-crossed, starred, unlucky; **ill-fated,** accident-prone, accursed, cursed, curst; **hard-hit,** in a bad way, in deep water, in dire straits, in the poo, in the shit, in the wars, in trouble, smitten, up against it; **down-and-out,** deadbeat, down on one's arse, down on one's luck
unfortunate *adj* → **1** bad **2** incongruous **3** inconvenient **4** unhappy
UNFORTUNATENESS *n* inauspiciousness, unfavourableness, unluckiness; **calamitousness,** disastrousness, ruggedness, ruinousness, tragicalness; **agony,** distress, misery, unhappiness, woe, wretchedness; **lucklessness,** haplessness
UNFRIENDLINESS *n* animosity, animus, bad feeling, enmity, hostility, ill feeling, ill will, inimicality, malevolence, rivalry, virulence; **antipathy,** adverseness, antagonism, defiantness, opposition, quarrelsomeness; **alienation,** disaffection, estrangement, incompatibility; **bitterness,** jealousy, rancorousness, rancour, resentment, spite, spitefulness, the sulks. *See also* UNSOCIABILITY
UNFRIENDLY *adj* adverse, antagonistic, hostile, inimical, malevolent, oppositional; **quarrelsome,** aggressive, belligerent, defiant, fighting drunk, pugnacious; **traitorous,** disloyal, snaky, treacherous; **bitter,** rancorous, resentful, spiteful, spleenful, splenetic. *See also* UNSOCIABLE
unfurl *v* → open up
ungainly *adj* → **1** incompetent **2** ugly
ungodly *adj* → **1** bad **2** immoral **3** irreverent
ungracious *adj* → **1** discourteous **2** incompetent
UNGRAMMATICAL *adj* anacoluthic, incorrect, slipshod, solecistic, unidiomatic, wrong
UNGRATEFUL *adj* incapable of gratitude, ingrate, insensible of benefits, unappreciative, unthankful, whingeing; **forgetful,** oblivious, unmindful; **thankless**
UNGRATEFULNESS *n* indifference, ingratitude, thanklessness, unappreciativeness, unthankfulness; **grudging thanks,** a show of gratitude; **ingrate,** ungrateful wretch
unguent *n* → **1** fat **2** medication
UNHAPPINESS *n* cheerlessness, disconsolateness, disconsolation, downheartedness, dreariness *(Archaic)*, dumpishness, sadness, wistfulness; **misery,** bale *(Archaic)*, comfortlessness, crestfallenness, distress, dole *(Archaic)*, dolefulness, dolorousness, dolour, mournfulness, plaintiveness, rue *(Archaic)*, ruefulness, ruth *(Archaic)*, ruthfulness, sorrow, sorrowfulness, tearfulness, woe, woefulness, wretchedness; **depression,** blue devils, blues, damp, dejectedness, dejection, despondency, gloom, gloominess, glumness, leadenness, low-spiritedness, maudlinness, mopishness, pensiveness, pessimism, prostration, vapourishness *(Archaic)*, Weltschmerz; **midlife crisis,** male menopause, MLC; **melancholy,** atrabiliousness, Byronism, melancholia, moodiness, spleen *(Archaic)*; **sullenness; loneliness,** forlornness, homesickness, lonesomeness, lovelornness;

dismalness, depressiveness, dreariness, gloominess, infelicity, joylessness, mirthlessness, miserableness, oppressiveness, sunlessness, unblessedness; **distressfulness,** pathos, poignancy; **heartache,** anguish, heartbreak, heartbrokenness, heartsickness

UNHAPPY *adj* blue, cheerless, comfortless, disconsolate, distressful, doleful, doloroso, dolorous, dreary *(Archaic)*, droopy, dumpish, dumpy, forlorn, gloomy, glum, grievous, happy as a bastard on father's day, heavy, heavy-hearted, heavy-laden, in the miseries, joyless, maudlin, miserable, miserable as a bandicoot, mournful, sad, sorrowful, sorry, upset; **dejected,** chapfallen, chopfallen, crestfallen, damp *(Archaic)*, depressed, despondent, down, down in the dumps, down in the mouth, downcast, downhearted, exanimate, hipped, hippish, leaden, low, low-spirited, melancholiac, melancholic, melancholy, mopey, mopish, prostrate, ratshit, run-down, vapourish *(Archaic)*, wistful; **lonely,** homesick, like a bandicoot on a burnt ridge, like a shag on a rock, lonesome, lorn *(Archaic)*; **broken-hearted,** broken up, grief-stricken, heart-stricken, heartbroken, heartsick, heartsore, lovelorn; **weepy,** in tears, lachrymal, lachrymose, tearful, teary; **moody,** atrabilious, broody, Byronic, morose, saturnine, splenetic *(Obs.)*, sullen; **humourless,** mirthless; **unfortunate,** baleful *(Archaic)*, rueful, unblessed, woebegone, woeful, wretched

unhappy *adj* → **1** badly-done **2** incongruous **3** unfortunate

UNHAPPY PERSON *n* languisher, lemon, lonely heart, long face, martyr, mater dolorosa, miser *(Obs.)*, misery, miseryguts, mope, moper, sad sack, streak of misery, wet blanket, wowser; **melancholiac,** brooder, depressive; **wretch,** object of compassion, poor unfortunate

unhealthy *adj* → **1** damaged **2** dangerous **3** immoral **4** unwholesome

unheard-of *adj* → **1** nonconformist **2** rare **3** strange **4** unknown

unicorn *n* → **1** carriage **2** mythical beast

UNIFORM *n* cap and gown, gown, habit, livery, silks, vestment; **military clothing,** battle fatigues, battledress, class A's *(U.S.)*, dress uniform, fatigue dress, fatigues, full dress, gigglesuit, mess kit, number ones, order, Regimentals, service dress, tropical dress, tropical whites, tunic, undress; **spacesuit,** G-suit, pressure suit; **religious clothing,** alb, canonicals, cassock, chasuble, chimar, chimer, clericals, cloth *(Obs.)*, cope, cotta, dalmatic, ephod *(Judaism)*, epitrachelion *(Greek Orthodox Ch.)*, fanon, frock, Geneva gown, mantelletta *(Rom. Cath. Ch.)*, omophorion *(Eastern Ch.)*, pluvial, pontificals, rochet, scapular, soutane, surplice, tunicle, vestments; **prison clothing,** gigglesuit *(Obs.)*, magpie clothing; **hairshirt,** sanbenito

uniform *n* → **1** emblem of office **2** formal dress *adj* **3** boring **4** homogeneous **5** simple

unify *v* → combine

unilateral *adj* → **1** anarchic **2** genetic **3** intolerant **4** one **5** unequal

unimaginable *adj* → impossible

unimpeachable *adj* → **1** certain **2** correct

UNIMPORTANCE *n* immateriality, immaterialness, inessentiality, insignificance, irrelevance, worthlessness; **triviality,** bathos, impertinence, inconsequentiality, irrelevance, puerility, triflingness, trivialism, trivialness; **frivolity,** frivolousness, frothiness, lightsomeness, yeastiness; **pettiness,** insignificancy, littleness, nothingness, obscureness, obscurity, paltriness, puniness, tenuousness, veniality, venialness; **minimisation,** trivialisation

UNIMPORTANT *adj* foolish *(Archaic)*, forgettable, futile *(Obs.)*, inappreciable, insignificant, light, obscure, pint-size, simple, small, small-time, tenuous, two-by-four *(U.S.)*, unconsidered, uneventful; **unessential,** dispensable, expendable, inessential, non-essential, peripheral; **inconsequential,** immaterial, impertinent, irrelevant; **accidental,** circumstantial; **superficial,** shallow; **subordinate,** less, minor, paltry, petit *(Law)*, venial; **secondary,** subsidiary; **fiddling,** farting, mickey mouse, picayune, piddling, piffling, pimping, potty *(Brit.)*, tinhorn *(U.S.)*; **frivolous,** fallal *(Obs.)*, frothy, idle, jesting, light, lightsome, lightweight, slight, yeasty; **trivial,** footling, for the birds, frying pan, gewgaw, gimcrack, gingerbread, inconsiderable, nugatory, petty, puerile, puny, trifling, twopenny-halfpenny, worthless

UNIMPORTANT PERSON *n* also-ran, cipher, figurehead, insignificancy, insignificant, jackstraw, man of straw, nobody, nonperson, nonentity, nothing, obscurity; **trifler,** amateur, dabbler, dallier, dilettante, piddler; **lightweight,** minnow, peanut, picayune, pipsqueak, pygmy, shitkicker, small fry, snippet, twerp, zed

UNIMPORTANT THING *n* inessential, minim, non-essential, non-event, nothing, unessential; **side issue,** accident, accidental, afterthought, bye, circumstance, immateriality, indifference, insignificant, irrelevance, red herring, sideshow; **trifle,** bêtise, breath, falderal, fiddle-faddle, frivolity, impertinence, joke, petty detail, pinpoint, triviality; **bagatelle,** bauble, bit of tinsel, chip *(U.S.)*, fiddlestick, flummery, frippery, frivolity, gewgaw, gimcrack, gingerbread, kickshaw, knick-knack, peppercorn, picayune, straw, tinker's cuss, tinker's damn, toy, trinket, whatnot; **cavil,** fleabite, pinprick; **trivia,** minutiae; **chickenfeed,** kid-stakes, small beer, small change, small potatoes; **peccadillo,** venial sin; **insignificant place,** backstreet, byway, one-horse town, sideway, whistlestop *(U.S.)*

uninhibited *adj* → **1** informal **2** liberated

union *n* → **1** combination **2** combine **3** joining **4** marriage **5** society

UNIONISM *n* compulsory unionism, restrictive practice, syndicalism, trade unionism, unionisation; **union movement,** organised labour

unionist *n* → trade unionist

unique *adj* → **1** nonconformist **2** one **3** strange **4** unrelated

unison *n* → **1** congruity **2** music

unit *n* → **1** armed forces **2** flat **3** gradation **4** machine **5** one **6** train *adj* **7** one

unite *v* → **1** agree **2** associate **3** converge **4** cooperate **5** join **6** marry **7** stick together

unity *n* → **1** agreement **2** combination **3** congruity **4** oneness **5** wholeness

universal *adj* → **1** cosmic **2** general

universe *n* → **1** matter **2** sky

university *n* → college

UNKEMPT *adj* bedraggled, daggy, draggletailed, frowzy, grubby, scrubby, sleazy, slovenly, sluttish, wretched; **scruffy,** scabby, scrofulous, scurfy, snotty, snotty-nosed, unwashed; **flea-bitten,** buggy, chatty, crawling, lousy, mangy, pediculous, sordid, squalid; **piggish,** beastlike, hoggish, hoglike. *See also* DIRTY

unkempt *adj* → **1** ill-bred **2** untidy

UNKIND *adj* cutting, disobliging, incogitant, inconsiderate, thoughtless, uncharitable, unchristian, ungenerous, ungentle, unkindly, unpitying; **ill-willed,** cattish, catty, despiteful *(Archaic)*, ill-natured, malevolent, malicious, malignant, mean, misanthropic, nasty, poisonous, sharp-tongued, shrewd *(Archaic)*, snaky, spiteful, venomous, viper-like, viperish, viperous, virulent; **cruel,** bloody-minded, cold-blooded, crool, cutthroat, dispiteous *(Archaic)*, harsh, heartless, inhuman, inhumane, merciless, pitiless, remorseless, ruthless, sadistic, unmerciful, unrelenting, unsparing, unsympathetic; **brutal,** atrocious, beastly, brutish, butcherly, fell, fiendish, fierce, lupine, savage, tigerish, vicious, vulture-like

UNKINDNESS *n* cattiness, cattishness, disobligingness, harshness, ill-treatment, maltreatment, meanness, misanthropy, nastiness, soullessness, uncharitableness, ungentleness, unkindliness; **inconsiderateness,** insensitivity, thoughtlessness, unfeelingness; **cruelty,** bloody-mindedness, brutality, brutishness, cold-bloodedness, cruelness, flintiness, heartlessness, inhumanity, mental cruelty, mercilessness, pitilessness, remorselessness, ruthlessness, sadism, savageness, savagery, unmercifulness, unrelentingness, viciousness; **fiendishness,** atrociousness, fellness, tigerishness; **brutalisation,** dehumanisation

UNKIND PERSON *n* abuser, animal, brute, harmer, monster, sadist, savage, Turk, victimiser, vulture; **Job's comforter; cat,** tigress, viper

UNKNOWN *n* anon., anonymity, stranger; **closed book,** dark horse; **gamble,** pig in a poke

UNKNOWN *adj* strange, trackless, unbeknown *(Colloq.)*, uncharted, unco *(Scot.)*, unexplored, unfamiliar, unheard, unheard-of, unplumbed, unrecognised, unsounded, unsuspected; **unnamed,** anonymous, unbranded, unlisted

unknown *n* → **1** number **2** uncertain thing *adj* **3** uncertain

UNLAWFUL *adj* backstreet, backyard, illegal, illegitimate, illicit, non-legal, racketeering, unauthorized, wrongful; **contraband,** black, black-market; **law-breaking,** crim, criminal, criminological, crooked, felonious, malfeasant, recidivistic, recidivous; **indictable,** actionable, punishable, tortious; **lawless,** anarchic, chaotic; **above the law,** despotic, tyrannical; **outlawed,** out of bounds, outside the law; **fraudulent,** collusive, conspiratorial; **unconstitutional,** extrajudicial, irregular, unstatutory

UNLAWFULNESS *n* illegality, illegalness, illegitimacy, illicitness, law-breaking, unconstitutionality, wrong side of the law, wrongfulness; **criminality,** banditry, crookedness, delinquency, feloniousness, felonry, gangsterism, lawlessness, outlawry, racketeering, recidivism, standover tactics; **lynch law,** gang rule, kangaroo court, mob law, mob rule. *See also* CRIME

unless *conj* → on condition that

unlike *adj* → different

UNLIKELIHOOD *n* fishiness, improbability, unlikeliness; **an outside chance,** a hundred to one, a long chance, a poor chance, bare possibility, Buckley's chance, long shot, poor chance, remote possibility, small chance; **tall story,** exaggeration, shaggy dog story, the story about the one that got away

UNLIKELY *adj* at long odds, contrary to expectation, far-fetched, fishy, implausible, improbable, inconceivable

UNLIKELY *adv* hardly, improbably, scarcely, unlikely

unlikely *adj* → **1** unavailable *adv* **2** unlikely

unload *v* → **1** remove **2** sell **3** transport

unlucky *adj* → unfortunate

UNMANAGEABLE *adj* hard-mouthed *(Equestrian)*, mean, uncontrollable; **refractory,** bloody, bloody-minded, hard-set, impossible, impracticable, intractable, restive

unmannerly *adj* → discourteous

unmistakable *adj* → **1** blatant **2** certain **3** obvious **4** precise **5** visible

unmitigated *adj* → **1** most **2** thorough **3** unconditional

unmoved *adj* → **1** apathetic **2** callous

unnatural *adj* → **1** affected **2** incongruous **3** nonconformist **4** strange

unnecessary *adj* → **1** surplus **2** useless

unnerve *v* → alarm

unofficial *adj* → informal

UNPAID *adj* due, not yet payable, outstanding, undischarged; **deferring payment,** moratory; **complimentary,** free, gratis, tax-deductible, tax-free, untaxed; **honorary,** uncustomed, unpaid, unremunerated, unrewarded, voluntary

unparalleled *adj* → **1** perfect **2** strange **3** superior

UNPLEASANT *adj* awful, bad, beastly, bitter, dire, dislikeable, displeasing, forbidding, hard, hell of a, helluva, lousy, nasty, painful, perishing, rough, sharp, tough, ugly, unacceptable, uncomfortable, undesirable, unenviable, ungrateful, unpalatable, unpleasing, unsavoury, untoward; **disagreeable,** abhorrent, detestable, distasteful, execrable, hateful, loathly *(Archaic)*, loathsome, objectionable, obnoxious, odious, rebarbative, repellent, repugnant, repulsive, revolting, uninviting, vile, wicked *(Colloq.)*. *See also* UNBEARABLE; SICKENING; DREADFUL; PESTERING

UNPLEASANTNESS *n* awfulness, badness, disagreeableness, distastefulness, dreadfulness, frightfulness, harshness, insufferableness, intolerability, intolerableness, irksomeness, lousiness, meanness, monstrousness, nastiness, poisonousness, unbearableness, uncomfortableness; **obnoxiousness,** fulsomeness, repellence, repellency, repulsiveness; **gruesomeness,** creepiness, ghastliness, ghoulishness, grimness, grisliness, horribleness; **bloody-mindedness,** bad temper, bitchiness, cantankerousness, doggishness; **discomfort,** irritation, pain; **filthiness,** abominableness, beastliness, foulness, goo, guck, gunk, insalubrity, loathsomeness, muck, rottenness, slime, sourness, vileness

UNPLEASANT PERSON *n* bag, bastard, bête noire, bugger, cunt, cunthook *(N.Z.)*, deadshit, ghoul, hazer, heavy, iron maiden, mother-fucker *(U.S.)*, pill, prick, repeller, reptile, shocker, stinker, twat, varmint *(Archaic)*

UNPLEASANT PLACE *n* hell, hellhole, purgatory, the dead end, the end, the living end, the pits

UNPLEASANT THING *n* a bad scene, a cow of a something, a fair cow, a taste of one's own medicine, bitter cup, bitter pill, blow, dose, four-letter word, horror, incubus, lemon, nightmare, pain, pain in the arse, pain in the behind, pain in the bum, pain in the neck, sorry sight, thorn in one's flesh, wormwood and gall; **chore,** dirty work, nuisance, taskwork; **abomination,** anathema, detestable action, shameful vice, wickedness

unprincipled *adj* → **1** immoral **2** wrong

unprofessional *adj* → **1** incompetent **2** incorrect

unquestionable *adj* → certain

unravel *v* → **1** clarify **2** inquire into **3** separate **4** simplify **5** translate

UNREADINESS *n* improvidence, lack of preparation, neglect, unpreparedness; **rawness,** crudeness, crudity, rudeness

UNREADY *adj* cold, flat-footed, ill-equipped, ill-prepared, out of order, unarmed, unarranged, unorganised, unprepared; **half-baked,** sketchy; **on the anvil,** on the drawing-board, under discussion; **improvident,** happy-go-lucky, shiftless, unthrifty. *See also* RAW

unreal *adj* → **1** bad **2** delusive **3** good **4** intangible **5** unrealistic

UNREALISTIC *adj* airy-fairy, capricious *(Obs.)*, escapist, fairytale, fanciful, far-out, idealist, idealistic, moonshiny, notional, romantic, starry-eyed, unreal, utopian, vaporous, visionary

unreasonable *adj* → **1** illogical **2** prejudiced **3** rash **4** stubborn

UNRELATED *adj* dissociated, foreign, immaterial, impertinent, inconsequent, independent, irrelevant, unconnected; **absolute,** irrelative, positive, unique; **kinless; beside the point,** not to the purpose

UNRELATEDNESS *n* distance, foreignness, impertinence, inconsequence, independence, irrelativeness, irrelevance; **absoluteness,** uniqueness

unrelenting *adj* → **1** callous **2** continual **3** strict **4** unkind

unrelieved *adj* → **1** boring **2** continual

unremitting *adj* → **1** continual **2** persevering

unrest *n* → **1** discontentedness **2** turbulence

unruffled *adj* → **1** apathetic **2** composed **3** smooth

unruly *adj* → **1** anarchic **2** badly-behaved **3** disobedient

UNSAVOURY *adj* ill-flavoured, indigestible, inedible, unappetizing, uneatable, unpalatable; **rough,** astringent, austere, coarse, strong; **off,** corked, corky, nasty, noisome, on the turn, tinny; **rank,** acrid, brackish, fetid, gamy, rammish, rancid

unsavoury *adj* → unpleasant

unscrew *v* → **1** liberate **2** unfasten

unseat *v* → **1** dismiss **2** misplace

unsecured *adj* → vulnerable

unseen *adj* → invisible

UNSELFISH *adj* altruistic, benevolent, disinterested, high-minded, non-profitmaking, public-spirited, self-devotional, self-effacing, self-forgetful, self-renunciatory, self-sacrificing, selfless; **generous,** big, big-hearted, chivalrous, magnanimous, noble, philanthropic

UNSELFISH PERSON *n* altruist, humanitarian, martyr, noble soul, philanthropist, saint

unsettled *adj* → **1** changeable **2** climatic **3** disorderly **4** indecisive **5** uncertain

unsightly *adj* → ugly

unskilled *adj* → incompetent

UNSOCIABILITY *n* exclusiveness, inhospitableness, inhospitality; **surliness,** bearishness, moroseness, spleen, sulkiness, sullenness; **coldness,** chill, chillness, coolness, frostiness; **uncommunicativeness,** retirement, retreat, silence, undemonstrativeness, withdrawal; **reserve,** aloofness, distance, offishness, remoteness, reservedness, reticence, stand-offishness, unapproachableness. *See also* UNFRIENDLINESS

UNSOCIABLE *adj* antisocial, dissociable, dissocial, forbidding, ill-disposed, inhospitable, insociable, unwelcoming; **sullen,** bearish, farouche, morose, sulky, surly; **reserved,** in one's shell, indrawn, reticent, retiring, unforthcoming, withdrawn; **aloof,** distant, exclusive, inapproachable, offish, remote, stand-off, stand-offish, unapproachable, uncommunicative, undemonstrative; **cold,** chill, chilly, coldish, cool, frigid, frosty, frozen, icy; **antipathetic,** disaffected, incompatible, intolerant, unsympathetic; **alienated,** estranged, irreconcilable, isolated. *See also* UNFRIENDLY

unsound *adj* → **1** changeable **2** damaged **3** illogical **4** imperfect **5** misjudged **6** unwholesome

unspeakable *adj* → **1** bad **2** obscene

unstable *adj* → **1** changeable **2** indecisive **3** uncertain

unsteady *adj* → **1** changeable **2** indecisive **3** irregular

unsung *adj* → disreputable

unswerving *adj* → strict

untenable *adj* → **1** illogical **2** vulnerable

unthinkable *adj* → impossible

unthinking *adj* → **1** inattentive **2** stupid

UNTIDILY *adv* frowzily, seedily, shabbily, sleazily, sloppily; **chaotically,** all over the shop, at random, at sixes and sevens, higgledy-piggledy, topsy-turvy, willy-nilly; **helter-skelter,** hurly-burly, hurry-scurry, pell-mell; **confusedly,** confusingly, desultorily, discomposedly, immethodically; **riotously,** harum-scarum, rowdily, tempestuously, tumultuously, uproariously, wildly

UNTIDINESS *n* dishabille, dishevelment, dowdiness, frowziness, sleaze, sleaziness, sloppiness, slovenliness, tousle *(Rare)*, unkemptness; **pigsty,** brothel, disaster area, dump, fleapit, shambles

UNTIDY *v* dishevel, ruffle, rumple, tousle; **jumble,** clutter, derange, disarrange, disarray, litter, shuffle; **sprawl,** knock about, slummock; **confuse,** anarchise, discompose, embroil, fuddle, gum up the works, make hay, make the feathers fly, make the fur fly, put the cart before the horse, rock the boat, throw a spanner in the works, upset the applecart

UNTIDY *adj* bedraggled, blowzy, dishevelled, down at heel, frowzy, mussy *(U.S.)*, out at elbow, out at the elbow, raggle-taggle, scruffy, shaggy, slatternly, sleazy, slipshod, sloppy, slovenly, slummocky, sluttish, tatty, unkempt, warby, wild, wild and woolly, windblown, windswept

untidy *v* → **1** dirty *adj* **2** dirty

UNTIDY PERSON *n* chat, dag, derelict, dero, dowdy, ragamuffin, ragbag, scarecrow, scrubber, scruff, scunge, slattern, sleaze, sloven, slummock, slut, warb; **rowdy,** boyo, harum-scarum; **rabble,** mob; **disarranger,** disorganiser, disturber, jumbler, rifler

untie *v* → **1** liberate **2** separate **3** simplify

until *conj* → while

UNTIMELINESS *n* bad timing, inopportuneness, inopportunity, interruption, unseasonableness; **mistiming,** asynchronism; **false start,** miscue, wrong entry *(Music)*; **anachronism,** archaism, prolepsis; **obsolescence,** fustiness, obsoleteness

UNTIMELY *adj* abortive, early, ill-timed, inopportune, interruptive, late, out of season overhasty, premature, unseasonable; **mistimed,** asynchronous, fast, slow; **anachronous,** anachronistic, archaic, demoded, fusty, obsolescent, obsolete, old hat, old-fashioned, old-time, olde-worlde, out of fashion, out-of-date, outdated, outmoded, outworn

UNTIMELY *adv* inopportunely, out of turn; **out,** behind, out of season, out of time, unseasonably

untimely *adj* → early

untold *adj* → **1** infinite **2** many **3** uncertain

untoward *adj* → **1** inconvenient **2** stubborn **3** unpleasant

untrue *adj* → **1** fake **2** false **3** unfaithful

UNUSED *adj* unbeaten, unfired, untapped, untouched, untravelled, virgin; **at a loose end,** at liberty, free, loose, standing, vacant

unusual *adj* → **1** nonconformist **2** rare **3** strange

unveil *v* → **1** bare **2** reveal

unwarranted *adj* → **1** anarchic **2** unfair

UNWHOLESOME *adj* insalubrious, morbid, morbific, unhealthy, unsound; **septic,** abscessed, cankerous, infect *(Archaic)*, mature, purulent, scorbutic, ulcerative, ulcerous, watery; **cancerous,** carcinomatous, tumorous; **wasted,** atrophied, degenerate, waxy; **anaemic,** exsanguine; **inflamed,** angry, bloodshot; **dropsical,** hydropic; **acute,** afflictive, progressive; **subclinical; chronic,** confirmed; **incurable,** immedicable, remediless; **infectious,** catching, endemic, epidemic, pandemic; **inflammatory,** phlogistic; **deleterious; pathogenetic,** bacterial, germinal, viral; **cryptogenic,** iatrogenic, idiopathic, psychosomatic

unwieldy *adj* → incompetent

UNWILLING *adj* averse, difficult, disinclined, hesitant, indisposed, loath, negative, reluctant, reserved, scrupulous, uncooperative, unenthusiastic, uninclined; **involuntary,** automatic, autonomic, compulsive, matter-of-course, mechanical, mesmeric, reflex, semi-automatic; **backward,** bashful, shy, timid

UNWILLINGLY *adv* aversely, grudgingly, hesitatingly, loathly, reluctantly, with a bad grace; **involuntarily,** automatically, autonomically, by rote, compulsively, mechanically; **backwardly,** bashfully, shyly, timidly; **purposelessly,** idly, tardily; **unintentionally,** accidentally, in spite of oneself, unconsciously, unwittingly

UNWILLINGNESS *n* averseness, disinclination, indisposition, unenthusiasm; **reluctance,** hesitation, reservation, scrupulosity; **involuntariness,** automatism, mechanicalness; **automatic response,** compulsion, knee-jerk reaction; **idleness,** laziness, perfunctoriness, tardiness; **aimlessness,** purposelessness; **backwardness,** bashfulness, shyness, timidity; **obstacle,** difficulty, scruple; **unintentionality,** unconsciousness, unwittingness

unwind *v* → **1** compose oneself **2** separate **3** simplify **4** straighten

unwitting *adj* → **1** ignorant **2** purposeless **3** stupid

unworldly *adj* → **1** artless **2** ignorant **3** innocent **4** spiritual

UNWORTHY *adj* incompetent, undeserving, unfit, unqualified, would-be; **presumptuous,** assuming, self-styled, upstart

unworthy *adj* → **1** bad **2** incorrect

unwritten *adj* → **1** allusive **2** customary

UP *adv* airwards, heavenward, skyward, sunward, upstairs, upwardly, upwards

upbraid *v* → scold

upbringing *n* → care

up-bringing *n* → teaching

update *n* → **1** innovation *v* **2** improve **3** innovate

up-end *v* → **1** erect **2** lift

upgrade *n* → **1** slope *v* **2** improve **3** promote

upheaval *n* → **1** distortion **2** lifting **3** revolution

uphill *n* → **1** slope *adj* **2** difficult **3** effortful **4** high **5** sloping

uphold *v* → **1** assent to **2** be faithful to **3** support

upholster *v* → **1** cover **2** soften

upholstery *n* → manchester

upkeep *n* → care

uplift *n* → **1** distortion **2** happiness **3** hope **4** improvement **5** lifting *v* **6** glorify **7** improve **8** lift **9** raise up

up on *adj* → **1** educated **2** informed **3** knowing

upper *n* → **1** apex **2** footgear **3** pleasure *adj* **4** aristocratic **5** high

Upper *adj* → late

uppercut *n* → **1** hit *v* **2** hit

upright *adj* → **1** correct **2** erect **3** honest **4** postural *adv* **5** erectly

uprising *n* → **1** ascent **2** mutiny **3** revolution

uproar *n* → **1** commotion **2** loud sound **3** muddle

uproot *v* → remove

upset *n* → **1** disagreement **2** illness **3** jumble **4** losing **5** muddle **6** overturn *v* **7** defeat **8** disorder **9** displease **10** make unhappy **11** overturn *adj* **12** nauseous **13** overturned **14** unhappy **15** worried

upshot *n* → finish

upside down *adj* → **1** disorderly **2** overturned

upstage *v* → **1** call attention to *adj* **2** rear *adv* **3** behind **4** dramatically

upstairs *n* → **1** storey **2** tower *adj* **3** high *adv* **4** up

upstanding *adj* → **1** erect **2** honest

upstart *n* → **1** arrogant person **2** innovator **3** middle class **4** vulgarian *adj* **5** unworthy

upsurge *n* → **1** ascent **2** flow **3** stream **4** flow

uptake *n* → **1** knowledge **2** lifting **3** passageway

uptight *adj* → **1** angry **2** conservative **3** irritable **4** worried

up-to-date *adj* → **1** accomplished **2** current **3** educated **4** fashionable **5** informed **6** innovative

upturn *n* → **1** increase *v* **2** overturn

upward *adj* → ascending

upwards *adv* → **1** high **2** up

uranium *n* → fuel

URBAN *adj* burghal, citied, civic, cosmopolitan, intercity, interurban, megalopolitan, metropolitan; **citified,** townish; **suburban,** cross-town, downtown, slummy, uptown

urbane *adj* → **1** courteous **2** knowledgeable **3** tasteful

urchin *n* → **1** children **2** disobeyer **3** fairy **4** man **5** neglected person *adj* **6** disobedient **7** youthful

urethra *n* → bladder

urge *n* → **1** desire **2** incentive *v* **3** encourage **4** entreat **5** guide **6** persuade

urgent *adj* → **1** assertive **2** important **3** insistent **4** necessary

urinal *n* → **1** toilet **2** vessel

URINATE *v* cross swords, drain the dragon, have a Japanese bladder, have a pee, leak, make water, micturate, pee, piddle, piss, point Percy at the porcelain, pot, powder one's nose, relieve oneself, shake hands with the wife's best friend, splash the boots, strain the potatoes, tinkle, wash one's hands, water the horse, wee-wee, wet

URINATION *n* hey-diddle-diddle, Jimmy Riddle, Johnny Bliss, leak, micturition, number one, pee, piddle, piss, slash, snake's, snake's hiss, twinkle, wee, wee-wee, werris; **call of nature; urine,** piss, stale, water; **diuresis,** bed-wetting, enuresis, frequency

urine *n* → urination

urn *n* → **1** coffin **2** vessel

ursine *adj* → animal-like

u/s *adj* **1** inactive **2** useless

usage *n* → **1** conformist behaviour **2** custom **3** meaning **4** use

USE *n* appliance, application, employment, exercise, exertion, improvement, usage; **deployment,** exploitation, optimisation, telesis, utilisation; **consumption,** enjoyment, exhaustion, expenditure, usufruct *(Roman Law)*; **access,** break *(Radio)*, easement; **recovery,** reclamation, resurrection, revival; **wear,** wear and tear

USE *v* employ, make use of, ply, wield; **put to use,** bestow, dispose of, optimise, parlay, utilise; **bring into use,** deploy, find, mobilise, press into service; **apply,** bear, bring to bear, exercise, exert; **capitalise on,** get the best out of, improve, make the most of, turn to account, use to the full; **avail oneself of,** adopt, draw on, enjoy, seize, take up; **resort to,** fall back on, have recourse to, make do with, run to; **exploit,** milk, play, take advantage of, tap, trade on; **recycle,** recover, resurrect, revive

use *n* → **1** necessities **2** ownership **3** profit *v* **4** inhabit

USEABLE *adj* applicative, applicatory, effective, exercisable, functional, practicable, practical, serviceable, subservient, utilisable, viable; **exploitable,** deployable, employable, tappable; **consumable,** enjoyable, expendable; **available,** disposable, ready, ready-made; **recoverable,** reclaimable, recyclable; **valid,** good, good for

used *adj* → **1** dilapidated **2** own

USED UP *adj* exhausted, spent; **worn,** second-hand

USEFUL *adj* handy, helpful, of use, serviceable; **all-purpose,** adaptable, convertible, flexible, general-purpose, multipurpose, purposive; **beneficial,** advantageous, available *(Archaic)*, profitable, valuable

useful *n* → **1** waiter *adj* **2** expedient **3** fertile **4** helpful **5** operating

USEFULNESS *n* advantageousness, profitableness, valuableness, value, worth; **function,** advantage, avail, good, purpose, service; **practicability,** instrumentality, practicality, viability; **useableness,** serviceability, serviceableness, useability, utility; **availability,** readiness

USELESS *adj* functionless, ineffective, ineffectual, inutile, naught *(Obs.)*, non-effective, unemployable, unpractical; **worthless,** trashy, two-bob, valueless; **good-for-nothing,** fit for nothing, no-good, not worth a pinch of shit, not worth a whoop, not worth shucks *(U.S.)*, not worth the candle; **rubbishy,** bodgie, brashy, draffy, dreggy, drossy, dud, grotty, jerry-built, pathetic, r.s., ratshit, trumpery, u/s, up to mud, up to putty, up to shit, warby, weak; **worn-out,** broken-down, clapped-out, condemnable, done, effete, inoperable, on the blink, on the scrap heap, on the way out, out of order, out of plumb, played-out, unfit, unserviceable; **obsolete,** obsolescent, otiose; **ne'er-do-well,** vagabond; **waste,** refuse, scrap; **futile,** abortive, bootless, empty, futilitarian, idle, no use, of no use, purposeless, Sisyphean, unavailing, vain; **invalid,** informal, inoperative; **redundant,** superfluous, unnecessary

useless *adj* → **1** inconvenient **2** infertile **3** powerless

USELESSLY *adv* effetely, otiosely, potteringly; **futilely,** bootlessly, emptily, idly, in vain, unavailingly, vainly

USELESSNESS *n* bootlessness, inutility, unemployability, unserviceability; **unsuitability,** inconvenience, inoperativeness, unfitness; **worthlessness,** drossiness, effeteness, inadequacy, inefficiency, trashiness, valuelessness; **futility,** futileness, idleness, otiosity, purposelessness, superfluousness, unnecessariness, vainness, vanity; **stultification,** crippling, thwarting; **impracticability,** impracticableness, unpracticality, unpracticalness, unworkability; **disservice,** disadvantage

USER *n* applier, exerciser, utiliser; **consumer,** enjoyer, exhauster, expender, spender; **exploiter,** urger

USE UP *v* consume, do, expend, go through, run through, spend; **exhaust,** clean out, finish up, work out

usher *n* → **1** forerunner **2** teacher

usual *adj* → **1** conventional **2** customary **3** repetitive

usurp *v* → take

usury *n* → **1** loan **2** taking

utensil *n* → tool

uterus *n* → groin

utilise *v* → use

utilitarian *n* → **1** realist *adj* **2** expedient **3** realistic

utility *n* → **1** car **2** fertility **3** usefulness *adj* **4** expedient

utmost *n* → **1** much **2** remote place *adj* **3** distant **4** most

utopia *n* → **1** dream **2** perfect thing

utter *v* → **1** circulate **2** expel **3** finance **4** publicise **5** speak **6** write *adj* **7** most **8** thorough **9** unconditional

uvula *n* → mouth

Vv

vacancy *n* → **1** employment **2** emptiness **3** gap **4** inaction **5** job **6** rest **7** stupidity
vacant *adj* → **1** abandoned **2** absent **3** empty **4** unused
vacate *v* → **1** back out **2** deny **3** depart **4** empty
vacation *n* → **1** abandonment **2** emptiness **3** holiday **4** period of inaction *v* **5** rest
vaccinate *v* → **1** insert **2** medicate **3** protect
vaccine *n* → **1** medication *adj* **2** animal-like
VACILLATE *v* abstain, back and fill, balance, blow hot and cold, boggle, change one's tune, chop and change, dicker, fluctuate, halt, hang, have a bit both ways, hesitate, hover, oscillate, pause, sway, swing, tergiversate, um and ah, waver, whiffle, wobble; **agonise over,** be torn between, be up in the air; **shillyshally,** buggerise about, buggerise around, dillydally, frig around, give someone the run around, meander, pussyfoot, pussyfoot around; **prevaricate,** evade, procrastinate, temporise
vacillate *v* → **1** be uncertain **2** flutter
vacuous *adj* → **1** empty **2** idle **3** stupid
vacuum *n* → **1** emptiness **2** non-being **3** space *v* **4** clean *adj* **5** empty
vagabond *n* → **1** poor person **2** traveller *adj* **3** travelling **4** useless
vagary *n* → **1** caprice **2** freak **3** idea **4** image
vagina *n* → **1** groin **2** leaf
vagrant *n* → **1** traveller **2** unfortunate *adj* **3** changeable **4** poor **5** travelling **6** wandering
vague *adj* → **1** imprecise **2** uncertain
vain *adj* → **1** foolish **2** inappropriate **3** infertile **4** proud **5** unavailable **6** useless
vainglory *n* → **1** arrogance **2** braggartism
valediction *n* → **1** farewell **2** oration
valentine *n* → **1** lover **2** tryst
Valentine *n* → message
valet *n* → **1** butler **2** stand
valiant *adj* → courageous
valid *adj* → **1** healthy **2** lawful **3** logical **4** true **5** useable
valise *n* → case
valley *n* → **1** channel **2** gap **3** hollow
valour *n* → courage
valuable *adj* → **1** expensive **2** useful
valuation *n* → **1** assessment **2** tax
VALUE *n* money's worth, the full two bob, worth; **face value,** book value, nominal value, par value; **assessment,** appraisal, appraisement, appreciation, duty, estimate, transvaluation; **quotation,** forward quotation, quote; **exchange rate,** cable rate, ratio
value *n* → **1** assessment **2** colour **3** goodness **4** importance **5** meaning **6** number **7** reputation **8** respectability **9** superiority **10** usefulness *v* **11** appraise **12** approve **13** assess
valve *n* → **1** electrical device **2** flower **3** radio **4** tap
vamp *n* → **1** allurer **2** companionship **3** footgear **4** music **5** repair **6** sexual partner **7** woman *v* **8** allure **9** flirt **10** repair
vampire *n* → **1** bad person **2** devil **3** extortionist **4** opening **5** woman
van *n* → **1** advance **2** combat troops **3** forerunner **4** train **5** truck
vandal *n* → **1** destroyer *adj* **2** brutal **3** destructive
vane *n* → signpost
vanguard *n* → **1** advance **2** combat troops **3** forerunner **4** starter
vanish *v* → disappear
vanity *n* → **1** pride **2** uselessness
vanquish *v* → repress
vantage *n* → advantage
vapid *adj* → **1** boring **2** insipid
vaporise *v* → **1** cloud **2** etherealise
vapour *n* → **1** cloud **2** ephemeral **3** gas **4** smell **5** soul *v* **6** brag **7** cloud
VARIABLE *adj* adjustable, alterable, amendable, changeable, convertible, deformable, flexible, flexile, malleable, modifiable, permutable, pervertible, rectifiable, temperable, transformable, transmutable; **variational,** adaptational, dissimilative, gradational, mutational, mutative, revisional, sportive *(Biol.)*; **conversionary,** conversional, diversified, metabolic, transmutational; **transformational,** alchemic, alchemical, alchemistic, alchemistical, metamorphic, transilient, transitional, transitionary, transitive
variable *n* → **1** number **2** uncertain thing *adj* **3** changeable **4** irregular **5** strange
variance *n* → **1** anomaly **2** difference **3** disagreement
variant *adj* → changing
variation *n* → **1** astronomic point **2** change **3** deflection **4** difference **5** diversity
varied *adj* → **1** different **2** multicoloured
variety *n* → **1** choice **2** class **3** difference **4** something different *adj* **5** dramatic
various *adj* → **1** different **2** many
varnish *n* → **1** affectation **2** brightness **3** jewellery **4** paint *v* **5** coat **6** illuminate
vary *v* → **1** alternate **2** change **3** differ
vascular *adj* → channelled
vase *n* → vessel
vasectomy *n* → contraception
vaseline *n* → fat

assal *n* → 1 dependant 2 servant 3 subject *adj* 4 inferior
ast *adj* → 1 big 2 enormous
'.A.T. *n* → tax
audeville *n* → entertainment
ault *n* → 1 arch 2 grave 3 jump 4 room 5 treasury *v* 6 jump
'aunt *n* → 1 bragging *v* 2 brag
'eer *v* → swerve
'egetable *n* → 1 bore *adj* 2 floral
egetate *v* → be inactive
egetation *n* → inaction
ehement *adj* → 1 acrimonious 2 emotional 3 enthusiastic 4 ferocious
'ehicle *n* → method
'eil *n* → 1 covering 2 disguise 3 headband 4 monasticism 5 wall *v* 6 hide
'ein *n* → 1 blood vessel 2 character 3 diggings 4 line 5 mineral 6 multicolour 7 rock outcrop 8 stream *v* 9 channel 10 line
'ellum *n* → writing materials
'ELOCITY *n* airspeed, angular velocity, burnout velocity, characteristic velocity, critical velocity, escape velocity, flap speed, geostrophic wind speed, gradient wind speed, ground speed, group velocity, muzzle velocity, orbital velocity, phase velocity, radial velocity, stall speed, terminal velocity, velocity of light; **mach,** mach number, sound barrier, speed of sound; **knot,** k.p.h., m.p.h., r.p.m.. *See also* SPEED; RATE
velodrome *n* → sportsground
velvet *n* → 1 profit 2 smooth object *adj* 3 smooth 4 soft
venal *adj* → 1 bribable 2 dishonest 3 selfish
vend *v* → sell
vendetta *n* → 1 argument 2 fight 3 retaliation
veneer *n* → 1 affectation 2 coating 3 plaster 4 shallow 5 timber *v* 6 coat
venerable *adj* → 1 aged 2 highly regarded 3 past 4 reputable
venerate *v* → 1 glorify 2 respect 3 revere 4 worship
vengeance *n* → 1 punishment 2 retaliation
venial *adj* → 1 forgivable 2 justifiable 3 unimportant
venom *n* → 1 ill will 2 poison *v* 3 poison
vent *n* → 1 airway 2 exit 3 gap 4 means of escape *v* 5 discharge 6 display 7 expel 8 speak
ventilate *v* → 1 air 2 deodorise 3 speak
ventral *adj* → bottom
ventricle *n* → 1 head 2 heart
venture *n* → 1 attempt 2 danger 3 gamble 4 trade 5 undertaking *v* 6 brave 7 risk
venue *n* → position
veranda *n* → room
verb *n* → word
verbal *n* → 1 fake 2 revelation *v* 3 fake *adj* 4 precise 5 spoken
verbalise *v* → waffle
verbatim *adj* → 1 precise *adv* 2 precisely 3 strictly
verbiage *n* → 1 nonsense 2 waffle
VERBOSE *adj* diffuse, diffusive, gabby, garrulous, lengthy, long-drawn out, longwinded, loquacious, overblown, profusive, prolix, rambling, tedious, voluble, wordy; **amplificatory,** circumlocutionary, overelaborated, periphrastic, pretentious; **digressive,** apostrophic, discursive, divergent, episodic, excursive, prolegomenous, roundabout; **redundant,** empty, pleonastic, tautological
VERBOSITY *n* gabbiness, garrulity, garrulousness, gift of the gab, longwindedness, loquacity, overelaborateness, overelaboration, prolixity, surplusage, verboseness, volubility, volubleness, wordiness; **diffuseness,** diffusion, diffusiveness; **digressiveness,** discursiveness, vagrancy
verdant *adj* → 1 artless 2 floral 3 green 4 ignorant 5 living
verdict *n* → judgment
verdure *n* → 1 fertility 2 greenness
verge *n* → 1 apex 2 domain 3 edge 4 emblem of office 5 post 6 space *v* 7 come close 8 slope
verger *n* → 1 religious dignitary 2 servant
verify *v* → 1 authenticate 2 be true 3 examine
verily *adv* → 1 honestly 2 in fact *interj* 3 yes
veritable *adj* → 1 correct 2 essential 3 true
verity *n* → 1 actuality 2 truth
vermiform appendix *n* → abdomen
vermilion *adj* → red
vermin *n* → 1 bad person 2 working class
vernacular *n* → 1 language 2 name *adj* 3 public
vernal *adj* → 1 seasonal 2 youthful
versatile *adj* → 1 changeable 2 competent
verse *n* → poetry
versed *adj* → 1 accomplished 2 knowledgeable
VERSIFY *v* berhyme, metrify, poetise, sing; **rhyme,** clink, jingle; **scan**
version *n* → 1 misplacement 2 translation
vertex *n* → 1 apex 2 astronomic point 3 head 4 top
vertical *n* → 1 erectness *adj* 2 erect
verve *n* → 1 artistry 2 competence 3 sprightliness 4 vitality
VERY *adv* almightily, almighty, awfully, badly, bleeding, bloody, blooming, damned, darned, decidedly, deuced, deucedly, devilish, devilishly, effing, ever so *(Brit.)*, extra, frigging, fucking, full *(Archaic)*, how, jolly, mighty *(U.S.)*, molto, not a little, not half, particularly, passing *(Archaic)*, perishing, perishingly, piss, plenty, precious, pretty, rattling, real, remarkably, ruddy, signally, stinking, terribly, terrifically, thumpingly, thunderingly, too, uncommon, uncommonly
very *adj* → 1 correct 2 essential 3 lawful 4 precise 5 simple 6 true
vesicle *n* → 1 bag 2 bladder 3 bulge
VESSEL *n* amphora, ampulla, creamer, cruse, ewer, greybeard, hydria, jug, pitcher, potiche, toby jug, urn, vase; **jar,** Canopic vase, pipkin, pot; **crock,** pithos; **coffeepot,** teapot; **boat,** gravy boat, sauce boat; **bucket,** bale, baler, ice bucket, kibble, pail, piggin, pipkin *(U.S.)*, stoup *(Scot.)*, water-carrier, watering-can; **dipper,** clamshell; **jerry can,**

carboy, kerosene tin, milk can; **chamber-pot,** bedpan, bedroom mug, bottle, dry pan, gazunder, Melbourne Cup *(N.Z.)*, po, sanitary can, thunder-mug, urinal; **rocker,** banjo, cradle *(Mining)*, puddling tub, rumble, tumbling box, V-box. *See also* BASIN; BOTTLE; BARREL; DRINKING VESSEL

vessel *n* → **1** bladder **2** watercraft

vest *n* → **1** clothes **2** jacket **3** underwear *v* **4** cover **5** give

vestal *n* → **1** abstainer **2** monastic *adj* **3** abstinent

vestibule *n* → **1** entrance **2** hall

vestige *n* → **1** fossil **2** remnant **3** sign **4** small amount

vestment *n* → **1** overcoat **2** uniform

vestry *n* → **1** council **2** crowd **3** room

vet *n* → **1** healer **2** serviceman *v* **3** examine **4** investigate

veteran *n* → **1** serviceman **2** specialist *adj* **3** accomplished **4** antique **5** old

veterinary science *n* → healing

veterinary surgeon *n* → healer

veto *n* → **1** prohibition **2** refusal *v* **3** prohibit **4** refuse

vex *v* → **1** agitate **2** anger **3** damage **4** displease **5** irritate **6** pain

VEXING *adj* inciting, invidious, irritating, odious, provocative, provoking

viable *adj* → **1** feasible **2** living **3** useable

viaduct *n* → **1** bridge **2** path

viand *n* → food

vibes *n* → **1** emotion **2** percussion instrument **3** surroundings

vibrant *adj* → **1** energetic **2** exciting **3** fluttery **4** resonant

VIBRATE *v* beat, dandle, joggle, judder, pulsate, pulse, pump, shudder, thrill, throb; **shake,** dither, dodder, palpitate, pant, quake, quaver, shimmy, shiver, tremble, twitter, wobble; **go back and forth,** come and go, fishtail, go backwards and forwards, go to and fro, go up and down, rock, seesaw; **shake up,** bucket, concuss, jar, jig, jounce, welter; **buzz,** chatter, pound, quaver, rattle, resonate, twang, whirr

vibrate *v* → **1** feel emotion **2** flutter **3** ring

VIBRATING *adj* libratory, nutant, nutational, oscillating, oscillatory, pendulous, pulsatory, swinging, undulatory, up-and-down, vacillating, vacillatory; **shaky,** doddering, doddery, juddering, reeling, rocky, rolling, tottery, waggly, wobbling; **dithery,** agitated, all a-twitter, twittery; **earth-shaking,** seismic

VIBRATION *n* beat, drumming, judder, pulsation, pulse, throb, trepidation; **earthquake,** earth tremor, foreshock, microseism, moonquake, quake, seaquake, seiche, seism, shake, temblor; **shiver,** fremitus, shimmy, tremor, wobble; **quiver,** buzz, dither, palpitation, quaver, roll, shake, shiver, thrill, tremolo, twang, twitter, vibrato, whirr; **vibrancy,** shakiness, the shivers, tremulousness, vibratility, waviness; **buffeting,** concussion, jar, joggle, jounce, shake-up. *See als* FLUTTER

vibrato *n* → vibration

vicar *n* → **1** agent **2** ambassador **3** ecclesiasti

vicarious *adj* → agential

viceroy *n* → agent

vice versa *adv* → **1** head over heels **2** in contrast

vicinity *n* → **1** closeness **2** region

vicious *adj* → **1** immoral **2** imperfect **3** poisonous **4** promiscuous **5** unkind **6** wrong

vicissitude *n* → change

VICTIM *n* downtrodden people, forfeite kill, martyr, oppressed people, prey, protc martyr, sacrifice, scapegoat, sin offering, sufferer, willing sacrifice; **dupe,** cat's paw, cull *(Archaic)*, greenhorn, gudgeon, gull, mug new chum, pawn, pigeon, puppet, sucker tool, whipping boy. *See also* BUTT

victim *n* → **1** loser **2** patient **3** religious ceremony **4** unfortunate

VICTIMISATION *n* discrimination, frame-up harassment, racial discrimination, sexual discrimination, unfair treatment; **persecution,** genocide, holocaust, massacre, oppression, torment

VICTIMISE *v* come down heavily on, crack down on, deal hardly with, discriminate against, get tough with, punish selectively single out; **persecute,** be a scourge, decimate give no quarter, grind down, grind down the faces of the poor, harass, impose hardship upon, massacre, molest, oppress, spite, subdue, suppress

victimise *v* → **1** act unkindly **2** punish

VICTIMISED *adj* discriminated against, hard done by, ill-treated, ill-used, persecuted singled-out, stigmatised; **downtrodden** crushed, ground-down, heavy-laden, oppressed, stricken, under the whip, under the yoke

victor *n* → winner

victory *n* → success

video *n* → **1** film **2** television

vie *v* → **1** contest **2** gamble

VIEW *n* landscape, outlook, panorama, prospect, scene, vista; **range of vision,** command eyeshot, ken, prospect *(Archaic)*, purview

view *n* → **1** aim **2** conjecture **3** display **4** expected thing **5** investigation **6** look **7** opinion **8** painting **9** point of view *v* **10** investigate **11** see

viewpoint *n* → **1** lookout **2** opinion **3** point of view

vigil *n* → **1** evening **2** funeral rites **3** grieving **4** holy day

vigilante *n* → policeman

vignette *n* → **1** abridgment **2** bookbinding **3** drawing **4** photograph

vigour *n* → **1** health **2** power **3** sprightliness **4** strength **5** vitality

vile *adj* → **1** bad **2** immoral **3** inferior **4** obscene **5** unpleasant

vilify *v* → **1** disgrace **2** slander **3** swear

villa *n* → **1** cabin **2** house

village *n* → **1** population **2** town *adj* **3** rural

villain *n* → **1** actor **2** servant **3** wrongdoer
vim *n* → vitality
vindicate *v* → **1** acquit **2** justify **3** liberate **4** punish **5** retaliate
vindictive *adj* → punishing
vine *n* → plant
vinegar *n* → **1** irritableness **2** sourness
vineyard *n* → farm
vintage *n* → **1** fertilisation **2** winemaking *adj* **3** antique **4** good **5** old **6** tasty **7** vehicular
violate *v* → **1** be promiscuous **2** be violent **3** disobey **4** hold in low regard **5** ill-treat **6** profane **7** rape
VIOLENCE *n* bloodthirstiness, furiousness, rabidity, rabidness, rampancy, sanguinariness, sanguineness, vehemence; **boisterousness,** rampageousness, severeness, severity, storminess, turbulence, volcanicity; **aggression,** aggressiveness, aggro, bovver, hubris; **fierceness,** ferity, ferociousness, ferocity, forcibility, forcibleness, grimness, savageness, savagery, shrewishness, truculence; **barbarianism,** barbarity, loutishness, rudeness, wildness; **brutality,** bestiality, ruffianism, toughness
violence *n* → misrepresentation
VIOLENT *adj* driving, forceful, forcible, strongarm, terrorist; **boisterous,** blustery, rampageous, riotous, rough-and-tumble, uproarious, wild; **foul,** dirty, furious, rough, rugged *(Obs.)*; **drastic,** severe, slashing; **sensational,** blood-and-thunder, violent; **cataclysmic,** catastrophic, earth-shaking, earth-shattering; **stormy,** cyclonic, tornadic, tornado-like, torrential, turbulent, typhonic, volcanic, vulcanian. *See also* FEROCIOUS; BRUTAL
VIOLENTLY *adv* ferociously, savagely, truculently; **fiercely,** furiously, grimly, like fury, rabidly, rampantly, vehemently; **bloodthirstily,** sanguinarily, sanguinely; **brutally,** barbarically, bestially, ferociously, loutishly, rudely; **forcibly,** amain *(Archaic)*, hammer and tongs, heavily, slam-bang, slap-bang, with a vengeance; **stormily,** turbulently; **wildly,** roughly, tooth and nail, wild; **blusteringly,** aggressively, boisterously, swashingly, uproariously
VIOLENT OUTBURST *n* bluster, fury, heat, rage; **force,** brunt *(Archaic)*, main, shock; **cataclysm,** catastrophe; **storm,** blizzard, cloudburst, cyclone, dust squall, dust storm, gale, hailstorm, hurricane, maelstrom, sandstorm, snowstorm, squall, tempest, tornado, whirlwind, willy-willy; **paroxysm,** throes
VIOLENT PERSON *n* aggressor, assaulter, attacker, pirate, terrorist, trespasser, violator; **bully,** blusterer, brave *(Obs.)*, bruiser, dragon, swashbuckler; **lout,** barbarian, hoon; **Turk,** tartar; **ruffian,** apache, brute, bull, chokeman, gorilla, muscle man, nightrider *(U.S.)*, plug-ugly *(U.S.)*, poofter-basher, poofter-rorter, rowdy, thug, tough; **shrew,** fury, harridan, hell-cat, maenad, scold, spitfire, termagant, virago
violet *n* → **1** blue **2** purple *adj* **3** purple
violin *n* → instrumentalist
V.I.P. *n* → **1** famous person **2** important person
viper *n* → **1** bad person **2** betrayer **3** unkind person
virago *n* → **1** irritable person **2** strong person **3** violent person **4** woman
viral *adj* → unwholesome
virgin *n* → **1** abstainer **2** childless female **3** single person **4** woman *adj* **5** abstinent **6** clean **7** infertile **8** new **9** simple **10** single **11** unused
virginal *adj* → **1** abstinent **2** clean **3** infertile **4** innocent **5** new
virile *adj* → **1** energetic **2** male **3** strong
virtual *adj* → **1** capable **2** nonexistent
virtue *n* → **1** correctness **2** courage **3** good **4** honesty **5** innocence **6** manliness **7** power **8** reverence
virtuoso *n* → **1** aesthete **2** expert **3** musician **4** specialist *adj* **5** accomplished **6** knowledgeable
virulent *adj* → **1** acrimonious **2** poisonous **3** unkind
virus *n* → **1** illness **2** organism **3** poison
visa *n* → certificate
visage *n* → **1** appearance **2** face
vis-a-vis *n* → **1** carriage **2** equal **3** opposite position *adj* **4** opposite *adv* **5** opposite *prep* **6** concerning **7** opposite
viscera *n* → **1** abdomen **2** inside
viscount *n* → aristocrat
viscous *adj* → **1** sludgy **2** sticky
VISIBLE *adj* macroscopic, objective, observable, overt, viewable; **perceivable,** apparent, discernible, evident, obvious, perceptible; **in focus,** clear, clear-cut, plain, unblurred, unclouded, undisguised, unmistakable; **conspicuous,** exposed, eye-catching, for all to see, in full view, in view, marked, on view, open, open to view, plain as day, uncovered, under one's nose, within range; **bold,** full-faced *(Print.)*, in bold relief
visible *adj* → blatant
vision *n* → **1** delusion **2** fantasy **3** hope **4** image *v* **5** see
visionary *adj* → **1** delusive **2** unrealistic
VISIT *n* call, gam *(U.S. Naut.)*, social call, visitation; **stopover,** abode, sojourn, stay, stop, tarry *(Archaic)*; **tour,** tourism; **the rounds,** the traps; **visitors day,** open day
VISIT *v* blow in, call, call on, dance attendance, drop across, drop by, drop in, drop over, first-foot *(Scot.)*, go and see, go over to, leave one's card, look in, look in on, look up, make a call, pay a call, pay a visit, pop in, pop over, run across to, run over to, run round to, see, stop by, wait on, wait upon; **return a visit,** pay back the visit; **do the rounds,** do the calls, keep in touch, tour, visit the traps; **stay,** sojourn, stay with, stop off at, stop over, tarry; **frequent,** haunt
visit *n* → **1** inspection *v* **2** attack **3** help **4** inhabit **5** punish **6** talk
visitation *n* → **1** help **2** inspection **3** misfortune **4** punishment **5** visit

VISITOR *n* caller, first foot *(Scot.)*, guest, stranger, visitant; **frequenter,** habitué, haunter, roundsman; **tourer,** tourist

visor *n* → **1** armour **2** disguise *v* **3** secure

vista *n* → view

visual *n* → **1** drawing **2** photograph *adj* **3** optical

visualise *v* → **1** devise **2** fantasise **3** see

vital *adj* → **1** energetic **2** enthusiastic **3** fundamental **4** important **5** living **6** necessary

VITALITY *n* aliveness, animal spirits, animation, ardour, brio, ebullience, effervescence, exuberance, libido, liveliness, lustiness, spirit, spiritedness, sprightliness, vibrancy, vital force, vitalness, vivaciousness, vivacity; **invigoration,** energising, enlivenment, innervation, stimulation, vitalisation, vivification; **vigour,** bang *(U.S.)*, dash, elan, kick, nerve, pep, peppiness, red-bloodedness, snap, sthenia, verve, vigorousness, vim, zap, zest, zing, zip; **dynamism,** athleticism, briskness, freshness, rompishness, tirelessness, unweariedness; **get-up-and-go,** bustle, ginger, go, gumption, herbs, hustle, oomph, pull, push, spunk, steam; **drive,** aggressiveness, ambition, enterprise. *See also* ENERGY

vitiate *v* → **1** mix **2** spoil

viticulture *n* → farming

vitreous *adj* → **1** brittle **2** hard **3** transparent

vitrify *v* → harden

vitriol *n* → disapproval

vituperate *v* → **1** disapprove of **2** slander

vivacious *adj* → **1** energetic **2** happy **3** living

vivid *adj* → **1** artistic **2** bright **3** colourful **4** energetic **5** intense **6** living **7** obvious

viviparous *adj* → pregnant

vixen *n* → irritable person

VOCABULARY *n* accents *(Poetic)*, glossary, language, lexicon, lexis, text, vocab, wordage

vocabulary *n* → list

vocal *n* → **1** song *adj* **2** acoustic **3** musical **4** spoken **5** uncompromising

vocal cords *n* → neck

vocalise *n* → **1** song *v* **2** sing **3** speak

vocalist *n* → singer

vocation *n* → **1** employment **2** job **3** obligation

vociferous *adj* → **1** loud **2** shouting

vogue *n* → fashion

voice *n* → **1** election **2** singer **3** speaking *v* **4** publicise **5** speak

void *n* → **1** emptiness **2** gap **3** non-being **4** space *v* **5** annihilate **6** cancel **7** deny **8** depart **9** empty **10** expel *adj* **11** empty **12** ineffectual **13** powerless

volatile *adj* → **1** changeable **2** gaseous **3** impermanent

volcano *n* → **1** fire **2** mountain

volition *n* → **1** desire **2** will

volley *n* → **1** attack **2** explosion **3** shot **4** stroke *v* **5** be loud

volleyball *n* → ball

voltage *n* → electricity

voluble *adj* → **1** talkative **2** verbose

volume *n* → **1** book **2** loudness **3** much **4** size

voluminous *adj* → **1** big **2** enormous **3** twisting

VOLUNTARILY *adv* by choice, by one's own free will, volitionally; **at will,** as you like, when ready; **intentionally,** by design, consciously, deliberately, designingly, in cold blood, on purpose, premeditatedly, purposefully, purposely, purposively; **with a view to**

voluntary *n* → **1** introduction *adj* **2** agreeable **3** optional **4** unpaid **5** willing

volunteer *n* → **1** serviceman *v* **2** be willing **3** join up **4** offer *adj* **5** agreeable

VOLUPTUARY *n* bacchant, bacchante, epicure, epicurean, erotic, eroticist, erotologist, hedonist, sensualist, sybarite; **lecher,** beast, brute, d.o.m., dirty old man, goat, swine; **earthmother**

voluptuary *n* → **1** enjoyer *adj* **2** pleasure-loving **3** voluptuous

VOLUPTUOUS *adj* carnal, earthy, epicurean, erotic, erotogenic, erotological, fleshly, hedonistic, sensual, sensualistic, supersensual, sybaritic, voluptuary; **concupiscent,** hircine, hot, lascivious, lecherous, libidinous, lubricious, lustful, rampant, ruttish *(Obs.)*; **bacchanalian,** bacchanal, bacchic, dionysian; **bestial,** beastly, boarish, brute, brutish, debauched, swinish

voluptuous *adj* → **1** alluring **2** beautiful **3** pleasure-loving

VOLUPTUOUSNESS *n* bacchanalianism, carnality, earthiness, erotism, erotology, fleshliness, hedonism, luxuriousness, luxury, pleasure, pleasure principle, sensualism, sensuality, volupté, voluptuosity; **concupiscence,** goatishness, lecherousness, lechery, lewdness, libidinousness, lubricity, lustfulness; **lust,** eros, libido, sexual desire; **bestiality,** animalism, beastliness, debauchment, swinishness; **orgy,** bacchanal, bacchanalia; **fleshpots**

VOMIT *n* barf, berley, big spit, chuck, chunder, pellet, puke, sick, technicolour yawn, vomitus, yellow yawn

VOMIT *v* barf *(U.S.)*, bark, be sick, bring up, chuck, chunder, cry ruth, feed the fishes, fetch up, have a sale *(N.Z.)*, herk, hurl, keck, make a sale *(N.Z.)*, perk up, puke, regurgitate, reject, retch, sick up, throw up, spew

voodoo *n* → **1** magic *v* **2** bewitch

voracious *adj* → **1** enthusiastic **2** greedy **3** hungry

vortex *n* → **1** atmospheric pressure **2** current **3** spin **4** turbulence

votary *n* → **1** accomplice **2** believer **3** desirer **4** enthusiast **5** monastic **6** worshipper

vote *n* → **1** contract **2** election *v* **3** elect

votive *adj* → **1** desirous **2** optional

vouch *n* → **1** assertion **2** evidence *v* **3** assert **4** authenticate

voucher *n* → **1** authentication **2** cheque **3** label **4** testifier

vouchsafe *v* → **1** be meek **2** give **3** permit

vow *n* → **1** contract **2** religious ceremony *v* **3** assert **4** intend **5** promise

vowel *n* → letter

vox populi *n* → opinion

voyage *n* → **1** undertaking *v* **2** set sail **3** traverse

voyeur *n* → **1** looker **2** morbid curiosity **3** sexual type

vulcanise *v* → heat

VULGAR *adj* banausic, broad, coarse, coarse-grained, crass, crude, gross, heavy, indelicate, inelegant, unpolished, unrefined; **bawdy,** burlesque, earthy, profane, Rabelaisian, raunchy, ribald, scurrilous, strong; **unmentionable,** unparliamentary, unprintable, unrepeatable; **tasteless,** atrocious, outlandish, unaesthetic; **unfashionable,** dowdy, nunty, tatty; **garish,** cheap, chocolate-box, clinquant, commercial, common, flashy, fulsome, gaudy, gingerbread, meretricious, raffish, tarty, tawdry, tinsel, tinsel-like, tinselly, tizzy; **loud,** blatant, blushless, obtrusive; **kitsch,** Gothic, rococo. *See also* ILL-BRED

vulgar *n* → **1** language **2** working class *adj* **3** discourteous **4** obscene **5** ordinary **6** public **7** showy

VULGARIAN *n* bounder, cad, low-life; **philistine,** groundling, mucker *(Brit.)*, pleb, plebeian, rough diamond; **nouveau riche,** arriviste, parvenu, upstart; **peasant,** bushie, hayseed, yokel; **boor,** alf, buffoon, carl *(Archaic)*, churl, clown, ocker, rugger-bugger; **slob,** dick, dickhead, goon, oaf, swine, yob; **lair,** city slicker, masher *(Obs.)*, mug-lair, Teddy Bear, two-bob lair; **lout,** hector, hoon, rough, roughie, roughneck, rowdy, thug, yahoo, yegg *(U.S.)*; **barbarian,** apeman, beast, brute, caveman, savage, tramontane, trog, troglodyte; **vulgariser,** ribald, sensationalist

VULGARISE *v* cheapen, lower; **coarsen,** rusticate; **brutalise,** barbarise, brutify; **tart up,** commercialize, tinsel; **be vulgar,** lair it up, show bad taste

VULGARISM *n* burlesque, choice language, dirty word, ribaldry, slang; **kitsch,** gingerbread; **vulgarisation,** barbarisation, brutalisation, rustication

VULGARITY *n* commonness, grossness, low-mindedness, lowness, rudeness, rusticity, uncivility, uncouthness, vulgarism, vulgarness; **coarseness,** earthiness, ribaldry, sensuality, sensuism; **philistinism,** ill-breeding, illiberality, illiberalness, plebeianism; **bad taste,** no taste, tastelessness; **unmentionableness,** unparliamentariness, unrepeatability; **garishness,** blatancy, flashiness, fulsomeness, gaudiness, gothicism, loudness, outlandishness, sensationalism; **tawdriness,** dowdiness, frumpishness, unfashionableness, unkemptness; **indecorousness,** gaucherie, impropriety, indecorum, indelicacy, unbecomingness, unseemliness; **rowdiness,** bawdiness, boorishness, buffoonery, loutishness, oafishness, rowdyism, swinishness; **barbarism,** atrociousness, atrocity, barbarianism, barbarity, baseness, brutishness, harshness, heathenishness, heathenism, heathenry, life in the raw

VULNERABILITY *n* indefensibility, indefensibleness, nakedness, susceptibility, unguardedness, unsafeness, unsafety, untenability, unwariness, vulnerableness

VULNERABLE *adj* derelict, insecure, naked, obnoxious, unarmed, unassured, unattended, uncovered, undefended, unguarded, unsecured, unwary; **indefensible,** untenable

vulnerable *adj* → predisposed

vulture *n* → **1** extortionist **2** unkind person

vulva *n* → groin

Ww

wad *n* → **1** plug **2** wealth *v* **3** close
waddle *n* → **1** flutter **2** walking *v* **3** flutter **4** walk
waddy *n* → **1** club *v* **2** cudgel
wade *n* → **1** journey *v* **2** swim **3** travel
wafer *n* → **1** adhesive **2** coating **3** medication *v* **4** close
WAFFLE *n* all piss and wind, empty words, gabber, garbage, gush, load of old rubbish, mere words, nonsense, padding, palaver, rigamarole, sermonising, sound and fury signifying nothing, twaddle, verbiage; **amplification,** expansion, expatiation; **digression,** apostrophe, discursion, divagation, divergence, episode, excursus; **redundancy,** pleonasm, redundance, tautology; **circumlocution,** periphrasis, roundabout language
WAFFLE *v* bullshit, gasbag, gush, maunder, rabbit on, rant, rant and rave, rap on, run on and on, talk nonsense, talk someone blind, talk the leg off an iron pot, verbalise, yack on; **expatiate,** amplify, descant, dilate on, enlarge upon, expand, harp on, sermonise; **overelaborate,** draw out, pad out, protract; **digress,** divagate, diverge, ramble, wander
waffle *n* → **1** imprecision **2** nonsense *v* **3** talk nonsense
waft *n* → **1** quiet sound **2** sign **3** smell **4** wind *v* **5** float
wag *n* → **1** absentee **2** flutter **3** humorist *v* **4** be absent **5** flutter
wage *n* → **1** income **2** surety *v* **3** do **4** gamble
wager *n* → **1** contract **2** gamble *v* **3** be uncertain **4** gamble **5** promise
WAGE WAR *v* attack, commit hostilities, declare war, dig up the hatchet, engage in hostilities, give battle, go to war, invade, join battle, make war, raise one's banner, resort to war, take the offensive, take up arms, take up the cudgels; **be at war,** battle, be on the warpath, combat, contest, fight, make a stand, stand, stoush *(Colloq.)*, strive, war; **pillage,** burn, lay waste, put to the sword, ravage, scorch, shed blood, slaughter; **besiege,** beleaguer, blockade, dig in, lay siege to, siege; **barrage,** blitz, bomb, strafe, torpedo; **manoeuvre,** brush, counter-march, march, operate, outflank, skirmish, sortie; **deploy,** change front, deraign *(Archaic)*, enfilade, marshal
waggle *n* → **1** flutter *v* **2** flutter
WAGON *n* bullock dray, bullock wagon, camion, cart, dray, jinker, oxcart, telega, truck, tumbrel, wain *(Poetic)*; **sanitary cart,** dunny cart, night cart, sanny cart, seventeen door sedan, sullage tanker; **trailer,** band wagon *(U.S.)*, box-trailer, dog trailer, float, horse float, horsebox, tandem trailer; **barrow,** applecart, billycart, bogie, dolly, go-cart, golf buggy, handbarrow, handcart, noddy *(N.Z. Railways)*, pushcart, shopping buggy, shopping stroller, shopping trolley, soapbox, tea-trolley, tea-wagon, teacart *(U.S.)*, trolley, wheelbarrow. *See also* CARRIAGE
wagon *n* → **1** car **2** cell **3** train *v* **4** transport
waif *n* → **1** children **2** sign
wail *n* → **1** cry **2** shout *v* **3** be loud **4** call (of animals) **5** grieve **6** shrill
wainscot *n* → **1** plaster **2** timber
waist *n* → **1** abdomen **2** centre
waistcoat *n* → jacket
wait *n* → **1** expectation **2** interval **3** lateness **4** period of inaction **5** timepiece *v* **6** be patient **7** defer **8** idle
WAITER *n* Ganymede, garcon, server, waitress; **bartender,** bar useful, barkeep, barmaid, barman, drawer *(Archaic)*, drink waiter, tapster *(Archaic)*, useful, wine waiter; **kitchen hand,** bus boy *(U.S.)*, cupbearer, kitchener, kitchenman, scullion, tea lady; **flight attendant,** air hostess, hostess, hostie, steward, stewardess
waive *v* → abandon
wake *n* → **1** death **2** funeral rites **3** grieving **4** route **5** surf *v* **6** look **7** wake up
WAKE UP *v* awake, awaken, rouse, rub the sleep from one's eyes, wake, waken; **rise,** get out of bed, get up, hit the deck, rise and shine, surface, turn out; **arouse,** call, knock up, raise *(Archaic)*
WAKE UP *interj* rise and shine, wakey-wakey
WAKING *n* arousal, awakening, rouse; **wakefulness,** insomnia, restlessness, sleeplessness; **reveille,** early-morning call
WALK *n* airing, blow *(Colloq.)*, constitutional, promenade, roam, saunter, stroll, turn, wander; **march,** anabasis, cakewalk, forced march, route-march; **hike,** grind *(N.Z.)*, mush, rogaine, safari, tramp, trek, walkathon
WALK *v* amble, ambulate, defile, foot, foot it, footslog, goosestep, hoof it, leg it, march, mosey *(U.S. Colloq.)*, mush, pace, pad, parade, saunter, shamble, shank *(Scot.)*, slouch, somnambulate, step, stride, stroll, strut, swagger, swamp, sweep, toddle, tootle, tramp, tread, troop, truck, trundle, waddle; **promenade,** do the block, perambulate, stretch one's legs, take the air; **jaywalk; mince,** cakewalk, pansy, sashay, trip, waltz; **limp,** dot and carry one, hobble, hop, shuffle, stagger, stumble along, totter; **plod,** clamp, clump, lumber, pound, slog, thump, toil,

traipse, tramp, trample, trudge; **run,** breeze along, chase, double-time, jog, lope, pat, scour; **scramble,** slither, wriggle; **brachiate**

walk *n* → 1 field 2 move 3 path 4 pen *v* 5 accompany 6 advance 7 measure 8 move

walkabout *n* → travelling

WALKER *n* ambler, cakewalker, foot-passenger *(Archaic)*, footer, footslogger, marcher, passer-by, pedestrian, saunterer, stepper, strider, stroller, strutter, toddler, treader, trudger, waddler; **jaywalker; jogger,** galloper, loper, pacer, runner; **limper,** hobbler, shuffler, the walking wounded, totterer; **sleepwalker,** noctambulist, somnambulant, somnambulator, somnambulist

walkie-talkie *n* → radio

WALKING *n* ambulation, bushwalking, circumambulation, legwork, pedestrianism, perambulation; **sleepwalking,** somnambulation, somnambulism; **gait,** amble, dogtrot, double time, footing, goosestep, hobble, jog, lope, muddling pace, pace, plod, roll, saunter, shamble, shuffle, step, strut, stump, toddle, tread, waddle

WALKING *adj* ambulatory, heel-and-toe, high-stepping, pedestrian, perambulatory, strutting, unmounted; **sleepwalking,** noctivagant, somnambulant, somnambulistic; **gressorial,** digitigrade, gradient, plantigrade, unguligrade

walkout *n* → 1 departure 2 industrial action 3 stoppage 4 strike

walk out *v* → 1 depart 2 stop

walkover *n* → 1 easy thing 2 success

walk over *v* → 1 contest 2 do easily

WALL *n* ashlaring, brattice, bulkhead, cavity wall, firewall, partition, party wall, withe; **screen,** iconostasis, jube, reredos, transenna, veil; **curtain,** drop, drop curtain, drop scene, fire-curtain, safety curtain, tormentor; **diaphragm,** dissepiment, interface, mediastinum, septum, velum; **buffer,** cushion, fender, pudding fender, shock absorber, stopping; **deflector,** baffle, baffle plates, starling; **air-curtain,** airlock; **shield,** biological shield, butt, stone shield, washboard; **buffer zone,** Bamboo Curtain, border, frontier, Iron Curtain, no-man's-land. *See also* FENCE

wall *n* → 1 mountain 2 support *v* 3 separate

wallet *n* → case

wallop *n* → 1 alcohol 2 corporal punishment 3 hit 4 power *v* 5 beat 6 defeat 7 hit

wallow *n* → 1 binge 2 hollow 3 lake 4 show 5 swamp *v* 6 be pleased 7 get dirty 8 overindulge 9 roll

wallpaper *n* → plaster

walnut *n* → 1 timber *adj* 2 brown

waltz *v* → 1 dance 2 do easily 3 walk

wan *v* → 1 lose colour *adj* 2 colourless 3 ill 4 shadowy

wand *n* → 1 emblem of office 2 magic spell 3 stick

wander *n* → 1 walk *v* 2 become confused 3 be inattentive 4 travel 5 waffle

WANDERING *adj* itinerant, meandering, noctivagant, peripatetic, rambling, roving, vagarious, vagrant

WANDERINGLY *adv* errantly, excursively, from pillar to post, itinerantly, meanderingly, vagrantly; **on the road,** off, on the track, on the wallaby, on the wallaby track, on the wing; **aboard**

WANE *v* abate, fade out, fall, fall off, lag, peak, peak and pine, peter out, tail away, tail off, trail off; **depreciate,** break, drop, drop off, sag, slip, tumble; **decline,** crumble, decay, dwindle, ebb, fade away, subside, waste away, wear away. *See also* DECREASE

wane *n* → 1 abatement 2 decrease 3 powerlessness 4 slope *v* 5 age 6 finish 7 moderate

wangle *n* → 1 dishonesty 2 expedient 3 stratagem *v* 4 beguile 5 make do 6 swindle

want *n* → 1 absence 2 deficiency 3 desire 4 insufficiency 5 necessities 6 poverty 7 will *v* 8 desire 9 fall short 10 necessitate

wanton *n* → 1 promiscuous person 2 sexual partner *v* 3 be promiscuous 4 let oneself go 5 overindulge *adj* 6 capricious 7 extravagant 8 growing 9 happy 10 immoral 11 liberated 12 overindulgent 13 rash 14 uncompromising 15 unfair

WAR *n* appeal to arms, civil war, hostilities, resort to arms, shooting war, total war, trench warfare, war of attrition, war of nerves, war to the knife, warfare, world war; **state of war,** state of siege; **biological warfare,** chemical warfare, germ warfare; **atomic warfare,** nuclear warfare; **unconventional warfare,** evasion, guerilla warfare, subversion, terrorism; **psychological warfare,** propaganda; **economic warfare,** attrition, blockade, scorched earth policy; **gigantomachia,** theomachy; **holy war,** crusade, jihad. *See also* ACT OF WAR

war *n* → 1 argument 2 contest *v* 3 argue 4 wage war

warble *n* → 1 birdcall 2 song *v* 3 chirp 4 sing

ward *n* → 1 administrative area 2 care 3 city 4 dependant 5 domain 6 hospital 7 imprisonment 8 protection 9 room *v* 10 protect

warden *n* → 1 conservationist 2 gaoler 3 leader 4 policeman 5 religious dignitary

warder *n* → 1 emblem of office 2 gaoler 3 policeman 4 stick

wardrobe *n* → 1 clothes 2 container 3 cupboard

ware *v* → 1 be cautious *adj* 2 cautious 3 perceptive

warehouse *n* → 1 storehouse *v* 2 store

warfare *n* → war

warhead *n* → ammunition

WARLIKE *adj* armipotent, bellicose, belligerent, bloodthirsty, combatant, hawkish, martial, militant, pugnacious; **militaristic,** chauvinist, chauvinistic, jingoistic

warlock *n* → 1 bewitcher 2 occultist

warm *v* → 1 enthuse 2 heat *adj* 3 acrimonious 4 busy 5 close 6 emotional 7 energetic 8 enthusiastic 9 findable 10 friendly 11 hot 12 kind 13 reddish

WARMONGER *n* aggressor, campaigner, chauvinist, combater, crusader, fighter, hawk, militant, militarist
warmonger *n* → fighter
WARMONGERING *n* aggression, bellicosity, belligerence, combativeness, fight, hostility, militancy, pugnacity, warlikeness; **militarism; jingoism,** chauvinism, national prejudice
WARN *v* advertise *(Obs.)*, caution, exhort, forewarn, garnish *(Law)*, give someone a tip, premonish, previse, put wise, tip off; **alarm,** alert, gong; **patrol,** keep nit, keep watch
warn *v* → **1** guide **2** inform **3** predict
WARNER *n* cockatoo, exhorter, lookout, monitor, nit-keeper, patrol, sentinel, sentry, shark patrol, vedette, watchdog, watchman; **picket,** air picket *(Mil.)*, outrider; **monitor,** airborne early warning system *(Mil.)*, distant early warning system *(U.S. Mil.)*, early warning system, indicator, radar, sonobuoy; **alarmist,** Cassandra
WARNING *n* alarm, alarum *(Archaic)*, alert, appel *(Fencing)*, caution, Mayday *(Radio)*, red alert, red flag; **warning signal,** beacon, danger signal, distant signal *(Railways)*, exclamation mark *(Brit.)*, fog signal, hazard flasher, hazard lights, red light, seamark, skull and crossbones, stoplight, storm signals, storm warning; **alarm bell,** alarm clock, alarum, burglar alarm, curfew, foghorn *(Naut.)*, gong, horn, klaxon, shark bell, shark siren, siren, tocsin; **forewarning,** foreboding, omen, premonition, presentiment, symptom, the writing on the wall; **admonition,** caution, caveat *(Law)*, denunciation, exhortation, garnishment *(Law)*, lecture, memento mori, monition, notice, notification, threat, tip-off, warning; **example,** deterrent, lesson, object lesson
WARNING *adj* exemplary, instructive, monitory, premonitory, sematic, telltale; **threatening,** ominous; **admonitory,** cautionary, exhortative
warning *n* → **1** discouragement **2** guidance **3** information **4** warning *adj* **5** discouraging **6** guide
warp *n* → **1** cord **2** distortion **3** intolerance **4** soil *v* **5** distort **6** pull **7** swerve
warrant *n* → **1** account **2** authentication **3** insistence **4** justification **5** permission **6** surety *v* **7** authorise **8** justify **9** permit
warranty *n* → **1** contract **2** surety
warren *n* → **1** animal dwelling **2** cabin
warrigal *adj* → natural
warrior *n* → fighter
wart *n* → **1** bulge **2** disfigurement
wary *adj* → cautious
wash *n* → **1** airflow **2** channel **3** cleansing **4** coating **5** current **6** dirt **7** drink **8** dye **9** flow **10** liquid **11** medication **12** mineral **13** paint **14** painting **15** seaside **16** soil **17** splash **18** swamp *v* **19** clean **20** colour **21** flow
WASHER *n* face flannel, face washer, facecloth, flannel, loofah, washcloth, washrag; **toothbrush,** dental floss, dentifrice, tooth-stick, toothpaste, toothpick; **swab,** cotton bud; **napkin,** serviette, table napkin; **nappy,** diaper *(U.S.)*; **handkerchief,** hanky, nose rag, snot rag; **toilet paper,** bum fodder, dunny paper, lavatory paper; **doormat,** foot scraper; **dishcloth,** bottlebrush, dishrag, dishwasher, dolly mop, scourer, sponge, steel wool, washleather, wettex; **pull-through,** electric eel, four-by-two, pipe-cleaner, ramrod; **syringe,** syrette
washer *n* → **1** cleaner **2** filler **3** ring
wasp *n* → irritable person
WASP *n* → **1** conformer **2** ethnic *adj* **3** conservative
WASTE *n* chaff, debris, dregs, dross, effluent, husks, junk, leavings, lumber, mullock, off, scourings, scrap, skimmings, slack *(Coal Mining)*, slag, slash *(N.Z.)*, tailings, waste matter, waste product, wastepaper; **garbage,** gunk, litter, muck, outcast, refuse, rubbish, trash; **encumbrance,** cumbrance, deadwood, snuff, white elephant; **dead stock,** cast-offs, delenda, rags, rejectamenta, rejects, remainders
waste *n* → **1** deterioration **2** dirt **3** discard **4** extravagance **5** harm **6** misuse **7** nature **8** neglectfulness **9** remnant **10** textiles **11** wasteland *v* **12** contract **13** destroy **14** fall into disuse **15** ill-treat **16** kill **17** squander **18** weaken *adj* **19** disused **20** infertile **21** natural **22** surplus **23** useless
WASTELAND *n* desert, desolation, dust bowl, gumland *(N.Z.)*, no-man's-land, waste, wilderness; **duffer,** shicer *(Mining)*
WASTE ONE'S TIME *v* cry for the moon, flog a dead horse, labour in vain, labour the obvious, piss into the wind, whistle against the wind, whistle in the wind
wastrel *n* → **1** bad person **2** idler **3** squanderer
watch *n* → **1** looker **2** seeing **3** timepiece *v* **4** attend to **5** care for **6** look **7** worship *interj* **8** lo
water *n* → **1** extinguisher **2** rainfall **3** urination *v* **4** excrete **5** mix **6** wet *adj* **7** liquid
water-closet *n* → toilet
watercolour *n* → **1** dye **2** painting
watercourse *n* → **1** channel **2** stream
WATERCRAFT *n* boat, bottom, class boat, cockle, cockleshell, consort, craft, flatboat, flatiron, greyhound, hog, launch, monohull, pink, prow *(Poetic)*, shallop, ship, shipboard, skiff, vessel, whaleboat; **tub,** hulk, log, wreck; **jolly-boat,** cockboat, hoy, tender, yawl *(Obs.)*; **barge,** gondola *(U.S.)*, lighter, scow; **pirate ship,** corsair, rover *(Archaic)*, sea-rover; **training ship,** school ship, flagship, mother ship; **shipping,** flotage, marine, merchant navy, watercraft; **fleet,** argosy, armada, column, convoy, escadrille *(Obs.)*, fleet in being, flotilla, navy, screen, squadron; **warship,** aircraft-carrier, assault craft, battle cruiser, battleship, capital ship, caravel, carrier, corsair, cruiser, cutter, destroyer, destroyer escort, dreadnought, E-boat, fire ship, flag, flagship, flat-top, frigate, gunboat,

H.M.A.S., H.M.S., ironclad, landing craft, man-o'-war, man-of-war, mine-layer, mine-sweeper, minisub, monitor, pocket battleship, privateer, PT boat, Q-ship, R.A.N., razee *(Obs.)*, ship of the line, submarine, superdreadnought, three-decker, torpedo-boat, torpedo-boat destroyer, troop-carrier, trooper, troopship, U-boat, vedette; **merchant vessel,** argosy, bilander, bulk carrier, cargo boat, coaster, collier, container ship, factory ship, freighter, fruiter, Indiaman, liner, merchantman, oil tanker, packet (boat), pearler, sealer, sixty-miler, slaver, supertanker, tanker, trader, tramp, tramp steamer, whaler; **water taxi,** aquacab; **fishing vessel,** crabber, drifter, fisherman, fishing smack, hooker, smack, trawler; **ark,** bumboat, dredger, fireboat, hospital ship, iceboat, icebreaker, lifeboat, lightship, revenue cutter *(Brit.)*, showboat, snagger, surf rescue boat, transport, tug, tugboat, victualler, weathership. *See also* MOTOR VESSEL; SAILING SHIP; ROWING BOAT; RAFT

waterfall *n* → spring

waterfront *n* → **1** city **2** coastline **3** seaside

waterhole *n* → **1** hollow **2** lake

waterlog *v* → wet

watermark *n* → **1** apex **2** label *v* **3** label

waterproof *n* → **1** raincoat **2** textiles *v* **3** conserve *adj* **4** dry **5** preserved **6** safe

watershed *n* → **1** crucial moment **2** mountain **3** top

watertable *n* → **1** drain **2** layer **3** top

watertight *adj* → **1** dry **2** nautical **3** perfect

waterworks *n* → **1** bad mood **2** bladder **3** piping

watt *n* → energy

wattle *n* → **1** interlacement **2** plaster *v* **3** interlace **4** stick together

wave *n* → **1** advance **2** curve **3** flutter **4** gesture **5** hairdressing **6** outburst **7** point of view **8** sea **9** surf **10** water *v* **11** curve **12** flutter **13** gesture **14** twist

waver *v* → **1** flutter **2** lack courage **3** move **4** vacillate

wavy *adj* → curvilinear

wax *n* → **1** adhesive **2** angry act **3** fat **4** raw materials *v* **5** become greater **6** flower **7** illuminate **8** polish

waxwork *n* → portrait

way *n* → **1** access **2** advance **3** behaviour **4** characteristic **5** condition **6** custom **7** direction **8** method **9** move

wayfarer *n* → traveller

waylay *v* → **1** allure **2** rob

ways *n* → **1** behaviour **2** custom **3** propellant

wayward *adj* → **1** badly-behaved **2** capricious **3** changeable **4** strange

WEAK *adj* adynamic, asthenic, atonic, atrophic, atrophied, effete, enervate, enervated, expugnable, fatigable, helpless, infirm, invalid, nerveless, on one's last legs, sinewless, subduable, weak as gin's piss, weak as water; **frail,** delicate, dicky, faint, feckless, feeble, hothouse, languishing, languorous, limp, little, low, mushy, pimping, puny, sickly, silly *(Obs.)*, slight, small, soft, tender, thewless, thready, weedy, wet, wishy-washy; **pale,** anaemic, colourless, peaky, wispy; **effeminate,** anile, doting, dotty, female *(Obs.)*, feminine, sawney, womanish; **wonky,** doddered, doddering, doddery, groggy, rocky, shaky, tottery, tremulant, tremulous; **broken,** broken-down, decrepit, droopy, gone, perished, prostrate, wrecked; **loose,** flabby, flaccid, flagging, languid, limp, loose-jointed, slack, tenuous; **debilitative,** enervative, exhaustive

weak *adj* → **1** illogical **2** immoral **3** indecisive **4** insufficient **5** powerless **6** quiet **7** useless

WEAKEN *v* attenuate, blunt, deaden, debilitate, demoralise, devitalise, disable, enervate, enfeeble, prostrate, sap, slake *(Obs.)*, swamp, wilt; **collapse,** break down, conk out; **waste,** atrophy, die, die away, disintegrate, droop, fade, fail, faint *(Archaic)*, fall away, falter, flag, go soft, go to seed, languish, pass out, rot away, sink, subside, turn to jelly; **soften,** wilt; **loosen,** loose, open, relax, slack, slacken, unclasp, unlace, unlash, unloose, unstrap, unstring; **shake,** totter

WEAKLING *n* asthenic, broken reed, cream puff, cry-baby, dotard, gutless wonder, jellyfish, paper tiger, poofter *(Derog.)*, softie, sop, subman, wimp, wreck; **weak spot,** Achilles heel, breaking point, disability, failing, failure, foible, weak link

WEAKNESS *n* adynamia, anaemia, anergy, asthenia, atony, debility, decay, decrepitude, delicateness, dotage, effeteness, faintness, fecklessness, feebleness, frailness, helplessness, infirmness, languor, lassitude, littleness, lowness, malaise, mushiness, nervelessness, powerlessness, prostration, puniness, tremulousness; **enfeeblement,** anility, atrophy, brokenness, debilitation, devitalisation, disablement, disintegration, enervation, intolerance; **frailty,** caducity, destructibility, destructibleness, infirmity, pregnability, shakiness, sickliness, unsubstantiality, vincibility, vincibleness, violability; **paleness,** colourlessness, peakiness; **looseness,** flabbiness, flaccidity, flaccidness, flimsiness, languidness, languishment, limpness, slackness, tenuousness; **droop,** languish, tremor, wilt; **fatigue,** corrosion fatigue

weakness *n* → **1** ill health **2** immorality **3** imperfection **4** point of view **5** powerlessness **6** wrong **7** wrongfulness

weal *n* → **1** bulge **2** contentedness **3** disfigurement **4** good fortune **5** sore **6** wealth

WEALTH *n* cash in hand, dollars, filthy lucre, gold, gumtree money, lucre, Mammon, means, money, pelf, petrodollars, riches, the ready, the readies, weal *(Obs.)*; **fortune,** a pretty penny, big bickies, king's ransom, megabucks, mint, motser, pile, tidy sum, wad; **resources,** land *(Econ.)*, natural resources, resources boom; **treasure,** blue chip, bonanza, capital, goldmine, nest egg, private means, treasure-trove; **affluence,**

forehandedness *(U.S.)*, glory, prosperousness, solidity, soundness, substantiality; **richness,** abundance, opulence, sumptuousness; **enrichment,** aggrandisement, self-aggrandisement; **el dorado,** Babylon, Golconda, land of milk and honey

wealth *n* → **1** good fortune **2** much

WEALTHY *adj* affluent, brownstone *(U.S.)*, copper-bottomed, filthy rich, , flush, forehanded *(U.S.)*, in funds, in pocket, in the money, loaded, made of money, on easy street, opulent, prosperous, rich, rolling, solid, stinking, substantial, well-fixed, well-heeled, well-lined, well-off, well-to-do; **nouveau riche,** cashed-up, get-rich-quick, new-rich; **opulent,** Edwardian, palatial, palatine, ritzy, sumptuous, sybaritic; **capitalist,** capitalistic, chrematistic, mammonistic, nabobish, plutocratic

WEALTHY PERSON *n* billionaire, Croesus, dollar millionaire, fat cat, man of means, man of substance, Midas, millionaire, millionairess, moneybags, moneyed man, multimillionaire, pound millionaire, sugar daddy; **nouveau-riche,** new-rich, parvenu; **tycoon,** aggrandiser, baron, capitalist, king, magnate, merchant prince, money-maker, nabob, plutocrat; **mammonist,** mammonite; **playboy,** gilded youth, jetsetter, silvertail, sybarite, toff; **the rich,** plutocracy, the haves, the idle rich, the other half, the ruling class; **high society,** beautiful people, jet set, society

WEAR *v* dress in, have on, sport; **put on,** doll up, don, hop into, huddle on, invest *(Rare)*, try on; **rug up,** bundle up, cover up, do up, enrobe, get up, muffle up, re-dress, wrap up; **change,** disarray, shift *(Archaic)*; **overdress,** lair up, mocker up

wear *n* → **1** clothes **2** damage **3** use *v* **4** assent to **5** continue **6** deteriorate **7** display **8** swerve **9** tire

wearing *adj* → **1** boring **2** harmful **3** tiring

weary *v* → **1** bore **2** tire *adj* **3** bored **4** discontented **5** effortful **6** tired

weasel *n* → **1** betrayer **2** cunning person *v* **3** betray

WEATHER *n* elements, meteor *(Obs.)*; **climate,** clime, microclimate, regime, seasonal pattern; **continental climate,** equatorial climate, insular climate, maritime climate, Mediterranean climate, polar climate, temperate climate, tropical climate; **fair weather,** balminess, fairness, halcyon days, shine; **calm weather,** doldrums; **rough weather,** inclemency, intemperateness, storm, storminess, sultriness, thunder, tornado, unsettledness, wintriness. *See also* ATMOSPHERIC PRESSURE; CLIMATOLOGY

weather *v* → **1** continue **2** deteriorate **3** dry **4** slope

weatherboard *n* → side

weathervane *n* → indicator

weave *v* → **1** flutter **2** interlace **3** sew **4** twist

web *n* → **1** combine **2** feather **3** skin **4** stratagem **5** textiles *v* **6** cover

webbing *n* → **1** interlacement **2** skin

WEDDING *n* bridal, espousal, nuptials, spousals; **church wedding,** civil marriage, double wedding, elopement, shotgun wedding, white wedding; **marriage rites,** nuptial mass, solemnisation, wedding service; **marriage celebrant,** celebrant, solemniser, uniter; **bridal party,** best man, bridesmaid, flowergirl, groomsman, maid of honour, matron of honour, paranymph; **banns,** lines *(Brit.)*, marriage certificate; **reception,** wedding breakfast; **wedding march,** charivari, epithalamium, nuptial song, prothalamion, wedding song; **honeymoon; proposal,** offer; **engagement,** affiance, betrothal, contract, precontract; **troth,** hand, promise; **dowry,** marriage portion, marriage settlement; **matchmaker,** go-between, marriage broker. *See also* MARRIAGE

wedge *n* → **1** armed forces **2** atmospheric pressure **3** machine **4** nail **5** obstacle **6** part *v* **7** fill **8** obstruct **9** separate

wedlock *n* → marriage

wee *n* → **1** urination *adj* **2** small

weed *n* → **1** thin person **2** tobacco

weedy *adj* → **1** ill **2** thin **3** weak

weekend *n* → holiday

weekender *n* → **1** cabin **2** prisoner

weekly *n* → **1** magazine **2** newspaper

weep *n* → **1** cry *v* **2** be unhappy **3** discharge **4** excrete **5** grieve **6** wet

weeping *adj* → grieving

WEIGH *v* bulk, tip the scales at, weigh a ton, weigh in at; **outweigh,** outbalance, overbalance, overweigh, preponderate; **balance,** poise *(Obs.)*, scale, tare; **burden,** break the back of, charge, cumber, encumber, load, lumber, overbear, overburden, overcharge, overlade, overload, overweight, overwhelm, pack, surcharge, tax

weigh *v* → **1** assess **2** be important **3** hinder **4** respect

weight *n* → **1** atom **2** class **3** difficulty **4** heaviness **5** hindrance **6** importance **7** influence

weir *n* → **1** chute **2** dam **3** obstacle

weird *adj* → **1** fateful **2** strange **3** supernatural

WELCOME *v* be sociable, entertain, receive; **keep in with,** be all over, cultivate, familiarise *(Rare)*, ingratiate, make one's marble good with, make up to, smother, smother with kindness; **heap coals of fire on someone's head**

welcome *n* → **1** courtesy **2** friendship **3** sociability *v* **4** be sociable **5** enjoy *adj* **6** pleasant **7** rightful

weld *n* → **1** yellow pigment *v* **2** work metal

welfare *n* → **1** good **2** good fortune **3** health **4** income

WELL *adv* amazingly, bonnily, capitally, excellently, fabulously, famously, finely, grandly, magnificently, marvellously, sensationally, soundly, splendidly, superbly, swingingly, tremendously, unreally, wizardly *(Brit.)*, wonderfully; **exquisitely,** choicely, divinely, elegantly; **uncommonly,** exceptionally, extremely, peerlessly, remarkably, supremely, ultra, unco *(Scot.)*, uncommon

(Archaic); **fine,** all cush, great, okay, right; **beneficially,** advantageously

well-being *n* → **1** good fortune **2** health **3** pleasure

WELL DONE *interj* attaboy, beaut, beauty, bewdy, bully, curl the mo, good egg, good for you, good iron, good on you, good show, that's the shot, your blood's worth bottling; **goodo,** good, great, hot dog *(U.S.)*; **right on,** hear hear, no risk, spot-on, touché; **hip hip hooray,** alleluia, hallelujah, hooray, huzza *(Archaic)*, kapai *(N.Z.)*, pie *(N.Z.)*, three cheers, viva; **bravo,** encore

well-heeled *adj* → wealthy

wellington boot *n* → boot

wellnigh *adv* → almost

well-off *adj* → **1** content **2** wealthy

well-read *adj* → knowledgeable

well-to-do *adj* → **1** content **2** wealthy

welsh *v* → **1** fail to pay **2** report on

welt *n* → **1** bulge **2** coating **3** disfigurement **4** hit **5** injury *v* **6** cudgel

welter *n* → **1** turbulence *v* **2** toss **3** vibrate **4** wet

wench *n* → **1** country dweller **2** promiscuous person **3** prostitute **4** woman *v* **5** be promiscuous **6** prostitute oneself

wend *v* → advance

werewolf *n* → devil

west *n* → region

western *n* → story

WET *v* baptise, water; **bedew,** dew; **moisten,** baste, damp, dampen, embrocate, foment, humidify, irrigate, moisturise, water down; **impregnate,** imbibe *(Obs.)*, imbrue, imbue; **sweat,** reek, slobber, weep; **sprinkle,** asperse, drop *(Archaic)*, hose, shower; **splash,** dabble, dash, plash, slop, spat, splatter, squirt; **drench,** ret, rot, sop, swamp, waterlog; **soak,** macerate, marinade, marinate, sodden, souse, steep, water-soak, welter *(Archaic)*; **irrigate,** float, flood, inundate, subirrigate, water; **immerse,** bathe, douse, duck, immerge *(Rare)*, submerge; **dip,** dap, puddle, sop; **bathe,** go for a swim, have a dip, swim

WET *adj* humorous *(Obs.)*, hydric, moist, soggy, sticky, sweaty; **damp,** clammy, dampish, dank, humid, hygric, mesic; **dewy,** lachrymose, rainy, slobbery; **lush,** juicy, sappy, succulent; **boggy,** fenny *(Brit.)*, marshy, muddy, oozy, plashy, sloppy, sloshy, splashy; **irrigational,** irrigative; **hygrophilous; sodden,** dozy *(N.Z.)*, impregnate, soggy, sopping, soppy, waterlogged, wringing wet; **awash,** swimming, water-sick, watery; **immersed,** submerged, submersed

wet *n* → **1** brewer **2** economics **3** liquid **4** rainfall **5** wetness *v* **6** urinate *adj* **7** licensed **8** weak

wet blanket *n* → **1** bore **2** discourager **3** hinderer **4** sobersides **5** unhappy person

wet-blanket *v* → discourage

WETNESS *n* clamminess, dewiness, drench, moistness, ooziness, sloppiness, soddenness, sogginess, soppiness, stickiness, wet; **dampness,** dankness, humidness, sweatiness; **lushness,** succulence, succulency; **humidity,** regain *(Textiles)*, relative humidity, vapour concentration; **moisture,** damp, rising damp; **bog,** fen *(Brit.)*, wet ground; **seepage,** seep

WETTING *n* drench, marinade, soak, soakage, souse, steep; **saturation,** calcification *(Geol.)*, inundation, rinsing; **irrigation,** aspersion, drip irrigation, flood irrigation, subirrigation, watering, wild flooding; **immersion,** affusion, baptism, bath, bogie *(Colloq.)*, duck, immergence, rinse, submergence, submersion; **fomentation,** embrocation, humidification, imbuement; **maceration,** marination; **splash,** dash, plash, splosh

whack *n* → **1** attempt **2** click **3** hit **4** part **5** share *v* **6** hit **7** tire

whale *v* → **1** beat **2** fish

wham *n* → **1** boom **2** hit *v* **3** hit

wharf *n* → **1** harbour **2** seaside *v* **3** store

wharfie *n* → **1** labourer **2** transporter

what *adj* → **1** particular *adv* **2** how *interj* **3** bullshit **4** how about that **5** oh

whatnot *n* → **1** any **2** bad person **3** rack **4** shelf **5** unimportant thing

what not *n* → any

wheat *n* → yellow

wheedle *v* → **1** allure **2** beguile **3** flatter **4** persuade

WHEEL *n* cartwheel; **waterwheel,** millwheel, paddlewheel *(Naut.)*, windmill; **spinning wheel,** charka, potter's wheel; **roulette,** chocolate wheel, wheel of fortune; **cogwheel,** epicycloidal wheel, flywheel, gearwheel, gipsy, pinion, pinwheel, planet wheel, ratchet wheel, rowel, sheave, sprocket wheel, spur wheel; **castor,** rundle, truck *(Gunnery)*, trundle; **tyre,** inner tube, pneumatic tyre, radial, radial-ply tyre, slick *(Colloq.)*, tubeless tyre, whitewall, widey; **catherine-wheel,** pinwheel; **gyroscope,** gyrostat. *See also* CIRCLE; RING

wheel *n* → **1** important person *v* **2** roll **3** rotate **4** swerve **5** thrust

wheelbarrow *n* → **1** wagon *v* **2** transport

wheeze *n* → **1** breathing **2** joke **3** stratagem *v* **4** breathe **5** shrill

whelk *n* → sore

whelp *n* → **1** animal offspring **2** knob *v* **3** give birth

when *conj* → while

whenever *conj* → while

WHERE *adv* where'er *(Poetic)*, whereabout *(Rare)*, whereat, wherein, wheresoever, wherever, whither; **wherefrom**

WHERE *conj* where'er *(Poetic)*, wherein, wherever; **whence,** whencesoever, wherefrom; **whereto,** whither *(Archaic)*; **whereabouts**

whereabouts *n* → **1** position *conj* **2** where

wherefore *n* → **1** cause *adv* **2** why

whereupon *conj* → while

wherever *adv* → **1** where *conj* **2** where

wherewithal *n* → **1** expedient **2** method **3** supplies

whet *v* → **1** enthuse **2** rub **3** sharpen

whey *n* → drink

which *adj* → **1** particular **2** preceding

whiff *n* → **1** absorption **2** breathing **3** cloud **4** outburst **5** rowing boat **6** smell **7** tobacco *v* **8** absorb **9** breathe **10** smell out

WHILE *conj* as, whiles *(Archaic)*, whilst; **when,** once, whene'er *(Poetic)*, whenever, whensoever *(Archaic)*; **until,** till; **whereupon,** against *(Archaic)*

whim *n* → **1** caprice **2** desire **3** machine **4** puller

whimper *n* → **1** animal call **2** cry **3** shout *v* **4** grieve **5** shout

whimsical *adj* → **1** capricious **2** changeable **3** humorous **4** indecisive

whimsy *n* → **1** caprice **2** desire **3** humour **4** image

whine *n* → **1** animal call **2** click **3** complaint **4** cry **5** quiet sound **6** shout *v* **7** call (of animals) **8** complain **9** grieve **10** shrill **11** speak

whinge *n* → **1** complaint *v* **2** be ungrateful **3** complain

whinny *n* → **1** animal call *v* **2** call (of animals)

whip *n* → **1** club **2** cord **3** driver **4** gunfire **5** hit **6** incentive **7** leader **8** machine **9** move **10** propellant *v* **11** agitate **12** cook **13** cover **14** cudgel **15** defeat **16** fish **17** scold **18** speed **19** spin **20** twist

whiplash *n* → club

whirl *n* → **1** rate **2** spin *v* **3** speed **4** spin **5** swerve **6** throw

whirlpool *n* → **1** current **2** spin

whirlwind *n* → **1** advance **2** spin **3** violent outburst **4** wind

whirr *n* → **1** click **2** vibration *v* **3** click **4** spin **5** vibrate

whisk *n* → **1** accumulation **2** rate *v* **3** agitate **4** capture **5** cook

whisker *n* → **1** hair **2** small amount

whisper *n* → **1** hiss **2** news **3** quiet sound **4** speaking *v* **5** hiss **6** speak

whist *interj* → silence

whistle *n* → **1** hiss **2** siren *v* **3** call (of animals) **4** hiss **5** make music **6** shout **7** shrill **8** signal

whit *n* → small amount

WHITE *n* alabaster, chalk, cream, flour, ivory, lily, milk, mother-of-pearl, nacre, off-white, pearl, snow; **silver,** argent; **albino**

WHITE *adj* blank, candid *(Obs.)*, floury, lilied, lily-white, pale, white as a ghost, white as a sheet; **snowy,** frosty, snow-white, snowlike; **creamy,** cream, cream-coloured; **ivory,** alabaster, chalky, eburnean; **milky,** lacteous, milk-white, opalescent, opaline; **off-white,** albescent, broken white, fair, light, oyster white, whitish; **foaming,** sudsy; **silver,** argent, silvern *(Archaic)*, silvery; **blond,** albino, ash-blond, bald *(Zool.)*, blonde, canescent *(Biol.)*, hoar *(Archaic)*, hoary, platinum blonde, towheaded, white-haired; **pearly,** nacreous

white *n* → **1** emptiness **2** eye *v* **3** print **4** whiten *adj* **5** cold **6** colourless **7** empty **8** faithful **9** frightened **10** innocent **11** perfect

white-ant *v* → damage

whitecap *n* → surf

white-collar *adj* → working

white elephant *n* → waste

white flag *n* → **1** mediation **2** pacification

white heat *n* → **1** excitement **2** heat

white lie *n* → **1** hiding **2** lie

WHITEN *v* blanch, bleach, blench, etiolate; **chalk,** blanco, calcimine, do one's sandshoes, pipeclay, powder one's face, white *(Obs.)*, whitewash

whitewash *n* → **1** hiding **2** losing **3** paint *v* **4** coat **5** defeat **6** hide **7** justify **8** whiten

whither *adv* → **1** where *conj* **2** where

whiting *n* → cleanser

whittle *v* → **1** cut **2** decrease **3** shape **4** subtract

whiz *n* → **1** click **2** expert **3** hiss **4** wise person *v* **5** click **6** hiss **7** speed

whoever *n* → any

WHOLE *n* alpha and omega, entire, synthesis, synthesisation, tale *(Archaic)*, total, totality; **all,** the lot, the whole bang lot, the whole boodle, the whole box and dice, the whole caboodle, the whole hog, the whole kit and caboodle, the whole shooting match, the works; **whole amount,** aggregation, altogether, ensemble, full amount, sum, summation; **full set,** complement, corpus, full board *(Shearing)*, full house, series, system; **gamut,** circle, continuum, cycle, range

WHOLE *adj* all, compleat *(Archaic)*, complete, entire, full, livelong, plenary, total; **intact,** acatalectic, full-length, inedited, inviolate, unabbreviated, unabridged, unbroken, uncensored, uncut, undivided, unexpurgated, uninterrupted; **absolute,** consummate, dead, diametrical, living, perfect, plenipotentiary, unconditional, unconditioned, unqualified; **finished,** made-up, mature, rounded, well-rounded; **hundred-per-cent,** full on, full out, undamped; **inclusive,** integrated, integrative, round, sum, tutti, tutto; **self-contained,** self-sufficient, self-sufficing. *See also* THOROUGH

whole *adj* → **1** healthy **2** numerical **3** perfect

wholehearted *adj* → agreeable

whole number *n* → number

wholesale *v* → **1** sell *adj* **2** inclusive **3** thorough *adv* **4** commercially **5** sizeably **6** wholly

WHOLESOME *adj* clean, healthful, hygienic, macrobiotic, salubrious, salutary, salutiferous, sanatory, sanitary; **tonic,** analeptic, recuperative

WHOLLY *adv* absolutely, completely, consummately, entirely, every bit, every inch, first and last, grossly, heartily, hundred-percent, on the whole, perfectly, point-device *(Archaic)*, properly, thoroughly, totally, unconditionally, utterly; **unbrokenly,** undividedly, uninterruptedly; **altogether,** all, all told, as a whole, bodily, in all, in full, in sum, in the aggregate, in toto, inclusively, integrally *(Rare)*, overall, tout ensemble; **to the full,** bag and baggage, boots and all, cap-a-pie, down to the ground, from head to foot, holus-bolus, lock stock and barrel, neck and crop, root and branch, to the backbone, to the bitter end, to the hilt, to the letter, to the teeth; **head over heels,** head over tail, head over turkey, heart and soul, hook line and sinker; **downright,** dead, deathly, fair, fairly, hard *(U.S.)*, outright, quite, simply, stark, starkly, straight, wholesale; **with a vengeance,** and then some, in full force; **radically,** diametrically. *See also* THOROUGHLY

whoop *n* → **1** challenge **2** shout *v* **3** chirp **4** encourage **5** shout

whoops *interj* → oh

whoosh *n* → **1** hiss *v* **2** hiss

whopper *n* → **1** giant **2** lie

whorl *n* → **1** spiral **2** twist

WHY *adv* forwhy *(Archaic or Joc.)*, how, how come *(Colloq.)*, what for, whence *(Archaic)*, whencesoever *(Archaic)*, wherefore

why *n* → **1** cause *interj* **2** oh

wick *n* → **1** cord **2** explosive **3** fuel **4** groin **5** lighter

wicked *adj* → **1** annoying **2** bad **3** immoral **4** unpleasant **5** wrong

wicket *n* → **1** door **2** entrance **3** interlacement

wide *adj* → **1** deflective **2** distant **3** open **4** spacious **5** thick *adv* **6** deflectively **7** open **8** remotely **9** thoroughly

widespread *adj* → **1** dispersed **2** flooding **3** general

widow *n* → single person

width *n* → thickness

wield *v* → use

wife *n* → **1** spouse **2** woman

wig *n* → **1** hairpiece *v* **2** scold **3** shear

wiggle *n* → flutter

wigwam *n* → camp

wild *adj* → **1** animal-like **2** disorderly **3** enthusiastic **4** excited **5** foolish **6** liberated **7** muddled **8** natural **9** rash **10** untidy **11** violent *adv* **12** deflectively **13** naturally **14** violently

wildcat *n* → **1** angry person *v* **2** search *adj* **3** rash

wilderness *n* → **1** accumulation **2** commotion **3** garden **4** nature **5** wasteland

wile *n* → dishonesty

wilful *adj* → **1** capricious **2** disobedient **3** stubborn **4** uncompromising

WILFULNESS *n* an iron hand, iron will, resoluteness, resolution, single-mindedness, strength of purpose, strength of will, willpower; **decisiveness,** decidedness, decision, deliberateness, determinateness, determination, determinedness, earnestness, firmness, heart of oak, immovability, immovableness, intension, intentness, killer instinct, premeditation, purposefulness, purposiveness, seriousness, seriousness of purpose, stability, stableness, steadfastness, steadiness; **a will of one's own,** headstrongness

WILL *n* choice, craving, desire, inclination, pleasure, velleity, volition, want, wish, yen; **intention,** animus *(Law)*, frame of mind, gleam in one's eye, intent, purpose, tendency *(Lit.)*; **voluntarism,** conation *(Psychol.)*, free will, pleasure principle

will *n* → **1** choice **2** command **3** desire **4** record *v* **5** desire **6** determine **7** give **8** intend

WILLING *adj* desirous, longing; **voluntarist,** voluntaristic; **intended,** conative *(Psychol.)*, conscious, deliberate, intentional, intentioned, planned, premeditated, premeditative, prepense, purposeful, purposive; **voluntary,** free-will, self-determined, volitional, volitionary, volitive

willing *adj* → **1** agreeable **2** assenting **3** desirous **4** enthusiastic

WILLINGLY *adv* as lief, as soon, fain *(Archaic)*, gladly, readily, with a will, with open arms; **voluntarily,** of one's own accord, of one's own free will, ultroneously; **wholeheartedly,** con amore, heart and soul, ungrudgingly, unmurmuringly, with all one's heart, with good grace

WILLINGNESS *n* alacrity, desire, eagerness, enthusiasm, inclination, promptness, readiness, wholeheartedness; **agreeability,** a willing heart, complaisance; **free will,** ultroneousness, voluntariness

willow *n* → **1** club **2** timber *v* **3** harvest **4** sew

willowy *adj* → **1** arboreal **2** pliable **3** soft **4** thin

willpower *n* → wilfulness

wilt *n* → **1** weakness *v* **2** weaken

wily *adj* → cunning

wimple *n* → **1** headgear *v* **2** agitate

win *n* → **1** success *v* **2** dry **3** gain **4** gamble **5** get **6** marry **7** prepare **8** succeed

wince *n* → **1** reaction *v* **2** feel pain **3** react

winch *n* → **1** lift **2** machine **3** puller *v* **4** lift **5** pull

WIND *n* advection, air current, airflow, airstream, convection, cross-wind, current, current of air, down draught, draught, headwind, overdraught, standing wave, tail wind, up draught, windage; **breeze,** air, breath, cat's-paw, doctor, fresh breeze, gale *(Archaic)*, gentle breeze, land breeze, moderate breeze, sea-breeze, slight breeze, strong breeze, trade wind *(Archaic)*, variable wind, zephyr; **strong wind,** blow, buster, gale, high wind, near gale, stiff wind, strong gale, whole gale, windstorm; **gust,** blast, flaw, flurry, puff, waft; **whirlwind,** dust devil, tornado, tourbillion, twister *(U.S.)*, williwaw *(N.Z.)*, willy-willy; **storm,** blizzard, buran, cyclone, dust squall, dust storm, hurricane, magnetic storm, monsoon, squall, tempest, typhoon, white squall; **seasonal winds,** equinoctial, etesian winds, north-easter, north-wester, sou'wester, south, south-easter, south-wester, southerly, southerly buster, westerly; **regional winds,** Albany doctor, barber *(N.Z.)*, bora, brickfielder, Esperance doctor, Fremantle doctor, gregale, levanter; **mistral,** chili, föhn, north, samiel, simoom, sirocco; **trades,** anti-trades, roaring forties; **easterly,** Zephyrus

wind *n* → **1** abdomen **2** airflow **3** bombast **4** breathing **5** burp **6** gas **7** point of view **8** pride **9** twist *v* **10** flow **11** pursue **12** tangle **13** turn **14** twist

windbag *n* → **1** gasbag **2** talker
windbreak *n* → **1** obstacle **2** screen
windcheater *n* → jumper
windfall *n* → luck
WINDINESS *n* breeziness, draughtiness, gustiness
winding *n* → **1** circuitousness **2** complexity **3** spin **4** twist *adj* **5** complex **6** deflective **7** twisting
windlass *n* → **1** lift **2** machine **3** puller *v* **4** lift **5** pull
windmill *n* → **1** machine **2** spin **3** wheel *v* **4** rotate
WINDOW *n* ancient light *(Law)*, bay, bay window, bow window, bullseye, casement, catherine-wheel, dormer window, drop window, fanlight, fenestella, fenestra, French window, gable window, hopper window, Jesse window, lancet window, light, louvre window, lunette, luthern, picture window, quarter-vent window, rose, rose window, sash-window, sidelight, skylight, transom; **porthole,** flipper window *(Colloq.)*, port
window *v* → open
windpipe *n* → neck
windsurfer *n* → **1** mariner **2** sailing ship
WINDWARD *adv* aweather, downwind, upwind; **before the wind,** close to the wind, downwind, in the teeth of the wind, large, near, upwind, windrode; **onshore,** katabatic, offshore, quartering; **windily,** breezily
WINDY *adj* blowy, breezy, draughty, puffy; **blustery,** Aeolian, boreal, favonian, flawy, gusty, monsoonal, squally; **fair,** free, large *(Obs.)*; **stiff,** cyclonal, cyclonic, cyclonical, strong, tempestuous, tornadic, tornado-like, typhonic; **windswept**
WINE *n* bulk wine, plonk, quaffing wine, red wine, steam, the grape, vin bianco, vin ordinaire, vin rouge, vino, white wine; **champagne,** bubbly, champers, fizz. *See also* ALCOHOL
wine *v* → **1** intoxicate *adj* **2** red
wing *n* → **1** addition **2** aeroplane **3** arm **4** bird part **5** building **6** combat troops **7** door **8** feather **9** flight **10** flower **11** fruit **12** knob **13** political spectrum **14** side **15** stage *v* **16** fly **17** injure **18** perform
wink *n* → **1** gesture **2** light **3** moment *v* **4** gesture **5** shine
WINNER *n* ace, champ, champion, conqueror, giant-killer, knockout, master, scorer, vanquisher, victor, victress; **bolter,** boom galloper, goer, knocktaker, mudlark, skinner; **placegetter; winning hit,** boomer, bottler, score, trump card; **whiz-kid,** natural *(Colloq.)*, prodigy, wunderkind
winning *n* → **1** mineral **2** opening **3** successfulness *adj* **4** alluring **5** pleasant **6** successful **7** superior
winnow *v* → **1** discriminate **2** exclude **3** fly **4** harvest **5** inquire into **6** move
winsome *adj* → **1** alluring **2** pleasant
winter *n* → **1** coldness **2** season *adj* **3** cold **4** seasonal
wipe *v* → **1** coat **2** dry **3** repel
wipe out *v* → **1** annihilate **2** destroy **3** massacre **4** remove
wipe-out *n* → **1** failure **2** fall
WIRE *n* cheese-cutter, crosshair, crosswire, haywire, piano wire, tie wire, wire rope; **electric cord,** cable, cablet, cabling, coaxial cable, cord, flex, fuse wire, lead, line, main, pigtail wire, wiring; **chain,** chain cable, sling. *See also* CORD
wire *n* → **1** allure **2** fence **3** finish **4** hair **5** message **6** wire *v* **7** cord **8** hunt **9** restrain **10** send a message
wireless *n* → **1** radio **2** sound system
wiry *adj* → **1** corded **2** hard **3** resonant **4** strong **5** thin
WISDOM *n* counsel *(Archaic)*, far-sightedness, judiciousness, long-headedness, prudence, sageness, sapience, sapiency; **shrewdness,** astuteness, canniness, policy, sagaciousness, sagacity, subtleness, subtlety, supersubtlety; **commonsense,** gumption, horse sense, level-headedness, mother wit, nous, reason, savvy, sense, sensibleness; **profundity,** deepness, profoundness. *See also* INTELLIGENCE
wisdom *n* → knowledge
WISE *adj* far-seeing, far-sighted, judicious, longheaded, old, prudent, quaint *(Archaic)*, sagacious, sage, sapient, sapiential, witty *(Obs.)*; **shrewd,** astute, canny, politic, statesmanlike, subtle, supersubtle; **commonsensical,** level-headed, reasonable, sensible; **profound,** deep. *See also* INTELLIGENT
wise *n* → **1** method *adj* **2** knowledgeable
wisecrack *n* → **1** joke *v* **2** joke
WISE GUY *n* clever dick, know-all, smart alec, smart arse, smartie, smartypants, wiseacre, witling *(Archaic)*
WISE PERSON *n* doctor, elder, greybeard, hakim *(Islam)*, intellectual, level-head, light, Nestor, owl, philosopher, sage, sapient, seer, Solon, tohunga *(N.Z.)*, wise virgin, wise woman, witch, wizard *(Archaic)*; **genius,** mastermind, prodigy, wit *(Archaic)*, wunderkind; **oracle,** brains trust, elder statesman, expert, guru, master, whiz; **intelligentsia,** illuminati
wish *n* → **1** desire **2** will *v* **3** desire **4** intend
wishbone *n* → lucky charm
wishy-washy *adj* → **1** insipid **2** liquid **3** weak
wisp *n* → **1** accumulation **2** small person **3** thin person *v* **4** roll up
wistful *adj* → **1** desirous **2** unhappy
wit *n* → **1** eloquence **2** humorist **3** humour **4** intelligence **5** mind **6** wise person *v* **7** know
witch *n* → **1** allurer **2** bad person **3** bewitcher **4** fairy **5** occultist **6** ugly person **7** wise person **8** woman **9** worshipper *v* **10** allure **11** bewitch
WITH DIFFICULTY *adv* awkwardly, cumbersomely, ill, painfully, stiffly, troublesomely
withdraw *v* → **1** be modest **2** cancel **3** depart **4** extract **5** go back **6** make peace **7** remove

WITH EFFORT *adv* agonisingly, arduously, burdensomely, drudgingly, grindingly, heavily, heavy, laboriously, labouringly, strenuously, sweatily, toilfully, toilsomely; **industriously,** ably, enthusiastically, for all one's worth, for the life of one, hard, operosely, with might and main; **athletically,** agilely, gymnastically

wither *v* → 1 contract 2 deteriorate 3 die 4 dry

withhold *v* → 1 be miserly 2 be reticent 3 keep secret 4 restrict

within *n* → 1 inside *adv* 2 inside

WITHOUT *prep* minus, off, sans *(Archaic)*, senza, sine, wanting

without *adj* → 1 poor *adv* 2 outside *prep* 3 less 4 outside *conj* 5 on condition that

withstand *v* → oppose

witness *n* → 1 evidence 2 litigant 3 looker 4 testifier *v* 5 see 6 testify

witticism *n* → 1 joke 2 mockery

witty *adj* → 1 humorous 2 wise

wizard *n* → 1 bewitcher 2 expert 3 occultist 4 wise person *adj* 5 good 6 magic 7 supernatural

wizened *adj* → 1 contracted 2 dry

wobble *n* → 1 vibration *v* 2 vacillate 3 vibrate

woe *n* → 1 grieving 2 unfortunateness 3 unhappiness *interj* 4 alas

woebegone *adj* → 1 grieving 2 unhappy

wog *n* → 1 Australian 2 foreigner 3 illness 4 organism

wolf *n* → 1 allurer 2 animal's coat 3 dissonance 4 extortionist 5 promiscuous person *v* 6 eat 7 gorge 8 hunt

WOMAN *n* donna, earthmother, fair *(Archaic)*, female, feme *(Law)*, femme, gentlewoman, lady, she, squaw, wife; **womankind,** distaff side, fair sex, feminie *(Archaic)*, femininity, gentle sex, weaker sex, womenfolk; **sheila,** babe, baby, bart *(Obs.)*, bint, bird, bit, bit of fluff, broad, brush, bush, charlie, Charlie Wheeler, chick, chook, clinah *(Obs.)*, dame, donah *(Obs.)*, filly, flapper, heifer, hen, j.t., jam tart, jane, judy, ockerina, petticoat, piece, potato peeler, puss, quean *(Scot.)*, skirt, sort, tabby, tabo, tart, wench, widgie; **black woman,** gin, lubra, mary, wahine *(N.Z.)*; **white woman,** albino, mem-sahib; **seductress,** carnie, corpus delicti, enchantress, femme fatale, foxy lady, hot stuff, houri, kitten, mantrap, minx, nymphette, popsy, sex kitten, sexpot, siren, temptress, vamp, vamper, vampire; **beauty,** a good sort, bathing beauty, bathing belle, beauty queen, belle, charmer, doll, goddess, Juno, nymph, sylph, Venus, witch; **amazon,** butch, dyke, Lesbian, virago; **feminist,** suffragette, suffragist, women's libber; **girl,** damsel *(Archaic)*, demoiselle, lass, lassie, mademoiselle, maid, maiden, missy, virgin; **tomboy,** hoyden, romp; **old woman,** beldam, biddy, boiler, carline *(Scot.)*, crone, dowager, granny, matron, old chook, old duck, old girl, old maid

woman *n* → 1 lover 2 servant 3 sexual partner 4 spouse *v* 5 feminise

womanise *v* → 1 be promiscuous 2 feminise

WOMANLINESS *n* anima, femaleness, femineity, feminineness, femininity, gentlewomanliness, ladylikeness, matronliness, muliebrity, unmanliness, womanhood; **effeminacy,** effeminateness, womanishness; **feminisation,** emasculation, emollition

womb *n* → 1 abdomen 2 breeding ground 3 groin 4 reproductive organs 5 start

won *v* → inhabit

WONDER *v* gape, gawp, gaze, marvel

wonder *n* → 1 freak 2 surprise *v* 3 be curious 4 be uncertain 5 think

wonderful *adj* → 1 astonishing 2 good

wondrous *adj* → 1 astonishing *adv* 2 astonishingly

wonky *adj* → 1 ill 2 misplaced 3 weak

woo *v* → 1 desire 2 entreat 3 flirt

wood *n* → 1 timber *adj* 2 angry

wooden *v* → 1 bowl over 2 lower *adj* 3 hard 4 ringing

woodwind *n* → musical band

woodwork *n* → sculpture

woof *n* → 1 animal call 2 click *v* 3 call (of animals)

woofer *n* → sound system

wool *n* → animal's coat

wool-gathering *n* → 1 fantasy 2 inattentiveness 3 thinking

woolly *n* → 1 jumper 2 sheep *adj* 3 imprecise

woolshed *n* → stable

woomera *n* → spear

Woop Woop *n* → remote place

woozy *adj* → drunk

WORD *n* content word, element, expression, function word, lexeme, particle, substitute, term, vocable; **noun,** adjective, adverb, article, conjunction, gerund, participle, preposition, pronoun, substantive, verb; **monosyllable,** tetragram, triliteral; **polysyllable,** jaw-breaker, sesquipedalian, tonguetwister; **coinage,** back formation, ghost word, neologism, neology, non-word; **Australianism,** inkhorn term, Latinism; **euphemism,** genteelism; **blend,** contraction, haplography, portmanteau word; **malapropism,** catachresis, corruption, parapraxis; **archaism,** counterword, literalism; **colloquialism,** dialecticism, vernacularism, vulgarism; **expletive,** interjection, swearword; **catchcry,** battle cry, buzz word, catchphrase, catchword, cry, epithet, slogan, watchword; **byword,** household word; **qualifier,** attributive, complement, definitive, distributive, prepositive

word *n* → 1 allusion 2 command 3 information 4 message 5 proverb 6 signal

word processor *n* → computer

wordy *adj* → verbose

WORK *n* darg, employment, handiwork, industry, labour, legwork, piecework, workload, yakka; **bonus work,** dirty work, hackwork, mixed functions, overwork, taskwork; **task,** assignment, care, charge, chore, commission, duty, errand, job, job of work, mission, piece of work; **working bee,**

corvée, fatigue *(Mil.)*, fatigue duty, working party; **working holiday,** busman's holiday

WORK *v* devil, do hackwork, labour, moil, outwork, sweat, toil, work off a dead horse; **be employed,** carry a cut-lunch, carry on a business, drive a trade, have a steady job, have an honest job, ply one's trade, turn an honest penny, turn an honest quid; **serve,** lackey; **freelance,** fag, job, moonlight, scab

work *n* → **1** book **2** building **3** drama **4** effort **5** finished product **6** job **7** musical piece **8** undertaking *v* **9** accomplish **10** brew **11** make **12** make an effort **13** move **14** operate **15** sew **16** undertake

workable *adj* → **1** expedient **2** feasible

workaday *adj* → simple

WORKER *n* industrial, operative, tradesman, tradeswoman, working girl, workingman, workman; **employee,** breadwinner, jobholder, wage-earner; **casual,** day labourer, extra, floater, hobo, journeyman *(Obs.)*, supernumerary, temp, temporary; **hard worker,** a tiger for punishment, compulsive worker, glutton for punishment, grafter, wheel-horse *(U.S.)*, willing horse, workaholic, workhorse; **toiler,** battler, dogsbody, drudge, drudger, moiler, old soldier, slave, slogger; **bad worker,** clock-watcher, cobbler, dilutee, slopworker; **freelance,** backyarder, freelancer, independent contractor, moonlighter; **pieceworker,** jobber, outworker; **white-collar worker,** clerk, pen-pusher, shiny-arse; **professional,** career girl, career woman. *See also* LABOURER

worker *n* → prostitute

WORKERS *n* labour, labour force, labour market, shop floor, workfolk, workpeople; **staff,** cadre, general staff, office, personnel; **shift,** day shift, night shift, quick shift; **gang,** assembly line, chain-gang, crew, learners' chain, squad, the chain, working party; **coworker,** colleague, fellow servant *(Law)*, fellow worker, offsider, partner

WORKING *adj* at work, busy, employed, engaged, in a job, in harness, labouring, occupied, on duty, on fatigue *(Mil.)*, on the job; **blue-collar,** factory-floor, flunkeyish, sweated; **white-collar,** clerical, managerial, professional

working *n* → **1** making *adj* **2** employed **3** impermanent **4** operating

WORKING CLASS *n* humbler orders, lower class, lower orders, lumpenproletariat, proletariat, rank and file, the masses, third estate, white trash *(U.S.)*; **commonfolk,** all the world and his wife, common *(Obs.)*, commonage, commonalty, commons, crowd, demos, every man and his dog, every Tom Dick and Harry, folk, hoi polloi, mobile vulgus, multitude, plebs, populace, small fry, the many, the million, Tom Dick and Harry, vulgar *(Archaic)*; **rabble,** canaille, cattle, doggery, dregs of society, gutter, herd, mob, raff, ragtag and bobtail, rout, ruck, scum, tag *(Obs.)*, the great unwashed, varletry *(Archaic)*, vermin

WORKING-CLASS *adj* lower-class, lumpenproletarian, plebeian, proletarian, underprivileged; **lowborn,** base *(Archaic)*, baseborn, ceorlish *(Archaic)*, churlish, dunghill, ignoble, low, lowbred, obscure, of low birth, of low parentage, of mean birth, of mean parentage, peasant, simple, ungentle *(Archaic)*, unpolished

workman *n* → worker

WORK OF ART *n* chef-d'oeuvre, classic, creation, magnum opus, masterpiece, oeuvre, opus, production; **objet d'art,** antique, collectable, museum piece, old master, period piece, virtu; **set piece; found object,** ready-made; **collage,** assemblage, combine painting, montage, papier collé; **collection,** loan collection

work out *v* → **1** compute **2** solve **3** use up

work-out *n* → **1** exercise **2** test

WORKPLACE *n* work station, workhouse, workshop; **workroom,** atelier, studio, study; **office,** bureau, business, chambers, head office; **regional office,** branch, district office, local office; **laboratory,** lab, research laboratory

world *n* → **1** heavenly body **2** matter **3** much **4** sky **5** surroundings **6** the public

worldly *adj* → **1** irreverent **2** realistic

worm *n* → **1** crawler **2** insect **3** twist *v* **4** smooth

worn *adj* → **1** blunt **2** dilapidated **3** tired **4** used up

WORRIED *adj* anxious, apprehensive, drawn, exercised, overanxious; **trembly,** in a funk, shaky, tremulous, wobbly; **tense,** high-strung, highly strung, highly-wrought, on tenterhooks, overstrung, uptight; **nervous,** edgy, fidgety, fretful, hyper, hypersensitive, jittery, jumpy, like a cat on a hot tin-roof, like a cat on hot bricks, nappy *(Equestrian)*, nervy, scratchy, skittish, toey, twitchy, uneasy, unquiet; **fraught,** distressful, feverish, feverous, frantic, frenetic, frenzied, hag-ridden, het-up, like a blue-arsed fly, on the rack, overwrought, unstrung, upset; **agitated,** flustered, fluttery, hot and bothered, in a flap, in a tizz; **ill-at-ease,** uncomfortable; **self-conscious,** paranoid

WORRIER *n* fidget, flutterer, fusser, jitterbug, worrywart; **panic merchant,** mouse; **nervous wreck,** basket case

worrisome *adj* → **1** annoying **2** frightened

WORRY *n* anxiety, anxiousness, disquiet, disquietude, franticness, fussing, jimjams, nervousness, overanxiety, overanxiousness; **trepidation,** agitation, consternation, distress, feverishness, perturbation, tremulousness; **nerves,** butterflies, flutter, gooseflesh, goosepimples, tremor; **the twitches,** creeps, fidgets, jitters, jumps, shakes, shivers, willies; **tenseness,** self-consciousness, tension, tensity; **jumpiness,** boggle, dysphoria, edginess, fidgetiness, restlessness, skittishness, twitchiness, uneasiness; **fuss,** bother, flurry, fluster, flustration, needle, trouble, worriment; **flap**

dither, fever, funk, stew, sweat, tizz, tizzy, twit, twitter

WORRY *v* bother, come unstuck, flap, flurry, fluster, flutter, fret, fuss, get one's knickers in a knot, get one's knickers in a twist, lose sleep over, overreact, pother, stew, sweat; **have the jitters,** boggle, funk, go to pieces, have a willy, jump, shy, start, startle; **fidget,** have ants in one's pants, have got 'em bad, hop up and down; **jitter,** chatter, rattle; **sweat blood,** go hot and cold all over, tear one's hair out

worry *n* → **1** annoyer *v* **2** agitate **3** alarm **4** annoy **5** discontent

worse *n* → **1** inferiority *adj* **2** deteriorating **3** inferior

WORSHIP *n* adoration, blessing, celebration, ceremonial, extolment, latria, love, prayer, worshipfulness; **veneration,** apotheosis, canonisation, dulia, ennoblement, enshrinement, enthronement, glorification, hierolatry, hyperdulia, iconolatry, idolatry, Mariolatry *(Derog.)*, piety, reverence, transfigurement; **prostration,** bow, genuflection, sacramental, sign of the cross

WORSHIP *v* adore, extol, glorify; **pray,** count one's beads, magnify *(Archaic)*, make a novena, praise, psalm, say one's beads, tell one's beads; **meditate,** contemplate, go on retreat, watch; **humble oneself,** bow, cross, fall on one's knees, genuflect, go down on one's knees, kneel, kowtow, prostrate oneself, sain *(Archaic)*; **exalt,** beatify, canonise, ennoble, enshrine, enthrone, hallow, honour, mysticise, revere, reverence, saint, transfigure, venerate; **deify,** apotheosise, divinise

worship *n* → **1** mister **2** reputation *v* **3** respect **4** revere

WORSHIPFUL *adj* adoring, reverend, reverent, reverential; **prayerful,** churchgoing, dedicated, devotional, hierodulic *(Antiq.)*, practising; **hagiolatrous,** hierolatrous, Mariolatrous; **idolatrous,** fetishistic, haggy, pagan; **heliolatrous,** druidic, druidical, heliolithic, ophiolatrous

WORSHIPPER *n* adorer, consecrator, devotee, extoller, fanatic, genuflector, glorifier, kowtower, mystic, palmer, petitionary *(Archaic)*, pilgrim, praiser, votaress, votary, votress; **psalmist,** cantor *(Judaism)*, caroller, lauder, muezzin *(Islam)*, psalmodist, reader; **churchgoer,** celebrant, communicant, congregation, invoker, kirkman *(Scot.)*, watcher; **hierolater,** iconolater, Marian; **sacrificer,** flagellant, flagellator, immolator; **cultist,** coven, deifier, demonist, demonolater, diabolist, Druid, Druidess, fetishist, firewalker, hag, heliolater, Magi, Magus, pagan, paynim *(Archaic)*, phallicist, rainmaker, Rastafarian, Satanist, shaman, shamanist, sunworshipper, tohunga *(N.Z.)*, votary, witch

worst *n* → **1** inferiority *v* **2** defeat *adj* **3** bad **4** inferior

worth *n* → **1** character **2** goodness **3** importance **4** reputation **5** respectability **6** superiority **7** usefulness **8** value *v* **9** occur

worthwhile *adj* → **1** fertile **2** profitable

worthy *n* → **1** famous person **2** person *adj* **3** highly regarded **4** reputable

would-be *adj* → **1** desirous **2** fake **3** hopeful **4** unworthy

wound *n* → **1** injury *v* **2** displease **3** injure **4** pain

wowser *n* → **1** abstainer **2** discourager **3** intolerant person **4** moraliser **5** prohibiter **6** sobersides **7** unhappy person

wrack *n* → ruin

wraith *n* → **1** phantom **2** soul **3** thin person

wrangle *n* → **1** disagreement **2** fight *v* **3** contest **4** disagree **5** farm **6** persuade

wrap *n* → **1** cloak *v* **2** cover **3** fasten **4** fold **5** secure **6** surround **7** twist

WRAPPER *n* envelope, enveloper, folder, wrapping; **wrapping paper,** aluminium foil, cellophane, gift-wrapping, gladwrap, shrink-wrap, silver foil, silver paper, tinfoil; **book cover,** binder, binding, board, bookbinder, bookbinding, case, doublure, dust jacket, dustcover, dustsheet, full binding, headband, jacket, mull, self-cover, spine

wrath *n* → **1** anger **2** punishment **3** retaliation *adj* **4** angry

wreak *v* → **1** do **2** impose

wreath *n* → **1** commemoration **2** interlacement **3** plant **4** ring

wreathe *v* → **1** decorate **2** surround

wreck *n* → **1** casualty **2** damage **3** patient **4** remnant **5** ruin **6** unfortunate **7** watercraft **8** weakling *v* **9** ruin **10** spoil

wrench *n* → **1** distortion **2** extraction **3** pull *v* **4** break **5** capture **6** distort **7** pull **8** twist

wrest *n* → **1** distortion **2** pull *v* **3** capture **4** distort **5** gain **6** pull

wrestle *n* → **1** fight **2** hold *v* **3** fight

wretch *n* → **1** bad person **2** immoral person **3** unfortunate **4** unhappy person

wretched *adj* → **1** bad **2** pitiable **3** poor **4** unfortunate **5** unhappy **6** unkempt

wrick *v* → distort

wriggle *n* → **1** circuitousness **2** move *v* **3** flutter **4** make do **5** move **6** twist **7** walk

wring *n* → **1** circuitousness *v* **2** distort **3** pain **4** twist

wrinkle *n* → **1** fold **2** furrow **3** idea **4** innovation **5** stratagem **6** trick *v* **7** contract **8** fold **9** furrow

writ *n* → **1** imprisonment **2** insistence **3** litigation **4** record **5** restraining order

WRITE *v* character *(Archaic)*, doodle, print, scratch, scrawl, scribble, scribe *(Rare)*, scrive, scroll, trace, write out; **pencil,** chalk, charcoal, pen; **type,** touch-type; **author,** co-author, compose, contribute, ghost, indite, lucubrate, make, pen, rewrite, utter; **write down,** dash down, dash off, draft, jot down, knock off, minute, set down, take down, write up; **portray,** depict, express, limn *(Archaic)*

write *v* → **1** mark **2** narrate **3** portray **4** send a message

write off *v* → **1** abandon **2** account **3** counteract **4** despair

write-off *n* → **1** account **2** casualty **3** failure **4** incompetent

WRITER *n* annotator, author, authoress, co-author, columnist, composer, contributor, copywriter, essayist, inditer, littérateur, stylist, wordsmith; **portrayer,** depicter; **dialogist,** colloquist, librettist; **hack,** devil, garreteer, ghost, ghost writer, jotter, pamphleteer, paragrapher, penny-a-liner, scribbler; **scriptwriter; penman,** calligrapher, calligraphist, hieroglyphist; **scribe,** amanuensis, clerk, copy typist, copyist, court reporter, Hansard reporter, inscriber, pen-pusher, penciller *(Horseracing)*, scrivener *(Archaic)*, stenographer, stenographist, tachygrapher, tachygraphist, transcriber; **scrawler,** cacographer, scratcher, scribbler; **secretary,** private secretary; **typist,** typiste

writhe *n* → **1** circuitousness **2** distortion **3** move *v* **4** distort **5** feel pain **6** move **7** toss **8** twist

WRITING *n* calligraphy, chirography, manuscript; **handwriting,** fist, hand; **penmanship,** clerkship, pencraft; **longhand,** copperplate, court hand, cursive, roundhand, running writing, script; **shorthand,** dictation, logography, phonography, stenography, stenotypy, tachygraphy; **typewriting,** typing; **scrawl,** cacography, scratch, scribble; **writing style,** character, expression, fluency, language, literariness, stylisation, stylistics; **literature,** belles-lettres, humanism, letters, prose, republic of letters; **philology,** diplomatics, palaeography

WRITING MATERIALS *n* jotter, letter paper, notepad, notepaper, onion skin, pad, papyrus, parchment, scribble block, scribble pad, scroll, stationery, table-book, vellum, writing pad, writing paper; **slate,** diptych, tablet, tablets, triptych; **blackboard,** chalkboard, whiteboard; **pen,** ballpoint pen, biro, dip-pen, felt pen, fountain pen, graphos, micrograph, quill, speedball nib, stylo pen, stylograph, stylus; **pencil,** lead pencil; **chalk,** charcoal, crayon

written *adj* → readable

WRITTEN COMPOSITION *n* cameo, holograph, inditement, opus, opuscule, sketch, text; **manuscript,** codex, document, draft, inedita, MS., schedule *(Obs.)*, script, treatise, typescript; **scroll,** palimpsest, parchment; **jottings,** adversaria, notes, screed; **extract,** analects, chapter, excerpt, gobbet, par, paragraph, passage, pericope, quotation, selection, tag, tirade; **annotation,** comment, cross-index, cross-reference, end note, footnote, gloss, induction, interlineation, interlining, note, preface, rubric, scholium, sidenote, subtitle, superscription; **rewrite,** adaptation, redaction, revision, rifacimento; **caption,** balloon, banderol, chronogram, circumscription, epigraph, inscription

WRONG *n* aberration, error, fault, misdeed, misprision, misstep; **crime,** delict, felony, malefaction, outrage, tort, victimless crime; **transgression,** abuse, malpractice, offence, trespass; **minor transgression,** peccadillo, slip, stumble, trip; **misbehaviour,** misdemeanour; **sin,** actual sin, cardinal sin, mortal sin, seven deadly sins, venial sin; **vice,** besetting sin, weakness

WRONG *v* abuse, aggrieve, do the dirty on, grieve *(Obs.)*, harm, offend against; **offend,** sail close to the wind, scandalise; **debauch,** corrupt; **err,** go to the bad, misplay, sin, trespass, trip; **compound one's error,** add insult to injury

WRONG *adj* delinquent, erring, peccant; **immoral,** aberrant, aberrational, inofficious, unconscionable, unethical, unprincipled, unscrupulous; **criminal,** crim, illegal, lawless, unlawful, wrongful; **outrageous,** heinous, reprehensible; **villainous,** black-hearted, blackguardly, conscienceless; **vicious,** debauched, depraved, perverse, perverted, unclean, uncleanly; **unrepentant,** incorrigible, unreformed, unregenerate; **evil,** evildoing, harmful, wicked; **bad,** black, damnable, flagitious, foul, indefensible, obnoxious *(Obs.)*, piacular, putrid, shameful, unwarrantable; **base,** bastardly, caitiff, cheap, contemptible, currish, deadshit, ignominious, low, low-down, mean, scabby, scurvy, whoreson. *See also* INCORRECT

wrong *n* → **1** crime **2** evildoing **3** unfairness *v* **4** damage **5** rape *adj* **6** badly-behaved **7** false **8** illogical **9** incongruous **10** incorrect **11** misjudged **12** ungrammatical

WRONGDOER *n* blackguard, evildoer, malpractitioner, villain; **transgressor,** sinner, trespasser; **criminal,** crim, first offender, malfeasor, tortfeasor

WRONGFULNESS *n* badness, blameworthiness, censurableness, depravity, peccancy, sinfulness, sordidness, uncleanliness, unregeneracy, wickedness; **evil,** evildoing, evilness, flagitiousness, foulness, heinousness, outrageousness, viciousness; **immorality,** aberrance, aberrancy, delinquency, disgracefulness, obliquity, perverseness, perversity, unconscionableness, unprincipledness, unscrupulousness; **baseness,** blackguardism, contemptibility, contemptibleness, currishness, damnableness, despicability, despicableness, villainousness, villainy; **criminality,** illegality, reprehensibility, suability; **mens rea,** cold-blooded murder, malice aforethought, premeditated murder; **frailty,** turpitude, weakness; **impropriety,** bad form, improperness, incorrectness, inexcusability, inexcusableness, irregularity, offensiveness, shabbiness, unacceptableness, unbecomingness

wrought *adj* → **1** angry **2** decorative **3** made

wry *adj* → **1** cunning **2** deflective **3** discontented **4** displeased **5** distorted **6** humorous

Xx

enophobia *n* → hate
erox *n* → **1** copy **2** imitation **3** repetition *v* **4** copy

X-ray *n* → **1** physical examination *v* **2** examine **3** portray

Y y

yabber *n* → **1** talk *v* **2** talk
yacht *n* → sailing ship
yahoo *n* → **1** discourteous person **2** vulgarian
yak *n* → **1** nonsense *v* **2** talk nonsense
yakka *n* → work
yank *n* → **1** pull *v* **2** pull
yap *n* → **1** angry act **2** animal call **3** loud sound **4** speaking *v* **5** be angry **6** be loud **7** call (of animals) **8** speak
YARD *n* allotment, battleaxe block, block, building block, curtilage, lot, plot, vacant allotment; **industrial estate,** industrial park, trading estate *(Brit.)*; **car park,** parking area, parking lot; **goods yard,** car yard, shipyard, stockyard, timber yard; **airfield,** flying field, pad *(Aeron.)*; **gas field,** goldfield, oilfield
yard *n* → **1** factory **2** field **3** length **4** pole
yardstick *n* → **1** conformist behaviour **2** rule **3** stick **4** tester
yarn *n* → **1** story **2** talk **3** thread *v* **4** narrate **5** talk
yaw *n* → **1** turn *v* **2** rotate **3** swerve
yawl *n* → **1** sailing ship **2** watercraft
yawn *n* → **1** bore **2** gap **3** opening **4** sleepiness *v* **5** become sleepy **6** gape **7** open up
yea *n* → **1** affirmation *adv* **2** additionally *interj* **3** yes
yeah *interj* → yes
year *n* → grade
yearling *n* → animal offspring
yearly *n* → book
yeast *n* → **1** bubbling *v* **2** bubble
yell *n* → **1** shout *v* **2** shout **3** speak
YELLOW *n* butter, buttercup, cadmium yellow, canary-yellow, citrine, daffodil, lemon, lemon-yellow, ochre, primrose; **yellow-brown,** buff, isabel, maize, sand, tawny, wheat; **mustard,** crocus, gamboge, saffron, saffron-yellow; **yellow-green,** chartreuse, lime-green, sulphur; **cream,** champagne, eggshell, honey; **blond,** blonde; **gold**
YELLOW *v* gild; **turn yellow,** jaundice, sallow
YELLOW *adj* canary, chartreuse, citreous, citrine, lemon, quercetic, sulphurous, sulphury, xanthic, xanthous, yellowish; **ochre,** ochreous, ochroid, ochrous, ochry, rutilant *(Rare)*; **ash-blond,** blond, blonde; **buff,** cor[n-]coloured, fallow, flaxen, flaxy, isabel, sand[y], stramineous, straw-coloured, tawny, to[w]; **creamy,** champagne, cream, cream-coloure[d], eggshell; **yellowing,** flavescent; **sallow,** chlo[r]otic, jaundiced, sallowish; **gold,** aureat[e], brass, brazen, coppery, gilt, golden. *S[ee] also* ORANGE
yellow *adj* → cowardly
yelp *n* → **1** shout *v* **2** call (of animals) **3** sho[ut]
yen *n* → **1** desire **2** will
YES *interj* amen, ay, yair, yea, yeah; **certai[n]ly,** absolutely, all right, blood oath, by a[ll] manner of means, can do, dicken, exactl[y], fair enough, granted, my colonial oath, m[y] oath, no sweat, not half, O.K., par[de] *(Archaic)*, quite, quite so, rather *(Brit.)*, righ[t] on, so be it, sure thing *(U.S.)*, that's the stu[ff], to be sure, truly, verily, very well, you bet
yes *n* → affirmation
yes-man *n* → **1** accomplice **2** conform[ist] **3** obeyer
yesterday *n* → **1** past *adj* **2** past *adv* **3** befo[re] **4** in the past
yet *adv* → **1** additionally **2** continually **3** i[n] the future **4** nevertheless **5** now *conj* **6** still
yew *n* → timber
yield *n* → **1** amount **2** atomic radiatio[n] **3** finished product **4** profit *v* **5** abandon **6** b[e] fertile **7** be lenient **8** capitulate **9** give **10** los[e] **11** pay
yob *n* → **1** adolescent **2** vulgarian
yodel *n* → **1** song *v* **2** sing
yoga *n* → exercise
yoke *n* → **1** bond **2** two *v* **3** repress
yokel *n* → **1** ignoramus **2** vulgarian *a[dj]* **3** provincial
yolk *n* → **1** centre **2** fat **3** important thing
yonder *adj* → **1** distant *adv* **2** here **3** remotel[y]
yore *n* → past
young *n* → **1** offspring *adj* **2** ignorant **3** inferior **4** new **5** youthful
YOUTH *n* boyhood, early years, girlhoo[d], salad days, sweet sixteen, tender ag[e], youthhood; **adolescence,** awkward age, puberty, pubescence; **infancy,** babyhood, childhood, infanthood, preadolescence, swaddling clothes, the cradle; **minority,** nonage
youth *n* → **1** adolescent **2** innovator **3** ma[n] **4** start
YOUTHFUL *adj* juvenescent, prentice, rejuvenescent, vernal, youngish, youngling[;] **ageless,** evergreen, fresh, young-eyed; **childish,** babyish, infantile, infantine, puerile; **urchin,** boyish, coltish, cubbish, girlish; **callow[,]** beardless, green, immature, undeveloped[,] unfledged, wet behind the ears; **infant,** baby in arms, neonatal, newborn, preschool[,] yeanling; **preadolescent,** prepubescent[,] school-age; **adolescent,** hebetic, juvenile[,] kidult, preadult, pubescent, teen, teenage[;] **young,** small, tender; **younger,** baby, cade[t,] junior, kid, minor, puisne *(Law)*; **youngest[,]** minimus *(Brit.)*; **under-age,** minor *(Brit.)*
yowl *n* → **1** shout *v* **2** shout
YUK *interj*

Zz

zany *n* → **1** butt **2** stupid person *adj* **3** foolish **4** humorous
zeal *n* → **1** desire **2** enthusiasm
zealot *n* → **1** believer **2** enthusiast
zenith *n* → **1** apex **2** astronomic point **3** top
zephyr *n* → wind
zeppelin *n* → aircraft
zero *n* → nothing
zest *n* → **1** allure **2** artistry **3** enthusiasm **4** pleasure **5** savour **6** skin **7** vitality *v* **8** energise **9** make pleasant
zigzag *n* → **1** bend **2** road *v* **3** turn *adj* **4** bent
zinc *v* → **1** coat **2** work metal *adj* **3** metallic
zip *n* → **1** button **2** enthusiasm **3** hiss **4** vitality *v* **5** hiss **6** speed
zipper *n* → button
zombie *n* → **1** apathetic person **2** idol **3** living **4** occultist **5** phantom **6** the dead
zone *n* → **1** coating **2** dwelling **3** region *v* **4** class **5** limit
zoom *n* → **1** ascent **2** click *v* **3** ascend **4** speed
zounds *interj* → God
zzz *n* → sleepiness

Special Lists

These special lists consist of terms which are not synonyms but which are nevertheless closely related. For example, the words 'lyrebird' and 'bellbird' are not synonyms – they are not interchangeable – but they *are* both indigenous Australian birds.

The lists are divided into five groups: Plants, Animals, Matter, Sport and Language. Each group has its own contents page giving all the sub-divisions of each group and the paragraphs in which they are to be found.

Plants 451
Animals 469
Matter 483
Sport 488
Language 492

Plants

Gum-trees 1
Wattles 2
Rainforest trees 3
Legumes (trees) 4
Conifers 5
Palms 6
Trees – Australian 7
Trees – N.Z. 8
Trees – miscellaneous 9
Shrubs – Australian 10
Shrubs – N.Z. 11
Legumes (shrubs) 12
Shrubs – other 13
Herbaceous legumes – Australian 14
Herbaceous legumes – other 15
Bulbs, corms and tubers – Australian 16
Bulbs, corms and tubers – other 17
Grasses – Australian 18
Grasses – other 19
Sedges and rushes 20
Orchids – Australian 21
Orchids – other 22
Succulents – Australian 23
Succulents – other 24
Insectivores 25
Herbaceous plants – Australian 26
Herbaceous plants – N.Z 27
Herbaceous plants – other 28
Aquatic plants – Australian 29
Aquatic plants – other 30
Climbing plants – Australian 31
Climbing plants – other 32
Bacteria 33
Fungi 33
Lichens 33
Liverworts 33
Mosses 33
Algae 34
Ferns 35
Cycads 36
Cereals and grains 37
Vegetable and root crops 38
Fruits 39
Nuts 40
Herbs and spices 41
Beverage plants 42
Medicinal plants 43
Perfumery plants 44
Dye plants 45
Fibre plants 46
Timber plants 47
Timber and barks 48
Fodder and pasture plants 49
Plant oils and resins 40
Weeds 51
Poisonous plants 52
Plants used by Aborigines 53

1. GUM-TREES (EUCALYPTUS and ANGOPHORA), alpine ash, angophora, apple, apple box, apple gum, Argyle apple, bangalay, bimble box, black box, black gum, black sally, blackbutt, bloodwood, blue gum, blue mallee, box, brittle gum, brown barrel, brown mallet, bundy, but but, cabbage gum, cadagi, candle bark, carbeen, coolabah, coolabah apple, coolibah, Darwin stringbark, Darwin woollybutt, eucalypt, eucalyptus, eurabbie, flame-gum, flooded gum, ghost gum, giant mallee, gimlet, green mallee, grey box, grey gum, grey ironbark, gum, gum coolibah, gum tree, iron gum, ironbark, jarrah, karri, lemon-scented gum, mahogany, mallee, mallet, manna gum, marble gum, marlock, marri, messmate, moort, Moreton Bay ash, morrell, mountain ash, mugga, muttlegar, narrow-leaf ironbark, peppermint, red bloodwood, red stringbark, ribbon gum, river red gum, rivergum, rough-barked apple, rusty gum, sally, salmon gum, scribbly gum, silver box, silver-leaf ironbark, slaty gum, snappy gum redwood, snow gum, spotted gum, stinking gum, stringy-bark, sugar gum, swamp gum, swamp mahogony, Sydney blue gum, Sydney red gum, tallowwood, Tasmanian blue gum, tingle tingle, tuart, wandoo, white bloodwood, white box, white gum, white mahogony, white sally weeping box, woolly butt, yapunyah, yate, yellow box, yellow gum, yellow jacket, yertchuk, yorrell
2. WATTLES (ACACIA), acacia, bastard myall, belalie, black gidgee, black wattle, blackwood, blue skin, boree, bowyakka bendee, brigalow, Broughton willow, cedar wattle, cooba, Cootamundra wattle, curracabah, currawong, dead finish, desert oak, doolan, dune wattle, eumung, Georgina gidgee, gidgee, golden wattle, green wattle, gundabluey, hickory, ironwood, jam tree, kangaroo-thorn, karri, kurara, lancewood, Maitland's wattle, miljee, mimosa *(Obs.)*, mimosa bush, minni-ritchi, motherumbah, mountain cedar wattle, mudgerabah, mulga, myall, myall-gidgee, native willow, nealie, nelia, pin bush, prickly Moses, prickly wattle, purplewood, Queensland silver wattle, ranji bush, raspberry-jam tree, red mulga, river cooba, sally, sandhill wattle, silver wattle, stinking wattle, sunshine wattle, Sydney golden wattle, turpentine, umbrella bush, umbrella mulga, waddy-wood, wait-a-while, wattle, weeping myall, wirewood, wirilda, witchetty bush, wyrilda, yarran
3. RAINFOREST TREES, Antarctic beech, axe-handle wood, banyalla, basswood, beech, birch, birdlime tree, black apple, black bean, bleeding-heart, bolly gum, booyong, bopple nut, Brisbane box, brush bloodwood, brush box, bumpy ash, Burdekin plum, camphorwood, canary sassafras, carabeen, carrol, cedar, celerywood, cheese-tree, cheesewood, coachwood, corkwood, crow's ash, crowsfoot elm, cudgerie, cudjerie, deep yellowwood, djelwuck, durobby, featherwood, fig, finger cherry, firewheel tree, flame-tree, ghittoe, gympie nettle, Herbert River cherry, hickory, horizontal *(Tas.)*, Illawarra flame-tree, ironwood, Kerosene wood, lacebark, lancewood, leatherwood, lignum-vitae, lilly pilly, macadamia nut, mahogany, milk-wood, milky pine, mira mahogany, Moreton Bay chestnut, Moreton Bay fig, mutton-wood, myrtle, myrtle beech, na-

tive elm, native teak, nettle tree, nigger-head beech, Oliver's sassafras, onionwood, penda, pigeonberry ash, prickly ash, quandong, Queensland ebony, Queensland maple, Queensland nut, Queensland walnut, red bean, red cedar, robby, rose mahogany, rose satinash, rosewood, saffron heart, sassafras, satinwood, scrub beefwood, scrub stringybark, silky oak, socketwood, southern sassafras, stinging tree, tallowwood, Tasmanian myrtle, thorny yellowwood, tulip oak, tulipwood, umbrella tree, whalebone tree, white bean, white beech, white cedar, yellow boxwood, yellow carrabeen, yellow sassafras, yellowwood, yiel-yiel

4. LEGUMES (TREES) – AUSTRALIAN, bats-wing coral-tree, bauhinia, bean tree, black bean, cassia, Cooktown ironwood, corkwood, crested wattle, ironwood, Leichhardt bean, Moreton Bay chestnut, Queensland bean, white dragon tree, yalbah; LEGUMES – OTHER, acacia, algarroba, babul, bauhinia, bean tree, camwood, Cape teak, carob, cassia, coral tree, divi-divi, fever-tree, flamboyant, golden chain, golden rain, honey-locust, Judas tree, laburnum, locust, marble wood, mesquite, pagoda tree, poinciana, redbud, rose acacia, sappanwood, sassy, sassy bark, tagasaste, tamarind, tonka bean, tree lucerne

5. CONIFERS – AUSTRALIAN, araucaria, black cypress pine, black pine, brown pine, bunya-bunya, celery-top pine, cypress, cypress pine, hoop pine, Huon pine, kauri, King Billy pine, King William pine, pine, plum pine, Port Jackson pine, Queensland kauri, she-pine, white pine; CONIFERS – N.Z., black pine, celery-top pine, kahikatea, kauri, kawaka, matai, miro, mountain pine, red pine, ricker, rimu, silver pine, tanekaha, toatoa, totara, white pine; CONIFERS – OTHER, araucaria, arbor vitae, balsam fir, balsam spruce, black spruce, blue spruce, cade, cedar, cypress, deodar, Douglas fir, Douglas pine, Douglas spruce, fir, hemlock, hemlock spruce, insignis pine, Irish yew, jack pine, Japanese cedar, juniper, larch, loblolly, longleaf pine, macrocarpa, maritime pine, monkey-puzzle tree, Monterey pine, Norfolk Island pine, Norway spruce, nut pine, Oregon pine, pine, pitch pine, radiata pine, red cedar, red fir, redwood, sandarac, savin, Scotch fir, Scots pine, sequoia, sequoiadendron, silver fir, slash pine, spruce, tamarack, thuja, western hemlock, Western red cedar, white cedar, white pine, white spruce, yellowwood, yew

6. PALMS – AUSTRALIAN, bangalow palm, cabbage palm, cabbage tree, kentia palm, piccabeen *(Qld)*, walking-stick palm; PALMS – OTHER, areca, betel nut, betel palm, cabbage palm, cabbage tree, carnauba, coconut, cohune, coquilla nut, coquito, date palm, doum-palm, gomuti *(S.E. Asia)*, grugru, ivory palm, nipa, oil-palm, palmetto, palmyra, piassava, raffia, royal palm, sago, talipot *(India)*, Washington palm, wax-palm, wine palm

7. OTHER AUSTRALIAN TREES, agonis, apple, ash, ballart, banksia, baobab, barringtonia, beefwood, belah, bell-fruit tree, berrigan, bitterbark, black oak, black tea-tree, blackwattle, blanket-leaf, blind-your-eyes, blueberry ash, bollygum, boonery, bottle tree,

budda, bull oak, cadjeput, cajuput, casuarina, cherry ballart, Christmas bush, Christmas tree, cockatoo apple, colane, corkwood, cottontree, cow-itch tree, desert kurrajong, desert lemon, desert oak, desert poplar, desert walnut, durin, emu-apple, forest oak, grey mangrove, gruie, he-oak, jack-in-the-box, kanooka, katunga, kurrajong, Leichhardt tree, leopard tree, leopard wood, mangrove, melaleuca, milk-wood, mock-olive, moonah, native apricot, native cherry, native mulberry, native oak, native poplar, native willow, needlewood, nonda, Norfolk Island hibiscus, pandanus, paperbark, pigeonberry, pittosporum, poison peach, poison-tree, Port Jackson fig, quandong, quinine bush, red ash, red satinay, river mangrove, river oak, rosewood, rusty fig, sandalwood, santal, screw-pine, she-oak, silk-cotton tree, sugarwood, supplejack, swamp box, swamp oak, turpentine, warrior bush, watergum, whitewood, wild Irishman, wild orange, wilga, willow myrtle, wooden pear, woody pear

8. NEW ZEALAND TREES, aka, Antarctic beech, beech, birch, black beech, broadleaf, bucket-of-water-wood, clinker beech, cottonwood, cracker, hard beech, hinau, honeysuckle, houhere, ironwood, kamahi, karaka, karo, kohekohe, kotukutuku, kowhai, lace-wood, lacebark, lancewood, lemonwood, maire, makomako, mapou, matipo, milk tree, New Zealand beech, ngaio, nikau, pigeonwood, pittosporum, pohutukawa, pukatea, puriri, rata, red beech, rewarewa, ribbonwood, silver beech, silver birch, taraire, tarata, tawa, tawhai, thousand-jacket, ti, ti-palm, ti-tree, titoki, towai, whau, whiteywood, wineberry

9. MISCELLANEOUS TREES, abele, acajou, ailanthus, alamo, alder, allspice, almond, amarelle *(U.S.)*, anchovy pear, antiar, apricot, arbutus, ash, aspen, assegai, athel, azedarach, balm of Gilead, balsam poplar, bamboo, banyan, barringtonia, basswood, bay, bayberry, bebeeru, ben, benzoin, bergamot, birch, bird-cherry, bitterwood, black elder, black oak, black walnut, bo tree, box elder, buckeye, bully tree, button tree, buttonwood, cajuput, calabash, calabash nutmeg, camphor laurel, candleberry, candlenut, candletree, Cape ash, Cape chestnut, catalpa, champak, cherry laurel, cherry-plum, Chinese elm, chinquapin, chokecherry, copper beech, cork oak, cornel, cottontree, cottonwood, crepe myrtle, cucumber tree, dita, dogwood, dracaena, dragon tree, durmast, elder, elderberry, elm, English elm, fiddlewood, fig, frangipanni, fringe tree, gingerbread tree, gum tree, hackberry, hawthorn, Hercules'-club, hognut, holly, holly oak, holm, holm oak, hornbeam, horse chestnut, horseradish tree, ilex, jacaranda, jack-in-the-box, Joshua tree, Juneberry, karee, lagerstroemia, laurel, lime tree, linden, liquidambar, liriodendron, live oak, Lombardy poplar, madrona, magnolia, mahoe, mahogany, mahonia, mamey, mammee, maple, may, maytree, mazard, milk-wood, monkey-bread, mountain ash, oak, Osage orange, pandanus, paper birch, paulownia, pawpaw *(U.S.)*, pepperina, peppertree, pignut, pipal, plane tree, poplar, port wine magnolia, prunus, pussy willow, quercitron, red oak, rhus tree, roble, rowan, rubber plant, sacred fig tree, saguaro, sallow, sally *(Brit.)*, sandalwood, sandbox tree, santal, saskatoon, sassafras, screw-pine, seringa, service tree, serviceberry, silk-cotton tree, silver maple, silver tree, silverbell, simarouba, sloe, snowdrop tree, soapbark, soapberry, sorrel tree, sour gourd, sour gum, spindle tree, star-anise, stinkwood, storax, strawberry tree, sugar maple, sumach, sweet bay, sweet gum, sycamore, tacamahac, tamarisk, terebinth, thorn, toothache tree, traveller's tree, tree of heaven, trifoliata, trifoliate orange, tulip tree, tulipwood, tupelo, turkey oak, turpentine tree, ule, umbrella tree, upas, vitex, wallum, water-oak, watergum, wax tree, wedding bush, weeping willow, western catalpa, white beam, white birch, white cedar, white poplar, whitethorn, whitewood, wicopy *(U.S.)*, wild cherry, wilga, willow, wych-elm, yellow poplar

10. SHRUBS – AUSTRALIAN, abutilon, amulla, Australian boxthorn, ballart, banksia, bauera, Baw-Baw berry *(Vic.)*, beard-heath, berry saltbush, black boy, black gin, black wattle, black-eyed Susan, blackfellow's hemp, blackthorn, bladder saltbush, blanket bush, bluebush, bolwarra, boobialla, bootlace bush, boronia, bottlebrush, buck bush, cherry ballart, Chinese lantern, chucky chucky, coast rosemary, coastal saltbush, conebush, conker berry, conkle berry, copper burr, correa, cottonbush, cottonwood, cough-bush, crowea, cucurbit, daisy-bush, desert jasmine, desert lantern, desert lime, desert rose, dillon bush, dogrose, drumsticks, dryandra, Ellangowan poison bush, emu bush, epacris, eriostemon, Esperance waxflower, feather flower, five-corners, fringe-myrtle, fuchsia, gaultheria, geebung, Geraldton waxflower, giant saltbush, goathead burr, goodenia, grasstree, green bush, grevillea, grey saltbush, guinea flower, gunyang, hakea, heath, heath-myrtle, helichrysum, hibbertia, hibiscus, honey flower, honeysuckle, hopbush, jam tarts, jerry-jerry, jockey's cap, kangaroo apple, leptospermum, leschenaultia, lignum, mallee saltbush, manatoka, manuka, marsh saltbush, mealy saltbush, melaleuca, mint-bush, mistletoe, mock-olive, Mondurup bell, morrison, mountain devil, muntries, mustard bush, narrawa burr, native elder, native rose, native rosella, native sorrel, needlewood, nepine, nightshade, nitre bush, old-man saltbush, olearia, oondoroo, pearl bluebush, pink heath, pituri, plum bush, Port Jackson rose, potato bush, poverty bush, qualup bell, Queensland bluebush, rice-flower, ruby saltbush, saltbush, sand spurge, smoke-bush, snake vine, snowberry, solanum, spider flower, Sturt's desert rose, styphelia, Sydney rose, tea-tree, tickbush, turkey bush, turpentine bush, waratah, wax, waxberry, waxflower, waxplant, wedding bush, westringia, white elder, wild lime, wild parsnip, yacca, yakka

11. SHRUBS – N.Z., akeake, bull-a-bull, coffee bush, coprosma, dracaena, horopito, Irishman, kahikatoa, kanuka, karamu, kawakawa, koromiko, leptospermum, manuka, matagouri, neinei, New Zealand lilac, parrot's beak, peppertree, poroporo, ramarama, rangiora, snowberry, tauhinu, taupata, tawine, tea-tree, ti, ti-palm, ti-tree, toot, tumatakuru, tutu, vegetable sheep, veronica

12. LEGUMES (SHRUBS) – AUSTRALIAN, bacon-and-eggs, bitter-pea, bossiaea, box poison, broom brush, brother-brother, bush-pea, cassia, chorizema, cockroach bush, eggs-and-bacon, false sarsaparilla, fire bush, flat-pea, Flinders River poison, globe-pea, golden-tip, gompholobium, green birdflower, heart-leaf poison, hop, hovea, indigo, karalla, mountain beauty, native indigo, native senna, oxylobium, parrot pea, poison sage, poison-bush, prickly poison, punty bush, sarsaparilla, senna, shaggy pea, silver cassia, Sturt's pea, wattleflower poison, wedge-pea, wild indigo, yellow pea, york-road poison; LEGUMES – OTHER, bird flower, broom, camel's-thorn, cassia, dillwynia, dyer's greenwood, furze, genista, gorse, ground plum, mimosa, psoralea, rattlepod, rhatany, scurf-pea, senna, sensitive plant, Spanish broom, tragacanth, whin, wisteria

13. SHRUBS – OTHER, abelia, abutilon, acalypha, ambary, aralia, arbutus, azalea, balm of Gilead, barberry, bayberry, bell heather, blackthorn, bog myrtle, boneseed, box, boxthorn, bramble, briar, buckthorn, buddleia, camellia, candleberry, candletree, cane, caper, cascarilla, cestrum, cherry-pie, China rose, Chinese lantern, chokeberry, Christ's-thorn, common sallow, cornel, cotoneaster, creosote bush, croton, crowberry, damask rose, daphne, diosma, dogberry, dogrose, dogwood, eglantine, elder, elderberry, erica, euonymus, euphorbia, firethorn, floribunda, flowering dogwood, fly honeysuckle, forsythia, fuchsia, gale, gardenia, gaultheria, geranium, germander, goldfussia, granny's bonnet, greasebush, greasewood, guelder-rose, gum plant, hardhack, heath, heather, Hercules'-club, hibiscus, honeysuckle, hydrangea, Japan laurel, japonica, jasmine, Jerusalem cherry, Jerusalem sage, kalmia, lantana, lasiandra, laurel, laurustinus, lavender, leatherwood, lemon geranium, lemon verbena, lilac, ling, luculia, marula, matrimony vine, may, mezereon, milk-bush, milkwort, mistletoe, mock orange, moss rose, mountain laurel, musk rose, myrtle, nandina, nightshade, num-num, ochna, oleander, oleaster, osier, pelargonium, philadelphus, plumbago, poinciana, poinsettia, poison oak, poison sumach, polygala, prickly ash, privet, protea, pyracantha, rhododendron, rhodora, rhus, rockrose, rose, rose mallow, rose of Sharon, rosemary, rubber tree, sage, sagebrush, sallow, sally *(Brit.)*, saltbush, saltwort, salvia, Scotch heather, serviceberry, smoke tree, snowball, solanum, southernwood, Spanish bayonet, spicebush, spider flower, spike lavender, spiraea, spotted laurel, spurge laurel, stagger-bush, stinkwood, strophanthus, sugar bush, sumach, sweet gale, sweetbriar, syringa, tea-rose, titi, trailing arbutus, tree heath, trumpet flower, viburnum, vitex, wax-myrtle, wayfaring tree, weigela, whortleberry, wicopy *(U.S.)*, wild rose, wild thyme, wintergreen, wintersweet, witch-hazel, withy, wormwood, yaupon, yucca

14. HERBACEOUS LEGUMES – AUSTRALIAN, Broughton pea, clianthus, Cooper's clover, coral-pea, crotalaria, Darling clover, Darling pea, dwarf swainsona, kidney vetch, Menindie clover, psoralea, rattlepod, running postman, scurf-pea, Sturt's desert pea, swainson pea, yam

15. HERBACEOUS LEGUMES – OTHER, alfalfa *(U.S.)*, alsike, alsike clover, barrel medic, bird flower, bird's-foot, bird's-foot trefoil, blue lupin, Bokhara clover, burr medic, chickpea, clianthus, clover, cowpea, crotalaria, cut-leaf medic, Dutch clover, five-finger, glory pea, Hexham scent, hop-clover, horseshoe vetch, Indian liquorice,

King Island melilot, ladies' fingers, lespedeza, liquorice, loco *(U.S.)*, locoweed, lotus, lucerne, lupin, melilot, milk vetch, mimosa, nonesuch, psoralea, rattlepod, rest-harrow, sainfoin, scurf-pea, serradella, shamrock, sola *(India)*, stylo, subterranean clover, sweet clover, sweet lupin, sweet pea, tare, telegraph plant, trefoil, trifolium, vetch, white clover, wild indigo

16. BULBS/CORMS/TUBERS – AUSTRALIAN, blackfellow's yam, blackman's potatoes, bloodroot, crinum, cunjevoi, curcuma, Darling lily, early Nancy, garland lily, milkmaid, Murray lily, murrnong, native dandelion, vanilla flower, yam, yam daisy

17. BULBS/CORMS/TUBERS – OTHER, agapanthus, allium, amaryllis, arum, asphodel, autumn crocus, belladonna lily, bluebell, calla, camass, Cape tulip, chincherinchee, clivia, colchicum, crinum, crocus, crow garlic, cyclamen, daff *(Colloq.)*, daffodil, daffodilly *(Poetic)*, daffodowndilly *(Poetic)*, daffydowndilly *(Poetic)*, dogtooth violet, eucharis, flame lily, freesia, fritillary, gladiolus, grape hyacinth, hippeastrum, hyacinth, ixia, jonquil, Madonna lily, martagon lily, meadow saffron, narcissus, nerine, oxalis, pheasant's-eye, polyanthus, saffron, scilla, sea-onion, sea-squill, snowdrop, snowflake, sowbread, sparaxis, spider lily, squill, star-of-Bethlehem, sword lily, tiger lily, tuberose, tulip, Turk's-cap lily, wake-robin, watsonia, wood hyacinth

18. GRASSES – AUSTRALIAN, aristida, astrebla, Balcarra grass, bamboo grass, bandicoot grass, barbwire grass, beard grass, beetle grass, blady grass, blown grass, blue couch, blue grass, bottlewashers, bunch spear grass, button grass, cane, cane grass, comet grass, common reed, corkscrew grass, cotton panic grass, danthonia, eight-day grass, fairy grass, fescue, festuca, five minute grass, Flinders grass, hare's-foot grass, hare's-tail, kangaroo grass, kerosene grass, Landsborough grass, lovegrass, Mitchell grass, Mossman River grass, mulga grass, mulga oats, mulka grass, native millet, native oat, neverfail grass, oatgrass, panic, pepper grass, pigeon grass, plains grass, porcupine grass, Queensland blue, Queensland blue couch, rats tail couch, river grass, sago grass, salt couch, salt grass, sand brome, sandhill canegrass, satin top, scented grass, shot grass, silky browntop, silky-heads, small burr grass, snowgrass, spear grass, spider grass, spike grass, spinifex, spiny mud-grass, stink grass, sugar grass, swamp grass, three-awn grass, tropical reed, tussocky poa, umbrella cane-grass, umbrella grass, variable spear grass, wallaby grass, wanderrie, Warrego grass, water couch, wheat grass, wild rubber, windmill grass, wire grass, woolly butt, yakka grass

19. GRASSES – OTHER, barb-grass, barley grass, barnyard grass, beard grass, bent grass, bermuda grass, birdwood grass, blowfly grass, blown grass, blue couch, blue grass, bristlegrass, brome, browntop, buffalo grass, buffel grass, burr grass, canary grass, cane, carpet grass, cat's-tail, Chewings fescue, cocksfoot, cockspur, cogon, cord grass, couch, crabgrass, creeping bent grass, creeping red fescue, crowsfoot, darnel, dog's-tail, dog's-tooth grass, dropseed, English couch grass, esparto, false brome, feather-grass, fescue, festuca, fingergrass, flote-

grass, fog, foxtail, giant panic, grama grass, guinea grass, hairgrass, hare's-tail, heath grass, holy-grass, Indian rice, Italian rye, job's-tears, Johnson grass, kikuyu, lyme grass, marram grass, mat-grass, meadow grass, nasella tussock, Natal red-grass, nitgrass, pampas grass, panic, para grass, Parramatta grass, paspalum, perennial rye, phalaris, pigeon grass, quack grass, quaking grass, quick grass, quitch grass, rat's-tail fescue, rat-tail grass, reed, reed grass, rhodes grass, Rhodes grass, ribbon grass, rye-grass, scutch, serrated tussock, sheep's fescue, shivery grass, snowgrass *(N.Z.)*, softgrass, stink grass, sweet vernal grass, teosinte, timothy, twitch, umbrella grass, veldt grass, vetiver, water meadow grass, whangee, whitlow grass, wild oat, Wimmera rye, Yass river tussock, Yorkshire fog

20. SEDGES/RUSHES – AUSTRALIAN, arrow-grass, Bergalia tussock, bog-rush, bulrush, button grass, cat's-tail, club rush, cumbungi, cutting-grass, drooping sedge, finger rush, flag, hook grass, nalgoo, reed mace, rush, sag *(Tas.)*, saw sedge, sawgrass, sea rush, spike-rush, toad-rush; SEDGES/RUSHES – N.Z., cooper's flag, cutty-grass, Maori-head, pingao, raupo, toetoe; SEDGES/RUSHES – OTHER, bulrush, chufa, club rush, deergrass, flag, galingale, hammer sedge, hard-rush, hook grass, Mullumbimby couch, papyrus, reed mace, rush, sawgrass, spike-rush, toad-rush, woodrush

21. ORCHIDS – AUSTRALIAN, ant orchid, babe-in-a-cradle, beardy, bee orchid, beech orchid, bird orchid, caladenia, Cooktown orchid, cowslip orchid, cucumber orchid, cymbidium, dagger orchid, dendrobium, diuris, donkey orchid, double tails, elbow orchid, enamel orchid, flying-duck orchid, golden moths, green bird orchid, greenhood, helmet orchid, hyacinth orchid, ironbark orchid, leek orchid, midge orchid, mignonette orchid, mosquito orchid, onion orchid, orange-blossom orchid, orchis, parson's bands, pencil orchid, potato orchid, praying virgin, raspy-root, rat's-tail orchid, rock lily, rock orchid, spider-orchid, sugar orchid, sun orchid, tangle orchid, white feather orchid

22. ORCHIDS – OTHER, bee orchid, calypso, crucifix orchid, cymbidium, cypripedium, dead men's fingers, dendrobium, odontoglossum, vanilla

23. SUCCULENTS – AUSTRALIAN, ant-house plant, bottletree caustic, caustic bush, caustic vine, desert spurge, galvanised burr, Gascoyne spurge, karkalla, milk bush, New Zealand spinach, parakeelya, pigface, prickly saltwort, purslane, roly-poly

24. SUCCULENTS – OTHER, agave, aloe, American aloe, amole, artillery-plant, barilla, cactus, carrion flower, century plant, cereus, euphorbia, glasswort, halfmens, hen-and-chickens, Hottentot fig, houseleek, ice plant, kali, livelong, Livingstone daisy, maguey, milkbush, navelwort, New Zealand spinach, nopal, opuntia, pigface, portulaca, prickly pear, quiver tree, samphire, sansevieria, sedum, sisal, sour fig, spurge, stapelia, stonecrop, tuna, wall pepper

25. INSECTIVORES – AUSTRALIAN, bladderwort, flytrap, pitcher plant, sundew; INSECTIVORES – OTHER, bladderwort, flytrap, huntsman's-cup, pitcher plant, sarracenia, sundew, Venus flytrap

26. HERBACEOUS PLANTS – AUSTRALIAN, apple bush, Australian centaury, Australian edelweiss, bachelor's button, baldoo, biddy-biddy, billy button, bindi-eye, blue parsnip, blue rod, blue tinsel lily, bluebell, bogan flea, boggabri, bottle-washers, Brown's dock, bulbine lily, burr-daisy, buttons, caltrop, Caraweena clover, caterpillar-flower, cattle bush, caustic weed, chocolate lily, Christmas bell, claytonia, cotton fireweed, cranesbill, crowfoot, cudweed, cunjevoi, daisy-burr, dianella, digger's speedwell, dog's-tongue, duckweed, euphrasy, everlasting, eyebright, fairy lanterns, fairy spectacles, fan-flower, feather heads, fireweed, flannel flower, flax-lily, forget-me-not, fringe lily, fringed lily, fruit-salad plant, fuzz weed, giant lily, giant pigweed, goodenia, Gymea lily, helichrysum, helipterum, hogweed, hop lily, hound's-tongue, incense plant, jersey cudweed, kangaroo-paw, kidney weed, knawel, Koonamore daisy, lagoon spurge, lamb's-tail, leek lily, life-saver burr, mat-rush, minnie-daisy, mud-mat, mudwort, mulga cabbage, mulga nettle, mulga spinach, mulla-mulla, myosotis, native crowfoot, native hollyhock, New Zealand spinach, paperdaisy, pelargonium, poached-egg daisy, pop saltbush, potato bush, prickly poppy, prickly saltwort, Prince of Wales' feather, purslane, pussycat's tails, pussytails, quena, roly-poly, sand lily, selfheal, settler's flax, settler's twine, silver bush, silver tails, sneeze weed, snow daisy, snow flower, solanum, Southern Cross, spear lily, speedwell, squash bush, stinging nettle, stork's-bill, Swan River daisy, tar-vine, tassel top, tomato bush, trigger flower, trigger plant, vanilla lily, variable groundsel, vernonia, Ward's weed, Warrigal cabbage, waterbuttons, white foxtail, white-root, wild carrot, wild gooseberry, wild parsnip, woolly buttons, woolly mat-rush, yellow tails

27. HERBACEOUS PLANTS – N.Z., bayonet grass, brachycome, Chatham Island lily, cotton plant, hemp, kaka beak, korari, Mount Cook lily, mountain daisy, New Zealand flax, penwiper plant, piripiri, snow daisy, spaniard, spear grass

28. HERBACEOUS PLANTS – OTHER, abelmosk, acanthus, aconite, Adam's-needle, adder's-meat, African lily, African violet, ageratum, agrimony, alexanders, alkanet, allseed, althaea, alumroot, alyssum, amaranth, ambrosia, anemone, angelica, aniseed, antirrhinum, apple of Peru, apple of Sodom, aquilegia, archangel, arnica, arrow-grass, arrowhead, arrowroot, artichoke thistle, aspidistra, aster, astilbe, aubrietia, auricula, babies'-breath, baby's tears, baldmoney, balsam, baneberry, bear's-breech, bedstraw, begonia, bellflower, bells-of-Ireland, bennet, bergamot, billbergia, bird of paradise, bishop's weed, bistort, bittercress, bladder campion, bleeding-heart, blinks, bloodroot, blue borage, bluebell, borage, bouncing Bess, bouncing Bett, brooklime, brookweed, broomrape, bugle, bugloss, buttercup, caladium, calamus, calceolaria, calendula, Californian poppy, calliopsis, camomile, campanula, campion, candytuft, canna, Canterbury bell, cardinal flower, carline, carnation, catchfly, catmint, catnip, celandine, celosia, centaury, chamomile, Christmas rose, chrysanthemum, cineraria, cinquefoil, clarkia, claytonia, cleavers, cleome, clockweed, clove pink, cockscomb, cockspur, coleus, columbine, coneflower, coreopsis, corn poppy, cornflower, corydalis, cosmos, cow-parsley, cow-parsnip, cow-wheat, cowslip *(U.S.)*, coxcomb, cranesbill, crowfoot, cuckooflower, cuckoopint, curly pondweed, dahlia, dame's violet, day lily, deadnettle, delphinium, Deptford pink, dianthus, dimorphotheca, dittander, dittany, dog fennel, dog's mercury, dog's-tongue, dogbane, dumb cane, dwarf mallow, earthnut, edelweiss, elecampane, elephant's-ear, enchanter's nightshade, erigeron, eryngo, eupatorium, euphorbia, euphrasy, evening primrose, eyebright, fennelflower, ferula, feverfew, figwort, five-finger, flag, flamingo-flower, Flanders poppy, flax, fleawort, fleur-de-lis, Florida moss, flower of Jove, flower-de-luce, fool's parsley, fool's watercress, forget-me-not, four-o'clock, foxglove, fraxinella, gaillardia, garlic mustard, gazania, gentian, geranium, gerbera, German ivy, germander, geum, gillyflower *(Archaic)*, ginger, gipsywort, gladdon, globe amaranth, globe thistle, globeflower, gloxinia, goat's-rue, godetia, gold-of-pleasure, golden aster, golden saxifrage, goldenrod, goldenseal, goldilocks, goldthread, goosegrass, granny's bonnet, grass of Parnassus, green dragon, grindelia, gromwell, ground cherry, ground ivy, groundsel, guayule, gypsophila, harebell, hawk's-beard, hawkbit, hawkweed, heart's-ease, hedge parsley, hedge-hyssop, helianthus, heliotrope, hellebore, hemp agrimony, hen-and-chickens, hepatica, herb bennet, herb Paris, herb Peter, herb Robert, hog's-fennel, hognut, hollyhock, honesty, horned poppy, horse nettle, horsemint, hound's-tongue, Iceland poppy, immortelle, impatiens, Indian pipe, Indian shot, Indian tobacco, iris, Jacob's-ladder, keck, kingcup, knapweed, knawel, lad's-love, lamb's ear, lamb's tongue, larkspur, lily-of-the-valley, lobelia, London pride, loosestrife, lousewort, love-in-a-mist, love-in-idleness, love-lies-bleeding, lungwort, lychnis, maiden pink, mallow, marguerite, marigold, marsh mallow, marsh marigold, marvel-of-Peru, May apple, May blobs, May lily, meadow rue, meadowsweet, mercury, Michaelmas daisy, mignonette, milfoil, military fern, milk bush, milkweed, milkwort, mind-your-own-business, Molucca balm, monkey-flower, monkshood, moon daisy, moonwort, mother-of-thousands, mousetail, mudsill, mugwort, musk, myosotis, nasturtium, nemesia, nipplewort, orpine, ox-eye, ox-eye daisy, oxlip, oxtongue, paigle, pansy, paschal flower, pasqueflower, pearlwort, pennywort, pentstemon, peony, periwinkle, petunia, pheasant's-eye, phlox, picotee, pignut, pimpernel, pink, pipewort, ploughman's spikenard, poison creeper, polyanthus, polygala, polygonum, poor-man's orchid, poppy, portulaca, pot marigold, potentilla, primrose, primula, Prince of Wales' feather, prince's-feather, pulsatilla, pyrethrum, Queen Anne's lace, rafflesia, ragged robin, ragweed, ragwort, rampion, ranunculus, red valerian, red-hot poker, reseda, ribbon-weed, rock-cress, rocket, Roman nettle, rose campion, rose mallow, rose of Jericho, rose of Sharon, rosebay willowherb, rudbeckia, salad burnet, saltwort, salvia, samphire, sand spurry, sandwort, santonica, saxifrage, scabious, scammony, schizanthus, Scotch bluebell, Scotch thistle, sea tassel, sea-campion, sea-heath, sea-holly, sea-kale, sea-lavender, sea-pink, sea-rocket, seablite, selfheal, shamrock, shasta daisy, sheep's bit, shepherd's cress, shooting star, Siberian wallflower, silkweed, silverweed, skullcap, smartweed, snakeroot, snapdragon, sneeze weed, sneezewort, snow-in-summer, soapwort, solanum, solidago, Solomon's-seal, Spanish moss, speedwell, spider flower, spiderwort, spignel, spurge, spurry, St John's wort, St Peters wort, starwort, statice, stinging nettle, stitchwort, stork's-bill, strelitzia, sun spurge, sunflower, swallow-wort, swamp lily, sweet alyssum, sweet cicely, sweet flag, sweet william, tansy, tape vine, tar-vine, taraxacum, teasel, thistle, thrift, tillandsia, toadflax, tormentil, touch-me-not, tradescantia, trillium, tropaeolum, truelove, tutsan, twinflower, valerian, verbena, veronica, viola, violet, viper's bugloss, Virginia stock, wait-a-bit, wake-robin, wall rocket, wallflower, Wandering Jew, water nymph, water primrose, water-betony, water-chickweed, water-dropwort, water-hemlock, water-mat, water-parsnip, waterpepper, Welsh poppy, wicopy *(U.S.)*, wild carrot, wild parsley, wild parsnip, wild sorghum, willowherb, windflower, winter aconite, winter cress, winter heliotrope, wolf's-bane, wood sorrel, woodruff, woundwort, yarrow, yucca, zinnia

29. AQUATIC PLANTS – AUSTRALIAN, bladderwort, duckweed, eelgrass, floating heart, fringed waterlily, grass-wrack, lotus, milfoil, nelumbo, pondweed, seagrass, starwort, water blinks, water ribbons, water thyme, water-milfoil, water-starwort, waterbuttons, waterlily

30. AQUATIC PLANTS – OTHER, azolla, bladderwort, Canadian pondweed, Cape pondweed, duckweed, eelgrass, elodea, flote-grass, flowering rush, fringed waterlily, horned pondweed, hornwort, lotus, mare's-tail, milfoil, naiad, nelumbo, pickerelweed, pondweed, seagrass, spatterdock, star fruit, starwort, tape-grass, victoria, water hyacinth, water starwort, water thyme, water-chestnut, water-milfoil, water-nymph, water-plantain, water-shield, water-soldier, water-speedwell, water-violet, waterlily, waterweed, yellow waterlily

31. CLIMBING PLANTS – AUSTRALIAN, apple-berry, barrister, bluebell creeper, burny bean, bush-lawyer, button orchid, calamus, cane, caustic vine, clematis, coral-pea, derris, devil's guts, devil's twine, dodder laurel, doubah, dumplings, false sarsaparilla, ipomoea, jequirity, kangaroo vine, lawyer-cane, matchbox bean, monkey rope, passionflower, Queensland bean, sarsaparilla, scimitar pod, smilax, watervine, waxplant, weir vine, wombat berry, wonga-wonga

32. CLIMBING PLANTS – OTHER, ampelopsis, balloon vine, banana passionfruit, Banksia rose, bell-vine, bignonia, bindweed, bine, birthwort, bittersweet, black bindweed, black bryony, black-eyed Susan, bryony, butterfly pea, calabash, calamus, canary creeper, cane, Cape ivy, Carolina jasmine, ceriman, clematis, convolvulus, cow-itch, cowage, cross vine, derris, dodder, Dutchman's-pipe, five-finger, fruit salad plant, giegie *(N.Z.)*, gourd, heartseed, hog peanut, honeysuckle, ipomoea, ivy, Japanese ivy, jasmine, kiekie *(N.Z.)*, lamb's-tail, Madeira vine, matchbox bean, mignonette vine, monstera deliciosa, moonflower, moonseed, morning glory, Mysore thorn, passionflower, philodendron, poison ivy, poison oak, rata *(N.Z.)*, rattan, sarsaparilla, scimitar pod, smilax, squirting cucumber, stephanotis, thunbergia, traveller's joy, trumpet flower, trumpet honeysuckle, virgin's-bower, Virginia creeper, waxplant, white bryony, wisteria, woodbine, woody nightshade, yellow jasmine

33. FUNGI/BACTERIA/LICHENS, agaric, amanita, ambrosia, ascomycete, aspergillus, beech orange, blackfellow's bread, blewits, boletus, botrytis cinerea, breadmould, chanterelle, coral fungus, death cup, downy mildew, earthstar, ergot, fairies' closet, fly agaric, gill fungus, gold cap, gold top, grey mould, hairy jew's ear, horse mushroom, Iceland moss, ink-cap, jew's ear, magic mushroom, microphyte, mildew, morel, mould, mushroom, myxomycete, net fungus, orchil, penicillium, phytophthora, puffball, reindeer moss, rust, slime mould, sooty blotch, sooty mould, stinkhorn, toadstool, truffle, tuckahoe, vegetable caterpillar, yeast, yeast plant; MOSSES AND LIVERWORTS, bog moss, hepatic, sphagnum

34. ALGAE, anabaena, black scum, blackfish-weed, bladderwrack, carrageen, Ceylon moss, coralline, desmid, diatom, dulse, frogspawn, frogspit, fucoid, fucus, green weed, gulfweed, Irish moss, jelly plant, kelp, laver, microphyte, Neptune's necklace, nullipore, phytoplankton, pond scum, red algae, rock weed, sargasso, sargassum, sea lettuce, sea-wrack, seaware, seaweed, spirogyra, stonewort, wrack

35. FERNS AND FERN ALLIES, adder's-tongue, azolla, bird's-nest fern, bladder fern, bracken, brake, club moss, Dutch rush, elkhorn fern, equisetum, filmy fern, fishbone fern, hare's-foot, hart's-tongue, hen-and-chicken fern, holly fern, horseshoe fern, horsetail, lace-fern, lycopodium, maidenhair, male fern, marsh fern, moonwort, nardoo, osmund, pillwort, polypody, Prince of Wales feather, quillwort, rasp fern, rock-fern, royal fern, scouring rush, selaginella, shield-fern, sickle fern, spleenwort, stag's-horn moss, staghorn fern, tender brake, umbrella fern, Venus's hair, walking fern, wall rue, waterfern, woolly cloak-fern; N.Z. FERNS, bunger, crape fern, gully fern, kidney fern, king-fern, mamaku, mangemange, necklace fern, pig fern, ponga, silver fern, tree fern

36. CYCADS AND MINOR GYMNOSPERM, burrawang, coontie, ginkgo, macrozamia, maidenhair tree, sago, welwitschia, zamia

37. GRAINS/CEREALS/PULSES/OILSEEDS, amaranth, arrowroot, barley, barleycorn, bean, benne, black gram, bran, buckwheat, butterbean, butternut, camellia, canary grass, carob, chickpea, coconut, cohune, colza, corn *(U.S.)*, cowpea, durra, durum wheat, einkorn, emmer, farina, frijol, gingili, grain, gram, groundnut, guinea corn, haricot, helianthus, Indian corn, Indian millet, Indian rice, job's-tears, Kaffir, kaoliang, kidney bean, lentil, lima bean, lupin, maize, mealie *(S. African)*, millet, milo, mung bean, oat, oil-palm, olive, paddy, palm sugar, panic, pea, peanut, pearl millet, pigeon pea, pollard, ragi, rape, rapeseed, red bean, rice, rye, safflower, semolina, sesame, shea, shell bean *(U.S.)*, sorghum, sorgo, soya bean, spelt, sunflower, til, wheat, white bean

38. VEGETABLE/ROOT CROPS, artichoke, artichoke thistle, asparagus, aubergine, baby marrow, bean, bean shoot, beansprout, beet, beetroot, bell pepper, black gram, brassicas, brinjal, broad bean, broccoli, brussels sprout, burdock, burnet, butternut pumpkin, cabbage, calabash, capsicum, cardoon, carrot, casaba, cassava, caulie *(Colloq.)*, cauliflower, celeriac, celery, celery cabbage, chicory, Chinese cabbage, choko, chufa, cole, collard, coontie, cos lettuce, courgette, cress, cucumber, dasheen, day lily, dolichos, eddo, eggfruit, eggplant, elephant's-ear, endive, eschalot, French bean, frijol, garden orach, garlic, gherkin, globe artichoke, gram, gramma, green pepper, greens, gumbo *(U.S.)*, hairy jew's ear, haricot, hognut, horse bean, jack bean, jam melon, Jerusalem artichoke, kale, kidney bean, kohlrabi, lablab, leek, lettuce, lima bean, Maori cabbage *(N.Z.)*, marrow, marrow squash *(U.S.)*, merino, mung bean, mushroom, New Zealand spinach, okra, onion, orach, oyster plant, palm-cabbage, parsley, parsnip, pea, pepper, pigeon pea, pimiento, plantain, potato, puha, pumpkin, purslane, radish, rampion, rauriki *(N.Z.)*, red beet, red cabbage, rhubarb, rocambole, rosella, rosella bush, runner bean, rutabaga *(U.S.)*, sago, salad burnet, salsify, samphire, savoy, scallion *(U.S.)*, scarlet runner, sea-kale, shallot, shell bean *(U.S.)*, silver beet, skirret, smallage *(Obs.)*, snapbean *(U.S.)*, snow pea, sorrel, Spanish onion, spinach, spring onion, strawberry tomato, string bean, sugar beet, sugar pea, swede, sweet corn, sweet pepper, sweet potato, Swiss chard, sword bean, taro, tomato, trombone, turnip, udo, vegetable marrow, vegetable oyster, water-chestnut, watercress, wax-bean *(U.S.)*, white bean, white potato, winged bean, yam, yam bean, zucchini

39. FRUITS, alligator pear, amarelle *(U.S.)*, anchovy pear, apple, apricot, avocado, banana, banana passionfruit, bilberry, blackcap *(U.S.)*, blackcurrant, blackerry, blaeberry, blueberry, boysenberry, bramble, breadfruit, cainite, Cape gooseberry, ceriman, cherimoya, cherry, cherry guava, cherry-plum, Chinese gooseberry, citron, citrus, clementine, cling peach, codling, crab-apple, cranberry, cucumber tree, currant, custard-apple, damson, date, date palm, date plum, dewberry, durian, feijoa, fig, foxgrape, freestone, fruit salad plant, gage, gean, genipap, gingerbread tree, gooseberry, granadilla, Granny Smith, grape, grapefruit, grapevine, greengage, ground cherry, guanabana, guava, hanepoot, Hottentot fig, huckleberry, jaboticaba, jackfruit, jonathan, jujube, Kaffir orange, kaki, katunga, Kiwi fruit, konini, kumquat, ladyfinger, lemon, lime, loganberry, longan, loquat, lotus *(Greek Legend)*, love apple, lungan, lychee, malvoisie, mammee, mandarin, mandarine, mango, mangosteen, marmalade tree, May apple, medlar, melon, miraculous fruit, monstera deliciosa, morello, mulberry, muscat, muscatel, muskmelon, naseberry, nopal, olive, opuntia, orange, papaya, passionfruit, pawpaw, peach, peanut, pear, persimmon, pili, pineapple, pineapple guava, pippin, plantain, plum, pomegranate, pomelo, poor-man's orange, prune, quandong, quince, raisin, rambutan, raspberry, redcurrant, rennet, rockmelon, rose-apple, rough lemon, russet, sapodilla, service tree,

Seville orange, shaddock, sorb, sour fig, soursop, squash, star-apple, strawberry, sultana, sweet cherry, sweeting *(U.S. Brit.)*, sweetsop, tamarillo, tamarind, tangelo, tangerine, teaberry, thornapple, tree tomato, tuna, ugli fruit, victoria, warden, watermelon, white currant, whiteheart, whortleberry, youngberry

40. NUTS, almond, American chestnut, Barcelona nut, bauple nut, beech mast, beechnut, black walnut, bopple nut, brazil nut, cashew, chestnut, chinquapin, cobnut, coconut, coquilla nut, filbert, groundnut, hazel, hazelnut, hickory, Japanese chestnut, Jordan almond, macadamia nut, marron, nut pine, nutwood, oyster nut, peanut, pecan, pili, pine nut, pinyon, pistache, pistachio, Queensland nut, shagbark *(U.S.)*, Spanish chestnut, walnut, water chestnut

41. HERBS AND SPICES, allspice, angelica, anise, aniseed, balm, basil, bay, bay tree, borage, calabash nutmeg, canella, caper, capsicum, caraway, cardamom, cassia, caterpillar-flower, catmint, catnip, Ceylon cinnamon, chervil, chilli, chive, cicely, cinnamon, clary, clove, costmary, crocus, cumin, curcuma, dill, dittander, estragon, fennel, fennelflower, fenugreek, galangal, gherkin, ginger, gingerroot, grains of paradise, hop, horseradish, hyssop, lad's-love, laos, laurel, lemon balm, lemon grass, liquorice, lovage, mace, marasca, marjoram, mint, nasturtium, nutmeg, opium poppy, oregano, origan, paprika, parsley, pennyroyal, pepper, peppercorn, peppermint, pimento, pot marigold, race ginger, ramson, red pepper, rosemary, rue, saffron, sage, savory, spearmint, star-anise, sweet basil, sweet bay, sweet cicely, tamarind, tarragon, thyme, turmeric, vanilla

42. BEVERAGE PLANTS, absinth, black elder, burdock, cacao, camomile, chamomile, chicory, cocoa bean, coffee, coffee tree, cola, coquito, dandelion, elder, elderberry, gomuti *(S.E. Asia)*, grape, hop, horehound, hyson, juniper, kat, kava, mate, mint, qat, sarsaparilla, smilax, souchong, tea, wormwood, yaupon, yeast

43. DRUG AND MEDICINAL PLANTS, aconite, alkaloid, aloe, alumroot, areca, arnica, asafoetida, asthma-plant, atropine, bayberry, belladonna, benzoin, betel nut, betel palm, betel pepper, betony, bhang *(India)*, bitterbark, bitterwood, bloodroot, bryony, buckthorn, bull-a-bull, cade, cajuput, calendula, camomile, canella, cannabis, cardinal flower, carrageen, cascara, cascara sagrada, cascarilla, cascarilla bark, cassia, castor bean *(U.S.)*, castor seed, castor-oil plant, cevadilla, chamomile, chaulmoogra, cinchona, citronella, cocaine, cola, colchicum, colocynth, coltsfoot, comfrey, contrayerva, copaiba, corkwood, corn silk, croton, cubeb, Culver's root, curare, dagga *(S. African)*, datura, digitalis, dogbane, dragon's blood, ergot, eucalypt, fennel, fennelflower, fenugreek, ferula, fever-root, fever-tree, feverfew, fimble, fleawort, foxglove, fumitory, gagroot, galbanum, ganga, gentian, ginseng, gold cap, gold top, goldenseal, goldthread, grains of paradise, greenheart, grindelia, guaco, guaiacum, gunyang, hedge-hyssop, hemp, henbane, herb Paris, hop, horehound, Hottentot fig, Iceland moss, Indian hemp, ipecacuanha, jaborandi, jalap, jimson weed, kangaroo apple, kat, lavender, lignum vitae, liquorice, mandragora, mandrake, marijuana, May apple, mescal, milfoil, morphine, moxa, nard, nicotine, nightshade, nux-vomica, opium poppy, pagoda tree, pan, pareira, pellitory, penicillin, penicillium, pennyroyal, peppermint, Peruvian bark, pinkroot, pituri, poke, pokeweed, poppy, pyrethrum, qat, quebracho, quinine, quinine bush, rauwolfia, rhatany, rhubarb, rue, sabadilla, safflower, Saigon cinnamon, sanguinaria, sarsaparilla, sassafras, scammony, sea-onion, sea-squill, senega, senna, simarouba, slippery elm, smilax, snakeroot, solanum, spikenard, squill, stramonium, strophanthus, strychnine, swallow-wort, taraxacum, thornapple, thuja, tobacco, tonka bean, toothache tree, tormentil, tragacanth, turpeth, valerian, wall pellitory, witch-hazel, wormseed, wormwood, woundwort, yarrow, zanthoxylum

44. PERFUMERY PLANTS AND MATERIALS, abelmosk, aspic, bay, bdellium, bergamot, boronia, cassie-flower, champak, citronella, damask rose, eaglewood, frangipanni, gardenia, iris, jasmine, labdanum, lavender, lemon geranium, lemon grass, lemon-scented gum, lily-of-the-valley, marigold, mignonette, mimosa, myrrh, orange blossom, orris, orrisroot, patchouli, pennyroyal, peppermint, pimento, potpourri, rose, sandalwood, spike lavender, spikenard, stinking roger, tonka bean, tuberose, vetiver, ylang-ylang

45. DYE PLANTS, alkanet, anil, annatto, betony, bloodroot, camwood, divi-divi, dyer's greenweed, dyer's rocket, fustic, haemotoxylin, henna, indigo, logwood, madder, pastel, puccoon, quebracho, quercitron, redwood, weld, woad; DYES, anchusin, anil, annatto, brazil, fustic, madder, orchil, quercetin, safflower, sappanwood, valonia

46. FIBRE PLANTS, abaca, ambari, bhang *(India)*, bowstring hemp, broom millet, broomcorn, coconut palm, cogon, cottontree, dishcloth gourd, esparto, fimble, flax, ganga, gomuti *(S.E. Asia)*, hemp, Indian Hemp, jute, kenaf, korari, maguey, millet, New Zealand flax, osier, palmiet, papyrus, pita, ramie, sansevieria, silk-cotton tree, sisal, sunn, tapa, teasel, vetiver; FIBRES, abaca, bast, coir, cotton, cottonwool, hemp, kapok, loofah, piassava, pulp, raffia, wood pulp

47. TIMBER PLANTS, acajou, alamo, alpine ash, araucaria, arbor vitae, ash, balsa, balsam fir, banyalla, basswood, bebeeru, beech, birch, black bean, black walnut, blackbutt, blackwood, blue gum, bolly gum, box, briar, brush box, calamus, camphor laurel, canary sassafras, cedar, celery-top pine, clinker beech, cottonwood, cudgerie, cypress pine, Douglas fir, Douglas pine, Douglas spruce, durmast, durobby, ebony, eucalyptus, flooded gum, greenheart, guaiacum, haematoxylin, hemlock spruce, hickory, hoop pine, Huon pine, insignis pine, Japanese cedar, jarrah, karri, kauri, larch, laurel, lignum vitae, loblolly, locust, longleaf pine, mahogany, marmalade tree, miro, Monterey pine, Moreton bay chestnut, mountain ash, Norway spruce, oak, Oregon pine, padauk, partridge-wood, penda, persimmon, pine, poon, poplar, Queensland kauri, Queensland maple, radiata pine, red cedar, red fir, red pine, redwood, rimu, river red gum, satinwood, Scots pine, sequoia, shagbark *(U.S.)*, silky oak, silver fir, slash pine, sneezewood, spotted gum, spruce, sugar maple, tallowwood, Tasmanian blue gum, Tasmanian oak, teak, thuja, toon, turpentine, walnut, western hemlock, Western red cedar, white pine, white spruce, yellow sassafras, yew

48. TIMBERS/BARKS etc, balsawood, bamboo, boxwood, brazil, brushwood, bullswool, camphorwood, candle bark, cane, cork, fiddlewood, jacaranda, kingwood, pulpwood, rattan, rosewood, sandalwood, settler's matches, sola *(India)*, violet wood, whangee, withe, withy, zebrawood

49. FODDER AND PASTURE PLANTS, alfalfa *(U.S.)*, algarroba, alsike, alsike clover, baldoo, barley grass, beech mast, beet, bird's-foot trefoil, birdwood grass, bladder saltbush, blue grass, blue lupin, Bokhara clover, brome, browntop, buffel grass, burr medic, canary grass, chou moellier, chow *(N.Z. Colloq.)*, clover, coastal saltbush, cocksfoot, cole, comfrey, Cooper's clover, cottonbush, cowpea, Darling clover, dolichos, Dutch clover, fenugreek, field pea, Flinders grass, giant panic, giant saltbush, grey saltbush, guinea grass, herbage, kikuyu, King Island melilot, lablab, Landsborough grass, lespedeza, lucerne, lupin, maize, mangel-wurzel, mangold, mealy saltbush, melilot, Menindie clover, mesquite, millet, Mitchell grass, mustard bush, oat, old-man saltbush, panic, para grass, paspalum, Paterson's curse, pearl millet, perennial rye, phalaris, Queensland blue, rape, red clover, rhodes grass, rutabaga *(U.S.)*, rye-grass, sago grass, sainfoin, saltbush, salvation Jane, serradella, shot grass, small burr grass, sorghum, sorgo, soya bean, stylo, subterranean clover, sugar grass, sugarcane, swede, sweet clover, sweet lupin, teosinte, timothy, Townsville lucerne, Townsville stylo, trifolium, turnip, veldt grass, vetch, water meadow grass, wheat grass, white clover, wild sorghum, wilga, Wimmera rye, windmill grass

50. OILS/RESINS/CHEMICALS etc, agar, agar-agar, Aleppo gall, babul, balata, balm, balm of Gilead, balsam, barilla, bdellium, benzoin, camphor, candleberry, candlenut, candlewood, carnauba, carrageen, cashew, castor bean *(U.S.)*, castor seed, castor-oil, cutch, dragon's blood, galbanum, gallipot, gibberellin, guar gum, guayule, gum, latex, linseed, mastic, palm oil, papain, quillai bark, rubber, sandarac, shellac, soapbark, soapberry, storax, tacamahac, tannin, tragacanth, turpentine, ule, varnish, wattlebark, wintergreen

51. WEEDS, Aaron's-rod, African boxthorn, ailanthus, alexanders, allseed, amaranth, anabaena, apple of Peru, apple of Sodom, asphodel, asthma-plant, azolla, balloon vine, barley grass, barnyard grass, Bathurst burr, bearded oat, beggar's tick, Bergalia tussock, billygoat weed, bindi-eye, bindii, bindweed, bitter melon, bittercress, black bindweed, black nightshade, black oat, black thistle, blackberry, blue borage, blue couch, blue devil, blue thistle, blue top, blue weed, boneseed, boxthorn, bracken, bramble, briar, brome, Brown's dock, buffalo burr, burdock, burr grass, burr-marigold, calliopsis, caltrop, camphor laurel, Cape gooseberry, Cape ivy, capeweed, carpet grass, castor-oil plant, cat's head, cat's-ear, caterpillar weed, charlock, chickweed, chinee apple, cleavers, cockspur, cogon, colocynth, coltsfoot, compass plant, conium, convolvulus, coreopsis, corn poppy, corn spurry, corncockle, cornflower, cottonbush, couch, crabgrass, cracker *(N.Z.)*, creeping oxalis, creeping thistle, crofton weed, crowfoot, crown beard, crowsfoot grass, cudweed, dandelion, darnel, datura, deadly nightshade, devil's claw, dock, dodder, dog fennel, double gee, drooping sedge, duckweed, dwarf mallow, elodea, English couch grass, eryngo, eupatorium, evening primrose, fat-hen, fennel, field madder, fierce thornapple, fireweed, Flanders poppy, flat weed, flatweed, fleabane, flixweed, fluellen, fumitory, furze, gallant soldier, galvanised burr, Good-King-Henry, goose grass, goosefoot, gorse, gromwell, ground elder, groundsel, groundsel bush, hairy bittercress, hardheads, hare's-ear, hare's-foot, hawk's-beard, hawkweed, hedgemustard, heliotrope, hemlock, henbit, herb Gerard, Hexham scent, hoary cress, hogweed, horehound, horned poppy, Indian hedge-mustard, Indian weed, inkweed, jalap, Japanese honeysuckle, jelly-leaf, Jerusalem cherry, jimson weed, jo-jo, Johnson grass, joy-weed, khaki weed, King Island melilot, knapweed, lamb's tongue, lamb's-tail, land cress, lantana, London rocket, Madeira vine, mallow, Maltese cockspur, mayweed, mesquite, Mexican poppy, Mexican tea, milk thistle, milk vetch, milkweed, mimosa, mintweed, missionary *(N.Z.)*, mist flower, moon daisy, mouse-ear, mullein, Mullumbimby couch, Mysore thorn, nassella tussock, native hops, needle burr, nettle, Noogoora burr, nopal, nutgrass, oatgrass, onion grass, onion weed, opuntia, ox-eye daisy, oxalis, Paddy's lucerne, paddymelon, pampas grass, pampas lily-of-the-valley, Parramatta grass, parsley piert, pascalia weed, Paterson's curse, pearlwort, pellitory, penny-cress, pennywort, peppercress, pest pear, petty spurge, pheasant's-eye, pimpernel, plantain, polygonum, portulaca, prairie grass, prickly lettuce, prickly pear, prickly pear melon, prickly poppy, privet, purple top, purslane, quaking grass, Queensland hemp, ragweed, ragwort, rat's-tail fescue, Rhodes grass, ribwort, rocket, rubber vine, saffron thistle, Saint Barnaby's thistle, salvation Jane, scarlet pimpernel, Scotch thistle, sensitive plant, serrated tussock, sheep's sorrel, shepherd's needle, shepherd's-purse, shivery grass, sida weed, silkweed, skeleton weed, slender celery, small crofton weed, smartweed, smilax, snakeweed, sorrel, soursob, sow-thistle, sowbane, spear thistle, spiny burr grass, spiny emex, spurge, spurry, St John's wort, stagger-weed, star thistle, star-of-Bethlehem, starwort, stemless thistle, sticktight, stink grass, stinking roger, stinkweed, stinkwort, summer grass, sun spurge, swamp dock, sweetbriar, swinecress, taraxacum, tare, thistle, thornapple, three-cornered jack, tiger pear, tobacco tree, tradescantia, treacle mustard, tree of heaven, tulip, turnip-weed, tutsan, twitch, variable groundsel, variegated thistle, verbena, vetch, viper's bugloss, wall pellitory, Wandering Jew, wartcress, water hyacinth, waterpepper, whin, whitlow grass, wild carrot, wild lettuce, wild mustard, wild oat, wild onion, willowherb, winter grass, wireweed, witchweed, wood sorrel, xanthium, Yass river tussock, yellow sorrel, yellow wood sorrel, yellow-flowered oxalis

52. POISONOUS AND IRRITANT PLANTS, aconite, amanita, antiar, autumn crocus, baneberry, barringtonia, belladonna, blind-your-eyes, blue rod, bottletree caustic, box poison, brother-brother, buttercup, Calabar bean, Cape tulip, capeweed, castor-oil plant, caustic weed, cestrum, cherry laurel, cockatoo apple, colchicum, conium, Cooktown ironwood, cottonbush, cow-itch, cow-parsnip, cowage, cowbane, curare, Darling pea, datura, deadly nightshade, death cup, delphinium, derris, dumb cane, dwale, Ellangowan poison bush, ergot, euphorbia, finger cherry, flame lily, fly agaric, fool's parsley, foxglove, Gascoyne spurge, gidgee, gympie nettle, heart-leaf poison, heliotrope, hellebore, hemlock, henbane, herb Christopher, Indian liquorice, jequirity, jimson weed, Johnson grass, kalmia, karaka, lantana, larkspur, laurel, loco, locoweed, macrozamia, manchineel, mignonette vine, mintweed, monkshood, mountain laurel, narcissus, nettle, nettle tree, nightshade, oleander, poison ivy, poison oak, poison sumach, poison-bush, prickly poison, ragweed, ranunculus, rhus tree, rock-fern, sassy, sassy bark, smartweed, stagger-bush, stavesacre, stinging nettle, stinging tree, strophanthus, sugar gum, thornapple, toadstool, toot *(N.Z.)*, tutu, upas, wallflower poison, wax tree, weir vine, wolf's bane, yew, york-road poison

53. PLANTS USED BY ABORIGINES, amulla, apple-berry, Australian boxthorn, ballart, bats-wing coral-tree, bauhinia, beech orange, berrigan, black bean, black boy, blackfellow's bread, blackfellow's hemp, blackfellow's yam, blackman's potatoes, bloodroot, bolwarra, boobialla, bottle tree, bunya-bunya, Burdekin plum, burrawang, cabbage palm, cabbage tree, calamus, caterpillar-flower, cherry ballart, chucky chucky, colane, condoroo, cunjevoi, desert lemon, desert lime, doubah, early Nancy, Ellangowan poison bush, emu bush, emu-apple, gunyang, Herbert River cherry, kangaroo apple, katunga, kurrajong, lilly pilly, manatoka, mat-rush, Mitchell grass, Moreton bay chestnut, Moreton bay fig, murrnong, nalgoo, nardoo, native cherry, native dandelion, native millet, native mulberry, native rosella, native sorrel, native willow, nelumbo, nonda, panic, pigface, pitcheri, pituri, potato bush, quandong, quena, settler's flax, settler's twine, snowberry, tomato bush, warrigal cabbage, waterlily, waxberry, wild goosebery, wild lime, wild orange, wild tomato, yam, yam daisy

Animals

Bandicoots 1
Bilbies 1
Carnivorous marsupials 1
Dogs – Australasian 1
Kangaroos 1
Koalas 1
Marine mammals – Australasian 1
Mice – Australasian 1
Monotremes 1
Possums – Australasian 1
Rats – Australasian 1
Wallabies 1
Wombats 1
Artiodactyla 2
Primates 3
Edentata 4
Carnivora 5
Rodentia 6
Perissodactyls 7
Cetaceans 8
Dugongs 8
Chiroptera 9
Pinnipedia 10
Insectivora 11
Elephants 12
Hyracoidea 13
Lagomorphs 13
Pholidota 13
Birds – indigenous 14
Parrots – Australasian 15
Birds of prey – Australasian 16
Ocean birds – Australasian 17
Shore birds – Australasian 18
Water birds – Australasian 19
Birds – introduced 20
Birds – non-Australian 21
Lizards – Australasian 22
Lizards – other 23
Snakes – Australasian 24
Snakes – other 25
Tortoises – Australasian 26
Tortoises – other 27
Crocodiles 28
Amphibia 29
Fish 30
Rays 31
Sharks 31
Agnatha 32
Lancelets 33
Protochordates 33
Tunicates 33
Brittle stars 34
Sea cucumbers 34
Sea-lilies 34
Starfish 34
Urchins 34
Centipedes 35
Crustacea 35
Millipedes 35
Insects 36
Insects – Australasian 37
Butterflies 38
Moths 38
Beetles 39
Flies 40
Horseshoe crabs 41
Seaspiders 41
Spiders 41
Earthworms 42
Leeches 42
Onychophora 42
Tube worms 42
Chitons 43
Octopus 43
Oysters 43
Snails 43
Brachiopoda 44
Ectoprocta 45
Acanthocephala 46
Flukes 46
Free-living flatworms 46
Horsehair worms 46
Nematodes 46
Nemertea 46
Rotifers 46
Tapeworms 46
Ctenophores 47
Anemones 48
Bluebottles 48
Hard corals 48
Jellyfish 48
Sea wasps 48
Soft corals 48
Amoebae 49
Ciliates 49
Flagellates 49
Sponges 49
Sporozoa 49
Dinosaurs 50
Fossil birds 50

1. AUSTRALASIAN MAMMALS – MONOTREMES: anteater, duckbill, echidna, ornithorhynchus, platypus, porcupine *(Obs.)*, spiny anteater; CARNIVOROUS MARSUPIALS: banded anteater, Canning's little dog, cynocephalus, dibbler, dunnart, kowari, kultarr, larapinta, mardo, marsupial cat, marsupial mole, marsupial mouse, native cat, native mouse, northern native cat, numbat, phascogale, pitchi-pitchi, planigale, quoll, satanellus, spotted native cat, Tasmanian devil, Tasmanian tiger, Tasmanian wolf, thylacine, tiger cat, tuan, ursine dasyure, wambenger, wuhl-wuhl; BANDICOOTS AND BILBIES: Gunn's bandicoot, bandicoot, barred bandicoot, bilby, brindled bandicoot, brown bandicoot, dalgyte, desert bandicoot, golden bandicoot, long-eared bandicoot, long-nosed bandicoot, Malabar rat, marl, pig rat, quenda, rabbit-eared bandicoot, short-eared bandicoot, short-nosed bandicoot, Tasmanian barred bandicoot, wintarro, yallara; KOALAS AND WOMBATS: Australian badger, hairy-nosed wombat, koala, naked-nose wombat, native bear, New Holland sloth *(Obs.)*, wombat; POSSUMS AND GLIDERS: bobuck, brush-tailed possum, burramys, cuscus, feather-tail glider, fluffy glider, flying mouse, flying phalanger, flying possum, gliding possum, greater glider, green ringtail possum, mongan, mountain possum, mundarda, noolbenger, phalanger, pygmy glider, ringtail possum, rock possum, squirrel glider, striped possum, sugar glider, tait, toolah, wogoit, yellow-bellied glider; KANGAROOS AND WALLABIES: agile wallaby, antelope kangaroo, Bennett's tree-kangaroo, Bennett's wallaby, bettong, big red, biggada, black wallaby, black-faced kangaroo, black-tailed wallaby, blue flier, boodie rat, boongary, brush kangaroo, brush-tailed bettong, burrowing rat-kangaroo, dama, desert rat-kangaroo, eastern brush wallaby, euro, forester, great grey kangaroo, grey forester, Grey's brush wallaby, hare-wallaby, joey *(N.Z.)*, jungle kangaroo, kanga, kangaroo rat, karrabul, Lesueur's rat-kangaroo, Lumholtz's tree-kangaroo, mallee kangaroo, merrin, munning, musk rat-kangaroo, nail-tailed wallaby, pademelon, parma wallaby, plains kangaroo, potoroo, pretty-face wallaby, quokka, rat-kangaroo, red kangaroo, red wallaby, red-necked wallaby, river wallaby, rock wallaby, rufous rat-kangaroo, rufous wallaby, sandy wallaby, scrub wallaby, sooty kangaroo, squeaker, swamp wallaby, tammar, tcharibeena, toolache, tree-kangaroo, tungoo, uroo, wallaby, wallaroo, western grey kangaroo, whiptail wallaby, woylie, wurrung, wurrup; RATS AND MICE: Maori rat, broad-toothed rat, bush rat, dargawarra, false swamp-rat, hopping-mouse, kiore *(N.Z.)*, mosaic-tailed rat, native rat, oorarrie, rock-rat, spinifex hopping-mouse, stick-nest rat, tillikin, tree-rat, water-rat, wilkintie; MARINE MAMMALS: Australian fur seal, wig; DOGS AND DINGOS: Maori dog, dingo, warrigal

2. NON-AUSTRALIAN MAMMALS – ARTIODACTYLA: addax, alpaca, ammon, anoa, antelope, aoudad, argali, ariel, aurochs, axis, babiroussa, Bactrian camel, banteng, bharal, bighorn, bison, bongo, brocket, bubal, camelopard *(Obs.)*, Cape buffalo, caribou, cattle, chamois, chevrotain, chital, deer, dik-dik, dinoceras, dromedary, duiker, eland, elk, fallow deer, gaur *(India)*, gazelle, gemsbok, gerenuk, giraffe, gnu, goa, goat, goat antelope, goral, grysbok, guanaco, hart, hartebeest, hind, ibex, inyala, izard, kudu, llama, markhor, moose, mouflon, mountain goat, mountain ibex, mousedeer, mule deer, muntjac, musk deer, nilgai, okapi, oribi, oryx, peccary, pig, pronghorn, puku, red deer, reedbuck, reindeer, river-horse, Rocky Mountain goat, roebuck, roedeer, royal, rusa deer, sable antelope, saiga, sasin, sassaby, serow, spiker, springbok, stag, steenbok, steinbok, swine, tahr, tamarau, topi, uintatherium, urus, vicuna, wapiti, wart-hog, water-ox, waterbuck, white-tailed deer, wild boar, wildebeest, wisent, yak, yeanling

3. PRIMATES: anthropoid ape, ape, australopithecine *(Palaeontol.)*, aye-aye, baboon, Barbary ape, bushbaby, capuchin, chacma, chimp, chimpanzee, colugo, douc, douroucouli, drill, entellus, gelada, gibbon, gorilla, great ape, green monkey, grivet, guenon, hanuman, howler, howling monkey, indri, jackanapes *(Archaic)*, jocko, langur, lemur, lemuroid, loris, macaque, man, mandrill, mangabey, marmoset, monkey, orang-outang, pithecanthrope, pongid, pongo, potto, proboscis monkey, rhesus, saki, sapajou, siamang, simian, spider monkey, talapoin, tamarin, tarsier, titi, uakari, vervet, wanderoo; DERMOPTERA: flying lemur

4. EDENTATA: ai, ant-bear, anteater, armadillo, edentate, great anteater, lesser anteater, pichiciago, shrewmouse, silky anteater, sloth, tamandua, tatouay, Texas armadillo, two-toed anteater, unau; TUBULIDENTATA: aardvark

5. CARNIVORA: aardwolf, badger, bear, binturong, black bear, black buck, blue fox, bobcat, brock, brown bear, bruin, cacomistle, canis, caracal, carcajou, catamountain, cheetah, cinnamon bear, civet, coati, cougar, coyote, creodont, dhole *(India)*, earthwolf, ermine, eyra, felid, fennec, ferret, ferret badger, fisher, fitch, genet, glutton, golden cat, grey wolf, grison, grizzly, grizzly bear, honey bear, hyena, ichneumon, jackal, jaguar, jaguarondi, kinkajou, kolinsky, laughing hyena, leopard, liger, linsang, lion, lioness, lobo, lynx, maned wolf, margay, marten, meerkat *(S. African)*, mink, mongoose, mountain cat, mountain lion, ocelot, olingo, otter, ounce, painter *(U.S.)*, palm civet, panda, panther, pantheress, pard *(Archaic)*, pine marten, polar bear, polecat, prairie wolf, puma, raccoon, ratel, sable, sambar, sea-otter, serval, silver fox, skunk, sloth-bear, snow leopard, spotted hyena, stoat, striped hyena, suricate, tayra, teledu, tiger, tigon, tigress, timber wolf, viverrine, weasel, white bear, wildcat, wolf, wolverine, zoril

6. RODENTIA: acouchi, agouti, beaver, bunny, cane rat, capybara, castor, cavy, chickaree, chinchilla, chipmunk, coypu, deer-mouse, desert rat, dormouse, fat mouse, fieldmouse, flying squirrel, gerbil, golden hamster, gopher, grey squirrel, ground hog, ground squirrel, guineapig, hamster, harvest mouse, jerboa, jerboa rat, lemming, marmot, mouse, murine, muskrat, nutria, paca, pocket gopher, porcupine *(Obs.)*, prairie dog, rat, red squirrel, spermophile, squirrel, suslik, taguan, trade rat, tree-mouse, viscacha, vole, waltzing mouse, water mole, water-rat, water-vole, white rat, wood rat, woodchuck

7. PERISSODACTYLS: ass, barrow, black rhinoceros, eohippus *(Palaeontol.)*, hippo, hippopotamus, horse, jackass, jennet, kiang, mule, onager, perissodactyl, quagga, rhinoceros, sea-cow *(Obs.)*, tapir, tarpan, white rhinoceros, zebra

8. CETACEANS: baleen, bay whale, beluga, black whale, blackfish, blue whale, bottlenose, bowhead, cachalot, cetacean, dolphin, finback, finner, finwhale, grampus, humpback, killer whale, leveret, narwhal, orc *(Obs.)*, pika, pilot whale, porpoise, right whale, rorqual, sea-canary, sea-unicorn, sei whale, sperm whale, unicorn *(Obs.)*, whale, white whale; DUGONGS: dugong, manatee, sea-cow, sirenian

9. CHIROPTERA: bat, chiropter, false vampire, flittermouse *(Obs.)*, flying fox, fox-bat, fruit-bat, kalong, noctule, pipistrelle, serotine, vampire bat

10. PINNIPEDIA: bladdernose, clapmatch, eared seal, elephant seal, fur seal, hair seal, harbour seal, hooded seal, leopard seal, pinniped, sea elephant, sea leopard, sea lion, sea-dog, seal, walrus

11. INSECTIVORA: desman, elephant shrew, hedgehog, hedgepig, mole, moonrat, otter shrew, shrew, solenodon, tana, tenrec, tree shrew, water-shrew

12. ELEPHANTS: dinothere, African elephant, elephant, Indian elephant, jumbo, mammoth *(Palaeontol.)*, mastodon *(Palaeontol.)*, pachyderm

13. LAGOMORPHS: bunny, hare, jack rabbit, lagomorph, pika, rabbit; MARSUPIALS: opossum, yapok; PHOLIDOTA: pangolin, scaly anteater; HYRACOIDEA: daman, hyracoidean, hyrax, rock hyrax, tree hyrax

14. INDIGENOUS AUSTRALASIAN BIRDS: Albert lyrebird, anvil bird, apostle bird, apteryx, auctioneer bird, Australian coot, Australian courser, Australian ground-thrush, Australian pipit, Australian pratincole, babbler, barking jackass, barn owl, barn swallow, bell-miner, bellbird, berrin-berrin, bifcus, bird of paradise, black cuckoo, black-faced cuckoo-shrike, Black-headed honeyeater, blackhead, blightbird, blue jay, blue wren, blue-eye, blue-faced honeyeater, boobook, boomer, bowerbird, brain-fever bird, bristlebird, broad-billed roller, broadbill, brolga, bronze-wing, brown fieldlark, brush turkey, bubbly Jock, bubbly Mary, bush canary, bush robin *(N.Z.)*, bush stone curlew, bush wren *(N.Z.)*, bush-hen, bushlark, bustard, bustard quail, butcher bird, button quail, cassowary, catbird, caterpillar-eater, channel-billed cuckoo, chat, chatterer, chiffchaff, chimney swallow, chimney swift, chockalott, chough, cicada bird, coach-whip bird, coachman, cock, cooee bird, corncrake, coucal, courser, crake, crow, cuckoo, currawong, desert chat, diamond bird, diamond firetail, diamond sparrow, dinornis, dollar bird, dove, dragoon bird, drongo, eastern spinebill, emu, emu wren, fantail, field-wren, figbird, finch, finfoot, firetail, flock pigeon, flycatcher, flying coachman, four-o'clock, friar-bird, fringilline, frogmouth, gallinacean, gibber bird, goatsucker, golden-headed cisticola, goldfinch, Gouldian finch, grass-finch, grassbird, green catbird, greenfinch, grey-crowned babbler, groundlark, halcydon, happy family, Happy Jack, Hawkesbury clock *(Obs.)*, honey-sucker, honeyeater, Horsfield's bushlark, howling jackass, huia, Jacky Winter, jay, jungle fowl, kereru *(N.Z.)*, kite, kiwi, koel, kokako, korimako *(N.Z.)*, kotuku *(N.Z.)*, kuku, lapwing, leatherhead, Lewin honeyeater, logrunner, long-tail finch, lowan, lyrebird, maggie, magpie, magpie lark, makomako *(N.Z.)*, mallee fowl, manucode, Maori hen *(N.Z.)*, martin, matuku *(N.Z.)*, megapode, metallic starling, micky, miner, mistletoe bird, moa, mocker, mockingbird, moonbird, mopoke, mound bird, mudlark, mulberry bird, native companion, native pheasant, nighthawk, nightjar, noisy friar-bird, noisy miner, noisy pitta, northern chowchilla, notornis, nun, olive-backed oriole, orange-winged sittella, oriole, owlet-nightjar, painted finch, pallid cuckoo, pardalote, parson-bird *(N.Z.)*, peaceful dove, peewee, peewit, phalarope, pheasant coucal, pictorella mannikin, pigeon, pilot bird, piopio *(N.Z.)*, pipit, pitta, piwakawaka *(N.Z.)*, plain turkey, plains wanderer, plover, poll, pratincole, pukeko *(N.Z.)*, purple-breasted finch, quail, quail-thrush, rail, rainbird, rainbow bee-eater, raven, red grouse, red throat, red-necked avocet, redbill, redhead, reeve, regent bower-bird, regent honeyeater, restless flycatcher, Richard's pipit, riflebird, rifleman *(N.Z.)*, robin, roller, ruff, ruru *(N.Z.)*, sacred kingfisher, saddleback, satin bower-bird, satin flycatcher, satin sparrow, scalebird, scissors grinder, screech owl, scrub fowl, scrub robin, scrub turkey, scrub-bird, semitone-bird, shrike-thrush, sicklebill, silver-eye, singing bushlark, sittella, soldier bird, song lark, southern chowchilla, southern figbird, spangled drongo, spine-tailed chowchilla, spinebill, spinifex bird, spotted pardalote, spur-winged plover, squeaker, star finch, starling, sugarbird, sunbird, superb blue wren, superb lyrebird, swallow, swamp pheasant, swift, tailorbird, takahe *(N.Z.)*, tang, tawny frogmouth, teal, thickhead, thornbill, thrush, thunderbird, tit, titi *(N.Z.)*, topknot pigeon, tree runner, treecreeper, triller, tui, turkey quail, twelve apostle bird, wagtail, warbler, water-pipit, wattlebird, wax-eye, waybung, wedgebill, wee juggler, weka *(N.Z.)*, welcome swallow, whipbird, whistler, white-breasted finch, white-browed babbler, white-eye, white-fronted chat, white-naped honeyeater, white-quilled rock pigeon, white-throated warbler, white-winged chough, white-winged triller, whiteface, willaroo, Willie wagtail, wompoo pigeon, wonga pigeon, wood swallow, woodhen *(N.Z.)*, wren, wrybill *(N.Z.)*, yellowhead, zebra finch

15. ENDEMIC AUSTRALASIAN BIRDS – AUSTRALASIAN PARROTS, bluey *(Qld)*, Bourke parrot, budgerigar, budgie, bullen-bullen, buln-buln, cockatiel, cockatoo, cockatoo-parrot, cocklerina, cocky, corella, fig-parrot, galah, gang-gang, grass parrot, kaka, kakapo, kea, keet, Leadbeater's cockatoo, lorikeet, lorilet, lory, lovebird, lowry, Major Mitchell, Marshall's fig-parrot, night parrot, orange-breasted parrot, parakeet, parrot, quarrion, rainbow lorikeet, regent parrot, ringneck parrot, rock parakeet, rock pebbler, rosella, sulphur-crested cockatoo, twenty-eight parrot, white cockatoo, zebra parrot

16. AUSTRALASIAN BIRDS OF PREY: Australian goshawk, black-breasted buzzard, buzzard, chicken-hawk, duckhawk, eagle, eagle-hawk, falcon, falcon-gentle, goshawk, harrier, hawk, kestrel, marsh harrier, nankeen kestrel, osprey, peregrine, peregrine falcon, red goshawk, rufous-bellied buzzard, sea-eagle, sea-hawk, sparrowhawk, wedge-tailed eagle, wedgie, white-breasted sea-eagle, windhover

17. AUSTRALASIAN OCEAN BIRDS: Adelie penguin, Australian gannet, booby, crested tern, darter, diving petrel, fairy penguin, fairy prion, fairy tern, frigatebird, fulmar, gannet, gull, jaeger, king mutton-bird, korora *(N.Z.)*, larine, little penguin, little tern, mallemuck, Mother Carey's chicken, mutton-bird, oystercatcher, penguin, petrel, prion, sea-swallow, seagull, shearwater, short-tailed shearwater, silver gull, skua, sooty shearwater, stinker, storm-petrel, takapu *(N.Z.)*, Tasmanian mutton-bird, tropic bird, wandering albatross, Wilson's petrel

18. AUSTRALASIAN SHORE BIRDS: beach stone curlew, cob, curlew, dotterel, eastern curlew, godwit, greenshank, grey plover, knot, kuaka *(N.Z.)*, little whimbrel, red-necked stint, reedwarbler, sanderling, sandpiper, snipe, sooty oystercatcher, southern stone curlew, stint, stone-curlew, tattler, thick-knee, turnstone, wader, wading bird, whimbrel

19. AUSTRALASIAN WATER BIRDS: bald coot, baldyhead, banded landrail, bittern, black duck, black swan, blue crane, blue duck *(N.Z.)*, brown bittern, Cape Barren goose, coot, cormorant, crane, dabchick, didapper, diver, duck, dusky moorhen, egret, gallinule, goose, great crested grebe, grebe, greenhead, heron, ibis, jabiru, landrail, loom, loon, magpie goose, marsh hen, moorhen, nankeen night heron, night heron, paradise duck *(N.Z.)*, pelican, pied goose, policeman bird, shag, shoveler, snakebird, spoonbill, spotted crake, stilt, stork, swamphen, swan, water rail, water-crake, waterhen, white-eyed duck, white-faced heron, wood duck

20. INTRODUCED AUSTRALIAN BIRDS: blackbird, bulbul, Common myna, house sparrow, Indian Myna, mallard, ostrich, quail, skylark, spadger, spag, sparrow, spotted turtledove, starling, tree sparrow

21. BIRDS (GENERAL): accentor, accipiter, Adelie penguin, adjutant bird, aigrette, alarm bird, albatross, amadavat, American eagle, Andean condor, anhinga, ani, archangel, argus, auk, auklet, avocet, axebird, babbler, bald coot, bald eagle, banana-bird, banded landrail, banded tintac, barb, barbet, barebelly, barn owl, barn swallow, barnacle goose, bateleur eagle, bearded tit, bearded vulture, beccafico, bee-eater, bell magpie, bird of peace, bird of prey, black cuckoo, black grouse, blackbird, blackcap, blackhead, blightbird, blue crane, blue-winged teal, bluebird, bluecap, bluetit, boatbill, bobolink, booby, brain-fever bird, brambling, brant goose, brent, broad-billed roller, broadbill, brown owl, bufflehead, bulbul, bullbat, bullfinch, bunting, burrowing owl, bushtit, bustard, butcher bird, butterball, buzzard, cacique, cagebird, California condor, Canada goose, canary, canvasback, Cape Sparrow, Cape wren-warbler, capercailzie, caracara, cardinal, carrier, carrier pigeon, carrion crow, catbird, caterpillar-eater, chaffinch, channel-billed cuckoo, chanticleer, chaparral cock, chat, chatterer, chick, chickadee, chicken, chipping sparrow, chook, chough, cliff swallow, cob, cock, cock sparrow, cock-of-the-rock, cockatoo, cocky, coly, condor, conure, coot, corbie *(Scot.)*, cormorant, corncrake, cotinga, coucal, courser, cowbird, crake, crane, crested flycatcher, crested tern, crocodile bird, cropper, crossbill, crow, crow blackbird, cuckoo, culver *(Poetic)*, curassow, curlew, dabchick, darter, daw, demoiselle, didapper, dipper, diver, diving petrel, dodo, dollar bird, dotterel, dove, dovekie, drongo, duck, duckhawk, duckling, duiker, dunlin, dunnock, dusky moorhen, eagle, eagle owl, eaglet, eared owl, eastern curlew, egret, eider, emperor penguin, erne, eyas, fairy prion, falcon, falcon-gentle, falconet, fantail, finch, firebird, firecrest, firetail, flycatcher, fowl, francolin, frigatebird, fringilline, fulmar, gallinacean, gallinule, game bird, game fowl, gamecock, gander, gannet, garden warbler, garefowl, gerfalcon, glaucous gull, goatsucker, gobbler, godwit, goldcrest, golden eagle, golden pheasant, golden-headed cisticola, goldfinch, goliath heron, goony bird *(U.S.)*, goosander, goose, goshawk, grass parrot, grass-finch, grassbird, great auk, great crested grebe, great white heron, grebe, green plover, greenfinch, greenhead, greenshank, grey duck, grey parrot, grey plover, griffon, grosbeak, ground owl, grouse, guacharo, guan, guillemot, guinea, guinea hen, guineafowl, gull, gyrfalcon, hadada, halcyon, hamerkop, hammerhead, hangbird, harlequin duck, harpy eagle, harrier, hawk, hawk-owl, hedge-sparrow, hen, heron, herring gull, hoatzin, hobby *(Archaic)*, homer, homing pigeon, honey buzzard, honey-guide, honey-sucker, honeyeater, hoopoe, hornbill, house martin, house sparrow, hummingbird, ibis, Indian myna, Indian runner duck, indigo bunting, ivory gull, jabiru, jacamar, jackdaw, jacksnipe, jacobin, jaeger, Java sparrow, jay, jungle fowl, keet, kelly, kestrel, king mutton-bird, kinglet, kite, kittiwake, knot, koel, lammergeyer, landrail, lanner, lanneret, lapwing, larine, lark, leucosticte, limpkin, linnet, lintwhite *(Scot.)*, little auk, little greenshank, loggerhead, loggerhead shrike, loom, loon, lorikeet, lory, lourie, lovebird, macaw, magpie, mallard, mallemuck, man-o'-war bird, manakin, mandarin duck, marabou, marsh harrier, marsh hen, martin, martlet, meadow lark, merle *(Scot. Poetic)*, mew, missel thrush, mockingbird, monkey-faced owl, moorhen, mosquito hawk, mossie, Mother Carey's chicken, motmot, mound bird, mousebird, murre, murrelet, musket, mutton-bird, night heron, night raven, night-bird, nighthawk, nightingale, nightjar, noddy, Numidian crane, nutcracker, nuthatch, oilbird, old squaw, oldwife, oriole, ortolan, osprey, ostrich, ouzel, owl, oxpecker, oystercatcher, parrot, partridge, pastor, peaceful dove, peacock, peafowl, peahen, pecker, peetweet *(U.S.)*, pelican, pen, penguin, percher, peregrine, peregrine falcon, petrel, pewit, phalarope, pheasant, philomel *(Poetic)*, pie, pigeon, pigeon-hawk, pileated woodpecker, pipit, plantain-eater, plover, poll, popinjay, pouter, prairie chicken, pratincole, prion, ptarmigan, puffin, pyrrhuloxia, quail, quetzal, rail, raptor, raven, razorbill, red-backed sandpiper, red-necked stint, redbill, redbreast, redpoll, redshank, redstart, redwing, reedbird, reedling, reedwarbler, reeve, rhea, Richard's pipit, ring ouzel, ring-necked pheasant, ringdove, roadrunner, robin, robin redbreast, rock hopper, rock thrush, rock-dove, rockjumper, roller, rook, rookery, ruff, sacred ibis, sacred kingfisher, saddlebill, saker, sand-grouse, sand-martin, sanderling, sandpiper, sawbill, scaup duck, scoter, screamer, screech owl, sea-duck, sea-eagle, sea-hawk, sea-lark, sea-mew, sea-snipe, sea-swallow, seabird, seafowl, seagull, secretary bird, sedge warbler, seed-eater, seriema, serin, shag, shearwater, sheathbill, sheldrake, shelduck, shoebill, shorebird, short-tailed shearwater, shovelbill, shrike, shrike-tit, sicklebill, silver gull, silver-eye, singer, siskin, skimmer, skua, skylark, smew, snakebird, snipe, snow goose, snow-bunting, snowy owl, solan, song thrush, sooty shearwater, spadger, spag, sparrow, sparrowhawk, spoonbill, spotted turtledove, squab, starling, stilt, stinker, stint, stock dove, stone-curlew, stone-marten, stork, storm-cock, storm-petrel, sugarbird, sultana bird, sun-bittern, sunbird, swallow, swamphen, swan, swift, swordbill, syrinx, tailorbird, tanager, tang, tattler, teal, tercel, tern, thick-knee, thrasher, throstle, thrush, tick-bird, tinamou, tinktinkie, tit, titlark, titmouse, tody, topknot, toucan, touraco, tragopan, tree sparrow, treecreeper, triller, trochilus, trogon, tropic bird, troupial, trumpet bird, trumpeter, tumbler, turkey buzzard, turnstone, turtledove, umbrella bird, vulture, wader, wading bird, wagtail, wall creeper, wandering albatross, warbler, water rail, water-crake, water-ouzel, water-pipit, water-wagtail, waterbird, waterfowl, waterhen, wax-eye, waxbill, waxwing, weaver, weaverbird, weep, whimbrel, whippoorwill, whistler, whistling swan, white-eye, white-eyed duck, white-faced heron, whitethroat, whooper, whydah, widgeon, widowbird, wild goose, wildfowl, willet, willow warbler, Wilson's petrel, windhover, wood duck, wood ibis, wood swallow, woodchat, woodcock, woodgrouse, woodlark, woodpecker, woodpigeon, wren, wryneck, yellowbird, yellowhammer

22. AUSTRALASIAN LIZARDS: bearded dragon, bearded lizard, bicycle lizard, black rock skink, black skink, blue-tongue, blue-tongue lizard, bobtail lizard, bungarra, Burton's legless lizard, Cunningham's skink, double-ender, dtella, frill-necked lizard, frilled dragon, frilled lizard, frillie, garden lizard, giant skink, goanna, Gould's goanna, ground goanna, illchiljera, jacky lizard, jew lizard, knob-tailed gecko, lace monitor, land mullet, moloch, mountain devil, Myall snake, perentie, pine-cone lizard, sand goanna, scaly foot, sleepy lizard, stump-tailed skink, sun lizard, thorn devil, thorn lizard, tree dragon, tree goanna, water dragon; tuatara

23. NON-AUSTRALIAN LIZARDS: agama, amphisbaena, anole, basilisk, blindworm, bloodsucker, chameleon, chelonian, chuckwalla, cockatrice *(Bible)*, cycling lizard, draco lizard, dragon *(Rare)*, fence lizard, flying dragon, flying lizard, gecko, Gila monster, glass snake, horned toad, iguana, iguanid, iguanodon, komodo dragon, lacertilian, lance-head lizard, legless lizard, lizard, monitor, sand-lizard, scincoid, skink, slow-worm, snake-lizard, swift, three-toed skink, tokay, varan

24. AUSTRALASIAN SNAKES: Schneider python, amethystine python, bandy-bandy, black snake, black-headed python, blind snake, blindworm, blue-bellied black snake, broad-headed snake, brown snake, carpet snake, coral snake, deaf adder, death adder, diamond snake, dugite, fierce snake, gwardar, mallee snake, mulga snake, myall snake, night tiger, red-bellied black snake, rock python, salt-bush snake, snake-eater, spotted black snake, taipan, tarpot, tiger snake, water-snake, woma

25. NON-AUSTRALIAN SNAKES: adder, anaconda, asp, aspic, banded sea-snake, boa, boa constrictor, bushmaster, Cape cobra, constrictor, copperhead, cottonmouth, diamondback, elapid, fer-de-lance, gopher, grass snake, harlequin, herald snake, hognose snake, hoop snake, horned viper, king cobra, king snake, krait, mamba, massasauga, moccasin, ophidian, pit viper, puff adder, python, rattle, rattler, rattlesnake, ringed sea-snake, ringhals, serpent, sidewinder, spitting snake, viper, whip snake, worm snake

26. AUSTRALASIAN TORTOISES: long-necked tortoise, saw-tooth tortoise, snake-necked tortoise, ware, water tortoise

27. NON-AUSTRALIAN TORTOISES: chelonian, green turtle, hawk's-bill, leatherback, leathery turtle, loggerhead, loggerhead turtle, luth, matamata, mud turtle, snapper, snapping turtle, soft-shelled turtle, terrapin, tortoise *(U.S.)*, turtle

28. CROCODILES: alligator, caiman, croc, crocodile, crocodilian, garial, gavial, mugger

29. AMPHIBIA: aglossa, amphibian, anuran, arrow-poison frog, axolotl, batrachian, bufo, bullfrog, caecilian, cane toad, congo snake, dendrobates, escuerzo, frog, frogspawn, goliath frog, mud puppy, natterjack, newt, pipa, platanna, polliwog, rana, salamander, siren, Surinam toad, taddie, tadpole, toad, tongueless frog, tree frog, triton, xenopus

30. FISH: John Dory, acanthopterygian *(Palaeontol.)*, albacore, alevin, amberjack, anabantid, anabas, anchovy, anemone fish, angelfish, angler, arapaima, archerfish, armed bullhead, Australian salmon, bald-fish, ballahoo, barb, barbel, barra, barracouta, barracuda, barramundi, bass, batfish, bay trout *(Vic.)*, beardie, beluga, belut, bichir, billfish, black bass, black bream, black drummer, black king-fish, black perch, blackfish, bleak, blenny, blindfish, blowfish, blue-eye, blue-throated parrot fish, bluecap, bluefin tuna, bluefish, bluegill, bluenose, boarfish, bonefish, bonito, bony bream, bowfin, box fish, bream, brill, brisling, brit, broadbill, brown trout, brown-banded mullet, bull-trout, bullhead, bullrout, bullseye, bully mullet, bumble-bee, burbot, butterfish, butterfly cod, butterfly fish, callop, candlefish, capelin, carangid, carp, cat, catfish, cavally, ceratodus, cero, char, characin, cichlid, cisco, climbing perch, clingfish, clownfish, clupeid, coalfish, cobbler, cockney bream, cod, codfish, codling, coelacanth, conger, conger eel, congolli, coral trout, coralfish, count-fish, couta, cowfish, crossopterygian, cuckoo wrasse, cyprinid, cyprinodont, dab,

dace, damselfish, darkie, dart, dealfish, Derwent smelt, dewfish, dhufish, diamond fish, dipnoan, doctor fish, dog-tooth tuna, doggie, dolphin, dory, dragonet, drum, drummer, eel, eelpout, electric eel, elver, emperor, eulachon, fantail, fighting fish, filefish, fishing frog, flat *(N.Z. Colloq.)*, flat-tail mullet, flatfish, flathead, flattie, flounder, fluke, flying fish, flying gurnard, fortescue, four-eyes, freshwater bream, freshwater flathead, freshwater herring, frogfish, gadid, gadoid, galaxias, game fish, gar, garfish, garpike, gemfish, giant perch, gilthead, globefish, goatfish, goby, golden perch, goldfish, gouramy, grayling, greenbone *(N.Z.)*, grenadier, grilse, groper, grouper, grunt, grunter, gudgeon, gunnel, guppy, gurnard, haddock, hake, halfbeak, halibut, hapuku, harder, herring, herring cale, hogfish, horse mackerel, houting, inanga *(N.Z.)*, jack, jackass fish, jackfish, javelin fish, jewelfish, jewfish, jollytail, kabeljou, kahawai *(N.Z.)*, kelpfish, killifish, king barracouta, king of the herrings, kingfish, labroid, lake herring, lancet fish, lantern-fish, latchet, launce, lax, leatherjacket, lemon sole, ling, lizard fish, loach, long tom, luce, luderick *(Aborig.)*, lumpfish, lumpsucker, lungfish, mackerel, mado, mangrove Jack, marble fish, marlin, meagre, menhaden, milkfish, miller's thumb, minnow, mirror carp, mirror dory, moki *(N.Z.)*, molly, mooneye, moonfish, moorish idol, moray, morwong, mudskipper, mullet, mulloway, Murray cod, Murray perch, nannygai, native trout, needlefish, nigger, oarfish, opah, ox-eye herring, paddlefish, paradise fish, parore *(N.Z.)*, parr, parrotfish, patiki *(N.Z.)*, pearl perch, peppermint cod, perch, pickerel, pig drummer, pigfish, pike, pike eel, pike-perch, pilchard, pillie, pilot fish, pipefish, piranha, plaice, poddy mullet, pogge, pollack, pompano, pope, porae *(N.Z.)*, porcupine fish, pout, powan, puffer, pumpkin-seed, Queensland halibut, Queensland kingfish, Queensland lungfish, Queensland trumpeter, rainbow trout, red emperor, red mullet, red rock cod, redfin, redfish, remora, ribbonfish, river blackfish, roach, robalo, rock blackfish, rock cod, rock-bass, rock-hopper, rockling, roughie, rudd, ruff, ruffe, sailfish, saithe, salmon, salmon catfish, salmon trout, samlet, samson fish, sand trout, sand-dab, sand-eel, sand-launce, saratoda, sardine, sauger, saury, scabbard fish, scalare, schnapper, school mackerel, sciaenoid, scorpion-fish, scrod *(U.S.)*, sculpin, sea mullet, sea perch, sea pike, sea-bass, sea-bream, sea-cock, sea-dragon, sea-fox, sea-raven, sea-scorpion, sea-trout, sea-wife, sea-wolf, seahorse, sergeant baker, sergeant fish, serranoid, shad, sheatfish, shiner, Siamese fighting fish, sild, silurid, silver belly, silverfish, skipjack, sleepy cod, smelt, smolt, snapper, snoek, snook, snub-nosed dart, sockeye, sole, Spanish mackerel, sparid, sparling, spearfish, spinefoot, spoonbill, sportfish, spotted mackerel, sprat, springer, squeteague, squire, squirrelfish, stargazer, stickleback, stinkfish *(S.A.)*, stone-bass, stonefish, stranger, sturgeon, sucker, suckerfish, sunfish, surgeon, surgeonfish, surmullet, sweep, sweetlips, swellfish, swordfish, swordtail, tailor, tandan, tang, tarpon, tarwhine, Tasmanian kingfish, tassel-fish, tautog, taylor, tench, teraglin, terakihi *(N.Z.)*, tetra, threadfin, tigerfish, tilefish, tinker, toadfish, toado, toady, tommy ruff, top minnow, topknot, torsk, trevalla, trevally, triggerfish, tripletail, trout, trumpet-fish, trumpeter, trunkfish, tuna, tunny, tupong *(Aborig.)*, turbot, turrum, tusk fish, vendace, wahoo, walleye, weever, whitebait, whitefish, wirra, witch, wolf, wolf-fish, wollomai, wrasse, Yarra herring, yellow jack, yellow mullet, yellow-belly, yellowfin tuna, yellowtail, yellowtail kingfish, zebra-fish

31. SHARKS AND RAYS: angel shark, angelfish, basking shark, blue pointer, blue shark, bronze whaler, bull-head shark, carpet shark, cat's-eye, chimaera, chub, devil ray, devilfish, dog shark, dogfish, elasmobranch, electric ray, ghost shark, grey nurse shark, gummy shark, hammerhead, Joan of Arc *(Colloq.)*, leopard shark, mackerel shark, mako, manta, manta ray, monkfish, Noahs *(Colloq.)*, numbfish, nurse shark, porbeagle, Port Jackson shark, rabbit-fish, ray, saw shark, sawfish, school shark, selachian, seven-gill shark, shovel-nose ray, skate, stingaree, stingray, thrasher, thresher, tiger shark, torpedo, whale shark, whaler shark, white pointer, white shark, wobbegong, zebra shark

32. AGNATHA: ammocete, borer, cyclostome, hag, hagfish, lamper eel, lamprey, mulgara, rosella *(Colloq.)*

33. CHORDATES – PROTOCHORDATES: hemichordate, TUNICATES: ascidian, cunjevoi, salpa, sea-squirt; LANCELETS: amphioxus, cephalochordate

34. ECHINODERMS – SEA-LILIES: crinite, crinoid, encrinite, feather-star, sea-fan, sea-feather, sea-lily; STARFISH: asteroid, asteroidean, crown-of-thorns starfish, star, starfish; BRITTLE STARS: brittle-star; URCHINS: echinoid, echinus, kina, sand-dollar, sea-hedgehog, sea-urchin; SEA CUCUMBERS: beche-de-mer, holothurian, sea-cucumber, trepang

35. MANDIBULATA – CRUSTACEA: Balmain bug, amphipod, anomuran, banana prawn, barnacle, beach flea, blue manna, blue swimmer, bluey, brachyuran, branchiopod, cirriped, coconut crab, copepod, crab, crawbob, crawchie *(Qld)*, crawfish *(U.S.)*, cray, craybob, crayfish, crustacean, cuttlefish, decapod, euphausiasiid, fairy shrimp, fiddler crab, fish-louse, frog crab, ghost nipper, gilgie *(W.A.)*, gribble, hermit crab, isopod, isopodan, king crab, king prawn, kingie, krill, land crab, lobby *(Qld)*, lobster, macruran, malacostracan, mantis crab, marron, Moreton Bay bug, mud crab, opossum shrimp, oyster-crab, pagurian, pea crab, phyllopod, prawn, robber crab, sand crab, sandflea, sandhopper, sandie, schizopod, school prawn, schoolie, sea crayfish, shellfish, shovel-nosed lobster, shrimp, slater, soft-shelled crab, soldier crab, sowbug *(U.S.)*, spanner crab, spider crab, spiny lobster, squilla, stomatopod, tiger prawn, trilobite, water-flea, wood-borer, woodlouse, yabby; CENTIPEDES: centipede, chilopod, daddy-long-legs, house centipede, myriapod; MILLIPEDES: diplopod, millipede, myriapod, wireworm

36. INSECTS: alderfly, Amazon ant, ambrosia, ant-lion, aphid, Argentine ant, army ant, assassin bug, bedbug, bee, beef ant, bloodworm, blue ant, booklouse, bookworm, borer, bot, breeze, bristletail, bug, bull ant, bull Joe, bulldog ant, bumblebee, butcher's canary, caddice fly, caddis worm, carpenter bee, chalcid fly, chat, chigoe, chinch bug, chironomid, cicada hunter, cimex, click beetle, coccid, cochineal, cockroach, collembolan, cootie, cottony-cushion scale, crablouse, cricket, cuckoo-spit, culex, culicid, damsel fly, dayfly, demoiselle, devil's darning needle, dor, dragonfly, driver ant, drone, dun, earwig, ephemera, ephemerid, ergate, field cricket, firebrat, flea, flower wasp, froghopper, gall midge, gall wasp, gallfly, gnat, grasshopper, greenhead, grub, haustellum, hive bee, honeybee, hornet, horntail, horse-stinger, humblebee, hymenopteron, ichneumon, ichneumon fly, insect, isopteran, jumper ant, jumping plant louse, katydid, lac insect, lacewing, leaf-hopper, locust, longicorn, louse, maggot, mantis, Maori beetle *(N.Z.)*, mason bee, mason wasp, mayfly, mealworm, mealy bug, meat ant, midge, miller, mole cricket, mound ant, mud dauber, mud eye, myrmecophile, naiad, nit, nymph, orthopteron, phylloxera, pisser, pisswhacker, plague locust, plant-louse, policeman fly, pond-skater, praying mantis, psyllid, pupa, queen, roach, Rutherglen bug, sandflea, sawfly, scale insect, scorpion-fly, silverfish, skater, skipper, slave-ant, soldier, soldier ant, spittle insect, springtail, squeaker, stick insect, stonefly, swarm, sweat bee, termite, thrips, thynnid, thysanuran, vespid, walking-stick *(N.Z. Colloq.)*, wasp, water-boatman, water-scorpion, water-strider, wax-insect, white ant, wingless grasshopper, wood ant, woodworm, worker, yellow jacket, zygopteran

37. AUSTRALASIAN INSECTS: awheto, coon bug, cotton-feed bug, emperor gum moth, Hexham grey, honey-pot ant, huhu *(N.Z.)*, kootchar, magnetic termite, pink bollworm, taipo *(N.Z.)*, thynnid, vedalia, weta *(N.Z.)*, witchetty

38. MOTHS AND BUTTERFLIES: admiral, army worm, Atlas moth, bag moth, bagworm, bardy, bee-moth, bentwing swift moth, blue fanny, blue triangle, bogong, bollworm, bombycid, brimstone, burnet, burnet moth, butterfly, cabbage butterfly, cabbage moth, cabbage white butterfly, cabbage worm, cacto, cactoblastis, Camberwell beauty, cankerworm, case moth, caseworm, caterpillar, chrysalid, chrysalis, cinnabar, clothes moth, codling moth, comma butterfly, corn earworm *(U.S.)*, cup moth, cutworm, death's-head moth, diamondback moth, double-headed hawk, egger, emperor moth, flutter-by, forester, fritillary, geometrid, ghost moth, giant wood moth, gipsy moth, grayling, ground beetle, hairstreak, hawkmoth, hepialid, hornworm, hummingbird moth, inchworm, Io moth, lepidopteron, looper, luna moth, measuring worm, meloid, monarch, moth, mountain blue butterfly, mourning cloak, noctuid, nymphalid, painted applemoth, painted lady, pyralid, red admiral, saturniid, satyr, Saunder's case moth, silkworm, skipper, sphinx-moth, spitfire, sting moth, swallowtail, swift moth, tent caterpillar, tineid moth, tortoiseshell, tussock moth, Ulysses butterfly, wanderer, wax-moth, whistling moth, white, white admiral, woolly bear

39. BEETLES: bardy, ambrosia beetle, bark beetle, bee-beetle, beetle, black beetle, blister beetle, boll weevil, bombardier beetle, borer, buprestid, burying beetle, cadelle, cane-beetle, cantharid, carpet beetle, chafer, clavicorn, click beetle, cockchafer, coleopteron, Colorado beetle, curculio, deathwatch beetle, diamond beetle, dorbeetle, dung beetle, elaterid, fiddle-back, fiddler beetle, firefly, flea-beetle, glow-worm, goldsmith beetle, jewel beetle, June bug, kurrajong-pod beetle, ladybird, lamellicorn, lightning bug, pie-dish beetle, potato beetle, rhinoceros beetle, rove-beetle, scarab, scarabaeid, snapping beetle, snout-beetle, soldier beetle, Spanish fly, stag-beetle, tiger beetle, water-beetle, whirligig beetle, wireworm

40. FLIES etc.: aedes, anopheles, bee-fly, bee-killer, beetfly, black fly, blowfly, blowie, blue-arsed fly, bluebottle, botfly, bush fly, cabbage fly, cleg, cranefly, daddy-long-legs, drosophila, flesh-fly, flies, fly, fruit-fly, fungus fly, gadfly, glow-worm, greenfly, Hessian fly, horsefly, housefly, hoverfly, march fly, mosquito, mozzie, muscid, robber fly, sandfly, sandie, screw-worm, sheep tick, skeeter, syrphid, tabanid, tachina fly, tsetse fly, vinegar fly, warble fly

41. CHELICERATA – HORSESHOE CRABS: eurypterid, horseshoe crab, king crab, limuloid, limulus, xiphosuran; SPIDERS etc.: acarid, acaridan, arachnid, bird-eating spider, bird-spider, black house spider, black widow, book scorpion, brown spider, cattle tick, cheese mite, chigger, crab spider, daddy-long-legs, diadem spider, fiddle-back, funnel-web, harvest mite, harvest tick, harvester, harvestman, house centipede, huntsman, itch mite, jigger, jockey spider, jumping spider, katipo, ked, mite, money spider, mouse spider, orb-weaver, red mite, red-back spider, redbug *(U.S.)*, retiarius spider, scorpion, St Andrew's Cross spider, tarantula, tick, trapdoor spider, triantelope, vinegarroon, water-spider, whip scorpion, white-tailed spider, wolf spider; SEASPIDERS: sea-spider

42. ANNELIDS – TUBE WORMS: baitworm, beachworm, bluey, bungum worm, carbora *(Obs.)*, chaetopod, feather-worm, giant beachworm, hairy Mary, kingie, kingworm, lob, lobworm, lug, lugworm, palolo worm, polychaete, sandworm, sea-mouse, tube worm, wiry, wood-borer; EARTHWORMS: angleworm, annelid, brandling, chaetopod, earthworm, oligochaete, sipunculid, slimy, worm; LEECHES: bloodsucker, Hirudinea, horseleech, leech; ONYCHOPHORA: onychophoran, peripatus

43. MOLLUSCS – CHITONS: chiton, mollusc, pteropod; SNAILS etc.: abalone, australwink, cockle, cockleshell, conch, cone shell, cowry, dogwhelk, drill, ear fish, gastropod, Glavert's land snail, keyhole limpet, limpet, murex, mutton-fish, nudibranch, opisthobranch, paua *(N.Z.)*, periwinkle, pulmonate, sea hare, sea-butterfly, sea-ear, sea-lemon, shellfish, slug, snail, tooth shell, towershell, triton, trochus, volute, wentletrap, whelk, winkle; OYSTERS etc.: cherry-stone, clam, clamshell, lamellibranch, mussel, oyster, pearl oyster, piddock, pipi, razorshell, rock oyster, scallop, shipworm, spat, Tasmanian scallop, teredo, toheroa, ugari, univalve, wood-borer; OCTOPUS etc.: ammonite, argonaut, blue-ringed octopus, cephalopod, decapod, devilfish, dibranchiate, nautilus, octopod, octopus, paper nautilus, pearly nautilus, sepia, spirula, squid

44. BRACHIOPODA: brachiopod, lamp-shell, lophophore

45. ECTOPROCTA: bryozoan, lophophore, polyzoan, retepore, seamoss

46. PLATYHELMINTHES – FREE-LIVING FLATWORMS: flatworm, planarian, platyhelminth, turbellarian; FLUKES: bilharzia, cercaria, fluke, liver fluke, redia, trematode; TAPEWORMS: bladder worm, cestode, cysticercoid, hydatid, stomach worm, taenia, tapeworm; NEMERTEA: nemertean, ribbon worm; ACANTHOCEPHALA: acanthocephalan; ASCHELMINTHES – ROTIFERS etc.: gastrotrich, rotifer, tardigrade; NEMATODES: ascarid, eelworm, filaria, gapeworm, guinea worm, heartworm, hookworm, kidney worm, lungworm, nemathelminth, nematode, pinworm, roundworm, stomach worm, strongyle, threadworm, trichina, vinegar eel, wheatworm, whipworm, wireworm; HORSEHAIR WORMS: hairworm

47. CTENOPHORES: comb jelly, ctenophore, sea-gooseberry, Venus's girdle

48. COELENTERATES – ANEMONES: actinia, alcyonarian, anemone, anthozoan, bloodsucker, sea waratah, sea-anemone, sea-feather, sea-pen, sertularian, waratah anemone; SOFT CORALS: dead men's fingers, gorgonian, sea-fan; HARD CORALS: coral, coralline, gorgonian, madrepore, millepore, stony coral; JELLYFISH: hydra, hydroid, hydromedusa, hydrozoan, jelly blubber, jellyfish, medusa, medusan, polyp, Portuguese man-of-war, scyphozoan, velella; BLUEBOTTLES: Portuguese man-of-war, bluebottle, by-the-wind sailor, man-of-war, sallee rover, siphonophore; SEA WASPS etc.: box jellyfish, marine stinger, sea wasp

49. PROTOZOA – AMOEBAE: amoeba, endamoeba, foraminifer, heliozoan, nummulite, protozoan; CILIATES: ciliate, paramecium; SPOROZOA: gregarine, sporozoan; FLAGELLATES: flagellate, noctiluca, trichomonad, vorticella; SPONGES: sponge

50. DINOSAURS: brachiosaur, brontosaurus, dinosaur, diplodocus, ichthyosaur, megalosaur, megalosaurian, ornithopod, plesiosaur, pterodactyl, sauropod, stegosaur, titanosaurus, triceratops, tyrannosaurus; FOSSIL BIRDS: archaeopteryx, ichthyornis, teratorn

Matter

The elements 1
Imaginary substances 2
Elementary particles 3
Acids 4
Common compounds 5
Biochemicals 6
Salts 7
Minerals and ores 8
Igneous rocks 9
Metamorphic rocks 9
Sedimentary rocks 9
Gemstones 10
Ornamental stones 10

1. THE ELEMENTS: 1. Hydrogen (H), 2. Helium (He), 3. Lithium (Li), 4. Beryllium (Be), 5. Boron (B), 6. Carbon (C), 7. Nitrogen (N), 8. Oxygen (O), 9. Fluorine (F), 10. Neon (Ne), 11. Sodium (Na – natrium), 12. Magnesium (Mg), 13. Aluminium (Al), 14. Silicon (Si), 15. Phosphorus (P), 16. Sulphur (S), 17. Chlorine (Cl), 18. Argon (Ar), 19. Potassium (K – kalium), 20. Calcium (Ca), 21. Scandium (Sc), 22. Titanium (Ti), 23. Vanadium (V), 24. Chromium (Cr), 25. Manganese (Mn), 26. Iron (Fe – ferrum), 27. Cobalt (Co), 28. Nickel (Ni), 29. Copper (Cu – cuprum), 30. Zinc (Zn), 31. Gallium (Ga), 32. Germanium (Ge), 33. Arsenic (As), 34. Selenium (Se), 35. Bromine (Br), 36. Krypton (Kr), 37. Rubidium (Rb), 38. Strontium (Sr), 39. Yttrium (Y), 40. Zirconium (Zr), 41. Niobium (Nb), 42. Molybdenum (Mo), 43. Technetium (Tc), 44. Ruthenium (Ru), 45. Rhodium (Rh), 46. Palladium (Pd), 47. Silver (Ag – argentum), 48. Cadmium (Cd), 49. Indium (In), 50. Tin (Sn – stannum), 51. Antimony (Sb – stibium), 52. Tellurium (Te), 53. Iodine (I), 54. Xenon (Xe), 55. Caesium (Cs), 56. Barium (Ba), 57. Lanthanum (La), 58. Cerium (Ce), 59. Praseodymium (Pr), 60. Neodymium (Nd), 61. Promethium (Pm), 62. Samarium (Sm), 63. Europium (Eu), 64. Gadolinium (Gd), 65. Terbium (Tb), 66. Dysprosium (Dy), 67. Holmium (Ho), 68. Erbium (Er), 69. Thulium (Tm), 70. Ytterbium (Tb), 71. Lutetium (Lu), 72. Hafnium (Hf), 73. Tantalum (Ta), 74. Tungsten (W – Wolfram), 75. Rhenium (Re), 76. Osmium (Os), 77. Iridium (Ir), 78. Platinum (Pt), 79. Gold (Au – aurum), 80. Mercury (Hg – hydrargyrum), 81. Thallium (Tl), 82. Lead (Pb – plumbum), 83. Bismuth (Bi), 84. Polonium (Po), 85. Astatine (At), 86. Radon (Rn), 87. Francium (Fr), 88. Radium (Ra), 89. Actinium (Ac), 90. Thorium (Th), 91. Protactinium (Pa), 92. Uranium (U), 93. Neptunium (Np), 94. Plutonium (Pu), 95. Americium (Am), 96. Curium (Cm), 97. Berkelium (Bk), 98. Californium (Cf), 99. Einsteinium (Es), 100. Fermium (Fm), 101. Mendelevium (Md), 102. Nobelium (No), 103. Lawrencium (Lw), 104. Rutherfordium (Rf), 105. Hahnium (Ha); OBSOLETE NAMES FOR ELEMENTS, argent, azote, brimstone, columbium, silicium, Venus

2. IMAGINARY SUBSTANCES, elixir, ether, kryptonite, philosopher's stone, phlogiston

3. ELEMENTARY PARTICLE, alpha particle, antineutrino, antineutron, antiparticle, antiproton, baryon, beta particle, delayed neutron, deuteron, electron, fast neutron, fermion, graviton, hadron, hyperon, K-meson, kaon, meson, negatron, neutretto, neutrino, neutron, nucleon, nucleor, orbital electron, photomeson, photoneutron, photoproton, pimeson, pion, positron, positronium, prompt neutron, proton, quark, slow neutron, strange particle, tachyon, thermal neutron, triton

4. ACIDS: acetic acid, aqua fortis, aqua regia, boric acid, carbolic acid, carbonic acid, carboxylic acid, chromic acid, citric acid, cyanuric acid, disulphuric acid, dithionic acid, dithionous acid, fatty acid, fluorophosphoric acid, fluorosilicic acid, formic acid, glacial acetic acid, hydrochloric acid, nitric acid, Nordhausen acid, perchloric acid, perchromic acid, peroxyacid, silicic acid, spirits of salt, suberic acid, sulphuric acid, sulphuric ether, tartaric acid, xylic acid; ALKALIS: ammonia, aqua ammoniae, calcium hydroxide, caustic, caustic potash, caustic soda, spirits of hartshorn

5. COMMON COMPOUNDS: acetone, acetaldehyde, alcohol, alum, alumina, ammonia, amyl nitrite, arsenic, benzene, borax, calcium carbonate, calcium chloride, camphor, carbamide, carbohydrate, carbon dioxide, carbon monoxide, carbon silicide, carbon tetrachloride, carbonic acid gas, carborundum, cellulose, cellulose nitrate, chloroform, creosote, cresol, dextrose, dichlorodifluoromethane, dichlorodiphenyltrichloroethane (DDT), dichloromethane, dicyandiamide, diphenylamine, dripstone, epoxy, ethanal, ethanol, ethanolamine, ethene, ether, ethine, ethyl acetate, ethyl alcohol, ethyl ether, ethylene, ethylene glycol, ferric oxide, ferrite, fluorescein, fluorocarbon, formaldehyde, formalin, freon, gas black, gas carbon, gelatine, guanidine, lime, methane, naphtha, naphthalene, nitrous oxide, oxalate, oxalic acid, peroxide, potash, silicon carbide, silicone, silver bromide, silver chloride, silver iodide, tartrazine, toluene, trichloroacetic acid, tungsten carbide, urea, urea formaldehyde, vitriol, washing soda, zein, zinc chloride, zinc oxide

6. BIOCHEMICALS: adenosine triphosphate (ATP), adrenalin, alphahelix, amino acid, arginine, carbohydrate, catecholamine, chlorophyll, cholesterol, creatine, cystine, cytochrome, cytosine, deoxyribonucleic acid (DNA), diethylstilboestrol, dopa, enzyme, enzymogen, epinephrine, flavin adenine dinucleotide, flavin mononucleotide, guanosine, haemoglobin, hormone, lipid, noradrenaline, peptide, peptone, phenylalanine, phospholipid, protein, ribonucleic acid (RNA), steroid, thymine, tyrosine, valine

7. SALTS: carbonate, amine, carbide, carbonyl, carboxyl group, chlorate, chloride, chlorite, chromate, diazonium salts, dichromate, dioxide, disulphate, disulphide, ester, ether, fluoride, formate, oxide, perchlorate, peroxide, silicide, sulphate, sulphide

8. MINERALS AND ORES, adularia, aegerite, albite, allanite, allophane, alumina, alunite, amber potch, amblygonite, amianthus, amphibole, analcite, anatase, apophyllite, aragonite, argentite, arsenopyrite, asbestos, azurite, bandstone, barytes, bauxite, bay salt, biotite, blackfellow's button, blackjack, blende, blue asbestos, boracite, bornite, bort, bournonite, braunite, brocatelle, calamine *(U.S.)*, calaverite, calcine, calcite, calcspar, calx, carbonado, carnallite, cassiterite, celestite, cerargyrite, chabazite, chalcedony, chiastolite, chlorargyrite, chlorite, choline, chromite, chrysoberyl, chrysolite, chrysoprase, chrysotile, cinnabar, citrine, cleveite, cobaltite, columbite, copper pyrites, cordierite, corundum, covellite, crocidolite, crocoisite, crocoite, cryolite, cuprite, cymophane, diopside, dioptase, diorite, dolomite, dripstone, emerald copper, emery, enargite, endomorph, enstatite, epidote, erythrite, euclasite, euxenite, fayalite, felspar, felspathoid, ferberite, ferromagnesian, fibrolite, flos feri, fluor, fluorite, fluorspar, fool's gold, forsterite, fracture filling, franklinite, fuchsite, gadolinite, gahnite, gahnite, galena, garnierite, gehlenite, gibbsite, glass, glauberite, glauconite, gossan, graphite, Greenland spar, grossularite, gummite, gypsum, haematite, halite, hauerite, heavy spar, hedenbergite, hornblende, indianite, iron glance, iron olivine, iron ore, iron pyrites, ironstone, kamacite, kaolinite, labradorite, laterite, lazulite, lazurite, lodestone, macle, magnesite, magnetite, malachite, mica, microcline, minette, molybdenite, morion, mundic, muscovite, nepheline, nephrite, octahederite, oligoclase, olivenite, olivine, oolite, opacite, orpiment, orthite, orthoclase, pentlandite, periclase, perimorph, phenacite, pitchblende, plasma, potch, prase, prasine, proustite, pyrargyrite, pyrope, quartz, realgar, red-lead ore, rhodochrosite, rhyacolite, rocksalt, roscoelite, ruby silver, salt, sand, scapolite, scheelite, scolecite, sepiolite, sericite, shoad, siderite, silica, silica gel, silicate, sillimanite, silver glance, sinhalite, smaltite, smithsonite, soapstone, sperrylite, sphalerite, sphene, spinel, spodumene, stannite, steatite, steelband, stibnite, sunstone, sylvanite, sylvanite, sylvinite, sylvite, taconite *(U.S.)*, talc, tantalite, tarbuttite, tennantite, tenorite, tetradymite, tetrahedrite, thenardite, thorianite, thorite, tin pyrites, tin pyrites, tinstone, titanate, titanite, torbanite, tremolite, trichite, trona, tungstite, ulexite, uraninite, vermiculite, vesuvianite, vivianite, wavellite, wernerite, wheel ore, white mundic, white nickel, willemite, witherite, wolfram, wolframite, wolframium, wulfenite, wurtzite, xenotime, yellow quartz, yellowcake, ytterbite, yttria, yttrotantalite, zeolite, zinc blende, zinc-spinel, zincite, zinkenite, zirconia, zoisite

9. SEDIMENTARY ROCKS, argil, argillite, arkose, bind, bluestone, breccia, burr, burstone, calc-sinter, calc-tufa, chalk, chert, china stone, clay, claystone, conglomerate, coquina, coral, cornbrash, cuckoo sandstone, flint, flookan, geyserite, greensand, greywacke, grit, ironstone, itacolumite, kaolin, limestone, malm, marl, mottled sandstone, mudstone, niggerhead, novaculite, oil shale, oolite, papa *(N.Z.)*, pelite, pipestone, pisolite, Portland stone, psammite, psephite, pudding stone, quartzite, rottenstone, sandstone, scaglia, shale, silicified wood, siltstone, sinter, skarn, speckled hen, stinkstone, touchstone, travertine, tufa, wacke; IGNEOUS ROCKS, agglomerate, andesite, basalt, block lava, blue ground, breccia, clinkstone, diabase, dolerite, dunite, elvan, elvanite, felsite, gabbro, granite, granitite, granophyre, greenstone, ignimbrite, lava, margarite, monzonite, nephelinite, obsidian, ophite, pegmatite, peridotite, perlite, phonolite, pitchstone, porphyry, pounamu, pozzuolana, propylite, pumice, rhyolite, scoria, slag, syenite, tachylyte, taxite, tephrite, theralite, trachyte, trap, traprock, trass, tuff, volcanic glass, whin, whinstone; METAMORPHIC ROCKS, amphibolite, billy, biotite schist, eclogite, gneiss, granulite, groundmass, marble, metasediment, metavolcanic, potstone, schist, serpentinite, slate

10. GEMSTONES, agate, alexandrite, almandine, amethyst, aquamarine, asteria, azurite, beryl, bloodstone, cairngorm, carbuncle, cat's-eye, chrysoberyl, cinnamon stone, cornelian, emerald, garnet, greenstone *(N.Z.)*, heliodor, heliotrope, hessonite, hiddenite, hyacinth, jacinth, jargon, kunzite, marcasite, moonstone, oriental amethyst, peridot, phenacite, pounamu, pyrope, rhodolite, rubellite, ruby, sapphire, sard, scarab, schorl, star sapphire, star stone, topaz, tourmaline, turquoise, water-sapphire, white sapphire, zircon; ORNAMENTAL STONES, alabaster, amazon-stone, amazonite, calc-sinter, cipolin, crystal, hawk's-eye, jade, jasper, jet *(Obs.)*, lapis lazuli, marble, murrhine, onyx, porphyry, rhodonite, rock-crystal, sardonyx, serpentine, tiger's-eye, travertine, verd antique

Sport

Ball sports 1
Cricket 1
Football 1
Athletics 2
Footballers 3
Hockey players 3
Cricketers 4
International sporting teams 5
Soccer teams 6
Australian Rules teams 7
Rugby League teams 8
Rugby Union teams 9

1. BALL SPORTS, badminton, bandy-ball *(Obs.)*, baseball, basketball, battledore and shuttlecock, bocce, boule, bowling, bowls, bumble puppy, captain ball, carpet bowls, clock-golf, court tennis *(U.S.)*, croquet, curling, field hockey, fives, golf, hand tennis, handball, hockey, hurling, lawn bowls, lawn tennis, mall, minigolf, netball, overhead ball, pall-mall, pelota, ping-pong, real tennis, rounders, royal tennis, shinty, shuttlecock, softball, sphairee, squash, squash racquets, squash tennis, table tennis, tennis, tether tennis, vigoro, volleyball; FOOTBALL, aerial ping-pong, American football, association, Association Football, Aussie Rules, Australian Football, Australian National Football, Australian Rules, footer, footie, gridiron, League, national code, Rugby football, Rugby League, Rugby Union, rugger, Rules, soccer, touch football, wogball; CRICKET, cricko, French cricket, tip-and-run
2. ATHLETICS, broad jump, decathlon, discus, field event, hammer, heat, heptathlon, high jump, hop step and jump, hurdles, javelin, jump, long jump, marathon, medley relay, middle distance, pentathlon, pole vault, relay, running, shot-put, sprint, track, track event, triple jump
3. FOOTBALL AND HOCKEY PLAYERS, back, back line *(Rugby)*, back man *(Aus. Rules)*, back pocket *(Aus. Rules)*, centre, centre half-back, centre half-forward, centre three-quarter, centre-forward, centre-half, centre-line, centre-man, defence, emergency *(Aus. Rules)*, first five-eighth *(N.Z. Rugby)*, five-eighth *(Rugby)*, flank *(Aus. Rules)*, flank forward *(N.Z. Rugby Union)*, flanker *(N.Z. Rugby Union)*, fly half *(N.Z. Brit.)*, follower *(Aus. Rules)*, forward, forward line *(Soccer Hockey)*, forward pocket *(Aus. Rules)*, front-row forward *(Rugby)*, full-back, full-forward *(Aus. Rules)*, goalie, goalkeeper, guard *(American Football)*, half, half-back, half-back flanker *(Aus. Rules)*, half-forward *(Aus. Rules)*, half-forward flanker *(Aus. Rules)*, head *(Rugby)*, hooker *(Rugby)*, inside *(Soccer)*, inside centre *(Rugby)*, inside left *(Soccer Hockey)*, inside right *(Soccer Hockey)*, interchange *(Aus. Rules)*, key position *(Aus. Rules)*, kicker, left back, left half, left inner *(Hockey)*, left wing, lock *(Rugby)*, lock forward, loose *(Rugby)*, loose forward *(Rugby Union)*, loose man *(Aus. Rules)*, loosehead (prop) *(Rugby Union)*, nineteenth man *(Aus. Rules)*, number eight forward *(N.Z. Rugby)*, outside *(Rugby)*, outside half *(Rugby)*, outside left *(Hockey)*, outside right *(Hockey)*, pack *(Rugby)*, pig *(Rugby Union)*, pivot, placed man *(Aus. Rules)*, prop *(Rugby)*, prop-forward *(Rugby)*, right inner *(Hockey)*, rover *(Aus. Rules)*, ruck *(Aus. Rules)*, ruck-rover *(Aus. Rules)*, ruckman *(Aus. Rules)*, scrum-half *(Brit. Rugby)*, second five-eighth *(N.Z. Rugby)*, second rower *(Rugby)*, spearhead *(Aus. Rules)*, stand-off *(Brit. Rugby)*, stand-off half *(Brit. Rugby)*, sweeper *(Soccer)*, three-quarter *(Rugby)*, tighthead (prop) *(Rugby)*, twentieth man *(Aus. Rules)*, utility player, wing, wing-forward, wing-half *(Soccer)*, wing-three-quarter *(Rugby)*, winger, wingman *(Aus. Rules)*
4. CRICKETERS, all-rounder, attack, backward square leg, bat, batsman, bowler, change bowler, cover, cover-point, deep cover, deep extra cover, deep fine leg, deep mid wicket, deep mid-off, deep

mid-on, deep square leg, deep third man, extra cover, fast bowle fielder, fieldsman, fine leg, fly slip, forward short leg, glovemar grave-digger, gully, infielder, keeper, leg slip, leg spinner, leggie, lon leg, long-off, long-on, long-stop, medium pacer, mid wicket, mid-of mid-on, middle-order batsman, nightwatchman, non-striker, off spir ner, opener, outfielder, pace bowler, paceman, point, quickie, rabbi seam bowler, short fine leg, short leg, short point, short third mar silly mid-off, silly mid-on, silly point, slip, spin bowler, spinne square leg, stonewaller, straight hit, striker, swing bowler, tail-ende third man, topspinner, twelfth man, wicket-keeper

5. INTERNATIONAL TEAMS – AUSTRALIAN, Kangaroos *(Rugb League)*, Socceroos *(Soccer)*, Wallabies *(Rugby Union)*; OTHER, A Blacks *(N.Z. Rugby Union)*, Lions *(Brit. Rugby Union)*, MCC *(Bri Cricket)*, Springboks *(South Africa Rubgy Union)*, Windies *(We Indies Cricket)*

6. NATIONAL SOCCER LEAGUE, Adamstown *(Rosebuds)*, Adelaid City *(Giants)*, Blacktown *(Demons)*, Brisbane City *(Gladiators)*, Bris bane Lions *(Lions)*, Canberra Arrows *(Arrows)*, Footscray *(Eagles* Heidelberg United *(Warriors)*, Leichhardt *(Strikers)*, Marconi *(Leop ards)*, Newcastle K.B. United *(Raiders)*, Parramatta Melita, Presto *(Rams)*, Saints *(St George)*, South Melbourne *(Gunners)*, Sydney Cit *(Slickers)*, Sydney Olympic *(Olympians)*, West Adelaide *(Hawks* Wollongong City *(Wolves)*

7. AUSTRALIAN RULES TEAMS: VICTORIA, Collingwood *(Mag pies)*, Carlton *(Blues)*, Essendon *(Bombers (Dons))*, Fitzroy *(Lions* Footscray *(Bulldogs)*, Geelong *(Cats)*, Hawthorn *(Hawks)*, Melbourn *(Demons)*, North Melbourne *(Kangas (Roos))*, orig. South Melbourn *(Swans (Sydney Swans))*, Richmond *(Tigers)*, St Kilda *(Saints)*; TAS MANIA, Clarence *(Roos)*, Glenorchy *(Magpies (The Pies))*, Hobar *(Tigers)*, New Norfolk *(Eagles (Norfik))*, North Hobart *(Demon (North))*, Sandy Bay *(Seagulls (The Bay))*; NORTHERN TERRI TORY, Darwin *(Buffaloes)*, Nightcliff *(Tigers)*, North Darwin *(Mag pies)*, St Marys F.C. *(Saints)*, Wanderers F.C. *(Eagles)*, Waratah F.C *(Warriors)*; SOUTH AUSTRALIA, Central Districts *(Bulldogs)* Glenelg *(Tigers)*, North Adelaide *(Roosters)*, Norwood *(Redlegs)*, Por Adelaide *(Magpies)*, South Adelaide *(Panthers)*, Sturt *(Double Blues)* West Adelaide *(Bloods)*, West Torrens *(Eagles)*, Woodville *(War riors)*; WESTERN AUSTRALIA, Claremont *(Tigers)*, East Fre mantle *(Sharks)*, East Perth *(Royals)*, Perth *(Demons)*, South Fre mantle *(Bulldogs)*, Subiaco *(Lions)*, Swan District *(Swans)*, West Pertl *(Falcons)*; V.F.A., Berwick *(Wickers)*, Box Hill *(Mustangs)*, Brunswick *(Magpies)*, Camberwell *(Cobras)*, Caulfield *(Bears)*, Coburg *(Lions)* Dandenong *(Redlegs)*, Frankston *(Dolphins)*, Geelong West *(Roost ers)*, Kilsyth *(Cougars)*, Moorabbin *(Kangaroos)*, Mordialloc *(Bloods)* Northcote *(Dragons)*, Oakleigh *(Oaks)*, Port Melbourne *(Boroughs)* Prahran *(Two Blues)*, Preston *(Bullants)*, Sandringham *(Zebras)* Springvale *(Vales)*, Sunshine *(Shiners)*, Waverley *(Panthers)*, Werri-bee *(Tigers)*, Williamstown *(Seagulls)*, Yarraville *(Eagles)*

8. RUGBY LEAGUE TEAMS: N.S.W., Balmain *(Tigers)*, Canberra

(Raiders), Canterbury-Bankstown *(Bulldogs)*, Cronulla-Sutherland *(Sharks)*, Eastern Suburbs *(Roosters)*, Illawarra *(Steelers)*, Manly-Warringah *(Sea Eagles)*, N.S.W. State *(Blues)*, Newtown *(Jets)*, North Sydney *(Bears)*, Parramatta *(Eels)*, Penrith *(Panthers)*, South Sydney *(Rabbitohs)*, St George *(Saints (Dragons))*, Western Suburbs *(Magpies)*; QUEENSLAND, Central Queensland *(Capras)*, Eastern Suburbs *(Tigers)*, Gold Coast *(Vikings)*, Ipswich *(Jets)*, North Queensland *(Marlins)*, Northern Suburbs *(Devils)*, Past Brothers *(Brethren)*, Queensland State *(Maroons)*, Redcliffe *(Dolphins)*, Southern Suburbs *(Magpies)*, Toowoomba *(Clydesdales)*, Valleys *(Diehards)*, Western Suburbs *(Panthers)*, Wide Bay *(Bulls)*, Wynnum-Manly *(Seagulls)*

9. RUGBY UNION TEAMS: N.S.W., Eastern Suburbs *(Tricolours)*, Eastwood *(Woods)*, Gordon *(Highlanders)*, Manly *(Blues)*, N.S.W. State *(Blues)*, N.S.W. University *(Students)*, Northern Suburbs *(Norths)*, Parramatta *(Two Blues)*, Port Hacking *(Hackers)*, Randwick *(Galloping Greens)*, Sydney University *(Students)*, Warringah *(Green Rats)*, Western Suburbs *(Wests)*; QUEENSLAND, Brothers *(Paddies)*, Eastern Districts *(Tigers)*, G.P.S. *(Galloping Greens)*, Queensland State *(Maroons)*, Redcliffe *(Demons)*, Southern Districts *(Magpies)*, Teachers-Norths *(Teachers)*, University *(Varsity/Red Heavies)*, Western Districts *(Bulldogs)*

Language

Language families 1
Languages 2
English dialects 3
Australian (Aboriginal) languages 4
Amerindian languages 5
Languages of the Indian sub-continent 6
Computer languages 7
Artificial languages 8

. LANGUAGE FAMILY, Algonquian, Amerindian, Anatolian, Aryan, Athapaskan, Australian, Austronesian, Baltic, Bantu, Berber, Brythonic, Bushman, Caucasian, Celtic, Dravidian, Eskimo-Aleut, Eskimoan, Finno-Ugrian, Finno-Ugric, Germanic, Goidelic, Hamitic, Hellenic, Indic, Indo-European, Indo-Iranian, Indonesian, Iranian, Iroquoian, Italic, Japhetic, Latin, Malayo-Indonesian, Malayo-Polynesian, Manchu, Mayan, Melanesian, Micronesian, Mon-Khmer, Mongolian, Mongolic, Nahuatlan, Osco-Umbrian, Pama-Nyungan, Papuan, Polynesian, Rhaeto-Romanic, Romance, Romanic, Salishan, Samoyed, Sanskritic, Scandinavian, Semitic, Shoshonean, Sino-Tibetan, Siouan, Slavic (Slavonic), South Caucasian, Sudanic, Teutonic, Tibeto-Burman, Tocharian, Ugric, Ural-Altaic, Uralian, Uralic, Uto-Aztecan, Yuman

2. LANGUAGES, Afghan (Afghani), Afrikaans, Ainu, Akkadian, Albanian, Aleut, Amharic, Anglo-French, Anglo-Norman, Anglo-Saxon, Annamese, Arabic, Aramaic, Armenian, Aztec, Bahasa Indonesia, Balinese, Baluchi, Basque, Berber, Biblical Latin, Bohemian, Breton, Bulgarian, Burmese, Byelorussian, Cantonese, Carib, Castilian, Catalan, Chinese, Coptic, Cornish, Creole, Czech, Dalmatian, Danish, Dano-Norwegian, Demotic, Dinka, dog Latin, Dutch, Dyak, Edo, Egyptian, English, Epic, Erse, Eskimo, Esperanto, Estonian, Ethiopic, Etruscan, Ewe, Faeroese, Fijian, Finnish, Flemish, French, Frisian, Friulian, Gaelic, Galibi, Gallo-Roman, Gaulish, Georgian, German, Gothic, Greek, Guaraní, Gypsy, Hausa, Hawaiian, Hebrew, High German, Hittite, Hottentot, Hungarian, Ibo, Icelandic, Illyrian, Irish Gaelic, Italian, Japanese, Javanese, Jewish, Kaffir, Kalmuck, Khmer, Kiribas, Koine, Kongo, Korean, Kurdish, Ladin, Ladino, Landsmal, Langobardic, langue d'oc, langue d'oïl, Lao, Lapp, Late Greek, Late Latin, Latin, Latvian, Lettish, Libyan, Lithuanian, Livonian, Low German, Lydian, Macedonian, Magyar, Malagasy, Malay, Maltese, Manchu, Mandarin, Mandingo, Manx, Maori, Maya, Medieval Greek, Medieval Latin, Melanesian, Micronesian, Middle English, Middle French, Middle Greek, Middle High German, Middle Irish, Middle Low German, Miskito, Modern Hebrew, Mon, Mongol, Mongolian, Moriori, Moro, Nepalese, Norse, Norwegian, Nubian, Nynorsk, Occitanian, Old Church Slavonic, Old French, Old High German, Old Icelandic, Old Irish, Old Norse, Old Persian, Old Prussian, Old Saxon, Oscan, Ottoman Turkish, Pahlavi, Persian, Phrygian, pidgin English, pig Latin, Plattdeutsch, Polish, Portuguese, Provençal, Quechua, Quiché, Rabbinic, Riksmal, Romaic, Romanian, Romansh (Rhaeto-Romanic), Romany, Rumanian, Russian, Samoan, Sardinian, Saxon, Scottish Gaelic, Serbian, Serbo-Croat, Shan, Shelta, Slovak, Slovenian, Somali, South African Dutch, Spanish, Sumerian, Swahili, Swedish, Syriac, Tagalog, Tahitian, Tatar, Thai (Siamese), Thracian, Tibetan, Tocharian, Tonga, Tuareg, Turkish, Turkoman, Ukrainian, Umbrian, Uzbek, Vietnamese, Vulgar Latin, Walloon, Welsh, White Russian, Xhosa, Yakut, Yiddish, Yoruba, Zulu

3. OLD ENGLISH DIALECTS, Anglian, Kentish, Mercian,

Northumbrian, West Saxon; MIDDLE ENGLISH DIALECTS, East Midland, Northern, South Eastern, South Western, West Midland; MODERN ENGLISH DIALECTS OF THE BRITISH ISLES, Cockney, Geordie, Irish, Midlands, Received Pronunciation (R.P.), Scots (Scottish), Scouse, South Eastern, Welsh, West Country; MODERN ENGLISH DIALECTS NOT OF THE BRITISH ISLES, American, Australian, Bislama (Beach-la-mar), Canadian, Indian, Melanesian (Pidgin), Mid-Atlantic, Neo-Melanesian, New Zealand, Singaporean English, South African, Strine, Tok Pisin, West Indian; AUSTRALIAN ENGLISH VARIETIES, Aboriginal, Broad, Cultivated, General, Kriol, Modified, Ocker; AMERICAN ENGLISH DIALECTS, Black English, General, Gullah, Midland, New England, Northern, Southern, West Coast

4. AUSTRALIAN (ABORIGINAL) LANGUAGES, Alyawarra, Anindilyakwa, Burarra, Gunwinygu, Gurindji, Guugu Yimidhirr, Kala Lagan Ya, Kameraigal, Kamilaroi, Larakia, Pintupi, Pitjantjatjara, Tiwi, Walpiri, Western Desert, Wik-Munkan, Yolngu

5. AMERINDIAN LANGUAGES, Apache, Blackfoot, Cherokee, Chickasaw, Chinook, Choctaw, Creek, Crow, Dakota, Delaware (Lenape), Hopi, Kickapoo, Kiowa, Micmac, Mohawk, Mohican, Navaho, Nez Percé, Nootka, Pequot, Seminole, Shoshone, Yaqui, Zuñi

6. LANGUAGES OF THE INDIAN SUB-CONTINENT, Bengali, Gujarati, Hindi (Hindustani), Kannada (Kannarese), Lepcha, Malayam, Marathi, Punjabi, Rajasthani, Sanskrit, Sinhala (Sinhalese), Telegu, Urdu, Vedic

7. COMPUTER LANGUAGES, ADA, ALGOL, BASIC, C, COBOL, compiler, FORTH, FORTRAN, high-level language, LISP, low-level language, MODULA-2, PASCAL

8. ARTIFICIAL LANGUAGES, Basic English, Esperanto, Newspeak, Volapük